The Glorious American Essay

PANTHEON BOOKS, NEW YORK

The Glorious American Essay

One Hundred Essays
from Colonial Times
to the Present

Edited and with an introduction by

Phillip Lopate

Introduction, headnotes, and compilation copyright © 2020 by Phillip Lopate

Permissions acknowledgments appear following the acknowledgments.

Library of Congress Cataloging-in-Publication Data
Name: Lopate, Phillip, [date] editor.
Title: The glorious American essay : one hundred essays from colonial times
to the present / edited and with an introduction by Phillip Lopate.
Description: First edition. New York : Pantheon Books, 2020
Identifiers: LCCN 2020002258 (print). LCCN 2020002259 (ebook).
ISBN 9781524747268 (hardcover). ISBN 9781524747275 (ebook).
Subjects: LCSH: American essays.
Classification: LCC PS682 .G58 2020 (print) | LCC PS682 (ebook) | DDC 814/.009—dc23
LC record available at lccn.loc.gov/2020002258
LC ebook record available at lccn.loc.gov/2020002259

www.pantheonbooks.com

Jacket design by Sarahmay Wilkinson

Printed in the United States of America

First Edition

9 8 7 6 5 4 3 2 1

CONTENTS

Contents [ix]

INTRODUCTION

I

The essay is a literary form dating back to ancient times, with a long and glorious history. As the record *par excellence* of a mind tracking its thoughts, it can be considered the intellectual bellwether of any modern society. The great promise of essays is the freedom they offer to explore, digress, acknowledge uncertainty; to evade dogmatism and embrace ambivalence and contradiction; to engage in intimate conversation with one's readers and literary forebears; and to uncover some unexpected truth, preferably via a sparkling literary style. Flexible, shape-shifting, experimental, as befits its name derived from the French (*essai* = "attempt"), it is nothing if not versatile.

In the United States, the essay has had a particularly illustrious if underexamined career. In fact, it is possible to see the dual histories of the country and the literary form as running on parallel tracks, the essay mulling current issues and thereby reflecting the story of the United States in each succeeding period. And just as American democracy has been an ongoing experiment, with no guarantees of perfection, so has the essay been, as William Dean Howells argued, an innately democratic form inviting all comers to say their piece, however imperfectly.

The Puritans, some of our earliest settlers, chose the essay over fiction and poetry as their preferred mode of expression. In both sermons and texts explicitly labeled "essays," men like Cotton Mather and Jonathan Edwards articulated their religious and ethical values. Many later American commentators would take them to task for being sexually prudish, intolerant, and repressive. H. L. Mencken, in a scathing extended essay entitled "Puritanism as a Literary Force," blamed that heritage for holding back American literature by overstressing behavioral proprieties while understressing aesthetics. Edmund Wilson wittily noted that Mencken himself was something of a Puritan. The bohemian wing of American literature, from Walt Whitman to the present, has engaged in protracted guerrilla warfare with Puritanism and offered itself as an alternative. On the other hand, Marilynne Robinson defends the Puritans from what she regards as a caricature of their positions. Say what you will about their rigid morality: these Puritan thinkers were highly learned, with sophisticated prose styles, and we are fortunate in having them set so high an intellectual standard for later American essayists to follow.

Skip ahead to the Founding Fathers, including George Washington, Thomas Jefferson, Benjamin Franklin, Alexander Hamilton, and Thomas Paine, all of whom seem to have been superb writers. In their treatises, pamphlets, speeches, letters, and broadsides, they tested their tentative views on politics and governance, hoping to move from conviction to certainty. Theirs was a self-conscious rhetoric influenced by the French Enlightenment authors and the orators of ancient Greece and Rome, as well as the polished eighteenth-century nonfiction prose writers of their opponent, Great Britain.

In the decades following independence, United States authors labored to free themselves from subservience to English parental literary influence and to establish a national culture that would sound somehow unmistakably American. Washington Irving, perhaps the first freelance American author to support himself by his pen, was ridiculed by British critics such as William Hazlitt for imitating the English periodical essayists. He, in turn, wrote an essay entitled "English Writers in America," which began: "It is with feelings of deep regret that I observe the literary animosity daily growing up between England and America." He went on to analyze the condescending travel accounts of English authors in America, which were then all the rage in Great Britain: "That such men should give prejudiced accounts of America is not a matter of surprize. The themes it offers for contemplation are too vast and elevated for their capacities. The national character is yet in a state of fermentation: it may have its frothings and sediment, but its ingredients are sound and wholesome; it has already given proofs of powerful and generous qualities, and the whole promises to settle down into something substantially excellent." Edgar Allan Poe bristled at the canard that Americans were too materialistic and engineering-minded to produce literature: "Our necessities have been mistaken for our propensities. Having been forced to make rail-roads, it has been deemed impossible that we should make verse. . . . But this is the purest insanity. The principles of the poetic sentiment lie deep within the immortal nature of man, and have little necessary reference to the worldly circumstances which surround him . . . nor can any social, or political, or moral, or physical conditions do more than momentarily repress the impulses which glow in our own bosoms as fervently as in those of our progenitors."

But it was Ralph Waldo Emerson, our greatest nineteenth-century essayist, who sounded the alarm most famously in his speech "The American Scholar." Acknowledging that up to then the Americans were "a people too busy to give to letters more," he nevertheless prophesied that the time was coming "when the sluggard intellect of this continent will look from under its iron lids, and fill the postponed expectations of the world with something better than the exertions of mechanical skill. Our day of dependence, our long apprenticeship to the learning of other lands, draws to a close. The millions, that around us are rushing into life, cannot always be fed on the sere remains of foreign harvests." He concluded by saying: "We have listened too long to the courtly muses of Europe. . . . We will walk on our own feet; we will work with our own hands; we will speak with our own minds." It's worthwhile remembering that this author who called for independence from foreign culture was probably the best-read person of his time and had imbibed not only most of British, French, and German literature but Eastern religious classics as well.

Emerson developed a kind of essay that was quirky, densely complex, speculative, digressive, and epigrammatic. He was part of that extraordinary flowering of literary culture in the mid-nineteenth century, the so-called American Renaissance, which included Nathaniel Hawthorne, Poe, Henry David Thoreau, Herman Melville, Whitman, Margaret Fuller, and Emily Dickinson. By the time it had run its course, there was no longer any doubt that America had itself a national culture. But there was more at stake than just the development of literary talent. The nation was facing enormous political and moral challenges from the twin oppressions of blacks and women. The Fugitive Slave Act of 1850, which called for runaway slaves to be captured by northerners and returned as property to their southern slave owners, converted many of these writers to the abolitionist cause. Some of the most eloquent essays attacking slavery were penned by African Americans, such as Frederick Douglass and Martin R. Delany. They engendered an essayistic discourse on race that would be taken up by a distinguished lineage of black authors, including W. E. B. Du Bois, James Weldon Johnson, Zora Neale Hurston, Alain Locke, Ralph Ellison, and James Baldwin, continuing into our present day.

Meanwhile, women of the nineteenth century, still denied the vote and other rights, were barred from many professions, patronized, physically abused, and oppressed. It is remarkable how far back in America feminist voices were heard, from Judith Sargent Murray's 1790 "On the Equality of the Sexes" to Margaret Fuller to Sarah Moore Grimké and Fanny Fern, reaching a high point in the suffragist Elizabeth Cady Stanton's great essay, "The Solitude of Self," and sweeping forward to the twentieth century. The essay, once considered a male province, has been nourished by the mental toughness and emotional honesty of so many bold, brilliant women in the last hundred years: think of Mary McCarthy, Hannah Arendt, Elizabeth Hardwick, Susan Sontag, Adrienne Rich, Joan Didion, Cynthia Ozick, Zadie Smith. . . .

Even when suffrage was extended to blacks and women, there was still the problem of completing democracy by transforming it from a merely legal form to an everyday reality for all classes and groups. So John Dewey argued for students and teachers to have more of a voice in determining educational policy; Jane Addams addressed in her settlement house movement the problems of young people thrown together as strangers in big cities; and Randolph Bourne put forward his vision of a "trans-national America" that would embrace the diversity of immigrants from other than Anglo-Saxon backgrounds.

Whenever the American essay has been unhitched from the urgent political and moral issues of the day, it has had to battle to stay commercially relevant. A specialty of the personal or familiar essay, in the tradition of Michel de Montaigne, Hazlitt, Charles Lamb, and Robert Louis Stevenson, is to focus on some seemingly small, trivial curiosity or annoyance of daily life, and to coax a larger significance from it. Some of the essayists of the late nineteenth and early twentieth centuries, such as Agnes Repplier and Katharine Fullerton Gerould, excelled at this miniaturist belletristic form and found a home in magazines, but they also had to defend their work from charges that it was "genteel" or old-fashioned. The death of the essay was frequently if prematurely predicted. In 1919 Robert Cortes Holliday wrote good-humoredly: "It is said that essays are coming in again. Every once in a while someone says that. It is like prophecies concerning the immediate end of the world. However, it (either one of these prophecies) may be so this time." (How pertinent those remarks are may be seen by examining our own recent history. Publishers twenty-five years ago treated essay collections as pariahs and would not touch the stuff. Since then, essays have come roaring back, and today there are dozens of collections exciting popular interest. But that could easily change, in which case essayists would again have to package their wares in some other disguise.)

One of the ways that the American essay kept alive in the 1910s, '20s, and '30s was to gravitate to the newspaper or magazine column, often in the guise of humor pieces. A fraternal order of such practitioners, which included Christopher Morley, Don Marquis, and Heywood Broun, called themselves facetiously the "colyumnists." Masters of the six-hundred-word essay, they were very popular, especially in metropolitan settings, and set the agenda for the talk of the town. Their seemingly casual throwaway tone, "typical Joe" persona, and modest claims as literary artists belied the fact that they were all highly educated in the traditions of the English periodical essay.

At the opposite end of the journalistic spectrum, as far from the average Joe as possible, was H. L. Mencken, who employed an elevated, at times comically baroque, diction and took every opportunity to sneer at the provincial ignorance of the average American. In the Age of Mencken, roughly the 1920s, many writers felt alienated from American mass culture: some went abroad to Europe, like F. Scott Fitzgerald and Gertrude Stein, to absorb a more sophisticated, worldly ambience, while others stayed home and tried to raise the cultural level. (The critic Alfred Kazin spoke of "our writers' absorption in every last detail of their American world together with their deep and subtle alienation from it.") This lovers' quarrel between America and its writers initially took the form of a mistrust of the masses and, later on, a wary suspicion about how consumerist mass culture would shape the people's mentalities. It was also a protest against the shortcomings of the American dream, or at least its bland, self-satisfied complacencies. The discordant note struck by many native essayists regarding the mythologies of American exceptionalism may have sprung from the artists' felt obligation to question received opinion.

Many of the essays chosen for this anthology address themselves specifically—sometimes lovingly, sometimes critically—to American values. (See, for instance, the pieces by George Santayana, Mary McCarthy, and Wallace Stegner, each taking America's temperature.) But even those that do not do so have a secondary, if inadvertent, subtext about being American. E. B. White was an influential example of an essayist who conveyed, in a down-to-earth American tone, the average citizen's preoccupations at home, while remaining aware of the larger challenges facing society.

In a United States where various groups have felt marginalized because of their ethnicity, national origin, gender, geographical location, or disability, members of these groups have increasingly turned to the essay as a means of asserting identity (or complicating it). Gerald Early, in his anthology *Speech and Power,* wrote: "Since black writing came of age in this country in the 1920s, the essay seems to be the informing genre behind it. . . . It is not surprising that many black writers have been attracted to the essay as a literary form since the essay is the most exploitable mode of the confession and the polemic, the two variants of the essay that black writers have mostly used." The same could be said for other minority groups in American society, who have benefited the essay form immeasurably by adapting it to their purposes, enriching the American language with their dialect-flavored speech. They have contributed to the "cultural unity within diversity" ideal that Ralph Ellison envisioned for this country. At the same time, the American essay has taken a turn toward greater autobiographical frankness, thanks in part to their efforts.

Another skein of essay writing, of unarguable importance now that the planet finds itself endangered by climate change, is nature writing. In America, that tradition goes back at least as far as J. Hector St. John de Crèvecoeur and extends to John James Audubon, Henry David Thoreau, John Muir, Mary Austin, John Burroughs, Edward Abbey, Rachel Carson, and Annie Dillard, among others. We see in it an attempt to balance the factual and descriptive elements of flora and fauna with a fresh emotional access to wonder and awe. However alarmed these essayists may sound in their warnings of the threats to nature, there is still looming underneath an appeal to the original myth of America as the New World, a second Garden of Eden where humankind could finally get it right.

II

But wait: What *is* an essay? Many definitions have been proffered, none conclusive. Samuel Johnson called it "a loose sally of the mind." Marilynne Robinson said it was "thought in the pure enjoyment of itself." Chris Arthur wrote that "an essay is a literary electrocardiogram that traces out in words the pulse of thoughts" and "an essay arranges words with one eye on sense, one eye on style, and a third eye on wisdom." R. P. Blackmur called it a form of "unindoctrinated thinking," making it especially well suited to doubt, inconclusiveness, skepticism, and contrarian views. Not that it necessarily has to be inconclusive. We deduce from all this that it has something to do with tracking thought. Some have maintained that the essay must have an argument, must instruct; others, that essays must *not* do either. According to Agnes Repplier, "It offers no instruction, save through the medium of enjoyment, and one saunters lazily along with a charming unconsciousness of effort." That is one kind of essay, the informal essay, which depends less on reasoning than on authorial voice, what Elizabeth Hardwick called "the soloist's personal signature flowing through the text." But what about the formal essay? Doesn't it too need personal style of a sort?

Many have tried to limit the field. William Dean Howells drew a strict border between the essay and the article. William H. Gass forbade the scholarly paper from consideration as an essay. Cynthia Ozick wrote: "A genuine essay has no educational, polemical, or sociopolitical use; it is the movement of a free mind at play. . . . A genuine essay is not a doctrinaire tract or a propaganda effort or a broadside. Thomas Paine's 'Common Sense' and Emile Zola's 'J'Accuse' are heroic landmark writings, but to call them essays, though they may resemble the form, is to misunderstand. The essay is not meant for the barricades; it is a stroll through someone's mazy mind."

Much as I revere Howells, Gass, and Ozick, I respectfully disagree. We are just as privy to Thomas Paine's mind working through reasons to rebel as we are to his contemporary Hazlitt on the pleasures of hating, and why should a piece of writing be excluded from the essay kingdom simply because it follows a coherent line of reasoning? Even the lightest of familiar essays usually has an implicit armature of argumentation, just as essays that may not be overtly political invariably reflect an underlying politics. There are those who would seek to exclude criticism as a form of essay; but in my own experience, having taught and written a good deal of the stuff, I came to see that the best critics were all cobbling together a highly specific voice or persona through which their evaluations and insights could resound.

So, for this anthology I have taken the position of opening it to every type of the beast: the familiar essay, the personal essay, the critical essay, the biographical essay, the dialogue-essay, the humor essay, the philosophical essay, the academic essay, and the polemic. I have included essays that occurred in the form of speeches (George Washington, Abraham Lincoln, Martin Luther King Jr.), letters (Frederick Douglass), sermons (Jonathan Edwards), papers (Jane Addams), dialogue-essays (Finley Peter Dunne, Oliver Wendell Holmes), newspaper columns (Fanny Fern). While belletrists would like to exclude journalists, I don't see how I could have left out such remarkable prose stylists from any compendium of the American essay.

More, I have sought out essays from every walk of life, not just the ostensibly literary, based on my conviction that every discipline has exceptionally gifted writers who have tried to work out their thoughts on the page: in science (Albert Einstein, Loren Eiseley, Lewis Thomas), geography (John Brinckerhoff Jackson), social work (Jane Addams), education (John Dewey), theology (Paul Tillich), food (M. F. K. Fisher), art criticism (Clement Greenberg), and so on.

In the main I have given preference to pieces of writing that began as stand-alone essays, but I have not hesitated to take a chapter from a book if I thought it functioned perfectly as an autonomous essay (Thomas Paine, W. E. B. Du Bois). Another criterion for selection was that the author needed to be American either by birth or emigration.

Lest you infer that I have become utterly promiscuous in my embrace of any piece of writing that may lay claim to being an essay, out of some imperialistic land grab, let me reassure you that that is not the case. I have resisted fiction, including pieces that invent the facts or that attempt a hybrid form of fiction and nonfiction. On the other hand, there is room for speculation and imaginative flights of fancy in an essay, as witness James Thurber's "The Nature of the American Male: A Study of Pedestalism."

It is no accident that some of our greatest fiction writers and poets have also tried their hand at essays with excellent results: Hawthorne, Poe, Melville, Whitman, Howells, Twain, James, Dreiser, Cather, Wharton, Fitzgerald, Welty, Mailer, et cetera. A shorter list might be composed of those major American novelists and poets who did *not* excel at essay writing.

Many of the choices here are no-brainers, the names one might expect: Thoreau, Baldwin, Mencken, White, Didion. (I have made it a rule not to repeat selections from my *Art of the Personal Essay* anthology when dealing with the same author.) But it has also been my special delight to try to rescue from oblivion such estimable figures as John Jay Chapman, Randolph Bourne, and Mary Austin, who seem in danger of sinking into that American night of historical amnesia. In general, blessed or cursed as I am with a historical sense, I have given the nod here to the past over the present—not just out of filial loyalty to the dead, but in the interests of creating "a usable past," to quote Van Wyck Brooks's apt phrase. There is another reason: many of these essays not only are in conversation with one another but speak vividly to our present moment by showing how often the same conflicts, over, say, immigration, minority rights, land use, or degree of cultural maturity, keep recurring on the national stage.

Consider this anthologizing effort, then, not so much the assertion of a canon as a smorgasbord of treats, a place to begin to sample the endless riches of the American essay. I have tried to include representatives from different ethnicities, genders, regions, and aesthetic camps—not just to be politically correct, but simply because they deserve a place at the table for the quality of their prose. Still, editing an anthology is a chump's game: no matter how inclusive you may try to be, you will be criticized for various omissions, and some critics may even go through the table of contents with a calculator and total up the statistics, finding, say, too many dead white males. It can't be helped. Yes, there are regrettable omissions, given the stark reality of page limits: a binding can only hold so much. Where's Gore Vidal? Oliver Sacks? Philip Roth? (Phillip Lopate, for that matter?) The lyric essay? Fear not, reader: this is only the first of three volumes; the other two are forthcoming and should correct many of the worst omissions. Volume 2, *The Golden Age of the American Essay,* will focus more intensively on the postwar era, 1945–1970. Volume 3 will be dedicated to the contemporary essay, that is, the twenty-first century.

The
Glorious
American
Essay

COTTON MATHER

Cotton Mather (1663–1728) straddled the seventeenth and eighteenth centuries. Descended from illustrious ministers, he too became a prominent Puritan pastor in Massachusetts. An inveterate writer, he penned more than four hundred books, as well as tracts and pamphlets on various subjects. Fascinated by medicine and botany, he championed smallpox inoculation, performed plant hybridization experiments, and wrote disquisitions on vegetables. He was steeped in theology and the ancients but also familiar with essayists such as Erasmus, Michel de Montaigne, and Blaise Pascal. It's hard to reconcile that the same man, so open to new scientific ideas, who corresponded with learned Europeans, could promote the Salem witchcraft trials and claim that the Devil was about to invade New England. On his essaying, he declared in The Christian Philosopher: *"The works of the Glorious GOD in the Creation of the World, are what I now propose to exhibit; in brief Essays to enumerate some of them, that He may be glorified in them." Here, he is at pains to square his love of poetry with his Puritanical disapproval of its potential for what he sees as immorality.*

Of Poetry, and of Style

(1726)

Poetry, whereof we have now even an antediluvian piece in our hands, has from the beginning been in such request, that I must needs recommend unto you some acquaintance with it. Though some have had a soul so unmusical, that they have decried all verse, as being but a mere playing and fiddling upon words; all versifying, as if it were more unnatural than if we should choose dancing instead of walking; and rhyme, as if it were but a sort of Morisco dancing with bells: yet I cannot wish you a soul that shall be wholly unpoetical. And old Horace has left us an *Art of Poetry*, which you may do well to bestow a perusal on. And besides your lyric hours, I wish you may so far understand an epic poem, that the beauties of an Homer and a Virgil may be discerned with you. As to the moral part of Homer, 'tis true, and let me not be counted a Zoilus for saying so, that by first exhibiting their gods as no better than rogues, he set open the floodgates for a prodigious inundation of wickedness to break in upon the nations, and was one of the greatest apostles the Devil ever had in the world. Among the rest that felt the ill impressions of this universal corrupter (as men of the best sentiments have called him), one was that overgrown robber, of execrable memory, whom we celebrate under the name of Alexander the Great; who by his continual admiring and studying of his *Iliad*, and by following that false model of heroic virtue set before him in his Achilles, became one of the worst of men, and at length inflated with the ridiculous pride of being himself a deity, exposed himself to all the scorn that could belong unto a lunatic. And hence, notwithstanding the veneration which this idol has had, yet Plato banishes him out of a commonwealth, the welfare whereof he was concerned for. Nevertheless, custom or conscience obliges him to bear testimonies unto many points of morality. And it is especially observable, that he commonly propounds prayer to heaven as a most necessary preface unto all important enterprises; and when the action comes on too suddenly for a more extended supplication, he yet will not let it come on without an ejaculation; and he never speaks of any supplication but he brings in a gracious answer to it. I have seen a travesteering highflyer, not much to our dishonor, scoff at Homer for this; as making his actors to be like those whom the English call Dissenters. But then, we are so much led into the knowledge of antiquities, by reading of this poet, and into so many parts of the recondite learning, that notwithstanding some little nods in him, not a few acute pens beside the old Bishop of Thessalonica's, have got a reputation by regaling us with annotations upon him. Yea, though one can't but smile at the fancy of Croese, who tries with much ostentation of erudition, to show, that Homer has all along tendered us in a disguise and fable, the history of the Old Testament, yet many illustrations of the sacred scriptures, I find are to be fetched from him; who indeed had probably read what was extant of them in his days: particularly, our eighteenth Psalm is what he has evidently imitated. Virgil too, who so much lived upon him, as well as after him, is unaccountably mad upon his fate, which he makes to be he knows not what himself, but superior to gods as well as to men, and through his whole composures he so asserts the doctrine of this nonsensical power, as is plainly inconsistent with all virtue. And what fatal mischief did Fascinator do to the Roman Empire, when by deifying one great emperor, he taught the successors to claim the adoration of gods, while they were perpetrating the crimes of devils? I will not be a Carbilius upon him; nor will I say anything, how little the married state owes unto one who writes as if he were a woman hater: nor what his blunders are about his poor-spirited and inconsistent hero, for which many have taxed him. Nevertheless, 'tis observed, that the pagans had no rules of manners, that were more laudable and regular than what are to be found in him. And some have said, it is hardly possible seriously to read his works without being more disposed unto goodness, as well as being agreeably entertained. Be sure, had Virgil writ before Plato, his works had not been any of the books prohibited. But then, this poet also has abundance of rare antiquities for us: and such things, as others besides a Servius, have imagined that they have instructed and obliged mankind, by employing all their days upon. Wherefore if his *Aeneis,* which though it were once near twenty times as big as he has left it, yet he has left it unfinished, may not appear so valuable to you, that you may think twenty-seven verses of the part that is the most finished in it, worth one and twenty hundred pounds and odd money, yet his *Georgics,* which he put his left hand unto, will furnish you with many things far from despicable. But after all, when I said, I was willing that the beauties of these two poets, might become visible to your visive faculty in poetry, I did not mean, that you should judge nothing to be admittable into an epic poem, which is not authorized by their example; but I perfectly concur with one who is inexpressibly more capable to be a judge of such a matter than I can be: that it is a false critic who with a petulant air, will insult reason itself, if it presumes to oppose such authority.

I proceed now to say, that if (under the guidance of a Vida) you try your young wings now and then to see what flights you can make, at least for an epigram, it may a little sharpen your sense, and polish your style, for more important performances; for this purpose you are now even overstocked with patterns, and *poemata passim.* You may, like Nazianzen, all your days, make a little recreation of poetry in the midst of your more painful studies. Nevertheless, I cannot but advise you, withhold thy throat from thirst. Be not so set upon poetry, as to be always poring on the passionate and measured pages. Let not what should be sauce rather than food for you, engross all your application. Beware of a boundless and sickly appetite, for the reading of the poems, which now the rickety nation swarms withal: and let not the Circaean cup intoxicate you. But especially preserve the chastity of your soul from the dangers you may incur, by a conversation with Muses that are no better than harlots: among which are others besides Ovid's epistles, which for their tendency to excite and foment impure flames, and cast coals into your bosom, deserve rather to be thrown into the fire, than to be laid before the eye which a covenant

should be made withal. Indeed, not merely for the impurities which they
convey, but also on some other accounts, the powers of darkness have a
library among us, whereof the poets have been the most numerous as well
as the most venomous authors. Most of the modern plays, as well as the
romances and novels and fictions, which are a sort of poems, do belong to
the catalogue of this cursed library. The plays, I say, in which there are so
many passages, that have a tendency to overthrow all piety, that one whose
name is Bedford, has extracted near seven thousand instances of them,
from the plays chiefly of but five years preceding; and says awfully upon
them, "They are national sins, and therefore call for national plagues; and
if God should enter into judgment, all the blood in the nation would not
be able to atone for them." How much do I wish that such pestilences,
and indeed all those worse than Egyptian toads (the spawns of a Butler,
and a Brown, and a Ward, and a company whose name is legion!) might
never crawl into your chamber! The unclean spirits that come like frogs
out of the mouth of the dragon, and of the beast; which go forth unto
the young people of the earth, and expose them to be dealt withal as the
enemies of God, in the battle of the great day of the Almighty. As for
those wretched scribbles of madmen, My Son, touch them not, taste them
not, handle them not: thou wilt perish in the using of them. They are, the
dragons whose contagious breath peoples the dark retreats of death. To
much better purpose will an excellent but an envied Blackmore feast you,
than those vile rhapsodies (of that *vinum daemonum*) which you will find
always leave a taint upon your mind, and among other ill effects, will sensibly indispose you to converse with the holy oracles of God your Saviour.

But there is, what I may rather call a parenthesis, than a digression,
which this may be not altogether an improper place for the introducing of.

(There has been a deal of ado about a style; so much, that I must offer
you my sentiments upon it. There is a way of writing, wherein the author
endeavors, that the reader may have something to the purpose in every
paragraph. There is not only a vigor sensible in every sentence, but the
paragraph is embellished with profitable references, even to something
beyond what is directly spoken. Formal and painful quotations are not
studied; yet all that could be learnt from them is insinuated. The writer
pretends not unto reading, yet he could not have writ as he does if he had
not read very much in his time; and his composures are not only a cloth
of gold, but also struck with as many jewels, as the gown of a Russian
ambassador. This way of writing has been decried by many, and is at
this day more than ever so, for the same reason, that in the old story, the
grapes were decried: that they were not ripe. A lazy, ignorant, conceited
set of authors, would persuade the whole tribe, to lay aside that way of
writing, for the same reason that one would have persuaded his brethren
to part with the encumbrance of their bushy tails. But however fashion

and humour may prevail, they must not think that the club at their coffee-house is all the world, but there will always be those, who will in this case be governed by indisputable reason: and who will think, that the real excellency of a book will never lie in saying of little; that the less one has for his money in a book, 'tis really the more valuable for it; and that the less one is instructed in a book, and the more of superfluous margin, and superficial harangue, and the less of substantial matter one has in it, the more 'tis to be accounted of? And if a more massy way of writing be never so much disgusted at this day, a better gust will come on, as will some other thing, *quae jam cecidere.* In the meantime, nothing appears to me more impertinent and ridiculous than the modern way (I cannot say rule: for they have none!) of criticizing. The blades that set up for critics, I know not who constituted or commissioned 'em!—they appear to me, for the most part as contemptible, as they are a supercilious generation. For indeed no two of them have the same style; and they are as intolerably cross-grained and severe in their censures one upon another, as they are upon the rest of mankind. But while each of them, conceitedly enough, sets up for the standard of perfection, we are entirely at a loss which fire to follow. Nor can you easily find any one thing wherein they agree for their style, except perhaps a perpetual care to give us jejune and empty pages, without such touches of erudition (so to speak in the style of an ingenious traveler) as may make the discourses less tedious, and more enriching, to the mind of him that peruses them. There is much talk of a florid style, obtaining among the pens, that are most in vogue; but how often would it puzzle one, even with the best glasses to find the flowers! And if they were to be chastised for it, it would be with as much of jus-tice, as Jerome was, for being a Ciceronian. After all, every man will have his own style, which will distinguish him as much as his gait: and if you can attain to that which I have newly described, but always writing so as to give an easy conveyance unto your ideas, I would not have you by any scourging be driven out of your gait; but if you must confess a fault in it, make a confession like that of the lad unto his father while he was beating him for his versifying.

However, since every man will have his own style, I would pray, that we may learn to treat one another with mutual civilities, and condescensions, and handsomely indulge one another in this, as gentlemen do in other matters.

I wonder what ails people that they can't let Cicero write in the style of Cicero, and Seneca write in the (much other!) style of Seneca; and own that both may please in their several ways. But I will freely tell you; what has made me consider the humourists that set up for critics upon style, as the most unregardable set of mortals in the world, is this! Far more illustrious critics than any of those to whom I am now bidding defiance, and no less men than your Erasmus's, and your Crotius's, have taxed the

Greek style of the New Testament, with I know not what solecisms and barbarisms; and, how many learned folks have obsequiously run away with the notion! Whereas 'tis an ignorant and an insolent whimsy; which they have been guilty of. It may be (and particularly by an ingenious Blackwall, it has been) demonstrated, that the gentlemen are mistaken in every one of their pretended instances; all the unquestionable classics, may be brought in, to convince them of their mistakes. Those glorious oracles are as pure Greek as ever was written in the world; and so correct, so noble, so sublime in their style, that never anything under the cope of heaven, but the Old Testament, has equaled it.

JONATHAN EDWARDS

Jonathan Edwards (1703–1758) was, according to scholar Perry Miller, the first homegrown American philosopher. A pastor in Northampton, Massachusetts, he published several collections of sermons, his most famous (and perhaps the most famous in American history) being "Sinners in the Hands of an Angry God." Though Edwards was a learned intellectual, versed in Enlightenment ideas, "Sinners" is an atypically fierce performance, giving no quarter. Calvinist pastors of the seventeenth century had been less inclined to threaten punishments that might await their congregants after death. The eighteenth-century turn to hellfire sermons was a by-product of the First Great Awakening, an evangelical movement that swept up Edwards and was meant to stir listeners' emotions to conversion. Some today may think his willingness to consign little children to damnation monstrous; others may find curious his presumption to inhabit the mind of God. But none can dispute his rhetorical powers, drawing on psychology and logic to expose sinners' rationalizations, and using trenchant images to pile climax upon climax.

Sinners in the Hands
of an Angry God

(1741)

Their foot shall slide in due time. (Deut. XXXII. 35)

In this verse is threatened the vengeance of God on the wicked unbeliev-ing Israelites, who were God's visible people, and who lived under the means of grace; but who, notwithstanding all God's wonderful works towards them, remained (as ver. 28.) void of counsel, having no under-standing in them. Under all the cultivations of heaven, they brought forth bitter and poisonous fruit: as in the two verses next preceding the text.— The expression I have chosen for my text, *Their foot shall slide in due time,* seems to imply the following things, relating to the punishment and destruction to which these wicked Israelites were exposed.

1. That they were always exposed to *destruction;* as one that stands or walks in slippery places is always exposed to fall. This is implied in the manner of their destruction coming upon them, being represented by their foot sliding. The same is expressed. Psalm lxxiii. 18. "Surely thou didst set them in slippery places; thou castedst them down into destruc-tion."

2. It implies, that they were always exposed to sudden unexpected destruction. As he that walks in slippery places is every moment liable to fall, he cannot foresee one moment whether he shall stand or fall the next; and when he does fall, he falls at once without warning: Which is also expressed in Psalm lxxiii. 18, 19. "Surely thou didst set them in slippery places; thou castedst them down into destruction: How are they brought into desolation as in a moment!"

3. Another thing implied is, that they are liable to fall of the selves, without being thrown down by the hand of another; as he that stands or walks on slippery ground needs nothing but his own weight to throw him down.

4. That the reason why they are not fallen already, and do not fall now, is only that God's appointed time is not come. For it is said, that when that due time, or appointed times comes, *their foot shall slide.* Then they shall be left to fall, as they are inclined by their own weight. God will not hold them up in these slippery places any longer, but will let them go; and then, at that very instant, they shall fall into destruction; as he that stands on such slippery declining ground, on the edge of a pit, he cannot stand alone, when he is let go he immediately falls and is lost.

The observation from the words that I would now insist upon is this.—"There is nothing that keeps wicked men at any one moment out of hell, but the mere pleasure of God"—By the *mere* pleasure of God, I mean his *sovereign* pleasure, his arbitrary will, restrained by no obligation, hindered by no manner of difficulty, any more than if nothing else but God's mere will had in the least degree, or in any respect whatsoever, any hand in the preservation of wicked men one moment.—The truth of this observation may appear by the following considerations.

1. There is no want of *power* in God to cast wicked men into hell at any moment. Men's hands cannot be strong when God rises up. The strongest have no power to resist him, nor can any deliver out of his hands.—He is not only able to cast wicked men into hell, but he can most easily do it. Sometimes an earthly prince meets with a great deal of difficulty to subdue a rebel, who has found means to fortify himself, and has made himself strong by the numbers of his followers. But it is not so with God. There is no fortress that is any defence from the power of God. Though hand join in hand, and vast multitudes of God's enemies combine and associate themselves, they are easily broken in pieces. They are as great heaps of light chaff before the whirlwind; or large quantities of dry stubble before devouring flames. We find it easy to tread on and crush a worm that we see crawling on the earth; so it is easy for us to cut or singe a slender thread that any thing hangs by: thus easy is it for God, when he pleases, to cast his enemies down to hell. What are we, that we should think to stand before him, whose rebuke the earth trembles, and before whom the rocks are thrown down?

2. They *deserve* to be cast into hell; so that divine justice never stands in the way, it makes no objection against God's using his power at any moment to destroy them. Yea, on the contrary, justice calls aloud for an infinite punishment of their sins. Divine justice says of the tree that brings forth such grapes of Sodom, "Cut it down, why cumbereth it the ground?" Luke xiii. 7. The sword of divine justice is every moment brandished over their heads, and it is nothing but the hand of arbitrary mercy, and God's mere will, that holds it back.

3. They are already under a sentence of *condemnation* to hell. They do not only justly deserve to be cast down thither, but the sentence of the law of God, that eternal and immutable rule of righteousness that God has fixed between him and mankind, is gone out against them, and stands against them; so that they are bound over already to hell. John iii. 18. "He that believeth not is condemned already." So that every unconverted man properly belongs to hell; that is his place; from thence he is, John viii. 23. "Ye are from beneath": And thither he is bound; it is the place that justice, and God's word, and the sentence of his unchangeable law assign to him.

4. They are now the objects of that very same *anger* and wrath of God, that is expressed in the torments of hell. And the reason why they do not go down to hell at each moment, is not because God, in whose power

they are, is not then very angry with them; as he is with many miserable creatures now tormented in hell, who there feel and bear the fierceness of his wrath. Yea, God is a great deal more angry with great numbers that are now on earth: yea, doubtless, with many that are now in this congregation, who it may be are at ease, than he is with many of those who are now in the flames of hell.

So that it is not because God is unmindful of their wickedness and does not resent it, that he does not let loose his hand and cut them off. God is not altogether such an one as themselves though they may imagine him to be so. The wrath of God burns against them, their damnation does not slumber; the pit is prepared, the fire is made ready, the furnace is now hot, ready to receive them; the flames do now rage and glow. The glittering sword is whet, and held over them, and the pit hath opened its mouth under them.

5. The *devil* stands ready to fall upon them, and seize them as his own, at what moment God shall permit him. They belong to him; he has their souls in his possession, and under his dominion. The scripture represents them as his goods, Luke xi. 12. The devils watch them; they are ever by them at their right hand; they stand waiting for them, like greedy hungry lions that see their prey, and expect to have it, but are for the present kept back. If God should withdraw his hand, by which they are restrained, they would in one moment fly upon their poor souls. The old serpent is gaping for them; hell opens its mouth wide to receive them; and if God should permit it, they would be hastily swallowed up and lost.

6. There are in the souls of wicked men those hellish *principles* reigning, that would presently kindle and flame out into hell fire, if it were not for God's restraints. There is laid in the very nature of carnal men, a foundation for the torments of hell. There are those corrupt principles, in reigning power in them, and in full possession of them; that are seeds of hell fire. These principles are active and powerful exceeding violent in their nature, and if it were not for the restraining hand of God upon them, they would soon break out, they would flame out after the same manner as the same corruptions, the same enmity does in the hearts of damned souls, and would beget the same torments as they do in them. The souls of the wicked are in scripture compared to the troubled sea, Isa, lvii. 20. For the present, God restrains their wickedness by his mighty power, as he does the raging waves of the troubled sea, saying, "Hitherto shalt thou come, but no further": but if God should withdraw that restraining power, it would soon carry all before it. Sin is the ruin and misery of the soul; it is destructive in its nature; and if God should leave it without restraint, there would need nothing else to make the soul perfectly miserable. The corruption of the heart of man is immoderate and boundless in its fury; and while wicked men live here, it is like fire pent up by God's restraints, whereas if it were let loose, it would set on fire

the course of nature; and as the heart is now a sink of sin, so if sin was not restrained, it would immediately turn the soul into a fiery oven, or a furnace of fire and brimstone.

7. It is no security to wicked men for one moment, that there are no visible means of death at hand. It is no security to a natural man, that he is now in health, and that he does not see which way he should now immediately go out of the world by any accident, and that there is no visible danger in any respect in his circumstances. The manifold and continual experience of the world in all ages, shows this is no evidence, that a man is not on the very brink of eternity, and that the next step will not be into another world. The unseen, unthought-of ways and means of persons going suddenly out of the world are innumerable and inconceivable. Unconverted men walk over the pit of hell on a rotten covering, and there are innumerable places in this covering so weak that they will not bear their weight, and these places are not seen. The arrows of death fly unseen at noonday; the sharpest sight cannot discern them. God has so many different unsearchable ways of taking wicked men out of the world and sending them to hell, that there is nothing to make it appear, that God had need to be at the expence of a miracle, or go out of the ordinary course of his providence, to destroy any wicked man, at any moment. All the means that there are of sinners going out of the world, are so in God's hands, and so universally and absolutely subject to his power and determination, that it does not depend at all the less on the mere will of God, whether sinners shall at any moment go to hell, than if means were never made use of, or at all concerned in the case.

8. Natural men's prudence and care to preserve their own lives, or the care of others to preserve them, do not secure them a moment. To this, divine providence and universal experience do also bear testimony. There is this clear evidence that men's own wisdom is no security to them from death; that if it were otherwise we should see some difference between the wise and politic men of the world, and others, with regard to their liableness to early and unexpected death: but how is it in fact? Eccles. ii. 16. "How dieth the wise man? even as the fool."

9. All wicked men's pains and *contrivance* which they use to escape hell, while they continue to reject Christ, and so remain wicked men, do not secure them from hell one moment. Almost every natural man that hears of hell, flatters himself that he shall escape it; he depends upon himself for his own security; he flatters himself in what he has done, in what he is now doing, or what he intends to do. Every one lays out matters in his own mind how he shall avoid damnation, and flatters himself that he contrives well for himself, and that his schemes will not fail. They hear indeed that there are but few saved, and that the greater part of men that have died heretofore are gone to hell; but each one imagines that he lays out matters better for his own escape than others have done. He does

not intend to come to that place of torment; he says within himself, that he intends to take effectual care, and to order matters so for himself as not to fail.

But the foolish children of men miserably delude themselves in their own schemes, and in confidence in their own strength and wisdom; they trust to nothing but a shadow. The greater part of those who heretofore have lived under the same means of grace, and are now dead, are undoubtedly gone to hell; and it was not because they were not as wise as those who are now alive: it was not because they did not lay out matters as well for themselves to secure their own escape. If we could speak with them, and inquire of them, one by one, whether they expected, when alive, and when they used to hear about hell, ever to be the subjects of that misery: we doubtless, should hear one and another reply, "No, I never intended to come here: I had laid out matters otherwise in my mind; I thought I should contrive well for myself: I thought my scheme good. I intended to take effectual care; but it came upon me unexpected; I did not look for it at that time, and in that manner; it came as a thief: Death outwitted me: God's wrath was too quick for me. Oh, my cursed foolishness! I was flattering myself, and pleasing myself with vain dreams of what I would do hereafter; and when I was saying, Peace and safety, then suddenly destruction came upon me."

10. God has laid himself under no *obligation,* by any promise, to keep any natural man out of hell one moment. God certainly has made no promises either of eternal life, or of any deliverance or preservation from eternal death, but what are contained in the covenant of grace, the promises that are given in Christ, in whom all the promises yea and amen. But surely they have no interest in the promises of the covenant of grace who are not the children of the covenant, who do not believe in any of the promises, and have no interest in the Mediator of the covenant.

So that, whatever some have imagined and pretended about promises made to natural men's earnest seeking and knocking, it is plain and manifest, that whatever pains a natural man takes in religion, whatever prayers he makes, till he believes in Christ, God is under no manner of obligation to keep him a moment from eternal destruction.

So that, thus it is that natural men are held in the hand of God, over the pit of hell; they have deserved the fiery pit, and are already sentenced to it; and God is dreadfully provoked, his anger is as great towards them as to those that are actually suffering the executions of the fierceness of his wrath in hell, and they have done nothing in the least to appease or abate that anger, neither is God in the least bound by any promise to hold them up one moment; the devil is waiting for them, hell is gaping for them, the flames gather and flash about them, and would fain lay hold on them, and swallow them up; the fire pent up in their own hearts is struggling to break out: and they have no interest in any Mediator, there are no means within reach that can be any security to them. In short, they have no refuge, nothing to take hold of; all that preserves them every moment is the mere arbitrary will, and uncovenanted, unobliged forbearance of an incensed God.

Application

The use of this awful subject may be for awakening unconverted persons in this congregation. This that you have heard is the case of every one of you that are out of Christ.—That world of misery, that lake of burning brimstone, is extended abroad under you. There is the dreadful pit of the glowing flames of the wrath of God; there is hell's wide gaping mouth open; and you have nothing to stand upon, nor any thing to take hold of; there is nothing between you and hell but the air; it is only the power and mere pleasure of God that holds you up.

You probably are not sensible of this; you find you are kept out of hell, but do not see the hand of God in it; but look at other things, as the good state of your bodily constitution, your care of your own life, and the means you use for your own preservation. But indeed these things are nothing; if God should withdraw his hand, they would avail no more to keep you from falling, than the thin air to hold up a person that is suspended in it.

Your wickedness makes you as it were heavy as lead, and to tend downwards with great weight and pressure towards hell; and if God should let you go, you would immediately sink and swiftly descend and plunge into the bottomless gulf, and your healthy constitution, and your own care and prudence, and best contrivance, and all your righteousness, would have no more influence to uphold you and keep you out of hell, than a spider's web would have to stop a fallen rock. Were it not for the sovereign pleasure of God, the earth would not bear you one moment; for you are a burden to it; the creation groans with you; the creature is made subject to the bondage of your corruption, not willingly; the sun does not willingly shine upon you to give you light to serve sin and Satan; the earth does not willingly yield her increase to satisfy your lusts; nor is it willingly a stage for your wickedness to be acted upon; the air does not willingly serve you for breath to maintain the flame of life in your vitals, while you spend your life in the service of God's enemies. God's creatures are good, and were made for men to serve God with, and do not willingly subserve to any other purpose, and groan when they are abused to purposes so directly contrary to their nature and end. And the world would spew you out, were it not for the sovereign hand of him who hath subjected it in hope. There are black clouds of God's wrath now hanging directly over your heads, full of the dreadful storm, and big with thunder; and were it not for the restraining hand of God, it would immediately burst forth upon you. The sovereign pleasure of God, for the present, stays his rough wind; otherwise it would come with fury, and your destruction would come like a whirlwind, and you would be like the chaff of the summer threshing floor.

The wrath of God is like great waters that are dammed for the present; they increase more and more, and rise higher and higher, till an outlet is given; and the longer the stream is stopped, the more rapid and mighty is its course, when once it is let loose. It is true, that judgment against your evil works has not been executed hitherto; the floods of God's vengeance have been withheld; but your guilt in the mean time is constantly increasing, and you are every day treasuring up more wrath; the waters are constantly rising, and waxing more and more mighty; and there is nothing but the mere pleasure of God, that holds the waters back, that are unwilling to be stopped, and press hard to go forward. If God should only withdraw his hand from the floodgate, it would immediately fly open, and the fiery floods of the fierceness and wrath of God, would rush forth with inconceivable fury, and would come upon you with omnipotent power; and if your strength were ten thousand times greater than it is, yea, ten thousand times greater than the strength of the stoutest, sturdiest devil in hell, it would be nothing to withstand or endure it.

The bow of God's wrath is bent, and the arrow made ready on the string, and justice bends the arrow at your heart, and strains the bow, and it is nothing but the mere pleasure of God, and that of an angry God, without any promise or obligation at all, that keeps the arrow one moment from being made drunk with your blood. Thus all you that never passed under a great change of heart, by the mighty power of the Spirit of God upon your souls; all you that were never born again, and made new creatures, and raised from being dead in sin, to a state of new, and before altogether unexperienced light and life, are in the hands of an angry God. However you may have reformed your life in many things, and may have had religious affections, and may keep up a form of religion in your families and closets, and in the house of God, it is nothing but his mere pleasure that keeps you from being this moment swallowed up in everlasting destruction. However unconvinced you may now be of the truth of what you hear, by and by you will be fully convinced of it. Those that are gone from being in the like circumstances with you, see that it was so with them; for destruction came suddenly upon most of them; when they expected nothing of it, and while they were saying, Peace and safety: now they see, that those things on which they depended for peace and safety, were nothing but thin air and empty shadows.

The God that holds you over the pit of hell, much as one holds a spider, or some loathsome insect over the first, abhors you, and is dreadfully provoked: his wrath towards you burns like fire; he looks upon you as worthy of nothing else, but to be cast into the fire; he is of purer eyes than to bear to have you in his sight; you are ten thousand times more abominable in his eyes, than the most hateful venomous serpent is in ours. You have offended him infinitely more than ever a stubborn rebel did his prince; and yet it is nothing but his hand that holds you from falling into the fire every moment. It is to be ascribed to nothing else, that you did not go to hell the last night; that you was suffered to awake again in this world, after you closed your eyes to sleep. And there is no other reason to be given, why you have not dropped into hell since you arose in the morning, but that God's hand has held you up. There is no other reason to be given why you have not gone to hell, since you have sat here in the house of God, provoking his pure eyes by your sinful wicked manner of attending his solemn worship. Yea, there is nothing else that is to be given as a reason why you do not this very moment drop down into hell.

O sinner! Consider the fearful danger you are in: it is a great furnace of wrath, a wide and bottomless pit, full of the fire of wrath, that you are held over in the hand of that God, whose wrath is provoked and incensed as much against you, as against many of the damned in hell. You hang by a slender thread, with the flames of divine wrath flashing about it, and ready every moment to singe it, and burn it asunder; and you have no interest in any Mediator, and nothing to lay hold of to save yourself, nothing to keep off the flames of wrath, nothing of your own, nothing that you ever have done, nothing that you can do, to induce God to spare you one moment.—And consider here more particularly,

1. *Whose* wrath it is: it is the wrath of the infinite God. If it were only the wrath of man, though it were of the most potent prince, it would be comparatively little to be regarded. The wrath of kings is very much dreaded, especially of absolute monarchs, who have the possessions and lives of their subjects wholly in their power, to be disposed of at their mere will. Prov. xx. 2. "The fear of a king is as the roaring of a lion: Whoso provoketh him to anger, sinneth against his own soul." The subject that very much enrages an arbitrary prince, is liable to suffer the most extreme torments that human art can invent, or human power can inflict. But the greatest earthly potentates in their greatest majesty and strength, and when clothed in their greatest terrors, are but feeble, despicable worms of the dust, in comparison of the great and almighty Creator and King of heaven and earth. It is but little that they can do, when most enraged, and when they have exerted the utmost of their fury. All the kings of the earth, before God, are as grasshoppers; they are nothing, and less than nothing: both their love and their hatred is to be despised. The wrath of the great King of kings, is as much more terrible than theirs, as his majesty is greater. Luke xii. 4, 5. "And I say unto you, my friends, Be not

afraid of them that kill the body, and after that, have no more that they can do. But I will forewarn you whom you shall fear: fear him, which after he hath killed, hath power to cast into hell: yea, I say unto you, Fear him."

2. It is the *fierceness* of his wrath that you are exposed to. We often read of the fury of God; as in Isaiah lix. 18. "According to their deeds, accordingly he will repay fury to his adversaries." So Isaiah lxvi. 15. "For behold, the Lord will come with fire, and with his chariots like a whirl-wind, to render his anger with fury, and his rebuke with flames of fire." And in many other places. So, Rev. xix. 15. we read of "the wine press of the fierceness and wrath of Almighty God." The words are exceeding ter-rible. If it had only been said, "the wrath of God," the words would have implied that which is infinitely dreadful: but it is "the fierceness and wrath of God." The fury of God! the fierceness of Jehovah! Oh, how dread-ful must that be! Who can utter or conceive what such expressions carry in them! But it is also "the fierceness and wrath of *Almighty* God." As though there would be a very great manifestation of his almighty power in what the fierceness of his wrath should inflict, as though omnipotence should be as it were enraged, and exerted, as men are wont to exert their strength in the fierceness of their wrath. Oh! then, what will be the conse-quence. What will become of the poor worms that shall suffer it! Whose hands can be strong? And whose heart can endure? To what a dreadful, inexpressible, inconceivable depth of misery must the poor creature be sunk who shall be the subject of this!

Consider this, you that are here present, that yet remain in an unregen-erate state. That God will execute the fierceness of his anger, implies, that he will inflict wrath without any pity. When God beholds the ineffable extremity of your case, and sees your torment to be so vastly dispropor-tioned to your strength, and sees how your poor soul is crushed, and sinks down, as it were, into an infinite gloom; he will have no compassion upon you, he will not forbear the executions of his wrath, or in the least lighten his hand; there shall be no moderation or mercy, nor will God then at all stay his rough wind; he will have no regard to your welfare, nor be at all careful lest you should suffer too much in any other sense, than only that you shall *not suffer beyond what strict justice requires.* Nothing shall be withheld, because it is so hard for you to bear. Ezek. viii. 18. "Therefore will I also deal in fury: mine eye shall not spare, neither will I have pity; and though they cry in mine ears with a loud voice, yet I will not hear them." Now God stands ready to pity you; this is a day of mercy; you may cry now with some encouragement of obtaining mercy. But when once the day of mercy is past, your most lamentable and dolorous cries and shrieks will be in vain; you will be wholly lost and thrown away of God, as to any regard to your welfare. God will have no other use to put you to, but to suffer misery; you shall be continued in being to no other end; for you will be a vessel of wrath fitted to destruction; and there will be no other use of this vessel, but to be filled full of wrath. God will be so far from pitying you when you cry to him, that it is said he will only "laugh and mock," Prov. i. 25, 26, &c.

How awful are those words, Isa. lxiii. 3, which are the words of the great God. "I will tread them in mine anger, and will trample them in my fury, and their blood shall be sprinkled upon my garments, and I will stain all my raiment." It is perhaps impossible to conceive of words that carry in them greater manifestations of these three things, *viz.* contempt, and hatred, and fierceness of indignation. If you cry to God to pity you, he will be so far from pitying you in your doleful case, or showing you the least regard or favour, that instead of that, he will only tread you under foot. And though he will know that you cannot bear the weight of omnipotence treading upon you, yet he will not regard that, but he will crush you under his feet without mercy: he will crush out your blood, and make it fly, and it shall be sprinkled on his garments, so as to stain all his raiment. He will not only hate you, but he will have you, in the utmost contempt: no place shall be thought fit for you, but under his feet to be trodden down as the mire of the streets.

3. The misery you are exposed to is that which God will inflict to that end, that he might show what that wrath of Jehovah is. God hath had it on his heart to show to angels and men, both how excellent his love is, and also how terrible his wrath is. Sometimes earthly kings have a mind to show how terrible their wrath is, by the extreme punishments they would execute on those that would provoke them. Nebuchadnezzar, that mighty and haughty monarch of the Chaldean empire, was willing to show his wrath when enraged with Shadrach, Meshech, and Abednego. and accordingly gave orders that the burning fiery furnace should be heated seven times hotter than it was before; doubtless, it was raised to the utmost degree of fierceness that human art could raise it. But the great God is also willing to show his wrath, and magnify his awful majesty and mighty power in the extreme sufferings of his enemies. Rom. ix. 22. "What if God, willing to show his wrath, and to make his power known, endure with much long-suffering the vessels of wrath fitted to destruction?" And seeing this is his design, and what he has determined, even to show how terrible the unrestrained wrath, the fury and fierceness of Jehovah is, he will do it to effect. There will be something accomplished and brought to pass that will be dreadful with a witness. When the great and angry God hath risen up and executed his awful vengeance on the poor sinner, and the wretch is actually suffering the infinite weight and power of his indignation, then will God call upon the whole universe to behold that awful majesty and mighty power that is to be seen in it. Isa. xxxiii. 12–14. "And the people shall be as the burnings of lime, as thorns

cut up shall they be burnt in the fire. Hear ye that are far off, what I have done; and ye that are near, acknowledge my might. The sinners in Zion are afraid; fearfulness hath surprised the hypocrites," &c.

Thus it will be with you that are in an unconverted state, if you continue in it; the infinite might, and majesty, and terribleness of the omnipotent God shall be magnified upon you, in the ineffable strength of your torments. You shall be tormented in the presence of the holy angels, and in the presence of the Lamb; and when you shall be in this state of suffering, the glorious inhabitants of heaven shall go forth and look on the awful spectacle, that they may see what the wrath and fierceness of the Almighty is; and when they have seen it, they will fall down and adore that great power and majesty. Isa. lxvi. 23, 24. "And it shall come to pass, that from one new moon to another, and from one sabbath to another, shall all flesh come to worship before me, saith the Lord. And they shall go forth and look upon the carcasses of the men that have transgressed against me; for their worm shall not die, neither shall their fire be quenched, and they shall be an abhorring unto all flesh."

4. It is *everlasting* wrath. It would be dreadful to suffer this fierceness and wrath of Almighty God one moment; but you must suffer it to all eternity. There will be no end to this exquisite horrible misery. When you look forward, you shall see a long for ever, a boundless duration before you, which will swallow up your thoughts, and amaze your soul; and you will absolutely despair of ever having any deliverance, any end, any miti-gation, any rest at all. You will know certainly that you must wear out long ages, millions of millions of ages, in wrestling and conflicting with this almighty merciless vengeance; and then when you have so done, when so many ages have actually been spent by you in this manner, you will know that all is but a point to what remains. So that your punishment will indeed be infinite. Oh, who can express what the state of a soul in such circumstances is! All that we can possibly say about it, gives but a very feeble, faint representation of it; it is inexpressible and inconceivable: For "who knows the power of God's anger?"

How dreadful is the state of those that are daily and hourly in the danger of this great wrath and infinite misery! But this is the dismal case of every soul in this congregation that has not been born again, however moral and strict, sober and religious, they may otherwise be. Oh that you would consider it, whether you be young or old! There is reason to think, that there are many in this congregation now hearing this discourse, that will actually be the subjects of this very misery to all eternity. We know not who they are, or in what seats they sit, or what thoughts they now have. It may be they are now at ease, and hear all these things without much disturbance, and are now flattering themselves that they are not the persons, promising themselves that they shall escape. If we knew that there was one person, and but one, in the whole congregation, that was to be the subject of this misery, what an awful thing would it be to think of! If we knew who it was, what an awful sight would it be to see such a person! How might all the rest of the congregation lift up a lamentable and bitter cry over him! But, alas! instead of one, how many is it likely will remember this discourse in hell? And it would be a wonder, if some that are now present should not be in hell in a very short time, even before this year is out. And it would be no wonder if some persons, that now sit here, in some seats of this meeting-house, in health, quiet and secure, should be there before to-morrow morning. Those of you that finally continue in a natural condition, that shall keep out of hell longest will be there in a little time! your damnation does not slumber; it will come swiftly, and, in all probability, very suddenly upon many of you. You have reason to wonder that you are not already in hell. It is doubtless the case of some whom you have seen and known, that never deserved hell more than you, and that heretofore appeared as likely to have been now alive as you. Their case is past all hope; they are crying in extreme misery and perfect despair; but here you are in the land of the living and in the house of God, and have an opportunity to obtain salvation. What would not those poor damned hopeless souls give for one day's opportunity such as you now enjoy!

And now you have an extraordinary opportunity, a day wherein Christ has thrown the door of mercy wide open, and stands in calling and crying with a loud voice to poor sinners; a day wherein many are flocking to him, and pressing into the kingdom of God. Many are daily coming from the east, west, north and south; many that were very lately in the same miserable condition that you are in, are now in a happy state, with their hearts filled with love to him who has loved them, and washed them from their sins in his own blood, and rejoicing in hope of the glory of God. How awful is it to be left behind at such a day! To see so many others feasting, while you are pining and perishing! To see so many rejoicing and singing for joy of heart, while you have cause to mourn for sorrow of heart, and howl for vexation of spirit! How can you rest one moment in such a condition? Are not your souls as precious as the souls of the people at Suffield, where they are flocking from day to day to Christ?

Are there not many here who have lived long in the world, and are not to this day born again? and so are aliens from the commonwealth of Israel, and have done nothing ever since they have lived, but treasure up wrath against the day of wrath? Oh, sirs, your case, in an especial manner, is extremely dangerous. Your guilt and hardness of heart is extremely great. Do you not see how generally persons of your years are passed over and left, in the present remarkable and wonderful dispensation of God's mercy? You had need to consider yourselves, and awake thoroughly out of sleep. You cannot bear the fierceness and wrath of the infinite God.—And you, young men, and young women, will you neglect this precious season which you now enjoy, when so many others of your age are renouncing all youthful vanities, and flocking to Christ? You especially have now an extraordinary opportunity; but if you neglect it, it will soon be with you as with those persons who spent all the precious days of youth in sin, and are now come to such a dreadful pass in blindness and hardness.—And you, children, who are unconverted, do not you know that you are going down to hell, to bear the dreadful wrath of that God, who is now angry with you every day and every night? Will you be content to be the children of the devil, when so many other children in the land are converted, and are become the holy and happy children of the King of kings?

And let every one that is yet of Christ, and hanging over the pit of hell, whether they be old men and women, or middle aged, or young people, or little children, now hearken to the loud calls of God's word and providence. This acceptable year of the Lord, a day of such great favours to some, will doubtless be a day of as remarkable vengeance to others. Men's hearts harden, and their guilt increases apace at such a day as this, if they neglect their souls; and never was there so great danger of such persons being given up to hardness of heart and blindness of mind. God seems now to be hastily gathering in his elect in all parts of the land: and probably the greater part of adult persons that ever shall be saved, will be brought in now in a little time, and that it will be as it was on the great out-pouring of the Spirit upon the Jews in the apostles' days; the election will obtain, and the rest will be blinded. If this should be the case with you, you will eternally curse this day, and will curse the day that ever you was born, to see such a season of the pouring out of God's Spirit, and will wish that you had died and gone to hell before you had seen it. Now undoubtedly it is, as it was in the days of John the Baptist, the axe is in an extraordinary manner laid at the root of the trees, that every tree which brings not forth good fruit, may be hewn down and cast into the fire.

Therefore, let every one that is out of Christ, now awake and fly from the wrath to come. The wrath of Almighty God is now undoubtedly hanging over a great part of this congregation: Let every one fly out of Sodom: "Haste and escape for your lives, look not behind you, escape to the mountain, lest you be consumed."

THOMAS PAINE

Thomas Paine (1737–1809) began life as an Englishman, but at the age of thirty-seven, after a succession of failed enterprises, he migrated to America in 1774. Two years later, the American Revolution began, and he published the pamphlet Common Sense *to rally the troops. It sold more than one hundred thousand copies and bolstered the resolve of the colonials to separate from Great Britain. The pamphlet's title enunciated Paine's democratic belief that ordinary people were fully capable of reasoning and self-rule. Its style—clear, vigorous, refusing deference toward the monarch—underscored his desire to address the masses. In the section below, Paine works through a set of negations that deflate each excuse loyalists to the British Crown might proffer, arguing that it is too late, the fight for independence is joined, what counts is the future, not tradition, and America is poised to offer the world a sanctuary for freedom and republicanism. Paine continued to propound radical ideas in his* Rights of Man *and* The Age of Reason, *sometimes getting into trouble as a result. John Adams wrote: "I know not whether any man in the world has had more influence on its inhabitants or affairs for the last thirty years than Tom Paine."*

Thoughts on the Present State of American Affairs

(1776)

In the following pages I offer nothing more than simple facts, plain arguments, and common sense; and have no other preliminaries to settle with the reader, than that he will divest himself of prejudice and prepossession, and suffer his reason and his feelings to determine for themselves; that he will put on, or rather that he will not put *off*, the true character of a man, and generously enlarge his views beyond the present day.

Volumes have been written on the subject of the struggle between England and America. Men of all ranks have embarked in the controversy, from different motives, and with various designs; but all have been ineffectual, and the period of debate is closed. Arms, as the last resource, decide the contest; the appeal was the choice of the king, and the continent hath accepted the challenge.

It hath been reported of the late Mr. Pelham (who tho' an able minister was not without his faults) that on his being attacked in the house of commons, on the score, that his measures were only of a temporary kind, replied *"they will last my time."* Should a thought so fatal and unmanly possess the colonies in the present contest, the name of ancestors will be remembered by future generations with detestation.

The sun never shined on a cause of greater worth. 'Tis not the affair of a city, a country, a province, or a kingdom, but of a continent—of at least one eighth part of the habitable globe. 'Tis not the concern of a day, a year, or an age; posterity are virtually involved in the contest, and will be more or less affected, even to the end of time, by the proceedings now. Now is the seed time of continental union, faith and honor. The least fracture now will be like a name engraved with the point of a pin on the tender rind of a young oak; the wound will enlarge with the tree, and posterity read it in full grown characters.

By referring the matter from argument to arms, a new era for politics is struck; a new method of thinking hath arisen. All plans, proposals, &c. prior to the nineteenth of April, i. e. to the commencement of hostilities, are like the almanacks of the last year; which, though proper then, are superceded and useless now. Whatever was advanced by the advocates on either side of the question then, terminated in one and the same point, viz. a union with Great-Britain; the only difference between the parties was the method of effecting it; the one proposing force, the other friendship; but it hath so far happened that the first hath failed, and the second hath withdrawn her influence.

As much hath been said of the advantages of reconciliation, which, like an agreeable dream, hath passed away and left us as we were, it is but right, that we should examine the contrary side of the argument, and inquire into some of the many material injuries which these colonies sustain, and always will sustain, by being connected with, and dependant on Great-Britain. To examine that connexion and dependance, on the principles of nature and common sense, to see what we have to trust to, if separated, and what we are to expect, if dependant.

I have heard it asserted by some, that as America hath flourished under her former connexion with Great-Britain, that the same connexion is necessary towards her future happiness, and will always have the same effect. Nothing can be more fallacious than this kind of argument. We may as well assert that because a child has thrived upon milk, that it is never to have meat, or that the first twenty years of our lives is to become a precedent for the next twenty. But even this is admitting more than is true, for I answer roundly, that America would have flourished as much, and probably much more, had no European power had any thing to do with her. The commerce, by which she hath enriched herself are the necessaries of life, and will always have a market while eating is the custom of Europe.

But she has protected us, say some. That she hath engrossed us is true, and defended the continent at our expence as well as her own is admitted, and she would have defended Turkey from the same motive, viz. the sake of trade and dominion.

Alas, we have been long led away by ancient prejudices, and made large sacrifices to superstition. We have boasted the protection of Great-Britain, without considering, that her motive was *interest* not *attachment;* that she did not protect us from *our enemies* on *our account,* but from *her enemies* on *her own account,* from those who had no quarrel with us on any other account, and who will always be our enemies on the *same account.* Let Britain wave her pretensions to the continent, or the continent throw off the dependance, and we should be at peace with France and Spain were they at war with Britain. The miseries of Hanover last war ought to warn us against connexions.

It hath lately been asserted in parliament, that the colonies have no relation to each other but through the parent country, i. e. that Pennsylvania and the Jerseys, and so on for the rest, are sister colonies by the way of England; this is certainly a very round-about way of proving relationship, but it is the nearest and only true way of proving enemyship, if I may so call it. France and Spain never were, nor perhaps ever will be our enemies as *Americans,* but as our being the *subjects of Great-Britain.*

But Britain is the parent country, say some. Then the more shame upon her conduct. Even brutes do not devour their young, nor savages make war upon their families; wherefore the assertion, if true, turns to her reproach; but it happens not to be true, or only partly so, and the phrase *parent* or *mother country* hath been jesuitically adopted by the king and his parasites, with a low papistical design of gaining an unfair bias on the credulous weakness of our minds. Europe, and not England, is the parent country of America. This new world hath been the asylum for the persecuted lovers of civil and religious liberty from *every part* of Europe. Hither have they fled, not from the tender embraces of the mother, but from the cruelty of the monster; and it is so far true of England, that the same tyranny which drove the first emigrants from home, pursues their descendants still.

In this extensive quarter of the globe, we forget the narrow limits of three hundred and sixty miles (the extent of England) and carry our friendship on a larger scale; we claim brotherhood with every European Christian, and triumph in the generosity of the sentiment.

It is pleasant to observe by what regular gradations we surmount the force of local prejudice, as we enlarge our acquaintance with the world. A man born in any town in England divided into parishes, will naturally associate most with his fellow parishioners (because their interests in many cases will be common) and distinguish him by the name of *neighbour;* if he meet him but a few miles from home, he drops the narrow idea of a street, and salutes him by the name of *townsman;* if he travel out of the county, and meet him in any other, he forgets the minor divisions of street and town, and calls him *countryman,* i. e. *county-man;* but if in their foreign excursions they should associate in France or any other part of *Europe,* their local remembrance would be enlarged into that of *Englishmen.* And by a just parity of reasoning, all Europeans meeting in America, or any other quarter of the globe, are *countrymen;* for England, Holland, Germany, or Sweden, when compared with the whole, stand in the same places on the larger scale, which the divisions of street, town, and county do on the smaller ones; distinctions too limited for continental minds. Not one third of the inhabitants, even of this province, are of English descent. Wherefore I reprobate the phrase of parent or mother country applied to England only, as being false, selfish, narrow and ungenerous.

But admitting, that we were all of English descent, what does it amount to? Nothing. Britain, being now an open enemy, extinguishes every other name and title: And to say that reconciliation is our duty, is truly farcical. The first king of England, of the present line (William the Conqueror) was a Frenchman, and half the Peers of England are descendants from the same country; wherefore, by the same method of reasoning, England ought to be governed by France.

Much hath been said of the united strength of Britain and the colonies, that in conjunction they might bid defiance to the world. But this is mere presumption; the fate of war is uncertain, neither do the expressions mean any thing; for this continent would never suffer itself to be drained of inhabitants, to support the British arms in either Asia, Africa, or Europe.

Besides, what have we to do with setting the world at defiance? Our plan is commerce, and that, well attended to, will secure us the peace and friendship of all Europe; because, it is the interest of all Europe to have America a *free port*. Her trade will always be a protection, and her barrenness of gold and silver secure her from invaders.

I challenge the warmest advocate for reconciliation, to shew, a single advantage that this continent can reap, by being connected with Great-Britain. I repeat the challenge, not a single advantage is derived. Our corn will fetch its price in any market in Europe, and our imported goods must be paid for buy them where we will.

But the injuries and disadvantages we sustain by that connection, are without number; and our duty to mankind at large, as well as to ourselves, instruct us to renounce the alliance: Because, any submission to, or dependance on Great-Britain, tends directly to involve this continent in European wars and quarrels; and sets us at variance with nations, who would otherwise seek our friendship, and against whom, we have neither anger nor complaint. As Europe is our market for trade, we ought to form no partial connection with any part of it. It is the true interest of America to steer clear of European contentions, which she never can do, while by her dependance on Britain, she is made the make-weight in the scale of British politics.

Europe is too thickly planted with kingdoms to be long at peace, and whenever a war breaks out between England and any foreign power, the trade of America goes to ruin, *because of her connection with Britain.* The next war may not turn out like the last, and should it not, the advocates for reconciliation now will be wishing for separation then, because, neutrality in that case, would be a safer convoy than a man of war. Every thing that is right or natural pleads for separation. The blood of the slain, the weeping voice of nature cries, 'TIS TIME TO PART. Even the distance at which the Almighty hath placed England and America, is a strong and natural proof, that the authority of the one, over the other, was never the design of Heaven. The time likewise at which the continent was discovered, adds weight to the argument, and the manner in which it was peopled encreases the force of it. The reformation was preceded by the discovery of America, as if the Almighty graciously meant to open a sanctuary to the persecuted in future years, when home should afford neither friendship nor safety.

The authority of Great-Britain over this continent, is a form of government, which sooner or later must have an end: And a serious mind can draw no true pleasure by looking forward, under the painful and positive conviction, that what he calls "the present constitution" is merely temporary. As parents, we can have no joy, knowing that *this government* is not sufficiently lasting to ensure any thing which we may bequeath to posterity: And by a plain method of argument, as we are running the next generation into debt, we ought to do the work of it, otherwise we use them meanly and pitifully. In order to discover the line of our duty rightly, we should take our children in our hand, and fix our station a few years farther into life; that eminence will present a prospect, which a few present fears and prejudices conceal from our sight.

Though I would carefully avoid giving unnecessary offence, yet I am inclined to believe, that all those who espouse the doctrine of reconciliation, may be included within the following descriptions. Interested men, who are not to be trusted; weak men, who cannot see; prejudiced men, who will not see; and a certain set of moderate men, who think better of the European world than it deserves; and this last class, by an ill-judged deliberation, will be the cause of more calamities to this continent, than all the other three.

It is the good fortune of many to live distant from the scene of sorrow; the evil is not sufficiently brought to their doors to make them feel the precariousness with which all American property is possessed. But let our imaginations transport us for a few moments to Boston, that seat of wretchedness will teach us wisdom, and instruct us for ever to renounce a power in whom we can have no trust. The inhabitants of that unfortunate city, who but a few months ago were in ease and affluence, have now, no other alternative than to stay and starve, or turn out to beg. Endangered by the fire of their friends if they continue within the city, and plundered by the soldiery if they leave it. In their present condition they are prisoners without the hope of redemption, and in a general attack for their relief, they would be exposed to the fury of both armies.

Men of passive tempers look somewhat lightly over the offences of Britain, and, still hoping for the best, are apt to call out, *"Come, come, we shall be friends again, for all this."* But examine the passions and feelings of mankind, Bring the doctrine of reconciliation to the touchstone of nature, and then tell me, whether you can hereafter love, honour, and faithfully serve the power that hath carried fire and sword into your land? If you cannot do all these, then are you only deceiving yourselves, and by your delay bringing ruin upon posterity. Your future connection with Britain, whom you can neither love nor honour, will be forced and unnatural, and being formed only on the plan of present convenience, will in a little time fall into a relapse more wretched than the first. But if you say, you can still pass the violations over, then I ask, Hath your house been burnt? Hath your property been destroyed before your face? Are your wife and children destitute of a bed to lie on, or bread to live on? Have you lost a parent or a child by their hands, and yourself the ruined and wretched survivor? If you have not, then are you not a judge of those who have. But if you have, and still can shake hands with the murderers, then are you unworthy the name of husband, father, friend, or lover, and whatever may be your rank or tide in life, you have the heart of a coward, and the spirit of a sycophant.

This is not inflaming or exaggerating matters, but trying them by those feelings and affections which nature justifies, and without which, we should be incapable of discharging the social duties of life, or enjoying the felicities of it. I mean not to exhibit horror for the purpose of provoking revenge, but to awaken us from fatal and unmanly slumbers, that we may pursue determinately some fixed object. It is not in the power of Britain or of Europe to conquer America, if she do not conquer herself by *delay* and *timidity*. The present winter is worth an age if rightly employed, but if lost or neglected, the whole continent will partake of the misfortune; and there is no punishment which that man will not deserve, be he who, or what, or where he will, that may be the means of sacrificing a season so precious and useful.

It is repugnant to reason, to the universal order of things to all examples from former ages, to suppose, that this continent can longer remain subject to any external power. The most sanguine in Britain does not think so. The utmost stretch of human wisdom cannot, at this time, compass a plan short of separation, which can promise the continent even a year's security. Reconciliation is *now* a falacious dream. Nature hath deserted the connexion, and Art cannot supply her place. For, as Milton wisely expresses, "never can true reconcilement grow where wounds of deadly hate have pierced so deep."

Every quiet method for peace hath been ineffectual. Our prayers have been rejected with disdain; and only tended to convince us, that nothing flatters vanity, or confirms obstinacy in Kings more than repeated petitioning—and nothing hath contributed more than that very measure to make the Kings of Europe absolute: Witness Denmark and Sweden. Wherefore, since nothing but blows will do, for God's sake, let us come to a final separation, and not leave the next generation to be cutting throats, under the violated unmeaning names of parent and child.

To say, they will never attempt it again is idle and visionary, we thought so at the repeal of the stamp-act, yet a year or two undeceived us; as well may we suppose that nations, which have been once defeated, will never renew the quarrel.

As to government matters, it is not in the power of Britain to do this continent justice: The business of it will soon be too weighty, and intricate, to be managed with any tolerable degree of convenience, by a power, so distant from us, and so very ignorant of us; for if they cannot conquer us, they cannot govern us. To be always running three or four thousand miles with a tale or a petition, waiting four or five months for an answer, which when obtained requires five or six more to explain it in, will in a few years be looked upon as folly and childishness—There was a time when it was proper, and there is a proper time for it to cease.

Small islands not capable of protecting themselves, are the proper objects for kingdoms to take under their care; but there is something very absurd, in supposing a continent to be perpetually governed by an island. In no instance hath nature made the satellite larger than its primary planet, and as England and America, with respect to each other, reverses the common order of nature, it is evident they belong to different systems: England to Europe, America to itself.

I am not induced by motives of pride, party, or resentment to espouse the doctrine of separation and independence; I am clearly, positively, and conscientiously persuaded that it is the true interest of this continent to be so; that every thing short of *that* is mere patchwork, that it can afford no lasting felicity,—that it is leaving the sword to our children, and shrinking back at a time, when, a little more, a little farther, would have rendered this continent the glory of the earth.

As Britain hath not manifested the least inclination towards a compromise, we may be assured that no terms can be obtained worthy the acceptance of the continent, or any ways equal to the expence of blood and treasure we have been already put to.

The object, contended for, ought always to bear some just proportion to the expence. The removal of North, or the whole detestable junto, is a matter unworthy the millions we have expended. A temporary stoppage of trade, was an inconvenience, which would have sufficiently ballanced the repeal of all the acts complained of, had such repeals been obtained; but if the whole continent must take up arms, if every man must be a soldier, it is scarcely worth our while to fight against a contemptible ministry only. Dearly, dearly, do we pay for the repeal of the acts, if that is all we fight for; for in a just estimation, it is as great a folly to pay a Bunker-hill price for law, as for land. As I have always considered the independancy of this continent, as an event, which sooner or later must arrive, so from the late rapid progress of the continent to maturity, the event could not be far off. Wherefore, on the breaking out of hostilities, it was not worth the while to have disputed a matter, which time would have finally redressed, unless we meant to be in earnest; otherwise, it is like wasting an estate on a suit at law, to regulate the trespasses of a tenant, whose lease is just expiring. No man was a warmer wisher for reconciliation than myself, before the fatal nineteenth of April 1775, but the moment the event of that day was made known, I rejected the hardened, sullen tempered Pharoah of England for ever; and disdain the wretch, that with the pretended title of FATHER OF HIS PEOPLE can unfeelingly hear of their slaughter, and composedly sleep with their blood upon his soul.

But admitting that matters were now made up, what would be the event? I answer, the ruin of the continent. And that for several reasons.

First. The powers of governing still remaining in the hands of the king, he will have a negative over the whole legislation of this continent. And as he hath shewn himself such an inveterate enemy to liberty, and discovered such a thirst for arbitrary power; is he, or is he not, a proper man to say to these colonies, *"You shall make no laws but what I please."* And is there any inhabitant in America so ignorant, as not to know, that according to what is called the *present constitution,* that this continent can make no laws but what the king gives leave to; and is there any man so unwise, as not to see, that (considering what has happened) he will suffer no law to be made here, but such as suit *his* purpose. We may be as effectually enslaved by the want of laws in America, as by submitting to laws made for us in England. After matters are made up (as it is called) can there be any doubt, but the whole power of the crown will be exerted, to keep this continent as low and humble as possible? Instead of going forward we shall go backward, or be perpetually quarrelling or ridiculously petitioning.—We are already greater than the king wishes us to be, and will he not hereafter endeavour to make us less? To bring the matter to one point. Is the power who is jealous of our prosperity, a proper power to govern us? Whoever says *No* to this question is an *independant,* for independancy means no more, than, whether we shall make our own laws, or, whether the king, the greatest enemy this continent hath, or can have, shall tell us *"there shall be no laws but such as I like."*

But the king you will say has a negative in England; the people there can make no laws without his consent. In point of right and good order, there is something very ridiculous, that a youth of twenty-one (which hath often happened) shall say to several millions of people, older and wiser than himself, I forbid this or that act of yours to be law. But in this place I decline this sort of reply, though I will never cease to expose the absurdity of it, and only answer, that England being the King's residence, and America not so, makes quite another case. The king's negative *here* is ten times more dangerous and fatal than it can be in England, for *there* he will scarcely refuse his consent to a bill for putting England into as strong a state of defence as possible, and in America he would never suffer such a bill to be passed.

America is only a secondary object in the system of British politics, England consults the good of *this* country, no farther than it answers her *own* purpose. Wherefore, her own interest leads her to suppress the growth of *ours* in every case which doth not promote her advantage, or in the least interferes with it. A pretty state we should soon be in under such a second-hand government, considering what has happened! Men do not change from enemies to friends by the alteration of a name: And in order to shew that reconciliation now is a dangerous doctrine, I affirm, *that it would be policy in the king at this time, to repeal the acts for the sake of reinstating himself in the government of the provinces;* in order, that HE MAY ACCOMPLISH BY CRAFT AND SUBTILTY, IN THE LONG RUN, WHAT HE CANNOT DO BY FORCE AND VIOLENCE IN THE SHORT ONE. Reconciliation and ruin are nearly related.

Secondly. That as even the best terms, which we can expect to obtain, can amount to no more than a temporary expedient, or a kind of government by guardianship, which can last no longer than till the colonies come of age, so the general face and state of things, in the interim, will be unsettled and unpromising. Emigrants of property will not choose to come to a country whose form of government hangs but by a thread, and who is every day tottering on the brink of commotion and disturbance; and numbers of the present inhabitants would lay hold of the interval, to dispose of their effects, and quit the continent.

But the most powerful of all arguments, is, that nothing but independence, i. e. a continental form of government, can keep the peace of the continent and preserve it inviolate from civil wars. I dread the event of a reconciliation with Britain now, as it is more than probable, that it will be followed by a revolt somewhere or other, the consequences of which may be far more fatal than all the malice of Britain.

Thousands are already ruined by British barbarity; (thousands more will probably suffer the same fate). Those men have other feelings than us who have nothing suffered. All they now possess is liberty, what they before enjoyed is sacrificed to its service, and having nothing more to lose, they disdain submission. Besides, the general temper of the colonies, towards a British government, will be like that of a youth, who is nearly out of his time; they will care very little about her. And a government which cannot preserve the peace, is no government at all, and in that case we pay our money for nothing; and pray what is it that Britain can do, whose power will be wholly on paper, should a civil tumult break out the very day after reconciliation? I have heard some men say, many of whom I believe spoke without thinking, that they dreaded an independence, fearing that it would produce civil wars. It is but seldom that our first thoughts are truly correct, and that is the case here; for there are ten times more to dread from a patched up connexion than from independence. I make the sufferers case my own, and I protest, that were I driven from house and home, my property destroyed, and my circumstances ruined, that as a man, sensible of injuries, I could never relish the doctrine of reconciliation, or consider myself bound thereby.

The colonies have manifested such a spirit of good order and obedience to continental government, as is sufficient to make every reasonable person easy and happy on that head. No man can assign the least pretence for his fears, on any other grounds, than such as are truly childish and ridiculous, viz. that one colony will be striving for superiority over another.

Where there are no distinctions there can be no superiority, perfect equality affords no temptation. The republics of Europe are all (and we may say always) in peace. Holland and Swisserland are without wars, foreign or domestic: Monarchical governments, it is true, are never long at rest; the crown itself is a temptation to enterprizing ruffians at *home;*

and that degree of pride and insolence ever attendant on regal authority, swells into a rupture with foreign powers, in instances, where a republican government, by being formed on more natural principles, would negotiate the mistake.

If there is any true cause of fear respecting independance, it is because no plan is yet laid down. Men do not see their way out—Wherefore, as an opening into that business, I offer the following hints; at the same time modestly affirming, that I have no other opinion of them myself, than that they may be the means of giving rise to something better. Could the straggling thoughts of individuals be collected, they would frequently form materials for wise and able men to improve into useful matter.

Let the assemblies be annual, with a President only. The representation more equal. Their business wholly domestic, and subject to the authority of a Continental Congress.

Let each colony be divided into six, eight, or ten, convenient districts, each district to send a proper number of delegates to Congress, so that each colony send at least thirty. The whole number in Congress will be at least 390. Each Congress to sit and to choose a president by the following method. When the delegates are met, let a colony be taken from the whole thirteen colonies by lot, after which, let the whole Congress choose (by ballot) a president from out of the delegates of that province. In the next Congress, let a colony be taken by lot from twelve only, omitting that colony from which the president was taken in the former Congress, and so proceeding on till the whole thirteen shall have had their proper rotation. And in order that nothing may pass into a law but what is satisfactorily just, not less than three fifths of the Congress to be called a majority.—He that will promote discord, under a government so equally formed as this, would have joined Lucifer in his revolt.

But as there is a peculiar delicacy, from whom, or in what manner, this business must first arise, and as it seems most agreeable and consistent that it should come from some intermediate body between the governed and the governors, that is, between the Congress and the people, let a CONTINENTAL CONFERENCE be held, in the following manner, and for the following purpose.

A committee of twenty-six members of Congress, viz. two for each colony. Two members from each House of Assembly, or Provincial Convention; and five representatives of the people at large, to be chosen in the capital city or town of each province, for, and in behalf of the whole province, by as many qualified voters as shall think proper to attend from all parts of the province for that purpose; or, if more convenient, the representatives may be chosen in two or three of the most populous parts thereof. In this conference, thus assembled, will be united, the two grand principles of business, *knowledge* and *power*. The members of Congress, Assemblies, or Conventions, by having had experience in national concerns, will be able and useful counsellors, and the whole, being impowered by the people, will have a truly legal authority.

The conferring members being met, let their business be to frame a CONTINENTAL CHARTER, or Charter of the United Colonies; (answering to what is called the Magna Charta of England) fixing the number and manner of choosing members of Congress, members of Assembly, with their date of sitting, and drawing the line of business and jurisdiction between them: (Always remembering, that our strength is continental, not provincial:) Securing freedom and property to all men, and above all things, the free exercise of religion, according to the dictates of conscience; with such other matter as is necessary for a charter to contain. Immediately after which, the said Conference to dissolve, and the bodies which shall be chosen comformable to the said charter, to be the legislators and governors of this continent for the time being: Whose peace and happiness, may God preserve, Amen.

Should any body of men be hereafter delegated for this or some similar purpose, I offer them the following extracts from that wise observer on governments *Dragonetti*. "The science" says he "of the politician consists in fixing the true point of happiness and freedom. Those men would deserve the gratitude of ages, who should discover a mode of government that contained the greatest sum of individual happiness, with the least national expense." (Dragonetti on virtue and rewards.)

But where says some is the King of America? I'll tell you Friend, he reigns above, and doth not make havoc of mankind like the Royal Brute of Britain. Yet that we may not appear to be defective even in earthly honors, let a day be solemnly set apart for proclaiming the charter; let it be brought forth placed on the divine law, the word of God; let a crown be placed thereon, by which the world may know, that so far as we approve of monarchy, that in America THE LAW IS KING. For as in absolute governments the King is law, so in free countries the law *ought* to be King; and there ought to be no other. But lest any ill use should afterwards arise, let the crown at the conclusion of the ceremony be demolished, and scattered among the people whose right it is.

A government of our own is our natural right: And when a man seriously reflects on the precariousness of human affairs, he will become convinced, that it is infinitely wiser and safer, to form a constitution of our own in a cool deliberate manner, while we have it in our power, than to trust such an interesting event to time and chance. If we omit it now, some Massanello may hereafter arise, who laying hold of popular disquietudes, may collect together the desperate and the discontented, and by assuming to themselves the powers of government, may sweep away the liberties of the continent like a deluge. Should the government of America return again into the hands of Britain, the tottering situation of things, will be a temptation for some desperate adventurer to try his fortune; and in such a case, what relief can Britain give? Ere she could hear the news, the fatal business might be done; and ourselves suffering like the wretched Britons under the oppression of the Conqueror. Ye that oppose independance now, ye know not what ye do; ye are opening a door to eternal tyranny, by keeping vacant the seat of government. There are thousands, and tens of thousands, who would think it glorious to expel from the continent, that barbarous and hellish power, which hath stirred up the Indians and Negroes to destroy us, the cruelty hath a double guilt, it is dealing brutally by us, and treacherously by them.

To talk of friendship with those in whom our reason forbids us to have faith, and our affections wounded through a thousand pores instruct us to detest, is madness and folly. Every day wears out the little remains of kindred between us and them, and can there be any reason to hope, that as the relationship expires, the affection will increase, or that we shall agree better, when we have ten times more and greater concerns to quarrel over than ever?

Ye that tell us of harmony and reconciliation, can ye restore to us the time that is past? Can ye give to prostitution its former innocence? Neither can ye reconcile Britain and America. The last cord now is broken, the people of England are presenting addresses against us. There are injuries which nature cannot forgive; she would cease to be nature if she did. As well can the lover forgive the ravisher of his mistress, as the continent forgive the murders of Britain. The Almighty hath implanted in us these unextinguishable feelings for good and wise purposes. They are the guardians of his image in our hearts. They distinguish us from the herd of common animals. The social compact would dissolve, and justice be extirpated from the earth, or have only a casual existence were we callous to the touches of affection. The robber, and the murderer, would often escape unpunished, did not the injuries which our tempers sustain, provoke us into justice.

O ye that love mankind! Ye that dare oppose, not only the tyranny, but the tyrant, stand forth! Every spot of the old world is overrun with oppression. Freedom hath been hunted round the globe. Asia, and Africa, have long expelled her.—Europe regards her like a stranger, and England hath given her warning to depart. O! receive the fugitive, and prepare in time an asylum for mankind.

J. HECTOR ST. JOHN DE CRÈVECOEUR

J. Hector St. John de Crèvecoeur (1735–1813) was born in France, the child of minor nobility; he moved first to Canada as a young man and subsequently to America, where he bought and worked a farm in upstate New York. His 1782 book, Letters from an American Farmer, *is a series of essays purported to be written by an agriculturist named James to an English minister. In the newly coined American tradition of self-invention, Crèvecoeur not only altered his name but constructed an idealized persona of a simple, unaffected Yankee who championed the good life of homebody self-sufficiency. Its author loved birds and was fascinated as well by bees, snakes, ants; the book is filled with charming nature descriptions that won over European readers, including William Hazlitt, Lord Byron, and Samuel Taylor Coleridge, who accepted his picture of the New World as pure and pristine. It was the first book by an American author to be universally praised abroad. Today Crèvecoeur is seen as a forerunner of Henry David Thoreau, Wendell Berry, and other American nature writers who expressed an attachment to the land.*

On the Situation, Feelings, and Pleasures, of an American Farmer

(1782)

As you are the first enlightened European I have ever had the pleasure of being acquainted with, you will not be surprised that I should, according to your earnest desire and my promise, appear anxious of preserving your friendship and correspondence. By your accounts, I observe a material difference subsists between your husbandry, modes, and customs, and ours; everything is local; could we enjoy the advantages of the English farmer, we should be much happier, indeed, but this wish, like many others, implies a contradiction; and could the English farmer have some of those privileges we possess, they would be the first of their class in the world. Good and evil I see is to be found in all societies, and it is in vain to seek for any spot where those ingredients are not mixed. I therefore rest satisfied, and thank God that my lot is to be an American farmer, instead of a Russian boor, or an Hungarian peasant. I thank you kindly for the idea, however dreadful, which you have given me of their lot and condition; your observations have confirmed me in the justness of my ideas, and I am happier now than I thought myself before. It is strange that misery, when viewed in others, should become to us a sort of real good, though I am far from rejoicing to hear that there are in the world men so thoroughly wretched; they are no doubt as harmless, industrious, and willing to work as we are. Hard is their fate to be thus condemned to a slavery worse than that of our negroes. Yet when young I entertained some thoughts of selling my farm. I thought it afforded but a dull repetition of the same labours and pleasures. I thought the former tedious and heavy, the latter few and insipid; but when I came to consider myself as divested of my farm, I then found the world so wide, and every place so full, that I began to fear lest there would be no room for me. My farm, my house, my barn, presented to my imagination objects from which I adduced quite new ideas; they were more forcible than before. Why should not I find myself happy, said I, where my father was before? He left me no good books it is true, he gave me no other education than the art of reading and writing; but he left me a good farm, and his experience; he left me free from debts, and no kind of difficulties to struggle with.—I married, and this perfectly reconciled me to my situation; my wife rendered my house all at once cheerful and pleasing; it no longer appeared gloomy and solitary as before; when I went to work in my fields I worked with more alacrity and sprightliness; I felt that I did not work for myself alone, and this encouraged me much. My wife would often come with her knitting in her hand, and sit under the shady trees, praising the straightness of my furrows, and the docility of my horses; this swelled my heart and made everything light and pleasant, and I regretted that I had not married before.

I felt myself happy in my new situation, and where is that station which can confer a more substantial system of felicity than that of an American farmer, possessing freedom of action, freedom of thoughts, ruled by a mode of government which requires but little from us? I owe nothing, but a pepper corn to my country, a small tribute to my king, with loyalty, and due respect; I know no other landlord than the lord of all land, to whom I owe the most sincere gratitude. My father left me three hundred and seventy-one acres of land, forty-seven of which are good timothy meadow, an excellent orchard, a good house, and a substantial barn. It is my duty to think how happy I am that he lived to build and to pay for all these improvements; what are the labours which I have to undergo, what are my fatigues when compared to his, who had everything to do, from the first tree he felled to the finishing of his house? Every year I kill from 1500 to 2000 weight of pork, 1200 of beef, half a dozen of good wethers in harvest: of fowls my wife has always a great stock: what can I wish more? My negroes are tolerably faithful and healthy; by a long series of industry and honest dealings, my father left behind him the name of a good man; I have but to tread his paths to be happy and a good man like him. I know enough of the law to regulate my little concerns with propriety, nor do I dread its power; these are the grand outlines of my situation, but as I can feel much more than I am able to express, I hardly know how to proceed.

When my first son was born, the whole train of my ideas were suddenly altered; never was there a charm that acted so quickly and powerfully; I ceased to ramble in imagination through the wide world; my excursions since have not exceeded the bounds of my farm, and all my principal pleasures are now centred within its scanty limits: but at the same time there is not an operation belonging to it in which I do not find some food for useful reflections. This is the reason, I suppose, that when you was here, you used, in your refined style, to denominate me the farmer of feelings; how rude must those feelings be in him who daily holds the axe or the plough, how much more refined on the contrary those of the European, whose mind is improved by education, example, books, and by every acquired advantage! Those feelings, however, I will delineate as well as I can, agreeably to your earnest request.

When I contemplate my wife, by my fire-side, while she either spins, knits, darns, or suckles our child, I cannot describe the various emotions of love, of gratitude, of conscious pride, which thrill in my heart and often overflow in involuntary tears. I feel the necessity, the sweet pleasure of acting my part, the part of an husband and father, with an attention and propriety which may entitle me to my good fortune. It is true these pleasing images vanish with the smoke of my pipe, but though they disappear from my mind, the impression they have made on my heart is indelible. When I play with the infant, my warm imagination runs forward, and eagerly anticipates his future temper and constitution. I would willingly open the book of fate, and know in which page his destiny is delineated; alas! where is the father who in those moments of paternal ecstasy can delineate one half of the thoughts which dilate his heart? I am sure I cannot; then again I fear for the health of those who are become so dear to me, and in their sicknesses I severely pay for the joys I experienced while they were well. Whenever I go abroad it is always involuntary. I never return home without feeling some pleasing emotion, which I often suppress as useless and foolish. The instant I enter on my own land, the bright idea of property, of exclusive right, of independence exalt my mind. Precious soil, I say to myself, by what singular custom of law is it that thou wast made to constitute the riches of the freeholder? What should we American farmers be without the distinct possession of that soil? It feeds, it clothes us, from it we draw even a great exuberancy, our best meat, our richest drink, the very honey of our bees comes from this privileged spot. No wonder we should thus cherish its possession, no wonder that so many Europeans who have never been able to say that such portion of land was theirs, cross the Atlantic to realise that happiness. This formerly rude soil has been converted by my father into a pleasant farm, and in return it has established all our rights; on it is founded our rank, our freedom, our power as citizens, our importance as inhabitants of such a district. These images I must confess I always behold with pleasure, and extend them as far as my imagination can reach: for this is what may be called the true, and the only philosophy of an American farmer.

Pray do not laugh in thus seeing an artless countryman tracing himself through the simple modifications of his life; remember that you have required it, therefore with candour, though with diffidence, I endeavour to follow the thread of my feelings, but I cannot tell you all. Often when I plough my low ground, I place my little boy on a chair which screws to the beam of the plough—its motion and that of the horses please him, he is perfectly happy and begins to chat. As I lean over the handle, various are the thoughts which crowd into my mind. I am now doing for him, I say, what my father formerly did for me, may God enable him to live that he may perform the same operations for the same purposes when I am worn out and old! I relieve his mother of some trouble while I have him with me, the odoriferous furrow exhilarates his spirits, and seems to do the child a great deal of good, for he looks more blooming since I have adopted that practice; can more pleasure, more dignity be added to that primary occupation? The father thus ploughing with his child, and to feed his family, is inferior only to the emperor of China ploughing as an example to his kingdom. In the evening when I return home through my low grounds, I am astonished at the myriads of insects which I perceive dancing in the beams of the setting sun. I was before scarcely acquainted with their existence, they are so small that it is difficult to distinguish them; they are carefully improving this short evening space, not daring to expose themselves to the blaze of our meridian sun. I never see an egg brought on my table but I feel penetrated with the wonderful change it would have undergone but for my gluttony; it might have been a gentle useful hen leading her chickens with a care and vigilance which speaks shame to many women. A cock perhaps, arrayed with the most

majestic plumes, tender to its mate, bold, courageous, endowed with
an astonishing instinct, with thoughts, with memory, and every distinguishing characteristic of the reason of man. I never see my trees drop
their leaves and their fruit in the autumn, and bud again in the spring,
without wonder; the sagacity of those animals which have long been
the tenants of my farm astonish me: some of them seem to surpass even
men in memory and sagacity. I could tell you singular instances of that
kind. What then is this instinct which we so debase, and of which we
are taught to entertain so diminutive an idea? My bees, above any other
tenants of my farm, attract my attention and respect; I am astonished to
see that nothing exists but what has its enemy, one species pursue and live
upon the other: unfortunately our kingbirds are the destroyers of those
industrious insects; but on the other hand, these birds preserve our fields
from the depredation of crows which they pursue on the wing with great
vigilance and astonishing dexterity.

Thus divided by two interested motives, I have long resisted the desire
I had to kill them, until last year, when I thought they increased too
much, and my indulgence had been carried too far; it was at the time of
swarming when they all came and fixed themselves on the neighbouring trees, from whence they catched those that returned loaded from the
fields. This made me resolve to kill as many as I could, and I was just
ready to fire, when a bunch of bees as big as my fist, issued from one
of the hives, rushed on one of the birds, and probably stung him, for he
instantly screamed, and flew, not as before, in an irregular manner, but in
a direct line. He was followed by the same bold phalanx, at a considerable
distance, which unfortunately becoming too sure of victory, quitted their
military array and disbanded themselves. By this inconsiderate step they
lost all that aggregate of force which had made the bird fly off. Perceiving their disorder he immediately returned and snapped as many as he
wanted; nay, he had even the impudence to alight on the very twig from
which the bees had drove him. I killed him and immediately opened his
craw, from which I took 171 bees; I laid them all on a blanket in the sun,
and to my great surprise 54 returned to life, licked themselves clean, and
joyfully went back to the hive; where they probably informed their companions of such an adventure and escape, as I believe had never happened
before to American bees! I draw a great fund of pleasure from the quails
which inhabit my farm; they abundantly repay me, by their various notes
and peculiar tameness, for the inviolable hospitality I constantly show
them in the winter. Instead of perfidiously taking advantage of their great
and affecting distress, when nature offers nothing but a barren universal
bed of snow, when irresistible necessity forces them to my barn doors, I
permit them to feed unmolested; and it is not the least agreeable spectacle
which that dreary season presents, when I see those beautiful birds, tamed
by hunger, intermingling with all my cattle and sheep, seeking insecurity

for the poor scanty grain which but for them would be useless and lost. Often in the angles of the fences where the motion of the wind prevents the snow from settling, I carry them both chaff and grain; the one to feed them, the other to prevent their tender feet from freezing fast to the earth as I have frequently observed them to do.

I do not know an instance in which the singular barbarity of man is so strongly delineated, as in the catching and murthering those harmless birds, at that cruel season of the year. Mr. ——, one of the most famous and extraordinary farmers that has ever done honour to the province of Connecticut, by his timely and humane assistance in a hard winter, saved this species from being entirely destroyed. They perished all over the country, none of their delightful whistlings were heard the next spring, but upon this gentleman's farm; and to his humanity we owe the continuation of their music. When the severities of that season have dispirited all my cattle, no farmer ever attends them with more pleasure than I do; it is one of those duties which is sweetened with the most rational satisfaction. I amuse myself in beholding their different tempers, actions, and the various effects of their instinct now powerfully impelled by the force of hunger. I trace their various inclinations, and the different effects of their passions, which are exactly the same as among men; the law is to us precisely what I am in my barn yard, a bridle and check to prevent the strong and greedy from oppressing the timid and weak. Conscious of superiority, they always strive to encroach on their neighbours; unsatisfied with their portion, they eagerly swallow it in order to have an opportunity of taking what is given to others, except they are prevented. Some I chide, others, unmindful of my admonitions, receive some blows. Could victuals thus be given to men without the assistance of any language, I am sure they would not behave better to one another, nor more philosophically than my cattle do.

The same spirit prevails in the stable; but there I have to do with more generous animals, there my well-known voice has immediate influence, and soon restores peace and tranquillity. Thus by superior knowledge I govern all my cattle as wise men are obliged to govern fools and the ignorant. A variety of other thoughts crowd on my mind at that peculiar instant, but they all vanish by the time I return home. If in a cold night I swiftly travel in my sledge, carried along at the rate of twelve miles an hour, many are the reflections excited by surrounding circumstances. I ask myself what sort of an agent is that which we call frost? Our minister compares it to needles, the points of which enter our pores. What is become of the heat of the summer; in what part of the world is it that the N. W. keeps these grand magazines of nitre? when I see in the morning a river over which I can travel, that in the evening before was liquid, I am astonished indeed! What is become of those millions of insects which played in our summer fields, and in our evening meadows; they were so puny and so delicate, the period of their existence was so short, that one cannot help wondering how they could learn, in that short space, the sublime art to hide themselves and their offspring in so perfect a manner as to baffle the rigour of the season, and preserve that precious embryo of life, that small portion of ethereal heat, which if once destroyed would destroy the species! Whence that irresistible propensity to sleep so common in all those who are severely attacked by the frost. Dreary as this season appears, yet it has like all others its miracles, it presents to man a variety of problems which he can never resolve; among the rest, we have here a set of small birds which never appear until the snow falls; contrary to all others, they dwell and appear to delight in that element.

It is my bees, however, which afford me the most pleasing and extensive themes; let me look at them when I will, their government, their industry, their quarrels, their passions, always present me with something new; for which reason, when weary with labour, my common place of rest is under my locust-tree, close by my bee-house. By their movements I can predict the weather, and can tell the day of their swarming; but the most difficult point is, when on the wing, to know whether they want to go to the woods or not. If they have previously pitched in some hollow trees, it is not the allurements of salt and water, of fennel, hickory leaves, etc., nor the finest box, that can induce them to stay; they will prefer those rude, rough habitations to the best polished mahogany hive. When that is the case with mine, I seldom thwart their inclinations; it is in freedom that they work: were I to confine them, they would dwindle away and quit their labour. In such excursions we only part for a while; I am generally sure to find them again the following fall. This elopement of theirs only adds to my recreations; I know how to deceive even their superlative instinct; nor do I fear losing them, though eighteen miles from my house, and lodged in the most lofty trees, in the most impervious of our forests. I once took you along with me in one of these rambles, and yet you insist on my repeating the detail of our operations: it brings back into my mind many of the useful and entertaining reflections with which you so happily beguiled our tedious hours.

After I have done sowing, by way of recreation, I prepare for a week's jaunt in the woods, not to hunt either the deer or the bears, as my neighbours do, but to catch the more harmless bees. I cannot boast that this chase is so noble, or so famous among men, but I find it less fatiguing, and full as profitable; and the last consideration is the only one that moves me. I take with me my dog, as a companion, for he is useless as to this game; my gun, for no man you know ought to enter the woods without one; my blanket, some provisions, some wax, vermilion, honey, and a small pocket compass. With these implements I proceed to such woods as are at a considerable distance from any settlements. I carefully examine whether they abound with large trees, if so, I make a small fire on some flat stones, in a convenient place; on the fire I put some wax; close by this fire, on another stone, I drop honey in distinct drops, which I surround with small quantities of vermilion, laid on the stone; and then I retire carefully to watch whether any bees appear. If there are any in that neighbourhood, I rest assured that the smell of the burnt wax will unavoidably attract them; they will soon find out the honey, for they are fond of preying on that which is not their own; and in their approach they will necessarily tinge themselves with some particles of vermilion, which will adhere long to their bodies. I next fix my compass, to find out their course, which they keep invariably straight, when they are returning home loaded. By the assistance of my watch, I observe how long those are returning which are marked with vermilion. Thus possessed of the course, and, in some measure, of the distance, which I can easily guess at, I follow the first, and seldom fail of coming to the tree where those republics are lodged. I then mark it; and thus, with patience, I have found out sometimes eleven swarms in a season; and it is inconceivable what a quantity of honey these trees will sometimes afford. It entirely depends on the size of the hollow, as the bees never rest nor swarm till it is all replenished; for like men, it is only the want of room that induces them to quit the maternal hive. Next I proceed to some of the nearest settlements, where I procure proper assistance to cut down the trees, get all my prey secured, and then return home with my prize. The first bees I ever procured were thus found in the woods, by mere accident; for at that time I had no kind of skill in this method of tracing them. The body of the tree being perfectly sound, they had lodged themselves in the hollow of one of its principal limbs, which I carefully sawed off and with a good deal of labour and industry brought it home, where I fixed it up again in the same position in which I found it growing. This was in April; I had five swarms that year, and they have been ever since very prosperous. This business generally takes up a week of my time every fall, and to me it is a week of solitary ease and relaxation.

The seed is by that time committed to the ground; there is nothing very material to do at home, and this additional quantity of honey enables me to be more generous to my home bees, and my wife to make a due quantity of mead. The reason, Sir, that you found mine better than that of others is, that she puts two gallons of brandy in each barrel, which ripens it, and takes off that sweet, luscious taste, which it is apt to retain a long time. If we find anywhere in the woods (no matter on whose land) what is called a bee-tree, we must mark it; in the fall of the year when we propose to cut it down, our duty is to inform the proprietor of the land, who is entitled to half the contents; if this is not complied with we are exposed to an action of trespass, as well as he who should go and cut down a bee-tree which he had neither found out nor marked.

We have twice a year the pleasure of catching pigeons, whose numbers are sometimes so astonishing as to obscure the sun in their flight. Where is it that they hatch? for such multitudes must require an immense quantity of food. I fancy they breed toward the plains of Ohio, and those about lake Michigan, which abound in wild oats; though I have never killed any that had that grain in their craws. In one of them, last year, I found some undigested rice. Now the nearest rice fields from where I live must be at least 560 miles; and either their digestion must be suspended while they are flying, or else they must fly with the celerity of the wind. We catch them with a net extended on the ground, to which they are allured by what we call *tame wild pigeons,* made blind, and fastened to a long string; his short flights, and his repeated calls, never fail to bring them down. The greatest number I ever catched was fourteen dozen, though much larger quantities have often been trapped. I have frequently seen them at the market so cheap, that for a penny you might have as many as you could carry away; and yet from the extreme cheapness you must not conclude, that they are but an ordinary food; on the contrary, I think they are excellent. Every farmer has a tame wild pigeon in a cage at his door all the year round, in order to be ready whenever the season comes for catching them.

The pleasure I receive from the warblings of the birds in the spring, is superior to my poor description, as the continual succession of their tuneful notes is for ever new to me. I generally rise from bed about that indistinct interval, which, properly speaking, is neither night or day; for this is the moment of the most universal vocal choir. Who can listen unmoved to the sweet love tales of our robins, told from tree to tree? or to the shrill cat birds? The sublime accents of the thrush from on high always retard my steps that I may listen to the delicious music. The variegated appearances of the dew drops, as they hang to the different objects, must present even to a clownish imagination, the most voluptuous ideas. The astonishing art which all birds display in the construction of their nests, ill provided as we may suppose them with proper tools, their neatness, their convenience, always make me ashamed of the slovenliness of our houses; their love to their dame, their incessant careful attention, and the peculiar songs they address to her while she tediously incubates their eggs, remind me of my duty could I ever forget it. Their affection to their helpless little ones, is a lively precept; and in short, the whole economy of what we proudly call the brute creation, is admirable in every circumstance; and vain man, though adorned with the additional gift of reason, might learn from the perfection of instinct how to regulate the follies, and how to temper the errors which this second gift often makes him commit. This is a subject, on which I have often bestowed the most serious thoughts; I have often blushed within myself and been greatly astonished, when I have compared the unerring path they all follow, all just, all proper, all wise, up to the necessary degree of perfection, with the coarse, the imperfect systems of men, not merely as governors and kings, but as masters, as husbands, as fathers, as citizens. But this is a sanctuary in which an ignorant farmer must not presume to enter.

If ever man was permitted to receive and enjoy some blessings that might alleviate the many sorrows to which he is exposed, it is certainly in the country, when he attentively considers those ravishing scenes with which he is everywhere surrounded. This is the only time of the year in which I am avaricious of every moment, I therefore lose none that can add to this simple and inoffensive happiness. I roam early throughout all my fields; not the least operation do I perform, which is not accompanied with the most pleasing observations; were I to extend them as far as I have carried them, I should become tedious; you would think me guilty of affectation, and I should perhaps represent many things as pleasurable from which you might not perhaps receive the least agreeable emotions. But, believe me, what I write is all true and real.

Some time ago, as I sat smoking a contemplative pipe in my piazza, I saw with amazement a remarkable instance of selfishness displayed in a very small bird, which I had hitherto respected for its inoffensiveness. Three nests were placed almost contiguous to each other in my piazza: that of a swallow was affixed in the corner next to the house, that of a phebe in the other, a wren possessed a little box which I had made on purpose, and hung between. Be not surprised at their tameness, all my family had long been taught to respect them as well as myself. The wren had shown before signs of dislike to the box which I had given it, but I knew not on what account; at last it resolved, small as it was, to drive the swallow from its own habitation, and to my very great surprise it succeeded. Impudence often gets the better of modesty, and this exploit was no sooner performed, than it removed every material to its own box with the most admirable dexterity; the signs of triumph appeared very visible, it fluttered its wings with uncommon velocity, an universal joy was perceivable in all its movements. Where did this little bird learn that spirit of injustice? It was not endowed with what we term reason! Here then is a proof that both those gifts border very near on one another; for we see the perfection of the one mixing with the errors of the other! The peaceable swallow, like the passive Quaker, meekly sat at a small distance and never offered the least resistance; but no sooner was the plunder carried away, than the injured bird went to work with unabated ardour, and in a few days the depredations were repaired. To prevent however a repetition of the same violence, I removed the wren's box to another part of the house.

In the middle of my new parlour I have, you may remember, a curious republic of industrious hornets; their nest hangs to the ceiling, by the same twig on which it was so admirably built and contrived in the woods. Its removal did not displease them, for they find in my house plenty of food; and I have left a hole open in one of the panes of the window, which answers all their purposes. By this kind usage they are become quite harmless; they live on the flies, which are very troublesome to us throughout the summer; they are constantly busy in catching them, even on the eyelids of my children. It is surprising how quickly they smear them with a sort of glue, lest they might escape, and when thus prepared, they carry them to their nests, as food for their young ones. These globular nests are most ingeniously divided into many stories, all provided with cells, and proper communications. The materials with which this fabric is built, they procure from the cottony furze, with which our oak rails are coveted; this substance tempered with glue, produces a sort of pasteboard, which is very strong, and resists all the inclemencies of the weather. By their assistance, I am but little troubled with flies. All my family are so accustomed to their strong buzzing, that no one takes any notice of them; and though they are fierce and vindictive, yet kindness and hospitality has made them useful and harmless.

We have a great variety of wasps; most of them build their nests in mud, which they fix against the shingles of our roofs, as nigh the pitch as they can. These aggregates represent nothing, at first view, but coarse and irregular lumps, but if you break them, you will observe, that the inside of them contains a great number of oblong cells, in which they deposit their eggs, and in which they bury themselves in the fall of the year. Thus immured they securely pass through the severity of that season, and on the return of the sun are enabled to perforate their cells, and to open themselves a passage from these recesses into the sunshine. The yellow wasps, which build under ground, in our meadows, are much more to be dreaded, for when the mower unwittingly passes his scythe over their holes they immediately sally forth with a fury and velocity superior even to the strength of man. They make the boldest fly, and the only remedy is to lie down and cover our heads with hay, for it is only at the head they aim their blows; nor is there any possibility of finishing that part of the work until, by means of fire and brimstone, they are all silenced. But though I have been obliged to execute this dreadful sentence in my own defence, I have often thought it a great pity, for the sake of a little hay, to lay waste so ingenious a subterranean town, furnished with every conveniency, and built with a most surprising mechanism.

I never should have done were I to recount the many objects which involuntarily strike my imagination in the midst of my work, and spontaneously afford me the most pleasing relief. These appear insignificant trifles to a person who has travelled through Europe and America, and is acquainted with books and with many sciences; but such simple objects of contemplation suffice me, who have no time to bestow on more extensive observations. Happily these require no study, they are obvious, they gild the moments I dedicate to them, and enliven the severe labours which I perform. At home my happiness springs from very different objects; the gradual unfolding of my children's reason, the study of their dawning tempers attract all my paternal attention. I have to contrive little punishments for their little faults, small encouragements for their good actions, and a variety of other expedients dictated by various occasions. But these are themes unworthy your perusal, and which ought not to be carried beyond the walls of my house, being domestic mysteries adapted only to the locality of the small sanctuary wherein my family resides. Sometimes I delight in inventing and executing machines, which simplify my wife's labour. I have been tolerably successful that way; and these, Sir, are the narrow circles within which I constantly revolve, and what can I wish for beyond them? I bless God for all the good he has given me; I envy no man's prosperity, and with no other portion of my happiness than that I may live to teach the same philosophy to my children; and give each of them a farm, show them how to cultivate it, and be like their father, good substantial independent American farmers—an appellation which will be the most fortunate one a man of my class can possess, so long as our civil government continues to shed blessings on our husbandry. Adieu.

BENJAMIN FRANKLIN

Benjamin Franklin (1705–1790) is etched in our minds as the embodiment of those quintessential American virtues of hard work, persistence, optimism, and self-confidence. Inventor, scientist, printer, writer, Founder, diplomat, educator, and politician, he wrote fluidly and wittily, as his correspondence attests. Though his autobiography has sometimes been denigrated as a tissue of pious platitudes, he had a humorous streak and a keen sense of fair play. The piece below demonstrates his worldly, relativistic appreciation for the varying manners of different nations, the strengths of Native American orators, and the cruel ways that indigenous tribes were being fleeced.

Remarks Concerning the Savages of North America

(1784)

Savages we call them, because their manners differ from ours, which we think the perfection of civility; they think the same of theirs.

Perhaps, if we could examine the manners of different nations with impartiality, we should find no people so rude, as to be without any rules of politeness; nor any so polite, as not to have some remains of rudeness.

The Indian men, when young, are hunters and warriors; when old, counselors; for all their government is by counsel of the sages; there is no force, there are no prisons, no officers to compel obedience, or inflict punishment. Hence they generally study oratory, the best speaker having the most influence. The Indian women till the ground, dress the food, nurse and bring up the children, and preserve and hand down to posterity the memory of public transactions. These employments of men and women are accounted natural and honorable. Having few artificial wants, they have abundance of leisure for improvement by conversation. Our laborious manner of life, compared with theirs, they esteem slavish and base; and the learning, on which we value ourselves, they regard as frivolous and useless. An instance of this occurred at the Treaty of Lancaster, in Pennsylvania, *anno* 1744, between the government of Virginia and the Six Nations. After the principal business was settled, the commissioners from Virginia acquainted the Indians by a speech, that there was at Williamsburg a college, with a fund for educating Indian youth; and that, if the chiefs of the Six Nations would send down half a dozen of their sons to that college, the government would take care that they should be well provided for, and instructed in all the learning of the white people. It is one of the Indian rules of politeness not to answer a public proposition the same day that it is made; they think it would be treating it as a light matter, and that they show it respect by taking time to consider it, as of a matter important. They therefore deferred their answer till the day following; when their speaker began, by expressing their deep sense of the kindness of the Virginia government, in making them that offer; "for we know," says he, "that you highly esteem the kind of learning taught in those Colleges, and that the maintenance of our young men, while with you, would be very expensive to you. We are convinced, therefore, that you mean to do us good by your proposal, and we thank you heartily. But you, who are wise, must know that different nations have different conceptions of things; and you will therefore not take it amiss, if our ideas of this kind of education happen not to be the same with yours. We have had some experience of it. Several of our young people were formerly brought up at the colleges of the northern provinces; they were instructed in all your sciences; but, when they came back to us, they were bad runners, ignorant of every means of living in the woods, unable to bear either cold or hunger, knew neither how to build a cabin, take a deer, or kill an enemy, spoke our language imperfectly, were therefore neither fit for hunters, warriors, nor counselors; they were totally good for nothing. We are however not the less obliged by your kind offer, though we decline accepting it; and, to show our grateful sense of it, if the gentlemen of Virginia will send us a dozen of their sons, we will take great care of their education, instruct them in all we know, and make men of them."

Having frequent occasions to hold public councils, they have acquired great order and decency in conducting them. The old men sit in the foremost ranks, the warriors in the next, and the women and children in the hindmost. The business of the women is to take exact notice of what passes, imprint it in their memories, for they have no writing, and communicate it to their children. They are the records of the council, and they preserve tradition of the stipulations in treaties a hundred years back; which, when we compare with our writings, we always find exact. He that would speak, rises. The rest observe a profound silence. When he has finished and sits down, they leave him 5 or 6 minutes to recollect, that, if he has omitted anything he intended to say, or has anything to add, he may rise again and deliver it. To interrupt another, even in common conversation, is reckoned highly indecent. How different this is from the conduct of a polite British House of Commons, where scarce a day passes without some confusion that makes the speaker hoarse in calling *to order;* and how different from the mode of conversation in many polite companies of Europe, where, if you do not deliver your sentence with great rapidity, you are cut off in the middle of it by the impatient loquacity of those you converse with, and never suffered to finish it.

The politeness of these savages in conversation is indeed carried to excess, since it does not permit them to contradict or deny the truth of what is asserted in their presence. By this means they indeed avoid disputes, but then it becomes difficult to know their minds, or what impression you make upon them. The missionaries who have attempted to convert them to Christianity, all complain of this as one of the great difficulties of their mission. The Indians hear with patience the truths of the Gospel explained to them, and give their usual tokens of assent and approbation; you would think they were convinced. No such matter. It is mere civility.

A Swedish minister having assembled the chiefs of the Susquehanna Indians made a sermon to them, acquainting them with the principal historical facts on which our religion is founded; such as the fall of our first parents by eating an apple, the coming of Christ to repair the mischief, His miracles and suffering, &c. When he had finished, an Indian orator stood up to thank him. "What you have told us," says he, "is all very good. It is indeed bad to eat apples. It is better to make them all into cider. We are much obliged by your kindness in coming so far to tell us those things which you have heard from your mothers. In return, I will tell you some of those we have heard from ours.

"In the beginning, our fathers had only the flesh of animals to subsist on; and if their hunting was unsuccessful, they were starving. Two of our young hunters, having killed a deer, made a fire in the woods to broil some parts of it. When they were about to satisfy their hunger, they beheld a beautiful young woman descend from the clouds, and seat herself on that hill, which you see yonder among the blue mountains. They said to each other, it is a spirit that has smelled our broiling venison, and wishes to eat of it; let us offer some to her. They presented her with the tongue. She was pleased with the taste of it, and said, 'Your kindness shall be rewarded. Come to this place after thirteen moons, and you shall find something that will be of great benefit in nourishing you and your children to the latest generations.' They did so, and, to their surprise, found plants they had never seen before, but which, from that ancient time, have been constantly cultivated among us, to our great advantage. Where her right hand had touched the ground, they found maize; where her left hand had touched it, they found kidney-beans; and where her backside had sat on it, they found tobacco." The good missionary, disgusted with this idle tale, said, "What I delivered to you were sacred truths; but what you tell me is mere fable, fiction, and falsehood." The Indian, offended, replied, "My brother, it seems your friends have not done you justice in your education; they have not well instructed you in the rules of common civility. You saw that we, who understand and practice those rules, believed all your stories; why do you refuse to believe ours?"

When any of them come into our towns, our people are apt to crowd round them, gaze upon them, and incommode them, where they desire to be private; this they esteem great rudeness, and the effect of the want of instruction in the rules of civility and good manners. "We have," say they, "as much curiosity as you, and when you come into our towns, we wish for opportunities of looking at you; but for this purpose we hide ourselves behind bushes, where you are to pass, and never intrude ourselves into your company."

Their manner of entering one another's village has likewise its rules. It is reckoned uncivil in traveling strangers to enter a village abruptly, without giving notice of their approach. Therefore, as soon as they arrive within hearing, they stop and hollow, remaining there till invited to enter. Two old men usually come out to them, and lead them in. There is in every village a vacant dwelling, called the strangers' house. Here they are placed, while the old men go round from hut to hut acquainting the inhabitants that strangers are arrived, who are probably hungry and weary; and every one sends them what he can spare of victuals, and skins to repose on. When the strangers are refreshed, pipes and tobacco are brought; and then, but not before, conversation begins, with inquiries who they are, whither bound, what news, &c.; and it usually ends with offers of service, if the strangers have occasion of guides, or any necessaries for continuing their journey; and nothing is exacted for the entertainment.

The same hospitality, esteemed among them as a principal virtue, is practiced by private persons; of which Conrad Weiser, our interpreter, gave me the following instances. He had been naturalized among the Six Nations, and spoke well the Mohawk language. In going through the Indian country, to carry a message from our Governor to the Council at Onondaga, he called at the habitation of Canassatego, an old acquaintance, who embraced him, spread furs for him to sit on, placed before him some boiled beans and venison, and mixed some rum and water for his drink. When he was well refreshed, and had lit his pipe, Canassatego began to converse with him, asked how he had fared the many years since they had seen each other, whence he then came, what occasioned the journey, &c. Conrad answered all his questions; and when the discourse began to flag, the Indian, to continue it, said, "Conrad, you have lived long among the white people, and know something of their customs; I have been sometimes at Albany, and have observed that once in seven days they shut up their shops and assemble all in the great house; tell me what it is for? What do they do there?" "They meet there," says Conrad, "to hear and learn *good things*." "I do not doubt," says the Indian, "that they tell you so; they have told me the same; but I doubt the truth of what they say, and I will tell you my reasons. I went lately to Albany to sell my skins and buy blankets, knives, powder, rum, &c. You know I used generally to deal with Hans Hanson; but I was a little inclined this time to try some other merchant. However, I called first upon Hans, and asked him what he would give for beaver. He said he could not give any more than four shillings a pound; 'but,' says he, 'I cannot talk on business now; this is the day when we meet together to learn *good things*, and I am going to the meeting.' So I thought to myself, 'Since we cannot do any business today, I may as well go to the meeting too,' and I went with him. There stood up a man in black, and began to talk to the people very angrily. I did not understand what he said; but, perceiving that he looked much at me and at Hanson, I imagined he was angry at seeing me there; so I went out, sat down near the house, struck fire, and lit my pipe, waiting till the meeting should break up. I thought too, that the man had mentioned something of beaver, and I suspected it might be the subject of their meeting. So, when they came out, I accosted my merchant. 'Well, Hans,' says I, 'I hope you have agreed to give more than four shillings a pound.' 'No,' says he, 'I cannot give so much; I cannot give more than three shillings and sixpence.' I then spoke to several other dealers, but they all sung the same song, three and sixpence, three and sixpence. This made it clear to me, that my suspicion was right; and, that whatever they pretended of meeting to learn *good things*, the real purpose was to consult how to cheat Indians in the price of beaver. Consider but a little, Conrad, and you must be of my opinion. If they met so often to learn *good things*, they would certainly have learned some before this time. But they are still ignorant. You know our practice. If a white man, in traveling through our country, enters one of our cabins, we all treat him as I treat you; we dry him if he is wet, we warm him if he is cold, and give him meat and drink that he may allay his thirst and hunger; and we spread soft furs for him to rest and sleep on. We demand nothing in return. But, if I go into a white man's house at Albany, and ask for victuals and drink, they say, 'Where is your money?' and if I have none, they say, 'Get out, you Indian dog.'

You see they have not yet learned those little *good things,* that we need no meetings to be instructed in, because our mothers taught them to us when we were children. And therefore it is impossible their meetings should be, as they say, for any such purpose, or have any such effect; they are only to contrive *the cheating of Indians in the price of beaver.*"

ALEXANDER HAMILTON

After the Constitution was drawn up in 1787, it was sent to each of the thirteen states for ratification. Opposition was immediately raised in the press by articles signed "Cato" and "Brutus" (note the fashion for early American political writers to cloak themselves as ancient Romans). Alexander Hamilton launched a series of eighty-five essays in defense of the Constitution, which would come to be known as The Federalist Papers. *He composed more than half of them (including the one below), signing his with the name "Publius"; James Madison and John Jay wrote the others. In arguing for the union and for strong government, Hamilton acknowledges conflicts between special interests and the public good while posing this larger philosophical question: "whether societies of men are capable or not, of establishing good government from reflection and choice, or whether they are forever destined to depend, for their political constitutions, on accident and force." He does not demonize his opponents but hopes that "reflection" will have the final word; and by calmly laying out the grounds of contention and resistance to his position, he enacts the rhetoric of reason.* The Federalist Papers *may be the most influential set of essays in American history.*

The Federalist No. 1

(1787)

To the People of the State of New-York.

After an unequivocal experience of the inefficacy of the subsisting Federal Government, you are called upon to deliberate on a new Constitution for the United States of America. The subject speaks its own ⁚ .portance; comprehending in its consequences, nothing less than the existence of the UNION, the safety and welfare of the parts of which it is composed, the fate of an empire, in many respects, the most interesting in the world. It has been frequently remarked, that it seems to have been reserved to the people of this country, by their conduct and example, to decide the important question, whether societies of men are really capable or not, of establishing good government from reflection and choice, or whether they are forever destined to depend, for their political constitutions, on accident and force. If there be any truth in the remark, the crisis, at which we are arrived, may with propriety be regarded as the era in which that decision is to be made; and a wrong election of the part we shall act, may, in this view, deserve to be considered as the general misfortune of mankind.

This idea will add the inducements of philanthropy to those of patriotism to heighten the sollicitude, which all considerate and good men must feel for the event. Happy will it be if our choice should be decided by a judicious estimate of our true interests, unperplexed and unbiassed by considerations not connected with the public good. But this is a thing more ardently to be wished, than seriously to be expected. The plan offered to our deliberations, affects too many particular interests, innovates upon too many local institutions, not to involve in its discussion a variety of objects foreign to its merits, and of views, passions and prejudices little favourable to the discovery of truth.

Among the most formidable of the obstacles which the new Constitution will have to encounter, may readily be distinguished the obvious interests of a certain class of men in every State to resist all changes which may hazard a diminution of the power, emolument and consequence of the offices they hold under the State-establishments—and the perverted ambition of another class of men, who will either hope to aggrandise themselves by the confusions of their country, or will flatter themselves with fairer prospects of elevation from the subdivision of the empire into several partial confederacies, than from its union under one government.

It is not, however, my design to dwell upon observations of this nature. I am well aware that it would be disingenuous to resolve indiscriminately the opposition of any set of men (merely because their situations might subject them to suspicion) into interested or ambitious views: Candour will oblige us to admit, that even such men may be actuated by upright intentions; and it cannot be doubted, that much of the opposition which has made its appearance, or may hereafter make its appearance, will spring from sources, blameless at least, if not respectable, the honest errors of minds led astray by preconceived jealousies and fears. So numerous indeed and so powerful are the causes, which serve to give a false bias to the judgment, that we upon many occasions, see wise and good men on the wrong as well as on the right side of questions, of the first magnitude to society. This circumstance, if duly attended to, would furnish a lesson of moderation to those, who are ever so much persuaded of their being in the right, in any controversy. And a further reason for caution, in this respect, might be drawn from the reflection, that we are not always sure, that those who advocate the truth are influenced by purer principles than their antagonists. Ambition, avarice, personal animosity, party opposition, and many other motives, not more laudable than these, are apt to operate as well upon those who support as upon those who oppose the right side of a question. Were there not even these inducements to moderation, nothing could be more illjudged than that intolerant spirit, which has, at all times, characterised political parties. For, in politics as in religion, it is equally absurd to aim at making proselytes by fire and sword. Heresies in either can rarely be cured by persecution.

And yet however just these sentiments will be allowed to be, we have already sufficient indications, that it will happen in this as in all former cases of great national discussion. A torrent of angry and malignant passions will be let loose. To judge from the conduct of the opposite parties, we shall be led to conclude, that they will mutually hope to evince the justness of their opinions, and to increase the number of their converts by the loudness of their declamations, and by the bitterness of their invectives. An enlightened zeal for the energy and efficiency of government will be stigmatised, as the off-spring of a temper fond of despotic power and hostile to the principles of liberty. An overscrupulous jealousy of danger to the rights of the people, which is more commonly the fault of the head than of the heart, will be represented as mere pretence and artifice; the bait for popularity at the expence of public good. It will be forgotten, on the one hand, that jealousy is the usual concomitant of violent love, and that the noble enthusiasm of liberty is too apt to be infected with a spirit of narrow and illiberal distrust. On the other hand, it will be equally forgotten, that the vigour of government is essential to the security of liberty; that, in the contemplation of a sound and well informed judgment, their interest can never be separated; and that a dangerous ambition more often lurks behind the specious mask of zeal for the rights of the people, than under the forbidding appearance of zeal for the firmness and efficiency of government. History will teach us, that the former has been found a much more certain road to the introduction of despotism, than the latter, and that of those men who have overturned the liberties of republics the greatest number have begun their career, by paying an obsequious court to the people, commencing Demagogues and ending Tyrants.

In the course of the preceeding observations I have had an eye, my Fellow Citizens, to putting you upon your guard against all attempts, from whatever quarter, to influence your decision in a matter of the utmost moment to your welfare by any impressions other than those which may result from the evidence of truth. You will, no doubt, at the same time, have collected from the general scope of them that they proceed from a source not unfriendly to the new Constitution. Yes, my Countrymen, I own to you, that, after having given it an attentive consideration, I am clearly of opinion, it is your interest to adopt it. I am convinced, that this is the safest course for your liberty, your dignity, and your happiness. I affect not reserves, which I do not feel. I will not amuse you with an appearance of deliberation, when I have decided. I frankly acknowledge to you my convictions, and I will freely lay before you the reasons on which they are founded. The consciousness of good intentions disdains ambiguity. I shall not however multiply professions on this head. My motives must remain in the depositary of my own breast: My arguments will be open to all, and may be judged of by all. They shall at least be offered in a spirit, which will not disgrace the cause of truth.

I propose in a series of papers to discuss the following interesting particulars—*The utility of the* UNION *to your political prosperity—The insufficiency of the present Confederation to preserve that Union— The necessity of a government at least equally energetic with the one proposed to the attainment of this object—The conformity of the proposed Constitution to the true principles of republican government—Its analogy to your own state constitution—and lastly, The additional security, which its adoption will afford to the preservation of that species of government, to liberty and to property.*

In the progress of this discussion I shall endeavour to give a satisfactory answer to all the objections which shall have made their appearance that may seem to have any claim to your attention.

It may perhaps be thought superfluous to offer arguments to prove the utility of the UNION, a point, no doubt, deeply engraved on the hearts of the great body of the people in every state, and one, which it may be imagined has no adversaries. But the fact is, that we already hear it whispered in the private circles of those who oppose the new constitution, that the Thirteen States are of too great extent for any general system, and that we must of necessity resort to seperate confederacies of distinct portions of the whole. This doctrine will, in all probability, be gradually propagated, till it has votaries enough to countenance an open avowal of it. For nothing can be more evident, to those who are able to take an enlarged view of the subject, than the alternative of an adoption of the new Constitution, or a dismemberment of the Union. It will therefore be of use to begin by examining the advantages of that Union, the certain evils and the probable dangers, to which every State will be exposed from its dissolution. This shall accordingly constitute the subject of my next address.

PUBLIUS

THOMAS JEFFERSON

Though all the Founders wrote fairly well, Thomas Jefferson (1743–1826) probably had the best prose style. Principally responsible for the composition of the Declaration of Independence, he also wrote Notes on the State of Virginia *(1787), which demonstrated his wide-ranging knowledge of the history, geography, natural resources, and culture of his home state. In the chapter below, he argues for religious freedom and separation of church and state. He himself avoided organized religion and was a deist of Christian bent. A planter and slave owner, he warns elsewhere in the same book that slavery is immoral and undermines the liberty of a nation founded on the premise that, in his words, "all men are created equal."*

Religion

(1787)

The first settlers in this country were emigrants from England, of the English church, just at a point of time when it was flushed with complete victory over the religious of all other persuasions. Possessed, as they became, of the powers of making, administering, and executing the laws, they shewed equal intolerance in this country with their Presbyterian brethren, who had emigrated to the northern government. The poor Quakers were flying from persecution in England. They cast their eyes on these new countries as asylums of civil and religious freedom; but they found them free only for the reigning sect. Several acts of the Virginia assembly of 1659, 1662, and 1693, had made it penal in parents to refuse to have their children baptized; had prohibited the unlawful assembling of

Quakers; had made it penal for any master of a vessel to bring a Quaker into the state; had ordered those already here, and such as should come thereafter, to be imprisoned till they should abjure the country; provided a milder punishment for their first and second return, but death for their third; had inhibited all persons from suffering their meetings in or near their houses, entertaining them individually, or disposing of books which supported their tenets. If no capital execution took place here, as did in New-England, it was not owing to the moderation of the church, or spirit of the legislature, as may be inferred from the law itself; but to historical circumstances which have not been handed down to us. The Anglicans retained full possession of the country about a century. Other opinions began then to creep in, and the great care of the government to support their own church, having begotten an equal degree of indolence in its clergy, two-thirds of the people had become dissenters at the commencement of the present revolution. The laws indeed were still oppressive on them, but the spirit of the one party had subsided into moderation, and of the other had risen to a degree of determination which commanded respect.

The present state of our laws on the subject of religion is this. The convention of May 1776, in their declaration of rights, declared it to be a truth, and a natural right, that the exercise of religion should be free; but when they proceeded to form on that declaration the ordinance of government, instead of taking up every principle declared in the bill of rights, and guarding it by legislative sanction, they passed over that which asserted our religious rights, leaving them as they found them. The same convention, however, when they met as a member of the general assembly in October 1776, repealed all *acts of parliament* which had rendered criminal the maintaining any opinions in matters of religion, the forbearing to repair to church, and the exercising any mode of worship; and suspended the laws giving salaries to the clergy, which suspension was made perpetual in October 1779. Statutory oppressions in religion being thus wiped away, we remain at present under those only imposed by the common law, or by our own acts of assembly. At the common law, *heresy* was a capital offence, punishable by burning. Its definition was left to the ecclesiastical judges, before whom the conviction was, till the statute of the 1 El. c. 1. circumscribed it, by declaring, that nothing should be deemed heresy, but what had been so determined by authority of the canonical scriptures, or by one of the four first general councils, or by some other council having for the grounds of their declaration the express and plain words of the scriptures. Heresy, thus circumscribed, being an offence at the common law, our act of assembly of October 1777, c. 17. gives cognizance of it to the general court, by declaring, that the jurisdiction of that court shall be general in all matters at the common law. The execution is by the writ *de haeretico comburendo*. By our own act of assembly of 1705, c. 30, if a person brought up in the Christian religion denies the being of a God, or the Trinity, or asserts there are more gods than one, or denies the Christian religion to be true, or the scriptures to be of divine authority, he is punishable on the first offence by incapacity to hold any office or employment ecclesiastical, civil, or military; on the second by disability to sue, to take any gift or legacy, to be guardian, executor, or administrator, and by three years imprisonment, without bail. A father's right to the custody of his own children being founded in law on his right of guardianship, this being taken away, they may of course be severed from him, and put, by the authority of a court, into more orthodox hands. This is a summary view of that religious slavery, under which a people have been willing to remain, who have lavished their lives and fortunes for the establishment of their civil freedom.

The error seems not sufficiently eradicated, that the operations of the mind, as well as the acts of the body, are subject to the coercion of the laws. But our rulers can have authority over such natural rights only as we have submitted to them. The rights of conscience we never submitted, we could not submit. We are answerable for them to our God. The legitimate powers of government extend to such acts only as are injurious to others. But it does me no injury for my neighbour to say there are twenty gods, or no god. It neither picks my pocket nor breaks my leg. If it be said, his testimony in a court of justice cannot be relied on, reject it then, and be the stigma on him. Constraint may make him worse by making him a hypocrite, but it will never make him a truer man. It may fix him obstinately in his errors, but will not cure them. Reason and free inquiry are the only effectual agents against error. Give a loose to them, they will support the true religion, by bringing every false one to their tribunal, to the test of their investigation. They are the natural enemies of error, and of error only. Had not the Roman government permitted free inquiry, Christianity could never have been introduced. Had not free inquiry been indulged, at the era of the reformation, the corruptions of Christianity could not have been purged away. If it be restrained now, the present corruptions will be protected, and new ones encouraged. Was the government to prescribe to us our medicine and diet, our bodies would be in such keeping as our souls are now. Thus in France the emetic was once forbidden as a medicine, and the potatoe as an article of food. Government is just as infallible too when it fixes systems in physics. Galileo was sent to the inquisition for affirming that the earth was a sphere: the government had declared it to be as flat as a trencher, and Galileo was obliged to abjure his error. This error however at length prevailed, the earth became a globe, and Descartes declared it was whirled round its axis by a vortex. The government in which he lived was wise enough to see that this was no question of civil jurisdiction, or we should all have been involved by authority in vortices. In fact, the vortices have been exploded, and the Newtonian principle of gravitation is now more firmly established, on the basis of reason, than it would be were the government to step in, and to make it an article of necessary faith. Reason and experiment have been indulged, and error has fled before them. It is error alone which needs the support of government. Truth can stand by itself. Subject opinion to coercion: whom will you make your inquisitors? Fallible men; men governed by bad passions, by private as well as public reasons. And why subject it to coercion? To produce uniformity. But is uniformity of opinion desireable? No more than of face and stature. Introduce the bed of Procrustes then, and as there is danger that the large men may beat the small, make us all of a size, by lopping the former and stretching the latter. Difference of opinion is advantageous in religion. The several sects perform the office of a Censor morum over each other. Is uniformity attainable? Millions of innocent men, women, and children, since the introduction of Christianity, have been burnt, tortured, fined, imprisoned; yet we have not advanced one inch towards uniformity. What has been the effect of coercion? To make one half the world fools, and the other half hypocrites. To support roguery and error all over the earth. Let us reflect that it is inhabited by a thousand millions of people. That these profess probably a thousand different systems of religion. That ours is but one of that thousand. That if there be but one right, and ours that one, we should wish to see the 999 wandering sects gathered into the fold of truth. But against such a majority we cannot effect this by force. Reason and persuasion are the only practicable instruments. To make way for these, free inquiry must be indulged; and how can we wish others to indulge it while we refuse it ourselves. But every state, says an inquisitor, has established some religion. No two, say I, have established the same. Is this a proof of the infallibility of establishments? Our sister states of Pennsylvania and New York, however, have long subsisted without any establishment at all. The experiment was new and doubtful when they made it. It has answered beyond conception. They flourish infinitely. Religion is well supported; of various kinds, indeed, but all good enough; all sufficient to preserve peace and order: or if a sect arises, whose tenets would subvert morals, good sense has fair play, and reasons and laughs it out of doors, without suffering the state to be troubled with it. They do not hang more malefactors than we do. They are not more disturbed with religious dissensions. On the contrary, their harmony is unparalleled, and can be ascribed to nothing but their unbounded tolerance, because there is no other circumstance in which they differ from every nation on earth. They have made the happy discovery, that the way to silence religious disputes, is to take no notice of them. Let us too give this experiment fair play, and get rid, while we may, of those tyrannical laws. It is true, we are as yet secured against them by the spirit of the times. I doubt whether the people of this country would suffer an execution for heresy, or a three years imprisonment for not comprehending the mysteries of the Trinity. But is the spirit of the people an infallible, a permanent reliance? Is it government? Is this the kind of protection we receive in return for the rights we give up? Besides, the spirit of the times may alter, will alter. Our rulers will become corrupt, our people careless. A single zealot may commence persecutor, and better men be his victims. It can never be too often repeated, that the time for fixing every essential right on a legal basis is while our rulers are honest, and ourselves united. From, the conclusion of this war we shall be going down hill. It will not then be necessary to resort every moment to the people for support. They will be forgotten, therefore, and their rights disregarded. They will forget themselves, but in the sole faculty of making money, and will never think of uniting to effect a due respect for their rights. The shackles, therefore, which shall not be knocked off at the conclusion of this war, will remain on us long, will be made heavier and heavier, till our rights shall revive or expire in a convulsion.

JUDITH SARGENT MURRAY

The essayist, dramatist, and poet Judith Sargent Murray (1751–1820) was a pioneering feminist, and her most famous essay, "On the Equality of the Sexes," appeared in The Massachusetts Magazine *in 1790, two years before Mary Wollstonecraft's* Vindication of the Rights of Woman. *Born in Gloucester, Massachusetts, she married first a ship captain, who abandoned her, and then a Unitarian/Universalist minister, John Murray. Writing under the pen names Constantia, Honoria, and Martesia, she also assumed a male identity as "The Gleaner" so that her views would be taken more seriously. Her writings helped to support her family, and her essays and articles were collected in a widely read volume published in 1798. Along with Abigail Adams, she championed the patriotic notion of Republican Motherhood, which argued that the new nation needed educated women to raise sons to be intelligent citizens.*

On the Equality of the Sexes

(1790)

TO THE EDITORS OF THE MASSACHUSETTS MAGAZINE,

GENTLEMEN,

The following ESSAY is yielded to the patronage of Candour.—If it hath been anticipated, the testimony of many respectable persons, who saw it in manuscripts as early as the year 1779, can obviate the imputation of plagiarism.

Is it upon mature consideration we adopt the idea, that nature is thus partial in her distributions? Is it indeed a fact, that she hath yielded to one half of the human species so unquestionable a mental superiority? I know that to both sexes elevated understandings, and the reverse, are common. But, suffer me to ask, in what the minds of females are so notoriously deficient, or unequal. May not the intellectual powers be ranged under these four heads—imagination, reason, memory and judgment. The province of imagination hath long since been surrendered to us, and we have been crowned and undoubted sovereigns of the regions of fancy. Invention is perhaps the most arduous effort of the mind; this branch of imagination hath been particularly ceded to us, and we have been time out of mind invested with that creative faculty. Observe the variety of fashions (here I bar the contemptuous smile) which distinguish and adorn the female world: how continually are they changing, insomuch that they almost render the wise man's assertion problematical, and we are ready to say, *there is something new under the sun.* Now what a playfulness, what an exuberance of fancy, what strength of inventive imagination, doth this continual variation discover? Again, it hath been observed, that if the turpitude of the conduct of our sex, hath been ever so enormous, so extremely ready are we, that the very first thought presents us with an apology, so plausible, as to produce our actions even in an amiable light. Another instance of our creative powers, is our talent for slander; how ingenious are we at inventive scandal? what a formidable story can we in a moment fabricate merely from the force of a prolifick imagination? how many reputations, in the fertile brain of a female, have been utterly despoiled? how industrious are we at improving a hint? suspicion how easily do we convert into conviction, and conviction, embellished by the power of eloquence, stalks abroad to the surprise and confusion of unsuspecting innocence. Perhaps it will be asked if I furnish these facts as instances of excellency in our sex. Certainly not; but as proofs of a creative faculty, of a lively imagination. Assuredly great activity of mind is thereby discovered, and was this activity properly directed, what beneficial effects would follow. Is the needle and kitchen sufficient to employ the operations of a soul thus organized? I should conceive not, Nay, it is a truth that those very departments leave the intelligent principle vacant, and at liberty for speculation. Are we deficient in reason? we can only reason from what we know, and if an opportunity of acquiring knowledge hath been denied us, the inferiority of our sex cannot fairly be deduced from thence. Memory, I believe, will be allowed us in common, since everyone's experience must testify, that a loquacious old woman is as frequently met with, as a communicative man; their subjects are alike drawn from the fund of other times, and the transactions of their youth, or of maturer life, entertain, or perhaps fatigue you, in the evening of their lives.

"But our judgment is not so strong—we do not distinguish so well."—
Yet it may be questioned, from what doth this superiority, in this determining faculty of the soul, proceed. May we not trace its source in the
difference of education, and continued advantages? Will it be said that
the judgment of a male of two years old, is more sage than that of a
female's of the same age? I believe the reverse is generally observed to be
true. But from that period what partiality! how is the one exalted, and the
other depressed, by the contrary modes of education which are adopted!
the one is taught to aspire, and the other is early confined and limitted.
As their years increase, the sister must be wholly domesticated, while the
brother is led by the hand through all the flowery paths of science. Grant
that their minds are by nature equal, yet who shall wonder at the *apparent* superiority, if indeed custom becomes *second nature*; nay if it taketh
place of nature, and that it doth the experience of each day will evince.
At length arrived at womanhood, the uncultivated fair one feels a void,
which the employments allotted her are by no means capable of filling.
What can she do? to books she may not apply; or if she doth, *to those
only of the novel kind,* lest she merit the appellation of a *learned lady;*
and what ideas have been affixed to this term, the observation of many
can testify. Fashion, scandal, and sometimes what is still more reprehen-
sible, are then called in to her relief; and who can say to what lengths the
liberties she takes may proceed. Meantimes she herself is most unhappy;
she feels the want of a cultivated mind. Is she single, she in vain seeks to
fill up time from sexual employments or amusements. Is she united to a
person whose soul nature made equal to her own, education hath set him
so far above her, that in those entertainments which are productive of such
rational felicity, she is not qualified to accompany him. She experiences a
mortifying consciousness of inferiority, which embitters every enjoyment.
Doth the person to whom her adverse fate hath consigned her, possess
a mind incapable of improvement, she is equally wretched, in being so
closely connected with an individual whom she cannot but despise. Now,
was she permitted the same instructors as her brother, (with an eye however to their particular departments) for the employment of a rational
mind an ample field would be opened. In astronomy she might catch a
glimpse of the immensity of the Deity, and thence she would form amazing conceptions of the august and supreme Intelligence. In geography she
would admire Jehovah in the midst of his benevolence; thus adapting this
globe to the various wants and amusements of its inhabitants. In natural
philosophy she would adore the infinite majesty of heaven, clothed in
condescension; and as she traversed the reptile world, she would hail the
goodness of a creating God. A mind, thus filled, would have little room
for the trifles with which our sex are, with too much justice, accused of
amusing themselves, and they would thus be rendered fit companions
for those, who should one day wear them as their crown. Fashions, in

their variety, would then give place to conjectures, which might perhaps conduce to the improvements of the literary world; and there would be no leisure for slander or detraction. Reputation would not then be blasted, but serious speculations would occupy the lively imaginations of the sex. Unnecessary visits would only be indulged by way of relaxation, or to answer the demands of consanguinity and friendship. Females would become discreet, their judgments would be invigorated, and their partners for life being circumspectly chosen, an unhappy Hymen would then be as rare, as is now the reverse.

Will it be urged that those acquirements would supersede our domestick duties. I answer that every requisite in female economy is easily attained; and, with truth I can add, that when once attained, they require no further *mental attention*. Nay, while we are pursuing the needle, or the superintendency of the family, I repeat, that our minds are at full liberty for reflection; that imagination may exert itself in full vigor; and that if a just foundation is early laid, our ideas will then be worthy of rational beings. If we were industrious we might easily find time to arrange them upon paper, or should avocations press too hard for such an indulgence, the hours allotted for conversation would at least become more refined and rational. Should it still be vociferated, "Your domestick employments are sufficient"—I would calmly ask, is it reasonable, that a candidate for immortality, for the joys of heaven, an intelligent being, who is to spend an eternity in contemplating the works of the Deity, should at present be so degraded, as to be allowed no other ideas, than those which are suggested by the mechanism of a pudding, or the sewing the seams of a garment? Pity that all such censurers of female improvement do not go one step further, and deny their future existence; to be consistent they surely ought.

Yes, ye lordly, ye haughty sex, our souls are by nature *equal* to yours; the same breath of God animates, enlivens, and invigorates us; and that we are not fallen lower than yourselves, let those witness who have greatly towered above the various discouragements by which they have been so heavily oppressed; and though I am unacquainted with the list of celebrated characters on either side, yet from the observations I have made in the contracted circle in which I have moved, I dare confidently believe, that from the commencement of time to the present day, there hath been as many females, as males, who, by the *mere force of natural powers*, have merited the crown of applause; who, thus unassisted, have seized the wreath of fame. I know there are who assert, that as the animal power of the one sex are superiour, of course their mental faculties also must be stronger; thus attributing strength of mind to the transient organization of this earth born tenement. But if this reasoning is just, man must be content to yield the palm to many of the brute creation, since by not a few of his brethren of the field, he is far surpassed in bodily strength. Moreover, was this argument admitted, it would prove too much, for occular demonstration evinceth, that there are many robust masculine ladies, and effeminate gentlemen. Yet I fancy that Mr. Pope, though clogged with an enervated body, and distinguished by a diminutive stature, could nevertheless lay claim to greatness of soul; and perhaps there are many other instances which might be adduced to combat so unphilosophical an opinion. Do we not often see, that when the clay built tabernacle is well nigh dissolved, when it is just ready to mingle with the parent soil, the immortal inhabitant aspires to, and even attaineth heights the most sublime, and which were before wholly unexplored. Besides, were we to grant that animal strength proved any thing, taking into consideration the accustomed impartiality of nature, we should be induced to imagine, that she had invested the female mind with superiour strength as an equivalent for the bodily powers of man. But waving this however palpable advantage, for *equality only,* we wish to contend.

I am aware that there are many passages in the sacred oracles which seem to give the advantage to the other sex; but I consider all these as wholly metaphorical. Thus David was a man after God's own heart, yet see him enervated by his licentious passions! behold him following Uriah to the death, and shew me wherein could consist the immaculate Being's complacency. Listen to the curses which Job bestoweth upon the day of his nativity, and tell me where is his perfection, where his patience—*literally* it existed not. David and Job were types of him who was to come; and the superiority of man, as exhibited in scripture, being also emblematical, all arguments deduced from thence, of course fall to the ground. The exquisite delicacy of the female mind proclaimeth the exactness of its texture, while its nice sense of honour announceth its innate, its native grandeur. And indeed, in one respect, the preeminence seems to be tacitly allowed us; for after an education which limits and confines, and employments and recreations which naturally tend to enervate the body, and debilitate the mind; after we have from early youth been adorned with ribbons, and other gewgaws, dressed out like the ancient victims previous to a sacrifice, being taught by the care of our parents in collecting the most showy materials that the ornamenting our exteriour ought to be the principal object of our attention; after, I say, fifteen years thus spent, we are introduced into the world, amid the united adulation of every beholder. Praise is sweet to the soul; we are immediately intoxicated by large draughts of flattery, which being plentifully administered, is to the pride of our hearts, the most acceptable incense. It is expected that with the other sex we should commence immediate war, and that we should triumph over the machinations of the most artful. We must be constantly upon our guard; prudence and discretion must be our characteristiks; and we must rise superiour to, and obtain a complete victory over those who have been long adding to the native strength of their minds, by an unremitted study of men and books, and who have, moreover, conceived from the loose characters which they have seen portrayed in the extensive variety of their reading, a most contemptible opinion of the sex. Thus unequal, we are, notwithstanding, forced to the combat, and the infamy which is consequent upon the smallest deviation in our conduct, proclaims the high idea which was formed of our native strength; and thus, indirectly at least, is the preference acknowledged to be our due. And if we are allowed an equality of acquirements, let serious studies equally employ our minds, and we will bid our souls arise to equal strengths. We will meet upon even ground, the despot man; we will rush with alacrity to the combat, and, crowned by success, we shall then answer the exalted expectations, which are formed. Though sensibility, soft compassion, and gentle commiseration, are inmates in the female bosom, yet against every deep laid art, altogether fearless of the event, we will set them in array; for assuredly the wreath of victory will encircle the spotless brow. If we meet an equal, a sensible friend, we will reward him with the hand of amity, and through life we will be assiduous to promote his happiness; but from every deep laid scheme, for our ruin, retiring into ourselves, amid the flowery paths of science, we will indulge in all the refined and sentimental pleasures of contemplation: And should it still be urged, that the studies thus insisted upon would interfere with our more peculiar department, I must further reply, that *early hours*, and close application, will do wonders; and to her who is from the first dawn of reason taught to fill up time rationally, both the requisites will be easy. I grant that niggard fortune is too generally unfriendly to the mind; and that much of that valuable treasure, time, is necessarily expended upon the wants of the body; but it should be remembered; that in embarrassed circumstances our companions have as little leisure for literary improvements, as is afforded to us; for most certainly their provident care is at least as requisite as our exertions. Nay, we have even more leisure for sedentary pleasures, as our avocations are more retired, much less laborious, and, as hath been observed, by no means require that avidity of attention which is proper to the employments of the other sex. In high life, or, in other words, where the parties are in possession of affluence, the objection respecting time is wholly obviated, and of course falls to the ground; and it may also be repeated, that many of those hours which are at present swallowed up in fashion and scandal, might be redeemed, were we habituated to useful reflections. But in one respect, O ye arbiters of our fate! we confess that the superiority is indubitably yours; you are by nature formed for our protectors; we pretend not to vie with you in bodily strength; upon this point we will never contend for victory. Shield us then, we beseech you, from external evils, and in return we will transact *your* domestick affairs. Yes, *your*, for are you not equally interested in those matters with ourselves? Is not the elegancy of neatness as agreeable to your sight as to ours; is not the well favoured viand equally delightful to your taste; and doth not your sense of hearing suffer as much, from the discordant sounds prevalent in an ill regulated family, produced by the voices of children and many *et ceteras*?

CONSTANTIA.

GEORGE WASHINGTON

George Washington (1732–1799), first president of the United States, having been elected twice and offered a more or less open-ended reign, declined a third term and asked to retire to his home in Mount Vernon, Virginia. He wrote this Farewell Address, with input from Alexander Hamilton, as a letter to be printed in newspapers. With characteristic modesty he acknowledges his "fallible judgment," then goes on to offer advice to preserve the union. In doing so, he enunciates his vision of what America should aspire to be: nonaligned, prosperous, peaceful, and whole. As prose, the speech conveys his thoughts lucidly while showing a penchant for long list-sentences that pile clause upon clause, to cover all possibilities. Warning against "the fury of party spirit" and "the insidious wiles of foreign influence," Washington demonstrates a wisdom and foresight still relevant today.

Farewell Address

(1796)

United States, September 19, 1796.

Friends, and Fellow-Citizens: The period for a new election of a Citizen, to Administer the Executive government of the United States, being not far distant, and the time actually arrived, when your thoughts must be employed in designating the person, who is to be cloathed with that important trust, it appears to me proper, especially as it may conduce to a more distinct expression of the public voice, that I should now apprise you of the resolution I have formed, to decline being considered among the number of those, out of whom a choice is to be made.

I beg you, at the same time, to do me the justice to be assured, that this resolution has not been taken, without a strict regard to all the considerations appertaining to the relation, which binds a dutiful citizen to his country, and that, in withdrawing the tender of service which silence in my situation might imply, I am influenced by no diminution of zeal for your future interest, no deficiency of grateful respect for your past kindness; but am supported by a full conviction that the step is compatible with both.

The acceptance of, and continuance hitherto in, the office to which your Suffrages have twice called me, have been a uniform sacrifice of inclination to the opinion of duty, and to a deference for what appeared to be your desire. I constantly hoped, that it would have been much earlier in my power, consistently with motives, which I was not at liberty to disregard, to return to that retirement, from which I had been reluctantly drawn. The strength of my inclination to do this, previous to the last Election, had even led to the preparation of an address to declare it to you; but mature reflection on the then perplexed and critical posture of our Affairs with foreign Nations, and the unanimous advice of persons entitled to my confidence, impelled me to abandon the idea.

I rejoice, that the state of your concerns, external as well as internal, no longer renders the pursuit of inclination incompatible with the sentiment of duty, or propriety; and am persuaded whatever partiality may be retained for my services, that in the present circumstances of our country, you will not disapprove my determination to retire.

The impressions, with which I first undertook the arduous trust, were explained on the proper occasion. In the discharge of this trust, I will only say, that I have, with good intentions, contributed towards the Organization and Administration of the government, the best exertions of which a very fallible judgment was capable. Not unconscious, in the outset, of the inferiority of my qualifications, experience in my own eyes, perhaps still more in the eyes of others, has strengthened the motives to diffidence of myself; and every day the encreasing weight of years admonishes me more and more, that the shade of retirement is as necessary to me as it will be welcome. Satisfied that if any circumstances have given peculiar value to my services, they were temporary, I have the consolation to believe, that while choice and prudence invite me to quit the political scene, patriotism does not forbid it.

In looking forward to the moment, which is intended to terminate the career of my public life, my feelings do not permit me to suspend the deep acknowledgment of that debt of gratitude which I owe to my beloved country, for the many honors it has conferred upon me; still more for the stedfast confidence with which it has supported me; and for the opportunities I have thence enjoyed of manifesting my inviolable attachment, by services faithful and persevering, though in usefulness unequal to my zeal. If benefits have resulted to our country from these services, let it always be remembered to your praise, and as an instructive example in our annals, that, under circumstances in which the Passions agitated in every direction were liable to mislead, amidst appearances sometimes dubious, viscissitudes of fortune often discouraging, in situations in which not unfrequently want of Success has countenanced the spirit of criticism, the constancy of your support was the essential prop of the efforts, and a guarantee of the plans by which they were effected. Profoundly penetrated with this idea, I shall carry it with me to my grave, as a strong incitement to unceasing vows that Heaven may continue to you the choicest tokens of its beneficence; that your Union and brotherly affection may be perpetual; that the free constitution, which is the work of your hands, may be sacredly maintained; that its Administration in every department may be stamped with wisdom and Virtue; that, in fine, the happiness of the people of these States, under the auspices of liberty, may be made complete, by so careful a preservation and so prudent a use of this blessing as will acquire to them the glory of recommending it to the applause, the affection, and adoption of every nation which is yet a stranger to it.

Here, perhaps, I ought to stop. But a solicitude for your welfare, which cannot end but with my life, and the apprehension of danger, natural to that solicitude, urge me on an occasion like the present, to offer to your solemn contemplation, and to recommend to your frequent review, some sentiments; which are the result of much reflection, of no inconsiderable observation, and which appear to me all important to the permanency of your felicity as a People. These will be offered to you with the more freedom, as you can only see in them the disinterested warnings of a parting friend, who can possibly have no personal motive to biass his counsel. Nor can I forget, as an encouragement to it, your endulgent reception of my sentiments on a former and not dissimilar occasion.

Interwoven as is the love of liberty with every ligament of your hearts, no recommendation of mine is necessary to fortify or confirm the attachment.

The Unity of Government which constitutes you one people is also now dear to you. It is justly so; for it is a main Pillar in the Edifice of your real independence, the support of your tranquility at home; your peace abroad; of your safety of your prosperity; of that very Liberty which you so highly prize. But as it is easy to foresee, that from different causes and from different quarters, much pains will be taken, many artifices employed, to weaken in your minds the conviction of this truth; as this is the point in your political fortress against which the batteries of internal and external enemies will be most constantly and actively (though often covertly and insidiously) directed, it is of infinite moment, that you should properly estimate the immense value of your national Union to your collective and individual happiness; that you should cherish a cordial, habitual and immoveable attachment to it; accustoming yourselves to think and speak of it as of the Palladium of your political safety and prosperity; watching for its preservation with jealous anxiety; discountenancing whatever may suggest even a suspicion that it can in any event be abandoned, and indignantly frowning upon the first dawning of every attempt to alienate any portion of our Country from the rest, or to enfeeble the sacred ties which now link together the various parts.

For this you have every inducement of sympathy and interest. Citizens by birth or choice, of a common country, that country has a right to concentrate your affections. The name of AMERICAN, which belongs to you, in your national capacity, must always exalt the just pride of Patriotism, more than any appellation derived from local discriminations. With slight shades of difference, you have the same Religion, Manners, Habits and political Principles. You have in a common cause fought and triumphed together. The independence and liberty you possess are the work of joint councils, and joint efforts; of common dangers, sufferings and successes.

But these considerations, however powerfully they address themselves to your sensibility are greatly outweighed by those which apply more immediately to your Interest. Here every portion of our country finds the most commanding motives for carefully guarding and preserving the Union of the whole.

The *North,* in an unrestrained intercourse with the *South,* protected by the equal Laws of a common government, finds in the productions of the latter, great additional resources of Maratime and commercial enterprise and precious materials of manufacturing industry. The *South* in the same Intercourse, benefitting by the Agency of the *North,* sees its agriculture grow and its commerce expand. Turning partly into its own channels the seamen of the *North,* it finds its particular navigation envigorated; and while it contributes, in different ways, to nourish and increase the general mass of the National navigation, it looks forward to the protection of a Maratime strength, to which itself is unequally adapted. The *East,* in a like intercourse with the *West,* already finds, and in the progressive improvement of interior communications, by land and water, will more and more find a valuable vent for the commodities which it brings from abroad, or manufactures at home. The *West* derives from the *East* supplies requisite to its growth and comfort, and what is perhaps of still greater consequence, it must of necessity owe the *secure* enjoyment of indispensable *outlets* for its own productions to the weight, influence, and the future Maratime strength of the Atlantic side of the Union, directed by an indissoluble community of Interest as *one Nation.* Any other tenure by which the *West* can hold this essential advantage, whether derived from its own seperate strength, or from an apostate and unnatural connection with any foreign Power, must be intrinsically precarious.

While then every part of our country thus feels an immediate and particular Interest in Union, all the parts combined cannot fail to find in the united mass of means and efforts greater strength, greater resource, proportionably greater security from external danger, a less frequent interruption of their Peace by foreign Nations; and, what is of inestimable value! they must derive from Union an exemption from those broils and Wars between themselves, which so frequently afflict neighbouring countries, not tied together by the same government; which their own rivalships alone would be sufficient to produce, but which opposite foreign alliances, attachments and intrigues would stimulate and embitter. Hence likewise they will avoid the necessity of those overgrown Military establishments, which under any form of Government are inauspicious to liberty, and which are to be regarded as particularly hostile to Republican Liberty: In this sense it is, that your Union ought to be considered as a main prop of your liberty, and that the love of the one ought to endear to you the preservation of the other.

These considerations speak a persuasive language to every reflecting and virtuous mind, and exhibit the continuance of the UNION as a primary object of Patriotic desire. Is there a doubt, whether a common government can embrace so large a sphere? Let experience solve it. To listen to mere speculation in such a case were criminal. We are authorized to hope that a proper organization of the whole, with the auxiliary agency of governments for the respective Subdivisions, will afford a happy issue to the experiment. 'Tis well worth a fair and full experiment. With such powerful and obvious motives to Union, affecting all parts of our country, while experience shall not have demonstrated its impracticability, there will always be reason, to distrust the patriotism of those, who in any quarter may endeavour to weaken its bands.

In contemplating the causes which may disturb our Union, it occurs as matter of serious concern, that any ground should have been furnished for characterizing parties by *Geographical* discriminations: *Northern* and *Southern; Atlantic* and *Western;* whence designing men may endeavour to excite a belief that there is a real difference of local interests and views. One of the expedients of Party to acquire influence, within particular districts, is to misrepresent the opinions and aims of other Districts. You cannot shield yourselves too much against the jealousies and heart burnings which spring from these misrepresentations. They tend to render Alien to each other those who ought to be bound together by fraternal affection. The Inhabitants of our Western country have lately had a useful lesson on this head. They have seen, in the Negociation by the Executive, and in the unanimous ratification by the Senate, of the Treaty with Spain, and in the universal satisfaction at that event, throughout the United States, a decisive proof how unfounded were the suspicions propagated among them of a policy in the General Government and in the Atlantic States unfriendly to their Interests in regard to the MISSISSIPPI. They have been witnesses to the formation of two Treaties, that with G: Britain and that with Spain, which secure to them everything they could desire, in respect to our Foreign relations, towards confirming their prosperity. Will it not be their wisdom to rely for the preservation of these advantages on the UNION by which they were procured? Will they not henceforth be deaf to those advisers, if such there are, who would sever them from their Brethren and connect them with Aliens?

To the efficacy and permanency of Your Union, a Government for the whole is indispensable. No Alliances however strict between the parts can be an adequate substitute. They must inevitably experience the infractions and interruptions which all Alliances in all times have experienced. Sensible of this momentous truth, you have improved upon your first essay, by the adoption of a Constitution of Government, better calculated than your former for an intimate Union, and for the efficacious management of your common concerns. This government, the offspring of our own choice uninfluenced and unawed, adopted upon full investigation and mature deliberation, completely free in its principles, in the distribution of its powers, uniting security with energy, and containing within itself a provision for its own amendment, has a just claim to your confidence and your support. Respect for its authority, compliance with its Laws, acquiescence in its measures, are duties enjoined by the fundamental maxims of true Liberty. The basis of our political systems is the right of the people to make and to alter their Constitutions of Government. But the Constitution which at any time exists, till changed by an explicit and authentic act of the whole People, is sacredly obligatory upon all. The very idea of the power and the right of the People to establish Government presupposes the duty of every Individual to obey the established Government.

All obstructions to the execution of the Laws, all combinations and Associations, under whatever plausible character, with the real design to direct, controul, counteract, or awe the regular deliberation and action of the Constituted authorities are destructive of this fundamental principle and of fatal tendency. They serve to organize faction, to give it an artificial and extraordinary force; to put in the place of the delegated will of the Nation, the will of a party; often a small but artful and enterprizing minority of the Community; and, according to the alternate triumphs of different parties, to make the public administration the Mirror of the ill concerted and incongruous projects of faction, rather than the organ of consistent and wholesome plans digested by common councils and modefied by mutual interests. However combinations or Associations of the above description may now and then answer popular ends, they are likely, in the course of time and things, to become potent engines, by which cunning, ambitious and unprincipled men will be enabled to subvert the Power of the People, and to usurp for themselves the reins of Government; destroying afterwards the very engines which have lifted them to unjust dominion.

Towards the preservation of your Government and the permanency of your present happy state, it is requisite, not only that you steadily discountenance irregular oppositions to its acknowledged authority, but also that you resist with care the spirit of innovation upon its principles however specious the pretexts. One method of assault may be to effect, in the forms of the Constitution, alterations which will impair the energy of the system, and thus to undermine what cannot be directly overthrown. In all the changes to which you may be invited, remember that time and habit are at least as necessary to fix the true character of Governments, as of other human institutions; that experience is the surest standard, by which to test the real tendency of the existing Constitution of a country; that facility in changes upon the credit of mere hypotheses and opinion exposes to perpetual change, from the endless variety of hypotheses and opinion: and remember, especially, that for the efficient management of your common interests, in a country so extensive as ours, a Government of as much vigour as is consistent with the perfect security of Liberty is indispensable. Liberty itself will find in such a Government, with powers properly distributed and adjusted, its surest Guardian. It is indeed little else than a name, where the Government is too feeble to withstand the enterprises of faction, to confine each member of the Society within the limits prescribed by the laws and to maintain all in the secure and tranquil enjoyment of the rights of person and property.

I have already intimated to you the danger of Parties in the State, with particular reference to the founding of them on Geographical discriminations. Let me now take a more comprehensive view, and warn you in the most solemn manner against the baneful effects of the Spirit of Party, generally.

This spirit, unfortunately, is inseperable from our nature, having its root in the strongest passions of the human Mind. It exists under different shapes in all Governments, more or less stifled, controuled, or repressed; but, in those of the popular form it is seen in its greatest rankness and is truly their worst enemy.

The alternate domination of one faction over another, sharpened by the spirit of revenge natural to party dissention, which in different ages and countries has perpetrated the most horrid enormities, is itself a frightful despotism. But this leads at length to a more formal and permanent despotism. The disorders and miseries, which result, gradually incline the minds of men to seek security and repose in the absolute power of an Individual: and sooner or later the chief of some prevailing faction more able or more fortunate than his competitors, turns this disposition to the purposes of his own elevation, on the ruins of Public Liberty.

Without looking forward to an extremity of this kind (which nevertheless ought not to be entirely out of sight) the common and continual mischiefs of the spirit of Party are sufficient to make it the interest and the duty of a wise People to discourage and restrain it.

It serves always to distract the Public Councils and enfeeble the Public administration. It agitates the Community with ill-founded jealousies and false alarms, kindles the animosity of one part against another, foments occasionally riot and insurrection. It opens the door to foreign influence and corruption, which find a facilitated access to the government itself through the channels of party passions. Thus the policy and the will of one country, are subjected to the policy and will of another.

There is an opinion that parties in free countries are useful checks upon the Administration of the Government and serve to keep alive the spirit of Liberty. This within certain limits is probably true, and in Governments of a Monarchical cast Patriotism may look with endulgence, if not with favour, upon the spirit of party. But in those of the popular character, in Governments purely elective, it is a spirit not to be encouraged. From their natural tendency, it is certain there will always be enough of that spirit for every salutary purpose. And there being constant danger of excess, the effort ought to be, by force of public opinion, to mitigate and assuage it. A fire not to be quenched; it demands a uniform vigilance to prevent its bursting into a flame, lest instead of warming it should consume.

It is important, likewise, that the habits of thinking in a free Country should inspire caution in those entrusted with its administration, to confine themselves within their respective Constitutional spheres; avoiding in the exercise of the Powers of one department to encroach upon another. The spirit of encroachment tends to consolidate the powers of all the departments in one, and thus to create whatever the form of government, a real despotism. A just estimate of that love of power, and proneness to abuse it, which predominates in the human heart is sufficient to satisfy us of the truth of this position. The necessity of reciprocal checks in the exercise of political power; by dividing and distributing it into different depositories, and constituting each the Guardian of the Public Weal against invasions by the others, has been evinced by experiments ancient and modern; some of them in our country and under our own eyes. To preserve them must be as necessary as to institute them. If in the opinion of the People, the distribution or modification of the Constitutional powers be in any particular wrong, let it be corrected by an amendment in the way which the Constitution designates. But let there be no change by usurpation; for though this, in one instance, may be the instrument of good, it is the customary weapon by which free governments are destroyed. The precedent must always greatly overbalance in permanent evil any partial or transient benefit which the use can at any time yield.

Of all the dispositions and habits which lead to political prosperity, Religion and morality are indispensable supports. In vain would that man claim the tribute of Patriotism, who should labour to subvert these great Pillars of human happiness, these firmest props of the duties of Men and citizens. The mere Politician, equally with the pious man ought to respect and to cherish them. A volume could not trace all their connections with private and public felicity. Let it simply be asked where is the security for property, for reputation, for life, if the sense of religious obligation *desert* the oaths, which are the instruments of investigation in Courts of Justice? And let us with caution indulge the supposition, that morality can be maintained without religion. Whatever may be conceded to the influence of refined education on minds of peculiar structure, reason and experience both forbid us to expect that National morality can prevail in exclusion of religious principle.

'Tis substantially true, that virtue or morality is a necessary spring of popular government. The rule indeed extends with more or less force to every species of free Government. Who that is a sincere friend to it, can look with indifference upon attempts to shake the foundation of the fabric.

Promote then as an object of primary importance, Institutions for the general diffusion of knowledge. In proportion as the structure of a government gives force to public opinion, it is essential that public opinion should be enlightened.

As a very important source of strength and security, cherish public credit. One method of preserving it is to use it as sparingly as possible: avoiding occasions of expence by cultivating peace, but remembering also that timely disbursements to prepare for danger frequently prevent much greater disbursements to repel it; avoiding likewise the accumulation of debt, not only by shunning occasions of expence, but by vigorous exertions in time of Peace to discharge the Debts which unavoidable wars may have occasioned, not ungenerously throwing upon posterity the burthen which we ourselves ought to bear. The execution of these maxims belongs to your Representatives, but it is necessary that public opinion should cooperate. To facilitate to them the performance of their duty it is essential that you should practically bear in mind, that towards the payment of debts there must be Revenue; that to have Revenue there must be taxes; that no taxes can be devised which are not more or less inconvenient and unpleasant; that the intrinsic embarrassment inseperable from the selection of the proper objects (which is always a choice of difficulties) ought to be a decisive motive for a candid construction of the Conduct of the Government in making it, and for a spirit of acquiescence in the measures for obtaining Revenue which the public exigencies may at any time dictate.

Observe good faith and justice towards all Nations. Cultivate peace and harmony with all. Religion and morality enjoin this conduct; and can it be that good policy does not equally enjoin it? It will be worthy of a free, enlightened, and, at no distant period, a great Nation, to give to mankind the magnanimous and too novel example of a People always guided by an exalted justice and benevolence. Who can doubt that in the course of time and things the fruits of such a plan would richly repay any temporary advantages which might be lost by a steady adherence to it? Can it be, that Providence has not connected the permanent felicity of a Nation with its virtue? The experiment, at least, is recommended by every sentiment which ennobles human Nature. Alas! is it rendered impossible by its vices?

In the execution of such a plan nothing is more essential than that permanent, inveterate antipathies against particular Nations and passionate attachments for others should be excluded; and that in place of them just and amicable feelings towards all should be cultivated. The Nation, which indulges towards another an habitual hatred, or an habitual fondness, is in some degree a slave. It is a slave to its animosity or to its affection, either of which is sufficient to lead it astray from its duty and its interest. Antipathy in one Nation against another, disposes each more readily to offer insult and injury, to lay hold of slight causes of umbrage, and to be haughty and intractable, when accidental or trifling occasions of dispute occur. Hence frequent collisions, obstinate envenomed and bloody contests. The Nation, prompted by ill will and resentment sometimes impels to War the Government, contrary to the best calculations of policy. The Government sometimes participates in the national propensity, and adopts through passion what reason would reject; at other times, it makes the animosity of the Nation subservient to projects of hostility instigated by pride, ambition and other sinister and pernicious motives. The peace often, sometimes perhaps the Liberty, of Nations has been the victim.

So likewise, a passionate attachment of one Nation for another produces a variety of evils. Sympathy for the favourite nation, facilitating the illusion of an imaginary common interest, in cases where no real common interest exists, and infusing into one the enmities of the other, betrays the former into a participation in the quarrels and Wars of the latter, without adequate inducement or justification: It leads also to concessions to the favourite Nation of priviledges denied to others, which is apt doubly to injure the Nation making the concessions; by unnecessarily parting with what ought to have been retained; and by exciting jealousy, ill will, and a disposition to retaliate, in the parties from whom equal priviledges are withheld: And it gives to ambitious, corrupted, or deluded citizens (who devote themselves to the favourite Nation) facility to betray, or sacrifice the interests of their own country, without odium, sometimes even with popularity; gilding with the appearances of a virtuous sense of obligation a commendable deference for public opinion, or a laudable zeal for public good, the base or foolish compliances of ambition, corruption or infatuation.

As avenues to foreign influence in innumerable ways, such attachments are particularly alarming to the truly enlightened and independent Patriot. How many opportunities do they afford to tamper with domestic factions, to practice the arts of seduction, to mislead public opinion, to influence or awe the public Councils! Such an attachment of a small or weak, towards a great and powerful Nation, dooms the former to be the satellite of the latter.

Against the insidious wiles of foreign influence, (I conjure you to believe me fellow citizens), the jealousy of a free people ought to be *constantly* awake; since history and experience prove that foreign influence is one of the most baneful foes of Republican Government. But that jealousy to be useful must be impartial; else it becomes the instrument of the very influence to be avoided, instead of a defence against it. Excessive partiality for one foreign nation and excessive dislike of another, cause those whom they actuate to see danger only on one side, and serve to veil and even second the arts of influence on the other. Real Patriots, who may resist the intriegues of the favourite, are liable to become suspected and odious; while its tools and dupes usurp the applause and confidence of the people, to surrender their interests.

The Great rule of conduct for us, in regard to foreign Nations is in extending our commercial relations to have with them as little *political* connection as possible. So far as we have already formed engagedments let them be fulfilled, with perfect good faith. Here let us stop.

Europe has a set of primary interests, which to us have none, or a very remote relation. Hence she must be engaged in frequent controversies, the causes of which are essentially foreign to our concerns. Hence therefore it must be unwise in us to implicate ourselves, by artificial ties, in the ordinary vicissitudes of her politics, or the ordinary combinations and collisions of her friendships, or enmities.

Our detached and distant situation invites and enables us to pursue a different course. If we remain one People, under an efficient government, the period is not far off, when we may defy material injury from external annoyance; when we may take such an attitude as will cause the neutrality we may at any time resolve upon to be scrupulously respected; when belligerent nations, under the impossibility of making acquisitions upon us, will not lightly hazard the giving us provocation; when we may choose peace or war, as our interest guided by our justice shall Counsel.

Why forgo the advantages of so peculiar a situation? Why quit our own to stand upon foreign ground? Why, by interweaving our destiny with that of any part of Europe, entangle our peace and prosperity in the toils of European Ambition, Rivalship, Interest, Humour or Caprice?

'Tis our true policy to steer clear of permanent Alliances, with any portion of the foreign world. So far, I mean, as we are now at liberty to do it, for let me not be understood as capable of patronising infidelity to existing engagements (I hold the maxim no less applicable to public than to private affairs, that honesty is always the best policy). I repeat it therefore, let those engagements be observed in their genuine sense. But in my opinion, it is unnecessary and would be unwise to extend them.

Taking care always to keep ourselves, by suitable establishments, on a respectably defensive posture, we may safely trust to temporary alliances for extraordinary emergencies.

Harmony, liberal intercourse with all Nations, are recommended by policy, humanity and interest. But even our Commercial policy should hold an equal and impartial hand: neither seeking nor granting exclusive favours or preferences; consulting the natural course of things; diffusing and deversifying by gentle means the streams of Commerce, but forcing nothing; establishing with Powers so disposed; in order to give to trade a stable course, to define the rights of our Merchants, and to enable the Government to support them; conventional rules of intercourse, the best that present circumstances and mutual opinion will permit, but temporary, and liable to be from time to time abandoned or varied, as experience and circumstances shall dictate; constantly keeping in view, that 'tis folly in one Nation to look for disinterested favours from another; that it must pay with a portion of its Independence for whatever it may accept under that character; that by such acceptance, it may place itself in the condition of having given equivalents for nominal favours and yet of being reproached with ingratitude for not giving more. There can be no greater error than to expect, or calculate upon real favours from Nation to Nation. 'Tis an illusion which experience must cure, which a just pride ought to discard.

In offering to you, my Countrymen these counsels of an old and affectionate friend, I dare not hope they will make the strong and lasting impression, I could wish; that they will controul the usual current of the passions, or prevent our Nation from running the course which has hitherto marked the Destiny of Nations: But if I may even flatter myself, that they may be productive of some partial benefit, some occasional good; that they may now and then recur to moderate the fury of party spirit, to warn against the mischiefs of foreign Intriegue, to guard against the Impostures of pretended patriotism; this hope will be a full recompence for the solicitude for your welfare, by which they have been dictated.

How far in the discharge of my Official duties, I have been guided by the principles which have been delineated, the public Records and other evidences of my conduct must Witness to You and to the world. To myself, the assurance of my own conscience is, that I have at least believed myself to be guided by them.

In relation to the still subsisting War in Europe, my Proclamation of the 22d. of April 1793 is the index to my Plan. Sanctioned by your approving voice and by that of Your Representatives in both Houses of Congress, the spirit of that measure has continually governed me; uninfluenced by any attempts to deter or divert me from it.

After deliberate examination with the aid of the best lights I could obtain I was well satisfied that our Country, under all the circumstances of the case, had a right to take, and was bound in duty and interest, to take a Neutral position. Having taken it, I determined, as far as should depend upon me, to maintain it, with moderation, perseverence and firmness.

The considerations, which respect the right to hold this conduct, it is not necessary on this occasion to detail. I will only observe, that according to my understanding of the matter, that right, so far from being denied by any of the Belligerent Powers has been virtually admitted by all.

The duty of holding a Neutral conduct may be inferred, without anything more, from the obligation which justice and humanity impose on every Nation, in cases in which it is free to act, to maintain inviolate the relations of Peace and amity towards other Nations.

The inducements of interest for observing that conduct will best be referred to your own reflections and experience. With me, a predominant motive has been to endeavour to gain time to our country to settle and mature its yet recent institutions, and to progress without interruption, to that degree of strength and consistency, which is necessary to give it, humanly speaking, the command of its own fortunes.

Though in reviewing the incidents of my Administration, I am unconscious of intentional error, I am nevertheless too sensible of my defects not to think it probable that I may have committed many errors. Whatever they may be I fervently beseech the Almighty to avert or mitigate the evils to which they may tend. I shall also carry with me the hope that my Country will never cease to view them with indulgence; and that after forty-five years of my life dedicated to its Service, with an upright zeal, the faults of incompetent abilities will be consigned to oblivion, as myself must soon be to the Mansions of rest.

Relying on its kindness in this as in other things, and actuated by that fervent love towards it, which is so natural to a Man, who views in it the native soil of himself and his progenitors for several Generations; I anticipate with pleasing expectation that retreat, in which I promise myself to realize, without alloy, the sweet enjoyment of partaking, in the midst of my fellow Citizens, the benign influence of good Laws under a free Government, the ever favourite object of my heart, and the happy reward, as I trust, of our mutual cares, labours and dangers.

WASHINGTON IRVING

Washington Irving (1783–1859) was America's first professional man of letters. Other writers—clergymen, statesmen, housewives—preceded him, but Irving was the first to make a living entirely by his pen. The belletristic fiction, nonfiction, and travel writer's 1819 Sketch Book collection contains his most celebrated short stories, "Rip Van Winkle" and "The Legend of Sleepy Hollow." His familiar essays operate stylistically in the bachelor-spectator vein of Joseph Addison, Richard Steele, and Charles Lamb, complete with an invented persona (Geoffrey Crayon). Irving's patriotic love of America was balanced by his urge to take in the larger world, as he makes clear by this genially self-mocking defense in "The Author's Account of Himself."

The Author's Account of Himself

(1819)

> I am of this mind with Homer, that as the snaile that crept out of her shel was turned eftsoones into a Toad, and thereby was forced to make a stoole to sit on; so the traveller that stragleth from his owne country is in a short time transformed into so monstrous a shape that he is faine to alter his mansion with his manners and to live where he can, not where he would.
>
> —Lyly's *Euphues*

I was always fond of visiting new scenes and observing strange characters and manners. Even when a mere child I began my travels and made many tours of discovery into foreign parts and unknown regions of my native city; to the frequent alarm of my parents and the emolument of the town cryer. As I grew into boyhood I extended the range of my observations. My holyday afternoons were spent in rambles about the surrounding country. I made myself familiar with all its places famous in history or fable. I knew every spot where a murder or robbery had been committed or a ghost seen. I visited the neighbouring villages and added greatly to my stock of knowledge, by noting their habits and customs, and conversing with their sages and great men. I even journeyed one long summer's day to the summit of the most distant hill, from whence I stretched my eye over many a mile of terra incognita, and was astonished to find how vast a globe I inhabited.

This rambling propensity strengthened with my years. Books of voyages and travels became my passion, and in devouring their contents I neglected the regular exercises of the school. How wistfully would I wander about the pier heads in fine weather, and watch the parting ships, bound to distant climes. With what longing eyes would I gaze after their lessening sails, and waft myself in imagination to the ends of the earth.

Further reading and thinking, though they brought this vague inclination into more reasonable bounds, only served to make it more decided. I visited various parts of my own country, and had I been merely a lover of fine scenery, I should have felt little desire to seek elsewhere its gratification, for on no country have the charms of nature been more prodigally lavished. Her mighty lakes, like oceans of liquid silver; her mountains with their bright aerial tints; her valleys teeming with wild fertility; her tremendous cataracts thundering in their solitudes; her boundless plains waving with spontaneous verdure; her broad deep rivers, rolling in solemn silence to the ocean; her trackless forests, where vegetation puts forth all its magnificence; her skies kindling with the magic of summer clouds and glorious sunshine—no, never need an American look beyond his own country for the sublime and beautiful of natural scenery.

But Europe held forth the charms of storied and poetical association. There were to be seen the masterpieces of art, the refinements of highly cultivated society, the quaint peculiarities of ancient and local custom. My native country was full of youthful promise; Europe was rich in the accumulated treasures of age. Her very ruins told the history of times gone by, and every mouldering stone was a chronicle. I longed to wander over the scenes of renowned achievement—to tread as it were in the footsteps of antiquity—to loiter about the ruined castle—to meditate on the falling tower—to escape in short, from the commonplace realities of the present, and lose myself among the shadowy grandeurs of the past.

I had, beside all this, an earnest desire to see the great men of the earth. We have, it is true, our great men in America—not a city but has an ample share of them. I have mingled among them in my time, and been almost withered by the shade into which they cast me; for there is nothing so baleful to a small man as the shade of a great one, particularly the great man of a city. But I was anxious to see the great men of Europe; for I had read in the works of various philosophers, that all animals degenerated in America, and man among the number. A great man of Europe, thought I, must therefore be as superior to a great man of America, as a peak of the Alps to a highland of the Hudson; and in this idea I was confirmed by observing the comparative importance and swelling magnitude of many English travellers among us; who, I was assured, were very little people in their own country.—I will visit this land of wonders, thought I, and see the gigantic race from which I am degenerated.

It has been either my good or evil lot to have my roving passion gratified. I have wandered through different countries and witnessed many of the shifting scenes of life. I cannot say that I have studied them with the eye of a philosopher, but rather with the sauntering gaze with which humble lovers of the picturesque stroll from the window of one print shop to another; caught sometimes by the delineations of beauty, sometimes by the distortions of caricature and sometimes by the loveliness of landscape. As it is the fashion for modern tourists to travel pencil in hand, and bring home their portfolios filled with sketches, I am disposed to get up a few for the entertainment of my friends. When I look over, however, the hints and memorandums I have taken down for the purpose, my heart almost fails me at finding how my idle humour has led me aside from the great objects studied by every regular traveller who would make a book. I fear I shall give equal disappointment with an unlucky landscape painter, who had travelled on the continent, but following the bent of his vagrant inclination, had sketched in nooks and corners and bye places. His sketch book was accordingly crowded with cottages, and landscapes, and obscure ruins; but he had neglected to paint St. Peter's or the Coliseum; the cascade of Terni or the Bay of Naples; and had not a single Glacier or Volcano in his whole collection.

JOHN JAMES AUDUBON

Famous for his beautiful drawings and paintings of birds, which were displayed in his books Birds of America *and the five-volume* Ornithological Biography, *John James Audubon (1785–1851) has come to be appreciated also as a pioneering American nature writer. He was born in Haiti, grew up in France, and migrated to the United States at eighteen. In his many expeditions through the American wilderness, he brought the same marvelous precision and unquenchable sense of wonderment to his verbal descriptions of birds as he did to his portraits. From the report below on the passenger pigeons' then-astonishing abundance as well as their massive slaughter, one can foresee that Audubon would become an outspoken conservationist.*

The Passenger Pigeon

(1835)

The Passenger Pigeon, or, as it is usually named in America, the Wild Pigeon, moves with extreme rapidity, propelling itself by quickly repeated flaps of the wings, which it brings more or less near to the body, according to the degree of velocity which is required. Like the Domestic Pigeon, it often flies, during the love season, in a circling manner, supporting itself with both wings angularly elevated, in which position it keeps them until it is about to alight. Now and then, during these circular flights, the tips of the primary quills of each wing are made to strike against each other, producing a smart rap, which may be heard at a distance of thirty or forty yards. Before alighting, the Wild Pigeon, like the Carolina Parrot and a few other species of birds, breaks the force of its flight by repeated flappings, as if apprehensive of receiving injury from coming too suddenly into contact with the branch or the spot of ground on which it intends to settle.

I have commenced my description of this species with the above account of its flight, because the most important facts connected with its habits relate to its migrations. These are entirely owing to the necessity of procuring food, and are not performed with the view of escaping the severity of a northern latitude, or of seeking a southern one for the purpose of breeding. They consequently do not take place at any fixed period or season of the year. Indeed, it sometimes happens that a continuance of a sufficient supply of food in one district will keep these birds absent from another for years. I know, at least, to a certainty, that in Kentucky they remained for several years constantly, and were nowhere else to be found. They all suddenly disappeared one season when the mast was exhausted, and did not return for a long period. Similar facts have been observed in other States.

Their great power of flight enables them to survey and pass over an astonishing extent of country in a very short time. This is proved by facts well known. Thus, Pigeons have been killed in the neighbourhood of New York, with their crops full of rice, which they must have collected in the fields of Georgia and Carolina, these districts being the nearest in which they could possibly have procured a supply of that kind of food. As their power of digestion is so great that they will decompose food entirely in twelve hours, they must in this case have travelled between three and four hundred miles in six hours, which shews their speed to be at an average of about one mile in a minute. A velocity such as this would enable one of these birds, were it so inclined, to visit the European continent in less than three days.

This great power of flight is seconded by as great a power of vision, which discover their food with facility, and thus attain the object for which their journey has been undertaken. This I have also proved to be the case, by having observed them, when passing over a sterile part of the country, or one scantily furnished with food suited to them, keep high in the air, flying with an extended front, so as to enable them to survey hundreds of acres at once. On the contrary, when the land is richly covered with food, or the trees abundantly hung with mast, they fly low, in order to discover the part most plentifully supplied.

Their body is of an elongated oval form, steered by a long well-plumed tail, and propelled by well-set wings, the muscles of which are very large and powerful for the size of the bird. When an individual is seen gliding through the woods and close to the observer, it passes like a thought, and on trying to see it again, the eye searches in vain; the bird is gone.

The multitudes of Wild Pigeons in our woods are astonishing. Indeed, after having viewed them so often, and under so many circumstances, I even now feel inclined to pause, and assure myself that what I am going to relate is fact. Yet I have seen it all, and that too in the company of persons who, like myself, were struck with amazement.

In the autumn of 1813, I left my house at Dameron, on the banks of the Ohio, on my way to Louisville. In passing over the Barrens a few miles beyond Hardensburgh, I observed the Pigeons flying from north-east to south-west, in greater numbers than I thought I had ever seen them before, and feeling an inclination to count the flocks that might pass within the reach of my eye in one hour, I dismounted, seated myself on an eminence, and began to mark with my pencil, making a dot for every flock that passed. In a short time finding the task which I had undertaken impracticable, as the birds poured in in countless multitudes, I rose, and counting the dots then put down, found that 163 had been made in twenty-one minutes. I travelled on, and still met more the farther I proceeded. The air was literally filled with Pigeons; the light of noon-day was obscured as by an eclipse, the dung fell in spots, not unlike melting flakes of snow; and the continued buzz of wings had a tendency to lull my senses to repose.

Whilst waiting for dinner at YOUNG's inn at the confluence of Salt river with the Ohio, I saw, at my leisure, immense legions still going by, with a front reaching far beyond the Ohio on the west, and the beech-wood forests directly on the east of me. Not a single bird alighted; for not a nut or acorn was that year to be seen in the neighbourhood. They consequently flew so high, that different trials to reach them with a capital rifle proved ineffectual; nor did the reports disturb them in the least. I cannot describe to you the extreme beauty of their aerial evolutions, when a Hawk chanced to press upon the rear of a flock. At once, like a torrent, and with a noise like thunder, they rushed into a compact mass, pressing upon each other towards the centre. In these almost solid masses, they darted forward in undulating and angular lines, descended and swept close over the earth with inconceivable velocity, mounted perpendicularly so as to resemble a vast column, and, when high, were seen wheeling and twisting within their continued lines, which then resembled the coils of a gigantic serpent.

Before sunset I reached Louisville, distant from Hardensburgh fifty-five miles. The Pigeons were still passing in undiminished numbers, and continued to do so for three days in succession. The people were all in arms. The banks of the Ohio were crowded with men and boys, incessantly shooting at the pilgrims, which there flew lower as they passed the river. Multitudes were thus destroyed. For a week or more, the population fed on no other flesh than that of Pigeons, and talked of nothing but Pigeons.

It is extremely interesting to see flock after flock performing exactly the same evolutions which had been traced as it were in the air by a preceding flock. Thus, should a Hawk have charged on a group at a certain spot, the angles, curves, and undulations that have been described by the birds, in their efforts to escape from the dreaded talons of the plunderer, are unde-viatingly followed by the next group that comes up. Should the bystander happen to witness one of these affrays, and, struck with the rapidity and elegance of the motions exhibited, feel desirous of seeing them repeated, his wishes will be gratified if he only remain in the place until the next group comes up.

As soon as the Pigeons discover a sufficiency of food to entice them to alight, they fly around in circles, reviewing the country below. Dur-ing their evolutions, on such occasions, the dense mass which they form exhibits a beautiful appearance, as it changes its direction, now displaying a glistening sheet of azure, when the backs of the birds come simulta-neously into view, and anon, suddenly presenting a mass of rich deep purple. They then pass lower, over the woods, and for a moment are lost among the foliage, but again emerge, and are seen gliding aloft. They now alight, but the next moment, as if suddenly alarmed, they take to wing, producing by the flappings of their wing a noise like the roar of distant thunder, and sweep through the forests to see if danger is near. Hunger, however, soon brings them to the ground. When alighted, they are seen industriously throwing up the withered leaves in quest of the fallen mast. The rear ranks are continually rising, passing over the main-body, and alighting in front, in such rapid succession, that the whole flock seems still on wing. The quantity of ground thus swept is astonishing, and so completely has it been cleared, that the gleaner who might follow in their rear would find his labour completely lost. Whilst feeding, their avidity is at times so great that in attempting to swallow a large acorn or nut, they are seen gasping for a long while, as if in the agonies of suffocation.

On such occasions, when the woods are filled with these Pigeons, they are killed in immense numbers, although no apparent diminution ensues. About the middle of the day, after their repast is finished, they settle on the trees, to enjoy rest, and digest their food. On the ground they walk with ease, as well as on the branches, frequently jerking their beautiful tail, and moving the neck backwards and forwards in the most graceful manner. As the sun begins to sink beneath the horizon, they depart en masse for the roosting-place, which not unfrequently is hundreds of miles distant, as has been ascertained by persons who have kept an account of their arrivals and departures.

Let us now, kind reader, inspect their place of nightly rendezvous. One of these curious roosting-places, on the banks of the Green river in Kentucky, I repeatedly visited. It was, as is always the case, in a portion of the forest where the trees were of great magnitude, and where there was little under-wood. I rode through it upwards of forty miles, and, crossing it in different parts, found its average breadth to be rather more than three miles. My first view of it was about a fortnight subsequent to the period when they had made choice of it, and I arrived there nearly two hours before sunset. Few Pigeons were then to be seen, but a great number of persons, with horses and wagons, guns and ammunition, had already established encampments on the borders. Two farmers from the vicinity of Russelsville, distant more than a hundred miles, had driven upwards of three hundred hogs to be fattened on the pigeons which were to be slaughtered. Here and there, the people employed in plucking and salting what had already been procured, were seen sitting in the midst of large piles of these birds. The dung lay several inches deep, covering the whole extent of the roosting-place. Many trees two feet in diameter, I observed, were broken off at no great distance from the ground; and the branches of many of the largest and tallest had given way, as if the forest had been swept by a tornado. Every thing proved to me that the number of birds resorting to this part of the forest must be immense beyond conception. As the period of their arrival approached, their foes anxiously prepared to receive them. Some were furnished with iron-pots containing sulphur, others with torches of pine-knots, many with poles, and the rest with guns. The sun was lost to our view, yet not a Pigeon had arrived. Every thing was ready, and all eyes were gazing on the clear sky, which appeared in glimpses amidst the tall trees. Suddenly there burst forth a general cry of "Here they come!" The noise which they made, though yet distant, reminded me of a hard gale at sea, passing through the rigging of a close-reefed vessel. As the birds arrived and passed over me, I felt a current of air that surprised me. Thousands were soon knocked down by the pole-men. The birds continued to pour in. The fires were lighted, and a magnificent, as well as wonderful and almost terrifying, sight presented itself. The Pigeons, arriving by thousands, alighted everywhere, one above another, until solid masses were formed on the branches all round. Here and there the perches gave way under the weight with a crash, and, falling to the ground, destroyed hundreds of the birds beneath, forcing down the dense groups with which every stick was loaded. It was a scene of uproar and confusion. I found it quite useless to speak, or even to shout to those persons who were nearest to me. Even the reports of the guns were seldom heard, and I was made aware of the firing only by seeing the shooters reloading.

No one dared venture within the line of devastation. The hogs had been penned up in due time, the picking up of the dead and wounded being left for the next morning's employment. The Pigeons were constantly coming, and it was past midnight before I perceived a decrease in the number of those that arrived. The uproar continued the whole night; and as I was anxious to know to what distance the sound reached, I sent off a man, accustomed to perambulate the forest, who, returning two hours afterwards, informed me he had heard it distinctly when three miles distant from the spot. Towards the approach of day, the noise in some measure subsided: long before objects were distinguishable, the Pigeons began to move off in a direction quite different from that in which they had arrived the evening before, and at sunrise all that were able to fly had disappeared. The howlings of the wolves now reached our ears, and the foxes, lynxes, cougars, bears, racoons, opossums and pole-cats were seen sneaking off, whilst eagles and hawks of different species, accompanied by a crowd of vultures, came to supplant them, and enjoy their share of the spoil.

It was then that the authors of all this devastation began their entry amongst the dead, the dying, and the mangled. The Pigeons were picked up and piled in heaps, until each had as many as he could possibly dispose of, when the hogs were let loose to feed on the remainder.

Persons unacquainted with these birds might naturally conclude that such dreadful havoc would soon put an end to the species. But I have satisfied myself, by long observation, that nothing but the gradual diminution of our forests can accomplish their decrease, as they not unfrequently quadruple their numbers yearly, and always at least double it. In 1805 I saw schooners loaded in bulk with Pigeons caught up the Hudson river, coming in to the wharf at New York, when the birds sold for a cent a piece. I knew a man in Pennsylvania, who caught and killed upwards of 500 dozens in a clap-net in one day, sweeping sometimes twenty dozens or more at a single haul. In the month of March 1830, they were so abundant in the markets of New York, that piles of them met the eye in every direction. I have seen the Negroes at the United States' Salines or Saltworks of Shawanee Town, wearied with killing Pigeons, as they alighted to drink the water issuing from the leading pipes, for weeks at a time; and yet in 1826, in Louisiana, I saw congregated flocks of these birds as numerous as ever I had seen them before, during a residence of nearly thirty years in the United States.

The breeding of the Wild Pigeons, and the places chosen for that purpose, are points of great interest. The time is not much influenced by season, and the place selected is where food is most plentiful and most attainable, and always at a convenient distance from water. Forest-trees of great height are those in which the Pigeons form their nests. Thither the countless myriads resort, and prepare to fulfil one of the great laws of nature. At this period the note of the Pigeon is a soft coo-coo-coo-coo, much shorter than that of the domestic species. The common notes resemble the monosyllables kee-kee-kee-kee, the first being the loudest, the others gradually diminishing in power. The male assumes a pompous demeanour, and follows the female, whether on the ground or on the branches, with spread tail and drooping wings, which it rubs against the part over which it is moving. The body is elevated, the throat swells, the eyes sparkle. He continues his notes, and now and then rises on the wing, and flies a few yards to approach the fugitive and timorous female.

Like the domestic Pigeon and other species, they caress each other by bill-ing, in which action, the bill of the one is introduced transversely into that of the other, and both parties alternately disgorge the contents of their crop by repeated efforts. These preliminary affairs are soon settled, and the Pigeons commence their nests in general peace and harmony. They are composed of a few dry twigs, crossing each other, and are supported by forks of the branches. On the same tree from fifty to a hundred nests may frequently be seen:—I might say a much greater number, were I not anxious, kind reader, that however wonderful my account of the Wild Pigeon is, you may not feel disposed to refer it to the marvellous. The eggs are two in number, of a broadly elliptical form, and pure white. During incubation, the male supplies the female with food. Indeed, the tender-ness and affection displayed by these birds towards their mates, are in the highest degree striking. It is a remarkable fact, that each brood generally consists of a male and a female.

Here again, the tyrant of the creation, man, interferes, disturbing the harmony of this peaceful scene. As the young birds grow up, their enemies, armed with axes, reach the spot, to seize and destroy all they can. The trees are felled, and made to fall in such a way that the cut-ting of one causes the overthrow of another, or shakes the neighbouring trees so much, that the young Pigeons, or squabs, as they are named, are violently hurried to the ground. In this manner also, immense quantities are destroyed.

The young are fed by the parents in the manner described above; in other words, the old bird introduces its bill into the mouth of the young one in a transverse manner, or with the back of each mandible opposite the separations of the mandibles of the young bird, and disgorges the contents of its crop. As soon as the young birds are able to shift for them-selves, they leave their parents, and continue separate until they attain maturity. By the end of six months they are capable of reproducing their species.

The flesh of the Wild Pigeon is of a dark colour, but affords tolerable eating. That of young birds from the nest is much esteemed. The skin is covered with small white filmy scales. The feathers fall off at the least touch, as has been remarked to be the case in the Carolina Turtle-dove. I have only to add, that this species, like others of the same genus, immerses its head up to the eyes while drinking.

In March 1830, I bought about 350 of these birds in the market of New York, at four cents a piece. Most of these I carried alive to England, and distributed them amongst several noblemen, presenting some at the same time to the Zoological Society.

SARAH MOORE GRIMKÉ

Sarah Moore Grimké (1792–1873) was a dedicated abolitionist and feminist who saw the two causes as intertwined. Born to a rich, slave-owning planter in South Carolina, she came to hate slavery and the oppression of women. Intellectually gifted, she resented deeply the better education that her brothers received, and the relegation of girls to be consecrated "to the pleasure of man." In her Letters on the Equality of the Sexes, and the Condition of Woman, *addressed to her younger sister Angelina, which first ran in newspapers, she embedded her views on women's rights in the Quaker faith she had embraced. Speaking as a single woman on the abolitionist lecture circuit, she encountered opposition from her coreligionists, but her writings and example inspired later advocates of women's suffrage, such as Elizabeth Cady Stanton and Lucretia Mott.*

On the Condition of Women in the United States

(1837)

My Dear Sister,—I have now taken a brief survey of the condition of woman in various parts of the world. I regret that my time has been so much occupied by other things, that I have been unable to bestow that attention upon the subject which it merits, and that my constant change of place has prevented me from having access to books, which might probably have assisted me in this part of my work. I hope that the principles I have asserted will claim the attention of some of my sex, who may be able to bring into view, more thoroughly than I have done, the situation and degradation of woman. I shall now proceed to make a few remarks on the condition of women in my own country.

During the early part of my life, my lot was cast among the butterflies of the *fashionable* world; and of this class of women, I am constrained to say, both from experience and observation, that their education is miserably deficient; that they are taught to regard marriage as the one thing needful, the only avenue to distinction; hence to attract the notice and win the attentions of men, by their external charms, is the chief business of fashionable girls. They seldom think that men will be allured by intellectual acquirements, because they find, that where any mental superiority exists, a woman is generally shunned and regarded as stepping out of her "appropriate sphere," which, in their view, is to dress, to dance, to set out to the best possible advantage her person, to read the novels which inundate the press, and which do more to destroy her character as a rational creature, than any thing else. Fashionable women regard themselves, and are regarded by men, as pretty toys or as mere instruments of pleasure; and the vacuity of mind, the heartlessness, the frivolity which is the necessary result of this false and debasing estimate of women, can only be fully understood by those who have mingled in the folly and wickedness of fashionable life; and who have been called from such pursuits by the voice of the Lord Jesus, inviting their weary and heavy laden souls to come unto Him and learn of Him, that they may find something worthy of their immortal spirit, and their intellectual powers; that they may learn the high and holy purposes of their creation, and consecrate themselves unto the service of God; and not, as is now the case, to the pleasure of man.

There is another and much more numerous class in this country, who are withdrawn by education or circumstances from the circle of fashionable amusements, but who are brought up with the dangerous and absurd idea, that *marriage* is a kind of preferment; and that to be able to keep their husband's house, and render his situation comfortable, is the end of her being. Much that she does and says and thinks is done in reference to this situation; and to be married is too often held up to the view of girls as the sine qua non of human happiness and human existence. For this purpose more than for any other, I verily believe the majority of girls are trained. This is demonstrated by the imperfect education which is bestowed upon them, and the little pains taken to cultivate their minds, after they leave school, by the little time allowed them for reading, and by the idea being constantly inculcated, that although all household concerns should be attended to with scrupulous punctuality at particular seasons, the improvement of their intellectual capacities is only a secondary consideration, and may serve as an occupation to fill up the odds and ends of time. In most families, it is considered a matter of far more consequence to call a girl off from making a pie, or a pudding, than to

interrupt her whilst engaged in her studies. This mode of training necessarily exalts, in their view, the animal above the intellectual and spiritual
nature, and teaches women to regard themselves as a kind of machinery,
necessary to keep the domestic engine in order, but of little value as the
intelligent companions of men.

Let no one think, from these remarks, that I regard a knowledge of
housewifery as beneath the acquisition of women. Far from it: I believe
that a complete knowledge of household affairs is an indispensable requisite in a woman's education,—that by the mistress of a family, whether
married or single, doing her duty thoroughly and *understandingly,* the
happiness of the family is increased to an incalculable degree, as well as
a vast amount of time and money saved. All I complain of is, that our
education consists so almost exclusively in culinary and other manual
operations. I do long to see the time, when it will no longer be necessary
for women to expend so many precious hours in furnishing "a well spread
table," but that their husbands will forgo some of their accustomed indul-
gences in this way, and encourage their wives to devote some portion of
their time to mental cultivation, even at the expense of having to dine
sometimes on baked potatoes, or bread and butter. . . .

The influence of women over the minds and character of *children*
of both sexes, is allowed to be far greater than that of men. This being
the case by the very ordering of nature, women should be prepared by
education for the performance of their sacred duties as mothers and as
sisters. . . .

There is another way in which the general opinion, that women are
inferior to men, is manifested, that bears with tremendous effect on the
laboring class, and indeed on almost all who are obliged to earn a subsistence, whether it be by mental or physical exertion—I allude to the
disproportionate value set on the time and labor of men and of women.
A man who is engaged in teaching, can always, I believe, command a
higher price for tuition than a woman—even when he teaches the same
branches, and is not in any respect superior to the woman. This I know is
the case in boarding and other schools with which I have been acquainted,
and it is so in every occupation in which the sexes engage indiscriminately. As for example, in tailoring, a man has twice, or three times as
much for making a waistcoat or pantaloons as a woman, although the
work done by each may be equally good. In those employments which are
peculiar to women, their time is estimated at only half the value of that
of men. A woman who goes out to wash, works as hard in proportion as a
wood sawyer, or a coal heaver, but she is not generally able to make more
than half as much by a day's work. The low remuneration which women
receive for their work, has claimed the attention of a few philanthropists,
and I hope it will continue to do so until some remedy is applied for this
enormous evil. I have known a widow, left with four or five children, to

provide for, unable to leave home because her helpless babes demand her attention, compelled to earn a scanty subsistence, by making coarse shirts at 12½ cents a piece, or by taking in washing, for which she was paid by some wealthy persons 12½ cents per dozen. All these things evince the low estimation in which woman is held. There is yet another and more disastrous consequence arising from this unscriptural notion—women being educated, from the earliest childhood, to regard themselves as inferior creatures, have not that self-respect which conscious equality would engender, and hence when their virtue is assailed, they yield to temptation with facility, under the idea that it rather exalts than debases them, to be connected with a superior being.

There is another class of women in this country, to whom I cannot refer, without feelings of the deepest shame and sorrow. I allude to our female slaves. Our southern cities are helmed beneath a tide of pollution; the virtue of female slaves is wholly at the mercy of responsible tyrants, and women are bought and sold in our slave markets, to gratify the brutal lust of those who bear the name of Christians. In our slave States, if amid all her degradation and ignorance, a woman desires to preserve her virtue unsullied, she is either bribed or whipped into compliance, or if she dares resist her seducer, her life by the laws of some of the slave States may be, and has actually been sacrificed to the fury of disappointed passion. Where such laws do not exist, the power which is necessarily vested in the master over his property, leaves the defenceless slave entirely at his mercy, and the sufferings of some females on this account, both physical and mental, are intense. . . .

. . . Nor does the colored woman suffer alone: the moral purity of the white woman is deeply contaminated. In the daily habit of seeing the virtue of her enslaved sister sacrificed without hesitancy or remorse, she looks upon the crimes of seduction and illicit intercourse without horror, and although not personally involved in the guilt, she loses that value for innocence in her own, as well as the other sex, which is one of the strongest safeguards to virtue. She lives in habitual intercourse with men, whom she knows to be polluted by licentiousness, and often is she compelled to witness in her own domestic circle, those disgusting and heart-sickening jealousies and strifes which disgraced and distracted the family of Abraham. In addition to all this, the female slaves suffer every species of degradation and cruelty, which the most wanton barbarity can inflict; they are indecently divested of their clothing, sometimes tied up and severely whipped, sometimes prostrated on the earth while their naked bodies are torn by the scorpion lash.

> "The whip on woman's shrinking flesh!
> Our soil yet reddening with the stains
> Caught from her scourging warm and fresh."

Can any American woman look at these scenes of shocking licentious-ness and cruelty, and fold her hands in apathy, and say, "I have nothing to do with slavery"? *She cannot and be guiltless.*

I cannot close this letter, without saying a few words on the benefits to be derived men, as well as women, from the opinions I advocate relative to the equality of the sexes. Many women are now supported, in idleness and extravagance, by the industry of their husbands, fathers, or broth-ers, who are compelled to toil out their existence, at the counting house, or in the printing office, or some other laborious occupation, while the wife and daughters and sisters take no part in the support of the family, and appear to think that their sole business is to spend the hard bought earnings of their male friends. I deeply regret such a state of things, because I believe that if women felt their responsibility, for the support of themselves, or their families it would add strength and dignity to their characters, and teach them more true sympathy for their husbands, than is now generally manifested,—a sympathy which would be exhibited by actions as well as words. Our brethren may reject my doctrine, because it runs counter to common opinions, and because it wounds their pride; but I believe they would be "partakers of the benefit" resulting from the Equality of the Sexes, and would find that woman, as their equal, was unspeakably more valuable than woman as their inferior, both as a moral and an intellectual being.

Thine in the bonds of womanhood,

Sarah M. Grimke

EDGAR ALLAN POE

We would not necessarily expect Edgar Allan Poe (1809–1849), the great teller of grisly tales, to be an arbiter of interior decoration, yet "The Philosophy of Furniture" shows him making cultivated distinctions on the subject while deploring the vulgarity of American social climbers. Like many critics of the young republic, he thought his countrymen materialistic and obsessed with making money. Poe was no democrat; he rued the country's lack of an inherited aristocracy to pass down standards of taste.

The Philosophy of Furniture

(1840)

In the internal decoration, if not in the external architecture, of their residences, the English are supreme. The Italians have but little sentiment beyond marbles and colors. In France *meliora probant, deteriora sequuntur*—the people are too much a race of gad-abouts to study and maintain those household proprieties, of which indeed they have a delicate appreciation, or at least the elements of a proper sense. The Chinese, and most of the Eastern races, have a warm but inappropriate fancy. The Scotch are poor decorists. The Dutch have merely a vague idea that a curtain is not a cabbage. In Spain they are all curtains—a nation of hangmen. The Russians do not furnish. The Hottentots and Kickapoos are very well in their way—the Yankees alone are preposterous.

How this happens it is not difficult to see. We have no aristocracy of blood, and having, therefore, as a natural and, indeed as an inevitable thing, fashioned for ourselves an aristocracy of dollars, the display of wealth has here to take the place, and perform the office, of the heraldic display in monarchical countries. By a transition readily understood, and which might have been easily foreseen, we have been brought to merge in simple show our notions of taste itself.

To speak less abstractedly. In England, for example, no mere parade of costly appurtenances would be so likely as with us to create an impression of the beautiful in respect to the appurtenances themselves, or of taste as respects the proprietor—this for the reason, first, that wealth is not in England, the loftiest object of ambition, as constituting a nobility; and, secondly, that there the true nobility of blood rather avoids than affects costliness in which a *parvenu* rivalry may be successfully attempted, confining itself within the rigorous limits, and to the analytical investigation, of legitimate taste. The people naturally imitate the nobles, and the result is a thorough diffusion of a right feeling. But, in America, dollars being the supreme insignia of aristocracy, their display may be said, in general terms, to be the sole means of aristocratic distinction; and the populace, looking up for models, are insensibly led to confound the two entirely separate ideas of magnificence and beauty. In short, the cost of an article of furniture has, at length, come to be, with us, nearly the sole test of its merit in a decorative point of view. And this test, once established, has led the way to many analogous errors, readily traceable to the one primitive folly.

There could be scarcely any thing more directly offensive to the eye of an artist than the interior of what is termed, in the United States, a well furnished apartment. Its most usual defect is a preposterous want of keeping. We speak of the keeping of a room as we would of the keeping of a picture; for both the picture and the room are amenable to those undeviating principles which regulate all varieties of art; and very nearly the same laws by which we decide upon the higher merits of a painting, suffice for a decision upon the adjustment of a chamber. A want of keeping is observable sometimes in the character of the several pieces of furniture, but generally in their colors or modes of adaptation to use. Very often the eye is offended by their inartistic arrangement. Straight lines are too prevalent, too uninterruptedly continued, or clumsily interrupted at right angles. If curved lines occur, they are repeated into unpleasant uniformity. Undue precision spoils the appearance of many a room.

Curtains are rarely well disposed, or well chosen, in respect to the other decorations. With formal furniture curtains are out of place, and an excessive volume of drapery of any kind is, under any circumstances, irreconcilable with good taste; the proper quantum, as well as the proper adjustment, depends upon the character of the general effect.

Carpets are better understood of late than of ancient days, but we still very frequently err in their patterns and colors. A carpet is the soul of the apartment. From it are deduced not only the hues but the forms of all objects incumbent. A judge at common law may be an ordinary man; a good judge of a carpet must be a genius. Yet I have heard fellows discourse of carpets with the visage of a sheep in reverie—*"d'un mouton qui rêve"*—who should not and who could not be entrusted with the management of their own moustachios. Every one knows that a large floor should have a covering of large figures, and a small one must have a covering of small; yet this is not all the knowledge in the world. As regards texture the Saxony is alone admissible. Brussels is the preter-pluperfect tense of fashion, and Turkey is taste in its dying agonies. Touching pattern, a carpet should not be bedizzened out like a Riccaree Indian—all red chalk, yellow ochre and cock's feathers. In brief, distinct grounds and vivid circular figures, of no meaning, are here Median laws. The abomination of flowers, or representations of well known objects of any kind should never be endured within the limits of Christendom. Indeed, whether on carpets, or curtains, or paper-hangings, or ottoman coverings, all upholstery of this nature should be rigidly Arabesque. Those antique floor-cloths which are still seen occasionally in the dwellings of the rabble—cloths of huge, sprawling and radiating devices, stripe-interspersed, and glorious with all hues, among which no ground is intelligible—are but the wicked invention of a race of time servers and money lovers—children of Baal and worshippers of Mammon—men who, to save trouble of thought and exercise of fancy, first cruelly invented the Kaleidoscope, and then established a patent company to twirl it by steam.

Glare is a leading error in the philosophy of American household decoration—an error easily recognized as deduced from the perversion of taste just specified. We are violently enamoured of gas and of glass. The former is totally inadmissible within doors. Its harsh and unsteady light is positively offensive. No man having both brains and eyes will use it. A mild, or what artists term a cool light, with its consequent warm shadows, will do wonders for even an ill-furnished apartment. Never was a more lovely thought than that of the astral lamp. I mean, of course, the astral lamp proper, and do not wish to be misunderstood—the lamp of Argand with its original plain ground-glass shade, and its tempered and uniform moonlight rays. The cut-glass shade is a weak invention of the enemy. The eagerness with which we have adopted it, partly on account of its flashiness, but principally on account of its greater cost, is a good commentary upon the proposition with which I began. It is not too much to say that the deliberate employer of a cut-glass shade, is a person either radically deficient in taste, or blindly subservient to the caprices of fashion. The light proceeding from one of these gaudy abominations is unequal, broken, and painful. It alone is sufficient to mar a world of good effect in the furniture subjected to its influence. Female loveliness in especial is more than one half disenchanted beneath its evil eye.

In the matter of glass, generally, we proceed upon false principles. Its leading feature is glitter—and in that one word how much of all that is detestable do we express! Flickering, unquiet lights are sometimes pleasing—to children and idiots always so—but in the embellishment of a room they should be scrupulously avoided. In truth even strong steady lights are inadmissible. The huge and unmeaning glass chandeliers, prism-cut, gas-litten, and without shade, which dangle by night in our most fashionable drawing-rooms, may be cited as the quintessence of false taste, as so many concentrations of preposterous folly.

The rage for glitter—because its idea has become, as I before observed, confounded with that of magnificence in the abstract—has led also to the exaggerated employment of mirrors. We line our dwellings with great British plates, and then imagine we have done a fine thing. Now the slightest thought will be sufficient to convince any one who has an eye at all, of the ill effect of numerous looking-glasses, and especially of large ones. Regarded apart from its reflection the mirror presents a continuous, flat, colorless, unrelieved surface—a thing always unpleasant, and obviously so. Considered as a reflector it is potent in producing a monstrous and odious uniformity—and the evil is here aggravated in no direct proportion with the augmentation of its sources, but in a ratio constantly increasing. In fact a room with four or five mirrors arranged at random is, for all purposes of artistical show, a room of no shape at all. If we add to this the attendant glitter upon glitter, we have a perfect farrago of discordant and displeasing effects. The veriest bumpkin, not addle-headed, upon entering an apartment so bedizzened, would be instantly aware of something wrong, although he might be altogether unable to assign a cause for his dissatisfaction. But let the same individual be led into a room tastefully furnished, and he would be startled into an exclamation of surprise and of pleasure.

It is an evil growing out of our republican institutions, that here a man of large purse has usually a very little soul which he keeps in it. The corruption of taste is a portion and a pendant of the dollar-manufacture. As we grow rich our ideas grow rusty. It is therefore not among our aristocracy that we must look if at all, in the United States, for the spirituality of a British boudoir. But I have seen apartments in the tenure of Americans—men of exceedingly moderate means—which, in negative merit at least, might vie with any of the or-molu'd cabinets of our friends across the water. Even now there is present to my mind's eye a small and not ostentatious chamber with whose decorations no fault can be found. The proprietor lies asleep upon a sofa—the weather is cool—the time is near midnight—I will make a sketch of the room ere he awakes. It is oblong—some thirty feet in length and twenty-five in breadth—a shape affording the best opportunities for the adjustment of furniture. It has but one door, which is at one end of the parallelogram, and but two windows, which are at the other. These latter are large, reaching downwards to the floor, are situated in deep recesses, and open upon an Italian veranda. Their panes are of a crimson-tinted glass, set in rose-wood framings, of a kind somewhat broader than usual. They are curtained, within the recess, by a thick silver tissue, adapted to the shape of the window and hanging loosely, but having no volumes. Without the recess are curtains of an exceedingly rich crimson silk, fringed with a deep network of gold, and lined with the silver tissue, which forms the exterior blind. There are no cornices; but the folds of the whole fabric, (which are sharp rather than massive, and have an airy appearance) issue from beneath a broad entablature of rich gilt-work, which encircles the room at the junction of the ceiling and walls. The drapery is thrown open, also, or closed, by means of a thick rope of gold loosely enveloping it, and resolving itself readily into a knot—no pins or other such devices are apparent. The colors of the curtains and their fringe—the tints of crimson and gold—form the character of the room, and appear everywhere in profusion. The carpet, of Saxony material, is quite half an inch thick, and is of the same crimson ground, relieved simply by the appearance of a gold cord (like that festooning the curtains) thrown upon it in such a manner as to form a succession of short irregular curves, no one overlaying the other. This carpet has no border. The paper on the walls is of a glossy, silvery hue, intermingled with small Arabesque devices of a fainter tint of the prevalent crimson. Many paintings relieve the expanse of the paper. These are chiefly landscapes of an imaginative cast, such as the fairy grottoes of Stanfield, or the Lake of the Dismal Swamp of our own Chapman. The tone of each is warm, but dark—there are no brilliant effects. Not one of the pictures is of small size. Diminutive paintings give that spotty look to a room which is the blemish of so many a fine work of art overtouched. The frames are broad but not deep, and richly carved, without being fillagreed. Their profuse gilding gives them the whole lustre of gold. They lie flat upon the walls, and do not hang off with cords. The designs themselves may, sometimes, be best seen in this latter position, but the general appearance of the chamber is injured. No mirror is visible—nor chairs. Two large sofas, of rose-wood and crimson silk, form the only seats. An octagonal table, formed entirely of the richest gold-threaded marble, is placed near one of the sofas—this table is also without cover—the drapery of the curtains has been thought sufficient. Four large and gorgeous Sèvres vases, in which grow a number of sweet and vivid flowers in full bloom, occupy the angles of the room. A tall and magnificent candelabrum, bearing a small antique lamp with highly perfumed oil, is standing near the head of my sleeping friend. Some light and graceful hanging shelves, with golden edges and crimson silk cords with gold tassels, sustain two or three hundred magnificently-bound books. Beyond these things there is no furniture, if we except an Argand lamp, with a plain crimson-tinted ground glass shade, which depends from the lofty ceiling by a single gold chain, and throws a subdued but magical radiance over all.

NATHANIEL HAWTHORNE

Nathaniel Hawthorne (1804–1864), New England's austere, brooding master of sin and psychological guilt, was fascinated with the past, as witness his fictions set in Puritan times (The Scarlet Letter, "Young Goodman Brown," The House of the Seven Gables). *His nonfiction style, lighter and friendlier, can be seen in the* "The Custom House," *an extended personal essay that introduces* The Scarlet Letter; *in his notebooks, including the delightful* "Twenty Days with Julian & Little Bunny, by Papa"; *and in the essays he often sprinkled into his collected tales and sketches. One,* "Fire-Worship," *is squarely in the English tradition of facetious essays deploring new fashions. Here he seems to be having fun playing the nostalgic cranky conservative, personifying fire as a trusty retainer, and working up an outrage at fireplaces being replaced by iron stoves.*

Fire-Worship

(1843)

It is a great revolution in social and domestic life, and no less so in the life of a secluded student, this almost universal exchange of the open fireplace for the cheerless and ungenial stove. On such a morning as now lowers around our old gray parsonage, I miss the bright face of my ancient friend, who was wont to dance upon the hearth and play the part of more familiar sunshine. It is sad to turn from the cloudy sky and sombre landscape; from yonder hill, with its crown of rusty, black pines, the foliage of which is so dismal in the absence of the sun; that bleak pasture-land, and the broken surface of the potato-field, with the brown clods partly concealed by the snowfall of last night; the swollen and sluggish river, with ice-incrusted borders, dragging its bluish-gray stream along the verge of our orchard like a snake half torpid with the cold,—it is sad to turn from an outward scene of so little comfort and find the same sullen influences brooding within the precincts of my study. Where is that brilliant guest, that quick and subtle spirit, whom Prometheus lured from heaven to civilize mankind and cheer them in their wintry desolation; that comfortable inmate, whose smile, during eight months of the year, was our sufficient consolation for summer's lingering advance and early flight? Alas! blindly inhospitable, grudging the food that kept him cheery and mercurial, we have thrust him into an iron prison, and compel him to smoulder away his life on a daily pittance which once would have been too scanty for his breakfast. Without a metaphor, we now make our fire in an air-tight stove, and supply it with some half a dozen sticks of wood between dawn and nightfall.

I never shall be reconciled to this enormity. Truly may it be said that the world looks darker for it. In one way or another, here and there and all around us, the inventions of mankind are fast blotting the picturesque, the poetic, and the beautiful out of human life. The domestic fire was a type of all these attributes, and seemed to bring might and majesty, and wild nature and a spiritual essence, into our inmost home, and yet to dwell with us in such friendliness that its mysteries and marvels excited no dismay. The same mild companion that smiled so placidly in our faces was he that comes roaring out of Etna and rushes madly up the sky like a fiend breaking loose from torment and fighting for a place among the upper angels. He it is, too, that leaps from cloud to cloud amid the crashing thunder-storm. It was he whom the Gheber worshipped with no unnatural idolatry; and it was he who devoured London and Moscow and many another famous city, and who loves to riot through our own dark forests and sweep across our prairies, and to whose ravenous maw, it is said, the universe shall one day be given as a final feast. Meanwhile he is the great artisan and laborer by whose aid men are enabled to build a world within a world, or, at least, to smooth down the rough creation which nature flung to it. He forges the mighty anchor and every lesser instrument; he drives the steamboat and drags the rail-car; and it was he—this creature of terrible might, and so many-sided utility and all-comprehensive destructiveness—that used to be the cheerful, homely friend of our wintry days, and whom we have made the prisoner of this iron cage.

How kindly he was! and, though the tremendous agent of change, yet bearing himself with such gentleness, so rendering himself a part of all life-long and age-coeval associations, that it seemed as if he were the great conservative of nature. While a man was true to the fireside, so long would he be true to country and law, to the God whom his fathers worshipped, to the wife of his youth, and to all things else which instinct or religion has taught us to consider sacred. With how sweet humility did this elemental spirit perform all needful offices for the household in which he was domesticated! He was equal to the concoction of a grand dinner, yet scorned not to roast a potato or toast a bit of cheese. How humanely did he cherish the school-boy's icy fingers, and thaw the old man's joints with a genial warmth which almost equalled the glow of youth! And how carefully did he dry the cowhide boots that had trudged through mud and snow, and the shaggy outside garment stiff with frozen sleet! taking heed, likewise, to the comfort of the faithful dog who had followed his master through the storm. When did he refuse a coal to light a pipe, or even a part of his own substance to kindle a neighbor's fire? And then, at twilight, when laborer, or scholar, or mortal of whatever age, sex, or degree, drew a chair beside him and looked into his glowing face, how acute, how profound, how comprehensive was his sympathy with the mood of each and all! He pictured forth their very thoughts. To the youthful he showed the scenes of the adventurous life before them; to the aged the shadows of departed love and hope; and, if all earthly things had grown distasteful, he could gladden the fireside muser with golden glimpses of a better world. And, amid this varied communion with the human soul, how busily would the sympathizer, the deep moralist, the painter of magic pictures, be causing the teakettle to boil!

Nor did it lessen the charm of his soft, familiar courtesy and help-fulness that the mighty spirit, were opportunity offered him, would run riot through the peaceful house, wrap its inmates in his terrible embrace, and leave nothing of them save their whitened bones. This possibility of mad destruction only made his domestic kindness the more beautiful and touching. It was so sweet of him, being endowed with such power, to dwell day after day, and one long lonesome night after another, on the dusky hearth, only now and then betraying his wild nature by thrusting his red tongue out of the chimney-top! True, he had done much mischief in the world, and was pretty certain to do more; but his warm heart atoned for all. He was kindly to the race of man; and they pardoned his characteristic imperfections.

The good old clergyman, my predecessor in this mansion, was well acquainted with the comforts of the fireside. His yearly allowance of wood, according to the terms of his settlement, was no less than sixty cords. Almost an annual forest was converted from sound oak logs into ashes, in the kitchen, the parlor, and this little study, where now an unwor-thy successor, not in the pastoral office, but merely in his earthly abode, sits scribbling beside an air-tight stove. I love to fancy one of those fireside days while the good man, a contemporary of the Revolution, was in his early prime, some five-and-sixty years ago. Before sunrise, doubtless, the blaze hovered upon the gray skirts of night and dissolved the frostwork that had gathered like a curtain over the small window-panes. There is something peculiar in the aspect of the morning fireside; a fresher, brisker glare; the absence of that mellowness which can be produced only by half-consumed logs, and shapeless brands with the white ashes on them, and mighty coals, the remnant of tree-trunks that the hungry elements have gnawed for hours. The morning hearth, too, is newly swept, and the brazen andirons well brightened, so that the cheerful fire may see its face in them. Surely it was happiness, when the pastor, fortified with a substantial breakfast, sat down in his arm-chair and slippers and opened the Whole Body of Divinity, or the Commentary on Job, or whichever of his old folios or quartos might fall within the range of his weekly sermons. It must have been his own fault if the warmth and glow of this abundant hearth did not permeate the discourse and keep his audience comfortable in spite of the bitterest northern blast that ever wrestled with the church-steeple. He reads while the heat warps the stiff covers of the volume; he writes without numbness either in his heart or fingers; and, with unstinted hand, he throws fresh sticks of wood upon the fire.

A parishioner comes in. With what warmth of benevolence—how should he be otherwise than warm in any of his attributes?—does the minister bid him welcome, and set a chair for him in so close proximity to the hearth, that soon the guest finds it needful to rub his scorched shins with his great red hands! The melted snow drips from his steaming boots and bubbles upon the hearth. His puckered forehead unravels its entanglement of crisscross wrinkles. We lose much of the enjoyment of fireside heat without such an opportunity of marking its genial effect upon those who have been looking the inclement weather in the face. In the course of the day our clergyman himself strides forth, perchance to pay a round of pastoral visits; or, it may he, to visit his mountain of a wood-pile and cleave the monstrous logs into billets suitable for the fire. He returns with fresher life to his beloved hearth. During the short afternoon the western sunshine comes into the study and strives to stare the ruddy blaze out of countenance but with only a brief triumph, soon to be succeeded by brighter glories of its rival. Beautiful it is to see the strengthening gleam, the deepening light that gradually casts distinct shadows of the human figure, the table, and the high-backed chairs upon the opposite wall, and at length, as twilight comes on, replenishes the room with living radiance and makes life all rose-color. Afar the wayfarer discerns the flickering flame as it dances upon the windows, and hails it as a beacon-light of humanity, reminding him, in his cold and lonely path, that the world is not all snow, and solitude, and desolation. At eventide, probably, the study was peopled with the clergyman's wife and family, and children tumbled themselves upon the hearth-rug, and grave puss sat with her back to the fire, or gazed, with a semblance of human meditation, into its fervid depths. Seasonably the plenteous ashes of the day were raked over the mouldering brands, and from the heap came jets of flame, and an incense of night-long smoke creeping quietly up the chimney.

Heaven forgive the old clergyman! In his later life, when for almost ninety winters he had been gladdened by the firelight,—when it had gleamed upon him from infancy to extreme age, and never without brightening his spirits as well as his visage, and perhaps keeping him alive so long,—he had the heart to brick up his chimney-place and bid farewell to the face of his old friend forever, why did he not take an eternal leave of the sunshine too? His sixty cords of wood had probably dwindled to a far less ample supply in modern times; and it is certain that the parsonage had grown crazy with time and tempest and pervious to the cold; but still it was one of the saddest tokens of the decline and fall of open fireplaces that, the gray patriarch should have deigned to warm himself at an air-tight stove.

And I, likewise,—who have found a home in this ancient owl's-nest since its former occupant took his heavenward flight,—I, to my shame, have put up stoves in kitchen and parlor and chamber. Wander where you will about the house, not a glimpse of the earth-born, heaven-aspiring fiend of Etna,—him that sports in the thunder-storm, the idol of the Ghebers, the devourer of cities, the forest-rioter and prairie-sweeper, the future destroyer of our earth, the old chimney-corner companion who mingled himself so sociably with household joys and sorrows,—not a glimpse of this mighty and kindly one will greet your eyes. He is now an invisible presence. There is his iron cage. Touch it, and he scorches your fingers. He delights to singe a garment or perpetrate any other little unworthy mischief; for his temper is ruined by the ingratitude of mankind, for whom he cherished such warmth of feeling, and to whom he taught all their arts, even that of making his own prison-house. In his fits of rage he puffs volumes of smoke and noisome gas through the crevices of the door, and shakes the iron walls of his dungeon so as to overthrow the ornamental urn upon its summit. We tremble lest he should break forth amongst us. Much of his time is spent in sighs, burdened with unutterable grief, and long drawn through the funnel. He amuses himself, too, with repeating all the whispers, the moans, and the louder utterances or tempestuous howls of the wind; so that the stove becomes a microcosm of the aerial world. Occasionally there are strange combinations of sounds,—voices talking almost articulately within the hollow chest of iron,—insomuch that fancy beguiles me with the idea that my firewood must have grown in that infernal forest of lamentable trees which breathed their complaints to Dante. When the listener is half asleep he may readily take these voices for the conversation of spirits and assign them an intelligible meaning. Anon there is a pattering noise,—drip, drip, drip,—as if a summer shower were falling within the narrow circumference of the stove.

These barren and tedious eccentricities are all that the air-tight stove can bestow in exchange for the invaluable moral influences which we have lost by our desertion of the open fireplace. Alas! is this world so very bright that we can afford to choke up such a domestic fountain of gladsomeness, and sit down by its darkened source without being conscious of a gloom?

It is my belief that social intercourse cannot long continue what it has been, now that we have subtracted from it so important and vivifying an element as firelight. The effects will be more perceptible on our children and the generations that shall succeed them than on ourselves, the mechanism of whose life may remain unchanged, though its spirit be far other than it was. The sacred trust of the household fire has been transmitted in unbroken succession from the earliest ages, and faithfully cherished in spite of every discouragement such as the curfew law of the Norman conquerors, until in these evil days physical science has nearly succeeded in extinguishing it. But we at least have our youthful recollections tinged with the glow of the hearth, and our life-long habits and associations arranged on the principle of a mutual bond in the domestic fire. Therefore, though the sociable friend be forever departed, yet in a degree he will be spiritually present with us; and still more will the empty forms which were once full of his rejoicing presence continue to rule our manners. We shall draw our chairs together as we and our forefathers have been wont for thousands of years back, and sit around some blank and empty corner of the room, babbling with unreal cheerfulness of topics suitable to the homely fireside. A warmth from the past—from the ashes of bygone years and the raked-up embers of long ago—will sometimes thaw the ice about our hearts; but it must be otherwise with our successors. On the most favorable supposition, they will be acquainted with the fireside in no better shape than that of the sullen stove; and more probably they will have grown up amid furnace heat in houses which might be fancied to have their foundation over the infernal pit, whence sulphurous steams and unbreathable exhalations ascend through the apertures of the floor. There will be nothing to attract these poor children to one centre. They will never behold one another through that peculiar medium of vision the ruddy gleam of blazing wood or bituminous coal—which gives the human spirit so deep an insight into its fellows and melts all humanity into one cordial heart of hearts. Domestic life, if it may still be termed domestic, will seek its separate corners, and never gather itself into groups. The easy gossip; the merry yet unambitious jest; the life-like, practical discussion of real matters in a casual way; the soul of truth which is so often incarnated in a simple fireside word,—will disappear from earth. Conversation will contract the air of debate, and all mortal intercourse be chilled with a fatal frost.

In classic times, the exhortation to fight "pro axis et focis," for the altars and the hearths, was considered the strongest appeal that could be made to patriotism. And it seemed an immortal utterance; for all subsequent ages and people have acknowledged its force and responded to it with the full portion of manhood that nature had assigned to each. Wisely were the altar and the hearth conjoined in one mighty sentence; for the hearth, too, had its kindred sanctity. Religion sat down beside it, not in the priestly robes which decorated and perhaps disguised her at the altar, but arrayed in a simple matron's garb, and uttering her lessons with the tenderness of a mother's voice and heart. The holy hearth! If any earthly and material thing, or rather a divine idea embodied in brick and mortar, might be supposed to possess the permanence of moral truth, it was this. All revered it. The man who did not put off his shoes upon this holy ground would have deemed it pastime to trample upon the altar. It has been our task to uproot the hearth. What further reform is left for our children to achieve, unless they overthrow the altar too? And by what appeal hereafter, when the breath of hostile armies may mingle with the pure, cold breezes of our country, shall we attempt to rouse up native valor? Fight for your hearths? There will be none throughout the land.

FIGHT FOR YOUR STOVES! Not I, in faith. If in such a cause I strike a blow, it shall be on the invader's part; and Heaven grant that it may shatter the abomination all to pieces!

RALPH WALDO EMERSON

Ralph Waldo Emerson (1803–1882) was nineteenth-century America's foremost public intellectual and, during his lifetime, the nation's greatest essayist. An ex-schoolmaster and ex-minister, he supported his family and himself by giving lectures based on his essays. Emerson kept private journals in which he recorded "the meteorology of thought": his practice was to track his consciousness wherever it went, and he quarried these journals for use in his essays. Following Socrates and Michel de Montaigne, he asserted that "the purpose of life seems to be to acquaint a man with himself," and he chose writing as his means to do so, converting every scrap of daily life into speculation and wisdom seeking. His essays, unsystematically philosophical and aphoristic, contain one amazing sentence after another, without necessarily providing transitional banisters. In one of his greatest, "Experience," which was provoked by grief at the death of his son Waldo, he oscillates between despair and hope, assertion and irresolution, daring to squint into the darkest places of uncertainty where life is "a flux of moods."

Experience

(1844)

Where do we find ourselves? In a series of which we do not know the extremes, and believe that it has none. We wake and find ourselves on a stair; there are stairs below us, which we seem to have ascended; there are stairs above us, many a one, which go upward and out of sight. But the

Genius which, according to the old belief, stands at the door by which we enter, and gives us the lethe to drink, that we may tell no tales, mixed the cup too strongly, and we cannot shake off the lethargy now at noonday. Sleep lingers all our lifetime about our eyes, as night hovers all day in the boughs of the fir-tree. All things swim and glitter. Our life is not so much threatened as our perception. Ghostlike we glide through nature, and should not know our place again. Did our birth fall in some fit of indigence and frugality in nature, that she was so sparing of her fire and so liberal of her earth, that it appears to us that we lack the affirmative principle, and though we have health and reason, yet we have no superflu-ity of spirit for new creation? We have enough to live and bring the year about, but not an ounce to impart or to invest. Ah that our Genius were a little more of a genius! We are like millers on the lower levels of a stream, when the factories above them have exhausted the water. We too fancy that the upper people must have raised their dams.

If any of us knew what we were doing, or where we are going, then when we think we best know! We do not know today whether we are busy or idle. In times when we thought ourselves indolent, we have afterwards discovered, that much was accomplished, and much was begun in us. All our days are so unprofitable while they pass, that 'tis wonderful where or when we ever got anything of this which we call wisdom, poetry, virtue. We never got it on any dated calendar day. Some heavenly days must have been intercalated somewhere, like those that Hermes won with dice of the Moon, that Osiris might be born. It is said, all martyrdoms looked mean when they were suffered. Every ship is a romantic object, except that we sail in. Embark, and the romance quits our vessel, and hangs on every other sail in the horizon. Our life looks trivial, and we shun to record it. Men seem to have learned of the horizon the art of perpetual retreating and reference. "Yonder uplands are rich pasturage, and my neighbor has fertile meadow, but my field," says the querulous farmer, "only holds the world together." I quote another man's saying; unluckily, that other withdraws himself in the same way, and quotes me. 'Tis the trick of nature thus to degrade today; a good deal of buzz, and some-where a result slipped magically in. Every roof is agreeable to the eye, until it is lifted; then we find tragedy and moaning women, and hard-eyed husbands, and deluges of lethe, and the men ask, "What's the news?" as if the old were so bad. How many individuals can we count in society? how many actions? how many opinions? So much of our time is preparation, so much is routine, and so much retrospect, that the pith of each man's genius contracts itself to a very few hours. The history of literature—take the net result of Tiraboschi, Warton, or Schlegel,—is a sum of very few ideas, and of very few original tales,—all the rest being variation of these. So in this great society wide lying around us, a critical analysis would find very few spontaneous actions. It is almost all custom and gross sense. There are even few opinions, and these seem organic in the speakers, and do not disturb the universal necessity.

What opium is instilled into all disaster! It shows formidable as we approach it, but there is at last no rough rasping friction, but the most slippery sliding surfaces. We fall soft on a thought. *Ate Dea* is gentle,

> "Over men's heads walking aloft,
> With tender feet treading so soft."

People grieve and bemoan themselves, but it is not half so bad with them as they say. There are moods in which we court suffering, in the hope that here, at least, we shall find reality, sharp peaks and edges of truth. But it turns out to be scene-painting and counterfeit. The only thing grief has taught me, is to know how shallow it is. That, like all the rest, plays about the surface, and never introduces me into the reality, for contact with which, we would even pay the costly price of sons and lovers. Was it Boscovich who found out that bodies never come in contact? Well, souls never touch their objects. An innavigable sea washes with silent waves between us and the things we aim at and converse with. Grief too will make us idealists. In the death of my son, now more than two years ago, I seem to have lost a beautiful estate,—no more. I cannot get it nearer to me. If tomorrow I should be informed of the bankruptcy of my principal debtors, the loss of my property would be a great inconvenience to me, perhaps, for many years; but it would leave me as it found me,—neither better nor worse. So is it with this calamity: it does not touch me: some thing which I fancied was a part of me, which could not be torn away without tearing me, nor enlarged without enriching me, falls off from me, and leaves no scar. It was caducous. I grieve that grief can teach me nothing, nor carry me one step into real nature. The Indian who was laid under a curse, that the wind should not blow on him, nor water flow to him, nor fire burn him, is a type of us all. The dearest events are summer-rain, and we the Para coats that shed every drop. Nothing is left us now but death. We look to that with a grim satisfaction, saying, there at least is reality that will not dodge us.

I take this evanescence and lubricity of all objects, which lets them slip through our fingers then when we clutch hardest, to be the most unhandsome part of our condition. Nature does not like to be observed, and likes that we should be her fools and playmates. We may have the sphere for our cricket-ball, but not a berry for our philosophy. Direct strokes she never gave us power to make; all our blows glance, all our hits are accidents. Our relations to each other are oblique and casual.

—

Dream delivers us to dream, and there is no end to illusion. Life is a train of moods like a string of beads, and, as we pass through them, they prove to be many-colored lenses which paint the world their own hue, and each shows only what lies in its focus. From the mountain you see the mountain. We animate what we can, and we see only what we animate. Nature and books belong to the eyes that see them. It depends on the mood of the man, whether he shall see the sunset or the fine poem. There are always sunsets, and there is always genius; but only a few hours so serene that we can relish nature or criticism. The more or less depends on structure or temperament. Temperament is the iron wire on which the beads are strung. Of what use is fortune or talent to a cold and defective nature? Who cares what sensibility or discrimination a man has at some time shown, if he falls asleep in his chair? or if he laugh and giggle? or if he apologize? or is affected with egotism? or thinks of his dollar? or cannot go by food? or has gotten a child in his boyhood? Of what use is genius, if the organ is too convex or too concave, and cannot find a focal distance within the actual horizon of human life? Of what use, if the brain is too cold or too hot, and the man does not care enough for results, to stimulate him to experiment, and hold him up in it? or if the web is too finely woven, too irritable by pleasure and pain, so that life stagnates from too much reception, without due outlet? Of what use to make heroic vows of amendment, if the same old law-breaker is to keep them? What cheer can the religious sentiment yield, when that is suspected to be secretly dependent on the seasons of the year, and the state of the blood? I knew a witty physician who found theology in the biliary duct, and used to affirm that if there was disease in the liver, the man became a Calvinist, and if that organ was sound, he became a Unitarian. Very mortifying is the reluctant experience that some unfriendly excess or imbecility neutralizes the promise of genius. We see young men who owe us a new world, so readily and lavishly they promise, but they never acquit the debt; they die young and dodge the account: or if they live, they lose themselves in the crowd.

Temperament also enters fully into the system of illusions, and shuts us in a prison of glass which we cannot see. There is an optical illusion about every person we meet. In truth, they are all creatures of given temperament, which will appear in a given character, whose boundaries they will never pass: but we look at them, they seem alive, and we presume there is impulse in them. In the moment it seems impulse; in the year, in the lifetime, it turns out to be a certain uniform tune which the revolving barrel of the music-box must play. Men resist the conclusion in the morning, but adopt it as the evening wears on, that temper prevails over everything of time, place, and condition, and is inconsumable in the flames of religion. Some modifications the moral sentiment avails to impose, but the individual texture holds its dominion, if not to bias the moral judgments, yet to fix the measure of activity and of enjoyment.

I thus express the law as it is read from the platform of ordinary life, but must not leave it without noticing the capital exception. For temperament is a power which no man willingly hears any one praise but himself. On the platform of physics, we cannot resist the contracting influences of so-called science. Temperament puts all divinity to rout. I know the mental proclivity of physicians. I hear the chuckle of the phrenologists. Theoretic kidnappers and slave-drivers, they esteem each man the victim of another, who winds him round his finger by knowing the law of his being, and by such cheap signboards as the color of his beard, or the slope of his occiput, reads the inventory of his fortunes and character. The grossest ignorance does not disgust like this impudent knowing-ness. The physicians say, they are not materialists; but they are:—Spirit is matter reduced to an extreme thinness: O *so* thin!—But the definition of *spiritual* should be, *that which is its own evidence.* What notions do they attach to love! what to religion! One would not willingly pronounce these words in their hearing, and give them the occasion to profane them. I saw a gracious gentleman who adapts his conversation to the form of the head of the man he talks with! I had fancied that the value of life lay in its inscrutable possibilities; in the fact that I never know, in addressing myself to a new individual, what may befall me. I carry the keys of my castle in my hand, ready to throw them at the feet of my lord, whenever and in what disguise soever he shall appear. I know he is in the neighbor-hood hidden among vagabonds. Shall I preclude my future, by taking a high seat, and kindly adapting my conversation to the shape of heads? When I come to that, the doctors shall buy me for a cent.—"But, sir, medical history; the report to the Institute; the proven facts!"—I distrust the facts and the inferences. Temperament is the veto or limitation-power in the constitution, very justly applied to restrain an opposite excess in the constitution, but absurdly offered as a bar to original equity. When virtue is in presence, all subordinate powers sleep. On its own level, or in view of nature, temperament is final. I see not, if one be once caught in this trap of so-called sciences, any escape for the man from the links of the chain of physical necessity. Given such an embryo, such a history must follow. On this platform, one lives in a sty of sensualism, and would soon come to suicide. But it is impossible that the creative power should exclude itself. Into every intelligence there is a door which is never closed, through which the creator passes. The intellect, seeker of absolute truth, or the heart, lover of absolute good, intervenes for our succor, and at one whisper of these high powers, we awake from ineffectual struggles with this nightmare. We hurl it into its own hell, and cannot again contract ourselves to so base a state.

—

The secret of the illusoriness is in the necessity of a succession of moods or objects. Gladly we would anchor, but the anchorage is quicksand. This onward trick of nature is too strong for us: *Pero si muove*. When, at night, I look at the moon and stars, I seem stationary, and they to hurry. Our love of the real draws us to permanence, but health of body consists in circulation, and sanity of mind in variety or facility of association. We need change of objects. Dedication to one thought is quickly odious. We house with the insane, and must humor them; then conversation dies out. Once I took such delight in Montaigne, that I thought I should not need any other book; before that, in Shakespeare; then in Plutarch; then in Plotinus; at one time in Bacon; afterwards in Goethe; even in Bettine; but now I turn the pages of either of them languidly, whilst I still cherish their genius. So with pictures; each will bear an emphasis of attention once, which it cannot retain, though we fain would continue to be pleased in that manner. How strongly I have felt of pictures, that when you have seen one well, you must take your leave of it; you shall never see it again. I have had good lessons from pictures, which I have since seen without emotion or remark. A deduction must be made from the opinion, which even the wise express of a new book or occurrence. Their opinion gives me tidings of their mood, and some vague guess at the new fact but is nowise to be trusted as the lasting relation between that intellect and that thing. The child asks, "Mamma, why don't I like the story as well as when you told it me yesterday?" Alas, child, it is even so with the oldest cherubim of knowledge. But will it answer thy question to say, Because thou wert born to a whole, and this story is a particular? The reason of the pain this discovery causes us (and we make it late in respect to works of art and intellect), is the plaint of tragedy which murmurs from it in regard to persons, to friendship and love.

That immobility and absence of elasticity which we find in the arts, we find with more pain in the artist. There is no power of expansion in men. Our friends early appear to us as representatives of certain ideas, which they never pass or exceed. They stand on the brink of the ocean of thought and power, but they never take the single step that would bring them there. A man is like a bit of Labrador spar, which has no lustre as you turn it in your hand, until you come to a particular angle; then it shows deep and beautiful colors. There is no adaptation or universal applicability in men, but each has his special talent, and the mastery of successful men consists in adroitly keeping themselves where and when that turn shall be oftenest to be practised. We do what we must, and call it by the best names we can, and would fain have the praise of having intended the result which ensues. I cannot recall any form of man who is not superfluous sometimes. But is not this pitiful? Life is not worth the taking, to do tricks in.

Of course, it needs the whole society, to give the symmetry we seek. The parti-colored wheel must revolve very fast to appear white. Something is learned too by conversing with so much folly and defect. In fine, whoever loses, we are always of the gaining party. Divinity is behind our failures and follies also. The plays of children are nonsense, but very educative nonsense. So it is with the largest and solemnest things, with commerce, government, church, marriage, and so with the history of every man's bread, and the ways by which he is to come by it. Like a bird which alights nowhere, but hops perpetually from bough to bough, is the Power which abides in no man and in no woman, but for a moment speaks from this one, and for another moment from that one.

But what help from these fineries or pedantries? What help from thought? Life is not dialectics. We, I think, in these times, have had lessons enough of the futility of criticism. Our young people have thought and written much on labor and reform, and for all that they have written, neither the world nor themselves have got on a step. Intellectual tasting of life will not supersede muscular activity. If a man should consider the nicety of the passage of a piece of bread down his throat, he would starve. At Education-Farm, the noblest theory of life sat on the noblest figures of young men and maidens, quite powerless and melancholy. It would not rake or pitch a ton of hay; it would not rub down a horse; and the men and maidens it left pale and hungry. A political orator wittily compared our party promises to western roads, which opened stately enough, with planted trees on either side, to tempt the traveller, but soon became narrow and narrower, and ended in a squirrel-track, and ran up a tree. So does culture with us; it ends in head-ache. Unspeakably sad and barren does life look to those, who a few months ago were dazzled with the splendor of the promise of the times. "There is now no longer any right course of action, nor any self-devotion left among the Iranis." Objections and criticism we have had our fill of. There are objections to every course of life and action, and the practical wisdom infers an indifferency, from the omnipresence of objection. The whole frame of things preaches indifferency. Do not craze yourself with thinking, but go about your business anywhere. Life is not intellectual or critical, but sturdy. Its chief good is for well-mixed people who can enjoy what they find, without question. Nature hates peeping, and our mothers speak her very sense when they say, "Children, eat your victuals, and say no more of it." To fill the hour,—that is happiness; to fill the hour, and leave no crevice for a repentance or an approval. We live amidst surfaces, and the true art of life is to skate well on them. Under the oldest mouldiest conventions, a man of native force prospers just as well as in the newest world, and that by skill of handling and treatment. He can take hold anywhere. Life itself is a mixture of power and form, and will not bear the least excess of either. To finish the moment, to find the journey's end in every step of the road, to live the greatest number of good hours, is wisdom. It is not the part of men, but of fanatics, or of mathematicians, if you will, to say, that, the shortness of life considered, it is not worth caring whether for so short a duration we were sprawling in want, or sitting high. Since our office is with moments, let us husband them. Five minutes of today are worth as much to me, as five minutes in the next millennium. Let u be poised, and wise, and our own, today. Let us treat the men and women well: treat them as if they were real: perhaps they are. Men live in their fancy, like drunkards whose hands are too soft and tremulous for successful labor. It is a tempest of fancies, and the only ballast I know, is a respect to the present hour. Without any shadow of doubt, amidst this vertigo of shows and politics, I settle myself ever the firmer in the creed, that we should not postpone and refer and wish, but do broad justice where we are, by whomsoever we deal with, accepting our actual companions and circumstances, however humble or odious, as the mystic officials to whom the universe has delegated its whole pleasure for us. If these are mean and malignant, their contentment, which is the last victory of justice, is a more satisfying echo to the heart, than the voice of poets and the casual sympathy of admirable persons. I think that however a thoughtful man may suffer from the defects and absurdities of his company, he cannot without affectation deny to any set of men and women, a sensibility to extraordinary merit. The coarse and frivolous have an instinct of superiority, if they have not a sympathy, and honor it in their blind capricious way with sincere homage.

The fine young people despise life, but in me, and in such as with me are free from dyspepsia, and to whom a day is a sound and solid good, it is a great excess of politeness to look scornful and to cry for company. I am grown by sympathy a little eager and sentimental, but leave me alone, and I should relish every hour and what it brought me, the pot-luck of the day, as heartily as the oldest gossip in the bar-room. I am thankful for small mercies. I compared notes with one of my friends who expects everything of the universe, and is disappointed when anything is less than the best, and I found that I begin at the other extreme, expecting nothing, and am always full of thanks for moderate goods. I accept the clangor and jangle of contrary tendencies. I find my account in sots and bores also. They give a reality to the circumjacent picture, which such a vanishing meteorous appearance can ill spare. In the morning I awake, and find the old world, wife, babes, and mother, Concord and Boston, the dear old spiritual world, and even the dear old devil not far off. If we will take the good we find, asking no questions, we shall have heaping measures. The great gifts are not got by analysis. Everything good is on the highway. The middle region of our being is the temperate zone. We may climb into the thin and cold realm of pure geometry and lifeless science, or sink into that of sensation. Between these extremes is the equator of life, of thought, of spirit, of poetry,—a narrow belt. Moreover, in popular experience, everything good is on the highway. A collector peeps into all the picture-shops of Europe, for a landscape of Poussin, a crayon-sketch of Salvator; but the Transfiguration, the Last Judgment, the Communion of St. Jerome, and what are as transcendent as these, are on the walls of the Vatican, the Uffizi, or the Louvre, where every footman may see them; to say nothing of nature's pictures in every street, of sunsets and sunrises every day, and the sculpture of the human body never absent. A collector recently bought at public auction, in London, for one hundred and fifty-seven guineas, an autograph of Shakespeare: but for nothing a school-boy can read Hamlet, and can detect secrets of highest concernment yet unpublished therein. I think I will never read any but the commonest books,—the Bible, Homer, Dante, Shakespeare, and Milton. Then we are impatient of so public a life and planet, and run hither and thither for nooks and secrets. The imagination delights in the wood-craft of Indians, trappers, and bee-hunters. We fancy that we are strangers, and not so intimately domesticated in the planet as the wild man, and the wild beast and bird. But the exclusion reaches them also; reaches the climbing, fly-ing, gliding, feathered and four-footed man. Fox and woodchuck, hawk and snipe, and bittern, when nearly seen, have no more root in the deep world than man, and are just such superficial tenants of the globe. Then the new molecular philosophy shows astronomical interspaces betwixt atom and atom, shows that the world is all outside: it has no inside.

The mid-world is best. Nature, as we know her, is no saint. The lights of the church, the ascetics, Gentoos and Grahamites, she does not dis-tinguish by any favor. She comes eating and drinking and sinning. Her darlings, the great, the strong, the beautiful, are not children of our law, do not come out of the Sunday School, nor weigh their food, nor punctu-ally keep the commandments. If we will be strong with her strength, we must not harbor such disconsolate consciences, borrowed too from the consciences of other nations. We must set up the strong present tense against all the rumors of wrath, past or to come. So many things are unsettled which it is of the first importance to settle,—and, pending their settlement, we will do as we do. Whilst the debate goes forward on the equity of commerce, and will not be closed for a century or two, New and Old England may keep shop. Law of copyright and international copy-right is to be discussed, and, in the interim, we will sell our books for the most we can. Expediency of literature, reason of literature, lawfulness of writing down a thought, is questioned; much is to say on both sides, and, while the fight waxes hot, thou, dearest scholar, stick to thy foolish task, add a line every hour, and between whiles add a line. Right to hold land, right of property, is disputed, and the conventions convene, and before the vote is taken, dig away in your garden, and spend your earnings as a waif or godsend to all serene and beautiful purposes. Life itself is a bubble and a skepticism, and a sleep within a sleep. Grant it, and as much more as they will,—but thou, God's darling! heed thy private dream: thou wilt not be missed in the scorning and skepticism: there are enough of them: stay there in thy closet, and toil, until the rest are agreed what to do about it. Thy sickness, they say, and thy puny habit, require that thou do this or avoid that, but know that thy life is a flitting state, a tent for a night, and do thou, sick or well, finish that stint. Thou art sick, but shalt not be worse, and the universe, which holds thee dear, shall be the better.

Human life is made up of the two elements, power and form, and the proportion must be invariably kept, if we would have it sweet and sound. Each of these elements in excess makes a mischief as hurtful as its defect. Everything runs to excess: every good quality is noxious, if unmixed, and, to carry the danger to the edge of ruin, nature causes each man's peculiarity to superabound. Here, among the farms, we adduce the scholars as examples of this treachery. They are nature's victims of expression. You who see the artist, the orator, the poet, too near, and find their life no more excellent than that of mechanics or farmers, and themselves victims of partiality, very hollow and haggard, and pronounce them failures,— not heroes, but quacks,—conclude very reasonably, that these arts are not for man, but are disease. Yet nature will not bear you out. Irresistible nature made men such, and makes legions more of such, every day. You love the boy reading in a book, gazing at a drawing, or a cast: yet what are these millions who read and behold, but incipient writers and sculptors? Add a little more of that quality which now reads and sees, and they will seize the pen and chisel. And if one remembers how innocently he began to be an artist, he perceives that nature joined with his enemy. A man is a golden impossibility. The line he must walk is a hair's breadth. The wise through excess of wisdom is made a fool.

How easily, if fate would suffer it, we might keep forever these beautiful limits, and adjust ourselves, once for all, to the perfect calculation of the kingdom of known cause and effect. In the street and in the newspapers, life appears so plain a business, that manly resolution and adherence to the multiplication-table through all weathers, will insure success. But ah! presently comes a day, or is it only a half-hour, with its angel-whispering,— which discomfits the conclusions of nations and of years! Tomorrow again, everything looks real and angular, the habitual standards are reinstated, common sense is as rare as genius,—is the basis of genius, and experience is hands and feet to every enterprise;—and yet, he who should do his business on this understanding, would be quickly bankrupt. Power keeps quite another road than the turnpikes of choice and will, namely, the subterranean and invisible tunnels and channels of life. It is ridiculous that we are diplomatists, and doctors, and considerate people: there are no dupes like these. Life is a series of surprises, and would not be worth taking or keeping, if it were not. God delights to isolate us every day, and hide from us the past and the future. We would look about us, but with grand politeness he draws down before us an impenetrable screen of purest sky, and another behind us of purest sky. "You will not remember," he seems to say, "and you will not expect." All good conversation, manners, and action, come from a spontaneity which forgets usages, and makes the moment great. Nature hates calculators; her methods are saltatory and impulsive. Man lives by pulses; our organic movements are such; and the chemical and ethereal agents are undulatory and alternate; and the mind goes antagonizing on, and never prospers but by fits. We thrive by casualties. Our chief experiences have been casual. The most attractive class of people are those who are powerful obliquely, and not by the direct stroke: men of genius, but not yet accredited: one gets the cheer of their light, without paying too great a tax. Theirs is the beauty of the bird, or the morning light, and not of art. In the thought of genius there is always a surprise; and the moral sentiment is well called "the newness," for it is never other; as new to the oldest intelligence as to the young child,—"the kingdom that cometh without observation." In like manner, for practical success, there must not be too much design. A man will not be observed in doing that which he can do best. There is a certain magic about his properest action, which stupefies your powers of observation, so that though it is done before you, you wist not of it. The art of life has a pudency, and will not be exposed. Every man is an impossibility, until he is born; every thing impossible, until we see a success. The ardors of piety agree at last with the coldest skepticism,—that nothing is of us or our works,—that all is of God. Nature will not spare us the smallest leaf of laurel. All writing comes by the grace of God, and all doing and having. I would gladly be moral, and keep due metes and bounds, which I dearly love, and allow the most to the will of man, but I have set my heart on honesty in this chapter, and I can see nothing at last, in success or failure, than more or less of vital force supplied from the Eternal. The results of life are uncalculated and uncalculable. The years teach much which the days never know. The persons who compose our company, converse, and come and go, and design and execute many things, and somewhat comes of it all, but an unlooked for result. The individual is always mistaken. He designed many things, and drew in other persons as coadjutors, quarrelled with some or all, blundered much, and something is done; all are a little advanced, but the individual is always mistaken. It turns out somewhat new, and very unlike what he promised himself.

—

The ancients, struck with this irreducibleness of the elements of human life to calculation, exalted Chance into a divinity, but that is to stay too long at the spark,—which glitters truly at one point,—but the universe is warm with the latency of the same fire. The miracle of life which will not be expounded, but will remain a miracle, introduces a new element. In the growth of the embryo, Sir Everard Home, I think, noticed that the evolution was not from one central point, but co-active from three or more points. Life has no memory. That which proceeds in succession might be remembered, but that which is coexistent, or ejaculated from a deeper cause, as yet far from being conscious, knows not its own tendency. So is it with us, now skeptical, or without unity, because immersed in forms and effects all seeming to be of equal yet hostile value, and now religious, whilst in the reception of spiritual law. Bear with these distractions, with this coetaneous growth of the parts: they will one day be *members,* and obey one will. On that one will, on that secret cause, they nail our attention and hope. Life is hereby melted into an expectation or a religion. Underneath the inharmonious and trivial particulars, is a musical perfection, the Ideal journeying always with us, the heaven without rent or seam. Do but observe the mode of our illumination. When I converse with a profound mind, or if at any time being alone I have good thoughts, I do not at once arrive at satisfactions, as when, being thirsty, I drink water, or go to the fire, being cold: no! but I am at first apprised of my vicinity to a new and excellent region of life. By persisting to read or to think, this region gives further sign of itself, as it were in flashes of light, in sudden discoveries of its profound beauty and repose, as if the clouds that covered it parted at intervals, and showed the approaching traveller the inland mountains, with the tranquil eternal meadows spread at their base, whereon flocks graze, and shepherds pipe and dance. But every insight from this realm of thought is felt as initial, and promises a sequel. I do not make it; I arrive there, and behold what was there already. I make! O no! I clap my hands in infantine joy and amazement, before the first opening to me of this august magnificence, old with the love and homage of innumerable ages, young with the life of life, the sunbright Mecca of the desert. And what a future it opens! I feel a new heart beating with the love of the new beauty. I am ready to die out of nature, and be born again into this new yet unapproachable America I have found in the West.

> "Since neither now nor yesterday began
> These thoughts, which have been ever, nor yet can
> A man be found who their first entrance knew."

If I have described life as a flux of moods, I must now add, that there is that in us which changes not, and which ranks all sensations and states of mind. The consciousness in each man is a sliding scale, which identifies him now with the First Cause, and now with the flesh of his body; life above life, in infinite degrees. The sentiment from which it sprung determines the dignity of any deed, and the question ever is, not, what you have done or forborne, but, at whose command you have done or forborne it.

Fortune, Minerva, Muse, Holy Ghost,—these are quaint names, too narrow to cover this unbounded substance. The baffled intellect must still kneel before this cause, which refuses to be named,—ineffable cause, which every fine genius has essayed to represent by some emphatic symbol, as, Thales by water, Anaximenes by air, Anaxagoras by (Nous) thought, Zoroaster by fire, Jesus and the moderns by love: and the metaphor of each has become a national religion. The Chinese Mencius has not been the least successful in his generalization. "I fully understand language," he said, "and nourish well my vast-flowing vigor."—"I beg to ask what you call vast-flowing vigor?"—said his companion. "The explanation," replied Mencius, "is difficult. This vigor is supremely great, and in the highest degree unbending. Nourish it correctly, and do it no injury, and it will fill up the vacancy between heaven and earth. This vigor accords with and assists justice and reason, and leaves no hunger."—In our more correct writing, we give to this generalization the name of Being, and thereby confess that we have arrived as far as we can go. Suffice it for the joy of the universe, that we have not arrived at a wall, but at interminable oceans. Our life seems not present, so much as prospective; not for the affairs on which it is wasted, but as a hint of this vast-flowing vigor. Most of life seems to be mere advertisement of faculty: information is given us not to sell ourselves cheap; that we are very great. So, in particulars, our greatness is always in a tendency or direction, not in an action. It is for us to believe in the rule, not in the exception. The noble are thus known from the ignoble. So in accepting the leading of the sentiments, it is not what we believe concerning the immortality of the soul, or the like, but *the universal impulse to believe,* that is the material circumstance, and is the principal fact in the history of the globe. Shall we describe this cause as that which works directly? The spirit is not helpless or needful of mediate organs. It has plentiful powers and direct effects. I am explained without explaining, I am felt without acting, and where I am not. Therefore all just persons are satisfied with their own praise. They refuse to explain themselves, and are content that new actions should do them that office. They believe that we communicate without speech, and above speech, and that no right action of ours is quite unaffecting to our friends, at whatever distance; for the influence of action is not to be measured by miles. Why should I fret myself, because a circumstance has occurred, which hinders my presence where I was expected? If I am not at the meeting, my presence where I am, should be as useful to the commonwealth of friendship and wisdom, as would be my presence in that place. I exert the same quality of power in all places. Thus journeys the mighty Ideal before us; it never was known to fall into the rear. No man ever came to an experience which was satiating, but his good is tidings of a better. Onward and onward! In liberated moments, we know that a new picture of life and duty is already possible; the elements already exist in many minds around you, of a doctrine of life which shall transcend any written record we have. The new statement will comprise the skepticisms, as well as the faiths of society, and out of unbeliefs a creed shall be formed. For, skepticisms are not gratuitous or lawless, but are limitations of the affirmative statement, and the new philosophy must take them in, and make affirmations outside of them, just as much as it must include the oldest beliefs.

It is very unhappy, but too late to be helped, the discovery we have made, that we exist. That discovery is called the Fall of Man. Ever afterwards, we suspect our instruments. We have learned that we do not see directly, but mediately, and that we have no means of correcting these colored and distorting lenses which we are, or of computing the amount of their errors. Perhaps these subject-lenses have a creative power; perhaps there are no objects. Once we lived in what we saw; now, the rapaciousness of this new power, which threatens to absorb all things, engages us. Nature, art, persons, letters, religions,—objects, successively tumble in, and God is but one of its ideas. Nature and literature are subjective phenomena; every evil and every good thing is a shadow which we cast. The street is full of humiliations to the proud. As the fop contrived to dress his bailiffs in his livery, and make them wait on his guests at table, so the chagrins which the bad heart gives off as bubbles, at once take form as ladies and gentlemen in the street, shopmen or barkeepers in hotels, and threaten or insult whatever is threatenable and insultable in us. 'Tis the same with our idolatries. People forget that it is the eye which makes the horizon, and the rounding mind's eye which makes this or that man a type or representative of humanity with the name of hero or saint. Jesus the "providential man," is a good man on whom many people are agreed that these optical laws shall take effect. By love on one part, and by forbearance to press objection on the other part, it is for a time settled, that we will look at him in the centre of the horizon, and ascribe to him the properties that will attach to any man so seen. But the longest love or aversion has a speedy term. The great and crescive self, rooted in absolute nature, supplants all relative existence, and ruins the kingdom of mortal friendship and love. Marriage (in what is called the spiritual world) is impossible, because of the inequality between every subject and every object. The subject is the receiver of Godhead, and at every comparison must feel his being enhanced by that cryptic might. Though not in energy, yet by presence, this magazine of substance cannot be otherwise than felt: nor can any force of intellect attribute to the object the proper deity which sleeps or wakes forever in every subject. Never can love make consciousness and ascription equal in force. There will be the same gulf between every me and thee, as between the original and the picture. The universe is the bride of the soul. All private sympathy is partial. Two human beings are like globes, which can touch only in a point, and, whilst they remain in contact, all other points of each of the spheres are inert; their turn must also come, and the longer a particular union lasts, the more energy of appetency the parts not in union acquire.

Life will be imaged, but cannot be divided nor doubled. Any invasion of its unity would be chaos. The soul is not twin-born, but the only begotten, and though revealing itself as child in time, child in appearance, is of a fatal and universal power, admitting no co-life. Every day, every act betrays the ill-concealed deity. We believe in ourselves, as we do not believe in others. We permit all things to ourselves, and that which we call sin in others, is experiment for us. It is an instance of our faith in ourselves, that men never speak of crime as lightly as they think: or, every man thinks a latitude safe for himself, which is nowise to be indulged to another. The act looks very differently on the inside, and on the outside; in its quality, and in its consequences. Murder in the murderer is no such ruinous thought as poets and romancers will have it; it does not unsettle him, or fright him from his ordinary notice of trifles: it is an act quite easy to be contemplated, but in its sequel, it turns out to be a horrible jangle and confounding of all relations. Especially the crimes that spring from love, seem right and fair from the actor's point of view, but, when acted, are found destructive of society. No man at last believes that he can be lost, nor that the crime in him is as black as in the felon. Because the intellect qualifies in our own case the moral judgments. For there is no crime to the intellect. That is antinomian or hypernomian, and judges law as well as fact. "It is worse than a crime, it is a blunder," said Napoleon, speaking the language of the intellect. To it, the world is a problem in mathematics or the science of quantity, and it leaves out praise and blame, and all weak emotions. All stealing is comparative. If you come to absolutes, pray who does not steal? Saints are sad, because they behold sin, (even when they speculate,) from the point of view of the conscience, and not of the intellect; a confusion of thought. Sin seen from the thought, is a diminution or less: seen from the conscience or will, it is pravity or *bad*. The intellect names it shade, absence of light, and no essence. The conscience must feel it as essence, essential evil. This it is not: it has an objective existence, but no subjective.

Thus inevitably does the universe wear our color, and every object fall successively into the subject itself. The subject exists, the subject enlarges; all things sooner or later fall into place. As I am, so I see; use what language we will, we can never say anything but what we are;

Hermes, Cadmus, Columbus, Newton, Buonaparte, are the mind's ministers. Instead of feeling a poverty when we encounter a great man, let us treat the new comer like a travelling geologist, who passes through our estate, and shows us good slate, or limestone, or anthracite, in our brush pasture. The partial action of each strong mind in one direction, is a telescope for the objects on which it is pointed. But every other part of knowledge is to be pushed to the same extravagance, ere the soul attains her due sphericity. Do you see that kitten chasing so prettily her own tail? If you could look with her eyes, you might see her surrounded with hundreds of figures performing complex dramas, with tragic and comic issues, long conversations, many characters, many ups and downs of fate,—and meantime it is only puss and her tail. How long before our masquerade will end its noise of tamborines, laughter, and shouting, and we shall find it was a solitary performance?—A subject and an object,—it takes so much to make the galvanic circuit complete, but magnitude adds nothing. What imports it whether it is Kepler and the sphere; Columbus and America; a reader and his book; or puss with her tail?

It is true that all the muses and love and religion hate these developments, and will find a way to punish the chemist, who publishes in the parlor the secrets of the laboratory. And we cannot say too little of our constitutional necessity of seeing things under private aspects, or saturated with our humors. And yet is the God the native of these bleak rocks. That need makes in morals the capital virtue of self-trust. We must hold hard to this poverty, however scandalous, and by more vigorous self-recoveries, after the sallies of action, possess our axis more firmly. The life of truth is cold, and so far mournful; but it is not the slave of tears, contritions, and perturbations. It does not attempt another's work, nor adopt another's facts. It is a main lesson of wisdom to know your own from another's. I have learned that I cannot dispose of other people's facts; but I possess such a key to my own, as persuades me against all their denials, that they also have a key to theirs. A sympathetic person is placed in the dilemma of a swimmer among drowning men, who all catch at him, and if he give so much as a leg or a finger, they will drown him. They wish to be saved from the mischiefs of their vices, but not from their vices. Charity would be wasted on this poor waiting on the symptoms. A wise and hardy physician will say, *Come out of that,* as the first condition of advice.

In this our talking America, we are ruined by our good nature and listening on all sides. This compliance takes away the power of being greatly useful. A man should not be able to look other than directly and forthright. A preoccupied attention is the only answer to the importunate frivolity of other people: an attention, and to an aim which makes their wants frivolous. This is a divine answer, and leaves no appeal, and no hard thoughts. In Flaxman's drawing of the Eumenides of Aeschylus, Orestes supplicates Apollo, whilst the Furies sleep on the threshold. The face of the god expresses a shade of regret and compassion, but calm with the conviction of the irreconcilableness of the two spheres. He is born into other politics, into the eternal and beautiful. The man at his feet asks for his interest in turmoils of the earth, into which his nature cannot enter. And the Eumenides there lying express pictorially this disparity. The god is surcharged with his divine destiny.

Illusion, Temperament, Succession, Surface, Surprise, Reality, Subjectiveness,—these are threads on the loom of time, these are the lords of life. I dare not assume to give their order, but I name them as I find them in my way. I know better than to claim any completeness for my picture. I am a fragment, and this is a fragment of me. I can very confidently announce one or another law, which throws itself into relief and form, but I am too young yet by some ages to compile a code. I gossip for my hour concerning the eternal politics. I have seen many fair pictures not in vain. A wonderful time I have lived in. I am not the novice I was fourteen, nor yet seven years ago. Let who will ask, where is the fruit? I find a private fruit sufficient. This is a fruit,—that I should not ask for a rash effect from meditations, counsels, and the hiving of truths. I should feel it pitiful to demand a result on this town and county, an overt effect on the instant month and year. The effect is deep and secular as the cause. It works on periods in which mortal lifetime is lost. All I know is reception; I am and I have: but I do not get, and when I have fancied I had gotten anything, I found I did not. I worship with wonder the great Fortune. My reception has been so large, that I am not annoyed by receiving this or that superabundantly. I say to the Genius, if he will pardon the proverb, *In for a mill, in for a million.* When I receive a new gift, I do not macerate my body to make the account square, for, if I should die, I could not make the account square. The benefit overran the merit the first day, and has overran the merit ever since. The merit itself, so-called, I reckon part of the receiving.

Also, that hankering after an overt or practical effect seems to me an apostasy. In good earnest, I am willing to spare this most unnecessary deal of doing. Life wears to me a visionary face. Hardest, roughest action is visionary also. It is but a choice between soft and turbulent dreams. People disparage knowing and the intellectual life, and urge doing. I am very content with knowing, if only I could know. That is an august entertainment, and would suffice me a great while. To know a little, would be worth the expense of this world. I hear always the law of Adrastia, "that every soul which had acquired any truth, should be safe from harm until another period."

I know that the world I converse with in the city and in the farms, is not the world I *think*. I observe that difference and shall observe it. One day, I shall know the value and law of this discrepance. But I have not found that much was gained by manipular attempts to realize the world of thought. Many eager persons successively make an experiment in this way, and make themselves ridiculous. They acquire democratic manners, they foam at the mouth, they hate and deny. Worse, I observe, that, in the history of mankind, there is never a solitary example of success,—taking their own tests of success. I say this polemically, or in reply to the inquiry, why not realize your world? But far be from me the despair which prejudges the law by a paltry empiricism,—since there never was a right endeavor, but it succeeded. Patience and patience, we shall win at the last. We must be very suspicious of the deceptions of the element of time. It takes a good deal of time to eat or to sleep, or to earn a hundred dollars, and a very little time to entertain a hope and an insight which becomes the light of our life. We dress our garden, eat our dinners, discuss the household with our wives, and these things make no impression, are forgotten next week; but in the solitude to which every man is always returning, he has a sanity and revelations, which in his passage into new worlds he will carry with him. Never mind the ridicule, never mind the defeat: up again, old heart!—it seems to say,—there is victory yet for all justice; and the true romance which the world exists to realize, will be the transformation of genius into practical power.

MARGARET FULLER

Margaret Fuller (1810–1850)—a charismatic speaker and literary critic; friend of Ralph Waldo Emerson and member of his transcendentalist circle; the editor of its journal, The Dial; *and a contributor to Horace Greeley's newspaper, the* New-York Daily Tribune—*is best known today for her feminist tract,* Woman in the Nineteenth Century. *In the excerpt below, she dismantles the notion that women cannot reason as well as men, offering the example of an outspoken, free woman, Miranda, whom many have surmised is a self-portrait. Consistently evident in her championing of abolition, women's rights, Chinese immigrants, and better treatment of the poor and the mentally ill is an acute sympathy for the Other. Fuller tragically drowned in a nautical accident while returning to America from Europe.*

from *Woman in the Nineteenth Century*

(1845)

The numerous party, whose opinions are already labeled and adjusted too much to their mind to admit of any new light, strive, by lectures on some model-woman of bride-like beauty and gentleness, by writing and lending little treatises, intended to mark out with precision the limits of Woman's sphere, and Woman's mission, to prevent other than the rightful shepherd from climbing the wall, or the flock from using any chance to go astray.

Without enrolling ourselves at once on either side, let us look upon the subject from the best point of view which to-day offers; no better, it is to be feared, than a high house-top. A high hill-top, or at least a cathedral-spire, would be desirable.

It may well be an Anti-Slavery party that pleads for Woman, if we consider merely that she does not hold property on equal terms with men; so that, if a husband dies without making a will, the wife, instead of taking at once his place as head of the family, inherits only a part of his fortune, often brought him by herself, as if she were a child, or ward only, not an equal partner.

We will not speak of the innumerable instances in which profligate and idle men live upon the earnings of industrious wives; or if the wives leave them, and take with them the children, to perform the double duty of mother and father, follow from place to place, and threaten to rob them of the children, if deprived of the rights of a husband, as they call them, planting themselves in their poor lodgings, frightening them into paying tribute by taking from them the children, running into debt at the expense of these otherwise so overtasked helots. Such instances count up by scores within my own memory. I have seen the husband who had stained himself by a long course of low vice, till his wife was wearied from her heroic forgiveness, by finding that his treachery made it useless, and that if she would provide bread for herself and her children, she must be separate from his ill fame—I have known this man come to install himself in the chamber of a woman who loathed him, and say she should never take food without his company. I have known these men steal their children, whom they knew they had no means to maintain, take them into dissolute company, expose them to bodily danger, to frighten the poor woman, to whom, it seems, the fact that she alone had borne the pangs of their birth, and nourished their infancy, does not give an equal right to them. I do believe that this mode of kidnapping—and it is frequent enough in all classes of society—will be by the next age viewed as it is by Heaven now, and that the man who avails himself of the shelter of men's laws to steal from a mother her own children, or arrogate any superior right in them, save that of superior virtue, will bear the stigma he deserves, in common with him who steals grown men from their mother-land, their hopes, and their homes.

I said, we will not speak of this now; yet I have spoken, for the subject makes me feel too much. I could give instances that would startle the most vulgar and callous; but I will not, for the public opinion of their own sex is already against such men, and where cases of extreme tyranny are made known, there is private action in the wife's favor. But she ought not to need this, nor, I think, can she long. Men must soon see that as, on their own ground, Woman is the weaker party, she ought to have legal protection, which would make such oppression impossible. But I would

not deal with "atrocious instances," except in the way of illustration, neither demand from men a partial redress in some one matter, but go to the
root of the whole. If principles could be established, particulars would
adjust themselves aright. Ascertain the true destiny of Woman; give her
legitimate hopes, and a standard within herself; marriage and all other
relations would by degrees be harmonized with these.

But to return to the historical progress of this matter. Knowing that
there exists in the minds of men a tone of feeling toward women as toward
slaves, such as is expressed in the common phrase, "Tell that to women
and children"; that the infinite soul can only work through them in
already ascertained limits; that the gift of reason, Man's highest prerogative, is allotted to them in much lower degree; that they must be kept from
mischief and melancholy by being constantly engaged in active labor,
which is to be furnished and directed by those better able to think, &c.,
&c.,—we need not multiply instances, for who can review the experience
of last week without recalling words which imply, whether in jest or earnest, these views, or views like these,—knowing this, can we wonder that
many reformers think that measures are not likely to be taken in behalf
of women, unless their wishes could be publicly represented by women?

"That can never be necessary," cry the other side. All men are privately
influenced by women; each has his wife, sister, or female friends, and is
too much biased by these relations to fail of representing their interests;
and, if this is not enough, let them propose and enforce their wishes with
the pen. The beauty of home would be destroyed, the delicacy of the sex
be violated, the dignity of halls of legislation degraded, by an attempt to
introduce them there. Such duties are inconsistent with those of a mother;
"and then we have ludicrous pictures of ladies in hysterics at the polls,
and senate-chambers filled with cradles."

But if, in reply, we admit as truth that Woman seems destined by nature
rather for the inner circle, we must add that the arrangements of civilized life have not been, as yet, such as to secure it to her. Her circle, if
the duller, is not the quieter. If kept from "excitement," she is not from
drudgery. Not only the Indian squaw carries the burdens of the camp, but
the favorites of Louis XIV accompany him in his journeys, and the wash-
erwoman stands at her tub, and carries home her work at all seasons,
and in all states of health. Those who think the physical circumstances
of Woman would make a part in the affairs of national government
unsuitable, are by no means those who think it impossible for negresses
to endure field-work, even during pregnancy, or for sempstresses to go
through their killing labors.

As to the use of the pen, there was quite as much opposition to
Woman's possessing herself of that help to free agency as there is now to
her seizing on the rostrum or the desk; and she is likely to draw, from a

permission to plead her cause that way, opposite inferences to what might be wished by those who now grant it.

As to the possibility of her filling with grace and dignity any such position, we should think those who had seen the great actresses, and heard the Quaker preachers of modern times, would not doubt that Woman can express publicly the fulness of thought and creation, without losing any of the peculiar beauty of her sex. What can pollute and tarnish is to act thus from any motive except that something needs to be said or done. Woman could take part in the processions, the songs, the dances of old religion; no one fancied her delicacy was impaired by appearing in public for such a cause.

As to her home, she is not likely to leave it more than she now does for balls, theatres, meetings for promoting missions, revival meetings, and others to which she flies, in hope of an animation for her existence commensurate with what she sees enjoyed by men. Governors of ladies' fairs are no less engrossed by such a charge, than the governor of a state by his; presidents of Washingtonian societies no less away from home than presidents of conventions. If men look straitly to it, they will find that, unless their lives are domestic, those of the women will not be. A house is no home unless it contain food and fire for the mind as well as for the body. The female Greek, of our day, is as much in the street as the male to cry, "What news?" We doubt not it was the same in Athens of old. The women, shut out from the market-place, made up for it at the religious festivals. For human beings are not so constituted that they can live without expansion. If they do not get it in one way, they must in another, or perish.

As to men's representing women fairly at present, while we hear from men who owe to their wives not only all that is comfortable or graceful, but all that is wise, in the arrangement of their lives, the frequent remark, "You cannot reason with a woman,"—when from those of delicacy, nobleness, and poetic culture, falls the contemptuous phrase "women and children," and that in no light sally of the hour, but in works intended to give a permanent statement of the best experiences,—when not one man, in the million, shall I say? no, not in the hundred million, can rise above the belief that Woman was made for Man,—when such traits as these are daily forced upon the attention, can we feel that Man will always do justice to the interests of Woman? Can we think that he takes a sufficiently discerning and religious view of her office and destiny ever to do her justice, except when prompted by sentiment,—accidentally or transiently, that is, for the sentiment will vary according to relations in which he is placed? The lover, the poet, the artist, are likely to view her nobly. The father and the philosopher have some chance of liberality; the man of the world, the legislator for expediency, none.

Under these circumstances, without attaching importance, in themselves, to the changes demanded by the champions of Woman, we hail
them as signs of the times. We would have every arbitrary barrier thrown
down. We would have every path laid open to Woman as freely as to Man.
Were this done, and a slight temporary fermentation allowed to subside,
we should see crystallizations more pure and of more various beauty. We
believe the divine energy would pervade nature to a degree unknown in
the history of former ages, and that no discordant collision, but a ravishing harmony of the spheres, would ensue.

Yet, then and only then will mankind be ripe for this, when inward and
outward freedom for Woman as much as for Man shall be acknowledged
as a right, not yielded as a concession. As the friend of the negro assumes
that one man cannot by right hold another in bondage, so should the
friend of Woman assume that Man cannot by right lay even well-meant
restrictions on Woman. If the negro be a soul, if the woman be a soul,
apparelled in flesh, to one Master only are they accountable. There is but
one law for souls, and, if there is to be an interpreter of it, he must come
not as man, or son of man, but as son of God.

Were thought and feeling once so far elevated that Man should esteem
himself the brother and friend, but nowise the lord and tutor, of Woman,—
were he really bound with her in equal worship,—arrangements as to
function and employment would be of no consequence. What Woman
needs is not as a woman to act or rule, but as a nature to grow, as an
intellect to discern, as a soul to live freely and unimpeded, to unfold such
powers as were given her when we left our common home. If fewer talents
were given her, yet if allowed the free and full employment of these, so
that she may render back to the giver his own with usury, she will not
complain; nay, I dare to say she will bless and rejoice in her earthly birthplace, her earthly lot. Let us consider what obstructions impede this good
era, and what signs give reason to hope that it draws near.

I was talking on this subject with Miranda, a woman, who, if any in
the world could, might speak without heat and bitterness of the position
of her sex. Her father was a man who cherished no sentimental reverence
for Woman, but a firm belief in the equality of the sexes. She was his
eldest child, and came to him at an age when he needed a companion.
From the time she could speak and go alone, he addressed her not as a
plaything, but as a living mind. Among the few verses he ever wrote was a
copy addressed to this child, when the first locks were cut from her head;
and the reverence expressed on this occasion for that cherished head, he
never belied. It was to him the temple of immortal intellect. He respected
his child, however, too much to be an indulgent parent. He called on her
for clear judgment, for courage, for honor and fidelity; in short, for such
virtues as he knew. In so far as he possessed the keys to the wonders of
this universe, he allowed free use of them to her, and, by the incentive of

a high expectation, he forbade, so far as possible, that she should let the privilege lie idle.

Thus this child was early led to feel herself a child of the spirit. She took her place easily, not only in the world of organized being, but in the world of mind. A dignified sense of self-dependence was given as all her portion, and she found it a sure anchor. Herself securely anchored, her relations with others were established with equal security. She was fortunate in a total absence of those charms which might have drawn to her bewildering flatteries, and in a strong electric nature, which repelled those who did not belong to her, and attracted those who did. With men and women her relations were noble,—affectionate without passion, intellectual without coldness. The world was free to her, and she lived freely in it. Outward adversity came, and inward conflict; but that faith and self-respect had early been awakened which must always lead, at last, to an outward serenity and an inward peace.

Of Miranda I had always thought as an example, that the restraints upon the sex were insuperable only to those who think them so, or who noisily strive to break them. She had taken a course of her own, and no man stood in her way. Many of her acts had been unusual, but excited no uproar. Few helped, but none checked her; and the many men who knew her mind and her life, showed to her confidence as to a brother, gentleness as to a sister. And not only refined, but very coarse men approved and aided one in whom they saw resolution and clearness of design. Her mind was often the leading one, always effective.

When I talked with her upon these matters, and had said very much what I have written, she smilingly replied: "And yet we must admit that I have been fortunate, and this should not be. My good father's early trust gave the first bias, and the rest followed, of course. It is true that I have had less outward aid, in after years, than most women; but that is of little consequence. Religion was early awakened in my soul,—a sense that what the soul is capable to ask it must attain, and that, though I might be aided and instructed by others, I must depend on myself as the only constant friend. This self-dependence, which was honored in me, is deprecated as a fault in most women. They are taught to learn their rule from without, not to unfold it from within.

"This is the fault of Man, who is still vain, and wishes to be more important to Woman than, by right, he should be."

"Men have not shown this disposition toward you," I said.

"No; because the position I early was enabled to take was one of self-reliance. And were all women as sure of their wants as I was, the result would be the same. But they are so overloaded with precepts by guardians, who think that nothing is so much to be dreaded for a woman as originality of thought or character, that their minds are impeded by doubts till they lose their chance of fair, free proportions. The difficulty is to get them to the point from which they shall naturally develop self-respect, and learn self-help.

"Once I thought that men would help to forward this state of things more than I do now. I saw so many of them wretched in the connections they had formed in weakness and vanity. They seemed so glad to esteem whenever they could.

"'The soft arms of affection,' said one of the most discerning spirits, 'will not suffice for me, unless on them I see the steel bracelets of strength.'

"But early I perceived that men never, in any extreme of despair, wished to be women. On the contrary, were ever ready to taunt one another, at any sign of weakness, with, "Art thou not like the women, who,' "—

The passage ends various ways, according to the occasion and rhetoric of the speaker. When they admired any woman, they were inclined to speak of her as "above her sex." Silently I observed this, and feared it argued a rooted scepticism, which for ages had been fastening on the heart, and which only an age of miracles could eradicate. Ever I have been treated with great sincerity; and I look upon it as a signal instance of this, that an intimate friend of the other sex said, in a fervent moment, that I "deserved in some star to be a man." He was much surprised when I disclosed my view of my position and hopes, when I declared my faith that the feminine side, the side of love, of beauty, of holiness, was now to have its full chance, and that, if either were better, it was better now to be a woman for even the slightest achievement of good was furthering an especial work of our time.

FREDERICK DOUGLASS

Frederick Douglass (1818–1895), after escaping slavery, served the abolitionist cause invaluably as an orator, a memoirist, and a model of the vast literary and intellectual capabilities of African Americans given an opportunity to learn. Douglass had been taught to read and write by a white woman who owned him for a while in Maryland, and by the time she came to regret that favor, having been warned that literate slaves would hanker for freedom, it was too late. Douglass tried again and again to escape and was finally successful. That dramatic story was told in his 1845 Narrative of the Life of Frederick Douglass, an American Slave and retold in two subsequent autobiographies. What makes "To My Old Master, Thomas Auld," a letter-essay, so effective is the controlled ironic application of traditional forms of respect for this man he clearly regards as a monster. By addressing someone who already knows parts of the story, he is able to compress it in places and spring graphic passages of guilt-inducing description with mounting indignation, all the while keeping up his calm, reasonable epistolary tone.

To My Old Master, Thomas Auld

(1848)

SIR—The long and intimate, though by no means friendly, relation which unhappily subsisted between you and myself, leads me to hope that you will easily account for the great liberty which I now take in addressing you in this open and public manner. The same fact may remove any disagreeable surprise which you may experience on again finding your name coupled with mine, in any other way than in an advertisement, accurately describing my person, and offering a large sum for my arrest. In thus dragging you again before the public, I am aware that I shall subject myself to no inconsiderable amount of censure. I shall probably be charged with an unwarrantable, if not a wanton and reckless disregard of the rights and properties of private life. There are those north as well as south who entertain a much higher respect for rights which are merely conventional, than they do for rights which are personal and essential. Not a few there are in our country, who, while they have no scruples against robbing the laborer of the hard earned results of his patient industry, will be shocked by the extremely indelicate manner of bringing your name before the public. Believing this to be the case, and wishing to meet every reasonable or plausible objection to my conduct, I will frankly state the ground upon which I justify myself in this instance, as well as on former occasions when I have thought proper to mention your name in public. All will agree that a man guilty of theft, robbery, or murder, has forfeited the right to concealment and private life; that the community have a right to subject such persons to the most complete exposure. However much they may desire retirement, and aim to conceal themselves and their movements from the popular gaze, the public have a right to ferret them out, and bring their conduct before the proper tribunals of the country for investigation. Sir, you will undoubtedly make the proper application of these generally admitted principles, and will easily see the light in which you are regarded by me; I will not therefore manifest ill temper, by calling you hard names. I know you to be a man of some intelligence, and can readily determine the precise estimate which I entertain of your character. I may therefore indulge in language which may seem to others indirect and ambiguous, and yet be quite well understood by yourself.

I have selected this day on which to address you, because it is the anniversary of my emancipation; and knowing no better way, I am led to this as the best mode of celebrating that truly important event. Just ten years ago this beautiful September morning, yon bright sun beheld me a slave—a poor degraded chattel—trembling at the sound of your voice, lamenting that I was a man, and wishing myself a brute. The hopes which I had treasured up for weeks of a safe and successful escape from your grasp, were powerfully confronted at this last hour by dark clouds of doubt and fear, making my person shake and my bosom to heave with the heavy contest between hope and fear. I have no words to describe to you the deep agony of soul which I experienced on that never-to-be-forgotten morning—for I left by daylight. I was making a leap in the dark. The probabilities, so far as I could by reason determine them, were stoutly against the undertaking. The preliminaries and precautions I had adopted previously, all worked badly. I was like one going to war without weapons—ten chances of defeat to one of victory. One in whom I had confided, and one who had promised me assistance, appalled by fear at the trial hour, deserted me, thus leaving the responsibility of success or failure solely with myself. You, sir, can never know my feelings. As I look back to them, I can scarcely realize that I have passed through a scene so trying. Trying, however, as they were, and gloomy as was the prospect, thanks be to the Most High, who is ever the God of the oppressed, at the moment which was to determine my whole earthly career, His grace was sufficient; my mind was made up. I embraced the golden opportunity, took the morning tide at the flood, and a free man, young, active, and strong, is the result.

I have often thought I should like to explain to you the grounds upon which I have justified myself in running away from you. I am almost ashamed to do so now, for by this time you may have discovered them yourself. I will, however, glance at them. When yet but a child about six years old, I imbibed the determination to run away. The very first mental effort that I now remember on my part, was an attempt to solve the mystery—why am I a slave? and with this question my youthful mind was troubled for many days, pressing upon me more heavily at times than others. When I saw the slave-driver whip a slave-woman, cut the blood out of her neck, and heard her piteous cries, I went away into the corner of the fence, wept and pondered over the mystery. I had, through some medium, I know not what, got some idea of God, the Creator of all mankind, the black and the white, and that he had made the blacks to serve the whites as slaves. How he could do this and be *good,* I could not tell. I was not satisfied with this theory, which made God responsible for slavery, for it pained me greatly, and I have wept over it long and often. At one time, your first wife, Mrs. Lucretia, heard me sighing and saw me shedding tears, and asked of me the matter, but I was afraid to tell her. I was puzzled with this question, till one night while sitting in the kitchen, I heard some of the old slaves talking of their parents having been stolen from Africa by white men, and were sold here as slaves. The whole mystery was solved at once. Very soon after this, my Aunt Jinny and Uncle Noah ran away, and the great noise made about it by your father-in-law, made me for the first time acquainted with the fact, that there were free states as well as slave states. From that time, I resolved that I would some day run away. The morality of the act I dispose of as follows: I am myself; you are yourself; we are two distinct persons, equal persons. What you are, I am. You are a man, and so am I. God created both, and made us separate beings. I am not by nature bond to you, or you to me. Nature does not make your existence depend upon me, or mine to depend upon yours. I cannot walk upon your legs, or you upon mine. I cannot breathe for you, or you for me; I must breathe for myself, and you for yourself. We are distinct persons, and are each equally provided with faculties necessary to our individual existence. In leaving you, I took nothing but what belonged to me, and in no way lessened your means for obtaining an *honest* living. Your faculties remained yours, and mine became useful to their rightful owner. I therefore see no wrong in any part of the transaction. It is true, I went off secretly; but that was more your fault than mine. Had I let you into the secret, you would have defeated the enterprise entirely; but for this, I should have been really glad to have made you acquainted with my intentions to leave.

You may perhaps want to know how I like my present condition. I am free to say, I greatly prefer it to that which I occupied in Maryland. I am, however, by no means prejudiced against the state as such. Its geography, climate, fertility, and products, are such as to make it a very desirable abode for any man; and but for the existence of slavery there, it is not impossible that I might again take up my abode in that state. It is not that I love Maryland less, but freedom more. You will be surprised to learn that people at the north labor under the strange delusion that if the slaves were emancipated at the south, they would flock to the north. So far from this being the case, in that event, you would see many old and familiar faces back again to the south. The fact is, there are few here who would not return to the south in the event of emancipation. We want to live in the land of our birth, and to lay our bones by the side of our fathers; and nothing short of an intense love of personal freedom keeps us from the south. For the sake of this, most of us would live on a crust of bread and a cup of cold water.

Since I left you, I have had a rich experience. I have occupied stations which I never dreamed of when a slave. Three out of the ten years since I left you, I spent as a common laborer on the wharves of New Bedford, Massachusetts. It was there I earned my first free dollar. It was mine. I could spend it as I pleased. I could buy hams or herring with it, without asking any odds of anybody. That was a precious dollar to me. You remember when I used to make seven, or eight, or even nine dollars a week in Baltimore, you would take every cent of it from me every Saturday night, saying that I belonged to you, and my earnings also. I never liked this conduct on your part—to say the best, I thought it a little mean. I would not have served you so. But let that pass. I was a little awkward about counting money in New England fashion when I first landed in New Bedford. I came near betraying myself several times. I caught myself saying phip, for fourpence; and at one time a man actually charged me with being a runaway, whereupon I was silly enough to become one by running away from him, for I was greatly afraid he might adopt measures to get me again into slavery, a condition I then dreaded more than death.

I soon learned, however, to count money, as well as to make it, and got on swimmingly. I married soon after leaving you; in fact, I was engaged to be married before I left you; and instead of finding my companion a burden, she was truly a helpmate. She went to live at service, and I to work on the wharf, and though we toiled hard the first winter, we never lived more happily. After remaining in New Bedford for three years, I met with William Lloyd Garrison, a person of whom you have *possibly* heard, as he is pretty generally known among slaveholders. He put it into my head that I might make myself serviceable to the cause of the slave, by devoting a portion of my time to telling my own sorrows, and those of other slaves, which had come under my observation. This was the commencement of a higher state of existence than any to which I had ever aspired. I was thrown into society the most pure, enlightened, and benevolent, that the country affords. Among these I have never forgotten you, but have invariably made you the topic of conversation—thus giving you all the notoriety I could do. I need not tell you that the opinion formed of you in these circles is far from being favorable. They have little respect for your honesty, and less for your religion.

But I was going on to relate to you something of my interesting experience. I had not long enjoyed the excellent society to which I have referred, before the light of its excellence exerted a beneficial influence on my mind and heart. Much of my early dislike of white persons was removed, and their manners, habits, and customs, so entirely unlike what I had been used to in the kitchen-quarters on the plantations of the south, fairly charmed me, and gave me a strong disrelish for the coarse and degrading customs of my former condition. I therefore made an effort so to improve my mind and deportment, as to be somewhat fitted to the station to which I seemed almost providentially called. The transition from degradation to respectability was indeed great, and to get from one to the other without carrying some marks of one's former condition, is truly a difficult matter. I would not have you think that I am now entirely clear of all plantation peculiarities, but my friends here, while they entertain the strongest dislike to them, regard me with that charity to which my past life somewhat entitles me, so that my condition in this respect is exceedingly pleasant. So far as my domestic affairs are concerned, I can boast of as comfortable a dwelling as your own. I have an industrious and neat companion, and four dear children—the oldest a girl of nine years, and three fine boys, the oldest eight, the next six, and the youngest four years old. The three oldest are now going regularly to school—two can read and write, and the other can spell, with tolerable correctness, words of two syllables. Dear fellows! they are all in comfortable beds, and are sound asleep, perfectly secure under my own roof. There are no slaveholders here to rend my heart by snatching them from my arms, or blast a mother's dearest hopes by tearing them from her bosom. These dear children are ours—not to work up into rice, sugar, and tobacco, but to watch over, regard, and protect, and to rear them up in the nurture and admonition of the gospel—to train them up in the paths of wisdom and virtue, and, as far as we can, to make them useful to the world and to themselves. Oh! sir, a slaveholder never appears to me so completely an agent of hell, as when I think of and look upon my dear children. It is then that my feelings rise above my control. I meant to have said more with respect to my own prosperity and happiness, but thoughts and feelings which this recital has quickened, unfit me to proceed further in that direction. The grim horrors of slavery rise in all their ghastly terror before me; the wails of millions pierce my heart and chill my blood. I remember the chain, the gag, the bloody whip; the death-like gloom overshadowing the broken spirit of the fettered bondman; the appalling liability of his being torn away from wife and children, and sold like a beast in the market. Say not that this is a picture of fancy. You well know that I wear stripes on my back, inflicted by your direction; and that you, while we were brothers in the same church, caused this right hand, with which I am now penning this letter, to be closely tied to my left, and my person dragged, at the pistol's mouth, fifteen miles, from the Bay Side to Easton, to be sold like a beast in the market, for the alleged crime of intending to escape from your possession. All this, and more, you remember, and know to be perfectly true, not only of yourself, but of nearly all of the slaveholders around you.

At this moment, you are probably the guilty holder of at least three of my own dear sisters, and my only brother, in bondage. These you regard as your property. They are recorded on your ledger, or perhaps have been sold to human flesh-mongers, with a view to filling our own ever-hungry purse. Sir, I desire to know how and where these dear sisters are. Have you sold them? or are they still in your possession? What has become of them? are they living or dead? And my dear old grandmother, whom you turned out like an old horse to die in the woods—is she still alive? Write and let me know all about them. If my grandmother be still alive, she is of no service to you, for by this time she must be nearly eighty years old—too old to be cared for by one to whom she has ceased to be of service; send her to me at Rochester, or bring her to Philadelphia, and it shall be the crowning happiness of my life to take care of her in her old age. Oh! she was to me a mother and a father, so far as hard toil for my comfort could make her such. Send me my grandmother! that I may watch over and take care of her in her old age. And my sisters—let me know all about them. I would write to them, and learn all I want to know of them, without disturbing you in any way, but that, through your unrighteous conduct, they have been entirely deprived of the power to read and write. You have kept them in utter ignorance, and have therefore robbed them of the sweet enjoyments of writing or receiving letters from absent friends and relatives. Your wickedness and cruelty, committed in this respect on your fellow-creatures, are greater than all the stripes you have laid upon my back or theirs. It is an outrage upon the soul, a war upon the immortal spirit, and one for which you must give account at the bar of our common Father and Creator.

The responsibility which you have assumed in this regard is truly awful, and how you could stagger under it these many years is marvelous. Your mind must have become darkened, your heart hardened, your conscience seared and petrified, or you would have long since thrown off the accursed load, and sought relief at the hands of a sin-forgiving God. How, let me ask, would you look upon me, were I, some dark night, in company with a band of hardened villains, to enter the precincts of your elegant dwelling, and seize the person of your own lovely daughter, Amanda, and carry her off from your family, friends, and all the loved ones of her youth—make her my slave—compel her to work, and I take her wages—place her name on my ledger as property—disregard her personal rights—fetter the powers of her immortal soul by denying her the right and privilege of learning to read and write—feed her coarsely—clothe her scantily, and whip her on the naked back occasionally; more, and still more horrible, leave her unprotected—a degraded victim to the brutal lust of fiendish overseers, who would pollute, blight, and blast her fair soul—rob her of all dignity—destroy her virtue, and annihilate in her person all the graces that adorn the character of virtuous womanhood? I ask, how would you regard me, if such were my conduct? Oh! the vocabulary of the damned would not afford a word sufficiently infernal to express your idea of my God-provoking wickedness. Yet, sir, your treatment of my beloved sisters is in all essential points precisely like the case I have now supposed. Damning as would be such a deed on my part, it would be no more so than that which you have committed against me and my sisters.

I will now bring this letter to a close; you shall hear from me again unless you let me hear from you. I intend to make use of you as a weapon with which to assail the system of slavery—as a means of concentrating public attention on the system, and deepening the horror of trafficking in the souls and bodies of men. I shall make use of you as a means of exposing the character of the American church and clergy—and as a means of bringing this guilty nation, with yourself, to repentance. In doing this, I entertain no malice toward you personally. There is no roof under which you would be more safe than mine, and there is nothing in my house which you might need for your comfort, which I would not readily grant. Indeed, I should esteem it a privilege to set you an example as to how mankind ought to treat each other.

I am your fellow-man, but not your slave.

HERMAN MELVILLE

In 1850, the same year he was working on Moby-Dick, *Herman Melville (1819–1891) took time off to write this review-essay of Nathaniel Hawthorne's story collection* Mosses from an Old Manse. *In a free and easy manner, curiously pretending to be a Virginian, he bestowed one of the most generous, insightful appreciations an American writer has ever given a contemporary. Espousing the need for a mature national literature, he anointed Hawthorne its pioneer. Singling out Hawthorne's "darker" side also connected it with Melville's own: Melville credited his reading of Hawthorne with "dropping germinous seeds into my soul" and spurring him to expand and deepen* Moby-Dick. *The essay was published anonymously in* The Literary World; *Hawthorne's wife, reading it, declared it the first time anyone had really "apprehended" her husband's work in print. When the article writer's identity became known, Melville tried to bring about a personal friendship with this author he so admired, but the shy, self-contained Hawthorne put up barriers. In the end, this essay may have been the closest these two giants would ever come to communicating successfully with each other.*

Hawthorne and His Mosses

By a Virginian Spending July in Vermont

(1850)

A papered chamber in a fine old farm-house—a mile from any other dwelling, and dipped to the eaves in foliage—surrounded by mountains, old woods, and Indian ponds,—this, surely, is the place to write of Hawthorne. Some charm is in this northern air, for love and duty seem both impelling to the task. A man of a deep and noble nature has seized me in this seclusion. His wild, witch voice rings through me; or, in softer cadences, I seem to hear it in the songs of the hill-side birds, that sing in the larch trees at my window.

Would that all excellent books were foundlings, without father or mother, that so it might be, we could glorify them, without including their ostensible authors. Nor would any true man take exception to this;—least of all, he who writes,—"When the Artist rises high enough to achieve the Beautiful, the symbol by which he makes it perceptible to mortal senses becomes of little value in his eyes, while his spirit possesses itself in the enjoyment of the reality."

But more than this. I know not what would be the right name to put on the title-page of an excellent book, but this I feel, that the names of all fine authors are fictitious ones, far more so than that of Junius,—simply standing, as they do, for the mystical, ever-eluding Spirit of all Beauty, which ubiquitously possesses men of genius. Purely imaginative as this fancy may appear, it nevertheless seems to receive some warranty from the fact, that on a personal interview no great author has ever come up to the idea of his reader. But that dust of which our bodies are composed, how can it fitly express the nobler intelligences among us? With reverence be it spoken, that not even in the case of one deemed more than man, not even in our Saviour, did his visible frame betoken anything of the augustness of the nature within. Else, how could those Jewish eyewitnesses fail to see heaven in his glance.

It is curious, how a man may travel along a country road, and yet miss the grandest, or sweetest of prospects, by reason of an intervening hedge, so like all other hedges, as in no way to hint of the wide landscape beyond. So has it been with me concerning the enchanting landscape in the soul of this Hawthorne, this most excellent Man of Mosses. His "Old Manse" has been written now four years, but I never read it till a day or two since. I had seen it in the book-stores—heard of it often—even had it recommended to me by a tasteful friend, as a rare, quiet book, perhaps too deserving of popularity to be popular. But there are so many books called "excellent," and so much unpopular merit, that amid the thick stir of other things, the hint of my tasteful friend was disregarded; and for four years the Mosses on the old Manse never refreshed me with their perennial green. It may be, however, that all this while, the book, like wine, was only improving in flavor and body. At any rate, it so chanced that this long procrastination eventuated in a happy result. At breakfast the other day, a mountain girl, a cousin of mine, who for the last two weeks has every morning helped me to strawberries and raspberries,—which, like the roses and pearls in the fairy-tale, seemed to fall into the saucer from those strawberry-beds her cheeks,—this delightful creature, this charming Cherry says to me—"I see you spend your mornings in the hay mow; and yesterday I found there 'Dwight's Travels in New England.' Now I have something far better than that,—something more congenial to our summer on these hills. Take these raspberries, and then I will give you some moss."—"Moss!" said I.—"Yes, and you must take it to the barn with you, and good-bye to 'Dwight.'"

With that she left me, and soon returned with a volume, verdantly bound, and garnished with a curious frontispiece in green,—nothing less, than a fragment of real moss cunningly pressed to a fly-leaf.—"Why this," said I spilling my raspberries, "this is the 'Mosses from an Old Manse.'" "Yes" said cousin Cherry "yes, it is that flowery Hawthorne."—"Hawthorne and Mosses" said I "no more: it is morning: it is July in the country: and I am off for the barn."

Stretched on that new mown clover, the hill-side breeze blowing over me through the wide barn door, and soothed by the hum of the bees in the meadows around, how magically stole over me this Mossy Man! and how amply, how bountifully, did he redeem that delicious promise to his guests in the Old Manse, of whom it is written—"Others could give them pleasure, or amusement, or instruction—these could be picked up anywhere—but it was for me to give them rest. Rest, in a life of trouble! What better could be done for weary and world-worn spirits? what better could be done for anybody, who came within our magic circle, than to throw the spell of a magic spirit over him?"—So all that day, half-buried in the new clover, I watched this Hawthorne's "Assyrian dawn, and Paphian sunset and moonrise, from the summit of our Eastern Hill."

The soft ravishments of the man spun me round about in a web of dreams, and when the book was closed, when the spell was over, this wizard "dismissed me with but misty reminiscences, as if I had been dreaming of him."

What a mild moonlight of contemplative humor bathes that Old Manse!—the rich and rare distilment of a spicy and slowly-oozing heart. No rollicking rudeness, no gross fun fed on fat dinners, and bred in the lees of wine,—but a humor so spiritually gentle, so high, so deep, and yet so richly relishable, that it were hardly inappropriate in an angel. It is the very religion of mirth; for nothing so human but it may be advanced to that. The orchard of the Old Manse seems the visible type of the fine mind that has described it. Those twisted, and contorted old trees, "that stretch out their crooked branches, and take such hold of the imagination, that we remember them as humorists, and odd-fellows." And then, as surrounded by these grotesque forms, and hushed in the noon-day repose of this Hawthorne's spell, how aptly might the still fall of his ruddy thoughts into your soul be symbolized by "the thump of a great apple, in the stillest afternoon, falling without a breath of wind, from the mere necessity of perfect ripeness"! For no less ripe than ruddy are the apples of the thoughts and fancies in this sweet Man of Mosses.

"Buds and Bird-voices"—What a delicious thing is that!—"Will the world ever be so decayed, that Spring may not renew its greenness?"— And the "Fire-Worship." Was ever the hearth so glorified into an altar before? The mere title of that piece is better than any common work in fifty folio volumes. How exquisite is this:—"Nor did it lessen the charm of his soft, familiar courtesy and helpfulness, that the mighty spirit, were opportunity offered him, would run riot through the peaceful house, wrap its inmates in his terrible embrace, and leave nothing of them save their whitened bones. This possibility of mad destruction only made his domestic kindness the more beautiful and touching. It was so sweet of him, being endowed with such power, to dwell, day after day, and one long, lonesome night after another, on the dusky hearth, only now and then betraying his wild nature, by thrusting his red tongue out of the chimney-top! True, he had done much mischief in the world, and was pretty certain to do more, but his warm heart atoned for all. He was kindly to the race of man."

But he has still other apples, not quite so ruddy, though full as ripe;— apples, that have been left to wither on the tree, after the pleasant autumn gathering is past. The sketch of "The Old Apple Dealer" is conceived in the subtlest spirit of sadness; he whose "subdued and nerveless boyhood prefigured his abortive prime, which, likewise, contained within itself the prophecy and image of his lean and torpid age." Such touches as are in this piece can not proceed from any common heart. They argue such a depth of tenderness, such a boundless sympathy with all forms of being, such an omnipresent love, that we must needs say, that this Hawthorne is here almost alone in his generation,—at least, in the artistic manifestation of these things. Still more. Such touches as these,—and many, very many similar ones, all through his chapters—furnish clews, whereby we enter a little way into the intricate, profound heart where they originated. And we see, that suffering, some time or other and in some shape or other,—this only can enable any man to depict it in others. All over him, Hawthorne's melancholy rests like an Indian Summer, which though bathing a whole country in one softness, still reveals the distinctive hue of every towering hill, and each far-winding vale.

But it is the least part of genius that attracts admiration. Where Haw-thorne is known, he seems to be deemed a pleasant writer, with a pleasant style,—a sequestered, harmless man, from whom any deep and weighty thing would hardly be anticipated:—a man who means no meanings. But there is no man, in whom humor and love, like mountain peaks, soar to such a rapt height, as to receive the irradiations of the upper skies;— there is no man in whom humor and love are developed in that high form called genius; no such man can exist without also possessing, as the indispensable complement of these, a great, deep intellect, which drops down into the universe like a plummet. Or, love and humor are only the eyes, through which such an intellect views this world. The great beauty in such a mind is but the product of its strength. What, to all readers, can be more charming than the piece entitled "Monsieur du Miroir"; and to a reader at all capable of fully fathoming it, what, at the same time, can possess more mystical depth of meaning?—Yes, there he sits, and looks at me,—this "shape of mystery," this "identical Monsieur du Miroir."—"Methinks I should tremble now, were his wizard power of gliding through all impediments in search of me, to place him suddenly before my eyes."

How profound, nay appalling, is the moral evolved by the "Earth's Holocaust"; where—beginning with the hollow follies and affectations of the world,—all vanities and empty theories and forms, are, one after another, and by an admirably graduated, growing comprehensiveness, thrown into the allegorical fire, till, at length, nothing is left but the all-engendering heart of man; which remaining still unconsumed, the great conflagration is nought.

Of a piece with this, is the "Intelligence Office," a wondrous symbolizing of the secret workings in men's souls. There are other sketches, still more charged with ponderous import.

"The Christmas Banquet" and "The Bosom Serpent" would be fine subjects for a curious and elaborate analysis, touching the conjectural parts of the mind that produced them. For spite of all the Indian-summer sunlight on the hither side of Hawthorne's soul, the other side—like the dark half of the physical sphere—is shrouded in a blackness, ten times black. But this darkness but gives more effect to the ever-moving dawn, that forever advances through it, and circumnavigates his world. Whether Hawthorne has simply availed himself of this mystical blackness as a means to the wondrous effects he makes it to produce in his lights and shades; or whether there really lurks in him, perhaps unknown to himself, a touch of Puritanic gloom,—this, I cannot altogether tell. Certain it is, however, that this great power of blackness in him derives its force from its appeals to that Calvinistic sense of Innate Depravity and Original Sin, from whose visitations, in some shape or other, no deeply thinking mind is always and wholly free. For, in certain moods, no man can weigh this world, without throwing in something, somehow like Original Sin, to strike the uneven balance. At all events, perhaps no writer has ever wielded this terrific thought with greater terror than this same harmless Hawthorne. Still more: this black conceit pervades him, through and through. You may be witched by his sunlight,—transported by the bright gildings in the skies he builds over you;—but there is the blackness of darkness beyond; and even his bright gildings but fringe, and play upon the edges of thunder-clouds.—In one word, the world is mistaken in this

Nathaniel Hawthorne. He himself must often have smiled at its absurd misconception of him. He is immeasurably deeper than the plummet of the mere critic. For it is not the brain that can test such a man; it is only the heart. You cannot come to know greatness by inspecting it; there is no glimpse to be caught of it, except by intuition; you need not ring it, you but touch it, and you find it is gold.

Now it is that blackness in Hawthorne, of which I have spoken, that so fixes and fascinates me. It may be, nevertheless, that it is too largely developed in him. Perhaps he does not give us a ray of his light for every shade of his dark. But however this may be, this blackness it is that furnishes the infinite obscure of his back-ground,—that back-ground, against which Shakespeare plays his grandest conceits, the things that have made for Shakespeare his loftiest, but most circumscribed renown, as the profoundest of thinkers. For by philosophers Shakespeare is not adored as the great man of tragedy and comedy.—"Off with his head! so much for Buckingham!" this sort of rant, interlined by another hand, brings down the house,—those mistaken souls, who dream of Shakespeare as a mere man of Richard-the-Third humps, and Macbeth daggers. But it is those deep far-away things in him; those occasional flashings-forth of the intuitive Truth in him; those short, quick probings at the very axis of reality;—these are the things that make Shakespeare, Shakespeare. Through the mouths of the dark characters of Hamlet, Timon, Lear, and Iago, he craftily says, or sometimes insinuates the things, which we feel to be so terrifically true, that it were all but madness for any good man, in his own proper character, to utter, or even hint of them. Tormented into desperation, Lear the frantic King tears off the mask, and speaks the sane madness of vital truth. But, as I before said, it is the least part of genius that attracts admiration. And so, much of the blind, unbridled admiration that has been heaped upon Shakespeare, has been lavished upon the least part of him. And few of his endless commentators and critics seem to have remembered, or even perceived, that the immediate products of a great mind are not so great, as that undeveloped (and sometimes undevelopable) yet dimly-discernable greatness, to which these immediate products are but the infallible indices. In Shakespeare's tomb lies infinitely more than Shakespeare ever wrote. And if I magnify Shakespeare, it is not so much for what he did do, as for what he did not do, or refrained from doing. For in this world of lies, Truth is forced to fly like a scared white doe in the woodlands; and only by cunning glimpses will she reveal herself, as in Shakespeare and other masters of the great Art of Telling the Truth,—even though it be covertly, and by snatches.

But if this view of the all-popular Shakespeare be seldom taken by his readers, and if very few who extol him, have ever read him deeply, or, perhaps, only have seen him on the tricky stage, (which alone made, and is still making him his mere mob renown)—if few men have time, or patience, or palate, for the spiritual truth as it is in that great genius;—it is, then, no matter of surprise that in a contemporaneous age, Nathaniel Hawthorne is a man, as yet, almost utterly mistaken among men. Here and there, in some quiet arm-chair in the noisy town, or some deep nook among the noiseless mountains, he may be appreciated for something of what he is. But unlike Shakespeare, who was forced to the contrary course by circumstances, Hawthorne (either from simple disinclination, or else from inaptitude) refrains from all the popularizing noise and show of broad farce, and blood-besmeared tragedy; content with the still, rich utterances of a great intellect in repose, and which sends few thoughts into circulation, except they be arterialized at his large warm lungs, and expanded in his honest heart.

Nor need you fix upon that blackness in him, if it suit you not. Nor, indeed, will all readers discern it, for it is, mostly, insinuated to those who may best understand it, and account for it; it is not obtruded upon every one alike.

Some may start to read of Shakespeare and Hawthorne on the same page. They may say, that if an illustration were needed, a lesser light might have sufficed to elucidate this Hawthorne, this small man of yesterday. But I am not, willingly, one of those, who, as touching Shakespeare at least, exemplify the maxim of Rochefoucault, that "we exalt the reputation of some, in order to depress that of others";—who, to teach all noble-souled aspirants that there is no hope for them, pronounce Shakespeare absolutely unapproachable. But Shakespeare has been approached. There are minds that have gone as far as Shakespeare into the universe. And hardly a mortal man, who, at some time or other, has not felt as great thoughts in him as any you will find in Hamlet. We must not inferentially malign mankind for the sake of any one man, whoever he may be. This is too cheap a purchase of contentment for conscious mediocrity to make. Besides, this absolute and unconditional adoration of Shakespeare has grown to be a part of our Anglo Saxon superstitions. The Thirty Nine articles are now Forty. Intolerance has come to exist in this matter. You must believe in Shakespeare's unapproachability, or quit the country. But what sort of a belief is this for an American, a man who is bound to carry republican progressiveness into Literature, as well as into Life? Believe me, my friends, that Shakespeares are this day being born on the banks of the Ohio. And the day will come, when you shall say who reads a book by an Englishman that is a modern? The great mistake seems to be, that even with those Americans who look forward to the coming of a great literary genius among us, they somehow fancy he will come in the costume of Queen Elizabeth's day,—be a writer of dramas founded upon old English history, or the tales of Boccaccio. Whereas, great geniuses are parts of the times; they themselves are the times; and possess a correspondent coloring. It is of a piece with the Jews, who while their Shiloh was meekly walking in their streets, were still praying for his magnificent coming; looking for him in a chariot, who was already among them on an ass. Nor must we forget, that, in his own lifetime, Shakespeare was not Shakespeare, but only Master William Shakespeare of the shrewd, thriving, business firm of Condell, Shakespeare & Co., proprietors of the Globe Theatre in London; and by a courtly author, of the name of Greene, was hooted at, as an "upstart crow" beautified "with other birds' feathers." For, mark it well, imitation is often the first charge brought against real originality. Why this is so, there is not space to set forth here. You must have plenty of sea-room to tell the Truth in; especially, when it seems to have an aspect of newness, as America did in 1492, though it was then just as old, and perhaps older than Asia, only those sagacious philosophers, the common sailors, had never seen it before; swearing it was all water and moonshine there.

Now, I do not say that Nathaniel of Salem is a greater than William of Avon, or as great. But the difference between the two men is by no means immeasurable. Not a very great deal more, and Nathaniel were verily William.

This, too, I mean, that if Shakespeare has not been equalled, he is sure to be surpassed, and surpassed by an American born now or yet to be born. For it will never do for us who in most other things out-do as well as out-brag the world, it will not do for us to fold our hands and say, In the highest department advance there is none. Nor will it at all do to say, that the world is getting grey and grizzled now, and has lost that fresh charm which she wore of old, and by virtue of which the great poets of past times made themselves what we esteem them to be. Not so. The world is as young today, as when it was created; and this Vermont morning dew is as wet to my feet, as Eden's dew to Adam's. Nor has Nature been all over ransacked by our progenitors, so that no new charms and mysteries remain for this latter generation to find. Far from it. The trillionth part has not yet been said; and all that has been said, but multiplies the avenues to what remains to be said. It is not so much paucity, as superabundance of material that seems to incapacitate modern authors.

Let America then prize and cherish her writers; yea, let her glorify them. They are not so many in number, as to exhaust her good-will. And while she has good kith and kin of her own, to take to her bosom, let her not lavish her embraces upon the household of an alien. For believe it or not England, after all, is, in many things, an alien to us. China has more bowels of real love for us than she. But even were there no Hawthorne, no Emerson, no Whittier, no Irving, no Bryant, no Dana, no Cooper, no Willis (not the author of the "Dashes," but the author of the "Belfry Pigeon")—were there none of these, and others of like calibre among us, nevertheless, let America first praise mediocrity even, in her own children, before she praises (for everywhere, merit demands acknowledgment from every one) the best excellence in the children of any other land. Let her own authors, I say, have the priority of appreciation. I was much pleased with a hot-headed Carolina cousin of mine, who once said,—"If there were no other American to stand by, in Literature,—why, then, I would stand by Pop Emmons and his 'Fredoniad,' and till a better epic came along, swear it was not very far behind the Iliad." Take away the words, and in spirit he was sound.

Not that American genius needs patronage in order to expand. For that explosive sort of stuff will expand though screwed up in a vice, and burst it, though it were triple steel. It is for the nation's sake, and not for her authors' sake, that I would have America be heedful of the increasing greatness among her writers. For how great the shame, if other nations should be before her, in crowning her heroes of the pen. But this is almost the case now. American authors have received more just and discriminating praise (however loftily and ridiculously given, in certain cases) even from some Englishmen, than from their own countrymen. There are hardly five critics in America; and several of them are asleep. As for patronage, it is the American author who now patronizes his country, and not his country him. And if at times some among them appeal to the people for more recognition, it is not always with selfish motives, but patriotic ones.

It is true, that but few of them as yet have evinced that decided originality which merits great praise. But that graceful writer, who perhaps of all Americans has received the most plaudits from his own country for his productions,—that very popular and amiable writer, however good, and self-reliant in many things, perhaps owes his chief reputation to the self-acknowledged imitation of a foreign model, and to the studied avoidance of all topics but smooth ones. But it is better to fail in originality, than to succeed in imitation. He who has never failed somewhere, that man can not be great. Failure is the true test of greatness. And if it be said, that continual success is a proof that a man wisely knows his powers,—it is only to be added, that, in that case, he knows them to be small. Let us believe it, then, once for all, that there is no hope for us in these smooth pleasing writers that know their powers. Without malice, but to speak the plain fact, they but furnish an appendix to Goldsmith, and other English authors. And we want no American Goldsmiths; nay, we want no American Miltons. It were the vilest thing you could say of a true American author, that he were an American Tompkins. Call him an American, and have done; for you can not say a nobler thing of him.— But it is not meant that all American writers should studiously cleave to nationality in their writings; only this, no American writer should write like an Englishman, or a Frenchman; let him write like a man, for then he will be sure to write like an American. Let us away with this Bostonian leaven of literary flunkeyism towards England. If either must play the

flunkey in this thing, let England do it, not us. And the time is not far
off when circumstances may force her to it. While we are rapidly preparing for that political supremacy among the nations, which prophetically
awaits us at the close of the present century; in a literary point of view,
we are deplorably unprepared for it; and we seem studious to remain so.
Hitherto, reasons might have existed why this should be; but no good
reason exists now. And all that is requisite to amendment in this matter, is
simply this: that, while freely acknowledging all excellence, everywhere,
we should refrain from unduly lauding foreign writers and, at the same
time, duly recognize the meritorious writers that are our own;—those
writers, who breathe that unshackled, democratic spirit of Christianity in
all things, which now takes the practical lead in this world, though at the
same time led by ourselves—us Americans. Let us boldly contemn all imitation, though it comes to us graceful and fragrant as the morning; and
foster all originality, though, at first, it be crabbed and ugly as our own
pine knots. And if any of our authors fail, or seem to fail, then, in the
words of my enthusiastic Carolina cousin, let us clap him on the shoulder,
and back him against all Europe for his second round. The truth is, that
in our point of view, this matter of a national literature has come to such
a pass with us, that in some sense we must turn bullies, else the day is lost,
or superiority so far beyond us, that we can hardly say it will ever be ours.

And now, my countrymen, as an excellent author, of your own flesh
and blood,—an unimitating, and, perhaps, in his way, an inimitable
man—whom better can I commend to you, in the first place, than
Nathaniel Hawthorne. He is one of the new, and far better generation of
your writers. The smell of your beeches and hemlocks is upon him; your
own broad prairies are in his soul; and if you travel away inland into his
deep and noble nature, you will hear the far roar of his Niagara. Give not
over to future generations the glad duty of acknowledging him for what
he is. Take that joy to your self, in your own generation; and so shall he
feel those grateful impulses in him, that may possibly prompt him to the
full flower of some still greater achievement in your eyes. And by confess-
ing him, you thereby confess others; you brace the whole brotherhood.
For genius, all over the world, stands hand in hand, and one shock of
recognition runs the whole circle round.

In treating of Hawthorne, or rather of Hawthorne in his writings (for
I never saw the man; and in the chances of a quiet plantation life, remote
from his haunts, perhaps never shall) in treating of his works, I say, I have
thus far omitted all mention of his "Twice Told Tales" and "Scarlet Letter." Both are excellent; but full of such manifold, strange and diffusive
beauties, that time would all but fail me, to point the half of them out.
But there are things in those two books, which, had they been written in
England a century ago, Nathaniel Hawthorne had utterly displaced many
of the bright names we now revere on authority. But I am content to leave

Hawthorne to himself, and to the infallible finding of posterity; and however great may be the praise I have bestowed upon him, I feel, that in so doing, I have more served and honored myself, than him. For, at bottom, great excellence is praise enough to itself; but the feeling of a sincere and appreciative love and admiration towards it, this is relieved by utterance; and warm, honest praise ever leaves a pleasant flavor in the mouth; and it is an honorable thing to confess to what is honorable in others.

But I cannot leave my subject yet. No man can read a fine author, and relish him to his very bones, while he reads, without subsequently fancying to himself some ideal image of the man and his mind. And if you rightly look for it, you will almost always find that the author himself has somewhere furnished you with his own picture.—For poets (whether in prose or verse), being painters of Nature, are like their brethren of the pencil, the true portrait-painters, who, in the multitude of likenesses to be sketched, do not invariably omit their own; and in all high instances, they paint them without any vanity, though, at times, with a lurking something, that would take several pages to properly define.

I submit it, then, to those best acquainted with the man personally, whether the following is not Nathaniel Hawthorne;—and to himself, whether something involved in it does not express the temper of his mind,—that lasting temper of all true, candid men—a seeker, not a finder yet:—

"A man now entered, in neglected attire, with the aspect of a thinker, but somewhat too rough-hewn and brawny for a scholar. His face was full of sturdy vigor, with some finer and keener attribute beneath; though harsh at first, it was tempered with the glow of a large, warm heart, which had force enough to heat his powerful intellect through and through. He advanced to the Intelligencer, and looked at him with a glance of such stern sincerity, that perhaps few secrets were beyond its scope.

"'I seek for Truth,' said he."

Twenty-four hours have elapsed since writing the foregoing. I have just returned from the hay mow, charged more and more with love and admiration of Hawthorne. For I have just been gleaning through the Mosses, picking up many things here and there that had previously escaped me. And I found that but to glean after this man, is better than to be in at the harvest of others. To be frank (though, perhaps, rather foolish) notwithstanding what I wrote yesterday of these Mosses, I had not then culled them all; but had, nevertheless, been sufficiently sensible of the subtle essence, in them, as to write as I did. To what infinite height of loving wonder and admiration I may yet be borne, when by repeatedly banquetting on these Mosses, I shall have thoroughly incorporated their whole stuff into my being,—that, I can not tell. But already I feel that this Hawthorne has dropped germinous seeds into my soul. He expands and deepens down, the more I contemplate him; and further, and further, shoots his strong New-England roots into the hot soil of my Southern soul.

By careful reference to the "Table of Contents," I now find, that I have gone through all the sketches; but that when I yesterday wrote, I had not at all read two particular pieces, to which I now desire to call special attention,—"A Select Party" and "Young Goodman Brown." Here, be it said to all those whom this poor fugitive scrawl of mine may tempt to the perusal of the "Mosses," that they must on no account suffer themselves to be trifled with, disappointed, or deceived by the triviality of many of the titles to these Sketches. For in more than one instance, the title utterly belies the piece. It is as if rustic demijohns containing the very best and costliest of Falernian and Tokay, were labelled "Cider," "Perry," and "Elderberry wine." The truth seems to be, that like many other geniuses, this Man of Mosses takes great delight in hoodwinking the world,—at least, with respect to himself. Personally, I doubt not, that he rather prefers to be generally esteemed but a so-so sort of author; being willing to reserve the thorough and acute appreciation of what he is, to that party most qualified to judge—that is, to himself. Besides, at the bottom of their natures, men like Hawthorne, in many things, deem the plaudits of the public such strong presumptive evidence of mediocrity in the object of them, that it would in some degree render them doubtful of their own powers, did they hear much and vociferous braying concerning them in the public pastures. True, I have been braying myself (if you please to be witty enough, to have it so) but then I claim to be the first that has so brayed in this particular matter; and therefore, while pleading guilty to the charge still claim all the merit due to originality.

But with whatever motive, playful or profound, Nathaniel Hawthorne has chosen to entitle his pieces in the manner he has, it is certain, that some of them are directly calculated to deceive—egregiously deceive, the superficial skimmer of pages. To be downright and candid once more, let me cheerfully say, that two of these titles did dolefully dupe no less an eagle-eyed reader than myself; and that, too, after I had been impressed with a sense of the great depth and breadth of this American man. "Who in the name of thunder" (as the country-people say in this neighborhood) "who in the name of thunder," would anticipate any marvel in a piece entitled "Young Goodman Brown"? You would of course suppose that it was a simple little tale, intended as a supplement to "Goody Two Shoes." Whereas, it is deep as Dante; nor can you finish it, without addressing the author in his own words—"It is yours to penetrate, in every bosom, the deep mystery of sin." And with Young Goodman, too, in allegorical pursuit of his Puritan wife, you cry out in your anguish,—

" 'Faith!' shouted Goodman Brown, in a voice of agony and desperation; and the echoes of the forest mocked him, crying—'Faith! Faith!' as if bewildered wretches were seeking her all through the wilderness."

Now this same piece, entitled "Young Goodman Brown," is one of the two that I had not all read yesterday; and I allude to it now, because it is, in itself, such a strong positive illustration of that blackness in Hawthorne, which I had assumed from the mere occasional shadows of it, as revealed in several of the other sketches. But had I previously perused "Young Goodman Brown," I should have been at no pains to draw the conclusion, which I came to, at a time, when I was ignorant that the book contained one such direct and unqualified manifestation of it.

The other piece of the two referred to, is entitled "A Select Party," which, in my first simplicity upon originally taking hold of the book, I fancied must treat of some pumpkin-pie party in Old Salem, or some chowder party on Cape Cod. Whereas, by all the gods of Peedee! it is the sweetest and sublimest thing that has been written since Spencer wrote. Nay, there is nothing in Spencer that surpasses it, perhaps, nothing that equals it. And the test is this: read any canto in "The Faery Queen," and then read "A Select Party," and decide which pleases you the most,—that is, if you are qualified to judge. Do not be frightened at this; for when Spencer was alive, he was thought of very much as Hawthorne is now,—was generally accounted just such a "gentle" harmless man. It may be, that to common eyes, the sublimity of Hawthorne seems lost in his sweetness,—as perhaps in this same "Select Party" of his; for whom, he has builded so august a dome of sunset clouds, and served them on richer plate, than Belshazzar's when he banquetted his lords in Babylon.

But my chief business now, is to point out a particular page in this piece, having reference to an honored guest, who under the name of "The Master Genius" but in the guise of "a young man of poor attire, with no insignia of rank or acknowledged eminence," is introduced to the Man of Fancy, who is the giver of the feast. Now the page having reference to this "Master Genius," so happily expresses much of what I yesterday wrote, touching the coming of the literary Shiloh of America, that I cannot but be charmed by the coincidence; especially, when it shows such a parity of ideas, at least in this one point, between a man like Hawthorne and a man like me.

And here, let me throw out another conceit of mine touching this American Shiloh, or "Master Genius," as Hawthorne calls him. May it not be, that this commanding mind has not been, is not, and never will be, individually developed in any one man? And would it, indeed, appear so unreasonable to suppose, that this great fullness and overflowing may be, or may be destined to be, shared by a plurality of men of genius? Surely, to take the very greatest example on record, Shakespeare cannot be regarded as in himself the concretion of all the genius of his time; nor as so immeasurably beyond Marlowe, Webster, Ford, Beaumont, Jonson,

that those great men can be said to share none of his power? For one, I
conceive that there were dramatists in Elizabeth's day, between whom and
Shakespeare the distance was by no means great. Let anyone, hitherto
little acquainted with those neglected old authors, for the first time read
them thoroughly, or even read Charles Lamb's Specimens of them, and
he will be amazed at the wondrous ability of those Anaks of men, and
shocked at this renewed example of the fact, that Fortune has more to do
with fame than merit,—though, without merit, lasting fame there can be
none.

Nevertheless, it would argue too illy of my country were this maxim
to hold good concerning Nathaniel Hawthorne, a man, who already, in
some few minds, has shed "such a light, as never illuminates the earth,
save when a great heart burns as the household fire of a grand intellect."

The words are his,—in the "Select Party"; and they are a magnificent
setting to a coincident sentiment of my own, but ramblingly expressed
yesterday, in reference to himself. Gainsay it who will, as I now write, I
am Posterity speaking by proxy—and after times will make it more than
good, when I declare—that the American, who up to the present day, has
evinced, in Literature, the largest brain with the largest heart, that man
is Nathaniel Hawthorne. Moreover, that whatever Nathaniel Hawthorne
may hereafter write, "The Mosses from an Old Manse" will be ultimately
accounted his masterpiece. For there is a sure, though a secret sign in
some works which prove the culmination of the powers (only the develop-
able ones, however) that produced them. But I am by no means desirous
of the glory of a prophet. I pray Heaven that Hawthorne may yet prove
me an impostor in this prediction. Especially, as I somehow cling to the
strange fancy, that, in all men, hiddenly reside certain wondrous, occult
properties—as in some plants and minerals—which by some happy but
very rare accident (as bronze was discovered by the melting of the iron
and brass in the burning of Corinth) may chance to be called forth here
on earth; not entirely waiting for their better discovery in the more congenial, blessed atmosphere of heaven.

Once more—for it is hard to be finite upon an infinite subject, and all
subjects are infinite. By some people, this entire scrawl of mine may be
esteemed altogether unnecessary, inasmuch, "as years ago" (they may say)
"we found out the rich and rare stuff in this Hawthorne, whom you now
parade forth, as if only *yourself* were the discoverer of this Portuguese
diamond in our Literature."—But even granting all this; and adding to
it, the assumption that the books of Hawthorne have sold by the five-
thousand,—what does that signify? They should be sold by the hundred-
thousand; and read by the million; and admired by every one who is
capable of admiration.

MARTIN R. DELANY

Martin R. Delany (1812–1885) was one of the major African American figures in the nineteenth century. Dynamic and multitalented—a polemicist, novelist, physician, soldier, politician, and educator—he was born a freeman but faced racism stringent enough to make him become the first spokesman for Black Nationalism. Though he collaborated with Frederick Douglass on their newspaper, The North Star, *they came to represent opposite sides in the struggle: Delany argued for the Colonizationalists, who asserted that Negroes had no future in the United States and their best hope was for settlement elsewhere (Liberia and Canada being possibilities), while Douglass spoke for the anti-slavery faction, which insisted that they should stay in this country and fight for liberation. In his 1852 book,* The Condition, Elevation, Emigration, and Destiny of the Colored People in the United States, *from which the essay below was taken, Delany puts forward the view that racial prejudice is part of a larger historical pattern by which one group oppresses a subservient class for its economic benefit, justifying it with bogus claims that the subordinates are innately inferior. Delany's literary style is cutting, refined, bracingly sarcastic, and provocative—as when he twits his white anti-slavery "friends" for not hiring more colored workers to staff their abolitionist headquarters.*

Comparative Condition of the Colored People of the United States

(1852)

The United States, untrue to her trust and unfaithful to her professed principles of republican equality, has also pursued a policy of political degradation to a large portion of her native born countrymen, and that class is the Colored People. Denied an equality not only of political but of natural rights, in common with the rest of our fellow citizens, there is no species of degradation to which we are not subject.

Reduced to abject slavery is not enough, the very thought of which should awaken every sensibility of our common nature; but those of their descendants who are freemen even in the non-slaveholding States, occupy the very same position politically, religiously, civilly and socially, (with but few exceptions,) as the bondman occupies in the slave States.

In those States, the bondman is disfranchised, and for the most part so are we. He is denied all civil, religious, and social privileges, except such as he gets by mere sufferance, and so are we. They have no part nor lot in the government of the country, neither have we. They are ruled and governed without representation, existing as mere nonentities among the citizens, and excrescences on the body politic—a mere dreg in community, and so are we. Where then is our political superiority to the enslaved? none, neither are we superior in any other relation to society, except that we are defacto masters of ourselves and joint rulers of our own domestic household, while the bondman's self is claimed by another, and his relation to his family denied him. What the unfortunate classes are in Europe, such are we in the United States, which is folly to deny, insanity not to understand, blindness not to see, and surely now full time that our eyes were opened to these startling truths, which for ages have stared us full in the face.

It is time that we had become politicians, we mean, to understand the political economy and domestic policy of nations; that we had become as well as moral theorists, also the practical demonstrators of equal rights and self-government. Except we do, it is idle to talk about rights, it is mere chattering for the sake of being seen and heard—like the slave, saying something because his so called "master" said it, and saying just what he told him to say. Have we not now sufficient intelligence among us to understand our true position, to realise our actual condition, and determine for ourselves what is best to be done? If we have not now, we never shall have, and should at once cease prating about our equality, capacity, and all that.

Twenty years ago, when the writer was a youth, his young and yet uncultivated mind was aroused, and his tender heart made to leap with anxiety in anticipation of the promises then held out by the prime movers in the cause of our elevation.

In 1830 the most intelligent and leading spirits among the colored men in the United States, such as James Forten, Robert Douglass, I. Bowers, A. D. Shadd, John Peck, Joseph Cassey, and John B. Vashon of Pennsylvania; John T. Hilton, Nathaniel and Thomas Paul, and James G. Barbodoes of Massachusetts; Henry Sipkins, Thomas Hamilton, Thomas L. Jennings, Thomas Downing, Samuel E. Cornish, and others of New York; R. Cooley and others of Maryland, and representatives from other States which cannot now be recollected, the data not being at hand, assembled in the city of Philadelphia, in the capacity of a National Convention, to "devise ways and means for the bettering of our condition." These Conventions determined to assemble annually, much talent, ability, and energy of character being displayed; when in 1831 at a sitting of the Convention in September, from their previous pamphlet reports, much interest having been created throughout the country, they were favored by the presence of a number of whites, some of whom were able and distinguished men, such as Rev. R. R. Gurley, Arthur Tappan, Elliot Cresson, John Rankin, Simeon Jocelyn and others, among them William Lloyd Garrison, then quite a young man, all of whom were staunch and ardent Colonizationists, young Garrison at that time, doing his mightiest in his favorite work.

Among other great projects of interest brought before the Convention at a previous sitting, was that of the expediency of a general emigration, as far as it was practicable, of the colored people to the British Provinces of North America. Another was that of raising sufficient means for the establishment and erection of a College for the proper education of the colored youth. These gentlemen long accustomed to observation and reflection on the condition of their people saw at once, that there must necessarily be means used adequate to the end to be attained—that end being an unqualified equality with the ruling class of their fellow citizens. He saw that as a class, the colored people of the country were ignorant, degraded and oppressed, by far the greater portion of them being abject slaves in the South, the very condition of whom was almost enough, under the circumstances, to blast the remotest hope of success, and those who were freemen, whether in the South or North, occupied a subservient, servile, and menial position, considering it a favor to get into the service of the whites, and do their degrading offices. That the difference between the whites and themselves, consisted in the superior advantages of the one over the other, in point of attainments. That if a knowledge of the arts and sciences, the mechanical occupations, the industrial occupations, as farming, commerce, and all the various business enterprises, and learned professions were necessary for the superior position occupied by their rulers, it was also necessary for them. And very reasonably too, the first suggestion which occurred to them was, the advantages of a location, then the necessity of a qualification. They reasoned with themselves, that all distinctive differences made among men on account of their origin, is wicked, unrighteous, and cruel, and never shall receive countenance in any shape from us, therefore, the first acts of the measure entered into by them, was to protest, solemnly protest, against every unjust measure and policy in the country, having for its object the proscription of the colored people, whether state, national, municipal, social, civil, or religious.

But being far-sighted, reflecting, discerning men, they took a political view of the subject, and determined for the good of their people to be governed in their policy according to the facts as they presented themselves. In taking a glance at Europe, they discovered there, however unjustly, as we have shown in another part of this pamphlet, that there are and have been numerous classes proscribed and oppressed, and it was not for them to cut short their wise deliberations, and arrest their proceedings in contention, as to the cause, whether on account of language, the color of eyes, hair, skin, or their origin of country—because all this is contrary to reason, a contradiction to common sense, at war with nature herself, and at variance with facts as they stare us every day in the face, among all nations, in every country—this being made the pretext as a matter of *policy* alone—a fact worthy of observation, that wherever the objects of oppression are the most easily distinguished by any peculiar or general characteristics, these people are the more easily oppressed, because the war of oppression is the more easily waged against them. This is the case with the modern Jews and many other people who have strongly-marked, peculiar, or distinguishing characteristics. This arises in this wise. The policy of all those who proscribe any people, induces them to select as the objects of proscription, those who differed as much as possible, in some particulars, from themselves. This is to ensure the greater success, because it engenders the greater prejudice, or in other words, elicits less interest on the part of the oppressing class, in their favor. This fact is well understood in national conflicts, as the soldier or civilian, who is distinguished by his dress, mustache, or any other peculiar appendage, would certainly prove himself a madman, if he did not take the precaution to change his dress, remove his mustache, and conceal as much as possible his peculiar characteristics, to give him access among the repelling party. This is mere policy, nature having nothing to do with it. Still, it is a fact, a great truth well worthy of remark, and as such as adduce it for the benefit of those of our readers, unaccustomed to an enquiry into the policy of nations.

In view of these truths, our fathers and leaders in our elevation, discovered that as a policy, we the colored people were selected as the subordinate class in this country, not on account of any actual or supposed inferiority on their part, but simply because, in view of all the circumstances of the case, they were the very best class that could be selected. They would have as readily had any other class as subordinates in the country, as the colored people, but the condition of society *at the time,* would not admit of it. In the struggle for American Independence, there were among those who performed the most distinguished parts, the most common-place peasantry of the Provinces. English, Danish, Irish, Scotch, and others, were among those whose names blazoned forth as heroes in the American Revolution. But a single reflection will convince us, that no course of policy could have induced the proscription of the parentage and relatives of such men as Benjamin Franklin the printer, Roger Sherman the cobbler, the tinkers, and others of the signers of the Declaration of Independence. But as they were determined to have a subservient class, it will readily be conceived, that according to the state of society at the time, the better policy on their part was, to select some class, who from their political position—however much they may have contributed their aid as we certainly did, in the general struggle for liberty by force of arms—who had the least claims upon them, or who had the *least chance,* or was the *least potent* in urging their claims. This class of course was the colored people and Indians.

The Indians who in the early settlement of the continent, before an African captive had ever been introduced thereon, were reduced to the most abject slavery, toiling day and night in the mines, under the relentless hands of heartless Spanish taskmasters, but being a race of people raised to the sports of fishing, the chase, and of war, were wholly unaccustomed to labor, and therefore sunk under the insupportable weight, two millions and a half having fallen victims to the cruelty of oppression and toil suddenly placed upon their shoulders. And it was only this that prevented their farther enslavement as a class, after the provinces were absolved from the British Crown. It is true that their general enslavement took place on the islands and in the mining districts of South America, where indeed, the Europeans continued to enslave them, until a comparatively recent period; still, the design, the feeling, and inclination from policy, was the same to do so here, in this section of the continent.

Nor was it until their influence became too great, by the political position occupied by their brethren in the new republic, that the German and Irish peasantry ceased to be sold as slaves for a term of years fixed by law, for the repayment of their passage-money, the descendants of these classes of people for a long time being held as inferiors, in the estimation of the ruling class, and it was not until they assumed the rights and privileges guaranteed to them by the established policy of the country, among the leading spirits of whom were their relatives, that the policy towards them was discovered to be a bad one, and accordingly changed. Nor was it, as is frequently very erroneously asserted, by colored as well as white persons, that it was on account of hatred to the African, or in other words, on account of hatred to his color, that the African was selected as the subject of oppression in this country. This is sheer nonsense; being based on policy and nothing else, as shown in another place. The Indians, who being the most foreign to the sympathies of the Europeans on this continent, were selected in the first place, who, being unable to withstand the hardships, gave way before them.

But the African race had long been known to Europeans, in all ages of the world's history, as a long-lived, hardy race, subject to toil and labor of various kinds, subsisting mainly by traffic, trade, and industry, and consequently being as foreign to the sympathies of the invaders of the continent as the Indians, they were selected, captured, brought here as a laboring class, and as a matter of policy held as such. Nor was the absurd idea of natural inferiority of the African ever dreamed of, until recently adduced by the slave-holders and their abettors, in justification of the policy. This, with contemptuous indignation, we fling back into their face, as a scorpion to a vulture. And so did our patriots and leaders in the cause of regeneration know better, and never for a moment yielded to the base doctrine. But they had discovered the great fact, that a cruel policy was pursued towards our people, and that they possessed distinctive characteristics which made them the objects of proscription. These characteristics being strongly marked in the colored people, as in the Indians, by color, character of hair and so on, made them the more easily distinguished from other Americans, and the policies more effectually urged against us. For this reason they introduced the subject of emigration to Canada, and a proper institution for the education of the youth.

At this important juncture of their proceedings, the afore named white gentlemen were introduced to the notice of the Convention, and after gaining permission to speak, expressed their gratification and surprise at the qualification and talent manifested by different members of the Convention, all expressing their determination to give the cause of the colored people more serious reflection. Mr. Garrison, the youngest of them all, and none the less honest on account of his youthfulness, being but 26 years of age at the time (1831), expressed his determination to change his course of policy at once, and espouse the cause of the elevation of the colored people here in their own country. We are not at present well advised upon this point, it now having escaped our memory, but we are under the impression that Mr. Jocelyn also, at once changed his policy.

—

During the winter of 1832, Mr. Garrison issued his "Thoughts on African Colonization," and near about the same time or shortly after, issued the first number of the "Liberator," in both of which, his full convictions of the enormity of American slavery, and the wickedness of their policy towards the colored people, were fully expressed. At the sitting of the Convention in this year, a number, perhaps all of these gentlemen were present, and those who had denounced the Colonization scheme, and espoused the cause of the elevation of the colored people in this country, or the Anti-Slavery cause, as it was now termed, expressed themselves openly and without reserve.

Sensible of the high-handed injustice done to the colored people in the United States, and the mischief likely to emanate from the unchristian proceedings of the deceptious Colonization scheme, like all honest hearted penitents, with the ardor only known to new converts, they entreated the Convention, whatever they did, not to entertain for a moment, the idea of recommending emigration to their people, nor the establishment of separate institutions of learning. They earnestly contended, and doubtless honestly meaning what they said, that they (the whites) had been our oppressors and injurers, they had obstructed our progress to the high positions of civilization, and now, it was their bounden duty to make full amends for the injuries thus inflicted on an unoffending people. They exhorted the Convention to cease; as they had laid on the burden, they would also take it off; as they had obstructed our pathway, they would remove the hindrance. In a word, as they had oppressed and trampled down the colored people, they would now elevate them. These suggestions and promises, good enough to be sure, after they were made, were accepted by the Convention—though some gentlemen were still in favor of the first project as the best policy, Mr. A. D. Shadd of West Chester, Pa., as we learn from himself, being one among that number—ran through the country like wild-fire, no one thinking, and if he thought, daring to speak above his breath of going anywhere out of certain prescribed limits, or of sending a child to school, if it should but have the name of "colored" attached to it, without the risk of being termed a "traitor" to the cause of his people, or an enemy to the Anti-Slavery cause.

At this important point in the history of our efforts, the colored men stopped suddenly, and with their hands thrust deep in their breeches-pockets, and their mouths gaping open, stood gazing with astonishment, wonder, and surprise, at the stupendous moral colossal statues of our Anti-Slavery friends and brethren, who in the heat and zeal of honest hearts, from a desire to make atonement for the many wrongs inflicted, promised a great deal more than they have ever been able half to fulfill, in thrice the period in which they expected it. And in this, we have no fault to find with our Anti-Slavery friends, and here wish it to be understood, that we are not laying any thing to their charge as blame, neither do we desire for a moment to reflect on them, because we heartily believe that all that they did at the time, they did with the purest and best of motives, and further believe that they now are, as they then were, the truest friends we have among the whites in this country. And hope, and desire, and request, that our people should always look upon *true* Anti-Slavery people, Abolitionists we mean, as their friends, until they have just cause for acting otherwise. It is true, that the Anti-Slavery, like all good causes, has produced some recreants, but the cause itself is no more to be blamed for that, than Christianity is for the malconduct of any professing hypocrite, nor the society of Friends, for the conduct of a broad-brimmed hat and shad-belly coated horsethief, because he spoke *thee* and *thou* before stealing the horse. But what is our condition even amidst our Anti-Slavery friends? And here, as our sole intention is to contribute to the elevation of our people, we must be permitted to express our opinion freely, without being thought uncharitable.

In the first place, we should look at the objects for which the Anti-Slavery cause was commenced, and the promises or inducements it held out at the commencement. It should be borne in mind, that Anti-Slavery took its rise among *colored men,* just at the time they were introducing their greatest projects for their own elevation, and that our Anti-Slavery brethren were converts of the colored men, in behalf of their elevation. Of course, it would be expected that being baptized into the new doctrines, their faith would induce them to embrace the principles therein contained, with the strictest possible adherence.

The cause of dissatisfaction with our former condition, was, that we were proscribed, debarred, and shut out from every respectable position, occupying the places of inferiors and menials.

It was expected that Anti-Slavery, according to its professions, would extend to colored persons, as far as in the power of its adherents, those advantages nowhere else to be obtained among white men. That colored boys would get situations in their shops and stores, and every other advantage tending to elevate them as far as possible, would be extended to them. At least, it was expected, that in Anti-Slavery establishments, colored men would have the preference. Because, there was no other ostensible object in view, in the commencement of the Anti-Slavery enterprise, than the *elevation* of the *colored man,* by facilitating his efforts in attaining to equality with the white man. It was urged, and it was true, that the colored people were susceptible of all that the whites were, and all that was required was to give them a fair opportunity, and they would prove their capacity. That it was unjust, wicked, and cruel, the result of an unnatural prejudice, that debarred them from places of respectability, and that public opinion could and should be corrected upon this subject. That it was only necessary to make a sacrifice of feeling, and an innovation on the customs of society, to establish a different order of things,—

that as Anti-Slavery men, they were willing to make these sacrifices, and
determined to take the colored man by the hand, making common cause
with him in affliction, and bear a part of the odium heaped upon him.
That his cause was the cause of God—that "In as much as ye did it not
unto the least of these my little ones, ye did it not unto me," and that as
Anti-Slavery men, they would "do right if the heavens fell." Thus, was
the cause espoused, and thus did we expect much. But in all this, we were
doomed to disappointment, sad, sad disappointment. Instead of realising
what we had hoped for, we find ourselves occupying the very same position in relation to our Anti-Slavery friends, as we do in relation to the
pro-slavery part of the community—a mere secondary, underling position, in all our relations to them, and any thing more than this, is not a
matter of course affair—it comes not by established Anti-Slavery custom
or right, but like that which emanates from the pro-slavery portion of the
community by mere sufferance.

It is true, that the "Liberator" office, in Boston, has got Elijah Smith,
a colored youth, at the cases—the "Standard," in New York, a young
colored man, and the "Freeman," in Philadelphia, William Still, another,
in the publication office, as "packing clerk"; yet these are but three out of
the hosts that fill these offices in their various departments, all occupying
places that could have been, and as we once thought, would have been,
easily enough, occupied by colored men. Indeed, we can have no other
idea about Anti-Slavery in this country, than that the legitimate persons
to fill any and every position about an Anti-Slavery establishment are
colored persons. Nor will it do to argue in extenuation, that white men
are as justly entitled to them as colored men; because white men do not
from necessity become Anti-Slavery men in order to get situations; they
being white men, may occupy any position they are capable of filling—in
a word, their chances are endless, every avenue in the country being
opened to them. They do not therefore become abolitionists, for the sake
of employment—at least, it is not the song that Anti-Slavery sung, in the
first love of the new faith, proclaimed by its disciples.

And if it be urged that colored men are incapable as yet to fill these
positions, all that we have to say is, that the cause has fallen far short;
almost equivalent to a failure, of a tithe, of what it promised to do in half
the period of its existence, to this time, if it have not as yet, now a period
of twenty years, raised up colored men enough, to fill the offices within
its patronage. We think it is not unkind to say, if it had been half as faithful to itself, as it should have been—its professed principles we mean;
it could have reared and tutored from childhood, colored men enough
by this time, for its own especial purpose. These we know could have
been easily obtained, because colored people in general, are favorable to
the Anti-Slavery cause, and wherever there is an adverse manifestation,
it arises from sheer ignorance; and we have now but comparatively few

such among us. There is one thing certain, that no colored person, except such as would reject education altogether, would be adverse to putting their child with an Anti-Slavery person, for educational advantages. This then could have been done. But it has not been done, and let the cause of it be whatever it may, and let whoever may be to blame, we are willing to let all that pass, and extend to our Anti-Slavery brethren the right-hand of fellowship, bidding them God-speed in the propagation of good and wholesome sentiments—for whether they are practically carried out or not, the profession are in themselves all right and good. Like Christianity, the principles are holy and of divine origin. And we believe, if ever a man started right, with pure and holy motives, Mr. Garrison did; and that, had he the power of making the cause what it should be, it would all be right, and there never would have been any cause for the remarks we have made, though in kindness, and with the purest of motives. We are nevertheless, still occupying a miserable position in the community, wherever we live; and what we most desire is, to draw the attention of our people to this fact, and point out what, in our opinion, we conceive to be a proper remedy.

HENRY DAVID THOREAU

Few books have had as deep and lasting an impact on America as Walden; or, Life in the Woods, *the bible of nature writers and environmentalists. "I went to the woods because I wished to live deliberately, to front only the essential facts of life, and see if I could not learn what it had to teach, and not, when I came to die, discover that I had not lived," Henry David Thoreau (1817–1862) wrote in the book's second chapter. Intriguingly, Thoreau claimed he did not think much about literary style, but only about what he had to say. Note his attachment to concrete names and precise observations of nature; his penchant for moving from the specific to the general; his long paragraphs; his advocacy of "Simplicity!" while employing a rhetorical syntactical complexity befitting Cicero; his warm intimacy with the reader, alongside an aggressive, reclusive stance toward the common run of humanity. Thoreau's passion for freedom and unspoiled landscapes speaks to the dream of America as offering a new start for humanity, while his essay "Civil Disobedience" argues for attending to individual conscience over legal authority.*

Where I Lived, and What I Lived For

(1854)

At a certain season of our life we are accustomed to consider every spot as the possible site of a house. I have thus surveyed the country on every side within a dozen miles of where I live. In imagination I have bought all the farms in succession, for all were to be bought, and I knew their price. I walked over each farmer's premises, tasted his wild apples, discoursed on husbandry with him, took his farm at his price, at any price, mortgaging it to him in my mind; even put a higher price on it,—took everything but a deed of it,—took his word for his deed, for I dearly love to talk,— cultivated it, and him too to some extent, I trust, and withdrew when I had enjoyed it long enough, leaving him to carry it on. This experience entitled me to be regarded as a sort of real-estate broker by my friends. Wherever I sat, there I might live, and the landscape radiated from me accordingly. What is a house but a *sedes,* a seat?—better if a country seat. I discovered many a site for a house not likely to be soon improved, which some might have thought too far from the village, but to my eyes the village was too far from it. Well, there I might live, I said; and there I did live, for an hour, a summer and a winter life; saw how I could let the years run off, buffet the winter through, and see the spring come in. The future inhabitants of this region, wherever they may place their houses, may be sure that they have been anticipated. An afternoon sufficed to lay out the land into orchard, woodlot, and pasture, and to decide what fine oaks or pines should be left to stand before the door, and whence each blasted tree could be seen to the best advantage; and then I let it lie, fallow, perchance, for a man is rich in proportion to the number of things which he can afford to let alone.

My imagination carried me so far that I even had the refusal of several farms,—the refusal was all I wanted,—but I never got my fingers burned by actual possession. The nearest that I came to actual possession was when I bought the Hollowell place, and had begun to sort my seeds, and collected materials with which to make a wheelbarrow to carry it on or off with; but before the owner gave me a deed of it, his wife—every man has such a wife—changed her mind and wished to keep it, and he offered me ten dollars to release him. Now, to speak the truth, I had but ten cents in the world, and it surpassed my arithmetic to tell, if I was that man who had ten cents, or who had a farm, or ten dollars, or all together. However, I let him keep the ten dollars and the farm too, for I had carried it far enough; or rather, to be generous, I sold him the farm for just what I gave for it, and, as he was not a rich man, made him a present of ten dollars, and still had my ten cents, and seeds, and materials for a wheelbarrow left. I found thus that I had been a rich man without any damage to my poverty. But I retained the landscape, and I have since annually carried off what it yielded without a wheelbarrow. With respect to landscapes,—

"I am monarch of all I *survey,*
My right there is none to dispute."

I have frequently seen a poet withdraw, having enjoyed the most valuable part of a farm, while the crusty farmer supposed that he had got a few wild apples only. Why, the owner does not know it for many years when a poet has put his farm in rhyme, the most admirable kind of invisible fence, has fairly impounded it, milked it, skimmed it, and got all the cream, and left the farmer only the skimmed milk.

The real attractions of the Hollowell farm, to me, were; its complete retirement, being about two miles from the village, half a mile from the nearest neighbor, and separated from the highway by a broad field; its bounding on the river, which the owner said protected it by its fogs from frosts in the spring, though that was nothing to me; the gray color and ruinous state of the house and barn, and the dilapidated fences, which put such an interval between me and the last occupant; the hollow and lichen-covered apple trees, gnawed by rabbits, showing what kind of neighbors I should have; but above all, the recollection I had of it from my earliest voyages up the river, when the house was concealed behind a dense grove of red maples, through which I heard the house-dog bark. I was in haste to buy it, before the proprietor finished getting out some rocks, cutting down the hollow apple trees, and grubbing up some young birches which had sprung up in the pasture, or, in short, had made any more of his improvements. To enjoy these advantages I was ready to carry it on; like Atlas, to take the world on my shoulders,—I never heard what compensation he received for that,—and do all those things which had no other motive or excuse but that I might pay for it and be unmolested in my possession of it; for I knew all the while that it would yield the most abundant crop of the kind I wanted, if I could only afford to let it alone. But it turned out as I have said.

All that I could say, then, with respect to farming on a large scale (I have always cultivated a garden) was, that I had had my seeds ready. Many think that seeds improve with age. I have no doubt that time discriminates between the good and the bad; and when at last I shall plant, I shall be less likely to be disappointed. But I would say to my fellows, once for all, As long as possible live free and uncommitted. It makes but little difference whether you are committed to a farm or the county jail.

Old Cato, whose "De Re Rustica" is my "Cultivator," says, and the only translation I have seen makes sheer nonsense of the passage, "When you think of getting a farm, turn it thus in your mind, not to buy greedily; nor spare your pains to look at it, and do not think it enough to go round it once. The oftener you go there the more it will please you, if it is good." I think I shall not buy greedily, but go round and round it as long as I live, and be buried in it first, that it may please me the more at last.

—

The present was my next experiment of this kind, which I purpose to describe more at length, for convenience putting the experience of two years into one. As I have said, I do not propose to write an ode to dejection, but to brag as lustily as chanticleer in the morning, standing on his roost, if only to wake my neighbors up.

When first I took up my abode in the woods, that is, began to spend my nights as well as days there, which, by accident, was on Independence Day, or the fourth of July, 1845, my house was not finished for winter, but was merely a defence against the rain, without plastering or chimney, the walls being of rough, weather-stained boards, with wide chinks, which made it cool at night. The upright white hewn studs and freshly planed door and window casings gave it a clean and airy look, especially in the morning, when its timbers were saturated with dew, so that I fancied that by noon some sweet gum would exude from them. To my imagination it retained throughout the day more or less of this auroral character, reminding me of a certain house on a mountain which I had visited a year before. This was an airy and unplastered cabin, fit to entertain a travelling god, and where a goddess might trail her garments. The winds which passed over my dwelling were such as sweep over the ridges of mountains, bearing the broken strains, or celestial parts only, of terrestrial music. The morning wind forever blows, the poem of creation is uninterrupted; but few are the ears that hear it. Olympus is but the outside of the earth everywhere.

The only house I had been the owner of before, if I except a boat, was a tent, which I used occasionally when making excursions in the summer, and this is still rolled up in my garret; but the boat, after passing from hand to hand, has gone down the stream of time. With this more substantial shelter about me, I had made some progress toward settling in the world. This frame, so slightly clad, was a sort of crystallization around me, and reacted on the builder. It was suggestive somewhat as a picture in outlines. I did not need to go outdoors to take the air, for the atmosphere within had lost none of its freshness. It was not so much within doors as behind a door where I sat, even in the rainiest weather. The Harivansa says, "An abode without birds is like a meat without seasoning." Such was not my abode, for I found myself suddenly neighbor to the birds; not by having imprisoned one, but having caged myself near them. I was not only nearer to some of those which commonly frequent the garden and the orchard, but to those smaller and more thrilling songsters of the forest which never, or rarely, serenade a villager,—the wood-thrush, the veery, the scarlet tanager, the field-sparrow, the whippoorwill, and many others.

I was seated by the shore of a small pond, about a mile and a half south of the village of Concord and somewhat higher than it, in the midst of an extensive wood between that town and Lincoln, and about two miles south of that our only field known to fame, Concord Battle Ground; but

I was so low in the woods that the opposite shore, half a mile off, like the rest, covered with wood, was my most distant horizon. For the first week, whenever I looked out on the pond it impressed me like a tarn high up on the side of a mountain, its bottom far above the surface of other lakes, and, as the sun arose, I saw it throwing off its nightly clothing of mist, and here and there, by degrees, its soft ripples or its smooth reflecting surface was revealed, while the mists, like ghosts, were stealthily withdrawing in every direction into the woods, as at the breaking up of some nocturnal conventicle. The very dew seemed to hang upon the trees later into the day than usual, as on the sides of mountains.

This small lake was of most value as a neighbor in the intervals of a gentle rain storm in August, when, both air and water being perfectly still, but the sky overcast, mid-afternoon had all the serenity of evening, and the wood-thrush sang around, and was heard from shore to shore. A lake like this is never smoother than at such a time; and the clear portion of the air above it being shallow and darkened by clouds, the water, full of light and reflections, becomes a lower heaven itself so much the more important. From a hill top near by, where the wood had been recently cut off, there was a pleasing vista southward across the pond, through a wide indentation in the hills which form the shore there, where their opposite sides sloping toward each other suggested a stream flowing out in that direction through a wooded valley, but stream there was none. That way I looked between and over the near green hills to some distant and higher ones in the horizon, tinged with blue. Indeed, by standing on tiptoe I could catch a glimpse of some of the peaks of the still bluer and more distant mountain ranges in the northwest, those true-blue coins from heaven's own mint, and also of some portion of the village. But in other directions, even from this point, I could not see over or beyond the woods which surrounded me. It is well to have some water in your neighborhood, to give buoyancy to and float the earth. One value even of the smallest well is, that when you look into it you see that earth is not continent but insular. This is as important as that it keeps butter cool. When I looked across the pond from this peak toward the Sudbury meadows, which in time of flood I distinguished elevated perhaps by a mirage in their seething valley, like a coin in a basin, all the earth beyond the pond appeared like a thin crust insulated and floated even by this small sheet of intervening water, and I was reminded that this on which I dwelt was but *dry land*.

Though the view from my door was still more contracted, I did not feel crowded or confined in the least. There was pasture enough for my imagination. The low shrub oak plateau to which the opposite shore arose stretched away toward the prairies of the West and the steppes of Tartary, affording ample room for all the roving families of men. "There are none happy in the world but beings who enjoy freely a vast horizon,"—said Damodara, when his herds required new and larger pastures.

Both place and time were changed, and I dwelt nearer to those parts of the universe and to those eras in history which had most attracted me. Where I lived was as far off as many a region viewed nightly by astronomers. We are wont to imagine rare and delectable places in some remote and more celestial corner of the system, behind the constellation of Cassiopeia's Chair, far from noise and disturbance. I discovered that my house actually had its site in such a withdrawn, but forever new and unprofaned, part of the universe. If it were worth the while to settle in those parts near to the Pleiades or the Hyades, to Aldebaran or Altair, then I was really there, or at an equal remoteness from the life which I had left behind, dwindled and twinkling with as fine a ray to my nearest neighbor, and to be seen only in moonless nights by him. Such was that part of creation where I had squatted;—

"There was a shepherd that did live,
And held his thoughts as high
As were the mounts whereon his flocks
Did hourly feed him by."

What should we think of the shepherd's life if his flocks always wandered to higher pastures than his thoughts?

Every morning was a cheerful invitation to make my life of equal simplicity, and I may say innocence, with Nature herself. I have been as sincere a worshipper of Aurora as the Greeks. I got up early and bathed in the pond; that was a religious exercise, and one of the best things which I did. They say that characters were engraven on the bathing tub of King Tching-thang to this effect: "Renew thyself completely each day; do it again, and again, and forever again." I can understand that. Morning brings back the heroic ages. I was as much affected by the faint burn of a mosquito making its invisible and unimaginable tour through my apartment at earliest dawn, when I was sailing with door and windows open, as I could be by any trumpet that ever sang of fame. It was Homer's requiem; itself an Iliad and Odyssey in the air, singing its own wrath and wanderings. There was something cosmical about it; a standing advertisement, till forbidden, of the everlasting vigor and fertility of the world. The morning, which is the most memorable season of the day, is the awakening hour. Then there is least somnolence in us; and for an hour, at least, some part of us awakes which slumbers all the rest of the day and night. Little is to be expected of that day, if it can be called a day, to which we are not awakened by our Genius, but by the mechanical nudgings of some servitor, are not awakened by our own newly-acquired force and aspirations from within, accompanied by the undulations of celestial music, instead of factory bells, and a fragrance filling the air—to a higher life than we fell asleep from; and thus the darkness bear its fruit, and prove itself to be good, no less than the light. That man who does not believe that each day contains an earlier, more sacred, and auroral hour than he has yet profaned, has despaired of life, and is pursuing a descending and darkening way. After a partial cessation of his sensuous life, the soul of man, or its organs rather, are reinvigorated each day, and his Genius tries again what noble life it can make. All memorable events, I should say, transpire in morning time and in a morning atmosphere. The Vedas say, "All intelligences awake with the morning." Poetry and art, and the fairest and most memorable of the actions of men, date from such an hour. All poets and heroes, like Memnon, are the children of Aurora, and emit their music at sunrise. To him whose elastic and vigorous thought keeps pace with the sun, the day is a perpetual morning. It matters not what the clocks say or the attitudes and labors of men. Morning is when I am awake and there is a dawn in me. Moral reform is the effort to throw off sleep. Why is it that men give so poor an account of their day if they have not been slumbering? They are not such poor calculators. If they had not been overcome with drowsiness, they would have performed something. The millions are awake enough for physical labor; but only one in a million is awake enough for effective intellectual exertion, only one in a hundred millions to a poetic or divine life. To be awake is to be alive. I have never yet met a man who was quite awake. How could I have looked him in the face?

We must learn to reawaken and keep ourselves awake, not by mechanical aids, but by an infinite expectation of the dawn, which does not forsake us in our soundest sleep. I know of no more encouraging fact than the unquestionable ability of man to elevate his life by a conscious endeavor. It is something to be able to paint a particular picture, or to carve a statue, and so to make a few objects beautiful; but it is far more glorious to carve and paint the very atmosphere and medium through which we look, which morally we can do. To affect the quality of the day, that is the highest of arts. Every man is tasked to make his life, even in its details, worthy of the contemplation of his most elevated and critical hour. If we refused, or rather used up, such paltry information as we get, the oracles would distinctly inform us how this might be done.

I went to the woods because I wished to live deliberately, to front only the essential facts of life, and see if I could not learn what it had to teach, and not, when I came to die, discover that I had not lived. I did not wish to live what was not life, living is so dear; nor did I wish to practise resignation, unless it was quite necessary. I wanted to live deep and suck out all the marrow of life, to live so sturdily and Spartan-like as to put to rout all that was not life, to cut a broad swath and shave close, to drive life into a corner, and reduce it to its lowest terms, and, if it proved to be mean, why then to get the whole and genuine meanness of it, and publish its meanness to the world; or if it were sublime, to know it by experience, and be able to give a true account of it in my next excursion. For most men, it appears to me, are in a strange uncertainty about it, whether it is of the devil or of God, and have somewhat hastily concluded that it is the chief end of man here to "glorify God and enjoy him forever."

Still we live meanly, like ants; though the fable tells us that we were long ago changed into men; like pygmies we fight with cranes; it is error upon error, and clout upon clout, and our best virtue has for its occasion a superfluous and evitable wretchedness. Our life is frittered away by detail. An honest man has hardly need to count more than his ten fingers, or in extreme cases he may add his ten toes, and lump the rest. Simplicity, simplicity, simplicity! I say, let your affairs be as two or three, and not a hundred or a thousand; instead of a million count half a dozen, and keep your accounts on your thumb nail. In the midst of this chopping sea of civilized life, such are the clouds and storms and quicksands and thousand-and-one items to be allowed for, that a man has to live, if he would not founder and go to the bottom and not make his port at all, by dead reckoning, and he must be a great calculator indeed who succeeds. Simplify, simplify. Instead of three meals a day, if it be necessary eat but one; instead of a hundred dishes, five; and reduce other things in proportion. Our life is like a German Confederacy, made up of petty states, with its boundary forever fluctuating, so that even a German cannot tell you how it is bounded at any moment. The nation itself, with all its so-called internal improvements, which, by the way are all external and superficial, is just such an unwieldy and overgrown establishment, cluttered with furniture and tripped up by its own traps, ruined by luxury and heedless expense, by want of calculation and a worthy aim, as the million households in the land; and the only cure for it, as for them, is in a rigid economy, a stern and more than Spartan simplicity of life and elevation of purpose. It lives too fast. Men think that it is essential that the *Nation* have commerce, and export ice, and talk through a telegraph, and ride thirty miles an hour, without a doubt, whether *they* do or not; but whether we should live like baboons or like men, is a little uncertain. If we do not get out sleepers, and forge rails, and devote days and nights to the work, but go to tinkering upon our *lives* to improve *them*, who will build railroads? And if railroads are not built, how shall we get to heaven in season? But if we stay at home and mind our business, who will want railroads? We do not ride on the railroad; it rides upon us. Did you ever think what those sleepers are that underlie the railroad? Each one is a man, an Irishman, or a Yankee man. The rails are laid on them, and they are covered with sand, and the cars run smoothly over them. They are sound sleepers, I assure you. And every few years a new lot is laid down and run over; so that, if some have the pleasure of riding on a rail, others have the misfortune to be ridden upon. And when they run over a man that is walking in his sleep, a supernumerary sleeper in the wrong position, and wake him up, they suddenly stop the cars, and make a hue and cry about it, as if this were an exception. I am glad to know that it takes a gang of men for every five miles to keep the sleepers down and level in their beds as it is, for this is a sign that they may sometime get up again.

Why should we live with such hurry and waste of life? We are determined to be starved before we are hungry. Men say that a stitch in time saves nine, and so they take a thousand stitches today to save nine tomorrow. As for *work,* we haven't any of any consequence. We have the Saint Vitus' dance, and cannot possibly keep our heads still. If I should only give a few pulls at the parish bell-rope, as for a fire, that is, without setting the bell, there is hardly a man on his farm in the outskirts of Concord, notwithstanding that press of engagements which was his excuse so many times this morning, nor a boy, nor a woman, I might almost say, but would forsake all and follow that sound, not mainly to save property from the flames, but, if we will confess the truth, much more to see it burn, since burn it must, and we, be it known, did not set it on fire,—or to see it put out, and have a hand in it, if that is done as handsomely; yes, even if it were the parish church itself. Hardly a man takes a half-hour's nap after dinner, but when he wakes he holds up his head and asks, "What's the news?" as if the rest of mankind had stood his sentinels. Some give directions to be waked every half-hour, doubtless for no other purpose; and then, to pay for it, they tell what they have dreamed. After a night's sleep the news is as indispensable as the breakfast. "Pray tell me anything new that has happened to a man anywhere on this globe,"—and he reads it over his coffee and rolls, that a man has had his eyes gouged out this morning on the Wachito River; never dreaming the while that he lives in the dark unfathomed mammoth cave of this world, and has but the rudiment of an eye himself.

For my part, I could easily do without the post-office. I think that there are very few important communications made through it. To speak critically, I never received more than one or two letters in my life—I wrote this some years ago—that were worth the postage. The penny-post is, commonly, an institution through which you seriously offer a man that penny for his thoughts which is so often safely offered in jest. And I am sure that I never read any memorable news in a newspaper. If we read of one man robbed, or murdered, or killed by accident, or one house burned, or one vessel wrecked, or one steamboat blown up, or one cow run over on the Western Railroad, or one mad dog killed, or one lot of grasshoppers in the winter,—we never need read of another. One is enough. If you are acquainted with the principle, what do you care for a myriad instances and applications? To a philosopher all *news,* as it is called, is gossip, and they who edit and read it are old women over their tea. Yet not a few are greedy after this gossip. There was such a rush, as I hear, the other day at one of the offices to learn the foreign news by the last arrival, that several large squares of plate glass belonging to the establishment were broken by the pressure,—news which I seriously think a ready wit might write a twelve-month, or twelve years, beforehand with sufficient accuracy. As for Spain, for instance, if you know how to throw in Don Carlos and the Infanta, and Don Pedro and Seville and Granada, from time to time in the right proportions,—they may have changed the names a little since I saw the papers,—and serve up a bull-fight when other entertainments fail, it will be true to the letter, and give us as good an idea of the exact state or ruin of things in Spain as the most succinct and lucid reports under this head in the newspapers: and as for England, almost the last significant scrap of news from that quarter was the revolution of 1649; and if you have learned the history of her crops for an average year, you never need attend to that thing again, unless your speculations are of a merely pecuniary character. If one may judge who rarely looks into the newspapers, nothing new does ever happen in foreign parts, a French revolution not excepted.

What news! How much more important to know what that is which was never old! "Kieou-he-yu (great dignitary of the state of Wei) sent a man to Khoung-tseu to know his news. Khoung-tseu caused the messenger to be seated near him, and questioned him in these terms: What is your master doing? The messenger answered with respect: My master desires to diminish the number of his faults, but he cannot come to the end of them. The messenger being gone, the philosopher remarked: What a worthy messenger! What a worthy messenger!" The preacher, instead of vexing the ears of drowsy farmers on their day of rest at the end of the week,—for Sunday is the fit conclusion of an ill-spent week, and not the fresh and brave beginning of a new one,—with this one other draggletail of a sermon, should shout with thundering voice,—"Pause! Avast! Why so seeming fast, but deadly slow?"

Shams and delusions are esteemed for soundest truths, while reality is fabulous. If men would steadily observe realities only, and not allow themselves to be deluded, life, to compare it with such things as we know, would be like a fairy tale and the Arabian Nights' Entertainments. If we respected only what is inevitable and has a right to be, music and poetry would resound along the streets. When we are unhurried and wise, we perceive that only great and worthy things have any permanent and absolute existence, that petty fears and petty pleasures are but the shadow of the reality. This is always exhilarating and sublime. By closing the eyes and slumbering, and consenting to be deceived by shows, men establish and confirm their daily life of routine and habit everywhere, which still is built on purely illusory foundations. Children, who play life, discern its true law and relations more clearly than men, who fail to live it worthily, but who think that they are wiser by experience, that is, by failure. I have read in a Hindoo book, that "there was a king's son, who, being expelled in infancy from his native city, was brought up by a forester, and, growing up to maturity in that state, imagined himself to belong to the barbarous race with which he lived. One of his father's ministers having discovered him, revealed to him what he was, and the misconception of his character was removed, and he knew himself to be a prince. So soul," continues the Hindoo philosopher, "from the circumstances in which it is placed, mistakes its own character, until the truth is revealed to it by some holy teacher, and then it knows itself to be *Brahme*." I perceive that we inhabitants of New England live this mean life that we do because our vision does not penetrate the surface of things. We think that that *is* which *appears* to be. If a man should walk through this town and see only the reality, where, think you, would the "Mill-dam" go to? If he should give us an account of the realities he beheld there, we should not recognize the place in his description. Look at a meeting-house, or a court-house, or a jail, or a shop, or a dwelling-house, and say what that thing really is before a true gaze, and they would all go to pieces in your account of them. Men esteem truth remote, in the outskirts of the system, behind the farthest star, before Adam and after the last man. In eternity there is indeed something true and sublime. But all these times and places and occasions are now and here. God himself culminates in the present moment, and will never be more divine in the lapse of all the ages. And we are enabled to apprehend at all what is sublime and noble only by the perpetual instilling and drenching of the reality that surrounds us. The universe constantly and obediently answers to our conceptions; whether we travel fast or slow, the track is laid for us. Let us spend our lives in conceiving then. The poet or the artist never yet had so fair and noble a design but some of his posterity at least could accomplish it.

Let us spend one day as deliberately as Nature, and not be thrown off the track by every nutshell and mosquito's wing that falls on the rails. Let us rise early and fast, or break fast, gently and without perturbation; let company come and let company go, let the bells ring and the children cry,—determined to make a day of it. Why should we knock under and go with the stream? Let us not be upset and overwhelmed in that terrible rapid and whirlpool called a dinner, situated in the meridian shallows. Weather this danger and you are safe, for the rest of the way is down hill. With unrelaxed nerves, with morning vigor, sail by it, looking another way, tied to the mast like Ulysses. If the engine whistles, let it whistle till it is hoarse for its pains. If the bell rings, why should we run? We will consider what kind of music they are like. Let us settle ourselves, and work and wedge our feet downward through the mud and slush of opinion, and prejudice, and tradition, and delusion, and appearance, that alluvion which covers the globe, through Paris and London, through New York and Boston and Concord, through Church and State, through poetry and philosophy and religion, till we come to a hard bottom and rocks in place, which we can call *reality*, and say, This is, and no mistake; and then begin, having a *point d'appui*, below freshet and frost and fire, a place where you might found a wall or a state, or set a lamp-post safely, or perhaps a gauge, not a Nilometer, but a Realometer, that future ages might know how deep a freshet of shams and appearances had gathered from time to time. If you stand right fronting and face to face to a fact, you will see the sun glimmer on both its surfaces, as if it were a cimeter, and feel its sweet edge dividing you through the heart and marrow, and so you will happily conclude your mortal career. Be it life or death, we crave only reality. If we are really dying, let us hear the rattle in our throats and feel cold in the extremities; if we are alive, let us go about our business.

Time is but the stream I go a-fishing in. I drink at it; but while I drink I see the sandy bottom and detect how shallow it is. Its thin current slides away, but eternity remains. I would drink deeper; fish in the sky, whose bottom is pebbly with stars. I cannot count one. I know not the first letter of the alphabet. I have always been regretting that I was not as wise as the day I was born. The intellect is a cleaver; it discerns and rifts its way into the secret of things. I do not wish to be any more busy with my hands than is necessary. My head is hands and feet. I feel all my best faculties concentrated in it. My instinct tells me that my head is an organ for burrowing, as some creatures use their snout and fore-paws, and with it I would mine and burrow my way through these hills. I think that the richest vein is somewhere hereabouts; so by the divining rod and thin rising vapors I judge; and here I will begin to mine.

OLIVER WENDELL HOLMES

Oliver Wendell Holmes (1809–1894) was a poet, novelist, and physician who wrote a book of dramatic essays entitled The Autocrat of the Breakfast-Table, *in which residents of a boardinghouse discuss topics humorous and serious. So popular was the table-talk formula that he followed it up with* The Professor at the Breakfast-Table *and* The Poet at the Breakfast-Table, *even milking it one last time with* Over the Teacups, *which moved the prandial setting to the afternoon. Essays being an intrinsically conversational form, talk itself as a system of manners proved a favorite topic. Holmes was one of the Fireside Poets, a congenial if tame set of American versifiers, and a friend of all the literary Boston Brahmins, including James Russell Lowell, Henry Wadsworth Longfellow, and Ralph Waldo Emerson (whose biography he wrote). He also made key contributions to medical procedure with his paper "The Contagiousness of Puerperal Fever" in support of the germ theory of illness. As the dean of Harvard Medical School, he initially admitted Martin R. Delany and several other black students but later backed down in the face of vociferous white student protest. It sometimes seems as though all the important writers in nineteenth-century America at some point ran into one another.*

from *The Autocrat of the Breakfast-Table*

(1858)

—What are the great faults of conversation? Want of ideas, want of words, want of manners, are the principal ones, I suppose you think. I don't doubt it, but I will tell you what I have found spoil more good talks than anything else;—long arguments on special points between people who differ on the fundamental principles upon which these points depend. No men can have satisfactory relations with each other until they have agreed on certain *ultimata* of belief not to be disturbed in ordinary conversation, and unless they have sense enough to trace the secondary questions depending upon these ultimate beliefs to their source. In short, just as a written constitution is essential to the best social order, so a code of finalities is a necessary condition of profitable talk between two persons. Talking is like playing on the harp; there is as much in laying the hand on the strings to stop their vibrations as in twanging them to bring out their music.

—Do you mean to say the pun-question is not clearly settled in your minds? Let me lay down the law upon the subject. Life and language are alike sacred. Homicide and *verbicide*—that is, violent treatment of a word with fatal results to its legitimate meaning, which is its life—are alike forbidden. Manslaughter, which is the meaning of the one, is the same as man's laughter, which is the end of the other. A pun is *prima facie* an insult to the person you are talking with. It implies utter indifference to or sublime contempt for his remarks, no matter how serious. I speak of total depravity, and one says all that is written on the subject is deep raving. I have committed my self-respect by talking with such a person. I should like to commit him, but cannot, because he is a nuisance. Or I speak of geological convulsions, and he asks me what was the cosine of Noah's ark; also, whether the Deluge was not a deal huger than any modern inundation.

A pun does not commonly justify a blow in return. But if a blow were given for such cause, and death ensued, the jury would be judges both of the facts and of the pun, and might, if the latter were of an aggravated character, return a verdict of justifiable homicide. Thus, in a case lately decided before Miller, J., Doe presented Roe a subscription paper, and urged the claims of suffering humanity. Roe replied by asking, When charity was like a top? It was in evidence that Doe preserved a dignified silence. Roe then said, "When it begins to hum." Doe then—and not till then—struck Roe, and his head happening to hit a bound volume of the

Monthly Rag-Bag and Stolen Miscellany, intense mortification ensued, with a fatal result. The chief laid down his notions of the law to his brother justices, who unanimously replied, "Jest so." The chief rejoined, that no man should jest so without being punished for it, and charged for the prisoner, who was acquitted, and the pun ordered to be burned by the sheriff. The bound volume was forfeited as a deodand, but not claimed.

People that make puns are like wanton boys that put coppers on the railroad tracks. They amuse themselves and other children, but their little trick may upset a freight train of conversation for the sake of a battered witticism.

I will thank you, B. F., to bring down two books, of which I will mark the places on this slip of paper. (While he is gone, I may say that this boy, our landlady's youngest, is called BENJAMIN FRANKLIN, after the celebrated philosopher of that name. A highly merited compliment.)

I wished to refer to two eminent authorities. Now be so good as to listen. The great moralist says: "To trifle with the vocabulary which is the vehicle of social intercourse is to tamper with the currency of human intelligence. He who would violate the sanctities of his mother tongue would invade the recesses of the paternal till without remorse, and repeat the banquet of Saturn without an indigestion."

And, once more, listen to the historian. "The Puritans hated puns. The Bishops were notoriously addicted to them. The Lords Temporal carried them to the verge of license. Majesty itself must have its Royal quibble. 'Ye be burly, my Lord of Burleigh,' said Queen Elizabeth, 'but ye shall make less stir in our realm than my Lord of Leicester.' The gravest wisdom and the highest breeding lent their sanction to the practice. Lord Bacon playfully declared himself a descendant of 'Og, the King of Bashan. Sir Philip Sidney, with his last breath, reproached the soldier who brought him water, for wasting a casque full upon a dying man. A courtier, who saw Othello performed at the Globe Theatre, remarked, that the blackamoor was a brute, and not a man. 'Thou hast reason,' replied a great Lord, 'according to Plato his saying; for this be a two-legged animal *with* feathers.' The fatal habit became universal. The language was corrupted. The infection spread to the national conscience. Political double-dealings naturally grew out of verbal double meanings. The teeth of the new dragon were sown by the Cadmus who introduced the alphabet of equivocation. What was levity in the time of the Tudors grew to regicide and revolution in the age of the Stuarts."

Who was that boarder that just whispered something about the Macaulay-flowers of literature?—There was a dead silence.—I said calmly, I shall henceforth consider any interruption by a pun as a hint to change my boarding-house. Do not plead my example. If *I* have used any such, it has been only as a Spartan father would show up a drunken helot. We have done with them. . . .

—

The "Atlantic" obeys the moon, and its LUNIVERSARY has come round again. I have gathered up some hasty notes of my remarks made since the last high tides, which I respectfully submit. Please to remember this is *talk*; just as easy and just as formal as I choose to make it.

—I never saw an author in my life—saving, perhaps, one— at did not purr as audibly as a full-grown domestic cat (*Fells Catus,* LINN.) on having his fur smoothed in the right way by a skilful hand.

But let me give you a caution. Be very careful how you tell an author he is *droll*. Ten to one he will hate you; and if he does, be sure he can do you a mischief, and very probably will. Say you *cried* over his romance or his verses, and he will love you and send you a copy. You can laugh over that as much as you like,—in private.

—Wonder why authors and actors are ashamed of being funny?—Why, there are obvious reasons, and deep philosophical ones. The clown knows very well that the women are not in love with him, but with Hamlet, the fellow in the black cloak and plumed hat. Passion never laughs. The wit knows that his place is at the tail of a procession.

If you want the deep underlying reason, I must take more time to tell it. There is a perfect consciousness in every form of wit,—using that term in its general sense,—that its essence consists in a partial and incomplete view of whatever it touches. It throws a single ray, separated from the rest,—red, yellow, blue, or any intermediate shade,—upon an object; never white light; that is the province of wisdom. We get beautiful effects from wit,—all the prismatic colors,—but never the object as it is in fair daylight. A pun, which is a kind of wit, is a different and much shallower trick in mental optics; throwing the *shadows* of two objects so that one overlies the other. Poetry uses the rainbow tints for special effects, but always keeps its essential object in the purest white light of truth.—Will you allow me to pursue this subject a little farther?

[They didn't allow me at that time, for somebody happened to scrape the floor with his chair just then; which accidental sound, as all must have noticed, has the instantaneous effect that the cutting of the yellow hair by Iris had upon infelix Dido. It broke the charm, and that breakfast was over.]

—Don't flatter yourselves that friendship authorizes you to say disagreeable things to your intimates. On the contrary, the nearer you come into relation with a person, the more necessary do tact and courtesy become. Except in cases of necessity, which are rare, leave your friend to learn unpleasant truths from his enemies; they are ready enough to tell them. Good-breeding *never* forgets that *amour-propre* is universal! When you read the story of the Archbishop and Gil Bias, you may laugh, if you will, at the poor old man's delusion; but don't forget that the youth was the greater fool of the two, and that his master served such a booby rightly in turning him out of doors.

—You need not get up a rebellion against what I say, if you find everything in my sayings is not exactly new. You can't possibly mistake a man who means to be honest for a literary pickpocket. I once read an introductory lecture that looked to me too learned for its latitude. On examination, I found all its erudition was taken ready-made from Disraeli. If I had been ill-natured, I should have shown up the little great man, who had once belabored me in his feeble way. But one can generally tell these wholesale thieves easily enough, and they are not worth the trouble of putting them in the pillory. I doubt the entire novelty of my remarks just made on telling unpleasant truths, yet I am not conscious of any larceny.

Neither make too much of flaws and occasional overstatements. Some persons seem to think that absolute truth, in the form of rigidly stated propositions, is all that conversation admits. This is precisely as if a musician should insist on having nothing but perfect chords and simple melodies,—no diminished fifths, no flat sevenths, no flourishes, on any account. Now it is fair to say, that, just as music must have all these, so conversation must have its partial truths, its embellished truths, its exaggerated truths. It is in its higher forms an artistic product, and admits the ideal element as much as pictures or statues. One man who is a little too literal can spoil the talk of a whole tableful of men of *esprit.*—"Yes," you say, "but who wants to hear fanciful people's nonsense? Put the facts to it, and then see where it is!"—Certainly, if a man is too fond of paradox,—if he is flighty and empty,—if, instead of striking those fifths and sevenths, those harmonious discords, often so much better than the twinned octaves, in the music of thought,—if, instead of striking these, he jangles the chords, stick a fact into him like a stiletto,. But remember that talking is one of the fine arts,—the noblest, the most important, and the most difficult,—and that its fluent harmonies may be spoiled by the intrusion of a single harsh note. Therefore conversation which is suggestive rather than argumentative, which lets out the most of each talker's results of thought, is commonly the pleasantest and the most profitable.

ABRAHAM LINCOLN

The Civil War was coming to an end when Abraham Lincoln (1809–1865) delivered his second inaugural address, considered by many his greatest speech, and which he himself thought his best. Garry Wills, in a brilliant analysis of the speech, pointed out that its very brevity signaled a modest refusal to commit the country to divisive punitive strategies, but to take the future course pragmatically, step by step. Slavery is named as an evil, yet the guilt for it is shared by both North and South. Wills wrote: "Lincoln summoned no giddy feelings of victory. A chastened sense of man's limits was the only proper attitude to bring to the rebuilding of the nation, looking to God for guidance but not aspiring to replace him as the arbiter of national fate. . . . Lincoln had been growing as a writer and deepening as a thinker under the pressure of the war, which made him weight every word with the fateful events impending on it." The ex-slave Frederick Douglass was in attendance, and after the speech was over, Lincoln went up to him and asked what he thought. "Mr. Lincoln, that was a sacred effort," he replied.

Second Inaugural Address

(1865)

Fellow Countrymen:

At this second appearing to take the oath of the Presidential office there is less occasion for an extended address than there was at the first. Then a statement somewhat in detail of a course to be pursued seemed fitting and proper. Now, at the expiration of four years, during which public declarations have been constantly called forth on every point and phase of the great contest which still absorbs the attention and engrosses the energies of the nation, little that is new could be presented. The progress of our arms, upon which all else chiefly depends, is as well known to the public as to myself, and it is, I trust, reasonably satisfactory and encouraging to all. With high hope for the future, no prediction in regard to it is ventured.

On the occasion corresponding to this four years ago all thoughts were anxiously directed to an impending civil war. All dreaded it, all sought to avert it. While the inaugural address was being delivered from this place, devoted altogether to saving the Union without war, insurgent agents were in the city seeking to destroy it without war—seeking to dissolve the Union and divide effects by negotiation. Both parties deprecated war, but one of them would make war rather than let the nation survive, and the other would accept war rather than let it perish, and the war came.

One-eighth of the whole population were colored slaves, not distributed generally over the Union, but localized in the southern part of it. These slaves constituted a peculiar and powerful interest. All knew that this interest was somehow the cause of the war. To strengthen, perpetuate, and extend this interest was the object for which the insurgents would rend the Union even by war, while the Government claimed no right to do more than to restrict the territorial enlargement of it. Neither party expected for the war the magnitude or the duration which it has already attained. Neither anticipated that the cause of the conflict might cease with or even before the conflict itself should cease. Each looked for an easier triumph, and a result less fundamental and astounding. Both read the same Bible and pray to the same God, and each invokes His aid against the other. It may seem strange that any men should dare to ask a just God's assistance in wringing their bread from the sweat of other men's faces, but let us judge not, that we be not judged. The prayers of both could not be answered. That of neither has been answered fully. The Almighty has His own purposes. "Woe unto the world because of offenses; for it must needs be that offenses come, but woe to that man by whom the offense cometh." If we shall suppose that American slavery is one of those offenses which, in the providence of God, must needs come, but which, having continued through His appointed time, He now wills to remove, and that He gives to both North and South this terrible war as the woe due to those by whom the offense came, shall we discern therein any departure from those divine attributes which the believers in a living God always ascribe to Him? Fondly do we hope, fervently do we pray, that this mighty scourge of war may speedily pass away. Yet, if God wills that it continue until all the wealth piled by the bondsman's two hundred and fifty years of unrequited toil shall be sunk, and until every drop of blood drawn with the lash shall be paid by another drawn with the sword, as was said three thousand years ago, so still it must be said "the judgments of the Lord are true and righteous altogether."

With malice toward none, with charity for all, with firmness in the right as God gives us to see the right, let us strive on to finish the work we are in, to bind up the nation's wounds, to care for him who shall have borne the battle and for his widow and his orphan, to do all which may achieve and cherish a just and lasting peace among ourselves and with all nations.

FANNY FERN

Sara Payson Willis (1811–1872) used the pen name Fanny Fern, in part to distance herself from her noted writer-editor brother, Nathaniel Parker Willis, who—either from sibling rivalry or sheer meanness—refused to publish her in the magazine he owned. He and her father, who was a newspaper owner, also did everything to discourage her, but she triumphed in the end, becoming the best-paid and most widely read newspaper columnist of her time. With a tart, satirical voice, she skewered "masculine obtuseness" and championed the allegedly "little" concerns of her women readers. The essay form has historically gravitated to daily, overlooked subjects, finding in those materials the germ of a larger understanding. Fern, by calling her collection of newspaper columns (including the one below) Ginger-Snaps, *underlined her faith in the small.*

"Delightful Men"

(1870)

Isn't he a delightful man? This question was addressed to me by a lady in company concerning a gentleman who had rendered himself during the evening, peculiarly agreeable. Before I answer that question, I said, I would like to see him at home. I would like to know if, when he jars his wife's feelings, he says, "Beg pardon" as willingly and promptly as when he stepped upon yonder lady's dress. I would like to know if, when he comes home at night, he has some pleasant little things to say, such as he has scattered about so lavishly since he entered this room this evening; and whether if the badly cooked dish, which he gallantly declared to the hostess at the table, "could not have been improved," would have found a similar verdict on his own table, and to his own wife. *That is the test.* I am sorry to say that some of the most agreeable society-men, who could, by no possibility, be guilty of a rudeness abroad, could never be suspected in their own homes of ever doing anything else. The man who will invariably meet other ladies with "How very well you are looking!" will often never, from one day to another, take notice of his own wife's appearance, or, if so, only to find fault. How bright that home would be to his wife with one half the courtesy and toleration he invariably shows to strangers. "Allow me to differ"—he blandly remarks to an opponent with whom he argues in company. "Pshaw! what do *you* know about it?" he says at his own fireside and to his wife. Children are "angels" when they belong to his neighbors; his own are sent out of the room whenever he enters it, or receive so little recognition that they are glad to leave. "Permit me," says the gallant male *vis-a-vis* in the omnibus or car, as he takes your fare; while *his* wife often hands up her own fare, even with her husband by her side. No wonder she is not "looking well" when she sees politeness is for every place but for home-consumption.

"Oh, how men miss it in disregarding these little matters," said a sad-eyed wife to me one day. And she said truly; for these little kindnesses are like a breath of fresh air from an open window in a stifled room; we lift our drooping heads and breathe again! "Little!" did I say! *Can* that be little which makes or mars the happiness of a human being? A man says a rough, rude word, or neglects the golden opportunity to say a kind one, and goes his selfish way and thinks it of no account. Then he marvels when he comes back,—in sublime forgetfulness of the past,—that the familiar eye does not brighten at his coming, or the familiar tongue voice a welcome. Then, on inquiry, if he is told of the rough word, he says: "O-o-h! *that's* it—is it? Now it isn't possible that you gave *that* a second thought? Why, *I* forgot all about it!" as if this last were really a palliation and a merit.

It would be ludicrous, this masculine obtuseness, were it not for the tragic consequences—were it not for the loving hearts that are chilled—the homes that are darkened—the lives that are blighted—and the dew and promise of the morning that are so needlessly turned into sombre night.

"Little things!" There *are* no little things. "Little things," so called, are the hinges of the universe. They are happiness, or misery; they are poverty, or riches; they are prosperity or adversity; they are life, or death. Not a human being of us all, can afford to despise "the day of *small* things."

Yes, husbands, *be cheerful at home.* I daresay, sir, your Bible may belong to an expurgated edition; but this sentiment is in mine. I have unfortunately loaned it to a neighbor, so that I cannot at this minute point to the exact chapter, but that's neither here nor there.

In every "Guide for Wives" I find "cheerfulness" the first article set down in the creed; with no margin left for crying babies, or sleepless nights, or incompetent "help," or any of the small miseries which men wave off with their hands as "not worth minding, my dear!" So when the time comes for John's return from the shop or office, they begin the cheerful dodge, just as they are bid, by the *single* men and women, who usually write these "Guides for Wives." They hurry to wash the children's faces, or to have them washed, and stagger round, though they may not have had a breath of fresh air for a week, to make things "cheerful" for John. John's beef and vegetables and dessert are all right. He accepts them, and eats them. Then he lies down on the sofa to digest them, which he does silently—cow-fashion. The children, one by one, are sent to bed. Now, does it occur to John that he might try *his* hand at a little "cheerfulness"? Not a bit. He asks his wife, coolly, if there's anything in the evening paper.

She is so tired of the house and its cares, which have cobwebbed her all over till she is half smothered, soul and body, that this question seems the cruelest one that could be put, in her nervous condition. She *ought* to answer as he does, when she asks him what is in the *morning* paper, the while she is feeding Tommy—*his* Tommy as well as hers: "Read it, my dear; it is full of interest!"

Instead, she takes up the evening paper wearily; and though the telltale, exhausted tones of her voice as she reads, are sufficiently suggestive of her inability for reading aloud, yet he graciously listens well pleased, and goes to sleep just as she gets down to the advertisements, which is a good place!

Now that woman *ought* just then, quietly to put on her bonnet and shawl, and run into one of the neighbors', and stay till *she* has got a little "cheerfulness"; but the "Guide to Wives" insists that, instead, she sit down and look at her John, so that no unlucky noise may disturb his slumber; and half the wives do it too, and that's the way they make, and perpetuate, these very Johns.

The way men nurse up *their* frail bodies is curious to witness, in contrast with the little care they take of their wives. Now it never occurs to most wives that being "tired," is an excuse for not doing anything that, half dead, they are drummed up to do. Now there's just where I blame them. If they wait for their Johns to *see* it, or to *say* it, they may wait till the millennium. There's no need of a fight about it either. *He* wants to lie there and be read to. Well—let him lie there; but don't you read to him, or talk to him either, when you feel that way. If he is so stupid or indifferent, as not to see that you can't begin another day of worry like that, without a reprieve of some kind, bid him a pleasant good-evening, and go to some pleasant neighbor's, as he would do, if he felt like it, for the same reason—as he *did* do the evening before, without consulting your preference or tiredness.

Now this may sound vixenish, but it is simply *justice;* and it is time women learned that, as mothers of families, it is just as much their duty to consult their physical needs, as it is for the fathers of families to consult theirs, and more too, since the nervous organization of women is more delicate, and the pettiness of their household cares more exhaustive and wearing, than a man's can possibly be; and this I will insist on, spite of Todd and Bushnell, and every clerical pussy-cat who ever mewed "Let us have peace!" Peace, reverend sirs, is of no sex. *We* like it too; but too dear a price may be paid even for "peace."

Now I know there are instances, for I have seen them, in which the husband is the only cheerful element in the house—when his step, his countenance, like the sunrise, irradiates and warms every nook and corner. But ah! how rare is this! I know too that cheerfulness is greatly a thing of temperament; but I also know, that it is just as much a man's duty to cultivate it by reading to his wife, and conversing with his wife, as it is hers to amuse and cheer him when the day's cares are over. And in this regard I must say that men, as a general thing, are disgustingly selfish. Absorbing, but never giving out—accepting, but seldom returning. It is for women to assert their right to fresh air, to relaxation, to relief from care, whenever the physical system breaks down, just as men always do; for the Johns seldom wake up to it till a coffin is ordered—and pocket-handkerchiefs are too late!

And, speaking of that, nothing is more comical to me, in my journeyings to and fro in the earth, than the blundering way in which most men legislate their domestic affairs. Mr. Jones, for instance, is attracted to a delicate, timid, nervous little lady, and moves heaven and earth, and upsets several families who have a special objection to her becoming Mrs. Jones, in order to bring about this desirable result. After an immense besieging outlay, he gets her. We will leave a margin for the honeymoon. Then commences life in earnest. The little wife stands aghast to find that her husband's whole aim, is to transform her into the direct opposite to that which he formerly admired. In short, that to retain his love and respect, she must make herself, by some process or other only known to herself, entirely over. For instance, she is so constituted that the sight of blood has always given her a deadly faintness, and she never was able to assist, in any emergency or accident, where physical pain was involved. Now this is not an affectation with her—*she really can not* do it. Now Mr. Jones, with masculine acumen, immediately sets in motion a series of little tyrannies, to force what a lifetime could never bring about, no more than it could change his wife's hair from jet to flaxen color. Does their child break a leg, or arm, he insists, although other aid is at hand, that she shall not only be present, but assist in the dressing and binding up of the same, by way of eradicating and overcoming what he calls a "folly." To this end he uses sarcasm, ridicule, threats, every thing which he thinks the "head of the family" is justified in using, to force this child-woman's nature, which once had such fragile attractions for him, into an up-hill course, in which it is impossible for it ever to go, with all the tyranny he can bring to bear upon it; and thus he keeps on trying,—year after year,—with an amount of persistence which should entitle him to a lunatic's cell, and which is gradually preparing his wife for one, through mortification and wounded affection.

Again—a man is attracted to a woman of marked individuality of character. He admires her decision and self-poise, her energy and self-reliance, and stamps them, with one hand on his heart, with the conjugal seal. Directly upon possession, that which seemed to him so admirable conflicts with his opinions, wounds his self-love, and even though gradually and properly expressed, seems to breathe defiance. Now *this* woman he, too, strives to *make over.* He disputes her positions and opinions with acidity, because they differ from his own, and therefore must be wrong. Perhaps he looks at her, and at them, more through the eyes of impertinent outsiders who have nothing to do with it, than through his own spectacles. Many a man will perpetrate a great injustice in his own household, rather than bear the slightest meddling imputation that he is not its master. So, year after year, this fruitless effort goes on, to transform a full-grown tree to a little sapling, capable of being bent in any and every direction, according to the moulder's capricious whim or fancy, with not the ghost of a result, so far as success is concerned.

I might cite many other instances to illustrate the absurd manner in which men persist in marring their own happiness; committing those flagrant injustices of which women either die, and make no sign, or break into what is called *"unwomanly"* rebellion, when their sense of justice is outraged, by the *love* which has proved weaker than *pride.*

It is pitiful to think how frequent are these life-mistakes, and more pitiful still to think, that women themselves are responsible in a great measure for them. Let parents see to it, especially let *mothers* see to it, that the little boy is to yield equally with his sisters in their games and plays. Let the maxim, "Give it to your *sister,*" issue as often from your lips as "Give it to your *brother.*" Let the father say as often to his son, "Prepare to become the excellent husband of some good woman," as the mother to her daughter, "Prepare to be the worthy wife of some good man." In other words, begin at the fireside. Remember that you are training that little boy to make or mar the happiness of some woman, according as you teach him self-government—justice—and the contrary. This is an idea which even abused wives seldom think of. It might be well for them, and some now happy girl, who may lose through that boy, heart and hope in the future, did they do so.

WALT WHITMAN

*Walt Whitman (1819–1892), our greatest poet, was a consummate
list maker. In his epic* Leaves of Grass, *he furnished a preface that was
itself a dizzying dithyrambic itinerary. "The United States themselves
are essentially the greatest poem," he declared. Whitman was a passionate democrat, a celebrant of crowds and average Americans. Not that
all Americans met his approval: he was horrified by the shenanigans of
nineteenth-century politicians, except for Abraham Lincoln, for whom
he felt a near-idolatrous respect. "Death of Abraham Lincoln" is a more
sober account that draws on his prior reportorial training, as well as his
capacity for deep soulful feeling.*

Death of Abraham Lincoln

(1879)

How often since that dark and dripping Saturday—that chilly April day,
now fifteen years bygone—my heart has entertain'd the dream, the wish,
to give of Abraham Lincoln's death, its own special thought and memorial. Yet now the sought-for opportunity offers, I find my notes incompetent, (why, for truly profound themes, is statement so idle? why does the
right phrase never offer?) and the fit tribute I dream'd of, waits unprepared as ever. My talk here indeed is less because of itself or anything in
it, and nearly altogether because I feel a desire, apart from any talk, to
specify the day, the martyrdom. It is for this, my friends, I have call'd you
together. Oft as the rolling years bring back this hour, let it again, however
briefly, be dwelt upon. For my own part, I hope and desire, till my own

dying day, whenever the 14th or 15th of April comes, to annually gather a few friends, and hold its tragic reminiscence. No narrow or sectional reminiscence. It belongs to these States in their entirety—not the North only, but the South—perhaps belongs most tenderly and devoutly to the South, of all; for there, really, this man's birth-stock. There and thence his antecedent stamp. Why should I not say that thence his manliest traits—his universality—his canny, easy ways and words upon the surface—his inflexible determination and courage at heart? Have you never realized it, my friends, that Lincoln, though grafted on the West, is essentially, in personnel and character, a Southern contribution?

And though by no means proposing to resume the Secession war to-night, I would briefly remind you of the public conditions preceding that contest. For twenty years, and especially during the four or five before the war actually began, the aspect of affairs in the United States, though without the flash of military excitement, presents more than the survey of a battle, or any extended campaign, or series, even of Nature's convulsions. The hot passions of the South—the strange mixture at the North of inertia, incredulity, and conscious power—the incendiarism of the abolitionists—the rascality and *grip* of the politicians, unparalle'd in any land, any age. To these I must not omit adding the honesty of the essential bulk of the people everywhere—yet with all the seething fury and contradiction of their natures more arous'd than the Atlantic's waves in wildest equinox. In politics, what can be more ominous, (though generally unappreciated then)—what more significant than the Presidentiads of Fillmore and Buchanan? proving conclusively that the weakness and wickedness of elected rulers are just as likely to afflict us here, as in the countries of the Old World, under their monarchies, emperors, and aristocracies. In that Old World were everywhere heard underground rumblings, that died out, only to again surely return. While in America the volcano, though civic yet, continued to grow more and more convulsive—more and more stormy and threatening.

In the height of all this excitement and chaos, hovering on the edge at first, and then merged in its very midst, and destined to play a leading part, appears a strange and awkward figure. I shall not easily forget the first time I ever saw Abraham Lincoln. It must have been about the 18th or 19th of February, 1861. It was rather a pleasant afternoon, in New York city, as he arrived there from the West, to remain a few hours, and then pass on to Washington, to prepare for his inauguration. I saw him in Broadway, near the site of the present Post-office. He came down, I think from Canal street, to stop at the Astor House. The broad spaces, sidewalks, and street in the neighborhood, and for some distance, were crowded with solid masses of people, many thousands. The omnibuses and other vehicles had all been turn'd off, leaving an unusual hush in that busy part of the city. Presently two or three shabby hack barouches made their way with some difficulty through the crowd, and drew up at the Astor House entrance. A tall figure step'd out of the centre of these barouches, paus'd leisurely on the sidewalk, look'd up at the granite walls and looming architecture of the grand old hotel—then, after a relieving stretch of arms and legs, turn'd round for over a minute to slowly and good-humoredly scan the appearance of the vast and silent crowds. There were no speeches—no compliments—no welcome—as far as I could hear, not a word said. Still much anxiety was conceal'd in that quiet. Cautious persons had fear'd some mark'd insult or indignity to the President-elect—for he possess'd no personal popularity at all in New York city, and very little political. But it was evidently tacitly agreed that if the few political supporters of Mr. Lincoln present would entirely abstain from any demonstration on their side, the immense majority, who were any thing but supporters, would abstain on their side also. The result was a sulky, unbroken silence, such as certainly never before characterized so great a New York crowd.

Almost in the same neighborhood I distinctly remember'd seeing Lafayette on his visit to America in 1825. I had also personally seen and heard, various years afterward, how Andrew Jackson, Clay, Webster, Hungarian Kossuth, Filibuster Walker, the Prince of Wales on his visit, and other celebres, native and foreign, had been welcom'd there—all that indescribable human roar and magnetism, unlike any other sound in the universe—the glad exulting thunder-shouts of countless unloos'd throats of men! But on this occasion, not a voice—not a sound. From the top of an omnibus, (driven up one side, close by, and block'd by the curbstone and the crowds,) I had, I say, a capital view of it all, and especially of Mr. Lincoln, his look and gait—his perfect composure and coolness—his unusual and uncouth height, his dress of complete black, stovepipe hat push'd back on the head, dark-brown complexion, seam'd and wrinkled yet canny-looking face, black, bushy head of hair, disproportionately long neck, and his hands held behind as he stood observing the people. He look'd with curiosity upon that immense sea of faces, and the sea of faces return'd the look with similar curiosity. In both there was a dash of comedy, almost farce, such as Shakspere puts in his blackest tragedies. The crowd that hemm'd around consisted I should think of thirty to forty thousand men, not a single one his personal friend—while I have no doubt, (so frenzied were the ferments of the time,) many an assassin's knife and pistol lurk'd in hip or breast-pocket there, ready, soon as break and riot came.

But no break or riot came. The tall figure gave another relieving stretch or two of arms and legs; then with moderate pace, and accompanied by a few unknown looking persons, ascended the portico-steps of the Astor House, disappear'd through its broad entrance—and the dumb-show ended.

I saw Abraham Lincoln often the four years following that date. He changed rapidly and much during his Presidency—but this scene, and him in it, are indelibly stamped upon my recollection. As I sat on the top of my omnibus, and had a good view of him, the thought, dim and inchoate then, has since come out clear enough, that four sorts of genius, four mighty and primal hands, will be needed to the complete limning of this man's future portrait—the eyes and brains and finger-touch of Plutarch and Eschylus and Michel Angelo, assisted by Rabelais.

And now—(Mr. Lincoln passing on from this scene to Washington, where he was inaugurated, amid armed cavalry, and sharpshooters at every point—the first instance of the kind in our history—and I hope it will be the last)—now the rapid succession of well-known events, (too well known—I believe, these days, we almost hate to hear them mention'd)—the national flag fired on at Sumter—the uprising of the North, in paroxysms of astonishment and rage—the chaos of divided councils—the call for troops—the first Bull Run—the stunning cast-down, shock, and dismay of the North—and so in full flood the Secession war. Four years of lurid, bleeding, murky, murderous war. Who paint those years, with all their scenes?—the hard-fought engagements—the defeats, plans, failures—the gloomy hours, days, when our Nationality seem'd hung in pall of doubt, perhaps death—the Mephistophelean sneers of foreign lands and attachés—the dreaded Scylla of European interference, and the Charybdis of the tremendously dangerous latent strata of secession sympathizers throughout the free States, (far more numerous than is supposed)—the long marches in summer—the hot sweat, and many a sunstroke, as on the rush to Gettysburg in '63—the night battles in the woods, as under Hooker at Chancellorsville—the camps in winter—the military prisons—the hospitals—(alas! alas! the hospitals).

The Secession war? Nay, let me call it the Union war. Though whatever call'd, it is even yet too near us—too vast and too closely overshadowing—its branches unform'd yet, (but certain,), shooting too far into the future—and the most indicative and mightiest of them yet ungrown. A great literature will yet arise out of the era of those four years, those scenes—era compressing centuries of native passion, first-class pictures, tempests of life and death—an inexhaustible mine for the histories, drama, romance, and even philosophy, of peoples to come—indeed the verteber of poetry and art, (of personal character too,) for all future America—far more grand, in my opinion, to the hands capable of it, than Homer's siege of Troy, or the French wars to Shakspere.

But I must leave these speculations, and come to the theme I have assign'd and limited myself to. Of the actual murder of President Lincoln, though so much has been written, probably the facts are yet very indefinite in most persons' minds. I read from my memoranda, written at the time, and revised frequently and finally since.

The day, April 14, 1865, seems to have been a pleasant one throughout the whole land—the moral atmosphere pleasant too—the long storm, so dark, so fratricidal, full of blood and doubt and gloom, over and ended at last by the sun-rise of such an absolute National victory, and utter break-down of Secessionism—we almost doubted our own senses! Lee had capitulated beneath the apple-tree of Appomattox. The other armies, the flanges of the revolt, swiftly follow'd. And could it really be, then? Out of all the affairs of this world of woe and failure and disorder, was there really come the confirm'd, unerring sign of plan, like a shaft of pure light—of rightful rule—of God? So the day, as I say, was propitious. Early herbage, early flowers, were out. (I remember where I was stopping at the time, the season being advanced, there were many lilacs in full bloom. By one of those caprices that enter and give tinge to events without being at all a part of them, I find myself always reminded of the great tragedy of that day by the sight and odor of these blossoms. It never fails.)

But I must not dwell on accessories. The deed hastens. The popular afternoon paper of Washington, the little "Evening Star," had spatter'd all over its third page, divided among the advertisements in a sensational manner, in a hundred different places, *The President and his Lady will be at the Theatre this evening*. . . . (Lincoln was fond of the theatre. I have myself seen him there several times. I remember thinking how funny it was that he, in some respects the leading actor in the stormiest drama known to real history's stage through centuries, should sit there and be so completely interested and absorb'd in those human jack-straws, moving about with their silly little gestures, foreign spirit, and flatulent text.)

On this occasion the theatre was crowded, many ladies in rich and gay costumes, officers in their uniforms, many well-known citizens, young folks, the usual clusters of gas-lights, the usual magnetism of so many people, cheerful, with perfumes, music of violins and flutes—(and over all, and saturating all, that vast, vague wonder, *Victory*, the nation's victory, the triumph of the Union, filling the air, the thought, the sense, with exhilaration more than all music and perfumes.)

The President came betimes, and, with his wife, witness'd the play from the large stage-boxes of the second tier, two thrown into one, and profusely draped with the National flag. The acts and scenes of the pieces—one of those singularly written compositions which have at least the merit of giving entire relief to an audience engaged in mental action or business excitements and cares during the day, as it makes not the slightest call on either the moral, emotional, esthetic, or spiritual nature—a piece, ("Our American Cousin,") in which, among other characters, so call'd, a Yankee, certainly such a one as was never seen, or the least like it ever seen, in North America, is introduced in England, with a varied fol-de-rol of talk, plot, scenery, and such phantasmagoria as goes to make up a modern popular drama—had progress'd through perhaps a couple of its acts, when in the midst of this comedy, or non-such, or whatever it is to be call'd, and to offset it, or finish it out, as if in Nature's and the great Muse's mockery of those poor mimes, came interpolated that scene, not really or exactly to be described at all, (for on the many hundreds who were there it seems to this hour to have left a passing blur, a dream, a blotch)—and yet partially to be described as I now proceed to give it. There is a scene in the play representing a modern parlor, in which two unprecedented English ladies are inform'd by the impossible Yankee that he is not a man of fortune, and therefore undesirable for marriage-catching purposes; after which, the comments being finish'd, the dramatic trio make exit, leaving the stage clear for a moment. At this period came the murder of Abraham Lincoln. Great as all its manifold train, circling round it, and stretching into the future for many a century, in the politics, history, art, &c., of the New World, in point of fact the main thing, the actual murder, transpired with the quiet and simplicity of any commonest occurrence—the bursting of a bud or pod in the growth of vegetation, for instance. Through the general hum following the stage pause, with the change of positions, came the muffled sound of a pistol-shot, which not one-hundredth part of the audience heard at the time—and yet a moment's hush—somehow, surely, a vague startled thrill—and then, through the ornamented, draperied, starr'd and striped space-way of the President's box, a sudden figure, a man, raises himself with hands and feet, stands a moment on the railing, leaps below to the stage, (a distance of perhaps fourteen or fifteen feet,) falls out of position, catching his boot-heel in the copious drapery, (the American flag,) falls on one knee, quickly recovers himself, rises as if nothing had happen'd, (he really sprains his ankle, but unfelt then)—and so the figure, Booth, the murderer, dress'd in plain black broadcloth, bare-headed, with full, glossy, raven hair, and his eyes like some mad animal's flashing with light and resolution, yet with a certain strange calmness, holds aloft in one hand a large knife—walks along not much back from the footlights— turns fully toward the audience his face of statuesque beauty, lit by those basilisk eyes, flashing with desperation, perhaps insanity—launches out in a firm and steady voice the words *Sic semper tyrannis*—and then walks with neither slow nor very rapid pace diagonally across to the back of the stage, and disappears. (Had not all this terrible scene—making the mimic ones preposterous—had it not all been rehears'd, in blank, by Booth, beforehand?)

A moment's hush—a scream—the cry of murder—Mrs. Lincoln leaning out of the box, with ashy cheeks and lips, with involuntary cry, pointing to the retreating figure, *He has kill'd the President.* And still a moment's strange, incredulous suspense—and then the deluge!—then that mixture of horror, noises, uncertainty—(the sound, somewhere back, of a horse's hoofs clattering with speed)—the people burst through chairs and railings, and break them up—there is inextricable confusion and terror—women faint—quite feeble persons fall, and are trampled on—many cries of agony are heard—the broad stage suddenly fills to suffocation with a dense and motley crowd, like some horrible carnival— the audience rush generally upon it, at least the strong men do—the actors and actresses are all there in their play-costumes and painted faces, with mortal fright showing through the rouge—the screams and calls, confused talk—redoubled, trebled—two or three manage to pass up water from the stage to the President's box—others try to clamber up—&c., &c.

In the midst of all this, the soldiers of the President's guard, with others, suddenly drawn to the scene, burst in—(some two hundred altogether)—they storm the house, through all the tiers, especially the upper ones, inflamed with fury, literally charging the audience with fix'd bayonets, muskets and pistols, shouting *Clear out! clear out! you sons of* ——— . . . Such the wild scene, or a suggestion of it rather, inside the play-house that night.

Outside, too, in the atmosphere of shock and craze, crowds of people, fill'd with frenzy, ready to seize any outlet for it, come near committing murder several times on innocent individuals. One such case was especially exciting. The infuriated crowd, through some chance, got started against one man, either for words he utter'd, or perhaps without any cause at all, and were proceeding at once to actually hang him on a neighboring lamp-post, when he was rescued by a few heroic policemen, who placed him in their midst, and fought their way slowly and amid great peril toward the station house. It was a fitting episode of the whole affair. The crowd rushing and eddying to and fro—the night, the yells, the pale faces, many frighten'd people trying in vain to extricate themselves— the attack'd man, not yet freed from the jaws of death, looking like a corpse—the silent, resolute, half-dozen policemen, with no weapons but their little clubs, yet stern and steady through all those eddying swarms— made a fitting side-scene to the grand tragedy of the murder. They gain'd the station house with the protected man, whom they placed in security for the night, and discharged him in the morning.

And in the midst of that pandemonium, infuriated soldiers, the audience and the crowd, the stage, and all its actors and actresses, its paint-pots, spangles, and gas-lights—the life blood from those veins, the best and sweetest of the land, drips slowly down, and death's ooze already begins its little bubbles on the lips.

Thus the visible incidents and surroundings of Abraham Lincoln's murder, as they really occur'd. Thus ended the attempted secession of these States; thus the four years' war. But the main things come subtly and invisibly afterward, perhaps long afterward—neither military, political, nor (great as those are,) historical. I say, certain secondary and indirect results, out of the tragedy of this death, are, in my opinion, greatest. Not the event of the murder itself. Not that Mr. Lincoln strings the principal points and personages of the period, like beads, upon the single string of his career. Not that his idiosyncrasy, in its sudden appearance and disappearance, stamps this Republic with a stamp more mark'd and enduring than any yet given by any one man—(more even than Washington's;)—but, join'd with these, the immeasurable value and meaning of that whole tragedy lies, to me, in senses finally dearest to a nation, (and here all our own)—the imaginative and artistic senses—the literary and dramatic ones. Not in any common or low meaning of those terms, but a meaning precious to the race, and to every age. A long and varied series of contradictory events arrives at last at its highest poetic, single, central, pictorial denouement. The whole involved, baffling, multiform whirl of the secession period comes to a head, and is gather'd in one brief flash of lightning-illumination—one simple, fierce deed. Its sharp culmination, and as it were solution, of so many bloody and angry problems, illustrates those climax-moments on the stage of universal Time, where the historic Muse at one entrance, and the tragic Muse at the other, suddenly ringing down the curtain, close an immense act in the long drama of creative thought, and give it radiation, tableau, stranger than fiction. Fit radiation—fit close! How the imagination—how the student loves these things! America, too, is to have them. For not in all great deaths, nor far or near—not Caesar in the Roman senate-house, or Napoleon passing away in the wild night-storm at St. Helena—not Paleologus, falling, desperately fighting, piled over dozens deep with Grecian corpses—not calm old Socrates, drinking the hemlock—outvies that terminus of the Secession war, in one man's life, here in our midst, in our own time—that seal of the emancipation of three million slaves—that parturition and delivery of our at last really free Republic, born again, henceforth to commence its career of genuine homogeneous Union, compact, consistent with itself.

Nor will ever future American Patriots and Unionists, indifferently over the whole land, or North or South, find a better moral to their lesson. The final use of the greatest men of a Nation is, after all, not with reference to their deeds in themselves, or their direct bearing on their times or lands. The final use of a heroic-eminent life—especially of a heroic-eminent death—is its indirect filtering into the Nation and the race, and to give, often at many removes, but unerringly, age after age, color and fibre to the personalism of the youth and maturity of that age, and of mankind. Then there is a cement to the whole people, subtler, more underlying, than any thing in written constitution, or courts or armies—namely, the cement of a death identified thoroughly with that people, at its head, and for its sake. Strange, (is it not?) that battles, martyrs, agonies, blood, even assassination, should so condense—perhaps only really, lastingly condense—a Nationality.

I repeat it—the grand deaths of the race—the dramatic deaths of every nationality—are its most important inheritance-value—in some respects beyond its literature and art—(as the hero is beyond his finest portrait, and the battle itself beyond its choicest song or epic). Is not here indeed the point underlying all tragedy? the famous pieces of the Grecian masters—and all masters? Why, if the old Greeks had had this man, what trilogies of plays—what epics—would have been made out of him! How the rhapsodes would have recited him! How quickly that quaint tall form would have enter'd into the region where men vitalize gods, and gods divinify men! But Lincoln, his times, his death—great as any, any age—belong altogether to our own, and are autochthonic. (Sometimes indeed I think our American days, our own stage—the actors we know and have shaken hands, or talk'd with—more fateful than any thing in Eschylus—more heroic than the fighters around Troy—afford kings of men for our Democracy prouder than Agamemnon—models of character cute and hardy as Ulysses—deaths more pitiful than Priam's.)

When, centuries hence, (as it must, in my opinion, be centuries hence before the life of these States, or of Democracy, can be really written and illustrated,) the leading historians and dramatists seek for some personage, some special event, incisive enough to mark with deepest cut, and mnemonize, this turbulent Nineteenth century of ours, (not only these States, but all over the political and social world)—something, perhaps, to close that gorgeous procession of European feudalism, with all its pomp and caste-prejudices, (of whose long train we in America are yet so inextricably the heirs)—something to identify with terrible identification, by far the greatest revolutionary step in the history of the United States, (perhaps the greatest of the world, our century)—the absolute extirpation and erasure of slavery from the States—those historians will seek in vain for any point to serve more thoroughly their purpose, than Abraham Lincoln's death.

Dear to the Muse—thrice dear to Nationality—to the whole human race—precious to this Union—precious to Democracy—unspeakably and forever precious—their first great Martyr Chief.

HENRY JAMES

Henry James (1843–1916) was not only one of the greatest American novelists but a perceptive literary critic. His prefaces constitute a major aesthetic formulation about fiction, especially the kind of psychological realism he was attempting in novels such as The Portrait of a Lady, The Ambassadors, and The Wings of the Dove. In his 1884 talk, "The Art of Fiction," he gives us, along with his views on fiction, a master class in essay writing by circling a subject, opening it through questions that complicate the usual platitudes, sparring with a worthy if limited contemporary (Walter Besant), making nuanced distinctions that invite uncertainty, and then supplying illuminating hints about the overlap of moral and aesthetic values, and the importance of having a superior mind (no problem for Mr. James).

The Art of Fiction

(1884)

I should not have affixed so comprehensive a title to these few remarks, necessarily wanting in any completeness, upon a subject the full consideration of which would carry us far, did I not seem to discover a pretext for my temerity in the interesting pamphlet lately published under this name by Mr. Walter Besant. Mr. Besant's lecture at the Royal Institution—the original form of his pamphlet—appears to indicate that many persons are interested in the art of fiction and are not indifferent to such remarks as those who practise it may attempt to make about it. I am therefore anxious not to lose the benefit of this favourable association, and to edge in a few words under cover of the attention which Mr. Besant is sure to have excited. There is something very encouraging in his having put into form certain of his ideas on the mystery of story-telling.

It is a proof of life and curiosity—curiosity on the part of the brother-hood of novelists, as well as on the part of their readers. Only a short time ago it might have been supposed that the English novel was not what the French call *discutable*. It had no air of having a theory, a conviction, a consciousness of itself behind it—of being the expression of an artistic faith, the result of choice and comparison. I do not say it was necessarily the worse for that; it would take much more courage than I possess to intimate that the form of the novel, as Dickens and Thackeray (for instance) saw it had any taint of incompleteness. It was, however, *naïf* (if I may help myself out with another French word); and, evidently, if it is destined to suffer in any way for having lost its *naïveté* it has now an idea of making sure of the corresponding advantages. During the period I have alluded to there was a comfortable, good-humoured feeling abroad that a novel is a novel, as a pudding is a pudding, and that our only business with it could be to swallow it. But within a year or two, for some reason or other, there have been signs of returning animation—the era of discussion would appear to have been to a certain extent opened. Art lives upon discussion, upon experiment, upon curiosity, upon variety of attempt, upon the exchange of views and the comparison of standpoints; and there is a presumption that those times when no one has anything particular to say about it, and has no reason to give for practice or preference, though they may be times of genius, are not times of development, are times possibly even, a little, of dulness. The successful application of any art is a delightful spectacle, but the theory, too, is interesting; and though there is a great deal of the latter without the former, I suspect there has never been a genuine success that has not had a latent core of conviction. Discussion, suggestion, formulation, these things are fertilizing when they are frank and sincere. Mr. Besant has set an excellent example in saying what he thinks, for his part, about the way in which fiction should be written, as well as about the way in which it should be published; for his view of the "art," carried on into an appendix, covers that too. Other labourers in the same field will doubtless take up the argument, they will give it the light of their experience, and the effect will surely be to make our interest in the novel a little more what it had for some time threatened to fail to be—a serious, active, inquiring interest, under protection of which this delightful study may, in moments of confidence, venture to say a little more what it thinks of itself.

It must take itself seriously for the public to take it so. The old superstition about fiction being "wicked" has doubtless died out in England; but the spirit of it lingers in a certain oblique regard directed toward any story which does not more or less admit that it is only a joke. Even the most jocular novel feels in some degree the weight of the proscription that was formerly directed against literary levity; the jocularity does not always succeed in passing for orthodoxy. It is still expected, though perhaps people are ashamed to say it, that a production which is after all only a "make believe" (for what else is a "story"?) shall be in some degree apologetic—shall renounce the pretension of attempting really to represent life. This, of course, any sensible wide-awake story declines to do, for it quickly perceives that the tolerance granted to it on such a condition is only an attempt to stifle it, disguised in the form of generosity. The old evangelical hostility to the novel, which was as explicit as it was narrow, and which regarded it as little less favourable to our immortal part than a stage-play, was in reality far less insulting. The only reason for the existence of a novel is that it does attempt to with life. When it ceases to compete as the canvas of the painter competes, it will have arrived at a very strange pass. It is not expected of the picture that it will make itself humble in order to be forgiven; and the analogy between the art of the painter and the art of the novelist is, so far as I am able to see, complete. Their inspiration is the same, their process (allowing for the different quality of the vehicle) is the same, their success is the same. They may learn from each other, they may explain and sustain each other. Their cause is the same, and the honour of one is the honour of another. Peculiarities of manner, of execution, that correspond on either side, exist in each of them and contribute to their development. The Mahometans think a picture an unholy thing, but it is a long time since any Christian did, and it is therefore the more odd that in the Christian mind the traces (dissimulated though they may be) of a suspicion of the sister art should linger to this day. The only effectual way to lay it to rest is to emphasise the analogy to which I just alluded—to insist on the fact that as the picture is reality, so the novel is history. That is the only general description (which does it justice) that we may give the novel. But history also is allowed to compete with life, as I say; it is not, any more than painting, expected to apologise. The subject-matter of fiction is stored up likewise in documents and records, and if it will not give itself away, as they say in California, it must speak with assurance, with the tone of the historian. Certain accomplished novelists have a habit of giving themselves away which must often bring tears to the eyes of people who take their fiction seriously. I was lately struck, in reading over many pages of Anthony Trollope, with his want of discretion in this particular. In a digression, a parenthesis or an aside, he concedes to the reader that he and this trusting friend are only "making believe." He admits that the events he narrates have not really happened, and that he can give his narrative any turn the reader may like best. Such a betrayal of a sacred office seems to me, I confess, a terrible crime; it is what I mean by the attitude of apology, and it shocks me every whit as much in Trollope as it would have shocked me in Gibbon or Macaulay. It implies that the novelist is less occupied in looking for the truth (the truth, of course I mean, that he assumes, the premises that we must grant him, whatever they may be) than the historian, and in doing so it deprives him at a stroke of all his standing-room. To represent and illustrate the past, the actions of men, is the task of either writer, and the only difference that I can see is, in proportion as he succeeds, to the honour of the novelist, consisting as it does in his having more difficulty in collecting his evidence, which is so far from being purely literary. It seems to me to give him a great character, the fact that he has at once so much in common with the philosopher and the painter; this double analogy is a magnificent heritage.

It is of all this evidently that Mr. Besant is full when he insists upon the fact that fiction is one of the *fine* arts, deserving in its turn of all the honours and emoluments that have hitherto been reserved for the successful profession of music, poetry, painting, architecture. It is impossible to insist too much on so important a truth, and the place that Mr. Besant demands for the work of the novelist may be represented, a trifle less abstractly, by saying that he demands not only that it shall be reputed artistic, but that it shall be reputed very artistic indeed. It is excellent that he should have struck this note, for his doing so indicates that there was need of it, that his proposition may be to many people a novelty. One rubs one's eyes at the thought; but the rest of Mr. Besant's essay confirms the revelation. I suspect, in truth, that it would be possible to confirm it still further, and that one would not be far wrong in saying that in addition to the people to whom it has never occurred that a novel ought to be artistic, there are a great many others who, if this principle were urged upon them, would be filled with an indefinable mistrust. They would find it difficult to explain their repugnance, but it would operate strongly to put them on their guard. "Art," in our Protestant communities, where so many things have got so strangely twisted about, is supposed, in certain circles, to have some vaguely injurious effect upon those who make it an important consideration, who let it weigh in the balance. It is assumed to be opposed in some mysterious manner to morality, to amusement, to instruction. When it is embodied in the work of the painter (the sculptor is another affair!) you know what it is; it stands there before you, in the honesty of pink and green and a gilt frame; you can see the worst of it at a glance, and you can be on your guard. But when it is introduced into literature it becomes more insidious—there is danger of its hurting you before you know it. Literature should be either instructive or amusing, and there is in many minds an impression that these artistic preoccupations, the search for form, contribute to neither end, interfere indeed with both. They are too frivolous to be edifying, and too serious to be diverting; and they are, moreover, priggish and paradoxical and superfluous. That, I think, represents the manner in which the latent thought of many people who read novels as an exercise in skipping would explain itself if it were to become articulate. They would argue, of course, that a novel ought to be "good," but they would interpret this term in a fashion of their own, which, indeed would vary considerably from one critic to another. One would say that being good means representing virtuous and aspiring characters, placed in prominent positions; another would say that it depends for a "happy ending" on a distribution at the last of prizes, pensions, husbands, wives, babies, millions, appended paragraphs and cheerful remarks. Another still would say that it means being full of incident and movement, so that we shall wish to jump ahead, to see who was the mysterious stranger, and if the stolen will was ever found, and shall not be distracted from this pleasure by any tiresome analysis or "description." But they would all agree that the "artistic" idea would spoil some of their fun. One would hold it accountable for all the description, another would see it revealed in the absence of sympathy. Its hostility to a happy ending would be evident, and it might even, in some cases, render any ending at all impossible. The "ending" of a novel is, for many persons, like that of a good dinner, a course of dessert and ices, and the artist in fiction is regarded as a sort of meddlesome doctor who forbids agreeable aftertastes. It is therefore true that this conception of Mr. Besant's of the novel as a superior form encounters not only a negative but a positive indifference. It matters little that, as a work of art, it should really be as little or as much concerned to supply happy endings, sympathetic characters, and an objective tone, as if it were a work of mechanics; the association of ideas, however incongruous, might easily be too much for it if an eloquent voice were not sometimes raised to call attention to the fact that it is at once as free and as serious a branch of literature as any other.

Certainly, this might sometimes be doubted in presence of the enormous number of works of fiction that appeal to the credulity of our generation, for it might easily seem that there could be no great character in a commodity so quickly and easily produced. It must be admitted that good novels are somewhat compromised by bad ones, and that the field, at large, suffers discredit from overcrowding. I think, however, that this injury is only superficial, and that the superabundance of written fiction proves nothing against the principle itself. It has been vulgarised, like all other kinds of literature, like everything else, to-day, and it has proved more than some kinds accessible to vulgarisation. But there is as much difference as there ever was between a good novel and a bad one: the bad is swept, with all the daubed canvases and spoiled marble, into some unvisited limbo or infinite rubbish-yard, beneath the back-windows of the world, and the good subsists and emits its light and stimulates our desire for perfection. As I shall take the liberty of making but a single criticism of Mr. Besant, whose tone is so full of the love of his art, I may as well have done with it at once. He seems to me to mistake in attempting to say so definitely beforehand what sort of an affair the good novel will be. To indicate the danger of such an error as that has been the purpose of these few pages; to suggest that certain traditions on the subject, applied *a priori*, have already had much to answer for, and that the good health of an art which undertakes so immediately to reproduce life must demand that it be perfectly free. It lives upon exercise, and the very meaning of exercise is freedom. The only obligation to which in advance we may hold a novel without incurring the accusation of being arbitrary, is that it be interesting. That general responsibility rests upon it, but it is the only one I can think of. The ways in which it is at liberty to accomplish this result (of interesting us) strike me as innumerable and such as can only suffer from being marked out, or fenced in, by prescription. They are as various as the temperament of man, and they are successful in proportion as they reveal a particular mind, different from others. A novel is in its broadest definition a personal impression of life; that, to begin with, constitutes its value, which is greater or less according to the intensity of the impression. But there will be no intensity at all, and therefore no value, unless there is freedom to feel and say. The tracing of a line to be followed, of a tone to be taken, of a form to be filled out, is a limitation of that freedom and a suppression of the very thing that we are most curious about. The form, it seems to me, is to be appreciated after the fact; then the author's choice has been made, his standard has been indicated; then we can follow lines and directions and compare tones. Then, in a word, we can enjoy one of the most charming of pleasures, we can estimate quality, we can apply the test of execution. The execution belongs to the author alone; it is what is most personal to him, and we measure him by that. The advantage, the luxury, as well as the torment and responsibility of the novelist, is that there is no limit to what he may attempt as an executant—no limit to his possible experiments, efforts, discoveries, successes. Here it is especially that he works, step by step, like his brother of the brush, of whom we may always say that he has painted his picture in a manner best known to himself. His manner is his secret, not necessarily a deliberate one. He cannot disclose it, as a general thing, if he would; he would be at a loss to teach it to others. I say this with a due recollection of having insisted on the community of method of the artist who paints a picture and the artist who writes a novel. The painter is able to teach the rudiments of his practice, and it is possible, from the study of good work (granted the aptitude), both to learn how to paint and to learn how to write. Yet it remains true, without injury to the *rapprochement*, that the literary artist would be obliged to say to his pupil much more than the other, "Ah, well, you must do it as you can!" It is a question of degree, a matter of delicacy. If there are exact sciences there are also exact arts, and the grammar of painting is so much more definite that it makes the difference.

I ought to add, however, that if Mr. Besant says at the beginning of his essay that the "laws of fiction may be laid down and taught with as much precision and exactness as the laws of harmony, perspective, and proportion," he mitigates what might appear to be an extravagance by applying his remark to "general" laws, and by expressing most of these rules in a manner with which it would certainly be unaccommodating to disagree. That the novelist must write from his experience, that his "characters must be real and such as might be met with in actual life"; that "a young lady brought up in a quiet country village should avoid descriptions of garrison life," and "a writer whose friends and personal experiences belong to the lower middle-class should carefully avoid introducing his characters into society"; that one should enter one's notes in a common-place book; that one's figures should be clear in outline; that making them clear by some trick of speech or of carriage is a bad method, and "describing them at length" is a worse one; that English Fiction should have a "conscious moral purpose"; that "it is almost impossible to estimate too highly the value of careful workmanship—that is, of style"; that "the most important point of all is the story," that "the story is everything"—these are principles with most of which it is surely impossible not to sympathise. That remark about the lower middle-class writer and his knowing his place is perhaps rather chilling; but for the rest, I should find it difficult to dissent from any one of these recommendations. At the same time I should find it difficult positively to assent to them, with the exception, perhaps, of the injunction as to entering one's notes in a common-place book. They scarcely seem to me to have the quality that Mr. Besant attributes to the rules of the novelist—the "precision and exactness" of "the laws of harmony, perspective, and proportion." They are suggestive, they are even inspiring, but they are not exact, though they are doubtless as much so as the case admits of; which is a proof of that liberty of interpretation for which I just contended. For the value of these different injunctions—so beautiful and so vague—is wholly in the meaning one attaches to them. The characters, the situation, which strike one as real will be those that touch and interest one most, but the measure of reality is very difficult to fix. The reality of Don Quixote or of Mr. Micawber is a very delicate shade; it is a reality so coloured by the author's vision that, vivid as it may be, one would hesitate to propose it as a model; one would expose one's self to some very embarrassing questions on the part of a pupil. It goes without saying that you will not write a good novel unless you possess the sense of reality; but it will be difficult to give you a recipe for calling that sense into being. Humanity is immense and reality has a myriad forms; the most one can affirm is that some of the flowers of fiction have the odour of it, and others have not; as for telling you in advance how your nosegay should be composed, that is another affair. It is equally excellent and inconclusive to say that one must write from experience; to our supposititious aspirant such a declaration might savour of mockery. What kind of experience is intended, and where does it begin and end? Experience is never limited and it is never complete; it is an immense sensibility, a kind of huge spider-web, of the finest silken threads, suspended in the chamber of consciousness and catching every air-borne particle in its tissue. It is the very atmosphere of the mind; and when the mind is imaginative—much more when it happens to be that of a man of genius—it takes to itself the faintest hints of life, it converts the very pulses of the air into revelations. The young lady living in a village has only to be a damsel upon whom nothing is lost to make it quite unfair (as it seems to me) to declare to her that she shall have nothing to say about the military. Greater miracles have been seen than that, imagination assisting, she should speak the truth about some of these gentlemen. I remember an English novelist, a woman of genius, telling me that she was much commended for the impression she had managed to give in one of her tales of the nature and way of life of the French Protestant youth. She had been asked where she learned so much about this recondite being, she had been congratulated on her peculiar opportunities. These opportunities consisted in her having once, in Paris, as she ascended a staircase, passed an open door where, in the household of a *pasteur,* some of the young Protestants were seated at table round a finished meal. The glimpse made a picture; it lasted only a moment, but that moment was experience. She had got her impression, and she evolved her type. She knew what youth was, and what Protestantism; she also had the advantage of having seen what it was to be French; so that she converted these ideas into a concrete image and produced a reality. Above all, however, she was blessed with the faculty which when you give it an inch takes an ell, and which for the artist is a much greater source of strength than any accident of residence or of place in the social scale. The power to guess the unseen from the seen, to trace the implication of things, to judge the whole piece by the pattern, the condition of feeling life, in general, so completely that you are well on your way to knowing any particular corner of it—this cluster of gifts may almost be said to constitute experience, and they occur in country and in town, and in the most differing stages of education. If experience consists of impressions, it may be said that impressions are experience, just as (have we not seen it?) they are the very air we breathe. Therefore, if I should certainly say to a novice, "Write from experience, and experience only," I should feel that this was a rather tantalising monition if I were not careful immediately to add, "Try to be one of the people on whom nothing is lost!"

I am far from intending by this to minimise the importance of exactness—of truth of detail. One can speak best from one's own taste, and I may therefore venture to say that the air of reality (solidity of specification) seems to me to be the supreme virtue of a novel—the merit on which all its other merits (including that conscious moral purpose of which Mr.

Besant speaks) helplessly and submissively depend. If it be not there, they are all as nothing, and if these be there, they owe their effect to the success with which the author has produced the illusion of life. The cultivation of this success, the study of this exquisite process, form, to my taste, the beginning and the end of the art of the novelist. They are his inspiration, his despair, his reward, his torment, his delight. It is here, in very truth, that he competes with life; it is here that he competes with his brother the painter in *his* attempt to render the look of things, the look that conveys their meaning, to catch the colour, the relief, the expression, the surface, the substance of the human spectacle. It is in regard to this that Mr. Besant is well inspired when he bids him take notes. He cannot possibly take too many, he cannot possibly take enough. All life solicits him, and to "render" the simplest surface, to produce the most momentary illusion, is a very complicated business. His case would be easier, and the rule would be more exact, if Mr. Besant had been able to tell him what notes to take. But this I fear he can never learn in any hand-book; it is the business of his life. He has to take a great many in order to select a few, he has to work them up as he can, and even the guides and philosophers who might have most to say to him must leave him alone when it comes to the application of precepts, as we leave the painter in communion with his palette. That his characters "must be clear in outline," as Mr. Besant says—he feels that down to his boots; but how he shall make them so is a secret between his good angel and himself. It would be absurdly simple if he could be taught that a great deal of "description" would make them so, or that, on the contrary, the absence of description and the cultivation of dialogue, or the absence of dialogue and the multiplication of "incident," would rescue him from his difficulties. Nothing, for instance, is more possible than that he be of a turn of mind for which this odd, literal opposition of description and dialogue, incident and description, has little meaning and light. People often talk of these things as if they had a kind of internecine distinctness, instead of melting into each other at every breath and being intimately associated parts of one general effort of expression. I cannot imagine composition existing in a series of blocks, nor conceive, in any novel worth discussing at all, of a passage of description that is not in its intention narrative, a passage of dialogue that is not in its intention descriptive, a touch of truth of any sort that does not partake of the nature of incident, and an incident that derives its interest from any other source than the general and only source of the success of a work of art—that of being illustrative. A novel is a living thing, all one and continuous, like every other organism, and in proportion as it lives will it be found, I think, that in each of the parts there is something of each of the other parts. The critic who over the close texture of a finished work will pretend to trace a geography of items will mark some frontiers as artificial, I fear, as any that have been known to history. There is an old-fashioned distinction between the novel of character and the novel of incident, which must have cost many a smile to the intending romancer who was keen about his work. It appears to me as little to the point as the equally celebrated distinction between the novel and the romance—to answer as little to any reality. There are bad novels and good novels, as there are bad pictures and good pictures; but that is the only distinction in which I see any meaning, and I can as little imagine speaking of a novel of character as I can imagine speaking of a picture of character. When one says picture, one says of character, when one says novel, one says of incident, and the terms may be transposed. What is character but the determination of incident? What is incident but the illustration of character? What is a picture or a novel that is *not* of character? What else do we seek in it and find in it? It is an incident for a woman to stand up with her hand resting on a table and look out at you in a certain way; or if it be not an incident, I think it will be hard to say what it is. At the same time it is an expression of character. If you say you don't see it (character in that—*allons donc!*), this is exactly what the artist who has reasons of his own for thinking he *does* see it undertakes to show you. When a young man makes up his mind that he has not faith enough, after all, to enter the Church, as he intended, that is an incident, though you may not hurry to the end of the chapter to see whether perhaps he doesn't change once more. I do not say that these are extraordinary or startling incidents. I do not pretend to estimate the degree of interest proceeding from them, for this will depend upon the skill of the painter. It sounds almost puerile to say that some incidents are intrinsically much more important than others, and I need not take this precaution after having professed my sympathy for the major ones in remarking that the only classification of the novel that I can understand is into the interesting and the uninteresting.

The novel and the romance, the novel of incident and that of character—these separations appear to me to have been made by critics and readers for their own convenience, and to help them out of some of their difficulties, but to have little reality or interest for the producer, from whose point of view it is, of course, that we are attempting to consider the art of fiction. The case is the same with another shadowy category, which Mr. Besant apparently is disposed to set up—that of the "modern English novel"; unless, indeed, it be that in this matter he has fallen into an accidental confusion of standpoints. It is not quite clear whether he intends the remarks in which he alludes to it to be didactic or historical. It is as difficult to suppose a person intending to write a modern English, as to suppose him writing an ancient English, novel; that is a label which begs the question. One writes the novel, one paints the picture, of one's language and of one's time, and calling it modern English will not, alas! make the difficult task any easier. No more, unfortunately, will calling this or that work of one's fellow artist a romance—unless it be, of course, simply for the pleasantness of the thing, as, for instance, when Hawthorne gave this heading to his story of *Blithedale*. The French, who have brought the theory of fiction to remarkable completeness, have but one word for the novel, and have not attempted smaller things in it, that I can see, for that. I can think of no obligation to which the "romancer" would not be held equally with the novelist; the standard of execution is equally high for each. Of course it is of execution that we are talking— that being the only point of a novel that is open to contention. This is perhaps too often lost sight of, only to produce interminable confusions and cross-purposes. We must grant the artist his subject, his idea, what the French call his *donnée;* our criticism is applied only to what he makes of it. Naturally I do not mean that we are bound to like it or find it inter- esting: in case we do not our course is perfectly simple—to let it alone. We may believe that of a certain idea even the most sincere novelist can make nothing at all, and the event may perfectly justify our belief; but the failure will have been a failure to execute, and it is in the execution that the fatal weakness is recorded. If we pretend to respect the artist at all we must allow him his freedom of choice, in the face, in particular cases, of innumerable presumptions that the choice will not fructify. Art derives a considerable part of its beneficial exercise from flying in the face of presumptions, and some of the most interesting experiments of which it is capable are hidden in the bosom of common things. Gustave Flaubert has written a story about the devotion of a servant-girl to a parrot, and the production, highly finished as it is, cannot on the whole be called a success. We are perfectly free to find it flat, but I think it might have been interesting; and I, for my part, am extremely glad he should have written it; it is a contribution to our knowledge of what can be done or what can- not. Ivan Turgénieff has written a tale about a deaf and dumb serf and a lap-dog, and the thing is touching, loving, a little masterpiece. He struck the note of life where Gustave Flaubert missed it—he flew in the face of a presumption and achieved a victory.

Nothing, of course, will ever take the place of the good old fashion of "liking" a work of art or not liking it; the more improved criticism will not abolish that primitive, that ultimate, test. I mention this to guard myself from the accusation of intimating that the idea, the subject, of a novel or a picture, does not matter. It matters, to my sense, in the highest degree, and if I might put up a prayer it would be that artists should select none but the richest. Some, as I have already hastened to admit, are much more substantial than others, and it would be a happily arranged world in which persons intending to treat them should be exempt from confusions and mistakes. This fortunate condition will arrive only, I fear, on the same day that critics become purged from error. Meanwhile, I repeat, we do not judge the artist with fairness unless we say to him, "Oh, I grant you your starting-point, because if I did not I should seem to prescribe to you, and heaven forbid I should take that responsibility. If I pretend to tell you what you must not take, you will call upon me to tell you then what you must take; in which case I shall be prettily caught! Moreover, it isn't till I have accepted your data that I can begin to measure you. I have the pitch; I have no right to tamper with your flute and then criticise your music.

I judge you by what you propose, and you must look out for me there. Of course I may not care for your idea at all; I may think it silly, or stale, or unclean; in which case I wash my hands of you altogether. I may content myself with believing that you will not have succeeded in being interesting, but I shall of course not attempt to demonstrate it, and you will be as indifferent to me as I am to you. I needn't remind you that there are all sorts of tastes: who can know it better? Some people, for excellent reasons, don't like to read about carpenters; others, for reasons even better, don't like to read about courtesans. Many object to Americans. Others (I believe they are mainly editors and publishers) won't look at Italians. Some readers don't like quiet subjects; others don't like bustling ones. Some enjoy a complete illusion; others revel in a complete deception. They choose their novels accordingly, and if they don't care about your idea they won't, *a fortiori*, care about your treatment.

So that it comes back very quickly, as I have said, to the liking; in spite of M. Zola, who reasons less powerfully than he represents, and who will not reconcile himself to this absoluteness of taste, thinking that there are certain things that people ought to like, and that they can be made to like. I am quite at a loss to imagine anything (at any rate in this matter of fiction) that people *ought* to like or to dislike. Selection will be sure to take care of itself, for it has a constant motive behind it. That motive is simply experience. As people feel life, so they will feel the art that is most closely related to it. This closeness of relation is what we should never forget in talking of the effort of the novel. Many people speak of it as a factitious, artificial form, a product of ingenuity, the business of which is to alter and arrange the things that surround us, to translate them into conventional, traditional moulds. This, however, is a view of the matter which carries us but a very short way, condemns the art to an eternal repetition of a few familiar clichés, cuts short its development, and leads us straight up to a dead wall. Catching the very note and trick, the strange irregular rhythm of life, that is the attempt whose strenuous force keeps Fiction upon her feet. In proportion as in what she offers us we see life without rearrangement do we feel that we are touching the truth; in proportion as we see it with rearrangement do we feel that we are being put off with a substitute, a compromise and convention. It is not uncommon to hear an extraordinary assurance of remark in regard to this matter of rearranging, which is often spoken of as if it were the last word of art. Mr. Besant seems to me in danger of falling into this great error with his rather unguarded talk about "selection." Art is essentially selection, but it is a selection whose main care is to be typical, to be inclusive. For many people art means rose-coloured windows, and selection means picking a bouquet for Mrs. Grundy. They will tell you glibly that artistic considerations have nothing to do with the disagreeable, with the ugly; they will rattle off shallow commonplaces about the province of art and the limits of art, till you are moved to some wonder in return as to the province and the limits of ignorance. It appears to me that no one can ever have made a seriously artistic attempt without becoming conscious of an immense increase—a kind of revelation—of freedom. One perceives, in that case—by the light of a heavenly ray—that the province of art is all life, all feeling, all observation, all vision. As Mr. Besant so justly intimates, it is all experience. That is a sufficient answer to those who maintain that it must not touch the painful, who stick into its divine unconscious bosom little prohibitory inscriptions on the end of sticks, such as we see in public gardens—"It is forbidden to walk on the grass; it is forbidden to touch the flowers; it is not allowed to introduce dogs, or to remain after dark; it is requested to keep to the right." The young aspirant in the line of fiction, whom we continue to imagine, will do nothing without taste, for in that case his freedom would be of little use to him; but the first advantage of his taste will be to reveal to him the absurdity of the little sticks and tickets. If he have taste, I must add, of course he will have ingenuity, and my disrespectful reference to that quality just now was not meant to imply that it is useless in fiction. But it is only a secondary aid; the first is a vivid sense of reality.

Mr. Besant has some remarks on the question of "the story," which I shall not attempt to criticise, though they seem to me to contain a singular ambiguity, because I do not think I understand them. I cannot see what is meant by talking as if there were a part of a novel which is the story and part of it which for mystical reasons is not—unless indeed the distinction be made in a sense in which it is difficult to suppose that anyone should attempt to convey anything. "The story," if it represents anything, represents the subject, the idea, the data of the novel; and there is surely no "school"—Mr. Besant speaks of a school—which urges that a novel should be all treatment and no subject. There must assuredly be something to treat; every school is intimately conscious of that. This sense of the story being the idea, the starting-point, of the novel is the only one that I see in which it can be spoken of as something different from its organic whole; and since, in proportion as the work is successful, the idea permeates and penetrates it, informs and animates it, so that every word and every punctuation-point contribute directly to the expression, in that proportion do we lose our sense of the story being a blade which may be drawn more or less out of its sheath. The story and the novel, the idea and the form, are the needle and thread, and I never heard of a guild of tailors who recommended the use of the thread without the needle or the needle without the thread. Mr. Besant is not the only critic who may be observed to have spoken as if there were certain things in life which constitute stories and certain others which do not. I find the same odd implication in an entertaining article in the *Pall Mall Gazette*, devoted, as it happens, to Mr. Besant's lecture. "The story is the thing!" says this graceful writer, as if with a tone of opposition to another idea. I should think it was, as every painter who, as the time for "sending in" his picture looms in the distance, finds himself still in quest of a subject—as every belated artist, not fixed about his *donnée,* will heartily agree. There are some subjects which speak to us and others which do not, but he would be a clever man who should undertake to give a rule by which the story and the no-story should be known apart. It is impossible (to me at least) to imagine any such rule which shall not be altogether arbitrary. The writer in the *Pall Mall* opposes the delightful (as I suppose) novel of *Margot la Balafrée* to certain tales in which "Bostonian nymphs" appear to have "rejected English dukes for psychological reasons." I am not acquainted with the romance just designated, and can scarcely forgive the *Pall Mall* critic for not mentioning the name of the author, but the title appears to refer to a lady who may have received a scar in some heroic adventure. I am inconsolable at not being acquainted with this episode, but am utterly at a loss to see why it is a story when the rejection (or acceptance) of a duke is not, and why a reason, psychological or other, is not a subject when a cicatrix is. They are all particles of the multitudinous life with which the novel deals, and surely no dogma which pretends to make it lawful to touch the one and unlawful to touch the other will stand for a moment on its feet. It is the special picture that must stand or fall, according as it seems to possess truth or to lack it. Mr. Besant does not, to my sense, light up the subject by intimating that a story must, under penalty of not being a story, consist of "adventures." Why of adventures more than of green spectacles? He mentions a category of impossible things, and among them he places "fiction without adventure." Why without adventure, more than without matrimony, or celibacy, or parturition, or cholera, or hydropathy, or Jansenism? This seems to me to bring the novel back to the hapless little *rôle* of being an artificial, ingenious thing—bring it down from its large, free character of an immense and exquisite correspondence with life. And what is adventure, when it comes to that, and by what sign is the listening pupil to recognise it? It is an adventure—an immense one—for me to write this little article; and for a Bostonian nymph to reject an English duke is an adventure only less stirring, I should say, than for an English duke to be rejected by a Bostonian nymph. I see dramas within dramas in that, and innumerable points of view. A psychological reason is, to my imagination, an object adorably pictorial; to catch the tint of its complexion—I feel as if that idea might inspire one to Titian-esque efforts. There are few things more exciting to me, in short, than a psychological reason, and yet, I protest, the novel seems to me the most magnificent form of art. I have just been reading, at the same time, the delightful story of *Treasure Island,* by Mr. Robert Louis Stevenson, and the last tale from M. Edmond de Goncourt, which is entitled *Chérie.* One of these works treats of murders, mysteries, islands of dreadful renown, hairbreadth escapes, miraculous coincidences and buried doubloons. The other treats of a little French girl who lived in a fine house in Paris and died of wounded sensibility because no one would marry her. I call *Treasure Island* delightful, because it appears to me to have succeeded wonderfully in what it attempts; and I venture to bestow no epithet upon *Chérie,* which strikes me as having failed in what it attempts—that is, in tracing the development of the moral consciousness of a child. But one of these productions strikes me as exactly as much of a novel as the other, and as having a "story" quite as much. The moral consciousness of a child is as much a part of life as the islands of the Spanish Main, and the one sort of geography seems to me to have those "surprises" of which Mr. Besant speaks quite as much as the other. For myself (since it comes back in the last resort, as I say, to the preference of the individual), the picture of the child's experience has the advantage that I can at successive steps (an immense luxury, near to the "sensual pleasure" of which Mr. Besant's critic in the *Pall Mall* speaks) say Yes or No, as it may be, to what the artist puts before me. I have been a child, but I have never been on a quest for a buried treasure, and it is a simple accident that with M. de Goncourt I should have for the most part to say No. With George Eliot, when she painted that country, I always said Yes.

The most interesting part of Mr. Besant's lecture is unfortunately the briefest passage—his very cursory allusion to the "conscious moral purpose" of the novel. Here again it is not very clear whether he is recording a fact or laying down a principle; it is a great pity that in the latter case he should not have developed his idea. This branch of the subject is of immense importance, and Mr. Besant's few words point to considerations of the widest reach, not to be lightly disposed of. He will have treated the art of fiction but superficially who is not prepared to go every inch of the way that these considerations will carry him. It is for this reason that at the beginning of these remarks I was careful to notify the reader that my reflections on so large a theme have no pretension to be exhaustive. Like Mr. Besant, I have left the question of the morality of the novel till the last, and at the last I find I have used up my space. It is a question surrounded with difficulties, as witness the very first that meets us, in the form of a definite question, on the threshold. Vagueness, in such a discussion, is fatal, and what is the meaning of your morality and your conscious moral purpose? Will you not define your terms and explain how (a novel being a picture) a picture can be either moral or immoral? You wish to paint a moral picture or carve a moral statue; will you not tell us how you would set about it? We are discussing the Art of Fiction; questions of art are questions (in the widest sense) of execution; questions of morality are quite another affair, and will you not let us see how it is that you find it so easy to mix them up? These things are so clear to Mr. Besant that he has deduced from them a law which he sees embodied in English Fiction and which is "a truly admirable thing and a great cause for congratulation." It is a great cause for congratulation, indeed, when such thorny problems become as smooth as silk. I may add that, in so far as Mr. Besant perceives that in point of fact English Fiction has addressed itself preponderantly to these delicate questions, he will appear to many people to have made a vain discovery. They will have been positively struck, on the contrary, with the moral timidity of the usual English novelist; with his (or with her) aversion to face the difficulties with which, on every side, the treatment of reality bristles. He is apt to be extremely shy (whereas the picture that Mr. Besant draws is a picture of boldness), and the sign of his work, for the most part, is a cautious silence on certain subjects. In the English novel (by which I mean the American as well), more than in any other, there is a traditional difference between that which people know and that which they agree to admit that they know, that which they see and that which they speak of, that which they feel to be a part of life and that which they allow to enter into literature. There is the great difference, in short, between what they talk of in conversation and what they talk of in print. The essence of moral energy is to survey the whole field, and I should directly reverse Mr. Besant's remark, and say not that the English novel has a purpose, but that it has a diffidence. To what degree a purpose in a work of art is a source of corruption I shall not attempt to inquire; the one that seems to me least dangerous is the purpose of making a perfect work. As for our novel, I may say, lastly, on this score, that, as we find it in England to-day, it strikes me as addressed in a large degree to "young people," and that this in itself constitutes a presumption that it will be rather shy. There are certain things which it is generally agreed not to discuss, not even to mention, before young people. That is very well, but the absence of discussion is not a symptom of the moral passion. The purpose of the English novel—"a truly admirable thing, and a great cause for congratulation"—strikes me, therefore, as rather negative.

There is one point at which the moral sense and the artistic sense lie very near together; that is, in the light of the very obvious truth that the deepest quality of a work of art will always be the quality of the mind of the producer. In proportion as that mind is rich and noble will the novel, the picture, the statue, partake of the substance of beauty and truth. To be constituted of such elements is, to my vision, to have purpose enough. No good novel will ever proceed from a superficial mind; that seems to me an axiom which, for the artist in fiction, will cover all needful moral ground; if the youthful aspirant take it to heart it will illuminate for him many of the mysteries of "purpose." There are many other useful things that might be said to him, but I have come to the end of my article, and can only touch them as I pass. The critic in the *Pall Mall Gazette*, whom I have already quoted, draws attention to the danger, in speaking of the art of fiction, of generalising. The danger that he has in mind is rather, I imagine, that of particularising, for there are some comprehensive remarks which, in addition to those embodied in Mr. Besant's suggestive lecture, might, without fear of misleading him, be addressed to the ingenuous student. I should remind him first of the magnificence of the form that is open to him, which offers to sight so few restrictions and such innumerable opportunities. The other arts, in comparison, appear confined and hampered; the various conditions under which they are exercised are so rigid and definite. But the only condition that I can think of attaching to the composition of the novel is, as I have already said, that it be interesting. This freedom is a splendid privilege, and the first lesson of the young novelist is to learn to be worthy of it. "Enjoy it as it deserves," I should say to him; "take possession of it, explore it to its utmost extent, reveal it, rejoice in it. All life belongs to you, and don't listen either to those who would shut you up into corners of it and tell you that it is only here and there that art inhabits, or to those who would persuade you that this heavenly messenger wings her way outside of life altogether, breathing a superfine air and turning away her head from the truth of things. There is no impression of life, no manner of seeing it and feeling it, to which the plan of the novelist may not offer a place; you have only to remember that talents so dissimilar as those of Alexandre Dumas and Jane Austen, Charles Dickens and Gustave Flaubert, have worked in this field with equal glory. Don't think too much about optimism and pessimism; try and catch the colour of life itself. In France to-day we see a prodigious effort (that of Emile Zola, to whose solid and serious work no explorer of the capacity of the novel can allude without respect), we see an extraordinary effort vitiated by a spirit of pessimism on a narrow basis. M. Zola is magnificent, but he strikes an English reader as ignorant; he has an air of working in the dark; if he had as much light as energy his results would be of the highest value. As for the aberrations of a shallow optimism, the ground (of English fiction especially) is strewn with their brittle particles as with broken glass. If you must indulge in conclusions let them have the taste of a wide knowledge. Remember that your first duty is to be as complete as possible—to make as perfect a work. Be generous and delicate, and pursue the prize."

CHARLOTTE PERKINS GILMAN

Charlotte Perkins Gilman (1860–1935) was a feminist author, social reformer, editor, and orator. Of her hundreds of essays, poems, novels, and nonfiction tracts, best known today are the classic short story "The Yellow Wallpaper," about a woman suffering from postpartum depression who is essentially imprisoned by her patriarchal doctor-husband, and the utopian novel Herland, *about a world without men. She also wrote* Women and Economics, *in which she argues that mothers should be allowed to enter the workforce and the public sphere. Her own first marriage ended in divorce, which may account for the wry skepticism about that institution in her essay "On Advertising for Marriage." Were she alive today, she might very well approve of online dating.*

On Advertising for Marriage

(1885)

Why not? Why not take every means in one's power to discover so important a person as one's husband or wife? What is the prejudice that exists against it? To say that such advertisements are used for improper purposes is saying nothing against using them properly. To say that "marriages are made in heaven"; that it is "tempting Providence" to speak of mysterious laws which bring people together, needs only for answer, Look at the majority of marriages now existing! If they are made in heaven let us try some earth-made ones. *The Alpha* and all common sense teaches that we should use reason and discrimination in a selection like this; and if one is desirous to marry and fails to find a fit mate in one's neighborhood or acquaintance, what reason is there that he or she should not look farther? They have no surety that fate will bring them the desired one without effort on their part, for behold! Many of their friends are unmarried and many more mismarried. What certainty have they of a better lot? I do believe that if we obeyed all the laws of our life as the birds do, we should find mates as they do; but we do not. One reasonable argument may be adduced against me, namely, that people brought together from different parts of the country would be dissimilar in their tastes and habits, and so suffer when united; also that one must be separated from home and friends. To the latter I reply that in the case of true marriage it would be a small evil, that under ordinary circumstances the separation need not be complete, and that it frequently happens under the present method. To the former, that people whose local tastes and habits were stronger than their individualities, who shared the feelings of the neighborhood to such an extent that change would be painful, would not be likely to miss mating, for they would be satisfied with local character. Conversely, those who found no mate in the home influence and were so constituted as to demand something different would find full compensation in what they gained for all they lost. It may be said that if the match proved unhappy they would bitterly regret having meddled with fate, and wish they had waited patiently; but in like cases those who meet by chance, or are thrown together in the natural course of events, as bitterly curse fortune, or their own folly, and wish the same. Errors of judgment need be no more frequent than now, and even in case of mistaking, surely it is better to look back on an earnest attempt to choose wisely than the usual much-extolled drifting. Surely *The Alpha* teaches that marriage should result not from the will and judgment led by passion, but the opposite. If a man sees a fair woman before he knows her; feels the charm of her presence before he begins to understand her character; if first aroused to the necessity of judging by his strong inclination; surely he stands less chance of a cool and safe decision than one who begins knowingly, learns a character from earnest letters, loves the mind before he does the body. And that first love would improve and be more to him yearly, growing ever richer, stronger, and more lovely with advancing age. The other does not. I see in writing still another consideration. It would if it became a general custom, teach both sexes to cultivate the mind and the power of expression in writing more than the beauty of the body and its sexual attraction. Also when marriage was seen to depend more upon real value and worth coolly inquired into than upon feminine charms and snares and masculine force and persistence, that would be a huge power enlisted on the side of good. Young women would take more interest in the affairs of the world if they knew the chance of a happy marriage might depend on such knowledge; that they might be written to by such a man as they would love and honor, and expected to sympathize with his ideas,

appreciate his work, understand and help him; and man might conde-
scend to think a women's nature worth studying a little if their hopes
rested also in genuine sympathy and appreciation. (Not her sexual nature!
Heaven defend us! They have studied that long and well, but the *rest* of
her, the "ninety-nine parts human"!) Will some one explain what harm
would result from Advertising for Marriage?

SUI SIN FAR

Edith Maude Eaton (1865–1914), born of an English merchant father and a Chinese mother, took the pseudonym Sui Sin Far in solidarity with her mother's people, though her appearance did not identify her clearly as Asian. Appalled by the prejudice in the United States against Chinese immigrants, thousands of whom had been imported as indentured laborers to build railroads and work in mines, she wrote impassioned articles in their defense. The following personal essay is a pioneering effort by a biracial Asian American woman to examine the enigma of identity, and the conflict between a minority member's racial pride and her ability to pass, however inadvertently, as part of the white majority.

Leaves from the Mental Portfolio of an Eurasian

(1890)

When I look back over the years I see myself, a little child of scarcely four years of age, walking in front of my nurse, in a green English lane, and listening to her tell another of her kind that my mother is Chinese. "Oh Lord!" exclaims the informed. She turns around and scans me curiously from head to foot. Then the two women whisper together. Tho the word "Chinese" conveys very little meaning to my mind, I feel that they are talking about my father and mother and my heart swells with indignation. When we reach home I rush to my mother and try to tell her what I have heard. I am a young child. I fail to make myself intelligible. My mother does not understand, and when the nurse declares to her, "Little Miss Sui is a story-teller," my mother slaps me.

Many a long year has past over my head since that day—the day on which I first learned I was something different and apart from other children, but tho my mother has forgotten it, I have not.

I see myself again, a few years older. I am playing with another child in a garden. A girl passes by outside the gate. "Mamie," she cries to my companion. "I wouldn't speak to Sui if I were you. Her mamma is Chinese."

"I don't care," answers the little one beside me. And then to me, "Even if your mamma is Chinese, I like you better than I like Annie."

"But I don't like you," I answer, turning my back on her. It is my first conscious lie.

I am at a children's party, given by the wife of an Indian officer whose children were schoolfellows of mine. I am only six years of age, but have attended a private school for over a year, and have already learned that China is a heathen country, being civilized by England. However, for the time being, I am a merry romping child. There are quite a number of grown people present. One, a white haired old man, has his attention called to me by the hostess. He adjusts his eyeglasses and surveys me critically. "Ah, indeed!" he exclaims. "Who would have thought it at first glance? Yet now I see the difference between her and other children. What a peculiar coloring! Her mother's eyes and hair and her father's features, I presume. Very interesting little creature!"

I had been called from play for the purpose of inspection. I do not return to it. For the rest of the evening I hide myself behind a hall door and refuse to show myself until it is time to go home.

My parents have come to America. We are in Hudson City, N.Y., and we are very poor. I am out with my brother, who is ten months older than myself. We pass a Chinese store, the door of which is open. "Look!" says Charlie. "Those men in there are Chinese!" Eagerly I gaze into the long low room. With the exception of my mother, who is English bred with English ways and manner of dress, I have never seen a Chinese person. The two men within the store are uncouth specimens of their race, drest in working blouses and pantaloons with queues hanging down their backs. I recoil with a sense of shock.

"Oh, Charlie," I cry. "Are we like that?"

"Well, we're Chinese, and they're Chinese, too, so we must be!" returns my seven year old brother.

"Of course you are," puts in a boy who has followed us down the street, and who lives near us and has seen my mother: "Chinky, Chinky, Chinaman, yellow-face, pig-tail, rat-eater." A number of other boys and several little girls join in with him.

"Better than you," shouts my brother, facing the crowd. He is younger and smaller than any there, and I am even more insignificant than he; but my spirit revives.

"I'd rather be Chinese than anything else in the world," I scream.

They pull my hair, they tear my clothes, they scratch my face, and all but lame my brother; but the white blood in our veins fights valiantly for the Chinese half of us. When it is all over, exhausted and bedraggled, we crawl home, and report to our mother that we have "won the battle."

"Are you sure?" asks my mother doubtfully.

"Of course. They ran from us. They were frightened," returns my brother.

My mother smiles with satisfaction.

"Do you hear?" she asks my father.

"Umm," he observes, raising his eyes from his paper for an instant. My childish instinct, however, tells me that he is more interested than he appears to be.

It is tea time, but I cannot eat. Unobserved, I crawl away. I do not sleep that night. I am too excited and I ache all over. Our opponents had been so very much stronger and bigger than we. Toward morning, however, I fall into a doze from which I awake myself, shouting:

> "Sound the battle cry;
> See the foe is nigh."

My mother believes in sending us to Sunday school. She has been brought up in a Presbyterian college.

The scene of my life shifts to Eastern Canada. The sleigh which has carried us from the station stops in front of a little French Canadian hotel. Immediately we are surrounded by a number of villagers, who stare curiously at my mother as my father assists her to alight from the sleigh. Their curiosity, however, is tempered with kindness, as they watch, one after another, the little black heads of my brothers and sisters and myself emerge out of the buffalo robe, which is part of the sleigh's outfit. There are six of us; four girls and two boys; the eldest, my brother, being only seven years of age. My father and mother are still in their twenties. "Les pauvres enfants," the inhabitants murmur, as they help to carry us into the hotel. Then in lower tones: "Chinoise, Chinoise."

For some time after our arrival, whenever children are sent for a walk, our footsteps are dogged by a number of young French and English Canadians, who amuse themselves with speculations as to whether, we being Chinese, are susceptible to pinches and hair pulling, while older persons pause and gaze upon us, very much in the same way that I have seen people gaze upon strange animals in a menagerie. Now and then we are stopt and plied with questions as to what we eat and drink, how we go to sleep, if my mother understands what my father says to her, if we sit on chairs or squat on floors, etc., etc., etc.

There are many pitched battles, of course, and we seldom leave the house without being armed for conflict My mother takes a great interest in our battles, and usually cheers us on, tho I doubt whether she understands the depth of the troubled waters thru which her little children wade. As to my father, peace is his motto, and he deems it wisest to be blind and deaf to many things.

School days are short, but memorable. I am in the same class with my brother, my sister next to me in the class below. The little girl whose desk my sister shares shrinks close to the wall as my sister takes her place. In a little while she raises her hand.

"Please, teacher!"

"Yes, Annie."

"May I change my seat?"

"No, you may not!"

The little girl sobs. "Why should I have to sit beside a ——"

Happily, my sister does not seem to hear, and before long the two little girls become great friends. I have many such experiences.

My brother is remarkably bright; my sister next to me has a wonderful head for figures, and when only eight years of age helps my father with his night work accounts. My parents compare her with me. She is of sturdier build than I, and, as my father says, "Always has her wits about her." He thinks her more like my mother, who is very bright and interested in every little detail of practical life. My father tells me that I will never make half the woman that my mother is or that my sister will be. I am not as strong as my sisters, which makes me feel somewhat ashamed, for I am the eldest little girl, and more is expected of me. I have no organic disease, but the strength of my feelings seems to take from me the strength of my body. I am prostrated at times with attacks of nervous sickness. The doctor says that my heart is unusually large; but in the light of the present I know that the cross of the Eurasian bore too heavily upon my childish shoulders. I usually hide my weakness from the family until I cannot stand. I do not understand myself, and I have an idea that the others will despise me for not being as strong as they. Therefore, I like to wander away alone, either by the river or in the bush. The green fields and flowing water have a charm for me. At the age of seven, as it is today, a bird on the wing is my emblem of happiness.

I have come from a race on my mother's side which is said to be the most stolid and insensible to feeling of all races, yet I look back over the years and see myself so keenly alive to every shade of sorrow and suffering that it is almost a pain to live.

If there is any trouble in the house in the way of a difference between my father and mother, or if any child is punished, how I suffer! And when harmony is restored, heaven seems to be around me. I can be sad, but I can also be glad. My mother's screams of agony when a baby is born almost drive me wild, and long after her pangs have subsided I feel them in my own body. Sometimes it is a week before I can get to sleep after such an experience.

A debt owing by my father fills me with shame. I feel like a criminal when I pass by the creditor's door. I am only ten years old. And all the while the question of nationality perplexes my little brain. Why are we what we are? I and my brothers and sisters. Why did God make us to be hooted and stared at? Papa is English, mamma is Chinese. Why couldn't we have been either one thing or the other? Why is my mother's race despised? I look into the faces of my father and mother. Is she not every bit as dear and good as he? Why? Why? She sings us the song she learned at her English school. She tells us tales of China. Tho a child when she left her native land she remembers it well, and I am never tired of listening to the story of how she was stolen from her home. She tells us over and over again of her meeting with my father in Shanghai and the romance of their marriage. Why? Why?

I do not confide in my father and mother. They would not understand. How could they? He is English, she is Chinese. I am different to both of them—a stranger, tho their own child. "What are we?" I ask my brother. "It doesn't matter, sissy," he responds. But it does. I love poetry, particularly heroic pieces. I also love fairy tales. Stories of everyday life do not appeal to me. I dream dreams of being great and noble; my sisters and brothers also. I glory in the idea of dying at the stake and a great genie arising from the flames and declaring to those who have scorned us: "Behold, how great and glorious and noble are the Chinese people!"

My sisters are apprenticed to a dressmaker; my brother is entered in an office. I tramp around and sell my father's pictures, also some lace which I make myself. My nationality, if I had only know it at that time, helps to make sales. The ladies who are my customers call me "The Little Chinese Lace Girl." But it is a dangerous life for a very young girl. I come near to "mysteriously disappearing" many a time. The greatest temptation was in the thought of getting far away from where I was known, to where no mocking cries of "Chinese!" "Chinese!" could reach.

Whenever I have the opportunity I steal away to the library and read every book I can find on China and the Chinese. I learn that China is the oldest civilized nation on the face of the earth and a few other things. At eighteen years of age what troubles me is not that I am what I am, but that others are ignorant of my superiority. I am small, but my feelings are big—and great is my vanity.

My sisters attend dancing classes, for which they pay their own fees. In spite of covert smiles and sneers, they are glad to meet and mingle with other young folk. They are not sensitive in the sense that I am. And yet they understand. One of them tells me that she overheard a young man say to another that he would rather marry a pig than a girl with Chinese blood in her veins.

In course of time I too learn shorthand and take a position in an office. The local papers patronize me and give me a number of assignments, including most of the local Chinese reporting. I meet many Chinese persons, and when they get into trouble am often called upon to fight their battles in the papers. This I enjoy. My heart leaps for joy when I read one day an article by a New York Chinese in which he declares, "The Chinese in America owe an everlasting debt of gratitude to Sui Sin Far for the bold stand she has taken in their defense."

The Chinaman who wrote the article seeks me out and calls upon me. He is a clever and witty man, a graduate of one of the American colleges and as well a Chinese scholar. I learn that he has an American wife and several children. I am very much interested in these children, and when I meet them my heart throbs in sympathetic tune with the tales they relate of their experiences as Eurasians. "Why did papa and mamma born us?" asks one. Why?

I also meet other Chinese men who compare favorably with the white men of my acquaintance in mind and heart qualities. Some of them are quite handsome. They have not as finely cut noses and as well developed chins as the white men, but they have smoother skins and their expression is more serene; their hands are better shaped and their voices softer.

Some little Chinese women whom I interview are very anxious to know whether I would marry a Chinaman. I do not answer No. They clap their hands delightedly, and assure me that the Chinese are much the finest and best of all men. They are, however, a little doubtful as to whether one could be persuaded to care for me, full-blooded Chinese people having a prejudice against the half white.

Fundamentally, I muse, people are all the same. My mother's race is as prejudiced as my father's. Only when the whole world becomes as one family will human beings be able to see clearly and hear distinctly. I believe that some day a great part of the world will be Eurasian. I cheer myself with the thought that I am but a pioneer. A pioneer should glory in suffering.

"You were walking with a Chinaman yesterday," accuses an acquaintance.

"Yes, what of it?"

"You ought not to. It isn't right."

"Not right to walk with one of my mother's people? Oh, indeed!"

I cannot reconcile his notion of righteousness with my own.

—

I am living in a little town away off on the north shore of a big lake. Next to me at the dinner table is the man for whom I work as a stenographer. There are also a couple of business men, a young girl and her mother.

Some one makes a remark about the cars full of Chinamen that past that morning. A transcontinental railway runs thru the town.

My employer shakes his rugged head. "Somehow or other," says he, "I cannot reconcile myself to the thought that the Chinese are humans like ourselves. They may have immortal souls, but their faces seem to be so utterly devoid of expression that I cannot help but doubt."

"Souls," echoes the town clerk. "Their bodies are enough for me. A Chinaman is, in my eyes, more repulsive than a nigger."

"They always give me such a creepy feeling," puts in the young girl with a laugh.

"I wouldn't have one in my house," declares my landlady.

"Now, the Japanese are different altogether. There is something bright and likeable about those men," continues Mr. K.

A miserable, cowardly feeling keeps me silent. I am in a Middle West town. If I declare what I am, every person in the place will hear about it the next day. The population is in the main made up of working folks with strong prejudices against my mother's countrymen. The prospect before me is not an enviable one—if I speak. I have no longer an ambition to die at the stake for the sake of demonstrating the greatness and nobleness of the Chinese people.

Mr. K turns to me with a kindly smile.

"What makes Miss Far so quiet?" he asks.

"I don't suppose she finds the 'washee washee men' particularly interesting subjects of conversation," volunteers the young manager of the local bank.

With a great effort I raise my eyes from my plate. "Mr. K.," I say, addressing my employer, "the Chinese people may have no souls, no expression on their faces, be altogether beyond the pale of civilization, but whatever they are, I want you to understand that I am—I am a Chinese."

There is silence in the room for a few minutes. Then Mr. K. pushes back his plate and standing up beside me, says:

"I should have not spoken as I did. I know nothing whatever about the Chinese. It was pure prejudice. Forgive me!"

I admire Mr. K.'s moral courage in apologizing to me; he is a conscientious Christian man, but I do not remain much longer in the little town.

I am under a tropic sky, meeting frequently and conversing with persons who are almost as high up in the world as birth, education, and money can set them. The environment is peculiar, for I am also surrounded by a race of people, the reputed descendants of Ham, the son of Noah, whose offspring, it was prophesied, should be the servants of the sons of Shem and Japheth. As I am a descendant, according to the Bible, of both Shem and Japheth, I have a perfect right to set my heel upon the Ham people; but tho I see others around me following out the Bible suggestion, it is not in my nature to be arrogant to any but those who seek to impress me with their superiority, which the poor black maid who has been assigned to me by the hotel certainly does not. My employer's wife takes me to task for this. "It is unnecessary," she says, "to thank a black person for service."

The novelty of life in the West Indian island is not without its charm. The surroundings, people, manner of living, are so entirely different from what I have been accustomed to up North that I feel as if I were "born again." Mixing with people of fashion, and yet not of them, I am not of sufficient importance to create comment or curiosity. I am busy nearly all day and often well into the night. It is not monotonous work, but it is certainly strenuous. The planters and business men of the island take me as a matter of course and treat me with kindly courtesy. Occasionally an Englishman will warn me against the "brown boys" of the island, little dreaming that I too am of the "brown people" of the earth.

When it begins to be whispered about the place that I am not all white, some of the "sporty" people seek my acquaintance. I am small and look much younger than my years. When, however, they discover that I am a very serious and sober-minded spinster indeed, they retire quite gracefully, leaving me a few amusing reflections.

One evening a card is brought to my room. It bears the name of some naval officer. I go down to my visitor, thinking he is probably some one who, having been told that I am a reporter for the local paper, has brought me an item of news. I find him lounging in an easy chair on the veranda of the hotel—a big, blond, handsome fellow, several years younger than I.

"You are Lieutenant ——?" I inquire.

He bows and laughs a little. The laugh doesn't suit him somehow— and it doesn't suit me, either.

"If you have anything to tell me, please tell it quickly, because I'm very busy."

"Oh, you don't really mean that," he answers, with another silly and offensive laugh. "There's always plenty of time for good times. That's what I am here for. I saw you at the races the other day and twice at King's House. My ship will be here for —— weeks."

"Do you wish that noted?" I ask.

"Oh, no! Why—I came just because I had an idea that you might like to know me. I would like to know you. You look such a nice little body. Say, wouldn't you like to go for a sail this lovely night? I will tell you all about the sweet little Chinese girls I met when we were at Hong Kong. They're not so shy!"

—

I leave Eastern Canada for the Far West, so reduced by another attack of rheumatic fever that I only weigh eighty-four pounds. I travel on an advertising contract. It is presumed by the railway company that in some way or other I will give them full value for their transportation across the continent. I have been ordered beyond the Rockies by the doctor, who declares that I will never regain my strength in the East. Nevertheless, I am but two days in San Francisco when I start out in search of work. It is the first time that I have sought work as a stranger in a strange town. Both of the other positions away from home were secured for me by home influence. I am quite surprised to find that there is no demand for my services in San Francisco and that no one is particularly interested in me. The best I can do is accept an offer from a railway agency to typewrite their correspondence for $5 a month. I stipulate, however, that I shall have the privilege of taking in outside work and that my hours shall be light. I am hopeful that the sale of a story or newspaper article may add to my income, and I console myself with the reflection that, considering that I still limp and bear traces of sickness, I am fortunate to secure any work at all.

The proprietor of one of the San Francisco papers, to whom I have a letter of introduction, suggests that I obtain some subscriptions from the people of Chinatown, that district of the city having never been canvassed. This suggestion I carry out with enthusiasm, tho I find that the Chinese merchants and people generally are inclined to regard me with suspicion. They have been imposed upon so many times by unscrupulous white people. Another drawback—save for a few phrases, I am unacquainted with my mother tongue. How, then, can I expect these people to accept me as their own countrywoman? The Americanized Chinamen actually laugh in my face when I tell them that I am of their race. However, they are not all "doubting Thomases." Some little women discover that I have Chinese hair, color of eyes and complexion, also that I love rice and tea. This settles the matter for them—and for their husbands.

I meet a half Chinese, half white girl. Her face is plastered with a thick white coat of paint and her eyelids and eyebrows are blackened so that the shape of her eyes and the whole expression of her face is changed. She was born in the East, and at the age of eighteen came West to answer an advertisement. Living for many years among the working class, she had heard little but abuse of the Chinese. It is not difficult, in a land like California, for a half Chinese, half white girl to pass as one of Spanish or Mexican origin. This the poor child does, tho she lives in nervous dread of being "discovered." She becomes engaged to a young man, but fears to tell him what she is, and only does so when compelled by a fearless American girl friend. This girl, who knows her origin, realizing that the truth sooner or later must be told, and better soon than late, advises the Eurasian to confide in the young man, assuring her that he loves her well enough to not allow her nationality to stand, a bar sinister, between them. But the Eurasian prefers to keep her secret, and only reveals it to the man who is to be her husband when driven to bay by the American girl, who declares that if the half-breed will not tell the truth, she will. When the young man hears that the girl he is engaged to has Chinese blood in her veins, he exclaims: "Oh, what will my folks say?" But that is all. Love is stronger than prejudice with him, and neither he nor she deems it necessary to inform his "folks."

The Americans, having for many years manifested a much higher regard for the Japanese than for the Chinese, several half Chinese young men and women, thinking to advance themselves, both in a social and business sense, pass as Japanese. They continue to be known as Eurasians; but a Japanese Eurasian does not appear in the same light as a Chinese Eurasian. The unfortunate Chinese Eurasians! Are not those who compel them to thus cringe more to be blamed than they?

People, however, are not all alike. I meet white men, and women, too, who are proud to mate with those who have Chinese blood in their veins, and think it a great honor to be distinguished by the friendship of such. There are also Eurasians and Eurasians. I know of one who allowed herself to become engaged to a white man after refusing him nine times. She had discouraged him in every way possible, had warned him that she was half Chinese; that her people were poor, that every week or month she sent home a certain amount of her earnings, and that the man she married would have to do as much, if not more; also, most uncompromising truth of all, that she did not love him and never would. But the resolute and undaunted lover swore that it was a matter of indifference to him whether she was a Chinese or a Hottentot, that it would be his pleasure and privilege to allow her relations double what it was in her power to bestow, and as to not loving him—that did not matter at all. He loved her. So, because the young woman had a married mother and married sisters, who were always picking at her and gossiping over her independent manner of living, she finally consented to marry him, recording the agreement in her diary thus:

"I have promised to become the wife of —— —— on —— ——, 189—, because the world is so cruel and sneering to a single woman—and for no other reason."

Everything went smoothly until one day. The young man was driving a pair of beautiful horses and she was seated by his side, trying very hard to imagine herself in love with him, when a Chinese vegetable gardener's cart came rumbling along. The Chinaman was a jolly-looking individual in blue cotton blouse and pantaloons, his rakish looking hat being kept in place by a long queue which was pulled upward from his neck and wound around it. The young woman was suddenly possest with the spirit of mischief. "Look!" she cried, indicating the Chinaman, "there's my brother. Why don't you salute him?"

The man's face fell a little. He sank into a pensive mood. The wicked one by his side read him like an open book.

"When we are married," said she, "I intend to give a Chinese party every month."

No answer.

"As there are very few aristocratic Chinese in this city, I shall fill up with the laundrymen and the vegetable farmers. I don't believe in being exclusive in democratic America, do you?"

He hadn't a grain of humor in his composition, but a sickly smile contorted his features as he replied:

"You shall do just as you please, my darling. But—but—consider a moment. Wouldn't it just be a little pleasanter for us if, after we are married, we allowed it to be presumed that you were—er—Japanese? So many of my friends have inquired of me if that is not your nationality. They would be so charmed to meet a little Japanese lady."

"Hadn't you better oblige them by finding one?"

"Why—er—what do you mean?"

"Nothing much in particular. Only—I am getting a little tired of this," taking off the ring.

"You don't mean what you say! Oh, put it back, dearest! You know I would not hurt your feelings for the world!"

"You haven't. I'm more than pleased. But I do mean what I say."

That evening, the "ungrateful" Chinese Eurasian diaried, among other things, the following:

"Joy, oh, joy! I'm free once more. Never again shall I be untrue to my own heart. Never again will I allow any one to 'hound' or 'sneer' me into matrimony."

I secure transportation to many California points. I meet some literary people, chief among whom is the editor of the magazine who took my first Chinese stories. He and his wife give me a warm welcome to their ranch. They are broad-minded people, whose interest in me is sincere and intelligent, not affected and vulgar. I also meet some funny people who advise me to "trade" upon my nationality. They tell me that if I wish to succeed in literature in America I should dress in Chinese costume, carry a fan in my hand, wear a pair of scarlet beaded slippers, live in New York, and come of high birth. Instead of making myself familiar with the Chinese Americans around me, I should discourse on my spirit acquaintance with Chinese ancestors and quote in between the "Good mornings" and "How d'ye dos" of editors, Confucius, Confucius, how great is Confucius. Before Confucius, there never was Confucius. After Confucius, there never came Confucius," etc., etc., etc., or something like that, both illuminating and obscuring, don't you know. They forget, or perhaps they are not aware that the old Chinese sage taught "The way of sincerity is the way of heaven."

My experiences as a Eurasian never cease; but people are not now as prejudiced as they have been. In the West, too, my friends are more advanced in all lines of thought than those whom I knew in Eastern Canada—more genuine, more sincere, with less of the form of religion, but more of its spirit.

So I roam backward and forward across the continent. When I am East, my heart is West. When I am West, my heart is East. Before long I hope to be in China. As my life began in my father's country it may end in my mother's.

After all I have no nationality and am not anxious to claim any. Individuality is more than nationality. "You are you and I am I," says Confucius. I give my right hand to the Occidentals and my left to the Orientals, hoping that between them they will not utterly destroy the insignificant "connecting link." And that's all.

JANE ADDAMS

Jane Addams (1860–1935) was a towering figure in the field of social work. She started the settlement house movement "to provide," in her words, "a center for a higher civic and social life, to institute and maintain educational and philanthropic enterprises and to investigate and improve the conditions in the industrial districts of Chicago." She was especially concerned about the estrangement of thousands of young people thrown together in big cities without an anchor. Her books and essays, in line with her life's work, can be seen as an attempt to take democracy further, from the mere formality of voting to a true empowerment of ordinary citizens. An outspoken advocate for women's suffrage, as well as an ardent pacifist, she was awarded the Nobel Peace Prize in 1931.

The Subjective Necessity of Social Settlements

(1892)

Hull House, which was Chicago's first Settlement, was established in September, 1889. It represented no association, but was opened by two women, backed by many friends, in the belief that the mere foothold of a house, easily accessible, ample in space, hospitable and tolerant in spirit, situated in the midst of large foreign colonies which so easily isolated themselves in American cities, would be in itself a serviceable thing for Chicago. Hull House endeavors to make social intercourse express the growing sense of the economic unity of society. It is an effort to add the social function to democracy. It was opened on the theory that the dependence of classes on each other is reciprocal; and that as "the social relation is essentially a reciprocal relation, it gave a form of expression that has peculiar value."

This paper is an attempt to treat of the subjective necessity for Social Settlements, to analyze the motives which underlie a movement based not only upon conviction, but genuine emotion. Hull House of Chicago is used as an illustration, but so far as the analysis is faithful, it obtains wherever educated young people are seeking an outlet for that sentiment of universal brotherhood which the best spirit of our times is forcing from an emotion into a motive.

I have divided the motives which constitute the subjective pressure toward Social Settlements into three great lines: the first contains the desire to make the entire social organism democratic, to extend democracy beyond its political expression; the second is the impulse to share the race life, and to bring as much as possible of social energy and the accumulation of civilization to those portions of the race which have little; the third springs from a certain renaissance of Christianity, a movement toward its early humanitarian aspects.

It is not difficult to see that although America is pledged to the democratic ideal, the view of democracy has been partial, and that its best achievement thus far has been pushed along the line of the franchise. Democracy has made little attempt to assert itself in social affairs. We have refused to move beyond the position of its eighteenth-century leaders, who believed that political equality alone would secure all good to all men. We conscientiously followed the gift of the ballot hard upon the gift of freedom to the negro, but we are quite unmoved by the fact that he lives among us in a practical social ostracism. We hasten to give the franchise to the immigrant from a sense of justice, from a tradition that he ought to have it, while we dub him with epithets deriding his past life or present occupation, and feel no duty to invite him to our houses. We are forced to acknowledge that it is only in our local and national politics that we try very hard for the ideal so dear to those who were enthusiasts when the century was young. We have almost given it up as our ideal in social intercourse. There are city wards in which many of the votes are sold for drinks and dollars; still there is a remote pretence, at least a fiction current, that a man's vote is his own. The judgment of the voter is consulted and an opportunity for remedy given. There is not even a theory in the social order, not a shadow answering to the polls in politics. The time may come when the politician who sells one by one to the highest bidder all the offices in his grasp, will not be considered more base in his code of morals, more hardened in his practice, than the woman who constantly invites to her receptions those alone who bring her an equal social return, who shares her beautiful surroundings only with those who

minister to a liking she has for successful social events. In doing this is she
not just as unmindful of the common weal, as unscrupulous in her use of
power, as is any city "boss" who consults only the interests of the "ring"?

In politics "bossism" arouses a scandal. It goes on in society constantly
and is only beginning to be challenged. Our consciences are becoming
tender in regard to the lack of democracy in social affairs. We are perhaps
entering upon the second phase of democracy, as the French philosophers
entered upon the first, somewhat bewildered by its logical conclusions.
The social organism has broken down through large districts of our great
cities. Many of the people living there are very poor, the majority of
them without leisure or energy for anything but the gain of subsistence.
They move often from one wretched lodging to another. They live for the
moment side by side, many of them without knowledge of each other,
without fellowship, without local tradition or public spirit, without social
organization of any kind. Practically nothing is done to remedy this.
The people who might do it, who have the social tact and training, the
large houses, and the traditions and custom of hospitality, live in other
parts of the city. The clubhouses, libraries, galleries, and semi-public
conveniences for social life are also blocks away. We find working-men
organized into armies of producers because men of executive ability and
business sagacity have found it to their interests thus to organize them.
But these working-men are not organized socially; although living in
crowded tenement-houses, they are living without a corresponding social
contact. The chaos is as great as it would be were they working in huge
factories without foreman or superintendent. Their ideas and resources
are cramped. The desire for higher social pleasure is extinct. They have
no share in the traditions and social energy which make for progress. Too
often their only place of meeting is a saloon, their only host a bartender;
a local demagogue forms their public opinion. Men of ability and refinement, of social power and university cultivation, stay away from them.
Personally, I believe the men who lose most are those who thus stay away.
But the paradox is here: when cultivated people do stay away from a certain portion of the population, when all social advantages are persistently
withheld, it may be for years, the result itself is pointed at as a reason, is
used as an argument, for the continued withholding.

It is constantly said that because the masses have never had social
advantages they do not want them, that they are heavy and dull, and that
it will take political or philanthropic machinery to change them. This
divides a city into rich and poor; into the favored, who express their
sense of the social obligation by gifts of money, and into the unfavored,
who express it by clamoring for a "share"—both of them actuated by a
vague sense of justice. This division of the city would be more justifiable,
however, if the people who thus isolate themselves on certain streets and
use their social ability for each other gained enough thereby and added

sufficient to the sum total of social progress to justify the withholding of the pleasures and results of that progress from so many people who ought to have them. But they cannot accomplish this. "The social spirit discharges itself in many forms, and no one form is adequate to its total expression." We are all uncomfortable in regard to the sincerity of our best phrases, because we hesitate to translate our philosophy into the deed.

It is inevitable that those who feel most keenly this insincerity and partial living should be our young people, our so-called educated young people who accomplish little toward the solution of this social problem, and who bear the brunt of being cultivated into unnourished, oversensitive lives. They have been shut off from the common labor by which they live and which is a great source of moral and physical health. They feel a fatal want of harmony between their theory and their lives, a lack of coordination between thought and action. I think it is hard for us to realize how seriously many of them are taking to the notion of human brotherhood, how eagerly they long to give tangible expression to the democratic ideal. These young men and women, longing to socialize their democracy, are animated by certain hopes.

These hopes may be loosely formulated thus: that if in a democratic country nothing can be permanently achieved save through the masses of the people, it will be impossible to establish a higher political life than the people themselves crave; that it is difficult to see how the notion of a higher civic life can be fostered save through common intercourse; that the blessings which we associate with a life of refinement and cultivation can be made universal and must be made universal if they are to be permanent; that the good we secure for ourselves is precarious and uncertain, is floating in mid-air, until it is secured for all of us and incorporated into our common life.

These hopes are responsible for results in various directions, preeminently in the extension of educational advantages. We find that all educational matters are more democratic in their political than in their social aspects. The public schools in the poorest and most crowded wards of the city are inadequate to the number of children, and many of the teachers are ill prepared and overworked; but in each ward there is an effort to secure public education. The schoolhouse itself stands as a pledge that the city recognizes and endeavors to fulfill the duty of educating its children. But what becomes of these children when they are no longer in public schools? Many of them never come under the influence of a professional teacher nor a cultivated friend after they are twelve. Society at large does little for their intellectual development. The dream of transcendentalists that each New England village would be a university, that every child taken from the common school would be put into definite lines of study and mental development, had its unfulfilled beginning in the village lyceum and lecture courses, and has its feeble representative now in the multitude of clubs for study which are so sadly restricted to educators, to the leisure class, or only to the advanced and progressive wage-workers.

The University Extension movement—certainly when it is closely identified with Settlements—would not confine learning to those who already want it, or to those who, by making an effort, can gain it, or to those among whom professional educators are already at work, but would take it to the tailors of East London and the dock-laborers of the Thames. It requires tact and training, love of learning, and the conviction of the justice of its diffusion to give it to people whose intellectual faculties are untrained and disused. But men in England are found who do it successfully, and it is believed there are men and women in America who can do it. I also believe that the best work in University Extension can be done in Settlements, where the teaching will be further socialized, where the teacher will grapple his students, not only by formal lectures, but by every hook possible to the fuller intellectual life which he represents. This teaching requires distinct methods, for it is true of people who have been allowed to remain undeveloped and whose faculties are inert and sterile, that they cannot take their learning heavily. It has to be diffused in a social atmosphere. Information held in solution, a medium of fellowship and goodwill can be assimilated by the dullest.

If education is, as Froebel defined it, "deliverance," deliverance of the forces of the body and mind, then the untrained must first be delivered from all constraint and rigidity before their faculties can be used. Possibly one of the most pitiful periods in the drama of the much-praised young American who attempts to rise in life is the time when his educational requirements seem to have locked him up and made him rigid. He fancies himself shut off from his uneducated family and misunderstood by his friends. He is bowed down by his mental accumulations and often gets no farther than to carry them through life as a great burden. Not once has he had a glimpse of the delights of knowledge. Intellectual life requires for its expansion and manifestation the influence and assimilation of the interests and affections of others. Mazzini, that greatest of all democrats, who broke his heart over the condition of the South European peasantry, said: "Education is not merely a necessity of true life by which the individual renews his vital force in the vital force of humanity; it is a Holy Communion with generations dead and living, by which he fecundates all his faculties. When he is withheld from this Communion for generations, as the Italian peasant has been, we point our finger at him and say, 'He is like a beast of the field; he must be controlled by force.'" Even to this it is sometimes added that it is absurd to educate him, immoral to disturb his content. We stupidly use again the effect as an argument for a continuance of the cause. It is needless to say that a Settlement is a protest against a restricted view of education, and makes it possible for every educated man or woman with a teaching faculty to find out those who are ready to be taught. The social and educational activities of a Settlement are but differing manifestations of the attempt to socialize democracy, as is the existence of the Settlement itself.

I find it somewhat difficult to formulate the second line of motives which I believe to constitute the trend of the subjective pressure toward the Settlement. There is something primordial about these motives, but I am perhaps over-bold in designating them as a great desire to share the race life. We all bear traces of the starvation struggle which for so long made up the life of the race. Our very organism holds memories and glimpses of that long life of our ancestors which still goes on among so many of our contemporaries. Nothing so deadens the sympathies and shrivels the power of enjoyment as the persistent keeping away from the great opportunities for helpfulness and a continual ignoring of the starvation struggle which makes up the life of at least half the race. To shut one's self away from that half of the race life is to shut one's self away from the most vital part of it; it is to live out but half the humanity which we have been born heir to and to use but half our faculties. We have all had longings for a fuller life which should include the use of these faculties. These longings are the physical complement of the "Intimations of Immortality" on which no ode has yet been written. To portray these would be the work of a poet, and it is hazardous for any but a poet to attempt it.

You may remember the forlorn feeling which occasionally seizes you when you arrive early in the morning a stranger in a great city. The stream of laboring people goes past you as you gaze through the plate-glass window of your hotel. You see hard-working men lifting great burdens; you hear the driving and jostling of huge carts. Your heart sinks with a sudden sense of futility. The door opens behind you and you turn to the man who brings you in your breakfast with a quick sense of human fellowship. You find yourself praying that you may never lose your hold on it at all. A more poetic prayer would be that the great mother breasts of our common humanity, with its labor and suffering and its homely comforts, may never be withheld from you. You turn helplessly to the waiter. You feel that it would be almost grotesque to claim from him the sympathy you crave. Civilization has placed you far apart, but you resent your position with a sudden sense of snobbery. Literature is full of portrayals of these glimpses. They come to shipwrecked men on rafts; they overcome the differences of an incongruous multitude when in the presence of a great danger or when moved by a common enthusiasm. They are not, however, confined to such moments, and if we were in the habit of telling them to each other, the recital would be as long as the tales of children are, when they sit down on the green grass and confide to each other how many times they have remembered that they lived once before. If these tales are the stirring of inherited impressions, just so surely is the other the striving of inherited powers.

"There is nothing after disease, indigence, and a sense of guilt so fatal to health and to life itself as the want of a proper outlet for active faculties." I have seen young girls suffer and grow sensibly lowered in vitality in the first years after they leave school. In our attempt then to give a girl pleasure and freedom from care we succeed, for the most part, in making her pitifully miserable. She finds "life" so different from what she expected it to be. She is besotted with innocent little ambitions, and does not understand this apparent waste of herself, this elaborate preparation, if no work is provided for her. There is a heritage of noble obligation which young people accept and long to perpetuate. The desire for action, the wish to right wrong and alleviate suffering, haunts them daily. Society smiles at it indulgently instead of making it of value to itself.

The wrong to them begins even farther back, when we restrain the first childish desires for "doing good" and tell them that they must wait until they are older and better fitted. We intimate that social obligation begins at a fixed date, forgetting that it begins with birth itself. We treat them as children who, with strong-growing limbs, are allowed to use their legs but not their arms, or whose legs are daily carefully exercised that after awhile their arms may be put to high use. We do this in spite of the protest of the best educators, Locke and Pestalozzi. We are fortunate in the mean time if their unused members do not weaken and disappear. They do sometimes. There are a few girls who, by the time they are "educated," forget their old childish desires to help the world and to play with poor little girls "who haven't playthings." Parents are often inconsistent. They deliberately expose their daughters to knowledge of the distress in the world. They send them to hear missionary addresses on famines in India and China; they accompany them to lectures on the suffering in Siberia; they agitate together over the forgotten region of East London. In addition to this, from babyhood the altruistic tendencies of these daughters are persistently cultivated. They are taught to be self-forgetting and self-sacrificing, to consider the good of the Whole before the good of the Ego. But when all this information and culture show results, when the daughter comes back from college and begins to recognize her social claim to the "submerged tenth," and to evince a disposition to fulfill it, the family claim is strenuously asserted; she is told that she is unjustified, ill-advised in her efforts. If she persists the family too often are injured and unhappy, unless the efforts are called missionary, and the religious zeal of the family carry them over their sense of abuse. When this zeal does not exist the result is perplexing. It is a curious violation of what we would fain believe a fundamental law—that the final return of the Deed is upon the head of the Doer. The deed is that of exclusiveness and caution, but the return instead of falling upon the head of the exclusive and cautious, falls upon a young head full of generous and unselfish plans. The girl loses something vital out of her life which she is entitled to. She is restricted and unhappy; her elders, meanwhile, are unconscious of the situation, and we have all the elements of a tragedy.

We have in America a fast-growing number of cultivated young people who have no recognized outlet for their active faculties. They hear constantly of the great social maladjustment, but no way is provided for them to change it, and their uselessness hangs about them heavily. Huxley declares that the sense of uselessness is the severest shock which the human system can sustain, and that, if persistently sustained, it results in atrophy of function. These young people have had advantages of college, of European travel and economic study, but they are sustaining this shock of inaction. They have pet phrases, and they tell you that the things that make us all alike are stronger than the things that make us different. They say that all men are united by needs and sympathies far more permanent and radical than anything that temporarily divides them and sets them in opposition to each other. If they affect art, they say that the decay in artistic expression is due to the decay in ethics, that art when shut away from the human interests and from the great mass of humanity is self-destructive. They tell their elders with all the bitterness of youth that if they expect success from them in business, or politics, or in whatever lines their ambition for them has run, they must let them consult all of humanity; that they must let them find out what the people want and how they want it. It is only the stronger young people, however, who formulate this. Many of them dissipate their energies in so-called enjoyment. Others, not content with that, go on studying and go back to college for their second degrees, not that they are especially fond of study, but because they want something definite to do, and their powers have been trained in the direction of mental accumulation. Many are buried beneath mere mental accumulation with lowered vitality and discontent. Walter Besant says they have had the vision that Peter had when he saw the great sheet let down from heaven, wherein was neither clean nor unclean. He calls it the sense of humanity. It is not philanthropy nor benevolence. It is a thing fuller and wider than either of these. This young life, so sincere in its emotion and good phrases and yet so undirected, seems to me as pitiful as the other great mass of destitute lives. One is supplementary to the other, and some method of communication can surely be devised. Mr. Barnett, who urged the first Settlement,—Toynbee Hall, in East London,—recognized this need of outlet for the young men of Oxford and Cambridge, and hoped that the Settlement would supply the communication. It is easy to see why the Settlement movement originated in England, where the years of education are more constrained and definite than they are here, where class distinctions are more rigid. The necessity of it was greater there, but we are fast feeling the pressure of the need and meeting the necessity for Settlements in America. Our young people feel nervously the need of putting theory into action, and respond quickly to the Settlement form of activity.

The third division of motives which I believe make toward the Settlement is the result of a certain renaissance going forward in Christianity. The impulse to share the lives of the poor, the desire to make social service, irrespective of propaganda, express the spirit of Christ, is as old as Christianity itself. We have no proof from the records themselves that the early Roman Christians, who strained their simple art to the point of grotesqueness in their eagerness to record a "good news" on the walls of the catacombs, considered this "good news" a religion. Jesus had no set of truths labelled "Religious." On the contrary, his doctrine was that all truth is one, that the appropriation of it is freedom. His teaching had no dogma to mark it off from truth and action in general. He himself called it a revelation—a life. These early Roman Christians received the Gospel message, a command to love all men, with a certain joyous simplicity. The image of the Good Shepherd is blithe and gay beyond the gentlest shepherd of Greek mythology; the heart no longer pants, but rushes to the water brooks. The Christians looked for the continuous revelation, but believed what Jesus said, that this revelation to be held and made manifest must be put into terms of action; that action is the only medium man has for receiving and appropriating truth. "If any man will do His will, he shall know of the doctrine."

That Christianity has to be revealed and embodied in the line of social progress is a corollary to the simple proposition that man's action is found in his social relationships in the way in which he connects with his fellows, that his motives for action are the zeal and affection with which he regards his fellows. By this simple process was created a deep enthusiasm for humanity, which regarded man as at once the organ and object of revelation; and by this process came about that wonderful fellowship, that true democracy of the early Church, that so captivates the imagination. The early Christians were pre-eminently nonresistant. They believed in love as a cosmic force. There was no iconoclasm during the minor peace of the Church. They did not yet denounce, nor tear down temples, nor preach the end of the world. They grew to a mighty number, but it never occurred to them, either in their weakness or their strength, to regard other men for an instant as their foes or as aliens. The spectacle of the Christians loving all men was the most astounding Rome had ever seen. They were eager to sacrifice themselves for the weak, for children and the aged. They identified themselves with slaves and did not avoid the plague. They longed to share the common lot that they might receive the constant revelation. It was a new treasure which the early Christians added to the sum of all treasures, a joy hitherto unknown in the world, the joy of finding the Christ which lieth in each man, but which no man can unfold save in fellowship. A happiness ranging from the heroic to the pastoral enveloped them. They were to possess a revelation as long as life had new meaning to unfold, new action to propose.

I believe that there is a distinct turning among many young men and women toward this simple acceptance of Christ's message. They resent the assumption that Christianity is a set of ideas which belong to the religious consciousness, whatever that may be, that it is a thing to be proclaimed and instituted apart from the social life of the community. They insist that it shall seek a simple and natural expression in the social organism itself. The Settlement movement is only one manifestation of that wider humanitarian movement which throughout Christendom, but pre-eminently in England, is endeavoring to embody itself, not in a sect, but in society itself. Tolstoi has reminded us all very forcibly of Christ's principle of non-resistance. His formulation has been startling and his expression has deviated from the general movement, but there is little doubt that he has many adherents; men and women who are philosophically convinced of the futility of opposition, we believe that evil can be overcome only with good and cannot be opposed. If love is the creative force of the universe, the principle which binds men together, and by their interdependence on each other makes them human, just so surely is anger and the spirit of opposition the destructive principle of the universe, that which tears down, thrusts men apart, and makes them isolated and brutal.

I cannot, of course, speak for other Settlements, but it would, I think, be unfair to Hull House not to emphasize the conviction with which the first residents went there, that it would be a foolish and an unwarrantable expenditure of force to oppose or to antagonize any individual or set of people in the neighborhood; that whatever of good the House had to offer should be put into positive terms; that its residents should live with opposition to no man, with recognition of the good in every man, even the meanest. I believe that this turning, this renaissance of the early Christian humanitarianism, is going on in America, in Chicago, if you please, without leaders who write or philosophize, without much speaking, but with a bent to express in social service, in terms of action, the spirit of Christ. Certain it is that spiritual force is found in the Settlement movement, and it is also true that this force must be evoked and must be called into play before the success of any Settlement is assured. There must be the overmastering belief that all that is noblest in life is common to men as men, in order to accentuate the likenesses and ignore the differences which are found among the people whom the Settlement constantly brings into juxtaposition. It may be true, as Frederic Harrison insists, that the very religious fervor of man can be turned into love for his race and his desire for a future life into content to live in the echo of his deeds. How far the Positivists' formula of the high ardor for humanity can carry the Settlement movement, Mrs. Humphry Ward's house in London may in course of time illustrate. Paul's formula of seeking for the Christ which lieth in each man and founding our likenesses on him seems a simpler formula to many of us.

If you have heard a thousand voices singing in the Hallelujah Chorus in Handel's "Messiah," you have found that the leading voices could still be distinguished, but that the differences of training and cultivation between them and the voices of the chorus were lost in the unity of purpose and the fact that they were all human voices lifted by a high motive. This is a weak illustration of what a Settlement attempts to do. It aims, in a measure, to lead whatever of social life its neighborhood may afford, to focus and give form to that life, to bring to bear upon it the results of cultivation and training; but it receives in exchange for the music of isolated voices the volume and strength of the chorus. It is quite impossible for me to say what proportion or degree the subjective necessity, which led to the opening of Hull House, combined the three trends: first the desire to interpret democracy in social terms; secondly, the impulse beating at the very source of our lives urging us to aid in the race progress; and, thirdly, the Christian movement toward Humanitarianism. It is difficult to analyze a living thing; the analysis is at best imperfect. Many more motives may blend with the three trends; possibly the desire for a new form of social success due to the nicety of imagination, which refuses worldly pleasures unmixed with the joys of self-sacrifice; possibly a love of approbation, so vast that is it not content with the treble clapping of delicate hands, but wishes also to hear the bass notes from toughened palms, may mingle with these.

ELIZABETH CADY STANTON

Elizabeth Cady Stanton (1815–1902) has been called the greatest feminist thinker of the nineteenth century, "equal in intellectual stature," wrote Vivian Gornick, "to the two feminist greats who preceded and followed her: Mary Wollstonecraft and Simone de Beauvoir." In her 1892 speech delivered to the Committee of the Judiciary of the U.S. Congress, "The Solitude of Self," Stanton went far beyond the single issue of women's suffrage to argue existentially that each of us is profoundly alone, and therefore cannot rely on the other sex to protect us. According to Gornick, "the thing that she wanted her audience to consider, she said, was the individuality of a human being: that which Protestant American culture held as a first value. In one sense, the idea of the individual is a declaration of proud independence; in another, it is the recognition that we are, in fact, a world of Robinson Crusoes, each of us alone in the island of life." Stanton's balancing of this paradox—solitude as both a bereft condition and a consolation—constitutes the triumph of her essay.

The Solitude of Self

(1892)

Mr. Chairman and gentlemen of the committee: We have been speaking before Committees of the Judiciary for the last twenty years, and we have gone over all the arguments in favor of a sixteenth amendment which are familiar to all you gentlemen; therefore, it will not be necessary that I should repeat them again.

The point I wish plainly to bring before you on this occasion is the individuality of each human soul; our Protestant idea, the right of individual conscience and judgment—our republican idea, individual citizenship. In discussing the rights of woman, we are to consider, first, what belongs to her as an individual, in a world of her own, the arbiter of her own destiny, an imaginary Robinson Crusoe with her woman Friday on a solitary island. Her rights under such circumstances are to use all her faculties for her own safety and happiness.

Secondly, if we consider her as a citizen, as a member of a great nation, she must have the same rights as all other members, according to the fundamental principles of our Government.

Thirdly, viewed as a woman, an equal factor in civilization, her rights and duties are still the same—individual happiness and development.

Fourthly, it is only the incidental relations of life, such as mother, wife, sister, daughter, that may involve some special duties and training. In the usual discussion in regard to woman's sphere, such men as Herbert Spencer, Frederic Harrison, and Grant Allen uniformly subordinate her rights and duties as an individual, as a citizen, as a woman, to the necessities of these incidental relations, some of which a large class of women may never assume. In discussing the sphere of man we do not decide his rights as an individual, as a citizen, as a man by his duties as a father, a husband, a brother, or a son, relations some of which he may never fill. Moreover he would be better fitted for these very relations and whatever special work he might choose to do to earn his bread by the complete development of all his faculties as an individual.

Just so with woman. The education that will fit her to discharge the duties in the largest sphere of human usefulness will best fit her for whatever special work she may be compelled to do.

The isolation of every human soul and the necessity of self-dependence must give each individual the right to choose his own surroundings.

The strongest reason for giving woman all the opportunities for higher education, for the full development of her faculties, forces of mind and body; for giving her the most enlarged freedom of thought and action; a complete emancipation from all forms of bondage, of custom, dependence, superstition; from all the crippling influences of fear, is the solitude and personal responsibility of her own individual life. The strongest reason why we ask for woman a voice in the government under which she lives; in the religion she is asked to believe; equality in social life, where she is a chief factor; a place in the trades and professions, where she may earn her bread, is because of her birthright to self-sovereignty; because, as an individual, she must rely on herself. No matter how much women prefer to lean, to be protected and supported, nor how much men desire to have them do so, they must make the voyage of life alone, and for safety in an emergency they must know something of the laws of navigation. To guide our own craft, we must be captain, pilot, engineer; with chart and compass to stand at the wheel; to watch the wind and waves and know when to take in the sail, and to read the signs in the firmament over all. It matters not whether the solitary voyager is man or woman.

Nature having endowed them equally, leaves them to the own skill and judgment in the hour of danger, and, if not equal to the occasion, alike they perish.

To appreciate the importance of fitting every human soul for independent action, think for a moment of the immeasurable solitude of self. We come into the world alone, unlike all who have gone before us; we leave it alone under circumstances peculiar to ourselves. No mortal ever has been, no mortal ever will be like the soul just launched on the sea of life. There can never again be just such a combination of prenatal influences; never again just such environments as make up the infancy, youth, and manhood of this one. Nature never repeats herself, and the possibilities of one human soul will never be found in another. No one has ever found two blades of ribbon grass alike, and no one will ever find two human beings alike. Seeing, then, what must be the infinite diversity in human character, we can in a measure appreciate the loss to a nation when any large class of the people is uneducated and unrepresented in the government. We ask for the complete development of every individual, first, for his own benefit and happiness. In fitting out an army we give each soldier his own knapsack, arms, powder, his blanket, cup, knife, fork and spoon. We provide alike for all their individual necessities, then each man bears his own burden.

Again we ask complete individual development for the general good; for the consensus of the competent on the whole round of human interests; on all questions of national life, and here each man must bear his share of the general burden. It is sad to see how soon friendless children are left to bear their own burdens before they can analyze their feelings; before they can even tell their joys and sorrows, they are thrown on their own resources. The great lesson that nature seems to teach us at all ages is self-dependence, self-protection, self-support. What a touching instance of a child's solitude; of that hunger of the heart for love and recognition, in the case of the little girl who helped to dress a Christmas tree for the children of the family in which she served. On finding there was no present for herself she slipped away in the darkness and spent the night in an open field sitting on a stone, and when found in the morning was weeping as if her heart would break. No mortal will ever know the thoughts that passed through the mind of that friendless child in the long hours of that cold night, with only the silent stars to keep her company. The mention of her case in the daily papers moved many generous hearts to send her presents, but in the hours of her keenest suffering she was thrown wholly on herself for consolation.

In youth our most bitter disappointment, our brightest hopes and ambitions are known only to ourselves; even our friendship and love we never fully share with another; there is something of every passion in every situation we conceal. Even so in our triumphs and our defeats.

The successful candidate for the Presidency and his opponent each have a solitude peculiarly his own, and good form forbids either to speak of his pleasure or regret. The solitude of the king on his throne and the prisoner in his cell differs in character and degree, but it is solitude nevertheless.

We ask no sympathy from others in the anxiety and agony of a broken friendship or shattered love. When death sunders our nearest ties, alone we sit in the shadow of our affliction. Alike mid the greatest triumphs and darkest tragedies of life we walk alone. On the divine heights of human attainments, eulogized and worshiped as a hero or saint, we stand alone. In ignorance, poverty, and vice, as a pauper or criminal, alone we starve or steal; alone we suffer the sneers and rebuffs of our fellows; alone we are hunted and hounded through dark courts and alleys, in by-ways and highways; alone we stand in the judgment seat; alone in the prison cell we lament our crimes and misfortunes; alone we expiate them on the gallows. In hours like these we realize the awful solitude of individual life, its pains, its penalties, its responsibilities; hours in which the youngest and most helpless are thrown on their own resources for guidance and consolation. Seeing then that life must ever be a march and a battle, that each soldier must be equipped for his own protection, it is the height of cruelty to rob the individual of a single natural right.

To throw obstacles in the way of a complete education is like putting out the eyes; to deny the rights of property, like cutting off the hands. To deny political equality is to rob the ostracised of all self-respect; of credit in the market place; of recompense in the world of work; of a voice in those who make and administer the law; a choice in the jury before whom they are tried, and in the judge who decides their punishment. Shakespeare's play of Titus and Andronicus contains a terrible satire on woman's position in the nineteenth century—"Rude men" (the play tells us) "seized the king's daughter, cut out her tongue, cut off her hands, and then bade her go call for water and wash her hands." What a picture of woman's position. Robbed of her natural rights, handicapped by law and custom at every turn, yet compelled to fight her own battles, and in the emergencies of life to fall back on herself for protection.

The girl of sixteen, thrown on the world to support herself, to make her own place in society, to resist the temptations that surround her and maintain a spotless integrity, must do all this by native force or superior education. She does not acquire this power by being trained to trust others and distrust herself. If she wearies of the struggle, finding it hard work to swim upstream, and allows herself to drift with the current, she will find plenty of company, but not one to share her misery in the hour of her deepest humiliation. If she tries to retrieve her position, to conceal the past, her life is hedged about with fears lest willing hands should tear the veil from what she fain would hide. Young and friendless, she knows the bitter solitude of self.

How the little courtesies of life on the surface of society, deemed so important from man towards woman, fade into utter insignificance in view of the deeper tragedies in which she must play her part alone, where no human aid is possible.

The young wife and mother, at the head of some establishment with a kind husband to shield her from the adverse winds of life, with wealth, fortune and position, has a certain harbor of safety, secure against the ordinary ills of life. But to manage a household, have a desirable influence in society, keep her friends and the affections of her husband, train her children and servants well, she must have rare common sense, wisdom, diplomacy, and a knowledge of human nature. To do all this she needs the cardinal virtues and the strong points of character that the most successful statesman possesses.

An uneducated woman, trained to dependence, with no resources in herself must make a failure of any position in life. But society says women do not need a knowledge of the world; the liberal training that experience in public life must give, all the advantages of collegiate education; but when for the lack of all this, the woman's happiness is wrecked, alone she bears her humiliation; and the solitude of the weak and the ignorant is indeed pitiable. In the wild chase for the prizes of life they are ground to powder.

In age, when the pleasures of youth are passed, children grown up, married and gone, the hurry and bustle of life in a measure over, when the hands are weary of active service, when the old armchair and the fireside are the chosen resorts, then men and women alike must fall back on their own resources. If they cannot find companionship in books, if they have no interest in the vital questions of the hour, no interest in watching the consummation of reforms, with which they might have been identified, they soon pass into their dotage. The more fully the faculties of the mind are developed and kept in use, the longer the period of vigor and active interest in all around us continues. If from a lifelong participation in public affairs a woman feels responsible for the laws regulating our system of education, the discipline of our jails and prisons, the sanitary condition of our private homes, public buildings, and thoroughfares, an interest in commerce, finance, our foreign relations, in any or all these questions, her solitude will at least be respectable, and she will not be driven to gossip or scandal for entertainment.

The chief reason for opening to every soul the doors to the whole round of human duties and pleasures is the individual development thus attained, the resources thus provided under all circumstances to mitigate the solitude that at times must come to everyone. I once asked Prince Krapotkin, a Russian nihilist, how he endured his long years in prison, deprived of books, pen, ink, and paper. "Ah," he said, "I thought out many questions in which I had a deep interest. In the pursuit of an idea I took no note of time. When tired of solving knotty problems I recited all the beautiful passages in prose or verse I had ever learned. I became acquainted with myself and my own resources. I had a world of my own, a vast empire, that no Russian jailor or Czar could invade." Such is the value of liberal thought and broad culture when shut off from all human companionship, bringing comfort and sunshine within even the four walls of a prison cell.

As women ofttimes share a similar fate, should they not have all the consolation that the most liberal education can give? Their suffering in the prisons of St. Petersburg; in the long, weary marches to Siberia, and in the mines, working side by side with men, surely call for all the self-support that the most exalted sentiments of heroism can give. When suddenly roused at midnight, with the startling cry of "fire! fire!" to find the house over their heads in flames, do women wait for men to point the way to safety? And are the men, equally bewildered and half suffocated with smoke, in a position to do more than try to save themselves?

At such times the most timid women have shown a courage and heroism in saving their husbands and children that has surprised everybody. Inasmuch, then, as woman shares equally the joys and sorrows of time and eternity, is it not the height of presumption in man to propose to represent her at the ballot box and the throne of grace, to do her voting in the state, her praying in the church, and to assume the position of high priest at the family altar?

Nothing strengthens the judgment and quickens the conscience like individual responsibility. Nothing adds such dignity to character as the recognition of one's self-sovereignty; the right to an equal place, everywhere conceded; a place earned by personal merit, not an artificial attainment, by inheritance, wealth, family, and position. Seeing, then, that the responsibilities of life rest equally on man and woman, that their destiny is the same, they need the same preparation for time and eternity. The talk of sheltering woman from the fierce storms of life is the sheerest mockery, for they beat on her from every point of the compass, just as they do on man, and with more fatal results, for he has been trained to protect himself, to resist, to conquer. Such are the facts in human experience, the responsibilities of individual sovereignty. Rich and poor, intelligent and ignorant, wise and foolish, virtuous and vicious, man and woman, it is ever the same, each soul must depend wholly on itself.

Whatever the theories may be of woman's dependence on man, in the supreme moments of her life he can not bear her burdens. Alone she goes to the gates of death to give life to every man that is born into the world.

No one can share her fears, no one can mitigate her pangs; and if her sorrow is greater than she can bear, alone she passes beyond the gates into the vast unknown.

From the mountain tops of Judea, long ago, a heavenly voice bade His disciples, "Bear ye one another's burdens," but humanity has not yet risen to that point of self-sacrifice and if ever so willing, how few the burdens are that one soul can bear for another. In the highways of Palestine; in prayer and fasting on the solitary mountain top; in the Garden of Gethsemane; before the judgment seat of Pilate; betrayed by one of His trusted disciples at His last supper; in His agonies on the cross, even Jesus of Nazareth, in those last sad days on earth, felt the awful solitude of self. Deserted by man, in agony He cries, "My God! My God! Why hast Thou forsaken me?" And so it ever must be in the conflicting scenes of life, in the long, weary march, each one walks alone. We may have many friends, love, kindness, sympathy, and charity to smooth our pathway in everyday life, but in the tragedies and triumphs of human experience each mortal stands alone.

But when all artificial trammels are removed, and women are recognized as individuals, responsible for their own environments, thoroughly educated for all positions in life they may be called to fill; with all the resources in themselves that liberal thought and broad culture can give; guided by their own conscience and judgment; trained to self-protection by a healthy development of the muscular system and skill in the use of weapons of defense, and stimulated to self-support by a knowledge of the business world and the pleasure that pecuniary independence must ever give; when women are trained in this way they will, in a measure, be fitted for those hours of solitude that come alike to all, whether prepared or otherwise. As in our extremity we must depend on ourselves, the dictates of wisdom point to complete individual development.

In talking of education how shallow the argument that each class must be educated for the special work it proposes to do, and all those faculties not needed in this special work must lie dormant and utterly wither for want of use, when, perhaps, these will be the very faculties needed in life's greatest emergencies. Some say, Where is the use of drilling girls in the languages, the sciences, in law, medicine, theology? As wives, mothers, housekeepers, cooks, they need a different curriculum from boys who are to fill all positions. The chief cooks in our great hotels and ocean steamers are men. In our large cities men run the bakeries; they make our bread, cake and pies. They manage the laundries; they are now considered our best milliners and dressmakers. Because some men fill these departments of usefulness, shall we regulate the curriculum in Harvard and Yale to their present necessities? If not, why this talk in our best colleges of a curriculum for girls who are crowding into the trades and professions; teachers in all our public schools, rapidly filling many lucrative and honorable positions in life? They are showing, too, their calmness and courage in the most trying hours of human experience.

You have probably all read in the daily papers of the terrible storm in the Bay of Biscay when a tidal wave made such havoc on the shore, wrecking vessels, unroofing houses, and carrying destruction everywhere. Among other buildings the woman's prison was demolished. Those who escaped saw men struggling to reach the shore. They promptly by clasping hands made a chain of themselves and pushed out into the sea, again and again, at the risk of their lives, until they had brought six men to shore, carried them to a shelter, and did all in their power for their comfort and protection.

What special school training could have prepared these women for this sublime moment in their lives? In times like this humanity rises above all college curriculums and recognizes Nature as the greatest of all teachers in the hour of danger and death. Women are already the equals of men in the whole realm of thought, in art, science, literature, and government. With telescopic vision they explore the starry firmament and bring back the history of the planetary world. With chart and compass they pilot ships across the mighty deep, and with skillful finger send electric messages around the globe. In galleries of art the beauties of nature and the virtues of humanity are immortalized by them on canvas and by their inspired touch dull blocks of marble are transformed into angels of light.

In music they speak again the language of Mendelssohn, Beethoven, Chopin, Schumann, and are worthy interpreters of their great thoughts. The poetry and novels of the century are theirs, and they have touched the keynote of reform in religion, politics, and social life. They fill the editor's and professor's chair, and plead at the bar of justice, walk the wards of the hospital, and speak from the pulpit and the platform; such is the type of womanhood that an enlightened public sentiment welcomes today, and such the triumph of the facts of life over the false theories of the past.

Is it, then, consistent to hold the developed woman of this day within the same narrow political limits as the dame with the spinning wheel and knitting needle occupied in the past? No! no! Machinery has taken the labors of woman as well as man on its tireless shoulders; the loom and the spinning wheel are but dreams of the past; the pen, the brush, the easel, the chisel, have taken their places, while the hopes and ambitions of women are essentially changed.

We see reason sufficient in the outer conditions of human beings for individual liberty and development, but when we consider the self-dependence of every human soul we see the need of courage, judgment, and the exercise of every faculty of mind and body, strengthened and developed by use, in woman as well as man.

Whatever may be said of man's protecting power in ordinary conditions, mid all the terrible disasters by land and sea, in the supreme moments of danger, alone woman must ever meet the horrors of the situation; the Angel of Death even makes no royal pathway for her. Man's love and sympathy enter only into the sunshine of our lives. In that solemn solitude of self, that links us with the immeasurable and the eternal, each soul lives alone forever. A recent writer says:

> I remember once, in crossing the Atlantic, to have gone upon the deck of the ship at midnight, when a dense black cloud enveloped the sky, and the great deep was roaring madly under the lashes of demoniac winds. My feeling was not of danger or fear (which is a base surrender of the immortal soul), but of utter desolation and loneliness; a little speck of life shut in by a tremendous darkness. Again I remember to have climbed the slopes of the Swiss Alps, up beyond the point where vegetation ceases, and the stunted conifers no longer struggle against the unfeeling blasts. Around me lay a huge confusion of rocks, out of which the gigantic ice peaks shot into the measureless blue of the heavens, and again my only feeling was the awful solitude.

And yet, there is a solitude, which each and every one of us has always carried with him more inaccessible than the ice-cold mountains, more profound than the midnight sea; the solitude of self. Our inner being, which we call ourself, no eye nor touch of man or angel has ever pierced. It is more hidden than the caves of the gnome; the sacred adytum of the oracle; the hidden chamber of Eleusinian mystery, for to it only omniscience is permitted to enter.

Such is individual life. Who, I ask you, can take, dare take, on himself the rights, the duties, the responsibilities of another human soul?

JOHN MUIR

John Muir (1838–1914) is considered the father of the American envi-
ronmental movement. Emigrating from Scotland to the United States
in 1849, he brought an enthusiasm for natural history to explorations
of the West, which resulted in his books The Mountains of California,
My First Summer in the Sierra, *and* The Yosemite. *Muir's campaign for*
wildlife conservation ultimately led to the national park system. He is
also recognized as a superb American prose writer. In "A Wind-Storm in
the Forests," we see him orchestrating the various senses into rhythmic
crescendos that mimic the hurricane's progress. Muir's enjoyment of the
storm is singular: not many of us would choose to climb a hundred-foot
tree to be buffeted in a gale and find the view beautiful.

A Wind-Storm in the Forests

(1894)

The mountain winds, like the dew and rain, sunshine and snow, are measured and bestowed with love on the forests to develop their strength and
beauty. However restricted the scope of other forest influences, that of
the winds is universal. The snow bends and trims the upper forests every
winter, the lightning strikes a single tree here and there, while avalanches
mow down thousands at a swoop as a gardener trims out a bed of flowers. But the winds go to every tree, fingering every leaf and branch and
furrowed bole; not one is forgotten; the Mountain Pine towering with
outstretched arms on the rugged buttresses of the icy peaks, the lowliest and most retiring tenant of the dells; they seek and find them all,

caressing them tenderly, bending them in lusty exercise, stimulating their growth, plucking off a leaf or limb as required, or removing an entire tree or grove, now whispering and cooing through the branches like a sleepy child, now roaring like the ocean; the winds blessing the forests, the forests the winds, with ineffable beauty and harmony as the sure result.

After one has seen pines six feet in diameter bending like grasses before a mountain gale, and ever and anon some giant falling with a crash that shakes the hills, it seems astonishing that any, save the lowest thickset trees, could ever have found a period sufficiently stormless to establish themselves; or, once established, that they should not, sooner or later, have been blown down. But when the storm is over, and we behold the same forests tranquil again, towering fresh and unscathed in erect majesty, and consider what centuries of storms have fallen upon them since they were first planted,—hail, to break the tender seedlings; lightning, to scorch and shatter; snow, winds, and avalanches, to crush and overwhelm,—while the manifest result of all this wild storm-culture is the glorious perfection we behold; then faith in Nature's forestry is established, and we cease to deplore the violence of her most destructive gales, or of any other storm-implement whatsoever.

There are two trees in the Sierra forests that are never blown down, so long as they continue in sound health. These are the Juniper and the Dwarf Pine of the summit peaks. Their stiff, crooked roots grip the storm-beaten ledges like eagles' claws, while their lithe, cord-like branches bend round compliantly, offering but slight holds for winds, however violent. The other alpine conifers—the Needle Pine, Mountain Pine, Two-leaved Pine, and Hemlock Spruce—are never thinned out by this agent to any destructive extent, on account of their admirable toughness and the closeness of their growth. In general the same is true of the giants of the lower zones. The kingly Sugar Pine, towering aloft to a height of more than 200 feet, offers a fine mark to storm-winds; but it is not densely foliaged, and its long, horizontal arms swing round compliantly in the blast, like tresses of green, fluent algae in a brook; while the Silver Firs in most places keep their ranks well together in united strength. The Yellow or Silver Pine is more frequently overturned than any other tree on the Sierra, because its leaves and branches form a larger mass in proportion to its height, while in many places it is planted sparsely, leaving open lanes through which storms may enter with full force. Furthermore, because it is distributed along the lower portion of the range, which was the first to be left bare on the breaking up of the ice-sheet at the close of the glacial winter, the soil it is growing upon has been longer exposed to post-glacial weathering, and consequently is in a more crumbling, decayed condition than the fresher soils farther up the range, and therefore offers a less secure anchorage for the roots.

While exploring the forest zones of Mount Shasta, I discovered the path of a hurricane strewn with thousands of pines of this species. Great and small had been uprooted or wrenched off by sheer force, making a clean gap, like that made by a snow avalanche. But hurricanes capable of doing this class of work are rare in the Sierra, and when we have explored the forests from one extremity of the range to the other, we are compelled to believe that they are the most beautiful on the face of the earth, however we may regard the agents that have made them so.

There is always something deeply exciting, not only in the sounds of winds in the woods, which exert more or less influence over every mind, but in their varied water-like flow as manifested by the movements of the trees, especially those of the conifers. By no other trees are they rendered so extensively and impressively visible, not even by the lordly tropic palms or tree-ferns responsive to the gentlest breeze. The waving of a forest of the giant Sequoias is indescribably impressive and sublime, but the pines seem to me the best interpreters of winds. They are mighty waving goldenrods, ever in tune, singing and writing wind-music all their long century lives. Little, however, of this noble tree-waving and tree-music will you see or hear in the strictly alpine portion of the forests. The burly Juniper, whose girth sometimes more than equals its height, is about as rigid as the rocks on which it grows. The slender lash-like sprays of the Dwarf Pine stream out in wavering ripples, but the tallest and slenderest are far too unyielding to wave even in the heaviest gales. They only shake in quick, short vibrations. The Hemlock Spruce, however, and the Mountain Pine, and some of the tallest thickets of the Two-leaved species bow in storms with considerable scope and gracefulness. But it is only in the lower and middle zones that the meeting of winds and woods is to be seen in all its grandeur.

One of the most beautiful and exhilarating storms I ever enjoyed in the Sierra occurred in December, 1874, when I happened to be exploring one of the tributary valleys of the Yuba River. The sky and the ground and the trees had been thoroughly rain-washed and were dry again. The day was intensely pure, one of those incomparable bits of California winter, warm and balmy and full of white sparkling sunshine, redolent of all the purest influences of the spring, and at the same time enlivened with one of the most bracing wind-storms conceivable. Instead of camping out, as I usually do, I then chanced to be stopping at the house of a friend. But when the storm began to sound, I lost no time in pushing out into the woods to enjoy it. For on such occasions Nature has always something rare to show us, and the danger to life and limb is hardly greater than one would experience crouching deprecatingly beneath a roof.

It was still early morning when I found myself fairly adrift. Delicious sunshine came pouring over the hills, lighting the tops of the pines, and setting free a steam of summery fragrance that contrasted strangely with the wild tones of the storm. The air was mottled with pine-tassels and bright green plumes, that went flashing past in the sunlight like birds pursued. But there was not the slightest dustiness, nothing less pure than leaves, and ripe pollen, and flecks of withered bracken and moss. I heard trees falling for hours at the rate of one every two or three minutes; some uprooted, partly on account of the loose, water-soaked condition of the ground; others broken straight across, where some weakness caused by fire had determined the spot. The gestures of the various trees made a delightful study. Young Sugar Pines, light and feathery as squirrel-tails, were bowing almost to the ground; while the grand old patriarchs, whose massive boles had been tried in a hundred storms, waved solemnly above them, their long, arching branches streaming fluently on the gale, and every needle thrilling and ringing and shedding off keen lances of light like a diamond. The Douglas Spruces, with long sprays drawn out in level tresses, and needles massed in a gray, shimmering glow, presented a most striking appearance as they stood in bold relief along the hilltops. The madroños in the dells, with their red bark and large glossy leaves tilted every way, reflected the sunshine in throbbing spangles like those one so often sees on the rippled surface of a glacier lake. But the Silver Pines were now the most impressively beautiful of all. Colossal spires 200 feet in height waved like supple goldenrods chanting and bowing low as if in worship, while the whole mass of their long, tremulous foliage was kindled into one continuous blaze of white sun-fire. The force of the gale was such that the most steadfast monarch of them all rocked down to its roots with a motion plainly perceptible when one leaned against it. Nature was holding high festival, and every fiber of the most rigid giants thrilled with glad excitement.

I drifted on through the midst of this passionate music and motion, across many a glen, from ridge to ridge; often halting in the lee of a rock for shelter, or to gaze and listen. Even when the grand anthem had swelled to its highest pitch, I could distinctly hear the varying tones of individual trees,—Spruce, and Fir, and Pine, and leafless Oak,—and even the infinitely gentle rustle of the withered grasses at my feet. Each was expressing itself in its own way,—singing its own song, and making its own peculiar gestures,—manifesting a richness of variety to be found in no other forest I have yet seen. The coniferous woods of Canada, and the Carolinas, and Florida, are made up of trees that resemble one another about as nearly as blades of grass, and grow close together in much the same way. Coniferous trees, in general, seldom possess individual character, such as is manifest among Oaks and Elms. But the California forests are made up of a greater number of distinct species than any other in the world. And in them we find, not only a marked differentiation into special groups, but also a marked individuality in almost every tree, giving rise to storm effects indescribably glorious.

Toward midday, after a long, tingling scramble through copses of hazel

and ceanothus, I gained the summit of the highest ridge in the neighborhood; and then it occurred to me that it would be a fine thing to climb one
of the trees to obtain a wider outlook and get my ear close to the Aeolian
music of its topmost needles. But under the circumstances the choice of a
tree was a serious matter. One whose instep was not very strong seemed
in danger of being blown down, or of being struck by others in case they
should fall; another was branchless to a considerable height above the
ground, and at the same time too large to be grasped with arms and legs
in climbing; while others were not favorably situated for clear views. After
cautiously casting about, I made choice of the tallest of a group of Douglas Spruces that were growing close together like a tuft of grass, no one
of which seemed likely to fall unless all the rest fell with it. Though comparatively young, they were about 100 feet high, and their lithe, brushy
tops were rocking and swirling in wild ecstasy. Being accustomed to climb
trees in making botanical studies, I experienced no difficulty in reaching
the top of this one, and never before did I enjoy so noble an exhilaration
of motion. The slender tops fairly flapped and swished in the passionate
torrent, bending and swirling backward and forward, round and round,
tracing indescribable combinations of vertical and horizontal curves,
while I clung with muscles firm braced, like a bobolink on a reed.

In its widest sweeps my tree-top described an arc of from twenty to
thirty degrees, but I felt sure of its elastic temper, having seen others of
the same species still more severely tried—bent almost to the ground
indeed, in heavy snows—without breaking a fiber. I was therefore safe,
and free to take the wind into my pulses and enjoy the excited forest from
my superb outlook. The view from here must be extremely beautiful in
any weather. Now my eye roved over the piny hills and dales as over fields
of waving grain, and felt the light running in ripples and broad swelling
undulations across the valleys from ridge to ridge, as the shining foliage was stirred by corresponding waves of air. Oftentimes these waves
of reflected light would break up suddenly into a kind of beaten foam,
and again, after chasing one another in regular order, they would seem to
bend forward in concentric curves, and disappear on some hillside, like
sea-waves on a shelving shore. The quantity of light reflected from the
bent needles was so great as to make whole groves appear as if covered
with snow, while the black shadows beneath the trees greatly enhanced
the effect of the silvery splendor.

Excepting only the shadows there was nothing somber in all this wild
sea of pines. On the contrary, notwithstanding this was the winter season,
the colors were remarkably beautiful. The shafts of the pine and libo-
cedrus were brown and purple, and most of the foliage was well tinged
with yellow; the laurel groves, with the pale undersides of their leaves
turned upward, made masses of gray; and then there was many a dash of
chocolate color from clumps of manzanita, and jet of vivid crimson from

the bark of the madroños, while the ground on the hillsides, appearing here and there through openings between the groves, displayed masses of pale purple and brown.

The sounds of the storm corresponded gloriously with this wild exuberance of light and motion. The profound bass of the naked branches and boles booming like waterfalls; the quick, tense vibrations of the pine-needles, now rising to a shrill, whistling hiss, now falling to a silky murmur; the rustling of laurel groves in the dells, and the keen metallic click of leaf on leaf—all this was heard in easy analysis when the attention was calmly bent.

The varied gestures of the multitude were seen to fine advantage, so that one could recognize the different species at a distance of several miles by this means alone, as well as by their forms and colors, and the way they reflected the light. All seemed strong and comfortable, as if really enjoying the storm, while responding to its most enthusiastic greetings. We hear much nowadays concerning the universal struggle for existence, but no struggle in the common meaning of the word was manifest here; no recognition of danger by any tree; no deprecation; but rather an invincible gladness as remote from exultation as from fear.

I kept my lofty perch for hours, frequently closing my eyes to enjoy the music by itself, or to feast quietly on the delicious fragrance that was streaming past. The fragrance of the woods was less marked than that produced during warm rain, when so many balsamic buds and leaves are steeped like tea; but, from the chafing of resiny branches against each other, and the incessant attrition of myriads of needles, the gale was spiced to a very tonic degree. And besides the fragrance from these local sources there were traces of scents brought from afar. For this wind came first from the sea, rubbing against its fresh, briny waves, then distilled through the redwoods, threading rich ferny gulches, and spreading itself in broad undulating currents over many a flower-enameled ridge of the coast mountains, then across the golden plains, up the purple foot-hills, and into these piny woods with the varied incense gathered by the way.

Winds are advertisements of all they touch, however much or little we may be able to read them; telling their wanderings even by their scents alone. Mariners detect the flowery perfume of land-winds far at sea, and sea-winds carry the fragrance of dulse and tangle far inland, where it is quickly recognized, though mingled with the scents of a thousand land-flowers. As an illustration of this, I may tell here that I breathed sea-air on the Firth of Forth, in Scotland, while a boy; then was taken to Wisconsin, where I remained nineteen years; then, without in all this time having breathed one breath of the sea, I walked quietly, alone, from the middle of the Mississippi Valley to the Gulf of Mexico, on a botanical excursion, and while in Florida, far from the coast, my attention wholly bent on the splendid tropical vegetation about me, I suddenly recognized a sea-breeze, as it came sifting through the palmettos and blooming vine-tangles, which at once awakened and set free a thousand dormant associations, and made me a boy again in Scotland, as if all the intervening years had been annihilated.

Most people like to look at mountain rivers, and bear them in mind; but few care to look at the winds, though far more beautiful and sublime, and though they become at times about as visible as flowing water. When the north winds in winter are making upward sweeps over the curving summits of the High Sierra, the fact is sometimes published with flying snow-banners a mile long. Those portions of the winds thus embodied can scarce be wholly invisible, even to the darkest imagination. And when we look around over an agitated forest, we may see something of the wind that stirs it, by its effects upon the trees. Yonder it descends in a rush of water-like ripples, and sweeps over the bending pines from hill to hill. Nearer, we see detached plumes and leaves, now speeding by on level currents, now whirling in eddies, or, escaping over the edges of the whirls, soaring aloft on grand, upswelling domes of air, or tossing on flame-like crests. Smooth, deep currents, cascades, falls, and swirling eddies, sing around every tree and leaf, and over all the varied topography of the region with telling changes of form, like mountain rivers conforming to the features of their channels.

After tracing the Sierra streams from their fountains to the plains, marking where they bloom white in falls, glide in crystal plumes, surge gray and foam-filled in boulder-choked gorges, and slip through the woods in long, tranquil reaches—after thus learning their language and forms in detail, we may at length hear them chanting all together in one grand anthem, and comprehend them all in clear inner vision, covering the range like lace. But even this spectacle is far less sublime and not a whit more substantial than what we may behold of these storm-streams of air in the mountain woods.

We all travel the milky way together, trees and men; but it never occurred to me until this storm-day, while swinging in the wind, that trees are travelers, in the ordinary sense. They make many journeys, not extensive ones, it is true; but our own little journeys, away and back again, are only little more than tree-wavings—many of them not so much.

When the storm began to abate, I dismounted and sauntered down through the calming woods. The storm-tones died away, and, turning toward the east, I beheld the countless hosts of the forests hushed and tranquil, towering above one another on the slopes of the hills like a devout audience. The setting sun filled them with amber light, and seemed to say, while they listened, "My peace I give unto you."

As I gazed on the impressive scene, all the so-called ruin of the storm was forgotten, and never before did these noble woods appear so fresh, so joyous, so immortal.

STEPHEN CRANE

Before becoming celebrated as a leader of the American realist school for his novels Maggie: A Girl of the Streets *and* The Red Badge of Courage, *Stephen Crane (1871–1900) made his living as a journalist; he explored New York's lower depths and traveled through the Southwest and Mexico, filing travel pieces as he went. In "The Mexican Lower Classes" he provocatively questions the value of travel writing itself: "It perhaps might be said—if any one dared—that the most worthless literature of the world has been that which has been written by the men of one nation concerning the men of another." Paid to write just such literature, he seems to be biting the hand that feeds him; but this very self-consciousness, inviting readers to doubt whatever conclusions he then puts forth, lifts the text from a typical travel puff piece to a stimulating essay.*

The Mexican Lower Classes

(1895)

Above all things, the stranger finds the occupations of foreign peoples to be trivial and inconsequent. The average mind utterly fails to comprehend the new point of view and that such and such a man should be satisfied to carry bundles or mayhap sit and ponder in the sun all his life in this far-away country seems an abnormally stupid thing. The visitor feels scorn. He swells with a knowledge of his geographical experience. "How futile are the lives of these people," he remarks, "and what incredible ignorance that they should not be aware of their futility." This is the arrogance of the man who has not yet solved himself and discovered his own actual futility.

Yet, indeed, it requires wisdom to see a brown woman in one garment crouched listlessly in the door of a low adobe hut while a naked brown baby sprawls on his stomach in the dust of the roadway—it requires wisdom to see this thing and to see it a million times and yet to say: "Yes, this is important to the scheme of nature. This is part of her economy. It would not be well if it had never been."

It perhaps might be said—if any one dared—that the most worthless literature of the world has been that which has been written by the men of one nation concerning the men of another.

It seems that a man must not devote himself for a time to attempts at psychological perception. He can be sure of two things, form and color. Let him then see all he can but let him not sit in literary judgment on this or that manner of the people. Instinctively he will feel that there are similarities but he will encounter many little gestures, tones, tranquilities, rages, for which his blood, adjusted to another temperature, can possess no interpreting power. The strangers will be indifferent where he expected passion; they will be passionate where he expected calm. These subtle variations will fill him with contempt.

At first it seemed to me the most extraordinary thing that the lower classes of Indians in this country should insist upon existence at all. Their squalor, their ignorance seemed so absolute that death—no matter what it has in store—would appear as freedom, joy.

The people of the slums of our own cities fill a man with awe. That vast army with its countless faces immovably cynical, that vast army that silently confronts eternal defeat, it makes one afraid. One listens for the first thunder of the rebellion, the moment when this silence shall be broken by a roar of war. Meanwhile one fears this class, their numbers, their wickedness, their might—even their laughter. There is a vast national respect for them. They have it in their power to become terrible. And their silence suggests everything.

They are becoming more and more capable of defining their condition and this increase of knowledge evinces itself in the deepening of those savage and scornful lines which extend from near the nostrils to the corners of the mouth. It is very distressing to observe this growing appreciation of the situation.

I am not venturing to say that this appreciation does not exist in the lower classes of Mexico. No, I am merely going to say that I cannot perceive any evidence of it. I take this last position in order to preserve certain handsome theories which I advanced in the fore part of the article.

It is so human to be envious that of course even these Indians have envied everything from the stars of the sky to the birds, but you cannot ascertain that they feel at all the modern desperate rage at the accident of birth. Of course the Indian can imagine himself a king but he does not apparently feel that there is an injustice in the fact that he was not born a king any more than there is in his not being born a giraffe.

As far as I can perceive him, he is singularly meek and submissive. He has not enough information to be unhappy over his state. Nobody seeks to provide him with it. He is born, he works, he worships, he dies, all on less money than would buy a thoroughbred Newfoundland dog and who dares to enlighten him? Who dares cry out to him that there are plums, plums, plums in the world which belong to him? For my part, I think the apostle would take a formidable responsibility. I would remember that there really was no comfort in the plums after all as far as I had seen them and I would esteem no orations concerning the glitter of plums.

A man is at liberty to be virtuous in almost any position of life. The virtue of the rich is not so superior to the virtue of the poor that we can say that the rich have a great advantage. These Indians are by far the most poverty-stricken class with which I have met but they are not morally the lowest by any means. Indeed, as far as the mere form of religion goes, they are one of the highest. They are exceedingly devout, worshipping with a blind faith that counts a great deal among the theorists.

But according to my view this is not the measure of them. I measure their morality by what evidences of peace and contentment I can detect in the average countenance.

If a man is not given a fair opportunity to be virtuous, if his environment chokes his moral aspirations, I say that he has got the one important cause of complaint and rebellion against society. Of course it is always possible to be a martyr but then we do not wish to be martyrs. Martyrdom offers no inducements to the average mind. We prefer to be treated with justice and then martyrdom is not required. I never could appreciate those grey old gentlemen of history. Why did not they run? I would have run like mad and still respected myself and my religion.

I have said then that a man has the right to rebel if he is not given a fair opportunity to be virtuous. Inversely then, if he possesses this fair opportunity, he cannot rebel, he has no complaint. I am of the opinion that poverty of itself is no cause. It is something above and beyond. For example, there is Collis P. Huntington and William D. Rockefeller—as virtuous as these gentlemen are, I would not say that their virtue is any ways superior to mine for instance. Their opportunities are no greater. They can give more, deny themselves more in quantity but not relatively. We can each give all that we possess and there I am at once their equal.

I do not think however that they would be capable of sacrifices that would be possible to me. So then I envy them nothing. Far from having a grievance against them, I feel that they will confront an ultimate crisis that I, through my opportunities, may altogether avoid. There is in fact no advantage of importance which I can perceive them possessing over me.

It is for these reasons that I refuse to commit judgment upon these lower classes of Mexico. I even refuse to pity them. It is true that at night many of them sleep in heaps in door-ways, and spend their days squatting upon the pavements. It is true that their clothing is scant and thin. All manner of things of this kind is true but yet their faces have almost always a certain smoothness, a certain lack of pain, a serene faith. I can feel the superiority of their contentment.

WILLIAM DEAN HOWELLS

*As a major novelist of the realist school (*A Hazard of New Fortunes, The
Rise of Silas Lapham*), editor of* The Atlantic Monthly, *and influential
literary critic (through his "Easy Chair" column for* Harper's Magazine*),
William Dean Howells (1837–1920) was so highly esteemed that when he
moved from Boston to New York, he was said to have tilted the whole
national literary scene. Engaging and receptive, perhaps the only man
alive who could have stayed friends with both Mark Twain and Henry
James, as a critic he championed the work of authors as diverse as the
black poet Paul Laurence Dunbar and the Jewish writer Abraham Cahan.
In this lovely, too little known memoir-essay, "The Country Printer," he
was speaking in effect for all the midwestern autodidact artisans and
hopeful literati laboring to improve their minds far from the East Coast
publishing centers.*

The Country Printer

(1896)

My earliest memories, or those which I can make sure are not the sort
of early hearsay that we mistake for remembrance later in life, concern a
country newspaper, or, rather, a country printing-office. The office was in
my childish consciousness some years before the paper was; the compositors rhythmically swaying before their cases of type; the pressman flinging
himself back on the bar that made the impression, with a swirl of his long
hair; the apprentice rolling the forms, and the foreman bending over the
imposing-stone were familiar to me when I could not grasp the notion

of any effect from their labors. In due time I came to know all about it, and to understand that these activities went to the making of the Whig newspaper which my father edited to the confusion of the Locofocos, and in the especial interest of Henry Clay; I myself supported this leader so vigorously for the presidency in my seventh year that it was long before I could realize that the election of 1844 had resulted in his defeat. My father had already been a printer for a good many years, and sometime in the early thirties he had led a literary forlorn-hope, in a West-Virginian town, with a monthly magazine, which he printed himself and edited with the help of his sister.

As long as he remained in business he remained a country editor and a country printer; he began to study medicine when he was a young man, but he abandoned it for the calling of his life without regret, and, though with his speculative and inventive temperament he was tempted to experiment in other things, I do not think he would ever have lastingly forsaken his newspaper for them. In fact, the art of printing was in our blood; it never brought us great honor or profit; and we were always planning and dreaming to get out of it, or get it out of us; but we are all in some sort bound up with it still. To me it is now so endeared by the associations of childhood that I cannot breathe the familiar odor of types and presses without emotion; and I should not be surprised if I found myself trying to cast a halo of romance about the old-fashioned country office in what I shall have to say of it here.

I

Our first newspaper was published in southwestern Ohio, but after a series of varying fortunes, which I need not dwell upon, we found ourselves in possession of an office in the northeastern corner of the state, where the prevalent political feeling promised a prosperity to one of my father's antislavery opinions which he had never yet enjoyed. He had no money, but in those days it was an easy matter to get an interest in a country paper on credit, and we all went gladly to work to help him pay for the share that he acquired in one by this means. An office which gave a fair enough living, as living was then, could be bought for twelve or fifteen hundred dollars; but this was an uncommonly good office, and I suppose the half of it which my father took was worth one sum or the other. Afterward, within a few months, when it was arranged to remove the paper from the village where it had always been published to the county-seat, a sort of joint-stock company was formed, and the value of his moiety increased so much, nominally at least, that he was nearly ten years paying for it. By this time I was long out of the story, but at the beginning I was very vividly in it, and before the world began to call me with that voice which the heart of youth cannot resist, it was very interesting; I felt its charm then, and now, as I turn back to it, I feel its charm again, though it was always a story of steady work, if not hard work.

The county-seat, where it had been judged best to transfer the paper lest some other paper of like politics should be established there, was a village of only six or seven hundred inhabitants. But, as the United States senator who was one of its citizens used to say, it was "a place of great political privileges." The dauntless man who represented the district in the House for twenty years, and who had fought the antislavery battle from the first, was his fellow-villager and more than compeer in distinction; and, besides these, there was nearly always a state senator or representative among us. The county officers, of course, lived at the county-seat, and the leading lawyers, who were the leading politicians, made their homes in the shadow of the court-house, where one of them was presently elected to preside as judge of the common pleas. In politics, the county was always overwhelmingly Freesoil, as the forerunner of the Republican party was then called; the Whigs had hardly gathered themselves together since the defeat of General Scott for the presidency; the Democrats, though dominant in state and nation, and faithful to slavery at every election, did not greatly outnumber among us the zealots called Comeouters, who would not vote at all under a Constitution recognizing the right of men to own men. Our paper was Freesoil, and its field was large among that vast majority of the people who believed that slavery would finally perish if kept out of the territories and confined to the old Slave States. With the removal of the press to the county-seat there was a hope that this field could be widened till every Freesoil voter became a subscriber. It did not fall out so; even of those who subscribed in the ardor of their political sympathies, many never paid; but our list was nevertheless handsomely increased, and numbered fifteen or sixteen hundred. I do not know how it may be now, but then most country papers had a list of four or five hundred subscribers; a few had a thousand, a very few twelve hundred, and these were fairly decimated by delinquents. We were so flown with hope that I remember there was serious talk of risking the loss of the delinquents on our list by exacting payment in advance; but the measure was thought too bold, and we compromised by demanding two dollars a year for the paper, and taking a dollar and a half if paid in advance. Twenty-five years later my brother, who had followed my father in the business, discovered that a man who never meant to pay for his paper would as lief owe two dollars as any less sum, and he at last risked the loss of the delinquents by requiring advance payment; it was an heroic venture, but it was perhaps time to make it.

The people of the county were mostly farmers, and of these nearly all were dairymen. The few manufactures were on a small scale, except perhaps the making of oars, which were shipped all over the world from the heart of the primeval forests densely wooding the vast levels of the region. The portable steam-sawmills dropped down on the borders of the woods have long since eaten their way through and through them, and devoured every stick of timber in most places, and drunk up the water-courses that the woods once kept full; but at that time half the land was in the shadow of those mighty poplars and hickories, elms and chestnuts, ashes and hemlocks; and the meadows that pastured the herds of red cattle were dotted with stumps as thick as harvest stubble. Now there are not even stumps; the woods are gone, and the water-courses are torrents in spring and beds of dry clay in summer. The meadows themselves have vanished, for it has been found that the strong yellow soil will produce more in grain than in milk. There is more money in the hands of the farmers there, though there is still so little that by any city scale it would seem comically little, pathetically little; but forty years ago there was so much less that fifty dollars seldom passed through a farmer's hands in a year. Payment was made in kind rather than in coin, and every sort of farm produce was legal tender at the printing-office. Wood was welcome in any quantity, for the huge box-stove consumed it with inappeasable voracity, and then did not heat the wide, low room which was at once editorial-room, composing-room, and press-room. Perhaps this was not so much the fault of the stove as of the building. In that cold, lake-shore country the people dwelt in wooden structures almost as thin and flimsy as tents; and often in the first winter of our sojourn the type froze solid with the water which the compositor put on it when he wished to distrib-ute his case; the inking-rollers had to be thawed before they could be used on the press; and, if the current of the editor's soul had not been the most genial that ever flowed in this rough world, it must have been congealed at its source. The cases of type had to be placed very near the windows so as to get all the light there was, and they got all the cold there was, too. From time to time the compositor's fingers became so stiff that blowing on them would not avail; he passed the time in excursions between his stand and the stove; in very cold weather he practised the device of warm-ing his whole case of types by the fire, and, when it lost heat, warming it again. The man at the press-wheel was then the enviable man; those who handled the chill, damp sheets of paper were no more fortunate than the compositors.

II

The first floor of our office-building was used by a sash-and-blind fac-tory; there was a machine-shop somewhere in it, and a mill for sawing out shingles; and it was better fitted to the exercise of these robust industries than to the requirements of our more delicate craft. Later, we had a more comfortable place, in a new wooden "business block," and for several years before I left it the office was domiciled in an old dwelling-house, which we bought, and which we used without much change. It could never have been a very luxurious dwelling, and my associations with it are of a wintry cold, scarcely less polar than that we were inured to elsewhere. In fact, the climate of that region is rough and fierce; and the lake winds have a malice sharper than the saltest gales of the North Shore of Massachusetts. I know that there were lovely summers and lovelier autumns in my time there, full of sunsets of a strange, wild, melancholy splendor, I suppose from some atmospheric influence of the lake; but I think chiefly of the winters, so awful to us after the mild seasons of southern Ohio; the frosts of ten and twenty below; the village streets and the country roads drowned in snow, the consumptives in the thin houses, and the "slippin'," as the sleighing was called, that lasted from December to April with hardly a break. At first our family was housed on a farm a little way out, because there was no tenement to be had in the village, and my father and I used to walk to and from the office together in the morning and evening. I had taught myself to read Spanish, in my passion for *Don Quixote,* and I was then, at the age of fifteen, preparing to write a life of Cervantes. This scheme occupied me a good deal in those bleak walks, and perhaps it was because my head was so hot with it that my feet were always very cold; but my father assured me that they would get warm as soon as my boots froze. If I have never yet written that life of Cervantes, on the other hand I have never been quite able to make it clear to myself why my feet should have got warm when my boots froze.

III

It may have been only a theory of his; it may have been a joke. He had a great many theories and a great many jokes, and together these always kept life interesting and sunshiny to him. With his serene temperament and his happy doubt of disaster in any form, he was singularly well fitted to encounter the hardships of a country editor's lot. But for the moment, and for what now seems a long time after the removal of our paper to the county-seat, these seem to have vanished. The printing-office was the centre of civic and social interest; it was frequented by visitors at all times, and on publication day it was a scene of gayety that looks a little incredible in the retrospect. The place was as bare and rude as a printing-office seems always to be: the walls were splotched with ink and the floor littered with refuse newspapers; but lured by the novelty of the affair, and perhaps attracted by a natural curiosity to see what manner of strange men the printers were, the school-girls and young ladies of the village flocked in and made it like a scene of comic opera, with their pretty dresses and faces, their eager chatter and lively energy in folding the papers and addressing them to the subscribers, while our fellow-citizens of the place, like the bassos and barytones and tenors of the chorus, stood about and looked on with faintly sarcastic faces. It would not do to think now of what sorrow life and death have since wrought for all those happy young creatures, but I may recall without too much pathos the sensation when some citizen volunteer relaxed from his gravity far enough to relieve the regular mercenary at the crank of our huge power-press wheel, amid the applause of the whole company.

We were very vain of that press, which replaced the hand-press hitherto employed in printing the paper. This was of the style and make of the hand-press which superseded the Ramage press of Franklin's time; but it had been decided to signalize our new departure by the purchase of a power-press of modern contrivance and of a speed fitted to meet the demands of a subscription-list which might be indefinitely extended. A deputation of the leading politicians accompanied the editor to New York, where he went to choose the machine, and where he bought a second-hand Adams press of the earliest pattern and patent. I do not know, or at this date I would not undertake to say, just what principle governed his selection of this superannuated veteran; it seems not to have been very cheap; but possibly he had a prescience of the disabilities which were to task his ingenuity to the very last days of that press. Certainly no man of less gift and skill could have coped with its infirmities, and I am sure that he thoroughly enjoyed nursing it into such activity as carried it hysterically through those far-off publication days. It had obscure functional disorders of various kinds, so that it would from time to time cease to act, and would have to be doctored by the hour before it would go on. There was probably some organic trouble, too, for, though it did not really fall to pieces on our hands, it showed itself incapable of profiting by several improvements which he invented, and could, no doubt, have successfully applied to the press if its constitution had not been undermined. It went with a crank set in a prodigious fly-wheel which revolved at a great rate, till it came to the moment of making the impression, when the whole mechanism was seized with such a reluctance as nothing but an heroic effort at the crank could overcome. It finally made so great a draught upon our forces that it was decided to substitute steam for muscle in its operation, and we got a small engine which could fully sympathize with the press in having seen better days. I do not know that there was anything the matter with the engine itself, but the boiler had some peculiarities which might well mystify the casual spectator. He could easily have satisfied himself that there was no danger of its blowing up when he saw my brother feeding bran or corn-meal into its safety-valve in order to fill up certain seams or fissures in it which caused it to give out at the moments of the greatest reluctance in the press. But still he must have had his misgivings of latent danger of some other kind, though nothing ever actually happened of a hurtful character. To this day I do not know just where those seams or fissures were, but I think they were in the boiler-head, and that it was therefore suffering from a kind of chronic fracture of the skull. What is certain is that, somehow, the engine and the press did always get us through publication day, and not only with safety, but often with credit; so that not long ago, when I was at home, and my brother and I were looking over an old file of his paper, we found it much better printed than either of us expected; as well printed, in fact, as if it had been done on an old hand-press, instead of the steam power-press which it vaunted the use of. The wonder was that, under all the disadvantages, the paper was ever printed on our steam power-press at all; it was little short of miraculous that it was legibly printed, and altogether unaccountable that such impressions as we found in that file could come from it. Of course, they were not average impressions; they were the very best out of the whole edition, and were as creditable as the editorial make-up of the sheet.

IV

On the first page was a poem, which I suppose I must have selected, and then a story, filling all the rest of the page, which my brother more probably chose; for he had a decided fancy in fiction, and had a scrap-book of inexhaustible riches, which he could draw upon indefinitely for old personal or family favorites. The next page was filled with selections of various kinds, and with original matter interesting to farmers. Then came a page of advertisements, and then the editorial page, where my father had given his opinions of the political questions which interested him, and which he thought it the duty of the country press to discuss, with sometimes essays in the field of religion and morals. There was a letter of two columns from Washington, contributed every week by the congress-man who represented our district; and there was a letter from New York, written by a young lady of the county who was studying art under a master of portraiture then flourishing in the metropolis if that is not stating it too largely for the renown of Thomas Hicks, as we see it in a vanishing perspective. The rest of this page, as well as the greater part of the next, was filled with general news clipped from the daily papers and partly condensed from them. There was also such local intelligence as offered itself, and communications on the affairs of village and county; but the editor did not welcome tidings of new barns and abnormal vegetation, or flatter hens to lay eggs of unusual size or with unusual frequency by undue public notice. All that order of minute neighborhood gossip which now makes the country paper a sort of open letter was then unknown. He published marriages and deaths, and such obituary notices as the sorrowing fondness of friends prompted them to send him; and he introduced the custom of publishing births, after the English fashion, which the people took to kindly.

We had an ambition, even so remotely as that day, in the direction of the illustration which has since so flourished in the newspapers. Till then we had never gone further in the art than to print a jubilant raccoon over the news of some Whig victory, or, what was to the same purpose, an inverted cockerel in mockery of the beaten Democrats; but now we rose to the notion of illustrated journalism. We published a story with a woodcut in it, and we watched to see how that cut came out all through the edition with a pride that was perhaps too exhaustive; at any rate, we never tried another.

Of course, much of the political writing in the paper was controversial, and was carried on with editors of other opinions elsewhere in the county, for we had no rival in our own village. In this, which has always been the vice of American journalism, the country press was then fully as provincial as the great metropolitan journals are now. These may be more pitilessly personal in the conduct of their political discussions, and a little more skilled in obloquy and insult; but the bickering went on in the country papers quite as idly and foolishly. I fancy nobody really cared for our quarrels, and that those who followed them were disgusted when they were more than merely wearied.

The space given to them might better have been given even to original poetry. This was sometimes accepted, but was not invited; though our sixth page commonly began with verse of some kind. Then came more prose selections, but never at any time accounts of murder or violent crimes, which the editor abominated in themselves and believed thoroughly corrupting. Advertisements of various kinds filled out the sheet, which was simple and quiet in typography, wholly without the hand-bill display which now renders nearly all newspapers repulsive to the eye. I am rather proud, in my quality of printer, that this was the style which I established; and we maintained it against all advertisers, who then as now wished to outshriek one another in large type and ugly woodcuts.

It was by no means easy to hold a firm hand with the "live business men" of our village and county, who came out twice a year with the spring and fall announcements of their fresh stocks of goods, which they had personally visited New York to lay in; but one of the moral advantages of an enterprise so modest as ours was that the counting-room and the editorial-room were united under the same head, and this head was the editor's. After all, I think we lost nothing by the bold stand we made in behalf of good taste, and, at any rate, we risked it when we had not the courage to cut off our delinquent subscribers.

We had business advertising from all the villages in the county, for the paper had a large circle of readers in each, and a certain authority, in virtue of representing the county-seat. But a great deal of our advertising was of patent medicines, as the advertising still is in the country papers. It was very profitable, and so was the legal advertising, when we could get the money for it. The money had to come by order of court, and about half the time the order of court failed to include the costs of advertising. Then we did not get it, and we never got it, though we were always glad to get the legal advertising on the chance of getting the pay. It was not official, but was made up of the lawyers' notices to defendants of the suits brought against them. If it had all been paid for, I am not sure that we should now be in a position to complain of the ingratitude of the working-classes, or prepared to discuss, from a vantage of personal experience, the duty of vast wealth to the community; but still we should have been better off for that money, as well as the money we lost by a large and loyal list of delinquent subscribers. From time to time there were stirring appeals to these adherents in the editorial columns, which did not stir them, and again the most flattering offers to take any kind of produce in payment of subscription. Sometimes my brother boldly tracked the delinquents to their lairs. In most cases I fancy they escaped whatever arts he used to take them; many died peacefully in their beds afterward, and their debts follow them to this day. Still, he must now and then have got money from them, and I am sure he did get different kinds of "trade." Once, I remember, he brought back in the tail of his wagon a young pig, a pig so very young that my father pronounced it "merely an organization." Whether it had been wrought to frenzy or not by the strange experiences of its journey I cannot say, but as soon as it was set down on the ground it began to run madly, and it kept on running till it fell down and perished miserably. It had been taken for a year's subscription, and it was quite as if we had lost a delinquent subscriber.

V

Upon the whole, our paper was an attempt at conscientious and self-respecting journalism; it addressed itself seriously to the minds of its readers; it sought to form their tastes and opinions. I do not know how much it influenced them, if it influenced them at all, and as to any effect beyond the circle of its subscribers, that cannot be imagined, even in a fond retrospect. But since no good effort is altogether lost, I am sure that this endeavor must have had some tacit effect; and I am sure that no one got harm from a sincerity of conviction that devoted itself to the highest interest of the reader, that appealed to nothing base, and flattered nothing foolish in him. It went from our home to the homes of the people in a very literal sense, for my father usually brought his exchanges from the office at the end of his day there, and made his selections or wrote his editorials while the household work went on around him, and his children gathered about the same lamp, with their books or their jokes; there were apt to be a good many of both.

Our county was the most characteristic of that remarkable group of counties in northern Ohio called the Western Reserve, and forty years ago the population was almost purely New England in origin, either by direct settlement from Connecticut, or indirectly after the sojourn of a generation in New York State. We were ourselves from southern Ohio, where the life was then strongly tinged by the adjoining life of Kentucky and Virginia, and we found these transplanted Yankees cold and blunt in their manners; but we did not undervalue their virtues. They formed in that day a leaven of right thinking and feeling which was to leaven the whole lump of the otherwise proslavery or indifferent state; and I suppose that outside of the antislavery circles of Boston there was nowhere in the country a population so resolute and so intelligent in its political opinions. They were very radical in every way, and hospitable to novelty of all kinds. I imagine that they tested more new religions and new patents than have been even heard of in less inquiring communities. When we came among them they had lately been swept by the fires of spiritualism, which left behind a great deal of smoke and ashes where the inherited New England orthodoxy had been. A belief in the saving efficacy of spirit phenomena still exists among them, but not, I fancy, at all in the former measure, when nearly every household had its medium, and the tables that tipped outnumbered the tables that did not tip. The old New York *Tribune,* which was circulated in the country almost as widely as our own paper, had deeply schooled the people in the economics of Horace Greeley, and they were ready for any sort of millennium, religious or industrial, that should arrive, while they looked very wisely after the main chance in the mean time. They were temperate, hard-working, hard-thinking folks, who dwelt on their scattered farms, and came up to the county fair once a year, when they were apt to visit the printing-office and pay for their papers. In spite of the English superstition to the contrary, the average American is not very curious, if one may judge from his reticence in the presence of things strange enough to excite question; and if our craft surprised these witnesses they rarely confessed it.

They thought it droll, as people of the simpler occupations are apt to think all the more complex arts; and one of them once went so far in expression of his humorous conception as to say, after a long stare at one of the compositors dodging and pecking at the type in his case, "Like an old hen pickin' up millet." This sort of silence, and this sort of comment, both exasperated the printers, who took their revenge as they could. They fed it full, once, when a country subscriber's horse, tied before the office, crossed his hind-legs and sat down in his harness like a tired man, and they proposed to go out and offer him a chair, to take him a glass of water, and ask him to come inside. But fate did not often give them such innings; they mostly had to create their chances of reprisal, but they did not mind that.

There was always a good deal of talk going on, but, although we were very ardent politicians, the talk was not political. When it was not mere banter, it was mostly literary; we disputed about authors among ourselves and with the village wits who dropped in. There were several of these who were readers, and they liked to stand with their backs to our stove and challenge opinion concerning Holmes and Poe, Irving and Macaulay, Pope and Byron, Dickens and Shakespeare.

It was Shakespeare who was oftenest on our tongues; indeed, the printing-office of former days had so much affinity with the theatre that compositors and comedians were easily convertible; and I have seen our printers engaged in hand-to-hand combats with column-rules, two up and two down, quite like the real bouts on the stage. Religion entered a good deal into our discussions, which my father, the most tolerant of men, would not suffer to become irreverent, even on the lips of law students bathing themselves in the fiery spirit of Tom Paine. He was willing to meet any one in debate of moral, religious, or political questions, and the wildest-haired Comeouters, the most ruthless sceptic, the most credulous spiritualist, found him ready to take them seriously, even when it was hard not to take them in joke.

It was part of his duty, as publisher of the paper, to bear patiently with another kind of frequenter—the type of farmer who thought he wished to discontinue his paper, and really wished to be talked into continuing it. I think he rather enjoyed letting the subscriber talk himself out, and carrying him from point to point in his argument, always consenting that he knew best what he wanted to do, but skilfully persuading him at last that a home-paper was more suited to his needs than any city substitute. Once I could have given the heads of his reasoning, but they are gone from me now. The editor was especially interested in the farming of the region, and I think it was partly owing to the attention he called to the question that its character was so largely changed. It is still a dairy country, but now it exports grain, and formerly the farmers had to buy their flour.

He did not neglect any real local interest in his purpose of keeping his readers alive to matters of more general importance, but he was fortunate in addressing himself to people who cared for the larger, if remoter, themes he loved. In fact, as long as slavery remained a question in our politics, they had a seriousness and dignity which the present generation can hardly imagine; and men of all callings felt themselves uplifted by the appeal this question made to their reason and conscience. My father constantly taught in his paper that if slavery could be kept out of the territories it would perish, and, as I have said, this was the belief of the vast majority of his readers. They were more or less fervid in it, according to their personal temperaments; some of them were fierce in their convictions and some humorous, but they were all in earnest. The editor sympathized more with those who took the true faith gayly. All were agreed that the Fugitive-slave Law was to be violated at any risk; it would not have been possible to take an escaping slave out of that county without bloodshed, but the people would have enjoyed outwitting his captors more than destroying them. Even in the great John Brown times, when it was known that there was a deposit of his impracticable pikes somewhere in our woods, and he and his followers came and went among us on some mysterious business of insurrectionary aim, the affair had its droll aspects which none appreciated more keenly than the Quaker-born editor. With his cheerful scepticism, he could never have believed that any harm or danger would come of it all; and I think he would have been hardly surprised to wake up any morning and find that slavery had died suddenly during the night of its own iniquity.

He was like all country editors then, and I dare say now, in being a printer as well as an editor, and he took a full share in the mechanical labors. These were formerly much more burdensome, for twice or thrice the present typesetting was then done in the country offices. At the present day the country printer buys of a city agency his paper already printed on one side, and he gets it for the cost of the blank paper, the agency finding its account in the advertisements it puts in. Besides this patent inside, as it is called, the printer buys stereotyped selections of other agencies, which offer him almost as wide a range of matter as the exchange newspapers he used to choose from. The few columns left for local gossip and general news, and for whatever editorial comment he cares to make on passing events, can be easily filled up by two compositors. But in my time we had three journeymen at work and two or three girl-compositors, and commonly a boy-apprentice besides. The paper was richer in a personal quality, and the printing-office was unquestionably more of a school. After we began to take girl-apprentices it became coeducative, as far as they cared to profit by it; but I think it did not serve to widen their thoughts or quicken their wits as it did those of the men. They looked to their craft as a living, not as a life, and they had no pride in it. They did not learn the whole trade, as the journeymen had done, and served only such apprenticeship as fitted them to set type. They were then paid by the thousand ems, and their earnings were usually as great at the end of a month as at the end of a year. But the boy who came up from his father's farm, with the wish to be a printer because Franklin had been one, and with the intent of making the office his university, began by sweeping it out, by hewing wood and carrying water for it. He became a roller-boy, and served long behind the press before he was promoted to the case, where he learned slowly and painfully to set type. His wage was forty dollars a year and two suits of clothes, for three years, when his apprenticeship ended, and his wander-years (too often literally) began. He was glad of being inky and stained with the marks of his trade; he wore a four-cornered paper cap, in the earlier stages of his service, and even an apron. When he became a journeyman, he clothed himself in black doeskin and broadcloth, and put on a silk hat and the thinnest-soled fine boots that could be found, and comported himself as much like a man of the world as he knew how to do. His work brought him acquainted with a vast variety of interests, and kept his mind as well as hands employed; he could not help thinking about them, and he did not fail to talk about them. His comments had generally a slightly acid flavor, and his constant survey of the world, in the "map of busy life" always under his eye, bred in him the contempt of familiarity. He was none the less agreeable for that, and the jokes that flew about from case to case in our office were something the editor would have been the last man to interfere with. He read or wrote on through them all, and now and then turned from his papers to join in them.

VI

The journeyman of that time and place was much better than the printer whom we had known earlier and in a more lax civilization, who was too apt to be sober only when he had not the means to be otherwise, and who arrived out of the unknown with nothing in his pocket, and departed into it with only money enough to carry him to the next printing-office. If we had no work for him it was the custom to take up a collection in the office, and he accepted it as a usage of the craft, without loss of self-respect. It could happen that his often infirmity would overtake him before he got out of town, but in this case he did not return for a second collection; I suppose that would not have been good form. Now and then a printer of this earlier sort appeared among us for a little time, but the air of the Western Reserve was somehow unfriendly to him, and he soon left us for the kindlier clime of the Ohio River, or for the more southerly region which we were ourselves sometimes so homesick for, and which his soft, rolling accent so pleasantly reminded us of. Still, there was something about the business—perhaps the arsenic in the type-metal—which everywhere affected the morals as it was said sometimes to affect the nerves.

There was one of our printers who was a capital compositor, a most engaging companion, and of unimpeachable Western Reserve lineage, who would work along in apparent perpetuity on the line of duty, and then suddenly deflect from it. If he wanted a day off, or several days, he would take the time, without notice, and with a princely indifference to any exigency we might be in. He came back when he chose and offered to go to work again, and I do not remember that he was ever refused. He was never in drink; his behavior was the effect of some obscure principle of conduct, unless it was that moral contagion from the material he wrought in.

I do not know that he was any more characteristic, though, than another printer of ours, who was dear to my soul from the quaintness of his humor and his love of literature. I think he was, upon the whole, the most original spirit I have known, and it was not the least part of his originality that he was then aiming to become a professor in some college, and was diligently training himself for the calling in all the leisure he could get from his work. The usual thing would have been to read law and crowd forward in political life, but my friend despised this common ideal. We were both studying Latin, he quite by himself, as he studied Greek and German, and I with such help as I could find in reciting to a kindly old minister, who had forgotten most of his own Latin, and whom I do not now wish to blame for falling asleep over the lessons in my presence; I did not know them well enough to keep him up to the work. My friend and I read the language, he more and I less, and we tried to speak it together, to give ourselves consequence, and to have the pleasure of saying before some people's faces what we should otherwise have said behind their backs; I should not now undertake to speak Latin to achieve either of these aims. Besides this, we read a great deal together, mainly Shakespeare and Cervantes. I had a task of a certain number of thousand ems a day, and when I had finished that I was free to do what I liked; he would stop work at the same time, and then we would take our *Don Quixote* into some clean, sweet beech-woods there were near the village, and laugh our hearts out over it. I can see my friend's strange face now, very regular, very fine, and smooth as a girl's, with quaint blue eyes, shut long, long ago, to this *dolce lome;* and some day I should like to tell all about him; but this is not the place. When the war broke out he left the position he had got by that time in some college or academy farther west and went into the army. One morning, in Louisiana, he was killed by a guerilla who got a shot at him when he was a little way from his company, and who was probably proud of picking off the Yankee captain. But as yet such a fate was unimaginable. He was the first friend of my youth; he was older than I by five or six years; but we met in an equality of ambition and purpose, though he was rather more inclined to the severity of the scholar's ideal, and I hoped to slip through somehow with a mere literary use of my learning.

VII

As I have tried to say, the printers of that day had nearly all some affinity with literature, if not some love of it; it was in a sort always at their fingers-ends, and they must have got some touch of it whether they would or not. They thought their trade a poor one moneywise, but they were fond of it and they did not often forsake it. Their hope was somehow to get hold of a country paper and become editors and publishers; and my friend and I, when he was twenty-four and I eighteen, once crossed over into Pennsylvania, where we had heard there was a paper for sale; but we had not the courage to offer even promises to pay for it. The craft had a repute for insolvency which it merited, and it was at odds with the community at large by reason of something not immediately intelligible in it, or at least not classifiable. I remember that when I began to write a certain story of mine, I told Mark Twain, who was once a printer, that I was going to make the hero a printer, and he said: "Better not. People will not understand him. Printing is something every village has in it, but it is always a sort of mystery, and the reader does not like to be perplexed by something that he thinks he knows about." This seemed very acute and just, though I made my hero a printer all the same, and I offer it to the public as a light on the anomalous relation the country printer bears to his fellow-citizens. They see him following his strange calling among them, but to neither wealth nor worship, and they cannot understand why he does not take up something else, something respectable and remunerative; they feel that there must be something weak, something wrong in a man who is willing to wear his life out in a vocation which keeps him poor and dependent on the favor they grudge him. It is like the relation which all the arts bear to the world, and which is peculiarly thankless in a purely commercial civilization like ours; though I cannot pretend that printing is an art in the highest sense. I have heard old journeymen claim that it was a profession and ought to rank with the learned professions, but I am afraid that was from too fond a pride in it. It is in one sort a handicraft, like any other, like carpentering or stone-cutting; but it has its artistic delight, as every handicraft has. There is the ideal in all work; and I have had moments of unsurpassed gladness in feeling that I had come very near the ideal in what I had done in my trade. This joy is the right of every worker, and in so far as modern methods have taken it from him they have wronged him. I can understand Ruskin in his wish to restore it to some of the handicrafts which have lost it in the "base mechanical" operations of the great manufactories, where men spend their lives in making one thing, or a part of a thing, and cannot follow their work constructively. If that were to be the end, the operative would forever lose the delight in work which is the best thing in the world. But I hope this is not to be the end, and that when people like again to make things for use and not merely for profit the workman will have again the reward that is more than wages.

I know that in the old-fashioned country printing-office we had this, and we enjoyed our trade as the decorative art it also is. Questions of taste constantly arose in the arrangement of a title-page, the display of a placard or a hand-bill, the use of this type or that. They did not go far, these questions, but they employed the critical faculty and the aesthetic instinct, and they allied us, however slightly and unconsciously, with the creators of the beautiful.

But now, it must be confessed, printing has shared the fate of all other handicrafts. Thanks to united labor, it is better paid in each of its sub-divisions than it once was as a whole. In my time, the hire of a first-rate country printer, who usually worked by the week, was a dollar a day; but of course this was not so little in 1862 as it would be in 1892. My childish remembrance is of the journeymen working two hours after supper, every night, so as to make out a day of twelve hours; but at the time I write of the day of ten hours was the law and the rule, and nobody worked longer, except when the President's Message was to be put in type, or on some other august occasion.

The pay is not only increased in proportion to the cost of living, but it is really greater, and the conditions are all very much better. But I believe no apprentice now learns the whole trade, and each of our printers, forty years ago, would have known how to do everything in the kind of office he hoped to own. He would have had to make a good many things which the printer now buys, and first among them the rollers which are used for ink-ing the type on the press. These were of a composition of glue and molas-ses, and were of an india-rubbery elasticity and consistency, as long as they were in good condition. But with use and time they became hard, the ink smeared on them, and they failed to impart evenly to the type; they had to be thrown away or melted over again. This was done on the office stove, in a large bucket which they were cut up into, with fresh glue and molasses added. It seems in the retrospect to have been rather a simple affair, and I do not now see why casting a roller should have involved so much absolute failure and rarely have given a satisfactory result. The mould was a large copper cylinder, and the wooden core of the roller was fixed in place by an iron cap and foot-piece. The mixture boiled away, as it now seems to me, for days, and far into the sleepy nights, when as a child I was proud of sitting up with it very late. Then at some weird hour my father or my brother poured it into the mould, and we went home and left the rest with fate. The next morning the whole office crowded round to see the roller drawn from the mould, and it usually came out with such long hollows and gaps in its sides that it had to be cut up at once and melted over again. At present, all rollers are bought somewhere in New York or Chicago, I believe, and a printer would no more think of making a roller than of making any other part of his press. "And you know," said my brother, who told me of this change, "we don't wet the paper now." "Good Heavens," said I, "you don't print it *dry*!" "Yes, and it doesn't blur any more than if it were wet." I suppose wetting the paper was a usage that antedated the invention of movable type. It used to be drawn, quire by quire, through a vat of clear water, and then the night before publication day it was turned and sprinkled. Now it was printed dry, I felt as if it were time to class Benjamin Franklin with the sun-myths.

VIII

Publication day was always a time of great excitement. We were busy all the morning getting the last editorials and the latest news in type, and when the paper went to press in the afternoon the entire force was drafted to the work of helping the engine and the press through their various disabilities and reluctances. Several hands were needed to run the press, even when it was in a willing frame; others folded the papers as they came from it; as many more were called from their wonted work to address them to the subscribers, for with the well-known fickleness of their sex, the young ladies of the village ceased to do this as soon as the novelty of the affair wore off. Still, the office was always rather a lively scene, for the paper was not delivered at the village houses, and each subscriber came and got his copy; the villagers began to come about the hour we went to press, the neighboring farmers called next day and throughout the week. Nearly everybody who witnessed the throes of our machinery had advice or sympathy to offer, and in a place where many people were of a mechanical turn the spectacular failure of the editor's additions and improvements was naturally a source of public entertainment; perhaps others got as much pleasure out of his inventions as he did.

Of course, about election-time the excitement was intensified; we had no railroad or telegraphic communication with the outer world, but it was felt that we somehow had the news, and it was known that we had the latest papers from Cleveland, and that our sheet would report the intelligence from them. After all, however, there was nothing very burning or seething in the eagerness of our subscribers. They could wait; their knowledge of the event would not change it, or add or take away one vote either way. I dare say it is not so very different now, when the railroad and the telegraph have made the little place simultaneous with New York and London. We people who fret our lives out in cities do not know how tranquil life in the country still is. We talk of the whirl and rush, as if it went on everywhere, but if you will leave the express train anywhere and pass five miles into the country, away from the great through lines, you will not find the whirl and rush. People sometimes go mad there from the dulness and ennui, as in the cities they sometimes go mad from the stress and the struggle; and the problem of equalizing conditions has no phase more interesting than that of getting the good of the city and the country out of the one into the other. The old-fashioned country newspaper formed almost the sole intellectual experience of the remote and quiet folks who dwelt in their lonely farmsteads on the borders of the woods, with few neighbors and infrequent visits to the township centre, where the church, a store or two, and a tavern constituted a village. They got it out of the post-office there once a week, and read it in the scanty leisure left them by their farmwork or their household drudgery, and I dare say they found it interesting. There were some men in every neighborhood, tongueyer than the rest, who, when they called on us, seemed to have got it by heart, and who were ready to defend or combat its positions with all comers; this sort usually took some other paper, too—an agricultural paper, or the New York *Trybune,* as they called it, or a weekly edition of a Cleveland journal. It was generally believed that Horace Greeley wrote everything in the *Trybune,* and when a country subscriber unfolded his *Trybune* he said, with comfortable expectation, "Well, let's see what old Horace says *this* week." But by far the greater number of our subscribers took no paper but our own. I do not know whether there is much more reading done now on the farms, but I doubt it. In the villages, however, the circulation of the nearest city dailies is pretty general, and there is a large sale of the Sunday editions. I am not sure that this is an advantage, but in the undeniable decay of interest in the local preaching, some sort of mental relish for the only day of leisure is necessary. It is not so much a pity that they read the Sunday papers, as that the Sunday papers are so bad. If they were carefully and conscientiously made up, they would be of great use; they wait their reformer, and they do not seem impatient for him.

In the old time, we printers were rather more in touch with the world outside on the journalistic lines than most of our fellow-villagers, but otherwise we were as remote as any of them, and the weekly issue of the paper had not often anything tumultuously exciting for us. The greatest event of our year was the publication of the President's Message, which was a thrill in my childish life long before I had any conception of its meaning. I fancy that the patent inside, now so universally used by the country papers, originated in the custom which the printers within easy reach of a large city had of supplying themselves with an edition of the President's Message, to be folded into their own sheet, when they did not print their outside on the back of it. There was always a hot rivalry between the local papers in getting out the message, whether it was bought ready printed, or whether it was set up in the office and printed in the body of the paper. We had no local rival, but all the same we made haste when it was a question of the message. The printers filled their cases with type, ready for the early copy of the message, which the editor used every device to secure; when it was once in hand they worked day and night till it was all up, and then the paper was put to press at once, without regard to the usual publication day; and the community was as nearly electrified as could be with our journalistic enterprise, which was more important in our eyes than the matters the message treated of.

There is no longer the eager popular expectation of the President's Message that there once seemed to be; and I think it is something of a loss, that ebb of the high tide of political feeling which began with the era of our immense material prosperity. It was a feeling that formed a solidarity of all the citizens, and if it was not always, or often, the highest interest which can unite men, it was at least not that deadly and selfish cult of business which centres each of us in his own affairs and kills even our curiosity about others. Very likely people were less bent on the pursuit of wealth in those days, because there was less chance to grow rich, but the fact remains that they *were* less bent in that direction, and that they gave their minds to other things more than they do now. I think those other things were larger things, and that our civic type was once nobler than it is. It was before the period of corruption, when it was not yet fully known that dollars can do the work of votes, when the votes as yet rather outnumbered the dollars, and more of us had the one than the other. The great statesman, not the great millionaire, was then the American ideal, and all about in the villages and on the farms the people were eager to know what the President had said to Congress. They are not eager to know now, and that seems rather a pity. Is it because in the war which destroyed slavery, the American Democracy died, and by operation of the same fatal anomaly the American Plutocracy, which Lincoln foreboded, was born; and the people instinctively feel that they have no longer the old interest in President or Congress?

There are those that say so, and, whether they are right or not, it is certain that into the great centres where money is heaped up the life of the country is drained, and the country press has suffered with the other local interests. The railroads penetrate everywhere, and carry the city papers seven times a week, where the home paper pays its tardy visit once, with a patent inside imported from the nearest money centre, and its few columns of neighborhood gossip, too inconsiderable to be gathered up by the correspondents of the invasive dailies. Other causes have worked against the country press. In counties where there were once two or three papers there are now eight or ten, without a material increase of population to draw upon for support. The county printing, which the paper of the dominant party could reckon upon, is now shared with other papers of the same politics, and the amateur printing-offices belonging to ingenious boys in every neighborhood get much of the small job-work which once came to the publisher.

It is useless to quarrel with the course of events, for which no one is more to blame than another, though human nature loves a scape-goat, and from time to time we load up some individual with the common sins and drive him into a wilderness where he seems rather to enjoy himself than otherwise. I suppose that even if the conditions had continued favorable, the country press could never have become the influence which our editor fondly hoped and earnestly strove to make it. Like all of us who work at all, the country printer had to work too hard; and he had little time to think or to tell how to make life better and truer in any sort. His paper had once perhaps as much influence as the country pulpit; its support was certainly of the same scanty and reluctant sort, and it was without consecration by an avowed self-devotion. He was concerned with the main chance first, and after that there was often no other chance, or he lost sight of it. I should not instance him as an exemplary man, and I should be very far from idealizing him; I should not like even to undertake the task of idealizing a city journalist; and yet, in the retrospect at least, the country printer has his pathos for me—the pathos of a man who began to follow a thankless calling because he loved it, and kept on at it because he loved it, or else because its service had warped and cramped him out of form to follow any other.

JOHN BURROUGHS

It seems strange that an essayist once so popular and well-known as John Burroughs (1837–1921) would today be largely forgotten, but recently he has been undergoing a modest revival. In his books he would take readers on walks, pointing out with scientific knowledge and poetic appreciation the markings of birds, the odors of flowers. He taught generations of future nature writers how to work such humble material. Descending from generations of farmers, he wrote about country life rather than wilderness. "Burroughs had little use for the sublime," writes Bill McKibben. "Instead, he filled his many volumes of essays with the most local, small-scale, homey glimpses of nature. . . . He was blessed with an unrivaled talent for the familiar." In "The Art of Seeing Things," he invites us to learn how to read "the book of nature" by slowing down.

The Art of Seeing Things

(1899)

I

I do not purpose to attempt to tell my reader how to see things, but only to talk about the art of seeing things, as one might talk of any other art. One might discourse about the art of poetry, or of painting, or of oratory, without any hope of making one's readers or hearers poets or painters or orators.

The science of anything may be taught or acquired by study; the art of it comes by practice or inspiration. The art of seeing things is not something that may be conveyed in rules and precepts; it is a matter vital in the eye and ear, yea, in the mind and soul, of which these are the organs. I have as little hope of being able to tell the reader how to see things as I would have in trying to tell him how to fall in love or to enjoy his dinner. Either he does or he does not, and that is about all there is of it. Some people seem born with eyes in their heads, and others with buttons or painted marbles, and no amount of science can make the one equal to the other in the art of seeing things. The great mass of mankind are, in this respect, like the rank and file of an army: they fire vaguely in the direction of the enemy, and if they hit, it is more a matter of chance than of accurate aim. But here and there is the keen-eyed observer; he is the sharpshooter; his eye selects and discriminates, his purpose goes to the mark.

Even the successful angler seems born, and not made; he appears to know instinctively the ways of trout. The secret is, no doubt, love of the sport. Love sharpens the eye, the ear, the touch; it quickens the feet, it steadies the hand, it arms against the wet and the cold. What we love to do, that we do well. To know is not all; it is only half. To love is the other half. Wordsworth's poet was contented if he might enjoy the things which others understood. This is generally the attitude of the young and of the poetic nature. The man of science, on the other hand, is contented if he may understand the things that others enjoy: that is his enjoyment. Contemplation and absorption for the one; investigation and classification for the other. We probably all have, in varying degrees, one or the other of these ways of enjoying Nature: either the sympathetic and emotional enjoyment of her which the young and the artistic and the poetic temperament have, or the enjoyment through our knowing faculties afforded by natural science, or, it may be, the two combined, as they certainly were in such a man as Tyndall.

But nothing can take the place of love. Love is the measure of life: only so far as we love do we really live. The variety of our interests, the width of our sympathies, the susceptibilities of our hearts—if these do not measure our lives, what does? As the years go by, we are all of us more or less subject to two dangers, the danger of petrifaction and the danger of putrefaction; either that we shall become hard and callous, crusted over with customs and conventions till no new ray of light or of joy can reach us, or that we shall become lax and disorganized, losing our grip upon the real and vital sources of happiness and power. Now, there is no preservative and antiseptic, nothing that keeps one's heart young, like love, like sympathy, like giving one's self with enthusiasm to some worthy thing or cause.

If I were to name the three most precious resources of life, I should say books, friends, and nature; and the greatest of these, at least the most constant and always at hand, is nature. Nature we have always with us, an inexhaustible storehouse of that which moves the heart, appeals to the mind, and fires the imagination,—health to the body, a stimulus to the intellect, and joy to the soul. To the scientist Nature is a storehouse of facts, laws, processes; to the artist she is a storehouse of pictures; to the poet she is a storehouse of images, fancies, a source of inspiration; to the moralist she is a storehouse of precepts and parables; to all she may be a source of knowledge and joy.

II

There is nothing in which people differ more than in their powers of observation. Some are only half alive to what is going on around them. Others, again, are keenly alive: their intelligence, their powers of recognition, are in full force in eye and ear at all times. They see and hear everything, whether it directly concerns them or not. They never pass unseen a familiar face on the street; they are never oblivious of any interesting feature or sound or object in the earth or sky about them. Their power of attention is always on the alert, not by conscious effort, but by natural habit and disposition. Their perceptive faculties may be said to be always on duty. They turn to the outward world a more highly sensitized mind than other people. The things that pass before them are caught and individualized instantly. If they visit new countries, they see the characteristic features of the people and scenery at once. The impression is never blurred or confused. Their powers of observation suggest the sight and scent of wild animals; only, whereas it is fear that sharpens the one, it is love and curiosity that sharpens the other. The mother turkey with her brood sees the hawk when it is a mere speck against the sky; she is, in her solicitude for her young, thinking of hawks, and is on her guard against them. Fear makes keen her eye. The hunter does not see the hawk till his attention is thus called to it by the turkey, because his interests are not endangered; but he outsees the wild creatures of the plain and mountain,—the elk, the antelope, and the mountain-sheep,—he makes it his business to look for them, and his eyes carry farther than do theirs.

We may see coarsely and vaguely, as most people do, noting only masses and unusual appearances, or we may see finely and discriminatingly, taking in the minute and the specific. In a collection of stuffed birds, the other day, I observed that a wood thrush was mounted as in the act of song, its open beak pointing straight to the zenith. The taxidermist had not seen truly. The thrush sings with its beak but slightly elevated. Who has not seen a red squirrel or a gray squirrel running up and down the trunk of a tree? But probably very few have noticed that the position of the hind feet is the reverse in the one case from what it is in the other. In descending they are extended to the rear, the toe-nails hooking to the bark, checking and controlling the fall. In most pictures the feet are shown well drawn up under the body in both cases.

People who discourse pleasantly and accurately about the birds and flowers and external nature generally are not invariably good observers. In their walks do they see anything they did not come out to see? Is there any spontaneous or unpremeditated seeing? Do they make discoveries? Any bird or creature may be hunted down, any nest discovered, if you lay siege to it; but to find what you are not looking for, to catch the shy winks and gestures on every side, to see all the by-play going on around you, missing no significant note or movement, penetrating every screen with your eye-beams—that is to be an observer; that is to have "an eye practiced like a blind man's touch,"—a touch that can distinguish a white horse from a black,—a detective eye that reads the faintest signs. When Thoreau was at Cape Cod, he noticed that the horses there had a certain muscle in their hips inordinately developed by reason of the insecure footing in the ever-yielding sand. Thoreau's vision at times fitted things closely. During some great fête in Paris, the Empress Eugénie and Queen Victoria were both present. A reporter noticed that when the royal personages came to sit down, Eugénie looked behind her before doing so, to see that the chair was really there, but Victoria seated herself without the backward glance, knowing there must be a seat ready: there always had been, and there always would be, for her. The correspondent inferred that the incident showed the difference between born royalty and hastily made royalty. I wonder how many persons in that vast assembly made this observation; probably very few. It denoted a gift for seeing things.

If our powers of observation were quick and sure enough, no doubt we should see through most of the tricks of the sleight-of-hand man. He fools us because his hand is more dexterous than our eye. He captures our attention, and then commands us to see only what he wishes us to see.

In the field of natural history, things escape us because the actors are small, and the stage is very large and more or less veiled and obstructed. The movement is quick across a background that tends to conceal rather than expose it. In the printed page the white paper plays quite as important a part as the type and the ink; but the book of nature is on a different plan: the page rarely presents a contrast of black and white, or even black and brown, but only of similar tints, gray upon gray, green upon green, or drab upon brown.

By a close observer I do not mean a minute, cold-blooded specialist,—

"a fingering slave,
One who would peep and botanize
Upon his mother's grave,"—

but a man who looks closely and steadily at nature, and notes the individual features of tree and rock and field, and allows no subtle flavor of the night or day, of the place and the season, to escape him. His senses are so delicate that in his evening walk he feels the warm and the cool streaks in the air, his nose detects the most fugitive odors, his ears the most furtive sounds. As he stands musing in the April twilight, he hears that fine, elusive stir and rustle made by the angleworms reaching out from their holes for leaves and grasses; he hears the whistling wings of the woodcock as it goes swiftly by him in the dusk; he hears the call of the killdee come down out of the March sky; he hears far above him in the early morning the squeaking cackle of the arriving blackbirds pushing north; he hears the soft, prolonged, lulling call of the little owl in the cedars in the early spring twilight; he hears at night the roar of the distant waterfall, and the rumble of the train miles across the country when the air is "hollow"; before a storm he notes how distant objects stand out and are brought near on those brilliant days that we call "weather-breeders." When the mercury is at zero or lower, he notes how the passing trains hiss and simmer as if the rails or wheels were red-hot. He reads the subtile signs of the weather. The stars at night forecast the coming day to him; the clouds at evening and at morning are a sign. He knows there is the wet-weather diathesis and the dry-weather diathesis, or, as Goethe said, water affirmative and water negative, and he interprets the symptoms accordingly. He is keenly alive to all outward impressions. When he descends from the hill in the autumn twilight, he notes the cooler air of the valley like a lake about him; he notes how, at other seasons, the cooler air at times settles down between the mountains like a vast body of water, as shown by the level line of the fog or the frost upon the trees.

The modern man looks at nature with an eye of sympathy and love where the earlier man looked with an eye of fear and superstition. Hence he sees more closely and accurately; science has made his eye steady and clear. To a hasty traveler through the land, the farms and country homes all seem much alike, but to the people born and reared there, what a difference! They have read the fine print that escapes the hurried eye and that is so full of meaning. Every horizon line, every curve in hill or valley, every tree and rock and spring run, every turn in the road and vista in the landscape, has its special features and makes its own impression.

Scott wrote in his journal: "Nothing is so tiresome as walking through some beautiful scene with a minute philosopher, a botanist, or a pebble-gatherer, who is eternally calling your attention from the grand features of the natural picture to look at grasses and chuckie-stanes." No doubt Scott's large, generous way of looking at things kindles the imagination and touches the sentiments more than does this minute way of the specialist. The nature that Scott gives us is like the air and the water that all may absorb, while what the specialist gives us is more like some particular element or substance that only the few can appropriate. But Scott had his specialties, too, the specialties of the sportsman: he was the first to see the hare's eyes as she sat in her form, and he knew the ways of grouse and pheasants and trout. The ideal observer turns the enthusiasm of the sportsman into the channels of natural history, and brings home a finer game than ever fell to shot or bullet. He too has an eye for the fox and the rabbit and the migrating water-fowl, but he sees them with loving and not with murderous eyes.

III

So far as seeing things is an art, it is the art of keeping your eyes and ears open. The art of nature is all in the direction of concealment. The birds, the animals, all the wild creatures, for the most part try to elude your observation. The art of the bird is to hide her nest; the art of the game you are in quest of is to make itself invisible. The flower seeks to attract the bee and the moth by its color and perfume, because they are of service to it; but I presume it would hide from the excursionists and the picnickers if it could, because they extirpate it. Power of attention and a mind sensitive to outward objects, in these lies the secret of seeing things. Can you bring all your faculties to the front, like a house with many faces at the doors and windows; or do you live retired within yourself, shut up in your own meditations? The thinker puts all the powers of his mind in reflection: the observer puts all the powers of his mind in perception; every faculty is directed outward; the whole mind sees through the eye and hears through the ear. He has an objective turn of mind as opposed to a subjective. A person with the latter turn of mind sees little. If you are occupied with your own thoughts, you may go through a museum of curiosities and observe nothing.

Of course one's powers of observation may be cultivated as well as anything else. The senses of seeing and hearing may be quickened and trained as well as the sense of touch. Blind persons come to be marvelously acute in their powers of touch. Their feet find the path and keep it. They come to know the lay of the land through this sense, and recognize the roads and surfaces they have once traveled over. Helen Keller reads your speech by putting her hand upon your lips, and is thrilled by the music of an instrument through the same sense of touch. The perceptions of school-children should be trained as well as their powers of reflection and memory. A teacher in Connecticut, Miss Aiken,—whose work on mind-training I commend to all teachers,—has hit upon a simple and ingenious method of doing this. She has a revolving blackboard upon which she writes various figures, numbers, words, sentences, which she exposes to the view of the class for one or two or three seconds, as the case may be, and then asks them to copy or repeat what was written. In time they become astonishingly quick, especially the girls, and can take in a multitude of things at a glance. Detectives, I am told, are trained after a similar method; a man is led quickly by a show-window, for instance, and asked to name and describe the objects he saw there. Life itself is of course more or less a school of this kind, but the power of concentrated attention in most persons needs stimulating. Here comes in the benefit of manual-training schools. To *do* a thing, to make something, the powers of the mind must be focused. A boy in building a boat will get something that all the books in the world cannot give him. The concrete, the definite, the discipline of real things, the educational values that lie here, are not enough appreciated.

IV

The book of nature is like a page written over or printed upon with different-sized characters and in many different languages, interlined and crosslined, and with a great variety of marginal notes and references. There is coarse print and fine print; there are obscure signs and hiero-glyphics. We all read the large type more or less appreciatively, but only the students and lovers of nature read the fine lines and the footnotes. It is a book which he reads best who goes most slowly or even tarries long by the way. He who runs may read some things. We may take in the general features of sky, plain, and river from the express train, but only the pedestrian, the saunterer, with eyes in his head and love in his heart, turns every leaf and peruses every line. One man sees only the migrating water-fowls and the larger birds of the air; another sees the passing king-lets and hurrying warblers as well. For my part, my delight is to linger long over each page of this marvelous record, and to dwell fondly upon its most obscure text.

I take pleasure in noting the minute things about me. I am interested even in the ways of the wild bees, and in all the little dramas and tragedies that occur in field and wood. One June day, in my walk, as I crossed a rather dry, high-lying field, my attention was attracted by small mounds of fresh earth all over the ground, scarcely more than a handful in each. On looking closely, I saw that in the middle of each mound there was a hole not quite so large as a lead-pencil. Now, I had never observed these mounds before, and my curiosity was aroused. "Here is some fine print," I said, "that I have overlooked." So I set to work to try to read it; I waited for a sign of life. Presently I saw here and there a bee hovering about over the mounds. It looked like the honey-bee, only less pronounced in color and manner. One of them alighted on one of the mounds near me, and was about to disappear in the hole in the centre when I caught it in my hand. Though it stung me, I retained it and looked it over, and in the process was stung several times; but the pain was slight. I saw it was one of our native wild bees, cousin to the leaf-rollers, that build their nests under stones and in decayed fence-rails. (In Packard I found it described under the name of *Andrena*.) Then I inserted a small weed-stalk into one of the holes, and, with a little trowel I carried, proceeded to dig out the nest. The hole was about a foot deep; at the bottom of it I found a little semi-transparent, membranous sac or cell, a little larger than that of the honey-bee; in this sac was a little pellet of yellow pollen—a loaf of bread for the young grub when the egg should have hatched. I explored other nests and found them all the same. This discovery was not a great addition to my sum of natural knowledge, but it was something. Now when I see the signs in a field, I know what they mean: they indicate the tiny earthen cradles of *Andrena*.

Near by I chanced to spy a large hole in the turf, with no mound of soil about it. I could put the end of my little finger into it. I peered down, and saw the gleam of two small, bead-like eyes. I knew it to be the den of the wolf-spider. Was she waiting for some blundering insect to tumble in? I say she, because the real ogre among the spiders is the female. The male is small and of little consequence. A few days later I paused by this den again and saw the members of the ogress scattered about her own door. Had some insect Jack the Giant-Killer been there, or had a still more formidable ogress, the sand-hornet, dragged her forth and carried away her limbless body to her den in the bank?

What the wolf-spider does with the earth it excavates in making its den is a mystery. There is no sign of it anywhere about. Does it force its way down by pushing the soil to one side and packing it there firmly? The entrance to the hole usually has a slight rim or hem to keep the edge from crumbling in.

As it happened, I chanced upon another interesting footnote that very day. I was on my way to a muck swamp in the woods, to see if the showy lady's-slipper was in bloom. Just on the margin of the swamp, in the deep shade of the hemlocks, my eye took note of some small, unshapely creature crawling hurriedly over the ground. I stooped down, and saw it was some large species of moth just out of its case, and in a great hurry to find a suitable place in which to hang itself up and give its wings a chance to unfold before the air dried them. I thrust a small twig in its way, which it instantly seized upon. I lifted it gently, carried it to drier ground, and fixed the stick in the fork of a tree, so that the moth hung free a few feet from the ground. Its body was distended nearly to the size of one's little finger, and surmounted by wings that were so crumpled and stubby that they seemed quite rudimentary. The creature evidently knew what it wanted, and knew the importance of haste. Instantly these rude, stubby wings began to grow. It was a slow process, but one could see the change from minute to minute. As the wings expanded, the body contracted. By some kind of pumping arrangement air was being forced from a reservoir in the one into the tubes of the other. The wings were not really growing, as they at first seemed to be, but they were unfolding and expanding under this pneumatic pressure from the body. In the course of about half an hour the process was completed, and the winged creature hung there in all its full-fledged beauty. Its color was checked black and white like a loon's back, but its name I know not. My chief interest in it, aside from the interest we feel in any new form of life, arose from the creature's extreme anxiety to reach a perch where it could unfold its wings. A little delay would doubtless have been fatal to it. I wonder how many human geniuses are hatched whose wings are blighted by some accident or untoward circumstance. Or do the wings of genius always unfold, no matter what the environment may be?

One seldom takes a walk without encountering some of this fine print on nature's page. Now it is a little yellowish-white moth that spreads itself upon the middle of a leaf as if to imitate the droppings of birds; or it is the young cicadas working up out of the ground, and in the damp, cool places building little chimneys or tubes above the surface to get more warmth and hasten their development; or it is a wood-newt gorging a tree-cricket, or a small snake gorging the newt, or a bird song with some striking peculiarity—a strange defect, or a rare excellence. Now it is a shrike impaling his victim, or blue jays mocking and teasing a hawk and dropping quickly into the branches to avoid his angry blows, or a robin hustling a cuckoo out of the tree where her nest is, or a vireo driving away a cowbird, or the partridge blustering about your feet till her young are hidden. One October morning I was walking along the road on the edge of the woods, when I came into a gentle shower of butternuts; one of them struck my hat-brim. I paused and looked about me; here one fell, there another, yonder a third. There was no wind blowing, and I wondered what was loosening the butternuts. Turning my attention to the top of the tree, I soon saw the explanation: a red squirrel was at work gathering his harvest. He would seize a nut, give it a twist, when down it would come; then he would dart to another and another. Farther along I found where he had covered the ground with chestnut burs; he could not wait for the frost and the winds; did he know that the burs would dry and open upon the ground, and that the bitter covering of the butternuts would soon fall away from the nut?

There are three things that perhaps happen near me each season that I have never yet seen—the toad casting its skin, the snake swallowing its young, and the larvae of the moth and butterfly constructing their shrouds. It is a mooted question whether or not the snake does swallow its young, but if there is no other good reason for it, may they not retreat into their mother's stomach to feed? How else are they to be nourished? That the moth larva can weave its own cocoon and attach it to a twig seems more incredible. Yesterday, in my walk, I found a firm, silver-gray cocoon, about two inches long and shaped like an Egyptian mummy (probably *Promethea*), suspended from a branch of a bush by a narrow, stout ribbon twice as long as itself. The fastening was woven around the limb, upon which it turned as if it grew there. I would have given something to have seen the creature perform this feat, and then incase itself so snugly in the silken shroud at the end of this tether. By swinging free, its firm, compact case was in no danger from woodpeckers, as it might have been if resting directly upon a branch or tree-trunk. Near by was the cocoon of another species (*Cecropia*) that was fastened directly to the limb; but this was vague, loose, and much more involved and net-like. I have seen the downy woodpecker assaulting one of these cocoons, but its yielding surface and webby interior seemed to puzzle and baffle him.

I am interested even in the way each climbing plant or vine goes up the pole, whether from right to left, or from left to right,—that is, with the hands of a clock or against them,—whether it is under the law of the great cyclonic storms of the northern hemisphere, which all move against the hands of a clock, or in the contrary direction, like the cyclones in the southern hemisphere. I take pleasure in noting every little dancing whirl-wind of a summer day that catches up the dust or the leaves before me, and every little funnel-shaped whirlpool in the swollen stream or river, whether or not they spin from right to left or the reverse. If I were in the southern hemisphere, I am sure I should note whether these things were under the law of its cyclones in this respect or under the law of ours. As a rule, our twining plants and toy whirlwinds copy our revolving storms and go against the hands of the clock. But there are exceptions. While the bean, the bittersweet, the morning glory, and others go up from left to right, the hop, the wild buckwheat, and some others go up from right to left. Most of our forest trees show a tendency to wind one way or the other, the hard woods going in one direction, and the hemlocks and pines and cedars and butternuts and chestnuts in another. In different localities, or on different geological formations, I find these directions reversed. I recall one instance in the case of a hemlock six or seven inches in diam-eter, where this tendency to twist had come out of the grain, as it were, and shaped the outward form of the tree, causing it to make, in an ascent of about thirty feet, one complete revolution about a larger tree close to which it grew. On a smaller scale I have seen the same thing in a pine.

Persons lost in the woods or on the plains, or traveling at night, tend, I believe, toward the left. The movements of men and women, it is said, differ in this respect, one sex turning to the right and the other to the left.

I had lived in the world more than fifty years before I noticed a pecu-liarity about the rays of light one often sees diverging from an opening, or a series of openings, in the clouds, namely, that they are like spokes in a wheel, the hub, or centre, of which appears to be just there in the vapory masses, instead of being, as is really the case, nearly ninety-three millions of miles beyond. The beams of light that come through cracks or chinks in a wall do not converge in this way, but to the eye run parallel to one another. There is another fact: this fan-shaped display of converging rays is always immediately in front of the observer; that is, exactly between him and the sun, so that the central spoke or shaft in his front is always perpendicular. You cannot see this fan to the right or left of the sun, but only between you and it. Hence, as in the case of the rainbow, no two persons see exactly the same rays.

The eye sees what it has the means of seeing, and its means of seeing are in proportion to the love and desire behind it. The eye is informed and sharpened by the thought. My boy sees ducks on the river where and when I cannot, because at certain seasons he thinks ducks and dreams ducks. One season my neighbor asked me if the bees had injured my grapes. I said, "No; the bees never injure my grapes."

"They do mine," he replied; "they puncture the skin for the juice, and at times the clusters are covered with them."

"No," I said, "it is not the bees that puncture the skin; it is the birds."

"What birds?"

"The orioles."

"But I haven't seen any orioles," he rejoined.

"We have," I continued, "because at this season we think orioles; we have learned by experience how destructive these birds are in the vineyard, and we are on the lookout for them; our eyes and ears are ready for them."

If we think birds, we shall see birds wherever we go; if we think arrow-heads, as Thoreau did, we shall pick up arrowheads in every field. Some people have an eye for four-leaved clovers; they see them as they walk hastily over the turf, for they already have them in their eyes. I once took a walk with the late Professor Eaton of Yale. He was just then specially interested in the mosses, and he found them, all kinds, everywhere. I can see him yet, every few minutes upon his knees, adjusting his eye-glasses before some rare specimen. The beauty he found in them, and pointed out to me, kindled my enthusiasm also. I once spent a summer day at the mountain home of a well-known literary woman and editor. She lamented the absence of birds about her house. I named a half-dozen or more I had heard or seen in her trees within an hour—the indigo-bird, the purple finch, the yellowbird, the veery thrush, the red-eyed vireo, the song sparrow.

"Do you mean to say you have seen or heard all these birds while sitting here on my porch?" she inquired.

"I really have," I said.

"I do not see them or hear them," she replied, "and yet I want to very much."

"No," said I; "you only *want to want* to see and hear them."

You must have the bird in your heart before you can find it in the bush.

I was sitting in front of a farmhouse one day in company with the local Nimrod. In a maple tree in front of us I saw the great crested flycatcher. I called the hunter's attention to it, and asked him if he had ever seen that bird before. No, he had not; it was a new bird to him. But he probably had seen it scores of times,—seen it without regarding it. It was not the game he was in quest of, and his eye heeded it not.

Human and artificial sounds and objects thrust themselves upon us; they are within our sphere, so to speak: but the life of nature we must meet halfway; it is shy, withdrawn, and blends itself with a vast neutral background. We must be initiated; it is an order the secrets of which are well guarded.

WILLIAM JAMES

William James (1842–1910) was a philosopher associated with pragma-
tism, and a psychologist who coined the term "stream of conscious-
ness." His book The Varieties of Religious Experience *discussed belief*
in open, nondogmatic fashion. The elder brother of Henry James, he
was as masterly a literary stylist in his own right as his sibling. Given his
straightforward candor and habit of thinking against himself, he excelled
at essay writing, tackling the largest questions without presuppositions.
Elizabeth Hardwick wrote admiringly: "He is usually thought to be the
most significant thinker America has produced, and everyone who knew
him liked him, and since his death everyone has liked him, too, because
our history has not left a single man, except perhaps Jefferson, with so
much wisdom and so much sheer delight, such tolerance for the embar-
rassments of mankind, such a high degree of personal attractiveness and
spiritual generosity."

What Makes a Life Significant?

(1900)

In my previous talk, "On a Certain Blindness," I tried to make you feel
how soaked and shot-through life is with values and meanings which we
fail to realize because of our external and insensible point of view. The
meanings are there for the others, but they are not there for us. There lies
more than a mere interest of curious speculation in understanding this.
It has the most tremendous practical importance. I wish that I could convince you of it as I feel it myself. It is the basis of all our tolerance, social,

religious, and political. The forgetting of it lies at the root of every stupid and sanguinary mistake that rulers over subject-peoples make. The first thing to learn in intercourse with others is non-interference with their own peculiar ways of being happy, provided those ways do not assume to interfere by violence with ours. No one has insight into all the ideals. No one should presume to judge them off-hand. The pretension to dogmatize about them in each other is the root of most human injustices and cruelties, and the trait in human character most likely to make the angels weep.

Every Jack sees in his own particular Jill charms and perfections to the enchantment of which we stolid onlookers are stone-cold. And which has the superior view of the absolute truth, he or we? Which has the more vital insight into the nature of Jill's existence, as a fact? Is he in excess, being in this matter a maniac? or are we in defect, being victims of a pathological anesthesia as regards Jill's magical importance? Surely the latter; surely to Jack are the profounder truths revealed; surely poor Jill's palpitating little life-throbs *are* among the wonders of creation, *are* worthy of this sympathetic interest; and it is to our shame that the rest of us cannot feel like Jack. For Jack realizes Jill concretely, and we do not. He struggles toward a union with her inner life, divining her feelings, anticipating her desires, understanding her limits as manfully as he can, and yet inadequately, too; for he is also afflicted with some blindness, even here. Whilst we, dead clods that we are, do not even seek after these things, but are contented that that portion of eternal fact named Jill should be for us as if it were not. Jill, who knows her inner life, knows that Jack's way of taking it—so importantly—is the true and serious way; and she responds to the truth in him by taking him truly and seriously, too. May the ancient blindness never wrap its clouds about either of them again! Where would any of *us* be, were there no one willing to know us as we really are or ready to repay us for *our* insight by making recognizant return? We ought, all of us, to realize each other in this intense, pathetic, and important way.

If you say that this is absurd, and that we cannot be in love with everyone at once, I merely point out to you that, as a matter of fact, certain persons do exist with an enormous capacity for friendship and for taking delight in other people's lives; and that such persons know more of truth than if their hearts were not so big. The vice of ordinary Jack and Jill affection is not its intensity, but its exclusions and its jealousies. Leave those out, and you see that the ideal I am holding up before you, however impracticable to-day, yet contains nothing intrinsically absurd.

We have unquestionably a great cloud-bank of ancestral blindness weighing down upon us, only transiently riven here and there by fitful revelations of the truth. It is vain to hope for this state of things to alter much. Our inner secrets must remain for the most part impenetrable by others, for beings as essentially practical as we are necessarily short of sight. But, if we cannot gain much positive insight into one another, cannot we at least use our sense of our own blindness to make us more cautious in going over the dark places? Cannot we escape some of those hideous ancestral intolerances; and cruelties, and positive reversals of the truth?

For the remainder of this hour I invite you to seek with me some principle to make our tolerance less chaotic. And, as I began my previous lecture by a personal reminiscence, I am going to ask your indulgence for a similar bit of egotism now.

A few summers ago I spent a happy week at the famous Assembly Grounds on the borders of Chautauqua Lake. The moment one treads that sacred enclosure, one feels one's self in an atmosphere of success. Sobriety and industry, intelligence and goodness, orderliness and ideality, prosperity and cheerfulness, pervade the air. It is a serious and studious picnic on a gigantic scale. Here you have a town of many thousands of inhabitants, beautifully laid out in the forest and drained, and equipped with means for satisfying all the necessary lower and most of the superfluous higher wants of man. You have a first-class college in full blast. You have magnificent music—a chorus of seven hundred voices, with possibly the most perfect open-air auditorium in the world. You have every sort of athletic exercise from sailing, rowing, swimming, bicycling, to the ball-field and the more artificial doings which the gymnasium affords. You have kindergartens and model secondary schools. You have general religious services and special club-houses for the several sects. You have perpetually running soda-water fountains, and daily popular lectures by distinguished men. You have the best of company, and yet no effort. You have no zymotic diseases, no poverty, no drunkenness, no crime, no police. You have culture, you have kindness, you have cheapness, you have equality, you have the best fruits of what mankind has fought and bled and striven for under the name of civilization for centuries. You have, in short, a foretaste of what human society might be, were it all in the light, with no suffering and no dark corners.

I went in curiosity for a day. I stayed for a week, held spell-bound by the charm and ease of everything, by the middle-class paradise, without a sin, without a victim, without a blot, without a tear.

And yet what was my own astonishment, on emerging into the dark and wicked world again, to catch myself quite unexpectedly and involuntarily saying: "Ouf! what a relief! Now for something primordial and savage, even though it were as bad as an Armenian massacre, to set the balance straight again. This order is too tame, this culture too second-rate, this goodness too uninspiring. This human drama without a villain or a pang; this community so refined that ice-cream soda-water is the utmost offering it can make to the brute animal in man; this city simmering in the tepid lakeside sun; this atrocious harmlessness of all things,—I cannot abide with them. Let me take my chances again in the big outside worldly wilderness with all its sins and sufferings. There are the heights and depths, the precipices and the steep ideals, the gleams of the awful and the infinite; and there is more hope and help a thousand times than in this dead level and quintessence of every mediocrity."

Such was the sudden right-about-face performed for me by my lawless fancy! There had been spread before me the realization—on a small, sample scale of course—of all the ideals for which our civilization has been striving: security, intelligence, humanity, and order; and here was the instinctive hostile reaction, not of the natural man, but of a so-called cultivated man upon such a Utopia. There seemed thus to be a self-contradiction and paradox somewhere, which I, as a professor drawing a full salary, was in duty bound to unravel and explain, if I could.

So I meditated. And, first of all, I asked myself what the thing was that was so lacking in this Sabbatical city, and the lack of which kept one forever falling short of the higher sort of contentment. And I soon recognized that it was the element that gives to the wicked outer world all its moral style, expressiveness and picturesqueness,—the element of precipitousness, so to call it, of strength and strenuousness, intensity and danger. What excites and interests the looker-on at life, what the romances and the statues celebrate and the grim civic monuments remind us of, is the everlasting battle of the powers of light with those of darkness; with heroism, reduced to its bare chance, yet ever and anon snatching victory from the jaws of death. But in this unspeakable Chautauqua there was no potentiality of death in sight anywhere, and no point of the compass visible from which danger might possibly appear. The ideal was so completely victorious already that no sign of any previous battle remained, the place just resting on its oars. But what our human emotions seem to require is the sight of the struggle going on. The moment the fruits are being merely eaten, things become ignoble. Sweat and effort, human nature strained to its uttermost and on the rack, yet getting through alive, and then turning its back on its success to pursue another more rare and arduous still—this is the sort of thing the presence of which inspires us, and the reality of which it seems to be the function of all the higher forms of literature and fine art to bring home to us and suggest. At Chautauqua there were no racks, even in the place's historical museum; and no sweat, except possibly the gentle moisture on the brow of some lecturer, or on the sides of some player in the ball-field.

Such absence of human nature *in extremis* anywhere seemed, then, a sufficient explanation for Chautauqua's flatness and lack of zest.

But was not this a paradox well calculated to fill one with dismay? It looks indeed, thought I, as if the romantic idealists with their pessimism about our civilization were, after all, quite right. An irremediable flatness is coming over the world. Bourgeoisie and mediocrity, church sociables and teachers' conventions, are taking the place of the old heights and depths and romantic *chiaroscuro*. And, to get human life in its wild intensity, we must in future turn more and more away from the actual, and forget it, if we can, in the romancer's or the poet's pages. The whole world, delightful and sinful as it may still appear for a moment to one just escaped from the Chautauquan enclosure, is nevertheless obeying more and more just those ideals that are sure to make of it in the end a mere Chautauqua Assembly on an enormous scale. *Was im Gesang soll leben muss im Leben untergehn.* Even now, in our own country, correctness, fairness, and compromise for every small advantage are crowding out all other qualities. The higher heroisms and the old rare flavors are passing out of life.

With these thoughts in my mind, I was speeding with the train toward Buffalo, when, near that city, the sight of a workman doing something on the dizzy edge of a sky-scaling iron construction brought me to my senses very suddenly. And now I perceived, by a flash of insight, that I had been steeping myself in pure ancestral blindness, and looking at life with the eyes of a remote spectator. Wishing for heroism and the spectacle of human nature on the rack, I had never noticed the great fields of heroism lying round about me, I had failed to see it present and alive. I could only think of it as dead and embalmed, labelled and costumed, as it is in the pages of romance. And yet there it was before me in the daily lives of the laboring classes. Not in clanging fights and desperate marches only is heroism to be looked for, but on every railway bridge and fire-proof building that is going up to-day. On freight-trains, on the decks of vessels, in cattleyards and mines, on lumber-rafts, among the firemen and the policemen, the demand for courage is incessant; and the supply never fails. There, every day of the year somewhere, is human nature in extremis for you. And wherever a scythe, an axe, a pick, or a shovel is wielded, you have it sweating and aching and with its powers of patient endurance racked to the utmost under the length of hours of the strain.

As I awoke to all this unidealized heroic life around me, the scales seemed to fall from my eyes; and a wave of sympathy greater than anything I had ever before felt with the common life of common men began to fill my soul. It began to seem as if virtue with horny hands and dirty skin were the only virtue genuine and vital enough to take account of. Every other virtue poses; none is absolutely unconscious and simple, and unexpectant of decoration or recognition, like this. These are our soldiers, thought I, these our sustainers, these the very parents of our life.

Many years ago, when in Vienna, I had had a similar feeling of awe and reverence in looking at the peasant women, in from the country on their business at the market for the day. Old hags many of them were, dried and brown and wrinkled, kerchiefed and short-petticoated, with thick wool stockings on their bony shanks, stumping through the glittering thoroughfares, looking neither to the right nor the left, bent on duty, envying nothing, humble-hearted, remote;—and yet at bottom, when you came to think of it, bearing the whole fabric of the splendors and corruptions of that city on their laborious backs. For where would any of it have been without their unremitting, unrewarded labor in the fields? And so with us: not to our generals and poets, I thought, but to the Italian and Hungarian laborers in the Subway, rather, ought the monuments of gratitude and reverence of a city like Boston to be reared.

If any of you have been readers of Tolstoï, you will see that I passed into a vein of feeling similar to his, with its abhorrence of all that conventionally passes for distinguished, and its exclusive deification of the bravery, patience, kindliness, and dumbness of the unconscious natural man.

Where now is our Tolstoï, I said, to bring the truth of all this home to our American bosoms, fill us with a better insight, and wean us away from that spurious literary romanticism on which our wretched culture—as it calls itself—is fed? Divinity lies all about us, and culture is too hidebound to even suspect the fact. Could a Howells or a Kipling be enlisted in this mission? or are they still too deep in the ancestral blindness, and not humane enough for the inner joy and meaning of the laborer's existence to be really revealed? Must we wait for some one born and bred and living as a laborer himself, but who, by grace of Heaven, shall also find a literary voice?

And there I rested on that day, with a sense of widening of vision, and with what it is surely fair to call an increase of religious insight into life. In God's eyes the differences of social position, of intellect, of culture, of cleanliness, of dress, which different men exhibit and all the other rarities and exceptions on which they so fantastically pin their pride, must be so small as practically quite to vanish; and all that should remain is the common fact that here we are, a countless multitude of vessels of life, each of us pent in to peculiar difficulties, with which we must severally struggle by using whatever of fortitude and goodness we can summon up. The exercise of the courage, patience, and kindness, must be the significant portion of the whole business; and the distinctions of position can only be a manner of diversifying the phenomenal surface upon which these underground virtues may manifest their effects. At this rate, the deepest human life is everywhere, is eternal. And, if any human attributes exist only in particular individuals, they must belong to the mere trapping and decoration of the surface-show.

Thus are men's lives levelled up as well as levelled down,—levelled up in their common inner meaning, levelled down in their outer gloriousness and show. Yet always, we must confess, this levelling insight tends to be obscured again; and always the ancestral blindness returns and wraps us up, so that we end once more by thinking that creation can be for no other purpose than to develop remarkable situations and conventional distinctions and merits. And then always some new leveller in the shape of a religious prophet has to arise—the Buddha, the Christ, or some Saint Francis, some Rousseau or Tolstoï—to redispel our blindness. Yet, little by little, there comes some stable gain; for the world does get more humane, and the religion of democracy tends toward permanent increase.

This, as I said, became for a time my conviction, and gave me great content. I have put the matter into the form of a personal reminiscence, so that I might lead you into it more directly and completely, and so save time. But now I am going to discuss the rest of it with you in a more impersonal way.

Tolstoï's levelling philosophy began long before he had the crisis of melancholy commemorated in that wonderful document of his entitled *My Confession*, which led the way to his more specifically religious works. In his masterpiece *War and Peace*,—assuredly the greatest of human novels,—the rôle of the spiritual hero is given to a poor little soldier named Karataïeff, so helpful, so cheerful, and so devout that, in spite of his ignorance and filthiness, the sight of him opens the heavens, which have been closed, to the mind of the principal character of the book; and his example evidently is meant by Tolstoï to let God into the world again for the reader. Poor little Karataïeff is taken prisoner by the French; and, when too exhausted by hardship and fever to march, is shot as other prisoners were in the famous retreat from Moscow. The last view one gets of him is his little figure leaning against a white birch-tree, and uncomplainingly awaiting the end.

"The more," writes Tolstoï in the work *My Confession,* "the more I examined the life of these laboring folks, the more persuaded I became that they veritably have faith, and get from it alone the sense and the possibility of life. . . . Contrariwise to those of our own class, who protest against destiny and grow indignant at its rigor, these people receive maladies and misfortunes without revolt, without opposition, and with a firm and tranquil confidence that all had to be like that, could not be otherwise, and that it is all right so. . . . The more we live by our intellect, the less we understand the meaning of life. We see only a cruel jest in suffering and death, whereas these people live, suffer, and draw near to death with tranquillity, and oftener than not with joy. . . . There are enormous multitudes of them happy with the most perfect happiness, although deprived of what for us is the sole good of life. Those who understand life's meaning, and know how to live and die thus, are to be counted not by twos, threes, tens, but by hundreds, thousands, millions. They labor quietly, endure privations and pains, live and die, and throughout everything see the good without seeing the vanity. I had to love these people. The more I entered into their life, the more I loved them; and the more it became possible for me to live, too. It came about not only that the life of our society, of the learned and of the rich, disgusted me—more than that,

it lost all semblance of meaning in my eyes. All our actions, our deliberations, our sciences, our arts, all appeared to me with a new significance.
I understood that these things might be charming pastimes, but that one
need seek in them no depth, whereas the life of the hardworking populace,
of that multitude of human beings who really contribute to existence,
appeared to me in its true light. I understood that there veritably is life,
that the meaning which life there receives is the truth; and I accepted it."

In a similar way does Stevenson appeal to our piety toward the elemental virtue of mankind.

"What a wonderful thing," he writes, "is this Man! How surprising
are his attributes! Poor soul, here for so little, cast among so many hardships, savagely surrounded, savagely descended, irremediably condemned
to prey upon his fellow-lives,—who should have blamed him, had he
been of a piece with his destiny and a being merely barbarous? . . . [Yet]
it matters not where we look, under what climate we observe him, in
what stage of society, in what depth of ignorance, burdened with what
erroneous morality; in ships at sea, a man inured to hardship and vile
pleasures, his brightest hope a fiddle in a tavern, and a bedizened trull
who sells herself to rob him, and be, for all that, simple, innocent, cheerful, kindly like a child, constant to toil, brave to drown, for others; . . .
in the slums of cities, moving among indifferent millions to mechanical
employments, without hope of change in the future, with scarce a pleasure in the present, and yet true to his virtues, honest up to his lights, kind
to his neighbors, tempted perhaps in vain by the bright gin-palace, . . .
often repaying the world's scorn with service, often standing firm upon
a scruple; . . . everywhere some virtue cherished or affected, everywhere
some decency of thought and courage, everywhere the ensign of man's
ineffectual goodness,—ah! if I could show you this! If I could show you
these men and women all the world over, in every stage of history, under
every abuse of error, under every circumstance of failure, without hope,
without help, without thanks, still obscurely fighting the lost fight of
virtue, still clinging to some rag of honor, the poor jewel of their souls."

All this is as true as it is splendid, and terribly do we need our Tolstoïs
and Stevensons to keep our sense for it alive. Yet you remember the Irishman who, when asked, "Is not one man as good as another?" replied,
"Yes; and a great deal better, too!" Similarly (it seems to me) does Tolstoï
overcorrect our social prejudices, when he makes his love of the peasant
so exclusive, and hardens his heart toward the educated man as absolutely
as he does. Grant that at Chautauqua there was little moral effort, little
sweat or muscular strain in view. Still, deep down in the souls of the participants we may be sure that something of the sort was hid, some inner
stress, some vital virtue not found wanting when required. And, after all,
the question recurs, and forces itself upon us, Is it so certain that the
surroundings and circumstances of the virtue do make so little difference

in the importance of the result? Is the functional utility, the worth to the universe of a certain definite amount of courage, kindliness, and patience, no greater if the possessor of these virtues is in an educated situation, working out far-reaching tasks, than if he be an illiterate nobody, hewing wood and drawing water, just to keep himself alive? Tolstoï's philosophy, deeply enlightening though it certainly is, remains a false abstraction. It savors too much of that Oriental pessimism and nihilism of his, which declares the whole phenomenal world and its facts and their distinctions to be a cunning fraud.

A mere bare fraud is just what our Western common sense will never believe the phenomenal world to be. It admits fully that the inner joys and virtues are the *essential* part of life's business, but it is sure that some positive part is also played by the adjuncts of the show. If it is idiotic in romanticism to recognize the heroic only when it sees it labelled and dressed-up in books, it is really just as idiotic to see it only in the dirty boots and sweaty shirt of some one in the fields. It is with us really under every disguise: at Chautauqua; here in your college; in the stock-yards and on the freight-trains; and in the czar of Russia's court. But, instinctively, we make a combination of two things in judging the total significance of a human being. We feel it to be some sort of a product (if such a product only could be calculated) of his inner virtue *and* his outer place,—neither singly taken, but both conjoined. If the outer differences had no meaning for life, why indeed should all this immense variety of them exist? They must be significant elements of the world as well.

Just test Tolstoï's deification of the mere manual laborer by the facts. This is what Mr. Walter Wyckoff, after working as an unskilled laborer in the demolition of some buildings at West Point, writes of the spiritual condition of the class of men to which he temporarily chose to belong:—

> The salient features of our condition are plain enough. We are grown men, and are without a trade. In the labor-market we stand ready to sell to the highest bidder our mere muscular strength for so many hours each day. We are thus in the lowest grade of labor. And, selling our muscular strength in the open market for what it will bring, we sell it under peculiar conditions. It is all the capital that we have. We have no reserve means of subsistence, and cannot, therefore, stand off for a "reserve price." We sell under the necessity of satisfying imminent hunger. Broadly speaking, we must sell our labor or starve; and, as hunger is a matter of a few hours, and we have no other way of meeting this need, we must sell at once for what the market offers for our labor.
>
> Our employer is buying labor in a dear market, and he will certainly get from us as much work as he can at the price. The gang-boss is secured for this purpose, and thoroughly does he know his

business. He has sole command of us. He never saw us before, and he will discharge us all when the debris is cleared away. In the mean time he must get from us, if he can, the utmost of physical labor which we, individually and collectively, are capable of. If he should drive some of us to exhaustion, and we should not be able to continue at work, he would not be the loser; for the market would soon supply him with others to take our places.

We are ignorant men, but so much we clearly see,—that we have sold our labor where we could sell it dearest, and our employer has bought it where he could buy it cheapest. He has paid high, and he must get all the labor that he can; and, by a strong instinct which possesses us, we shall part with as little as we can. From work like ours there seems to us to have been eliminated every element which constitutes the nobility of labor. We feel no personal pride in its progress, and no community of interest with our employer. There is none of the joy of responsibility, none of the sense of achievement, only the dull monotony of grinding toil, with the longing for the signal to quit work, and for our wages at the end.

And being what we are, the dregs of the labor-market, and having no certainty of permanent employment, and no organization among ourselves, we must expect to work under the watchful eye of a gang-boss, and be driven, like the wage-slaves that we are, through our tasks.

All this is to tell us, in effect, that our lives are hard, barren, hopeless lives.

And such hard, barren, hopeless lives, surely, are not lives in which one ought to be willing permanently to remain. And why is this so? Is it because they are so dirty? Well, Nansen grew a great deal dirtier on his polar expedition; and we think none the worse of his life for that. Is it the insensibility? Our soldiers have to grow vastly more insensible, and we extol them to the skies. Is it the poverty? Poverty has been reckoned the crowning beauty of many a heroic career. Is it the slavery to a task, the loss of finer pleasures? Such slavery and loss are of the very essence of the higher fortitude, and are always counted to its credit,—read the records of missionary devotion all over the world. It is not any one of these things, then, taken by itself,—no, nor all of them together,—that make such a life undesirable. A man might in truth live like an unskilled laborer, and do the work of one, and yet count as one of the noblest of God's creatures. Quite possibly there were some such persons in the gang that our author describes; but the current of their souls ran underground; and he was too steeped in the ancestral blindness to discern it.

If there *were* any such morally exceptional individuals, however, what made them different from the rest? It can only have been this,—that their souls worked and endured in obedience to some inner *ideal,* while their comrades were not actuated by anything worthy of that name. These ideals of other lives are among those secrets that we can almost never penetrate, although something about the man may often tell us when they are there. In Mr. Wyckoff's own case we know exactly what the self-imposed ideal was. Partly he had stumped himself, as the boys say, to carry through a strenuous achievement; but mainly he wished to enlarge his sympathetic insight into fellow-lives. For this his sweat and toil acquire a certain heroic significance, and make us accord to him exceptional esteem. But it is easy to imagine his fellows with various other ideals. To say nothing of wives and babies, one may have been a convert of the Salvation Army, and had a nightingale singing of expiation and forgiveness in his heart all the while be labored. Or there might have been an apostle like Tolstoï himself, or his compatriot Bondaïeff, in the gang, voluntarily embracing labor as their religious mission. Class-loyalty was undoubtedly an ideal with many. And who knows how much of that higher manliness of poverty, of which Phillips Brooks has spoken so penetratingly, was or was not present in that gang?

"A rugged, barren land," says Phillips Brooks, "is poverty to live in,—a land where I am thankful very often if I can get a berry or a root to eat. But living in it really, letting it bear witness to me of itself, not dishonoring it all the time by judging it after the standard of the other lands, gradually there come out its qualities. Behold! no land like this barren and naked land of poverty could show the moral geology of the world. See how the hard ribs . . . stand out strong and solid. No life like poverty could so get one to the heart of things and make men know their meaning, could so let us feel life and the world with all the soft cushions stripped off and thrown away. . . . Poverty makes men come very near each other, and recognize each other's human hearts; and poverty, highest and best of all, demands and cries out for faith in God. . . . I know how superficial and unfeeling, how like mere mockery, words in praise of poverty may seem. . . . But I am sure that the poor man's dignity and freedom, his self-respect and energy, depend upon his cordial knowledge that his poverty is a true region and kind of life, with its own chances of character, its own springs of happiness and revelations of God. Let him resist the characterlessness which often goes with being poor. Let him insist on respecting the condition where he lives. Let him learn to love it, so that by and by, [if] he grows rich, he shall go out of the low door of the old familiar poverty with a true pang of regret, and with a true honor for the narrow home in which he has lived so long."

The barrenness and ignobleness of the more usual laborer's life consist in the fact that it is moved by no such ideal inner springs. The backache, the long hours, the danger, are patiently endured—for what? To gain a

quid of tobacco, a glass of beer, a cup of coffee, a meal, and a bed, and to
begin again the next day and shirk as much as one can. This really is why
we raise no monument to the laborers in the Subway, even though they be
our conscripts, and even though after a fashion our city is indeed based
upon their patient hearts and enduring backs and shoulders. And this is
why we do raise monuments to our soldiers, whose outward conditions
were even brutaller still. The soldiers are supposed to have followed an
ideal, and the laborers are supposed to have followed none.

You see, my friends, how the plot now thickens; and how strangely the
complexities of this wonderful human nature of ours begin to develop
under our hands. We have seen the blindness and deadness to each other
which are our natural inheritance; and, in spite of them, we have been led
to acknowledge an inner meaning which passeth show, and which may
be present in the lives of others where we least descry it. And now we are
led to say that such inner meaning can be *complete* and valid for us also,
only when the inner joy, courage, and endurance are joined with an ideal.

But what, exactly, do we mean by an ideal? Can we give no definite
account of such a word?

To a certain extent we can. An ideal, for instance, must be something
intellectually conceived, something of which we are not unconscious, if
we have it; and it must carry with it that sort of outlook, uplift, and
brightness that go with all intellectual facts. Secondly, there must be *novelty* in an ideal,—novelty at least for him whom the ideal grasps. Sodden
routine is incompatible with ideality, although what is sodden routine
for one person may be ideal novelty for another. This shows that there
is nothing absolutely ideal: ideals are relative to the lives that entertain
them. To keep out of the gutter is for us here no part of consciousness at
all, yet for many of our brethren it is the most legitimately engrossing of
ideals.

Now, taken nakedly, abstractly, and immediately, you see that mere ideals are the cheapest things in life. Everybody has them in some shape or
other, personal or general, sound or mistaken, low or high; and the most
worthless sentimentalists and dreamers, drunkards, shirks and verse-
makers, who never show a grain of effort, courage, or endurance, possibly
have them on the most copious scale. Education, enlarging as it does our
horizon and perspective, is a means of multiplying our ideals, of bringing
new ones into view. And your college professor, with a starched shirt and
spectacles, would, if a stock of ideals were all alone by itself enough to
render a life significant, be the most absolutely and deeply significant of
men. Tolstoï would be completely blind in despising him for a prig, a pedant and a parody; and all our new insight into the divinity of muscular
labor would be altogether off the track of truth.

But such consequences as this, you instinctively feel, are erroneous.
The more ideals a man has, the more contemptible, on the whole, do you

continue to deem him, if the matter ends there for him, and if none of the laboring man's virtues are called into action on his part,—no courage shown, no privations undergone, no dirt or scars contracted in the attempt to get them realized. It is quite obvious that something more than the mere possession of ideals is required to make a life significant in any sense that claims the spectator's admiration. Inner joy, to be sure, it may *have,* with its ideals; but that is its own private sentimental matter. To extort from us, outsiders as we are, with our own ideals to look after, the tribute of our grudging recognition, it must back its ideal visions with what the laborers have, the sterner stuff of manly virtue; it must multiply their sentimental surface by the dimension of the active will, if we are to have *depth,* if we are to have anything cubical and solid in the way of character.

The significance of a human life for communicable and publicly recognizable purposes is thus the offspring of a marriage of two different parents, either of whom alone is barren. The ideals taken by themselves give no reality, the virtues by themselves no novelty. And let the orientalists and pessimists say what they will, the thing of deepest—or, at any rate, of comparatively deepest—significance in life does seem to be its character of progress, or that strange union of reality with ideal novelty which it continues from one moment to another to present. To recognize ideal novelty is the task of what we call intelligence. Not every one's intelligence can tell which novelties are ideal. For many the ideal thing will always seem to cling still to the older more familiar good. In this case character, though not significant totally, may be still significant pathetically. So, if we are to choose which is the more essential factor of human character, the fighting virtue or the intellectual breadth, we must side with Tolstoï, and choose that simple faithfulness to his light or darkness which any common unintellectual man can show.

But, with all this beating and tacking on my part, I fear you take me to be reaching a confused result. I seem to be just taking things up and dropping them again. First I took up Chautauqua, and dropped that; then Tolstoï and the heroism of common toil, and dropped them; finally, I took up ideals, and seem now almost dropping those. But please observe in what sense it is that I drop them. It is when they pretend singly to redeem life from insignificance. Culture and refinement all alone are not enough to do so. Ideal aspirations are not enough, when uncombined with pluck and will. But neither are pluck and will, dogged endurance and insensibility to danger enough, when taken all alone. There must be some sort of fusion, some chemical combination among these principles, for a life objectively and thoroughly significant to result.

Of course, this is a somewhat vague conclusion. But in a question of significance, of worth, like this, conclusions can never be precise. The answer of appreciation, of sentiment, is always a more or a less, a balance struck by sympathy, insight, and good will. But it is an answer, all the same a real conclusion. And, in the course of getting it, it seems to me that our eyes have been opened to many important things. Some of you are, perhaps, more livingly aware than you were an hour ago of the depths of worth that lie around you, hid in alien lives. And, when you ask how much sympathy you ought to bestow, although the amount is, truly enough, a matter of ideal on your own part, yet in this notion of the combination of ideals with active virtues you have a rough standard for shaping your decision. In any case, your imagination is extended. You divine in the world about you matter for a little more humility on your own part, and tolerance, reverence, and love for others; and you gain a certain inner joyfulness at the increased importance of our common life. Such joyfulness is a religious inspiration and an element of spiritual health, and worth more than large amounts of that sort of technical and accurate information which we professors are supposed to be able to impart.

To show the sort of thing I mean by these words, I will just make one brief practical illustration, and then close.

We are suffering to-day in America from what is called the labor-question; and, when you go out into the world, you will each and all of you be caught up in its perplexities. I use the brief term labor-question to cover all sorts of anarchistic discontents and socialistic projects, and the conservative resistances which they provoke. So far as this conflict is unhealthy and regrettable,—and I think it is so only to a limited extent,— the unhealthiness consists solely in the fact that one-half of our fellow countrymen remain entirely blind to the internal significance of the lives of the other half. They miss the joys and sorrows, they fail to feel the moral virtue, and they do not guess the presence of the intellectual ideals. They are at cross-purposes all along the line, regarding each other as they might regard a set of dangerously gesticulating automata, or, if they seek to get at the inner motivation, making the most horrible mistakes. Often all that the poor man can think of in the rich man is a cowardly greediness for safety, luxury, and effeminacy, and a boundless affectation. What he is, is not a human being, but a pocket-book, a bank-account. And a similar greediness, turned by disappointment into envy, is all that many rich men can see in the state of mind of the dissatisfied poor. And, if the rich man begins to do the sentimental act over the poor man, what senseless blunders does he make, pitying him for just those very duties and those very immunities which, rightly taken, are the condition of his most abiding and characteristic joys! Each, in short, ignores the fact that happiness and unhappiness and significance are a vital mystery; each pins them absolutely on some ridiculous feature of the external situation; and everybody remains outside of everybody else's sight.

Society has, with all this, undoubtedly got to pass toward some newer and better equilibrium, and the distribution of wealth has doubtless slowly got to change: such changes have always happened, and will happen to the end of time. But if, after all that I have said, any of you expect that they will make any *genuine vital difference* on a large scale, to the lives of our descendants, you will have missed the significance of my entire lecture. The solid meaning of life is always the same eternal thing,—the marriage, namely, of some unhabitual ideal, however special, with some fidelity, courage, and endurance; with some man's or woman's pains.—And, whatever or wherever life may be, there will always be the chance for that marriage to take place.

Fitz-James Stephen wrote many years ago words to this effect more eloquent than any I can speak: "The 'Great Eastern,' or some of her successors," he said, "will perhaps defy the roll of the Atlantic, and cross the seas without allowing their passengers to feel that they have left the firm land. The voyage from the cradle to the grave may come to be performed with similar facility. Progress and science may perhaps enable untold millions to live and die without a care, without a pang, without an anxiety. They will have a pleasant passage and plenty of brilliant conversation. They will wonder that men ever believed at all in clanging fights and blazing towns and sinking ships and praying hands; and, when they come to the end of their course, they will go their way, and the place thereof will know them no more. But it seems unlikely that they will have such a knowledge of the great ocean on which they sail, with its storms and wrecks, its currents and icebergs, its huge waves and mighty winds, as those who battled with it for years together in the little craft, which, if they had few other merits, brought those who navigated them full into the presence of time and eternity, their maker and themselves, and forced them to have some definite view of their relations to them and to each other."

In this solid and tridimensional sense, so to call it, those philosophers are right who contend that the world is a standing thing, with no progress, no real history. The changing conditions of history touch only the surface of the show. The altered equilibriums and redistributions only diversify our opportunities and open chances to us for new ideals. But, with each new ideal that comes into life, the chance for a life based on some old ideal will vanish; and he would needs be a presumptuous calculator who should with confidence say that the total sum of significances is positively and absolutely greater at any one epoch than at any other of the world.

I am speaking broadly, I know, and omitting to consider certain qualifications in which I myself believe. But one can only make one point in one lecture, and I shall be well content if I have brought my point home to you this evening in even a slight degree. *There are compensations* and no outward changes of condition in life can keep the nightingale of its eternal meaning from singing in all sorts of different men's hearts. That is the main fact to remember. If we could not only admit it with our lips, but really and truly believe it, how our convulsive insistencies, how our antipathies and dreads of each other, would soften down! If the poor and the rich could look at each other in this way, *sub specie aeternitatis,* how gentle would grow their disputes! what tolerance and good humor, what willingness to live and let live, would come into the world!

W. E. B. DU BOIS

*"The problem of the twentieth century is the problem of the color-line."
So begins* The Souls of Black Folk, *a landmark collection of fourteen
essays, the first of which is included below. W. E. B. Du Bois (1868–1963)
was an accomplished sociologist, professor, and civil rights activist, the
first African American to earn a PhD from Harvard University, and a
cofounder of the National Association for the Advancement of Colored
People (NAACP), whose magazine,* The Crisis, *he edited. Du Bois also
wrote autobiographies and several novels, as well as countless essays
intended to spur political action against racism. "Of Our Spiritual
Strivings" explores his seminal idea of a "double consciousness" among
African Americans, through personal narrative about his own encounters
with racism and through large-picture analysis, employing powerfully
lyrical language in the process.*

Of Our Spiritual Strivings

(1903)

> O water, voice of my heart, crying in the sand,
> All night long crying with a mournful cry,
> As I lie and listen, and cannot understand
> The voice of my heart in my side or the voice of the sea,
> O water, crying for rest, is it I, is it I?
> All night long the water is crying to me.
> Unresting water, there shall never be rest
> Till the last moon droop and the last tide fail,

And the fire of the end begin to burn in the west;
And the heart shall be weary and wonder and cry like the sea,
All life long crying without avail,
As the water all night long is crying to me.

—Arthur Symons

Between me and the other world there is ever an unasked question: unasked by some through feelings of delicacy; by others through the difficulty of rightly framing it. All, nevertheless, flutter round it. They approach me in a half-hesitant sort of way, eye me curiously or compassionately, and then, instead of saying directly, How does it feel to be a problem? they say, I know an excellent colored man in my town; or, I fought at Mechanicsville; or, Do not these Southern outrages make your blood boil? At these I smile, or am interested, or reduce the boiling to a simmer, as the occasion may require. To the real question, How does it feel to be a problem? I answer seldom a word.

And yet, being a problem is a strange experience,—peculiar even for one who has never been anything else, save perhaps in babyhood and in Europe. It is in the early days of rollicking boyhood that the revelation first bursts upon one, all in a day, as it were. I remember well when the shadow swept across me. I was a little thing, away up in the hills of New England, where the dark Housatonic winds between Hoosac and Taghkanic to the sea. In a wee wooden schoolhouse, something put it into the boys' and girls' heads to buy gorgeous visiting-cards—ten cents a package—and exchange. The exchange was merry, till one girl, a tall newcomer, refused my card,—refused it peremptorily, with a glance. Then it dawned upon me with a certain suddenness that I was different from the others; or like, mayhap, in heart and life and longing, but shut out from their world by a vast veil. I had thereafter no desire to tear down that veil, to creep through; I held all beyond it in common contempt, and lived above it in a region of blue sky and great wandering shadows. That sky was bluest when I could beat my mates at examination-time, or beat them at a foot-race, or even beat their stringy heads. Alas, with the years all this fine contempt began to fade; for the words I longed for, and all their dazzling opportunities, were theirs, not mine. But they should not keep these prizes, I said; some, all, I would wrest from them. Just how I would do it I could never decide: by reading law, by healing the sick, by telling the wonderful tales that swam in my head,—some way. With other black boys the strife was not so fiercely sunny: their youth shrunk into tasteless sycophancy, or into silent hatred of the pale world about them and mocking distrust of everything white; or wasted itself in a bitter cry, Why did God make me an outcast and a stranger in mine own house? The shades of the prison-house closed round about us all: walls strait and stubborn to the whitest, but relentlessly narrow, tall, and unscalable to sons of night who must plod darkly on in resignation, or beat unavailing palms against the stone, or steadily, half hopelessly, watch the streak of blue above.

After the Egyptian and Indian, the Greek and Roman, the Teuton and Mongolian, the Negro is a sort of seventh son, born with a veil, and gifted with second-sight in this American world,—a world which yields him no true self-consciousness, but only lets him see himself through the revelation of the other world. It is a peculiar sensation, this double-consciousness, this sense of always looking at one's self through the eyes of others, of measuring one's soul by the tape of a world that looks on in amused contempt and pity. One ever feels his twoness,—an American, a Negro; two souls, two thoughts, two unreconciled strivings; two warring ideals in one dark body, whose dogged strength alone keeps it from being torn asunder.

The history of the American Negro is the history of this strife—this longing to attain self-conscious manhood, to merge his double self into a better and truer self. In this merging he wishes neither of the older selves to be lost. He would not Africanize America, for America has too much to teach the world and Africa. He would not bleach his Negro soul in a flood of white Americanism, for he knows that Negro blood has a message for the world. He simply wishes to make it possible for a man to be both a Negro and an American, without being cursed and spit upon by his fellows, without having the doors of Opportunity closed roughly in his face.

This, then, is the end of his striving: to be a co-worker in the kingdom of culture, to escape both death and isolation, to husband and use his best powers and his latent genius. These powers of body and mind have in the past been strangely wasted, dispersed, or forgotten. The shadow of a mighty Negro past flits through the tale of Ethiopia the Shadowy and of Egypt the Sphinx. Through history, the powers of single black men flash here and there like falling stars, and die sometimes before the world has rightly gauged their brightness. Here in America, in the few days since Emancipation, the black man's turning hither and thither in hesitant and doubtful striving has often made his very strength to lose effectiveness, to seem like absence of power, like weakness. And yet it is not weakness,—it is the contradiction of double aims. The double-aimed struggle of the black artisan—on the one hand to escape white contempt for a nation of mere hewers of wood and drawers of water, and on the other hand to plough and nail and dig for a poverty-stricken horde—could only result in making him a poor craftsman, for he had but half a heart in either cause. By the poverty and ignorance of his people, the Negro minister or doctor was tempted toward quackery and demagogy; and by the criticism of the other world, toward ideals that made him ashamed of his lowly tasks. The would-be black *savant* was confronted by the paradox that the knowledge his people needed was a twice-told tale to his white neighbors, while the knowledge which would teach the white world was Greek to his own flesh and blood. The innate love of harmony and beauty that set the ruder souls of his people a-dancing and a-singing raised but confusion and doubt in the soul of the black artist; for the beauty revealed to him was the soul-beauty of a race which his larger audience despised, and he could not articulate the message of another people. This waste of double aims, this seeking to satisfy two unreconciled ideals, has wrought sad havoc with the courage and faith and deeds of ten thousand thousand people,—has sent them often wooing false gods and invoking false means of salvation, and at times has even seemed about to make them ashamed of themselves.

Away back in the days of bondage they thought to see in one divine event the end of all doubt and disappointment; few men ever worshipped Freedom with half such unquestioning faith as did the American Negro for two centuries. To him, so far as he thought and dreamed, slavery was indeed the sum of all villainies, the cause of all sorrow, the root of all prejudice; Emancipation was the key to a promised land of sweeter beauty than ever stretched before the eyes of wearied Israelites. In song and exhortation swelled one refrain—Liberty; in his tears and curses the God he implored had Freedom in his right hand. At last it came,—suddenly, fearfully, like a dream. With one wild carnival of blood and passion came the message in his own plaintive cadences:—

> "Shout, O children!
> Shout, you're free!
> For God has bought your liberty!"

Years have passed away since then,—ten, twenty, forty; forty years of national life, forty years of renewal and development, and yet the swarthy spectre sits in its accustomed seat at the Nation's feast. In vain do we cry to this our vastest social problem:—

> "Take any shape but that, and my firm nerves
> Shall never tremble!"

The Nation has not yet found peace from its sins; the freedman has not yet found in freedom his promised land. Whatever of good may have come in these years of change, the shadow of a deep disappointment rests upon the Negro people,—a disappointment all the more bitter because the unattained ideal was unbounded save by the simple ignorance of a lowly people.

The first decade was merely a prolongation of the vain search for freedom, the boon that seemed ever barely to elude their grasp,—like a tantalizing will-o'-the-wisp, maddening and misleading the headless host. The holocaust of war, the terrors of the Ku-Klux Klan, the lies of carpet-baggers, the disorganization of industry, and the contradictory advice of friends and foes, left the bewildered serf with no new watch-word beyond the old cry for freedom. As the time flew, however, he began to grasp a new idea. The ideal of liberty demanded for its attainment powerful means, and these the Fifteenth Amendment gave him. The ballot, which before he had looked upon as a visible sign of freedom, he now regarded as the chief means of gaining and perfecting the liberty with which war had partially endowed him. And why not? Had not votes made war and emancipated millions? Had not votes enfranchised the freedmen? Was anything impossible to a power that had done all this? A million black men started with renewed zeal to vote themselves into the kingdom. So the decade flew away, the revolution of 1876 came, and left the half-free serf weary, wondering, but still inspired. Slowly but steadily, in the follow-ing years, a new vision began gradually to replace the dream of political power,—a powerful movement, the rise of another ideal to guide the un-guided, another pillar of fire by night after a clouded day. It was the ideal of "book-learning"; the curiosity, born of compulsory ignorance, to know and test the power of the cabalistic letters of the white man, the longing to know. Here at last seemed to have been discovered the mountain path to Canaan; longer than the highway of Emancipation and law, steep and rugged, but straight, leading to heights high enough to overlook life.

Up the new path the advance guard toiled, slowly, heavily, doggedly; only those who have watched and guided the faltering feet, the misty minds, the dull understandings, of the dark pupils of these schools know how faithfully, how piteously, this people strove to learn. It was weary work. The cold statistician wrote down the inches of progress here and there, noted also where here and there a foot had slipped or some one had fallen. To the tired climbers, the horizon was ever dark, the mists were often cold, the Canaan was always dim and far away. If, however, the vistas disclosed as yet no goal, no resting-place, little but flattery and criticism, the journey at least gave leisure for reflection and self-examination; it changed the child of Emancipation to the youth with dawning self-consciousness, self-realization, self-respect. In those sombre forests of his striving his own soul rose before him, and he saw himself,—darkly as through a veil; and yet he saw in himself some faint revelation of his power, of his mission. He began to have a dim feeling that, to attain his place in the world, he must be himself, and not another. For the first time he sought to analyze the burden he bore upon his back, that dead-weight of social degradation partially masked behind a half-named Negro problem. He felt his poverty; without a cent, without a home, without land, tools, or savings, he had entered into competition with rich, landed, skilled neighbors. To be a poor man is hard, but to be a poor race in a land of dollars is the very bottom of hardships. He felt the weight of his ignorance,—not simply of letters, but of life, of business, of the humanities; the accumulated sloth and shirking and awkwardness of decades and centuries shackled his hands and feet. Nor was his burden all poverty and ignorance. The red stain of bastardy, which two centuries of systematic legal defilement of Negro women had stamped upon his race, meant not only the loss of ancient African chastity, but also the hereditary weight of a mass of corruption from white adulterers, threatening almost the obliteration of the Negro home.

A people thus handicapped ought not to be asked to race with the world, but rather allowed to give all its time and thought to its own social problems. But alas! while sociologists gleefully count his bastards and his prostitutes, the very soul of the toiling, sweating black man is darkened by the shadow of a vast despair. Men call the shadow prejudice, and learnedly explain it as the natural defence of culture against barbarism, learning against ignorance, purity against crime, the "higher" against the "lower" races. To which the Negro cries Amen! and swears that to so much of this strange prejudice as is founded on just homage to civilization, culture, righteousness, and progress, he humbly bows and meekly does obeisance. But before that nameless prejudice that leaps beyond all this he stands helpless, dismayed, and well-nigh speechless; before that personal disrespect and mockery, the ridicule and systematic humiliation, the distortion of fact and wanton license of fancy, the cynical ignoring of the better and the boisterous welcoming of the worse, the all-pervading desire to inculcate disdain for everything black, from Toussaint to the devil,—before this there rises a sickening despair that would disarm and discourage any nation save that black host to whom "discouragement" is an unwritten word.

But the facing of so vast a prejudice could not but bring the inevitable self-questioning, self-disparagement, and lowering of ideals which ever accompany repression and breed in an atmosphere of contempt and hate. Whisperings and portents came home upon the four winds: Lo! we are diseased and dying, cried the dark hosts; we cannot write, our voting is vain; what need of education, since we must always cook and serve? And the Nation echoed and enforced this self-criticism, saying: Be content to be servants, and nothing more; what need of higher culture for half-men? Away with the black man's ballot, by force or fraud,—and behold the suicide of a race! Nevertheless, out of the evil came something of good,— the more careful adjustment of education to real life, the clearer perception of the Negroes' social responsibilities, and the sobering realization of the meaning of progress.

So dawned the time of *Sturm und Drang:* storm and stress to-day rocks our little boat on the mad waters of the world-sea; there is within and without the sound of conflict, the burning of body and rending of soul; inspiration strives with doubt, and faith with vain questionings. The bright ideals of the past,—physical freedom, political power, the training of brains and the training of hands,—all these in turn have waxed and waned, until even the last grows dim and overcast. Are they all wrong,— all false? No, not that, but each alone was over-simple and incomplete,— the dreams of a credulous race-childhood, or the fond imaginings of the other world which does not know and does not want to know our power. To be really true, all these ideals must be melted and welded into one. The training of the schools we need to-day more than ever,—the training of deft hands, quick eyes and ears, and above all the broader, deeper, higher culture of gifted minds and pure hearts. The power of the ballot we need in sheer self-defence,—else what shall save us from a second slavery? Freedom, too, the long-sought, we still seek,—the freedom of life and limb, the freedom to work and think, the freedom to love and aspire. Work, culture, liberty,—all these we need, not singly but together, not successively but together, each growing and aiding each, and all striving toward that vaster ideal that swims before the Negro people, the ideal of human brotherhood, gained through the unifying ideal of Race; the ideal of fostering and developing the traits and talents of the Negro, not in opposition to or contempt for other races, but rather in large conformity to the greater ideals of the American Republic, in order that some day on American soil two world-races may give each to each those characteristics both so sadly lack. We the darker ones come even now not altogether empty-handed: there are to-day no truer exponents of the pure human spirit of the Declaration of Independence than the American Negroes; there is no true American music but the wild sweet melodies of the Negro slave; the American fairy tales and folklore are Indian and African; and, all in all, we black men seem the sole oasis of simple faith and reverence in a dusty desert of dollars and smartness. Will America be poorer if she replace her brutal dyspeptic blundering with light-hearted but determined Negro humility? or her coarse and cruel wit with loving jovial good-humor? or her vulgar music with the soul of the Sorrow Songs?

Merely a concrete test of the underlying principles of the great republic is the Negro Problem, and the spiritual striving of the freedmen's sons is the travail of souls whose burden is almost beyond the measure of their strength, but who bear it in the name of an historic race, in the name of this the land of their fathers' fathers, and in the name of human opportunity.

And now what I have briefly sketched in large outline let me on coming pages tell again in many ways, with loving emphasis and deeper detail, that men may listen to the striving in the souls of black folk.

JOHN DEWEY

John Dewey (1859–1952) was a philosopher of the American pragmatic school, a pioneering psychologist, and an educational reformer. Believing unreservedly in democracy as an ethical ideal as well as a political system, he sought to make schools more democratic by questioning their top-down organization and their rigidly imposed curricula transmitted to passive receptors, which, he thought, suppressed the independence and creativity of teachers and students. A key element of progressive education, he stressed, was hands-on learning, or education through experience. His ideas have had a profound influence on liberal American thought, though they still remain largely unrealized in the classroom today, as witness the persistence of pedagogical practices that he impatiently decried in his forcefully argued 1903 essay, "Democracy in Education."

Democracy in Education

(1903)

Modern life means democracy, democracy means freeing intelligence for independent effectiveness—the emancipation of mind as an individual organ to do its own work. We naturally associate democracy, to be sure, with freedom of action, but freedom of action without freed capacity of thought behind it is only chaos. If external authority in action is given up, it must be because internal authority of truth, discovered and known to reason, is substituted.

How does the school stand with reference to this matter? Does the school as an accredited representative exhibit this trait of democracy as a spiritual force? Does it lead and direct the movement? Does it lag behind and work at cross-purpose? I find the fundamental need of the school today dependent upon its limited recognition of the principle of freedom of intelligence. This limitation appears to me to affect both of the elements of school life: teacher and pupil. As to both, the school has lagged behind the general contemporary social movement; and much that is unsatisfactory, much of conflict and of defect, comes from the discrepancy between the relatively undemocratic organization of the school, as it affects the mind of both teacher and pupil, and the growth and extension of the democratic principle in life beyond school doors.

The effort of the last two-thirds of a century has been successful in building up the machinery of a democracy of mind. It has provided the ways and means for housing and equipping intelligence. What remains is that the thought-activity of the individual, whether teacher or student, be permitted and encouraged to take working possession of this machinery: to substitute its rightful lordship for an inherited servility. In truth, our public-school system is but two-thirds of a century old. It dates, so far as such matters can be dated at all, from 1837, the year that Horace Mann became secretary of the state board of Massachusetts; and from 1843, when Henry Barnard began a similar work in Connecticut. At this time began that growing and finally successful warfare against all the influences, social and sectarian, which would prevent or mitigate the sway of public influence over private ecclesiastical and class interests. Between 1837 and 1850 grew up all the most characteristic features of the American public-school system: from this time date state normal schools, city training schools, county and state institutes, teachers' associations, teachers' journals, the institution of city superintendencies, supervisory officers, and the development of state universities as the crown of the public-school system of the commonwealth. From this time date the striving for better schoolhouses and grounds, improved text-books, adequate material equipment in maps, globes, scientific apparatus, etc. As an outcome of the forces thus set in motion, democracy has in principle, subject to relative local restrictions, developed an organized machinery of public education. But when we turn to the aim and method which this magnificent institution serves, we find that our democracy is not yet conscious of the ethical principle upon which it rests—the responsibility and freedom of mind in discovery and proof—and consequently we find confusion where there should be order, darkness where there should be light. The teacher has not the power of initiation and constructive endeavor which is necessary to the fulfilment of the function of teaching. The learner finds conditions antagonistic (or at least lacking) to the development of individual mental power and to adequate responsibility for its use.

1. *As to the teacher.*—If there is a single public-school system in the United States where there is official and constitutional provision made for

submitting questions of methods of discipline and teaching, and the questions of the curriculum, text-books, etc., to the discussion and decision of those actually engaged in the work of teaching, that fact has escaped my notice. Indeed, the opposite situation is so common that it seems, as a rule, to be absolutely taken for granted as the normal and final condition of affairs. The number of persons to whom any other course has occurred as desirable, or even possible—to say nothing of necessary—is apparently very limited. But until the public-school system is organized in such a way that every teacher has some regular and representative way in which he or she can register judgment upon matters of educational importance, with the assurance that this judgment will somehow affect the school system, the assertion that the present system is not, from the internal standpoint, democratic seems to be justified. Either we come here upon some fixed and inherent limitation of the democratic principle, or else we find in this fact an obvious discrepancy between the conduct of the school and the conduct of social life—a discrepancy so great as to demand immediate and persistent effort at reform.

The more enlightened portions of the public have, indeed, become aware of one aspect of this discrepancy. Many reformers are contending against the conditions which place the direction of school affairs, including the selection of text-books, etc., in the hands of a body of men who are outside the school system itself, who have not necessarily any expert knowledge of education and who are moved by non-educational motives. Unfortunately, those who have noted this undemocratic condition of affairs, and who have striven to change it, have, as a rule, conceived of but one remedy, namely, the transfer of authority to the school superintendent. In their zeal to place the center of gravity inside the school system, in their zeal to decrease the prerogatives of a non-expert school board, and to lessen the opportunities for corruption and private pull which go with that, they have tried to remedy one of the evils of democracy by adopting the principle of autocracy. For no matter how wise, expert, or benevolent the head of the school system, the one-man principle is autocracy.

The logic of the argument goes farther, very much farther, than the reformer of this type sees. The logic which commits him to the idea that the management of the school system must be in the hands of an expert commits him also to the idea that every member of the school system, from the first-grade teacher to the principal of the high school, must have some share in the exercise of educational power. The remedy is not to have one expert dictating educational methods and subject-matter to a body of passive, recipient teachers, but the adoption of intellectual initiative, discussion, and decision throughout the entire school corps. The remedy of the partial evils of democracy, the implication of the school system in municipal politics, is in appeal to a more thoroughgoing democracy.

The dictation, in theory at least, of the subject-matter to be taught, to the teacher who is to engage in the actual work of instruction, and frequently, under the name of close supervision, the attempt to determine the methods which are to be used in teaching, mean nothing more or less than the deliberate restriction of intelligence, the imprisoning of the spirit. Every well graded system of schools in this country rejoices in a course of study. It is no uncommon thing to find methods of teaching such subjects as reading, writing, spelling, and arithmetic officially laid down; outline topics in history and geography are provided ready-made for the teacher; gems of literature are fitted to the successive ages of boys and girls. Even the domain of art, songs and methods of singing, subject-matter and technique of drawing and painting, come within the region on which an outside authority lays its sacrilegious hands.

I have stated the theory, which is also true of the practice to a certain extent and in certain places. We may thank our heavens, however, that the practice is rarely as bad as the theory would require. Superintendents and principals often encourage individuality and thoughtfulness in the invention and adoption of methods of teaching; and they wink at departures from the printed manual of study. It remains true, however, that this great advance is personal and informal. It depends upon the wisdom and tact of the individual supervisory official; he may withdraw his concession at any moment; or it may be ruthlessly thrown aside by his successor who has formed a high ideal of "system."

I know it will be said that this state of things, while an evil, is a necessary one; that without it confusion and chaos would reign; that such regulations are the inevitable accompaniments of any graded system. It is said that the average teacher is incompetent to take any part in laying out the course of study or in initiating methods of instruction or discipline. Is not this the type of argument which has been used from time immemorial, and in every department of life, against the advance of democracy? What does democracy mean save that the individual is to have a share in determining the conditions and the aims of his own work; and that, upon the whole, through the free and mutual harmonizing of different individuals, the work of the world is better done than when planned, arranged, and directed by a few, no matter how wise or of how good intent that few? How can we justify our belief in the democratic principle elsewhere, and then go back entirely upon it when we come to education?

Moreover, the argument proves too much. The more it is asserted that the existing corps of teachers is unfit to have voice in the settlement of important educational matters, and their unfitness to exercise intellectual initiative and to assume the responsibility for constructive work is emphasized, the more their unfitness to attempt the much more difficult and delicate task of guiding souls appears. If this body is so unfit, how can it be trusted to carry out the recommendations or the dictations of the wisest body of experts? If teachers are incapable of the intellectual responsibility which goes with the determination of the methods they are to use in teaching, how can they employ methods when dictated by others, in other than a mechanical, capricious, and clumsy manner? The argument, I say, proves too much.

Moreover, if the teaching force is as inept and unintelligent and irresponsible as the argument assumes, surely the primary problem is that of their improvement. Only by sharing in some responsible task does there come a fitness to share in it. The argument that we must wait until men and women are fully ready to assume intellectual and social responsibilities would have defeated every step in the democratic direction that has ever been taken. The prevalence of methods of authority and of external dictation and direction tends automatically to perpetuate the very conditions of inefficiency, lack of interest, inability to assume positions of self-determination, which constitute the reasons that are depended upon to justify the regime of authority.

The system which makes no great demands upon originality, upon invention, upon the continuous expression of individuality, works automatically to put and to keep the more incompetent teachers in the school. It puts them there because, by a natural law of spiritual gravitation, the best minds are drawn to the places where they can work most effectively. The best minds are not especially like to be drawn where there is danger that they may have to submit to conditions which no self-respecting intelligence likes to put up with; and where their time and energy are likely to be so occupied with details of external conformity that they have no opportunity for free and full play of their own vigor.

I have dwelt at length upon the problem of the recognition of the intellectual and spiritual individuality of the teacher. I have but one excuse. All other reforms are conditioned upon reform in the quality and character of those who engage in the teaching profession. The doctrine of the man behind the gun has become familiar enough, in recent discussion, in every sphere of life. Just because education is the most personal, the most intimate, of all human affairs, there, more than anywhere else, the sole ultimate reliance and final source of power are in the training, character, and intelligence of the individual. If any scheme could be devised which would draw to the calling of teaching persons of force of character, of sympathy with children, and consequent interest in the problems of teaching and of scholarship, no one need be troubled for a moment about other educational reforms, or the solution of other educational problems. But as long as a school organization which is undemocratic in principle tends to repel from all but the higher portions of the school system those of independent force, of intellectual initiative, and of inventive ability, or tends to hamper them in their work after they find their way into the schoolroom, so long as all other reforms are compromised at their source and postponed indefinitely for fruition.

2. *As to the learner.*—The undemocratic suppression of the individuality of the teacher goes naturally with the improper restriction of the intelligence of the mind of the child. The mind, to be sure, is that of a child, and yet, after all, it is mind. To subject mind to an outside and ready-made material is a denial of the ideal of democracy, which roots itself ultimately in the principle of moral, self-directing individuality. Misunderstanding regarding the nature of the freedom that is demanded for the child is so common that it may be necessary to emphasize the fact that it is primarily intellectual freedom, free play of mental attitude, and operation which are sought. If individuality were simply a matter of feelings, impulses, and outward acts independent of intelligence, it would be more than a dubious matter to urge a greater degree of freedom for the child in the school. In that case much, and almost exclusive, force would attach to the objections that the principle of individuality is realized in the more exaggerated parts of Rousseau's doctrines: sentimental idealization of the child's immaturity, irrational denial of superior worth in the knowledge and mature experience of the adult, deliberate denial of the worth of the ends and instruments embodied in social organization. Deification of childish whim, unripened fancy, and arbitrary emotion is certainly a piece of pure romanticism. The would-be reformers who emphasize out of due proportion and perspective these aspects of the principle of individualism betray their own cause. But the heart of the matter lies not there. Reform of education in the direction of greater play for the individuality of the child means the securing of conditions which will give outlet, and hence direction, to a growing intelligence. It is true that this freed power of mind with reference to its own further growth cannot be obtained without a certain leeway, a certain flexibility, in the expression of even immature feelings and fancies. But it is equally true that it is not a riotous loosening of these traits which is needed, but just that kind and degree of freedom from repression which are found to be necessary to secure the full operation of intelligence.

Now, no one need doubt as to what mental activity or the freed expression of intelligence means. No one need doubt as to the conditions which are conducive to it. We do not have to fall back upon what some regard as the uncertain, distracting, and even distressing voice of psychology. Scientific methods, the methods pursued by the scientific inquirer, give us an exact and concrete exhibition of the path which intelligence takes when working most efficiently, under most favorable conditions. What is primarily required for that direct inquiry which constitutes the essence of science is first-hand experience; an active and vital participation through the medium of all the bodily organs with the means and materials of building up first-hand experience. Contrast this first and most fundamental of all the demands for an effective use of mind with what we find in so many of our elementary and high schools. There first-hand experience is at a discount; in its stead are summaries and formulas of the results of other people. Only very recently has any positive provision been made within the schoolroom for any of the modes of activity and for any of the equipment and arrangement which permit and require the extension of original experiences on the part of the child. The school has literally been dressed out with hand-me-down garments—with intellectual suits which other people have worn.

Secondly, in that freed activity of mind which we term "science" there is always a certain problem which focuses effort, which controls the collecting of facts that bear upon the question, the use of observation to get further data, the employing of memory to supply relevant facts, the calling into play of imagination, to yield fertile suggestion and construct possible solutions of the difficulty.

Turning to the school, we find too largely no counterpart to this mental activity. Just because a second-handed material has been supplied wholesale and retail, but anyway ready-made, the tendency is to reduce the activity of mind to a docile or passive taking in of the material presented—in short, to memorizing, with simply incidental use of judgment and of active research. As is frequently stated, acquiring takes the place of inquiring. It is hardly an exaggeration to say that the sort of mind-activity which is encouraged in the school is a survival from the days in which science had not made much headway; when education was mainly concerned with learning, that is to say, the preservation and handing down of the acquisitions of the past. It is true that more and more appeal is made every day in schools to judgment, reasoning, personal efficiency, and the calling up of personal, as distinct from merely book, experiences. But we have not yet got to the point of reversing the total method. The burden and the stress still fall upon learning in the sense of becoming possessed of the second-hand and ready-made material referred to. As Mrs. Young has recently said, the prevailing ideal is a perfect recitation, an exhibition without mistake, of a lesson learned. Until the emphasis changes to the conditions which make it necessary for the child to take an active share in the personal building up of his own problems and to participate in methods of solving them (even at the expense of experimentation and error), mind is not really freed.

In our schools we have freed individuality in many modes of outer expression without freeing intelligence, which is the vital spring and guarantee of all of these expressions. Consequently we give opportunity to the unconverted to point the finger of scorn, and to clamor for a return to the good old days when the teacher, the representative of social and moral authority, was securely seated in the high places of the school. But the remedy here, as in other phases of our social democracy, is not to turn back, but to go farther—to carry the evolution of the school to a point where it becomes a place for getting and testing experience, as real and adequate to the child upon his existing level as all the resources of laboratory and library afford to the scientific man upon his level. What is needed is not any radical revolution, but rather an organization of agencies already found in the schools. It is hardly too much to say that not a single subject or instrumentality is required which is not already found in many schools of the country. All that is required is to gather these materials and forces together and unify their operation. Too often they are used for a multitude of diverse and often conflicting aims. If a single purpose is provided, that of freeing the processes of mental growth, these agencies will at once fall into their proper classes and reinforce each other.

A catalogue of the agencies already available would include at least all of the following: Taking the child out of doors, widening and organizing his experience with reference to the world in which he lives; nature study when pursued as a vital observation of forces working under their natural conditions, plants and animals growing in their own homes, instead of mere discussion of dead specimens. We have also school gardens, the introduction of elementary agriculture, and more especially of horticulture—a movement that is already making great headway in many of the western states. We have also means for the sake of studying physiographic conditions, such as may be found by rivers, ponds or lakes, beaches, quarries, gulleys, hills, etc.

As similar agencies within the school walls, we find a very great variety of instruments for constructive work, or, as it is frequently, but somewhat unfortunately termed, "manual training." Under this head come cooking, which can be begun in its simpler form in the kindergarten; sewing, and what is of even greater educational value, weaving, including designing and the construction of simple apparatus for carrying on various processes of spinning, etc. Then there are also the various forms of tool-work directed upon cardboard, wood, and iron; in addition there are clay-modeling and a variety of ways of manipulating plastic material to gain power and larger experience.

Such matters pass readily over into the simpler forms of scientific experimentation. Every schoolroom from the lowest primary grade up should be supplied with gas, water, certain chemical substances and reagents. To experiment in the sense of trying things or to see what will happen is the most natural business of the child; it is, indeed, his chief concern. It is one which the school has largely either ignored or actually suppressed, so that it has been forced to find outlet in mischief or even in actually destructive ways. This tendency could find outlet in the construction of simple apparatus and the making of simple tests, leading constantly into more and more controlled experimentation, with greater insistense upon definiteness of intellectual result and control of logical process.

Add to these three typical modes of active experimenting, various forms of art expression, beginning with music, clay-modeling, and story-telling as foundation elements, and passing on to drawing, painting, designing in various mediums, we have a range of forces and materials which connect at every point with the child's natural needs and powers, and which supply the requisites for building up his experience upon all sides. As fast as these various agencies find their way into the schools, the center of gravity shifts, the regime changes from one of subjection of mind to an external and ready-made material, into the activity of mind directed upon the control of the subject-matter and thereby its own upbuilding.

Politically we have found that this country could not endure half free and half slave. We shall find equally great difficulty in encouraging freedom, independence, and initiative in every sphere of social life, while perpetuating in the school dependence upon external authority. The forces of social life are already encroaching upon the school institutions which we have inherited from the past, so that many of its main stays are crumbling. Unless the outcome is to be chaotic, we must take hold of the organic, positive principle involved in democracy, and put that in entire possession of the spirit and work of the school.

In education meet the three most powerful motives of human activity. Here are found sympathy and affection, the going out of the emotions to the most appealing and the most rewarding object of love—a little child. Here is found also the flowering of the social and institutional motive, interest in the welfare of society and in its progress and reform by the surest and shortest means. Here, too, is found the intellectual and scientific motive, the interest in knowledge, in scholarship, in truth for its own sake, unhampered and unmixed with any alien ideal. Copartnership of these three motives—of affection, of social growth, and of scientific inquiry—must prove as nearly irresistible as anything human when they are once united. And, above all else, recognition of the spiritual basis of democracy, the efficacy and responsibility of freed intelligence, is necessary to secure this union.

MARY AUSTIN

In the gorgeous collection of essays, The Land of Little Rain, *that Mary Austin (1868–1934) published in 1903, she wrote knowledgeably, exuberantly, and lovingly about the land bordering California and Arizona and its flora and fauna. "Mary Austin invested the land with magic, and yet looked at it with level eyes, relying upon history and science in her descriptions of her desert and celebrating its human nature with an eloquence which was also analytical," wrote Carl Van Doren. Maybe it is not too late to celebrate her as one of the pioneering American nature writers and environmentalists, along with Henry David Thoreau, John Muir, and John Burroughs. "The Basket Maker" displays her sympathetic respect for Native Americans; her precise, densely knotted descriptions of place and artisanal process; her spiritual bent; and her feminist outlook.*

The Basket Maker

(1903)

"A man," says Seyavi of the campoodie, "must have a woman, but a woman who has a child will do very well."

That was perhaps why, when she lost her mate in the dying struggle of his race, she never took another, but set her wit to fend for herself and her young son. No doubt she was often put to it in the beginning to find food for them both. The Paiutes had made their last stand at the border of the Bitter Lake; battle-driven they died in its waters, and the land filled with cattle-men and adventurers for gold: this while Seyavi and the boy lay up in the caverns of the Black Rock and ate tule roots and fresh-water clams that they dug out of the slough bottoms with their toes. In the interim, while the tribes swallowed their defeat, and before the rumor of war died out, they must have come very near to the bare core of things. That was the time Seyavi learned the sufficiency of mother wit, and how much more easily one can do without a man than might at first be supposed.

To understand the fashion of any life, one must know the land it is lived in and the procession of the year. This valley is a narrow one, a mere trough between hills, a draught for storms, hardly a crow's flight from the sharp Sierras of the Snows to the curled, red and ochre, uncomforted, bare ribs of Waban. Midway of the groove runs a burrowing, dull river, nearly a hundred miles from where it cuts the lava flats of the north to its widening in a thick, tideless pool of a lake. Hereabouts the ranges have no foothills, but rise up steeply from the bench lands above the river. Down from the Sierras, for the east ranges have almost no rain, pour glancing white floods toward the lowest land, and all beside them lie the campoodies, brown wattled brush heaps, looking east.

In the river are mussels, and reeds that have edible white roots, and in the soddy meadows tubers of joint grass; all these at their best in the spring. On the slope the summer growth affords seeds; up the steep the one-leafed pines, an oily nut. That was really all they could depend upon, and that only at the mercy of the little gods of frost and rain. For the rest it was cunning against cunning, caution against skill, against quacking hordes of wild-fowl in the tulares, against pronghorn and bighorn and deer. You can guess, however, that all this warring of rifles and bowstrings, this influx of overlording whites, had made game wilder and hunters fearful of being hunted. You can surmise also, for it was a crude time and the land was raw, that the women became in turn the game of the conquerors.

There used to be in the Little Antelope a she dog, stray or outcast, that had a litter in some forsaken lair, and ranged and foraged for them, slinking savage and afraid, remembering and mistrusting humankind, wistful, lean, and sufficient for her young. I have thought Seyavi might have had days like that, and have had perfect leave to think, since she will not talk of it. Paiutes have the art of reducing life to its lowest ebb and yet saving it alive on grasshoppers, lizards, and strange herbs; and that time must have left no shift untried. It lasted long enough for Seyavi to have evolved the philosophy of life which I have set down at the beginning. She had gone beyond learning to do for her son, and learned to believe it worth while.

In our kind of society, when a woman ceases to alter the fashion of her hair, you guess that she has passed the crisis of her experience. If she goes on crimping and uncrimping with the changing mode, it is safe to suppose she has never come up against anything too big for her. The Indian woman gets nearly the same personal note in the pattern of her baskets. Not that she does not make all kinds, carriers, water-bottles, and cradles,—these are kitchen ware,—but her works of art are all of the same piece. Seyavi made flaring, flat-bottomed bowls, cooking pots really, when cooking was done by dropping hot stones into water-tight food baskets, and for decoration a design in colored bark of the procession of plumed crests of the valley quail. In this pattern she had made cooking pots in the golden spring of her wedding year, when the quail went up two and two to their resting places about the foot of Oppapago. In this fashion she made them when, after pillage, it was possible to reinstate the housewifely crafts. Quail ran then in the Black Rock by hundreds,—so you will still find them in fortunate years,—and in the famine time the women cut their long hair to make snares when the flocks came morning and evening to the springs.

Seyavi made baskets for love and sold them for money, in a generation that preferred iron pots for utility. Every Indian woman is an artist,— sees, feels, creates, but does not philosophize about her processes. Seyavi's bowls are wonders of technical precision, inside and out, the palm finds no fault with them, but the subtlest appeal is in the sense that warns us of humanness in the way the design spreads into the flare of the bowl.

There used to be an Indian woman at Olancha who made bottle-neck trinket baskets in the rattlesnake pattern, and could accommodate the design to the swelling bowl and flat shoulder of the basket without sensible disproportion, and so cleverly that you might own one a year without thinking how it was done; but Seyavi's baskets had a touch beyond cleverness. The weaver and the warp lived next to the earth and were saturated with the same elements. Twice a year, in the time of white butterflies and again when young quail ran neck and neck in the chaparral, Seyavi cut willows for basketry by the creek where it wound toward the river against the sun and sucking winds. It never quite reached the river except in far-between times of summer flood, but it always tried, and the willows encouraged it as much as they could. You nearly always found them a little farther down than the trickle of eager water. The Paiute fashion of counting time appeals to me more than any other calendar. They have no stamp of heathen gods nor great ones, nor any succession of moons as have red men of the East and North, but count forward and back by the progress of the season; the time of *taboose*, before the trout begin to leap, the end of the piñon harvest, about the beginning of deep snows. So they get nearer the sense of the season, which runs early or late according as the rains are forward or delayed. But whenever Seyavi cut willows for baskets was always a golden time, and the soul of the weather went into the wood. If you had ever owned one of Seyavi's golden russet cooking bowls with the pattern of plumed quail, you would understand all this without saying anything.

Before Seyavi made baskets for the satisfaction of desire,—for that is a house-bred theory of art that makes anything more of it,—she danced and dressed her hair. In those days, when the spring was at flood and the blood pricked to the mating fever, the maids chose their flowers, wreathed themselves, and danced in the twilights, young desire crying out to young desire. They sang what the heart prompted, what the flower expressed, what boded in the mating weather.

"And what flower did you wear, Seyavi?"

"I, ah,—the white flower of twining [clematis], on my body and my hair, and so I sang:—

"I am the white flower of twining,
Little white flower by the river,
Oh, flower that twines close by the river;
Oh, trembling flower!
So trembles the maiden heart."

So sang Seyavi of the campoodie before she made baskets, and in her later days laid her arms upon her knees and laughed in them at the recollection. But it was not often she would say so much, never understanding the keen hunger I had for bits of lore and the "fool talk" of her people. She had fed her young son with meadowlarks' tongues, to make him quick of speech; but in late years was loath to admit it, though she had come through the period of unfaith in the lore of the clan with a fine appreciation of its beauty and significance.

"What good will your dead get, Seyavi, of the baskets you burn?" said I, coveting them for my own collection.

Thus Seyavi, "As much good as yours of the flowers you strew."

Oppapago looks on Waban, and Waban on Coso and the Bitter Lake, and the campoodie looks on these three; and more, it sees the beginning of winds along the foot of Coso, the gathering of clouds behind the high ridges, the spring flush, the soft spread of wild almond bloom on the mesa. These first, you understand, are the Paiute's walls, the other his furnishings. Not the wattled hut is his home, but the land, the winds, the hill front, the stream. These he cannot duplicate at any furbisher's shop as you who live within doors, who, if your purse allows, may have the same home at Sitka and Samarcand. So you see how it is that the homesickness of an Indian is often unto death, since he gets no relief from it; neither wind nor weed nor sky-line, nor any aspect of the hills of a strange land sufficiently like his own. So it was when the government reached out for the Paiutes, they gathered into the Northern Reservation only such poor tribes as could devise no other end of their affairs. Here, all along the river, and south to Shoshone Land, live the clans who owned the earth, fallen into the deplorable condition of hangers-on. Yet you hear them laughing at the hour when they draw in to the campoodie after labor, when there is a smell of meat and the steam of the cooking pots goes up against the sun. Then the children lie with their toes in the ashes to hear tales; then they are merry, and have the joys of repletion and the nearness of their kind. They have their hills, and though jostled are sufficiently free to get some fortitude for what will come. For now you shall hear of the end of the basket maker.

In her best days Seyavi was most like Deborah, deep bosomed, broad in the hips, quick in counsel, slow of speech, esteemed of her people. This was that Seyavi who reared a man by her own hand, her own wit, and none other. When the townspeople began to take note of her—and it was some years after the war before there began to be any towns—she was then in the quick maturity of primitive women; but when I knew her she seemed already old. Indian women do not often live to great age, though they look incredibly steeped in years. They have the wit to win sustenance from the raw material of life without intervention, but they have not the sleek look of the women whom the social organization conspires to nourish. Seyavi had somehow squeezed out of her daily round a spiritual ichor that kept the skill in her knotted fingers long after the accustomed time, but that also failed. By all counts she would have been about sixty years old when it came her turn to sit in the dust on the sunny side of the wickiup, with little strength left for anything but looking. And in time she paid the toll of the smoky huts and became blind. This is a thing so long expected by the Paiutes that when it comes they find it neither bitter nor sweet, but tolerable because common. There were three other blind women in the campoodie, withered fruit on a bough, but they had memory and speech. By noon of the sun there were never any left in the campoodie but these or some mother of weanlings, and they sat to keep the ashes warm upon the hearth. If it were cold, they burrowed in the blankets of the hut; if it were warm, they followed the shadow of the wickiup around. Stir much out of their places they hardly dared, since one might not help another; but they called, in high, old cracked voices, gossip and reminder across the ash heaps.

Then, if they have your speech or you theirs, and have an hour to spare, there are things to be learned of life not set down in any books, folk tales, famine tales, love and long-suffering and desire, but no whimpering. Now and then one or another of the blind keepers of the camp will come across to where you sit gossiping, tapping her way among the kitchen middens, guided by your voice that carries far in the clearness and stillness of mesa afternoons. But suppose you find Seyavi retired into the privacy of her blanket, you will get nothing for that day. There is no other privacy possible in a campoodie. All the processes of life are carried on out of doors or behind the thin, twig-woven walls of the wickiup, and laughter is the only corrective for behavior. Very early the Indian learns to possess his countenance in impassivity, to cover his head with his blanket. Something to wrap around him is as necessary to the Paiute as to you your closet to pray in.

So in her blanket Seyavi, sometime basket maker, sits by the unlit hearths of her tribe and digests her life, nourishing her spirit against the time of the spirit's need, for she knows in fact quite as much of these matters as you who have a larger hope, though she has none but the certainty that having borne herself courageously to this end she will not be reborn a coyote.

MARK TWAIN

Samuel Langhorne Clemens (1835–1910), who was known by the pen name Mark Twain, was an indispensably irreverent humorist and man of letters. Ernest Hemingway credited The Adventures of Huckleberry Finn *as the foundational text of modern American literature, placing all future authors in its debt. Certainly Hemingway was indebted to Twain's speedy, colloquial, and economical prose style. Twain wrote hundreds of stories, sketches, and essays imbued with his devilish voice. "The Turning Point of My Life" begins by undercutting the very premise of the assignment, then harking back to ancient Rome before settling into his own anti-heroic account, a mixed salad of absurdity, anecdote, and sensible generalization—all in the interest of tracing how he "came to be literary." Of course, Twain would have probably been the first to shrug off the literary mantle as pretentious snootiness.*

The Turning Point of My Life

(1910)

If I understand the idea, the *bazar* invites several of us to write upon the above text. It means the change in my life's course which introduced what must be regarded by me as the most *important* condition of my career. But it also implies—without intention, perhaps—that that turning-point *itself* was the creator of the new condition. This gives it too much distinction, too much prominence, too much credit. It is only the *last* link in a very long chain of turning-points commissioned to produce the cardinal result; it is not any more important than the humblest of its ten thousand predecessors. Each of the ten thousand did its appointed share, on its appointed date, in forwarding the scheme, and they were all necessary; to have left out any one of them would have defeated the scheme and brought about *some other* result. I know we have a fashion of saying "such and such an event was the turning-point in my life," but we shouldn't say it. We should merely grant that its place as *last* link in the chain makes it the most *conspicuous* link; in real importance it has no advantage over any one of its predecessors.

Perhaps the most celebrated turning-point recorded in history was the crossing of the Rubicon. Suetonius says:

> Coming up with his troops on the banks of the Rubicon, he halted for a while, and, revolving in his mind the importance of the step he was on the point of taking, he turned to those about him and said, "We may still retreat; but if we pass this little bridge, nothing is left for us but to fight it out in arms."

This was a stupendously important moment. And all the incidents, big and little, of Caesar's previous life had been leading up to it, stage by stage, link by link. This was the *last* link—merely the last one, and no bigger than the others; but as we gaze back at it through the inflating mists of our imagination, it looks as big as the orbit of Neptune.

You, the reader, have a *personal* interest in that link, and so have I; so has the rest of the human race. It was one of the links in your life-chain, and it was one of the links in mine. We may wait, now, with bated breath, while Caesar reflects. Your fate and mine are involved in his decision.

> While he was thus hesitating, the following incident occurred. A person remarked for his noble mien and graceful aspect appeared close at hand, sitting and playing upon a pipe. When not only the shepherds, but a number of soldiers also, flocked to listen to him, and some trumpeters among them, he snatched a trumpet from one of them, ran to the river with it, and, sounding the advance with a piercing blast, crossed to the other side. Upon this, Caesar exclaimed: "Let us go whither the omens of the gods and the iniquity of our enemies call up. *The die is cast.*"

So he crossed—and changed the future of the whole human race, for all time. But that stranger was a link in Caesar's life-chain, too; and a necessary one. We don't know his name, we never hear of him again; he was very casual; he acts like an accident; but he was no accident, he was there by compulsion of *his* life-chain, to blow the electrifying blast that was to make up Caesar's mind for him, and thence go piping down the aisles of history forever.

If the stranger hadn't been there! But he *was*. And Caesar crossed. With such results! Such vast events—each a link in the *human race's* life-chain; each event producing the next one, and that one the next one, and so on: the destruction of the republic; the founding of the empire; the breaking up of the empire; the rise of Christianity upon its ruins; the spread of the religion to other lands—and so on; link by link took its appointed place at its appointed time, the discovery of America being one of them; our Revolution another; the inflow of English and other immigrants another; their drift westward (my ancestors among them) another; the settlement of certain of them in Missouri, which resulted in *me*. For I was one of the unavoidable results of the crossing of the Rubicon. If the stranger, with his trumpet blast, had stayed away (which he *couldn't*, for he was the appointed link) Caesar would not have crossed. What would have happened, in that case, we can never guess. We only know that the things that did happen would not have happened. They might have been replaced by equally prodigious things, of course, but their nature and results are beyond our guessing. But the matter that interests me personally is that I would not be *here* now, but somewhere else; and probably black—there is no telling. Very well, I am glad he crossed. And very really and thankfully glad, too, though I never cared anything about it before.

II

To me, the most important feature of my life is its literary feature. I have been professionally literary something more than forty years. There have been many turning-points in my life, but the one that was the link in the chain appointed to conduct me to the literary guild is the most *conspicuous* link in that chain. *Because* it was the last one. It was not any more important than its predecessors. All the other links have an inconspicuous look, except the crossing of the Rubicon; but as factors in making me literary they are all of the one size, the crossing of the Rubicon included.

I know how I came to be literary, and I will tell the steps that lead up to it and brought it about.

The crossing of the Rubicon was not the first one, it was hardly even a recent one; I should have to go back ages before Caesar's day to find the first one. To save space I will go back only a couple of generations and start with an incident of my boyhood. When I was twelve and a half years old, my father died. It was in the spring. The summer came, and brought with it an epidemic of measles. For a time a child died almost every day. The village was paralyzed with fright, distress, despair. Children that were not smitten with the disease were imprisoned in their homes to save them from the infection. In the homes there were no cheerful faces, there was no music, there was no singing but of solemn hymns, no voice but of prayer, no romping was allowed, no noise, no laughter, the family moved spectrally about on tiptoe, in a ghostly hush. I was a prisoner. My soul was steeped in this awful dreariness—and in fear. At some time or other every day and every night a sudden shiver shook me to the marrow, and I said to myself, "There, I've got it! and I shall die." Life on these miserable terms was not worth living, and at last I made up my mind to get the disease and have it over, one way or the other. I escaped from the house and went to the house of a neighbor where a playmate of mine was very ill with the malady. When the chance offered I crept into his room and got into bed with him. I was discovered by his mother and sent back into captivity. But I had the disease; they could not take that from me. I came near to dying. The whole village was interested, and anxious, and sent for news of me every day; and not only once a day, but several times. Everybody believed I would die; but on the fourteenth day a change came for the worse and they were disappointed.

This was a turning-point of my life. For when I got well my mother closed my school career and apprenticed me to a printer. She was tired of trying to keep me out of mischief, and the adventure of the measles decided her to put me into more masterful hands than hers.

I became a printer, and began to add one link after another to the chain which was to lead me into the literary profession. A long road, but I could not know that; and as I did not know what its goal was, or even that it had one, I was indifferent. Also contented.

A young printer wanders around a good deal, seeking and finding work; and seeking again, when necessity commands. N. B. Necessity is a *Circumstance;* Circumstance is man's master—and when Circumstance commands, he must obey; he may argue the matter—that is his privilege, just as it is the honorable privilege of a falling body to argue with the attraction of gravitation—but it won't do any good, he must *obey.* I wandered for ten years, under the guidance and dictatorship of Circumstance, and finally arrived in a city of Iowa, where I worked several months. Among the books that interested me in those days was one about the Amazon. The traveler told an alluring tale of his long voyage up the great river from Para to the sources of the Madeira, through the heart of an enchanted land, a land wastefully rich in tropical wonders, a romantic land where all the birds and flowers and animals were of the museum varieties, and where the alligator and the crocodile and the monkey seemed as much at home as if they were in the Zoo. Also, he told an astonishing tale about *coca,* a vegetable product of miraculous powers, asserting that it was so nourishing and so strength-giving that the native of the mountains of the Madeira region would tramp up hill and down all day on a pinch of powdered coca and require no other sustenance.

I was fired with a longing to ascend the Amazon. Also with a longing to open up a trade in coca with all the world. During months I dreamed that dream, and tried to contrive ways to get to Para and spring that splendid enterprise upon an unsuspecting planet. But all in vain. A person may *plan* as much as he wants to, but nothing of consequence is likely to come of it until the magician *Circumstance* steps in and takes the matter off his hands. At last Circumstance came to my help. It was in this way. Circumstance, to help or hurt another man, made him lose a fifty-dollar bill in the street; and to help or hurt me, made me find it. I advertised the find, and left for the Amazon the same day. This was another turning-point, another link.

Could Circumstance have ordered another dweller in that town to go to the Amazon and open up a world-trade in coca on a fifty-dollar basis and been obeyed? No, I was the only one. There were other fools there— shoals and shoals of them—but they were not of my kind. I was the only one of my kind.

Circumstance is powerful, but it cannot work alone; it has to have a partner. Its partner is man's *temperament*—his natural disposition. His temperament is not his invention, it is *born* in him, and he has no authority over it, neither is he responsible for its acts. He cannot change it, nothing can change it, nothing can modify it—except temporarily. But it won't stay modified. It is permanent, like the color of the man's eyes and the shape of his ears. Blue eyes are gray in certain unusual lights; but they resume their natural color when that stress is removed.

A Circumstance that will coerce one man will have no effect upon a man of a different temperament. If Circumstance had thrown the bank-note in Caesar's way, his temperament would not have made him start for the Amazon. His temperament would have compelled him to do something with the money, but not that. It might have made him advertise the note—and *wait*. We can't tell. Also, it might have made him go to New York and buy into the Government, with results that would leave Tweed nothing to learn when it came his turn.

Very well, Circumstance furnished the capital, and my temperament told me what to do with it. Sometimes a temperament is an ass. When that is the case the owner of it is an ass, too, and is going to remain one. Training, experience, association, can temporarily so polish him, improve him, exalt him that people will think he is a mule, but they will be mistaken. Artificially he IS a mule, for the time being, but at bottom he is an ass yet, and will remain one.

By temperament I was the kind of person that *does* things. Does them, and reflects afterward. So I started for the Amazon without reflecting and without asking any questions. That was more than fifty years ago. In all that time my temperament has not changed, by even a shade. I have been punished many and many a time, and bitterly, for doing things and reflecting afterward, but these tortures have been of no value to me; I still do the thing commanded by Circumstance and Temperament, and reflect afterward. Always violently. When I am reflecting, on these occasions, even deaf persons can hear me think.

I went by the way of Cincinnati, and down the Ohio and Mississippi. My idea was to take ship, at New Orleans, for Para. In New Orleans I inquired, and found there was no ship leaving for Para. Also, that there never had *been* one leaving for Para. I reflected. A policeman came and asked me what I was doing, and I told him. He made me move on, and said if he caught me reflecting in the public street again he would run me in.

After a few days I was out of money. Then Circumstance arrived, with another turning-point of my life—a new link. On my way down, I had made the acquaintance of a pilot. I begged him to teach me the river, and he consented. I became a pilot.

By and by Circumstance came again—introducing the Civil War, this time, in order to push me ahead another stage or two toward the literary profession. The boats stopped running, my livelihood was gone.

Circumstance came to the rescue with a new turning-point and a fresh link. My brother was appointed secretary to the new Territory of Nevada, and he invited me to go with him and help him in his office. I accepted.

In Nevada, Circumstance furnished me the silver fever and I went into the mines to make a fortune, as I supposed; but that was not the idea. The idea was to advance me another step toward literature. For amusement I scribbled things for the Virginia City *Enterprise*. One isn't a printer ten years without setting up acres of good and bad literature, and learning—unconsciously at first, consciously later—to discriminate between the two, within his mental limitations; and meantime he is unconsciously acquiring what is called a "style." One of my efforts attracted attention, and the *Enterprise* sent for me and put me on its staff.

And so I became a journalist—another link. By and by Circumstance and the Sacramento *Union* sent me to the Sandwich Islands for five or six months, to write up sugar. I did it; and threw in a good deal of extraneous matter that hadn't anything to do with sugar. But it was this extraneous matter that helped me to another link.

It made me notorious, and San Francisco invited me to lecture. Which I did. And profitably. I had long had a desire to travel and see the world, and now Circumstance had most kindly and unexpectedly hurled me upon the platform and furnished me the means. So I joined the "Quaker City Excursion."

When I returned to America, Circumstance was waiting on the pier—with the *last* link—the conspicuous, the consummating, the victorious link: I was asked to *write a book,* and I did it, and called it *The Innocents Abroad.* Thus I became at last a member of the literary guild. That was forty-two years ago, and I have been a member ever since. Leaving the Rubicon incident away back where it belongs, I can say with truth that the reason I am in the literary profession is because I had the measles when I was twelve years old.

III

Now what interests me, as regards these details, is not the details themselves, but the fact that none of them was foreseen by me, none of them was planned by me, I was the author of none of them. Circumstance, working in harness with my temperament, created them all and compelled them all. I often offered help, and with the best intentions, but it was rejected—as a rule, uncourteously. I could never plan a thing and get it to come out the way I planned it. It came out some other way—some way I had not counted upon.

And so I do not admire the human being—as an intellectual marvel—as much as I did when I was young, and got him out of books, and did not know him personally. When I used to read that such and such a general did a certain brilliant thing, I believed it. Whereas it was not so. Circumstance did it by help of his temperament. The circumstances would have failed of effect with a general of another temperament: he might see the chance, but lose the advantage by being by nature too slow or too quick or too doubtful. Once General Grant was asked a question about a matter which had been much debated by the public and the newspapers; he answered the question without any hesitancy. "General, who planned the march through Georgia?" "The enemy!" He added that the enemy usually makes your plans for you. He meant that the enemy by neglect or through force of circumstances leaves an opening for you, and you see your chance and take advantage of it.

Circumstances do the planning for us all, no doubt, by help of our temperaments. I see no great difference between a man and a watch, except that the man is conscious and the watch isn't, and the man *tries* to plan things and the watch doesn't. The watch doesn't wind itself and doesn't regulate itself—these things are done exteriorly. Outside influences, outside circumstances, wind the *man* and regulate him. Left to himself, he wouldn't get regulated at all, and the sort of time he would keep would not be valuable. Some rare men are wonderful watches, with gold case, compensation balance, and all those things, and some men are only simple and sweet and humble Waterburys. I am a Waterbury. A Waterbury of that kind, some say.

A nation is only an individual multiplied. It makes plans and Circumstance comes and upsets them—or enlarges them. Some patriots throw the tea overboard; some other patriots destroy a Bastille. The *plans* stop there; then Circumstance comes in, quite unexpectedly, and turns these modest riots into a revolution.

And there was poor Columbus. He elaborated a deep plan to find a new route to an old country. Circumstance revised his plan for him, and he found a new *world*. And *he* gets the credit of it to this day. He hadn't anything to do with it.

Necessarily the scene of the real turning-point of my life (and of yours) was the Garden of Eden. It was there that the first link was forged of the chain that was ultimately to lead to the emptying of me into the literary guild. Adam's *temperament* was the first command the Deity ever issued to a human being on this planet. And it was the only command Adam would *never* be able to disobey. It said, "Be weak, be water, be characterless, be cheaply persuadable." The latter command, to let the fruit alone, was certain to be disobeyed. Not by Adam himself, but by his *temperament*—which he did not create and had no authority over. For the *temperament* is the man; the thing tricked out with clothes and named Man is merely its Shadow, nothing more. The law of the tiger's temperament is, Thou shalt kill; the law of the sheep's temperament is, Thou shalt not kill. To issue later commands requiring the tiger to let the fat stranger alone, and requiring the sheep to imbue its hands in the blood of the lion is not worth while, for those commands *can't* be obeyed. They would invite to violations of the law of *temperament,* which is supreme, and take precedence of all other authorities. I cannot help feeling disappointed in Adam and Eve. That is, in their temperaments. Not in *them,* poor helpless young creatures—afflicted with temperaments made out of butter; which butter was commanded to get into contact with fire and *be melted.* What I cannot help wishing is, that Adam had been postponed, and Martin Luther and Joan of Arc put in their place—that splendid pair equipped with temperaments not made of butter, but of asbestos. By neither sugary persuasions nor by hell fire could Satan have beguiled *them* to eat the apple.

There would have been results! Indeed, yes. The apple would be intact today; there would be no human race; there would be no *you;* there would be no *me.* And the old, old creation-dawn scheme of ultimately launching me into the literary guild would have been defeated.

RANDOLPH BOURNE

Randolph Bourne (1886–1918) was a progressive thinker and social critic. Struck by a disease that left him with a double curvature of the spine, which inhibited his growth, and by a birth injury that had disfigured his face, he wrote movingly about these problems in an essay that originally appeared anonymously in The Atlantic Monthly, *"The Handicapped—By One of Them." Bourne also wrote many notable pieces for* The New Republic. *One, "The War and the Intellectual," criticized the country's entry into World War I. Another, "Trans-National America," argued that immigrants would enrich the United States more by retaining their culture than by surrendering to "melting pot" assimilation. He was cherished by his friends, including Max Eastman, who said, "He had a powerful mind, a philosophical erudition, a commanding prose style, and the courage of a giant." He died of the flu epidemic of 1918, in his early thirties.*

The Handicapped

(1911)

It would not perhaps be thought, ordinarily, that the man whom physical disabilities have made so helpless that he is unable to move around among his fellows can bear his lot more happily, even though he suffer pain, and face life with a more cheerful and contented spirit, than can the man whose deformities are merely enough to mark him out from the rest of his fellows without preventing him from entering with them into most of their common affairs and experiences. But the fact is that the former's very helplessness makes him content to rest and not to strive. I know a young man so helplessly deformed that he has to be carried about, who is happy in reading a little, playing chess, taking a course or two in college, and all with the sunniest goodwill in the world, and a happiness that seems strange and unaccountable to my restlessness. He does not cry for the moon.

When one, however, is in full possession of his faculties, and can move about freely, bearing simply a crooked back and an unsightly face, he is perforce drawn into all the currents of life. Particularly if he has his own way in the world to make, his road is apt to be hard and rugged, and he will penetrate to an unusual depth in his interpretation both of the world's attitude toward such misfortunes, and of the attitude toward the world which such misfortunes tend to cultivate in men like him. For he has all the battles of a stronger man to fight, and he is at a double disadvantage in fighting them. He has constantly with him the sense of being obliged to make extra efforts to overcome the bad impression of his physical defects, and he is haunted with a constant feeling of weakness and low vitality which makes effort more difficult and renders him easily fainthearted and discouraged by failure. He is never confident of himself, because he has grown up in an atmosphere where nobody has been very confident of him; and yet his environment and circumstances call out all sorts of ambitions and energies in him which, from the nature of his case, are bound to be immediately thwarted. This attitude is likely to keep him at a generally low level of accomplishment unless he have an unusually strong will, and a strong will is perhaps the last thing to develop under such circumstances.

That vague sense of physical uncomfortableness which is with him nearly every minute of his waking day serves, too, to make steady application for hours to any particular kind of work much more irksome than it is even to the lazy man. No one but the deformed man can realize just what the mere fact of sitting a foot lower than the normal means in discomfort and annoyance. For one cannot carry one's special chair everywhere, to theatre and library and train and schoolroom. This sounds trivial, I know, but I mention it because it furnishes a real, even though usually dim, "background of consciousness" which one had to reckon with during all one's solid work or enjoyment. The things that the world deems hardest for the deformed man to bear are perhaps really the easiest of all. I can truthfully say, for instance, that I have never suffered so much as a pang from the interested comments on my personal appearance made by urchins in the street, nor from the curious looks of people in the street and public places. To ignore this vulgar curiosity is the simplest and easiest thing in the world. It does not worry me in the least to appear on a platform if I have anything to say and there is anybody to listen. What one does get sensitive to is rather the inevitable way that people, acquaintances and strangers alike, have of discounting in advance what one does or says.

The deformed man is always conscious that the world does not expect very much from him. And it takes him a long time to see in this a challenge instead of a firm pressing down to a low level of accomplishment. As a result, he does not expect very much of himself; he is timid in approaching people, and distrustful of his ability to persuade and convince. He becomes extraordinarily sensitive to other people's first impressions of him. Those who are to be his friends he knows instantly, and further acquaintance adds little to the intimacy and warm friendship that he at once feels for them. On the other hand, those who do not respond to him immediately cannot by any effort either on his part or theirs overcome that first alienation.

This sensitiveness has both its good and bad sides. It makes friendship that most precious thing in the world to him, and he finds that he arrives at a much richer and wider intimacy with his friends than do ordinary men with their light, surface friendships, based on good fellowship or the convenience of the moment. But on the other hand this sensitiveness absolutely unfits him for business and the practice of a profession, where one must be "all things to all men," and the professional manner is indispensable to success. For here, where he has to meet a constant stream of men of all sorts and conditions, his sensitiveness to these first impressions will make his case hopeless. Except with those few who by some secret sympathy will seem to respond, his deformity will stand like a huge barrier between his personality and other men's. The magical good fortune of attractive personal appearance makes its way almost without effort in the world, breaking down all sorts of walls of disapproval and lack of interest. Even the homely person can attract by personal charm. But deformity cannot even be charming.

The doors of the deformed man are always locked, and the key is on the outside. He may have treasures of charm inside, but they will never be revealed unless the person outside cooperates with him in unlocking the door. A friend becomes, to a much greater degree than with the ordinary man, the indispensable means of discovering one's own personality. One only exists, so to speak, with friends. It is easy to see how hopelessly such a sensitiveness incapacitates a man for business, professional, or social life, where the hasty and superficial impression is everything, and disaster is the fate of the man who has not all the treasures of his personality in the front window, where they can be readily inspected and appraised.

It thus takes the deformed man a long time to get adjusted to his world. Childhood is perhaps the hardest time of all. As a child he is a strange creature in a strange land. It was my own fate to be just strong enough to play about with the other boys, and attempt all their games and "stunts" without being strong enough actually to succeed in any of them. It never used to occur to me that my failures and lack of skill were due to circumstances beyond my control, but I would always impute them, in consequence of my rigid Calvinistic bringing-up, I suppose, to some moral weakness of my own. I suffered tortures in trying to learn to skate, to climb trees, to play ball, to conform in general to the ways of the world. I never resigned myself to the inevitable, but overexerted myself constantly in a grim determination to succeed. I was good at my lessons, and through timidity rather than priggishness, I hope, a very well-behaved boy at school; I was devoted, too, to music, and learned to play the piano pretty well. But I despised my reputation for excellence in these things, and instead of adapting myself philosophically to the situation, I strove (and have been striving ever since) to do the things I could not.

As I look back now it seems perfectly natural that I should have followed the standards of the crowd, and loathed my high marks in lessons and deportment, and the concerts to which I was sent by my aunt, and the exhibitions of my musical skill that I had to give before admiring ladies. Whether or not such an experience is typical of handicapped children, there is tragedy there for those situated as I was. For had I been a little weaker physically, I should have been thrown back on reading omnivorously and cultivating my music, with some possible results; while if I had been a little stronger, I could have participated in the play on an equal footing with the rest. As it was, I simply tantalized myself, and grew up with a deepening sense of failure, and a lack of pride in what I really excelled at.

When the world became one of dances and parties and social evenings and boy-and-girl attachments—the world of youth—I was to find myself still less adapted to it. And this was the harder to bear because I was naturally sociable, and all these things appealed tremendously to me. This world of admiration and gayety and smiles and favors and quick interest and companionship, however, is only for the well-begotten and the debonair. It was not through any cruelty or dislike, I think, that I was refused admittance; indeed they were always very kind about inviting me. But it was more as if a ragged urchin had been asked to come and look through the window at the light and warmth of a glittering party; I was truly in the world, but not of the world. Indeed there were times when one would almost prefer conscious cruelty to this silent, unconscious, gentle oblivion. And this is the tragedy, I suppose, not only of the deformed, but of all the ill-favored and unattractive to a greater or less degree. The world of youth is a world of so many conventions, and the abnormal in any direction is so glaringly and hideously abnormal.

Although it took me a long time to understand this, and I continue to attribute my failure mostly to my own character, trying hard to compensate for my physical deficiencies by skill and cleverness, I suffered comparatively few pangs, and got much better adjusted to this world than to the other. For I was older, and I had acquired a lively interest in all the social politics; I would get so interested in watching how people behaved, and in sizing them up, that only at rare intervals would I remember that I was really having no hand in the game. This interest just in the ways people are human has become more and more a positive advantage in my life, and has kept sweet many a situation that might easily have cost me a pang. Not that a person with my disabilities should be a sort of detective, evil-mindedly using his social opportunities for spying out and analyzing his friends' foibles, but that, if he does acquire an interest in people quite apart from their relation to him, he may go into society with an easy conscience and a certainty that he will be entertained and possibly entertaining, even though he cuts a poor enough social figure. He must simply not expect too much.

Perhaps the bitterest struggles of the handicapped man come when he tackles the business world. If he has to go out for himself to look for work, without fortune, training, or influence, as I personally did, his way will indeed be rugged. His disability will work against him for any position where he must be much in the eyes of men, and his general insignificance has a subtle influence in convincing those to whom he applies that he is unfitted for any kind of work. As I have suggested, his keen sensitiveness to other people's impressions of him makes him more than unusually timid and unable to counteract that fatal first impression by any display of personal force and will. He cannot get his personality over across that barrier. The cards seem stacked against him from the start. With training and influence something might be done, but alone and unaided his case is almost hopeless. At least, this was my own experience. We were poor relations, and our prosperous relatives thought they had done quite enough for us without sending me through college, and I did not seem strong enough to work my way through (although I have since done it). I started out auspiciously enough, becoming a sort of apprentice to a musician who had invented a machine for turning out music-rolls. Here, with steady work, good pay, and the comfortable consciousness that I was "helping support the family," I got the first pleasurable sensation of self-respect, I think, that I ever had. But with the failure of this business I was precipitated against the real world.

It would be futile to recount the story of my struggles: how I besieged for nearly two years firm after firm, in search of a permanent position, trying everything in New York in which I thought I had the slightest chance of success, meanwhile making a precarious living by a few music lessons. The attitude toward me ranged from "You can't expect us to create a place for you," to, "How could it enter your head that we should find any use for a man like you?" My situation was doubtless unusual. Few men handicapped as I was would be likely to go so long without

arousing some interest and support in relative or friend. But my experience serves to illustrate the peculiar difficulties that a handicapped man
meets if he has his own way to make in the world. He is discounted at the
start: it is not business to make allowances for anybody; and while people
were not cruel or unkind, it was the hopeless finality of the thing that
filled one's heart with despair.

The environment of a big city is perhaps the worst possible that a man
in such a situation could have. For the thousands of seeming opportunities lead one restlessly on and on, and keep one's mind perpetually unsettled and depressed. There is a poignant mental torture that comes with
such an experience—the urgent need, the repeated failure, or rather the
repeated failure even to obtain a chance to fail, the realization that those
at home can ill afford to have you idle, the growing dread of encountering
people—all this is something that those who have never been through it
can never realize. Personally I know of no particular way of escape. One
can expect to do little by one's own unaided efforts. I solved my difficulties only by evading them, by throwing overboard some of my responsibility, and taking the desperate step of entering college on a scholarship.
Desultory work is not nearly so humiliating when one is using one's time
to some advantage, and college furnishes an ideal environment where the
things at which a man handicapped like myself can succeed really count.
One's self-respect can begin to grow like a weed.

For at the bottom of all the difficulties of a man like me is really the
fact that his self-respect is so slow in growing up. Accustomed from childhood to being discounted, his self-respect is not naturally very strong, and
it would require pretty constant success in a congenial line of work really
to confirm it. If he could only more easily separate the factors that are
due to his physical disability from those that are due to his weak will and
character, he might more quickly attain self-respect, for he would realize
what he is responsible for, and what he is not. But at the beginning he
rarely makes allowances for himself, he is his own severest judge. He longs
for a "strong will," and yet the experience of having his efforts promptly
nipped off at the beginning is the last thing on earth to produce that will.

Life, particularly if he is brought into harsh and direct touch with the
real world, is a much more complex thing to him than to the ordinary
man. Many of his inherited platitudes vanish at the first touch. Life
appears to him as a grim struggle, where ability does not necessarily
mean opportunity and success, nor piety sympathy, and where helplessness cannot count on assistance and kindly interest. Human affairs seem
to be running on a wholly irrational plan, and success to be founded on
chance as much as on anything. But if he can stand the first shock of
disillusionment, he may find himself enormously interested in discovering
how they actually do run, and he will want to burrow into the motives of
men, and find the reasons for the crass inequalities and injustices of the

world he sees around him. He has practically to construct anew a world of his own, and explain a great many things to himself that the ordinary person never dreams of finding unintelligible at all. He will be filled with a profound sympathy for all who are despised and ignored in the world. When he has been through the neglect and struggles of a handicapped and ill-favored man himself, he will begin to understand the feelings of all the horde of the unpresentable and the unemployable, the incompetent and the ugly, the queer and crotchety people who make up so large a proportion of human folk.

We are perhaps too prone to get our ideas and standards of worth from the successful, without reflecting that the interpretations of life which patriotic legend, copybook philosophy, and the sayings of the wealthy give us are pitifully inadequate for those who fall behind in the race. Surely there are enough people to whom the task of making a decent living and maintaining themselves and their families in their social class, or of winning and keeping the respect of their fellows, is a hard and bitter task, to make a philosophy gained through personal disability and failure as just and true a method of appraising the life around us as the cheap optimism of the ordinary professional man. And certainly a kindlier, for it has no shade of contempt or disparagement about it.

It irritates me as if I had been spoken of contemptuously myself, to hear people called "common" or "ordinary," or to see that deadly and delicate feeling for social gradations crop out, which so many of our upper-middle-class women seem to have. It makes me wince to hear a man spoken of as a failure, or to have it said of one that he "doesn't amount to much." Instantly I want to know why he has not succeeded, and what have been the forces that have been working against him. He is the truly interesting person, and yet how little our eager-pressing, onrushing world cares about such aspects of life, and how hideously though unconsciously cruel and heartless it usually is.

Often I had tried in arguments to show my friends how much of circumstance and chance go to the making of success; and when I reached the age of sober reading, a long series of the works of radical social philosophers, beginning with Henry George, provided me with the materials for a philosophy which explained why men were miserable and overworked, and why there was on the whole so little joy and gladness among us—and which fixed the blame. Here was suggested a goal, and a definite glorious future, toward which all good men might work. My own working hours became filled with visions of how men could be brought to see all that this meant, and how I in particular might work some great and wonderful thing for human betterment. In more recent years, the study of history and social psychology and ethics has made those crude outlines sounder and more normal, and brought them into a saner relation to other aspects of life and thought, but I have not lost the first glow of enthusiasm, nor my belief in social progress as the first right and permanent interest for every thinking and truehearted man or woman.

I am ashamed that my experience has given me so little chance to count in any way toward either the spreading of such a philosophy or toward direct influence and action. Nor do I yet see clearly how I shall be able to count effectually toward this ideal. Of one thing I am sure, however: that life will have little meaning for me except as I am able to contribute toward some such ideal of social betterment, if not in deed, then in word. For this is the faith that I believe we need today, all of us—a truly religious belief in human progress, a thorough social consciousness, an eager delight in every sign and promise of social improvement, and best of all, a new spirit of courage that will dare. I want to give to the young men whom I see—who, with fine intellect and high principles, lack just that light of the future on their faces that would give them a purpose and meaning in life—to them I want to give some touch of this philosophy— that will energize their lives, and save them from the disheartening effects of that poisonous counsel of timidity and distrust of human ideals which pours out in steady stream from reactionary press and pulpit.

It is hard to tell just how much of this philosophy has been due to my handicaps. If it is solely to my physical misfortunes that I owe its existence, the price has not been a heavy one to pay. For it has given me something that I should not know how to be without. For, however gained, this radical philosophy has not only made the world intelligible and dynamic to me, but has furnished me with the strongest spiritual support. I know that many people, handicapped by physical weakness and failure, find consolation and satisfaction in a very different sort of faith—in an evangelical religion, and a feeling of close dependence on God and close communion with him. But my experience has made my ideal of character militant rather than long-suffering.

I very early experienced a revulsion against the rigid Presbyterianism in which I had been brought up—a purely intellectual revulsion, I believe, because my mind was occupied for a long time afterward with theological questions, and the only feeling that entered into it was a sort of disgust at the arrogance of damning so great a proportion of the human race. I read T. W. Higginson's *The Sympathy of Religions* with the greatest satisfaction, and attended the Unitarian Church whenever I could slip away. This faith, while it still appeals to me, seems at times a little too static and refined to satisfy me with completeness. For some time there was a considerable bitterness in my heart at the narrowness of the people who could still find comfort in the old faith. Reading Buckle and Oliver Wendell Holmes gave me a new contempt for "conventionality," and my social philosophy still further tortured me by throwing the burden for the misery of the world on these same good neighbors. And all this, although I think I did not make a nuisance of myself, made me feel a spiritual and intellectual isolation in addition to my more or less effective physical isolation.

Happily these days are over. The world has righted itself, and I have been able to appreciate and realize how people count in a social and group capacity as well as in an individual and personal one, and to separate the two in my thinking. Really to believe in human nature while striving to know the thousand forces that warp it from its ideal development—to call for and expect much from men and women, and not to be disappointed and embittered if they fall short—to try to do good with people rather than to them—this is my religion on its human side. And if God exists, I think that He must be in the warm sun, in the kindly actions of the people we know and read of, in the beautiful things of art and nature, and in the closeness of friendships. He may also be in heaven, in life, in suffering, but it is only in these simple moments of happiness that I feel Him and know that He is there.

Death I do not understand at all. I have seen it in its cruelest, most irrational forms, where there has seemed no excuse, no palliation. I have only known that if we were more careful, and more relentless in fighting evil, if we knew more of medical science, such things would not be. I know that a sound body, intelligent care and training, prolong life, and that the death of a very old person is neither sad nor shocking, but sweet and fitting. I see in death a perpetual warning of how much there is to be known and done in the way of human progress and betterment. And equally, it seems to me, is this true of disease. So all the crises and deeper implications of life seem inevitably to lead back to that question of social improvement, and militant learning and doing.

This, then, is the goal of my religion—the bringing of fuller, richer life to more people on this earth. All institutions and all works that do not have this for their object are useless and pernicious. And this is not to be a mere philosophic precept which may well be buried under a host of more immediate matters, but a living faith, to permeate one's thought, and transfuse one's life. Prevention must be the method against evil. To remove temptation from men, and to apply the stimulus which shall call forth their highest endeavors—these seem to me the only right principles of ethical endeavor. Not to keep waging the agelong battle with sin and poverty, but to make the air around men so pure that foul lungs cannot breathe it—this should be our noblest religious aim.

Education—knowledge and training—I have felt so keenly my lack of these things that I count them as the greatest of means toward making life noble and happy. The lack of stimulus has tended with me to dissipate the power which might otherwise have been concentrated in some one productive direction. Or perhaps it was the many weak stimuli that constantly incited me and thus kept me from following one particular bent. I look back on what seems a long waste of intellectual power, time frittered away in groping and moping, which might easily have been spent constructively. A defect in one of the physical senses often means a keener sensitiveness in the others, but it seems that unless the sphere of action that the handicapped man has is very much narrowed, his intellectual ability will not grow in compensation for his physical defects. He will always feel that, had he been strong or even successful, he would have been further advanced intellectually, and would have attained greater command over his powers. For his mind tends to be cultivated extensively, rather than intensively. He has so many problems to meet, so many things to explain to himself, that he acquires a wide rather than a profound knowledge. Perhaps eventually, by eliminating most of these interests as practicable fields, he may tie himself down to one line of work; but at first he is pretty apt to find his mind rebellious. If he is eager and active, he will get a smattering of too many things, and his imperfect, badly trained organism will make intense application very difficult.

Now that I have talked a little of my philosophy of life, particularly about what I want to put into it, there is something to be said also of its enjoyment, and what I may hope to get out of it. I have said that my ideal of character was militant rather than long-suffering. It is true that my world has been one of failure and deficit—I have accomplished practically nothing alone, and can count only two or three instances where I have received kindly counsel and suggestion; moreover it still seems a miracle to me that money can be spent for anything beyond the necessities without being first carefully weighed and pondered over—but it has not been a world of suffering and sacrifice, my health has been almost criminally perfect in the light of my actual achievement, and life has appeared to me, at least since my more pressing responsibilities were removed, as a challenge and an arena, rather than a vale of tears. I do not like the idea of helplessly suffering one's misfortunes, of passively bearing one's lot. The Stoics depress me. I do not want to look on my life as an eternal making the best of a bad bargain. Granting all the circumstances, admitting all my disabilities, I want too to "warm both hands before the fire of life." What satisfactions I have, and they are many and precious, I do not want to look on as compensations, but as positive goods.

The difference between what the strongest of the strong and the most winning of the attractive can get out of life, and what I can, is after all so slight. Our experiences and enjoyments, both his and mine, are so infinitesimal compared with the great mass of possibilities; and there must be a division of labor. If he takes the world of physical satisfactions and of material success, I at least can occupy the far richer kingdom of mental effort and artistic appreciation. And on the side of what we are to put into life, although I admit that achievement on my part will be harder relatively to encompass than on his, at least I may have the field of artistic creation and intellectual achievement for my own. Indeed, as one gets older, the fact of one's disabilities fades dimmer and dimmer away from consciousness. One's enemy is now one's own weak will, and the struggle is to attain the artistic ideal one has set.

But one must have grown up, to get this attitude. And that is the best thing the handicapped man can do. Growing up will have given him one of the greatest, and certainly the most durable satisfaction of his life. It will mean at least that he is out of the woods. Childhood has nothing to offer him; youth little more. They are things to be gotten through with as soon as possible. For he will not understand, and he will not be understood. He finds himself simply a bundle of chaotic impulses and emotions and ambitions, very few of which, from the nature of the case, can possibly be realized or satisfied. He is bound to be at cross-grains with the world, and he has to look sharp that he does not grow up with a bad temper and a hateful disposition, and become cynical and bitter against those who turn him away. But grown up, his horizon will broaden; he will get a better perspective, and will not take the world so seriously as he used to, nor will failure frighten him so much. He can look back and see how inevitable it all was, and understand how precarious and problematic even the best regulated of human affairs may be. And if he feels that there were times when he should have been able to count upon the help and kindly counsel of relatives and acquaintances who remained dumb and uninterested, he will not put their behavior down as proof of the depravity of human nature, but as due to an unfortunate blindness which it will be his work to avoid in himself by looking out for others when he has the power.

When he has grown up, he will find that people of his own age and experience are willing to make those large allowances for what is out of the ordinary which were impossible to his younger friends, and that grown-up people touch each other on planes other than the purely superficial. With a broadening of his own interests, he will find himself overlapping other people's personalities at new points, and will discover with rare delight that he is beginning to be understood and appreciated—at least to a greater degree than when he had to keep his real interests hid as something unusual. For he will begin to see in his friends, his music and books, and his interest in people and social betterment, his true life; many of his restless ambitions will fade gradually away, and he will come to recognize all the more clearly some true ambition of his life that is within the range of his capabilities. He will have built up his world, and have sifted out the things that are not going to concern him, and participation in which will only serve to vex and harass him. He may well come to count his deformity even as a blessing, for it has made impossible to him at last many things in the pursuit of which he would only fritter away his time and dissipate his interest. He must not think of "resigning himself to his fate"; above all he must insist on his own personality. For once really grown up, he will find that he has acquired self-respect and personality. Grown-upness, I think, is not a mere question of age, but of being able to look back and understand and find satisfaction in one's experience, no matter how bitter it may have been.

So to all who are situated as I am, I would say—Grow up as fast as you can. Cultivate the widest interests you can, and cherish all your friends. Cultivate some artistic talent, for you will find it the most durable of satisfactions, and perhaps one of the surest means of livelihood as well. Achievement is, of course, on the knees of the gods; but you will at least have the thrill of trial, and, after all, not to try is to fail. Taking your disabilities for granted, and assuming constantly that they are being taken for granted, make your social intercourse as broad and as constant as possible. Do not take the world too seriously, nor let too many social conventions oppress you. Keep sweet your sense of humor, and above all do not let any morbid feelings of inferiority creep into your soul. You will find yourself sensitive enough to the sympathy of others, and if you do not find people who like you and are willing to meet you more than halfway, it will be because you have let your disability narrow your vision and shrink up your soul. It will be really your own fault, and not that of your circumstances. In a word, keep looking outward; look out eagerly for those things that interest you, for people who will interest you and be friends with you, for new interests and for opportunities to express yourself. You will find that your disability will come to have little meaning for you, that it will begin to fade quite completely out of your sight; you will wake up some fine morning and find yourself, after all the struggles that seemed so bitter to you, really and truly adjusted to the world.

I am perhaps not yet sufficiently out of the wilderness to utter all these brave words. For, I must confess, I find myself hopelessly dependent on my friends, and my environment. My friends have come to mean more to me than almost anything else in the world. If it is far harder work for a man in my situation to make friendships quickly, at least friendships once made have a depth and intimacy quite beyond ordinary attachments. For a man such as I am has little prestige; people do not want to impress him. They are genuine and sincere, talk to him freely about themselves, and are generally far less reticent about revealing their real personality and history and aspirations. And particularly is this so in friendships with young women. I have found their friendships the most delightful and satisfying of all. For all that social convention that insists that every friendship between a young man and woman must be on a romantic basis is necessarily absent in our case. There is no fringe around us to make our acquaintance anything but a charming companionship. With all my friends, the same thing is true. The first barrier of strangeness broken down, our interest is really in each other, and not in what each is going to think of the other, how he is to be impressed, or whether we are going to fall in love with each other. When one of my friends moves away, I feel as if a great hole had been left in my life. There is a whole side of my personality that I cannot express without him. I shudder to think of any change that will deprive me of their constant companionship. Without friends I feel as if even my music and books and interests would turn stale on my hands. I confess that I am not grown up enough to get along without them.

But if I am not yet out of the wilderness, at least I think I see the way to happiness. With health and a modicum of achievement, I shall not see my lot as unenviable. And if misfortune comes, it will only be something flowing from the common lot of men, not from my own particular disability. Most of the difficulties that flow from that I flatter myself I have met by this time of my twenty-fifth year, have looked full in the face, have grappled with, and find in nowise so formidable as the world usually deems them; no bar to my real ambitions and ideals.

JOHN JAY CHAPMAN

A year after a lynch mob in Coatesville, Pennsylvania, burned to death an African American man, a crime for which no one was punished, John Jay Chapman (1862–1933) rented a hall in that town for a penitential prayer meeting and delivered this searing address to the two people who bothered to show up. Chapman, a man of severe conscience, had as an undergraduate burned his hand so severely that it had to be amputated, in atonement for having unjustly thrashed a classmate. (See Edmund Wilson's superb biographical essay, on page 525.) Chapman tried everything he could to repudiate his WASP class privileges. He was an astute cultural critic; also a critic of America, which returned the favor by largely forgetting him. Jacques Barzun said, "His thought was too sinewy, too concentrated, and too simple. . . . He was at once a superior critic of his America and quite incomprehensible to it."

Coatesville

(1912)

We are met to commemorate the anniversary of one of the most dreadful crimes in history—not for the purpose of condemning it, but to repent of our share in it. We do not start any agitation with regard to that particular crime. I understand that an attempt to prosecute the chief criminals has been made, and entirely failed; because the whole community, and in a sense our whole people, are really involved in the guilt. The failure of the prosecution in this case, in all such cases, is only a proof of the magnitude of the guilt, and of the awful fact that everyone shares in it.

I will tell you why I am here; I will tell you what happened to me. When I read in the newspapers of August 14, a year ago, about the burning alive of a human being, and of how a few desperate, fiend-minded men had been permitted to torture a man chained to an iron bedstead, burning alive, thrust back by pitchforks when he struggled out of it, while around stood hundreds of well-dressed American citizens, both from the vicinity and from afar, coming on foot and in wagons, assembling on telephone call, as if by magic, silent, whether from terror or indifference, fascinated and impotent, hundreds of persons watching this awful sight and making no attempt to stay the wickedness, and no one man among them all who was inspired to risk his life in an attempt to stop it, no one man to name the name of Christ, of humanity, of government! As I read the newspaper accounts of the scene enacted here in Coatesville a year ago, I seemed to get a glimpse into the unconscious soul of this country. I saw a seldom revealed picture of the American heart and of the American nature. I seemed to be looking into the heart of the criminal—a cold thing, an awful thing.

I said to myself, "I shall forget this, we shall all forget it; but it will be there. What I have seen is not an illusion. It is the truth. I have seen death in the heart of this people." For to look at the agony of a fellow-being and remain aloof means death in the heart of the onlooker. Religious fanaticism has sometimes lifted men to the frenzy of such cruelty, political passion has sometimes done it, personal hatred might do it, the excitement of the amphitheater in the degenerate days of Roman luxury could do it. But here an audience chosen by chance in America has stood spellbound through an improvised *auto-da-fé,* irregular, illegal, having no religious significance, not sanctioned by custom, having no immediate provocation, the audience standing by merely in cold dislike.

I saw during one moment something beyond all argument in the depth of its significance. You might call it the paralysis of the nerves about the heart in a people habitually and unconsciously given over to selfish aims, an ignorant people who knew not what spectacle they were providing, or what part they were playing in a judgment-play which history was exhibiting on that day.

No theories about the race problem, no statistics, legislation, or mere educational endeavor, can quite meet the lack which that day revealed in the American people. For what we saw was death. The people stood like blighted things, like ghosts about Acheron, waiting for someone or something to determine their destiny for them.

Whatever life itself is, that thing must be replenished in us. The opposite of hate is love, the opposite of cold is heat; what we need is the love of God and reverence for human nature. For one moment I knew that I had seen our true need; and I was afraid that I should forget it and that I should go about framing arguments and agitations and starting schemes of education, when the need was deeper than education. And I became filled with one idea, that I must not forget what I had seen, and that I must do something to remember it. And I am here today chiefly that I may remember that vision. It seems fitting to come to this town where the crime occurred and hold a prayer-meeting, so that our hearts may be turned to God through whom mercy may flow into us.

Let me say one thing more about the whole matter. The subject we are dealing with is not local. The act, to be sure, took place at Coatesville and everyone looked to Coatesville to follow it up. Some months ago I asked a friend who lives not far from here something about the case, and about the expected prosecutions, and he replied to me: "It wasn't in my county," and that made me wonder whose county it was in. And it seemed to be in my county. I live on the Hudson River; but I knew that this great wickedness that happened in Coatesville is not the wickedness of Coatesville nor of to-day. It is the wickedness of all America and of three hundred years—the wickedness of the slave trade. All of us are tinctured by it. No special place, no special persons, are to blame. A nation cannot practice a course of inhuman crime for three hundred years and then suddenly throw off the effects of it. Less than fifty years ago domestic slavery was abolished among us; and in one way and another the marks of that vice are in our faces. There is no country in Europe where the Coatesville tragedy or anything remotely like it could have been enacted, probably no country in the world.

On the day of the calamity, those people in the automobiles came by the hundred and watched the torture, and passers-by came in a great multitude and watched it—and did nothing. On the next morning the newspapers spread the news and spread the paralysis until the whole country seemed to be helplessly watching this awful murder, as awful as anything ever done on earth; and the whole of our people seemed to be looking on helplessly, not able to respond, not knowing what to do next. That spectacle has been in my mind.

The trouble has come down to us out of the past. The only reason that slavery is wrong is that it is cruel and makes men cruel and leaves them cruel. Someone may say that you and I cannot repent because we did not do the act. But we are involved in it. We are still looking on. Do you not see that this whole event is merely the last parable, the most vivid, the most terrible illustration that ever was given by man or imagined by a Jewish prophet, of the relation between good and evil in this world, and of the relation of men to one another?

This whole matter has been an historic episode; but it is a part, not only of our national history, but of the personal history of each one of us. With the great disease (slavery) came the climax (the war), and after the climax gradually began the cure, and in the process of cure comes now the knowledge of what the evil was. I say that our need is new life, and that books and resolutions will not save us, but only such disposition in our hearts and souls as will enable the new life, love, force, hope, virtue, which surround us always, to enter into us.

This is the discovery that each man must make for himself—the discovery that what he really stands in need of he cannot get for himself, but must wait till God gives it to him. I have felt the impulse to come here today to testify to this truth.

The occasion is not small; the occasion looks back on three centuries and embraces a hemisphere. Yet the occasion is small compared with the truth it leads us to. For this truth touches all ages and affects every soul in the world.

AGNES REPPLIER

Agnes Repplier (1855–1950) was unusual among American authors in having devoted almost her entire literary output to the essay. In her fifty-year career, she wrote more than a thousand essays, which earned her the titles "our dean of essayists" and "the grand dame of the form." Versed in Michel de Montaigne and the English school of essayists, she readily incorporated literary references into her droll, worldly compositions. Repplier has been linked, in a critical and possibly misogynistic manner, with the genteel tradition in American literature; but as the tender yet clear-eyed observations and sharp, controlled prose of "The Grocer's Cat" indicate, there is much to be said for the best of that tradition.

The Grocer's Cat

(1912)

> Of all animals, the cat alone attains to the Contemplative Life.
> —Andrew Lang

The grocer's window—is not one of those gay and glittering enclosures which display only the luxuries of the table, and which give us the impression that there are favoured classes subsisting exclusively upon Malaga raisins, Russian chocolates, and Nuremberg gingerbread. It is an unassuming window, filled with canned goods and breakfast foods, wrinkled prunes devoid of succulence, and boxes of starch and candles. Its only ornament is the cat, and his beauty is more apparent to the artist than to the fancier. His splendid stripes, black and grey and tawny, are too wide for noble lineage. He has a broad benignant brow, like Benjamin Franklin's; but his brooding eyes, golden, unfathomable, deny benignancy. He is large and sleek,—the grocery mice must be many, and of an appetizing fatness,—and I presume he devotes his nights to the pleasures of the chase. His days are spent in contemplation, in a serene and wonderful stillness, which isolates him from the bustling vulgarities of the street.

Past the window streams the fretful crowd; in and out of the shop step loud-voiced customers. The cat is as remote as if he were drowsing by the waters of the Nile. Pedestrians pause to admire him, and many of them endeavour, with well-meant but futile familiarity, to win some notice in return. They tap on the window pane, and say, "Halloo, Pussy!" He does not turn his head, nor lift his lustrous eyes. They tap harder, and with more ostentatious friendliness. The stone cat of Thebes could not pay less attention. It is difficult for human beings to believe that their regard can be otherwise than flattering to an animal; but I did see one man intelligent enough to receive this impression. He was a decent and a good-tempered young person, and he had beaten a prolonged tattoo on the glass with the handle of his umbrella, murmuring at the same time vague words of cajolery. Then, as the cat remained motionless, absorbed in revery, and seemingly unconscious of his unwarranted attentions, he turned to me, a new light dawning in his eyes. "Thinks itself some," he said, and I nodded acquiescence. As well try to patronize the Sphinx as to patronize a grocer's cat.

Now, surely this attitude on the part of a small and helpless beast, dependent upon our bounty for food and shelter, and upon our sense of equity for the right to live, is worthy of note, and, to the generous mind, is worthy of respect. Yet there are people who most ungenerously resent it. They say the cat is treacherous and ungrateful, by which they mean that she does not relish unsolicited fondling, and that, like Mr. Chesterton, she will not recognize imaginary obligations. If we keep a cat because there are mice in our kitchen or rats in our cellar, what claim have we to gratitude? If we keep a cat for the sake of her beauty, and because our hearth is but a poor affair without her, she repays her debt with interest when she dozes by our fire. She is the most decorative creature the domestic world can show. She harmonizes with the kitchen's homely comfort, and with the austere seclusion of the library. She gratifies our sense of fitness and our sense of distinction, if we chance to possess these qualities. Did not Isabella d' Este, Marchioness of Mantua, and the finest exponent of distinction in her lordly age, send far and wide for cats to grace her palace? Did she not instruct her agents to make especial search through the Venetian convents, where might be found the deep-furred pussies of Syria and Thibet? Alas for the poor nuns, whose cherished pets were snatched away to gratify the caprice of a great and grasping lady, who habitually coveted all that was beautiful in the world.

The cat seldom invites affection, and still more seldom responds to it. A well-bred tolerance is her nearest approach to demonstration. The dog strives with pathetic insistence to break down the barriers between his intelligence and his master's, to understand and to be understood. The wise cat cherishes her isolation, and permits us to play but a secondary part in her solitary and meditative life. Her intelligence, less facile than the dog's, and far less highly differentiated, owes little to our tutelage; her character has not been moulded by our hands. The changing centuries have left no mark upon her; and, from a past inconceivably remote, she has come down to us, a creature self-absorbed and self-communing, undisturbed by our feverish activity, a dreamer of dreams, a lover of the mysteries of night.

And yet a friend. No one who knows anything about the cat will deny her capacity for friendship. Rationally, without enthusiasm, without illusions, she offers us companionship on terms of equality. She will not come when she is summoned,—unless the summons be for dinner,—but she will come of her own sweet will, and bear us company for hours, sleeping contentedly in her armchair, or watching with half-shut eyes the quiet progress of our work. A lover of routine, she expects to find us in the same place at the same hour every day; and when her expectations are fulfilled (cats have some secret method of their own for telling time), she purrs approval of our punctuality. What she detests are noise, confusion, people who bustle in and out of rooms, and the unpardonable intrusions of the housemaid. On those unhappy days when I am driven from my desk by the iron determination of this maid to "clean up," my cat is as comfortless as I am. Companions in exile, we wander aimlessly to and fro, lamenting our lost hours. I cannot explain to Lux that the fault is none of mine, and I am sure that she holds me to blame.

There is something indescribably sweet in the quiet, self-respecting friendliness of my cat, in her marked predilection for my society. The absence of exuberance on her part, and the restraint I put upon myself, lend an element of dignity to our intercourse. Assured that I will not presume too far on her good nature, that I will not indulge in any of those gross familiarities, those boisterous gambols which delight the heart of a dog, Lux yields herself more and more passively to my persuasions. She will permit an occasional caress, and acknowledge it with a perfunctory purr. She will manifest a patronizing interest in my work, stepping sedately among my papers, and now and then putting her paw with infinite deliberation on the page I am writing, as though the smear thus contributed spelt, "Lux, her mark," and was a reward of merit. But she never curls herself upon my desk, never usurps the place sacred to the memory of a far dearer cat. Some invisible influence restrains her. When her tour of inspection is ended, she returns to her chair by my side, stretching herself luxuriously on her cushions, and watching with steady, sombre stare the inhibited spot, and the little grey phantom which haunts my lonely hours by right of my inalienable love.

Lux is a lazy cat, wedded to a contemplative life. She cares little for play, and nothing for work,—the appointed work of cats. The notion that she has a duty to perform, that she owes service to the home which shelters her, that only those who toil are worthy of their keep, has never entered her head. She is content to drink the cream of idleness, and she does this in a spirit of condescension, wonderful to behold. The dignified distaste with which she surveys a dinner not wholly to her liking, carries confusion to the hearts of her servitors. It is as though Lucullus, having ordered Neapolitan peacock, finds himself put off with nightingales' tongues.

For my own part, I like to think that my beautiful and urbane companion is not a midnight assassin. Her profound and soulless indifference to mice pleases me better than it pleases my household. From an economic point of view, Lux is not worth her salt. Huxley's cat, be it remembered, was never known to attack anything larger and fiercer than a butterfly. "I doubt whether he has the heart to kill a mouse," wrote the proud possessor of this prodigy; "but I saw him catch and eat the first butterfly of the season, and I trust that the germ of courage thus manifested may develop with years into efficient mousing."

Even Huxley was disposed to take a utilitarian view of cathood. Even Cowper, who owed to the frolics of his kitten a few hours' respite from melancholy, had no conception that his adult cat could do better service than slay rats. "I have a kitten, my dear," he wrote to Lady Hesketh, "the drollest of all creatures that ever wore a cat's skin. Her gambols are incredible, and not to be described. She tumbles head over heels several times together. She lays her cheek to the ground, and humps her back at you with an air of most supreme disdain. From this posture she rises to dance on her hind feet, an exercise which she performs with all the grace imaginable; and she closes these various exhibitions with a loud smack of her lips, which, for want of greater propriety of expression, we call spitting. But, though all cats spit, no cat ever produced such a sound as she does. In point of size, she is likely to be a kitten always, being extremely small for her age; but time, that spoils all things, will, I suppose, make her also a cat. You will see her, I hope, before that melancholy period shall arrive; for no wisdom that she may gain by experience and reflection hereafter will compensate for the loss of her present hilarity. She is dressed in a tortoiseshell suit, and I know that you will delight in her."

Had Cowper been permitted to live more with kittens, and less with evangelical clergymen, his hours of gayety might have outnumbered his hours of gloom. Cats have been known to retain in extreme old age the "hilarity" which the sad poet prized. Nature has thoughtfully provided them with one permanent plaything; and Mr. Frederick Locker vouches for a light-hearted old Tom who, at the close of a long and ill-spent life, actually squandered his last breath in the pursuit of his own elusive tail. But there are few of us who would care to see the monumental calm of our fireside sphinx degenerate into senile sportiveness. Better far the measured slowness of her pace, the superb immobility of her repose. To watch an ordinary cat move imperceptibly and with a rhythmic waving of her tail through a doorway (while we are patiently holding open the door), is like looking at a procession. With just such deliberate dignity, in just such solemn state, the priests of Ra filed between the endless rows of pillars into the sunlit temple court.

The cat is a freebooter. She draws no nice distinctions between a mouse in the wainscot, and a canary swinging in its gilded cage. Her traducers, indeed, have been wont to intimate that her preference is for the forbidden quarry; but this is one of many libellous accusations. The cat, though she has little sympathy with our vapid sentiment, can be taught that a canary is a privileged nuisance, immune from molestation. The bird's shrill notes jar her sensitive nerves. She abhors noise, and a canary's pipe is the most piercing and persistent of noises, welcome to that large majority of mankind which prefers sound of any kind to silence. Moreover, a cage presents just the degree of hindrance to tempt a cat's agility. That Puss habitually refrains from ridding the household of canaries is proof of her innate reasonableness, of her readiness to submit her finer judgment and more delicate instincts to the common caprices of humanity.

As for wild birds, the robins and wrens and thrushes which are predestined prey, there is only one way to save them, the way which Archibald Douglas took to save the honour of Scotland,—"bell the cat." A good-sized sleigh-bell, if she be strong enough to bear it, a bunch of little bells, if she be small and slight,—and the pleasures of the chase are over. One little bell is of no avail, for she learns to move with such infinite precaution that it does not ring until she springs, and then it rings too late. There is an element of cruelty in depriving the cat of sport, but from the bird's point of view the scheme works to perfection. Of course rats and mice are as safe as birds from the claws of a belled cat, but, if we are really humane, we will not regret their immunity.

The boasted benevolence of man is, however, a purely superficial emotion. What am I to think of a friend who anathematizes the family cat for devouring a nest of young robins, and then tells me exultingly that the same cat has killed twelve moles in a fortnight. To a pitiful heart, the life of a little mole is as sacred as the life of a little robin. To an artistic eye, the mole in his velvet coat is handsomer than the robin, which is at best a bouncing, bourgeois sort of bird, a true suburbanite, with all the defects of his class. But my friend has no mercy on the mole because he destroys her garden,—her garden which she despoils every morning, gathering its fairest blossoms to droop and wither in her crowded rooms. To wax compassionate over a bird, and remain hard as flint to a beast, is possible only to humanity. The cat, following her predatory instincts, is at once more logical and less ruthless, because the question of property does not distort her vision. She has none of the vices of civilization.

> Cats I scorn, who, sleek and fat,
> Shiver at a Norway rat.
> Rough and hardy, bold and free,
> Be the cat that's made for me;
> He whose nervous paw can take
> My lady's lapdog by the neck,
> With furious hiss attack the hen,
> And snatch a chicken from the pen.

So sang Dr. Erasmus Darwin's intrepid pussy (a better poet than her master) to the cat of Miss Anna Seward, surely the last lady in all England to have encouraged such lawlessness on the part of a—presumably—domestic animal.

For the cat's domesticity is at best only a presumption. It is one of life's ironical adjustments that the creature who fits so harmoniously into the family group should be alien to its influences, and independent of its cramping conditions. She seems made for the fireside she adorns, and where she has played her part for centuries. Lamb, delightedly recording his "observations on cats," sees only their homely qualities. "Put 'em on a rug before the fire, they wink their eyes up, and listen to the kettle, and then purr, which is their music." The hymns which Shelley loved were sung by the roaring wind, the hissing kettle, and the kittens purring by his hearth. Heine's cat, curled close to the glowing embers, purred a soft accompaniment to the rhythms pulsing in his brain; but he at least, being a German, was not deceived by this specious show of impeccability. He knew that when the night called, his cat obeyed the summons, abandoning the warm fire for the hard-frozen snow, and the innocent companionship of a poet for the dancing of witches on the hill-tops.

The same grace of understanding—more common in the sixteenth than in the nineteenth century—made the famous Milanese physician, Jerome Cardan, abandon his students at the University of Pavia, in obedience to the decision of his cat. "In the year 1552," he writes with becoming gravity, "having left in the house a little cat of placid and domestic habits, she jumped upon my table, and tore at my public lectures; yet my Book of Fate she touched not, though it was the more exposed to her attacks. I gave up my chair, nor returned to it for eight years." Oh, wise physician, to discern so clearly that "placid and domestic habits" were but a cloak for mysteries too deep to fathom, for warnings too pregnant to be disregarded.

The vanity of man revolts from the serene indifference of the cat. He is forever lauding the dog, not only for its fidelity, which is a beautiful thing, but for its attitude of humility and abasement. A distinguished American prelate has written some verses on his dog, in which he assumes that, to the animal's eyes, he is as God,—a being whose word is law, and from whose sovereign hand flow all life's countless benefactions. Another complacent enthusiast describes his dog as sitting motionless in his presence, "at once tranquil and attentive, as a saint should be in the presence of God. He is happy with the happiness which we perhaps shall never know, since it springs from the smile and the approval of a life incomparably higher than his own."

Of course, if we are going to wallow in idolatry like this, we do well to choose the dog, and not the cat, to play the worshipper's part. I am not without a suspicion that the dog is far from feeling the rapture and the reverence which we so delightedly ascribe to him. What is there about any one of us to awaken such sentiments in the breast of an intelligent animal? We have taught him our vices, and he fools us to the top of our bent. The cat, however, is equally free from illusions and from hypocrisy. If we aspire to a petty omnipotence, she, for one, will pay no homage at our shrine. Therefore has her latest and greatest defamer, Maeterlinck, branded her as ungrateful and perfidious. The cat of "The Blue Bird" fawns and flatters, which is something no real cat was ever known to do. When and where did M. Maeterlinck encounter an obsequious cat? That the wise little beast should resent Tyltyl's intrusion into the ancient realms of night, is conceivable, and that, unlike the dog, she should see nothing godlike in a masterful human boy, is hardly a matter for regret; but the most subtle of dramatists should better understand the most subtle of animals, and forbear to rank her as man's enemy because she will not be man's dupe. Rather let us turn back and learn our lesson from Montaigne, serenely playing with his cat as friend to friend, for thus, and thus only, shall we enjoy the sweets of her companionship. If we want an animal to prance on its hind legs, and, with the over-faithful Tylo, cry out, "little god, little god," at every blundering step we take; if we are so constituted that we feel the need of being worshipped by something or somebody, we must feed our vanity as best we can with the society of dogs and men. The grocer's cat, enthroned on the grocer's starch-box, is no fitting friend for us.

As a matter of fact, all cats and kittens, whether royal Persians or of the lowliest estate, resent patronage, jocoseness (which they rightly hold to be in bad taste), and demonstrative affection,—those lavish embraces which lack delicacy and reserve. This last prejudice they carry sometimes to the verge of unkindness, eluding the caresses of their friends, and wounding the spirits of those who love them best. The little eight-year-old English girl who composed the following lines, when smarting from unrequited affection, had learned pretty much all there is to know concerning the capricious nature of cats:——

Oh, Selima shuns my kisses!
Oh, Selima hates her missus!
I never did meet
With a cat so sweet,
Or a cat so cruel as this is.

In such an instance I am disposed to think that Selima's coldness was ill-judged. No discriminating pussy would have shunned the kisses of such an enlightened little girl. But I confess to the pleasure with which I have watched other Selimas extricate themselves from well-meant but vulgar familiarities. I once saw a small black-and-white kitten playing with a judge, who, not unnaturally, conceived that he was playing with the kitten. For a while all went well. The kitten pranced and paddled, fixing her gleaming eyes upon the great man's smirking countenance, and pursued his knotted handkerchief so swiftly that she tumbled head over heels, giddy with her own rapid evolutions. Then the judge, being but human, and ignorant of the wide gap which lies between a cat's standard of good taste and the lenient standard of the court-room, ventured upon one of those doubtful pleasantries which a few pussies permit to privileged friends, but which none of the race ever endure from strangers. He lifted the kitten by the tail until only her forepaws touched the rug, which she clutched desperately, uttering a loud protesting mew. She looked so droll in her helplessness and wrath that several members of the household (her own household, which should have known better) laughed outright,—a shameful thing to do.

Here was a social crisis. A little cat of manifestly humble origin, with only an innate sense of propriety to oppose to a coarse-minded magistrate, and a circle of mocking friends. The judge, imperturbably obtuse, dropped the kitten on the rug, and prepared to resume their former friendly relations. The kitten did not run away, she did not even walk away; that would have been an admission of defeat. She sat down very slowly, as if first searching for a particular spot in the intricate pattern of the rug, turned her back upon her former playmate, faced her false friends, and tucked her outraged tail carefully out of sight. Her aspect was that of a cat alone in a desert land, brooding over the mystery of her nine lives. In vain the handkerchief was trailed seductively past her little nose, in vain her contrite family spoke words of sweetness and repentance. She appeared as aloof from her surroundings as if she had been wafted to Arabia; and presently began to wash her face conscientiously and methodically, with the air of one who finds solitude better than the companionship of fools. Only when the judge had put his silly handkerchief into his pocket, and had strolled into the library under the pretence of hunting for a book which he had never left there, did the kitten close her eyes, lower her obdurate little head, and purr herself tranquilly to sleep.

A few years afterwards I was permitted to witness another silent combat, another signal victory. This time the cat was, I grieve to say, a member of a troupe of performing animals, exhibited at the Folies-Bergère in Paris. Her fellow actors, poodles and monkeys, played their parts with relish and a sense of fun. The cat, a thing apart, condescended to leap twice through a hoop, and to balance herself very prettily on a large rubber ball. She then retired to the top of a ladder, made a deft and modest toilet, and composed herself for slumber. Twice the trainer spoke to her persuasively, but she paid no heed, and evinced no further interest in him nor in his entertainment. Her time for condescension was past.

The next day I commented on the cat's behaviour to some friends who had also been to the Folies-Bergère on different nights. "But," said the first friend, "the evening I went, that cat did wonderful things; came down the ladder on her ball, played the fiddle, and stood on her head."

"Really," said the second friend. "Well, the night I went, she did nothing at all except cuff one of the monkeys that annoyed her. She just sat on the ladder, and watched the performance. I presumed she was there by way of decoration."

All honour to the cat, who, when her little body is enslaved, can still preserve the freedom of her soul. The dogs and the monkeys obeyed their master; but the cat, like Montaigne's happier pussy long ago, had "her time to begin or to refuse," and showman and audience waited upon her will.

GEORGE SANTAYANA

George Santayana (1863–1952) was born in Madrid, immigrated to the United States to study philosophy, then went on to teach it at Harvard University for several decades before returning to Europe in his final years. Having retained Spanish citizenship, he was able to impart a skeptical if friendly outsider's perspective to America, as is manifest in the penetrating judgments of the country's mentality in his celebrated essay, "The Genteel Tradition in American Philosophy." The brilliant Santayana, also a skilled poet and novelist, brought a continental panache to his essays and his highly readable three-volume memoir.

The Genteel Tradition in American Philosophy

(1913)

Ladies and Gentlemen,—The privilege of addressing you to-day is very welcome to me, not merely for the honour of it, which is great, nor for the pleasures of travel, which are many, when it is California that one is visiting for the first time, but also because there is something I have long wanted to say which this occasion seems particularly favourable for saying. America is still a young country, and this part of it is especially so; and it would have been nothing extraordinary if, in this young country, material preoccupations had altogether absorbed people's minds, and they had been too much engrossed in living to reflect upon life, or to have any philosophy. The opposite, however, is the case. Not only have you already found time to philosophise in California, as your society proves, but the eastern colonists from the very beginning were a sophisticated race. As much as in clearing the land and fighting the Indians they were occupied, as they expressed it, in wrestling with the Lord. The country was new, but the race was tried, chastened, and full of solemn memories. It was an old wine in new bottles; and America did not have to wait for its present universities, with their departments of academic philosophy, in order to possess a living philosophy—to have a distinct vision of the universe and definite convictions about human destiny.

Now this situation is a singular and remarkable one, and has many consequences, not all of which are equally fortunate. America is a young country with an old mentality: it has enjoyed the advantages of a child carefully brought up and thoroughly indoctrinated; it has been a wise child. But a wise child, an old head on young shoulders, always has a comic and an unpromising side. The wisdom is a little thin and verbal, not aware of its full meaning and grounds; and physical and emotional growth may be stunted by it, or even deranged. Or when the child is too vigorous for that, he will develop a fresh mentality of his own, out of his observations and actual instincts; and this fresh mentality will interfere with the traditional mentality, and tend to reduce it to something perfunctory, conventional, and perhaps secretly despised. A philosophy is not genuine unless it inspires and expresses the life of those who cherish it. I do not think the hereditary philosophy of America has done much to atrophy the natural activities of the inhabitants; the wise child has not missed the joys of youth or of manhood; but what has happened is that the hereditary philosophy has grown stale, and that the academic philosophy afterwards developed has caught the stale odour from it. America is not simply, as I said a moment ago, a young country with an old mentality: it is a country with two mentalities, one a survival of the beliefs and standards of the fathers, the other an expression of the instincts, practice, and discoveries of the younger generations. In all the higher things of the mind—in religion, in literature, in the moral emotions—it is the hereditary spirit that still prevails, so much so that Mr. Bernard Shaw finds that America is a hundred years behind the times. The truth is that one-half of the American mind, that not occupied intensely in practical affairs, has remained, I will not say high-and-dry, but slightly becalmed; it has floated gently in the back-water, while, alongside, in invention and industry and social organisation, the other half of the mind was leaping down a sort of Niagara Rapids. This division may be found symbolised in American architecture: a neat reproduction of the colonial mansion—with some modern comforts introduced surreptitiously—stands beside the sky-scraper. The American Will inhabits the sky-scraper; the American Intellect inhabits the colonial mansion. The one is the sphere of the American man; the other, at least predominantly, of the American woman. The one is all aggressive enterprise; the other is all genteel tradition.

Now, with your permission, I should like to analyse more fully how this interesting situation has arisen, how it is qualified, and whither it tends. And in the first place we should remember what, precisely, that philosophy was which the first settlers brought with them into the country. In strictness there was more than one; but we may confine our attention to what I will call Calvinism, since it is on this that the current academic philosophy has been grafted. I do not mean exactly the Calvinism of Calvin, or even of Jonathan Edwards; for in their systems there was much that was not pure philosophy, but rather faith in the externals and history of revelation. Jewish and Christian revelation was interpreted by these men, however, in the spirit of a particular philosophy, which might have arisen under any sky, and been associated with any other religion as well as with Protestant Christianity. In fact, the philosophical principle of Calvinism appears also in the Koran, in Spinoza, and in Cardinal Newman; and persons with no very distinctive Christian belief, like Carlyle or like Professor Royce, may be nevertheless, philosophically, perfect Calvinists. Calvinism, taken in this sense, is an expression of the agonised conscience. It is a view of the world which an agonised conscience readily embraces, if it takes itself seriously, as, being agonised, of course it must. Calvinism, essentially, asserts three things: that sin exists, that sin is punished, and that it is beautiful that sin should exist to be punished. The heart of the Calvinist is therefore divided between tragic concern at his own miserable condition, and tragic exultation about the universe at large. He oscillates between a profound abasement and a paradoxical elation of the spirit. To be a Calvinist philosophically is to feel a fierce pleasure in the existence of misery, especially of one's own, in that this misery seems to manifest the fact that the Absolute is irresponsible or infinite or holy. Human nature, it feels, is totally depraved: to have the instincts and motives that we necessarily have is a great scandal, and we must suffer for it; but that scandal is requisite, since otherwise the serious importance of being as we ought to be would not have been vindicated.

To those of us who have not an agonised conscience this system may seem fantastic and even unintelligible; yet it is logically and intently thought out from its emotional premises. It can take permanent possession of a deep mind here and there, and under certain conditions it can become epidemic. Imagine, for instance, a small nation with an intense vitality, but on the verge of ruin, ecstatic and distressful, having a strict and minute code of laws, that paints life in sharp and violent chiaroscuro, all pure righteousness and black abominations, and exaggerating the consequences of both perhaps to infinity. Such a people were the Jews after the exile, and again the early Protestants. If such a people is philosophical at all, it will not improbably be Calvinistic. Even in the early American communities many of these conditions were fulfilled. The nation was small and isolated; it lived under pressure and constant trial; it was acquainted with but a small range of goods and evils. Vigilance over conduct and an absolute demand for personal integrity were not merely traditional things, but things that practical sages, like Franklin and Washington, recommended to their countrymen, because they were virtues that justified themselves visibly by their fruits. But soon these happy results themselves helped to relax the pressure of external circumstances, and indirectly the pressure of the agonised conscience within. The nation became numerous; it ceased to be either ecstatic or distressful; the high social morality which on the whole it preserved took another colour; people remained honest and helpful out of good sense and good will rather than out of scrupulous adherence to any fixed principles. They retained their instinct for order, and often created order with surprising quickness; but the sanctity of law, to be obeyed for its own sake, began to escape them; it seemed too unpractical a notion, and not quite serious. In fact, the second and native-born American mentality began to take shape. The sense of sin totally evaporated. Nature, in the words of Emerson, was all beauty and commodity; and while operating on it laboriously, and drawing quick returns, the American began to drink in inspiration from it aesthetically. At the same time, in so broad a continent, he had elbow-room. His neighbours helped more than they hindered him; he wished their number to increase. Good will became the great American virtue; and a passion arose for counting heads, and square miles, and cubic feet, and minutes saved—as if there had been anything to save them for. How strange to the American now that saying of Jonathan Edwards, that men are naturally God's enemies! Yet that is an axiom to any intelligent Calvinist, though the words he uses may be different. If you told the modern American that he is totally depraved, he would think you were joking, as he himself usually is. He is convinced that he always has been, and always will be, victorious and blameless.

Calvinism thus lost its basis in American life. Some emotional natures, indeed, reverted in their religious revivals or private searchings of heart to the sources of the tradition; for any of the radical points of view in philosophy may cease to be prevalent, but none can cease to be possible. Other natures, more sensitive to the moral and literary influences of the world, preferred to abandon parts of their philosophy, hoping thus to reduce the distance which should separate the remainder from real life.

Meantime, if anybody arose with a special sensibility or a technical genius, he was in great straits; not being fed sufficiently by the world, he was driven in upon his own resources. The three American writers whose personal endowment was perhaps the finest—Poe, Hawthorne, and Emerson—had all a certain starved and abstract quality. They could not retail the genteel tradition; they were too keen, too perceptive, and too independent for that. But life offered them little digestible material, nor were they naturally voracious. They were fastidious, and under the circumstances they were starved. Emerson, to be sure, fed on books. There was a great catholicity in his reading; and he showed a fine tact in his comments, and in his way of appropriating what he read. But he read transcendentally, not historically, to learn what he himself felt, not what others might have felt before him. And to feed on books, for a philosopher or a poet, is still to starve. Books can help him to acquire form, or to avoid pitfalls; they cannot supply him with substance, if he is to have any. Therefore the genius of Poe and Hawthorne, and even of Emerson, was employed on a sort of inner play, or digestion of vacancy. It was a refined labour, but it was in danger of being morbid, or tinkling, or self-indulgent. It was a play of intra-mental rhymes. Their mind was like an old music-box, full of tender echoes and quaint fancies. These fancies expressed their personal genius sincerely, as dreams may; but they were arbitrary fancies in comparison with what a real observer would have said in the premises. Their manner, in a word, was subjective. In their own persons they escaped the mediocrity of the genteel tradition, but they supplied nothing to supplant it in other minds.

The churches, likewise, although they modified their spirit, had no philosophy to offer save a new emphasis on parts of what Calvinism contained. The theology of Calvin, we must remember, had much in it besides philosophical Calvinism. A Christian tenderness, and a hope of grace for the individual, came to mitigate its sardonic optimism; and it was these evangelical elements that the Calvinistic churches now emphasised, seldom and with blushes referring to hell-fire or infant damnation. Yet philosophic Calvinism, with a theory of life that would perfectly justify hell-fire and infant damnation if they happened to exist, still dominates the traditional metaphysics. It is an ingredient, and the decisive ingredient, in what calls itself idealism. But in order to see just what part Calvinism plays in current idealism, it will be necessary to distinguish the other chief element in that complex system, namely, transcendentalism.

Transcendentalism is the philosophy which the romantic era produced in Germany, and independently, I believe, in America also. Transcendentalism proper, like romanticism, is not any particular set of dogmas about what things exist; it is not a system of the universe regarded as a fact, or as a collection of facts. It is a method, a point of view, from which any world, no matter what it might contain, could be approached by a self-conscious observer. Transcendentalism is systematic subjectivism. It studies the perspectives of knowledge as they radiate from the self; it is a plan of those avenues of inference by which our ideas of things must be reached, if they are to afford any systematic or distant vistas. In other words, transcendentalism is the critical logic of science. Knowledge, it says, has a station, as in a watch-tower; it is always seated here and now, in the self of the moment. The past and the future, things inferred and things conceived, lie around it, painted as upon a panorama. They cannot be lighted up save by some centrifugal ray of attention and present interest, by some active operation of the mind.

This is hardly the occasion for developing or explaining this delicate insight; suffice it to say, lest you should think later that I disparage transcendentalism, that as a method I regard it as correct and, when once suggested, unforgettable. I regard it as the chief contribution made in modern times to speculation. But it is a method only, an attitude we may always assume if we like and that will always be legitimate. It is no answer, and involves no particular answer, to the question: What exists; in what order is what exists produced; what is to exist in the future? This question must be answered by observing the object, and tracing humbly the movement of the object. It cannot be answered at all by harping on the fact that this object, if discovered, must be discovered by somebody, and by somebody who has an interest in discovering it. Yet the Germans who first gained the full transcendental insight were romantic people; they were more or less frankly poets; they were colossal egotists, and wished to make not only their own knowledge but the whole universe centre about themselves. And full as they were of their romantic isolation and romantic liberty, it occurred to them to imagine that all reality might be a transcendental self and a romantic dreamer like themselves; nay, that it might be just their own transcendental self and their own romantic dreams extended indefinitely. Transcendental logic, the method of discovery for the mind, was to become also the method of evolution in nature and history. Transcendental method, so abused, produced transcendental myth. A conscientious critique of knowledge was turned into a sham system of nature. We must therefore distinguish sharply the transcendental grammar of the intellect, which is significant and potentially correct, from the various transcendental systems of the universe, which are chimeras.

In both its parts, however, transcendentalism had much to recommend it to American philosophers, for the transcendental method appealed to the individualistic and revolutionary temper of their youth, while transcendental myths enabled them to find a new status for their inherited theology, and to give what parts of it they cared to preserve some semblance of philosophical backing. This last was the use to which the transcendental method was put by Kant himself, who first brought it into vogue, before the terrible weapon had got out of hand, and become the instrument of pure romanticism. Kant came, he himself said, to remove knowledge in order to make room for faith, which in his case meant faith in Calvinism. In other words, he applied the transcendental method to matters of fact, reducing them thereby to human ideas, in order to give

to the Calvinistic postulates of conscience a metaphysical validity. For
Kant had a genteel tradition of his own, which he wished to   move to a
place of safety, feeling that the empirical world had become too hot for
it; and this place of safety was the region of transcendental myth. I need
hardly say how perfectly this expedient suited the needs of philosophers
in America, and it is no accident if the influence of Kant soon became
dominant here. To embrace this philosophy was regarded as a sign of
profound metaphysical insight, although the most mediocre minds found
no difficulty in embracing it. In truth it was a sign of having been brought
up in the genteel tradition, of feeling it weak, and of wishing to save it.

But the transcendental method, in its way, was also sympathetic to the
American mind. It embodied, in a radical form, the spirit of Protestantism as distinguished from its inherited doctrines; it was autonomous,
undismayed, calmly revolutionary; it felt that Will was deeper than Intellect; it focussed everything here and now, and asked all things to show
their credentials at the bar of the young self, and to prove their value for
this latest born moment. These things are truly American; they would
be characteristic of any young society with a keen and discursive intelligence, and they are strikingly exemplified in the thought and in the person of Emerson. They constitute what he called self-trust. Self-trust, like
other transcendental attitudes, may be expressed in metaphysical fables.
The romantic spirit may imagine itself to be an absolute force, evoking
and moulding the plastic world to express its varying moods. But for a
pioneer who is actually a world-builder this metaphysical illusion has a
partial warrant in historical fact; far more warrant than it could boast
of in the fixed and articulated society of Europe, among the moonstruck
rebels and sulking poets of the romantic era. Emerson was a shrewd
Yankee, by instinct on the winning side; he was a cheery, child-like soul,
impervious to the evidence of evil, as of everything that it did not suit his
transcendental individuality to appreciate or to notice. More, perhaps,
than anybody that has ever lived, he practised the transcendental method
in all its purity. He had no system. He opened his eyes on the world every
morning with a fresh sincerity, marking how things seemed to him then,
or what they suggested to his spontaneous fancy. This fancy, for being
spontaneous, was not always novel; it was guided by the habits and training of his mind, which were those of a preacher. Yet he never insisted on
his notions so as to turn them into settled dogmas; he felt in his bones
that they were myths. Sometimes, indeed, the bad example of other transcendentalists, less true than he to their method, or the pressing questions
of unintelligent people, or the instinct we all have to think our ideas final,
led him to the very verge of system-making; but he stopped short. Had
he made a system out of his notion of compensation, or the over-soul,
or spiritual laws, the result would have been as thin and forced as it is in

other transcendental systems. But he coveted truth; and he returned to experience, to history, to poetry, to the natural science of his day, for new starting-points and hints toward fresh transcendental musings.

To covet truth is a very distinguished passion. Every philosopher says he is pursuing the truth, but this is seldom the case. As Mr. Bertrand Russell has observed, one reason why philosophers often fail to reach the truth is that often they do not desire to reach it. Those who are genuinely concerned in discovering what happens to be true are rather the men of science, the naturalists, the historians; and ordinarily they discover it, according to their lights. The truths they find are never complete, and are not always important; but they are integral parts of the truth, facts and circumstances that help to fill in the picture, and that no later interpretation can invalidate or afford to contradict. But professional philosophers are usually only apologists: that is, they are absorbed in defending some vested illusion or some eloquent idea. Like lawyers or detectives, they study the case for which they are retained, to see how much evidence or semblance of evidence they can gather for the defence, and how much prejudice they can raise against the witnesses for the prosecution; for they know they are defending prisoners suspected by the world, and perhaps by their own good sense, of falsification. They do not covet truth, but victory and the dispelling of their own doubts. What they defend is some system, that is, some view about the totality of things, of which men are actually ignorant. No system would have ever been framed if people had been simply interested in knowing what is true, whatever it may be. What produces systems is the interest in maintaining against all comers that some favourite or inherited idea of ours is sufficient and right. A system may contain an account of many things which, in detail, are true enough; but as a system, covering infinite possibilities that neither our experience nor our logic can prejudge, it must be a work of imagination and a piece of human soliloquy. It may be expressive of human experience, it may be poetical; but how should anyone who really coveted truth suppose that it was true?

Emerson had no system; and his coveting truth had another exceptional consequence: he was detached, unworldly, contemplative. When he came out of the conventicle or the reform meeting, or out of the rapturous close atmosphere of the lecture-room, he heard Nature whispering to him: "Why so hot, little sir?" No doubt the spirit or energy of the world is what is acting in us, as the sea is what rises in every little wave; but it passes through us, and cry out as we may, it will move on. Our privilege is to have perceived it as it moves. Our dignity is not in what we do, but in what we understand. The whole world is doing things. We are turning in that vortex; yet within us is silent observation, the speculative eye before which all passes, which bridges the distances and compares the combatants. On this side of his genius Emerson broke away from all conditions of age or country and represented nothing except intelligence itself.

There was another element in Emerson, curiously combined with transcendentalism, namely, his love and respect for Nature. Nature, for the transcendentalist, is precious because it is his own work, a mirror in which he looks at himself and says (like a poet relishing his own verses), "What a genius I am! Who would have thought there was such stuff in me?" And the philosophical egotist finds in his doctrine a ready explanation of whatever beauty and commodity nature actually has. No wonder, he says to himself, that nature is sympathetic, since I made it. And such a view, one-sided and even fatuous as it may be, undoubtedly sharpens the vision of a poet and a moralist to all that is inspiriting and symbolic in the natural world. Emerson was particularly ingenious and clear-sighted in feeling the spiritual uses of fellowship with the elements. This is something in which all Teutonic poetry is rich and which forms, I think, the most genuine and spontaneous part of modern taste, and especially of American taste. Just as some people are naturally enthralled and refreshed by music, so others are by landscape. Music and landscape make up the spiritual resources of those who cannot or dare not express their unfulfilled ideals in words. Serious poetry, profound religion (Calvinism, for instance), are the joys of an unhappiness that confesses itself; but when a genteel tradition forbids people to confess that they are unhappy, serious poetry and profound religion are closed to them by that; and since human life, in its depths, cannot then express itself openly, imagination is driven for comfort into abstract arts, where human circumstances are lost sight of, and human problems dissolve in a purer medium. The pressure of care is thus relieved, without its quietus being found in intelligence. To understand oneself is the classic form of consolation; to elude oneself is the romantic. In the presence of music or landscape human experience eludes itself; and thus romanticism is the bond between transcendental and naturalistic sentiment. The winds and clouds come to minister to the solitary ego.

Have there been, we may ask, any successful efforts to escape from the genteel tradition, and to express something worth expressing behind its back? This might well not have occurred as yet; but America is so precocious, it has been trained by the genteel tradition to be so wise for its years, that some indications of a truly native philosophy and poetry are already to be found. I might mention the humourists, of whom you here in California have had your share. The humourists, however, only half escape the genteel tradition; their humour would lose its savour if they had wholly escaped it. They point to what contradicts it in the facts; but not in order to abandon the genteel tradition, for they have nothing solid to put in its place. When they point out how ill many facts fit into it, they do not clearly conceive that this militates against the standard, but think it a funny perversity in the facts. Of course, did they earnestly respect the genteel tradition, such an incongruity would seem to them sad, rather than ludicrous. Perhaps the prevalence of humour in America, in and out of season, may be taken as one more evidence that the genteel tradition is present pervasively, but everywhere weak. Similarly in Italy, during the Renaissance, the Catholic tradition could not be banished from the intellect, since there was nothing articulate to take its place; yet its hold on the heart was singularly relaxed. The consequence was that humourists could regale themselves with the foibles of monks and of cardinals, with the credulity of fools, and the bogus miracles of the saints; not intending to deny the theory of the church, but caring for it so little at heart that they could find it infinitely amusing that it should be contradicted in men's lives and that no harm should come of it. So when Mark Twain says, "I was born of poor but dishonest parents," the humour depends on the parody of the genteel Anglo-Saxon convention that it is disreputable to be poor; but to hint at the hollowness of it would not be amusing if it did not remain at bottom one's habitual conviction.

The one American writer who has left the genteel tradition entirely behind is perhaps Walt Whitman. For this reason educated Americans find him rather an unpalatable person, who they sincerely protest ought not to be taken for a representative of their culture; and he certainly should not, because their culture is so genteel and traditional. But the foreigner may sometimes think otherwise, since he is looking for what may have arisen in America to express, not the polite and conventional American mind, but the spirit and the inarticulate principles that animate the community, on which its own genteel mentality seems to sit rather lightly. When the foreigner opens the pages of Walt Whitman, he thinks that he has come at last upon something representative and original. In Walt Whitman democracy is carried into psychology and morals. The various sights, moods, and emotions are given each one vote; they are declared to be all free and equal, and the innumerable commonplace moments of life are suffered to speak like the others. Those moments formerly reputed great are not excluded, but they are made to march in the ranks with their companions—plain foot-soldiers and servants of the hour. Nor does the refusal to discriminate stop there; we must carry our principle further down, to the animals, to inanimate nature, to the cosmos as a whole. Whitman became a pantheist; but his pantheism, unlike that of the Stoics and of Spinoza, was unintellectual, lazy, and self-indulgent; for he simply felt jovially that everything real was good enough, and that he was good enough himself. In him Bohemia rebelled against the genteel tradition; but the reconstruction that alone can justify revolution did not ensue. His attitude, in principle, was utterly disintegrating; his poetic genius fell back to the lowest level, perhaps, to which it is possible for poetic genius to fall. He reduced his imagination to a passive sensorium for the registering of impressions. No element of construction remained in it, and therefore no element of penetration. But his scope was wide; and his lazy, desultory apprehension was poetical. His work, for the very reason that it is so rudimentary, contains a beginning, or rather many beginnings, that might possibly grow into a noble moral imagination, a worthy filling for the human mind. An American in the nineteenth century who completely disregarded the genteel tradition could hardly have done more.

But there is another distinguished man, lately lost to this country, who has given some rude shocks to this tradition and who, as much as Whitman, may be regarded as representing the genuine, the long silent American mind—I mean William James. He and his brother Henry were as tightly swaddled in the genteel tradition as any infant geniuses could be, for they were born before 1850, and in a Swedenborgian household. Yet they burst those bands almost entirely. The ways in which the two brothers freed themselves, however, are interestingly different. Mr. Henry James has done it by adopting the point of view of the outer world, and by turning the genteel American tradition, as he turns everything else, into a subject-matter for analysis. For him it is a curious habit of mind, intimately comprehended, to be compared with other habits of mind, also well known to him. Thus he has overcome the genteel tradition in the classic way, by understanding it. With William James too this infusion of worldly insight and European sympathies was a potent influence, especially in his earlier days; but the chief source of his liberty was another. It was his personal spontaneity, similar to that of Emerson, and his personal vitality, similar to that of nobody else. Convictions and ideas came to him, so to speak, from the subsoil. He had a prophetic sympathy with the dawning sentiments of the age, with the moods of the dumb majority. His scattered words caught fire in many parts of the world. His way of thinking and feeling represented the true America, and represented in a measure the whole ultra-modern, radical world. Thus he eluded the genteel tradition in the romantic way, by continuing it into its opposite. The romantic mind, glorified in Hegel's dialectic (which is not dialectic at all, but a sort of tragi-comic history of experience), is always rendering its thoughts unrecognisable through the infusion of new insights, and through the insensible transformation of the moral feeling that accompanies them, till at last it has completely reversed its old judgments under cover of expanding them. Thus the genteel tradition was led a merry dance when it fell again into the hands of a genuine and vigorous romanticist like William James. He restored their revolutionary force to its neutralised elements, by picking them out afresh, and emphasising them separately, according to his personal predilections.

For one thing, William James kept his mind and heart wide open to all that might seem, to polite minds, odd, personal, or visionary in religion and philosophy. He gave a sincerely respectful hearing to sentimentalists, mystics, spiritualists, wizards, cranks, quacks, and impostors—for it is hard to draw the line, and James was not willing to draw it prematurely. He thought, with his usual modesty, that any of these might have something to teach him. The lame, the halt, the blind, and those speaking with tongues could come to him with the certainty of finding sympathy; and if they were not healed, at least they were comforted, that a famous professor should take them so seriously; and they began to feel that after all to have only one leg, or one hand, or one eye, or to have three, might be in itself no less beauteous than to have just two, like the stolid majority. Thus William James became the friend and helper of those groping, nervous, half-educated, spiritually disinherited, passionately hungry individuals of which America is full. He became, at the same time, their spokesman and representative before the learned world; and he made it a chief part of his vocation to recast what the learned world has to offer, so that as far as possible it might serve the needs and interests of these people.

Yet the normal practical masculine American, too, had a friend in William James. There is a feeling abroad now, to which biology and Darwinism lend some colour, that theory is simply an instrument for practice, and intelligence merely a help toward material survival. Bears, it is said, have fur and claws, but poor naked man is condemned to be intelligent, or he will perish. This feeling William James embodied in that theory of thought and of truth which he called pragmatism. Intelligence, he thought, is no miraculous, idle faculty, by which we mirror passively any or everything that happens to be true, reduplicating the real world to no purpose. Intelligence has its roots and its issue in the context of events; it is one kind of practical adjustment, an experimental act, a form of vital tension. It does not essentially serve to picture other parts of reality, but to connect them. This view was not worked out by William James in its psychological and historical details; unfortunately he developed it chiefly in controversy against its opposite, which he called intellectualism, and which he hated with all the hatred of which his kind heart was capable. Intellectualism, as he conceived it, was pure pedantry; it impoverished and verbalised everything, and tied up nature in red tape. Ideas and rules that may have been occasionally useful it put in the place of the full-blooded irrational movement of life which had called them into being; and these abstractions, so soon obsolete, it strove to fix and to worship for ever. Thus all creeds and theories and all formal precepts sink in the estimation of the pragmatist to a local and temporary grammar of action; a grammar that must be changed slowly by time, and may be changed quickly by genius. To know things as a whole, or as they are eternally, if there is anything eternal in them, is not only beyond our powers, but would prove worthless, and perhaps even fatal to our lives. Ideas are not mirrors, they are weapons; their function is to prepare us to meet events, as future experience may unroll them. Those ideas that disappoint us are false ideas; those to which events are true are true themselves.

This may seem a very utilitarian view of the mind; and I confess I think it a partial one, since the logical force of beliefs and ideas, their truth or falsehood as assertions, has been overlooked altogether, or confused with the vital force of the material processes which these ideas express. It is an external view only, which marks the place and conditions of the mind in nature, but neglects its specific essence; as if a jewel were defined as a round hole in a ring. Nevertheless, the more materialistic the pragmatist's theory of the mind is, the more vitalistic his theory of nature will have to become. If the intellect is a device produced in organic bodies to expedite their processes, these organic bodies must have interests and a chosen direction in their life; otherwise their life could not be expedited, nor could anything be useful to it. In other words—and this is a third point at which the philosophy of William James has played havoc with the genteel tradition, while ostensibly defending it—nature must be conceived anthropomorphically and in psychological terms. Its purposes are not to be static harmonies, self-unfolding destinies, the logic of spirit, the spirit of logic, or any other formal method and abstract law; its purposes are to be concrete endeavours, finite efforts of souls living in an environment which they transform and by which they, too, are affected. A spirit, the divine spirit as much as the human, as this new animism conceives it, is a romantic adventurer. Its future is undetermined. Its scope, its duration, and the quality of its life are all contingent. This spirit grows; it buds and sends forth feelers, sounding the depths around for such other centres of force or life as may exist there. It has a vital momentum, but no predetermined goal. It uses its past as a stepping-stone, or rather as a diving-board, but has an absolutely fresh will at each moment to plunge this way or that into the unknown. The universe is an experiment; it is unfinished. It has no ultimate or total nature, because it has no end. It embodies no formula or statable law; any formula is at best a poor abstraction, describing what, in some region and for some time, may be the most striking characteristic of existence; the law is a description *a posteriori* of the habit things have chosen to acquire, and which they may possibly throw off altogether. What a day may bring forth is uncertain; uncertain even to God. Omniscience is impossible; time is real; what had been omniscience hitherto might discover something more to-day. "There shall be news," William James was fond of saying with rapture, quoting from the unpublished poem of an obscure friend, "there shall be news in heaven!" There is almost certainly, he thought, a God now; there may be several gods, who might exist together, or one after the other. We might, by our conspiring sympathies, help to make a new one. Much in us is doubtless immortal; we survive death for some time in a recognisable form; but what our career and transformations may be in the sequel we cannot tell, although we may help to determine them by our daily choices. Observation must be continual if our ideas are to remain true. Eternal vigilance is the price of knowledge; perpetual hazard, perpetual experiment keep quick the edge of life.

This is, so far as I know, a new philosophical vista; it is a conception never before presented, although implied, perhaps, in various quarters, as in Norse and even Greek mythology. It is a vision radically empirical and radically romantic; and as William James himself used to say, the visions and not the arguments of a philosopher are the interesting and influential things about him. William James, rather too generously, attributed this vision to M. Bergson, and regarded him in consequence as a philosopher of the first rank, whose thought was to be one of the turning-points in history. M. Bergson had killed intellectualism. It was his book on creative evolution, said James with humorous emphasis, that had come at last to *"écraser l'infâme."* We may suspect, notwithstanding, that intellectualism, infamous and crushed, will survive the blow; and if the author of the Book of Ecclesiastes were now alive, and heard that there shall be news in heaven, he would doubtless say that there may possibly be news there, but that under the sun there is nothing new—not even radical empiricism or radical romanticism, which from the beginning of the world has been the philosophy of those who as yet had had little experience; for to the blinking little child it is not merely something in the world that is new daily, but everything is new all day.

I am not concerned with the rights and wrongs of that controversy; my point is only that William James, in this genial evolutionary view of the world, has given a rude shock to the genteel tradition. What! The world a gradual improvisation? Creation unpremeditated? God a sort of young poet or struggling artist? William James is an advocate of theism; pragmatism adds one to the evidences of religion; that is excellent. But is not the cool abstract piety of the genteel getting more than it asks for? This empirical naturalistic God is too crude and positive a force; he will work miracles, he will answer prayers, he may inhabit distinct places, and have distinct conditions under which alone he can operate; he is a neighbouring being, whom we can act upon, and rely upon for specific aids, as upon a personal friend, or a physician, or an insurance company. How disconcerting! Is not this new theology a little like superstition? And yet how interesting, how exciting, if it should happen to be true! I am far from wishing to suggest that such a view seems to me more probable than conventional idealism or than Christian orthodoxy. All three are in the region of dramatic system-making and myth to which probabilities are irrelevant. If one man says the moon is sister to the sun, and another that she is his daughter, the question is not which notion is more probable, but whether either of them is at all expressive. The so-called evidences are devised afterwards, when faith and imagination have prejudged the issue. The force of William James's new theology, or romantic cosmology, lies only in this: that it has broken the spell of the genteel tradition, and enticed faith in a new direction, which on second thoughts may prove no less alluring than the old. The important fact is not that the new fancy might possibly be true—who shall know that?—but that it has entered the heart of a leading American to conceive and to cherish it. The genteel tradition cannot be dislodged by these insurrections; there are circles to which it is still congenial, and where it will be preserved. But it has been challenged and (what is perhaps more insidious) it has been discovered. No one need be browbeaten any longer into accepting it. No one need be afraid, for instance, that his fate is sealed because some young prig may call him a dualist; the pint would call the quart a dualist, if you tried to pour the quart into him. We need not be afraid of being less profound, for being direct and sincere. The intellectual world may be traversed in many directions; the whole has not been surveyed; there is a great career in it open to talent. That is a sort of knell, that tolls the passing of the genteel tradition. Something else is now in the field; something else can appeal to the imagination, and be a thousand times more idealistic than academic idealism, which is often simply a way of white-washing and adoring things as they are. The illegitimate monopoly which the genteel tradition had established over what ought to be assumed and what ought to be hoped for has been broken down by the first-born of the family, by the genius of the race. Henceforth there can hardly be the same peace and the same pleasure in hugging the old proprieties. Hegel will be to the next generation what Sir William Hamilton was to the last. Nothing will have been disproved, but everything will have been abandoned. An honest man has spoken, and the cant of the genteel tradition has become harder for young lips to repeat.

With this I have finished such a sketch as I am here able to offer you of the genteel tradition in American philosophy. The subject is complex, and calls for many an excursus and qualifying footnote; yet I think the main outlines are clear enough. The chief fountains of this tradition were Calvinism and transcendentalism. Both were living fountains; but to keep them alive they required, one an agonised conscience, and the other a radical subjective criticism of knowledge. When these rare metaphysical preoccupations disappeared—and the American atmosphere is not favourable to either of them—the two systems ceased to be inwardly understood; they subsisted as sacred mysteries only; and the combination of the two in some transcendental system of the universe (a contradiction in principle) was doubly artificial. Besides, it could hardly be held with a single mind. Natural science, history, the beliefs implied in labour and invention, could not be disregarded altogether; so that the transcendental philosopher was condemned to a double allegiance, and to not letting his left hand know the bluff that his right hand was making. Nevertheless, the difficulty in bringing practical inarticulate convictions to expression is very great, and the genteel tradition has subsisted in the academic mind for want of anything equally academic to take its place.

The academic mind, however, has had its flanks turned. On the one side came the revolt of the Bohemian temperament, with its poetry of crude naturalism; on the other side came an impassioned empiricism, welcoming popular religious witnesses to the unseen, reducing science to an instrument of success in action, and declaring the universe to be wild and young, and not to be harnessed by the logic of any school.

This revolution, I should think, might well find an echo among you, who live in a thriving society, and in the presence of a virgin and prodigious world. When you transform nature to your uses, when you experiment with her forces, and reduce them to industrial agents, you cannot feel that nature was made by you or for you, for then these adjustments would have been pre-established. Much less can you feel it when she destroys your labour of years in a momentary spasm. You must feel, rather, that you are an offshoot of her life; one brave little force among her immense forces. When you escape, as you love to do, to your forests and your sierras, I am sure again that you do not feel you made them, or that they were made for you. They have grown, as you have grown, only more massively and more slowly. In their non-human beauty and peace they stir the sub-human depths and the superhuman possibilities of your own spirit. It is no transcendental logic that they teach; and they give no sign of any deliberate morality seated in the world. It is rather the vanity and superficiality of all logic, the needlessness of argument, the relativity of morals, the strength of time, the fertility of matter, the variety, the unspeakable variety, of possible life. Everything is measurable and conditioned, indefinitely repeated, yet, in repetition, twisted somewhat from its old form. Everywhere is beauty and nowhere permanence, everywhere an incipient harmony, nowhere an intention, nor a responsibility, nor a plan. It is the irresistible suasion of this daily spectacle, it is the daily discipline of contact with things, so different from the verbal discipline of the schools, that will, I trust, inspire the philosophy of your children. A Californian whom I had recently the pleasure of meeting observed that, if the philosophers had lived among your mountains their systems would have been different from what they are. Certainly, I should say, very different from what those systems are which the European genteel tradition has handed down since Socrates; for these systems are egotistical; directly or indirectly they are anthropocentric, and inspired by the conceited notion that man, or human reason, or the human distinction between good and evil, is the centre and pivot of the universe. That is what the mountains and the woods should make you at last ashamed to assert. From what, indeed, does the society of nature liberate you, that you find it so sweet?

It is hardly (is it?) that you wish to forget your past, or your friends, or that you have any secret contempt for your present ambitions. You respect these, you respect them perhaps too much; you are not suffered by the genteel tradition to criticise or to reform them at all radically. No; it is the yoke of this genteel tradition itself that these primeval solitudes lift from your shoulders. They suspend your forced sense of your own importance not merely as individuals, but even as men. They allow you, in one happy moment, at once to play and to worship, to take yourselves simply, humbly, for what you are, and to salute the wild, indifferent, non-censorious infinity of nature. You are admonished that what you can do avails little materially, and in the end nothing. At the same time, through wonder and pleasure, you are taught speculation. You learn what you are really fitted to do, and where lie your natural dignity and joy, namely, in representing many things, without being them, and in letting your imagination, through sympathy, celebrate and echo their life. Because the peculiarity of man is that his machinery for reaction on external things has involved an imaginative transcript of these things, which is preserved and suspended in his fancy; and the interest and beauty of this inward landscape, rather than any fortunes that may await his body in the outer world, constitute his proper happiness. By their mind, its scope, quality, and temper, we estimate men, for by the mind only do we exist as men, and are more than so many storage-batteries for material energy. Let us therefore be frankly human. Let us be content to live in the mind.

EDITH WHARTON

Edith Wharton (1861–1937), whose novels of manners, including The House of Mirth *and* The Age of Innocence, *earned her a permanent place in the American literary canon, was a Francophile who spent many of her later years in France. In 1918, she delivered a lecture in French to a Parisian audience about why the United States had enthusiastically chosen to enter World War I, a position she shared. The text of that talk, long considered lost, was rediscovered, edited, and translated by the scholar Virginia Ricard, who wrote: "It reveals Wharton's interest in the early American settlers' lasting contribution to democracy, and displays her wide—and generally unsuspected—knowledge of American history."*

America at War

(1918)

There is a profound difference, a fundamental difference, between the French and the Americans: a difference of language, far greater than that which exists between races of Latin origin, whose languages draw on a common linguistic fund. When an Italian or a Spaniard needs to translate his ideas into your language, he finds an equivalent, or even a synonym, far more easily than we do. For the person of purely Anglo-Saxon origin, there is, apart from the difficulty of pronunciation, that of finding exact equivalents in French for her American thoughts. If I call your attention to this obstacle, it is not merely to beg your indulgence. Rather, it is because I was invited to speak to you of my country and one of the most delicate questions concerning the relations between our two peoples is precisely the problem caused by the difference between our languages. If the United States and France were near neighbors, this obstacle would be less troublesome, but we are obliged to converse through the intermediary of the press and government statements. Each time I see the translation of a speech or an official American government statement in a French newspaper I fear a misunderstanding.

May I give you an example? When he arrived in Paris, Mr. House made a speech before the press, a simple, modest and dignified speech—provided it was read in English. Mr. House began by saying, "America is already mobilizing her *millions* in the factories, the fields, and the trenches." Now, the genius of English is essentially elliptic. We leave a great deal out, we imply words, whole phrases even, which could never be omitted in the French. So Mr. House did not say her millions of *men,* since the word "men" was implied by the meaning of the sentence. Anyone who knew English well could not possibly have misunderstood. But many French newspapers reported that Mr. House had said, *"L'Amérique a déjà mobilisé ses millions dans les usines,"* etc., which of course can only mean one thing in French: her millions of *dollars.* Thus poor Mr. House was recast as an *oncle d'Amérique* clinking the dollars in his pocket as he arrived at your doorstep. A small but very typical example, which I call to your attention to show you how difficult it is to translate us since in this particular case the translator rigorously followed the original.

You might object that, where there is a community of feeling, misunderstandings like these are always cleared up in the long run. I mention the problem nevertheless, because lexical discord is so often a sign of moral discord. Although they may have a common origin, words undergo mysterious changes as soon as they are absorbed by another language and these changes affect the soul, so that the emotions too are altered.

Our language is elliptic and sometimes our manners are too. We take shortcuts and byways, whereas you tread the paths traced by a long and glorious tradition. For more than a thousand years, you have had the use of wide roads, traced by the Roman Empire all over France, whereas our forefathers had to cut down trees and pull up shrubs in order to clear a path through the virgin forests. That analogy is a fairly exact symbol of the moral condition of our great-grandparents. Most of them, at least those who influenced the American character most deeply, were weary of well-trodden paths, of old institutions, and most of all, of old abuses. They left Europe to give their ideas a free rein—ideas that were not very interesting in themselves, since they remained within the narrow scope of theological quarrels. These people were, to put it bluntly, fanatics, the kind of boring, nasty, insufferable people that nature seems to produce from time to time in order to set in motion a widespread popular movement or to clear the land of a whole continent—because, of course, likable, reasonable people never change anything in the order of the universe.

And this brings me precisely to the subject I wish to discuss: the origins of my country and its deeps roots in the past. I was asked to talk today about "America at war," about the reasons why we entered the war. These reasons cannot be found in our need to defend a vulnerable border, nor even in the need for military or economic defense. They are to be found in the past. And since our entry into the war, I have come to realize that many French people have a very imperfect knowledge of that past.

I will not do you the injustice of supposing that you think all my compatriots are what you call *oncles d'Amérique*—fat planters who throw around gold by the fistful and, in the last act, solve disputes and misunderstandings with the help of their dollars—although, to be sure, at this particular moment, I can think of no better part for my country to play. . . . But are you really so far from believing that our grandparents went to America mainly to acquire dollars so that their grandsons could spend them merrily in the luxurious hotels of old Europe? Only a few of you have noticed that we also spend those dollars in antique shops and art galleries, and that we pack Fragonard panels, Boucher tapestries, and Rodin bronzes in our trunks. "The booty of barbarians," you might say. But little by little you have formed our taste and we now know where to purchase objects suitable for the decoration of a millionaire's house. Our impatience to enjoy European refinement is immense—and very childish, but that impatience, which you have observed a thousand times and recorded with exquisite irony, is also the result of our past, of our austere, arduous, and joyless past.

North America was colonized by people of different races, and at different times. Colonization, as you know, continues to this day, and over the past 150 years, we have become a testing ground for democracy. However, the deepest impression on the soul of our country was made by the English. Both the English Bible and English common law have nurtured the American soul. The Bible, in particular, has molded us, and my first task here is to help you understand the feelings that animated the *Mayflower* Pilgrims—the Pilgrims who left *old* England in 1620 to found *New* England. These were, as I have already said, fanatics—hard, cruel, and jealous people, eager to escape the persecution of the English national church, and perhaps in turn to persecute others. Those who have been persecuted are, alas, all too often the persecutors of tomorrow.

That said, we must not forget that the Puritans of the New World were sustained by perfectly disinterested motives. The colonization of the Atlantic states was not an economic undertaking. The Puritans did not go there seeking money or honors, nor even to conceal a depraved past. They were narrow-minded but honorable, respectable men, most of whom were fairly well-off, and who sacrificed everything—fortune, honor, friends, and well-being—to go and found a colony, beneath inclement skies, on inhospitable lands, peopled by artful and fierce natives, where each would be free to worship God according to the dogma of his sect, as well as to denounce neighbors suspected of worshiping differently. To achieve their purpose, they abandoned the pleasures of an organized society and all the dear beloved old ways that in England revolve around castle and church.

And while this theocracy was being founded on the rough stones of Massachusetts, Dutch merchants—all of them prosperous burghers and shrewd businessmen—established a warehouse for furs at the mouth of the Hudson and began to trade with the Red-Skins of the Great Lakes and the North. These intrepid Dutchmen were not at all interested in founding a theocracy. They had come to America in search of a new outlet for Dutch trade—in order to earn money, in other words. After a few years of dreadful struggle and terrible discouragement these tenacious merchants managed to establish a stable administration and to increase their fortunes. Their colony was governed by distinguished men, and when England took it over in 1664 the heirs of the old governors remained in New Amsterdam, later renamed New York and destined to become the main marketplace of the New World.

So right from the beginning of the seventeenth century, you had, side by side, dark and fanatic Massachusetts, founded in 1620 to establish "the reign of the spirit," and the state of New York founded seven years earlier to establish the dominion of the dollar. On the one hand, democratic equality, scorn for material wealth, and aversion for any reminders of the titles and privileges of old Europe; on the other hand, a society both mercantile and patrician, descended from an oligarchy founded by the Dutch West India Company. Thus, side by side, were two groups representing the two principal motives of human action: the will to sacrifice everything to intellectual and moral conviction, and the desire for wealth and the enjoyment of life. I, who am a descendant of the Dutch merchants and of their English successors, confess that I am glad not to have been brought up in the shadow of the gloomy theocracy of Massachusetts. Nevertheless, I must admit that those who sacrificed everything for their ideas are the ones who shaped the soul of my country most profoundly, more profoundly than those who faced similar dangers for material gain.

New York and the trends associated with New York—a fondness for profit, respect for rank and fortune, a taste for lavish meals and the comforts of rest beneath an eiderdown—provided a useful corrective to the somber ideology of the Puritans by contributing the healthy enjoyment of earthly goods to our national outlook. But it is written that the ideas that survive are always those that are born in disinterested sacrifice and it was the handful of fanatics thrown onto Plymouth Rock by the *May-flower* that has served to remind us of our national feeling at each crisis in our national history. Picture them, struggling alone, yet able not only to defend themselves and to resist, but also, even before they had even landed, to establish a plan for municipal administration, which was the first known written constitution in the history of the English-speaking peoples.

And what sort of society did they create? The settlers, whose ideas about government mostly harked back to earlier times, were innovators where municipal organization was concerned and many a democratic idea that had been smothered by the laws of the mother country prospered rapidly in the soil of the New World. In the wilderness, where each band of settlers formed an isolated center, cut off from their neighbors by forests inhabited by enemies, the only conceivable political unit was the "township"—a group of hamlets roughly corresponding to the French commune. According to their charter, every man admitted as a member of the colony had the right to take part in government. This plan resulted in the famous town meetings—community assemblies that were the origin of municipal liberties in Massachusetts. In fact, all the ideas that found local government in the United States were contained in this charter—all except the idea of religious freedom, which New England achieved only after a terrible struggle against the power of an uncompromising church.

And what sort of life did people lead in those bleak hamlets, the so-called townships of the New World? Stranded in the midst of immense forests, built on the edge of a stormy sea, and surrounded by ever-menacing natives, their humble wooden dwellings were buried in snow for six months a year. The inhabitants never left home except to go through the snow to listen to the minister who ruled over the parish. No one was allowed to miss the sermon, and in the flimsy wooden churches, where there was not even a stove to keep out the cold, everyone was chilled to the bone while the minister talked for hours on end. He taught that, according to the dogma of the Westminster Confession, children who died unbaptized burned forever in the depths of hell, that magistrates and ministers were bound to examine the doctrinal integrity of every Christian who attended the service, that any man who gathered firewood on a Sunday would be hanged, and that anyone who dared attribute the slightest sin to the Lord's elect would meet the same fate.

The ministers would preach for two or three hours running. The abuse grew so serious that the magistrates attempted to find a remedy, and argued that the frequency of the religious services, which took place every day, constantly compelled the settlers to interrupt their work and the women to neglect their domestic duties. The length of the sermons and prayers was such that the poor parishioners more often than not had to go home through a perilous forest in the middle of the night. The ministers responded that there were not enough hours in a day and night to name all the perils of heresy or to publicly condemn the sins of their flock. The magistrates were obliged to yield and the services went on as before.

As for the members of the flock, they seem to have responded to the uninterrupted flow of Christian eloquence in different ways. We read in Mr. X's diary that he attended a six-hour-long service in an unheated church in bone-numbing weather but did not feel the cold thanks to the force of the sermon—for which he praised God. On the other hand, a poor woman named Ursula Cole confessed to having told a neighbor that she would as soon hear a cat meow as hear Reverend Shepard preach, a blasphemy for which she was condemned either to pay a fine of 750 francs or be whipped. She was probably whipped. The ministers could and did avail themselves of the rod, shackles, stocks, gallows, and stake. You all know what tortures were inflicted on the so-called witches, some of whom were merely hysterics, others simply bonesetters such as can still be found in the French countryside. Others still were members of the Society of Friends who were disgusted with the tyranny of the clergy and certain they received their light directly from heaven. In such a climate, informers thrived and private grudges were settled mercilessly. If a regime of this sort had managed to ensure its continued existence, the United States would not have become the great country it is today.

I have paid so much attention to the bleakness of this picture because these men of iron, and the women who were their equals in stoic resilience, formed the kernel from which our civilization grew. Among them, right from the beginning, were a few individuals with wills equally strong, but with minds less narrow, who overthrew the all-powerful presbyteries and who founded schools and universities, and thus emancipated thought. A hundred years later, Americans were playing games, going to the theater, thinking about dress, dancing the passepied or the sarabande—and the ministers had begun to make shorter sermons. But long New England winters, fear of the Red-Skins, and continual dread of violent death and eternal punishment had left a shadow over the American soul. Americans danced, but on a volcano—the volcano of Presbyterian hell.

While New England was developing with difficulty, other settlers, who had arrived a few years earlier, took possession of the vast area that now extends from New Mexico to Pennsylvania. From 1620 onward, this colony of Virginia, named after Queen Elizabeth, was directly attached to the English Crown. It was divided up into large estates and conferred on certain aristocrats and gentlemen who wished to try their fortunes in the New World. The climate was mild, the land fertile, and the new colonies rapidly flourished economically. Under the benevolent dominion of the Anglican Church, a civilized society developed there, in comparison with which the New England settlers were like savages in the Stone Age. Alas, one day a Dutch merchant ship landed on the coast and unloaded amid its merchandise a few Negroes, who were sold with the rest.

That day, slavery came into being in the United States. That day too marks the beginning of the commercial and political ruin of the southern

States. Those poor dazed Africans, like the furies, came bearing the germs of disintegration and death. As you know, we did not die, and we did not even disintegrate, but our immense federation endured many moments of danger, for slavery introduced one of the elements which contributed, long afterward, to creating what I will call "statism"—that is, an attachment to the particular rights of a state rather than to the nation. The conflict came to a head only 150 years later with our Civil War, a war that had two causes, one remote and ideal, the other immediate and practical. The remote cause was the desire to end slavery. The immediate cause was the determination to thwart the separatist tendencies of certain states that had usurped the right to withdraw from the Union if their particular interests conflicted with those of the nation.

Right from the beginning, the American colonies, founded for different reasons by people of diverse races and with different ideas, were naturally suspicious of each other. The Revolution, which united them for an instant against a common enemy, did not put an end to their inevitable rivalry. And so it happened that at each national crisis there were two parties: one defending local interests, the freedom of choice of each state; the other constantly defending the idea that a federation of states cannot last and develop unless it places the interests of the country as a whole above local interests. It was only natural that at first local interests should be represented by the southern states, immersed as they were in the well-being of a quasi-patriarchal existence and unwilling to be disturbed. The settlers of the northern states—Pennsylvania, New York and New England—who had bought their freedom and their very lives at such a high price, more readily understood the need for national cohesion.

Yes, but why were the patrician planters of the South called Democrats during the Civil War, and why did the North—more plebeian in its ideas if not in its origin—choose a name that rings as though it was meant to disqualify its opponents? For visionary eighteenth-century minds, the federal union harked back to the monarchy, to feudal privileges, and to the power of a national church. The southern states declared with some justification, "You of the North say you represent the republic. Yet we are the real democrats since we defend the rights of states, and even the rights of individuals, against the threat of centralized power!" To which the federalists naturally responded with a greater sense of the facts of the matter: "On the contrary, we represent the republic, since we defend the public interest against the selfishness of separatists whose only goal is to make sure their private interests are not harmed." In spite of all the distortions that they have undergone with time, the terms "Democrat" and "Republican" still designate two conceptions, or rather two opposing influences: a centrifugal influence, inclined to break up the federation beneath the weight of conflicting state interests, and a centripetal influence, which continually subjects these interests to the powerful attraction of the federal idea, the idea of national unity.

The political ideas of the two parties are opposed on many other questions, but fortunately, in times of trouble, something else always prevails—the spirit of American patriotism. You can see evidence of this today. As the representative of the Democrats, President Wilson was wary of European alliances and military intervention abroad, and he was naturally influenced by his centrifugal environment. He hesitated to enter the war, and once he had made up his mind to do so, he expected as a matter of course to be thwarted in his efforts by a party that was hoping to see our vast country pursue its peaceful development without the risks involved in foreign intervention. You all know what happened in actual fact. General conscription, voted in a matter of two days and accepted without a murmur. Militarization of the railroads, rationing of food and raw materials, an agreement with the labor unions, which pledged not to strike during the war.

For a loose confederation made up of different races with sometimes conflicting interests, it is without question a surprising result. Less surprising for us than for our Allies, however. For the critical moments in our history have taught us how intense the patriotic spirit is in our country. Two major events have left their mark on our short history. Having shaken off the yoke of a clumsy (but not tyrannical as was once taught) government, we were able to develop, and so became a nation. In order to defend the integrity of that nation we shed the best of our blood and fought against our own brothers. Memories like these cannot be erased. They come to mind each time it is necessary to defend our own independence or the independence of other countries when it is threatened. We know it is our duty to fight for the liberty of our Allies because we bought our own at so high a price.

It may seem unbelievable to you that a country as remote from the scene of the war as ours should have accepted to take part in it for so-called ideal reasons. I admit that the word "ideal" unsettles me somewhat, but when it comes to explaining the motives of human behavior, I do not believe there is really such a difference between the ideal and the practical, or between interested and disinterested motives. We are certainly interested—immeasurably so; but not because we want to take over your industry, nor because, as the Germans say, we want, in payment of our aid, to take hold of a port on the Mediterranean. No, believe me, the real reason was given to me by an American officer, who was touched like so many others by the way you welcomed the American troops. "Tell the French," he said, "be sure to tell them, that we do not want to be thanked for having entered the war. Explain that we all know that by fighting for France, we will be fighting for ourselves." There you have, I think, the truth—clearly grasped by the more intelligent, and obscurely sensed by everyone.

Ladies and gentlemen, you can see why I wanted to describe our origins. I wanted above all to help you understand why our point of view, our ways, and our habits do not always resemble yours. How could it be otherwise? Think that while you were building Versailles, we were cutting down virgin forests, that while Descartes was writing his *Discourse on Method*, our scholars were drafting books on demonology, that while the king's players were putting on *Tartuffe* and *The School for Husbands*, the parishioners of Reverend Shepard were beaten for having criticized his sermons, and husbands in Connecticut had to pay a large fine if they kissed their wives on a Sunday. Think that while your great-grandfathers were polishing their manners in Madame de Rambouillet's bedroom and in Madame de Sévigné's beautiful painted salons, ours, in trappers' huts, surrounded by wild beasts, were doing their best to become laborers and merchants, blacksmiths and lawyers, fur traders or professors of rhetoric. Between these two pasts, one entirely improvised, the other founded on a long tradition of culture, there is no common measure. And yet, out of two such different histories patriotism and the love of liberty brought our two countries together once and has brought them together once again.

The continual stream of immigration has never, since our ghastly Civil War made a nation of us, diluted these feelings. You must not forget Lincoln's wisdom at the beginning of our Civil War. "It is doubtful that a democracy can conduct a great war to a happy conclusion," he said. But it can conduct a great war if the authors of its constitution have the courage to declare that as soon as the nation is in peril, all power will be placed in the hands of the head of state, and if the political education of the public is sufficiently advanced for it to accept temporary autocracy without being haunted by the specter of permanent dictatorship. Such is our situation and it explains why we are by your side today.

ROBERT CORTES HOLLIDAY

Robert Cortes Holliday (1880–1947) had, according to his writer friend Christopher Morley, "the genuine gift of the personal essay, mellow, fluent, and pleasantly eccentric." He could also be hilarious, as witness this send-up of an essayistic disquisition, which purports to improvise without an idea in its head. Like many of the newspaper columnists (or "colyumnists," as they were facetiously called) of his day, Holliday managed to play it both ways, displaying his considerable learning with a light touch while maintaining the guise of a lazy, slow-witted Everyman.

An Article Without an Idea

(1919)

William Makepeace Thackeray (if I correctly recall his name), William Makepeace Thackeray (to repeat) one time wrote a book described (in the sub-title) "A Novel Without a Hero." So, of course, you know. And so, too, of course you know that while the thing was a bit new at the time (in 1847, to be exact) that is to-day quite the correct way to write any novel pretending to any distinction. Indeed, the more unheroic your hero (or whatever you call him) the more distinction you may be said to have.

So much by way of leading up to this fact: There is an ancient convention regarding another, and an older form of literature, which still persists. And that is the notion that you should have an *idea* to write an essay, or what is now commonly called an article. Possibly this fact (as I have called it) is a fallacy. It may be that some (perhaps more than some) of the articles in our magazines do not turn on any idea. (I shall come to the subject of magazines presently.) Any idea, as I was saying, or at least any idea worth mentioning. However, if the writer of an article to-day does not have an idea what he does is this: He does the reverse of the novelist. If our novelist finds that he is getting a hero on his hands he contrives to throw him into a bad light somewhere and so take away the taint. What the writer of the article (with no idea in it) does is to attempt to dress up his absence of thought so that it may look (to some) like a perfectly stunning idea. He wants it to, as we say, make a noise like an idea. I have such a bad name for—I mean I have such a bad memory for names or I think I might be able to recall the titles and addresses of a number of such recent articles. And articles, we observe, are in this like people: it is not always so that a man is great, or wise, or even sensible because he lives in a smart house.

Anyhow, the upshot of the whole matter is this: that I, young and handsome, rich and famous, am now for the first time in the history of the world, according to the best of my knowledge and belief, writing an article (or essay) frankly and publicly announced by the writer thereof as being An Article Without an Idea. What I am writing is a paper containing a store of what a friend of mine refers to as glimpses into the obvious. It may become the fashion to do this. Things as curious have happened. There, for instance, is the case of contemporary book reviews. But we'll come to that subject presently.

It is said that essays are coming in again. Every once in a while somebody says that. 'Tis like prophecies concerning the immediate end of the world. However, it (either one of these prophecies) may be so this time. Still, as to essays, in view of the economy of ideas now going, as hand in hand we have seen is the case, that likelihood does not seem so probable. Because, whereas you can write an excellent article about something with only one idea, and a pretty fair one (such as this) with no idea at all, to write the best sort of essay, which is about nothing much, you really need any number of ideas.

We are all very much indebted to the month of March. It was, as every child knows, in the month of March that the essay was invented. (I always write much better myself in the month of March than in any other month of the year.) The year (of the invention), it is hardly necessary to say, was 1571. Don Marquis it was who discovered—I mean a gentleman of the name of Montaigne it was who discovered the process of just putting down ideas, one after another, in such a fashion that they blended into what is called an essay. It is, by the way, when you come to think of it, a curious thing, the relation of the letter "M" to the essay—March, Marquis, Montaigne, and Morley (Christopher).

The reason Mr. Marquis's recently published volume, "Prefaces," is so good a book (as essays) is that the instinctive essayist who proposes to write, say, on the Ten Commandments, begins quite naturally with a disquisition upon the importance of a good shape of human ear. And he concludes, perhaps with some warmth, with a denunciation of shell spectacles. Perhaps I should remark in passing that I recollect nothing in "Prefaces" about either the Ten Commandments, ears, or shell spectacles.

One word more as to essays. The mantle of the illustrious dead is always descending upon the peculiar cove who essays to write an essay. For a considerable spell in this country it was quite the thing to wrap anyone who announced that that which he had written was an essay in the mantle of Dr. Holmes. Now he is likely to get into the old clothes of Charles Lamb (Oh, Elia, of course!), of "R. L. S.," of the author of "The Reveries of a Bachelor," etc., etc., etc.

This may be said to bring us to the subject of book reviewing, and whether or not it is a good thing for reviews to contain any ideas. No, I'm getting on too fast. I'm quite out of breath. I meant to say, a few lines up, that if I had inadvertently given the impression of winding the mantle of Montaigne about Mr. Marquis I make all possible haste to unsheathe him. For in his own habit he is quite as he should be.

Peculiar thing about newspapers. That is, about their "book pages" and "literary supplements." Lately, more or less lately, there have been popping up here and there about the country, at any rate in the two principal cities, pages and supplements of a good deal of brightness, affairs of something of a rollicking nature, things with some dash and go to them, with a *flair* for the cheer-o. In fine, with jazz. These sheets have apparently caught on considerably. They undoubtedly "get advertising." They presumably "increase circulation." Now the point is as follows: some seven or eight years ago there was in this town a like organ, except that it was much better than any of these later ones. Even so. Or perhaps I think so because that was in my youth, or at any rate in my second youth. However, I refer you to the files. You'll see that it was a real doings, this. It failed. Nobody cared for it. Publishers themselves distinctly did not. Its editor was dropped. It changed its character completely. It is a thing most decidedly to reckon with now, probably the most powerful concern in its field. But it is an altogether different type of thing—and I take it that it couldn't go on at that time as it was. In those days we didn't know the word "jazz," and it seems we didn't know jazz in the fine art of literary journalism when we saw it.

I used to think that editing a magazine was quite a trick. Fell in the other day with a man who edits a magazine. Learned there was nothing to it at all. The way you edit a magazine, it seems, is this: First, you find out who died month after next. Say it was Casanova. Very good. Then all you have to do is to get up a Casanova "number" for month after next. There are a combination of ways in which you do this. You hire a man to sit down and cook up something about Casanova. Not because there is anything new to be said about the great memoirist, nor because everybody is going to be interested exclusively in Casanova throughout month after next. Not at all. But you have to get up a Casanova "number," haven't you? You sure have. That's the business of being a magazine editor. Then there are a lot of people going round to the library all the while looking up who died month after next. And they all cook up something about old Cas, and send it in to you because they know you'll be on the lookout for it in order to get up your "number." You get bunches and bunches of Casanova stuff. You take a few of these articles for your "number," such as will fit readily into the make-up. And there you are!

But about those book reviews, and whether or not they should have ideas in them, and a sense of the value of the books they discuss, and style in the treatment of all this. I see no harm in it, if the ideas are light, and the sense and style good. I notice, however, that one of our leading magazines has taken up this matter of reviews; taken it up, as Mr. Montaigne says, in a serious way. And it, this magazine, holds that all entertainment of any kind, all interest whatever, should be taken out of reviews; and then what you have left (this is the great principle of the thing) is just the review, and that's what people want.

DOROTHY PARKER

Dorothy Parker (1893–1967) was a poet, theater critic, screenwriter, frequent New Yorker *contributor, founding member of the Algonquin Round Table, which invited its members to top one another with witty comments, and famously one of the sharpest wits around. She did not suffer fools (or nice, pleasant people) gladly, as can be seen in her essay "Good Souls." It is a prime example of the contrarian essay, which inverts the usual pious assumptions about worthy behavior and dares to adopt a misanthropic or at least antisocial stance for the sake of laughter and surprise.*

Good Souls

(1919)

All about us, living in our families, it may be, there exists a race of curious creatures. Outwardly, they possess no marked peculiarities; in fact, at a hasty glance, they may be readily mistaken for regular human beings. They are built after the popular design; they have the usual number of features, arranged in the conventional manner; they offer no variations on the general run of things in their habits of dressing, eating, and carrying on their business.

Yet, between them and the rest of the civilized world, there stretches an impassable barrier. Though they live in the very thick of the human race, they are forever isolated from it. They are fated to go through life, congenial pariahs. They live out their little lives, mingling with the world, yet never a part of it. They are, in short, Good Souls.

And the piteous thing about them is that they are wholly unconscious of their condition. A Good Soul thinks he is just like anyone else. Nothing could convince him otherwise. It is heartrending to see him, going cheerfully about, even whistling or humming as he goes, all unconscious of his terrible plight. The utmost he can receive from the world is an attitude of good-humored patience, a perfunctory word of approbation, a praising with faint damns, so to speak—yet he firmly believes that everything is all right with him.

There is no accounting for Good Souls.

They spring up anywhere. They will suddenly appear in families which, for generations have had no slightest stigma attached to them. Possibly they are throw-backs. There is scarcely a family without at least one Good Soul somewhere in it at the present moment—maybe in the form of an elderly aunt, an unmarried sister, an unsuccessful brother, an indigent cousin. No household is complete without one.

The Good Soul begins early; he will show signs of his condition in extreme youth. Go now to the nearest window, and look out on the little children playing so happily below. Any group of youngsters that you may happen to see will do perfectly. Do you observe the child whom all other little dears make "it" in their merry games? Do you follow the child from whom the other little ones snatch the cherished candy, to consume it before his streaming eyes? Can you get a good look at the child whose precious toys are borrowed for indefinite periods by the other playful youngsters, and returned to him in fragments? Do you see the child upon whom all the other kiddies play their complete repertory of childhood's winsome pranks—throwing bags of water on him, running away and hiding from him, shouting his name in quaint rhymes, chalking coarse legends on his unsuspecting back?

Mark that child well. He is going to be a Good Soul when he grows up.

Thus does the doomed child go through early youth and adolescence. So does he progress towards the fulfillment of his destiny. And then, some day, when he is under discussion, someone will say of him, "Well, he means well, anyway." That settles it. For him, that is the end. Those words have branded him with the indelible mark of his pariahdom. He has come into his majority; he is a full-fledged Good Soul.

The activities of the adult of the species are familiar to us all. When you are ill, who is it that hastens to your beside bearing molds of blancmange, which, from infancy, you have hated with unspeakable loathing? As usual, you are way ahead of me, gentle reader—it is indeed the Good Soul. It is the Good Souls who efficiently smooth out your pillow when you have just worked it into the comfortable shape, who creak about the room on noisy tiptoe, who tenderly lay on your fevered brow damp cloths which drip ceaselessly down your neck. It is they who ask, every other minute, if there isn't something that they can do for you. It is they who, at great personal sacrifice, spend long hours sitting beside your bed, reading aloud the continued stories in the *Woman's Home Companion,* or chatting cozily on the increase in the city's death rate.

In health, as in illness, they are always right there, ready to befriend you. No sooner do you sit down, than they exclaim that they can see you aren't comfortable in that chair, and insist on your changing places with them. It is the Good Souls who just know that you don't like your tea that way, and who bear it masterfully away from you to alter it with cream and sugar until it is a complete stranger to you. At the table, it is they who always feel that their grapefruit is better than yours and who have to be restrained almost forcibly from exchanging with you. In a restaurant the waiter invariably makes a mistake and brings them something which they did not order—and which they refuse to have changed, choking it down with a wistful smile. It is they who cause traffic blocks, by standing in subway entrances arguing altruistically as to who is to pay the fare. At the theater, should they be members of a box-party, it is the Good Souls who insist on occupying the rear chairs; if the seats are in the orchestra, they worry audibly, all through the performance, about their being able to see better than you, until finally in desperation you grant their plea and change seats with them. If, by so doing, they can bring a little discomfort on themselves—sit in a draught, say, or behind a pillar—than their happiness is complete. To feel the genial glow of martyrdom—that is all they ask of life.

Good Souls are punctilious in their observation of correct little ceremonies. If, for example, they borrow a postage stamp, they immediately offer two pennies in return for it—they insist upon this business transaction. They never fail to remember birthdays—their little gift always brings with it a sharp stab of remembrance that you have blissfully ignored their own natal day. At the last moment, on Christmas Eve, comes a present from some Good Soul whose existence, in the rush of holiday shopping you have completely overlooked. When they go away, be it only for an overnight stay, they never neglect to send postcards bearing views of the principal buildings of the place to all their acquaintances; to their intimates, they always bring back some local souvenir—a tiny dish, featuring the gold-lettered name of the town; a thimble in an appropriate case, both bearing the name of their native city; a tie-rack with the name of its place of residence burned decoratively on its wood; or some such useful novelty.

The lives of Good Souls are crowded with Occasions, each with its own ritual which must be solemnly followed. On Mother's Day, Good Souls conscientiously wear carnations; on St. Patrick's Day, they faithfully don boutonnieres of shamrocks; on Columbus Day, they carefully pin on miniature Italian flags. Every feast must be celebrated by the sending out of cards—Valentine's Day, Arbor, Groundhog Day, and all the other important festivals, each is duly observed. They have a perfect genius for discovering appropriate cards of greeting for the event. It must take hours of research.

If it's too long a time between holidays, then the Good Soul will send little cards or little mementoes, just by way of surprises. He is strong on surprises anyway. It delights him to drop in unexpectedly on his friends. Who has not known the joy of those evenings when some Good Soul just runs in, as a surprise? It is particularly effective when a chosen company of other guests happens to be present—enough for two tables of bridge, say. This means that the Good Soul must cut in at intervals, volubly voicing his desolation at causing so much inconvenience, and apologizing constantly during the evening.

His conversation, admirable though it is, never receives its just due of attention and appreciation. He is one of those who believe and frequently quote the exemplary precept that there is good in everybody; hanging in his bedchamber is the whimsically phrased, yet vital, statement, done in burned leather—"There is so much good in the worst of us and so much bad in the best of us that it hardly behooves any of us to talk about the rest of us." This, too, he archly quotes on appropriate occasions. Two or three may be gathered together, intimately discussing some mutual acquaintance. It is just getting really absorbing, when comes the Good Soul, to utter his dutiful. "We mustn't judge harshly—after all, we must always remember that many times our own actions may be misconstrued." Somehow, after several of these little reminders, there seems to be a general waning of interest; the little gathering breaks up, inventing quaint excuses to get away and discuss the thing more fully, adding a few really good details, some place where the Good Soul will not follow. While the Good Soul pitifully ignorant of their evil purpose glows with the warmth of conscious virtue, and settles himself to read the Contributors' Club, in the *Atlantic Monthly,* with a sense of duty well done.

Yet it must not be thought that their virtue lifts Good Souls above the enjoyment of popular pastimes. Indeed, it does not; they are enthusiasts on the subject of good, wholesome fun. They lavishly patronize the drama, in its cleaner forms. They flock to the plays of Miss Rachel Crothers, Miss Eleanor Porter, and Mr. Edward Childs Carpenter. They are passionate admirers of the art of Mr. William Hodge. In literature, they worship at the chaste shrines of Harold Bell Wright, Gene Stratton-Porter, Eleanor Hallowell Abbott, Alice Hegan Rice, and the other triple-named apostles of optimism. The have never felt the same towards Arnold Bennett since he sprung "The Pretty Lady" on them; they no longer give "The Human Machine" and "How to Live on Twenty-four Hours a Day" as birthday offerings to their friends. In poetry, though Tennyson, Whittier, and Longfellow stand for the highest, of course, they have marked leaning towards the later works of Mrs. Ella Wheeler Wilcox. They are continually meeting people who know her, encounters of which they proudly relate. Among humorists, they prefer Mr. Ellis Parker Butler.

Good Souls, themselves, are no mean humorists. They have a time-honored formula of fun-making, which must be faithfully followed. Certain words or phrases must be whimsically distorted every time they are used. "Over the river," they dutifully say, whenever they take their leave. "Don't you cast any asparagus on me," they warn, archly; and they never fail to speak of "three times in concussion." According to their ritual, these screaming phrases must be repeated several times, for the most telling effect, and are invariably followed by hearty laughter from the speaker, to whom they seem eternally new.

Perhaps the most congenial role of the Good Soul is that of advice-giver. He loves to take people aside and have serious little personal talks, all for their own good. He thinks it only right to point out faults or bad habits which are, perhaps unconsciously, growing on them. He goes home and laboriously writes long, intricate letters, invariably beginning, "Although you may feel that this is no affair of mine, I think that you really ought to know," and so on, indefinitely. In his desire to help, he reminds one irresistibly of Marceline, who used to try so pathetically and so fruitlessly to be of some assistance in arranging the circus arena, and who brought such misfortunes on his own innocent person thereby.

The Good Souls will, doubtless, gain their reward in heaven: on this earth, certainly, theirs is what is technically known as a rough deal. The most hideous outrages are perpetrated on them. "Oh, he won't mind," people say. "He's a Good Soul." And then they proceed to heap the rankest impositions upon him. When Good Souls give a party, people who have accepted weeks in advance call up at the last second and refuse, without the shadow of an excuse save that of a subsequent engagement. Other people are invited to all sorts of entertaining affairs; the Good Soul, unasked, waves them a cheery good-bye and hopes wistfully that they will have a good time. His is the uncomfortable seat in the motor; he is the one to ride backwards in the train; he is the one who is always chosen to solicit subscriptions and make up deficits. People borrow his money, steal his servants, lose his golf balls, use him as a sort of errand boy, leave him flat whenever something more attractive offers—and carry it all off with their cheerful slogan, "Oh, he won't mind—he's a Good Soul."

And that's just it—Good Souls never do mind. After each fresh atrocity they are more cheerful, forgiving and virtuous, if possible, than they were before. There is simply no keeping them down—back they come, with their little gifts, and their little words of advice, and their little endeavors to be of service, always anxious for more.

Yes, there can be no doubt about it—their reward will come to them in the next world.

Would that they were even now enjoying it!

FINLEY PETER DUNNE

*Finley Peter Dunne (1867–1936) was a journalist who wrote topical sat-
ire in the character of a philosophical bartender named Mr. Dooley. In
channeling the voice of this barely literate Irish publican, he also gave
full rein to dialect humor, which necessitated frequent misspellings. These
essentially essayistic monologues, interrupted occasionally by a barfly,
were full of surprises: a reader who might initially assume the joke was
on Dooley as a vulgar, uneducated purveyor of popular opinion would be
brought up short by his shrewd, worldly insights. Often his targets were
politicians, and he was equally rough on the corrupt ones who had their
hands in the till as on the do-gooder reformers who had instituted the (to
his way of thinking) curse of Prohibition.*

The Prohibition Era

(1920)

Joshua Levering, John G. Woolley, and Silas C. Swallow were the candidates of the Prohibition party for president in 1896, 1900, and 1904.

"What's this Anti-Saloon League, annyhow?" Mr. Hennessy asked.

"Well," said Mr. Dooley, "it's like the Anti-Anti-Saloon League. It's
wan way iv makin' a livin'.

"D'ye know, Hinnissy, I niver wanted to be a liquor dealer. I drifted into
th' business because I was sociable be nature, an' had a joynt's strenth,
but didn't want to use it like a joynt be wurrukin' at a thrade. Besides,
it give me a great power an' inflooence. But, at that, me high position
didn't pay me f'r th' kind iv company I had to face an' inhale day after

day. It give me a great contimpt f'r human nature to be mixed up with me customers.

"In thim days I was a prohybitionist, an' talked th' good cause long before Willum Jennings Bryan opened his noble head about it. Ye niver heerd that great statesman shoutin' f'r Wooly or Levering or Swallow, did ye? No, faith. I'm prob'bly th' on'y man now livin' that raymimbers their cillybrated names. They were a fine lot iv ol' fellows, cornin' out year afther year, to lead their little foorces to certain defeat, an' ca'mly carryin' on their campaign with ivrybody laughin' at thim. That was th' hardest thing f'r th' old heroes. Manny a man can be stopped be a bullet.

"But they didn't mind, these inthrepid old geezers with their spectacles an' their throat whiskers. They smiled serenely, put for'ard argyments that no wan cud answer, sung 'Where is my wandhrin' boy tonight,' paid out their own money f'r hall rent, niver held a polytical job an' were niver heerd about between ilictions.

"Yes, sir, I was with thim at heart, an' I had a hundherd argymints in their favor. You, Hinnissy, were wan iv me sthrongist. I cud always pint to ye whin language failed me. Iv coorse I didn't vote f'r these good men. I like comp'ny whin I go to th' polls. But I was with thim, an' I am today.

"Thin why do I go on sellin' th' stuff? What is there f'r a veteran juggler iv bottles to do? I've got to break th' law or th' law will break me. But whin I look back at th' old days an' thin cast me eyes around this repulsive candy an' parfumery store, I wish that Andy Volstead had had th' heart to provide a Home f'r th' Victims iv his rash act. Ivry time a fellow comes in here an' ordhers wan iv thim mixtures iv marble dust an' coal tar pro-ducks that some wag has called soft dhrinks, I reach f'r th' bung-starter. But it isn't there!

"Th' scepter has gone with th' crown an' excipt that I have more money I'm no better off thin th' king in Greece. To see me, that was wanst a free an' law-abidin' citizen that cud give th' back iv me hand an' th' sole iv me fut to th' very loot at th' station now keepin' wan eye on th' customer an' th' other on th' dure, to see ye lurkin' in like a tom-cat an' me sellin' ye hop that Thomas A. Edison wuddn't handle with rubber gloves an' handin' it to ye as if I was passin' countherfeit money, is grajally breakin' me heart. 'Tis thrue I have more coin thin I iver see befure. But what is money, afther all? As Hogan says, where wealth accumylates man decays. What does it profit me, as th' good book says, if I gain th' whole wurruld be sellin' ye conthraband juice, if th' next I see iv ye a little dog is leadin' ye around at th' end iv a sthring. Oh, th' shame iv it! . . .

"An' there ye ar-re. I've got to go on in th' on'y business I know. Th' saloon desthroyed th' home, but th' home has turned like a rattle snake an' desthroyed th' saloon—th' home an' th' home brew. Where are all th' cheerful saloons ye used to know? Cobwebs hang on th' wall, th' cash registher chimes no more. Where are all me old customers most iv th' time? At home, be dad. Th' fam'ly don't see much iv thim. They're down in th' cellar stewin' hops.

"That's th' throuble us pro-hybitionists are up against. Ye can make alcohol out iv most annything. Ivry German an' most Englishmen know how to make beer. Give an Eyetalyan a bunch iv grapes an' he'll turn out a bottle iv wine. Th' Scotch make it out iv barley; th' Irish out iv potatoes an' th' Mexicans out iv cactus, which is full iv needles an' makes a noble stimylant. Th' Americans, a free, indipindant, injanyous an' law-defyin' people, make it out iv these things an' also corn, wheat, apples, cherries, and pine shavin's.

"Gallagher don't throuble with machinery. He gets his ingrejints at th' dhrug store.

"He was in here last night, so how-come-ye-so that I knew he'd been in th' bosom iv his family. 'Where did ye get it?' says I. 'At home,' says he. 'I've often warned ye again frequentin' that resort,' says I. 'It will be ye'er destruction.' 'Well, annyhow,' says he, 'me destruction don't cost me as much as it did,' he says. 'It makes me mad to think iv all th' money I've been robbed iv be th' distillers an' brewers. It amounts to a fortune. If I'd known what it costs thim I'd niver have took a dhrink.'

"I used to think gin was made out iv juniper berries an' I wondhered why all th' farmers in th' counthry raised hay whin they cud be harvestin' gin. Now I know that wan juniper berry will turn a bar'l iv alcohol into th' kind iv gin I used to get. If ye don't want gin stir it around with a piece iv charred wood an' ye have Scotch. Add a little proon juice an' its rye. It cost thim bandits a dollar a bar'l an' most iv that was f'r labels. If I ask him, a little Eyetalyan frind iv mine who used to run a two-dollar-bill facthry before he convarted it, will hand me anny label ye iver see or heerd about. So, when I intertain me frinds, I projooce a bottle iv 'superfin' Sour Mash, nineteen hundhred an' siven, aged in th' wood, McManus an' Comp'ny, Louisville, Ky.' An' whin th' boys choke it down an' with tears in their eyes say 'That's th' rale thing, where did ye get it?' I tell thim I see pro-hybition comin' an' laid in enough to last me th' rest iv me life.

"An' so it goes. I thought f'r awhile th' charackter iv th' dhrink wud stop dhrinkin'. But it seems as if a man that will dhrink annything will take what he can get. It's alcohol he's afther an' all booze is alcohol. If it's wood alcohol it will dhrop ye in ye'er thracks. If it's made out iv th' projooce iv our fair westhren farm lands, th' longer ye keep it th' longer ye'll last. What I have I'm savin' f'r me wake.

"Do I think pro-hybition is makin' pro-gress? Me boy, I'm no stasti-cyan. I hope to die without havin' that to do pinance f'r that. But if ye want me opinyon, I'll say it stands to reason that if it's hard to get an' costly th' poor won't have so much iv it, an' what they'll have will be worse f'r thim. But it's makin' sad inroads on th' rich.

"Ye see, Hinnissy, th' rich will accumylate annything that's scarce—

pictures, books, postage stamps or money. Now, whin booze was to be had be high an' low an' Jack alike, th' low got it an' th' high shunned it. Me frind Grogan, th' banker, niver wud look at it whin 'twas plintiful. Now he's up an' at it befure he goes to count his morgedges in th' mornin'. He's got a rare collection iv old masthers in his basemint. He was showin' thim to me th' other day, his eye lightin' up as he pinted th' bottles out. 'Here,' he says, 'is a ginooyine ol' Pepper. There ye have th' Dutch artist Overholt. This wan is atthributed to McBrayor. That fine spicimen over there is iv th' Maryland school,' says he. I didn't dare contradict him, Hinnissy. Him an' me are capytalists an' we've got to stand together. But may th' diwle take me if I didn't see me own bootlegger puttin' on thim very labels less thin a month ago. But what was th' use iv ondeceivin' him! They were as ginooyine, annyhow, as his pictures."

"Don't ye think prohybition has had anny effect?" Mr. Hennessy asked.

"Sure it has," said Mr. Dooley, "Iyry reform increases th' number iv jobs. Th' more reforms th' more laws, th' more laws th' more polismen, th' more polismen th' more crimes, th' more crimes th' more reformers, an' so on, till fin'lly th' counthry will be akelly divided—fifty per-cint tax payers an' fifty per-cint cops."

"There ain't as much dhrunkenness as there was. I know that," said Mr. Hennessy.

"No," said Mr. Dooley, "but what there is is a much more finished product."

WILLA CATHER

*Willa Cather (1873–1947), who captured Nebraska and the Southwest so well in her matchless novels (*My Ántonia, A Lost Lady, The Professor's House, Death Comes for the Archbishop*), lived most of her working life in New York City, initially drawn there by a job offer to edit* McClure's Magazine. *In "148 Charles Street," taken from her essay collection,* Not Under Forty, *she lovingly portrayed a house and its owner, Mrs. Fields, as a living bridge to the golden age of literary Boston. Cather, sometimes accused in her own day by modernist critics of being too attached to the lost past, ends this essay (years after the first part was written) with an impassioned personal lament about the transience of literary renown and the eradications of history.*

148 Charles Street

(1922)

Late in the winter of 1908 Mrs. Louis Brandeis conducted me along a noisy street in Boston and rang at a door hitherto unknown to me. Sometimes entering a new door can make a great change in one's life. That afternoon I had set out from the Parker House (the old, the real Parker House, before it was "modernized") to make a call on Mrs. Brandeis. When I reached her house in Otis Place she told me that we would go farther: she thought I would enjoy meeting a very charming old lady who was a near neighbour of hers, the widow of James T. Fields, of the publishing firm of Ticknor and Fields. The name of that firm meant something to me. In my father's bookcase there were little volumes of Longfellow and

Hawthorne with that imprint. I wondered how the widow of one of the partners could still be living. Mrs. Brandeis explained that when James T. Fields was a man in middle life, a publisher of international reputation and a widower, he married Annie Adams, then a girl of nineteen. She had naturally survived him by many years.

When the door at 148 Charles Street was opened we waited a few moments in a small reception-room just off the hall, then went up a steep, thickly carpeted stairway and entered the "long drawing-room," where Mrs. Fields and Miss Jewett sat at tea. That room ran the depth of the house, its front windows, heavily curtained, on Charles Street, its back windows looking down on a deep garden. Directly above the garden wall lay the Charles River and, beyond, the Cambridge shore. At five o'clock in the afternoon the river was silvery from a half-hidden sun; over the great open space of water the western sky was dove-coloured with little ripples of rose. The air was full of soft moisture and the hint of approaching spring. Against this screen of pale winter light were the two ladies: Mrs. Fields reclining on a green sofa, directly under the youthful portrait of Charles Dickens (now in the Boston Art Museum), Miss Jewett seated, the low tea-table between them.

Mrs. Fields wore the widow's lavender which she never abandoned except for black velvet, with a scarf of Venetian lace on her hair. She was very slight and fragile in figure, with a great play of animation in her face and a delicate flush of pink on her cheeks. Like her friend Mrs. John Gardner, she had a skin which defied age. As for Miss Jewett—she looked very like the youthful picture of herself in the game of "Authors" I had played as a child, except that she was fuller in figure and a little grey. I do not at all remember what we talked about. Mrs. Brandeis asked that I be shown some of the treasures of the house, but I had no eyes for the treasures, I was too intent upon the ladies.

That winter afternoon began a friendship, impoverished by Miss Jewett's death sixteen months later, but enduring until Mrs. Fields herself died, in February 1915.

In 1922 M. A. DeWolfe Howe, Mrs. Fields' literary executor, published a book of extracts from her diaries under the title *Memories of a Hostess*, a book which delighted all who had known her and many who had not, because of its vivid pictures of the Cambridge and Concord groups in the '60s and '70s, not as "celebrities" but as friends and fellow citizens. When Mr. Howe's book appeared, I wrote for *The Literary Review* an appreciation of it, very sketchy, but done with genuine enthusiasm, which I here incorporate without quotation marks.

In his book made up from the diaries of Mrs. James T. Fields, Mr. DeWolfe Howe presents a record of beautiful memories and, as its subtitle declares, "a chronicle of eminent friendships." For a period of sixty years Mrs. Fields' Boston house, at 148 Charles Street, extended its hospitality to the aristocracy of letters and art. During that long stretch of time there was scarcely an American of distinction in art or public life who was not a guest in that house; scarcely a visiting foreigner of renown who did not pay his tribute there.

It was not only men of letters, Dickens, Thackeray, and Matthew Arnold, who met Mrs. Fields' friends there; Salvini and Modjeska and Edwin Booth and Christine Nilsson and Joseph Jefferson and Ole Bull, Winslow Homer and Sargent, came and went, against the background of closely united friends who were a part of the very Charles Street scene.

Longfellow, Emerson, Whittier, Hawthorne, Lowell, Sumner, Norton, Oliver Wendell Holmes—the list sounds like something in a school-book; but in Mrs. Fields' house one came to believe that they had been very living people—to feel that they had not been long absent from the rooms so full of their thoughts, of their letters, their talk, their remembrances sent at Christmas to the hostess, or brought to her from foreign lands. Even in the garden flourished guelder roses and flowering shrubs which some of these bearers of school-book names had brought in from Cambridge or Concord and set out there. At 148 Charles Street an American of the Apache period and territory could come to inherit a Colonial past.

Although Mrs. Fields was past seventy when I was first conducted into the long drawing-room, she did not seem old to me. Frail, diminished in force, yes; but, emphatically, *not* old. "The personal beauty of her younger years, long retained, and even at the end of such a stretch of life not quite lost," to quote Henry James, may have had something to do with the impression she gave; but I think it was even more because, as he also said of her, "all her implications were gay." I had seldom heard so young, so merry, so musical a laugh; a laugh with countless shades of relish and appreciation and kindness in it. And, on occasion, a short laugh from that same fragile source could positively do police duty! It could put an end to a conversation that had taken an unfortunate turn, absolutely dismiss and silence impertinence or presumption. No woman could have been so great a hostess, could have made so many highly developed personalities happy under her roof, could have blended so many strongly specialized and keenly sensitive people in her drawing-room, without having a great power to control and organize. It was a power so sufficient that one seldom felt it as one lived in the harmonious atmosphere it created—an atmosphere in which one seemed absolutely safe from everything ugly. Nobody can cherish the flower of social intercourse, can give it sun and sustenance and a tempered clime, without also being able very completely to dispose of anything that threatens it—not only the slug, but even the cold draught that ruffles its petals.

Mrs. Fields was in her own person flower-like; the remarkable fineness of her skin and pinkness of her cheeks gave one the comparison—and the natural ruby of her lips she never lost. It always struck one afresh (along with her clear eyes and their quick flashes of humour), that large, generous, mobile mouth, with its rich freshness of colour. "A woman's mouth," I used to think as I watched her talking to someone who pleased her; "not an old woman's!" One rejoiced in her little triumphs over colour-destroying age and its infirmities, as at the play one rejoices in the escape of the beautiful and frail from the pursuit of things powerful and evil. It was a drama in which the heroine must be sacrificed in the end: but for how long did she make the outward voyage delightful, with how many a *divertissement* and bright scene did she illumine the respite and the long wait at Aulis!

Sixty years of hospitality, so smooth and unruffled for the recipients, cost the hostess something—cost her a great deal. The Fieldses were never people of liberal means, and the Charles Street house was not a convenient house to entertain in. The basement kitchen was a difficulty. On the first floor were the reception-room and the dining-room, on the second floor was the "long drawing-room," running the depth of the house. Mrs. Fields' own apartments were on the third floor, and the guest-rooms on the fourth. A house so constructed took a great deal of managing. Yet there was never an hour in the day when the order and calm of the drawing-room were not such that one might have sat down to write a sonnet or a sonata. The sweeping and dusting were done very early in the morning, the flowers arranged before the guests were awake.

Besides being distinctly young on the one hand, on the other Mrs. Fields seemed to me to reach back to Waterloo. As Mr. Howe reminds us, she had talked to Leigh Hunt about Shelley and his starlike beauty of face—and it is now more than a century since Shelley was drowned. She had known Severn well, and it was he who gave her a lock of Keats' hair, which, under glass with a drawing of Keats by the same artist, was one of the innumerable treasures of that house. With so much to tell, Mrs. Fields never became a set story-teller. She had no favourite stories—there were too many. Stories were told from time to time, but only as things of today reminded her of things of yesterday. When we came home from the opera, she could tell one what Chorley had said on such and such an occasion. And then if one did not "go at" her, but talked of Chorley just as if he were Philip Hale or W. J. Henderson, one might hear a great deal about him.

When one was staying at that house the past lay in wait for one in all the corners; it exuded from the furniture, from the pictures, the rare editions, and the cabinets of manuscript—the beautiful, clear manuscripts of a typewriterless age, which even the printers had respected and kept clean. The unique charm of Mrs. Fields' house was not that it was a place where one could hear about the past, but that it was a place where the past lived on—where it was protected and cherished, had sanctuary from the noisy push of the present. In casual conversation, at breakfast or tea, you might at any time unconsciously press a spring which liberated recollection, and one of the great shades seemed quietly to enter the room and to take the chair or the corner he had preferred in life.

One afternoon I showed her an interesting picture of Pauline Viardot I had brought from Paris, and my hostess gave me such an account of hearing Viardot sing Gluck's *Orpheus* that I felt I had heard it myself. Then she told me how, when she saw Dickens in London, just after he had returned from giving a reading in Paris, he said: "Oh, yes, the house was sold out. But the important thing is that Viardot came, and sat in a front seat and never took her glorious eyes off me. So, of course," with a flourish of his hand, "nothing else mattered!" A little-known Russian gentleman, Mr. Turgeniev, must have been staying at Madame Viardot's country house at that time. Did he accompany her to the reading, one wonders? If he had, it would probably have meant very little to "Mr. Dickens."

It was at tea-time, I used to think, that the great shades were most likely to appear; sometimes they seemed to come up the deeply carpeted stairs, along with living friends. At that hour the long room was dimly lighted, the fire bright, and through the wide windows the sunset was flaming, or softly brooding, upon the Charles River and the Cambridge shore beyond. The ugliness of the world, all possibility of wrenches and jars and wounding contacts, seemed securely shut out. It was indeed the peace of the past, where the tawdry and cheap have been eliminated and the enduring things have taken their proper, happy places.

Mrs. Fields read aloud beautifully, especially Shakespeare and Milton, for whom she had, even in age, a wonderful depth of voice. I loved to hear her read *Richard II,* or the great, melancholy speeches of *Henry IV* in the Palace at Westminster:

> "And changes fill the cup of altera-ti-on
> With diverse liquors."

Many of those lines I can only remember with the colour, the slight unsteadiness, of that fine old voice.

Once I was sitting on the sofa beside her, helping her to hold a very heavy, very old, calf-bound Milton, while she read:

> "In courts and palaces he also reigns,
> And in luxurious cities, where the noise
> Of riot ascends above their loftiest towers,
> And injury and outrage."

When she paused in the solemn evocation for breath, I tried to fill in the interval by saying something about such lines calling up the tumult of Rome and Babylon.

"Or New York," she said slyly, glancing sidewise, and then at once again attacked the mighty page.

Naturally, she was rich in reference and quotation. I recall how she once looked up from a long reverie and said: "You know, my dear, I think we sometimes forget how much we owe to Dryden's prefaces." To my shame, I have not to this day discovered the full extent of my indebtedness. On another occasion Mrs. Fields murmured something about *"A bracelet of bright hair about the bone."* "That's very nice," said I, "but I don't recognize it."

"Surely," she said, "that would be Dr. Donne."

I never pretended to Mrs. Fields—I would have had to pretend too much. "And who," I brazenly asked, "was Dr. Donne?"

I knew before morning. She had a beautiful patience with Boeotian ignorance, but I was strongly encouraged to take two fat volumes of Dr. Donne to bed with me that night.

I love to remember one charming visit in her summer house at Manchester-by-the-Sea, when Sarah Orne Jewett was there. I had just come from Italy bringing word of the places they most loved and about which they had often written me, entreating, nay, commanding me to visit them. Had I gone riding on the Pincian Hill? Mrs. Fields asked. No, I hadn't; I didn't think many people rode there now. Well, said Mrs. Fields, the Brownings' little boy used to ride there, in his velvets. When he complained to her that the Pincio was the same every day, no variety, she suggested that he might ride out into the Campagna. But he sighed and shook his head. "Oh, no! My pony and I have to go there. We are one of the sights of Rome, you know!" As this was the son of a friend, one didn't comment upon the child's speech or the future it suggested.

The second evening after my arrival happened to be a rainy one—no visitors. After dinner Mrs. Fields began to read a little—warmed to her work, and read all of Matthew Arnold's *Scholar Gypsy* and *Tristan and Iseult*. Miss Jewett said she didn't believe the latter poem had been read aloud in that house since Matthew Arnold himself read it there.

At Manchester, when there were no guests, Mrs. Fields had tea on the back veranda, overlooking a wild stretch of woodland. Down in this wood, directly beneath us, were a tea-table and seats built under the trees, where they used to have tea when the hostess was younger—now the climb was too steep for her. It was a little sad, perhaps, to sit and look out over a shrinking kingdom; but if she felt it, she never showed it. Miss Jewett and I went down into the wood, and she told me she hated to go there now, as it reminded her that much was already lost, and what was left was so at the mercy of chance! It seemed as if a strong wind might blow away that beloved friend of many years. We talked in low voices. Who could have believed that Mrs. Fields was to outlive Miss Jewett, so much the younger, by nearly six years, as she outlived Mr. Fields by thirty-four! She had the very genius of survival. She was not, as she once laughingly told me, "to escape anything, not even free verse or the Cubists!" She was not in the least dashed by either. Oh, no, she said, the Cubists weren't any queerer than Manet and the Impressionists were when they first came to Boston, and people used to run in for tea and ask her whether she had ever heard of such a thing as "blue snow," or a man's black hat being purple in the sun!

As in Boston tea was the most happy time for reminiscences, in Manchester it was at the breakfast hour that they were most likely to throng. Breakfasts were long, as country breakfasts have a right to be. We had always been out of doors first and were very hungry.

One morning when the cantaloupes were particularly fine Mrs. Fields began to tell me of Henry James' father,—apropos of the melons, though I forget whether it was that he liked them very much or couldn't abide them. She told me a great deal about him; but I was most interested in what she said regarding his faith in his son. When the young man's first essays and stories began to come back across the Atlantic from Rome and Paris they did not meet with approval in Boston; they were thought self-conscious, artificial, shallow. His father's friends feared the young man had mistaken his calling. Mr. James the elder, however, was altogether pleased. He came down to Manchester one summer to have a talk with the great publisher about Henry, and expressed his satisfaction and confidence. "Believe me," he said, sitting at this very table, "the boy will make his mark in letters, Fields."

The next summer I was visiting Mrs. Fields at Manchester in a season of intense heat. We were daily expecting the arrival of Henry James, Jr., himself. One morning came a spluttery letter from the awaited friend, containing bitter references to the "Great American summer," and saying that he was "lying at Nahant," prostrated by the weather. I was very much disappointed, but Mrs. Fields said wisely: "My dear, it is just as well. Mr. James is always greatly put about by the heat, and at Nahant there is the chance of a breeze."

The house at Manchester was called Thunderbolt Hill. Mr. Howe thinks the name incongruous, but that depends on what associations you choose to give it. When I went a-calling with Mrs. Fields and left her card with Thunderbolt Hill engraved in the corner, I felt that I was paying calls with the lady Juno herself. Why shouldn't such a name befit a hill of high decisions and judgments? Moreover, Mrs. Fields was not at all responsible for that name; it came, as she and Miss Jewett liked proverbs and place-names to come, from the native folk. Long years before James T. Fields bought the hill to build a summer cottage, some fine trees at the top of it had been destroyed by lightning; the country people thereabouts had ever afterward called it Thunderbolt Hill.

Mrs. Fields' Journal tells us how in her young married days she always moved from Boston to Manchester-by-the-Sea in early summer, just as she still did when I knew her. I remember one characteristic passage in the Journal, written at Manchester and dated July 16, 1870:

It is a perfect summer day, she says. Mr. Fields does not go up to town but stays at home with a bag full of MSS. He and his wife go to a favourite spot in a pasture by the sea, and she reads him a new story which has just come in from Henry James, Jr., then a very young man—*Compagnons de Voyage,* in "execrable" handwriting. They find the quality good. "I do not know," Mrs. Fields wrote in her diary that evening, "why success in work should affect one so powerfully, but I could have wept as I finished reading, not from the sweet, low pathos of the tale, but from the knowledge of the writer's success. It is so difficult to do anything well in this mysterious world."

Yes, one says to oneself, that is Mrs. Fields, at her best. She rose to meet a fine performance, always—to the end. At eighty she could still entertain new people, new ideas, new forms of art. And she brought to her greeting of the new all the richness of her rich past: a long, unbroken chain of splendid contacts, beautiful friendships.

As one follows the diary down through the years, the reader must feel a certain pride in the determined way in which the New England group refused to be patronized by glittering foreign celebrities—by any celebrities! At dinner Dr. Holmes holds himself a little apart from the actor guests, Jefferson and Warren, and addresses them as "you gentlemen of the stage" in a way that quite disturbed Longfellow and, one may judge, the hostess. They all come to dine with Dickens in his long stays with the Fieldses, come repeatedly, but they seem ever a little on their guard. Emerson cannot be got to believe him altogether genuine and sincere. He insists to Mrs. Fields that Dickens has "too much talent for his genius," and that he is "too consummate an artist to have a thread of nature left"! Thackeray made a long visit at 148 Charles Street. (It is said that he finished *Henry Esmond* there.) In the guest-room which he occupied, with an alcove study, hung a little drawing he had made of himself, framed with the note he had written the hostess telling her that, happy as he was here, he must go home to England for Christmas.

When Mrs. Fields was still a young woman, she noted in her diary that Aristotle says: "Virtue is concerned with action; art with production." "The problem in life," she adds, "is to harmonize these two." In a long life she went far toward working out this problem. She knew how to appreciate the noble in behaviour and the noble in art. In the patriot, the philanthropist, the statesman, she could forgive abominable taste. In the artist, the true artist, she could forgive vanity, sensitiveness, selfishness, indecision, and vacillation of will. She was generous and just in her judgment of men and women because she understood Aristotle's axiom. "With a great gift," I once heard her murmur thoughtfully, "we must be willing to bear greatly, because it has already greatly borne."

Today, in 1936, a garage stands on the site of 148 Charles Street. Only in memory exists the long, green-carpeted, softly lighted drawing-room, and the dining-table where Learning and Talent met, enjoying good food and good wit and rare vintages, looking confidently forward to the growth of their country in the finer amenities of life. Perhaps the garage and all it stands for represent the only real development, and have altogether taken the place of things formerly cherished on that spot. If we try to imagine those dinner-parties which Mrs. Fields describes, the scene is certainly not to us what it was to her: the lighting has changed, and the guests seem hundreds of years away from us. Their portraits no longer hang on the walls of our academies, nor are their "works" much discussed there. The English classes, we are told, can be "interested" only in contemporary writers, the newer the better. A letter from a prep-school boy puts it tersely: "D. H. Lawrence is rather rated a back-number here, but Faulkner keeps his end up."

Not the prep-school boys only are blithe to leave the past untroubled: their instructors pretty generally agree with them. And the retired professors who taught these instructors do not see Shelley plain as they once did. The faith of the elders has been shaken.

Just how did this change come about, one wonders. When and where were the Arnolds overthrown and the Brownings devaluated? Was it at the Marne? At Versailles, when a new geography was being made on paper? Certainly the literary world which emerged from the war used a new coinage. In England and America the "masters" of the last century diminished in stature and pertinence, became remote and shadowy.

But Mrs. Fields never entered this strange twilight. She rounded out her period, from Dickens and Thackeray and Tennyson, through Hardy and Meredith to the Great War, with her standards unshaken. For her there was no revaluation. She died with her world (the world of "letters" which mattered most to her) unchallenged. Marcel Proust somewhere said that when he came to die he would take all his great men with him: since his Beethoven and his Wagner could never be at all the same to anyone else, they would go with him like the captives who were slain at the funeral pyres of Eastern potentates. It was thus Mrs. Fields died, in that house of memories, with the material keepsakes of the past about her.

THEODORE DREISER

The Indiana-born Theodore Dreiser (1871–1945) came to New York and wandered penniless through its streets, awestruck by the contrasts between wealth and poverty. In 1904, a few years after he had published his great American novel, Sister Carrie, *Dreiser, at the behest of a newspaper, began writing the urban sketches that would ultimately make up his very fine collection,* The Color of a Great City. *Dreiser was recognized as a literary giant by virtue of his powerfully sympathetic portrayals of the winners and losers of the American dream, but he was also criticized for his florid prose style. Both are in evidence in this piece, but one is willing to forgive the somewhat dated character of the prose for the authenticity and urgency of the vision.*

The City of My Dreams

(1923)

It was silent, the city of my dreams, marble and serene, due perhaps to the fact that in reality I knew nothing of crowds, poverty, the winds and storms of the inadequate that blow like dust along the paths of life. It was an amazing city, so far-flung, so beautiful, so dead. There were tracks of iron stalking through the air, and streets that were as cañons, and stairways that mounted in vast flights to noble plazas, and steps that led down into deep places where were, strangely enough, underworld silences. And there were parks and flowers and rivers. And then, after twenty years, here it stood, as amazing almost as my dream, save that in the waking the flush of life was over it. It possessed the tang of contests and dreams and enthusiasms and delights and terrors and despairs. Through its ways and cañons and open spaces and underground passages were running, seething, sparkling, darkling, a mass of beings such as my dream-city never knew.

The thing that interested me then as now about New York—as indeed about any great city, but more definitely New York because it was and is so preponderantly large—was the sharp, and at the same time immense, contrast it showed between the dull and the shrewd, the strong and the weak, the rich and the poor, the wise and the ignorant. This, perhaps, was more by reason of numbers and opportunity than anything else, for of course humanity is much the same everywhere. But the number from which to choose was so great here that the strong, or those who ultimately dominated, were so very strong, and the weak so very, very weak—and so very, very many.

I once knew a poor, half-demented, and very much shriveled little seamstress who occupied a tiny hall-bedroom in a side-street rooming-house, cooked her meals on a small alcohol stove set on a bureau, and who had about space enough outside of this to take three good steps either way.

"I would rather live in my hall-bedroom in New York than in any fifteen-room house in the country that I ever saw," she commented once, and her poor little colorless eyes held more of sparkle and snap in them than I ever saw there, before or after. She was wont to add to her sewing income by reading fortunes in cards and tea-leaves and coffee-grounds, telling of love and prosperity to scores as lowly as herself, who would never see either. The color and noise and splendor of the city as a spectacle was sufficient to pay her for all her ills.

And have I not felt the glamour of it myself? And do I not still? Broadway, at Forty-second Street, on those selfsame spring evenings when the city is crowded with an idle, sightseeing cloud of Westerners; when the doors of all shops are open, the windows of nearly all restaurants wide to the gaze of the idlest passer-by. Here is the great city, and it is lush and dreamy. A May or June moon will be hanging like a burnished silver disc between the high walls aloft. A hundred, a thousand electric signs will blink and wink. And the floods of citizens and visitors in summer clothes and with gay hats; the street cars jouncing their endless carloads on indifferent errands; the taxis and private cars fluttering about like jeweled flies. The very gasoline contributes a distinct perfume. Life bubbles, sparkles; chatters gay, incoherent stuff. Such is Broadway.

And then Fifth Avenue, that singing, crystal street, on a shopping afternoon, winter, summer, spring or fall. What tells you as sharply of spring when, its windows crowded with delicate effronteries of silks and gay nothings of all description, it greets you in January, February and March? And how as early as November again, it sings of Palm Beach and Newport and the lesser or greater joys of the tropics and the warmer seas. And in September, how the haughty display of furs and rugs, in this same avenue, and costumes de luxe for ball and dinner, cry out of snows and blizzards, when you are scarcely ten days back from mountain or seaside. One might think, from the picture presented and the residences which line the upper section, that all the world was inordinately prosperous and exclusive and happy. And yet, if you but knew the tawdry underbrush of society, the tangle and mat of futile growth between the tall trees of success, the shabby chambers crowded with aspirants and climbers, the immense mansions barren of a single social affair, perfect and silent!

I often think of the vast mass of underlings, boys and girls, who, with nothing but their youth and their ambitions to commend them, are daily and hourly setting their faces New Yorkward, reconnoitering the city for what it may hold in the shape of wealth or fame, or, if not that, position and comfort in the future; and what, if anything, they will reap. Ah, their young eyes drinking in its promise! And then, again, I think of all the powerful or semi-powerful men and women throughout the world, toiling at one task or another—a store, a mine, a bank, a profession—somewhere outside of New York, whose one ambition is to reach the place where their wealth will permit them to enter and remain in New York, dominant above the mass, luxuriating in what they consider luxury.

The illusion of it, the hypnosis deep and moving that it is! How the strong and the weak, the wise and the fools, the greedy of heart and of eye, seek the nepenthe, the Lethe, of its something hugeness. I always marvel at those who are willing, seemingly, to pay any price—the price, whatever it may be—for one sip of this poison cup. What a stinging, quivering zest they display. How beauty is willing to sell its bloom, virtue its last rag, strength an almost usurious portion of that which it controls, youth its very best years, its hope or dream of fame, fame and power their dignity and presence, age its weary hours, to secure but a minor part of all this, a taste of its vibrating presence and the picture that it makes. Can you not hear them almost, singing its praises?

CHRISTOPHER MORLEY

One of the tribe of "colyumnists," along with Heywood Broun, Don Marquis, and Robert Cortes Holliday, Christopher Morley (1890–1957) was highly literate, later serving on the Book of the Month Club board. The author of the popular novel Kitty Foyle, *later made into a movie, he wrote hundreds of essays. Collected into eighteen volumes, most of them appeared originally as columns in magazines and newspapers. His literary appreciations of the classics were offered in genial, accessible form, with personal asides, to educate the average reader without much pain. He also wrote marvelous urban sketches of New York and Philadelphia. At a time when the fashion for American writers was to disparage their native land, Morley dissented in "Intellectuals and Roughnecks," pointing out how glib, ungrateful, and self-congratulatory that alienated stance could be.*

Intellectuals and Roughnecks

(1923)

I

We look forward with keen interest to reading *Civilization in the United States,* the work of thirty-three independent observers commenting upon various phases of the American scene. So far we have only glanced into it, and have already found much that looks as though it needed contradiction. It is obviously going to be a gloomy book, rather strongly flavoured with intellectual ammonia. Of course, it is a healthy thing that some of our Intellectuals are so depressed about America. It is a good thing for a nation, as it is for an individual, occasionally to go home at night cursing itself for being a boob, a numbskull, and a mental flounder. But we feel about some of our Extreme Intellectuals as we do about the Physical Culture restaurants. The people in these restaurants eat nothing but vitamines and plasms and protose; they live in an atmosphere of carefully planned Scandinavian hygiene; yet most of them look mysteriously pallid. And some of our most Conscientious Brows, in spite of leading lives of carefully regulated meditation, don't seem any too robust in the region of the wits.

However, we shall study this book with care. It contains articles by a number of people whom we admire specially. What we have been wondering is whether among its rather acid comments it gives any panoramic picture of the America we see daily and admire—an America which, in spite of comical simplicities and tragic misdirections of energy, seems to us, in vitality, curiosity, and surprising beauty, the most thrilling experiment of the human race.

In one article in this book we find the following:

> Everything in our society tends to check the growth of the spirit and to shatter the confidence of the individual in himself. Considered with reference to its higher manifestations, life itself has been thus far, in modern America, a failure. Of this the failure of our literature is merely emblematic. Mr. Mencken, who shares this belief, urges that the only hope of a change for the better lies in the development of a native aristocracy that will stand between the writer and the public, supporting him, appreciating him, forming as it were a *cordon sanitaire* between the individual and the mob.

Well, our confidence in ourself is not yet wholly shattered, in spite of the grinding horror of American life. We feel confident enough to venture that this theory is dubious. Greatness in literature does not need to be protected from the insanitary infection of the mob. How Charles Dickens would have roared at such a timid little bluesock doctrine! Great writers do not need any clique of private appreciators or supporters. They are not produced by plaintive patter about ideals and the pride of the "artist." They arise haphazard, and they carry in them an anger, an energy, and a fecundity that deny all classroom rules. And the mob, heaven help us! is the ground and source of their strength and their happiness. Nothing can "check the growth of their spirit," because the spirit is big enough to turn everything to its own inscrutable account. You might as well say that Shakespeare couldn't write great plays because the typewriter hadn't been invented.

Of course, if by "a native aristocracy that will stand between the writer and the public," we are to understand an efficient service of tactful office boys and mendacious telephone girls to keep the chance caller from cutting the mortal artery of Time, we applaud. But we fear that is not meant.

When we get weary of upstage comments about literature we go aloft and have a talk to the fellows in the composing room (who, by the way, are all reading *Moby Dick* nowadays). There is no priggishness in their criticism. They have the sound, sober, sincere instinct—as when one of them tells us, with magnificent insight, that Moby Dick is "Hamlet stuff." When professional connoisseurs can teach us as much as the composing room can about the human values that lie behind literature, then we will mend our manners.

The more we think about it, the more we are staggered by the statement that American life "tends to check the growth of the spirit." To us the exact opposite seems true. American life as we see it all round us seems to be crying aloud for a spirit great enough to grasp and express it. It seems the most prodigious and stimulating material that any writer ever had for his contemplation. It is a perpetual challenge to the imagination—a challenge that hardly any one since Whitman has been great enough, or daring enough, to deal with; but to say that it stunts the spirit can only be valid as a personal opinion. It is to say that a hungry man going into a restaurant loses his appetite.

II

We have ventured a little further into *Civilization in the United States* (which someone has said should really be called "Civilization between Fourteenth Street and Washington Square") and, to tell the truth, we are astounded. This time we are astounded by the extraordinary mellow gravity of the Young Intellectual. It is sad, by the way, that the editor of the volume is actually not much younger than ourself; but indeed he makes us feel immeasurably aged and decadent.

There are, of course, admirable things in the book. Mr. Mencken is at his best in his attack upon Congressional mediocrity. Messrs. Macy, Van Loon, Lardner, and Ernest Boyd carry us with them, as they very often do. Mr. Henry Longan Stuart's "As an Englishman Sees It" is the most quietly pregnant of the essays we have read. But we must confess that when the editor (Mr. Harold Stearns) writes on "The Intellectual Life" he leaves us puzzled and unhappy.

Perhaps Professor Colby's contribution on "Humour" affords a clue. At first we did not quite "get" it; we did not realize that Mr. Colby was having his little joke at the expense of some of the masculine Hermiones who met fortnightly (so Mr. Stearns assures us) at the editor's home "to clarify their individual fields, and contribute towards the advance of intellectual life in America." After reading the appalling solemnities of Mr. Stearns's Preface we realize how charmingly Mr. Colby is (as becomes a veteran) chaffing the young pyrophags. He remarks that the "upper literary class" in America is utterly devoid of humour. This intramural stab he must have meditated at one of those fortnightly meetings while the chairman was remarking that "the most moving and pathetic fact in the social life of America to-day is emotional and aesthetic starvation."

When young men of thirty or so begin to talk about "contributing to the advance of intellectual life in America" they should do it with a smile. Otherwise someone else will have to do the smiling for them.

Consider the weight of the Great Problems faced by the editor of *Civilization in America* at those fortnightly meetings, while (let us hope) the elder members, such as Jack Macy and Professor Colby, smiled a trifle wanly—

> . . . These larger points of policy were decided by common agreement or, on occasion, by majority vote, and to the end I settled no important question without consultation with as many members of the group as I could approach within the limited time we had agreed to have this volume in the hands of the publisher. But with the extension of the scope of the book, the negotiations with the publisher, and the mass of complexities and details that are inevitable in so difficult an enterprise, the authority to decide specific questions and the usual editorial powers were delegated as a matter of convenience to me, aided by a committee of three.

But you must read that Preface entire, to get the full humour of the matter, to get the self-destroying seriousness of the Young Intellectual. It ought to be reprinted as a pamphlet for the warning of college students. Consider the syntax of the first sentence quoted above, as a "contribution to intellectual life in America." For our own part, after reading that Preface we couldn't help turning to the quiet and modest little prefaces of some of the great books, e. g., *Leviathan* and *Religio Medici*.

We must not be ill humoured. The editor of the volume, we are told, has made his own contribution to the intellectual life in America by leaving for Paris as soon as the proofs were corrected. He is perhaps a victim of that oldest of American sophomore superstitions—the idea that Paris is the only city of the world where men of letters may enjoy true freedom of the body and the spirit. Mr. Stearns has for some time been threatening that the sterility and coarseness of American life will drive our sensitive young men overseas. Well, the rest of us must shuffle along as best we can, and see what we can do with this poor tawdry civilization of ours. And incidentally, as a gesture of divorce from American crass-ness, going to Paris and taking a job on the Parisian edition of the *New York Herald* seems to us inadequate. We are reminded of another Young Intellectual—in Chicago this time—who greatly yearned to write a mas-terpiece of obscenity, but could not spell Messalina correctly.

Mr. Stearns speaks of himself and his friends as "unhappy intellectu-als educated beyond our environment." There is a roaring risibility in this that leaves us prostrate. The tragedy is that they apparently mean it. We admire their sincerity, their high-mindedness, and all that, but even at the risk of seeming argumentative we cannot, as long as honesty and clear thinking mean anything, let that sort of remark go by unprotested. It is impossible for any man to be educated beyond his environment— whatever that environment may be. For no man can be greater than Life itself, and in whatever field of life he may be placed, if he has the true insight and the true humility, he will find material for his art. The extraor-dinary panorama of American life, whatever its cruelties and absurdities, should be glowing material for any artist with the genuine receptive and creative gift. The real "artist" (since our Intellectuals love that term) will not timidly crawl into a corner and squeak; nor need he run away to some imagined Utopia abroad.

Perhaps this is a more serious matter than we had supposed. We are one of the stoutest—one of the sincerest, let us say, to avoid misunderstanding—partisans of the Young Intellectual. We used to like, in our wilder moments, to think ourself almost one of them. But it looks now as though we should have to organize a new clique—the Young Roughnecks. The Young Intellectuals are too easily pleased with themselves. In the first place, we honestly believe that few men have any real critical balance and judgment before they are forty. In the second place, the Young Intellectuals are perilously devoid of humour. Of that rich, magical, grotesque, and savoury quality they have far too little. They have it, but it works spasmodically.

We welcome a book like *Civilization in America* because it shows in a clear cross-cutting what is wrong with a great many excellent young minds. They are quick to scoff, but they are not humorous; they are eager for human perfection, but want to escape from humanity itself. They say a great many admirable things, true things; but so condescendingly that, by some quaint perversion, they impel us to fly to the opposite view. Life itself, apparently, is too multitudinous, too terrible for them. They enjoy pouring ridicule upon the world of business and upon the business man. We should like to see them tackle their own tasks with the same devo-tion and lack of parade that the business man shows. Some of the most amazing beauties of American life have been the work of quiet business men who were not clamouring for admiration as "artists." Our friends the Intellectuals keep shouting that the "creative class" (so they call themselves) must be more admired, more respected, more appreciated. We answer, they are already respected and applauded as much as—perhaps more than—is good for them. Let them cease to consider themselves a class above and apart. They are too painfully conscious of being "artists." They make us feel like gathering a group of Young Roughnecks—let us say Heywood Broun and H. I. Phillips for a nucleus—and going off in a corner to be constructively and creatively vulgar.

H. L. MENCKEN

Newspaperman, editor, and incorrigible essayist H. L. Mencken (1880–1956) was a happy provocateur: typical of his contrarianism was his decision to entitle several of his collections Prejudices, *giving that pejorative term a positive tinge. Consistently criticizing Americans for their lack of sophistication, referring to his fellow countrymen as Boobus americanus, he managed in spite (or because) of his satiric takedowns to attract so wide a readership that Walter Lippmann called him "the most powerful influence upon his whole generation of American people." In one of his most celebrated essays, "The Hills of Zion," he covered the Scopes evolution trial, ridiculing the southern townspeople with his characteristic blend of high spirits, mandarin diction, and outrageously mocking caricature. The secret of Mencken's ability to get away with needling the American public was probably that he loved being amused by his country's vulgarity as much as he deplored it.*

The Hills of Zion

(1925)

It was hot weather when they tried the infidel Scopes at Dayton, Tenn., but I went down there very willingly, for I was eager to see something of evangelical Christianity as a going concern. In the big cities of the Republic, despite the endless efforts of consecrated men, it is laid up with a wasting disease. The very Sunday-school superintendents, taking jazz from the stealthy radio, shake their fire-proof legs; their pupils, moving into adolescence, no longer respond to the proliferating hormones by enlisting for missionary service in Africa, but resort to necking instead. Even in Dayton, I found, though the mob was up to do execution upon Scopes, there was a strong smell of antinomianism. The nine churches of the village were all half empty on Sunday, and weeds choked their yards. Only two or three of the resident pastors managed to sustain themselves by their ghostly science; the rest had to take orders for mail-order pantaloons or work in the adjacent strawberry fields; one, I heard, was a barber. On the courthouse green a score of sweating theologians debated the darker passages of Holy Writ day and night, but I soon found that they were all volunteers, and that the local faithful, while interested in their exegesis as an intellectual exercise, did not permit it to impede the indigenous debaucheries. Exactly twelve minutes after I reached the village I was taken in tow by a Christian man and introduced to the favorite tipple of the Cumberland Range: half corn liquor and half Coca-Cola. It seemed a dreadful dose to me, but I found that the Dayton illuminati got it down with gusto, rubbing their tummies and rolling their eyes. I include among them the chief local proponents of the Mosaic cosmogony. They were all hot for Genesis, but their faces were far too florid to belong to teetotalers, and when a pretty girl came tripping down the main street, which was very often, they reached for the places where their neckties should have been with all the amorous enterprise of movie actors. It seemed somehow strange.

An amiable newspaper woman of Chattanooga, familiar with those uplands, presently enlightened me. Dayton, she explained, was simply a great capital like any other. That is to say, it was to Rhea county what Atlanta was to Georgia or Paris to France. That is to say, it was predominantly epicurean and sinful. A country girl from some remote valley of the county, coming into town for her semi-annual bottle of Lydia Pinkham's Vegetable Compound, shivered on approaching Robinson's drug-store quite as a country girl from up-State New York might shiver on approaching the Metropolitan Opera House. In every village lout she saw a potential white-slaver. The hard sidewalks hurt her feet. Temptations of the flesh bristled to all sides of her, luring her to Hell. This newspaper woman told me of a session with just such a visitor, holden a few days before. The latter waited outside one of the town hot-dog and Coca-Cola shops while her husband negotiated with a hardware merchant across the street. The newspaper woman, idling along and observing that the stranger was badly used by the heat, invited her to step into the shop for a glass of Coca-Cola. The invitation brought forth only a gurgle of terror. Coca-Cola, it quickly appeared, was prohibited by the country lady's pastor, as a levantine and Hell-sent narcotic. He also prohibited coffee and tea—and pies! He had his doubts about white bread and boughten meat. The newspaper woman, interested, inquired about ice-cream. It was, she found, not specifically prohibited, but going into a Coca-Cola shop to get it would be clearly sinful. So she offered to get a saucer of it, and bring it out to the sidewalk. The visitor vacillated—and came near being lost. But God saved her in the nick of time. When the newspaper woman emerged from the place she was in full flight up the street. Later on her husband, mounted on a mule, overtook her four miles out the mountain pike.

This newspaper woman, whose kindness covered city infidels as well as Alpine Christians, offered to take me back in the hills to a place where the old-time religion was genuinely on tap. The Scopes jury, she explained, was composed mainly of its customers, with a few Dayton sophisticates added to leaven the mass. It would thus be instructive to climb the heights and observe the former at their ceremonies. The trip, fortunately, might be made by automobile. There was a road running out of Dayton to Morgantown, in the mountains to the westward, and thence beyond. But foreigners, it appeared, would have to approach the sacred grove cautiously, for the upland worshipers were very shy, and at the first sight of a strange face they would adjourn their orgy and slink into the forest. They were not to be feared, for God had long since forbidden them to practise assassination, or even assault, but if they were alarmed a rough trip would go for naught. So, after dreadful bumpings up a long and narrow road, we parked our car in a little woodpath a mile or two beyond the tiny village of Morgantown, and made the rest of the approach on foot, deployed like skirmishers. Far off in a dark, romantic glade a flickering light was visible, and out of the silence came the rumble of exhortation. We could distinguish the figure of the preacher only as a moving mote in the light: it was like looking down the tube of a dark-field microscope. Slowly and cautiously we crossed what seemed to be a pasture, and then we stealthily edged further and further. The light now grew larger and we could begin to make out what was going on. We went ahead on all fours, like snakes in the grass.

From the great limb of a mighty oak hung a couple of crude torches of the sort that car inspectors thrust under Pullman cars when a train pulls in at night. In the guttering glare was the preacher, and for a while we could see no one else. He was an immensely tall and thin mountaineer in blue jeans, his collarless shirt open at the neck and his hair a tousled mop. As he preached he paced up and down under the smoking flambeaux, and at each turn he thrust his arms into the air and yelled "Glory to God!" We crept nearer in the shadow of the cornfield, and began to hear more of his discourse. He was preaching on the Day of Judgment. The high kings of the earth, he roared, would all fall down and die; only the sanctified would stand up to receive the Lord God of Hosts. One of these kings he mentioned by name, the king of what he called Greece-y. The king of Greece-y, he said, was doomed to Hell. We crawled forward a few more yards and began to see the audience. It was seated on benches ranged round the preacher in a circle. Behind him sat a row of elders, men and women. In front were the younger folk. We crept on cautiously, and individuals rose out of the ghostly gloom. A young mother sat suckling her baby, rocking as the preacher paced up and down. Two scared little girls hugged each other, their pigtails down their backs. An immensely huge mountain woman, in a gingham dress, cut in one piece, rolled on her heels at every "Glory to God!" To one side, and but half visible, was what appeared to be a bed. We found afterward that half a dozen babies were asleep upon it.

The preacher stopped at last, and there arose out of the darkness a woman with her hair pulled back into a little tight knot. She began so quietly that we couldn't hear what she said, but soon her voice rose resonantly and we could follow her. She was denouncing the reading of books. Some wandering book agent, it appeared, had come to her cabin and tried to sell her a specimen of his wares. She refused to touch it. Why, indeed, read a book? If what was in it was true, then everything in it was already in the Bible. If it was false, then reading it would imperil the soul. This syllogism from the Caliph Omar complete, she sat down. There followed a hymn, led by a somewhat fat brother wearing silver-rimmed country spectacles. It droned on for half a dozen stanzas, and then the first speaker resumed the floor. He argued that the gift of tongues was real and that education was a snare. Once his children could read the Bible, he said, they had enough. Beyond lay only infidelity and damnation. Sin stalked the cities. Dayton itself was a Sodom. Even Morgantown had begun to forget God. He sat down, and a female aurochs in gingham got up. She began quietly, but was soon leaping and roaring, and it was hard to follow her. Under cover of the turmoil we sneaked a bit closer.

A couple of other discourses followed, and there were two or three hymns. Suddenly a change of mood began to make itself felt. The last hymn ran longer than the others, and dropped gradually into a monotonous, unintelligible chant. The leader beat time with his book. The faithful broke out with exultations. When the singing ended there was a brief palaver that we could not hear, and two of the men moved a bench into the circle of light directly under the flambeaux. Then a half-grown girl emerged from the darkness and threw herself upon it. We noticed with astonishment that she had bobbed hair. "This sister," said the leader, "has asked for prayers." We moved a bit closer. We could now see faces plainly, and hear every word. At a signal all the faithful crowded up to the bench and began to pray—not in unison, but each for himself. At another they all fell on their knees, their arms over the penitent. The leader kneeled facing us, his head alternately thrown back dramatically or buried in his hands. Words spouted from his lips like bullets from a machine-gun— appeals to God to pull the penitent back out of Hell, defiances of the demons of the air, a vast impassioned jargon of apocalyptic texts. Suddenly he rose to his feet, threw back his head and began to speak in the tongues—blub-blub-blub, gurgle-gurgle-gurgle. His voice rose to a higher register. The climax was a shrill, inarticulate squawk, like that of a man throttled. He fell headlong across the pyramid of supplicants.

From the squirming and jabbering mass a young woman gradually detached herself—a woman not uncomely, with a pathetic homemade cap on her head. Her head jerked back, the veins of her neck swelled, and her fists went to her throat as if she were fighting for breath. She bent backward until she was like half a hoop. Then she suddenly snapped forward. We caught a flash of the whites of her eyes. Presently her whole body began to be convulsed—great throes that began at the shoulders and ended at the hips. She would leap to her feet, thrust her arms in air, and then hurl herself upon the heap. Her praying flattened out into a mere delirious caterwauling. I describe the thing discreetly, and as a strict behaviorist. The lady's subjective sensations I leave to infidel pathologists, privy to the works of Ellis, Freud and Moll. Whatever they were, they were obviously not painful, for they were accompanied by vast heavings and gurglings of a joyful and even ecstatic nature. And they seemed to be contagious, too, for soon a second penitent, also female, joined the first, and then came a third, and a fourth, and a fifth. The last one had an extraordinary violent attack. She began with mild enough jerks of the head, but in a moment she was bounding all over the place, like a chicken with its head cut off. Every time her head came up a stream of hosannas would issue out of it. Once she collided with a dark, undersized brother, hitherto silent and stolid. Contact with her set him off as if he had been kicked by a mule. He leaped into the air, threw back his head, and began to gargle as if with a mouthful of BB shot. Then he loosed one tremendous, stentorian sentence in the tongues, and collapsed.

By this time the performers were quite oblivious to the profane universe and so it was safe to go still closer. We left our hiding and came up to the little circle of light. We slipped into the vacant seats on one of the rickety benches. The heap of mourners was directly before us. They bounced into us as they cavorted. The smell that they radiated, sweating there in that obscene heap, half suffocated us. Not all of them, of course, did the thing in the grand manner. Some merely moaned and rolled their eyes. The female ox in gingham flung her great bulk on the ground and jabbered an unintelligible prayer. One of the men, in the intervals between fits, put on his spectacles and read his Bible. Beside me on the bench sat the young mother and her baby. She suckled it through the whole orgy, obviously fascinated by what was going on, but never venturing to take any hand in it. On the bed just outside the light the half a dozen other babies slept peacefully. In the shadows, suddenly appearing and as suddenly going away, were vague figures, whether of believers or of scoffers I do not know. They seemed to come and go in couples. Now and then a couple at the ringside would step out and vanish into the black night.

After a while some came back, the males looking somewhat sheepish. There was whispering outside the circle of vision. A couple of Model T Fords lurched up the road, cutting holes in the darkness with their lights. Once someone out of sight loosed a bray of laughter.

All this went on for an hour or so. The original penitent, by this time, was buried three deep beneath the heap. One caught a glimpse, now and then, of her yellow bobbed hair, but then she would vanish again. How she breathed down there I don't know; it was hard enough six feet away, with a strong five-cent cigar to help. When the praying brothers would rise up for a bout with the tongues their faces were streaming with perspiration. The fat harridan in gingham sweated like a longshoreman. Her hair got loose and fell down over her face. She fanned herself with her skirt. A powerful old gal she was, plainly equal in her day to a bout with obstetrics and a week's washing on the same morning, but this was worse than a week's washing. Finally, she fell into a heap, breathing in great, convulsive gasps.

Finally, we got tired of the show and returned to Dayton. It was nearly eleven o'clock—an immensely late hour for those latitudes—but the whole town was still gathered in the courthouse yard, listening to the disputes of theologians. The Scopes trial had brought them in from all directions. There was a friar wearing a sandwich sign announcing that he was the Bible champion of the world. There was a Seventh Day Adventist arguing that Clarence Darrow was the beast with seven heads and ten horns described in Revelation xiii, and that the end of the world was at hand. There was an evangelist made up like Andy Gump, with the news that atheists in Cincinnati were preparing to descend upon Dayton, hang the eminent Judge Raulston, and burn the town. There was an ancient who maintained that no Catholic could be a Christian. There was the eloquent Dr. T. T. Martin, of Blue Mountain, Miss., come to town with a truck-load of torches and hymn-books to put Darwin in his place. There was a singing brother bellowing apocalyptic hymns. There was William Jennings Bryan, followed everywhere by a gaping crowd. Dayton was having a roaring time. It was better than the circus. But the note of devotion was simply not there; the Daytonians, after listening a while, would slip away to Robinson's drug-store to regale themselves with Coca-Cola, or to the lobby of the Aqua Hotel, where the learned Raulston sat in state, judicially picking his teeth. The real religion was not present. It began at the bridge over the town creek, where the road makes off for the hills.

JAMES WELDON JOHNSON

James Weldon Johnson (1871–1938), a major figure in the Harlem Renaissance, was a poet (God's Trombones), novelist (The Autobiography of an Ex-Colored Man), songwriter, cultural historian (Black Manhattan), diplomat, and civil rights activist (executive secretary of the National Association for the Advancement of Colored People). He spoke out strongly against the racial prejudice and lynching of his time. In "The Dilemma of the Negro Author," Johnson put forth with consummate clarity, dry humor, and dispassionate intelligence, without offering any definitive resolution, a conundrum—should the black writer address white America or black America?—which continues to engage African American authors to this day.

The Dilemma of the Negro Author

(1928)

I

The Negro author—the creative author—has arrived. He is here. He appears in the lists of the best publishers. He even breaks into the lists of the best-sellers. To the general American public he is a novelty, a strange phenomenon, a miracle straight out of the skies. Well, he *is* a novelty, but he is by no means a new thing.

The line of American Negro authors runs back for a hundred and fifty years, back to Phillis Wheatley, the poet. Since Phillis Wheatley there have been several hundred Negro authors who have written books of many kinds. But in all these generations down to within the past six years only seven or eight of the hundreds have ever been heard of by the general American public or even by the specialists in American literature. As many Negro writers have gained recognition by both in the past six years as in all the generations gone before. What has happened is that efforts which have been going on for more than a century are being noticed and appreciated at last, and that this appreciation has served as a stimulus to greater effort and output. America is aware today that there are such things as Negro authors. Several converging forces have been at work to produce this state of mind. Had these forces been at work three decades ago, it is possible that we then should have had a condition similar to the one which now exists.

Now that the Negro author has come into the range of vision of the American public eye, it seems to me only fair to point out some of the difficulties he finds in his way. But I wish to state emphatically that I have no intention of making an apology or asking any special allowances for him; such a plea would at once disqualify him and void the very recognition be has gained. But the Negro writer does face peculiar difficulties that ought to be taken into account when passing judgment upon him.

It is unnecessary to say that he faces every one of the difficulties common to all that crowd of demon-driven individuals who feel that they must write. But the Aframerican author faces a special problem which the plain American author knows nothing about—the problem of the double audience. It is more than a double audience; it is a divided audience, an audience made up of two elements with differing and often opposite and antagonistic points of view. His audience is always both white America and black America. The moment a Negro writer takes up his pen or sits down to his typewriter he is immediately called upon to solve, consciously or unconsciously, this problem of the double audience. To whom shall he address himself, to his own black group or to white America? Many a Negro writer has fallen down, as it were, between these two stools.

It may be asked why he doesn't just go ahead and write and not bother himself about audiences. That is easier said than done. It is doubtful if anything with meaning can be written unless the writer has some definite audience in mind. His audience may be as far away as the angelic host or the rulers of darkness, but an audience he must have in mind. As soon as he selects his audience he immediately falls, whether he wills it or not, under the laws which govern the influence of the audience upon the artist, laws that operate in every branch of art.

Now, it is axiomatic that the artist achieves his best when working at his best with the materials he knows best. And it goes without saying that the material which the Negro as a creative or general writer knows best comes out of the life and experience of the colored people in America. The overwhelming bulk of the best work done by Aframerican writers has some bearing on the Negro and his relations to civilization and society in the United States. Leaving authors, white or black, writing for coteries on special and technical subjects out of the discussion, it is safe to say that the white American author, when he sits down to write, has in mind a white audience—and naturally. The influence of the Negro as a group on his work is infinitesimal if not zero. Even when he talks about the Negro he talks to white people. But with the Aframerican author the case is different. When he attempts to handle his best known material he is thrown upon two, indeed, if it is permissible to say so, upon three horns of a dilemma. He must intentionally or unintentionally choose a black audience or a white audience or a combination of the two; and each of them presents peculiar difficulties.

If the Negro author selects white America as his audience he is bound to run up against many long-standing artistic conceptions about the Negro; against numerous conventions and traditions which through age have become binding; in a word, against a whole row of hard-set stereotypes which are not easily broken up. White America has some firm opinions as to what the Negro is, and consequently some pretty well fixed ideas as to what should be written about him, and how.

What is the Negro in the artistic conception of white America? In the brighter light, he is a simple, indolent, docile, improvident peasant; a singing, dancing, laughing, weeping child; picturesque beside his log cabin and in the snowy fields of cotton; naively charming with his banjo and his songs in the moonlight and along the lazy Southern rivers; a faithful, ever-smiling and genuflecting old servitor to the white folks of quality; a pathetic and pitiable figure. In a darker light, he is an impulsive, irrational, passionate savage, reluctantly wearing a thin coat of culture, sullenly hating the white man, but holding an innate and unescapable belief in the white man's superiority; an everlastingly alien and irredeemable element in the nation; a menace to Southern civilization; a threat to Nordic race purity; a figure casting a sinister shadow across the future of the country.

Ninety-nine one-hundredths of all that has been written about the Negro in the United States in three centuries and read with any degree of interest or pleasure by white America has been written in conformity to one or more of these ideas. I am not saying that they do not provide good material for literature; in fact, they make material for poetry and romance and comedy and tragedy of a high order. But I do say they have become stencils, and that the Negro author finds these stencils inadequate for the portrayal and interpretation of Negro life today. Moreover, when he does attempt to make use of them he finds himself impaled upon the second horn of his dilemma.

II

It is known that art—literature in particular, unless it be sheer fantasy—must be based on more or less well established conventions, upon ideas that have some roots in the general consciousness, that are at least somewhat familiar to the public mind. It is this that gives it verisimilitude and finality. Even revolutionary literature, if it is to have any convincing power, must start from a basis of conventions, regardless of how unconventional its objective may be. These conventions are changed by slow and gradual processes—except they be changed in a flash. The conventions held by white America regarding the Negro will be changed. Actually they are being changed, but they have not yet sufficiently changed to lessen to any great extent the dilemma of the Negro author.

It would be straining the credulity of white America beyond the breaking point for a Negro writer to put out a novel dealing with the wealthy class of colored people. The idea of Negroes of wealth living in a luxurious manner is still too unfamiliar. Such a story would have to be written in a burlesque vein to make it at all plausible and acceptable. Before Florence Mills and Josephine Baker implanted a new general idea in the public mind it would have been worse than a waste of time for a Negro author to write for white America the story of a Negro girl who rose in spite of all obstacles, racial and others, to a place of world success and acclaim on the musical revue stage. It would be proof of little less than supreme genius in a Negro poet for him to take one of the tragic characters in American Negro history—say Crispus Attucks or Nat Turner or Denmark Vesey—put heroic language in his mouth and have white America accept the work as authentic. American Negroes as heroes form no part of white America's concept of the race. Indeed, I question if three out of ten of the white Americans who will read these lines know anything of either Attucks, Turner or Vesey; although each of the three played a role in the history of the nation. The Aframerican poet might take an African chief or warrior, set him forth in heroic couplets or blank verse and present him to white America with infinitely greater chance of having his work accepted.

But these limiting conventions held by white America do not constitute the whole difficulty of the Negro author in dealing with a white audience. In addition to these conventions regarding the Negro as a race, white America has certain definite opinions regarding the Negro as an artist, regarding the scope of his efforts. White America has a strong feeling that Negro artists should refrain from making use of white subject matter. I mean by that, subject matter which it feels belongs to the white world. In plain words, white America does not welcome seeing the Negro competing with the white man on what it considers the white man's own ground.

In many white people this feeling is dormant, but brought to the test it flares up, if only faintly. During his first season in this country after his European success a most common criticism of Roland Hayes was provoked by the fact that his programme consisted of groups of English, French, German and Italian songs, closing always with a group of Negro Spirituals. A remark frequently made was, "Why doesn't he confine himself to the Spirituals?" This in face of the fact that no tenor on the American concert stage could surpass Hayes in singing French and German songs. The truth is that white America was not quite prepared to relish the sight of a black man in a dress suit singing French and German love songs, and singing them exquisitely. The first reaction was that there was something incongruous about it. It gave a jar to the old conventions and something of a shock to the Nordic superiority complex. The years have not been many since Negro players have dared to interpolate a love duet in a musical show to be witnessed by white people. The representation of romantic love-making by Negroes struck the white audience as somewhat ridiculous; Negroes were supposed to mate in a more primeval manner.

White America has for a long time been annexing and appropriating Negro territory, and is prone to think of every part of the domain it now controls as originally—and aboriginally—its own. One sometimes hears the critics in reviewing a Negro musical show lament the fact that it is so much like white musical shows. But a great deal of this similarity it would be hard to avoid because of the plain fact that two out of the four chief ingredients in the present day white musical show, the music and the dancing, are directly derived from the Negro. These ideas and opinions regarding the scope of artistic effort affect the Negro author, the poet in particular. So whenever an Aframerican writer addresses himself to white America and attempts to break away from or break through these conventions and limitations he makes more than an ordinary demand upon his literary skill and power.

At this point it would appear that a most natural thing for the Negro author to do would be to say, "Damn the white audience!" and devote himself to addressing his own race exclusively. But when he turns from the conventions of white America he runs afoul of the taboos of black America. He has no more absolute freedom to speak as he pleases addressing black America than he has in addressing white America. There are certain phases of life that he dare not touch, certain subjects that he dare not critically discuss, certain manners of treatment that he dare not use— except at the risk of rousing bitter resentment. It is quite possible for a Negro author to do a piece of work, good from every literary point of view, and at the same time bring down on his head the wrath of the entire colored pulpit and press, and gain among the literate element of his own people the reputation of being a prostitutor of his talent and a betrayer of his race—not by any means a pleasant position to get into.

This state of mind on the part of the colored people may strike white America as stupid and intolerant, but it is not without some justification and not entirely without precedent; the white South on occasion discloses a similar sensitiveness. The colored people of the United States are anomalously situated. They are a segregated and antagonized minority in a very large nation, a minority unremittingly on the defensive. Their faults and failings are exploited to produce exaggerated effects. Consequently, they have a strong feeling against exhibiting to the world anything but their best points. They feel that other groups may afford to do otherwise but, as yet, the Negro cannot. This is not to say that they refuse to listen to criticism of themselves, for they often listen to Negro speakers excoriating the race for its faults and foibles and vices. But these criticisms are not for the printed page. They are not for the ears or eyes of white America.

A curious illustration of this defensive state of mind is found in the Negro theatres. In those wherein Negro players give Negro performances for Negro audiences all of the Negro weaknesses, real and reputed, are burlesqued and ridiculed in the most hilarious manner, and are laughed at and heartily enjoyed. But the presence of a couple of dozen white people would completely change the psychology of the audience, and the players. If some of the performances so much enjoyed by strictly Negro audiences in Negro theatres were put on, say, in a Broadway theatre, a wave of indignation would sweep Aframerica from the avenues of Harlem to the canebrakes of Louisiana. These taboos of black America are as real and binding as the conventions of white America. Conditions may excuse if not warrant them; nevertheless, it is unfortunate that they exist, for their effect is blighting. In past years they have discouraged in Negro authors the production of everything but *nice* literature; they have operated to hold their work down to literature of the defensive, exculpatory sort. They have a restraining effect at the present time which Negro writers are compelled to reckon with.

This division of audience takes the solid ground from under the feet of the Negro writer and leaves him suspended. Either choice carries hampering and discouraging conditions. The Negro author may please one audience and at the same time rouse the resentment of the other; or he may please the other and totally fail to rouse the interest of the one. The situation, moreover, constantly subjects him to the temptation of posing and posturing for the one audience or the other; and the sincerity and soundness of his work are vitiated whether he poses for white or black.

The dilemma is not made less puzzling by the fact that practically it is an extremely difficult thing for the Negro author in the United States to address himself solely to either of these two audiences. If he analyzes what he writes he will find that on one page black America is his whole or main audience, and on the very next page white America. In fact, a psychoanalysis of the Negro authors of the defensive and exculpatory literature, written in strict conformity to the taboos of black America, would reveal that they were unconsciously addressing themselves mainly to white America.

III

I have sometimes thought it would be a way out, that the Negro author would be on surer ground and truer to himself, if he could disregard white America; if he could say to white America, "What I have written, I have written. I hope you'll be interested and like it. If not, I can't help it." But it is impossible for a sane American Negro to write with total disregard for nine-tenths of the people of the United States. Situated as his own race is amidst and amongst them, their influence is irresistible.

I judge there is not a single Negro writer who is not, at least secondarily, impelled by the desire to make his work have some effect on the white world for the good of his race. It may be thought that the work of the Negro writer, on account of this last named condition, gains in pointedness what it loses in breadth. Be that as it may, the situation is for the time one in which he is inextricably placed. Of course, the Negro author can try the experiment of putting black America in the orchestra chairs, so to speak, and keeping white America in the gallery, but he is likely at any moment to find his audience shifting places on him, and sometimes without notice.

And now, instead of black America and white America as separate or alternating audiences, what about the combination of the two into one? That, I believe, is the only way out. However, there needs to be more than a combination, there needs to be a fusion. In time, I cannot say how much time, there will come a gradual and natural rapprochement of these two sections of the Negro author's audience. There will come a breaking up and remodelling of most of white America's traditional stereotypes, forced by the advancement of the Negro in the various phases of our national life. Black America will abolish many of its taboos. A sufficiently large class of colored people will progress enough and become strong enough to render a constantly sensitive and defensive attitude on the part of the race unnecessary and distasteful. In the end, the Negro author will have something close to a common audience, and will be about as free from outside limitations as other writers.

Meanwhile, the making of a common audience out of white and black America presents the Negro author with enough difficulties to constitute a third horn of his dilemma. It is a task that is a very high test for all his skill and abilities, but it can be and has been accomplished. The equipped Negro author working at his best in his best known material can achieve this end; but, standing on his racial foundation, he must fashion something that rises above race, and reaches out to the universal in truth and beauty. And so, when a Negro author does write so as to fuse white and black America into one interested and approving audience he has performed no slight feat, and has most likely done a sound piece of literary work.

ZORA NEALE HURSTON

*I Love Myself When I Am Laughing, the title of a collection of work by Zora Neale Hurston (1891–1960), exactly sums up her ability to find joy in self-amusement and her refusal to play what she called "the tragic Negro." In "How It Feels to Be Colored Me," she boldly wonders about those who discriminate against her: "How can any deny themselves the pleasure of my company?" A prominent Harlem Renaissance figure, Hurston was a novelist (*Their Eyes Were Watching God*) who captured the mores of southern blacks. She also studied cultural anthropology under Franz Boas and collected folklore extensively.*

How It Feels to Be Colored Me

(1928)

I am colored but I offer nothing in the way of extenuating circumstances except the fact that I am the only Negro in the United States whose grandfather on the mother's side was *not* an Indian chief.

I remember the very day that I became colored. Up to my thirteenth year I lived in the little Negro town of Eatonville, Florida. It is exclusively a colored town. The only white people I knew passed through the town going to or coming from Orlando. The native whites rode dusty horses, the Northern tourists chugged down the sandy village road in automobiles. The town knew the Southerners and never stopped cane chewing when they passed. But the Northerners were something else again. They were peered at cautiously from behind curtains by the timid. The more venturesome would come out on the porch to watch them go past and got just as much pleasure out of the tourists as the tourists got out of the village.

The front porch might seem a daring place for the rest of the town, but it was a gallery seat to me. My favorite place was atop the gate-post. Proscenium box for a born first-nighter. Not only did I enjoy the show, but I didn't mind the actors knowing that I liked it. I actually spoke to them in passing. I'd wave at them and when they returned my salute, I would say something like this: "Howdy-do-well-I-thank-you-where-you-goin'?" Usually automobile or the horse paused at this, and after a queer exchange of compliments, I would probably "go a piece of the way" with them, as we say in farthest Florida. If one of my family happened to come to the front in time to see me, of course negotiations would be rudely broken off. But even so, it is clear that I was the first "welcome-to-our-state" Floridian, and I hope the Miami Chamber of Commerce will please take notice.

During this period, white people differed from colored to me only in that they rode through town and never lived there. They liked to hear me "speak pieces" and sing and wanted to see me dance the parse-me-la, and gave me generously of their small silver for doing these things, which seemed strange to me for I wanted to do them so much that I needed bribing to stop. Only they didn't know it. The colored people gave no dimes. They deplored any joyful tendencies in me, but I was their Zora nevertheless. I belonged to them, to the nearby hotels, to the county—everybody's Zora.

But changes came in the family when I was thirteen, and I was sent to school in Jacksonville. I left Eatonville, the town of the oleanders, as Zora. When I disembarked from the riverboat at Jacksonville, she was no more. It seemed that I had suffered a sea change. I was not Zora of Orange County any more, I was now a little colored girl. I found it out in certain ways. In my heart as well as in the mirror, I became a fast brown—warranted not to rub nor run.

But I am not tragically colored. There is no great sorrow dammed up in my soul, nor lurking behind my eyes. I do not mind at all. I do not belong to the sobbing school of Negro-hood who hold that nature somehow has given them a low-down dirty deal and whose feelings are all hurt about it. Even in the helter-skelter skirmish that is my life, I have seen that the world is to the strong regardless of a little pigmentation more or less. No, I do not weep at the world—I am too busy sharpening my oyster knife.

Someone is always at my elbow reminding me that I am the grand-daughter of slaves. It fails to register depression with me. Slavery is sixty years in the past. The operation was successful and the patient is doing well, thank you. The terrible struggle that made me an American out of a potential slave said "On the line!" The Reconstruction said "Get set!"; and the generation before said "Go!" I am off to a flying start and I must not halt in the stretch to look behind and weep. Slavery is the price I paid for civilization, and the choice was not with me. It is a bully adventure and worth all that I have paid through my ancestors for it. No one on earth ever had a greater chance for glory. The world to be won and nothing to be lost. It is thrilling to think—to know that for any act of mine, I shall get twice as much praise or twice as much blame. It is quite exciting to hold the center of the national stage, with the spectators not knowing whether to laugh or to weep.

The position of my white neighbor is much more difficult. No brown specter pulls up a chair beside me when I sit down to eat. No dark ghost thrusts its leg against mine in bed. The game of keeping what one has is never so exciting as the game of getting.

I do not always feel colored. Even now I often achieve the unconscious Zora of Eatonville before the Hegira. I feel most colored when I am thrown against a sharp white background.

For instance at Barnard. "Beside the waters of the Hudson" I feel my race. Among the thousand white persons, I am a dark rock surged upon, overswept by a creamy sea. I am surged upon and overswept, but through it all, I remain myself. When covered by the waters, I am; and the ebb but reveals me again.

Sometimes it is the other way around. A white person is set down in our midst, but the contrast is just as sharp for me. For instance, when I sit in the drafty basement that is The New World Cabaret with a white person, my color comes. We enter chatting about any little nothing that we have in common and are seated by the jazz waiters. In the abrupt way that jazz orchestras have, this one plunges into a number. It loses no time in circumlocutions, but gets right down to business. It constricts the thorax and splits the heart with its tempo and narcotic harmonies. This orchestra grows rambunctious, rears on its hind legs and attacks the tonal veil with primitive fury, rending it, clawing it until it breaks through to the jungle beyond. I follow those heathen—follow them exultingly. I dance wildly inside myself; I yell within, I whoop; I shake my assegai above my head, I hurl it true to the mark *yeeeeooww!* I am in the jungle and living in the jungle way. My face is painted red and yellow, and my body is painted blue. My pulse is throbbing like a war drum. I want to slaughter something—give pain, give death to what, I do not know. But the piece ends. The men of the orchestra wipe their lips and rest their fingers. I creep back slowly to the veneer we call civilization with the last tone and find the white friend sitting motionless in his seat, smoking calmly.

"Good music they have here," he remarks, drumming the table with his fingertips.

Music! The great blobs of purple and red emotion have not touched him. He has only heard what I felt. He is far away and I see him but dimly across the ocean and the continent that have fallen between us. He is so pale with his whiteness then and I am *so* colored.

At certain times I have no race, I am *me*. When I set my hat at a certain angle and saunter down Seventh Avenue, Harlem City, feeling as snooty as the lions in front of the Forty-Second Street Library, for instance. So far as my feelings are concerned, Peggy Hopkins Joyce on the Boule Mich with her gorgeous raiment, stately carriage, knees knocking together in a most aristocratic manner, has nothing on me. The cosmic Zora emerges. I belong to no race nor time, I am the eternal feminine with its string of beads.

I have no separate feeling about being an American citizen and colored. I am merely a fragment of the Great Soul that surges within the boundaries. My country, right or wrong.

Sometimes, I feel discriminated against, but it does not make me angry. It merely astonishes me. How *can* any deny themselves the pleasure of my company! It's beyond me.

But in the main, I feel like a brown bag of miscellany propped against a wall. Against a wall in company with other bags, white, red and yellow. Pour out the contents, and there is discovered a jumble of small things priceless and worthless. A first-water diamond, an empty spool, bits of broken glass, lengths of string, a key to a door long since crumbled away, a rusty knife-blade, old shoes saved for a road that never was and never will be, a nail bent under the weight of things too heavy for any nail, a dried flower or two, still a little fragrant. In your hand is the brown bag. On the ground before you is the jumble it held—so much like the jumble in the bags, could they be emptied, that all might be dumped in a single heap and the bags refilled without altering the content of any greatly. A bit of colored glass more or less would not matter. Perhaps that is how the Great Stuffer of Bags filled them in the first place—who knows?

JAMES THURBER

James Thurber (1894–1961) was a humorist and cartoonist, often associated with The New Yorker. *His sly portrayal of the American male as prone to daydreaming ("The Secret Life of Walter Mitty"), bossed around by superiors, and overmatched by the American female is a droll apotheosis of reverse machismo. We root for his antiheroic protagonists, even as we wish they would grow a spine. In "The Nature of the American Male: A Study of Pedestalism," Thurber deliciously parodies the sound of the detached research sociologist, complete with case histories, resulting in essay as farce.*

The Nature of the American Male: A Study of Pedestalism

(1929)

In no other civilized nation are the biological aspects of love so distorted and transcended by emphasis upon its sacredness as they are in the United States of America. In China it's all biology. In France it's a mixture of biology and humor. In America it's half, or two-thirds, *psyche*. The Frenchman's idea, by and large, is to get the woman interested in him as a male. The American idea is to point out, first of all, the great and beautiful part which the stars, and the infinite generally, play in Man's relationship to women. The French, Dutch, Brazilians, Danes, etc., can proceed in their amours on a basis entirely divorced from the psyche. The

Chinese give it no thought at all, and never have given it any thought. The American would be lost without the *psyche,* lost and a little scared.

As a result of all this there is more confusion about love in America than in all the other countries put together. As soon as one gets the psychical mixed up with the physical—a thing which is likely to happen quite easily in a composing-room, but which should not happen anywhere else at all—one is almost certain to get appetite mixed up with worship. This is a whole lot like trying to play golf with a basketball, and is bound to lead to maladjustments.

The phenomenon of the American male's worship of the female, which is not so pronounced now as it was, but is still pretty pronounced, is of fairly recent origin. It developed, in fact, or reached its apex, anyway, in the early years of the present century. There was nothing like it in the preceding century. Throughout the nineteenth century the American man's amatory instincts had been essentially economic. Marriage was basically a patriotic concern, the idea being to have children for the sake of the commonwealth. This was bad enough, but nevertheless it is far less dangerous to get the commonwealth mixed up with love than to get the infinite mixed up with love.

There was not a single case of nervous breakdown, or neurosis, arising from amatory troubles, in the whole cycle from 1800 to 1900, barring a slight flare-up just before the Mexican and Civil wars. This was because love and marriage and children stood for progress, and progress is—or was—a calm, routine business. "Mrs. Hopkins," a man would say to the lady of his choice (she was a widow in this case)—"Mrs. Hopkins, I am thinking, now that George has been dead a year, you and I should get married and have offspring. They are about to build the Union Pacific, you know, and they will need men." Because parents can't always have men-children when they want them, this led to almost as many women as men working on the Union Pacific, which in turn led to the greater stature of women in the present Northwest than in any other part of the nation. But that is somewhat beside the point. The point is that men and women, husbands and wives, suitors and sweethearts, in the last century lived without much sentiment and without any psycho-physical confusion at all. They missed a certain amount of fun, but they avoided an even greater amount of pother. They did not worry each other with emotional didoes. There was no hint of Pleasure-Principle. Everything was empiric, almost somatic.

This direct evasion of the Love Urge on the part of Americans of the last century was the nuclear complex of the psycho-neurosis as we know it today, and the basis for that remarkable reaction against patriotic sex which was to follow so soon after the Spanish-American war.

At the turn of the century, the nation was on a sound economic basis and men had the opportunity to direct their attention away from the mechanics of life to the pleasures of living. No race can leap lightly, however, from an economic value to an emotional value. There must be a long period of *Übertragung*, long and tedious. Men were not aware of this, thirty years ago, because the science of psychology was not far advanced, but nature came to their aid by supplying a temporary substitute for an emotional sex life, to tide them over during the period of *Übertragung*. This substitute took the form of games. Baseball assumed a new and enormous importance, prize-fighting reached its heyday; horse-racing became an absorption, bicycling a craze.

Now women, naturally intraverts, could not easily identify themselves with baseball or prize-fighting (they admired Christy Mathewson and Terry McGovern, but that was about all); they took but slowly to horse-racing; and they giggled and acted the fool when they first tried to balance themselves on a bicycle. They drew away from men and from men's concerns, therefore—there was no more of the old Union Pacific camaraderie—and began to surround the mere fact of their biological destiny with a nimbus of ineffability. It got so that in speaking of birth and other natural phenomena, women seemed often to be discussing something else, such as the Sistine Madonna or the aurora borealis. They became mysterious to themselves and to men; they became suddenly, in their own eyes, as capable of miracle and as worthy of worship as Juno and her sisters. This could not go on. The conflict was ineluctable.

When men, wearied of games, turned to women with that urgency so notable in the American male for its simplicity and directness, they found them unprepared for acceptance and surrender. The process of adjustment in courtship and in marriage became more involved than it had ever been before in the history of the country, if not in the history of the world. The new outdoors type of American man, with all his strength and impetuosity, was not easily to be put off. But the female, equipped with a Defense far superior in polymorphous ingenuities to the rather simple Attack of the male, was prepared. She developed and perfected the Diversion Subterfuge. Its purpose was to put Man in his place. Its first manifestation was fudge-making.

The effectiveness of fudge-making in fending off the male and impressing him with the female's divine unapproachability can not be over-estimated. Neither can its potentiality as a nuclear complex. The flitting from table to stove, the constant necessity of stirring the boiling confection, the running out-of-doors to see if the candy had cooled and hardened, served to abort any objective demonstrations at all on the part of the male. He met this situation with a strong Masculine Protest. He began to bring a box of candy with him when he called, so that there would not be any more fudge-making. These years constituted the great Lowney's era in this country. Brought back to where she had started, face to face with the male's simple desire to sit down and hold her, the female, still intent upon avoidance of the tactual, retaliated by suggesting Indoor Pastimes—one of the greatest of all Delay Mechanisms. All manner of parlor games came into being at this period, notably charades, which called for the presence of other persons in the room (Numerical Protection). The American male's repugnance to charades, which is equaled, perhaps, by his repugnance to nothing else at all, goes back to those years. The Masculine Protest, in this case, was a counter-suggestion of some games of his own, in which there was a greater possibility of personal contact. His first suggestions were quite primitive, such as that it would be fun to count up to a hundred by kissing. The female's response was the famous one of Osculatory Justification. There must be, she decreed, more elaborate reasons for kissing than a mere exhibition of purposeless arithmetical virtuosity. Thus Post Office and Pillow were finally devised, as a sort of compromise. Neither was satisfactory to either sex. The situation became considerably strained and relationships finally trailed off into the even less satisfactory expedient of going for long rides on a tandem bicycle, which has had its serious effects upon the nature of the American man. He liked, for one thing, to do tricks on a bicycle. The contraption was new to him, and he wanted to do tricks on it. One trick that he liked especially was riding backwards. But there wasn't one woman in ten thousand, riding frontwards on the rear seat of a tandem wheel, who would permit her consort to ride backwards on the front seat. The result of all this was not adjustment, but irritability. Man became frustrated.

Frustration wrought its inevitable results. Men began to act jumpy and strange. They were getting nowhere at all with women. The female gradually assumed, in men's eyes, as she had in her own, the proportions of an unattainable deity, something too precious to be touched. The seed of Pedestalism was sown. The male, in a sort of divine discontent, began to draw apart by himself. This produced that separation of the physical and the psychic which causes the adult to remain in a state of suspended love, as if he were holding a bowl of goldfish and had nowhere to put it. This condition nowadays would lead directly to a neurosis, but in those days men were unable to develop a neurosis because they didn't know how. Men withdrew, therefore, quietly and morosely, to their "dens." It was the epoch of the den in America. Some marvelous ones sprang into being. Their contents were curiously significant. Deprived of possessing the female, the male worked off his Possessive Complex by collecting all manner of bibelots and bric-à-brac. The average den contained a paper-weight from Lookout Mountain, a jagged shell from Chickamaugua, a piece of wood from the *Maine*, pictures of baseball players with beards, pictures of bicycle champions, a yellowing full-page photograph of Admiral Schley, a letter-opener from Niagara Falls, a lithograph of Bob Fitzsimmons, a musket-badge from the G. A. R. parade, a red tumbler from the state fair, a photograph of Julia Marlowe, a monk's head match-holder, a Malay kriss, five pipe racks, a shark's tooth, a starfish, a snapshot of the owner's father's bowling team, colored pictures of Natural Bridge and Balanced Rock, a leather table runner with an Indian chief on it, and the spangled jacket of a masquerade costume, softly shedding its sequins.

The den was the beginning of male sublimation in this country, but the fruits of that sublimation were slow in ripening. At the start, in fact, they were in a state of absolute suspension. Man began to preoccupy himself with anything, no matter how trivial, which might help him to "forget," as the lay expression has it. He thought up childish diversions, at which one person can amuse himself, and to justify his absorption in these futile pastimes he exaggerated their importance, as we shall see. These diversions included the diabolo, the jig-saw puzzle, linked nails and linked keys, which men took apart and put back together again, and most important of all, pigs-in-clover.

During this period almost no achievements of value, in art, science, or engineering, were forthcoming in the nation. Art, indeed, consisted chiefly of putting strange devices on boxes with the aid of a wood-burning set. The commonest device was the swastika, whose curiously distorted conformation bears no discernible relationship to any known phallic symbolism. Those years were blank, idle, lost years. Outside affairs of all lands were neglected. Men retired to their dens and were not seen for days. The panic of 1907 was a direct result. It might be interesting to examine into a typical case history of the period.

CASE HISTORY

George Smith, aged 32, real estate operator. Unmarried, lived with mother. No precocious mother fixation. Had freed his libido without difficulty from familial objects, and was eager to marry. Had formed an attachment in 1899, at the age of 29, with a young virgin. Her Protective Reactions had been immediate and lasted over a period of three years, during which he had never even held her hand. Defense Devices: usually euchre (four-handed), or pedro. Definite and frequent fudge-making subterfuge. Post Office and Pillow, both with low degree of success.

Smith's separation between the physical and the psychic occurred in 1902, the direct stimuli presenting themselves on June 6th of that year, examination (by Dr. Matthiessen) showed. On that day Smith ran, frightened, from a barbershop in Indianapolis, where he lived. Inside the shop, on the floor, a middle-aged man named Herschel Queeper had thrown a fit. Queeper had been trying for two days to get three little balls, under a glass in a tiny round box, to roll into an opening made for them (common pigs-in-clover puzzle). But no sooner would he get the third one in than one, or perhaps both, of the others would roll out. Mrs. Queeper was beginning to wonder where he was.

Smith withdrew to his den and pondered and fiddled around and made Unconscious Drawings. He turned his attention from the object of his amorous affections to a consideration of the problems of pigs-in-clover. The usual Justification of Occupation occurred. It took the form of exaggerating the importance of finding out whether the puzzle could possibly be solved, and of working out a methodology of solving it more readily, if it could be solved at all. The case procured one of the little boxes and began to roll the balls toward the opening. At first he set about it quite calmly. There were no immediate signs of mental deterioration, either malignant or benign. But although the case got all the balls into the opening, thus proving that it could be done, he never got them all in at the same time. In the second month he threw a brief fit. This, today, would ordinarily prove the first step toward a complete physico-psychic breakdown, but in those days neuroses were staved off longer, owing to the general ignorance of psychology, and Smith not only calmly examined the effect of the fit upon himself, without calling in any scientists, but determined to go on and examine the effect of fits upon others. He decided, however, that it would be difficult to examine the effects of puzzle-fits upon men, because men brooked no examination when they were intent upon puzzles, and so he hit on the idea of having his dog, an animal named Dewey, play with the little round box until it threw a fit. But when he called in his dog he found, after several experiments, that the dog could not hold the box in either its right or left paw. Furthermore, the animal was profoundly incurious about the puzzle.

Undismayed, Smith decided that somewhere in Indianapolis there must be a dog adroit enough to handle the box and sagacious enough to grasp the idea behind it, and with a view to finding such an animal, he determined to get all the dogs in town, and all the pigs-in-clover puzzles in town, into one room and see what would happen. (Apotheosis Complex, with Plurality Fallacy.)

Smith was able, however, to round up only about 85 per cent of the dogs of the city, because there were many who were too busy to get away at the time. Even so, 85 per cent of the dogs in Indianapolis was more than had ever been got together in one room before. The case attempted to explain the problem to the dogs in short, one-syllable talks, but the bedlam was too loud and too prolonged for him to make himself heard. Fifty or more St. Bernards and a few dozen Chesapeake spaniels listened, half-heartedly, but the others made holiday. Furthermore, eighty-four bulldogs would not permit themselves to be muzzled, and this added to Smith's difficulties. Thus, on the fifth day of the singular experiment, Smith, hearing a remarkable hullaballoo belowstairs (he worked in the attic), descended to the parlor, where he discovered the bulldogs engaged in a sort of tug-of-war, using a body Brussels carpet as a rope. (The case's mother had several days before retreated to French Lick, in a rundown condition.)

Smith grasped the carpet firmly, with some idea of wresting it away from the dogs, whereupon all of them save three began to pull against him. The Exaggeration Complex under which the case was laboring gave him strength enough to meet with some small success in his first efforts to take the carpet away from the dogs. He pulled them as far as the bay window in the parlor, largely because they had not settled down seriously to winning. When they did, however, the total of three hundred and twenty-four solidly implanted feet and the virtually immeasurable tugging potentiality were too much for Smith. He was slowly pulled out into the hall, through the front door, and into the street. He stubbornly contested every inch of the way until a drug store, three blocks away, was reached. Here some one had the presence of mind to call out the fire department.

Dr. Matthiessen, who took the case at about this period in its development, attempted to reduce the Magnification of Objective, first by Analytic Reasoning, and then by cold applications. Neither was successful. Matthiessen could not divert the libido. Smith declined to resume his interest in the feminine object of his affections, and insisted that his experiment with puzzles was a glorious project for the benefit of mankind.

It was sheer accident that saved the patient—not Dr. Matthiessen. Smith finally refused Dr. Matthiessen admittance to his house, nor would he go to the doctor's office, claiming that he did not believe in psychology, but one day he dropped one of the little pigs-in-clover puzzles and broke the glass in it. He then found that he did not have to roll the balls into the openings, *but could push them in with his finger.* He got a hammer and broke the glass in all the thousands of puzzles he had brought to his home for the dogs, and solved every one of the puzzles by pushing, not rolling. This instantly released him from his complex by the Gordian Knot principle of complex release. He thus gained the necessary confidence and sense of power to feel worthy of the woman with whom he was in love, and he finally married her. The marriage was of average success.

Marriages, however, were frequently delayed much longer than in the case of George Smith, and it was not, indeed, until 1909 that the usual norm was restored. Meanwhile, in between the time of the first general separation of the physical and the psychic in this country, and the final culmination in marriages, a period of sublimation set in. This followed directly on the heels of the remarkable and lamentable era of preoccupation with trivial diversions and was characterized by an extravert interest in truly important projects and activities. The airplane was brought to a high stage of development, the telephone transmitter was perfected, tungsten replaced carbon as a filament for incandescent lamps, better books were written, art progressed, there was a cultural advance generally and the birth of a new Aesthetic, and people began to get at the real facts in the Thaw case. Nevertheless, Pedestalism has left its serious effects. It is doubtful if they will fully wear off for another fifty or seventy-five years.

ALBERT EINSTEIN

Albert Einstein (1879–1955), whose theories of relativity led to his renown as the smartest man alive, also wrote articulate essays on morality and politics. Some of his topics included the question of disarmament, the relationship between religion and science, and "Why Socialism?" A refugee from Nazi Germany, he was a passionate defender of democracy and social justice. "The World as I See It" is surprisingly personal, giving us a window into the way the great physicist viewed himself.

The World as I See It

(1931)

How strange is the lot of us mortals! Each of us is here for a brief sojourn; for what purpose he knows not, though he sometimes thinks he senses it. But without deeper reflection one knows from daily life that one exists for other people—first of all for those upon whose smiles and well-being our own happiness is wholly dependent, and then for the many, unknown to us, to whose destinies we are bound by the ties of sympathy. A hundred times every day I remind myself that my inner and outer life are based on the labors of other men, living and dead, and that I must exert myself in order to give in the same measure as I have received and am still receiving. I am strongly drawn to a frugal life and am often oppressively aware that I am engrossing an undue amount of the labor of my fellow-men. I regard class distinctions as unjustified and, in the last resort, based on force. I also believe that a simple and unassuming life is good for everybody, physically and mentally.

I do not at all believe in human freedom in the philosophical sense. Everybody acts not only under external compulsion but also in accordance with inner necessity. Schopenhauer's saying, "A man can do what he wants, but not want what he wants," has been a very real inspiration to me since my youth; it has been a continual consolation in the face of life's hardships, my own and others', and an unfailing well-spring of tolerance. This realization mercifully mitigates the easily paralyzing sense of responsibility and prevents us from taking ourselves and other people all too seriously; it is conducive to a view of life which, in particular, gives humor its due.

To inquire after the meaning or object of one's own existence or that of all creatures has always seemed to me absurd from an objective point of view. And yet everybody has certain ideals which determine the direction of his endeavors and his judgments. In this sense I have never looked upon ease and happiness as ends in themselves—this ethical basis I call the ideal of a pigsty. The ideals which have lighted my way, and time after time have given me new courage to face life cheerfully, have been Kindness, Beauty, and Truth. Without the sense of kinship with men of like mind, without the occupation with the objective world, the eternally unattainable in the field of art and scientific endeavors, life would have seemed to me empty. The trite objects of human efforts—possessions, outward success, luxury—have always seemed to me contemptible.

My passionate sense of social justice and social responsibility has always contrasted oddly with my pronounced lack of need for direct contact with other human beings and human communities. I am truly a "lone traveler" and have never belonged to my country, my home, my friends, or even my immediate family, with my whole heart; in the face of all these ties, I have never lost a sense of distance and a need for solitude—feelings which increase with the years. One becomes sharply aware, but without regret, of the limits of mutual understanding and consonance with other people. No doubt, such a person loses some of his innocence and unconcern; on the other hand, he is largely independent of the opinions, habits, and judgments of his fellows and avoids the temptation to build his inner equilibrium upon such insecure foundations.

My political ideal is democracy. Let every man be respected as an individual and no man idolized. It is an irony of fate that I myself have been the recipient of excessive admiration and reverence from my fellow-beings, through no fault, and no merit, of my own. The cause of this may well be the desire, unattainable for many, to understand the few ideas to which I have with my feeble powers attained through ceaseless struggle. I am quite aware that it is necessary for the achievement of the objective of an organization that one man should do the thinking and directing and generally bear the responsibility. But the led must not be coerced, they must be able to choose their leader. An autocratic system of coercion, in my opinion, soon degenerates. For force always attracts men of low morality, and I believe it to be an invariable rule that tyrants of genius are succeeded by scoundrels. For this reason I have always been passionately opposed to systems such as we see in Italy and Russia today. The thing that has brought discredit upon the form of democracy as it exists in Europe today is not to be laid to the door of the democratic principle as such, but to the lack of stability of governments and to the impersonal character of the electoral system. I believe that in this respect the United States of America have found the right way. They have a President who is elected for a sufficiently long period and has sufficient powers really to exercise his responsibility. What I value, on the other hand, in the German political system is the more extensive provision that it makes for the individual in case of illness or need. The really valuable thing in the pageant of human life seems to me not the political state, but the creative, sentient individual, the personality; it alone creates the noble and the sublime, while the herd as such remains dull in thought and dull in feeling.

This topic brings me to that worst outcrop of herd life, the military system, which I abhor. That a man can take pleasure in marching in fours to the strains of a band is enough to make me despise him. He has only been given his big brain by mistake; unprotected spinal marrow was all he needed. This plague-spot of civilization ought to be abolished with all possible speed. Heroism on command, senseless violence, and all the loathsome nonsense that goes by the name of patriotism—how passionately I hate them! How vile and despicable seems war to me! I would rather be hacked in pieces than take part in such an abominable business. My opinion of the human race is high enough that I believe this bogey would have disappeared long ago, had the sound sense of the peoples not been systematically corrupted by commercial and political interests acting through the schools and the Press.

The most beautiful experience we can have is the mysterious. It is the fundamental emotion which stands at the cradle of true art and true science. Whoever does not know it and can no longer wonder, no longer marvel, is as good as dead, and his eyes are dimmed. It was the experience of mystery—even if mixed with fear—that engendered religion. A knowledge of the existence of something we cannot penetrate, our perceptions of the profoundest reason and the most radiant beauty, which only in their most primitive forms are accessible to our minds—it is this knowledge and this emotion that constitute true religiosity; in this sense, and in this alone, I am a deeply religious man. I cannot conceive of a God who rewards and punishes his creatures, or has a will of the kind that we experience in ourselves. Neither can I nor would I want to conceive of an individual that survives his physical death; let feeble souls, from fear or absurd egoism, cherish such thoughts. I am satisfied with the mystery of the eternity of life and with the awareness and a glimpse of the marvelous structure of the existing world, together with the devoted striving to comprehend a portion, be it ever so tiny, of the Reason that manifests itself in nature.

KENNETH BURKE

Kenneth Burke (1897–1993) was a major literary critic and thinker for most of the twentieth century. His writings went far beyond literature, encompassing aesthetics, music, and the social sciences, synthesizing everything that interested him via an integrated theory involving the rhetoric of symbolic action. In his first, heady essay collection, the 1931 Counter-Statement, *he wrote with skeptical wit about "The Status of Art," dismantling many of the field's presumptions, standards, and judgmental certainties, and concluding, in true essayist fashion, "We advocate nothing, then, but a return to inconclusiveness."*

The Status of Art

(1931)

In the nineteenth century, when much was brought into question, many things previously called good had to be defended—poetry among them. Wherefore the slogan of *Art for Art's Sake* which, though it was often pronounced with bravado, clearly had about it the element of a "justification." With the development of technology, "usefulness" was coming into prominence as a test of values, so that art's slogan was necessarily phrased to take the criterion of usefulness into account. The strategy of the artist is understandable enough. Against the accusation that art was "useless" he pitted the challenge that art was important to those to whom art was important. Nevertheless, his position could readily take on the appearance of a "last stand."

The original doctrines of art's "uselessness" were not offered as attacks upon art. Kant, in proposing "purposiveness without purpose" *(Zweck-mässigkeit ohne Zweck)* as a formula for the aesthetic, had no intention of providing a "refutation" of art. His formula did, however, mark the emergence of the "use" criterion which was subsequently to place all purely intellectual pursuits upon a defensive basis. His proposition could be readily perverted: if the aesthetic had no *purpose* outside itself, the corollary seemed to be that the aesthetic had no *result* outside itself. Logically there was no cogency in such an argument, but psychologically there was a great deal. And the damage was perhaps increased through attempts to justify art by the postulating of a special "art instinct" or "aesthetic sense."

On the face of it, this was a good move. For at a time when instincts were gaining considerably in repute, and no complicated human mind could arouse us to admiration so promptly as the routine acts of an insect, what could be more salubrious for the reputation of art than the contention that art satisfies an "instinctive need"? The trouble arose from the fact that the "art instinct" was associated with the "play instinct," thus becoming little more than an adult survival from childhood. The apologists, still in the Kantian scheme, associated art with play because both seemed, from the standpoint of utility, purposeless. But in an age when "work" was becoming one of society's basic catchwords, art could not very well be associated with play without some loss of prestige.

Perhaps Flaubert's constant talk of toil was prompted in part by a grudging awareness of the new criterion. At least, his complaints serve to make this form of "play" a colossal task. Remy de Gourmont saw the issue clearly enough to use a complete reversal of standards in his defense of art, ridiculing the "serious" as a democratic preference, and insisting that the things of essential human value were gratuitous, hardly more than unforeseen mutations, qualities obtained *in spite* of society, and worthy of cultivation even though they might be found, not merely useless, but positively subversive to social ends. The position was vigorously taken—and doubtless De Gourmont's able championship of the symbolists had much to do with the advancing of their experiments. De Gourmont was bright; he was very handy with ideas; he could carry the discussion aggressively into the territory of the enemy. He made one think of literature as a risk, a kind of outlawry, with the notable exception that the outlaws were in reality the true preservers of the good. Art would eventually be driven into the catacombs, he said, thus associating the artist with both rebellion and virtue at once. It was not until shortly before the war, however, that De Gourmont became an "authority"—and his influence collapsed soon afterwards as he was prevented by death from bolstering it up with new books. For many of the critical and philosophical matters he treated had since been handled in other terms and with more thoroughness by other men—and his fiction, necessarily restricted by his cloistered existence, could not bear the diffusion of his great productivity and his attempted breadth. Furthermore, ironic detachment is a difficult position to uphold when men are being copiously slaughtered—and De Gourmont's enlistment in the cause of the Allies implied the renunciation of his earlier doctrines. Disciples of Art for Art's Sake might advocate art as a refuge, a solace for the grimness about them, but the spirit of social mockery could no longer fit the scene. One can mock death, but one cannot mock men in danger of death. In the presence of so much disaster, there was no incentive to call art disastrous.

But if De Gourmont had seen the issues clearly enough to realize that one might best defend art by calling art "immoral," most critics attempted the compromise of defending art as "amoral" or "unmoral." Their invented adjective probably did wonders to assist the introduction of new social values and to procure, for many an artist's ethical innovations, asylum from the law. The word was needed, as the artist's position was a particularly difficult one. The scientists of the nineteenth century, despite the thoroughness of their attacks upon traditional values, could be very circumspect in their methods. Though the tenets of anthropology, for instance, might imply the discrediting of orthodox religion, one could discuss them adequately without handling the matter in this light at all. Art, on the other hand, must be first of all "forceful." The artist, in dealing with ethical revaluations (as he naturally would, since the characteristics of the century would be as fully represented in him as in a scientist or an inventor) had to make those conflicts explicit which the scientist could leave implicit. He got his effects by throwing into relief those very issues which the scientist could treat by circumlocution, implication, and the mystical protection of a technical vocabulary. Thus, whereas science for the most part was permitted to progress in peace, the artistic equivalents of this science produced a succession of scandals.

An incident in Flaubert's trial indicates the nature of the artist's predicament. The prosecuting attorney selected among others a passage from *Madame Bovary* which described Emma undressing in the presence of her lover. The rhythm of this passage very obviously contributed to the effect, since it suggested her impatience as she struggled with her garments, and her final impetuosity as she rushed across the room to embrace him. The prosecuting attorney read this passage with feeling—and the better he read it, the worse the case for Flaubert. The defense lawyer, however, sought to remove the impression by reading the same passage himself and interpolating remarks of his own which ruined the passage as literature. The more ineffective he made it, the more pardonable Flaubert became!

The term "unmoral" was a valuable discovery for handling the situation. By this subterfuge (surely no one thought of it as such) the artist could plead immunity from judgment by any code of practical ethics. In keeping with the doctrine of the "unmorality" of art, we must distinguish between virtuous conduct and virtuous sentences, we must not restrict art as we should restrict its equivalent in actual life, we must not limit the laws of the "beautiful" by the laws of social behavior. But "unmorality" was in the end a much greater danger to the prestige of art than "immorality" could ever have been, since it implied once again the ineffectiveness of art.

As a matter of fact, art exerted a tremendous influence upon the changing morals and customs of the Western world, but its contribution to the "transvaluation of values" was minimized because of this apologetic adjective. Art was, as De Gourmont said, "immoral." It was, that is, using its expressiveness as a means of making people seek what they customarily fled and flee what they customarily sought. And there is no greater evidence of art's "immorality" than the bourgeois-Bohemian conflict which characterized the century. The issue was indeterminate and fluctuant, but in the main the disciples of Art for Art's Sake were Bohemians, prepared on many occasions to outrage the bourgeois.

In some respects they were struggling to alter the moral code in keeping with the changes brought about by science and technology (a tendency which, in its purely artistic manifestations, is to be seen in the extending of the "beautiful" into the realm of the previously repugnant). In this they were really working for the bourgeois interests, though the bourgeois public was prompt to resist them. In other respects, however, they were not *devanciers* at all but were, like such men as T. S. Eliot today, the preservers of older standards which the bourgeois themselves were attempting to discredit. Baudelaire was attacked as a destroyer of the earlier moral code, but as a matter of fact he was opposing the new social code. Baudelaire is a "sinner" and what is more alien to the new social code than the concept of sin? Baudelaire courts poverty, lamentation, sullenness, a discipline of internal strife; his concerns are the concerns of an early Christian anchorite voluntarily placing himself in jeopardy—and what could be more "conservative" than this, what more unlike the young Californian with his benign circle of culture, progress, and prosperity, or his football conception of discipline? In most instances the division was not so intense, the artists being the defenders simply of older humanistic doctrines overlooked in the rising intensity of economic strife. In general they tended towards Pater's belief that ethics should be a subdivision of aesthetics. The artists were innovators and conservators at once, advocating many requisite alterations of morality while attempting to preserve many cultural values of the past which seemed equally requisite. Thus can such an innovator as Eliot be found saying: "We fight rather to keep something alive than in the expectation that anything will triumph."

In general, therefore, a division between artist and bourgeois was emphasized. And here again the alignment was greatly to the detriment of art, as many trivial artists, and even some artists of rank, chose to exploit this division by making their opposition more picturesque than ominous. Hence arose the "aesthete" whose adherence to the doctrine of Art for Art's Sake served to associate the doctrine with many effete mannerisms. Wilde is perhaps the purest symbol of the type—and Wilde is as responsible as anyone for the weakening of the bourgeois-Bohemian conflict. The next generation of authors married at twenty, courted the strictest conventionality of dress and manners, and tended to consider a few years in business as the new educational equivalent of the European tour.

The bourgeois-Bohemian conflict had another unfavorable feature in its alliance with the rise of symbolism. Symbolism contained one important alteration in method. In emphasizing the emotional connection of ideas and images, it tended to suppress their commoner experimental or "logical" connections. Instead of saying that something was like something else, the symbolist progressed from the one thing to the other by ellipsis. He would not tell us that a toothache is a raging storm—rather, he might advance directly from the mention of a diseased tooth to the account of a foundering ship. Objects are thus linked by their less obvious connectives. This is, of course, an over-simplification of symbolist methods, but it is roughly indicative. Whether it is correct or not, however, the fact remains that while the artist was attempting new departures in methodology, he was not matching his imaginative experiments with their equivalents in critical theory. To an extent he was probably uncertain as to the exact critical principles underlying the new tendencies. And taking his cue from the earlier moral conflict between bourgeois and Bohemian, he now widened the conflict to include questions of method. Far from pleading with his public, the artist heightened his antagonism: hence his readiness to *épater le bourgeois*. Art now took on a distinctly obscurantist trait, not because it was any more "obscure" than previous art (nothing is more obscure than an after-dinner speaker's distinctions between optimism and over-optimism, yet no one is troubled by them) but because the public had not been schooled as to just wherein the clarity of such art was to be sought. The vagueness of the issue made a good deal of slovenly work possible—and even men in sympathy with the movement had to confess themselves "defeated" by many of its proponents.

Closely allied with the "mystification" of the new movement, came the *tour d'ivoire* or "pure" art movement. The most pretentious writing, that is, was done by men whose methods and preoccupations seemed certain to limit their reading public considerably. They were "experts," and nothing was more abhorrent to a civilization of specialists than artists who likewise were specialists. (It seems that, beginning with the pre-historic bard, the artist had always been a specialist, but people never resented the fact until, by becoming specialists themselves, they became less fit to follow him.) In any event, the rarity and electness of "pure" art seemed—in an age of propaganda—negative, retiring, and powerless. What was the value of neglected excellence, when the world was glutted with crude fiction? Had not the spread of literacy through compulsory education made readers of people who had no genuine interest in literature? Would not this group henceforth form the majority of the reading public? And would not good books pale into insignificance, not because they had fewer readers than in the past (they had more) but because an overwhelming army of bad readers had been recruited? The Art for Art's Sake slogan now began to apply more specifically to the art of the minority, those writers for whom, so far as the vast public was concerned, the publication of a new work was like putting a bottle out to sea.

A masterpiece, privately printed in a limited edition of two hundred copies, seemed to furnish some cause for derision. Yet *The Little Review* had a much larger circulation than the magazine published by Goethe and Schiller. And one must recall that most of the works fed to the public are purely derivative, and as such can constitute the bridge between the "rare" writer and the public at large. The same basic patterns of thought can be exemplified either in subtle ways or in a crude form for the consumption of millions. Through such derivative processes, for instance, the public of today is undergoing the influence of nineteenth century writers whom, for one reason or another, it would not at all care to read. It is coming to accept methods which, but a few years ago, were confined to the most "abstruse." In general the "rare" writers will serve as "sources," for only a man whose attitudes arise from the persistency of his character can be expected to work with them until they have acquired a forbidding distinction and to express them with such thoroughness and penetration as makes his work unacceptable to the majority. The vulgarizers, however, the epigons, the "steppers-down" will adapt this source material for wider reception. Indeed, when we consider how few masters of theology there were in the early Church, how small was their reading public, yet how great was their influence upon the course of history, we realize that a work can, by devious ways, profoundly affect people who have never laid eyes upon it. A single book, were it greatly to influence one man in a position of authority, could thus indirectly alter the course of a nation; and similarly the group that turns to "minority" art may be a "pivotal" group. They need not be "pivotal" in the sense that they enjoy particular social, political, or economic prestige—but purely in the sense that they are more articulate and enterprising in the assertion of their views and the communication of their attitudes. Nor must we, recalling Eliot's statement, assume that one cannot be an influence except by "succeeding." The rôle of opposition is by no means negligible in the shaping of society. The victory of one "principle" in history is usually not the vanquishing, but the partial incorporation, of another.

As for the concerns of a "neglected minority," it is hard to understand

how any cultural movement could begin otherwise than in a very restricted quarter, spreading by radiation from the few who are quickest
to sense new factors in their incipient stages. Astute politicians, it is true,
will tell us that a political movement must arise "from the grass roots." It
must, they say, spring up spontaneously in various parts of the country,
a party serving merely to consolidate it into a united front. But the artist exploits human potentialities in a different way than a politician. If
thirty million people are eager for a trip to the country, a book might gain
great popularity through enabling them to imagine that they were in the
country. Yet not one of them would have to know that their weariness
with city living was the cause of the book's appeal. The politician, on
the other hand, could not safely back a new bond issue for the suburban-
izing of his city until his constituents' preferences were clearly and vocally
established. A politician seeks to ally himself, actually or apparently, with
issues which to his mind the people consciously advocate. An artist can
appeal tremendously by the utilization of motives which both he and they
are unaware of. It is obvious that a situation must be widespread before a
method for handling it can find general reception. But it is the *situation*,
not the *method*, that rises "from the grass roots." Let the situation be
tinder, and the method may "catch like wildfire"; but the spark is not integral to the situation, it must be added. The "times were ripe" for a Byron;
but Byronism radiated from an individual. A slogan is not widely effective
because it rises spontaneously in every part of the country (it is usually
one man's invention); a slogan is widely effective because it is appropriate to a widespread situation. And thus a work of art may at times be
confined to a minority, not because of either its virtues or its defects,
but purely because the particular situation with which it is dealing is not
generally felt. Indeed, by the time the situation has become generally felt,
this particular work of art may still be inappropriate for another reason:
it may happen to have dealt with the situation in conventions which have
since altered. And thus it will serve, not in itself, but in the suggestions it
gave to a writer of the day who "translates" them into his contemporary
conventions.

II

Perhaps none of the issues so far discussed had so adverse an effect upon
the status of art as certain "causation" theories which seemed to place
art as a kind of by-product, the result of more vital and important forces.
Doctrines of psychology, economics, and world history have all been used
with nearly evangelical zeal to undermine the sanctions of the "impractical." Thus, the psychoanalyst's analogies between art and dream-life,
while not formulated as an attack upon art, readily came to serve as one.

For how could we transfer to art the dream relationship between frustration and wish-fulfillment without seeming to indicate a fundamental ineffectualness on the part of the artist? The doctrine could be manipulated to reveal the artist purely as a "thwarted" individual who was compensating for his inabilities by dreaming of triumphs.

In noting the similarity between art and dream-life, the psychoanalytic critics failed to note the important dissimilarity, an oversight somewhat justified by the fact that the theorists of individualism in art had themselves made the same omission. They did not consider that, whereas a dream is wholly subjective, all competent art is a means of communication, however vague the artist's conception of his audience may be. Thus, the analogies summarily dismissed the important qualification that daydreaming generally makes exceptionally bad art. The many aspects of analysis, discovery, observation, diction, revision, tactics in presentation, which are anything but "day-dreaming," were wholly ignored. And in their eagerness to point out the artist's maladjustments, the psychoanalytic critics did not take into account the elements of strength often implicated in such maladjustments. Maladjustments were too readily assumed to be evidences of weakness. But there is much in Nietzsche, for instance, to indicate that his maladjustments arose from his searching perception of issues which were wholly unnoted by his more "fit" contemporaries. Is it a sign of "weakness" to see with such intensity that one can disclose "conflicts" and encounter "defeats" where hackmen find nothing?

Again, few considered the fact that, by psychoanalytic tenets, practical activities as well as imaginative ones can constitute "compensations" for frustrated conditions. To every poet who became a poet after failure in business, there are at least a hundred business men who became business men after failure in poetry. And psychoanalysis had given many instances of deflection and frustration in practical life. Nothing was more prevalent in its case histories than examples of intense practical activities stimulated by the pressure of an unsuccessful love affair or some unavowed desire. A cruel impulse can be "sublimated" into a philanthropic act as well as into a philanthropic poem. Napoleons themselves were credited with such "inferiority complexes" as were supposed to motivate the artist.*

And if the artist turns to art rather than to business or baseball, his

---

* Until psychoanalysis defines a social norm, we are logically at liberty to interpret any activity (either contemplative or practical) as an "avoidance" of some other contemplative or practical activity. A man chopping down trees can be said to avenge himself against the entanglements of an emotion by this vicarious cutting of Gordian knots; or we can look upon Rimbaud's flight into Africa as a practical means of avoiding the aesthetic dilemma into which he had placed himself. Let us further note the "heads I win, tails you lose" mechanism which the psychoanalysts have at their disposal. Having defined the nature of a man's psychosis, they can fit any act into the scheme. For if the act follows the same pattern as the psychosis, they can explain it as consistent—but if it does not follow this pattern, they can account for it as "sublimated" or "compensatory." With

choice need not have anything negative about it. Eliminate the medical terminology and you eliminate the disease. The great amount of annoyance which an artist generally undergoes to establish himself in his craft would indicate a very positive preference for this craft. Far from being "in retreat," he must master ways of exerting influence upon the minds and emotions of others. Could anything be less like regression, though one were to write on a desert island? True, one cannot devote himself greatly to a single pursuit without endangering his competence in others, though the predicament applies as much to engineering or farming as to art. An artist such as Beethoven, whose musical attainments seemed to require great specialization and concentration, would necessarily become a bungler in other aspects of social intercourse. The intensity of his character gave him greater turmoil than most men must learn to subdue by the compromises and tactics of social advantage, while the many hours devoted to music left him much less opportunity than most men require to perfect themselves in social matters. Thus his specialization in music could lead to his inadequacy in other things, and his inadequacy in other things could give him further incentive to specialize in that pursuit wherein he was a master—the interactions are too confusing for anyone to dare call the inadequacies exclusively a "cause" and the art exclusively an "effect." A man may become aesthetically entangled because of some sexual difficulty—but he may as truly become sexually entangled because of some aesthetic difficulty; and many a prowler would gladly sacrifice his night if he could but write a good paragraph by doing so.

Art must have a subject, and a spontaneous subject. And what could be a more spontaneous subject for the artist than the matter of his maladjustments? Is not every man concerned primarily with his "problems"? Is the case different with the scientist, the explorer, the business man? Is not genius, in whatever channel it appears, distinguished by the persistence of its preoccupations—and are not man's preoccupations essentially a matter of volition, and hence of frustration? And that a man, let us say incestuously troubled, should express this trouble in his art, is no more an indication of weakness than that a man raised in Australia should paint Australian landscapes.

And as for the "escape" of art, there is much to indicate that the artist is, of all men, equipped to confront an issue. The very conventions of art often provide him with a method for freely admitting experiences and situations which the practical man must conceal. And psychologists of other schools have noted that whereas intensity of fear or pain will generally produce in most people a kind of "stereotypy," a mental and physical numbing which leaves the individual almost without memory

---

such *vasticinium post eventum* (such explanation by epicycles) at their command, there is no reason why they should ever be at a loss for explanations in keeping with their tenets.

of the painful or terrifying event, great artists have shown capacity to keep themselves receptive at precisely such moments. They may bear the full brunt of an experience without psychological evasions, because their attitude enables them to feel partially as opportunity what others must feel solely as a menace. This ability does not, I believe, derive from exceptional strength; it probably arises purely from the "professional interest" the artist may take in his difficulties; and I cite the distinction, not as evidence of unusual power on the artist's part, but simply as evidence that the need of "escape" by subterfuge is more natural to the man whose problems are exclusively practical than to the man whose outlook upon his difficulties is partially aesthetic.*

Ironically enough, the point on which the psychoanalytic critics paid the highest tribute to art turned out to be perhaps the strongest attack of all. I refer to the great emphasis upon intensity of experience which such criticism associated with the work of art. There is no reason why the enjoyment of a work of art should not be intense, to be sure; the danger arose from the fact that actual and imaginative experiences were not distinguished. Now, once one is taught to seek in art such experiences as one gets in life itself, it is a foregone conclusion that one must discover how trivial are artistic experiences as compared with "real living." A mere headache is more "authentic" than a great tragedy; the most dismal love affair is more worth experiencing in actual life than the noblest one in a poem. When the appeal of art as method is eliminated and the appeal of art as experience is stressed, art seems futile indeed. Experience is less the aim of art than the subject of art; art is not experience, but something added to experience. But by making art and experience synonymous, a critic provides an unanswerable reason why a man of spirit should renounce art forever.

The economic attack upon art arose in an equally roundabout and unintended manner. It involved essentially a theory of meaning, though it might have become more defensible dialectically had it been developed with a clearer understanding of its basis. Noting that certain great works of the past were "imperiled" by subsequent changes of history, critics influenced by the tenets of evolutionism held that to appreciate a work

---

* Under extremely distasteful conditions one builds a wall of anaesthesia and forgetfulness, contrives mental ways of leaving the pain unregistered. Yet a man may, in undergoing stress, meet it without safeguards of this sort. He may accept its full impact, may let it pour down upon him, as though he were putting his face up into a thundershower. If he survives, the period of stress is not a period of blankness, but a period of great intricacy and subtlety which lives on in the memory and can be drawn upon. The artist's technique of articulation then enables him to admit what other men, by emotional subterfuges, deny.

we must understand the environmental conditions out of which it arose. The Greek tragedies are now unsatisfactory to most of us, the "genetic" critic argued, because we are too unfamiliar with the structure of Greek society implicated in these tragedies. To "restore" the full value of these tragedies, we must steep ourselves in their social context.

The point is irrefutable. Insofar as a social context changes, the work of art erected upon it is likely to change in evaluation (though the genetic critic does not tell us whether we should also apply his method to an artist whose reputation has risen with the years—whether we should, by placing Melville in his times, "restore" to him the inferior position he held among his contemporaries). If Swift, in *Gulliver's Travels,* makes a sly gibe at some current political intrigue now forgotten, the modern reader must have the relevant environmental facts of this intrigue restored for him by editorial annotation before he can appreciate the full "meaning" of Swift's sentence. It may also have "meaning" as fancy, which is its meaning for a child, or for a reader lacking the editorial annotation, or for one of Swift's contemporaries unaware of the political intrigue Swift had in mind; but for its full meaning as Swift meant it, we must perceive its equivocal nature. An element of Swift's social context was here involved in his meaning, the words themselves not being an adequate statement of the situation. Similarly a knowledge of Plato's archetypes may be useful in reading of Wordsworth's clouds of glory; the *Divine Comedy* uses aspects of scholastic thinking which are no longer current and the recovery of which is essential; when we read, "Speak to it, Horatio, you are a scholar," we must know, or be able to infer, that erudition was once supposed to enable its possessor to talk with ghosts.

In some cases the matter to be recovered is so remote, is in a channel of thinking or feeling so alien to our own, that even a savant's "restoration" of the environmental context is not adequate. This is always true in some degree—though historical relativists have tended to make too much of it. For in the last analysis, any reader surrounds each word and each act in a work of art with a *unique* set of his own previous experiences (and therefore a unique set of imponderable emotional reactions), communication existing in the "margin of overlap" between the writer's experience and the reader's. And while it is dialectically true that two people of totally different experiences must totally fail to communicate, it is also true that there are no two such people, the "margin of overlap" always being considerable (due, if to nothing else, to the fact that man's biologic functions are uniform). Absolute communication between ages is impossible in the same way that absolute communication between contemporaries is impossible. And conversely, as we communicate approximately though "imprisoned within the walls of our personality," so we communicate approximately though imprisoned within the walls of our age.

The historical approach may have affected the status of art slightly by questioning art's "permanence" (a roadbed was not expected to meet the same rigorous requirement). But the "practicality" shibboleth, as introduced by the economic critic, converted this genetic theory of social contexts into a causation theory, with economic forces as prime movers and art as a mere "result." If art arises out of a social context, the economic critic argued, art is "caused" by the social context. And thence, by simplifying the concept of social context to exclude all but political and economic factors, he could interpret art as the mere reflection of contemporary political and economic issues.

To begin with, the theories of meaning that underlie the historical or environmental approach could not properly be converted into a system of causation. If I say that "white" has certain connotations because snow is white, I certainly am not saying that a work of art using these connotations is "caused" by snow. I am simply saying that the meaning of white to an Eskimo will differ from its meaning to a mid-African, and that a work of art constructed about the mid-African's connotations of "white" may be inappropriate to a reader who approaches it with the "white" experiences of an Eskimo. Or if people hold a certain doctrine, a work of art can exploit their belief to make them, let us say, feel terror; if they hold the opposite doctrine, the work of art can similarly exploit this opposite belief to make them feel terror. The work that arouses terror by exploiting the one belief will be imperiled at the hands of any reader who holds to the opposite belief; but could we say that either work is "caused" by the belief which it exploits?

Reduced to its essentials, the encroachment of a causation doctrine here seems to be statable as follows: Changes in art occur concomitantly with changes in political and economic conditions; therefore the changes in art are caused by the changes in political and economic conditions. At times the process is removed one step further, the changes in art being attributed in turn to changes in economic conditions. Now, it is not very sound dialectic to assume that, because two things change concomitantly, one can be called exclusively a cause of the other. If mere concurrence can prove causation, why could not an opponent assume from the same facts that the changes in art and ideas caused the changes in economic conditions? We know, for example, that the feminist "aesthetic" served as preparation for the enfranchisement of women: here is an obvious example of an attitude's affecting a change in social structure.

In one sense, art or ideas do "reflect" a situation, since they are a way of dealing with a situation. When a man solves a problem, however, we should hardly say that his solution is "caused" by the problem to be solved. The problem may limit somewhat the *nature* of his solution, but the problem can remain unsolved forever unless he *adds* the solution. Similarly, the particular ways of feeling and seeing which the thinker or the artist develop to cope with a situation, the vocabulary they bring into prominence, the special kinds of intellectual and emotional adjustment which their works make possible by the discovery of appropriate symbols for encompassing the situation, the kinds of action they stimulate by their attitudes towards the situation, are not "caused" by the situation which they are designed to handle. The theory of economic causation seemed to rest upon the assumption that there is only one possible aesthetic response to a given situation, and that this situation is solely an economic one.

Our argument is not intended as a plea for free will. It may be true that, if we knew every single factor involved in a stimulus, we could infallibly predict the response. It may be true that, despite our "illusion of liberty" we are rigidly determined in both our thoughts and our actions. Even if we grant the validity of this principle, however, the doctrine of the economic determination of art need not be conceded. For by any principle of universal determinism, there would be no hierarchy of causes whereby economic manifestations could be called causally "prior" to aesthetic manifestations. Economic and aesthetic manifestations alike would be caused by the "nature of things." If determinism is extended to such cosmic proportions, art need have no complaint. For by the tenets of determinism as so extended, every factor of experience would be equally involved in the causal chain, being indeterminately cause and effect, the effect of one event and the cause of another. And in a scheme whereby we "all go down together," the appropriateness of art has long ago been established, as in the ethical teachings of the Roman Stoics. Drive the logic of economic causation to the point where economic determinism becomes cosmic determinism, and the detractors of art are necessarily silenced, for their own detractions become but the output of the universal mill, their preferences mere personal choices devoid of "absolute" sanction.

Yet recent years have witnessed an attempt to manipulate precisely this argument of cosmic determination in such a way that the pursuit of art can be discredited and the criterion of "use" once more put forward. I refer to Oswald Spengler's "morphology of history." While accepting the logical conclusion of cosmic determinism so far as the attempt at a hierarchy of causes is concerned, and thus placing economic and aesthetic manifestations on a par, he proposes nonetheless to draw forth an exhortation for the abandonment of art as ineffectual. The evidence by which he supports his thesis has been brought into question, but that need not concern us here, as we are examining primarily the dialectic of his proof. We are discussing the logical issue as to whether the thesis, even if established, would justify his exhortation to abandon art. The steps of his argument are worth following in detail, as his work is the most ambitious schematization of its sort, and its dilemma is typical of the dilemma confronting all such programs.

Over against the H. G. Wells concept of history as a straight line progressing from savagery to modernity, Spengler opposes the concept of numberless cultural systems, each of which has followed a cycle of its own, growing, flourishing, and decaying in a fixed order or "periodicity." These cultural cycles, by Spengler's doctrine, evolve in an irreversible sequence through "spring, summer, autumn, and winter" aspects, any "season" of one culture being comparable with the corresponding season of any other culture. These analogous stages of different cultural systems are called "contemporaneous"; and by aligning the stages of our own cultural cycle (that of Europe and European America, which Spengler dates from about 1000 A.D.) with the contemporaneous stages of other cultural cycles, Spengler claims to produce a series of co-ordinates for determining which of the cultural seasons is now upon us.

Homer, in the Greco-Roman cycle, would be contemporaneous with the northern sagas in our own, this era always being "rural and intuitive" and marked by the "birth of a myth in the grand style, expressing a new sense of divinity." Spring gradually metamorphoses into summer, a period of "ripening consciousness" and of the "earliest urban and critical stirrings"—the pre-Socratics of the sixth and fifth centuries being "contemporaneous" with Galileo, Bacon, and Descartes. In autumn the city assumes a leading position in the life of the culture. This is the age of "enlightenment" (Socrates and Rousseau) in which the traditional code is now subjected to a rigorous questioning, although it is still powerful as a religious and creative force. The mathematics characteristic of the culture is now definitely formulated, and the "great conclusive" metaphysical systems are constructed (Plato and Aristotle having their contemporaneous parallel in Goethe and Kant).

But each culture, while exemplifying the laws of growth and decay common to all cultures, is a self-contained unit, talking in a language addressed to itself alone. When it has passed, it leaves us its monuments and its scripts, but the experience which these works symbolized has vanished, so that subsequent cultures inherit a body of rigid symbols to which they are psychically alien—much the way one of Jung's typical extroverts would be alien to a typical introvert. In this sense, ancient Greek is as undecipherable a language as Etruscan, since there is no word in the Greek vocabulary which corresponds, in its cultural background, to the word which we select as its equivalent in any one of our modern languages. Consider, for instance, the difference in content between "man" as one of a race who stole the fire from heaven and "man" as a link in the evolutionary chain. It is not hard to imagine how a work of art arising out of the one attitude could be "alien" to a reader in whom the other attitude was ingrained.

Spengler lays great emphasis upon this cultural subjectivism, and even insists upon the subjective element in natural science. He characterizes the science of any given culture as the conversion of its religion into an irreligious field—such concepts as "force" and "energy," for instance, merely being an altered aspect of the omnipotent and omnipresent God conceived at an earlier stage in the same culture.

The growth of science is also the evidence of a radical change in a culture's evolution. At this stage, the intellectualistic, critical, and irreligious elements of the culture gradually rise to the ascendancy. The emotional certainty of the earlier epochs, when religious, metaphysical, and aesthetic systems were built up spontaneously, is now past. The culture becomes a civilization. "In the one period life *reveals* itself, the other has life as its *object*." In place of the city we have the metropolis, and the "ethical-practical tendencies of an irreligious and unmetaphysical cosmopolitanism." Winter, thereby, is upon us. Hellenistic-Roman Stoicism after 200—returning to our concept of the contemporaneous—is paralleled by ethical socialism after 1900. The theatricality of Pergamene art is matched by Liszt, Berlioz, and Wagner—and Hellenistic painting finds its equivalent in impressionism. The American skyscraper, instead of being looked upon as the evidence of a new "dawn," is interpreted by Spengler as the symptom of decay corresponding to the "architectural display in the cities of the Diadochi."

Spengler thus finds that the high point of our culture has been passed, while we go deeper into the closing period, the era of civilization. With intellectualistic elements predominant, we are no longer fitted for the production of great works of art, but for the technical exploits, for economic, commercial, political, and imperialistic activities. We are, like Rome, which was the civilization of the Greek culture, ordained to be superior as road-builders and inferior as artists. And by his doctrine of cultural subjectivism, even those great works of art which our culture in its more youthful and vigorous stages produced as the symbolization of Western-European experience will become alien as this experience itself, recedes before the rise of other cultures having other modes of experience to symbolize.

In conclusion, then: (*a*) Even the greatest works of art are couched, not in the language of "mankind," but in the language of a specific cultural tradition, and the loss of the tradition is like the loss of the dictionary; and (*b*) since art is inevitably inferior in an era of civilization, we are invited to abandon all hope of further artistic excellence in our cultural cycle.

Let us consider first Spengler's subjectivist argument. In discussing each cultural cycle, he finds some dominant trait which characterizes the entire mode of experience peculiar to the culture. Arabic culture, for instance, is "Magian," our own is "Faustian," and the Greco-Roman is "Apollonian." He then shows how these dominant traits manifest themselves in all the various aspects of a culture's "behavior." The Apollonian trait can be

expanded as a sense of the "pure present," a concrete "thisness and here-
ness," which is to be found equally in the repose of the Greek temple, the
"corporeality" of Greek mathematics, and the Greek indifference to time
(the Greeks had no system of chronological reckoning comparable to our
method of dating from the birth of Christ). The same attitude naturally
resulted in the development of sculpture into a major art. In contrast,
Faustian culture has a pronounced historic sense, a mathematics of function and time, an "aspiring" architecture; and it has developed music into
a major art. In painting, the "corporeal" mentality of the Greeks led to
the exclusion of sky-blue as a color, and the disinterest in perspective;
while the Faustian culture, with its feeling for distance, showed a marked
preference for this very blue, and developed perspective exhaustively.
Spengler considers this as evidence of totally different subjective states;
yet could it not, as well, be used to indicate a very fundamental kind
of similarity? If blue and perspective are employed by the Faustian for
the same reason that they are rejected by the Apollonian, does not this
argue a common basis of choice? It is to grant, categorically, that blue and
perspective symbolize for both cultures a sense of distance. A genuinely
subjective difference between cultures would be undetectable, for it would
involve a situation in which the symbols could be employed with directly
opposite content. Blue and perspective could then, for the Greek, mean
pure present; and we could have formed the Greek temple, rather than the
Gothic cathedral, as our symbol of aspiration. The aesthetic symbols of
an alien culture could give us no clue as to the mode of experience behind
them.

Furthermore, why should Spengler stop at cultural subjectivism? Why
not accept epochal subjectivism as well? If a difference in the traits of
a culture involves a difference in the content of its expressionistic symbols, does not his division of a culture into seasons indicate that each
season symbolizes a mode of experience peculiar to itself? If a culture
speaks a language of its own, then each season has its own dialect of that
language. What "vested interests" would this savant save who would so
willingly sacrifice an entire culture?

The fact is that epochal subjectivism would interfere with his two
major conclusions: cultural subjectivism and aesthetic defeatism. Spengler's division into spring, summer, autumn, and winter is at bottom the
formulation of four subjective types, four typical modes of experience
which occur in each cultural cycle. Thus, subjectivity is seen to produce
its alliances as well as its estrangements. And contemporeaneous epochs
of different cultural cycles might even be considered to have more in
common than different epochs of the same culture—our "irreligious and
cosmopolitan" winter, for instance, being nearer to the same mode of
experience in the Greco-Roman cycle than to its own "rural and intuitive"
spring. At least, there is more of Apuleius than of Beowulf in the modern

Weltanschauung. Epochal subjectivity, looked upon in this way, would tend to counteract the estrangements of cultural subjectivity. Cultural subjectivity would not be an *absolute* condition, but an *approximate* one—and the modes of experience in different eras of the world's history would be capable of an approach towards identity.

Epochal subjectivity, furthermore, would constitute a sanction of the modern artist. It would force us to recognize that winter, purely by being a different mode of experience from spring, summer, or autumn, is categorically entitled to symbolize this mode of experience in art. For we must remember that Spengler is applying the Hegelian concept of the *Zeitgeist.* He holds that every age has its particular character, which is manifested in all its activities. There is an *Urphenomen,* a kind of Reality x, a "time-spirit"—each specific activity of an age being a different mode of this time-spirit. As Pater once expressed the same idea: "In every age there is a peculiar *ensemble* of conditions which determines a common character in every product of that age, in business and art, in fashion and speculation, in religion and manners, in men's very faces." One might explain this *ensemble* or consistency (if there is such) in behavioristic terms as the result of mutual interaction, since certain attitudes developed in art can be converted into their equivalents in engineering, business, athletics, marriage customs, etc., while each of these in turn can similarly affect the others. Spengler prefers to discuss the matter in his vocabulary of metaphysical mysticism—whence the *Zeitgeist* concept which has made his entire project seem malapropos to more realistic thinkers. But whether one consider the consistency of an age as the manifold manifestation of a time-spirit or as the result of mutual interaction among all our modes of thinking, feeling, and acting, the fact remains that the entire concept places all manifestations of the age upon the same level: any activity, that is, be it intellectual, emotional, practical, or what not, is *symbolic* of the era in which it takes place.

The noteworthy point is: How does Spengler, out of his system, draw the conclusion that modern art must be "inferior"? Inferior to what? Inferior to the art of "spring," or "summer," or "autumn"? But spring art was a manifestation of the spring era, and thus why not winter art for a winter era? There is no question of superiority or inferiority here—the only problem Spengler's system equips him to discuss is not a matter of "excellence" but of the "symbolic" or the "representative." Which is "better"—a left shoe for a left foot or a right shoe for a right foot? There is no criterion of comparative excellence in his scheme of the symbolic or representative. He can ask only that a work of art typify the characteristics of the era out of which it arises. His logical machinery provides no step beyond the observation that in spring we must have the symbolizations of spring and in winter the symbolizations of winter. To emerge with a judgment in such a case would be like concluding, after an explanation of the earth's seasons as being caused by the planet's revolution about the sun, "therefore winter is 'inferior' to summer."

That art is beset by questions of method is undeniable. That much of our best art today has an "intellectual" aspect seems equally well established. That we are exposed to many conflicting influences, that tentatives have in many instances replaced canons, that our culture is no longer "thoroughbred"—all such can be admitted. In the mere listing of such issues, however, we must realize how much better "fitted" are our contemporaries for dealing with them than were the writers of the "rural and intuitive" era. The earlier writers omitted many aspects of thinking and feeling which, by Spengler's own schema, have since come to the fore. Their cultural "youth" did not equip them to symbolize the fundamental concerns of our cultural "senectitude."

The fact is that Spengler has loaded the dice against us. His analogy of the seasons contains an implicit judgment. If we but select another analogy, an analogy with the pejorative connotations reversed, the result is entirely different. We might, for instance, instead of accepting his interpretation of the culture-civilization dichotomy, consider the earlier stages of a cultural cycle as periods of upbuilding, of pioneering, of grim, hard-working zealotry. Culture, we could say, struggles and wrestles with its environment and its mental confusions to amass an inheritance which civilization, coming after, has the opportunity to squander and enjoy. When a culture is in full swing, it is not only politically and religiously intolerant, but aesthetically intolerant as well. In Leckey's studies of late Rome, for instance, there is much to indicate that living conditions in this decadent "era of peace," before the new turmoil that came with the growth of Christianity, were in many ways picturesque and delightful. Spengler's whole conception of values contains his conclusions in advance. Which may, it is true, be the predicament of us all—but is more vicious in his case because he masks his personal choice as the inescapable verdict of all history.

III

In times of revolution, it is usually the best features of the old régime that are attacked. Vandals, swarming upon a city, will select the finest monuments to topple and leave inferior things unharmed. It is, perhaps, some such psychology which has led many to bring up art for judgment while the harsh aspects of our civilization awaken them to joyful prophesyings.

Most remarkable of all, however, is the fact that the doctrines of art's ineffectualness have flourished in a period noted for its intense utilization of art. As rapidly as "pure" science became applied science (as technologists, carrying out the possibilities opened up by "pure" scientific speculations, utilized scientific principles for the invention of countless unnecessary commodities) just so fast has "pure" literature become applied literature, to the end of making people want these same commodities. For what is our advertising, what is our "success" fiction in the average commercial magazine, what are our cinematic representations of the "good life" but a vast method of determining the criteria of a nation, and thus its conduct, by the assistance of art? And if, as in modern warfare, the fundamental aspirations of our "pure" scientists are derided, similarly in the use of art to promote a belief in the primary cultural value of material acquisitions, the fundamental aspirations of the "pure" artist are derided. The proper complaint here, however, is not that art has been ineffective, but that a certain brand of art has been only too effective.

Still, we should not be driven by the excesses of our opponents into making too good a case for art. Such was, perhaps, much of the trouble in the first place. One cannot advocate art as a cure for toothache without disclosing the superiority of dentistry. Our program is simply to point out that the criterion of "usefulness" has enjoyed much more prestige than its underlying logic merited. Otherwise the issues are left precisely as vague as we would have them; thus:

No categorical distinction can possibly be made between "effective" and "ineffective" art. The most fanciful, "unreal" romance may stimulate by implication the same attitudes towards our environment as a piece of withering satire attempts explicitly. The rarest work may have more influence upon the shaping of society than a work read by millions. A book, as De Gourmont would say, is alive until the last copy is destroyed. We do not, however, presume to glorify "rare" art at the expense of "popular" art. And it would be unjust to assume that the "minority" interests of today are necessarily the "majority" interests of tomorrow. Minorities are not exclusively "ahead" of their times; they may be "behind" their times, "counter" to their times, "aside" from their times. They can arrogate to themselves no corner on worth. There are some forms of excellence (such as complexity, subtlety, remote inquiry, stylistic rigor) which may limit a book's public as surely as though it were a work on higher mathematics. But where directness, picturesqueness, humor, and power are concerned, such qualities seem to fall easily within the range of a general appeal. We ask only to leave the entire matter vague—to say that a work may be popular and good, popular and bad, unpopular and good, unpopular and bad. It may be widely read and ineffectual, widely read and influential, little read and ineffectual, little read and influential. It may usher in something of great value; it may "keep something alive"; it may represent the concerns of a few people living under exceptional conditions. It may, in fact, do all of these things at different times in its history, or in its action upon different kinds of readers.

We advocate nothing, then, but a return to inconclusiveness. A century of "refutations" is salutary at least in emphasizing the fact that art has not been "refuted." For the rest, the artist's ability to express himself in art would be enough, in most instances, to keep him at his vocation, though he felt it a positive offense against mankind. Art needs nothing by way of "sanction" but the neutralizing of its detractors. It needs no "dignity" beyond the mere zero of not being glibly vilified. To the artist, the belief that the ways of influence are devious and unpredictable, and that "anything can happen" should be sufficient justification for devoting himself to his purely aesthetic problems, solving them according to his lights, and letting all other eventualities take care of themselves.

F. SCOTT FITZGERALD

F. Scott Fitzgerald (1896–1940), one of America's most revered novelists and short story writers, narrates in this autobiographical essay, "My Lost City," his progression from a Minnesota provincial to an undergraduate at Princeton (where one of his classmates was the estimable Edmund Wilson, nicknamed "Bunny"), and his post-college elevation from anonymous drudge in the big city to celebrity chronicler of the Jazz Age. All the Fitzgeraldian trademarks are here: his lyrical anaphoric prose, his sharp visual details, his bifocal fusion of the romantic and the self-mocking— the desire to hold on to one's innocence and illusions at the same time one covets worldly disenchantment.

My Lost City

(1932)

There was first the ferry boat moving softly from the Jersey shore at dawn—the moment crystallized into my first symbol of New York. Five years later when I was fifteen I went into the city from school to see Ina Claire in *The Quaker Girl* and Gertrude Bryan in *Little Boy Blue*. Confused by my hopeless and melancholy love for them both, I was unable to choose between them—so they blurred into one lovely entity, the girl. She was my second symbol of New York. The ferry boat stood for triumph, the girl for romance. In time I was to achieve some of both, but there was a third symbol that I have lost somewhere, and lost forever.

I found it on a dark April afternoon after five more years.

"Oh, Bunny," I yelled. *"Bunny!"*

He did not hear me—my taxi lost him, picked him up again half a block down the street. There were black spots of rain on the sidewalk and I saw him walking briskly through the crowd wearing a tan raincoat over his inevitable brown get-up; I noted with a shock that he was carrying a light cane.

"Bunny!" I called again, and stopped. I was still an undergraduate at Princeton while he had become a New Yorker. This was his afternoon walk, this hurry along with his stick through the gathering rain, and as I was not to meet him for an hour it seemed an intrusion to happen upon him engrossed in his private life. But the taxi kept pace with him and as I continued to watch I was impressed: he was no longer the shy little scholar of Holder Court—he walked with confidence, wrapped in his thoughts and looking straight ahead, and it was obvious that his new background was entirely sufficient to him. I knew that he had an apartment where he lived with three other men, released now from all undergraduate taboos, but there was something else that was nourishing him and I got my first impression of that new thing—the Metropolitan spirit.

Up to this time I had seen only the New York that offered itself for inspection—I was Dick Whittington up from the country gaping at the trained bears, or a youth of the Midi dazzled by the boulevards of Paris. I had come only to stare at the show, though the designers of the Woolworth Building and the Chariot Race Sign, the producers of musical comedies and problem plays, could ask for no more appreciative spectator, for I took the style and glitter of New York even above its own valuation. But I had never accepted any of the practically anonymous invitations to debutante balls that turned up in an undergraduate's mail, perhaps because I felt that no actuality could live up to my conception of New York's splendor. Moreover, she to whom I fatuously referred as "my girl" was a Middle Westerner, a fact which kept the warm center of the world out there, so I thought of New York as essentially cynical and heartless—save for one night when she made luminous the Ritz Roof on a brief passage through.

Lately, however, I had definitely lost her and I wanted a man's world, and this sight of Bunny made me see New York as just that. A week before, Monsignor Fay had taken me to the Lafayette where there was spread before us a brilliant flag of food, called an *hors d'oeuvre,* and with it we drank claret that was as brave as Bunny's confident cane—but after all it was a restaurant, and afterwards we would drive back over a bridge into the hinterland. The New York of undergraduate dissipation, of Bustanoby's, Shanley's, Jack's, had become a horror, and though I returned to it, alas, through many an alcoholic mist, I felt each time a betrayal of a persistent idealism. My participance was prurient rather than licentious and scarcely one pleasant memory of it remains from those days; as Ernest Hemingway once remarked, the sole purpose of the cabaret is for unattached men to find complaisant women. All the rest is a wasting of time in bad air.

But that night, in Bunny's apartment, life was mellow and safe, a finer distillation of all that I had come to love at Princeton. The gentle playing of an oboe mingled with city noises from the street outside, which penetrated into the room with difficulty through great barricades of books; only the crisp tearing open of invitations by one man was a discordant note. I had found a third symbol of New York and I began wondering about the rent of such apartments and casting about for the appropriate friends to share one with me.

Fat chance—for the next two years I had as much control over my own destiny as a convict over the cut of his clothes. When I got back to New York in 1919 I was so entangled in life that a period of mellow monasticism in Washington Square was not to be dreamed of. The thing was to make enough money in the advertising business to rent a stuffy apartment for two in the Bronx. The girl concerned had never seen New York but she was wise enough to be rather reluctant. And in a haze of anxiety and unhappiness I passed the four most impressionable months of my life.

New York had all the iridescence of the beginning of the world. The returning troops marched up Fifth Avenue and girls were instinctively drawn East and North towards them—this was the greatest nation and there was gala in the air. As I hovered ghost-like in the Plaza Red Room of a Saturday afternoon, or went to lush and liquid garden parties in the East Sixties or tippled with Princetonians in the Biltmore Bar, I was haunted always by my other life—my drab room in the Bronx, my square foot of the subway, my fixation upon the day's letter from Alabama— would it come and what would it say?—my shabby suits, my poverty, and love. While my friends were launching decently into life I had muscled my inadequate bark into midstream. The gilded youth circling around young Constance Bennett in the Club de Vingt, the classmates in the Yale-Princeton Club whooping up our first after-the-war reunion, the atmosphere of the millionaires' houses that I sometimes frequented— these things were empty for me, though I recognized them as impressive scenery and regretted that I was committed to other romance. The most hilarious luncheon table or the most moony cabaret—it was all the same; from them I returned eagerly to my home on Claremont Avenue—home because there might be a letter waiting outside the door. One by one my great dreams of New York became tainted. The remembered charm of Bunny's apartment faded with the rest when I interviewed a blowsy landlady in Greenwich Village. She told me I could bring girls to the room, and the idea filled me with dismay—why should I want to bring girls to my room?—I had a girl. I wandered through the town of 127th Street, resenting its vibrant life; or else I bought cheap theatre seats at Gray's drugstore and tried to lose myself for a few hours in my old passion for

Broadway. I was a failure—mediocre at advertising work and unable to get started as a writer. Hating the city, I got roaring, weeping drunk on my last penny and went home . . .

. . . Incalculable city. What ensued was only one of a thousand success stories of those gaudy days, but it plays a part in my own movie of New York. When I returned six months later the offices of editors and publishers were open to me, impresarios begged plays, the movies panted for screen material. To my bewilderment, I was adopted, not as a Middle Westerner, not even as a detached observer, but as the archetype of what New York wanted. This statement requires some account of the metropolis in 1920.

There was already the tall white city of today, already the feverish activity of the boom, but there was a general inarticulateness. As much as anyone the columnist F.P.A. guessed the pulse of the individual crowd, but shyly, as one watching from a window. Society and the native arts had not mingled—Ellen Mackay was not yet married to Irving Berlin. Many of Peter Arno's people would have been meaningless to the citizen of 1920, and save for F.P.A.'s column there was no forum for metropolitan urbanity.

Then, for just a moment, the "younger generation" idea became a fusion of many elements in New York life. People of fifty might pretend there was still a four hundred, or Maxwell Bodenheim might pretend there was a Bohemia worth its paint and pencils—but the blending of the bright, gay, vigorous elements began then, and for the first time there appeared a society a little livelier than the solid mahogany dinner parties of Emily Price Post. If this society produced the cocktail party, it also evolved Park Avenue wit, and for the first time an educated European could envisage a trip to New York as something more amusing than a gold-trek into a formalized Australian Bush.

For just a moment, before it was demonstrated that I was unable to play the role, I, who knew less of New York than any reporter of six months' standing and less of its society than any hall-room boy in a Ritz stag line, was pushed into the position not only of spokesman for the time but of the typical product of that same moment. I, or rather it was "we" now, did not know exactly what New York expected of us and found it rather confusing. Within a few months after our embarkation on the Metropolitan venture we scarcely knew any more who we were and we hadn't a notion what we were. A dive into a civic fountain, a casual brush with the law, was enough to get us into the gossip columns, and we were quoted on a variety of subjects we knew nothing about. Actually our "contacts" included half a dozen unmarried college friends and a few new literary acquaintances—I remember a lonesome Christmas when we had not one friend in the city, nor one house we could go to. Finding no nucleus to which we could cling, we became a small nucleus ourselves and gradually we fitted our disruptive personalities into the contemporary scene of New York. Or rather New York forgot us and let us stay.

This is not an account of the city's changes but of the changes in this writer's feeling for the city. From the confusion of the year 1920 I remember riding on top of a taxicab along deserted Fifth Avenue on a hot Sunday night, and a luncheon in the cool Japanese gardens at the Ritz with the wistful Kay Laurel and George Jean Nathan, and writing all night again and again, and paying too much for minute apartments, and buying magnificent but broken-down cars. The first speakeasies had arrived, the toddle was *passé,* the Montmartre was the smart place to dance and Lillian Tashman's fair hair weaved around the floor among the enliquored college boys. The plays were *Declassée* and *Sacred and Profane Love,* and at the Midnight Frolic you danced elbow to elbow with Marion Davies and perhaps picked out the vivacious Mary Hay in the pony chorus. We thought we were apart from all that; perhaps everyone thinks they are apart from their milieu. We felt like small children in a great bright unexplored barn. Summoned out to Griffith's studio on Long Island, we trembled in the presence of the familiar face of the *Birth of a Nation;* later I realized that behind much of the entertainment that the city poured forth into the nation there were only a lot of rather lost and lonely people. The world of the picture actors was like our own in that it was in New York and not of it. It had little sense of itself and no center: when I first met Dorothy Gish I had the feeling that we were both standing on the North Pole and it was snowing. Since then they have found a home but it was not destined to be New York.

When bored we took our city with a Huysmans-like perversity. An afternoon alone in our "apartment" eating olive sandwiches and drinking a quart of Bushmill's whiskey presented by Zoë Atkins, then out into the freshly bewitched city, through strange doors into strange apartments with intermittent swings along in taxis through the soft nights. At last we were one with New York, pulling it after us through every portal. Even now I go into many flats with the sense that I have been there before or in the one above or below—was it the night I tried to disrobe in the *Scandals,* or the night when (as I read with astonishment in the paper next morning) "Fitzgerald Knocks Officer This Side of Paradise"? Successful scrapping not being among my accomplishments, I tried in vain to reconstruct the sequence of events which led up to this dénouement in Webster Hall. And lastly from that period I remember riding in a taxi one afternoon between very tall buildings under a mauve and rosy sky; I began to bawl because I had everything I wanted and knew I would never be so happy again.

It was typical of our precarious position in New York that when our child was to be born we played safe and went home to St. Paul—it seemed inappropriate to bring a baby into all that glamor and loneliness. But in a year we were back and we began doing the same things over again and not liking them so much. We had run through a lot, though we had retained an almost theatrical innocence by preferring the role of the observed to that of the observer. But innocence is no end in itself and as our minds unwillingly matured we began to see New York whole and try to save some of it for the selves we would inevitably become.

It was too late—or too soon. For us the city was inevitably linked up with Bacchic diversions, mild or fantastic. We could organize ourselves only on our return to Long Island and not always there. We had no incentive to meet the city half way. My first symbol was now a memory, for I knew that triumph is in oneself; my second one had grown commonplace—two of the actresses whom I had worshipped from afar in 1913 had dined in our house. But it filled me with a certain fear that even the third symbol had grown dim—the tranquillity of Bunny's apartment was not to be found in the ever-quickening city. Bunny himself was married, and about to become a father, other friends had gone to Europe, and the bachelors had become cadets of houses larger and more social than ours. By this time we "knew everybody"—which is to say most of those whom Ralph Barton would draw as in the orchestra on an opening night.

But we were no longer important. The flapper, upon whose activities the popularity of my first books was based, had become *passé* by 1923—anyhow in the East. I decided to crash Broadway with a play, but Broadway sent its scouts to Atlantic City and quashed the idea in advance, so I felt that, for the moment, the city and I had little to offer each other. I would take the Long Island atmosphere that I had familiarly breathed and materialize it beneath unfamiliar skies.

It was three years before we saw New York again. As the ship glided up the river, the city burst thunderously upon us in the early dusk—the white glacier of lower New York swooping down like a strand of a bridge to rise into uptown New York, a miracle of foamy light suspended by the stars. A band started to play on deck, but the majesty of the city made the march trivial and tinkling. From that moment I knew that New York, however often I might leave it, was home.

The tempo of the city had changed sharply. The uncertainties of 1920 were drowned in a steady golden roar and many of our friends had grown wealthy. But the restlessness of New York in 1927 approached hysteria. The parties were bigger—those of Condé Nast, for example, rivaled in their way the fabled balls of the nineties; the pace was faster—the catering to dissipation set an example to Paris; the shows were broader, the buildings were higher, the morals were looser and the liquor was cheaper; but all these benefits did not really minister to much delight. Young people wore out early—they were hard and languid at twenty-one, and save for

Peter Arno none of them contributed anything new; perhaps Peter Arno and his collaborators said everything there was to say about the boom days in New York that couldn't be said by a jazz band. Many people who were not alcoholics were lit up four days out of seven, and frayed nerves were strewn everywhere; groups were held together by a generic nervousness and the hangover became a part of the day as well allowed-for as the Spanish siesta. Most of my friends drank too much—the more they were in tune to the times the more they drank. And so effort *per se* had no dignity against the mere bounty of those days in New York, a depreciatory word was found for it: a successful programme became a racket—I was in the literary racket.

We settled a few hours from New York and I found that every time I came to the city I was caught into a complication of events that deposited me a few days later in a somewhat exhausted state on the train for Delaware. Whole sections of the city had grown rather poisonous, but invariably I found a moment of utter peace in riding south through Central Park at dark towards where the façade of 59th Street thrusts its lights through the trees. There again was my lost city, wrapped cool in its mystery and promise. But that detachment never lasted long—as the toiler must live in the city's belly, so I was compelled to live in its disordered mind.

Instead there were the speakeasies—the moving from luxurious bars, which advertised in the campus publications of Yale and Princeton, to the beer gardens where the snarling face of the underworld peered through the German good nature of the entertainment, then on to strange and even more sinister localities where one was eyed by granite-faced boys and there was nothing left of joviality but only a brutishness that corrupted the new day into which one presently went out. Back in 1920 I shocked a rising young business man by suggesting a cocktail before lunch. In 1929 there was liquor in half the downtown offices, and a speakeasy in half the large buildings.

One was increasingly conscious of the speakeasy and of Park Avenue. In the past decade Greenwich Village, Washington Square, Murray Hill, the châteaux of Fifth Avenue had somehow disappeared, or become unexpressive of anything. The city was bloated, gutted, stupid with cake and circuses, and a new expression "Oh yeah?" summed up all the enthusiasm evoked by the announcement of the last super-skyscrapers. My barber retired on a half million bet in the market and I was conscious that the head waiters who bowed me, or failed to bow me, to my table were far, far wealthier than I. This was no fun—once again I had enough of New York and it was good to be safe on shipboard where the ceaseless revelry remained in the bar in transport to the fleecing rooms of France.

"What news from New York?"

"Stocks go up. A baby murdered a gangster."

"Nothing more?"

"Nothing. Radios blare in the street."

I once thought that there were no second acts in American lives, but there was certainly to be a second act to New York's boom days. We were somewhere in North Africa when we heard a dull distant crash which echoed to the farthest wastes of the desert.

"What was that?"

"Did you hear it?"

"It was nothing."

"Do you think we ought to go home and see?"

"No—it was nothing."

In the dark autumn of two years later we saw New York again. We passed through curiously polite customs agents, and then with bowed head and hat in hand I walked reverently through the echoing tomb. Among the ruins a few childish wraiths still played to keep up the pretense that they were alive, betraying by their feverish voices and hectic cheeks the thinness of the masquerade. Cocktail parties, a last hollow survival from the days of carnival, echoed to the plaints of the wounded: "Shoot me, for the love of God, someone shoot me!," and the groans and wails of the dying: "Did you see that United States Steel is down three more points?" My barber was back at work in his shop; again the head waiters bowed people to their tables, if there were people to be bowed. From the ruins, lonely and inexplicable as the sphinx, rose the Empire State Building and, just as it had been a tradition of mine to climb to the Plaza Roof to take leave of the beautiful city, extending as far as eyes could reach, so now I went to the roof of the last and most magnificent of towers. Then I understood—everything was explained: I had discovered the crowning error of the city, its Pandora's box. Full of vaunting pride the New Yorker had climbed here and seen with dismay what he had never suspected, that the city was not the endless succession of canyons that he had supposed but that *it had limits*—from the tallest structure he saw for the first time that it faded out into the country on all sides, into an expanse of green and blue that alone was limitless. And with the awful realization that New York was a city after all and not a universe, the whole shining edifice that he had reared in his imagination came crashing to the ground. That was the rash gift of Alfred E. Smith to the citizens of New York.

Thus I take leave of my lost city. Seen from the ferry boat in the early morning, it no longer whispers of fantastic success and eternal youth. The whoopee mamas who prance before its empty parquets do not suggest to me the ineffable beauty of my dream girls of 1914. And Bunny, swinging along confidently with his cane towards his cloister in a carnival, has gone over to Communism and frets about the wrongs of southern mill workers and western farmers whose voices, fifteen years ago, would not have penetrated his study walls.

All is lost save memory, yet sometimes I imagine myself reading, with curious interest, a *Daily News* of the issue of 1945:

MAN OF FIFTY RUNS AMUCK IN NEW YORK
Fitzgerald Feathered Many Love Nests Cutie Avers
Bumped Off By Outraged Gunman

So perhaps I am destined to return some day and find in the city new experiences that so far I have only read about. For the moment I can only cry out that I have lost my splendid mirage. Come back, come back, O glittering and white!

EMMA GOLDMAN

Emma Goldman (1869–1940), known as "Red Emma," was a leading anarchist renowned for her firebrand speeches and agitating activities. Born in present-day Lithuania, then part of Russia, she immigrated to the United States at sixteen and almost immediately began organizing workers and fighting to improve conditions in the slums. She was imprisoned for inciting a riot and eventually deported, though her continuing affection for the American people, if not their government, comes through in her essay "Was My Life Worth Living?"

Was My Life Worth Living?

(1934)

I

How much a personal philosophy is a matter of temperament and how much it results from experience is a moot question. Naturally we arrive at conclusions in the light of our experience, through the application of a process we call reasoning to the facts observed in the events of our lives. The child is susceptible to fantasy. At the same time he sees life more truly in some respects than his elders do as he becomes conscious of his surroundings. He has not yet become absorbed by the customs and prejudices which make up the largest part of what passes for thinking. Each child responds differently to his environment. Some become rebels, refusing to be dazzled by social superstitions. They are outraged by every injustice perpetrated upon them or upon others. They grow ever more sensitive to the suffering round them and the restriction registering every convention and taboo imposed upon them. Others become rubber stamps, registering every convention and taboo imposed upon them.

I evidently belong to the first category. Since my earliest recollection of my youth in Russia I have rebelled against orthodoxy in every form. I could never bear to witness harshness whether on the part of our parents to us or in their dealings with the servants. I was outraged over the official brutality practiced on the peasants in our neighborhood. I wept bitter tears when the young men were conscripted into the army and torn from homes and hearths. I resented the treatment of our servants, who did the hardest work and yet had to put up with wretched sleeping quarters and the leavings of our table. I was indignant when I discovered that love between young people of Jewish and Gentile origin was considered the crime of crimes, and the birth of an illegitimate child the most depraved immorality.

On coming to America I had the same hopes as have most European immigrants and the same disillusionment, though the latter affected me more keenly and more deeply. The immigrant without money and without connections is not permitted to cherish the comforting illusion that America is a benevolent uncle who assumes a tender and impartial guardianship of nephews and nieces. I soon learned that in a republic there are myriad ways by which the strong, the cunning, the rich can seize power and hold it. I saw the many work for small wages which kept them always on the borderline of want for the few who made huge profits. I saw the courts, the halls of legislation, the press, and the schools—in fact every avenue of education and protection—effectively used as an instrument for the safeguarding of a minority, while the masses were denied every right. I found that the politicians knew how to befog every issue, how to control public opinion and manipulate votes to their own advantage and to that of their financial and industrial allies. This was the picture of democracy I soon discovered on my arrival in the United States. Fundamentally there have been few changes since that time.

This situation, which was a matter of daily experience, was brought home to me with a force that tore away shams and made reality stand out vividly and clearly by an event which occurred shortly after my coming to America. It was the so-called Haymarket riot, which resulted in the trial and conviction of eight men, among them five Anarchists. Their crime was an all-embracing love for their fellow-men and their determination to emancipate the oppressed and disinherited masses. In no way had the State of Illinois succeeded in proving their connection with the bomb that had been thrown at an open-air meeting in Haymarket Square in Chicago. It was their Anarchism which resulted in their conviction and execution on the 11th of November, 1887. This judicial crime left an indelible mark on my mind and heart and sent me forth to acquaint myself with the ideal for which these men had died so heroically. I dedicated myself to their cause.

It requires something more than personal experience to gain a philosophy or point of view from any specific event. It is the quality of our response to the event and our capacity to enter into the lives of others that help us to make their lives and experiences our own. In my own case my convictions have derived and developed from events in the lives of others as well as from my own experience. What I have seen meted out to others by authority and repression, economic and political, transcends anything I myself may have endured.

I have often been asked why I maintained such a non-compromising antagonism to government and in what way I have found myself oppressed by it. In my opinion every individual is hampered by it. It exacts taxes from production. It creates tariffs, which prevent free exchange. It stands ever for the status quo and traditional conduct and belief. It comes into private lives and into most intimate personal relations, enabling the superstitious, puritanical, and distorted ones to impose their ignorant prejudice and moral servitudes upon the sensitive, the imaginative, and the free spirits. Government does this by its divorce laws, its moral censorships, and by a thousand petty persecutions of those who are too honest to wear the moral mask of respectability. In addition, government protects the strong at the expense of the weak, provides courts and laws which the rich may scorn and the poor must obey. It enables the predatory rich to make wars to provide foreign markets for the favored ones, with prosperity for the rulers and wholesale death for the ruled. However, it is not only government in the sense of the state which is destructive of every individual value and quality. It is the whole complex of authority and institutional domination which strangles life. It is the superstition, myth, pretense, evasions, and subservience which support authority and institutional domination. It is the reverence for these institutions instilled in the school, the church and the home in order that man may believe and obey without protest. Such a process of devitalizing and distorting personalities of the individual and of whole communities may have been a part of historical evolution; but it should be strenuously combated by every honest and independent mind in an age which has any pretense to enlightenment.

It has often been suggested to me that the Constitution of the United States is a sufficient safeguard for the freedom of its citizens. It is obvious that even the freedom it pretends to guarantee is very limited. I have not been impressed with the adequacy of the safeguard. The nations of the world, with centuries of international law behind them, have never hesitated to engage in mass destruction when solemnly pledged to keep the peace; and the legal documents in America have not prevented the United States from doing the same. Those in authority have and always will abuse their power. And the instances when they do not do so are as rare as roses growing on icebergs. Far from the Constitution playing any liberating part in the lives of the American people, it has robbed them of the capacity to rely on their own resources or do their own thinking. Americans are so easily hoodwinked by the sanctity of law and authority. In fact, the pattern of life has become standardized, routinized, and mechanized like canned food and Sunday sermons. The hundred-percenter easily swallows syndicated information and factory-made ideas and beliefs. He thrives on the wisdom given him over the radio and cheap magazines by corporations whose philanthropic aim is selling America out. He accepts the standards of conduct and art in the same breath with the advertising of chewing gum, toothpaste, and shoe polish. Even songs are turned out like buttons or automobile tires—all cast from the same mold.

II

Yet I do not despair of American life. On the contrary, I feel that the freshness of the American approach and the untapped stores of intellectual and emotional energy resident in the country offer much promise for the future. The War has left in its wake a confused generation. The madness and brutality they had seen, the needless cruelty and waste which had almost wrecked the world made them doubt the values their elders had given them. Some, knowing nothing of the world's past, attempted to create new forms of life and art from the air. Others experimented with decadence and despair. Many of them, even in revolt, were pathetic. They were thrust back into submission and futility because they were lacking in an ideal and were further hampered by a sense of sin and the burden of dead ideas in which they could no longer believe.

Of late there has been a new spirit manifested in the youth which is growing up with the Depression. This spirit is more purposeful though still confused. It wants to create a new world, but is not clear as to how it wants to go about it. For that reason the young generation asks for saviors. It tends to believe in dictators and to hail each new aspirant for that honor as a messiah. It wants cut and dried systems of salvation with a wise minority to direct society on some one-way road to utopia. It has not yet realized that it must save itself. The young generation has not yet learned that the problems confronting them can be solved only by themselves and will have to be settled on the basis of social and economic freedom in co-operation with the struggling masses for the right to the table and joy of life.

As I have already stated, my objection to authority in whatever form has been derived from a much larger social view, rather than from anything I myself may have suffered from it. Government has, of course, interfered with my full expression, as it has with others. Certainly the powers have not spared me. Raids on my lectures during my thirty-five years' activity in the United States were a common occurrence, followed by innumerable arrests and three convictions to terms of imprisonment. This was followed by the annulment of my citizenship and my deportation. The hand of authority was forever interfering with my life. If I have none the less expressed myself, it was in spite of every curtailment and difficulty put in my path and not because of them. In that I was by no means alone. The whole world has given heroic figures to humanity, who in the face of persecution and obloquy have lived and fought for their right and the right of mankind to free and unstinted expression. America has the distinction of having contributed a large quota of native-born children who have most assuredly not lagged behind. Walt Whitman, Henry David Thoreau, Voltairine de Cleyre, one of America's great Anarchists, Moses Harman, the pioneer of woman's emancipation from sexual bondage, Horace Traubel, sweet singer of liberty, and quite an array of other brave souls have expressed themselves in keeping with their vision of a new social order based on freedom from every form of coercion. True, the price they had to pay was high. They were deprived of most of the comforts society offers to ability and talent, but denies when they will not be subservient. But whatever the price, their lives were enriched beyond the common lot. I, too, feel enriched beyond measure. But that is due to the discovery of Anarchism, which more than anything else has strengthened my conviction that authority stultifies human development, while full freedom assures it.

I consider Anarchism the most beautiful and practical philosophy that has yet been thought of in its application to individual expression and the relation it establishes between the individual and society. Moreover, I am certain that Anarchism is too vital and too close to human nature ever to die. It is my conviction that dictatorship, whether to the right or to the left, can never work—that it never has worked, and that time will prove this again, as it has been proved before. When the failure of modern dictatorship and authoritarian philosophies becomes more apparent and the realization of failure more general, Anarchism will be vindicated. Considered from this point, a recrudescence of Anarchist ideas in the near future is very probable. When this occurs and takes effect, I believe that humanity will at last leave the maze in which it is now lost and will start on the path to sane living and regeneration through freedom.

There are many who deny the possibility of such regeneration on the ground that human nature cannot change. Those who insist that human nature remains the same at all times have learned nothing and forgotten nothing. They certainly have not the faintest idea of the tremendous strides that have been made in sociology and psychology, proving beyond a shadow of a doubt that human nature is plastic and can be changed.

Human nature is by no means a fixed quantity. Rather, it is fluid and responsive to new conditions. If, for instance, the so-called instinct of self-preservation were as fundamental as it is supposed to be, wars would have been eliminated long ago, as would all dangerous and hazardous occupations.

Right here I want to point out that there would not be such great changes required as is commonly supposed to insure the success of a new social order, as conceived by Anarchists. I feel that our present equipment would be adequate if the artificial oppressions and inequalities and the organized force and violence supporting them were removed.

Again it is argued that if human nature can be changed, would not the love of liberty be trained out of the human heart? Love of freedom is a universal trait, and no tyranny has thus far succeeded in eradicating it. Some of the modern dictators might try it, and in fact are trying it with every means of cruelty at their command. Even if they should last long enough to carry on such a project—which is hardly conceivable—there are other difficulties. For one thing, the people whom the dictators are attempting to train would have to be cut off from every tradition in their history that might suggest to them the benefits of freedom. They would also have to isolate them from contact with any other people from whom they could get libertarian ideas. The very fact, however, that a person has a consciousness of self, of being different from others, creates a desire to act freely. The craving for liberty and self-expression is a very fundamental and dominant trait.

As is usual when people are trying to get rid of uncomfortable facts, I have often encountered the statement that the average man does not want liberty; that the love for it exists in very few; that the American people, for instance, simply do not care for it. That the American people are not wholly lacking in the desire for freedom was proved by their resistance to the late Prohibition Law, which was so effective that even the politicians finally responded to popular demand and repealed the amendment. If the American masses had been as determined in dealing with more important issues, much more might have been accomplished. It is true, however, that the American people are just beginning to be ready for advanced ideas. This is due to the historical evolution of the country. The rise of capitalism and a very powerful state are, after all, recent in the United States. Many still foolishly believe themselves back in the pioneer tradition when success was easy, opportunities more plentiful than now, and the economic position of the individual was not likely to become static and hopeless.

It is true, none the less, that the average American is still steeped in these traditions, convinced that prosperity will yet return. But because a number of people lack individuality and the capacity for independent thinking I cannot admit that for this reason society must have a special nursery to regenerate them. I would insist that liberty, real liberty, a freer and more flexible society, is the only medium for the development of the best potentialities of the individual.

I will grant that some individuals grow to great stature in revolt against existing conditions. I am only too aware of the fact that my own development was largely in revolt. But I consider it absurd to argue from this fact that social evils should be perpetrated to make revolt against them necessary. Such an argument would be a repetition of the old religious idea of purification. For one thing it is lacking in imagination to suppose that one who shows qualities above the ordinary could have developed only in one way. The person who under this system has developed along the lines of revolt might readily in a different social situation have developed as an artist, scientist, or in any other creative and intellectual capacity.

III

Now I do not claim that the triumph of my ideas would eliminate all possible problems from the life of man for all time. What I do believe is that the removal of the present artificial obstacles to progress would clear the ground for new conquests and joy of life. Nature and our own complexes are apt to continue to provide us with enough pain and struggle. Why then maintain the needless suffering imposed by our present social structure, on the mythical grounds that our characters are thus strengthened, when broken hearts and crushed lives about us every day give the lie to such a notion?

Most of the worry about the softening of human character under freedom comes from prosperous people. It would be difficult to convince the starving man that plenty to eat would ruin his character. As for individual development in the society to which I look forward, I feel that with freedom and abundance unguessed springs of individual initiative would be released. Human curiosity and interest in the world could be trusted to develop individuals in every conceivable line of effort.

Of course those steeped in the present find it impossible to realize that gain as an incentive could be replaced by another force that would motivate people to give the best that is in them. To be sure, profit and gain are strong factors in our present system. They have to be. Even the rich feel a sense of insecurity. That is, they want to protect what they have and to strengthen themselves. The gain and profit motives, however, are tied up with more fundamental motives. When a man provides himself with clothes and shelter, if he is the money-maker type, he continues to work to establish his status—to give himself prestige of the sort admired in the eyes of his fellow-men. Under different and more just conditions of life these more fundamental motives could be put to special uses, and the profit motive, which is only their manifestation, will pass away. Even today the scientist, inventor, poet, and artist are not primarily moved by the consideration of gain or profit. The urge to create is the first and most impelling force in their lives. If this urge is lacking in the mass of workers it is not at all surprising, for their occupation is deadly routine. Without any relation to their lives or needs, their work is done in the most appalling surroundings, at the behest of those who have the power of life and death over the masses. Why then should they be impelled to give of themselves more than is absolutely necessary to eke out their miserable existence?

In art, science, literature, and in departments of life which we believe to be somewhat removed from our daily living we are hospitable to research, experiment, and innovation. Yet, so great is our traditional reverence for authority that an irrational fear arises in most people when experiment is suggested to them. Surely there is even greater reason for experiment in the social field than in the scientific. It is to be hoped, therefore, that humanity or some portion of it will be given the opportunity in the not too distant future to try its fortune living and developing under an application of freedom corresponding to the early stages of an anarchistic society. The belief in freedom assumes that human beings can co-operate. They do it even now to a surprising extent, or organized society would be impossible. If the devices by which men can harm one another, such as private property, are removed and if the worship of authority can be discarded, co-operation will be spontaneous and inevitable, and the individual will find it his highest calling to contribute to the enrichment of social well-being.

Anarchism alone stresses the importance of the individual, his possibilities and needs in a free society. Instead of telling him that he must fall down and worship before institutions, live and die for abstractions, break his heart and stunt his life for taboos, Anarchism insists that the center of gravity in society is the individual—that he must think for himself, act freely, and live fully. The aim of Anarchism is that every individual in the world shall be able to do so. If he is to develop freely and fully, he must be relieved from the interference and oppression of others. Freedom is, therefore, the cornerstone of the Anarchist philosophy. Of course, this has nothing in common with a much boasted "rugged individualism." Such predatory individualism is really flabby, not rugged. At the least danger to its safety it runs to cover of the state and wails for protection of armies, navies, or whatever devices for strangulation it has at its command. Their "rugged individualism" is simply one of the many pretenses the ruling class makes to unbridled business and political extortion.

Regardless of the present trend toward the strong-armed man, the totalitarian states, or the dictatorship from the left, my ideas have remained unshaken. In fact, they have been strengthened by my personal experience and the world events through the years. I see no reason to change, as I do not believe that the tendency of dictatorship can ever successfully solve our social problems. As in the past, so I do now insist that freedom is the soul of progress and essential to every phase of life. I consider this as near a law of social evolution as anything we can postulate. My faith is in the individual and in the capacity of free individuals for united endeavor.

The fact that the Anarchist movement for which I have striven so long is to a certain extent in abeyance and overshadowed by philosophies of authority and coercion affects me with concern, but not with despair. It seems to me a point of special significance that many countries decline to admit Anarchists. All governments hold the view that while parties of the right and left may advocate social changes, still they cling to the idea of government and authority. Anarchism alone breaks with both and propagates uncompromising rebellion. In the long run, therefore, it is Anarchism which is considered deadlier to the present regime than all other social theories that are now clamoring for power.

Considered from this angle, I think my life and my work have been successful. What is generally regarded as success—acquisition of wealth, the capture of power or social prestige—I consider the most dismal failures. I hold when it is said of a man that he has arrived, it means that he is finished—his development has stopped at that point. I have always striven to remain in a state of flux and continued growth, and not to petrify in a niche of self-satisfaction. If I had my life to live over again, like anyone else, I should wish to alter minor details. But in any of my more important actions and attitudes I would repeat my life as I have lived it. Certainly I should work for Anarchism with the same devotion and confidence in its ultimate triumph.

KATHARINE FULLERTON GEROULD

Katharine Fullerton Gerould (1879–1944) was, in her day, a widely published short story writer and essayist. She defended the traditional meditative essay of Michel de Montaigne, Charles Lamb, William Hazlitt, and Robert Louis Stevenson, deploring what she saw as a takeover by factual articles and topical polemics. One of many practitioners who wished to delimit the form, Gerould has been relegated by her critics to the aesthetically conservative "genteel essay" mode, but her vigorous writing (ironically, she herself excelled at polemics) and her love of the essay as a "mental stimulant" remain worthy of revisionist consideration.

An Essay on Essays

(1935)

Some of the rhetoric books my generation used in college went back to Aristotle for many of their definitions. "Rhetoric," he says, "may be defined as a faculty of discovering all the possible means of persuasion in any subject." Persuasion, indeed, is more starkly and simply the purpose of the essay than of fiction or poetry, since the essay deals always with an idea. No true essay, however desultory or informal, but states a proposition which the writer hopes, temporarily at least, to make the reader accept. Though it be only the defense of a mood, subject and predicate are the bare bones of any essay. It may be of a complex nature (like many of Emerson's) stating several propositions; but unless it states at least one, it is not an essay. It may be a dream or a dithyramb; I repeat, it is not an essay.

Let us neglect the old rhetorical distinctions between exposition and argument. To sort all essays into those two types of writing would be more troublesome a task than the wicked stepmother ever set her step-daughter in a fairy-tale. We can no more do it without the help of magic than could the poor princess. When is an essay argument, and when is it exposition? That way lie aridity and the carving of cummin. In so far as the essay attempts to persuade, it partakes of the nature of argument. Yet who would call Lamb's "Dream Children" an argument? Or who shall say it is not an essay? It contains a proposition, if you will only look for it; yet to associate Lamb's persuading process with the forum would be prepos-terous. All writing presupposes an audience (which some of our younger writers seem to forget) but formal argument presupposes opponents, and I cannot find the faintest scent of an enemy at hand in "Dream Children."

I am sorry to kick the dust of the Schools about, even in this half-hearted way, yet some salutation had to be made to rhetoric, which is a noble science, too much neglected. Let us now forget the rhetoricians, and use our own terminology (our common sense too, if we have any). Let us say, first, that the object of the essay is, explicitly, persuasion; and that the essay states a proposition. Indeed, we need to be as rigorously simple as that, if we are going to consider briefly a type that is supposed to include Bacon's "Of Truth," De Quincey's "Murder as a Fine Art," Lamb's "In Praise of Chimney Sweeps," Hazlitt's "On Going a Journey," Irving's "Bachelors," Hunt's "Getting up on Cold Mornings," Poe's "The Poetic Principle," Emerson's "Self-Reliance," Arnold's "Function of Criti-cism," Stevenson's "Penny Plain and Twopence Coloured," Paul Elmer More's "The Demon of the Absolute," Chesterton's "On Leisure," Max Beerbohm's "No. 2. The Pines," Stephen Leacock's "People We Know," and James Truslow Adams' "The Mucker Pose."

The foregoing list, in itself, confesses our main difficulty in delimit-ing the essay. The most popular kind of essay, perhaps, is that known as "familiar." When people deplore the passing of the essay from the pages of our magazines, it is usually this that they are regretting. They are thinking wistfully of pieces of prose like Lamb's "Sarah Battle on Whist," Leigh Hunt's "The Old Gentleman," Stevenson's "El Dorado," Max Beer-bohm's "Mobled King." They mean the essay that is largely descriptive, more or less sentimental or humorous, in which it is sometimes difficult to find a stated proposition. This kind of prose has not been very popular since the war, and I for one, am not regretting it. It will come back—as long as the ghost of Montaigne is permitted to revisit the glimpses of the moon. But the familiar-essay-which-is-hardly-an-essay can be spared for a few years if necessary, since it demands literary gifts of a very high order, and the authors mentioned have at present no competitors in this field. If the bones of the essay are to be weak, the flesh must be exceeding fair and firm.

Are we to admit, at all, that "Sarah Battle" and "The Old Gentleman," and "El Dorado" and "Mobled King" are essays? Do they state a proposition to which they attempt to persuade us? Well, we can twist them to a proposition, if we are very keen on our definition—though I think most of us would admit that they are chiefly descriptive and that they are only gently directed to the creation of opinion. Must we then deny that they are essays? No, I think they are essays, though it is obvious that the familiar essayist goes about his business far otherwise than Arnold or Emerson or Macaulay. He attempts rather to sharpen our perceptions than to convince us of a statement; to win our sympathy rather than our suffrage. His proposition is less important to him than his mood. If put to it, we can sift a proposition out of each one of these—and they were especially chosen because they put our definition on its defense. Lamb states, if you like, that to abide by the rigor of the game is in its way an admirable thing; Leigh Hunt states, if you like, that growing old is a melancholy business; Stevenson states that it is better to travel hopefully than to arrive; Max Beerbohm states that no man is worthy to be reproduced as a statue. But the author's proposition, in such essays, is not our main interest. This brings us to another consideration which may clarify the matter.

Though an essay must state a proposition, there are other requirements to be fulfilled. The bones of subject and predicate must be clothed in a certain way. The basis of the essay is meditation, and it must in a measure admit the reader to the meditative process. (This procedure is frankly hinted in all those titles that used to begin with "Of" or "On": "Of Truth," "Of Riches," "On the Graces and Anxieties of Pig-Driving," "On the Knocking at the Gate in 'Macbeth,'" "On the Enjoyment of Unpleasant Places.") An essay, to some extent, thinks aloud; though not in the loose and pointless way to which the "stream of consciousness" addicts have accustomed us. The author must have made up his mind—otherwise, where is his proposition? But the essay, I think, should show how and why he made up his mind as he did; should engagingly rehearse the steps by which he came to his conclusions. ("Francis of Verulam reasoned thus with himself.") Meditation; but an oriented and fruitful meditation.

This is the most intimate of forms, because it permits you to see a mind at work. On the quality and temper of that mind depends the goodness of the production. Now, if the essay is essentially meditative, it cannot be polemical. No one, I think, would call Cicero's first oration against Catiline an essay; or Burke's Speech on the Conciliation of America; hardly more could we call Swift's "Modest Proposal" a true essay. The author must have made up his mind, but when he has made it up with a vengeance, he will not produce an essay. Because the process is meditative, the manner should be courteous; he should always, by implication, admit that there are good people who may not agree with him; his irony should never turn to the sardonic. Reasonableness, urbanity (as Matthew Arnold would have said) are prerequisites for a form whose temper is meditative rather than polemical.

We have said that this is the most intimate of forms. Not only for technical reasons, though obviously the essayist is less sharply controlled by his structure than the dramatist or the sonneteer or even the novelist. It is the most intimate because it is the most subjective. When people talk of "creative" and "critical" writing—dividing all literature thus—they always call the essay critical. In spite of Oscar Wilde, to call it critical is probably correct; for creation implies objectivity. The created thing, though the author have torn its raw substance from his very vitals, ends by being separate from its creator. The essay, however, is incurably subjective; even "Wuthering Heights" or "Manfred" is less subjective—strange though it sound—than "The Function of Criticism" or "The Poetic Principle." What Oscar Wilde really meant in "The Critic as Artist"—if, that is, you hold him back from his own perversities—is not that Pater's essay on Leonardo da Vinci was more creative than many a novel, but that it was more subjective than any novel; that Pater, by virtue of his style and his mentality, made of his conception of the Mona Lisa something that we could be interested in, regardless of our opinion of the painting. I do not remember that Pater saw himself as doing more than explain to us what he thought Leonardo had done—Pater, I think, would never have regarded his purple page as other than criticism. I, myself—because I like the fall of Pater's words, and do not much care for Mona Lisa's feline face—prefer Pater's page to Leonardo's portrait; but I am quite aware that I am merely preferring criticism, in this instance, to the thing criticized. I am, if you like, preferring Mr. Pecksniff's drunken dream—"Mrs. Todger's idea of a wooden leg"—to the wooden leg itself. Anything (I say to myself) rather than a wooden leg!

A lot of nineteenth century "impressionistic" criticism—Jules Lemaître, Anatole France, etc.—is more delightful than the prose or verse that is being criticized. It is none the less criticism. The famous definition of the "adventures of a soul among the masterpieces" does not put those adventures into the "creative" category; it merely stresses their subjectivity. Wilde is to some extent right when he says that criticism is the only civilized form of autobiography; but he is not so right when he says that the highest criticism is more creative than creation. No one would deny that the purple page Wilde quotes tells us more about Pater than it does about Leonardo, or even about Mona Lisa—as Macaulay's essay on Milton conceivably tells us more about Macaulay than about the author of "Paradise Lost." All Bacon's essays together but build up a portrait of Bacon—Francis of Verulam reasoning with himself; and what is the substance of *The Essays of Elia,* but Elia? "Subjective" is the word, however, rather than "creative."

It is this subjectivity—Montaigne's first of all, perhaps—that has confused many minds. It is subjectivity run wild that has tempted many people to believe that the familiar essay alone *is* the essay; which would make some people contend that an essay does not necessarily state a proposition. But we are talking of the essay itself; not of those bits of whimsical prose which are to the true essay what expanded anecdote is to the short story.

The essay, then, having persuasion for its object, states a proposition; its method is meditation; it is subjective rather than objective, critical rather than creative. It can never be a mere marshaling of facts; for it struggles, in one way or another, for truth; and truth is something one arrives at by the help of facts, not the facts themselves. Meditating on facts may bring one to truth; facts alone will not. Nor can there be an essay without a point of view and a personality. A geometrical proposition cannot be an essay, since, though it arranges facts in a certain pattern, there is involved no personal meditative process, conditioned by the individuality of the author. A geometrical proposition is not subjective. One is even tempted to say that its tone is not urbane!

Perhaps—with the essay thus defined—we shall understand without effort why it is being so little written at present. Dorothy Thompson has said that Germany is living in a state of war. The whole world is living more or less in a state of war; and a state of war produces any literary form more easily than the essay. It is not hard to see why. People in a state of war, whether the war be military or economic, express themselves polemically. A wise man said to me, many years ago, that, in his opinion, the worst by-product of the World War was propaganda. Many times, in the course of the years, I have had occasion to recall that statement. There are perhaps times and places where propaganda is justified—it is not for me to say. But I think we should all agree that the increasing habit of using the technique of propaganda is corrupting the human mind in its most secret and delicate processes. Propaganda has, in common with all other expression, the object of persuasion; but it pursues that legitimate object by illegitimate means—by *suggestio falsi* and *suppressio veri;* by the *argumentum ad hominem* and hitting below the belt; by demagogic appeal and the disregard of right reason. The victim of propaganda is not intellectually persuaded, but intellectually—if not emotionally—coerced. The essayist, whatever the limitations of his intelligence, is bound over to be honest; the propagandist is always dishonest.

To qualify a large number of the articles and pseudo-essays that appear at present in our serious periodicals, British and American, as "dishonest" calls for a little explaining. When one says that the propagandist is always dishonest, one means this: He is a man so convinced of the truth of a certain proposition that he dissembles the facts that tell against it. Occasionally, he is dishonest through ignorance—he is verily unaware of any facts save those that argue for him. Sometimes, having approached his subject with his decision already made, he is unable to appreciate the value of hostile facts, even though he is aware of them. In the latter case, instead of presenting those hostile facts fairly, he tends to suppress or distort them because he is afraid that his audience, readers or listeners, will not react to them precisely as he has done. The propagandist believes (when he is not a paid prostitute) that his conclusions are right; but, no more than any other demagogue, does he like to give other men and women a fair chance to decide for themselves. The last thing he will show them is Francis of Verulam reasoning with himself. He cannot encourage the meditative process. He is, at best, the special pleader.

It can have escaped no reader of British and American periodicals that there is very little urbane meditation going on in print. Half the articles published are propaganda—political, economic, social; the other half are purely informational, mere catalogues of fact. The essay is nowhere. Either there is no proposition, or evidence is suppressed. Above all, there is no meditation—no urbanity. All this is characteristic of the state of war in which we are unfortunately living; that state of war which, alas! permits us few unprejudiced hours.

Yet I think many people would agree that we need those unprejudiced hours rather particularly, just now. We need the essay rather particularly, just now, since fiction and poetry have suffered even more cruelly than critical prose from the corruption of propaganda on the one hand and the rage for "fact-finding" on the other. We need to get away from polemics; we even need to get away from statistics. Granted that we are in a state of war: are we positively so badly off that we must permit every sense save the economic to be atrophied; that we cannot afford to think about life in any terms except those of bread? The desperate determination to guarantee bread to every one—which seems to be the basis of all our political and economic quarreling—is perhaps our major duty. And after? As the French say, Is it not worth our while to keep ourselves complex and civilized, so that, when bread for every one is guaranteed, we shall be capable of entertaining other interests?

The preoccupation with bread alone is a savage's preoccupation; even when it concerns itself altruistically with other people's bread, it is still a savage's preoccupation. The preoccupation with facts to the exclusion of what can be done with them, and the incapacity for logical thinking, are both savage. Until a man begins to think—not merely to lose his temper or to learn by heart—he is, mentally, clothed in the skins of beasts. We are, I fear, under economic stress, de-civilizing ourselves. Between propaganda and "dope" there is little room for the meditative process and the subtler propositions.

I am not urging that we play the flute while Rome burns. I recall the sad entry in Dorothy Wordsworth's journal: "William wasted his mind all day in the magazines." I am not asking the magazines to waste the minds of our Williams. . . . The fact that the familiar essay of the whimsical type is not at the moment popular—that when people wish to be diverted, they prefer Wodehouse to Leacock, let us say—does not disturb me. But it seems a pity that meditative prose should suffer a total eclipse, if only because meditation is highly contagious. A good essay inevitably sets the reader to thinking. Just because it expresses a point of view, is limited by one personality, and cannot be exhaustive or wholly authoritative, it invites the reader to collaboration. A good essay is neither intoxicant nor purge nor anodyne; it is a mental stimulant.

Poetry may be, indeed, as Arnold said, "a criticism of life." But most of us need a different training in critical thinking from that which is offered to us by the poets. A vast amount of the detail of life, detail which preoccupies and concerns us all, is left out of great poetry. We do not spend all our time on the heights, or in the depths, and if we are to live we must reflect on many matters rather temporal than eternal. The essayist says, "Come, let us reason together." That is an invitation—whether given by word of mouth or on the printed page—that civilized people must encourage and, as often as possible in their burdened lives, accept.

GERTRUDE STEIN

Gertrude Stein (1874–1946) was one of the major experimental American writers of the twentieth century. William James, her professor at Radcliffe, saw with his characteristic receptiveness how uniquely intelligent she was and encouraged her to enter medical school; but she dropped out and moved to Paris, where she lived from then on, writing masterworks such as Three Lives *and* The Making of Americans, *and hosting a salon that included the leading modern artists and writers, among them Picasso, Matisse, and Hemingway. After a lecture tour in America in 1936, she delivered the following talk at Oxford and Cambridge, England. Though Stein was often accused of being incomprehensible, this essay demonstrates that, by dint of her patiently circling, reiterating, and linguistically teasing manner, she could make perfect sense and be analytically astute.*

What Are Master-pieces and Why Are There So Few of Them?

(1936)

I was almost going to talk this lecture and not write and read it because all the lectures that I have written and read in America have been printed and although possibly for you they might even being read be as if they had not been printed still there is something about what has been written having been printed which makes it no longer the property of the one who wrote it and therefore there is no more reason why the writer should say it out loud than anybody else and therefore one does not.

Therefore I was going to talk to you but actually it is impossible to talk about master-pieces and what they are because talking essentially has nothing to do with creation. I talk a lot I like to talk and I talk even more than that I may say I talk most of the time and I listen a fair amount too and as I have said the essence of being a genius is to be able to talk and listen to listen while talking and talk while listening but and this is very important very important indeed talking has nothing to do with creation. What are master-pieces and why after all are there so few of them. You may say after all there are a good many of them but in any kind of proportion with everything that anybody who does anything is doing there are really very few of them. All this summer I meditated and wrote about this subject and it finally came to be a discussion of the relation of human nature and the human mind and identity. The thing one gradually comes to find out is that one has no identity that is when one is in the act of doing anything. Identity is recognition, you know who you are because you and others remember anything about yourself but essentially you are not that when you are doing anything. I am I because my little dog knows me but, creatively speaking the little dog knowing that you are you and your recognizing that he knows, that is what destroys creation. That is what makes school. Picasso once remarked I do not care who it is that has or does influence me as long as it is not myself.

It is very difficult so difficult that it always has been difficult but even more difficult now to know what is the relation of human nature to the human mind because one has to know what is the relation of the act of creation to the subject the creator uses to create that thing. There is a great deal of nonsense talked about the subject of anything. After all there is always the same subject there are the things you see and there are human beings and animal beings and everybody you might say since the beginning of time knows practically commencing at the beginning and going to the end everything about these things. After all any woman in any village or men either if you like or even children know as much of human psychology as any writer that ever lived. After all there are things you do know each one in his or her way knows all of them and it is not this knowledge that makes master-pieces. Not at all not at all at all. Those who recognize master-pieces say that is the reason but it is not. It is not the way Hamlet reacts to his father's ghost that makes the master-piece, he might have reacted according to Shakespeare in a dozen other ways and everybody would have been as much impressed by the psychology of it. But there is no psychology in it, that is not probably the way any young man would react to the ghost of his father and there is no particular reason why they should. If it were the way a young man could react to the ghost of his father then that would be something anybody in any village would know they could talk about it talk about it endlessly but that would not make a master-piece and that brings us once more back to the subject of identity. At any moment when you are you you are you without the memory of yourself because if you remember yourself while you are you you are not for purposes of creating you. This is so important because it has so much to do with the question of a writer to his audience. One of the things that I discovered in lecturing was that gradually one ceased to hear what one said one heard what the audience hears one say, that is the reason that oratory is practically never a master-piece very rarely and very rarely history, because history deals with people who are orators who hear not what they are not what they say but what their audience hears them say. It is very interesting that letter writing has the same difficulty, the letter writes what the other person is to hear and so entity does not exist there are two present instead of one and so once again creation breaks down. I once wrote in writing *The Making of Americans* I write for myself and strangers but that was merely a literary formalism for if I did write for myself and strangers if I did I would not really be writing because already then identity would take the place of entity. It is awfully difficult, action is direct and effective but after all action is necessary and anything that is necessary has to do with human nature and not with the human mind. Therefore a master-piece has essentially not to be necessary, it has to be that is it has to exist but it does not have to be necessary it is not in response to necessity as action is because the minute it is necessary it has in it no possibility of going on.

To come back to what a master-piece has as its subject. In writing about painting I said that a picture exists for and in itself and the painter has to use objects landscapes and people as a way the only way that he is able to get the picture to exist. That is every one's trouble and particularly the trouble just now when everyone who writes or paints has gotten to be abnormally conscious of the things he uses that is the events the people the objects and the landscapes and fundamentally the minute one is conscious deeply conscious of these things as a subject the interest in them does not exist.

You can tell that so well in the difficulty of writing novels or poetry these days. The tradition has always been that you may more or less describe the things that happen you imagine them of course but you more or less describe the things that happen but nowadays everybody all day long knows what is happening and so what is happening is not really interesting, one knows it by radios cinemas newspapers biographies autobiographies until what is happening does not really thrill any one, it excites them a little but it does not really thrill them. The painter can no longer say that what he does is as the world looks to him because he cannot look at the world any more, it has been photographed too much and he has to say that he does something else. In former times a painter said he painted what he saw of course he didn't but anyway he could say it, now he does not want to say it because seeing it is not interesting. This has something to do with master-pieces and why there are so few of them but not everything.

So you see why talking has nothing to do with creation, talking is really human nature as it is and human nature has nothing to do with master-pieces. It is very curious but the detective story which is you might say the only really modern novel form that has come into existence gets rid of human nature by having the man dead to begin with the hero is dead to begin with and so you have so to speak got rid of the event before the book begins. There is another very curious thing about detective stories. In real life people are interested in the crime more than they are in detection, it is the crime that is the thing the shock the thrill the horror but in the story it is the detection that holds the interest and that is natural enough because the necessity as far as action is concerned is the dead man, it is another function that has very little to do with human nature that makes the detection interesting. And so always it is true that the master-piece has nothing to do with human nature or with identity, it has to do with the human mind and the entity that is with a thing in itself and not in relation. The moment it is in relation it is common knowledge and anybody can feel and know it and it is not a master-piece. At the same time every one in a curious way sooner or later does feel the reality of a master-piece. The thing in itself of which the human nature is only its clothing does hold the attention. I have meditated a great deal about that. Another curious thing about master-pieces is, nobody when it is created there is in the thing that we call the human mind something that makes it hold itself just the same. The manner and habits of Bible times or Greek or Chinese have nothing to do with ours today but the masterpieces exist just the same and they do not exist because of their identity, that is what any one remembering then remembered then, they do not exist by human nature because everybody always knows everything there is to know about human nature, they exist because they came to be as something that is an end in itself and in that respect it is opposed to the business of living which is relation and necessity. That is what a master-piece is not although it may easily be what a master-piece talks about. It is another one of the curious difficulties a master-piece has that is to begin and end, because actually a master-piece does not do that it does not begin and end if it did it would be of necessity and in relation and that is just what a master-piece is not. Everybody worries about that just now everybody that is what makes them talk about abstract and worry about punctuation and capitals and small letters and what a history is. Everybody worries about that not because everybody knows what a master-piece is but because a certain number have found out what a master-piece is not. Even the very master-pieces have always been very bothered about beginning and ending because essentially that is what a master-piece is not. And yet after all like the subject of human nature master-pieces have to use beginning and ending to become existing. Well anyway anybody who is trying to do anything today is desperately not having a beginning and an ending but nevertheless in some way one does have to stop. I stop.

I do not know whether I have made any of this very clear, it is clear, but unfortunately I have written it all down all summer and in spite of everything I am now remembering and when you remember it is never clear. This is what makes secondary writing, it is remembering, it is very curious you begin to write something and suddenly you remember something and if you continue to remember your writing gets very confused. If you do not remember while you are writing, it may seem confused to others but actually it is clear and eventually that clarity will be clear, that is what a master-piece is, but if you remember while you are writing it will seem clear at the time to any one but the clarity will go out of it that is what a master-piece is not.

All this sounds awfully complicated but it is not complicated at all, it is just what happens. Any of you when you write you try to remember what you are about to write and you will see immediately how lifeless the writing becomes that is why expository writing is so dull because it is all remembered, that is why illustration is so dull because you remember what somebody looked like and you make your illustration look like it. The minute your memory functions while you are doing anything it may be very popular but actually it is dull. And that is what a masterpiece is not, it may be unwelcome but it is never dull.

And so then why are there so few of them. There are so few of them because mostly people live in identity and memory that is when they think. They know they are they because their little dog knows them, and so they are not an entity but an identity. And being so memory is necessary to make them exist and so they cannot create master-pieces. It has been said of geniuses that they are eternally young. I once said what is the use of being a boy if you are going to grow up to be a man, the boy and the man have nothing to do with each other, except in respect to memory and identity, and if they have anything to do with each other in respect to memory and identity then they will never produce a master-piece. Do you do you understand well it really does not make much difference because after all masterpieces are what they are and the reason why is that there are very few of them. The reason why is any of you try it just not to be you are you because your little dog knows you. The second you are you because your little dog knows you you cannot make a masterpiece and that is all of that.

It is not extremely difficult not to have identity but it is extremely difficult the knowing not having identity. One might say it is impossible but that it is not impossible is proved by the existence of master-pieces which are just that. They are knowing that there is no identity and producing while identity is not.

That is what a master-piece is.

And so we do know what a master-piece is and we also know why there are so few of them. Everything is against them. Everything that makes life go on makes identity and everything that makes identity is of necessity a necessity. And the pleasures of life as well as the necessities help the necessity of identity. The pleasures that are soothing all have to do with identity and the pleasures that are exciting all have to do with identity and moreover there is all the pride and vanity which play about master-pieces as well as about every one and these too all have to do with identity, and so naturally it is natural that there is more identity that one knows about than anything else one knows about and the worst of all is that the only thing that any one thinks about is identity and thinking is something that does so nearly need to be memory and if it is then of course it has nothing to do with a master-piece.

But what can a master-piece be about mostly it is about identity and all it does and in being so it must not have any. I was just thinking about anything and in thinking about anything I saw something. In seeing that thing shall we see it without it turning into identity, the moment is not a moment and the sight is not the thing seen and yet it is. Moments are not important because of course master-pieces have no more time than they have identity although time like identity is what they concern themselves about of course that is what they do concern themselves about.

Once when one has said what one says it is not true or too true. That is what is the trouble with time. That is what makes what women say truer than what men say. That is undoubtedly what is the trouble with time and always in its relation to master-pieces. I once said that nothing could bother me more than the way a thing goes dead once it has been said. And if it does it it is because of there being this trouble about time.

Time is very important in connection with master-pieces, of course it makes identity time does make identity and identity does stop the creation of master-pieces. But time does something by itself to interfere with the creation of master-pieces as well as being part of what makes identity. If you do not keep remembering yourself you have no identity and if you have no time you do not keep remembering yourself and as you remember yourself you do not create anybody can and does know that.

Think about how you create if you do create you do not remember yourself as you do create. And yet time and identity is what you tell about as you create only while you create they do not exist. That is really what it is.

And do you create yes if you exist but time and identity do not exist. We live in time and identity but as we are we do not know time and identity everybody knows that quite simply. It is so simple that anybody does know that. But to know what one knows is frightening to live what one lives is soothing and though everybody likes to be frightened what they really have to have is soothing and so the master-pieces are so few not that the master-pieces themselves are frightening no of course not because if the creator of the master-piece is frightened then he does not exist without the memory of time and identity, and insofar as he is that then he is frightened and insofar as he is frightened the master-piece does not exist, it looks like it and it feels like it, but the memory of the fright destroys it as a master-piece. Robinson Crusoe and the footstep of the man Friday is one of the most perfect examples of the non-existence of time and identity which makes a master-piece. I hope you do see what I mean but anyway everybody who knows about Robinson Crusoe and the footstep of Friday knows that that is true. There is no time and identity in the way it happened and that is why there is no fright.

And so there are very few master-pieces of course there are very few master-pieces because to be able to know that is not to have identity and time but not to mind talking as if there was because it does not interfere with anything and to go on being not as if there were no time and identity but as if there were and at the same time existing without time and identity is so very simple that it is difficult to have many who are that. And of course that is what a master-piece is and that is why there are so few of them and anybody really anybody can know that.

What is the use of being a boy if you are going to grow up to be a man. And what is the use there is no use from the standpoint of master-pieces there is no use. Anybody can really know that.

There is really no use in being a boy if you are going to grow up to be a man because then man and boy you can be certain that that is continuing and a master-piece does not continue it is as it is but it does not continue. It is very interesting that no one is content with being a man and boy but he must also be a son and a father and the fact that they all die has something to do with time but it has nothing to do with a master-piece. The word timely as used in our speech is very interesting but you can any one can see that it has nothing to do with master-pieces we all readily know that. The word timely tells that master-pieces have nothing to do with time.

It is very interesting to have it be inside one that never as you know yourself you know yourself without looking and feeling and looking and feeling make it be that you are some one you have seen. If you have seen any one you know them as you see them whether it is yourself or any other one and so the identity consists in recognition and in recognizing you lose identity because after all nobody looks as they look like, they do not look like that we all know that of ourselves and of any one. And therefore in every way it is a trouble and so you write anybody does write to confirm what any one is and the more one does the more one looks like what one was and in being so identity is made more so and that identity is not what any one can have as a thing to be but as a thing to see. And it being a thing to see no master-piece can see what it can see if it does then it is timely and as it is timely it is not a master-piece.

There are so many things to say. If there was no identity no one could be governed, but everybody is governed by everybody and that is why they make no master-pieces, and also why governing has nothing to do with master-pieces it has completely to do with identity but it has nothing to do with master-pieces. And that is why governing is occupying but not interesting, governments are occupying but not interesting because master-pieces are exactly what they are not.

There is another thing to say. When you are writing before there is an audience anything written is as important as any other thing and you cherish anything and everything that you have written. After the audience begins, naturally they create something that is they create you, and so not everything is so important, something is more important than another thing, which was not true when you were you that is when you were not you as your little dog knows you.

And so there we are and there is so much to say but anyway I do not say that there is no doubt that master-pieces are master-pieces in that way and there are very few of them.

M. F. K. FISHER

M. F. K. Fisher (1908–1992), the doyenne of American food writing, had a refined, urbane prose style, producing vibrant personal essays about how to live in the guise of discoursing on the mundane subject of eating. In "Meals for Me," she is prescriptive if not downright persnickety, telling us in detail how the rituals of the table should be performed to her liking. She also demonstrates her historical sense of gastronomy, reaching back to ancient Rome. (Her scholarly researches led her to translate the French classic by Jean Anthelme Brillat-Savarin, The Physiology of Taste.) *If Fisher seems to advocate a sunny hedonism based on seizing whatever is pleasant in the moment's offerings, it is always shadowed by a darker recognition of life's limitations, unsatisfied hungers, and chagrins.*

Meals for Me

(1937)

"When shall we live, if not now?" asked Seneca before a table laid for his pleasure and his friends'. It is a question whose answer is almost too easily precluded. When indeed? We are alive, and now. When else live, and how more pleasantly than supping with sweet comrades?

Perhaps Landor, a little later, meant more than he said (but more than Seneca?) when he decided, "I shall dine late, but the dining-room will be well lighted, the guests few and selected."

Whatever his imputations, his tastes are mine. I too dine late by preference, and I too like my room clear and beautiful, and above all, my guests very few and even more selected.

It is true that in the beginnings of all cultures meals were served early in the day, as indeed they are now among simple folk. A banquet at noon leaves long waking-hours for digestion, conversation, and the easing and refilling of the body. It is practical, and early Greeks and Romans, as well as modern peasants, have appreciated the double festival of a day spent far from the fields before tables tottering under the rare dishes of a marriage or a birthday.

Not until ancient men leave their pastures and their vineyards for the vitiated air of cities; not until they stretch days longer with the false light of burning wax or electricity, and then sleep wastefully in artificial darkness when the sun is high; not until they have grown far away from simplicity do they leave their daytime feastings.

Then, as in old Rome and our own towns, we dine later. For us it is a comparatively recent progression; as few years ago as the early eighteenth century Alexander Pope stabbed scornful couplets at the dissolute Londoners who put off banqueting until well past three o'clock.

We soon grow used to the slow signs of corruption, so surrounded by them are we. In the beginning of the nineteenth century we dined at six, and today a good meal is wasted on most people unless the sun has long set.

What is more tedious for us than an early supper? It thrusts itself into the gathering speed of a day's life like a stick into the spokes of a turning wheel. It forces a pause, a stop, which acts as a kind of disequilibrium to the fine balance of the remaining hours of consciousness.

If the days are short, an early evening meal seems to cut them in two, leaving the second part hanging lifeless on the hardly realized beginning. And if the days are long, they are made twice as monotonously hot by the tired interruption of cooked food.

An early evening meal—a long evening. A long evening—what to do with it? There is a fairly good play, a passable movie, a game of bridge— surely *some* way to kill a few hours.

But an evening killed is murder of a kind, criminal like any disease, and like disease a thorough-going crime. If Time, so fleeting, must like humans die, let it be filled with good food and good talk, and then embalmed in the perfumes of conviviality.

Let us kill it in slow parley, over the leisured savourings of fare both simple and elaborate, in the tempered colour of a room lighted softly, clearly, by living fire of wax or oil or wood, or by the most artful disguises of electricity.

Let the death-chamber itself be airy, intimate, free of thick odours and the sensual distraction of high colour. It should he warmed by a fire in winter, cool with moving air in summer; and in summer too the soft comfortable rugs should be taken away, leaving the shadows of chair legs spidering, reflecting, into the polished floor.

The chair should be comfortable, not low and soft enough to slow digestion, as did the Roman couches, not hard as Cornish rocks, but well fitted to the average body. The best I ever sat in were wide, generous, solid, with high backs, made of ash, brought from England and polished in a log-cabin long before they ever set leg on a hardwood floor.

The table should he ample, and above all solid, with no squeaks and shiverings. Plates, too, should be large, and the silver heavy rather than light, with smooth simple lines to it. Plain linen, ample as the table, plain colours in the flowers and the fruits, glasses no more ornamented than the bubbles they imitate—all should be simple, and adequate as the food and drink served there.

The guests, "few and selected," are most important to Landor and to me, as they were to Archestratus long ago. He wrote, in a fragment of his lost poem on "Gastronomy":

> I write these precepts for immortal Greece,
> That round a table delicately spread,
> Or three, or four, may sit in choice repast,
> Or five at most. Who otherwise shall dine,
> Are like a troop marauding for their prey.

I would add one more person to his dictum, though, and say that six can dine well at a table. More, even one or two, are dangerous, and beyond ten deadly.

What is worse than the rigid right-left conversational etiquette of a formal banquet, unless it be the forced jollity of an annual feast of some modern "service" club, thick with the noise of too many people eating too much food cooked in too large quantities? In either case there is more than a faint likeness to Archestratus' "troop marauding for their prey."

Too few of us, perhaps, feel that the breaking of bread, the sharing of salt, the common dipping into one bowl, mean more than satisfaction of a need. We make such primal things as casual as tunes heard over a radio, forgetting the mystery and strength in both.

Very simple men still know that if you injure the food another leaves, you can thus injure him. The bones from his plate, the rice from his bowl, can be moulded into a little figurine, and then decay will eat into his own flesh as into the mannequin's. Or poison can be dropped into the bowl.

But it is obvious that none who plans to harm a man through food will himself partake of that same food. Thus, there is honour and sanctity in eating together, when you are simple.

So it should be now, although we have civilised ourselves away from the first rules of life. Sharing our meals should be a joyful and a trustful act, rather than the cursory fulfilment of our social obligations.

I know one man, however, the opposite of what I mean, who has so simplified his concept of human hunger and its quelling that he considers the act of taking food as necessary and intimate as any other function, like defecation or sexual play, and no more to be shared with several other beings. For him it is disgusting to eat even with his dear friends.

His viewpoint is exaggerated, and to my mind unhealthy. For me, there is no more agreeable relaxation than a quiet sharing of food with my few friends. My only approximation of his feeling is the irritation and revolt that rise in me at the thought of obligatory feeding with unknown or uncongenial people.

To such a lewd exhibition I should prefer Plato's solitary bowl of olives, but for neither of these would I forgo a slow meal with three or four—or six at most, sitting in "choice repast."

What six persons may consider choice is delicate to decide. Six tastes, six appetites, must be known, and fused by one memory and one skill into a mutually exciting whole. Old preferences must be converted into new. New flavours must be linked with old.

From this fusion should result meals as stimulating to the tongue as to the gastric fluids, meals to be remembered with pleasure, evocative of future delights.

And to concoct such meals and serve them is one of the most satisfying of all civilised amenities, I think. Nothing is much sweeter than the sincere gratification—and admiration—of a friend.

When Horace succoured a storm-bound traveller, he fed him a good chicken, a fat kid roasted, grapes, figs and nuts, and sweet Roman wine.

When we went to sup with Nell Coover, the small old etcher, often hungry in her rooms filled with Whistler's cushions and Heppelwhite's beautiful chairs and cupboards, she gave us a strange lovely salad of sea mosses and jewelled ice-plants from the cliffs, and a bowl of green wild spinach. It was all she had, but it was served forth with no apology, nor did it need one. Our eyes and our stomachs were pleased, and Miss Coover too, I think, sure in the pleasure of well-treated guests.

For my own meals I like simplicity above all. I like newness in what I serve, perhaps because any interest I may thus stir in my fellow-diners is indirect flattery of myself. I like leisure.

I like a mutual ease. For this reason I prefer not to have among my guests two people or more, of any sex, who are in the first wild tremours of love. It is better to invite them after their new passion has settled, has solidified into a quieter reciprocity of emotions. (It is also a waste of good food, to serve it to new lovers.)

I do not agree with the Greeks and Romans, that women should be reserved for the end of a meal and served with the final wines and music, nor do I think that Frenchman was right who stated that there are no blue eyes, no curls and dimpled shoulders, which can replace for a true gourmet the charms of a black truffle.

It is, though, very dull to be at a table with dull people, no matter what their sex.

Dining partners, regardless of gender, social standing, or the years they've lived, should be chosen for their ability to eat—and drink!—with the right mixture of abandon and restraint. They should enjoy food, and look upon its preparation and its degustation as one of the human arts. They should relish the accompanying drinks, whether they be ale from a bottle on a hillside or the ripe bouquet of a Chambertin 1919 in a great crystal globe on finest damask.

And above all, friends should possess the rare gift of sitting. They should be able, no, eager, to sit for hours—three, four, six—over a meal of soup and wine and cheese, as well as one of twenty fabulous courses.

Then, with good friends of such attributes, and good food on the board, and good wine in the pitcher, we may well ask, When shall we live if not now?

LEWIS MUMFORD

Lewis Mumford (1895–1990) was a leading urbanist thinker and architectural critic whose researches culminated in such magisterial tomes as The Culture of Cities *and* The City in History. *He also wrote a regular column for* The New Yorker. *One of those columns, the autobiographical sketch "A New York Adolescence," traces the roots of his love of urban form to growing up in Manhattan. His passion for exploring the streets of New York seems all tied up with discovering girls. Here he writes of getting the brush-off from one "ruthless beauty," with sufficient retrospective amusement to take the edge off that indignity. In Mumford's appreciation of the serendipitous New York of his youth lay a reproach to those coming technological interventions that he thought trapped the individual in a "megamachine." As he saw it, "the freedom of movement, the change of pace, the choice of alternative destinations, the spontaneous encounters . . . in fact, the multifarious life of a city, have been traded away for expressway, parking space, and vertical circulation."*

A New York Adolescence

(1937)

Toward the end of the first decade of the century, the horizons of New York visibly widened for me. My main activities ceased to be bounded by my neighborhood. Up to that time, one could be identified by the block one lived on. West Ninety-fourth Street boys were quite different in manner and social outlook and the ability to play one-old-cat from West Ninety-first Street boys, who were sissies, and we all would shrink into areaways or dive behind the portals of our apartment houses when the Ninety-eighth Street gang, tough, dirty, brutal, appeared on the scene. Occasionally friendships would break across block lines, but only rarely did they span a distance of more than a couple of blocks. It was like living in a walled town.

Adolescence and high school advanced together, although I don't think my voice broke or my legs became gangly till at least a year after I had left grammar school. When I was graduated from grammar school, we had sung a song at commencement about our eternal loyalty to dear old 166, but in our hearts we knew that in our part of the West Side one school was practically identical with another, whereas the high schools we had to choose from had names, not numbers, and each one had a collective character. Townsend Harris was almost collegiate in its standards, but, despite its playing fields on Convent Avenue, was terrible in sports. Commerce, at Sixty-fifth Street near Broadway, had a fine baseball team, and it turned out fellows who became bookkeepers, accountants, and male secretaries. De Witt Clinton, at Fifty-ninth Street near Tenth Avenue, was just literary, while Stuyvesant, which had a good basketball team and a new building, prepared people for engineering.

At the time the choice came to me, I was making clumsy models of airplanes on the lines of the Wright plane—models that would never fly in the air and would hardly even stay glued together in repose on my bedroom table. With the help of an old instrument-maker to whom Dr. Phillips, our family doctor, had introduced me, I had begun to rig up feeble little wireless sets with which I purposed to communicate with another ingenious lad in the next block, if either of us ever had the patience to master the Morse code. So I chose Stuyvesant. I think the good basketball team erased any lingering doubts I may have had about it.

Emerson used to say that the essence of a college education was having a room of one's own, with a fire, in a strange city. Going to high school on East Fifteenth Street, between Stuyvesant Square and First Avenue, gave me essentially the same sort of shock. In those days, the upper West Side had a fairly homogeneous population; there was the typical New York mixture of German and Irish stocks, interspersed with older branches of the American. Our fathers and mothers, at least, had usually been born in the United States, and in a class of forty boys, only eight or ten would be even identifiably Jewish, while the newer Russo-Polish migration was so sparsely represented that I can still remember the name of Malatzky, the bright, beady-eyed son of a glazier on Columbus Avenue.

Except for Broadway, which was very spottily built up until the opening of the subway in 1904 defined its new character, this part of the West Side had taken shape in the late eighties and nineties. The poorer classes lived on Amsterdam and Columbus Avenues: the cabmen and the clerks and the mechanics and the minor city employees. The rich lived in the big apartments on Central Park West or in the heavy, stone-encrusted mansions on Riverside Drive; between them, on the cross streets, and more sumptuously on West End Avenue, was the connecting tissue of the bourgeoisie, in brownstone rows whose dinginess was sometimes graced by some of the lighter-yellow, brick-and-limestone houses designed by Stanford White and his imitators. A boy growing up in such a neighborhood took middle-class comfort to be the dominant pattern of life, and except for an occasional twist of Irish, everyone spoke plain Manhattanese.

Suddenly I was thrown into a remote quarter of the city, and surrounded by a group of boys with foreign faces and uncouth, almost undecipherable accents and grubby, pushing manners: boys who ate strange food whose flavors pervaded their breath and seemed to hang about their clothes; boys whose aggressive vitality left me feeling like a sick goldfinch among a flock of greedy sparrows. One had to fend for oneself among people who had learned the art of survival in a far more difficult environment than I had come from, and in the lunch hour I would inevitably find myself near the tag end of the line that filed past the cafeteria counter, never capable of making decisions fast enough to get what I wanted before I was pushed beyond reach.

My school comrades were mostly the second generation of the great Russian and Polish Jewish immigration that had swept into the East Side after the assassination of Czar Alexander II. They had names like Moscowitz and Lefkowitz and Pinsky, and they had not merely learned in the settlement houses how to play circles round most of us in basketball or track sports, but they had an equally strenuous grip on the academic subjects. Indeed, most of them also excelled in the use of their hands, not having had so many of their manual opportunities shorn from them by solicitous parents and nursemaids. All in all, these boys were good stuff, but for one who had lived a more pallid existence, they were, during the first year, a little overwhelming.

My new schoolfellows brought the raw facts of life home to me with a rush. My own family knew the pinch of genteel poverty, but here was poverty on a grand scale, massive, extensive, blighting vast neighborhoods, altering the whole character of life, a poverty that, instead of shrinking submissively behind a false front, reached out into the city, creating its own forms, demanding, arguing, asserting, claiming its own, now busy with schemes for making money, now whispering the strange word Socialism as a key that would open the door. My political views were extremely conservative in those days; the rights of property seemed axiomatic; and I remember how shocked I was when I found out that one of my pals named Stamer, whose father was a Greenpoint cigarmaker of the old '48 German stock, was a Socialist. Stamer jarred my middle-class complacency with his scornful descriptions of what had hitherto seemed a reasonable and well-balanced world, and I was gradually unsettled in all my views, not so much through the strength of his arguments as through the obvious feebleness of my replies. Even a couple of teachers, quiet, upright men, were Socialists and would occasionally explain their views in class. I might have lived and died in my part of the upper West Side without realizing that neither the Democratic nor the Republican Party had ever recognized the Class Struggle.

Fourteenth Street, too, was something of an education for a provincial West Side boy. Tammany Hall still reigned in its dingy building near Third Avenue, embracing the old Tony Pastor's theatre, and almost across the way was Tom Sharkey's saloon, with a wide glass front, and the Dewey Theatre, painted white, where lurid posters of obese beauties, who did the belly dances that preceded strip tease, were spread before our gaze. "Don't do that dance I tell you Sadie, that ain't no business for a lady" was one of the popular songs of the period, and all of us knew, at least at second hand, how much farther Fourteenth Street went than Broadway's Sadie. My usual route to school was through Irving Place and along Fifteenth Street, because I discovered in my second year that a beautiful girl with austere white cheeks and black hair would pass me almost every morning on her way to the Quaker school at the corner of Stuyvesant Square. I can still see her graceful figure, in a blue serge dress, topped by a black hat with a jaunty feather, her poised, unhurried walk, and her slightly archaic inward smile, which was at once impenetrable and yet not indifferent, and I wonder now if I played anything of the part in her secret dream life that she did in mine.

When school was out, one would encounter in the same street, nearer Third Avenue, white-faced and heavily rouged prostitutes, no longer young, already on patrol. We knew what these ladies were, in a vague way; some of the boys, who lived on Forsythe or Chrystie Street, had even encountered them closer at hand in the halls of their own tenements; and we held a certain resentment against them because they were mainly responsible for the fact that we were not permitted to go out on the streets for lunch, but had to remain cooped in our building. The year after I was graduated, however, a new social ferment began to work in school. A group of boys rushed the teacher who was guarding the main door and broke for liberty during the lunch hour; this precipitated a school strike, and when the matter was settled the boys had won the right to eat outdoors. The squirrels in Stuyvesant Square benefited more by this arrangement, I am sure, than the painted ladies.

Often I preferred to spend my carfare on candy and walked home, usually with a couple of other lads. The path led diagonally across the city, sometimes up Broadway, sometimes around the open New York Central yards and across to Central Park. I watched the Public Library and the Grand Central Terminal during their building, and remember parts of Fifth Avenue below Fifty-ninth that were still lined with brownstone

dwellings and plushy-looking mansions before which victorias and han-
soms would stop, and the stages—as my mother still calls the buses—
would roll by. Yet visually these walks remain dim, because so much of
them, particularly when a sallow, evangelical boy named George Lush
was along, was spent in talks about God and immortality and True Christianity. The openness of the midtown district then, its low buildings and
the vast unbuilt spaces on Park Avenue, of course remain with me, for
they were still visible when the Shelton was erected as late as 1924, but I
dearly wish some heavenly stenographer would transcribe one of those
theological debates for me. Both Lush and I were still pious lads. Could
it be that we spent all those hours comparing the practices of the Baptists
and the Episcopalians? Or were we battling with the Higher Criticism? I
can't remember.

In grammar school, most of the male teachers were aged men, who
had grown old in a profession they conducted with dignity untouched
by inspiration—men who could remember the drafts riots, or the black-
walled city that celebrated Lincoln's funeral. In high school, there were a
lot of young teachers who brought into the place the contemporary flavor
of Cornell, Chicago, or Wisconsin, as well as nearer universities, people
who were stirred up over their subjects and who would break into their
routine demonstrations in physics with hints of exciting scientific news
that would not for a decade or more penetrate the textbooks—Einstein's
first theory of relativity, or the electronic theory of matter, which made
the old-fashioned doctrine of the indivisible atom look silly except as a
convenience in writing chemical equations. Our principal, a sweet, portly
man with a gray Vandyke beard and a bald head, was excited about science, too; he kept a class in physics for himself all through his principal-
ship, and he would beam on us when he had made a good demonstration.
Some of the more menial subjects in engineering, like mechanical drawing, seemed to attract routineers, but to make up for it, there were teachers in pattern-making or metal-turning who had worked with the Yale
& Towne lock company or in the Baldwin Locomotive Works, and who
were not tethered to the profession of teaching out of mere ineptitude for
worldly tasks or for the sake of premature repose. As for the man who
taught us forging, he was a German blacksmith of the old school, and his
iron roses and scrolly leaves were our envy.

That a school so strenuously dedicated to science and the mechanical
arts should have had a good English department was extremely fortunate
for a lad whose mathematical aptitude waned shortly after he wrote his
first love letter. The English teachers worked against odds, too, because
the Board of Regents had chosen a lot of pretty stale literature for our
edification, and it didn't help matters that, by some oversight, we had
already gone through "The Lady of the Lake" and "Julius Caesar" in
grammar school. But my teacher in freshman English, a rapt, brooding

young man with a freckled face and a huge mop of carroty hair, encouraged a group of us to write a play, and from his lips I first heard the name of Bernard Shaw. That was what was important, as one looks back on it, in all the classes. Not the lesson itself, but the overflow—a hint, a pat on the shoulder, the confession of a secret ambition, a fragment of unposed life as someone had actually lived it.

I hated quadratic equations and I wasn't overly fond of geometry, but high school had none of the close-packed boredom that remains the chief impress of my earlier education. It was a big chunk of life to swallow, and maybe we were stretched a little too hard at study during a period when our bodies demanded a larger share of idleness and relaxation than we gave them. But there was no lack of intellectual stimulus in this new milieu. By the time we had visited foundries on the East River, practiced tennis on courts in Staten Island, travelling two hours for the sake of playing one, cheered baseball games in the Bronx, and dickered with one-horse job printers on John Street, we knew our way about the city and we knew a lot about what life had to offer ourselves and our fellows.

When I left high school, however, my ambitions had changed. I wanted to be a newspaperman as a first step toward becoming a novelist. Shep Friedman was then the city editor of the *Morning Telegraph,* and since he was a friend of the family, I kept on politely nagging him for a job for the next year or two. I would usually drop in around 6 P.M., before he had started the heavy business or the heavy drinking of the day, and although I was palpably a callow and ratty adolescent, he was always decent enough to drag me down to the corner bar for a friendly beer. After this he would give me a note of introduction to the most recent occupant of the *Evening Journal*'s city desk. Being idiotic as well as honorable, I never examined these notes. I suspect now that they said, "For God's sake dump this kid somewhere or drown him." At the end of six months I compromised with my ambitions and went on the *Evening Telegram* as copy boy for the lobster trick. My feelings were a little like those of a broken-down gentleman I once knew who was finally reduced to taking a job as dishwasher in a big hotel. But, he proudly explained to his friends, he was not an ordinary dishwasher; he washed only the dishes of the guests who were served privately in their rooms. It was understood that I was to become a cub reporter the first time someone moved up or out.

The job forced me to get up at 2:50 A.M., make my own breakfast, and catch a Sixth Avenue "L" to Herald Square. The back of our flat faced Columbus Avenue, and I could tell by leaning out the kitchen window and noting whether the passing train had green or white lights how much time I had left for finishing my cocoa. It made one feel slightly superior to be abroad in the city at that hour, before the milkman started on his rounds. The cold white flare of the arc lights intensified one's feeling of aloofness, and an occasional light in the bedroom of an otherwise darkened tenement house might even add a touch of mystery, hinting of someone in pain, someone quarrelling, someone dying or being born. But often I would be oblivious of the sleeping city because I was reading, with an indescribable priggish elation, a few pages in Plato or William James. Reading "A Pluralistic Universe" at 3:25 in the morning almost wiped away the humiliation of sweeping the floor and setting out the flimsy in the stale air of the city room half an hour later. If I happened to catch a train ten minutes earlier, I would encounter the last of the reporters, winding up their poker game in a corner of our common city room.

The *Telegram* was even in 1913 a pretty seedy sheet, but James Gordon Bennett was still alive, and some faint, ridiculous spark of his vindictive energy would cause an editor or a reporter suddenly to jump out of his skin. (Bennett was the same insolent devil who offered Stanley his old job on the *Herald* after he had found Livingstone and made himself famous.) At this time, the name Roosevelt was taboo; he could be referred to only as the Third Termer. Among other examples of Bennett's crotchets, there was an ice chest in one corner of the city room, which was duly filled with ice every day, supposedly because the Old Boy himself might suddenly appear and want ice for his champagne. Bennett's alpaca coat, too, hung on a hook in his private office, waiting. I rushed the beer and sandwiches and coffee while the night city editor was marking up the morning papers for the rewrite men. Even at that hour, the saloon on the northeast corner of Thirty-fifth Street would have a few stragglers in it. The rewrite men, who averaged around thirty-five dollars a week then—the night city editor got only fifty—used to tip me, too, even if I did read William James and sometimes do a stick or two of rewrite myself when one of the men got in late. If any small story broke in the neighborhood, I would be sent out to cover it, but a sewer explosion and a burning mattress were about all that came my way, and my pride suffered as my boredom grew, so I chucked the job after a couple of months. It was a cheap and harmless inoculation. I never looked for Life in newspaper offices any more, and thenceforward I read newspapers with a scorn and a skepticism born of intimacy. Had I not, when a freighter without a wireless sank near Halifax, seen a big front-page story manufactured in three-quarters of an hour out of a rewrite man's stinking clay pipe and his otherwise unaided imagination?

All this time, and for the next few years, I was studying at City College at night, from 7:30 to 10:20. In every way that was a remarkable experience, and one that only New York could have offered. Even New York could offer it only once, for the college I knew, with some five hundred students and a close, intimate life, disappeared—under mere pressure of congestion—within half a dozen years after its inception. It was one of

those important experiments that the City College began before it went
the way of other metropolitan institutions by succumbing to giantism.
Dr. Stephen Duggan was the director and Dr. Frederick B. Robinson (he
of umbrella memory) was then his assistant, an affable, clever man who
was yet to disclose his remarkable talent for disingenuously setting a
whole institution by the ears.

The students were mostly mature men, and they spoiled me for any
other kind of undergraduate. One of them was a well-established mari-
time lawyer, with an argumentative Scotch tongue; another was a South
American consul; and there were doctors, brokers, accountants, engineers, as well as people almost as infirmly established as myself. Being
under no obligations to regularity, I took my college education backward,
skipping most of the freshman subjects and plunging into junior and
senior courses in politics, philosophy, and English. In all the new plans
for revising curricula that I have examined, not even Dr. Hutchins seems
to have hit on this particular dodge, but perhaps it would work no worse
for others than it did for me.

There is something amoeboid about the ordinary undergraduate, but
we night students had a shape and a backbone and a definite point of
view. Our discussions were battles, and though we often lived to change
sides, there was nothing tentative or hesitating in our espousals; we did
not suffer from the academic disease of evasive "open-mindedness." Our
professors were men of character—men like Morris Cohen, who thought
and taught out of a passion for things of the mind as pure as that of
a Socrates or a Spinoza. There was Alfred Compton, a slim, sardonic
gentleman with a touch of Robert Louis Stevenson about him. There
was John Pickett Turner, a handsome man with a massive dark head, a
wart on his cheek, and shoulders of Platonic dimensions; he spoke with a
Southern deliberation and enlivened his course on psychology with case
histories drawn undisguised from his own life and marital experience.
Even-handed and tolerant, he didn't quiver a hairbreadth when a sharp
little Rumanian, Jallver, in the ethics class, declared that the *summuifi
bonum* would be to die at the height of an orgasm in the arms of a
beautiful woman. There was J. Salwyn Schapiro, one of J. H. Robinson's
brilliant disciples, who filled the air with epigrams and paradoxes, one of
which seems even more startling in 1937 than it did in 1913—"The Constitution might be overthrown, but it could not be amended." And then
there was Earle Palmer, a little man with a drawn white face, hunched
shoulders, and dark eyes that smoldered behind his glasses. He took us
through Pancoast's anthology of poetry, living and enacting the poems,
with an acrid humor in commentary that sprang out of passion rather
than bitterness—a frail but ageless figure, half pixie, half demon, with
the sudden dark touch of one who had not lightly triumphed over terror
and wrath and pain. My Harvard friends have overfilled me with tales

about their famous Copey, but none of them has ever made me feel the least regretful that I missed the histrionic Harvard professor. One touch of Palmer's ruthless sincerity was at least half a college education.

The Trustees of City College had chosen a grand site for their new buildings when the college moved up from Twenty-third Street, and the architecture had a powerful effect when one climbed the hill past the Hebrew Orphan Asylum through the deepening October twilight and saw the college buildings, in their dark stone masses and white terra-cotta quoins and moldings, rising like a collection of crystals out of the form-less rocks on the crest. Below, the plain of Harlem spread, a vapor of light beneath the twinkle and flood of a large beer sign. In the afterglow, or on a dark night, these buildings could awaken nostalgic memory as easily as those of Brasenose or Magdalen. Often we would accompany one of our professors to his home, along Convent Avenue or Broadway, or sometimes a group of us, heady with the discussions started in the classroom, would stalk down Riverside Drive, matching outrageous puns, arguing about free will and determinism, bursting into irrelevant song. It had the inti-macy that only a small college can give, plus the variety and intensity of stimulus that come in a great city.

The other part of my adolescence, particularly in the earlier years, centred chiefly around the old tennis courts in Central Park on the south side of the transverse at Ninety-sixth Street. The courts were then covered with grass, and the most popular court, half-denuded by constant playing, was called the dirt court. An aged keeper, with a gray beard spattered with tobacco juice, had charge of the marking of the courts and the stowing away of the nets. He was probably one of those Civil War pensioners who were still favored on the public payrolls, and we called him "Captain," but he had a vile temper and carried on an uncivil war of his own with most of the people who played there. He was often drunk, and the white lines he marked with his sprinkler showed no disposition to follow the straight and narrow path, but this crusty character gave the place a certain fla-vor which contrasts with the colorless, antiseptic courtesy of today. We couldn't start playing till the Captain raised the flag on the flagpole.

It was a queer gang that hung around the courts in those days—a few newspaper reporters on the *American* and the *Press;* a theatrical agent whom we called Ted; a little hunchback with no visible occupation, whom we called Dirty Ferdie; a few semi-professional loafers who used to play for stakes; and a handful of young women who were usually attached to the older men, ancients who might be at least thirty years old, as well as a few boys of my own age who took tennis very seriously. Day after day through the muggy summer we would lounge around on the hill behind the dirt court, and play, and lounge, and play again till we could scarcely drag our feet around the court. This was a complete, self-contained world; even on a rainy day, we would come over to the courts with our racquets, sprawling on benches beneath the trees toward the reservoir, speculating on the weather. When the males were alone, the conversation would often descend to basement level, and I would go home with new words I couldn't find in the ten-volume Century Dictionary, sometimes with lickerish hints about aspects of life I hadn't the faintest clue to till I studied abnormal psychology. On the whole, perhaps it was a good thing we played so much tennis.

I don't know if I can convey the precise flavor of the city that one inhaled on those Central Park courts in my day. It was perhaps closest to what one feels on a clean, sunny beach onto which the ocean periodically washes stale watermelon rinds, mildewed oranges, and discarded paper boxes. There was nothing particular in my immediate life to make me look naturally for meanness or sordidness or dishonesty, but constant hints of these things seeped in from the world around me. By the time I was fifteen, I had acquired a layer of protective cynicism that would have honored the proverbial cub reporter, and my tennis coach in high school, an excellent English teacher named Quimby, once said in perfectly justifiable horror, "You talk like a disillusioned man of sixty." Yet with all my early knowingness, I went through the first experience of being in love at fifteen—with Sybil, a girl I met at the tennis courts—as if all my life had been spent among the innocents of Arcadia. The other day I attended a singing festival given by the girls in one of our municipal colleges, a charming mass of hussies whose dance routines would have done credit to Broadway. In the very alluring performance they put on, in the songs they had made up, I detected the same combination of virginity and cynicism, of chastity and shamelessness—the curious patina of hardness that forms over youth in the big city. They were exquisitely young and fresh, yet already they were a little cheapened, a little soiled.

My own girl was one of those ruthless beauties who are never at ease unless they put five or six men simultaneously in a state of torture. With one, she danced for tango prizes in the footsteps of Irene Castle; with another, she swam; with another, she went to football games. She had us all, in fact, pretty well specialized and subordinated, and it was usually for one of the older lads that she reserved her emotional complications. If I began earlier and remained on the scene longer than any of her other young admirers, it was because I served as a sort of fixed spar to mark the height of the incoming or the ebbing tide. Every once in a while she would cling to me to get her bearings. My specialty was playing tennis on the courts near Morningside Park, a few blocks from her apartment, at six in the morning, before she started her day as artist's model. It was perhaps the only time in my life, except in the Navy, that I visibly profited by my gift of waking up easily.

I can't pretend that there was anything very typical of New York in this relationship. The closest it came to taking on the color of the city was one hot summer night, on a street swarming with children and inundated by a hurdy-gurdy thumping out "Cavalleria Rusticana," when I told her I wanted to marry her. She was very self-possessed about that. She sent me round the corner for some ice cream, which the dealers then used to heap up in flimsy paper boxes, and then she took me up to the roof of her apartment house, a flight higher than the elevator went, so that we could talk matters over while we dipped, turn and turn, into the ice-cream box. The thick summer sky flared to the east with the lights of Harlem, and on this high roof one had a sense of separation from the rest of the world one usually doesn't achieve in Nature at a level lower than five thousand feet. But nobody ever succeeded in making love convincingly when his hands were all sticky from ice cream. Perhaps Sybil knew that when she complained about the heat. On her telling me what good friends we would always be—pals, in fact—I abruptly left her, and went down onto the steamy pavement, on which big raindrops were beginning to spatter, feeling dramatically solemn. The same tune—probably from the same hand organ—was still clanging in the distance. And I was already sketching in my mind the first act of a play to be called "Love on Morningside Heights."

EDMUND WILSON

Edmund Wilson (1895–1972) was one of our most distinguished, ven-
erated literary critics. He was an omnivorous reader whose curiosity
led him to subjects as varied as the Dead Sea Scrolls, Canada, the Civil
War, taxation, and the Bolshevik Revolution. A specialty of his was the
biographical essay (often using his review of someone else's biography
as a springboard), which allowed him to examine in depth the life and
work of figures he admired, without stinting on their contradictions and
flaws. His fascination with the intricacies of character was Balzacian,
and in fact, Wilson tried his hand several times at novel writing (largely
autobiographical), but was never as successful at it as he was with his
biographical essays, which allowed him to be sympathetically engaged
with complicated others.

John Jay Chapman: The Mute and the Open Strings

(1938)

Mr. M. A. DeWolfe Howe has done an excellent job with the letters and
papers of the late John Jay Chapman. Mr. Howe enjoyed the advantages
of having known Chapman personally and of already being thoroughly
at home in the latter's period and circle.

One's only complaint about Mr. Howe's book is that there is not anywhere near enough of it. I understand that he was induced by his publishers to cut down his original manuscript; and this seems to me to have

been a mistake. Anybody interested in Chapman at all would be able to read a book twice as long as the present one. My own impression from what is here published is that John Jay Chapman was probably the best letter-writer that we have ever had in this country. And it seems to me a pity that Mr. Howe did not include the whole text of the autobiographical document which Chapman prepared not long before his death, instead of only selections from it. My hope and belief is, in fact, that the future will be sufficiently interested in Chapman to print and read his letters as eagerly as has been done with Horace Walpole's—as well as to go back to his published works as we have done to those of Thoreau.

Yet at the present time hardly one reader in a million has heard of even the name of John Jay Chapman. His later books have had no circulation, and most of his earlier ones are out of print. How, then, is it possible to attach so much importance to a writer who has been persistently ignored by the historians of American literature and who has been read by almost nobody, even during these last twenty years when so much rummaging has been going on in the attic of our literary history? How has it been possible thus for a writer who was at one time a conspicuous figure and who is still valued so highly by a few readers, to become completely invisible to the general reading public even while he was still living and writing?

This essay will attempt to answer that question, on which Mr. Howe's biography has thrown a great deal of light.

I

Perhaps our most vivid impression as we read about Chapman in this book—especially through the first half of his life—is that we have encountered a personality who does not belong in his time and place and who by contrast makes us aware of the commonness, the provinciality and the timidity of most of his contemporaries. "Yes," we say to ourselves in our amazement, "people ought to be more like this!"

When John Jay Chapman was twenty-five and studying law at Harvard—it was the winter of 1886–7—he made the acquaintance of the half-Italian niece of the Brimmer family of Boston: "a swarthy, fiery large-eyed girl, who looked like the younger Sibyl of Michael Angelo" and "had the man-minded seriousness of women in classic myths, the regular brow, heavy dark hair, free gait of the temperament that lives in heroic thought and finds the world full of chimeras, of religious mysteries, sacrifice, purgation"—such a woman as had hardly existed outside "the imagination of Aeschylus and the poets."

"I had never abandoned my reading of Dante"—it would be a pity not to give it in his own words—"and it somehow came about that I read Dante with Minna. There was a large airy room at the top of the old

Athenaeum Library in Boston whose windows looked out on the church-yard. It was a bare and quiet place: no one ever came there. And during the winter we read Dante there together, and in the course of this she told me of her early life in Milan. There were five children, three of them boys, and there were tempestuous quarrels between the parents. I saw that it was from her mother that she had inherited her leonine temperament. The mother had been a fury. I could see this, though she did not say it . . . The Dante readings moved gradually like a cloud between me and the law, between me and the rest of life. It was done with few words. I had come to see that she was in love with someone. It never occurred to me that she might be in love with me. An onlooker might have said, 'You loved her for the tragedies of her childhood and she loved you that you did pity them.'

"The case was simple, but the tension was blind and terrible. I was completely unaware that I was in love."

But he did come to be aware that something was making her unhappy, and he decided that "an acquaintance of hers, a friend in whom she had little interest," had been trifling with her affections. One evening at "the most innocent kind of party that you can imagine at a country house," he suddenly, without conscious premeditation, invited the man outside and beat him.

"The next thing I remember is returning late at night to my room. At that time I was rooming alone in a desolate side-street in Cambridge. It was a small, dark, horrid little room. I sat down. There was a hard-coal fire burning brightly. I took off my coat and waistcoat, wrapped a pair of suspenders tightly on my left forearm above the wrist, plunged the left hand deep in the blaze and held it down with my right hand for some minutes. When I took it out, the charred knuckles and finger bones were exposed. I said to myself, 'This will never do.' I took an old coat, wrapped it about my left hand and arm, slipped my right arm into an overcoat, held the coat about me and started for Boston in the horsecars. On arriving at the Massachusetts General Hospital I showed the trouble to a surgeon, was put under ether, and the next morning waked up without the hand and very calm in my spirits. Within a few days I was visited by the great alienist, Dr. Reginald Heber Fitz, an extremely agreeable man. He asked me among other things whether I was insane. I said, 'That is for you to find out.' He reported me as sane. I took no interest in the scandal which my two atrocious acts must have occasioned."

He knew now that he was in love with Minna and that it was he whom Minna loved. "Do you know, Minna," he wrote her, before they were married, in the summer of the same year, "the one time in my life dur-ing which I lived was that twenty days of pain. I read *Henry Esmond,* Dickens' *Christmas Stories,* one morning—I never shall forget them—*Mr. Barnes of New York.* Every word of it is glowing with life and love. There was fire in everything I touched—the fire of the activity of that part of me which was meant to be used, which got suppressed all my life till it broke. The depth of the intentions and remote unkempt wells of life and feeling. Browning I used to read anywhere . . . Somehow I have known the meaning of things, if not for long, and all the while I thought I need rest, I need sleep. You see life is an experiment. I had not the least idea but what [if] I met you all this would run the other way and the pain turn into pleasure. I thought I had opened life forever—what matter if the entrance was through pain."

And later, three years after they were married, he wrote her in an extraordinary love letter on one of his business trips to the West: "It was not a waste desert in Colorado. It is not a waste time, for you are here and many lives packed into one life, and the green shoot out of the heart of the plant, springing up blossoms in the night, and many old things have put on immortality and lost things have come back knocking within, from before the time I was conceived in the womb, there were you, also. And what shall we say of the pain! it was false—and the rending, it was unnecessary. It was the breaking down of the dams that ought not to have been put up—but being up it was the sweeping away of them that the waters might flow together."*

They lived in New York, where he had been born. Chapman practiced and hated law. He was, on the other hand, passionately interested in politics. He had been a member of the City Reform Club, founded by Theodore Roosevelt and others, almost from its beginning in 1882; and later became president of the Good Government Club, which had grown out of the City Reform Club. The Good Government Club had been founded by another Harvard man, Edmond Kelly, for the purpose of fighting Tammany Hall. When Kelly found out that it was impossible to recruit the working-class to his movement, he gave it up and became a socialist. But Chapman and another Harvard man assumed the leadership of the Good Government movement, and from 1895 through 1900 he had an odd and very interesting career as a non-socialist political radical.

In the election of 1895, the "Goo-Goo's," unable to agree with the Republicans on a common ticket against Tammany, ran a campaign of their own and were defeated; and in all this John Jay Chapman played a spirited and provocative part. He made speeches from the cart-tail in the streets and created a great impression by getting down and manhandling hecklers who were trying to break him up—he was a man of formidable build—then going back and finishing his speech and afterwards buying his opponents drinks; and he was able, also, to upset the routine of such accepted professional reformers as Joseph Choate and Godkin of the *Post*. His announced policy at political dinners was "to say nothing that he would not regret"; and he is reported to have been the only person

---

* *John Jay Chapman and His Letters.*

who ever caused the venerable and cultivated Choate to lose his urbanity in public—by pointing out to him that the anti-Tammany organization to which Mr. Choate belonged had been guilty of a deal with the enemy. John Jay Chapman did not understand politics even as the political reformers did. He combined the extreme exhilaration of hope with the utmost contempt of compromise. He had at this period what the poet Yeats calls "the purity of a natural force," and he disturbed and frightened people.

But he was presently to collide with another personality, with whom he had supposed himself to be traveling, but of whom he turned out to be crossing the path. In the autumn of 1898, John Jay Chapman was one of the leaders of a group of political Independents who wanted to nominate Theodore Roosevelt for the governorship of New York. Chapman had an interview with Roosevelt: the latter accepted the nomination and continued to affirm his willingness to be run by the Independents even after the Republican Party had offered to nominate him, too. But, in the meantime, the Independents had drawn up a whole Independent ticket; and the Republican boss, Tom Platt, told Roosevelt that if he wanted the Republicans to run him, he would have to throw over the Independents— which Roosevelt immediately did. Chapman had been so unwary as to fail to extract a written promise from Roosevelt, because he had supposed a gentleman's word was enough. He had happened to start down to Oyster Bay to call on his supposed candidate just before the news of the defection broke in New York; and when he got there, he found there was no train back, so that he had to spend the evening with Roosevelt. It seems to have been a harrowing occasion, "for I was not going home leaving any mist or misunderstandings in the air as to how the Good Government Club group viewed the situation. But I went further. I unloaded the philosophy of agitation upon Roosevelt and pictured him as the broken-backed half-good man, the successor of the doughface and Northern man with Southern principles of Civil War times, the trimmer who wouldn't break with his party and so, morally speaking, it ended by breaking him."

Chapman knew very well what Roosevelt had promised him; and the incident gave him seriously to think. He observed that Roosevelt presently persuaded himself that he had never understood the original proposal; and that he thereafter became very vociferous over the damage done progressive movements by fanatics on their "lunatic fringe." Chapman had been publishing since March 1897 a review called the *Political Nursery* (originally, simply the *Nursery*), and he now used it to attack Roosevelt's subsequent activities and those of the reformist mayor, Seth Low, formerly a candidate of the Independents. It was the McKinley-Roosevelt era of American imperialist expansion, and Chapman fought the policy of the United States in Cuba and in the Philippines, as well as denounced the British in South Africa.

This review, which he carried on through January 1901, is one of the best written things of the kind which has ever been published anywhere. Chapman wrote most of it himself, and he dealt with philosophical and literary, as well as with political, subjects. Here he began the characteristic practice which William James described when he wrote of him: "He just looks at things and tells the truth about them—a strange thing even to *try* to do, and he doesn't always succeed." But he did succeed pretty often, and he is at his best during this early period. As I have not the files of the *Political Nursery* by me, I shall quote some portraits and comments from the letters of his later as well as of his earlier years.

Of James Russell Lowell, he wrote in 1896:

"I don't dislike the man. I think him a fine man, a little dandified and genteel perhaps, but still a good story character. His poetry is nothing but a fine talent, a fine ear, a fine facility—too much morality and an incredible deftness at imitating everybody from Milton down. I cannot read his poems with any comfort—but his early essays I still think the best things he ever did, witty, snappy, 'smart' to a degree, and quite natural—they are the only things he ever did that were quite natural. In later life he got all barnacled with quotations and leisure. He pulls out pocket-books and gold snuff boxes and carbuncled cigarette-cases, and emerald eye-glasses, and curls and pomatums himself and looks in pocket looking glasses, and smoothes his Vandyke beard and is a literary fop—f-o-p, fop. Too much culture—overnourished as Waddy Longfellow says—too many truffled essays and champagne odes and lobster sonnets, too much Spanish olives, potted proverbs—a gouty old cuss in his later essays. But in '54–'65 he wrote rapidly and most clearly. Belles Lettres is the devil after all. It spoils a man. His prefaces—sometimes very nice, in spirit—but his later prefaces are so expressive—O my! so expressive of hems and haws and creased literary trousers. I feel like running him in the belly and singing out Hulloo! old cockolorum."

Of President Eliot of Harvard (1898):

"Read the essays of (Pres.) Eliot. There's no offense in them. Two by six. Everything in Massachusetts is deal boards. You can put every man in a box—Smug, Smug. He has a good word for poetry too. It's the Dodgedom of Culture. My God, how I hate it. He's the very highest type of a most limited and inspiring pork-chopism. My God, he is hopeful—calls his book *American Contributions to Civilization*—thinks we don't understand small parks and drainage—but will learn and are doing nicely. Has a chapter on 'the pleasures of life.' It's all one size. Every word in this work is the same size. The Puritans—the war—the problems of labor and capital—education—all excite the same emotion—i.e. that of a woodchuck eating a carrot."

Of Eliot and J. Pierpont Morgan (1907):

"Pierpont Morgan is the actual apex as well as the type, of the commercial perversions of the era. The political corruption, etc., the power behind all . . . Now then, at the dedication of the New Medical School, Eliot goes about in a cab with Pierpont, hangs laurel wreaths on his nose, and gives him his papal kiss. Now what I want to know is this—what has Eliot got to say to the young man entering business or politics who is about to be corrupted by Morgan and his class? How eloquently can Eliot present the case for honesty? Can he say anything that will reverberate through the chambers of that young man's brain more loudly than that kiss?

"If Eliot is a great man, I want a small man."

Of Roosevelt and Wilson (1930):

"I have just read in type-writing a book about Roosevelt—which ought to be called the Night Side of T. R.; for it is wholly malignant—and to that extent ineffective. But it's true. He was very nearly mad at times—and broke down his mind by his egotism and mendacity. I had a quarrel with him—political, and personal, and deadly. He was a great genius for handling a situation, and with men, in such a way as to get credit—but he was a damned scoundrel. His genius was to flash a light, put someone down a well, raise a howl to heaven about honesty, and move on to the next thing. Such a genius for publicity as never was—and our people being boy-minded and extremely stupid found him lovely. His feebleness of intellect appears in his writings—which are dull and bombastic—and I doubt whether he will go down as a great man. He's more like a figure out of Dumas. Wilson, a character more odious still, will go down to history as the father of the League of Nations. Drat him! His writings also are dull and he also had the power of hypnotizing men. They idolized him—even those who didn't like him—obeyed—worshiped.

"Apropos—aren't great men apt to be horrid?"

In 1898, he published a volume of literary papers called *Emerson and Other Essays.* In this collection and in the *Political Nursery,* he wrote a commentary on authors then popular—Stevenson, Kipling, Browning, etc.—of which in our day the acumen seems startling. I cannot remember any other American critic of that period—except, in his more specialized field and his more circumlocutionary way, Henry James—who had anything like the same sureness of judgment, the same freedom from current prejudices and sentimentalities. Chapman was then, as, it seems to me, he was to remain, much our best writer on literature of his generation—who made the Babbitts and the Mores and the Brownells, for all the more formidable rigor of their systems and the bulkier mass of their work, look like colonial schoolmasters.

It is worth while to rescue a passage from one of his more ephemeral papers—an article on Kipling in the *Political Nursery* of April 1899—for its statement of his organic ideal for literature:

"Permanent interest cannot attach to anything which does not consist, from rind to seeds, of instructive truth. A thing must be interesting from every point of view, as history, as poetry, as philosophy; good for a sick man, just the thing for Sunday morning. It must be true if read backwards, true literally and true as a parable, true in fragments and true as a whole. It must be valuable as a campaign document, and it must make you laugh or cry at any time, day or night. Lasting literature has got to be so very good as to fulfill all these conditions. Kipling's work does not do so since the time he began making money out of it."

But the long study of Emerson had a special importance. It was something other than a mere essay on Emerson. It was rather an extension of Emerson, a re-creation of Emerson for a new generation, for it was really an expression—the first full expression—of Chapman's own point of view. And what Chapman got out of Emerson was something entirely different from the gentle and eupeptic personality—though that was a part of the real Emerson, too—of Van Wyck Brooks's recent portrayals. What Chapman got out of Emerson was a sort of beneficent Nietzscheanism, as electrical as Nietzsche's but less rhetorical. It had seemed to him at college, Chapman wrote, "as if Emerson were a younger brother of Shakespeare . . . I was intoxicated with Emerson. He let loose something within me which made me in my own eyes as good as anyone else." It was Emerson who had first made it possible for him to say to himself: "After all, it is just as well that there should be *one* person like *me* in the world." John Jay Chapman was thus a continuator of the individualist tradition of Emerson, which is also the tradition of Thoreau. (Chapman speaks of Thoreau less often, though it seems to me that he is in some ways even more closely akin to him.) He had carried this tradition to New York— for, in spite of the influence on his thought of Cambridge and Concord and Boston, he was distinctly to remain a New Yorker; and in his hands it was to undergo here an interesting variation.

"As I look back over my past," he writes, "the figure of Emerson looms up in my mind as the first modern man, and the city of Boston as the first living civilization which I knew. New York is not a civilization; it is a railway station." Yet the New Yorker, though beside the New Englanders, with their Concord flavor and color, he may seem a little abstract and steely (as Henry James does, also, beside Hawthorne), is the man of a larger world. He was to bring against Emerson a new criticism. "Our people are as thin-skinned as babies," he wrote in one of his lectures, "and the Massachusetts crowd has never been criticized." No one had ventured to stand up to Emerson on the issue of the sexual emotions since Walt Whitman had walked with him on Boston Common and, after listening to all his remonstrances against the *Children of Adam* section of *Leaves of Grass,* had replied that he couldn't answer Emerson's arguments, but that he felt sure of being right just the same. "If an inhabitant of another planet," wrote Chapman, "should visit the earth, he would receive, on the whole, a truer notion of human life by attending an Italian opera than he would by reading Emerson's volumes. He would learn from the Italian opera that there were two sexes; and this, after all, is probably the fact with which the education of such a stranger ought to begin. In a review of Emerson's personal character and opinions, we are thus led to see that his philosophy, which finds no room for the emotions, is a faithful exponent of his own and of the New England temperament, which distrusts and dreads the emotions. Regarded as a sole guide to life for a young person of strong conscience and undeveloped affections, his works might conceivably be even harmful because of their unexampled power of purely intellectual stimulation."

And he was to take the Thoreauvian intransigence into society instead of into solitude. John Jay Chapman's attitude toward politics is to develop with a curious logic, which is set forth in two other remarkable books: *Causes and Consequences* (1898) and *Practical Agitation* (1900). *Causes and Consequences* is one of the most powerful tracts ever written on the debasement of our politics and government by unscrupulous business interests. It begins with a pungent fable about the gradual but complete domination of a small American town by a railroad which passes through it. This, says Chapman, when he has told his story, is the whole history of America since the Civil War. And he shows the results of this process in the general cultural life with a force which was not later surpassed by Mencken or Van Wyck Brooks:

"We have seen that the retailer in the small town could not afford to think clearly upon the political situation. But this was a mere instance, a sample of his mental attitude. He dare not face any question. He must shuffle, qualify and defer. Here at last we have the great characteristic which covers our continent like a climate—intellectual dishonesty. This state of mind does not merely prevent a man having positive opinions. The American is incapable of taking a real interest in anything. The lack of passion in the American—noticeable in his books and in himself—comes from the same habitual mental distraction; for passion is concentration. Hence also the flippancy, superficiality and easy humor for which we are noted. Nothing except the dollar is believed to be worthy the attention of a serious man. People are even ashamed of their tastes. Until recently, we thought it effeminate for a man to play on the piano. When a man takes a living interest in anything, we call him a 'crank.' There is an element of self-sacrifice in any honest intellectual work which we detect at once and score with contumely.

"It was not solely commercial interest that made the biographers of Lincoln so thrifty to extend and veneer their books. It was that they themselves did not, could not, take an interest in the truth about him. The second-rate quality of all our letters and verse is due to the same cause. The intellectual integrity is undermined. The literary man is concerned for what 'will go,' like the reformer who is half politician. The attention of everyone in the United States is on someone else's opinion, not on truth."

What is one to do in such a world? The diagnosis of *Causes and Consequences* is followed by a program of action in *Practical Agitation;* but Chapman's practical agitation is of a special and unexpected kind. As a result of his experience as a reformer, he has ceased to believe in the possibility of organized political reform under the American conditions of the time. One of the most amusing and searching passages of *Practical Agitation* describes the rapid absorption and the complete neutralization of a reform movement by the forces it has set out to correct. The commercial solidarity of society has rendered such crusading futile.

Once arrived at such a recognition, one might expect a man like Chapman to turn socialist; but his position on socialism is stated as follows:

"The function of Socialism is clear. It is a religious reaction going on in an age which thinks in terms of money. We are very nearly at the end of it, because we are very nearly at the end of the age. Some people believe they hate the wealth of the millionaire. They denounce corporations and trusts, as if these things hurt them. They strike at the symbol. What they really hate is the irresponsible rapacity which these things typify, and which nothing but moral forces will correct. In so far as people seek the cure in property-laws they are victims of the plague. The cure will come entirely from the other side; for as soon as the millionaires begin to exert and enjoy the enormous power for good which they possess, everybody will be glad they have the money."

He does not, therefore, believe much in economics:

"The economic laws are valuable and suggestive, but they are founded on the belief that a man will pursue his own business interests exclusively. This is never entirely true even in trade, and the doctrines of the economists become more and more misleading when applied to fields of life where the money motive becomes incidental. The law of supply and demand does not govern the production of sonnets."

But, "when you see cruelty going on before you, you are put to the alternative of interposing to stop it, or of losing your sensibility."

What then? Here is where Emerson comes in. "If a soul," he wrote, "be taken and crushed by democracy till it utter a cry, that cry will be Emerson." And: "The thing seems to me about this," he wrote in a letter of this time, after finishing an essay on the *Social Results of Commercialism*— "Emerson made coherent. It's all Emerson. I should have had neither the ideas reduced so clearly nor the public to understand them if it hadn't been for Emerson. I can't imagine what I should have been if it hadn't been for Emerson." For he is thrown back on the individual conscience. Here is the situation with which the citizen finds himself confronted:

"Remember . . . that there is no such thing as abstract truth. You must talk facts, you must name names, you must impute motives. You must say what is in your mind. It is the only means you have of cutting yourself free from the body of this death. Innuendo will not do. Nobody minds innuendo. We live and breathe nothing else. If you are not strong enough to face the issue in private life, do not dream that you can do anything for public affairs. This, of course, means fight, not tomorrow, but now. It is only in the course of conflict that anyone can come to understand the system, the habit of thought, the mental condition, out of which all our evils arise. The first difficulty is to see the evils clearly; and when we do see them it is like fighting an atmosphere to contend against them. They are so universal and omnipresent that you have no terms to name them by. You must burn a disinfectant."

And one can take only individual action:

"You yourself cannot turn Niagara; but there is not a town in America where one single man cannot make his force felt against the whole torrent. He takes a stand on a practical matter. He takes action against some abuse. What does this accomplish? Everything. How many people are there in your town? Well, every one of them gets a thrill that strikes deeper than any sermon he ever heard. He may howl, but he hears. The grocer's boy, for the first time in his life, believes that the whole outfit of morality has any place in the practical world."

There can have been few codes of morality ever formulated so individualistic as John Jay Chapman's:

"If you want a compass at any moment in the midst of some difficult situation, you have only to say to yourself, 'Life is larger than this little imbroglio. I shall follow my instinct.' As you say this, your compass swings true. You may be surprised to find what course it points to. But what it tells you to do will be practical agitation."

This code, with high courage and immense energy, he attempted to put into practice. These were intent and tumultuous years, during which he was shaken by many emotions. At the beginning of 1897, after the birth of their second son, his wife suddenly and unexpectedly died while he was reading to her aloud as she lay in bed. The next year he married his friend, Elizabeth Chanler. Through all this he had been speaking, writing, organizing, getting out his paper, practicing law and leading an active social life—while the immovable magnitude of the forces against him was gradually but inexorably becoming clear to him. "My own family and connections," he wrote, "being a lot of well-meaning bourgeois, are horrified at me. But I enjoy it." Yet, "Politics takes physique," he wrote at another time, "and being odious takes physique. I feel like Atlas, lifting the entire universe. I hate this community and despise 'em—and fighting, fighting, fighting, fighting an atmospheric pressure gets tiresome." When his friends expressed apprehension: "As for insanity," he replied, "why, I was once examined for insanity by the two most distinguished physicians

in Boston [at the time when he had burned off his hand]. It has no terrors.
I talked to them like Plato."

In the summer of 1900, he went out to attend a convention in Indianapolis which nominated "Gold Democrat" candidates to run against
both McKinley and Bryan; and he worked hard to organize a "National
Party," the candidates proposed for which refused to run. That winter,
after an attack of grippe, at the time when his wife was expecting a baby,
he suddenly broke down in the midst of a speech in a small town in Pennsylvania. "Too much will and self-will," he wrote his mother.

He retreated to a darkened room. For a year he did not leave his bed,
and when he was finally able to get up, remained for two or three years
longer under the delusion that he was unable to walk without crutches.
Turned in on his own blackness, the sight of a beautiful sunset or the
interior of an Italian church, which he had been induced to come out to
see, would excite him to the point of collapse.

II

The second half of John Jay Chapman's life is quite distinct from the
first. In the August of 1903, one of his sons by his first wife Minna was
drowned in an Austrian river; and the shock seems to have brought him to
himself. He went back to the United States without his crutches.

He recovered, and thereafter for thirty years led the life of a well-to-do
country squire at Barrytown on the Hudson. His second wife's family, the
Chanlers, were among the most adventurous and gifted of that special
race, the Hudson River gentry; and John Jay Chapman took his place
in their world. Chapman's father had been president of the New York
Stock Exchange, but had lost heavily in the panic of the seventies, so that
John Jay had had partly to put himself through college by tutoring, and
he seems to have had a certain amount of difficulty in supporting his
family on his earnings from the law. In his youth he had had a variety
of social experience which verged at moments on the picaresque. In the
course of a trip to Europe after his graduation from Harvard, he had gone
to visit an aunt who had married the German minister to Russia and had
attended a ball at the Winter Palace, where he saw through the eyes of
Tolstoy the Grand Dukes and "the gorgeous ministers holding glittering
staves" and the "consoling duplicities" of the diplomats, and rescued a
pair of toboggans which seemed about to become untied on a chute by
throwing himself between them and holding them together while he was
dragged on his belly to the bottom; and not long afterwards, when he had
returned to America, he went to Canada and hired himself out as a farm-
hand: he "did chores, digged holes for posts, picked cherries on a ladder"
till his "head swam" and "the landscape reeled," but was so bad at it that

one farmer refused to pay him, and he finally came back to his family in such a condition of raggedness and shagginess that they were unable to recognize him; his whole exploit had netted him a dollar.

On the eve of his second marriage, he had been troubled by apprehensions at the prospect of being well-to-do. "The first thing you know we'll be drowned in possessions," he wrote at that time to Miss Chanler, "and then by thinking of our horses' health. It is not so easy to keep the keen vision which an empty stomach lends, if you have footmen. I fear a footman. I tremble before a man with hot water . . . Let's keep the New Testament open before us. The losing of wrath is to be feared . . . If I become classed with men at ease about money, the Lord protect me. It is a steel corselet against the heart of mankind and the knowledge of life." And there are indications in his later letters that he continued to shrink from allowing himself to be "classed with men at ease about money." "I take rides on the busses—for 4d.," he wrote a friend from London. "You can go at the rate of 10 m. per hour for half an hour. These things recall London—and student days. The cheap things give one most pleasure—when one is old and rich like me." And: "The food of the rich is disgusting to me . . . messes. Last night I had to go to Childs and eat cornbeef hash and poached eggs, which pulled me round."

Yet he is haunted by ideas of his affinities with royalty and aristocracy. "I never saw children like them," he wrote of his sons by his first wife. "They are King's children in disguise, and I am a stepfather to them." And, during a visit to an Italian noble, "I am having some gold fringe put on my pants and I have assumed the title of Monsignore. It is amazing how easily gentility sits on me. I believe some people are just naturally swells—you know what I mean—and fit well in palaces and eat good food naturally and without effort. I remember the first royal palace I saw—seemed to me—gave me a feeling—just like the old homestead. I often think that Grandma Jones used to say, 'the Chapmans were once Kings.' Dear old Grandpa, with his old cotton socks, wouldn't he be proud if he could see me he-hawing and chaw-chawing with Roman princes!" His plays are full of princes and counts and kings. He had himself something of a kingly presence, especially adorned with the magnificent beard with which he had emerged from his illness. And it is impossible to escape the impression that the comfort and security of his later years did to some degree dull his responses and cut him off from the active world. He succumbed to the Hudson Valley in becoming one of its principal ornaments—to Dutchess County, with its cupolaed castles on their towering dark-wooded hills, which do their best to give work or give alms to the humble feudal villages on the riverbank, to the thunderstorms that seem to crack the firmament and the heavy and slumbrous summers, to the tradition of public responsibility which Hamilton Fish shares with Franklin D. Roosevelt, to the culture which, where it occurs, is likely to range so much more widely and to seem to have so much more authenticity than that of most wealthy communities in America, and to the naturalness and amiability which merge quietly and not unpleasantly with smugness—and all, as it were, walled-in from the rest of the United States and alone with the noble river.

The young John Jay Chapman had plunged into the thick of the conflicts of his time. *Emerson* and *Causes and Consequences* had been talked about and read, had had their influence. In both his political and his literary writing, he had dealt with matters of current interest. But now, in his second period, he seems to have withdrawn from contemporary life, and tends to confine himself to history and the classics. He seems almost to be talking to himself, he seems hardly to expect or hope for an audience; and so people cease to listen to him. The second half of Chapman's career must inevitably be surprising and depressing, though not entirely disappointing, to one who has been stirred by the first. Though he had been able to throw away his crutches, he was to remain, in a deeper sense, a crippled man all the rest of his life. Yet the alternative to survival on these terms would, one supposes, have been madness or death; and it is the proof of the authenticity of his genius that, throughout this long period when he is turned toward the past, when, as a rule, he emerges into the present to raise only trivial or unreal issues, he keeps his power not merely to charm but also sometimes to stimulate.

The Americans who graduated from college in the eighties had to contend with a world that broke most of them. One can see the situation very clearly if one compares the men of the eighties even with those of the seventies. In the seventies, the universities were still turning out admirable professional men, who had had the old classical education, a culture much wider than their profession and the tradition of political idealism and public conscience which had presided at the founding of the Republic. The world which they had found when they got out had not yet become different enough from the world for which their education had fitted them so that they were not able, on the terms of that old education, to make for themselves positions of dignity in it. But by the later years of the eighties, the industrial and commercial development which followed the Civil War had reached a point where the old education was no longer an equipment for life. It had, in fact, become a troublesome handicap. The best of the men who had taken it seriously were launched on careers of tragic misunderstanding. They could no longer play the role in the professions of a trained and public-spirited caste: the new society did not recognize them. The rate of failure and insanity and suicide in some of the college "classes" of the eighties shows an appalling demoralization.

Some set themselves to learn the new methods and choked their scruples and did their best to cash in; but John Jay Chapman—who had John Jay among his ancestors—was too honest, too fastidious, too proud, and too violently impulsive, for this. Others compromised shrewdly, like Roosevelt; but the merest suggestion of compromise seems at that period to have driven Chapman into a frenzy. Almost all were compelled to accept in some way the values of the world of business; but how little this was possible for Chapman is indicated in one of his late letters when he insists that, let people say what they please, business can never be a profession. (I have heard a college man of as late as the nineties, who had spent fifty years with an importing firm, tell of his feelings of humiliation when he first started in to work there at a time when the business men, on their side, were supposed to have no use for college graduates. By the second decade of our century, probably the majority of college students had no higher object, on graduating, than to qualify for selling bonds or to slip behind some desk in a family concern and present a well-brushed appearance; and the movement for business courses in the colleges and the talk of the university as a "big business" were already well under way.)

Given the fineness of Chapman's equipment, the overpowering nature of his emotions and the relentless clarity of his insight—and given the inescapable conviction of his superiority which made him, for all the ardor of his patriotism, talk about "a soul crushed by democracy"—there was nothing for him to do but break. And the permanent psychological damage which he had inflicted upon himself by beating his head against the gilt of the Gilded Age was as much one of the scars of the heroism of his passionate and expiatory nature as the hand he had burnt off in his youth.

Let us see how he occupies himself. He begins by writing little plays for children—then, later, tries longer plays. *The Treason and Death of Benedict Arnold* (1910) is perhaps the best of these and has a certain personal interest—with its Coriolanian picture of a man of touchy pride and strong self-will driving through a perverse course of action, which will bring him, among his enemies, honor but no comfort and which will separate him forever from the cause for which he has fought:

> They must pet me then,
> To show that loyal treason reaps reward.
> 'Twas policy, not liking for my face,
> That made King George so sweet.
> What in this world of savage Englishmen,
> Strange monsters that they are, have you and I
> Found of a country? Friends, good hearts and true;
> But alien as the mountains of the moon,
> More unrelated than the Polander,
> Are Englishmen to us. They are a race,
> A selfish, brawling family of hounds,
> Holding a secret contract on each fang,

"For us," "for us," "for us" They'll fawn about;
But when the prey's divided;—Keep away!
I have some beef about me and bear up
Against an insolence as basely set
As mine own infamy; yet I have been
Edged to the outer cliff. I have been weak,
And played too much the lackey.
What am I In this waste, empty, cruel, land of England,
Save an old castaway,—a buccaneer,—
The hull of derelict Ambition,—
Without a mast or spar, the rudder gone,
A danger to mankind!

But, on the whole, as his biographer says, Chapman is unable to trans-
mit to his characters his own power of self-dramatization. He shrank
from and had little comprehension of the new dramatic forms of Ibsen
and Shaw, as he shrank from the world they reflected. The companion
of Shakespeare and Aeschylus, he followed their methods as a matter of
course, with results which are not hopelessly academic only because he
could not help getting some reality into everything that he wrote. His
plays were mostly in verse; and his verse—he also made some translations from the Greeks and published a certain amount of miscellaneous
poetry—is usually only effective when it approximates to the qualities of
his prose. There are a few exceptions to this, such as his fine translations
from Dante; but the poet that there undoubtedly was in Chapman—
perhaps some Puritan heritage had its blighting effect here—found
expression chiefly in preaching. As a moralist, John Jay Chapman is a
highly successful artist; and it is mainly as a moralist now that he will
continue to hold our attention.

With his illness, there emerges a new point of view—really a sort of
rarefication of his earlier one. It was before the days of psychoanalysis,
and he had been helped through his breakdown by "faith healers." In
a peculiar and personal way, he now becomes religious. "There was
never anyone with more practical notions, or less under the belief that
he was religious in his aims, than I," he wrote to a friend in 1922 of his
early political experience. "I wanted to attack practical evils—find out
about them anyway, affront and examine them, understand them—and
I set out by experiment and analysis to deal with them as a workaday
problem. And gradually under inspection and ratiocination they turned
into spiritual things—mystical elements, and went back into the envelope
of religious truth. Nothing else but religious truth was involved. It happened to me apropos of reform movements, to the next man in medicine,
to the next in hygiene, in education, in literary work—(look at Winston
Churchill). Surely all of us were toys in a shop, and were being turned by

the same dynamo—we all approach more nearly all the time to a common frame of mind and temperament—a common sense of helplessness—we who were going to be so powerful and triumphant." He had announced his new attitude in 1913 at the end of his book on William Lloyd Garrison: "At first," he says, "we desire to help vigorously, and we do all in our power to assist mankind. As time goes on, we perceive more and more clearly that the advancement of the world does not depend upon us, but that we, rather, are bound up in it, and can command no foothold of our own. At last we see that our very ambitions, desires and hopes in the matter are a part of the Supernal Machinery moving through all things, and that our souls can be satisfied and our power exerted only in so far as we are taken up into that original motion, and merged in that primal power. Our minds thus dissolve under the grinding analysis of life, and leave behind nothing except God. Towards him we stand and look: and we, who started out with so many gifts for men, have nothing left in our satchel for mankind except a blessing."

To one who, like the present writer, is fundamentally unsympathetic with all modern manifestations of religion, the books of John Jay Chapman on this subject—*Notes on Religion* (1922) and *Letters and Religion* (1924)—seem genuine and impressive in a way that most other such recent writings do not. There have been lately in fashion among literary people two main ways of being religious: one historical, philosophical and ritualistic—the convert turns to the Catholic Church; the other through a substitute pseudo-religion, like that proposed by H. G. Wells. But in the flashes of revelation that were intermittently noted by Chapman, we seem to touch a live spiritual experience as we do not often do with these writers. It is, of course, intensely Protestant: it is Emersonianism again. We are not to look for direction to any established church; each is to trust his own instinct and to interpret the Scriptures for himself:

"Christianity accomplishes itself; and this not through a grand, frontal attack on humanity, but rather through the story and sayings of Christ which dart through the earth, pierce men's ears and heal them, run like elixirs through the languages and habits of men. They are couriers, arrows that live in the ether and need no inns or baiting-places between their flights. The sayings have inexhaustible meanings, and many depths of meaning which the comfortable people of the world cannot hope to fathom—meanings that lie in ambush in the texts, and enter men's hearts in the wake of grief. A man must have been disgraced and in jail to know many of them." Yet the instincts of individuals are to unite in communion the whole of mankind. With the capacity for deep humility and the sympathy with American life which saved his sense of superiority from snobbery, he was able to interest himself in philanthropies and popular churches:

"I believe that if we could see the invisible church as it actually exists in the interlacing of all men in God and with each other through the force that makes them live, the alarm of those who are fostering religion for fear it will die out would appear ridiculous. Even the half-charlatan, half-illiterate American religious cults deserve our interest and respect."

"The new American mysticism, for all its eccentricities, dropped an anchor for a generation that had been living in continuous flotation; and being at anchor, the waves of life began to play against the souls of that generation, and beat them into faith. The breakdown of the older ecclesiastical authorities proved a blessing. All the barriers, the interpretations, the shopworn catechisms, the churchy miasmas of many centuries, had been blown away, and the bare text of the New Testament began to convert a new generation and to bring them rest. The new faith was purest in the most humble, as has been the case with all Christian revivals."

The later Chapman is a lesser Tolstoy, fighting out on his estate on the Hudson the same kind of long war with his conscience which Tolstoy fought at Yasnaya Polyana. And we feel about him somewhat as the contemporaries of Tolstoy seem to have felt about him: that, whatever his inconsistencies and his crusadings for mistaken causes, his spirit and example were a force of incalculable value.

"Truly," he wrote in one of his letters, "it is the decay in the American brain that is the real danger, and in my narrow philosophy I see the only cure in self-expression, passion, feeling—spiritual reality of some sort. We're about dead spiritually—that's my illusion." William James, the one of Chapman's contemporaries who probably appreciated him most, called him "a profound moralist." "I have a notion," he once wrote James, "that I could tell you what is the matter with pragmatism—if you would only stand still. A thing is not truth till it is so strongly believed in that the believer is convinced that its existence does not depend upon him. This cuts off the pragmatist from knowing what truth is." And: "It is utter nonsense," he wrote another correspondent, "this great passion and little passion—this upper clef and lower clef. All life is nothing but passion. From the great passion of love to the regard for a passing stranger is all one diapason, and is the same chord. The whole of it vibrates no matter where you touch it—tho' in different degrees." His ideal of practical agitation has in his later phase subsided to this: "I am saying things which will some day be thought of, rather than trying to get the attention of anyone." "It is an accident when I *do* right, but I *am* right," he once declared.

This rightness was due to some influence which took possession of him and was stronger than he. We may be puzzled at first by the language in which he writes to Minna Timmins, his future wife, after the experience of burning off his hand: "I do think there was something Promethean in it, in the capacity to yield." What fire had Chapman snatched from Heaven? And is it Promethean to yield? He means that a divine revelation had caused him to mutilate himself—the revelation of his love for Minna, which was unable to break through into his consciousness and to assert its authority over him save by compelling him to recognize, and hence to punish himself for, his mistake. And he wrote later on to Miss Chanler: "I . . . have broken and battered down the doors of silence once and forever years ago, and go about the world escaped from that prison, I thank the powers of life." Yet he must break out of prison again and again; and his language is always that of giving himself up to something that invades him from outside: "I'll tell you my philosophy—that there's only one real joy in life . . . —the joy of casting at the world the stone of an unknown world." His first love, his first wife and her children, with their fierce natures and their sudden or violent deaths, is itself like a power that seizes upon him, a current for which he acts as conductor and which will leave him partially shattered. And when it is not love, he calls it God.

Besides these religious *pensées,* Chapman publishes during this period several volumes of essays, literary, historical and social, and some memoirs of New York and Boston. He perfects himself now as a writer: in these books, the "style all splinters," of which William James wrote at the time of *Practical Agitation,* is hammered out into an instrument of perfect felicity, economy, limpidity, precision and point. Some of his most beautiful prose is in his very latest writings. And he can still take our breath away by laying hold of the root of some subject, by thrusting through, with a brusque direct gesture, all the familiar conventions and pretensions with which it has been enclosed.

In his relation to the literary classics, he was that almost unprecedented phenomenon, a highly intelligent and well-educated American who paid almost no attention to European criticism and scholarship. Well as he knew Europe, he was never afflicted with the nostalgia for it which seized so many of the cultivated Americans of his time. In his opinions on European culture, he was as naturally and uncompromisingly American as Walt Whitman or Mark Twain. The accepted apparatus of learning he either quarreled with or disregarded—characterizing, for example, the taking-over of Greek literature by the mandarins of the English universities as an incident in the expansion of the British Empire.

To Chapman, the great writers of the past were neither a pantheon nor a vested interest. He approached them open-mindedly and boldly, very much as he did living persons who he thought might entertain or instruct him. Not that he judged them by contemporary standards; but he would go straight to them across the ages in the role of an independent traveler, who was willing to pay his toll to the people that kept the roads but wished to linger with them as little as possible. He sometimes committed blunders: he got the relationships mixed up in the *Antigone,* and he never grasped the simple enough principles which govern, in the *Divine Comedy,* the assignment of the souls to the different worlds—complaining that Dante's arrangements involved a good deal of injustice. "You know," he says in a letter, "I've never known the literature of the subjects I wrote on. I never knew the Emerson literature—except Emerson himself." But Chapman has at least always got there and had a good look at the man; and he can always tell you about him something that you have not heard before. To me, Chapman's flashlighting and spotlighting in his studies of the Greeks, Dante, Shakespeare and Goethe (this last left unpublished at his death and unfortunately not yet published) are among the few real recent contributions to the knowledge of these familiar subjects. He cannot help bumping into aspects which, though they bulk very large in these authors, have so often been ignored or evaded that many people have never noticed they were there. He saw the basic barbarity of Greek tragedy, which he denounced Gilbert Murray for sentimentalizing; he saw the importance of the pederasty of Plato: Diotima, he writes, is "an odious creature, being a man in disguise"; he saw, through all the Dante commentaries, how impossible it is to interpret Dante in terms of medieval theology.

Here are passages from some of the latest of these essays, which show the freshness of Chapman's mind in his sixties:

"Plato soothes and rests. He takes the mind off its troubles and supplies it with imaginative solutions for problems which do not press. To read him is a solace and to write commentaries on him is an entrancing and enduring preoccupation. He is the patron saint of those who sit in armchairs and speculate. His wealth of information, myth and anecdote, the amenity and fluidity of his procedure, endear him to all book-lovers. He is enshrined in a civilization which will interest the world as long as intelligent men shall be born into it. Even the limitations and defects of the Athenians are stimulating. 'Athens,' we say, and surrender ourselves to romance. We sleep while awake; and if you point out that Plato deceives us by intellectual legerdemain which cheats the mind, nay, if you should prove it, this will make you no friends; for, as Mr. Barnum discovered to his profit many centuries later, the public likes to be fooled. A vision of truth which does not call upon us to get out of our armchair—why, this is the desideratum of mankind."

"Dante's frailty is the source of his power. Had he been truly a medieval theologian, or philosopher, or moralist, or historian, he would today be as dead as the rest of them . . . [His philosophy] is full of whimsies and cobwebs, private significances and key-words; and there is no philosophic instrument of thought which he does not distort as he touches it—even as all poets do, and must do." "The conceptions of Greek mythology spring out of a Supermind which harmonizes the fantasies of childhood with the thought of mature age. They are embedded in the ganglia of the brain as music is: no explanation touches them. They defy analysis, and Dante himself fails to interpret them: his metaphysics will not stick to them." "To raise the question whether Dante was technically or virtually a heretic . . . is to miss the human and important point of the whole question. Dante's attitude toward the Empire and the Papacy was that of a super-autocrat who is above both of them, and holds a commission from on high to regulate the affairs of each." "The truth is that one must gather Dante's meanings, as one gathers the meanings of other men, by putting two and two together, not by drawing pictures of his Supposed Universe, and then hanging his phrases on them as on a Christmas Tree." "He had invented the *terza rima,* a form in which a continuous lyric can float and be indefinitely sustained upon the narrative below it."

What a pity, one is moved to exclaim, that John Jay Chapman remained a dilettante! Yet "dilettante" is not the proper word for one who worked at his writing so diligently and so seriously. And his literary essays, after all, are only a part of his general commentary, which possesses a sort of center of its own, independent of the various subjects treated.

Aside from this purely literary activity, he carried on a certain amount of agitation, sporadically and in behalf of a strange diversity of causes. His rejection of economics, his failure, when he had recognized political corruption as a mere by-product of the industrial-commercial system, to study the mechanics and the history of that system, had left him without bearings in the political world.

First of all, he went back to the Civil War—he was very proud of one of his grandmothers, who had been a prominent Abolitionist—and in his book on William Lloyd Garrison fought the battle of slavery all over again with a spirit that would have been employed more usefully in fighting the battle of labor. It was the period of the rise of Bill Haywood's Wobblies, of the growth of Eugene Debs's Socialist Party, of Lincoln Steffens's muck-raking movement.

On August 13, 1911, a Negro who had shot and killed a special officer of the Worth Brothers Steel Company in Coatesville, Pennsylvania, was burned alive by a mob under circumstances of special horror. Chapman, who was full of the Civil War, brooded upon this incident till he "felt as if the whole country would be different if any one man did something in penance, and so I went to Coatesville and declared my intention of holding a prayer meeting to the various business men I could buttonhole." He had difficulty in getting a hall, but finally, four days after the anniversary of the lynching, succeeded in finding a place to speak. The address he delivered was strange and moving. He said that, when he had read in the papers how "hundreds of well-dressed American citizens" had stood by and watched the torture of the Negro, he had seemed to see into "the unconscious soul" of America. And what he had seen there was death— "the paralysis of the nerves about the heart in a people habitually and unconsciously given over to selfish aims." They had "stood like blighted things, like ghosts about Acheron, waiting for someone or something to determine their destiny for them." It was the old wickedness, not yet purged, of the slave trade, and all America was to blame for it. They could but open their hearts to God and pray that new life might flow into them.—The only persons who attended the meeting were an educated Negro woman from Boston and a stool pigeon sent by the police.

The World War, when it first broke out, aroused him to a new burst of agitation. He was in Europe in August 1914, and went immediately to Balfour, Haldane and Sir Edward Grey, and told them that it was of vital importance, in order to elicit the sympathy of the world, that the Allies should declare their aims to be non-aggressive and announce their intention, in the event of their victory, of calling a world disarmament congress; and he seems to have been deceived by the intelligence and kindness with which these statesmen heard him out. Later, he went to Wilson and urged him to elicit such a declaration. He also published a book, *Deutschland über Alles* (1914), in which he pointed out the propaganda methods by which the Germans had been worked up to the war, and advised the United States to stay out. "If America should enter the war, the world would lose the benevolence and commonsense which we now possess, and which is a strong factor in the whole situation. You and I would, in that case, become partisans, cruel, excited and bent on immediate results."

In the meantime, however, his son Victor, one of his children by his first wife, had, against his father's wishes, enlisted in the Foreign Legion and had later become one of the most daring pilots of the Lafayette Escadrille. He was killed—the first American aviator to die—on June 23, 1916; and his father now fell a victim to that war psychology which he had foreseen and dreaded for the country. Chapman was even betrayed temporarily into applauding his old enemy Roosevelt, whose pro-Ally bellowings and pawings of the ground were certainly no more to be taken seriously than the other Rooseveltian impostures which Chapman had so relentlessly exposed. Later, in 1920, when Siegfried Sassoon came to New York, and read his poems and made an anti-war speech at the Cosmopolitan Club, the former opponent of wartime fanaticism—who, no doubt, felt it a duty to speak for his dead son—got up and aroused consternation and hisses by denouncing what he characterized as a philosophy of fear and self-pity. The next day he tried to call on Sassoon and finally wrote him a letter: "Sorry to miss you this morning. It was a suffering occasion last night. I think I suffered as much as you did. If you will do it, why, you must." Had he remembered his early gospel of the value of the individual gesture and reflected that the young Sassoon had, after all, only been doing what he himself had done when, for example, at that political dinner in 1895, he had spoken out in a way that had made old Mr. Choate turn pale?

The most wrongheaded of all his crusades, but the one to which he devoted most energy, was his attack on the Roman Catholic Church. He had received no doubt a terrifying impression of the bad influence of the

Catholics in Boston; but he exaggerated its importance in the United States as a whole, and he had become, by 1925, so almost monomaniacally obsessed by it that it was thought best for him to go abroad to distract his mind from the subject and avoid another breakdown. At one period he was inclined to believe—in spite of the admiration for Jewish culture which had caused him once to call himself a "Hebraist"—that the Jews, also, were coming to be a sinister influence, and he even contributed a sonnet, anti-Catholic and anti-Semitic, to the organ of the Ku Klux Klan. ("The Jews," he had written in 1897, "have in my experience more faith than the Christians. They have clever heads, better hearts, and more belief in the power of good every way. They gave to the world all the religion it has got and are themselves the most religious people in it. I work with them day and night and most of the time is spent in prying up some Christian to do a half day's work.")

For two years he and Mrs. Chapman conducted a club-room for young people in the Hell's Kitchen section of New York. On one occasion, two boys whom he had had to put out, came back and blew kerosene in his beard and tried to set it afire. When they had failed, he handed them a handkerchief and told them to wipe themselves off.

Besides all this he was continually agitating against the influence of big business at Harvard and harrying with scolding letters the Head Master of St. Paul's School, as well as old friends in positions of prominence of whose activities he disapproved. One of his correspondents, Mr. T. B. Wells, the editor of *Harper's Magazine*, was finally goaded to ask what Chapman himself had accomplished any more than "a lot of other brilliant fellows who did not make full use of their talents" to give him the right to call everyone else to account over the way they handled their jobs. And it is true that one feels a touch of envy in his tone toward men like Shaw and Wells, even toward William James, whom he undoubtedly liked and admired—who were doing a kind of work that one would think he might have applauded. There is even an occasional accent of the ignorant and cutting Boston snootiness that he had disliked and ridiculed. As one goes through his later letters—as in reading his work of this period—one is made more and more uncomfortable by the feeling that one has been shut up in a chamber from which the air is being gradually withdrawn— shut in with a chafing spirit who, baffled of finding an outlet, is sometimes furious and sometimes faint. Then suddenly one recoils and stands outside the cell: one sees how Chapman's outlook has narrowed. One remembers all the things that have happened in the world of which there is almost no mention in these letters—almost the whole significant life of the time; and one realizes that Chapman's interests have come to be almost entirely confined to the horizons of his old Harvard circle. It is all Harvard College and St. Paul's School, Porcellian Club and Tavern Club. He writes to Dr. Drury of St. Paul's and E. S. Martin of *Life* as if they were among the great molders of thought of their age. We have the suspicion that even William James, as distinct from Wells and Shaw, is only admitted to the sphere of Chapman's interest because he, too, belongs to Harvard. It is the lost traveler's dream under the hill—the old conception of the caste of trained "college men" who were to preside over the arts and professions. It is the same point of view—we had not recognized it at first—that seemed so fatuous, that became so unconsciously comic, in Owen Wister's memoirs of Roosevelt. Mr. Wister, whose claim to celebrity consists in his having written novels, is wonderful when, after telling of his acquaintance with various personages of Philadelphia and Harvard of whom we have never heard, he says that, "Huysmans (if I recall the right name) had recently published a novel, in which were described the rites of the Black Mass"—and he is even more wonderful when, after a life "chiefly passed," as he says, "among the Alexander Cassatts, the George Baers and the Weir Mitchells" of Philadelphia, he goes West and discovers Coxey's army and the stoppage of trains due to the Pullman strike, and is obliged to spend two dreadful nights sleeping on the floor of a boat from San Pedro. But this failure of response to contemporary events, either artistic or economic is, in Chapman's case, simply depressing. Owen Wister thinks them still important, Olympians who dominate the world—Roosevelt and Henry Adams and Henry Cabot Lodge and the rest. John Jay Chapman has no illusions about them, but he has to go on nagging at them and abusing them. He does not seem to realize that they have all been either absorbed or left behind by a new world never contemplated by old Harvard. He himself—for all the piercing intuitions which still at moments strike through age and class—has been left behind by that world.

He believed in these later days that the society of the period after the war was on the eve of a great religious reawakening:

"Who shall say that this present era, when all the idols are broken, all the great traditions dead, and the fine arts have become mere wandering lights, while the mind of man seems to have passed into a tunnel of transition—who shall say that these apparent extinguishments and this twilight are not necessary? Our present incredulity as to all the explanations of life is very favorable to a direct vision of life itself. The floods have carried away our mills, and a thunderstorm has destroyed the wiring of our houses; but the powers of gravity and electricity are not abolished for a moment. The contrivances on which we had set so much store served but to obscure the phenomena. Like Job in the wreck of his homestead, we have been humbled. The war humbled that spirit which had ruled the nineteenth century. In scale the drama differed from the Book of Job, but in plot it was similar.

"In the meantime, though the arts have lost their message, religion stalks in upon us. The auld wives' tales about prayer and healing, which during many centuries had been regarded as ecstatic parables, are now taken literally: we live in them. This tunnel into which the age is running is one of the clairvoyant periods of history in which men are seen as trees walking. The actual world does not disappear, nor is it relegated to a life to come, or disparaged, or condemned as evil, it remains perfectly real, and yet visibly penetrated by the rays of an inner universe which are at play everywhere."

One used to see him, during those years, in New York, in company a figure of a distinction almost exotic for the United States, with his fine manners, his sensitive intelligence, his clothes with their attractive suggestion of the elegance of another era, his almost Jove-like beard and brow, his deep and genial laugh; or for a moment under a quite different aspect, when one had happened to meet him in the street: walking alone, head drooping and brooding, with his muffler around his neck, in his face dreadful darkness and sadness and fear, as if he were staring into some lidless abyss.

He died, after an operation, on November 4, 1933. He had loved music, and when he was a student at Harvard had had what he described as "an obsession, a sort of self-willed mania for learning to play the violin, for which I had no talent." He had worked at it two years, but his fellow students had discouraged him by throwing coal scuttles at his door and hanging alarm-clocks outside his windows. After his father's financial failure, he wrote home, "I shall sell the violin: it's no halfway business." But at the time he was recovering from his breakdown, he had taken up the study of harmony and tried to compose a little. Now two days before his death, writes Mrs. Chapman, he kept murmuring, "A soldier lay dying, a soldier lay dying." "I bent over him to catch the words, and he repeated the first four lines of 'A soldier of the Legion lay dying in Algiers,' adding, *'But there is lack of nothing here,'* in a voice of deep feeling." But later, when semi-conscious, he began saying, "plucking at my fingers, 'I want to take it away, I want to take it away!' 'What?' I asked. 'The pillow?' 'No,' he said. 'The mute, the mute. I want to play on the open strings.'"

WILLIAM SAROYAN

William Saroyan (1908–1981), born in California, trumpeted his Armenian roots, presenting himself as a tragicomic loner permanently perplexed by the optimistic American scene. His first short story collection, The Daring Young Man on the Flying Trapeze, *was a huge success, and he followed it up with the autobiographical* My Name Is Aram, *the hit play* The Time of Your Life, *and the novel* The Human Comedy. *Almost all of his prose, fiction and nonfiction, sounds like a memoir-essay verging on reverie. A sampling of his uniquely appealing voice can be garnered from these "Fragments."*

from Seven Fragments

(1938)

1. I'm Not Breaking Your Heart
Don't Start Breaking My Heart

It was the worst winter I could remember. There was heavy fog, or drizzle, or rain all the time, and one morning I read in the paper that a hurricane or something had come in from somewhere in the Pacific and wreaked havoc. I guess that's how it is with something like that. You don't know about it till you see the papers. Trees had been broken down or lifted up by the roots, roofs had been blown off, telephone poles had fallen, and about six people had been killed.

I read the names of the dead in the paper, but they were people I didn't know. I was afraid one of them would be Bess. That scared me at first, but afterward it gave me a laugh.

Maybe I got that kind of a feeling because I had been up all night and it was still raining. I can't remember exactly how I happened to get on that trapeze, unless it was nothing more than the bad weather all the time, the people I was seeing all the time I didn't want to see, and all the other little things you never pay any attention to until they put you on board and start carrying you away. In any case, I had been on that trapeze about ten days and nights when I read in the paper about the hurricane. I hadn't known about it when it happened because I had been living in another world. I had been in small barrooms until two in the morning and after that I had moved over to Joe's on Broadway where there was a little game of stud. I had been sitting in the game every night till daybreak.

After that I bought papers and magazines, as they came out, and got in a cab and went home.

It wasn't anything. It wasn't tragic. I guess I just wanted to go along that way for a while. I wanted her to be happy and that was the best way for me to keep from phoning her and starting everything all over again. The number was always in my mind, but I hardly ever went near a phone booth. I'd see her a lot too and feel glad about everything, and every once in a while I'd hear her and want her so badly I'd feel awfully proud of myself for being somebody who could behave intelligently, instead of romantically. We were through. We'd said so. We liked each other more than ever and we'd agreed to let it stay good and not let it get bad.

After that, she was the first to phone. She wanted me to know she was in love again.

You must fall in love again, she said.

I'll do my best, I said.

Etc. A story.

2. The Stillness of Night

February is gone, March is almost gone, spring is here, and the swallows of a certain monastery have returned and driven away another variety of birds from the eaves. So stillness finds a man at a new moment of nothing: February, March, spring, swallows, and so on. All it is, all of it, is sex and fury. Loneliness, art, religion, all of it, that's all. The hash of all things. The incurably alive, that's who we are: we long for the great glowing magic loveliness and power and delight that a woman is; we have it; then we long to function, to be artists, for instance, or something else; then once again we long for a new half-dozen things a woman is; then we long for the poise of labor; then for woman; then labor; then again; and again. I think tonight that I am the worst great writer that ever lived. I know everything; I have visions of everything not yet revealed, but I won't work; I won't report what I know, and I won't reveal to others what I have seen. I don't like to work. I walked along the ocean and it made me very hungry. There was nothing filling to eat, so I went to the grocer's and bought a can of Armour's hash and prepared it and sat down and ate it! I was very thirsty so I drank a quart of wine, and afterward six or seven glasses of water; and I'm still thirsty; perhaps I'm dying. I daresay I live too tensely, inwardly, although I am often very much at ease; as a matter of fact ease is my average. There is a tenseness within me, however, that has nothing to do with ease; I am at ease and yet tense, eager, curious; whether I ought to be or not; whether, I mean, there is anything around to be eager or curious about. Also planning is constant and endless within myself; I am continuously in the midst of plans; I instinctively insist that I shall create a future, a present, and a past; and I do so. I raise hell all the time doing things which will be sweet to me a year from when they are done; or two; or twenty. Of course I am too wise and honest to be other than tense and eager and full of plans: living at its best to a realist, to one who is wise, is a boring event; my job is to keep it from boring me; and I do so; I am not dreaming my time away; that's the difference; I could and won't. Anyhow, I really don't know: this is merely one of my moments of quiet, stillness, and disquiet and confusion.

3. Public Speech

Since I saw you last I have grown a moustache, as you see. I am going to make a one-hour speech in five minutes, I hope. Or else a five-minute speech in an hour. That depends on how lucky I am. My father was a preacher; if there's anything to this theory they're talking about, speech-making ought to be a cinch for me. The theory I'm referring to, I think, is Einstein's. At the outset let me say that as far as I know everything is worth saving. This leaves nothing to be said, so in order to go on speaking, I'll have to elaborate or modify or make reservations. What, for instance, do I mean by *everything*? That is a good question for a heckler. Everything, as far as I know, is nine times out of ten and sometimes ten times out of ten, *you*; that is, me. Everybody. One at a time. I think each of you is worth saving. I know I'm worth saving. Money is another thing, but I won't go into economics and all like that. Is Capitalism worth saving? Yes and no. Is Communism? Same. Is a man worth saving? Yes. And no maybe. Who shall save the man? Any man? His brother, or who? Well, I think I know the answer: his brother can't save him, nobody and nothing can save him. The question is, Who can save the man? The answer is, The man himself and nobody else. That seems very simple. But how's the man going to do it? I don't know. He's got to find out for himself. God's given him what it takes to find out; the rest is up to him. A rabid Communist, I believe, would not hesitate two seconds to say I'm talking nonsense. I, in turn, would not hesitate two seconds to say he's talking nonsense. I have no quarrel with the race of man; it is a good race; it's the best there is to have anyway. My quarrel is with one man at a time. That is said to be the Christian approach; it is in a way; and then again it isn't because you don't have to be a Christian to believe that every man should be answerable to himself; myself, I'm a Presbyterian. The thing to save is not, in short, civilization, and I'll tell you why; civilization never belonged to the millions anyway; it was made by and perpetuated by a handful of men; one at a time; the mob merely wallowed in it as it were; civilization is mostly the manners of an age, the mode of living, the pattern of feeling, believing, and so on, which the mob has gradually picked up from these few things, which are the work of men here and there: from music, from literature, from painting, from sculpture, and if I may, from the vigorous manner of living of somebody special—that is an art too; that is truly the main art of man; the one all the other arts hope to elevate. Since civilization is the work of only a handful of men, we don't need to save civilization; we need to save ourselves, that's all.

CLEMENT GREENBERG

Clement Greenberg (1909–1994) was the most dominant (some would say domineering) American art critic in the twentieth century. A member of the New York intellectual set, he regularly published essays in Partisan Review, The Nation, *and* Commentary. *One of his most influential, "Avant-Garde and Kitsch," delved into the differences between high and low, and sounded an early warning of the highbrows' alienation from popular culture. Writing in the 1930s from a Marxist perspective, which acknowledged that art is never created in a social vacuum, Greenberg nevertheless advocated a formalist reading of visual art. He would go on to champion the Abstract Expressionists, especially Jackson Pollock. Greenberg's prose style can be dense to navigate, perhaps because he is trying to express elusive, difficult, novel ideas that push at the boundaries of clarity, or because he is seeking a verbal equivalent on the page to "all-over" painting like Pollock's that filled the entire canvas.*

Avant-Garde and Kitsch

(1939)

One and the same civilization produces simultaneously two such different things as a poem by T. S. Eliot and a Tin Pan Alley song, or a painting by Braque and a *Saturday Evening Post* cover. All four are on the order of culture, and ostensibly, parts of the same culture and products of the same society. Here, however, their connection seems to end. A poem by Eliot and a poem by Eddie Guest—what perspective of culture is large enough to enable us to situate them in an enlightening relation to each other? Does the fact that a disparity such as this exists within the frame of a single cultural tradition, which is and has been taken for granted—does this fact indicate that the disparity is a part of the natural order of things? Or is it something entirely new, and particular to our age?

The answer involves more than an investigation in aesthetics. It appears to me that it is necessary to examine more closely and with more originality than hitherto the relationship between aesthetic experience as met by the specific—not the generalized—individual, and the social and historical contexts in which that experience takes place. What is brought to light will answer, in addition to the question posed above, other and perhaps more important questions.

I

A society, as it becomes less and less able, in the course of its development, to justify the inevitability of its particular forms, breaks up the accepted notions upon which artists and writers must depend in large part for communication with their audiences. It becomes difficult to assume anything. All the verities involved by religion, authority, tradition, style, are thrown into question, and the writer or artist is no longer able to estimate the response of his audience to the symbols and references with which he works. In the past such a state of affairs has usually resolved itself into a motionless Alexandrianism, an academicism in which the really important issues are left untouched because they involve controversy, and in which creative activity dwindles to virtuosity in the small details of form, all larger questions being decided by the precedent of the old masters. The same themes are mechanically varied in a hundred different works, and yet nothing new is produced: Statius, mandarin verse, Roman sculpture, Beaux-Arts painting, neo-republican architecture.

It is among the hopeful signs in the midst of the decay of our present society that we—some of us—have been unwilling to accept this last phase for our own culture. In seeking to go beyond Alexandrianism, a part of Western bourgeois society has produced something unheard of heretofore:—avant-garde culture. A superior consciousness of history—more precisely, the appearance of a new kind of criticism of society, an historical criticism—made this possible. This criticism has not confronted our present society with timeless utopias, but has soberly examined in the terms of history and of cause and effect the antecedents, justifications and functions of the forms that lie at the heart of every society. Thus our present bourgeois social order was shown to be, not an eternal, "natural" condition of life, but simply the latest term in a succession of social orders. New perspectives of this kind, becoming a part of the advanced intellectual conscience of the fifth and sixth decades of the nineteenth century, soon were absorbed by artists and poets, even if unconsciously for the most part. It was no accident, therefore, that the birth of the avant-garde coincided chronologically—and geographically, too—with the first bold development of scientific revolutionary thought in Europe.

True, the first settlers of bohemia—which was then identical with the avant-garde—turned out soon to be demonstratively uninterested in politics. Nevertheless, without the circulation of revolutionary ideas in the air about them, they would never have been able to isolate their concept of the "bourgeois" in order to define what they were *not*. Nor, without the moral aid of revolutionary political attitudes would they have had the courage to assert themselves as aggressively as they did against the prevailing standards of society. Courage indeed was needed for this, because the avant-garde's emigration from bourgeois society to bohemia meant also an emigration from the markets of capitalism, upon which artists and writers had been thrown by the falling away of aristocratic patronage. (Ostensibly, at least, it meant this—meant starving in a garret—although, as will be shown later, the avant-garde remained attached to bourgeois society precisely because it needed its money.)

Yet it is true that once the avant-garde had succeeded in "detaching" itself from society, it proceeded to turn around and repudiate revolutionary as well as bourgeois politics. The revolution was left inside society, a part of that welter of ideological struggle which art and poetry find so unpropitious as soon as it begins to involve those "precious" axiomatic beliefs upon which culture thus far has had to rest. Hence it developed that the true and most important function of the avant-garde was not to "experiment," but to find a path along which it would be possible to keep culture *moving* in the midst of ideological confusion and violence. Retiring from public altogether, the avant-garde poet or artist sought to maintain the high level of his art by both narrowing and raising it to the expression of an absolute in which all relativities and contradictions would be either resolved or beside the point. "Art for art's sake" and "pure poetry" appear, and subject matter or content becomes something to be avoided like a plague.

It has been in search of the absolute that the avant-garde has arrived at "abstract" or "nonobjective" art—and poetry, too. The avant-garde poet or artist tries in effect to imitate God by creating something valid solely on its own terms, in the way nature itself is valid, in the way a landscape—not its picture—is aesthetically valid; something *given,* increate, independent of meanings, similars or originals. Content is to be dissolved so completely into form that the work of art or literature cannot be reduced in whole or in part to anything not itself.

But the absolute is absolute, and the poet or artist, being what he is, cherishes certain relative values more than others. The very values in the name of which he invokes the absolute are relative values, the values of aesthetics. And so he turns out to be imitating, not God—and here I use "imitate" in its Aristotelian sense—but the disciplines and processes of art and literature themselves. This is the genesis of the "abstract."* In turning his attention away from subject matter of common experience, the poet or artist turns it in upon the medium of his own craft. The non-representational or "abstract," if it is to have aesthetic validity, cannot be arbitrary and accidental, but must stem from obedience to some worthy constraint or original. This constraint, once the world of common, extra-verted experience has been renounced, can only be found in the very pro-cesses or disciplines by which art and literature have already imitated the former. These themselves become the subject matter of art and literature. If, to continue with Aristotle, all art and literature are imitation, then what we have here is the imitation of imitating. To quote Yeats:

> Nor is there singing school but studying
> Monuments of its own magnificence.

Picasso, Braque, Mondrian, Miró, Kandinsky, Brancusi, even Klee, Matisse and Cézanne derive their chief inspiration from the medium they work in. The excitement of their art seems to lie most of all in its pure preoccupation with the invention and arrangement of spaces, surfaces, shapes, colors, etc., to the exclusion of whatever is not necessarily impli-cated in these factors. The attention of poets like Rimbaud, Mallarmé, Valéry, Pound, Hart Crane, Stevens, even Rilke and Yeats, appears to be centered on the effort to create poetry and on the "moments" themselves of poetic conversion, rather than on experience to be converted into poetry. Of course, this cannot exclude other preoccupations in their work, for poetry must deal with words, and words must communicate. Certain poets, such as Mallarmé and Valéry, are more radical in this respect than others—leaving aside those poets who have tried to compose poetry in pure sound alone. However, if it were easier to define poetry, modern

---

* The example of music, which has long been an abstract art, and which avant-garde poetry has tried so much to emulate, is interesting. Music, Aristotle said curiously enough, is the most imitative and vivid of all arts because it imitates its original—the state of the soul—with the greatest immediacy. Today this strikes us as the exact opposite of the truth, because no art seems to us to have less reference to something outside itself than music. However, aside from the fact that in a sense Aristotle may still be right, it must be explained that ancient Greek music was closely associated with poetry, and depended upon its character as an accessory to verse to make its imitative meaning clear. Plato, speaking of music, says: "For when there are no words, it is very difficult to recognize the meaning of the harmony and rhythm, or to see that any worthy object is imitated by them." As far as we know, all music originally served such an accessory function. Once, however, it was abandoned, music was forced to withdraw into itself to find a constraint or original. This is found in the various means of its own composition and performance.

poetry would be much more "pure" and "abstract." As for the other fields of literature—the definition of avant-garde aesthetics advanced here is no Procrustean bed. But aside from the fact that most of our best contemporary novelists have gone to school with the avant-garde, it is significant that Gide's most ambitious book is a novel about the writing of a novel, and that Joyce's *Ulysses* and *Finnegans Wake* seem to be, above all, as one French critic says, the reduction of experience to expression for the sake of expression, the expression mattering more than what is being expressed.

That avant-garde culture is the imitation of imitating—the fact itself—calls for neither approval nor disapproval. It is true that this culture contains within itself some of the very Alexandrianism it seeks to overcome. The lines quoted from Yeats referred to Byzantium, which is very close to Alexandria; and in a sense this imitation of imitating is a superior sort of Alexandrianism. But there is one most important difference: the avant-garde moves, while Alexandrianism stands still. And this, precisely, is what justifies the avant-garde's methods and makes them necessary. The necessity lies in the fact that by no other means is it possible today to create art and literature of a high order. To quarrel with necessity by throwing about terms like "formalism," "purism," "ivory tower" and so forth is either dull or dishonest. This is not to say, however, that it is to the *social* advantage of the avant-garde that it is what it is. Quite the opposite.

The avant-garde's specialization of itself, the fact that its best artists are artists' artists, its best poets, poets' poets, has estranged a great many of those who were capable formerly of enjoying and appreciating ambitious art and literature, but who are now unwilling or unable to acquire an initiation into their craft secrets. The masses have always remained more or less indifferent to culture in the process of development. But today such culture is being abandoned by those to whom it actually belongs—our ruling class. For it is to the latter that the avant-garde belongs. No culture can develop without a social basis, without a source of stable income. And in the case of the avant-garde, this was provided by an elite among the ruling class of that society from which it assumed itself to be cut off, but to which it has always remained attached by an umbilical cord of gold. The paradox is real. And now this elite is rapidly shrinking. Since the avant-garde forms the only living culture we now have, the survival in the near future of culture in general is thus threatened.

We must not be deceived by superficial phenomena and local successes. Picasso's shows still draw crowds, and T. S. Eliot is taught in the universities; the dealers in modernist art are still in business, and the publishers still publish some "difficult" poetry. But the avant-garde itself, already sensing the danger, is becoming more and more timid every day that passes. Academicism and commercialism are appearing in the strangest places. This can mean only one thing: that the avant-garde is becoming unsure of the audience it depends on—the rich and the cultivated.

Is it the nature itself of avant-garde culture that is alone responsible for the danger it finds itself in? Or is that only a dangerous liability? Are there other, and perhaps more important, factors involved?

II

Where there is an avant-garde, generally we also find a rear-guard. True enough—simultaneously with the entrance of the avant-garde, a second new cultural phenomenon appeared in the industrial West: that thing to which the Germans give the wonderful name of *Kitsch:* popular, commercial art and literature with their chromeotypes, magazine covers, illustrations, ads, slick and pulp fiction, comics, Tin Pan Alley music, tap dancing, Hollywood movies, etc., etc. For some reason this gigantic apparition has always been taken for granted. It is time we looked into its whys and wherefores.

Kitsch is a product of the industrial revolution which urbanized the masses of Western Europe and America and established what is called universal literacy.

Prior to this the only market for formal culture, as distinguished from folk culture, had been among those who, in addition to being able to read and write, could command the leisure and comfort that always goes hand in hand with cultivation of some sort. This until then had been inextricably associated with literacy. But with the introduction of universal literacy, the ability to read and write became almost a minor skill like driving a car, and it no longer served to distinguish an individual's cultural inclinations, since it was no longer the exclusive concomitant of refined tastes.

The peasants who settled in the cities as proletariat and petty bourgeois learned to read and write for the sake of efficiency, but they did not win the leisure and comfort necessary for the enjoyment of the city's traditional culture. Losing, nevertheless, their taste for the folk culture whose background was the countryside, and discovering a new capacity for boredom at the same time, the new urban masses set up a pressure on society to provide them with a kind of culture fit for their own consumption. To fill the demand of the new market, a new commodity was devised: ersatz culture, kitsch, destined for those who, insensible to the values of genuine culture, are hungry nevertheless for the diversion that only culture of some sort can provide.

Kitsch, using for raw material the debased and academicized simulacra of genuine culture, welcomes and cultivates this insensibility. It is the source of its profits. Kitsch is mechanical and operates by formulas. Kitsch is vicarious experience and faked sensations. Kitsch changes according to style, but remains always the same. Kitsch is the epitome of all that is spurious in the life of our times. Kitsch pretends to demand nothing of its customers except their money—not even their time.

The precondition for kitsch, a condition without which kitsch would be impossible, is the availability close at hand of a fully matured cultural tradition, whose discoveries, acquisitions, and perfected self-consciousness kitsch can take advantage of for its own ends. It borrows from it devices, tricks, stratagems, rules of thumb, themes, converts them into a system, and discards the rest. It draws its life blood, so to speak, from this reservoir of accumulated experience. This is what is really meant when it is said that the popular art and literature of today were once the daring, esoteric art and literature of yesterday. Of course, no such thing is true. What is meant is that when enough time has elapsed the new is looted for new "twists," which are then watered down and served up as kitsch. Self-evidently, all kitsch is academic; and conversely, all that's academic is kitsch. For what is called the academic as such no longer has an independent existence, but has become the stuffed-shirt "front" for kitsch. The methods of industrialism displace the handicrafts.

Because it can be turned out mechanically, kitsch has become an integral part of our productive system in a way in which true culture could never be, except accidentally. It has been capitalized at a tremendous investment which must show commensurate returns; it is compelled to extend as well as to keep its markets. While it is essentially its own salesman, a great sales apparatus has nevertheless been created for it, which brings pressure to bear on every member of society. Traps are laid even in those areas, so to speak, that are the preserves of genuine culture. It is not enough today, in a country like ours, to have an inclination towards the latter; one must have a true passion for it that will give him the power to resist the faked article that surrounds and presses in on him from the moment he is old enough to look at the funny papers. Kitsch is deceptive. It has many different levels, and some of them are high enough to be dangerous to the naive seeker of true light. A magazine like *The New Yorker*, which is fundamentally high-class kitsch for the luxury trade, converts and waters down a great deal of avant-garde material for its own uses. Nor is every single item of kitsch altogether worthless. Now and then it produces something of merit, something that has an authentic folk flavor; and these accidental and isolated instances have fooled people who should know better.

Kitsch's enormous profits are a source of temptation to the avant-garde itself, and its members have not always resisted this temptation. Ambitious writers and artists will modify their work under the pressure of kitsch, if they do not succumb to it entirely. And then those puzzling borderline cases appear, such as the popular novelist, Simenon, in France, and Steinbeck in this country. The net result is always to the detriment of true culture, in any case.

Kitsch has not been confined to the cities in which it was born, but has flowed out over the countryside, wiping out folk culture. Nor has it shown any regard for geographical and national-cultural boundaries. Another mass product of Western industrialism, it has gone on a triumphal tour of the world, crowding out and defacing native cultures in one colonial country after another, so that it is now by way of becoming a universal culture, the first universal culture ever beheld. Today the native of China, no less than the South American Indian, the Hindu, no less than the Polynesian, have come to prefer to the products of their native art, magazine covers, rotogravure sections and calendar girls. How is this virulence of kitsch, this irresistible attractiveness, to be explained? Naturally, machine-made kitsch can undersell the native handmade article, and the prestige of the West also helps; but why is kitsch a so much more profitable export article than Rembrandt? One, after all, can be reproduced as cheaply as the other.

In his last article on the Soviet cinema in the *Partisan Review,* Dwight Macdonald points out that kitsch has in the last ten years become the dominant culture in Soviet Russia. For this he blames the political regime—not only for the fact that kitsch is the official culture, but also that it is actually the dominant, most popular culture, and he quotes the following from Kurt London's *The Seven Soviet Arts:* ". . . the attitude of the masses both to the old and new art styles probably remains essentially dependent on the nature of the education afforded them by their respective states." Macdonald goes on to say: "Why after all should ignorant peasants prefer Repin (a leading exponent of Russian academic kitsch in painting) to Picasso, whose abstract technique is at least as relevant to their own primitive folk art as is the former's realistic style? No, if the masses crowd into the Tretyakov (Moscow's museum of contemporary Russian art: kitsch), it is largely because they have been conditioned to shun 'formalism' and to admire 'socialist realism.'"

In the first place it is not a question of a choice between merely the old and merely the new, as London seems to think—but of a choice between the bad, up-to-date old and the genuinely new. The alternative to Picasso is not Michelangelo, but kitsch. In the second place, neither in backward Russia nor in the advanced West do the masses prefer kitsch simply because their governments condition them toward it. Where state educational systems take the trouble to mention art, we are told to respect the old masters, not kitsch; and yet we go and hang Maxfield Parrish or his equivalent on our walls, instead of Rembrandt and Michelangelo. Moreover, as Macdonald himself points out, around 1925 when the Soviet regime was encouraging avant-garde cinema, the Russian masses continued to prefer Hollywood movies. No, "conditioning" does not explain the potency of kitsch.

All values are human values, relative values, in art as well as elsewhere. Yet there does seem to have been more or less of a general agreement among the cultivated of mankind over the ages as to what is good art and what bad. Taste has varied, but not beyond certain limits; contemporary connoisseurs agree with the eighteenth-century Japanese that Hokusai was one of the greatest artists of his time; we even agree with the ancient Egyptians that Third and Fourth Dynasty art was the most worthy of being selected as their paragon by those who came after. We may have come to prefer Giotto to Raphael, but we still do not deny that Raphael was one of the best painters of his time. There has been an agreement then, and this agreement rests, I believe, on a fairly constant distinction made between those values only to be found in art and the values which can be found elsewhere. Kitsch, by virtue of a rationalized technique that draws on science and industry, has erased this distinction in practice.

Let us see, for example, what happens when an ignorant Russian peasant such as Macdonald mentions stands with hypothetical freedom of choice before two paintings, one by Picasso, the other by Repin. In the first he sees, let us say, a play of lines, colors and spaces that represent a woman. The abstract technique—to accept Macdonald's supposition, which I am inclined to doubt—reminds him somewhat of the icons he has left behind him in the village, and he feels the attraction of the familiar. We will even suppose that he faintly surmises some of the great art values the cultivated find in Picasso. He turns next to Repin's picture and sees a battle scene. The technique is not so familiar—as technique. But that weighs very little with the peasant, for he suddenly discovers values in Repin's picture that seem far superior to the values he has been accustomed to find in icon art; and the unfamiliar itself is one of the sources of those values: the values of the vividly recognizable, the miraculous and the sympathetic. In Repin's picture the peasant recognizes and sees things in the way in which he recognizes and sees things outside of pictures—there is no discontinuity between art and life, no need to accept a convention and say to oneself, that icon represents Jesus because it intends to represent Jesus, even if it does not remind me very much of a man. That Repin can paint so realistically that identifications are self-evident immediately and without any effort on the part of the spectator—that is miraculous. The peasant is also pleased by the wealth of self-evident meanings which he finds in the picture: "it tells a story." Picasso and the icons are so austere and barren in comparison. What is more, Repin heightens reality and makes it dramatic: sunset, exploding shells, running and falling men. There is no longer any question of Picasso or icons. Repin is what the peasant wants, and nothing else but Repin. It is lucky, however, for Repin that the peasant is protected from the products of American capitalism, for he would not stand a chance next to a *Saturday Evening Post* cover by Norman Rockwell.

Ultimately, it can be said that the cultivated spectator derives the same values from Picasso that the peasant gets from Repin, since what the latter enjoys in Repin is somehow art too, on however low a scale, and he is sent to look at pictures by the same instincts that send the cultivated spectator. But the ultimate values which the cultivated spectator derives from Picasso are derived at a second remove, as the result of reflection upon the immediate impression left by the plastic values. It is only then that the recognizable, the miraculous and the sympathetic enter. They are not immediately or externally present in Picasso's painting, but must be projected into it by the spectator sensitive enough to react sufficiently to plastic qualities. They belong to the "reflected" effect. In Repin, on the other hand, the "reflected" effect has already been included in the picture, ready for the spectator's unreflective enjoyment.* Where Picasso paints *cause*, Repin paints *effect*. Repin predigests art for the spectator and spares him effort, provides him with a short cut to the pleasure of art that detours what is necessarily difficult in genuine art. Repin, or kitsch, is synthetic art.

The same point can be made with respect to kitsch literature: it provides vicarious experience for the insensitive with far greater immediacy than serious fiction can hope to do. And Eddie Guest and the *Indian Love Lyrics* are more poetic than T. S. Eliot and Shakespeare.

III

If the avant-garde imitates the processes of art, kitsch, we now see, imitates its effects. The neatness of this antithesis is more than contrived; it corresponds to and defines the tremendous interval that separates from each other two such simultaneous cultural phenomena as the avant-garde and kitsch.

This interval, too great to be closed by all the infinite gradations of popularized "modernism" and "modernistic" kitsch, corresponds in turn to a social interval, a social interval that has always existed in formal culture, as elsewhere in civilized society, and whose two termini converge and diverge in fixed relation to the increasing or decreasing stability of the given society. There has always been on one side the minority of the powerful—and therefore the cultivated—and on the other the great mass

---

* T. S. Eliot said something to the same effect in accounting for the shortcomings of English Romantic poetry. Indeed the Romantics can be considered the original sinners whose guilt kitsch inherited. They showed kitsch how. What does Keats write about mainly, if not the effect of poetry upon himself?

of the exploited and poor—and therefore the ignorant. Formal culture has always belonged to the first, while the last have had to content themselves with folk or rudimentary culture, or kitsch.

In a stable society that functions well enough to hold in solution the contradictions between its classes, the cultural dichotomy becomes somewhat blurred. The axioms of the few are shared by the many; the latter believe superstitiously what the former believe soberly. And at such moments in history the masses are able to feel wonder and admiration for the culture, on no matter how high a plane, of its masters. This applies at least to plastic culture, which is accessible to all.

In the Middle Ages the plastic artist paid lip service at least to the lowest common denominators of experience. This even remained true to some extent until the seventeenth century. There was available for imitation a universally valid conceptual reality, whose order the artist could not tamper with. The subject matter of art was prescribed by those who commissioned works of art, which were not created, as in bourgeois society, on speculation. Precisely because his content was determined in advance, the artist was free to concentrate on his medium. He needed not to be philosopher, or visionary, but simply artificer. As long as there was general agreement as to what were the worthiest subjects for art, the artist was relieved of the necessity to be original and inventive in his "matter" and could devote all his energy to formal problems. For him the medium became, privately, professionally, the content of his art, even as his medium is today the public content of the abstract painter's art—with that difference, however, that the medieval artist had to suppress his professional preoccupation in public—had always to suppress and subordinate the personal and professional in the finished, official work of art. If, as an ordinary member of the Christian community, he felt some personal emotion about his subject matter, this only contributed to the enrichment of the work's public meaning. Only with the Renaissance do the inflections of the personal become legitimate, still to be kept, however, within the limits of the simply and universally recognizable. And only with Rembrandt do "lonely" artists begin to appear, lonely in their art.

But even during the Renaissance, and as long as Western art was endeavoring to perfect its technique, victories in this realm could only be signalized by success in realistic imitation, since there was no other objective criterion at hand. Thus the masses could still find in the art of their masters objects of admiration and wonder. Even the bird that pecked at the fruit in Zeuxis' picture could applaud.

It is a platitude that art becomes caviar to the general when the reality it imitates no longer corresponds even roughly to the reality recognized by the general. Even then, however, the resentment the common man may feel is silenced by the awe in which he stands of the patrons of this art. Only when he becomes dissatisfied with the social order they administer does he begin to criticize their culture. Then the plebeian finds courage for the first time to voice his opinions openly. Every man, from the Tammany alderman to the Austrian house-painter, finds that he is entitled to his opinion. Most often this resentment toward culture is to be found where the dissatisfaction with society is a reactionary dissatisfaction which expresses itself in revivalism and puritanism, and latest of all, in fascism. Here revolvers and torches begin to be mentioned in the same breath as culture. In the name of godliness or the blood's health, in the name of simple ways and solid virtues, the statue-smashing commences.

IV

Returning to our Russian peasant for the moment, let us suppose that after he has chosen Repin in preference to Picasso, the state's educational apparatus comes along and tells him that he is wrong, that he should have chosen Picasso—and shows him why. It is quite possible for the Soviet state to do this. But things being as they are in Russia—and everywhere else—the peasant soon finds that the necessity of working hard all day for his living and the rude, uncomfortable circumstances in which he lives do not allow him enough leisure, energy and comfort to train for the enjoyment of Picasso. This needs, after all, a considerable amount of "conditioning." Superior culture is one of the most artificial of all human creations, and the peasant finds no "natural" urgency within himself that will drive him toward Picasso in spite of all difficulties. In the end the peasant will go back to kitsch when he feels like looking at pictures, for he can enjoy kitsch without effort. The state is helpless in this matter and remains so as long as the problems of production have not been solved in a socialist sense. The same holds true, of course, for capitalist countries and makes all talk of art for the masses there nothing but demagogy.*

Where today a political regime establishes an official cultural policy,

---

* It will be objected that such art for the masses as folk art was developed under rudimentary conditions of production and that a good deal of folk art is on a high level. Yes, it is—but folk art is not Athene, and it's Athene whom we want: formal culture with its infinity of aspects, its luxuriance, its large comprehension. Besides, we are now told that most of what we consider good in folk culture is the static survival of dead formal, aristocratic, cultures. Our old English ballads, for instance, were not created by the "folk," but by the post-feudal squirearchy of the English countryside, to survive in the mouths of the folk long after those for whom the ballads were composed had gone on to other forms of literature. Unfortunately, until the machine-age, culture was the exclusive prerogative of a society that lived by the labor of serfs or slaves. They were the real symbols of culture. For one man to spend time and energy creating or listening to poetry meant that another man had to produce enough to keep himself alive and the former in comfort. In Africa today we find that the culture of slave-owning tribes is generally much superior to that of the tribes that possess no slaves.

it is for the sake of demagogy. If kitsch is the official tendency of culture in Germany, Italy and Russia, it is not because their respective governments are controlled by philistines, but because kitsch is the culture of the masses in these countries, as it is everywhere else. The encouragement of kitsch is merely another of the inexpensive ways in which totalitarian regimes seek to ingratiate themselves with their subjects. Since these regimes cannot raise the cultural level of the masses—even if they wanted to—by anything short of a surrender to international socialism, they will flatter the masses by bringing all culture down to their level. It is for this reason that the avant-garde is outlawed, and not so much because a superior culture is inherently a more critical culture. (Whether or not the avant-garde could possibly flourish under a totalitarian regime is not pertinent to the question at this point.) As a matter of fact, the main trouble with avant-garde art and literature, from the point of view of fascists and Stalinists, is not that they are too critical, but that they are too "innocent," that it is too difficult to inject effective propaganda into them, that kitsch is more pliable to this end. Kitsch keeps a dictator in closer contact with the "soul" of the people. Should the official culture be one superior to the general mass-level, there would be a danger of isolation.

Nevertheless, if the masses were conceivably to ask for avant-garde art and literature, Hitler, Mussolini and Stalin would not hesitate long in attempting to satisfy such a demand. Hitler is a bitter enemy of the avant-garde, both on doctrinal and personal grounds, yet this did not prevent Goebbels in 1932–1933 from strenuously courting avant-garde artists and writers. When Gottfried Benn, an Expressionist poet, came over to the Nazis he was welcomed with a great fanfare, although at that very moment Hitler was denouncing Expressionism as *Kulturbolschewismus*. This was at a time when the Nazis felt that the prestige which the avant-garde enjoyed among the cultivated German public could be of advantage to them, and practical considerations of this nature, the Nazis being skillful politicians, have always taken precedence over Hitler's personal inclinations. Later the Nazis realized that it was more practical to accede to the wishes of the masses in matters of culture than to those of their paymasters; the latter, when it came to a question of preserving power, were as willing to sacrifice their culture as they were their moral principles; while the former, precisely because power was being withheld from them, had to be cozened in every other way possible. It was necessary to promote on a much more grandiose style than in the democracies the illusion that the masses actually rule. The literature and art they enjoy and understand were to be proclaimed the only true art and literature and any other kind was to be suppressed. Under these circumstances people like Gottfried Benn, no matter how ardently they support Hitler, become a liability; and we hear no more of them in Nazi Germany.

We can see then that although from one point of view the personal philistinism of Hitler and Stalin is not accidental to the political roles they play, from another point of view it is only an incidentally contributory factor in determining the cultural policies of their respective regimes. Their personal philistinism simply adds brutality and double-darkness to policies they would be forced to support anyhow by the pressure of all their other policies—even were they, personally, devotees of avant-garde culture. What the acceptance of the isolation of the Russian Revolution forces Stalin to do, Hitler is compelled to do by his acceptance of the contradictions of capitalism and his efforts to freeze them. As for Mussolini—his case is a perfect example of the *disponibilité* of a realist in these matters. For years he bent a benevolent eye on the Futurists and built modernistic railroad stations and government-owned apartment houses. One can still see in the suburbs of Rome more modernistic apartments than almost anywhere else in the world. Perhaps Fascism wanted to show its up-to-dateness, to conceal the fact that it was a retrogression; perhaps it so wanted to conform to the tastes of the wealthy elite it served. At any rate Mussolini seems to have realized lately that it would be more useful to him to please the cultural tastes of the Italian masses than those of their masters. The masses must be provided with objects of admiration and wonder; the latter can dispense with them. And so we find Mussolini announcing a "new Imperial style." Marinetti, Chirico, *et al.*, are sent into the outer darkness, and the new railroad station in Rome will not be modernistic. That Mussolini was late in coming to this only illustrates again the relative hesitancy with which Italian Fascism has drawn the necessary implications of its role.

Capitalism in decline finds that whatever of quality it is still capable of producing becomes almost invariably a threat to its own existence. Advances in culture, no less than advances in science and industry, corrode the very society under whose aegis they are made possible. Here, as in every other question today, it becomes necessary to quote Marx word for word. Today we no longer look toward socialism for a new culture—as inevitably as one will appear, once we do have socialism. Today we look to socialism *simply* for the preservation of whatever living culture we have right now.

EUDORA WELTY

Eudora Welty (1909–2001) was one of the United States' most celebrated and revered fiction writers. In her stories and novels, she explored the dynamic by which character is shaped by place—in her case, Jackson, Mississippi, where she lived most of her life. "Ida M'Toy" is an exemplary portrait-essay. Though the narrator doesn't tells us much about herself, in some ways it is a double portrait: her lively take on this old African American woman gives us a clear idea of her own curiosity, literary skill, and powers of observation. She makes Ida sound larger than life by finding her secondhand business "magnificent" and projecting prophetic if not unearthly powers onto the woman. In the process, Welty also subtly conveys how some blacks and whites were able to see each other as human beings in spite of the oppressive restrictions of the then-segregated South.

Ida M'Toy

(1942)

For one human being to point out another as "unforgettable" seems a trifle condescending, and in the ideal world we would all keep well aware of each other, but there are nevertheless a few persons one meets who are as inescapable of notice as skyrockets; it may be because like skyrockets they are radiant with their own substance and shower it about regardlessly. Ida M'Toy, an old Negro woman, for a long time a midwife in my Mississippi town and for another long time a dealer in secondhand clothes in the same place, has been a skyrocket as far back as most people remember. Or, rather, she is a kind of meteor (for she is not ephemeral, only sudden and startling). Her ways seem on a path of their own without regard to any course of ours and of a somewhat wider circuit; she will probably leave a glow behind and return in the far future on some other lap of her careening through all our duller and steadier bodies. She herself deals with the rest of us in this mighty and spacious way, calling in allegories and the elements, so it is owing to her nature that I may speak a little grandly.

The slave traders of England and New England, when they went capturing, took away the most royal of Africans along with their own slaves, and I have not much doubt that Ida has come down from a race of tall black queens. I wish I might have seen her when she was young. She has sharp clever features, light-filled black eyes, arched nostrils and fine thin mobile lips, and her hair, gray now, springs like a wild kind of diadem from the widow's peak over her forehead. Her voice is indescribable but it is a constant part of her presence and is filled with invocation. She never speaks lightly of any person or thing, but she flings out her arm and points at something and begins, "Oh, precious, I'm telling you to look at that—*look* at it!" and then she invokes about it, and tolerates no interruptions. I have heard long chants and utterances on the origin and history and destination of the smallest thing, any article or object her eye lights on; a bit of candle stuck on the mantelpiece will set her off, as if its little fire had ignited her whole mind. She invokes what she wishes to invoke and she has in all ways something of the seer about her. She wields a control over great numbers of her race by this power, which has an integrity that I believe nothing could break, and which sets her up, aloof and triumphant, above the rest. She is inspired and they are not. Maybe off by themselves they could be inspired, but nobody else could be inspired in the same room with Ida, it would be too crowded.

Ida is not a poor old woman, she is a rich old woman. She accepts it that she is held in envy as well as respect, but it is only another kind of tribute as far as she is concerned, and she expects to be gaped at for being rich, for having been married in the home of a white lady, "in her bay window," and for being very wise, all these things; but she is not vain in the usual sense.

Ida's life has been divided in two (it is, in many ways, eloquent of duality); but there is a thread that runs from one part into the other, and to trace this connection between delivering the child and clothing the man is an interesting speculation. Moreover, it has some excuse, for Ida herself helps it along by a wild and curious kind of talk that sashays from one part to the other and sounds to some of her customers like "ranting and raving." It is my belief that if Ida had not been a midwife, she would not be the same kind of secondhand-clothes dealer she is. Midwifery set her off, it gave her a hand in the mysteries, and she will never let go that flying hold merely because she is engaged in something else. An ex-alchemist would run a secondhand-clothes business with extra touches—a reminiscence of glitter would cling to the garments he sold, and it is the same with Ida. So it is well when you meet her to think what she was once.

Ida's memory goes back to her beginnings, when she was, she says, the first practical nurse in Jackson at the age of twenty-one, and she makes the past sound very dark and far back. She thanks God, she says, that today Capitol Street is not just three planks to walk on and is the prettiest place on earth, but that "people white and black is too high and don't they know Ida seen them when they carried a little tin coal-oil lamp that wasn't any bigger than their little fingers?" Ida speaks of herself in the third person and in indirect discourse often and especially when she says something good of herself or something of herself long ago. She will intone, "Ida say that she was good to the poor white people as she was to the rich, as she made a bargain to nurse a poor white lady in obstetrical case for a peck of peas. Ida said no, she couldn't see her suffer, and therefore a peck of black-eyed peas would be sufficient." She wants all she says to be listened to with the whole attention, and declares she does wish it were all written down. "Let her keep it straight, darling, if she remember Ida's true words, the angels will know it and be waiting around the throne for her." But Ida's true words are many and strange. When she talks about the old days it is almost like a story of combat against evil. "Ida fitted a duel from twenty-one to fifty-six, and then they operated on her right side and she was never able to stoop down to the floor again. She was never like those young devils, that pace around in those white shoes and those white clothes and up and down the streets of an evening while their patient is calling for a drink of water down poor parched throat—though I wore those white shoes and those white clothes. Only, my heart was in another direction."

Ida said, "I was nursing ever since there was a big road in Jackson. There was only nine doctors, and they were the best in all the world, all nine, right here in Jackson, but they were weak in finance. There wasn't nary hospital nowhere—there wasn't nary brick in Jackson, not one brick, no brick walk, no brick store, no brick nothing else. There wasn't no Old Ladies' Home at the end of the street, there wasn't no stopping place but the country. Town was as black as tar come night, and praise God they finally put some gas in bottles on the corners. There wasn't no such thing in the world as a nice buggy. Never heard tell of a cotton mattress, but tore up shucks and see the bed, so high, and the hay pillow stand up so beautiful! Now they got all this electric light and other electricity. Can't do nothing without the clickety-click. And bless God they fly just like buzzards up in the air, but Ida don't intend to ride till she ride to Glory."

In those early days when Jackson seems to have been a Slough of Despond with pestilence sticking out its head in the nights as black as

tar, Ida was not only a midwife, she nursed all diseases. "It was the yellow
fever first, and the next after that was the worst pox that there ever was
in this world—it would kill you then, in my girl-days, six or seven a day.
They had to stretch a rope across the road to keep the poor sick ones
apart and many's the day I've et at the rope and carried the food back to
the ones suffering." Ida remembers epidemics as major combats in which
she was a kind of giant-killer. She nursed through influenza "six at a blow,
until the doctor told me if I didn't quit nursing by sixes I would drop dead
in the room." She says the doctors wrote her a recommendation as long as
where she will show you up her arm, saying that when they called, it never
was too cold and it never was too hot for Ida to go, and that the whole
town would bow and say Amen, from the Jews on. "Bless my patients,"
she says, "nary one ever did die under my nursing, though plenty were
sick enough to die. But laugh here," she directs. "My husband stayed sick
on me twenty-one years and cost me one thousand whole dollars, but you
can't nurse the heart to do no good, and in the night he fallen asleep and
left me a widow, and I am a widow still."

When Ida found she could no longer stoop to the floor she stopped
being a midwife and began selling clothes. She was successful at once
in that too, for there is a natural flowering-ground for the secondhand-
clothes business in the small American community where the richest people are only a little richer than the poor people and the poorest have ways
to save pride and not starve or go naked. In Jackson the most respectable
matron, if she would like a little extra cash to buy a new camellia bush
or take the excursion to New Orleans, can run over to Ida's with her
husband's other suit and Ida will sell it to a customer as a bargain at five
dollars and collect twenty-five percent for herself, and everybody except
the husband ("Right off my back! Perfectly good suit!") will be satisfied.

It could be a grubby enough little business in actual fact, but Ida is not
a grubby person, and in her handling, it has become an affair of imagination and, to my notion, an expression of a whole attitude of life as
integrated as an art or a philosophy.

Ida's store is her house, a white-painted five-room house with a porch
across the front, a picket fence around, and the door-yard planted to
capacity in big flowers. Inside, it is a phantasmagoria of garments. Every
room except the kitchen is hung with dresses or suits (the sexes are segregated) three and four times around the walls, for the turnover is large and
unpredictable, though not always rapid—people have to save up or wait
for cotton-money. She has assumed all the ceremonies of Business and
employs its practices and its terms to a point within sight of madness. She
puts on a show of logic and executive order before which the customer is
supposed to quail; sometimes I think her customers take on worth with
her merely as witnesses of the miracles of her workings, though that is
unfair of me. Her house turns year by year into a better labyrinth, more

inescapable, and she delights in its complication of aisles and curtains and its mystery of closed doors with little signs on ruled paper, "Nobody can come in here." Someday some little colored girl is going to get lost in Ida's house. The richer she gets, the more "departments" she builds and adds on to the house, and each one is named for the color of its walls, the pink department, or the blue. Even now her side yard is filled with miscellaneous doors, glass panes, planks, and little stacks of bricks that she is accumulating for a new green department she says she will build in 1943.

Her cupboards and drawers are a progressive series of hiding places, which is her interpretation of the filing system. She hides trinkets of mysterious importance or bits of paper filled with abbreviated information; she does not hide money, however, and she tells how much she has on hand ($660.60 is the latest figure), and her life insurance policy is nailed up on the wall over the mantel. Everybody knows her to be an old woman living with only a small grandchild to guard her in a house full of cash money, and yet she has not been murdered. She never will be. I have wondered what Ida would do if she saw a burglar coming after her money. I am convinced that she has no ax or gun ready for him, but a flow of words will be unstoppered that will put the fear of God in him for life; and I think the would-be burglars have the same suspicion, and will continue to keep away, not wanting so much fear of God as that.

She keeps as strict and full a ledger of transaction as the Book of Judgment, and in as enthusiastic and exalted a spirit of accuracy as an angel bookkeeper should have. The only trouble is, it is almost impossible to find in it what she is looking for—but perhaps there will be confusion on Doomsday too. The book, a great black one, which she now has little William, her grandson, to hold for her while she consults it (and he will kneel under it like a little mural figure), covers a period of twenty-six years, concerns hundreds of people, "white and black," and innumerable transactions, all noted down in a strange code full of flourishes, for Ida properly considers all she does confidential. "You could find anything in the world in this book," she says reverently, then slamming it shut in your face, "if you turn enough pages and go in the right direction. Nothing in here is wrong," she says. Loose slips are always flying out of the ledger like notes in a sibyl's book, and she sets William flying to chase them and get them inside again.

She writes her own descriptions of the garments brought to her to sell, and a lady giving over her finest white dress of last summer must not be surprised, if she looks over Ida's shoulder, to see her pen the words "Rally Day, $2.00" or note down her best spring straw hat as "Tom Boy, 75c." The customer might be right, but Ida does not ever ask the customer. After a moment of concentration Ida goes and hangs the object for sale on the wall in the room of her choice, and a tag is pinned to the sleeve, saying simply "Mrs. So-and-So." Accuracy is a passion with Ida, and so is her belief in her own conscience, and I do not know what it must have cost her to pin a tag on one poor sagging dress that has hung there year in, year out, saying "Don't know who this is."

She bears respect to clothes in the same degree as she bears it to the people from whose backs they come; she treats them like these people, until indeed it seems that dignity is in them, shapeless and even ridiculous as they have seemed at first; she gives them the space on the wall and the room in the house that correspond to the honor in which she holds the human beings, and she even speaks in the proper tone of voice when she is in the room with them. They hang at human height from the hangers on the walls, the brighter and more important ones in front and on top. With the most serene impartiality she makes up her mind about client and clothes, and she has been known to say, "For God's sake, take it back. Wouldn't a man white or black wear that suit out of here."

There is a magnificence in Ida's business, an extent and an influence at which she hints without ceasing, that undoubtedly inspire the poorest or idlest customer with almost an anxiety to buy. It is almost like an appease-ment, and the one that goes off with nothing must feel mean, foolish and naked indeed, naked to scorn. "I clothe them," she says, "from Jackson to Vicksburg, Meridian to Jackson, Big Black to 'Azoo, Memphis to New Orleans—Clinton! Bolton! Edwards! Bovina! Pocahontas! Flora! Bento-nia! 'Azoo City! Everywhere. There ain't nobody hasn't come to Ida, or sooner or later will come."

If no one else had thought of the secondhand-clothes business, Ida would have originated it, for she did originate it as far as she is concerned; and likewise I am forced to believe that if there had never been any mid-wives in the world, Ida would have invented midwifery, so ingenious and delicate-handed and wise she is, and sure of her natural right to take charge. She loves transformation and bringing things about; she simply cannot resist it. The Negro midwives of this state have a kind of orga-nization these days and lesser powers, they do certain things in certain book-specified ways, and all memorize and sing at meetings a song about "First we put—Drops in their eyes," but in Ida's day a midwife was a lone person, invested with the whole charge of life; she had to draw upon her own resources and imagination. Ida's constant gestures today still involve a dramatic outthrust of the right hand, and let any prominent names be mentioned (and she mentions them), and she will fling out her palm and cry into the conversation, "Born in this hand!" "Four hundred little white babies—or more," she says. "My God, I was bringing them all the time. I got 'em everywhere—doctors, lawyers, school teachers and preachers, married ladies." She has been in the clothes business for twenty-six years, but she was a midwife for thirty-five.

She herself has been married, twice, and by her first husband she had one son, "the only one I ever did have and I want his name written down:

Julius Knight." Her mother (before she died) and her brothers live out in the country, and only one little grandson has lived with her for a long time. Her husband, Braddie M'Toy, whom she called Toy, is remembered collecting and delivering clothes in a wagon when he was young, and was to be seen always on some street if not another, moving very slowly on account of his heart.

Now without Toy, Ida uses a telephone down the road and a kind of deluxe grapevine service to rouse up her clients and customers. Anybody who is asked to by Ida feels it a duty to phone any stranger for her and "tell them for God's sake to come get their money and bring the change." Strange Negroes call people at dawn, giving news of a sale, white ladies call unknown white ladies, notes on small rolls or scraps of paper folded like doctors' "powders" are conscientiously delivered, and the whole town contrives in her own spirit of emergency to keep Ida's messages on their way. Ida takes twenty-five percent of the sales price, and if she sells your dress for a dollar, you have to take her a quarter when you go, or come back another time, for she will not make change for anybody. She will not violate her system of bookkeeping any more than she would violate her code of ethics or her belief in God—down to the smallest thing, all is absolute in Ida's sight.

Ida finds all Ornament a wonderful and appropriate thing, the proper materializing of the rejoicing or sorrowing soul. I believe she holds Ornament next to birth and somehow kin to it. She despises a drab color and welcomes bright clothes with a queenly and triumphant smile, as if she acknowledges the bold brave heart that chose that. Inferior color means inferior spirit, and an inferior person should not hope to get or spend more than four-bits for an outfit. She dearly loves a dress that is at once identifiable as either rich mourning or "rally-day"—the symbolic and celebrating kind appeal to her inevitably over the warm or the serviceable, and she will ask and (by oratory) get the finest prices for rather useless but splendid garments. "Girl, you buy this spangle-dress," she says to a customer, and the girl buys it and puts it on and shines. Ida's scale of prices would make a graph showing precisely the rise from her condemnation of the subdued and nondescript to her acclaim of the bright and glorious. It is nice on Saturdays to pass in front of Ida's house on the edge of town and see the customers emerge. With some little flash of scarf, some extra glitter of trimming for which they have paid dearly, dressed like some visions in Ida's speculations on the world, glorious or menial as befits their birth, merit and willingness, but all rampant and somehow fulfilled by this last touch of costume as though they have been tapped by a spirit when Ida's thimble rapped them, they float dizzily down the steps and through the flowers out the gate; and you could not help thinking of the phrase "going out into the world," as if Ida had just birthed them anew.

I used to think she must be, a little, the cross between a transcendentalist and a witch, with the happiness and kind of self-wonder that this
combination must enjoy. They say that all things we write could be; and
sometimes in amazement I wonder if a tiny spark of the wonderful Philosopher of Clothes, Diogenes Teufelsdröckh, could be flashing for an
instant, and somewhat barbarically, in the wild and enthusiastic spirit
of this old black woman. Her life, like his, is proudly emblematic—she
herself being the first to see her place in the world. It is she literally who
clothes her entire world, as far and wide as she knows—a hard-worked
midwife grown old, with a memory like a mill turning through it all the
lives that were born in her hand or have passed through her door.

When she stalks about, alternately clapping her hand over her forehead
and flinging out her palm and muttering "Born in this hand!" as she is
likely to do when some lady of the old days comes bringing a dress to
sell, you cannot help believing that she sees them all, her children and
her customers, in the double way, naked and clothed, young and then old,
with love and with contempt, with open arms or with a push to bar the
door. She is moody now, if she has not always been, and sees her customers as a procession of sweet supplicant spirits that she has birthed, who
have returned to her side, and again sometimes as a bunch of scarecrows
or even changelings, that she wishes were well gone out of sight. "They
would steal from their own mother," she says, and while she is pinning
up some purchase in a newspaper and the customer is still counting out
the pennies, she will shout in a deep voice to the grandchild that flutters
around like a little blackbird, "Hold the door, William."

I have never caught Ida doing anything except selling clothes or holding forth on her meditations, but she has a fine garden. "If you want to
carry me something I really like," she will say, bringing up the subject
first, "carry me dallion potatoes [dahlia bulbs] *first*, and old newspapers
second." Ida has the green finger from her mother, and she says, "You're
never going to see any flowers prettier than these right here." She adores
giving flowers away; under your protest she will cut every one in the garden, every red and white rose on the trellis, which is a wooden sunset
with painted rays, the blossoms with little two-inch stems the way a child
cuts them, and distribute them among all present and those passing in
the road. She is full of all the wild humors and extravagances of the godlike toward this entire town and its environs. Sometimes, owing to her
superior wisdom, she is a little malign, but much oftener she will become
excruciatingly tender, holding, as if in some responsibility toward all the
little ones of the world, the entire population to her great black cameoed
breast. Then she will begin to call people "It." "It's all hot and tired, it
is, coming so far to see Ida. Take these beautiful flowers Ida grew with
her own hand, *that's* what it would like. Put 'em in its bedroom," and
she presses forward all the flowers she has cut and then, not content, a

bouquet dripping from a vase, one of a kind of everything, all into your arms.

She loves music too, and in her house she has one room, also hung with clothes, called the music room. "I got all the music in the world in here," she used to say, jabbing a finger at a silent radio and an old Gramophone shut up tight, "but what's the use of letting those contrivances run when you can make your own music?" And ignoring the humble customers waiting, she would fling down at the old pump organ in the corner and tear into a frenzy of chords. "I make my own!" she would shout into the turmoil. She would send for little William, and he knew how to sing with her, though he would give out. "Bass, William!" she would shout, and in his tiny treble he sang bass, bravely.

When Ida speaks of her mother it is in a strange kind of pity, a tender amazement. She says she knew when her mother was going to die, and with her deep feeling for events and commemorations, she gave her a fine big party. Ida would no more shrink from doing anything the grand way than she would shrink from other demands upon her greatness. "Hush now," she told me, "don't say a word while I tell you this. All that day long I was cooking dinner between niggers. I had: four turkeys, four hens, four geese, four hams, red cake, white cake, chocolate cake, caramel cake, every color cake known. The table reached from the front door to the icebox. I had all the lights burning up electricity, and all the flowers cut. I had the plates changed seven times, and three waiters from the hotel. I'd got Mama a partner. Mama was eighty years old and I got her another old lady eighty years old to march with. I had everybody come. All her children—one son, the big shot, came all the way from Detroit, riding in a train, to be at Mama's grand dinner. We had somebody play Silent Night and march music to follow later. And there was Mama: look at Mama! Mama loved powder. Mama had on a little old-fashioned hat, but she wouldn't take it off—had nice hair, too. Mama did all right for the march, she marched all right, and sat down on time at the right place at the head of the table, but she wouldn't take off her hat. So the waiters, they served the chicken soup first, and Mama says, 'Where my coffee? Bring on turnip and cornbread. Didn't you make a blackberry pie?' I said, 'Mama, you don't eat coffee first.' But she said, 'Where my coffee? Bring on turnip and cornbread. Didn't you make a blackberry pie? What's the matter with you?' Everything was so fine, you know. It took her two big sons, one on each side, to quiet her, that's the way Mama acted!" And Ida ended the story laughing and crying. It was plain that there was one person who had no recognition of Ida's grandeur and high place in the world, and who had never yielded at all to the glamour as others did. It was a cruelty for Ida, but perhaps all vision has lived in the house with cruelty.

Nowadays she is carried to such heights of business and power, and its paraphernalia crowds her so, that she is overcome with herself, and suddenly gives way to the magnitude of it all. A kind of chaos comes over her. Now and then she falls down in a trance and stays "dead as that chair for three days." White doctors love her and by a little struggle take care of her. Ida bears with them. "They took my appendix," she will say. "Well, they took my teeth." She says she has a paralyzed heel, though it is hard to see how she can tell—perhaps, like Achilles, she feels that her end is coming by entering that way. "The doctor told me I got to rest until 1945," she declares, with a lifted hand warding you off. "Rest! Rest! Rest! I must rest." If a step is heard on the front porch, she instantly cries warning from within the house, "Don't set your heels down! When you speak to me, whisper!" When a lady that was a stranger came to see her, Ida appeared, but said in haste, "Don't tell me your name, for I'm resting my mind. The doctors don't want me to have any more people in my head than I got already." Now on Saturdays if a dusty battered car full of customers from across the cotton fields draws up, one by one all the shades in the house are yanked down. Ida wishes to see no one, she wishes to sell nothing.

Perhaps the truth is that she has expended herself to excess and now suffers with a corresponding emptiness that she does not want anyone to see. She can show you the track of the pain it gives her: her finger crosses her two breasts. She is as hard to see as a queen.

And I think she lives today the way she would rather be living, directly in symbols. People are their vestures now. Memories, the great memories of births and marriages and deaths, are nearly the same as the pieces of jewelry ("$147.65 worth") she has bought on anniversary days and wears on her person. "That's Mamma's death," she says—a silver watch on a silver chain. She holds out for your admiration the yellow hands that she asserts most of this county was born in, on which now seven signet rings flash. "Don't go to church any longer," she says, "or need to go. I just sit at home and enjoy my fingers."

HANNAH ARENDT

Hannah Arendt (1906–1975), a formidable philosopher and political theorist whose seminal books included The Origins of Totalitarianism, Men in Dark Times, *and* Eichmann in Jerusalem, *was part of that cache of European thinkers, artists, and scientists who fled Nazi Germany for the United States, in the process immeasurably deepening its level of intellectual culture. In her little-known essay, "We Refugees," she both acted as a spokesperson for the group and stood outside it, registering not without irony its prickly defensiveness and confusions around identity. Arendt herself escaped Europe in 1941 and settled in New York, where she befriended Mary McCarthy, taught, and wrote productively for the rest of her life.*

We Refugees

(1943)

In the first place, we don't like to be called "refugees." We ourselves call each other "newcomers" or "immigrants." Our newspapers are papers for "Americans of German language"; and, as far as I know, there is not and never was any club founded by Hitler-persecuted people whose name indicated that its members were refugees.

A refugee used to be a person driven to seek refuge because of some act committed or some political opinion held. Well, it is true we have had to seek refuge; but we committed no acts and most of us never dreamt of having any radical opinion. With us the meaning of the term "refugee" has changed. Now "refugees" are those of us who have been so unfortunate as to arrive in a new country without means and have to be helped by Refugee Committees.

Before this war broke out we were even more sensitive about being called refugees. We did our best to prove to other people that we were just ordinary immigrants. We declared that we had departed of our own free will to countries of our choice, and we denied that our situation had anything to do with "so-called Jewish problems." Yes, we were "immigrants" or "newcomers" who had left our country because, one fine day, it no longer suited us to stay, or for purely economic reasons. We wanted to rebuild our lives, that was all. In order to rebuild one's life one has to be strong and an optimist. So we are very optimistic.

Our optimism, indeed, is admirable, even if we say so ourselves. The story of our struggle has finally become known. We lost our home, which means the familiarity of daily life. We lost our occupation, which means the confidence that we are of some use in this world. We lost our language, which means the naturalness of reactions, the simplicity of gestures, the unaffected expression of feelings. We left our relatives in the Polish ghettos and our best friends have been killed in concentration camps, and that means the rupture of our private lives.

Nevertheless, as soon as we were saved—and most of us had to be saved several times—we started our new lives and tried to follow as closely as possible all the good advice our saviors passed on to us. We were told to forget; and we forgot quicker than anybody ever could imagine. In a friendly way we were reminded that the new country would become a new home; and after four weeks in France or six weeks in America, we pretended to be Frenchmen or Americans. The most optimistic among us would even add that their whole former life had been passed in a kind of unconscious exile and only their new country now taught them what a home really looks like. It is true we sometimes raise objections when we are told to forget about our former work; and our former ideals are usually hard to throw over if our social standard is at stake. With the language, however, we find no difficulties: after a single year optimists are convinced they speak English as well as their mother tongue; and after two years they swear solemnly that they speak English better than any other language—their German is a language they hardly remember.

In order to forget more efficiently we rather avoid any allusion to concentration or internment camps we experienced in nearly all European countries—it might be interpreted as pessimism or lack of confidence in the new homeland. Besides, how often have we been told that nobody likes to listen to all that; hell is no longer a religious belief or a fantasy, but something as real as houses and stones and trees. Apparently nobody wants to know that contemporary history has created a new kind of human beings—the kind that are put in concentration camps by their foes and in internment camps by their friends.

Even among ourselves we don't speak about this past. Instead, we have found our own way of mastering an uncertain future. Since everybody plans and wishes and hopes, so do we. Apart from the general human attitudes, however, we try to clear up the future more scientifically. After so much bad luck we want a course as sure as a gun. Therefore, we leave the earth with all its uncertainties behind and we cast our eyes up to the sky. The stars tell us—rather than the newspapers—when Hitler will be defeated and when we shall become American citizens. We think the stars more reliable advisers than all our friends; we learn from the stars when we should have lunch with our benefactors and on what day we have the best chances of filling out one of these countless questionnaires which accompany our present lives. Sometimes we don't rely even on the stars but rather on the lines of our hand or the signs of our handwriting. Thus we learn less about political events but more about our own dear selves, even though somehow psychoanalysis has gone out of fashion. Those happier times are past when bored ladies and gentlemen of high society conversed about the genial misdemeanors of their early childhood. They don't want ghost-stories any more; it is real experiences that make their flesh creep. There is no longer any need of bewitching the past; it is spell-bound enough in reality. Thus, in spite of our outspoken optimism, we use all sorts of magical tricks to conjure up the spirits of the future.

I don't know which memories and which thoughts nightly dwell in our dreams. I dare not ask for information, since I, too, had rather be an optimist. But sometimes I imagine that at least nightly we think of our dead or we remember the poems we once loved. I could even understand how our friends of the West coast, during the curfew, should have had such curious notions as to believe that we are not only "prospective citizens" but present "enemy aliens." In daylight, of course, we become only "technically" enemy aliens—all refugees know this. But when technical reasons prevented you from leaving your home during the dark hours, it certainly was not easy to avoid some dark speculations about the relation between technicality and reality.

No, there is something wrong with our optimism. There are those odd optimists among us who, having made a lot of optimistic speeches, go home and turn on the gas or make use of a skyscraper in quite an unexpected way. They seem to prove that our proclaimed cheerfulness is based on a dangerous readiness for death. Brought up in the conviction that life is the highest good and death the greatest dismay, we became witnesses and victims of worse terrors than death—without having been able to discover a higher ideal than life. Thus, although death lost its horror for us, we became neither willing nor capable to risk our lives for a cause. Instead of fighting—or thinking about how to become able to fight back—refugees have got used to wishing death to friends or relatives; if somebody dies, we cheerfully imagine all the trouble he has been saved.

Finally many of us end by wishing that we, too, could be saved some trouble, and act accordingly.

Since 1938—since Hitler's invasion of Austria—we have seen how quickly eloquent optimism could change to speechless pessimism. As time went on, we got worse—even more optimistic and even more inclined to suicide. Austrian Jews under Schuschnigg were such a cheerful people— all impartial observers admired them. It was quite wonderful how deeply convinced they were that nothing could happen to them. But when German troops invaded the country and Gentile neighbors started riots at Jewish homes, Austrian Jews began to commit suicide.

Unlike other suicides, our friends leave no explanation of their deed, no indictment, no charge against a world that had forced a desperate man to talk and to behave cheerfully to his very last day. Letters left by them are conventional, meaningless documents. Thus, funeral orations we make at their open graves are brief, embarrassed and very hopeful. Nobody cares about motives, they seem to be clear to all of us.

I speak of unpopular facts; and it makes things worse that in order to prove my point I do not even dispose of the sole arguments which impress modern people—figures. Even those Jews who furiously deny the existence of the Jewish people give us a fair chance of survival as far as figures are concerned—how else could they prove that only a few Jews are criminals and that many Jews are being killed as good patriots in wartime? Through their effort to save the statistical life of the Jewish people we know that Jews had the lowest suicide rate among all civilized nations. I am quite sure those figures are no longer correct, but I cannot prove it with new figures, though I can certainly with new experiences. This might be sufficient for those skeptical souls who never were quite convinced that the measure of one's skull gives the exact idea of its content, or that statistics of crime show the exact level of national ethics. Anyhow, wherever European Jews are living today, they no longer behave according to statistical laws. Suicides occur not only among the panic-stricken people in Berlin and Vienna, in Bucharest or Paris, but in New York and Los Angeles, in Buenos Aires and Montevideo.

On the other hand, there has been little reported about suicides in the ghettos and concentration camps themselves. True, we had very few reports at all from Poland, but we have been fairly well informed about German and French concentration camps.

At the camp of Gurs, for instance, where I had the opportunity of spending some time, I heard only once about suicide, and that was the suggestion of a collective action, apparently a kind of protest in order to vex the French. When some of us remarked that we had been shipped there *"pour crever"* in any case, the general mood turned suddenly into a violent courage of life. The general opinion held that one had to be abnormally asocial and unconcerned about general events if one was still able to interpret the whole accident as personal and individual bad luck and, accordingly, ended one's life personally and individually. But the same people, as soon as they returned to their own individual lives, being faced with seemingly individual problems, changed once more to this insane optimism which is next door to despair.

We are the first non-religious Jews persecuted—and we are the first ones who, not only *in extremis,* answer with suicide. Perhaps the philosophers are right who teach that suicide is the last and supreme guarantee of human freedom; not being free to create our lives or the world in which we live, we nevertheless are free to throw life away and to leave the world. Pious Jews, certainly, cannot realize this negative liberty: they perceive murder in suicide, that is, destruction of what man never is able to make, interference with the rights of the Creator. *Adonai nathan veadonai lakach* ("The Lord hath given and the Lord hath taken away"); and they would add: *baruch shem adonai* ("blessed be the name of the Lord"). For them suicide, like murder, means a blasphemous attack on creation as a whole. The man who kills himself asserts that life is not worth living and the world not worth sheltering him.

Yet our suicides are no mad rebels who hurl defiance at life and the world, who try to kill in themselves the whole universe. Theirs is a quiet and modest way of vanishing; they seem to apologize for the violent solution they have found for their personal problems. In their opinion, generally, political events had nothing to do with their individual fate; in good or bad times they would believe solely in their personality. Now they find some mysterious shortcomings in themselves which prevent them from getting along. Having felt entitled from their earliest childhood to a certain social standard, they are failures in their own eyes if this standard cannot be kept any longer. Their optimism is the vain attempt to keep head above water. Behind this front of cheerfulness, they constantly struggle with despair of themselves. Finally, they die of a kind of selfishness.

If we are saved we feel humiliated, and if we are helped we feel degraded. We fight like madmen for private existences with individual destinies, since we are afraid of becoming part of that miserable lot of *schnorrers* whom we, many of us former philanthropists, remember only too well. Just as once we failed to understand that the so-called *schnorrer* was a symbol of Jewish destiny and not a *shlemihl,* so today we don't feel entitled to Jewish solidarity; we cannot realize that we by ourselves are not so much concerned as the whole Jewish people. Sometimes this lack of comprehension has been strongly supported by our protectors. Thus, I remember a director of a great charity concern in Paris who, whenever he received the card of a German-Jewish intellectual with the inevitable

"Dr." on it, used to exclaim at the top of his voice, "Herr Doktor, Herr Doktor, Herr Schnorrer, Herr Schnorrer!"

The conclusion we drew from such unpleasant experiences was simple enough. To be a doctor of philosophy no longer satisfied us; and we learnt that in order to build a new life, one has first to improve on the old one. A nice little fairy-tale has been invented to describe our behavior; a forlorn émigré dachshund, in his grief, begins to speak: "Once, when I was a St. Bernard . . ."

Our new friends, rather overwhelmed by so many stars and famous men, hardly understand that at the basis of all our descriptions of past splendors lies one human truth: once we were somebodies about whom people cared, we were loved by friends, and even known by landlords as paying our rent regularly. Once we could buy our food and ride in the subway without being told we were undesirable. We have become a little hysterical since newspapermen started detecting us and telling us publicly to stop being disagreeable when shopping for milk and bread. We wonder how it can be done; we already are so damnably careful in every moment of our daily lives to avoid anybody guessing who we are, what kind of passport we have, where our birth certificates were filled out—and that Hitler didn't like us. We try the best we can to fit into a world where you have to be sort of politically minded when you buy your food.

Under such circumstances, St. Bernard grows bigger and bigger. I never can forget that young man who, when expected to accept a certain kind of work, sighed out, "You don't know to whom you speak; I was Section-manager in Karstadt's [a great department store in Berlin]." But there is also the deep despair of that middle-aged man who, going through count-less shifts of different committees in order to be saved, finally exclaimed, "And nobody here knows who I am!" Since nobody would treat him as a dignified human being, he began sending cables to great personalities and his big relations. He learnt quickly that in this mad world it is much easier to be accepted as a "great man" than as a human being.

The less we are free to decide who we are or to live as we like, the more we try to put up a front, to hide the facts, and to play roles. We were expelled from Germany because we were Jews. But having hardly crossed the French borderline, we were changed into "boches." We were even told that we had to accept this designation if we really were against Hitler's racial theories. During seven years we played the ridiculous role of try-ing to be Frenchmen—at least, prospective citizens; but at the beginning of the war we were interned as "boches" all the same. In the meantime, however, most of us had indeed become such loyal Frenchmen that we could not even criticize a French governmental order; thus we declared it was all right to be interned. We were the first *"prisonniers volontaires"* history has ever seen. After the Germans invaded the country, the French Government had only to change the name of the firm; having been jailed because we were Germans, we were not freed because we were Jews.

It is the same story all over the world, repeated again and again. In Europe the Nazis confiscated our property; but in Brazil we have to pay 30% of our wealth, like the most loyal member of the *Bund der Auslandsdeutschen*. In Paris we could not leave our homes after eight o'clock because we were Jews; but in Los Angeles we are restricted because we are "enemy aliens." Our identity is changed so frequently that nobody can find out who we actually are.

Unfortunately, things don't look any better when we meet with Jews. French Jewry was absolutely convinced that all Jews coming from beyond the Rhine were what they called *Polaks*—what German Jewry called *Ostjuden*. But those Jews who really came from eastern Europe could not agree with their French brethren and called us *Jaeckes*. The sons of these *Jaecke*-haters—the second generation born in France and already duly assimilated—shared the opinion of the French Jewish upper class. Thus, in the very same family, you could be called a *Jaecke* by the father and a *Polak* by the son.

Since the outbreak of the war and the catastrophe that has befallen European Jewry, the mere fact of being a refugee has prevented our mingling with native Jewish society, some exceptions only proving the rule. These unwritten social laws, though never publicly admitted, have the great force of public opinion. And such a silent opinion and practice is more important for our daily lives than all official proclamations of hospitality and good will.

Man is a social animal and life is not easy for him when social ties are cut off. Moral standards are much easier kept in the texture of a society. Very few individuals have the strength to conserve their own integrity if their social, political and legal status is completely confused. Lacking the courage to fight for a change of our social and legal status, we have decided instead, so many of us, to try a change of identity. And this curious behavior makes matters much worse. The confusion in which we live is partly our own work.

Some day somebody will write the true story of this Jewish emigration from Germany; and he will have to start with a description of that Mr. Cohn from Berlin who had always been a 150% German, a German super-patriot. In 1933 that Mr. Cohn found refuge in Prague and very quickly became a convinced Czech patriot—as true and loyal a Czech patriot as he had been a German one. Time went on and about 1937 the Czech Government, already under some Nazi pressure, began to expel its Jewish refugees, disregarding the fact that they felt so strongly as prospective Czech citizens. Our Mr. Cohn then went to Vienna; to adjust oneself there a definite Austrian patriotism was required. The German invasion forced Mr. Cohn out of that country. He arrived in Paris at a bad moment and he never did receive a regular residence-permit. Having already acquired a great skill in wishful thinking, he refused to take mere administrative measures seriously, convinced that he would spend his future life in France. Therefore, he prepared his adjustment to the French nation by identifying himself with "our" ancestor Vercingetorix. I think I had better not dilate on the further adventures of Mr. Cohn. As long as Mr. Cohn can't make up his mind to be what he actually is, a Jew, nobody can foretell all the mad changes he will have to go through.

A man who wants to lose his self discovers, indeed, the possibilities of human existence, which are infinite, as infinite as is creation. But the recovering of a new personality is as difficult—and as hopeless—as a new creation of the world. Whatever we do, whatever we pretend to be, we reveal nothing but our insane desire to be changed, not to be Jews. All our activities are directed to attain this aim: we don't want to be refugees, since we don't want to be Jews; we pretend to be English-speaking people, since German-speaking immigrants of recent years are marked as Jews; we don't call ourselves stateless, since the majority of stateless people in the world are Jews; we are willing to become loyal Hottentots, only to hide the fact that we are Jews. We don't succeed and we can't succeed; under the cover of our "optimism" you can easily detect the hopeless sadness of assimilationists.

With us from Germany the word assimilation received a "deep" philosophical meaning. You can hardly realize how serious we were about it. Assimilation did not mean the necessary adjustment to the country where we happened to be born and to the people whose language we happened to speak. We adjust in principle to everything and everybody. This attitude became quite clear to me once by the words of one of my compatriots who, apparently, knew how to express his feelings. Having just arrived in France, he founded one of these societies of adjustment in which German Jews asserted to each other that they were already Frenchmen. In his first speech he said: "We have been good Germans in Germany and therefore we shall be good Frenchmen in France." The public applauded enthusiastically and nobody laughed; we were happy to have learnt how to prove our loyalty.

If patriotism were a matter of routine or practice, we should be the most patriotic people in the world. Let us go back to our Mr. Cohn; he certainly has beaten all records. He is that ideal immigrant who always, and in every country into which a terrible fate has driven him, promptly sees and loves the native mountains. But since patriotism is not yet believed to be a matter of practice, it is hard to convince people of the sincerity of our repeated transformations. This struggle makes our own society so intolerant; we demand full affirmation without our own group because we are not in the position to obtain it from the natives. The natives, confronted with such strange beings as we are, become suspicious; from their point of view, as a rule, only a loyalty to our old countries is understandable. That makes life very bitter for us. We might overcome this suspicion if we could explain that, being Jews, our patriotism in our original countries had rather a peculiar aspect. Though it was indeed sincere and deep-rooted. We wrote big volumes to prove it; paid an entire bureaucracy to explore its antiquity and to explain it statistically. We had scholars write philosophical dissertations on the predestined harmony between Jews and Frenchmen, Jews and Germans, Jews and Hungarians, Jews and . . . Our so frequently suspected loyalty of today has a long history. It is the history of a hundred and fifty years of assimilated Jewry who performed an unprecedented feat: though proving all the time their non-Jewishness, they succeeded in remaining Jews all the same.

The desperate confusion of these Ulysses-wanderers who, unlike their great prototype, don't know who they are is easily explained by their perfect mania for refusing to keep their identity. This mania is much older than the last ten years which revealed the profound absurdity of our existence. We are like people with a fixed idea who can't help trying continually to disguise an imaginary stigma. Thus we are enthusiastically fond of every new possibility which, being new, seems able to work miracles. We are fascinated by every new nationality in the same way as a woman of tidy size is delighted with every new dress which promises to give her the desired waistline. But she likes the new dress only as long as she believes in its miraculous qualities, and she discovers that it does not change her stature—or, for that matter, her status.

One may be surprised that the apparent uselessness of all our odd disguises has not yet been able to discourage us. If it is true that men seldom learn from history, it is also true that they may learn from personal experiences which, as in our case, are repeated time and again. But before you cast the first stone at us, remember that being a Jew does not give any legal status in the world. If we should start telling the truth that we are nothing but Jews, it would mean that we expose ourselves to the fate of human beings who, unprotected by any specific law or political convention, are nothing but human beings. I can hardly imagine an attitude more dangerous, since we actually live in a world in which human beings as such have ceased to exist for quite a while, since society has discovered discrimination as the great social weapon by which one may kill men without any bloodshed; since passports or birth certificates, and sometimes even income tax receipts, are no longer formal papers but matters of social distinction. It is true that most of us depend entirely upon social standards; we lose confidence in ourselves if society does not approve us; we are—and always were—ready to pay any price in order to be accepted by society. But it is equally true that the very few among us who have tried to get along without all these tricks and jokes of adjustment and assimilation have paid a much higher price than they could afford: they jeopardized the few chances even our laws are given in a topsy-turvy world.

The attitude of these few whom, following Bernard Lazare, one may call "conscious pariahs," can as little be explained by recent events alone as the attitude of our Mr. Cohn who tried by every means to become an upstart. Both are sons of the nineteenth century which, not knowing legal or political outlaws, knew only too well social pariahs and their counterpart, social parvenus. Modern Jewish history, having started with court Jews and continuing with Jewish millionaires and philanthropists, is apt to forget about this other trend of Jewish tradition—the tradition of Heine, Rahel Varnhagen, Sholom Aleichem, of Bernard Lazare, Franz Kafka or even Charlie Chaplin. It is the tradition of a minority of Jews who have not wanted to become upstarts, who preferred the status of "conscious pariah." All vaunted Jewish qualities—the "Jewish heart," humanity, humor, disinterested intelligence—are pariah qualities. All Jewish shortcomings—tactlessness, political stupidity, inferiority complexes and money-grubbing—are characteristic of upstarts. There have always been Jews who did not think it worth while to change their humane attitude and their natural insight into reality for the narrowness of caste spirit or the essential unreality of financial transactions.

History has forced the status of outlaws upon both, upon pariahs and parvenus alike. The latter have not yet accepted the great wisdom of Balzac's *"On ne parvient pas deux fois";* thus they don't understand the wild dreams of the former and feel humiliated in sharing their fate. Those few refugees who insist upon telling the truth, even to the point of "indecency," get in exchange for their unpopularity one priceless advantage: history is no longer a closed book to them and politics is no longer the privilege of Gentiles. They know that the outlawing of the Jewish people in Europe has been followed closely by the outlawing of most European nations. Refugees driven from country to country represent the vanguard of their peoples—if they keep their identity. For the first time Jewish history is not separate but tied up with that of all other nations. The comity of European peoples went to pieces when, and because, it allowed its weakest member to be excluded and persecuted.

MARY MCCARTHY

*Long in the public eye as a novelist (*The Group*), essayist, and autobiographer, Mary McCarthy (1912–1989) recounted in her indelible* Memories of a Catholic Girlhood *the tale of losing her parents at an early age and being taken in by coldhearted relatives and classically educated in Catholic schools, where her love of Latin syntax and concision would serve her well as a polished prose writer. Coming from the West Coast to the East, she catapulted into the New York literary scene with mercilessly amusing critical pieces. The title of her essay collection* On the Contrary *foregrounded her love of contrariety; in that book, she alternated as a public intellectual weighing in on issues of the day, a gimlet-eyed cultural critic, and a frank confessor of personal vanities and mistakes. In her provocative essay "America the Beautiful," she strives with the aid of shrewd, paradoxical, sometimes questionable but always thought-provoking generalizations to characterize a victorious United States in the postwar era.*

America the Beautiful: The Humanist in the Bathtub

(1947)

A visiting Existentialist wanted recently to be taken to dinner at a really American place. This proposal, natural enough in a tourist, disclosed a situation thoroughly unnatural. Unless the visiting lady's object was suffering, there was no way of satisfying her demand. Sukiyaki joints, chop suey joints, Italian table d'hôte places, French provincial restaurants with the menu written on a slate, Irish chophouses, and Jewish delicatessens came abundantly to mind, but these were not what the lady wanted. Schrafft's or the Automat would have answered, yet to take her there would have been to turn oneself into a tourist and to present America as a spectacle—a *New Yorker* cartoon or a savage drawing in the *New Masses*. It was the beginning of an evening of humiliations. The visitor was lively and eager; her mind lay open and orderly, like a notebook ready for impressions. It was not long, however, before she shut it up with a snap. We had no recommendations to make to her. With movies, plays, current books, it was the same story as with the restaurants. *Open City, Les Enfants du Paradis,* Oscar Wilde, a reprint of Henry James were *paté de maison* to this lady who wanted the definitive flapjack. She did not believe us when we said that there were no good Hollywood movies, no good Broadway plays—only curios; she was merely confirmed in her impression that American intellectuals were "negative."

Yet the irritating thing was that we did not feel negative. We admired and liked our country; we preferred it to that imaginary America, land of the *peaux rouges* of Caldwell and Steinbeck, dumb paradise of violence and the detective story, which had excited the sensibilities of our visitor and of the up-to-date French literary world. But to found our preference, to locate it materially in some admirable object or institution, such as Chartres, say, or French café life, was for us, that night at any rate, an impossible undertaking. We heard ourselves saying that the real America was elsewhere, in the white frame houses and church spires of New England; yet we knew that we talked foolishly—we were not Granville Hicks and we looked ludicrous in his opinions. The Elevated, half a block away, interrupting us every time a train passed, gave us the lie on schedule, every eight minutes. But if the elm-shaded village green was a false or at least an insufficient address for the *genius loci* we honored, where then was it to be found? Surveyed from the vantage point of Europe, this large continent seemed suddenly deficient in objects of virtue. The Grand Canyon, Yellowstone Park, Jim Hill's mansion in St. Paul, Jefferson's Monticello, the blast furnaces of Pittsburgh, Mount Rainier, the yellow observatory at Amherst, the little-theatre movement in Cleveland, Ohio, a Greek revival house glimpsed from a car window in a lost river-town in New Jersey—these things were too small for the size of the country. Each of them, when pointed to, diminished in interest with the lady's perspective of distance. There was no sight that in itself seemed to justify her crossing of the Atlantic.

If she was interested in "conditions," that was a different matter. There are conditions everywhere; it takes no special genius to produce them. Yet would it be an act of hospitality to invite a visitor to a lynching? Unfortunately, nearly all the "sights" in America fall under the head of conditions. Hollywood, Reno, the sharecroppers' homes in the South, the mining towns of Pennsylvania, Coney Island, the Chicago stockyards, Macy's, the Dodgers, Harlem, even Congress, the forum of our liberties, are spectacles rather than sights, to use the term in the colloquial sense of "Didn't he make a holy spectacle of himself?" An Englishman of almost any political opinion can show a visitor through the Houses of Parliament with a sense of pride or at least of indulgence toward his national foibles and traditions. The American, if he has a spark of national feeling, will be humiliated by the very prospect of a foreigner's visit to Congress—these, for the most part, illiterate hacks whose fancy vests are spotted with gravy, and whose speeches, hypocritical, unctuous, and slovenly, are spotted also with the gravy of political patronage, these persons are a reflection on the democratic process rather than of it; they expose it in its underwear. In European legislation, we are told, a great deal of shady business goes on in private, behind the scenes. In America, it is just the opposite, anything good, presumably, is accomplished *in camera,* in the committee rooms.

It is so with all our institutions. For the visiting European, a trip through the United States has, almost inevitably, the character of an exposé, and the American, on his side, is tempted by love of his country to lock the inquiring tourist in his hotel room and throw away the key. His contention that the visible and material America is not the real or the only one is more difficult to sustain than was the presumption of the "other" Germany behind the Nazi steel.

To some extent a citizen of any country will feel that the tourist's view of his homeland is a false one. The French will tell you that you have to go into their homes to see what the French people are really like. The intellectuals in the Left Bank cafés are not the real French intellectuals, etc., etc. In Italy, they complain that the tourist must not judge by the *ristorantes;* there one sees only black-market types. But in neither of these cases is the native really disturbed by the tourist's view of his country. If Versailles or Giotto's bell-tower in Florence do not tell the whole story, they are still not incongruous with it; you do not hear a Frenchman or an Italian object when these things are noticed by a visitor. With the American, the contradiction is more serious. He must, if he is to defend his country, repudiate its visible aspect almost entirely. He must say that its parade of phenomenology, its billboards, super-highways, even its skyscrapers, not only fail to represent the inner essence of his country but in fact contravene it. He may point, if he wishes, to certain beautiful objects, but here too he is in difficulties, for nearly everything that is beautiful and has not been produced by Nature belongs to the eighteenth century, to a past with which he has very little connection, and which his ancestors, in many or most cases, had no part in. Beacon Street and the

Boston Common are very charming in the eighteenth-century manner, so are the sea captains' houses in the old Massachusetts ports, and the ruined plantations of Louisiana, but an American from Brooklyn or the Middle West or the Pacific Coast finds the style of life embodied in them as foreign as Europe; indeed, the first sensation of a Westerner, coming upon Beacon Hill and the gold dome of the State House, is to feel that at last he has traveled "abroad." The American, if he is to speak the highest truth about his country, must refrain from pointing at all. The virtue of American civilization is that it is unmaterialistic.

This statement may strike a critic as whimsical or perverse. Everybody knows, it will be said, that America has the most materialistic civilization in the world, that Americans care only about money, they have no time or talent for living; look at radio, look at advertising, look at life insurance, look at the tired business man, at the Frigidaires and the Fords. In answer, the reader is invited first to look instead into his own heart and inquire whether he personally feels himself to be represented by these things, or whether he does not, on the contrary, feel them to be irrelevant to him, a necessary evil, part of the conditions of life. Other people, he will assume, care about them very much: the man down the street, the entire population of Detroit or Scarsdale, the back-country farmer, the urban poor or the rich. But he himself accepts these objects as imposed on him by a collective "otherness" of desire, an otherness he has not met directly but whose existence he infers from the number of automobiles, Frigidaires, or television sets he sees around him. Stepping into his new Buick convertible, he knows that he would gladly do without it, but imagines that to his neighbor, who is just backing his out of the driveway, this car is the motor of life. More often, however, the otherness is projected farther afield, onto a different class or social group, remote and alien. Thus the rich, who would like nothing better, they think, than for life to be a perpetual fishing trip with the trout grilled by a native guide, look patronizingly upon the whole apparatus of American civilization as a cheap Christmas present to the poor, and city people see the radio and the washing machine as the farm-wife's solace.

It can be argued, of course, that the subjective view is prevaricating, possession of the Buick being nine-tenths of the social law. But who has ever met, outside of advertisements, a true parishioner of this church of Mammon? A man may take pride in a car, and a housewife in her new sink or wallpaper, but pleasure in new acquisitions is universal and eternal; an Italian man with a new gold tooth, a French bibliophile with a new edition, a woman with a new baby, a philosopher with a new thought, all these people are rejoicing in progress, in man's power to enlarge and improve. Before men showed off new cars, they showed off new horses; it is alleged against modern man that he as an individual craftsman did not make the car; but his grandfather did not make the horse either. What is imputed to Americans is something quite different, an abject dependence on material possessions, an image of happiness as packaged by the manufacturer, content in a can. This view of American life is strongly urged by advertising agencies. We know the "others," of course, because we meet them every week in full force in *The New Yorker* or the *Saturday Evening Post,* those brightly colored families of dedicated consumers, waiting in unison on the porch for the dealer to deliver the new car, gobbling the new cereal ("Gee, Mom, is it good for you too?"), lining up to bank their paychecks, or fearfully anticipating the industrial accident and the insurance-check that will "compensate" for it. We meet them also, more troll-like underground, in the subway placards, in the ferociously complacent One-A-Day family, and we hear their courtiers sing to them on the radio of Ivory or Supersuds. The thing, however, that repels us in these advertisements is their naïve falsity to life. Who are these advertising men kidding, besides the European tourist? Between the tired, sad, gentle faces of the subway riders and the grinning Holy Families of the Ad-Mass, there exists no possibility of even a wishful identification. We take a vitamin pill with the hope of feeling (possibly) a little less tired, but the superstition of buoyant health emblazoned in the bright, ugly pictures has no more power to move us than the blood of St. Januarius.

Familiarity has perhaps bred contempt in us Americans: until you have had a washing machine, you cannot imagine how little difference it will make to you. Europeans still believe that money brings happiness, witness the bought journalist, the bought politician, the bought general, the whole venality of European literary life, inconceivable in this country of the dollar. It is true that America produces and consumes more cars, soap, and bathtubs than any other nation, but we live among these objects rather than by them. Americans build skyscrapers; Le Corbusier worships them. Ehrenburg, our Soviet critic, fell in love with the Check-O-Mat in American railway stations, writing home paragraphs of song to this gadget—while deploring American materialism. When an American heiress wants to buy a man, she at once crosses the Atlantic. The only really materialistic people I have ever met have been Europeans.

The strongest argument for the un-materialistic character of American life is the fact that we tolerate conditions that are, from a materialistic point of view, intolerable. What the foreigner finds most objectionable in American life is its lack of basic comfort. No nation with any sense of material well-being would endure the food we eat, the cramped apartments we live in, the noise, the traffic, the crowded subways and buses. American life, in large cities, at any rate, is a perpetual assault on the senses and the nerves; it is out of asceticism, out of unworldliness, precisely, that we bear it.

—

This republic was founded on an unworldly assumption, a denial of "the facts of life." It is manifestly untrue that all men are created equal; interpreted in worldly terms, this doctrine has resulted in a pseudo-equality, that is, in standardization, in an equality of things rather than of persons. The inalienable rights to life, liberty, and the pursuit of happiness appear, in practice, to have become the inalienable right to a bathtub, a flush toilet, and a can of Spam. Left-wing critics of America attribute this result to the intrusion of capitalism; right-wing critics see it as the logical dead end of democracy. Capitalism, certainly, now depends on mass production, which depends on large-scale distribution of uniform goods, till the consumer today is the victim of the manufacturer who launches on him a regiment of products for which he must make house-room in his soul. The buying impulse, in its original force and purity, was not nearly so crass, however, or so meanly acquisitive as many radical critics suppose. The purchase of a bathtub was the exercise of a spiritual right. The immigrant or the poor native American bought a bathtub, not because he wanted to take a bath, but because he wanted to be in a *position* to do so. This remains true in many fields today; possessions, when they are desired, are not wanted for their own sakes but as tokens of an ideal state of freedom, fraternity, and franchise. "Keeping up with the Joneses" is a vulgarization of Jefferson's concept, but it too is a declaration of the rights of man, and decidedly unfeasible and visionary. Where for a European, a fact is a fact, for us Americans, the real, if it is relevant at all, is simply symbolic appearance. We are a nation of twenty million bathrooms, with a humanist in every tub. One such humanist I used to hear of on Cape Cod had, on growing rich, installed two toilets side by side in his marble bathroom, on the model of the two-seater of his youth. He was a clear case of Americanism, hospitable, gregarious, and impractical, a theorist of perfection. Was his dream of the conquest of poverty a vulgar dream or a noble one, a material demand or a spiritual insistence? It is hard to think of him as a happy man, and in this too he is characteristically American, for the parity of the radio, the movies, and the washing machine has made Americans sad, reminding them of another parity of which these things were to be but emblems.

The American does not enjoy his possessions because sensory enjoyment was not his object, and he lives sparely and thinly among them, in the monastic discipline of Scarsdale or the barracks of Stuyvesant Town. Only among certain groups where franchise, socially speaking, has not been achieved, do pleasure and material splendor constitute a life-object and an occupation. Among the outcasts—Jews, Negroes, Catholics, homosexuals—excluded from the communion of ascetics, the love of fabrics, gaudy show, and rich possessions still anachronistically flaunts itself.

Once a norm has been reached, differing in the different classes, financial ambition itself seems to fade away. The self-made man finds, to his anger, his son uninterested in money; you have shirtsleeves to shirtsleeves in three generations. The great financial empires are a thing of the past. Some recent immigrants—movie magnates and gangsters particularly— retain their acquisitiveness, but how long is it since anyone in the general public has murmured, wonderingly, "as rich as Rockefeller"?

If the dream of American fraternity had ended simply in this, the value of humanistic and egalitarian strivings would be seriously called into question. Jefferson, the Adamses, Franklin, Madison, would be in the position of Dostoevsky's Grand Inquisitor, who, desiring to make the Kingdom of God incarnate on earth, inaugurated the kingdom of the devil. If the nature of matter is such that the earthly paradise, once realized, becomes always the paradise of the earthly, and a spiritual conquest of matter becomes an enslavement of spirit, then the atomic bomb is, as has been argued, the logical result of the Enlightenment, and the land of opportunity is, precisely, the land of death. This position, however, is a strictly materialist one, for it asserts the Fact of the bomb as the one tremendous truth: subjective attitudes are irrelevant; it does not matter what we think or feel; possession again in this case is nine-tenths of the law.

It must be admitted that there is a great similarity between the nation with its new bomb and the consumer with his new Buick. In both cases, there is a disinclination to use the product, stronger naturally in the case of the bomb, but somebody has manufactured the thing, and there seems to be no way not to use it, especially when everybody else will be doing so. Here again the argument of the "others" is invoked to justify our own procedures: if we had not invented the bomb, the Germans would have; the Soviet Union will have it in a year, etc., etc. This is keeping up with the Joneses indeed, our national propagandists playing the role of the advertising men in persuading us of the "others'" intentions.

It seems likely at this moment that we will find no way of not using the bomb, yet those who argue theoretically that this machine is the true expression of our society leave us, in practice, with no means of opposing it. We must differentiate ourselves from the bomb if we are to avoid using it, and in private thought we do, distinguishing the bomb sharply from our daily concerns and sentiments, feeling it as an otherness that waits outside to descend on us, an otherness already destructive of normal life, since it prevents us from planning or hoping by depriving us of a future. And this inner refusal of the bomb is also a legacy of our past; it is a denial of the given, of the power of circumstances to shape us in their mold. Unfortunately, the whole asceticism of our national character, our habit of living in but not through an environment, our alienation from objects, prepare us to endure the bomb but not to confront it.

Passivity and not aggressiveness is the dominant trait of the American character. The movies, the radio, the super-highway have softened us up for the atom bomb; we have lived with them without pleasure, feeling them as a coercion on our natures, a coercion seemingly from nowhere and expressing nobody's will. The new coercion finds us without the habit of protest; we are dissident but apart.

The very "negativeness," then, of American intellectuals is not a mark of their separation from our society, but a true expression of its separation from itself. We too are dissident but inactive. Intransigent on paper, in "real life" we conform; yet we do not feel ourselves to be dishonest, for to us the real life is rustling paper and the mental life is flesh. And even in our mental life we are critical and rather unproductive; we leave it to the "others," the best-sellers, to create.

The fluctuating character of American life must, in part, have been responsible for this dissociated condition. Many an immigrant arrived in this country with the most materialistic expectations, hoping, not to escape from a world in which a man was the sum of his circumstances, but to become a new sum of circumstances himself. But this hope was self-defeating; the very ease with which new circumstances were acquired left insufficient time for a man to live into them: all along a great avenue in Minneapolis the huge stone chateaux used to be dark at night, save for a single light in each kitchen, where the family still sat, Swedish-style, about the stove. The pressure of democratic thought, moreover, forced a rising man often, unexpectedly, to recognize that he was *not* his position: a speeding ticket from a village constable could lay him low. Like the agitated United Nations delegates who got summonses on the Merritt Parkway, he might find the shock traumatic: a belief had been destroyed. The effect of these combined difficulties turned the new American into a nomad, who camped out in his circumstances, as it were, and was never assimilated to them. And, for the native American, the great waves of internal migration had the same result. The homelessness of the American, migrant in geography and on the map of finance, is the whole subject of the American realists of our period. European readers see in these writers only violence and brutality. They miss not only the pathos but the nomadic virtues associated with it, generosity, hospitality, equity, directness, politeness, simplicity of relations—traits which, together with a certain gentle timidity (as of very *unpracticed* nomads), comprise the American character. Unobserved also is a peculiar nakedness, a look of being shorn of everything, that is very curiously American, corresponding to the spare wooden desolation of a frontier town and the bright thinness of the American light. The American character looks always as if it had just had a rather bad haircut, which gives it, in our eyes at any rate, a greater humanity than the European, which even among its beggars has an all too professional air.

The openness of the American situation creates the pity and the terror; status is not protection; life for the European is a career; for the American, it is a hazard. Slaves and women, said Aristotle, are not fit subjects for tragedy, but kings, rather, and noble men, men, that is, not defined by circumstance but outside it and seemingly impervious. In America we have, subjectively speaking, no slaves and no women; the efforts of *PM* and the Stalinized playwrights to introduce, like the first step to servitude, a national psychology of the "little man" have been, so far, unrewarding. The little man is one who is embedded in status; things can be done for and to him generically by a central directive; his happiness flows from statistics. This conception mistakes the national passivity for abjection. Americans will not eat this humble pie; we are still nature's noblemen. Yet no tragedy results, though the protagonist is everywhere; dissociation takes the place of conflict, and the drama is mute.

This humanity, this plain and heroic accessibility, was what we would have liked to point out to the visiting Existentialist as our national glory. Modesty perhaps forbade and a lack of concrete examples—how could we point to ourselves? Had we done so she would not have been interested. To a European, the humanity of an intellectual is of no particular moment; it is the barber pole that announces his profession and the hair oil dispensed inside. Europeans, moreover, have no curiosity about American intellectuals; we are insufficiently representative of the brute. Yet this anticipated and felt disparagement was not the whole cause of our reticence. We were silent for another reason: we were waiting to be discovered. Columbus, however, passed on, and this, very likely, was the true source of our humiliation. But this experience also was peculiarly American. We all expect to be found in the murk of otherness; it looks to us very easy since we know we are there. Time after time, the explorers have failed to see us. We have been patient, for the happy ending is our national belief. Now, however, that the future has been shut off from us, it is necessary for us to declare ourselves, at least for the record.

What it amounts to, in verity, is that we are the poor. This humanity we would claim for ourselves is the legacy, not only of the Enlightenment, but of the thousands and thousands of European peasants and poor townspeople who came here bringing their humanity and their sufferings with them. It is the absence of a stable upper class that is responsible for much of the vulgarity of the American scene. Should we blush before the visitor for this deficiency? The ugliness of American decoration, American entertainment, American literature—is not this the visible expression of the impoverishment of the European masses, a manifestation of all the backwardness, deprivation, and want that arrived here in boatloads from Europe? The immense popularity of American movies abroad demonstrates that Europe is the unfinished negative of which America is the proof. The European traveler, viewing with distaste a movie palace or a Motorola, is only looking into the terrible concavity of his continent of hunger inverted startlingly into the convex. Our civilization, deformed as it is outwardly, is still an accomplishment; all this had to come to light.

America is indeed a revelation, though not quite the one that was planned. Given a clean slate, man, it was hoped, would write the future. Instead, he has written his past. This past, inscribed on billboards, ball parks, dance halls, is not seemly, yet its objectification is a kind of disburdenment. The past is at length outside. It does not disturb us as it does Europeans, for our relation with it is both more distant and more familiar. We cannot hate it, for to hate it would be to hate poverty, our eager ancestors, and ourselves.

If there were time, American civilization could be seen as a beginning, even a favorable one, for we have only to look around us to see what a lot of sensibility a little ease will accrue. The children surpass the fathers and Louis B. Mayer cannot be preserved intact in his descendants. . . . Unfortunately, as things seem now, posterity is not around the comer.

E. B. WHITE

*E. B. White (1899–1985), celebrated as the author of classic children's books (*Charlotte's Web, Stuart Little*), and as cowriter, with William Strunk Jr., of* The Elements of Style, *made his greatest mark as one of the half-dozen premier American essayists. His regularly appearing essays for* The New Yorker *and* Harper's Magazine *combined amusing, often self-deprecating peeks into his daily life with liberal reflections on the larger social and political issues of the times. While other personal essayists paraded their eccentricities, it was White's achievement to present himself as an ordinary American, confronting the challenges of life and death with bafflement if goodwill, before arriving at a wistful, kindly common sense. A masterly prose stylist, he did much to perfect the conversational personal essay in the American vernacular, deceptively casual but so artfully composed.*

Death of a Pig

(1947)

I spent several days and nights in mid-September with an ailing pig and I feel driven to account for this stretch of time, more particularly since the pig died at last, and I lived, and things might easily have gone the other way round and none left to do the accounting. Even now, so close to the event, I cannot recall the hours sharply and am not ready to say whether death came on the third night or the fourth night. This uncertainty afflicts me with a sense of personal deterioration; if I were in decent health I would know how many nights I had sat up with a pig.

The scheme of buying a spring pig in blossom time, feeding it through summer and fall, and butchering it when the solid cold weather arrives, is a familiar scheme to me and follows an antique pattern. It is a tragedy enacted on most farms with perfect fidelity to the original script. The murder, being premeditated, is in the first degree but is quick and skillful, and the smoked bacon and ham provide a ceremonial ending whose fitness is seldom questioned.

Once in a while something slips—one of the actors goes up in his lines and the whole performance stumbles and halts. My pig simply failed to show up for a meal. The alarm spread rapidly. The classic outline of the tragedy was lost. I found myself cast suddenly in the role of pig's friend and physician—a farcical character with an enema bag for a prop. I had a presentiment, the very first afternoon, that the play would never regain its balance and that my sympathies were now wholly with the pig. This was slapstick—the sort of dramatic treatment which instantly appealed to my old dachshund, Fred, who joined the vigil, held the bag, and, when all was over, presided at the interment. When we slid the body into the grave, we both were shaken to the core. The loss we felt was not the loss of ham but the loss of pig. He had evidently become precious to me, not that he represented a distant nourishment in a hungry time, but that he had suffered in a suffering world. But I'm running ahead of my story and shall have to go back.

My pigpen is at the bottom of an old orchard below the house. The pigs I have raised have lived in a faded building which once was an icehouse. There is a pleasant yard to move about in, shaded by an apple tree which overhangs the low rail fence. A pig couldn't ask for anything better—or none has, at any rate. The sawdust in the icehouse makes a comfortable bottom in which to root, and a warm bed. This sawdust, however, came under suspicion when the pig took sick. One of my neighbors said he thought the pig would have done better on new ground—the same principle that applies in planting potatoes. He said there might be something unhealthy about that sawdust, that he never thought well of sawdust.

It was about four o'clock in the afternoon when I first noticed that there was something wrong with the pig. He failed to appear at the trough for his supper, and when a pig (or a child) refuses supper a chill wave of fear runs through any household, or ice-household. After examining my pig, who was stretched out in the sawdust inside the building, I went to the phone and cranked it four times. Mr. Dameron answered. "What's good for a sick pig?" I asked. (There is never any identification needed on a country phone; the person on the other end knows who is talking by the sound of the voice and by the character of the question.)

"I don't know, I never had a sick pig," said Mr. Dameron, "but I can find out quick enough. You hang up and I'll call Henry."

Mr. Dameron was back on the line again in five minutes. "Henry says roll him over on his back and give him two ounces of castor oil or sweet oil, and if that doesn't do the trick give him an injection of soapy water. He says he's almost sure the pig's plugged up, and even if he's wrong, it can't do any harm."

I thanked Mr. Dameron. I didn't go right down to the pig, though. I sank into a chair and sat still for a few minutes to think about my troubles, and then I got up and went to the barn, catching up on some odds and ends that needed tending to. Unconsciously I held off, for an hour, the deed by which I would officially recognize the collapse of the performance of raising a pig; I wanted no interruption in the regularity of feeding, the steadiness of growth, the even succession of days. I wanted no interruption, wanted no oil, no deviation. I just wanted to keep on raising a pig, full meal after full meal, spring into summer into fall. I didn't even know whether there were two ounces of castor oil on the place.

Shortly after five o'clock I remembered that we had been invited out to dinner that night and realized that if I were to dose a pig there was no time to lose. The dinner date seemed a familiar conflict: I move in a desultory society and often a week or two will roll by without my going to anybody's house to dinner or anyone's coming to mine, but when an occasion does arise, and I am summoned, something usually turns up (an hour or two in advance) to make all human intercourse seem vastly inappropriate. I have come to believe that there is in hostesses a special power of divination, and that they deliberately arrange dinners to coincide with pig failure or some other sort of failure. At any rate, it was after five o'clock and I knew I could put off no longer the evil hour.

When my son and I arrived at the pigyard, armed with a small bottle of castor oil and a length of clothesline, the pig had emerged from his house and was standing in the middle of his yard, listlessly. He gave us a slim greeting. I could see that he felt uncomfortable and uncertain. I had brought the clothesline thinking I'd have to tie him (the pig weighed more than a hundred pounds) but we never used it. My son reached down, grabbed both front legs, upset him quickly, and when he opened his mouth to scream I turned the oil into his throat—a pink, corrugated area I had never seen before. I had just time to read the label while the neck of the bottle was in his mouth. It said Puretest. The screams, slightly muffled by oil, were pitched in the hysterically high range of pig-sound, as though torture were being carried out, but they didn't last long: it was all over rather suddenly, and, his legs released, the pig righted himself.

In the upset position the corners of his mouth had been turned down, giving him a frowning expression. Back on his feet again, he regained the set smile that a pig wears even in sickness. He stood his ground, sucking slightly at the residue of oil; a few drops leaked out of his lips while his wicked eyes, shaded by their coy little lashes, turned on me in disgust and hatred. I scratched him gently with oily fingers and he remained quiet, as though trying to recall the satisfaction of being scratched when in health, and seeming to rehearse in his mind the indignity to which he had just been subjected. I noticed, as I stood there, four or five small dark spots on his back near the tail end, reddish brown in color, each about the size of a housefly. I could not make out what they were. They did not look troublesome but at the same time they did not look like mere surface bruises or chafe marks. Rather they seemed blemishes of internal origin. His stiff white bristles almost completely hid them and I had to part the bristles with my fingers to get a good look.

Several hours later, a few minutes before midnight, having dined well and at someone else's expense, I returned to the pig-house with a flashlight. The patient was asleep. Kneeling, I felt his ears (as you might put your hand on the forehead of a child) and they seemed cool, and then with the light made a careful examination of the yard and the house for sign that the oil had worked. I found none and went to bed. We had been having an unseasonable spell of weather—hot, close days, with the fog shutting in every night, scaling for a few hours in midday, then creeping back again at dark, drifting in first over the trees on the point, then suddenly blowing across the fields, blotting out the world and taking possession of houses, men, and animals. Everyone kept hoping for a break, but the break failed to come. Next day was another hot one. I visited the pig before breakfast and tried to tempt him with a little milk in his trough. He just stared at it, while I made a sucking sound through my teeth to remind him of past pleasures of the feast. With very small, timid pigs, weanlings, this ruse is often quite successful and will encourage them to eat; but with a large, sick pig the ruse is senseless and the sound I made must have made him feel, if anything, more miserable. He not only did not crave food, he felt a positive revulsion to it. I found a place under the apple tree where he had vomited in the night. At this point, although a depression had settled over me, I didn't suppose that I was going to lose my pig. From the lustiness of a healthy pig a man derives a feeling of personal lustiness; the stuff that goes into the trough and is received with such enthusiasm is an earnest of some later feast of his own, and when this suddenly comes to an end and the food lies stale and untouched, souring in the sun, the pig's imbalance becomes the man's, vicariously, and life seems insecure, displaced, transitory.

As my own spirits declined, along with the pig's, the spirits of my vile old dachshund rose. The frequency of our trips down the footpath through the orchard to the pigyard delighted him, although he suffers greatly from arthritis, moves with difficulty, and would be bedridden if he could find anyone willing to serve him meals on a tray.

He never missed a chance to visit the pig with me, and he made many professional calls on his own. You could see him down there at all hours, his white face parting the grass along the fence as he wobbled and stumbled about, his stethoscope dangling—a happy quack, writing his villainous prescriptions and grinning his corrosive grin. When the enema bag appeared, and the bucket of warm suds, his happiness was complete, and he managed to squeeze his enormous body between the two lowest rails of the yard and then assumed full charge of the irrigation. Once, when I lowered the bag to check the flow, he reached in and hurriedly drank a few mouthfuls of the suds to test their potency. I have noticed that Fred will feverishly consume any substance that is associated with trouble—the bitter flavor is to his liking. When the bag was above reach, he concentrated on the pig and was everywhere at once, a tower of strength and inconvenience. The pig, curiously enough, stood rather quietly through this colonic carnival, and the enema, though ineffective, was not as difficult as I had anticipated.

I discovered, though, that once having given a pig an enema there is no turning back, no chance of resuming one of life's more stereotyped roles. The pig's lot and mine were inextricably bound now, as though the rubber tube were the silver cord. From then until the time of his death I held the pig steadily in the bowl of my mind; the task of trying to deliver him from his misery became a strong obsession. His suffering soon became the embodiment of all earthly wretchedness. Along toward the end of the afternoon, defeated in physicking, I phoned the veterinary twenty miles away and placed the case formally in his hands. He was full of questions, and when I casually mentioned the dark spots on the pig's back, his voice changed its tone.

"I don't want to scare you," he said, "but when there are spots, erysipelas has to be considered."

Together we considered erysipelas, with frequent interruptions from the telephone operator, who wasn't sure the connection had been established. "If a pig has erysipolas can he give it to a person?" I asked.

"Yes, he can," replied the vet.

"Have they answered?" asked the operator.

"Yes, they have," I said. Then I addressed the vet again. "You better come over here and examine this pig right away."

"I can't come myself," said the vet, "but McFarland can come this evening if that's all right. Mac knows more about pigs than I do anyway. You needn't worry too much about the spots. To indicate erysipelas they would have to be deep hemorrhagic infarcts."

"Deep hemorrhagic what?" I asked.

"Infarcts," said the vet.

"Have they answered?" asked the operator.

"Well," I said, "I don't know what you'd call these spots, except they're about the size of a housefly. If the pig has erysipelas I guess I have it, too, by this time, because we've been very close lately."

"McFarland will be over," said the vet.

I hung up. My throat felt dry and I went to the cupboard and got a bottle of whiskey. Deep hemorrhagic infarcts—the phrase began fastening its hooks in my head. I had assumed that there could be nothing much wrong with a pig during the months it was being groomed for murder; my confidence in the essential health and endurance of pigs had been strong and deep, particularly in the health of pigs that belonged to me and that were part of my proud scheme. The awakening had been violent and I minded it all the more because I knew that what could be true of my pig could be true also of the rest of my tidy world. I tried to put this distasteful idea from me, but it kept recurring. I took a short drink of the whiskey and then, although I wanted to go down to the yard and look for fresh signs, I was scared to. I was certain I had erysipelas.

It was long after dark and the supper dishes had been put away when a car drove in and McFarland got out. He had a girl with him. I could just make her out in the darkness—she seemed young and pretty. "This is Miss Owen," he said. "We've been having a picnic supper on the shore, that's why I'm late."

McFarland stood in the driveway and stripped off his jacket, then his shirt. His stocky arms and capable hands showed up in my flashlight's gleam as I helped him find his coverall and get zipped up. The rear seat of his car contained an astonishing amount of paraphernalia, which he soon overhauled, selecting a chain, a syringe, a bottle of oil, a rubber tube, and some other things I couldn't identify. Miss Owen said she'd go along with us and see the pig. I led the way down the warm slope of the orchard, my light picking out the path for them, and we all three climbed the fence, entered the pighouse, and squatted by the pig while McFarland took a rectal reading. My flashlight picked up the glitter of an engagement ring on the girl's hand.

"No elevation," said McFarland, twisting the thermometer in the light. "You needn't worry about erysipelas." He ran his hand slowly over the pig's stomach and at one point the pig cried out in pain.

"Poor piggledy-wiggledy!" said Miss Owen.

The treatment I had been giving the pig for two days was then repeated, somewhat more expertly, by the doctor, Miss Owen and I handing him things as he needed them—holding the chain that he had looped around the pig's upper jaw, holding the syringe, holding the bottle stopper, the end of the tube, all of us working in darkness and in comfort, working with the instinctive teamwork induced by emergency conditions, the pig unprotesting, the house shadowy, protecting, intimate. I went to bed tired but with a feeling of relief that I had turned over part of the responsibility of the case to a licensed doctor. I was beginning to think, though, that the pig was not going to live.

He died twenty-four hours later, or it might have been forty-eight—there is a blur in time here, and I may have lost or picked up a day in the telling and the pig one in the dying. At intervals during the last day I took cool fresh water down to him and at such times as he found the strength to get to his feet he would stand with head in the pail and snuffle his snout around. He drank a few sips but no more; yet it seemed to comfort him to dip his nose in water and bobble it about, sucking in and blowing out through his teeth. Much of the time, now, he lay indoors half buried in sawdust. Once, near the last, while I was attending him I saw him try to make a bed for himself but he lacked the strength, and when he set his snout into the dust he was unable to plow even the little furrow he needed to lie down in.

He came out of the house to die. When I went down, before going to bed, he lay stretched in the yard a few feet from the door. I knelt, saw that he was dead, and left him there: his face had a mild look, expressive neither of deep peace nor of deep suffering, although I think he had suffered a good deal. I went back up to the house and to bed, and cried internally—deep hemorrhagic intears. I didn't wake till nearly eight the next morning, and when I looked out the open window the grave was already being dug, down beyond the dump under a wild apple. I could hear the spade strike against the small rocks that blocked the way. Never send to know for whom the grave is dug, I said to myself, it's dug for thee. Fred, I well knew, was supervising the work of digging, so I ate breakfast slowly.

It was a Saturday morning. The thicket in which I found the gravediggers at work was dark and warm, the sky overcast. Here, among alders and young hackmatacks, at the foot of the apple tree, Lennie had dug a beautiful hole, five feet long, three feet wide, three feet deep. He was standing in it, removing the last spadefuls of earth while Fred patrolled the brink in simple but impressive circles, disturbing the loose earth of the mound so that it trickled back in. There had been no rain in weeks and the soil, even three feet down, was dry and powdery. As I stood and stared, an enormous earthworm which had been partially exposed by the spade at the bottom dug itself deeper and made a slow withdrawal, seeking even remoter moistures at even lonelier depths. And just as Lennie stepped out and rested his spade against the tree and lit a cigarette, a small green apple separated itself from a branch overhead and fell into the hole. Everything about this last scene seemed overwritten—the dismal sky, the shabby woods, the imminence of rain, the worm (legendary bed-fellow of the dead), the apple (conventional garnish of a pig).

But even so, there was a directness and dispatch about animal burial, I thought, that made it a more decent affair than human burial: there was no stopover in the undertaker's foul parlor, no wreath nor spray; and when we hitched a line to the pig's hind legs and dragged him swiftly from his yard, throwing our weight into the harness and leaving a wake of crushed grass and smoothed rubble over the dump, ours was a business-like procession, with Fred, the dishonorable pallbearer, staggering along in the rear, his perverse bereavement showing in every seam in his face; and the post mortem performed handily and swiftly right at the edge of the grave, so that the inwards which had caused the pig's death preceded him into the ground and he lay at last resting squarely on the cause of his own undoing.

I threw in the first shovelful, and then we worked rapidly and without talk, until the job was complete. I picked up the rope, made it fast to Fred's collar (he is a notorious ghoul), and we all three filed back up the path to the house, Fred bringing up the rear and holding back every inch of the way, feigning unusual stiffness. I noticed that although he weighed far less than the pig, he was harder to drag, being possessed of the vital spark.

The news of the death of my pig traveled fast and far, and I received many expressions of sympathy from friends and neighbors, for no one took the event lightly and the premature expiration of a pig is, I soon discovered, a departure which the community marks solemnly on its cal-endar, a sorrow in which it feels fully involved. I have written this account in penitence and in grief, as a man who failed to raise his pig, and to explain my deviation from the classic course of so many raised pigs. The grave in the woods is unmarked, but Fred can direct the mourner to it unerringly and with immense good will, and I know he and I shall often revisit it, singly and together, in seasons of reflection and despair, on fla-gless memorial days of our own choosing.

JAMES BALDWIN

James Baldwin (1924–1987) was arguably the greatest American essayist of the second half of the twentieth century. He dissected dilemmas of race and identity in a searing prose style that consisted of an amalgam of early influences: the rhythmic, mellifluous sermons of the African American church, in which he had been a boy minister; the streetwise, sardonic argot of the blues, which he knew well from growing up in Harlem; and the formal, self-reflective diction of Henry James, whom he had read extensively. Fearing that continual exposure to poisonous home-ground racial tension might kill him, he left for France, where he wrote some of his best essays and fiction but also found—as "Equal in Paris" shows— that there was no getting away from unwarranted trouble.

Equal in Paris: An Autobiographical Story

(1955)

On the 19th of December, in 1949, when I had been living in Paris for a little over a year, I was arrested as a receiver of stolen goods and spent eight days in prison. My arrest came about through an American tourist whom I had met twice in New York, who had been given my name and address and told to look me up. I was then living on the top floor of a ludicrously grim hotel on the rue du Bac, one of those enormous dark, cold, and hideous establishments in which Paris abounds that seem to breathe forth, in their airless, humid, stone-cold halls, the weak light, scurrying chambermaids, and creaking stairs, an odor of gentility long long dead. The place was run by an ancient Frenchman dressed in an elegant black suit which was green with age, who cannot properly be described as bewildered or even as being in a state of shock, since he had really stopped breathing around 1910. There he sat at his desk in the weirdly lit, fantastically furnished lobby, day in and day out, greeting each one of his extremely impoverished and *louche* lodgers with a stately inclination of the head that he had no doubt been taught in some impossibly remote time was the proper way for a *propriétaire* to greet his guests. If it had not been for his daughter, an extremely hard-headed *tricoteuse*—the inclination of *her* head was chilling and abrupt, like the downbeat of an axe—the hotel would certainly have gone bankrupt long before. It was said that this old man had not gone farther than the door of his hotel for thirty years, which was not at all difficult to believe. He looked as though the daylight would have killed him.

I did not, of course, spend much of my time in this palace. The moment I began living in French hotels I understood the necessity of French cafés. This made it rather difficult to look me up, for as soon as I was out of bed I hopefully took notebook and fountain pen off to the upstairs room of the Flore, where I consumed rather a lot of coffee and, as evening approached, rather a lot of alcohol, but did not get much writing done. But one night, in one of the cafés of St. Germain des Prés, I was discovered by this New Yorker and only because we found ourselves in Paris we immediately established the illusion that we had been fast friends back in the good old U.S.A. This illusion proved itself too thin to support an evening's drinking, but by that time it was too late. I had committed myself to getting him a room in my hotel the next day, for he was living in one of the nest of hotels near the Gare St. Lazare, where, he said, the *propriétaire* was a thief, his wife a repressed nymphomaniac, the chambermaids "pigs," and the rent a crime. Americans are always talking this way about the French and so it did not occur to me that he meant what he said or that he would take into his own hands the means of avenging himself on the French Republic. It did not occur to me, either, that the means which he *did* take could possibly have brought about such dire results, results which were not less dire for being also comic-opera.

It came as the last of a series of disasters which had perhaps been made inevitable by the fact that I had come to Paris originally with a little over forty dollars in my pockets, nothing in the bank, and no grasp whatever of the French language. It developed, shortly, that I had no grasp of the French character either. I considered the French an ancient, intelligent, and cultured race, which indeed they are. I did not know, however, that ancient glories imply, at least in the middle of the present century, present fatigue and, quite probably, paranoia; that there is a limit to the role of the intelligence in human affairs; and that no people come into possession of a culture without having paid a heavy price for it. This price they cannot, of course, assess, but it is revealed in their personalities and in their institutions. The very word "institutions," from my side of the ocean, where, it seemed to me, we suffered so cruelly from the lack of them, had a pleasant ring, as of safety and order and common sense; one had to come into contact with these institutions in order to understand that they were also outmoded, exasperating, completely impersonal, and very often cruel. Similarly, the personality which had seemed from a distance to be so large and free had to be dealt with before one could see that, if it was large, it was also inflexible and, for the foreigner, full of strange, high, dusty rooms which could not be inhabited. One had, in short, to come into contact with an alien culture in order to understand that a culture was not a community basket-weaving project, nor yet an act of God; was something neither desirable nor undesirable in itself, being inevitable, being nothing more or less than the recorded and visible effects on a body of people of the vicissitudes with which they had been forced to deal. And their great men are revealed as simply another of these vicissitudes, even if, quite against their will, the brief battle of their great men with them has left them richer.

When my American friend left his hotel to move to mine, he took with him, out of pique, a bedsheet belonging to the hotel and put it in his suitcase. When he arrived at my hotel I borrowed the sheet, since my own were filthy and the chambermaid showed no sign of bringing me any clean ones, and put it on my bed. The sheets belonging to *my* hotel I put out in the hall, congratulating myself on having thus forced on the attention of the Grand Hôtel du Bac the unpleasant state of its linen. Thereafter, since, as it turned out, we kept very different hours—I got up at noon, when, as I gathered by meeting him on the stairs one day, he was only just getting in—my new-found friend and I saw very little of each other.

On the evening of the 19th I was sitting thinking melancholy thoughts about Christmas and staring at the walls of my room. I imagine that I had sold something or that someone had sent me a Christmas present, for I remember that I had a little money. In those days in Paris, though I floated, so to speak, on a sea of acquaintances, I knew almost no one. Many people were eliminated from my orbit by virtue of the fact that they had more money than I did, which placed me, in my own eyes, in the humiliating role of a free-loader; and other people were eliminated by virtue of the fact that they enjoyed their poverty, shrilly insisting that this wretched round of hotel rooms, bad food, humiliating concierges, and unpaid bills was the Great Adventure. It couldn't, however, for me, end soon enough, this Great Adventure; there was a real question in my mind as to which would end soonest, the Great Adventure or me. This meant, however, that there were many evenings when I sat in my room, knowing that I couldn't work there, and not knowing what to do, or whom to see. On this particular evening I went down and knocked on the American's door.

There were two Frenchmen standing in the room, who immediately introduced themselves to me as policemen; which did not worry me. I had got used to policemen in Paris bobbing up at the most improbable times and places, asking to see one's *carte d'identité*. These policemen, however, showed very little interest in my papers. They were looking for something else. I could not imagine what this would be and, since I knew I certainly didn't have it, I scarcely followed the conversation they were having with my friend. I gathered that they were looking for some kind of gangster and since I wasn't a gangster and knew that gangsterism was not, insofar as he had one, my friend's style, I was sure that the two policemen would presently bow and say *Merci, messieurs,* and leave. For by this time, I remember very clearly, I was dying to have a drink and go to dinner.

I did not have a drink or go to dinner for many days after this, and when I did my outraged stomach promptly heaved everything up again. For now one of the policemen began to exhibit the most vivid interest in me and asked, very politely, if he might see my room. To which we mounted, making, I remember, the most civilized small talk on the way and even continuing it for some moments after we were in the room in which there was certainly nothing to be seen but the familiar poverty and disorder of that precarious group of people of whatever age, race, country, calling, or intention which Paris recognizes as *les étudiants* and sometimes, more ironically and precisely, as *les nonconformistes*. Then he moved to my bed, and in a terrible flash, not quite an instant before he lifted the bedspread, I understood what he was looking for. We looked at the sheet, on which I read, for the first time, lettered in the most brilliant scarlet I have ever seen, the name of the hotel from which it had been stolen. It was the first time the word *stolen* entered my mind. I had certainly seen the hotel monogram the day I put the sheet on the bed. It had simply meant nothing to me. In New York I had seen hotel monograms on everything from silver to soap and towels. Taking things from New York hotels was practically a custom, though, I suddenly realized, I had never known anyone to take a *sheet*. Sadly, and without a word to me, the inspector took the sheet from the bed, folded it under his arm, and we started back downstairs. I understood that I was under arrest.

And so we passed through the lobby, four of us, two of us very clearly criminal, under the eyes of the old man and his daughter, neither of whom said a word, into the streets where a light rain was falling. And I asked, in French, "But is this very serious?"

For I was thinking, it is, after all, only a sheet, not even new.

"No," said one of them. "It's not serious."

"It's nothing at all," said the other.

I took this to mean that we would receive a reprimand at the police station and be allowed to go to dinner. Later on I concluded that they were not being hypocritical or even trying to comfort us. They meant exactly what they said. It was only that they spoke another language.

In Paris everything is very slow. Also, when dealing with the bureaucracy, the man you are talking to is never the man you have to see. The man you have to see has just gone off to Belgium, or is busy with his family, or has just discovered that he is a cuckold; he will be in next Tuesday at three o'clock, or sometime in the course of the afternoon, or possibly tomorrow, or, possibly, in the next five minutes. But if he is coming in the next five minutes he will be far too busy to be able to see you today. So that I suppose I was not really astonished to learn at the commissariat that nothing could possibly be done about us before The Man arrived in the morning. But no, we could not go off and have dinner and come back in the morning. Of course he knew that we *would* come back—that was not the question. Indeed, there was no question: we would simply have to stay there for the night. We were placed in a cell which rather resembled a chicken coop. It was now about seven in the evening and I relinquished the thought of dinner and began to think of lunch.

I discouraged the chatter of my New York friend and this left me alone with my thoughts. I was beginning to be frightened and I bent all my energies, therefore, to keeping my panic under control. I began to realize that I was in a country I knew nothing about, in the hands of a people I did not understand at all. In a similar situation in New York I would have had some idea of what to do because I would have had some idea of what to expect. I am not speaking now of legality which, like most of the poor, I had never for an instant trusted, but of the temperament of the people with whom I had to deal. I had become very accomplished in New York at guessing and, therefore, to a limited extent manipulating to my advantage the reactions of the white world. But this was not New York. None of my old weapons could serve me here. I did not know what they saw when they looked at me. I knew very well what Americans saw when they looked at me and this allowed me to play endless and sinister variations on the role which they had assigned me; since I knew that it was, for them, of the utmost importance that they never be confronted with what, in their own personalities, made this role so necessary and gratifying to them, I knew that they could never call my hand or, indeed, afford to know what

I was doing; so that I moved into every crucial situation with the deadly and rather desperate advantages of bitterly accumulated perception, of pride and contempt. This is an awful sword and shield to carry through the world, and the discovery that, in the game I was playing, I did myself a violence of which the world, at its most ferocious, would scarcely have been capable, was what had driven me out of New York. It was a strange feeling, in this situation, after a year in Paris, to discover that my weapons would never again serve me as they had.

It was quite clear to me that the Frenchmen in whose hands I found myself were no better or worse than their American counterparts. Certainly their uniforms frightened me quite as much, and their impersonality, and the threat, always very keenly felt by the poor, of violence, was as present in that commissariat as it had ever been for me in any police station. And I had seen, for example, what Paris policemen could do to Arab peanut vendors. The only difference here was that I did not understand these people, did not know what techniques their cruelty took, did not know enough about their personalities to see danger coming, to ward it off, did not know on what ground to meet it. That evening in the commissariat I was not a despised black man. They would simply have laughed at me if I had behaved like one. For them, I was an American. And here it was they who had the advantage, for that word, *Américain,* gave them some idea, far from inaccurate, of what to expect from me. In order to corroborate none of their ironical expectations I said nothing and did nothing—which was not the way any Frenchman, white or black, would have reacted. The question thrusting up from the bottom of my mind was not *what* I was, but *who.* And this question, since a *what* can get by with skill but a *who* demands resources, was my first real intimation of what humility must mean.

In the morning it was still raining. Between nine and ten o'clock a black Citroën took us off to the Ile de la Cité, to the great, gray Préfecture. I realize now that the questions I put to the various policemen who escorted us were always answered in such a way as to corroborate what I wished to hear. This was not out of politeness, but simply out of indifference—or, possibly, an ironical pity—since each of the policemen knew very well that nothing would speed or halt the machine in which I had become entangled. They knew I did not know this and there was certainly no point in their telling me. In one way or another I would certainly come out at the other side—for they also knew that being found with a stolen bedsheet in one's possession was not a crime punishable by the guillotine. (They had the advantage over me there, too, for there were certainly moments later on when I was not so sure.) If I did *not* come out at the other side—well, that was just too bad. So, to my question, put while we were in the Citroën—"Will it be over today?"—I received a *"Oui, bien sûr."* He was not lying. As it turned out, the *procès-verbal* was over that day. Trying to be realistic, I dismissed, in the Citroën, all thoughts of lunch and pushed my mind ahead to dinner.

At the Préfecture we were first placed in a tiny cell, in which it was almost impossible either to sit or to lie down. After a couple of hours of this we were taken down to an office, where, for the first time, I encountered the owner of the bedsheet and where the *procès-verbal* took place. This was simply an interrogation, quite chillingly clipped and efficient (so that there was, shortly, no doubt in one's own mind that one *should* be treated as a criminal), which was recorded by a secretary. When it was over, this report was given to us to sign. One had, of course, no choice but to sign it, even though my mastery of written French was very far from certain. We were being held, according to the law in France, incommunicado, and all my angry demands to be allowed to speak to my embassy or to see a lawyer met with a stony *"Oui, oui. Plus tard."* The *procès-verbal* over we were taken back to the cell, before which, shortly, passed the owner of the bedsheet. He said he hoped we had slept well, gave a vindictive wink, and disappeared.

By this time there was only one thing clear: that we had no way of controlling the sequence of events and could not possibly guess what this sequence would be. It seemed to me, since what I regarded as the high point—the *procès-verbal*—had been passed and since the hotelkeeper was once again in possession of his sheet, that we might reasonably expect to be released from police custody in a matter of hours. We had been detained now for what would soon be twenty-four hours, during which time I had learned only that the official charge against me was *receleur*. My mental shifting, between lunch and dinner, to say nothing of the physical lack of either of these delights, was beginning to make me dizzy. The steady chatter of my friend from New York, who was determined to keep my spirits up, made me feel murderous; I was praying that some power would release us from this freezing pile of stone before the impulse became the act. And I was beginning to wonder what was happening in that beautiful city, Paris, which lived outside these walls. I wondered how long it would take before anyone casually asked, "But where's Jimmy? He hasn't been around"—and realized, knowing the people I knew, that it would take several days.

Quite late in the afternoon we were taken from our cells; handcuffed, each to a separate officer; led through a maze of steps and corridors to the top of the building; finger-printed; photographed. As in movies I had seen, I was placed against a wall, facing an old-fashioned camera, behind which stood one of the most completely cruel and indifferent faces I had ever seen, while someone next to me and, therefore, just outside my line of vision, read off in a voice from which all human feeling, even feeling of the most base description, had long since fled, what must be called my public characteristics—which, at that time and in that place, seemed anything but that. He might have been roaring to the hostile world secrets which I could barely, in the privacy of midnight, utter to myself. But he was only reading off my height, my features, my approximate weight, my color—that color which, in the United States, had often, odd as it may sound, been my salvation—the color of my hair, my age, my nationality. A light then flashed, the photographer and I staring at each other as though there was murder in our hearts, and then it was over. Handcuffed again, I was led downstairs to the bottom of the building, into a great enclosed shed in which had been gathered the very scrapings off the Paris streets. Old, old men, so ruined and old that life in them seemed really to prove the miracle of the quickening power of the Holy Ghost—for clearly their life was no longer their affair, it was no longer even their burden, they were simply the clay which had once been touched. And men not so old, with faces the color of lead and the consistency of oatmeal, eyes that made me think of stale *café-au-lait* spiked with arsenic, bodies which could take in food and water—any food and water—and pass it out, but which could not do anything more, except possibly, at midnight, along the riverbank where rats scurried, rape. And young men, harder and crueler than the Paris stones, older by far than I, their chronological senior by some five to seven years. And North Africans, old and young, who seemed the only living people in this place because they yet retained the grace to be bewildered. But they were not bewildered by being in this shed: they were simply bewildered because they were no longer in North Africa. There was a great hole in the center of this shed, which was the common toilet. Near it, though it was impossible to get very far from it, stood an old man with white hair, eating a piece of camembert. It was at this point, probably, that thought, for me, stopped, that physiology, if one may say so, took over. I found myself incapable of saying a word, not because I was afraid I would cry but because I was afraid I would vomit. And I did not think any longer of the city of Paris but my mind flew back to that home from which I had fled. I was sure that I would never see it anymore. And it must have seemed to me that my flight from home was the cruelest trick I had ever played on myself, since it had led me here, down to a lower point than any I could ever in my life have imagined—lower, far, than anything I had seen in that Harlem which I had so hated and so loved, the escape from which had soon become the greatest direction of my life. After we had been here an hour or so a functionary came and opened the door and called out our names. And I was sure that *this* was my release. But I was handcuffed again and led out of the Préfecture into the streets—it was dark now, it was still raining—and before the steps of the Préfecture stood the great police wagon, doors facing me, wide open. The handcuffs were taken off, I entered the wagon, which was peculiarly constructed. It was divided by a narrow aisle, and on each side of the aisle was a series of narrow doors. These doors opened on a narrow cubicle, beyond which was a door which opened onto another narrow cubicle: three or four cubicles, each private, with a locking door. I was placed in one of them; I remember there was a small vent just above my head which let in a little light. The door of my cubicle was locked from the outside. I had no idea where this wagon was taking me and, as it began to move, I began to cry. I suppose I cried all the way to prison, the prison called Fresnes, which is twelve kilometers outside of Paris.

For reasons I have no way at all of understanding, prisoners whose last initial is A, B, or C are always sent to Fresnes; everybody else is sent to a prison called, rather cynically it seemed to me, La Santé. I will, obviously, never be allowed to enter La Santé, but I was told by people who certainly seemed to know that it was infinitely more unbearable than Fresnes. This arouses in me, until today, a positive storm of curiosity concerning what I promptly began to think of as The Other Prison. My colleague in crime, occurring lower in the alphabet, had been sent there and I confess that the minute he was gone I missed him. I missed him because he was not French and because he was the only person in the world who knew that the story I told was true.

For, once locked in, divested of shoelaces, belt, watch, money, papers, nailfile, in a freezing cell in which both the window and the toilet were broken, with six other adventurers, the story I told of *l'affaire du drap de lit* elicited only the wildest amusement or the most suspicious disbelief. Among the people who shared my cell the first three days no one, it is true, had been arrested for anything much more serious—or, at least, not serious in my eyes. I remember that there was a boy who had stolen a knitted sweater from a *monoprix,* who would probably, it was agreed, receive a six-month sentence. There was an older man there who had been arrested for some kind of petty larceny. There were two North Africans, vivid, brutish, and beautiful, who alternated between gaiety and fury, not at the fact of their arrest but at the state of the cell. None poured as much emotional energy into the fact of their arrest as I did; they took it, as I would have liked to take it, as simply another unlucky happening in a very dirty world. For, though I had grown accustomed to thinking of myself as looking upon the world with a hard, penetrating eye, the truth was that they were far more realistic about the world than I, and more nearly right about it. The gap between us, which only a gesture I made could have bridged, grew steadily, during thirty-six hours, wider. I could not make any gesture simply because they frightened me. I was unable to accept my imprisonment as a fact, even as a temporary fact. I could not, even for a moment, accept my present companions as *my* companions. And they, of course, felt this and put it down, with perfect justice, to the fact that I was an American.

There was nothing to do all day long. It appeared that we would one day come to trial but no one knew when. We were awakened at seven-thirty by a rapping on what I believe is called the Judas, that small opening in the door of the cell which allows the guards to survey the prisoners. At this rapping we rose from the floor—we slept on straw pallets and each of us was covered with one thin blanket—and moved to the door of the cell. We peered through the opening into the center of the prison, which was, as I remember, three tiers high, all gray stone and gunmetal steel, precisely that prison I had seen in movies, except that, in the movies, I had not known that it was cold in prison. I had not known that when one's shoelaces and belt have been removed one is, in the strangest way, demoralized. The necessity of shuffling and the necessity of holding up one's trousers with one hand turn one into a rag doll. And the movies fail, of course, to give one any idea of what prison food is like. Along the corridor, at seven-thirty, came three men, each pushing before him a great garbage can, mounted on wheels. In the garbage can of the first was the bread—this was passed to one through the small opening in the door. In the can of the second was the coffee. In the can of the third was what was always called *la soupe,* a pallid paste of potatoes which had certainly been bubbling on the back of the prison stove long before that first, so momentous revolution. Naturally, it was cold by this time and, starving as I was, I could not eat it. I drank the coffee—which was not coffee—because it was hot, and spent the rest of the day, huddled in my blanket, munching on the bread. It was not the French bread one bought in bakeries. In the evening the same procession returned. At ten-thirty the lights went out. I had a recurring dream, each night, a nightmare which always involved my mother's fried chicken. At the moment I was about to eat it came the rapping at the door. Silence is really all I remember of those first three days, silence and the color gray.

I am not sure now whether it was on the third or the fourth day that I was taken to trial for the first time. The days had nothing, obviously, to distinguish them from one another. I remember that I was very much aware that Christmas Day was approaching and I wondered if I was really going to spend Christmas Day in prison. And I remember that the first trial came the day before Christmas Eve.

On the morning of the first trial I was awakened by hearing my name called. I was told, hanging in a kind of void between my mother's fried chicken and the cold prison floor, "*Vous préparez. Vous êtes extrait*"— which simply terrified me, since I did not know what interpretation to put on the word "*extrait,*" and since my cellmates had been amusing themselves with me by telling terrible stories about the inefficiency of French prisons, an inefficiency so extreme that it had often happened that someone who was supposed to be taken out and tried found himself on the wrong line and was guillotined instead. The best way of putting my reaction to this is to say that, though I knew they were teasing me, it was simply not possible for me to totally *dis*believe them. As far as I was concerned, once in the hands of the law in France, anything could happen. I shuffled along with the others who were *extrait* to the center of the prison, trying, rather, to linger in the office, which seemed the only warm spot in the whole world, and found myself again in that dreadful wagon, and was carried again to the Ile de la Cité, this time to the Palais de Justice. The entire day, except for ten minutes, was spent in one of the cells, first waiting to be tried, then waiting to be taken back to prison.

For I was *not* tried that day. By and by I was handcuffed and led through the halls, upstairs to the courtroom where I found my New York friend. We were placed together, both stage-whisperingly certain that this was the end of our ordeal. Nevertheless, while I waited for our case to be called, my eyes searched the courtroom, looking for a face I knew, hoping, anyway, that there was someone there who knew *me,* who would carry to someone outside the news that I was in trouble. But there was no one I knew there and I had had time to realize that there was probably only one man in Paris who could help me, an American patent attorney for whom I had worked as an office boy. He could have helped me because he had a quite solid position and some prestige and would have testified that, while working for him, I had handled large sums of money regularly, which made it rather unlikely that I would stoop to trafficking in bedsheets. However, he was somewhere in Paris, probably at this very moment enjoying a snack and a glass of wine and as far as the possibility of reaching him was concerned, he might as well have been on Mars. I tried to watch the proceedings and to make my mind a blank. But the proceedings were not reassuring. The boy, for example, who had stolen the sweater *did* receive a six-month sentence. It seemed to me that all the sentences meted out that day were excessive; though, again, it seemed that all the people who were sentenced that day had made, or clearly were going to make, crime their career. This seemed to be the opinion of the judge, who scarcely looked at the prisoners or listened to them; it seemed to be the opinion of the prisoners, who scarcely bothered to speak in their own behalf; it seemed to be the opinion of the lawyers, state lawyers for the most part, who were defending them. The great impulse of the courtroom seemed to be to put these people where they could not be seen—and not because they were offended at their crimes, unless, indeed, they were offended that the crimes were so petty, but because they did not wish to know that their society could be counted on to produce, probably in greater and greater numbers, a whole body of people for whom crime was the only possible career. Any society inevitably produces its criminals, but a society at once rigid and unstable can do nothing whatever to alleviate the poverty of its lowest members, cannot present to the hypothetical young man at the crucial moment that so-well-advertised right path. And the fact, perhaps, that the French are the earth's least sentimental people and must also be numbered among the most proud aggravates the plight of their lowest, youngest, and unluckiest members, for it means that the idea of rehabilitation is scarcely real to them. I confess that this attitude on their part raises in me sentiments of exasperation, admiration, and despair, revealing as it does, in both the best and the worst sense, their renowned and spectacular hard-headedness.

Finally our case was called and we rose. We gave our names. At the point that it developed that we were American the proceedings ceased, a hurried consultation took place between the judge and what I took to be several lawyers. Someone called out for an interpreter. The arresting officer had forgotten to mention our nationalities and there was, therefore, no interpreter in the court. Even if our French had been better than it was we would not have been allowed to stand trial without an interpreter. Before I clearly understood what was happening, I was handcuffed again and led out of the courtroom. The trial had been set back for the 27th of December.

I have sometimes wondered if I would ever have got out of prison if it had not been for the older man who had been arrested for the mysterious petty larceny. He was acquitted that day and when he returned to the cell—for he could not be released until morning—he found me sitting numbly on the floor, having just been prevented, by the sight of a man, all blood, being carried back to *his* cell on a stretcher, from seizing the bars and screaming until they let me out. The sight of the man on the stretcher proved, however, that screaming would not do much for me. The petty-larceny man went around asking if he could do anything in the world outside for those he was leaving behind. When he came to me I, at first, responded, "No, nothing"—for I suppose I had by now retreated into the attitude, the earliest I remember, that of my father, which was simply (since I had lost his God) that nothing could help me. And I suppose I will remember with gratitude until I die the fact that the man now insisted: "*Mais, êtes-vous sûr?*" Then it swept over me that he was going *outside* and he instantly became my first contact since the Lord alone knew how long with the outside world. At the same time, I remember, I did not really believe that he would help me. There was no reason why he should. But I gave him the phone number of my attorney friend and my own name.

—

So, in the middle of the next day, Christmas Eve, I shuffled downstairs again, to meet my visitor. He looked extremely well fed and sane and clean. He told me I had nothing to worry about any more. Only not even he could do anything to make the mill of justice grind any faster. He would, however, send me a lawyer of his acquaintance who would defend me on the 27th, and he would himself, along with several other people, appear as a character witness. He gave me a package of Lucky Strikes (which the turnkey took from me on the way upstairs) and said that, though it was doubtful that there would be any celebration in the prison, he would see to it that I got a fine Christmas dinner when I got out. And this, somehow, seemed very funny. I remember being astonished at the discovery that I was actually laughing. I was, too, I imagine, also rather disappointed that my hair had not turned white, that my face was clearly not going to bear any marks of tragedy, disappointed at bottom, no doubt, to realize, facing him in that room, that far worse things had happened to most people and that, indeed, to paraphrase my mother, if this was the worst thing that ever happened to me I could consider myself among the luckiest people ever to be born. He injected—my visitor—into my solitary nightmare common sense, the world, and the hint of blacker things to come.

The next day, Christmas, unable to endure my cell, and feeling that, after all, the day demanded a gesture, I asked to be allowed to go to Mass, hoping to hear some music. But I found myself, for a freezing hour and a half, locked in exactly the same kind of cubicle as in the wagon which had first brought me to prison, peering through a slot placed at the level of the eye at an old Frenchman, hatted, overcoated, muffled, and gloved, preaching in this language which I did not understand, to this row of wooden boxes, the story of Jesus Christ's love for men.

The next day, the 26th, I spent learning a peculiar kind of game, played with matchsticks, with my cellmates. For, since I no longer felt that I would stay in this cell forever, I was beginning to be able to make peace with it for a time. On the 27th I went again to trial and, as had been predicted, the case against us was dismissed. The story of the *drap de lit,* finally told, caused great merriment in the courtroom, whereupon my friend decided that the French were "great." I was chilled by their merriment, even though it was meant to warm me. It could only remind me of the laughter I had often heard at home, laughter which I had sometimes deliberately elicited. This laughter is the laughter of those who consider themselves to be at a safe remove from all the wretched, for whom the pain of the living is not real. I had heard it so often in my native land that I had resolved to find a place where I would never hear it any more. In some deep, black, stony, and liberating way, my life, in my own eyes, began during that first year in Paris, when it was borne in on me that this laughter is universal and never can be stilled.

NORMAN MAILER

Norman Mailer (1923–2007) was a leading novelist of his generation, though many critics have come to regard his nonfiction as his most signifi-cant work: the essays in Advertisements for Myself; *his book-length-essay masterpiece,* The Armies of the Night; *and* The Executioner's Song. *Pos-sessed of energy, observational power, and stylistic virtuosity, he wrote with authority about sports, politics, the space program, Marilyn Mon-roe, killers, and graffiti—but his favorite subject was Norman Mailer. While his public persona could be swaggering, macho, and churlish, he brought to his essays a balance of modesty, self-awareness, and comic candor. In "The Homosexual Villain," written for a gay periodical, he examines his own prejudices in hope of fostering "acceptance, tolerance and sympathy."*

The Homosexual Villain

(1955)

Those readers of *One* who are familiar with my work may be somewhat surprised to find me writing for this magazine. After all, I have been as guilty as any contemporary novelist in attributing unpleasant, ridiculous, or sinister connotations to the homosexual (or more accurately, bisexual) characters in my novels. Part of the effectiveness of General Cummings in *The Naked and the Dead*—at least for those people who thought him well conceived as a character—rested on the homosexuality I was obvi-ously suggesting as the core of much of his motivation. Again, in *Barbary Shore*, the "villain" was a secret police agent named Leroy Hollingsworth whose sadism and slyness were essentially combined with his sexual deviation.

At the time I wrote those novels, I was consciously sincere. I did believe—as so many heterosexuals believe—that there was an intrinsic relation between homosexuality and "evil," and it seemed perfectly natural to me, as well as *symbolically* just, to treat the subject in such a way.

The irony is that I did not know a single homosexual during all those years. I had met homosexuals of course, I had recognized a few as homosexual, I had "suspected" others, I was to realize years later that one or two close friends were homosexual, but I had never known one in the human sense of knowing, which is to look at your friend's feelings through his eyes and not your own. I did not *know* any homosexual because obviously I did not want to. It was enough for me to recognize someone as homosexual, and I would cease to consider him seriously as a person. He might be intelligent or courageous or kind or witty or virtuous or tortured—no matter. I always saw him as at best ludicrous and at worst—the word again—sinister. (I think it is by the way significant that just as many homosexuals feel forced and are forced to throw up protective camouflage, even boasting if necessary of women they have had, not to mention the thousand smaller subtleties, so heterosexuals are often eager to be so deceived for it enables them to continue friendships which otherwise their prejudices and occasionally their fears might force them to terminate.)

Now, of course, I exaggerate to a certain degree. I was never a roaring bigot, I did not go in for homosexual baiting, at least not face-to-face, and I never could stomach the relish with which soldiers would describe how they had stomped some faggot in a bar. I had, in short, the equivalent of a "gentleman's anti-Semitism."

The only thing remarkable about all this is that I was hardly living in a small town. New York, whatever its pleasures and discontents, is not the most uncivilized milieu, and while one would go too far to say that its attitude toward homosexuals bears correspondence to the pain of the liberal or radical at hearing someone utter a word like "nigger" or "kike," there is nonetheless considerable tolerance and considerable propinquity. The hard-and-fast separations of homosexual and heterosexual society are often quite blurred. Over the past seven or eight years I had had more than enough opportunity to learn something about homosexuals if I had wanted to, and obviously I did not.

It is a pity I do not understand the psychological roots of my change of attitude, for something valuable might be learned from it. Unfortunately, I do not. The process has seemed a rational one to me, rational in that the impetus apparently came from reading and not from any important personal experiences. The only hint of my bias mellowing was that my wife and I had gradually become friendly with a homosexual painter who lived next door. He was pleasant, he was thoughtful, he was a good neighbor, and we came to depend on him in various small ways. It was tacitly understood that he was homosexual, but we never talked about it. However, since so much of his personal life was not discussable between us, the friendship was limited. I accepted him the way a small-town banker fifty years ago might have accepted a "good" Jew.

About this time I received a free copy of *One* which was sent out by the editors to a great many writers. I remember looking at the magazine with some interest and some amusement. Parts of it impressed me unfavorably. I thought the quality of writing generally poor (most people I've talked to agree that it has since improved), and I questioned the wisdom of accepting suggestive ads in a purportedly serious magazine. (Indeed, I still feel this way no matter what the problems of revenue might be.) But there was a certain militancy and honesty to the editorial tone, and while I was not sympathetic, I think I can say that for the first time in my life I was not unsympathetic. Most important of all, my curiosity was piqued. A few weeks later I asked my painter friend if I could borrow his copy of Donald Webster Cory's *The Homosexual in America*.

Reading it was an important experience. Mr. Cory strikes me as being a modest man, and I think he would be the first to admit that while his book is very good, closely reasoned, quietly argued, it is hardly a great book. Nonetheless, I can think of few books which cut so radically at my prejudices and altered my ideas so profoundly. I resisted it, I argued its points as I read, I was often annoyed, but what I could not overcome was my growing depression that I had been acting as a bigot in this matter, and "bigot" was one word I did not enjoy applying to myself. With that came the realization I had been closing myself off from understanding a very large part of life. This thought is always disturbing to a writer. A writer has his talent, and for all one knows, he is born with it, but whether his talent develops is to some degree responsive to his use of it. He can grow as a person or he can shrink, and by this I don't intend any facile parallels between moral and artistic growth. The writer can become a bigger hoodlum if need be, but his alertness, his curiosity, his reaction to life must not diminish. The fatal thing is to shrink, to be interested in less, sympathetic to less, desiccating to the point where life itself loses its flavor, and one's passion for human understanding changes to weariness and distaste.

So, as I read Mr. Cory's book, I found myself thinking in effect, *My God, homosexuals are people too*. Undoubtedly, this will seem incredibly naïve to the homosexual readers of *One* who have been all too painfully aware that they are indeed people, but prejudice is wed to naïveté, and even the sloughing of prejudice, particularly when it is abrupt, partakes of the naïve. I have not tried to conceal that note. As I reread this article I find its tone ingenuous, but there is no point in trying to alter it. One does not become sophisticated overnight about a subject one has closed from oneself.

At any rate I began to face up to my homosexual bias. I had been a libertarian socialist for some years, and implicit in all my beliefs had been the idea that society must allow every individual his own road to discovering himself. Libertarian socialism (the first word is as important as the second) implies inevitably that one have respect for the varieties of human experience. Very basic to everything I had thought was that sexual relations, above everything else, demand their liberty, even if such liberty should amount to no more than compulsion or necessity. For, in the reverse, history has certainly offered enough examples of the link between sexual repression and political repression. (A fascinating thesis on this subject is *The Sexual Revolution* by Wilhelm Reich.) I suppose I can say that for the first time I understood homosexual persecution to be a political act and a reactionary act, and I was properly ashamed of myself.

On the positive side, I found over the next few months that a great deal was opening to me—to put it briefly, even crudely, I felt that I understood more about people, more about life. My life-view had been shocked and the lights and shadows were being shifted, which is equal to saying that I was learning a great deal. At a perhaps embarrassingly personal level, I discovered another benefit. There is probably no sensitive heterosexual alive who is not preoccupied at one time or another with his latent homosexuality, and while I had no conscious homosexual desires, I had wondered more than once if really there were not something suspicious in my intense dislike of homosexuals. How pleasant to discover that once one can accept homosexuals as real friends, the tension is gone with the acceptance. I found that I was no longer concerned with latent homosexuality. It seemed vastly less important, and paradoxically enabled me to realize that I am actually quite heterosexual. Close friendships with homosexuals had become possible without sexual desire or even sexual nuance—at least no more sexual nuance than is present in all human relations.

However, I had a peculiar problem at this time. I was on the way to finishing *The Deer Park,* my third novel. There was a minor character in it named Teddy Pope who is a movie star and a homosexual. Through the first and second drafts he had existed as a stereotype, a figure of fun; he was ludicrously affected and therefore ridiculous. One of the reasons I resisted Mr. Cory's book so much is that I was beginning to feel uneasy with the characterization I had drawn. In life there are any number of ridiculous people, but at bottom I was saying that Teddy Pope was ridiculous because he was homosexual. I found myself dissatisfied with the characterization even before I read *The Homosexual in America,* it had already struck me as being compounded too entirely of malice, but I think I would probably have left it that way. After Mr. Cory's book, it had become impossible. I no longer believed in Teddy Pope as I had drawn him.

Yet a novel which is almost finished is very difficult to alter. If it is at all a good book, the proportions, the meanings, and the interrelations of the characters have become integrated, and one does not violate them without injuring one's work. Moreover, I have developed an antipathy to using one's novels as direct expressions of one's latest ideas. I therefore had no desire to change Teddy Pope into a fine virtuous character. That would be as false, and as close to propaganda, as to keep him the way he was. Also, while a minor character, he had an important relation to the story, and it was obvious that he could not be transformed too radically without recasting much of the novel. My decision, with which I am not altogether happy, was to keep Teddy Pope more or less intact, but to try to add dimension to him. Perhaps I have succeeded. He will never be a character many readers admire, but it is possible that they will have feeling for him. At least he is no longer a simple object of ridicule, nor the butt of my malice, and I believe *The Deer Park* is a better book for the change. My hope is that some readers may possibly be stimulated to envisage the gamut of homosexual personality as parallel to the gamut of heterosexual personality even if Teddy Pope is a character from the lower half of the spectrum. However, I think it is more probable that the majority of homosexual readers who may get around to reading *The Deer Park* when it is published will be dissatisfied with him. I can only say that I am hardly satisfied myself. But this time, at least, I have discovered the edges of the rich theme of homosexuality rather than the easy symbolic equation of it to evil. And to that extent I feel richer and more confident as a writer. What I have come to realize is that much of my homosexual prejudice was a servant to my aesthetic needs. In the variety and contradiction of American life, the difficulty of finding a character who can serve as one's protagonist is matched only by the difficulty of finding one's villain, and so long as I was able to preserve my prejudices, my literary villains were at hand. Now, the problem will be more difficult, but I suspect it may be rewarding too, for deep down I was never very happy nor proud of myself at whipping homosexual straw boys.

A last remark. If the homosexual is ever to achieve real social equality and acceptance, he too will have to work the hard row of shedding his own prejudices. Driven into defiance, it is natural, if regrettable, that many homosexuals go to the direction of assuming that there is something intrinsically superior in homosexuality, and carried far enough it is a viewpoint which is as stultifying, as ridiculous, and as antihuman as the heterosexual's prejudice. Finally, heterosexuals are people too, and the hope of acceptance, tolerance, and sympathy must rest on this mutual appreciation.

RACHEL CARSON

Rachel Carson (1907–1964), considered one of the leading figures in the environmental movement, worked as a marine biologist before writing the exquisite essays that became her book The Sea Around Us. *Her poetic prose is infused with the precise nomenclature of living things, filled with active verbs, and tinctured with the colors of sea and sky. For all her scientific familiarity with this natural world, she retained a sense of its wonder and magic. Writing about that liminal edge, "The Marginal World," in different seasons and locales, she took the long evolutionary view, from the very beginning of life, when sea creatures crawled onto the land. In a later book,* Silent Spring, *Carson warned eloquently of the dangers of harmful pesticides polluting the food chain, and her advocacy resulted in legislation passed to ban such substances.*

The Marginal World

(1955)

The edge of the sea is a strange and beautiful place. All through the long history of Earth it has been an area of unrest where waves have broken heavily against the land, where the tides have pressed forward over the continents, receded, and then returned. For no two successive days is the shore line precisely the same. Not only do the tides advance and retreat in their eternal rhythms, but the level of the sea itself is never at rest. It rises or falls as the glaciers melt or grow, as the floor of the deep ocean basins shifts under its increasing load of sediments, or as the earth's crust along the continental margins warps up or down in adjustment to strain and tension. Today a little more land may belong to the sea, tomorrow a little less. Always the edge of the sea remains an elusive and indefinable boundary.

The shore has a dual nature, changing with the swing of the tides, belonging now to the land, now to the sea. On the ebb tide it knows the harsh extremes of the land world, being exposed to heat and cold, to wind, to rain and drying sun. On the flood tide it is a water world, returning briefly to the relative stability of the open sea.

Only the most hardy and adaptable can survive in a region so mutable, yet the area between the tide lines is crowded with plants and animals. In this difficult world of the shore, life displays its enormous toughness and vitality by occupying almost every conceivable niche. Visibly, it carpets the intertidal rocks; or half hidden, it descends into fissures and crevices, or hides under boulders, or lurks in the wet gloom of sea caves. Invisibly, where the casual observer would say there is no life, it lies deep in the sand, in burrows and tubes and passageways. It tunnels into solid rock and bores into peat and clay. It encrusts weeds or drifting spars or the hard, chitinous shell of a lobster. It exists minutely, as the film of bacteria that spreads over a rock surface or a wharf piling; as spheres of protozoa, small as pinpricks, sparkling at the surface of the sea; and as Lilliputian beings swimming through dark pools that lie between the grains of sand.

The shore is an ancient world, for as long as there has been an earth and sea there has been this place of the meeting of land and water. Yet it is a world that keeps alive the sense of continuing creation and of the relentless drive of life. Each time that I enter it, I gain some new awareness of its beauty and its deeper meanings, sensing that intricate fabric of life by which one creature is linked with another, and each with its surroundings.

In my thoughts of the shore, one place stands apart for its revelation of exquisite beauty. It is a pool hidden within a cave that one can visit only rarely and briefly when the lowest of the year's low tides fall below it, and perhaps from that very fact it acquires some of its special beauty. Choosing such a tide, I hoped for a glimpse of the pool. The ebb was to fall early in the morning. I knew that if the wind held from the northwest and no interfering swell ran in from a distant storm the level of the sea should drop below the entrance to the pool. There had been sudden ominous showers in the night, with rain like handfuls of gravel flung on the roof. When I looked out into the early morning the sky was full of a gray dawn light but the sun had not yet risen. Water and air were pallid. Across the bay the moon was a luminous disc in the western sky, suspended above the dim line of distant shore—the full August moon, drawing the tide to the low, low levels of the threshold of the alien sea world. As I watched, a gull flew by, above the spruces. Its breast was rosy with the fight of the unrisen sun. The day was, after all, to be fair.

Later, as I stood above the tide near the entrance to the pool, the promise of that rosy light was sustained. From the base of the steep wall of
rock on which I stood, a moss-covered ledge jutted seaward into deep
water. In the surge at the rim of the ledge the dark fronds of oarweeds
swayed, smooth and gleaming as leather. The projecting ledge was the
path to the small hidden cave and its pool. Occasionally a swell, stronger
than the rest, rolled smoothly over the rim and broke in foam against the
cliff. But the intervals between such swells were long enough to admit me
to the ledge and long enough for a glimpse of that fairy pool, so seldom
and so briefly exposed.

And so I knelt on the wet carpet of sea moss and looked back into the
dark cavern that held the pool in a shallow basin. The floor of the cave
was only a few inches below the roof, and a mirror had been created in
which all that grew on the ceiling was reflected in the still water below.

Under water that was clear as glass the pool was carpeted with green
sponge. Gray patches of sea squirts glistened on the ceiling and colonies
of soft coral were a pale apricot color. In the moment when I looked
into the cave a little elfin starfish hung down, suspended by the merest
thread, perhaps by only a single tube foot. It reached down to touch its
own reflection, so perfectly delineated that there might have been, not one
starfish, but two. The beauty of the reflected images and of the limpid
pool itself was the poignant beauty of things that are ephemeral, existing
only until the sea should return to fill the little cave.

Whenever I go down into this magical zone of the low water of the
spring tides, I look for the most delicately beautiful of all the shore's
inhabitants—flowers that are not plant but animal, blooming on the
threshold of the deeper sea. In that fairy cave I was not disappointed.
Hanging from its roof were the pendent flowers of the hydroid Tubularia,
pale pink, fringed and delicate as the wind flower. Here were creatures so
exquisitely fashioned that they seemed unreal, their beauty too fragile to
exist in a world of crushing force. Yet every detail was functionally useful, every stalk and hydranth and petal-like tentacle fashioned for dealing
with the realities of existence. I knew that they were merely waiting, in
that moment of the tide's ebbing, for the return of the sea. Then in the
rush of water, in the surge of surf and the pressure of the incoming tide,
the delicate flower heads would stir with life. They would sway on their
slender stalks, and their long tentacles would sweep the returning water,
finding in it all that they needed for life.

And so in that enchanted place on the threshold of the sea the realities
that possessed my mind were far from those of the land world I had left
an hour before. In a different way the same sense of remoteness and of a
world apart came to me in a twilight hour on a great beach on the coast
of Georgia. I had come down after sunset and walked far out over sands
that lay wet and gleaming, to the very edge of the retreating sea. Looking

back across that immense flat, crossed by winding, water-filled gullies and here and there holding shallow pools left by the tide, I was filled with awareness that this intertidal area, although abandoned briefly and rhythmically by the sea, is always reclaimed by the rising tide. There at the edge of low water the beach with its reminders of the land seemed far away. The only sounds were those of the wind and the sea and the birds. There was one sound of wind moving over water, and another of water sliding over the sand and tumbling down the faces of its own wave forms. The flats were astir with birds, and the voice of the willet rang insistently. One of them stood at the edge of the water and gave its loud, urgent cry; an answer came from far up the beach and the two birds flew to join each other.

The flats took on a mysterious quality as dusk approached and the last evening light was reflected from the scattered pools and creeks. Then birds became only dark shadows, with no color discernible. Sanderlings scurried across the beach like little ghosts, and here and there the darker forms of the willets stood out. Often I could come very close to them before they would start up in alarm—the sanderlings running, the willets flying up, crying. Black skimmers flew along the ocean's edge, silhouetted against the dull, metallic gleam, or they went flitting above the sand like large, dimly seen moths. Sometimes they "skimmed" the winding creeks of tidal water, where little spreading surface ripples marked the presence of small fish.

The shore at night is a different world, in which the very darkness that hides the distractions of daylight brings into sharper focus the elemental realities. Once, exploring the night beach, I surprised a small ghost crab in the searching beam of my torch. He was lying in a pit he had dug just above the surf, as though watching the sea and waiting. The blackness of the night possessed water, air, and beach. It was the darkness of an older world, before Man. There was no sound but the all-enveloping, primeval sounds of wind blowing over water and sand, and of waves crashing on the beach. There was no other visible life—just one small crab near the sea. I have seen hundreds of ghost crabs in other settings, but suddenly I was filled with the odd sensation that for the first time I knew the creature in its own world—that I understood, as never before, the essence of its being. In that moment time was suspended; the world to which I belonged did not exist and I might have been an onlooker from outer space. The little crab alone with the sea became a symbol that stood for life itself— for the delicate, destructible, yet incredibly vital force that somehow holds its place amid the harsh realities of the inorganic world.

The sense of creation comes with memories of a southern coast, where the sea and the mangroves, working together, are building a witness of thousands of small islands off the southwestern coast of Florida, separated from each other by a tortuous pattern of bays, lagoons, and narrow waterways. I remember a winter day when the sky was blue and drenched with sunlight; though there was no wind one was conscious of flowing air like cold clear crystal. I had landed on the surf-washed tip of one of those islands, and then worked my way around to the sheltered bay side. There I found the tide far out, exposing the broad mud flat of a cove bordered by the mangroves with their twisted branches, their glossy leaves, and their long prop roots reaching down, grasping and holding the mud, building the land out a little more, then again a little more.

The mud flats were strewn with the shells of that small, exquisitely colored mollusk, the rose tellin, looking like scattered petals of pink roses. There must have been a colony nearby, living buried just under the surface of the mud. At first the only creature visible was a small heron in gray and rusty plumage—a reddish egret that waded across the flat with the stealthy, hesitant movements of its kind. But other land creatures had been there, for a line of fresh tracks wound in and out among the mangrove roots, marking the path of a raccoon feeding on the oysters that gripped the supporting roots with projections from their shells. Soon I found the tracks of a shore bird, probably a sanderling, and followed them a little; then they turned toward the water and were lost, for the tide had erased them and made them as though they had never been.

Looking out over the cove I felt a strong sense of the interchangeability of land and sea in this marginal world of the shore, and of the links between the life of the two. There was also an awareness of the past and of the continuing flow of time, obliterating much that had gone before, as the sea had that morning washed away the tracks of the bird.

The sequence and meaning of the drift of time were quietly summarized in the existence of hundreds of small snails—the mangrove periwinkles—browsing on the branches and roots of the trees. Once their ancestors had been sea dwellers, bound to the salt waters by every tie of their life processes. Little by little over the thousands and millions of years the ties had been broken, the snails had adjusted themselves to life out of water, and now today they were living many feet above the tide to which they only occasionally returned. And perhaps, who could say how many ages hence, there would be in their descendants not even this gesture of remembrance for the sea.

The spiral shells of other snails—these quite minute—left winding tracks on the mud as they moved about in search of food. They were horn shells, and when I saw them I had a nostalgic moment when I wished I might see what Audubon saw, a century and more ago. For such little horn shells were the food of the flamingo, once so numerous on this coast, and when I half closed my eyes I could almost imagine a flock of these magnificent flame birds feeding in that cove, filling it with their color. It was a mere yesterday in the life of the earth that they were there; in nature, time and space are relative matters, perhaps most truly perceived subjectively in occasional flashes of insight, sparked by such a magical hour and place.

There is a common thread that links these scenes and memories—the spectacle of life in all its varied manifestations as it has appeared, evolved, and sometimes died out. Underlying the beauty of the spectacle there is meaning and significance. It is the elusiveness of that meaning that haunts us, that sends us again and again into the natural world where the key to the riddle is hidden. It sends us back to the edge of the sea, where the drama of life played its first scene on earth and perhaps even its prelude; where the forces of evolution are at work today, as they have been since the appearance of what we know as life; and where the spectacle of living creatures faced by the cosmic realities of their world is crystal clear.

JOHN BRINCKERHOFF JACKSON

John Brinckerhoff Jackson (1909–1996) was not only an esteemed geographer and interpreter of the American landscape but an essayist of originality and style. He started the magazine Landscape, *which analyzed the actual ways Americans were shaping the land; he called it the "vernacular" landscape. Far from decrying that interaction, or deploring the incursion of people into the countryside, Jackson stated that the beauty of the American landscape "derives from the human presence." "The Stranger's Path," his defense of the often shaggy neighborhoods around bus terminals and railroad stations, bespeaks his delight in the comings and goings of humanity and his resistance to the sterile prettifications and working-class displacements that were a product in his day of federally funded urban renewal programs.*

The Stranger's Path

(1957)

As one who is by way of being a professional tourist with a certain painfully acquired knowledge of how to appraise strange cities, I often find myself brought up short by citizens remarking that I can't really hope to *know* a town until I have seen the inside of one of its homes. I usually agree, expecting that there will then ensue an invitation to their house and a chance to admire one of these shrines of local culture, these epitomes of whatever it is the town or city has to offer. All that follows is an urgent suggestion that I investigate on my own the residential quarter before I presume to form a final opinion. "Ours is a city of homes," they add. "The downtown section is like that anywhere else, but our Country Club Heights"—or Snob Hill or West End or European Section or Villa Quarter, depending on where I am—"is considered unique."

I have accordingly set out to explore that part of the city, and many are the hours I have spent wandering through carefully labyrinthine suburbs, seeking to discover the *essential* city, as distinguished from that of the tourist or transient. In retrospect, these districts all seem indistinguishable: tree- and garden-lined avenues and lanes, curving about a landscape of hills with pretty views over other hills; the traffic becomes sparser, the houses retreat further behind tall trees and expensive flowers; every prospect is green, most prosperous and beautiful. The latest-model cars wait on the carefully raked driveway or at the immaculate curb, and there comes the sound of tennis being played. When evening falls, the softest, most domestic lights shine from upstairs windows; the only reminder of the nearby city is that dusty pink glow in the sky which in any case the trees all but conceal.

Yet why have I always been glad to leave? Was it a painful realization that I was excluded from these rows and rows of (presumably) happy and comfortable homes that has always ended by making me beat a retreat to the city proper? Or was it a conviction that I had actually seen this, experienced it, relished it after a fashion countless times and could no longer derive the slightest spark of inspiration from it? Ascribe it if you like to a kind of sour grapes, but in the course of years of travel I have come to believe that the home, the domestic establishment, far from being a unique symbol of the local way of life, is essentially the same wherever you go. The lovely higher-income residential zone of Spokane is, I suspect, hardly to be distinguished (except for a few interesting but not very significant architectural variations) from the corresponding zone of Oslo or Naples or Rio de Janeiro. Granted the sanctity of the home, its social, cultural, biological importance, is it necessarily the truest index of a society? Offhand, I would say the stranger could derive just as revealing an insight into a foreign way of life by listening to a country sermon or reading the classified ads in a popular newspaper or watching the behavior of a crowd during a street altercation—or, for that matter, by deciphering the graffiti on public walls.

At all events, the home is not everything. The residential quarter, despite its undeniable charms, is not the entire city, and if we poor lonely travelers are ignorant of the joys of existence on Monte Vista Terrace and Queen Alexandra Lane, we are on the other hand apt to know much more about some other aspects of the city than the lifelong resident does. I am thinking in particular of that part of the city devoted to the outsider, the transient, devoted to receiving him and satisfying his immediate needs. I am possibly prone to overemphasize this function of the city, for it is naturally the one I see most of; but who is it, I'd like to know, who keeps the city going, who makes it important to the outside world: the permanent resident with his predictable tastes and habits, or the stranger who brings money and business and new ideas? Both groups, of course, are vital to the community; their efforts are complementary; but there is a peculiar tendency among us to think of the city as a self-contained and even a sort of defensive unit forever struggling to keep its individuality intact. "Town" in English comes from a Teutonic word meaning "hedge" or "enclosure"; strange that this concept, obsolete a thousand years and more, should somehow have managed to stow away and cross the Atlantic, so that even in America we are reluctant to think of our cities as places where strangers come; with us the resident is always given preference. I gather it was quite the opposite in ancient Egypt; there the suffix corresponding to "town" or "ton" meant "the place one arrives at"—a notion I much prefer.

Anyhow, regardless of our hesitation to think of our cities as "places one arrives at" in pursuit of business or pleasure or new ideas, that is actually what most of them are. Every sizable community exists partly to satisfy the outsider who visits it. Not only that; there always evolves a special part of town devoted to this purpose. What name to give this zone of transients is something of a problem, for unlike the other subdivisions of the city, this one, I think, must be thought of in terms of movement along a pretty well defined axis. For the stranger progresses up a reasonably predictable route from his point of arrival to his final destination—and then, of course, he is likely to retrace his steps. Call it a path, in the sense that it is a way not deliberately constructed or planned for that purpose. Actually, the Strangers' Path is, in most cities, easily recognizable, once a few of its landmarks are known, and particularly (so I have found) in American cities of between, say, twenty and fifty thousand. Larger cities naturally possess a Strangers' Path of their own, but often it is so extensive and complex that it is exceedingly hard to define. As for towns of less than twenty thousand, the Path here is rarely fully developed, so that it is equally difficult to trace. Thus the Path I am most familiar with is the one in the smaller American city.

Where it begins is easy enough to establish, for it is the place where the stranger first disembarks. You may object that this can be almost anywhere, but the average stranger still arrives by bus or train or truck, and even if he arrives in his own car, he is likely to try to park somewhere outside the more congested downtown area. Arrival therefore signifies a change in the means of transportation: from train or truck or bus or car to something else, and this transfer is likely to take place either at the train station or the bus depot. Near these establishments (and for a variety of obvious reasons) you will also find the truck centers, the larger parking lots, and even a taxi stand or two.

So the beginning of the Path is marked by the abandoned means of transportation and the area near the railroad tracks. We are welcomed to the city by a smiling landscape of parking lots, warehouses, pot-holed and weed-grown streets, where isolated filling stations and quick-lunch counters are scattered among cinders like survivals of a bombing raid. But where does the Path lead from here? Directly to the center of town? To the hotels or the civic center or the main street? Not necessarily, and I believe we can only begin to follow the strangers' progress into the city when we have found out who these strangers are and what they are after. There are cities, to be sure, where most transients are well-heeled tourists and pleasure seekers: Las Vegas is one, and Monte Carlo is another; so are countless other resort towns all over the globe. The Path in such places usually leads directly to a hotel. But "stranger" does not always mean "tourist," and by and large the strangers who come to town for a day or two belong to a more modest class: not very prosperous, often with no money at all. They are men looking for a job or on their way to a job; men come to buy or sell one item in their line of business, men on a brief holiday. In terms of cash outlay in the local stores, no very brilliant public; in terms of labor and potential skills, in terms of experience of other ways of doing things, of other ways of thinking, a very valuable influx indeed. Besides, is it not one of the chief functions of the city to exchange as well as to receive? Furthermore, the greater part of these strangers would seem to be unattached men from some smaller town or from the country. These characteristics are worth bearing in mind, for they make the Path in the average small city what it now is: loud, tawdry, down-at-the-heel, full of dives and small catchpenny businesses, and (in the eyes of the uptown residential white-collar element) more than a little shady and dangerous.

Some urban geographer will be able to explain why the Strangers' Path becomes more respectable the further it gets from its point of origin; why the flophouses and brothels and the poorest among the second-hand shops (now euphemistically called loan establishments—the three golden balls are a thing of the past), the dirtiest and steamiest of greasy spoons tend to cluster around those first raffish streets near the depot and bus and truck terminals, and why the city's finest hotel, its most luxurious night club, its largest restaurant with a French name and illustrated menus are all at the other end. But so it is; one terminus of the Path is Skid Row, the other is the local Great White Way, and remote though they seem from each other, they are still organically and geographically linked. The moral is clear: the Path caters to every pocketbook, every taste, and what gives it its unifying quality and sets it off from the rest of the city is its eagerness to satisfy the unattached man from out of town, here either for a brief bout of pleasure or on some business errand.

Still, it would be foolish to maintain that the Path is everywhere identical; somewhere between its extremes, one of squalor, the other of opulence, it achieves its most characteristic and vigorous aspect, and it is in this middle region of the Path that the town seems to display all that it has to offer the outsider, though in a crude form. The City as Place of Exchange: such a definition in the residential section, even in the section devoted to public institutions, would seem incongruous, but here you learn its validity. Nearby on a converging street or in a square you find the local produce market. It is not so handsome and prosperous as it once was, for except in the more varied farming regions of the United States it has dwindled to a weekly display of potted plants and fryers and a few seasonal vegetables; Lancaster, Pennsylvania, has a noteworthy exception. But still the market, even in its reduced state, survives in most of the small cities I have visited, and it continues to serve as a center for a group of feed and grain stores, hardware stores, and an occasional tractor and farm implements agency. Here in fact is another one of those trans-shipment points; the streets surrounding the market are crowded with farm trucks, and with farmers setting out to explore the Path. Exchange is taking place everywhere you look: exchange of goods for cash; exchange of labor for cash (or the promise of cash) in the employment agencies, with their opportunities scrawled in chalk on blackboards; exchange of talk and drink and opinion in a dozen bars and beer parlors and lunch counters; exchange of mandolins and foreign pistols and diamond rings against cash—to be exchanged in turn against an hour or so with a girl. The Path bursts into a luxuriance of colored and lighted signs: *Chiliburgers. Red Hots. Unborn Calf Oxfords: They're New! They're Smart! They're Ivy! Double Feature: Bride of the Gorilla—Monster from Outer Space. Gospel Evangelical Mission. Checks Cashed. Snooker Parlor. The Best Shine in Town! Dr. Logan and His Amazing Europathic Method. Coney Islands. Fortunes Told: Madame LaFay.* And Army surplus stores, tattoo parlors, barbershops, poolrooms lined with pinball and slot machines, gift shops with Chinese embroidered coats and tea sets. Along one Path after another—in Paducah and Vicksburg and Poplar Bluff and Quincy—I have run across, to my amazement, strange little establishments (wedged in, perhaps, between a hotel with only a dark flight of steps on the street and a luggage store going out of business) where they sell joke books and party favors and comic masks—worthy reminders, that the Path, for all its stench of beer and burning grease, its bleary eyes and uncertain clutching of doorjams, its bedlam of jukeboxes and radios and barkers, is still dedicated to good times. And in fact the Path is at its gayest and noisiest and most popular from Saturday noon until midnight.

You may call this part of town what you like: Skid Row, the Jungle, the Tenderloin, Hell's Kitchen, or (in the loftier parlance of sociology) a depressed or obsolescent area; but you cannot accurately call it a slum. It is, as I have said, primarily a district for unattached men from out of town. This implies a minority of unattached women, but it does not imply that any families live here. No children are brought up here, no home has to struggle against the atmosphere of anarchy. That is why you find no grocery or household furniture or women's and children's clothing stores, though stores with gifts for women are numerous enough. Not being an urban morphologist, I have no inkling of why there are no slum dwellings here, nor, for that matter, of where in the city makeup slums are likely to occur; but I have yet to find anywhere even the remotest connection between an extensive slum area and the Strangers' Path.

But then there is much in the whole matter that mystifies me. I cannot understand why loan establishments always exist cheek by jowl with the large and pretentious small city bank buildings; why the Path merges almost without transition into the financial section of the city. Yet I have observed this too often to be entirely mistaken. Scollay Square in Boston is not far from State Street, New York's Bowery is not far (in metropolitan terms) from Wall Street, and Chicago's Skid Row, the classic of them all, is only a few blocks from the center of the financial district: and nowhere is there a slum between the two extremes. I imagine the connection here is one easily explained in terms of the nineteenth-century American city and its exchange function; perhaps the Path was originally a link between warehouse and counting house, between depot and Main Street. And there are other traits I find equally hard to fathom: why the Path rarely if ever touches on the fashionable retail district or the culturally conscious civic center with its monument and museum and library and welfare organizations housed in remodeled old mansions. These two parts of town are of course the favorite haunts of the residents of the city: is that why the Path avoids all contact with them?

When the Path has reached the region of banks and hotels—usually grouped around one or two intersections in the average small city—it has lost much of its loud proletarian quality, and about all that is left is a newsstand with out-of-town papers, a travel agency, and an airline office on the ground floor of the dressy hotel. Here at one of the busiest corners it seems to pause and hesitate: Main Street leads to the substantial older residential district, and eventually (if you're persistent and ambitious enough) to beautiful, restricted Country Club Heights. Broadway is the beginning of the retail shopping district. The Path finally makes its way to City Hall; and here it is, among the surrounding decrepit brick office buildings dating from the last century, that it touches upon another and final aspect of the city: the politico-legal. Lawyers, the legal aid society, bonding companies, insurance agents, a new (but no less rapacious) breed of finance establishments proliferate among dark, wainscoted corridors and behind transoms in high-ceilinged rooms. With a kind of artistic appropriateness, the initial hangdog atmosphere of the depot and flophouse reasserts itself around the last landmark on the Path, the City Hall. Groups of hastily sobered-up faces gather forlornly outside the traffic court and the police court, or on the steps of the City Hall itself, while grimy documents are passed about. From across the street, the YMCA, the Salvation Army, and the Guild of Temperance Women look on benevolently, wanting to make friends but never quite succeeding. The Red Cross, on the other hand, dwells in proud seclusion in the basement of the Federal Building, several blocks away.

Is it in this manner that the Strangers' Path comes to an end? If so, how sad, and how pointed the moral: Start your career in brothels and saloons and you wind up, hat in hand, before the police magistrate. But this is not invariably the case, and for all I have been able to discover the Path (or some portion of it) may go on to other, happier goals. Yet it is here that it ceases to be a distinct feature of the urban landscape; from now on it is dispersed among all the other currents of city life. And the simile which inevitably comes to mind is that of a river, a stream; a powerful, muddy, untidy, but immensely fertile stream which, after being joined by its tributaries, briefly cuts its own characteristic channel in the gaudy middle section of its course, then, arrived at the center of town, fans out to deposit its waters and their burden, and vanishes.

There are two reasons for my trying to describe this part of the average American city that I have called the Stranger's Path. First, I wanted to show the people of that city that while they may know the residential section and be immensely proud of it, there is probably something about the downtown section (something very valuable in its way) that they have never recognized. My second reason is that I have derived much pleasure from exploring the Path and learning a few of its landmarks; hours in unknown cities that might otherwise have been dull thereby became enjoyable. And indeed *every* city has such a section; there are remains of it among the ruins of Pompeii; it was an integral part of every medieval town, and I have run across it in its clearest form in Mexico and in the Balkans.

But what many people will ask is, how important is the Strangers' Path to the modern city? What sort of a future does it have? To such questions I can give no educated answer. When I likened it to a river, I was using no very original simile, yet a simile having the virtue of aptness and of suggesting two characteristics. The Path, as I see it, has the prime function of introducing new life to the city, of bringing the city into touch with the outside world. (That it also has the no less valuable function of bringing the villager, the lonely field worker or traveling salesman or trucker, or the inhabitant of a dehumanized commercial farming landscape into touch with urban culture goes without saying.) Granted that these contacts are not always on a very exalted or even worthwhile scale, and that they are increasingly confined to the lowest class of citizen; nevertheless, they are what keep an infinite number of businesses and arts and crafts alive, and they represent what is after all one of the chief purposes of the city: to serve as a place of general exchange. For my part, I cannot conceive of any large community surviving without this ceaseless influx of new wants, new ideas, new manners, new strength, and so I cannot conceive of a city without some section corresponding to the Path.

The simile was further that of a stream which empties into no basin or lake, merely evaporating into the city or perhaps rising to the surface once more outside of town along some highway strip; and it is this lack of a final, well-defined objective that prevents the Path from serving an even more important role in the community and that tends to make it a poor-man's district. For when the stranger, the transient, has finished his business, something in the layout of the city should invite him to linger and become part of the town, should impel him to pay his respects, as it were. In other words, the Path should open into the center of civic leisure, into a square or plaza where citizens gather.

"Well," says the city planner, "we have given that matter some thought. We have decided to demolish the depressed area of the city (including your so-called Path where the financial return is low, the sanitation bad, and the traffic hopeless) and erect a wonderful series of apartment houses for moderate-income white-collar workers, who are the backbone of our country. We will landscape the development with wading pools, flagstone walks, and groves of Chinese elms, and we are also putting in a series of neighborhood shopping centers. And that is not all," he continues enthusiastically. "The City Hall is being removed, a handsome park will take its place, with parking facilities for five hundred cars underneath, and *more* shops, as high-class as possible, will be built around the square." He then goes on to talk about the pedestrian traffic-free center, with frequent references to the Piazza San Marco in Venice.

All well and good; freedom from traffic is what we want, and no one can object to a pretty square where none existed before. But I am growing a little weary of the Piazza San Marco. I yield to no one in my admiration of its beauty and social utility, but it seems to me that those who hold it up as the prototype of all civic (traffic-free) centers are not always aware of what makes it what it is. The piazza is not an area carved out of a residential district; its animation comes not from the art monuments which surround it; on the contrary, it is enclosed on three sides by a maze of streets and alleys whose function is almost exactly that of the Path; moreover, the Piazza San Marco has a landing-place where farmers, fishermen, sailors, merchants, and travelers all first disembark—or used to disembark—in the city. These prosaic characteristics are what give life to it. And then, how about the *universal* absence of wheeled traffic in Venice? The Mediterranean plaza is a charming and healthy institution, which American cities would be wise to adopt, but the plaza is organically connected with the workaday life of the city. It has never served, it was never intended to serve, as a place of business. It is the center of group leisure; it is the civic parlor and it therefore adjoins the civic workroom or place of exchange. The notion of a pedestrian plaza in the center of every small American city is a good one, but if it is merely to serve as a focal point for smart shops and "culture," then I still do not see in it any substitute for the Path.

There are others who try to persuade us that the suburban or residential shopping center is the civic center of the future. Victor Gruen, who is justifiably happy over his enormous (and enormously successful) shopping centers in Detroit and Minneapolis, tells us that these establishments (or rather their handsomely landscaped surroundings) are already serving more and more as the scene of holiday festivities, art shows, and pageants, as well as of general sociability and of supervised play for children. I have no doubt of it; but the shopping center, no matter how big, how modern, how beautiful, is the *exact* opposite of the Path. Its public is almost exclusively composed of housewives and children, it imposes a uniformity of taste and income and interests, and its strenuous efforts to be self-contained mean that it automatically rejects anything from outside. And compared to any traditional civic center—market place, bazaar, agora—what bloodless places these shopping centers are! I cannot see a roustabout fresh from the oil fields, or (at the other extreme) a student of manners willingly passing an hour in one of them; though both could spend a day and a night in the Path with pleasure and a certain amount of profit. Art shows indeed! It strikes me that some of our planners need to acquire a more robust idea of city life. Perhaps I do them an injustice, but I often have the feeling that their emphasis on convenience, cleanliness, and safety, their distrust of everything vulgar and small and poor, is symptomatic of a very lopsided view of urban culture.

Possibly this is the price we have to pay for planning becoming respectable, but it would be well if a wider and more humane understanding of the city and its problems soon evolved in this country. There is much to be done, and planners are the only ones who can do it. No one, I suppose, would wish to see the Stranger's Path remain as it is: garish and dirty and decaying, forced to expend its vitality in mean and neglected streets, cheated of a final merger with the broader life of the city. Yet even in its present sad state it has the power to suggest the avenue it might become, given imaginative treatment. Among the famous and best-loved streets of the world, how many of them are simply glorifications of the Strangers' Path! The Rambla in Barcelona, more than a mile of tree-lined boulevard with more trees and a promenade down the center, is such a one; and the Cannebière in Marseilles is another. They both link the harbor (the point of arrival) with the uptown area; neither of them is a show street in terms of architecture, and they are not bordered by expensive or fashionable shops. The public which frequents them at every hour of the day and night is not a "class" public: it is composed of a large cross-section of the population of the city—men, women, and children, rich and poor, strangers and natives. It happens that the residential section of both of these cities contains architectural wonders which must be visited—Gaudi's church in Barcelona, Le Corbusier's Cité Radieuse in Marseilles—and here (as in so many other places) I have done my duty, only to return as fast as possible to the center of town and those marvelous avenues.

There are few greater delights than to walk up and down them in the evening along with thousands of other people; up and down, relishing the lights coming through the trees or shining from the facades, listening to the sounds of music and foreign voices and traffic, enjoying the smell of flowers and good food and the air from the nearby sea. The sidewalks are lined with small shops, bars, stalls, dance halls, movies, booths lighted by acetylene lamps; and everywhere are strange faces, strange costumes, strange and delightful impressions. To walk up such a street into the quieter, more formal part of town is to be part of a procession, part of a ceaseless ceremony of being initiated into the city and of rededicating the city itself. And that is how our first progress through even the smallest city and town should be: a succession of gay and beautiful streets and squares, all of them extending a universal welcome.

Unlike so many visions of the city of the future, this one has a firm basis in reality. The Stranger's Path exists in one form or another in every large community, either (as in most American cities) ignored, or, as in the case of Marseilles and Barcelona and many other cities in the Old World, preserved and cherished. Everywhere it is the direct product of our economic and social evolution. If we seek to dam or bury this ancient river, we will live to regret it.

PAUL TILLICH

Paul Tillich (1886–1965) was a Lutheran pastor and theologian whose opposition to Hitler caused him to flee Germany for the United States, where he became a naturalized citizen, taught in divinity schools, and wrote books. His probing existential philosophy, which acknowledged uncertainty and doubt while eschewing pat answers, followed a classic essayistic pattern, reconfirming the intertwined historical roots of the sermon and the essay. Tillich's theology, for all its complexity, often addressed itself to a general readership: his book The Courage to Be *was a best seller, and "The Lost Dimension of Religion" appeared first in* The Saturday Evening Post. *That essay mirrored the postwar uneasiness felt by many secular intellectuals about America's consumer culture, which seemed to threaten a flattening out of the psyche.*

Invocation: The Lost Dimension in Religion

(1958)

Being religious means asking passionately the question of the meaning of our existence and being willing to receive answers, even if the answers hurt. Such an idea of religion makes religion universally human, but it certainly differs from what is usually called religion. It does not describe religion as the belief in the existence of gods or one God, and as a set of activities and institutions for the sake of relating oneself to these beings in thought, devotion and obedience. No one can deny that the religions which have appeared in history are religions in this sense. Nevertheless, religion in its innermost nature is more than religion in this narrower sense. It is the state of being concerned about one's own being and being universally.

There are many people who are ultimately concerned in this way who feel far removed, however, from religion in the narrower sense, and therefore from every historical religion. It often happens that such people take the question of the meaning of their life infinitely seriously and reject any historical religion just for this reason. They feel that the concrete religions fail to express their profound concern adequately. They are religious while rejecting the religions. It is this experience which forces us to distinguish the meaning of religion as living in the dimension of depth from particular expressions of one's ultimate concern in the symbols and institutions of a concrete religion. If we now turn to the concrete analysis of the religious situation of our time, it is obvious that our key must be the basic meaning of religion and not any particular religion, not even Christianity. What does this key disclose about the predicament of man in our period?

If we define religion as the state of being grasped by an infinite concern we must say: Man in our time has lost such infinite concern. And the resurgence of religion is nothing but a desperate and mostly futile attempt to regain what has been lost.

How did the dimension of depth become lost? Like any important event, it has many causes, but certainly not the one which one hears often mentioned from ministers' pulpits and evangelists' platforms, namely that a widespread impiety of modern man is responsible. Modern man is neither more pious nor more impious than man in any other period. The loss of the dimension of depth is caused by the relation of man to his world and to himself in our period, the period in which nature is being subjected scientifically and technically to the control of man. In this period, life in the dimension of depth is replaced by life in the horizontal dimension. The driving forces of the industrial society of which we are a part go ahead horizontally and not vertically. In popular terms this is expressed in phrases like "better and better," "bigger and bigger," "more and more." One should not disparage the feeling which lies behind such speech. Man is right in feeling that he is able to know and transform the world he encounters without a foreseeable limit. He can go ahead in all directions without a definite boundary.

A most expressive symbol of this attitude of going ahead in the horizontal dimension is the breaking through of the space which is controlled by the gravitational power of the earth into the world-space. It is interesting that one calls this world-space simply "space" and speaks, for instance, of space travel, as if every trip were not travel into space. Perhaps one feels that the true nature of space has been discovered only through our entering into indefinite world-space. In any case, the predominance of the horizontal dimension over the dimension of depth has been immensely increased by the opening of the space beyond the space of earth.

If we now ask what does man do and seek if he goes ahead in the horizontal dimension, the answer is difficult. Sometimes one is inclined to say that the mere movement ahead without an end, the intoxication with speeding forward without limits, is what satisfies him. But this answer is by no means sufficient. For on his way into space and time man changes the world he encounters. And the changes made by him change himself. He transforms everything he encounters into a tool; and in doing so he himself becomes a tool. But if he asks, a tool for what, there is no answer.

One does not need to look far beyond everyone's daily experience in order to find examples to describe this predicament. Indeed our daily life in office and home, in cars and airplanes, at parties and conferences, while reading magazines and watching television, while looking at advertisements and hearing radio, are in themselves continuous examples of a life which has lost the dimension of depth. It runs ahead, every moment is filled with something which must be done or seen or said or planned. But no one can experience depth without stopping and becoming aware of himself. Only if he has moments in which he does not care about what comes next can he experience the meaning of this moment here and now and ask himself about the meaning of his life. As long as the preliminary, transitory concerns are not silenced, no matter how interesting and valuable and important they may be, the voice of the ultimate concern cannot be heard. This is the deepest root of the loss of the dimension of depth in our period—the loss of religion in its basic and universal meaning.

If the dimension of depth is lost, the symbols in which life in this dimension has expressed itself must also disappear. I am speaking of the great symbols of the historical religions in our Western world, of Judaism and Christianity. The reason that the religious symbols became lost is not primarily scientific criticism, but it is a complete misunderstanding of their meaning; and only because of this misunderstanding was scientific critique able, and even justified, in attacking them. The first step toward the nonreligion of the Western world was made by religion itself. When it defended its great symbols, not as symbols, but as literal stories, it had already lost the battle. In doing so the theologians (and today many religious laymen) helped to transfer the powerful expressions of the dimension of depth into objects or happenings on the horizontal plane. There the symbols lose their power and meaning and become an easy prey to physical, biological and historical attack.

If the symbol of creation which points to the divine ground of everything is transferred to the horizontal plane, it becomes a story of events in a removed past for which there is no evidence, but which contradicts every piece of scientific evidence. If the symbol of the Fall of Man, which points to the tragic estrangement of man and his world from their true being, is transferred to the horizontal plane, it becomes a story of a human couple a few thousand years ago in what is now present-day Iraq. One of the most profound psychological descriptions of the general human predicament becomes an absurdity on the horizontal plane. If the symbols of the Saviour and the salvation through Him which point to the healing power in history and personal life are transferred to the horizontal plane, they become stories of a half-divine being coming from a heavenly place and returning to it. Obviously, in this form, they have no meaning whatsoever for people whose view of the universe is determined by scientific astronomy.

If the idea of God (and the symbols applied to Him) which expresses man's ultimate concern is transferred to the horizontal plane, God becomes a being among others whose existence or nonexistence is a matter of inquiry. Nothing, perhaps, is more symptomatic of the loss of the dimension of depth than the permanent discussion about the existence or nonexistence of God—a discussion in which both sides are equally wrong, because the discussion itself is wrong and possible only after the loss of the dimension of depth.

When in this way man has deprived himself of the dimension of depth and the symbols expressing it, he then becomes a part of the horizontal plane. He loses his self and becomes a thing among things. He becomes an element in the process of manipulated production and manipulated consumption. This is now a matter of public knowledge. We have become aware of the degree to which everyone in our social structure is managed, even if one knows it and even if one belongs himself to the managing group. The influence of the gang mentality on adolescents, of the corporation's demands on the executives, of the conditioning of everyone by public communication, by propaganda and advertising under the guidance of motivation research, et cetera, have all been described in many books and articles.

Under these pressures, man can hardly escape the fate of becoming a thing among the things he produces, a bundle of conditioned reflexes without a free, deciding and responsible self. The immense mechanism, set up by man to produce objects for his use, transforms man himself into an object used by the same mechanism of production and consumption.

But man has not ceased to be man. He resists this fate anxiously, desperately, courageously. He asks the question, for what? And he realizes that there is no answer. He becomes aware of the emptiness which is covered by the continuous movement ahead and the production of means for ends which become means again without an ultimate end. Without knowing what has happened to him, he feels that he has lost the meaning of life, the dimension of depth.

Out of this awareness the religious question arises and religious answers are received or rejected. Therefore, in order to describe the contemporary attitude toward religion, we must first point to the places where the awareness of the predicament of Western man in our period is most sharply expressed. These places are the great art, literature and, partly at least, the philosophy of our time. It is both the subject matter and the style of these creations which show the passionate and often tragic struggle about the meaning of life in a period in which man has lost the dimension of depth. This art, literature, philosophy is not religious in the narrower sense of the word; but it asks the religious question more radically and more profoundly than most directly religious expressions of our time.

It is the religious question which is asked when the novelist describes a man who tries in vain to reach the only place which could solve the problem of his life, or a man who disintegrates under the memory of a guilt which persecutes him, or a man who never had a real self and is pushed by his fate without resistance to death, or a man who experiences a profound disgust of everything he encounters.

It is the religious question which is asked when the poet opens up the horror and the fascination of the demonic regions of his soul, or if he leads us into the deserts and empty places of our being, or if he shows the physical and moral mud under the surface of life, or if he sings the song of transitoriness, giving words to the ever-present anxiety of our hearts.

It is the religious question which is asked when the playwright shows the illusion of a life in a ridiculous symbol, or if he lets the emptiness of a life's work end in self-destruction, or if he confronts us with the inescapable bondage to mutual hate and guilt, or if he leads us into the dark cellar of lost hopes and slow disintegration.

It is the religious question which is asked when the painter breaks the visible surface into pieces, then reunites them into a great picture which has little similarity with the world at which we normally look, but which expresses our anxiety and our courage to face reality.

It is the religious question which is asked when the architect, in creating office buildings or churches, removes the trimmings taken over from past styles because they cannot be considered an honest expression of our own period. He prefers the seeming poverty of a purpose-determined style to the deceptive richness of imitated styles of the past. He knows that he gives no final answer, but he does give an honest answer. . . .

Is there an answer? There is always an answer, but the answer may not be available to us. We may be too deeply steeped in the predicament out of which the question arises to be able to answer it. To acknowledge this is certainly a better way toward a real answer than to bar the way to it by deceptive answers. And it may be that in this attitude the real answer (within available limits) is given. The real answer to the question of how to regain the dimension of depth is not given by increased church membership or church attendance, nor by conversion or healing experiences. But it is given by the awareness that we have lost the decisive dimension of life, the dimension of depth, and that there is no easy way of getting it back. Such awareness is in itself a state of being grasped by that which is symbolized in the term, dimension of depth. He who realizes that he is separated from the ultimate source of meaning shows by this realization that he is not only separated but also reunited. And this is just our situation. What we need above all—and partly have—is the radical realization of our predicament, without trying to cover it up by secular or religious ideologies. The revival of religious interest would be a creative power in our culture if it would develop into a movement of search for the lost dimension of depth.

This does not mean that the traditional religious symbols should be dismissed. They certainly have lost their meaning in the literalistic form into which they have been distorted, thus producing the critical reaction against them. But they have not lost their genuine meaning, namely, of answering the question which is implied in man's very existence in powerful, revealing and saving symbols. If the resurgence of religion would produce a new understanding of the symbols of the past and their relevance for our situation, instead of premature and deceptive answers, it would become a creative factor in our culture and a saving factor for many who live in estrangement, anxiety and despair. The religious answer has always the character of "in spite of." In spite of the loss of dimension of depth, its power is present, and most present in those who are aware of the loss and are striving to regain it with ultimate seriousness.

SUSAN SONTAG

Susan Sontag (1933–2004), cultural critic and novelist, inspired genera-
tions of essayists with her bold, fearless pronouncements and heady so-
phistication. Associating herself with European intellectuals like Roland
Barthes and Walter Benjamin rather than with American essayists, she
was drawn to an aphoristic style that courted generalization and rigor. In
the title essay of her first collection, Against Interpretation, *Sontag laid*
the groundwork for a formalist aesthetic that would respect a work of art
"as a thing in the world, not just a text or commentary on the world." It
is another fine example of the "Against X or Y" contrarian essay. Years
later, she admitted that of course one cannot be totally against interpreta-
tions, since the mind works to keep producing them, but insisted that she
still had a valid point, which was to honor the formal skin of an artwork
rather than plunder it for underlying meanings.

Against Interpretation

(1964)

> Content is a glimpse of something, an encounter like a flash. It's
> very tiny—very tiny, content.
>
> —Willem De Kooning, in an interview

> It is only shallow people who do not judge by appearances. The
> mystery of the world is the visible, not the invisible.
>
> —Oscar Wilde, in a letter

I

The earliest experience of art must have been that it was incantatory, magical; art was an instrument of ritual. (Cf. the paintings in the caves at Lascaux, Altamira, Niaux, La Pasiega, etc.) The earliest *theory* of art, that of the Greek philosophers, proposed that art was mimesis, imitation of reality.

It is at this point that the peculiar question of the value of art arose. For the mimetic theory, by its very terms, challenges art to justify itself.

Plato, who proposed the theory, seems to have done so in order to rule that the value of art is dubious. Since he considered ordinary material things as themselves mimetic objects, imitations of transcendent forms or structures, even the best painting of a bed would be only an "imitation of an imitation." For Plato, art is neither particularly useful (the painting of a bed is no good to sleep on) nor, in the strict sense, true. And Aristotle's arguments in defense of art do not really challenge Plato's view that all art is an elaborate *trompe l'oeil,* and therefore a lie. But he does dispute Plato's idea that art is useless. Lie or no, art has a certain value according to Aristotle because it is a form of therapy. Art is useful, after all, Aristotle counters, medicinally useful in that it arouses and purges dangerous emotions.

In Plato and Aristotle, the mimetic theory of art goes hand in hand with the assumption that art is always figurative. But advocates of the mimetic theory need not close their eyes to decorative and abstract art. The fallacy that art is necessarily a "realism" can be modified or scrapped without ever moving outside the problems delimited by the mimetic theory.

The fact is, all Western consciousness of and reflection upon art have remained within the confines staked out by the Greek theory of art as mimesis or representation. It is through this theory that art as such— above and beyond given works of art—becomes problematic, in need of defense. And it is the defense of art which gives birth to the odd vision by which something we have learned to call "form" is separated off from something we have learned to call "content," and to the well-intentioned move which makes content essential and form accessory.

Even in modern times, when most artists and critics have discarded the theory of art as representation of an outer reality in favor of the theory of art as subjective expression, the main feature of the mimetic theory persists. Whether we conceive of the work of art on the model of a picture (art as a picture of reality) or on the model of a statement (art as the statement of the artist), content still comes first. The content may have changed. It may now be less figurative, less lucidly realistic. But it is still assumed that a work of art is its content. Or, as it's usually put today, that a work of art by definition says something. ("What X is saying is . . ." "What X is trying to say is . . ." "What X said is . . ." etc., etc.)

II

None of us can ever retrieve that innocence before all theory when art knew no need to justify itself, when one did not ask of a work of art what it said because one knew (or thought one knew) what it did. From now to the end of consciousness, we are stuck with the task of defending art. We can only quarrel with one or another means of defense. Indeed, we have an obligation to overthrow any means of defending and justifying art which becomes particularly obtuse or onerous or insensitive to contemporary needs and practice.

This is the case, today, with the very idea of content itself. Whatever it may have been in the past, the idea of content is today mainly a hindrance, a nuisance, a subtle or not so subtle philistinism.

Though the actual developments in many arts may seem to be leading us away from the idea that a work of art is primarily its content, the idea still exerts an extraordinary hegemony. I want to suggest that this is because the idea is now perpetuated in the guise of a certain way of encountering works of art thoroughly ingrained among most people who take any of the arts seriously. What the overemphasis on the idea of content entails is the perennial, never-consummated project of *interpretation*. And, conversely, it is the habit of approaching works of art in order to *interpret* them that sustains the fancy that there really is such a thing as the content of a work of art.

III

Of course, I don't mean interpretation in the broadest sense, the sense in which Nietzsche (rightly) says, "There are no facts, only interpretations." By interpretation, I mean here a conscious act of the mind which illustrates a certain code, certain "rules" of interpretation.

Directed to art, interpretation means plucking a set of elements (the X, the Y, the Z, and so forth) from the whole work. The task of interpretation is virtually one of translation. The interpreter says, Look, don't you see that X is really—or, really means—A? That Y is really B? That Z is really C?

What situation could prompt this curious project for transforming a text? History gives us the materials for an answer. Interpretation first appears in the culture of late classical antiquity, when the power and credibility of myth had been broken by the "realistic" view of the world introduced by scientific enlightenment. Once the question that haunts post-mythic consciousness—that of the *seemliness* of religious symbols— had been asked, the ancient texts were, in their pristine form, no longer acceptable. Then interpretation was summoned, to reconcile the ancient texts to "modern" demands. Thus, the Stoics, to accord with their view that the gods had to be moral, allegorized away the rude features of Zeus and his boisterous clan in Homer's epics. What Homer really designated by the adultery of Zeus with Leto, they explained, was the union between power and wisdom. In the same vein, Philo of Alexandria interpreted the literal historical narratives of the Hebrew Bible as spiritual paradigms. The story of the exodus from Egypt, the wandering in the desert for forty years, and the entry into the promised land, said Philo, was really an allegory of the individual soul's emancipation, tribulations, and final deliverance. Interpretation thus presupposes a discrepancy between the clear meaning of the text and the demands of (later) readers. It seeks to resolve that discrepancy. The situation is that for some reason a text has become unacceptable; yet it cannot be discarded. Interpretation is a radical strategy for conserving an old text, which is thought too precious to repudiate, by revamping it. The interpreter, without actually erasing or rewriting the text, is altering it. But he can't admit to doing this. He claims to be only making it intelligible, by disclosing its true meaning. However far the interpreters alter the text (another notorious example is the rabbinic and Christian "spiritual" interpretations of the clearly erotic Song of Songs), they must claim to be reading off a sense that is already there.

Interpretation in our own time, however, is even more complex. For the contemporary zeal for the project of interpretation is often prompted not by piety toward the troublesome text (which may conceal an aggression) but by an open aggressiveness, an overt contempt for appearances. The old style of interpretation was insistent, but respectful; it erected another meaning on top of the literal one. The modern style of interpretation excavates, and as it excavates, destroys; it digs "behind" the text, to find a sub-text which is the true one. The most celebrated and influential modern doctrines, those of Marx and Freud, actually amount to elaborate systems of hermeneutics, aggressive and impious theories of interpretation. All observable phenomena are bracketed, in Freud's phrase, as *manifest content*. This manifest content must be probed and pushed aside to find the true meaning—the *latent content*—beneath. For Marx, social events like revolutions and wars; for Freud, the events of individual lives (like neurotic symptoms and slips of the tongue) as well as texts (like a dream or a work of art)—all are treated as occasions for interpretation. According to Marx and Freud, these events only *seem* to be intelligible.

Actually, they have no meaning without interpretation. To understand is to interpret. And to interpret is to restate the phenomenon, in effect to find an equivalent for it.

Thus, interpretation is not (as most people assume) an absolute value, a gesture of mind situated in some timeless realm of capabilities. Interpretation must itself be evaluated, within a historical view of human consciousness. In some cultural contexts, interpretation is a liberating act. It is a means of revising, of transvaluing, of escaping the dead past. In other cultural contexts, it is reactionary, impertinent, cowardly, stifling.

IV

Today is such a time, when the project of interpretation is largely reactionary, stifling. Like the fumes of the automobile and of heavy industry which befoul the urban atmosphere, the effusion of interpretations of art today poisons our sensibilities. In a culture whose already classical dilemma is the hypertrophy of the intellect at the expense of energy and sensual capability, interpretation is the revenge of the intellect upon art.

Even more. It is the revenge of the intellect upon the world. To interpret is to impoverish, to deplete the world—in order to set up a shadow world of "meanings." It is to turn *the* world into *this* world. ("This world"! As if there were any other.)

The world, our world, is depleted, impoverished enough. Away with all duplicates of it, until we again experience more immediately what we have.

V

In most modern instances, interpretation amounts to the philistine refusal to leave the work of art alone. Real art has the capacity to make us nervous. By reducing the work of art to its content and then interpreting *that,* one tames the work of art. Interpretation makes art manageable, comfortable.

This philistinism of interpretation is more rife in literature than in any other art. For decades now, literary critics have understood it to be their task to translate the elements of the poem or play or novel or story into something else. Sometimes a writer will be so uneasy before the naked power of his art that he will install within the work itself—albeit with a little shyness, a touch of the good taste of irony—the clear and explicit interpretation of it. Thomas Mann is an example of such an overcooperative author. In the case of more stubborn authors, the critic is only too happy to perform the job.

The work of Kafka, for example, has been subjected to a mass ravishment by no less than three armies of interpreters. Those who read Kafka as a social allegory see case studies of the frustrations and insanity of modern bureaucracy and its ultimate issuance in the totalitarian state. Those who read Kafka as a psychoanalytic allegory see desperate revelations of Kafka's fear of his father, his castration anxieties, his sense of his own impotence, his thralldom to his dreams. Those who read Kafka as a religious allegory explain that K. in *The Castle* is trying to gain access to heaven, that Joseph K. in *The Trial* is being judged by the inexorable and mysterious justice of God . . . Another body of work that has attracted interpreters like leeches is that of Samuel Beckett. Beckett's delicate dramas of the withdrawn consciousness—pared down to essentials, cut off, often represented as physically immobilized—are read as a statement about modern man's alienation from meaning or from God, or as an allegory of psychopathology.

Proust, Joyce, Faulkner, Rilke, Lawrence, Gide . . . one could go on citing author after author; the list is endless of those around whom thick encrustations of interpretation have taken hold. But it should be noted that interpretation is not simply the compliment that mediocrity pays to genius. It is, indeed, the modern way of understanding something, and is applied to works of every quality. Thus, in the notes that Elia Kazan published on his production of *A Streetcar Named Desire*, it becomes clear that, in order to direct the play, Kazan had to discover that Stanley Kowalski represented the sensual and vengeful barbarism that was engulfing our culture, while Blanche DuBois was Western civilization, poetry, delicate apparel, dim lighting, refined feelings and all, though a little the worse for wear, to be sure. Tennessee Williams's forceful psychological melodrama now became intelligible: it was about something, about the decline of Western civilization. Apparently, were it to go on being a play about a handsome brute named Stanley Kowalski and a faded mangy belle named Blanche DuBois, it would not be manageable.

VI

It doesn't matter whether artists intend, or don't intend, for their works to be interpreted. Perhaps Tennessee Williams thinks *Streetcar* is about what Kazan thinks it to be about. It may be that Cocteau in *The Blood of a Poet* and in *Orpheus* wanted the elaborate readings which have been given these films, in terms of Freudian symbolism and social critique. But the merit of these works certainly lies elsewhere than in their "meanings." Indeed, it is precisely to the extent that Williams's plays and Cocteau's films do suggest these portentous meanings that they are defective, false, contrived, lacking in conviction.

From interviews, it appears that Resnais and Robbe-Grillet consciously designed *Last Year at Marienbad* to accommodate a multiplicity of equally plausible interpretations. But the temptation to interpret *Marienbad* should be resisted. What matters in *Marienbad* is the pure, untranslatable, sensuous immediacy of some of its images, and its rigorous if narrow solutions to certain problems of cinematic form.

Again, Ingmar Bergman may have meant the tank rumbling down the empty night street in *The Silence* as a phallic symbol. But if he did, it was a foolish thought. ("Never trust the teller, trust the tale," said Lawrence.) Taken as a brute object, as an immediate sensory equivalent for the mysterious abrupt armored happenings going on inside the hotel, that sequence with the tank is the most striking moment in the film. Those who reach for a Freudian interpretation of the tank are only expressing their lack of response to what is there on the screen.

It is always the case that interpretation of this type indicates a dissatisfaction (conscious or unconscious) with the work, a wish to replace it by something else.

Interpretation, based on the highly dubious theory that a work of art is composed of items of content, violates art. It makes art into an article for use, for arrangement into a mental scheme of categories.

VII

Interpretation does not, of course, always prevail. In fact, a great deal of today's art may be understood as motivated by a flight from interpretation. To avoid interpretation, art may become parody. Or it may become abstract. Or it may become ("merely") decorative. Or it may become non-art.

The flight from interpretation seems particularly a feature of modern painting. Abstract painting is the attempt to have, in the ordinary sense, no content; since there is no content, there can be no interpretation. Pop Art works by the opposite means to the same result; using a content so blatant, so "what it is," it, too, ends by being uninterpretable.

A great deal of modern poetry as well, starting from the great experiments of French poetry (including the movement that is misleadingly called Symbolism) to put silence into poems and to reinstate the *magic* of the word, has escaped from the rough grip of interpretation. The most recent revolution in contemporary taste in poetry—the revolution that has deposed Eliot and elevated Pound—represents a turning away from content in poetry in the old sense, an impatience with what made modern poetry prey to the zeal of interpreters.

I am speaking mainly of the situation in America, of course. Interpretation runs rampant here in those arts with a feeble and negligible avant-garde: fiction and the drama. Most American novelists and play-wrights are really either journalists or gentlemen sociologists and psychologists. They are writing the literary equivalent of program music. And so rudimentary, uninspired, and stagnant has been the sense of what might be done with form in fiction and drama that even when the content isn't simply information, news, it is still peculiarly visible, handier, more exposed. To the extent that novels and plays (in America), unlike poetry and painting and music, don't reflect any interesting concern with changes in their form, these arts remain prone to assault by interpretation.

But programmatic avant-gardism—which has meant, mostly, experiments with form at the expense of content—is not the only defense against the infestation of art by interpretations. At least, I hope not. For this would be to commit art to being perpetually on the run.

(It also perpetuates the very distinction between form and content which is, ultimately, an illusion.) Ideally, it is possible to elude the interpreters in another way, by making works of art whose surface is so unified and clean, whose momentum is so rapid, whose address is so direct that the work can be . . . just what it is. Is this possible now? It does happen in films, I believe. This is why cinema is the most alive, the most exciting, the most important of all art forms right now. Perhaps the way one tells how alive a particular art form is is by the latitude it gives for making mistakes in it and still being good. For example, a few of the films of Bergman—though crammed with lame messages about the modern spirit, thereby inviting interpretations—still triumph over the pretentious intentions of their director. In *Winter Light* and *The Silence,* the beauty and visual sophistication of the images subvert before our eyes the callow pseudo-intellectuality of the story and some of the dialogue. (The most remarkable instance of this sort of discrepancy is the work of D. W. Griffith.) In good films, there is always a directness that entirely frees us from the itch to interpret. Many old Hollywood films, like those of Cukor, Walsh, Hawks, and countless other directors, have this liberating anti-symbolic quality, no less than the best work of the new European directors, like Truffaut's *Shoot the Piano Player* and *Jules and Jim,* Godard's *Breathless* and *Vivre sa Vie,* Antonioni's *L'Avventura,* and Olmi's *The Fiancés.*

The fact that films have not been overrun by interpreters is in part due simply to the newness of cinema as an art. It also owes to the happy accident that films for such a long time were just movies; in other words, that they were understood to be part of mass, as opposed to high, culture, and were left alone by most people with minds. Then, too, there is always something other than content in the cinema to grab hold of, for those who want to analyze. For the cinema, unlike the novel, possesses a vocabulary of forms—the explicit, complex, and discussable technology of camera movements, cutting, and composition of the frame that goes into the making of a film.

VIII

What kind of criticism, of commentary on the arts, is desirable today? For I am not saying that works of art are ineffable, that they cannot be described or paraphrased. They can be. The question is how. What would criticism look like that would serve the work of art, not usurp its place?

What is needed, first, is more attention to form in art. If excessive stress on *content* provokes the arrogance of interpretation, more extended and more thorough descriptions of *form* would silence. What is needed is a vocabulary—a descriptive, rather than prescriptive, vocabulary—for forms.* The best criticism, and it is uncommon, is of this sort that dissolves considerations of content into those of form. On film, drama, and painting respectively, I can think of Erwin Panofsky's essay "Style and Medium in the Motion Pictures," Northrop Frye's essay "A Conspectus of Dramatic Genres," Pierre Francastel's essay "The Destruction of a Plastic Space." Roland Barthes's book *On Racine* and his two essays on Robbe-Grillet are examples of formal analysis applied to the work of a single author. (The best essays in Erich Auerbach's *Mimesis,* like "The Scar of Odysseus," are also of this type.) An example of formal analysis applied simultaneously to genre and author is Walter Benjamin's essay "The Storyteller: Reflections on the Works of Nicolai Leskov."

Equally valuable would be acts of criticism which would supply a really accurate, sharp, loving description of the appearance of a work of art. This seems even harder to do than formal analysis. Some of Manny Farber's film criticism, Dorothy Van Ghent's essay "The Dickens World: A View from Todgers'," Randall Jarrell's essay on Walt Whitman are among the rare examples of what I mean. These are essays which reveal the sensuous surface of art without mucking about in it.

IX

Transparence is the highest, most liberating value in art—and in criticism—today. Transparence means experiencing the luminousness of

---

* One of the difficulties is that our idea of form is spatial (the Greek metaphors for form are all derived from notions of space). This is why we have a more ready vocabulary of forms for the spatial than for the temporal arts. The exception among the temporal arts, of course, is the drama; perhaps this is because the drama is a narrative (i.e., temporal) form that extends itself visually and pictorially, upon a stage. . . . What we don't have yet is a poetics of the novel, any clear notion of the forms of narration. Perhaps film criticism will be the occasion of a breakthrough here, since films are primarily a visual form, yet they are also a subdivision of literature.

the thing in itself, of things being what they are. This is the greatness of, for example, the films of Bresson and Ozu and Renoir's *The Rules of the Game*.

Once upon a time (say, for Dante), it must have been a revolutionary and creative move to design works of art so that they might be experienced on several levels. Now it is not. It reinforces the principle of redundancy that is the principal affliction of modern life.

Once upon a time (a time when high art was scarce), it must have been a revolutionary and creative move to interpret works of art. Now it is not. What we decidedly do not need now is further to assimilate Art into Thought, or (worse yet) Art into Culture.

Interpretation takes the sensory experience of the work of art for granted, and proceeds from there. This cannot be taken for granted now. Think of the sheer multiplication of works of art available to every one of us, super-added to the conflicting tastes and odors and sights of the urban environment that bombard our senses. Ours is a culture based on excess, on overproduction; the result is a steady loss of sharpness in our sensory experience. All the conditions of modern life—its material plenitude, its sheer crowdedness—conjoin to dull our sensory faculties. And it is in the light of the condition of our senses, our capacities (rather than those of another age), that the task of the critic must be assessed.

What is important now is to recover our senses. We must learn to *see* more, to *hear* more, to *feel* more.

Our task is not to find the maximum amount of content in a work of art, much less to squeeze more content out of the work than is already there. Our task is to cut back content so that we can see the thing at all.

The aim of all commentary on art now should be to make works of art—and, by analogy, our own experience—more, rather than less, real to us. The function of criticism should be to show *how it is what it is, even that it is what it is,* rather than to show *what it means.*

X

In place of a hermeneutics we need an erotics of art.

JOAN DIDION

Joan Didion (1934–) is the most influential essayist in America today. Starting out as a magazine writer, she became a leading representative of the New Journalism, which incorporated subjectivity and autobiography into researched reportage. One of her most notable creations is the "Joan" persona: stylish and glum, socially worldly and migrainously hermetic, topically minded and disillusioned, nostalgic for a lost Eden. Identifying her perspective as resolutely Californian, she has said she regards the East Coast as the home of narratives and the West Coast as anti-narrative (hence, truer to life). But her exquisitely fashioned prose intimates that everything does somehow connect and make ironic sense.

Notes from a Native Daughter

(1965)

It is very easy to sit at the bar in, say, La Scala in Beverly Hills, or Ernie's in San Francisco, and to share in the pervasive delusion that California is only five hours from New York by air. The truth is that La Scala and Ernie's are only five hours from New York by air. California is somewhere else.

Many people in the East (or "back East," as they say in California, although not in La Scala or Ernie's) do not believe this. They have been to Los Angeles or to San Francisco, have driven through a giant redwood and have seen the Pacific glazed by the afternoon sun off Big Sur, and they naturally tend to believe that they have in fact been to California. They have not been, and they probably never will be, for it is a longer and in many ways a more difficult trip than they might want to undertake, one of those trips on which the destination flickers chimerically on the horizon, ever receding, ever diminishing. I happen to know about that trip because I come from California, come from a family, or a congeries of families, that has always been in the Sacramento Valley.

You might protest that no family has been in the Sacramento Valley for anything approaching "always." But it is characteristic of Californians to speak grandly of the past as if it had simultaneously begun, *tabula rasa,* and reached a happy ending on the day the wagons started west. *Eureka*—"I Have Found It"—as the state motto has it. Such a view of history casts a certain melancholia over those who participate in it; my own childhood was suffused with the conviction that we had long outlived our finest hour. In fact that is what I want to tell you about: what it is like to come from a place like Sacramento. If I could make you understand that, I could make you understand California and perhaps something else besides, for Sacramento is California, and California is a place in which a boom mentality and a sense of Chekhovian loss meet in uneasy suspension; in which the mind is troubled by some buried but ineradicable suspicion that things had better work here, because here, beneath that immense bleached sky, is where we run out of continent.

In 1847 Sacramento was no more than an adobe enclosure, Sutter's Fort, standing alone on the prairie; cut off from San Francisco and the sea by the Coast Range and from the rest of the continent by the Sierra Nevada, the Sacramento Valley was then a true sea of grass, grass so high a man riding into it could tie it across his saddle. A year later gold was discovered in the Sierra foothills, and abruptly Sacramento was a town, a town any moviegoer could map tonight in his dreams—a dusty collage of assay offices and wagonmakers and saloons. Call that Phase Two. Then the settlers came—the farmers, the people who for two hundred years had been moving west on the frontier, the peculiar flawed strain who had cleared Virginia, Kentucky, Missouri; they made Sacramento a farm town. Because the land was rich, Sacramento became eventually a rich farm town, which meant houses in town, Cadillac dealers, a country club. In that gentle sleep Sacramento dreamed until perhaps 1950, when something happened. What happened was that Sacramento woke to the fact that the outside world was moving in, fast and hard. At the moment of its waking Sacramento lost, for better or for worse, its character, and that is part of what I want to tell you about.

But the change is not what I remember first. First I remember running a boxer dog of my brother's over the same flat fields that our great-great-grandfather had found virgin and had planted; I remember swimming (albeit nervously, for I was a nervous child, afraid of sinkholes and afraid of snakes, and perhaps that was the beginning of my error) the same rivers we had swum for a century: the Sacramento, so rich with silt that we could barely see our hands a few inches beneath the surface; the American, running clean and fast with melted Sierra snow until July, when it would slow down, and rattlesnakes would sun themselves on its newly exposed rocks. The Sacramento, the American, sometimes the Cosumnes, occasionally the Feather. Incautious children died every day in those rivers; we read about it in the paper, how they had miscalculated a current or stepped into a hole down where the American runs into the Sacramento, how the Berry Brothers had been called in from Yolo County to drag the river but how the bodies remained unrecovered. "They were from away," my grandmother would extrapolate from the newspaper stories. "Their parents had no *business* letting them in the river. They were visitors from Omaha." It was not a bad lesson, although a less than reliable one; children we knew died in the rivers too.

When summer ended—when the State Fair closed and the heat broke, when the last green hop vines had been torn down along the H Street road and the tule fog began rising off the low ground at night—we would go back to memorizing the Products of Our Latin American Neighbors and to visiting the great-aunts on Sunday, dozens of great-aunts, year after year of Sundays. When I think now of those winters I think of yellow elm leaves wadded in the gutters outside the Trinity Episcopal Pro-Cathedral on M Street. There are actually people in Sacramento now who call M Street Capitol Avenue, and Trinity has one of those featureless new buildings, but perhaps children still learn the same things there on Sunday mornings:

Q. In what way does the Holy Land resemble the Sacramento Valley?
A. In the type and diversity of its agricultural products.

And I think of the rivers rising, of listening to the radio to hear at what height they would crest and wondering if and when and where the levees would go. We did not have as many dams in those years. The bypasses would be full, and men would sandbag all night. Sometimes a levee would go in the night, somewhere upriver; in the morning the rumor would spread that the Army Engineers had dynamited it to relieve the pressure on the city.

After the rains came spring, for ten days or so; the drenched fields would dissolve into a brilliant ephemeral green (it would be yellow and dry as fire in two or three weeks) and the real-estate business would pick up. It was the time of year when people's grandmothers went to Carmel; it was the time of year when girls who could not even get into Stephens or Arizona or Oregon, let alone Stanford or Berkeley, would be sent to Honolulu, on the *Lurline*. I have no recollection of anyone going to New York, with the exception of a cousin who visited there (I cannot imagine why) and reported that the shoe salesmen at Lord & Taylor were "intolerably rude." What happened in New York and Washington and abroad seemed to impinge not at all upon the Sacramento mind. I remember being taken to call upon a very old woman, a rancher's widow, who was reminiscing (the favored conversational mode in Sacramento) about the son of some contemporaries of hers. "That Johnston boy never did amount to much," she said. Desultorily, my mother protested: Alva Johnston, she said, had won the Pulitzer Prize, when he was working for *The New York Times*. Our hostess looked at us impassively. "He never amounted to anything in Sacramento," she said.

Hers was the true Sacramento voice, and, although I did not realize it then, one not long to be heard, for the war was over and the boom was on and the voice of the aerospace engineer would be heard in the land, VETS NO DOWN! EXECUTIVE LIVING ON LOW FHA!

Later, when I was living in New York, I would make the trip back to Sacramento four and five times a year (the more comfortable the flight, the more obscurely miserable I would be, for it weighs heavily upon my kind that we could perhaps not make it by wagon), trying to prove that I had not meant to leave at all, because in at least one respect California— the California we are talking about—resembles Eden: it is assumed that those who absent themselves from its blessings have been banished, exiled by some perversity of heart. Did not the Donner-Reed Party, after all, eat its own dead to reach Sacramento?

I have said that the trip back is difficult, and it is—difficult in a way that magnifies the ordinary ambiguities of sentimental journeys. Going back to California is not like going back to Vermont, or Chicago; Vermont and Chicago are relative constants, against which one measures one's own change. All that is constant about the California of my childhood is the rate at which it disappears. An instance: on Saint Patrick's Day of 1948 I was taken to see the legislature "in action," a dismal experience; a handful of florid assemblymen, wearing green hats, were reading Pat-and-Mike jokes into the record. I still think of the legislators that way—wearing green hats, or sitting around on the veranda of the Senator Hotel fanning themselves and being entertained by Artie Samish's emissaries. (Samish was the lobbyist who said, "Earl Warren may be the governor of the state, but I'm the governor of the legislature.") In fact there is no longer a veranda at the Senator Hotel—it was turned into an airline ticket office, if you want to embroider the point—and in any case the legislature has largely deserted the Senator for the flashy motels north of town, where the tiki torches flame and the steam rises off the heated swimming pools in the cold Valley night.

It is hard to find California now, unsettling to wonder how much of it was merely imagined or improvised; melancholy to realize how much of anyone's memory is no true memory at all but only the traces of someone else's memory, stories handed down on the family network. I have an indelibly vivid "memory," for example, of how Prohibition affected the hop growers around Sacramento: the sister of a grower my family knew brought home a mink coat from San Francisco, and was told to take it back, and sat on the floor of the parlor cradling that coat and crying. Although I was not born until a year after Repeal, that scene is more "real" to me than many I have played myself.

I remember one trip home, when I sat alone on a night jet from New York and read over and over some lines from a W. S. Merwin poem I had come across in a magazine, a poem about a man who had been a long time in another country and knew that he must go home:

> . . . But it should be
> Soon. Already I defend hotly
> Certain of our indefensible faults,
> Resent being reminded; already in my mind
> Our language becomes freighted with a richness
> No common tongue could offer, while the mountains
> Are like nowhere on earth, and the wide rivers.

You see the point. I want to tell you the truth, and already I have told you about the wide rivers.

It should be clear by now that the truth about the place is elusive, and must be tracked with caution. You might go to Sacramento tomorrow and someone (although no one I know) might take you out to Aerojet-General, which has, in the Sacramento phrase, "something to do with rockets." Fifteen thousand people work for Aerojet, almost all of them imported; a Sacramento lawyer's wife told me, as evidence of how Sacramento was opening up, that she believed she had met one of them, at an open house two Decembers ago. ("Couldn't have been nicer, actually," she added enthusiastically. "I think he and his wife bought the house next door to Mary and Al, something like that, which of course was how they met him.") So you might go to Aerojet and stand in the big vendors' lobby where a couple of thousand components salesmen try every week to sell their wares and you might look up at the electrical wallboard that lists Aerojet personnel, their projects and their location at any given time, and you might wonder if I have been in Sacramento lately. MINUTEMAN, POLARIS, TITAN, the lights flash, and all the coffee tables are littered with airline schedules, very now, very much in touch.

But I could take you a few miles from there into towns where the banks still bear names like The Bank of Alex Brown, into towns where the one hotel still has an octagonal-tile floor in the dining room and dusty potted palms and big ceiling fans; into towns where everything—the seed business, the Harvester franchise, the hotel, the department store and the main street—carries a single name, the name of the man who built the town. A few Sundays ago I was in a town like that, a town smaller than that, really, no hotel, no Harvester franchise, the bank burned out, a river town. It was the golden anniversary of some of my relatives and it was 110° and the guests of honor sat on straight-backed chairs in front of a sheaf of gladioluses in the Rebekah Hall. I mentioned visiting Aerojet-General to a cousin I saw there, who listened to me with interested disbelief. Which is the true California? That is what we all wonder.

Let us try out a few irrefutable statements, on subjects not open to interpretation. Although Sacramento is in many ways the least typical of the Valley towns, it *is* a Valley town, and must be viewed in that context. When you say "the Valley" in Los Angeles, most people assume that you mean the San Fernando Valley (some people in fact assume that you mean Warner Brothers), but make no mistake: we are talking not about the valley of the sound stages and the ranchettes but about the real Valley, the Central Valley, the fifty thousand square miles drained by the Sacramento and the San Joaquin Rivers and further irrigated by a complex network of sloughs, cutoffs, ditches, and the Delta-Mendota and Friant-Kern Canals.

A hundred miles north of Los Angeles, at the moment when you drop from the Tehachapi Mountains into the outskirts of Bakersfield, you leave Southern California and enter the Valley. "You look up the highway and it is straight for miles, coming at you, with the black line down the center coming at you and at you . . . and the heat dazzles up from the white slab so that only the black line is clear, coming at you with the whine of the tires, and if you don't quit staring at that line and don't take a few deep breaths and slap yourself hard on the back of the neck you'll hypnotize yourself."

Robert Penn Warren wrote that about another road, but he might have been writing about the Valley road, U.S. 99, three hundred miles from Bakersfield to Sacramento, a highway so straight that when one flies on the most direct pattern from Los Angeles to Sacramento one never loses sight of U.S. 99. The landscape it runs through never, to the untrained eye, varies. The Valley eye can discern the point where miles of cotton seedlings fade into miles of tomato seedlings, or where the great corporation ranches—Kern County Land, what is left of DiGiorgio—give way to private operations (somewhere on the horizon, if the place is private, one sees a house and a stand of scrub oaks), but such distinctions are in the long view irrelevant. All day long, all that moves is the sun, and the big Rainbird sprinklers.

Every so often along 99 between Bakersfield and Sacramento there is a town: Delano, Tulare, Fresno, Madera, Merced, Modesto, Stockton. Some of these towns are pretty big now, but they are all the same at heart, one- and two- and three-story buildings artlessly arranged, so that what appears to be the good dress shop stands beside a W. T. Grant store, so that the big Bank of America faces a Mexican movie house. *Dos Peliculas, Bingo Bingo Bingo*. Beyond the downtown (pronounced *down*town, with the Okie accent that now pervades Valley speech patterns) lie blocks of old frame houses—paint peeling, sidewalks cracking, their occasional leaded amber windows overlooking a Foster's Freeze or a five-minute car wash or a State Farm Insurance office; beyond those spread the shopping centers and the miles of tract houses, pastel with redwood siding, the unmistakable signs of cheap building already blossoming on those houses which have survived the first rain. To a stranger driving 99 in an air-conditioned car (he would be on business, I suppose, any stranger driving 99, for 99 would never get a tourist to Big Sur or San Simeon, never get him to the California he came to see), these towns must seem, so flat, so impoverished, as to drain the imagination. They hint at evenings spent hanging around gas stations, and suicide pacts sealed in drive-ins.

But remember:

Q. In what way does the Holy Land resemble the Sacramento Valley?
A. In the type and diversity of its agricultural products.

U.S. 99 in fact passes through the richest and most intensely cultivated agricultural region in the world, a giant outdoor hothouse with a billion-dollar crop. It is when you remember the Valley's wealth that the monochromatic flatness of its towns takes on a curious meaning, suggests a habit of mind some would consider perverse. There is something in the Valley mind that reflects a real indifference to the stranger in his air-conditioned car, a failure to perceive even his presence, let alone his thoughts or wants. An implacable insularity is the seal of these towns. I once met a woman in Dallas, a most charming and attractive woman accustomed to the hospitality and social hypersensitivity of Texas, who told me that during the four war years her husband had been stationed in Modesto, she had never once been invited inside anyone's house. No one in Sacramento would find this story remarkable ("She probably had no *rel*atives there," said someone to whom I told it), for the Valley towns understand one another, share a peculiar spirit. They think alike and they look alike. *I* can tell Modesto from Merced, but I have visited there, gone to dances there; besides, there is over the main street of Modesto an arched sign which reads:

WATER WEALTH
CONTENTMENT HEALTH

There is no such sign in Merced.

I said that Sacramento was the least typical of the Valley towns, and it is—but only because it is bigger and more diverse, only because it has had the rivers and the legislature; its true character remains the Valley character, its virtues the Valley virtues, its sadness the Valley sadness. It is just as hot in the summertime, so hot that the air shimmers and the grass bleaches white and the blinds stay drawn all day, so hot that August comes on not like a month but like an affliction; it is just as flat, so flat that a ranch of my family's with a slight rise on it, perhaps a foot, was known for the hundred-some years which preceded this year as "the hill ranch." (It is known this year as a subdivision in the making, but that is another part of the story.) Above all, in spite of its infusions from outside, Sacramento retains the Valley insularity.

To sense that insularity a visitor need do no more than pick up a copy of either of the two newspapers, the morning *Union* or the afternoon *Bee*. The *Union* happens to be Republican and impoverished and the *Bee* Democratic and powerful ("THE VALLEY OF THE BEES!" as the McClatchys, who own the Fresno, Modesto, and Sacramento *Bees*, used to headline their advertisements in the trade press, "ISOLATED FROM ALL OTHER MEDIA INFLUENCE!"), but they read a good deal alike, and the tone of their chief editorial concerns is strange and wonderful and instructive. The *Union*, in a county heavily and reliably Democratic, frets mainly about the possibility of a local takeover by the John Birch Society; the *Bee*, faithful to the letter of its founder's will, carries on overwrought crusades against phantoms it still calls "the power trusts." Shades of Hiram Johnson, whom the *Bee* helped elect governor in 1910. Shades of Robert La Follette, to whom the *Bee* delivered the Valley in 1924. There is something about the Sacramento papers that does not quite connect with the way Sacramento lives now, something pronouncedly beside the point. The aerospace engineers, one learns, read the San Francisco *Chronicle*.

The Sacramento papers, however, simply mirror the Sacramento peculiarity, the Valley fate, which is to be paralyzed by a past no longer relevant. Sacramento is a town which grew up on farming and discovered to its shock that land has more profitable uses. (The chamber of commerce will give you crop figures, but pay them no mind—what matters is the feeling, the knowledge that where the green hops once grew is now

Larchmont Riviera, that what used to be the Whitney ranch is now Sunset City, thirty-three thousand houses and a country-club complex.) It is a town in which defense industry and its absentee owners are suddenly the most important facts; a town which has never had more people or more money, but has lost its *raison d'être*. It is a town many of whose most solid citizens sense about themselves a kind of functional obsolescence. The old families still see only one another, but they do not see even one another as much as they once did; they are closing ranks, preparing for the long night, selling their rights-of-way and living on the proceeds. Their children still marry one another, still play bridge and go into the real-estate business together. (There is no other business in Sacramento, no reality other than land—even I, when I was living and working in New York, felt impelled to take a University of California correspondence course in Urban Land Economics.) But late at night when the ice has melted there is always somebody now, some Julian English, whose heart is not quite in it. For out there on the outskirts of town are marshaled the legions of aerospace engineers, who talk their peculiar condescending language and tend their dichondra and plan to stay in the promised land; who are raising a new generation of native Sacramentans and who do not care, really do not care, that they are not asked to join the Sutter Club. It makes one wonder, late at night when the ice is gone; introduces some air into the womb, suggests that the Sutter Club is perhaps not, after all, the Pacific Union or the Bohemian; that Sacramento is not the city. In just such self-doubts do small towns lose their character.

I want to tell you a Sacramento story. A few miles out of town is a place, six or seven thousand acres, which belonged in the beginning to a rancher with one daughter. That daughter went abroad and married a title, and when she brought the title home to live on the ranch, her father built them a vast house—music rooms, conservatories, a ballroom. They needed a ballroom because they entertained: people from abroad, people from San Francisco, house parties that lasted weeks and involved special trains. They are long dead, of course, but their only son, aging and unmarried, still lives on the place. He does not live in the house, for the house is no longer there. Over the years it burned, room by room, wing by wing. Only the chimneys of the great house are still standing, and its heir lives in their shadow, lives by himself on the charred site, in a house trailer.

That is a story my generation knows; I doubt that the next will know it, the children of the aerospace engineers. Who would tell it to them? Their grandmothers live in Scarsdale, and they have never met a great-aunt. "Old" Sacramento to them will be something colorful, something they read about in *Sunset*. They will probably think that the Redevelopment has always been there, that the Embarcadero, down along the river, with its amusing places to shop and its picturesque fire houses turned into bars, has about it the true flavor of the way it was. There will be no reason for them to know that in homelier days it was called Front Street (the town was not, after all, settled by the Spanish) and was a place of derelicts and missions and itinerant pickers in town for a Saturday-night drunk: VICTORIOUS LIFE MISSION, JESUS SAVES, BEDS 25¢ A NIGHT, CROP INFORMATION HERE. They will have lost the real past and gained a manufactured one, and there will be no way for them to know, no way at all, why a house trailer should stand alone on seven thousand acres outside town.

But perhaps it is presumptuous of me to assume that they will be missing something. Perhaps in retrospect this has been a story not about Sacramento at all, but about the things we lose and the promises we break as we grow older; perhaps I have been playing out unawares the Margaret in the poem:

> Margaret, are you grieving
> Over Goldengrove unleaving? . . .
> It is the blight man was born for,
> It is Margaret you mourn for.

MARTIN LUTHER KING JR.

Martin Luther King Jr. (1929–1968), the great African American Baptist clergyman and civil rights leader, won the Nobel Peace Prize for his successful efforts to build an integration movement by using nonviolent tactics of protest and boycott. An inspiring orator who delivered his famous "I Have a Dream" speech at the March on Washington, he did not stop there but broadened his campaigns to include economic justice for workers and an antiwar crusade. In a lesser known but perhaps more daring speech, "Beyond Vietnam," he began by directly addressing the challenge—what right did he have to speak about the war, thereby threatening the purity of his civil rights message?—and worked through the reasons one by one. Dr. King is increasingly seen now as a political philosopher, whose writings outlined a radical vision of American society.

Beyond Vietnam

(1967)

Mr. Chairman, ladies and gentlemen, I need not pause to say how very delighted I am to be here tonight, and how very delighted I am to see you expressing your concern about the issues that will be discussed tonight by turning out in such large numbers. I also want to say that I consider it a great honor to share this program with Dr. Bennett, Dr. Commager, and Rabbi Heschel, some of the most distinguished leaders and personalities of our nation. And of course it's always good to come back to Riverside Church. Over the last eight years, I have had the privilege of preaching here almost every year in that period, and it's always a rich and rewarding experience to come to this great church and this great pulpit.

I come to this great magnificent house of worship tonight because my conscience leaves me no other choice. I join you in this meeting because I am in deepest agreement with the aims and work of the organization that brought us together, Clergy and Laymen Concerned About Vietnam. The recent statements of your executive committee are the sentiments of my own heart, and I found myself in full accord when I read its opening lines: "A time comes when silence is betrayal." That time has come for us in relation to Vietnam.

The truth of these words is beyond doubt, but the mission to which they call us is a most difficult one. Even when pressed by the demands of inner truth, men do not easily assume the task of opposing their government's policy, especially in time of war. Nor does the human spirit move without great difficulty against all the apathy of conformist thought within one's own bosom and in the surrounding world. Moreover, when the issues at hand seem as perplexing as they often do in the case of this dreadful conflict, we are always on the verge of being mesmerized by uncertainty. But we must move on.

Some of us who have already begun to break the silence of the night have found that the calling to speak is often a vocation of agony, but we must speak. We must speak with all the humility that is appropriate to our limited vision, but we must speak. And we must rejoice as well, for surely this is the first time in our nation's history that a significant number of its religious leaders have chosen to move beyond the prophesying of smooth patriotism to the high grounds of a firm dissent based upon the mandates of conscience and the reading of history. Perhaps a new spirit is rising among us. If it is, let us trace its movement, and pray that our inner being may be sensitive to its guidance. For we are deeply in need of a new way beyond the darkness that seems so close around us.

Over the past two years, as I have moved to break the betrayal of my own silences and to speak from the burnings of my own heart, as I have called for radical departures from the destruction of Vietnam, many persons have questioned me about the wisdom of my path. At the heart of their concerns, this query has often loomed large and loud: "Why are you speaking about the war, Dr. King? Why are you joining the voices of dissent?" "Peace and civil rights don't mix," they say. "Aren't you hurting the cause of your people?" they ask. And when I hear them, though I often understand the source of their concern, I am nevertheless greatly saddened, for such questions mean that the inquirers have not really known me, my commitment, or my calling. Indeed, their questions suggest that they do not know the world in which they live. In the light of such tragic misunderstanding, I deem it of signal importance to state clearly, and

I trust concisely, why I believe that the path from Dexter Avenue Baptist Church—the church in Montgomery, Alabama, where I began my pastorate—leads clearly to this sanctuary tonight.

I come to this platform tonight to make a passionate plea to my beloved nation. This speech is not addressed to Hanoi or to the National Liberation Front. It is not addressed to China or to Russia. Nor is it an attempt to overlook the ambiguity of the total situation and the need for a collective solution to the tragedy of Vietnam. Neither is it an attempt to make North Vietnam or the National Liberation Front paragons of virtue, nor to overlook the role they must play in the successful resolution of the problem. While they both may have justifiable reasons to be suspicious of the good faith of the United States, life and history give eloquent testimony to the fact that conflicts are never resolved without trustful give and take on both sides. Tonight, however, I wish not to speak with Hanoi and the National Liberation Front, but rather to my fellow Americans.

Since I am a preacher by calling, I suppose it is not surprising that I have seven major reasons for bringing Vietnam into the field of my moral vision. There is at the outset a very obvious and almost facile connection between the war in Vietnam and the struggle I and others have been waging in America. A few years ago there was a shining moment in that struggle. It seemed as if there was a real promise of hope for the poor, both black and white, through the poverty program. There were experiments, hopes, new beginnings. Then came the buildup in Vietnam, and I watched this program broken and eviscerated as if it were some idle political plaything on a society gone mad on war. And I knew that America would never invest the necessary funds or energies in rehabilitation of its poor so long as adventures like Vietnam continued to draw men and skills and money like some demonic, destructive suction tube. So I was increasingly compelled to see the war as an enemy of the poor and to attack it as such.

Perhaps a more tragic recognition of reality took place when it became clear to me that the war was doing far more than devastating the hopes of the poor at home. It was sending their sons and their brothers and their husbands to fight and to die in extraordinarily high proportions relative to the rest of the population. We were taking the black young men who had been crippled by our society and sending them eight thousand miles away to guarantee liberties in Southeast Asia which they had not found in southwest Georgia and East Harlem. So we have been repeatedly faced with the cruel irony of watching Negro and white boys on TV screens as they kill and die together for a nation that has been unable to seat them together in the same schools. So we watch them in brutal solidarity burning the huts of a poor village, but we realize that they would hardly live on the same block in Chicago. I could not be silent in the face of such cruel manipulation of the poor.

My third reason moves to an even deeper level of awareness, for it grows out of my experience in the ghettos of the North over the last three years, especially the last three summers. As I have walked among the desperate, rejected, and angry young men, I have told them that Molotov cocktails and rifles would not solve their problems. I have tried to offer them my deepest compassion while maintaining my conviction that social change comes most meaningfully through nonviolent action. But they asked, and rightly so, "What about Vietnam?" They asked if our own nation wasn't using massive doses of violence to solve its problems, to bring about the changes it wanted. Their questions hit home, and I knew that I could never again raise my voice against the violence of the oppressed in the ghettos without having first spoken clearly to the greatest purveyor of violence in the world today: my own government. For the sake of those boys, for the sake of this government, for the sake of the hundreds of thousands trembling under our violence, I cannot be silent.

For those who ask the question, "Aren't you a civil rights leader?" and thereby mean to exclude me from the movement for peace, I have this further answer. In 1957, when a group of us formed the Southern Christian Leadership Conference, we chose as our motto: "To save the soul of America." We were convinced that we could not limit our vision to certain rights for black people, but instead affirmed the conviction that America would never be free or saved from itself until the descendants of its slaves were loosed completely from the shackles they still wear. In a way we were agreeing with Langston Hughes, that black bard of Harlem, who had written earlier:

> O, yes, I say it plain,
> America never was America to me,
> And yet I swear this oath—
> America will be!

Now it should be incandescently clear that no one who has any concern for the integrity and life of America today can ignore the present war. If America's soul becomes totally poisoned, part of the autopsy must read "Vietnam." It can never be saved so long as it destroys the deepest hopes of men the world over. So it is that those of us who are yet determined that "America will be" are led down the path of protest and dissent, working for the health of our land.

As if the weight of such a commitment to the life and health of America were not enough, another burden of responsibility was placed upon me in 1954.* And I cannot forget that the Nobel Peace Prize was

---

* A slip of the tongue—King obviously meant 1964, the year he received the Nobel Peace Prize.

also a commission, a commission to work harder than I had ever worked before for the brotherhood of man. This is a calling that takes me beyond national allegiances.

But even if it were not present, I would yet have to live with the meaning of my commitment to the ministry of Jesus Christ. To me, the relationship of this ministry to the making of peace is so obvious that I sometimes marvel at those who ask me why I am speaking against the war. Could it be that they do not know that the Good News was meant for all men—for communist and capitalist, for their children and ours, for black and for white, for revolutionary and conservative? Have they forgotten that my ministry is in obedience to the one who loved his enemies so fully that he died for them? What then can I say to the Vietcong or to Castro or to Mao as a faithful minister of this one? Can I threaten them with death or must I not share with them my life?

Finally, as I try to explain for you and for myself the road that leads from Montgomery to this place, I would have offered all that was most valid if I simply said that I must be true to my conviction that I share with all men the calling to be a son of the living God. Beyond the calling of race or nation or creed is this vocation of sonship and brotherhood. Because I believe that the Father is deeply concerned, especially for His suffering and helpless and outcast children, I come tonight to speak for them. This I believe to be the privilege and the burden of all of us who deem ourselves bound by allegiances and loyalties which are broader and deeper than nationalism and which go beyond our nation's self-defined goals and positions. We are called to speak for the weak, for the voiceless, for the victims of our nation, for those it calls "enemy," for no document from human hands can make these humans any less our brothers.

And as I ponder the madness of Vietnam and search within myself for ways to understand and respond in compassion, my mind goes constantly to the people of that peninsula. I speak now not of the soldiers of each side, not of the ideologies of the Liberation Front, not of the junta in Saigon, but simply of the people who have been living under the curse of war for almost three continuous decades now. I think of them, too, because it is clear to me that there will be no meaningful solution there until some attempt is made to know them and hear their broken cries.

They must see Americans as strange liberators. The Vietnamese people proclaimed their own independence in 1954—in 1945 rather—after a combined French and Japanese occupation and before the communist revolution in China. They were led by Ho Chi Minh. Even though they quoted the American Declaration of Independence in their own document of freedom, we refused to recognize them. Instead, we decided to support France in its reconquest of her former colony. Our government felt then that the Vietnamese people were not ready for independence, and we again fell victim to the deadly Western arrogance that has poisoned the international atmosphere for so long. With that tragic decision we rejected a revolutionary government seeking self-determination and a government that had been established not by China—for whom the Vietnamese have no great love—but by clearly indigenous forces that included some communists. For the peasants this new government meant real land reform, one of the most important needs in their lives.

For nine years following 1945 we denied the people of Vietnam the right of independence. For nine years we vigorously supported the French in their abortive effort to recolonize Vietnam. Before the end of the war we were meeting eighty percent of the French war costs. Even before the French were defeated at Dien Bien Phu, they began to despair of their reckless action, but we did not. We encouraged them with our huge financial and military supplies to continue the war even after they had lost the will. Soon we would be paying almost the full costs of this tragic attempt at recolonization.

After the French were defeated, it looked as if independence and land reform would come again through the Geneva Agreement. But instead there came the United States, determined that Ho should not unify the temporarily divided nation, and the peasants watched again as we supported one of the most vicious modern dictators, our chosen man, Premier Diem. The peasants watched and cringed and Diem ruthlessly rooted out all opposition, supported their extortionist landlords, and refused even to discuss reunification with the North. The peasants watched as all of this was presided over by United States influence and then by increasing numbers of United States troops who came to help quell the insurgency that Diem's methods had aroused. When Diem was overthrown they may have been happy, but the long line of military dictators seemed to offer no real change, especially in terms of their need for land and peace.

The only change came from America as we increased our troop commitments in support of governments which were singularly corrupt, inept, and without popular support. All the while the people read our leaflets and received the regular promises of peace and democracy and land reform. Now they languish under our bombs and consider us, not their fellow Vietnamese, the real enemy. They move sadly and apathetically as we herd them off the land of their fathers into concentration camps where minimal social needs are rarely met. They know they must move on or be destroyed by our bombs.

So they go, primarily women and children and the aged. They watch as we poison their water, as we kill a million acres of their crops. They must weep as the bulldozers roar through their areas preparing to destroy the precious trees. They wander into the hospitals with at least twenty casualties from American firepower for one Vietcong-inflicted injury. So far we may have killed a million of them, mostly children. They wander into the towns and see thousands of the children, homeless, without clothes, running in packs on the streets like animals. They see the children degraded by our soldiers as they beg for food. They see the children selling their sisters to our soldiers, soliciting for their mothers.

What do the peasants think as we ally ourselves with the landlords and as we refuse to put any action into our many words concerning land reform? What do they think as we test out our latest weapons on them, just as the Germans tested out new medicine and new tortures in the concentration camps of Europe? Where are the roots of the independent Vietnam we claim to be building? Is it among these voiceless ones?

We have destroyed their two most cherished institutions: the family and the village. We have destroyed their land and their crops. We have cooperated in the crushing of the nation's only noncommunist revolutionary political force, the unified Buddhist Church. We have supported the enemies of the peasants of Saigon. We have corrupted their women and children and killed their men.

Now there is little left to build on, save bitterness. Soon the only solid physical foundations remaining will be found at our military bases and in the concrete of the concentration camps we call "fortified hamlets." The peasants may well wonder if we plan to build our new Vietnam on such grounds as these. Could we blame them for such thoughts? We must speak for them and raise the questions they cannot raise. These, too, are our brothers.

Perhaps a more difficult but no less necessary task is to speak for those who have been designated as our enemies. What of the National Liberation front, that strangely anonymous group we call "VC" or "communists"? What must they think of the United States of America when they realize that we permitted the repression and cruelty of Diem, which helped to bring them into being as a resistance group in the South? What do they think of our condoning the violence which led to their own taking up of arms? How can they believe in our integrity when now we speak of "aggression from the North" as if there was nothing more essential to the war? How can they trust us when now we charge them with violence after the murderous reign of Diem and charge them with violence while we pour every new weapon of death into their land? Surely we must understand their feelings, even if we do not condone their actions. Surely we must see that the men we supported pressed them to their violence. Surely we must see that our own computerized plans of destruction simply dwarf their greatest acts.

How do they judge us when our officials know that their membership is less than twenty-five percent communist, and yet insist on giving them the blanket name? What must they be thinking when they know that we are aware of their control of major sections of Vietnam, and yet we appear ready to allow national elections in which this highly organized political parallel government will not have a part? They ask how we can speak of free elections when the Saigon press is censored and controlled by the military junta. And they are surely right to wonder what kind of new government we plan to help form without them, the only real party in real touch with the peasants. They question our political goals and they deny the reality of a peace settlement from which they will be excluded. Their questions are frighteningly relevant. Is our nation planning to build on political myth again, and then shore it up upon the power of a new violence?

Here is the true meaning and value of compassion and nonviolence, when it helps us to see the enemy's point of view, to hear his questions, to know his assessment of ourselves. For from his view we may indeed see the basic weaknesses of our own condition, and if we are mature, we may learn and grow and profit from the wisdom of the brothers who are called the opposition.

So, too, with Hanoi. In the North, where our bombs now pummel the land, and our mines endanger the waterways, we are met by a deep but understandable mistrust. To speak for them is to explain this lack of confidence in the Western world, and especially their distrust of American intentions now. In Hanoi are the men who led this nation to independence against the Japanese and the French, the men who sought membership in the French Commonwealth and were betrayed by the weakness of Paris and the willfulness of the colonial armies. It was they who led a second struggle against French domination at tremendous costs, and then were persuaded to give up the land they controlled between the thirteenth and seventeenth parallel as a temporary measure at Geneva. After 1954 they watched us conspire with Diem to prevent elections which could have surely brought Ho Chi Minh to power over a unified Vietnam, and they realized they had been betrayed again. When we ask why they do not leap to negotiate, these things must be considered.

Also, it must be clear that the leaders of Hanoi considered the presence of American troops in support of the Diem regime to have been the initial military breach of the Geneva Agreement concerning foreign troops. They remind us that they did not begin to send troops in large numbers and even supplies into the South until American forces had moved into the tens of thousands.

Hanoi remembers how our leaders refused to tell us the truth about the earlier North Vietnamese overtures for peace, how the president claimed that none existed when they had clearly been made. Ho Chi Minh has watched as America has spoken of peace and built up its forces, and now he has surely heard the increasing international rumors of American plans for an invasion of the North. He knows the bombing and shelling and mining we are doing are part of traditional pre-invasion strategy. Perhaps only his sense of humor and of irony can save him when he hears the most powerful nation of the world speaking of aggression as it drops thousands of bombs on a poor, weak nation more than eight hundred, or rather, eight thousand miles away from its shores.

At this point I should make it clear that while I have tried to give a voice to the voiceless in Vietnam and to understand the arguments of those who are called "enemy," I am as deeply concerned about our own troops there as anything else. For it occurs to me that what we are submitting them to in Vietnam is not simply the brutalizing process that goes on in any war where armies face each other and seek to destroy. We are adding cynicism to the process of death, for they must know after a short period there that none of the things we claim to be fighting for are really involved. Before long they must know that their government has sent them into a struggle among Vietnamese, and the more sophisticated surely realize that we are on the side of the wealthy, and the secure, while we create a hell for the poor.

Surely this madness must cease. We must stop now. I speak as a child of God and brother to the suffering poor of Vietnam. I speak for those whose land is being laid waste, whose homes are being destroyed, whose culture is being subverted. I speak for the poor in America who are paying the double price of smashed hopes at home, and dealt death and corruption in Vietnam. I speak as a citizen of the world, for the world as it stands aghast at the path we have taken. I speak as one who loves America, to the leaders of our own nation: The great initiative in this war is ours; the initiative to stop it must be ours.

This is the message of the great Buddhist leaders of Vietnam. Recently one of them wrote these words, and I quote:

> Each day the war goes on the hatred increased in the hearts of the Vietnamese and in the hearts of those of humanitarian instinct. The Americans are forcing even their friends into becoming their enemies. It is curious that the Americans, who calculate so carefully on the possibilities of military victory, do not realize that in the process they are incurring deep psychological and political defeat. The image of America will never again be the image of revolution, freedom, and democracy, but the image of violence and militarism.

Unquote.

If we continue, there will be no doubt in my mind and in the mind of the world that we have no honorable intentions in Vietnam. If we do not stop our war against the people of Vietnam immediately, the world will be left with no other alternative than to see this as some horrible, clumsy, and deadly game we have decided to play. The world now demands a maturity of America that we may not be able to achieve. It demands that we admit we have been wrong from the beginning of our adventure in

Vietnam, that we have been detrimental to the life of the Vietnamese people. The situation is one in which we must be ready to turn sharply from our present ways. In order to atone for our sins and errors in Vietnam, we should take the initiative in bringing a halt to this tragic war.

I would like to suggest five concrete things that our government should do to begin the long and difficult process of extricating ourselves from this nightmarish conflict:

> Number one: End all bombing in North and South Vietnam.
>
> Number two: Declare a unilateral cease-fire in the hope that such action will create the atmosphere for negotiation.
>
> Three: Take immediate steps to prevent other battlegrounds in Southeast Asia by curtailing our military buildup in Thailand and our interference in Laos.
>
> Four: Realistically accept the fact that the National Liberation Front has substantial support in South Vietnam and must thereby play a role in any meaningful negotiations and any future Vietnam government.
>
> Five: Set a date that we will remove all foreign troops from Vietnam in accordance with the 1954 Geneva Agreement.

Part of our ongoing commitment might well express itself in an offer to grant asylum to any Vietnamese who fears for his life under a new regime which included the Liberation Front. Then we must make what reparations we can for the damage we have done. We must provide the medical aid that is badly needed, making it available in this country if necessary. Meanwhile, we in the churches and synagogues have a continuing task while we urge our government to disengage itself from a disgraceful commitment. We must continue to raise our voices and our lives if our nation persists in its perverse ways in Vietnam. We must be prepared to match actions with words by seeking out every creative method of protest possible.

As we counsel young men concerning military service, we must clarify for them our nation's role in Vietnam and challenge them with the alternative of conscientious objection. I am pleased to say that this is a path now chosen by more than seventy students at my own alma mater, Morehouse College, and I recommend it to all who find the American course in Vietnam a dishonorable and unjust one. Moreover, I would encourage all ministers of draft age to give up their ministerial exemptions and seek status as conscientious objectors. These are the times for real choices and not false ones. We are at the moment when our lives must be placed on the line if our nation is to survive its own folly. Every man of humane convictions must decide on the protest that best suits his convictions, but we must all protest.

Now there is something seductively tempting about stopping there and sending us all off on what in some circles has become a popular crusade against the war in Vietnam. I say we must enter that struggle, but I wish to go on now to say something even more disturbing.

The war in Vietnam is but a symptom of a far deeper malady within the American spirit, and if we ignore this sobering reality, we will find ourselves organizing "clergy and laymen concerned" committees for the next generation. They will be concerned about Guatemala and Peru. They will be concerned about Thailand and Cambodia. They will be concerned about Mozambique and South Africa. We will be marching for these and a dozen other names and attending rallies without end unless there is a significant and profound change in American life and policy. So such thoughts take us beyond Vietnam, but not beyond our calling as sons of the living God.

In 1957 a sensitive American official overseas said that it seemed to him that our nation was on the wrong side of a world revolution. During the past ten years we have seen emerge a pattern of suppression which has now justified the presence of U.S. military advisors in Venezuela. This need to maintain social stability for our investments accounts for the counterrevolutionary action of American forces in Guatemala. It tells why American helicopters are being used against guerrillas in Cambodia and why American napalm and Green Beret forces have already been active against rebels in Peru.

It is with such activity that the words of the late John F. Kennedy come back to haunt us. Five years ago he said, "Those who make peaceful revolution impossible will make violent revolution inevitable." Increasingly, by choice or by accident, this is the role our nation has taken, the role of those who make peaceful revolution impossible by refusing to give up the privileges and the pleasures that come from the immense profits of overseas investments. I am convinced that if we are to get on to the right side of the world revolution, we as a nation must undergo a radical revolution of values. We must rapidly begin the shift from a thing-oriented society to a person-oriented society. When machines and computers, profit motives and property rights, are considered more important than people, the giant triplets of racism, extreme materialism, and militarism are incapable of being conquered.

A true revolution of values will soon cause us to question the fairness and justice of many of our past and present policies. On the one hand we are called to play the Good Samaritan on life's roadside, but that will be only an initial act. One day we must come to see that the whole Jericho Road must be transformed so that men and women will not be constantly beaten and robbed as they make their journey on life's highway. True compassion is more than flinging a coin to a beggar. It comes to see that an edifice which produces beggars needs restructuring.

A true revolution of values will soon look uneasily on the glaring contrast of poverty and wealth. With righteous indignation, it will look across the seas and see individual capitalists of the West investing huge sums of money in Asia, Africa, and South America, only to take the profits out with no concern for the social betterment of the countries, and say, "This is not just." It will look at our alliance with the landed gentry of South America and say, "This is not just." The Western arrogance of feeling that it has everything to teach others and nothing to learn from them is not just.

A true revolution of values will lay hand on the world order and say of war, "This way of settling differences is not just." This business of burning human beings with napalm, of filling our nation's homes with orphans and widows, of injecting poisonous drugs of hate into the veins of peoples normally humane, of sending men home from dark and bloody battlefields physically handicapped and psychologically deranged, cannot be reconciled with wisdom, justice, and love. A nation that continues year after year to spend more money on military defense than on programs of social uplift is approaching spiritual death.

America, the richest and most powerful nation in the world, can well lead the way in this revolution of values. There is nothing except a tragic death wish to prevent us from reordering our priorities so that the pursuit of peace will take precedence over the pursuit of war. There is nothing to keep us from molding a recalcitrant status quo with bruised hands until we have fashioned it into a brotherhood.

This kind of positive revolution of values is our best defense against communism. War is not the answer. Communism will never be defeated by the use of atomic bombs or nuclear weapons. Let us not join those who shout war and, through their misguided passions, urge the United States to relinquish its participation in the United Nations. These are days which demand wise restraint and calm reasonableness. We must not engage in a negative anticommunism, but rather in a positive thrust for democracy, realizing that our greatest defense against communism is to take offensive action in behalf of justice. We must with positive action seek to remove those conditions of poverty, insecurity, and injustice, which are the fertile soil in which the seed of communism grows and develops.

These are revolutionary times. All over the globe men are revolting against old systems of exploitation and oppression, and out of the wounds of a frail world, new systems of justice and equality are being born. The shirtless and barefoot people of the land are rising up as never before. The people who sat in darkness have seen a great light. We in the West must support these revolutions.

It is a sad fact that because of comfort, complacency, a morbid fear of communism, and our proneness to adjust to injustice, the Western nations that initiated so much of the revolutionary spirit of the modern world have now become the arch antirevolutionaries. This has driven many to feel that only Marxism has a revolutionary spirit. Therefore, communism is a judgment against our failure to make democracy real and follow through on the revolutions that we initiated. Our only hope today lies in our ability to recapture the revolutionary spirit and go out into a sometimes hostile world declaring eternal hostility to poverty, racism, and militarism. With this powerful commitment we shall boldly challenge the status quo and unjust mores, and thereby speed the day when "every valley shall be exalted, and every mountain and hill shall be made low; the crooked shall be made straight, and the rough places plain."

A genuine revolution of values means in the final analysis that our loyalties must become ecumenical rather than sectional. Every nation must now develop an overriding loyalty to mankind as a whole in order to preserve the best in their individual societies.

This call for a worldwide fellowship that lifts neighborly concern beyond one's tribe, race, class, and nation is in reality a call for an all-embracing and unconditional love for all mankind. This oft misunderstood, this oft misinterpreted concept, so readily dismissed by the Nietzsches of the world as a weak and cowardly force, has now become an absolute necessity for the survival of man. When I speak of love I am not speaking of some sentimental and weak response. I'm not speaking of that force which is just emotional bosh. I am speaking of that force which all of the great religions have seen as the supreme unifying principle of life. Love is somehow the key that unlocks the door which leads to ultimate reality. This Hindu-Muslim-Christian-Jewish-Buddhist belief about ultimate reality is beautifully summed up in the first epistle of Saint John: "Let us love one another, for love is God. And every one that loveth is born of God and knoweth God. He that loveth not knoweth not God, for God is love. . . . If we love one another, God dwelleth in us and his love is perfected in us." Let us hope that this spirit will become the order of the day.

We can no longer afford to worship the god of hate or bow before the altar of retaliation. The oceans of history are made turbulent by the ever-rising tides of hate. History is cluttered with the wreckage of nations and individuals that pursued this self-defeating path of hate. As Arnold Toynbee says: "Love is the ultimate force that makes for the saving choice of life and good against the damning choice of death and evil. Therefore the first hope in our inventory must be the hope that love is going to have the last word." Unquote.

We are now faced with the fact, my friends, that tomorrow is today. We are confronted with the fierce urgency of now. In this unfolding conundrum of life and history, there is such a thing as being too late. Procrastination is still the thief of time. Life often leaves us standing bare, naked, and dejected with a lost opportunity. The tide in the affairs of men does not remain at flood—it ebbs. We may cry out desperately for time to pause in her passage, but time is adamant to every plea and rushes on. Over the bleached bones and jumbled residues of numerous civilizations are written the pathetic words, "Too late." There is an invisible book of life that faithfully records our vigilance or our neglect. Omar Khayyam is right: "The moving finger writes, and having writ moves on."

We still have a choice today: nonviolent coexistence or violent coannihilation. We must move past indecision to action. We must find new ways to speak for peace in Vietnam and justice throughout the developing world, a world that borders on our doors. If we do not act, we shall surely be dragged down the long, dark, and shameful corridors of time reserved for those who possess power without compassion, might without morality, and strength without sight.

Now let us begin. Now let us rededicate ourselves to the long and bitter, but beautiful, struggle for a new world. This is the calling of the sons of God, and our brothers wait eagerly for our response. Shall we say the odds are too great? Shall we tell them the struggle is too hard? Will our message be that the forces of American life militate against their arrival as full men, and we send our deepest regrets? Or will there be another message—of longing, of hope, of solidarity with their yearnings, of commitment to their cause, whatever the cost? The choice is ours, and though we might prefer it otherwise, we must choose in this crucial moment of human history.

As that noble bard of yesterday, James Russell Lowell, eloquently stated:

> Once to every man and nation comes a moment to decide,
> In the strife of Truth and Falsehood, for the good or evil side;
> Some great cause, God's new Messiah offering each the bloom
>   or blight,
> And the choice goes by forever 'twixt that darkness and that
>   light.
> Though the cause of Evil prosper, yet 'tis Truth alone is strong
> Though her portions be the scaffold, and upon the throne be
>   wrong
> Yet that scaffold sways the future, and behind the dim unknown
> Standeth God within the shadow, keeping watch above his own.

And if we will only make the right choice, we will be able to transform this pending cosmic elegy into a creative psalm of peace. If we will make the right choice, we will be able to transform the jangling discords of our world into a beautiful symphony of brotherhood. If we will but make the right choice, we will be able to speed up the day, all over America and all over the world, when justice will roll down like waters, and righteousness like a mighty stream.

RALPH ELLISON

Ralph Ellison (1914–1994) studied music at Tuskegee Institute and eventually moved to New York, where he wrote his masterpiece, Invisible Man, *which not only won the National Book Award but was later voted in a poll the most important American novel since World War II. Ellison's middle name was Waldo—he'd been named after Ralph Waldo Emerson—and he lived up to that suggestion with two splendid essay collections,* Shadow and Act *and* Going to the Territory. *While the literary world waited in vain for him to publish a second novel (*Juneteenth, *left unfinished), he refuted F. Scott Fitzgerald's claim that there are no second acts in American lives by switching genres and achieving a generous, full-bodied, expressive essay style, as demonstrated in the piece below.*

What America Would Be Like Without Blacks

(1970)

The fantasy of an America free of blacks is at least as old as the dream of creating a truly democratic society. While we are aware that there is something inescapably tragic about the cost of achieving our democratic ideals, we keep such tragic awareness segregated to the rear of our minds. We allow it to come to the fore only during moments of great national crisis.

On the other hand, there is something so embarrassingly absurd about the notion of purging the nation of blacks that it seems hardly a product of thought at all. It is more like a primitive reflex, a throwback to the dim past of tribal experience, which we rationalize and try to make respectable by dressing it up in the gaudy and highly questionable trappings of what we call the "concept of race." Yet, despite its absurdity, the fantasy of a blackless America continues to turn up. It is a fantasy born not merely of racism but of petulance, of exasperation, of moral fatigue. It is a boil bursting forth from impurities in the bloodstream of democracy.

In its benign manifestations, it can be outrageously comic—as in the picaresque adventures of Percival Brownlee who appears in William Faulkner's story "The Bear." Exasperating to his white masters because his aspirations and talents are for preaching and conducting choirs rather than for farming, Brownlee is "freed" after much resistance and ends up as the prosperous proprietor of a New Orleans brothel. In Faulkner's hands, the uncomprehending drive of Brownlee's owners to "get shut" of him is comically instructive. Indeed, the story resonates certain abiding, tragic themes of American history with which it is interwoven, and which are causing great turbulence in the social atmosphere today. I refer to the exasperation and bemusement of the white American with the black, the black American's ceaseless (and swiftly accelerating) struggle to escape the misconceptions of whites, and the continual confusing of the black American's racial background with his individual culture. Most of all, I refer to the recurring fantasy of solving one basic problem of American democracy by "getting shut" of the blacks through various wishful schemes that would banish them from the nation's bloodstream, from its social structure, and from its conscience and historical consciousness.

This fantastic vision of a lily-white America appeared as early as 1713, with the suggestion of a white "native American," thought to be from New Jersey, that all the Negroes be given their freedom and returned to Africa. In 1777, Thomas Jefferson, while serving in the Virginia legislature, began drafting a plan for the gradual emancipation and exportation of the slaves. Nor were Negroes themselves immune to the fantasy. In 1815, Paul Cuffe, a wealthy merchant, shipbuilder, and landowner from the New Bedford area, shipped and settled at his own expense thirty-eight of his fellow Negroes in Africa. It was perhaps his example that led in the following year to the creation of the American Colonization Society, which was to establish in 1821 the colony of Liberia. Great amounts of cash and a perplexing mixture of motives went into the venture. The slaveowners and many Border-state politicians wanted to use it as a scheme to rid the country not of slaves but of the militant free Negroes who were agitating against the "peculiar institution." The abolitionists, until they took a lead from free Negro leaders and began attacking the scheme, also participated as a means of righting a great historical injustice. Many blacks went along with it simply because they were sick of the black and white American mess and hoped to prosper in the quiet peace of the old ancestral home.

Such conflicting motives doomed the Colonization Society to failure, but what amazes one even more than the notion that anyone could have believed in its success is the fact that it was attempted during a period when the blacks, slave and free, made up eighteen percent of the total population. When we consider how long blacks had been in the New World and had been transforming it and being Americanized by it, the scheme appears not only fantastic, but the product of a free-floating irrationality. Indeed, a national pathology.

Nevertheless, some of the noblest of Americans were bemused. Not only Jefferson but later Abraham Lincoln was to give the scheme credence. According to historian John Hope Franklin, Negro colonization seemed as important to Lincoln as emancipation. In 1862, Franklin notes, Lincoln called a group of prominent free Negroes to the White House and urged them to support colonization, telling them, "Your race suffers greatly, many of them by living among us, while ours suffers from your presence. If this is admitted, it affords a reason why we should be separated."

In spite of his unquestioned greatness, Abraham Lincoln was a man of his times and limited by some of the less worthy thinking of his times. This is demonstrated both by his reliance upon the concept of race in his analysis of the American dilemma and by his involvement in a plan of purging the nation of blacks as a means of healing the badly shattered ideals of democratic federalism. Although benign, his motive was no less a product of fantasy. It envisaged an attempt to relieve an inevitable suffering that marked the growing pains of the youthful body politic by an operation which would have amounted to the severing of a healthy and indispensable member.

Yet, like its twin, the illusion of secession, the fantasy of a benign amputation that would rid the country of black men to the benefit of a nation's health not only persists; today, in the form of neo-Garveyism, it fascinates black men no less than it once hypnotized whites. Both fantasies become operative whenever the nation grows weary of the struggle toward the ideal of American democratic equality. Both would use the black man as a scapegoat to achieve a national catharsis, and both would, by way of curing the patient, destroy him.

What is ultimately intriguing about the fantasy of "getting shut" of the Negro American is the fact that no one who entertains it seems ever to have considered what the nation would have become had Africans *not* been brought to the New World, and had their descendants not played such a complex and confounding role in the creation of American history and culture. Nor do they appear to have considered with any seriousness the effect upon the nation of having any of the schemes for exporting blacks succeed beyond settling some fifteen thousand or so in Liberia.

We are reminded that Daniel Patrick Moynihan, who has recently aggravated our social confusion over the racial issue while allegedly attempting to clarify it, is co-author of a work which insists that the American melting pot didn't melt because our white ethnic groups have resisted all assimilative forces that appear to threaten their identities. The problem here is that few Americans know who and what they really are. That is why few of these groups—or at least few of the children of these groups—have been able to resist the movies, television, baseball, jazz, football, drum-majoretting, rock, comic strips, radio commercials, soap operas, book clubs, slang, or any of a thousand other expressions and carriers of our pluralistic and easily available popular culture. And it is here precisely that ethnic resistance is least effective. On this level the melting pot did indeed melt, creating such deceptive metamorphoses and blending of identities, values, and life-styles that most American whites are culturally part Negro American without even realizing it.

If we can resist for a moment the temptation to view everything having to do with Negro Americans in terms of their racially imposed status, we become aware of the fact that for all the harsh reality of the social and economic injustices visited upon them, these injustices have failed to keep Negroes clear of the cultural mainstream; Negro Americans are in fact one of its major tributaries. If we can cease approaching American social reality in terms of such false concepts as white and nonwhite, black culture and white culture, and think of these apparently unthinkable matters in the realistic manner of Western pioneers confronting the unknown prairie, perhaps we can begin to imagine what the United States would have been, or not been, had there been no blacks to give it—if I may be so bold as to say—color.

For one thing, the American nation is in a sense the product of the American language, a colloquial speech that began emerging long before the British colonials and Africans were transformed into Americans. It is a language that evolved from the king's English but, basing itself upon the realities of the American land and colonial institutions—or lack of institutions, began quite early as a vernacular revolt against the signs, symbols, manners, and authority of the mother country. It is a language that began by merging the sounds of many tongues, brought together in the struggle of diverse regions. And whether it is admitted or not, much of the sound of that language is derived from the timbre of the African voice and the listening habits of the African ear. So there is a *de'z* and *do'z* of slave speech sounding beneath our most polished Harvard accents, and if there is such a thing as a Yale accent, there is a Negro wail in it—doubtlessly introduced there by Old Yalie John C. Calhoun, who probably got it from his mammy.

Whitman viewed the spoken idiom of Negro Americans as a source for a native grand opera. Its flexibility, its musicality, its rhythms, freewheeling diction, and metaphors, as projected in Negro American folklore, were absorbed by the creators of our great nineteenth-century literature even when the majority of blacks were still enslaved. Mark Twain celebrated it in the prose of *Huckleberry Finn;* without the presence of blacks, the book could not have been written. No Huck and Jim, no American novel as we know it. For not only is the black man a co-creator of the language that Mark Twain raised to the level of literary eloquence, but Jim's condition as American and Huck's commitment to freedom are at the moral center of the novel.

In other words, had there been no blacks, certain creative tensions arising from the cross-purposes of whites and blacks would also not have existed. Not only would there have been no Faulkner; there would have been no Stephen Crane, who found certain basic themes of his writing in the Civil War. Thus, also, there would have been no Hemingway, who took Crane as a source and guide. Without the presence of Negro American style, our jokes, our tall tales, even our sports would be lacking in the sudden turns, the shocks, the swift changes of pace (all jazz-shaped) that serve to remind us that the world is ever unexplored, and that while a complete mastery of life is mere illusion, the real secret of the game is to make life swing. It is its ability to articulate this tragic-comic attitude toward life that explains much of the mysterious power and attractiveness of that quality of Negro American style known as "soul." An expression of American diversity within unity, of blackness with whiteness, soul announces the presence of a creative struggle against the realities of existence.

Without the presence of blacks, our political history would have been otherwise. No slave economy, no Civil War; no violent destruction of the Reconstruction; no K.K.K. and no Jim Crow system. And without the disenfranchisement of black Americans and the manipulation of racial fears and prejudices, the disproportionate impact of white Southern politicians upon our domestic and foreign policies would have been impossible. Indeed, it is almost impossible to conceive of what our political system would have become without the snarl of forces—cultural, racial, religious—that make our nation what it is today.

Absent, too, would be the need for that tragic knowledge which we try ceaselessly to evade: that the true subject of democracy is not simply material well-being but the extension of the democratic process in the direction of perfecting itself. And that the most obvious test and clue to that perfection is the inclusion—*not* assimilation—of the black man.

—

Since the beginning of the nation, white Americans have suffered from a deep inner uncertainty as to who they really are. One of the ways that has been used to simplify the answer has been to seize upon the presence of black Americans and use them as a marker, a symbol of limits, a metaphor for the "outsider." Many whites could look at the social position of blacks and feel that color formed an easy and reliable gauge for determining to what extent one was or was not American. Perhaps that is why one of the first epithets that many European immigrants learned when they got off the boat was the term "nigger"—it made them feel instantly American. But this is tricky magic. Despite his racial difference and social status, something indisputably American about Negroes not only raised doubts about the white man's value system but aroused the troubling suspicion that whatever else the true American is, he is also somehow black.

Materially, psychologically, and culturally, part of the nation's heritage is Negro American, and whatever it becomes will be shaped in part by the Negro's presence. Which is fortunate, for today it is the black American who puts pressure upon the nation to live up to its ideals. It is he who gives creative tension to our struggle for justice and for the elimination of those factors, social and psychological, which make for slums and shaky suburban communities. It is he who insists that we purify the American language by demanding that there be a closer correlation between the meaning of words and reality, between ideal and conduct, our assertions and our actions. Without the black American, something irrepressibly hopeful and creative would go out of the American spirit, and the nation might well succumb to the moral slobbism that has ever threatened its existence from within.

When we look objectively at how the dry bones of the nation were hung together, it seems obvious that some one of the many groups that compose the United States had to suffer the fate of being allowed no easy escape from experiencing the harsh realities of the human condition as they were to exist under even so fortunate a democracy as ours. It would seem that some one group had to be stripped of the possibility of escaping such tragic knowledge by taking sanctuary in moral equivocation, racial chauvinism, or the advantage of superior social status. There is no point in complaining over the past or apologizing for one's fate. But for blacks, there are no hiding places down here, not in suburbia or in penthouse, neither in country nor in city. They are an American people who are geared to what is and who yet are driven by a sense of what it is possible for human life to be in this society. The nation could not survive being deprived of their presence because, by the irony implicit in the dynamics of American democracy, they symbolize both its most stringent testing and the possibility of its greatest human freedom.

LOREN EISELEY

Loren Eiseley (1907–1977) was an eminent paleontologist who turned to the personal essay as a way of blending science and poetry. He perfected an essay form that would jump from remembered scenes and images to larger ideas about time, sometimes compassing millions of years in a few pages. His hero was Charles Darwin, whose evolutionary theories deeply inflected his vision. His voice was always quirky and personal, with a dark undertone veering toward the pessimistic. The poet W. H. Auden, wrote: "I have eagerly read anything of his I could lay my hands on. . . . Dr. Eiseley's autobiographical passages are, most of them, descriptions of numinous encounters—some joyful, some terrifying. After reading them, I get the impression of a wanderer who is often in danger of being ship-wrecked on the shores of dejection. . . . I suspect Dr. Eiseley of being a melancholic." In fact, one of Eiseley's favorite books was Robert Burton's The Anatomy of Melancholy. *Addressed to a general audience, his own essay collections, such as* The Immense Journey *and* The Night Country, *were best sellers in their day. An exacting stylist, he remains one of the modern masters of the scientific essay—or simply of the essay.*

The Brown Wasps

(1971)

There is a corner in the waiting room of one of the great Eastern stations where women never sit. It is always in the shadows and overhung by rows of lockers. It is, however, always frequented—not so much by genuine travelers as by the dying. It is here that a certain element of the abandoned poor seeks a refuge out of the weather, clinging for a few hours longer to the city that has fathered them. In a precisely similar manner I have seen, on a sunny day in midwinter, a few old brown wasps creep over an abandoned wasp nest in a thicket. Numbed and forgetful and frost-blackened, the hum of the spring hive still resounded faintly in their sodden tissues. Then the temperature would fall and they would drop away into the white oblivion of the snow. Here in the station it is in no way different save that the city is busy in its snows. But the old ones cling to their seats as though these were symbolic and could not be given up. Now and then they sleep, their gray old heads resting with painful awkwardness on the backs of the benches.

Also they are not at rest. For an hour they may sleep in the gasping exhaustion of the ill-nourished and aged who have to walk in the night. Then a policeman comes by on his rounds and nudges them upright.

"You can't sleep here," he growls.

A strange ritual then begins. An old man is difficult to awaken. After a muttered conversation the policeman presses a coin into his hand and passes fiercely along the benches prodding and gesturing toward the door. In his wake, like birds rising and settling behind the passage of a farmer through a cornfield, the men totter up, move a few paces and subside once more upon the benches.

One man, after a slight, apologetic lurch, does not move at all. Tubercularly thin, he sleeps on steadily. The policeman does not look back. To him, too, this has become a ritual. He will not have to notice it again officially for another hour.

Once in a while one of the sleepers will not awake. Like the brown wasps, he will have had his wish to die in the great droning center of the hive rather than in some lonely room. It is not so bad here with the shuffle of footsteps and the knowledge that there are others who share the bad luck of the world. There are also the whistles and the sounds of everyone, everyone in the world, starting on journeys. Amidst so many journeys somebody is bound to come out all right. Somebody.

Maybe it was on a like thought that the brown wasps fell away from the old paper nest in the thicket. You hold till the last, even if it is only to a public seat in a railroad station. You want your place in the hive more than you want a room or a place where the aged can be eased gently out of the way. It is the place that matters, the place at the heart of things. It is life that you want, that bruises your gray old head with the hard chairs; a man has a right to his place.

But sometimes the place is lost in the years behind us. Or sometimes it is a thing of air, a kind of vaporous distortion above a heap of rubble. We cling to a time and place because without them man is lost, not only man but life. This is why the voices, real or unreal, which speak from the floating trumpets at spiritualist seances are so unnerving. They are voices out of nowhere whose only reality lies in their ability to stir the memory of a living person with some fragment of the past. Before the medium's cabinet both the dead and the living resolve endlessly about an episode, a place, an event that has already been engulfed by time.

This feeling runs deep in my life; it brings stray cats running over endless miles, and birds homing from the ends of the earth. It is as though all living creatures, and particularly the more intelligent, can survive only by fixing or transforming a bit of time into space or by securing a bit of space with its objects immortalized and made permanent in time. For example, I once saw, on a flower pot in my own living room, the efforts of a field mouse to build a remembered field. I have lived to see this episode repeated in a thousand guises, and since I have spent a large portion of my life in the shade of a nonexistent tree, I think I am entitled to speak for the field mouse.

One day as I cut across the field which at that time extended on one side of our suburban shopping center, I found a giant slug feeding from a runnel of pink ice cream in an abandoned Dixie cup. I could see his eyes telescope and protrude in a kind of dim, uncertain ecstasy as his dark body bunched and elongated in the curve of the cup. Then, as I stood there at the edge of the concrete, contemplating the slug, I began to realize it was like standing on a shore where a different type of life creeps up and fumbles tentatively among the rocks and the sea wrack. It knows its place and will only creep so far until something changes. Little by little as I stood there I began to see more of this shore that surrounds the place of man. I looked with sudden care and attention at things I had been running over thoughtlessly for years. I even waded out a short way into the grass and the wild-rose thickets to see more. A huge black-belted bee went droning by and there were some indistinct scurryings in the underbrush.

Then I came to a sign which informed me that this field was to be the site of a new Wanamaker suburban store. Thousands of obscure lives were about to perish, the spores of puffballs would go smoking off to new fields, and the bodies of little white-footed mice would be crunched under the inexorable wheels of the bulldozers. Life disappears or modifies its appearances so fast that everything takes on an aspect of illusion—a momentary fizzing and boiling with smoke rings, like pouring dissident chemicals into a retort. Here man was advancing, but in a few years his plaster and bricks would be disappearing once more into the insatiable maw of the clover. Being of an archaeological cast of mind, I thought of this fact with an obscure sense of satisfaction and waded back through the rose thickets to the concrete parking lot. As I did so, a mouse scurried ahead in front of me, frightened by my steps if not of that ominous Wanamaker sign. I saw him vanish in the general direction of my apartment house, his little body quivering with fear in the great open sun on the blazing concrete. Blinded and confused, he was running straight away from his field. In another week scores would follow him.

I forgot the episode then and went home to the quiet of my living room. It was not until a week later, letting myself into the apartment, that I realized I had a visitor. I am fond of plants and had several ferns standing on the floor pots to avoid the noon glare by the south window.

As I snapped on the light and glanced carelessly around the room, I saw a little heap of earth on the carpet and a scrabble of pebbles that had been kicked merrily over the edge of one of the flower pots. To my astonishment I discovered a full-fledged burrow delving downward among the fern roots. I waited silently. The creature who had made the burrow did not appear. I remembered the wild field then, and the flight of the mice. No house mouse, no *Mus domesticus,* had kicked up this little heap of earth or sought refuge under a fern root in a flower pot. I thought of the desperate little creature I had seen fleeing from the wild-rose thicket. Through intricacies of pipes and attics, he, or one of his fellows, had climbed to this high green solitary room. I could visualize what had occurred. He had an image in his head, a world of seed pods and quiet, of green sheltering leaves in the dim light among the weed stems. It was the only world he knew and it was gone.

Somehow in his flight he had found his way to this room with drawn shades where no one would come till nightfall. And here he had smelled green leaves and run quickly up the flower pot to dabble his paws in common earth. He had even struggled half the afternoon to carry his burrow deeper and had failed. I examined the hole, but no whiskered twitching face appeared. He was gone. I gathered up the earth and refilled the burrow. I did not expect to find traces of him again.

Yet for three nights thereafter I came home to the darkened room and my ferns to find the dirt kicked gaily about the rug and the burrow reopened, though I was never able to catch the field mouse within it. I dropped a little food about the mouth of the burrow, but it was never touched. I looked under beds or sat reading with one ear cocked for rustlings in the ferns. It was all in vain; I never saw him. Probably he ended in a trap in some other tenant's room.

But before he disappeared I had come to look hopefully for his evening burrow. About my ferns there had begun to linger the insubstantial vapor of an autumn field, the distilled essence, as it were, of a mouse brain in exile from his home. It was a small dream, like our dreams, carried a long and weary journey along pipes and through spider webs, past holes over which loomed the shadows of waiting cats, and finally, desperately, into this room where he had played in the shuttered daylight for an hour among the green ferns on the floor. Every day these invisible dreams pass us on the street, or rise from beneath our feet, or look out upon us from beneath a bush.

Some years ago the old elevated railway in Philadelphia was torn down and replaced by a subway system. This ancient El with its barnlike stations containing nut-vending machines and scattered food scraps had, for generations, been the favorite feeding ground of flocks of pigeons, generally one flock to a station along the route of the El. Hundreds of pigeons were dependent upon the system. They flapped in and out of its stanchions and steel work or gathered in watchful little audiences about the feet of anyone who rattled the peanut-vending machines. They even watched people who jingled change in their hands, and prospected for food under the feet of the crowds who gathered between trains. Probably very few among the waiting people who tossed a crumb to an eager pigeon realized that this El was like a food-bearing river, and that the life which haunted its bank was dependent upon the running of the trains with their human freight.

I saw the river stop.

The time came when the underground tubes were ready; the traffic was transferred to a realm unreachable by pigeons. It was like a great river subsiding suddenly into desert sands. For a day, for two days, pigeons continued to circle over the El or stand close to the red vending machines. They were patient birds, and surely this great river which had flowed through the lives of unnumbered generations was merely suffering from some momentary drought.

They listened for the familiar vibrations that had always heralded an approaching train; they flapped hopefully about the head of an occasional workman walking along the steel runways. They passed from one empty station to another, all the while growing hungrier. Finally they flew away.

I thought I had seen the last of them about the El, but there was a revival and it provided a curious instance of the memory of living things for a way of life or a locality that has long been cherished. Some weeks after the El was abandoned workmen began to tear it down. I went to work every morning by one particular station, and the time came when the demolition crews reached this spot. Acetylene torches showered passers-by with sparks, pneumatic drills hammered at the base of the structure, and a blind man who, like the pigeons, had clung with his cup to a stairway, leading to the change booth, was forced to give up his place.

It was then, strangely, momentarily, one morning that I witnessed the return of a little band of the familiar pigeons. I even recognized one or two members of the flock that had lived around this particular station before they were dispersed into the streets. They flew in bravely in and out among the sparks and the hammers and the shouting workmen. They had returned—and they had returned because the hubbub of the wreckers had convinced them that the river was about to flow once more. For several hours they flapped in and out through empty windows, nodding their heads and watching the fall of girders with attentive little eyes.

By the following morning the station was reduced to some burned-off stanchions in the street. My birds had gone. It was plain, however, that they retained a memory for an insubstantial structure now compounded of air and time. Even the blind man clung to it. Someone had provided him with a chair, and he sat at the same corner staring sightlessly at an invisible stairway where, so far as he was concerned, the crowds were still ascending to the trains.

I have said my life has been passed in the shade of a nonexistent tree, so that such sights do not offend me. Prematurely I am one of the brown wasps and I often sit with them in the great droning hive of the station, dreaming sometimes of a certain tree. It was planted sixty years ago by a boy with a bucket and a toy spade in a little Nebraska town. That boy was myself. It was a cottonwood sapling and the boy remembered it because of some words spoken by his father and because everyone died or moved away who was supposed to wait and grow old under its shade. The boy was passed from hand to hand, but the tree for some intangible reason had taken root in his mind. It was under its branches that he sheltered; it was from this tree that his memories, which are my memories, led away into the world.

After sixty years the mood of the brown wasps grows heavier upon one. During a long inward struggle I thought it would do me good to go and look upon that actual tree. I found a rational excuse in which to clothe this madness. I purchased a ticket and at the end of the two thousand miles I walked another mile to an address that was still the same. The house had not been altered.

I came close to the white picket fence and reluctantly, with great effort, looked down the long vista of the yard. There was nothing there to see. For sixty years that cottonwood had been growing in my mind. Season by season its seeds had been floating farther on the hot prairie winds. We had planted it lovingly there, my father and I, because he had a great hunger for soil and live things growing, and because none of these things had long been ours to protect. We had planted the little sapling and watered it faithfully, and I remembered that I had run out with my small bucket to drench its roots the day we moved away. And all the years since it had been growing in my mind, a huge tree that somehow stood for my father and the love I bore him. I took a grasp on the picket fence and forced myself to look again.

A boy with the hard bird eye of youth pedaled a tricycle slowly up beside me.

"What'cha lookin' at?" he asked curiously.

"A tree," I said.

"What for?" he said.

"It isn't there," I said, to myself mostly, and began to walk away at a pace just slow enough not to seem to be running.

"What isn't there?" the boy asked. I didn't answer. It was obvious I was attached by a thread to a thing that had never been there, or certainly not for long. Something that had to be held in the air, or sustained in the mind, because it was part of my orientation in the universe and I could not survive without it. There was more than an animal's attachment to a place. There was something else, the attachment of the spirit to a grouping of events in time; it was part of our mortality.

So I had come home at last, driven by a memory in the brain as surely as the field mouse who had delved long ago in my flower pot or the pigeons flying forever amidst the rattle of nut-vending machines. These, the burrow under the greenery in my living room and the red-bellied bowls of peanuts now hovering in midair in the minds of pigeons, were all part of an elusive world that existed nowhere and yet everywhere. I looked once at the real world about me while the persistent boy pedaled at my heels.

It was without meaning, though my feet took a remembered path. In sixty years the house and street had rotted out of my mind. But the tree, the tree that no longer was, that had perished in its first season, bloomed on in my individual mind, unblemished as my father's words. "We'll plant a tree here, son, and we're not going to move any more. And when you're an old, old man you can sit under it and think how we planted it here, you and me, together."

I began to outpace the boy on the tricycle.

"Do you live here, Mister?" he shouted after me suspiciously. I took a firm grasp on airy nothing—to be precise, on the bole of the great tree. "I do," I said. I spoke for myself, one field mouse, and several pigeons. We were all out of touch but somehow permanent. It was the world that had changed.

NORA EPHRON

Nora Ephron (1941–2012), before becoming a successful screenwriter and film director (When Harry Met Sally, Sleepless in Seattle, You've Got Mail), *developed a devoted following as a journalist and cultural commentator. Her lifestyle essays sparkled with humor, often homing in on the insecurities of women like herself about aging, physical appearance, social status, or irregular male companionship. She was especially adept at generating a warmly conversational, trustworthy if cranky voice on the page, one that would hook the reader into an ostensibly minor topic and propel it forward to larger resonances. Known for her quips and friendly advice-giving, an unswerving feminist who urged women to take chances, she said: "Above all, be the heroine of your life, not the victim."*

A Few Words About Breasts

(1972)

I have to begin with a few words about androgyny. In grammar school, in the fifth and sixth grades, we were all tyrannized by a rigid set of rules that supposedly determined whether we were boys or girls. The episode in *Huckleberry Finn* where Huck is disguised as a girl and gives himself away by the way he threads a needle and catches a ball—that kind of thing. We learned that the way you sat, crossed your legs, held a cigarette, and looked at your nails—the way you did these things instinctively was absolute proof of your sex. Now obviously most children did not take this literally, but I did. I thought that just one slip, just one incorrect cross of my legs or flick of an imaginary cigarette ash would turn me from whatever I was into the other thing; that would be all it took, really. Even though I was outwardly a girl and had many of the trappings generally associated with girldom—a girl's name, for example, and dresses, my own telephone, an autograph book—I spent the early years of my adolescence absolutely certain that I might at any point gum it up. I did not feel at all like a girl. I was boyish. I was athletic, ambitious, outspoken, competitive, noisy, rambunctious. I had scabs on my knees and my socks slid into my loafers and I could throw a football. I wanted desperately not to be that way, not to be a mixture of both things, but instead just one, a girl, a definite indisputable girl. As soft and as pink as a nursery. And nothing would do that for me, I felt, but breasts.

I was about six months younger than everyone else in my class, and so for about six months after it began, for six months after my friends had begun to develop (that was the word we used, develop), I was not particularly worried. I would sit in the bathtub and look down at my breasts and know that any day now, any second now, they would start growing like everyone else's. They didn't. "I want to buy a bra," I said to my mother one night. "What for?" she said. My mother was really hateful about bras, and by the time my third sister had gotten to the point where she was ready to want one, my mother had worked the whole business into a comedy routine. "Why not use a Band-Aid instead?" she would say. It was a source of great pride to my mother that she had never even had to wear a brassiere until she had her fourth child, and then only because her gynecologist made her. It was incomprehensible to me that anyone could ever be proud of something like that. It was the 1950s, for God's sake. Jane Russell. Cashmere sweaters. Couldn't my mother see that? *I am too old to wear an undershirt.* Screaming. Weeping. Shouting. "Then don't wear an undershirt," said my mother. "But I want to buy a bra." "What for?"

I suppose that for most girls, breasts, brassieres, that entire thing, has more trauma, more to do with the coming of adolescence, with becoming a woman, than anything else. Certainly more than getting your period, although that, too, was traumatic, symbolic. But you could see breasts; they were there; they were visible. Whereas a girl could claim to have her period for months before she actually got it and nobody would ever know the difference. Which is exactly what I did. All you had to do was make a great fuss over having enough nickels for the Kotex machine and walk around clutching your stomach and moaning for three to five days a month about The Curse and you could convince anybody. There is a school of thought somewhere in the women's lib/women's mag/gynecology establishment that claims that menstrual cramps are purely psychological, and I lean toward it. Not that I didn't have them finally. Agonizing cramps, heating-pad cramps, go-down-to-the-school-nurse-and-lie-on-the-cot cramps. But unlike any pain I had ever suffered, I adored the pain of cramps, welcomed it, wallowed in it, bragged about it. "I can't go. I have cramps." "I can't do that. I have cramps." And most of all, gigglingly, blushingly: "I can't swim. I have cramps." Nobody ever used the hard-core word. Menstruation. God, what an awful word. Never that. "I have cramps."

The morning I first got my period, I went into my mother's bedroom to tell her. And my mother, my utterly-hateful-about-bras mother, burst into tears. It was really a lovely moment, and I remember it so clearly not just because it was one of the two times I ever saw my mother cry on my account (the other was when I was caught being a six-year-old kleptomaniac), but also because the incident did not mean to me what it meant to her. Her little girl, her firstborn, had finally become a woman. That was what she was crying about. My reaction to the event, however, was that I might well be a woman in some scientific, textbook sense (and could at least stop faking every month and stop wasting all those nickels). But in another sense—in a visible sense—I was as androgynous and as liable to tip over into boyhood as ever.

I started with a 28 AA bra. I don't think they made them any smaller in those days, although I gather that now you can buy bras for five-year-olds that don't have any cups whatsoever in them; trainer bras they are called. My first brassiere came from Robinson's Department Store in Beverly Hills. I went there alone, shaking, positive they would look me over and smile and tell me to come back next year. An actual fitter took me into the dressing room and stood over me while I took off my blouse and tried the first one on. The little puffs stood out on my chest. "Lean over," said the fitter. (To this day, I am not sure what fitters in bra departments do except to tell you to lean over.) I leaned over, with the fleeting hope that my breasts would miraculously fall out of my body and into the puffs. Nothing.

"Don't worry about it," said my friend Libby some months later, when things had not improved. "You'll get them after you're married."

"What are you talking about?" I said.

"When you get married," Libby explained, "your husband will touch your breasts and rub them and kiss them and they'll grow."

That was the killer. Necking I could deal with. Intercourse I could deal with. But it had never crossed my mind that a man was going to touch my breasts, that breasts had something to do with all that, petting, my God, they never mentioned petting in my little sex manual about the fertilization of the ovum. I became dizzy. For I knew instantly—as naive as I had been only a moment before—that only part of what she was saying was true: the touching, rubbing, kissing part, not the growing part. And I knew that no one would ever want to marry me. I had no breasts. I would never have breasts.

My best friend in school was Diana Raskob. She lived a block from me in a house full of wonders. English muffins, for instance. The Raskobs were the first people in Beverly Hills to have English muffins for breakfast. They also had an apricot tree in the back, and a badminton court, and a subscription to *Seventeen* magazine, and hundreds of games, like Sorry and Parcheesi and Treasure Hunt and Anagrams. Diana and I spent three or four afternoons a week in their den reading and playing and eating. Diana's mother's kitchen was full of the most colossal assortment of junk food I have ever been exposed to. My house was full of apples and peaches and milk and homemade chocolate-chip cookies—which were nice, and good for you, but-not-right-before-dinner-or-you'll-spoil-your-appetite. Diana's house had nothing in it that was good for you, and what's more, you could stuff it in right up until dinner and nobody cared. Bar-B-Q potato chips (they were the first in them, too), giant bottles of ginger ale, fresh popcorn with melted butter, hot fudge sauce on Baskin-Robbins Jamoca ice cream, powdered-sugar doughnuts from Van de Kamp's. Diana and I had been best friends since we were seven; we were about equally popular in school (which is to say, not particularly), we had about the same success with boys (extremely intermittent), and we looked much the same. Dark. Tall. Gangly.

It is September, just before school begins. I am eleven years old, about to enter the seventh grade, and Diana and I have not seen each other all summer. I have been to camp and she has been somewhere like Banff with her parents. We are meeting, as we often do, on the street midway between our two houses, and we will walk back to Diana's and eat junk and talk about what has happened to each of us that summer. I am walking down Walden Drive in my jeans and my father's shirt hanging out and my old red loafers with the socks falling into them and coming toward me is . . . I take a deep breath . . . a young woman. Diana. Her hair is curled and she has a waist and hips and a bust and she is wearing a straight skirt, an article of clothing I have been repeatedly told I will be unable to wear until I have the hips to hold it up. My jaw drops, and suddenly I am crying, crying hysterically, can't catch my breath sobbing. My best friend has betrayed me. She has gone ahead without me and done it. She has shaped up.

Here are some things I did to help:
  Bought a Mark Eden Bust Developer.

Slept on my back for four years.

Splashed cold water on them every night because some French actress said in *Life* magazine that that was what *she* did for her perfect bustline.

Ultimately, I resigned myself to a bad toss and began to wear padded bras. I think about them now, think about all those years in high school that I went around in them, my three padded bras, every single one of them with different-sized breasts. Each time I changed bras I changed sizes: one week nice perky but not too obtrusive breasts, the next medium-sized slightly pointy ones, the next week knockers, true knockers; all the time, whatever size I was, carrying around this rubberized appendage on my chest that occasionally crashed into a wall and was poked inward and had to be poked outward—I think about all that and wonder how anyone kept a straight face through it. My parents, who normally had no restraints about needling me—why did they say nothing as they watched my chest go up and down? My friends, who would periodically inspect my breasts for signs of growth and reassure me—why didn't they at least counsel consistency?

And the bathing suits. I die when I think about the bathing suits. That was the era when you could lay an uninhabited bathing suit on the beach and someone would make a pass at it. I would put one on, an absurd swimsuit with its enormous bust built into it, the bones from the suit stabbing me in the rib cage and leaving little red welts on my body, and there I would be, my chest plunging straight downward absolutely vertically from my collarbone to the top of my suit and then suddenly, wham, out came all that padding and material and wiring absolutely horizontally.

Buster Klepper was the first boy who ever touched them. He was my boyfriend my senior year of high school. There is a picture of him in my high-school yearbook that makes him look quite attractive in a Jewish, horn-rimmed-glasses sort of way, but the picture does not show the pimples, which were air-brushed out, or the dumbness. Well, that isn't really fair. He wasn't dumb. He just wasn't terribly bright. His mother refused to accept it, refused to accept the relentlessly average report cards, refused to deal with her son's inevitable destiny in some junior college or other. "He was tested," she would say to me, apropos of nothing, "and it came out a hundred and forty-five. That's near-genius." Had the word "underachiever" been coined, she probably would have lobbed that one at me, too. Anyway, Buster was really very sweet—which is, I know, damning with faint praise, but there it is. I was the editor of the front page of the high-school newspaper and he was editor of the back page; we had to work together, side by side, in the print shop, and that was how it started. On our first date, we went to see *April Love,* starring Pat Boone. Then we started going together. Buster had a green coupe, a 1950 Ford with an engine he had hand-chromed until it shone, dazzled, reflected the image of anyone who looked into it, anyone usually being Buster polishing it or the gas-station attendants he constantly asked to check the oil in order for them to be overwhelmed by the sparkle on the valves. The car also had a boot stretched over the back seat for reasons I never understood; hanging from the rearview mirror, as was the custom, was a pair of angora dice. A previous girlfriend named Solange, who was famous throughout Beverly Hills High School for having no pigment in her right eyebrow, had knitted them for him. Buster and I would ride around town, the two of us seated to the left of the steering wheel. I would shift gears. It was nice.

There was necking. Terrific necking. First in the car, overlooking Los Angeles from what is now the Trousdale Estates. Then on the bed of his parents' cabana at Ocean House. Incredibly wonderful, frustrating necking, I loved it, really, but no further than necking, please don't, please, because there I was absolutely terrified of the general implications of going-a-step-further with a near-dummy and also terrified of his finding out there was next to nothing there (which he knew, of course; he wasn't that dumb).

I broke up with him at one point. I think we were apart for about two weeks. At the end of that time, I drove down to see a friend at a boarding school in Palos Verdes Estates and a disc jockey played "April Love" on the radio four times during the trip. I took it as a sign. I drove straight back to Griffith Park to a golf tournament Buster was playing in (he was the sixth-seeded teenage golf player in Southern California) and presented myself back to him on the green of the eighteenth hole. It was all very dramatic. That night we went to a drive-in and I let him get his hand under my protuberances and onto my breasts. He really didn't seem to mind at all.

"Do you want to marry my son?" the woman asked me.

"Yes," I said.

I was nineteen years old, a virgin, going with this woman's son, this big strange woman who was married to a Lutheran minister in New Hampshire and pretended she was gentile and had this son, by her first husband, this total fool of a son who ran the hero-sandwich concession at Harvard Business School and whom for one moment one December in New Hampshire I said—as much out of politeness as anything else—that I wanted to marry.

"Fine," she said. "Now, here's what you do. Always make sure you're on top of him so you won't seem so small. My bust is very large, you see, so I always lie on my back to make it look smaller, but you'll have to be on top most of the time."

I nodded. "Thank you," I said.

"I have a book for you to read," she went on. "Take it with you when you leave. Keep it." She went to the bookshelf, found it, and gave it to me. It was a book on frigidity.

"Thank you," I said.

That is a true story. Everything in this article is a true story, but I feel I have to point out that that story in particular is true. It happened on December 30, 1960. I think about it often. When it first happened, I naturally assumed that the woman's son, my boyfriend, was responsible. I invented a scenario where he had had a little heart-to-heart with his mother and had confessed that his only objection to me was that my breasts were small; his mother then took it upon herself to help out. Now I think I was wrong about the incident. The mother was acting on her own, I think: that was her way of being cruel and competitive under the guise of being helpful and maternal. You have small breasts, she was saying; therefore you will never make him as happy as I have. Or you have small breasts; therefore you will doubtless have sexual problems. Or you have small breasts; therefore you are less woman than I am. She was, as it happens, only the first of what seems to me to be a never-ending string of women who have made competitive remarks to me about breast size. "I would love to wear a dress like that," my friend Emily says to me, "but my bust is too big." Like that. Why do women say these things to me? Do I attract these remarks the way other women attract married men or alcoholics or homosexuals? This summer, for example. I am at a party in East Hampton and I am introduced to a woman from Washington. She is a minor celebrity, very pretty and Southern and blond and outspoken, and I am flattered because she has read something I have written. We are talking animatedly, we have been talking no more than five minutes, when a man comes up to join us. "Look at the two of us," the woman says to the man, indicating me and her. "The two of us together couldn't fill an A cup." Why does she say that? It isn't even true, dammit, so why? Is she even more addled than I am on this subject? Does she honestly believe there is something wrong with her size breasts, which, it seems to me, now that I look hard at them, are just right? Do I unconsciously bring out competitiveness in women? In that form? What did I do to deserve it?

As for men.

There were men who minded and let me know that they minded. There were men who did not mind. In any case, *I* always minded.

And even now, now that I have been countlessly reassured that my figure is a good one, now that I am grown-up enough to understand that most of my feelings have very little to do with the reality of my shape, I am nonetheless obsessed by breasts. I cannot help it. I grew up in the terrible fifties—with rigid stereotypical sex roles, the insistence that men be men and dress like men and women be women and dress like women, the intolerance of androgyny—and I cannot shake it, cannot shake my feelings of inadequacy. Well, that time is gone, right? All those exaggerated examples of breast worship are gone, right? Those women were freaks, right? I know all that. And yet here I am, stuck with the psychological remains of it all, stuck with my own peculiar version of breast worship. You probably think I am crazy to go on like this: here I have set out to write a confession that is meant to hit you with the shock of recognition, and instead you are sitting there thinking I am thoroughly warped. Well, what can I tell you? If I had had them, I would have been a completely different person. I honestly believe that.

After I went into therapy, a process that made it possible for me to tell total strangers at cocktail parties that breasts were the hang-up of my life, I was often told that I was insane to have been bothered by my condition. I was also frequently told, by close friends, that I was extremely boring on the subject. And my girlfriends, the ones with nice big breasts, would go on endlessly about how their lives had been far more miserable than mine. Their bra straps were snapped in class. They couldn't sleep on their stomachs. They were stared at whenever the word "mountain" cropped up in geography. And *Evangeline,* good God what they went through every time someone had to stand up and recite the Prologue to Longfellow's *Evangeline:* ". . . stand like druids of eld . . . / With beards that rest on their bosoms." It was much worse for them, they tell me. They had a terrible time of it, they assure me. I don't know how lucky I was, they say.

I have thought about their remarks, tried to put myself in their place, considered their point of view. I think they are full of shit.

LEWIS THOMAS

Lewis Thomas (1913–1993), a biologist and physician, wrote essays that touched on scientific speculation—comfortingly urbane at first glance, then expanding in the mind. From the start, critics acknowledged his uncommon literary skill. His first book, The Lives of a Cell, *won the National Book Award, and he followed it up with five more collections. To call him simply a science writer would scant his appeal to readers who have no interest in science. Thomas's easy sense of authority may have derived initially from his specialist's knowledge, but he never played the pedant. Instead, he spoke in the voice of an amateur philosopher trying to figure out a puzzle. There was something of Michel de Montaigne in his skeptical stance, as well as a bit of E. B. White in his bemused geniality. By articulating how all living things are interdependent, he put the vanity of humans in its rightful place.*

The Lives of a Cell

(1974)

We are told that the trouble with Modern Man is that he has been trying to detach himself from nature. He sits in the topmost tiers of polymer, glass, and steel, dangling his pulsing legs, surveying at a distance the writhing life of the planet. In this scenario, Man comes on as a stupendous lethal force, and the earth is pictured as something delicate, like rising bubbles at the surface of a country pond, or flights of fragile birds.

But it is illusion to think that there is anything fragile about the life of the earth; surely this is the toughest membrane imaginable in the universe, opaque to probability, impermeable to death. We are the delicate part, transient and vulnerable as cilia. Nor is it a new thing for man to invent an existence that he imagines to be above the rest of life; this has been his most consistent intellectual exertion down the millennia. As illusion, it has never worked out to his satisfaction in the past, any more than it does today. Man is embedded in nature.

The biologic science of recent years has been making this a more urgent fact of life. The new, hard problem will be to cope with the dawning, intensifying realization of just how interlocked we are. The old, clung-to notions most of us have held about our special lordship are being deeply undermined.

Item. A good case can be made for our nonexistence as entities. We are not made up, as we had always supposed, of successively enriched packets of our own parts. We are shared, rented, occupied. At the interior of our cells, driving them, providing the oxidative energy that sends us out for the improvement of each shining day, are the mitochondria, and in a strict sense they are not ours. They turn out to be little separate creatures, the colonial posterity of migrant prokaryocytes, probably primitive bacteria that swam into ancestral precursors of our eukaryotic cells and stayed there. Ever since, they have maintained themselves and their ways, replicating in their own fashion, privately, with their own DNA and RNA quite different from ours. They are as much symbionts as the rhizobial bacteria in the roots of beans. Without them, we would not move a muscle, drum a finger, think a thought.

Mitochondria are stable and responsible lodgers, and I choose to trust them. But what of the other little animals, similarly established in my cells, sorting and balancing me, clustering me together? My centrioles, basal bodies, and probably a good many other more obscure tiny beings at work inside my cells, each with its own special genome, are as foreign, and as essential, as aphids in anthills. My cells are no longer the pure line entities I was raised with; they are ecosystems more complex than Jamaica Bay.

I like to think that they work in my interest, that each breath they draw for me, but perhaps it is they who walk through the local park in the early morning, sensing my senses, listening to my music, thinking my thoughts.

I am consoled, somewhat, by the thought that the green plants are in the same fix. They could not be plants, or green, without their chloroplasts, which run the photosynthetic enterprise and generate oxygen for the rest of us. As it turns out, chloroplasts are also separate creatures with their own genomes, speaking their own language.

We carry stores of DNA in our nuclei that may have come in, at one time or another, from the fusion of ancestral cells and the linking of ancestral organisms in symbiosis. Our genomes are catalogues of instructions from all kinds of sources in nature, filed for all kinds of contingencies. As for me, I am grateful for differentiation and speciation, but I cannot feel as separate an entity as I did a few years ago, before I was told these things, nor, I should think, can anyone else.

Item. The uniformity of the earth's life, more astonishing than its diversity, is accountable by the high probability that we derived, originally, from some single cell, fertilized in a bolt of lightning as the earth cooled. It is from the progeny of this parent cell that we take our looks; we still share genes around, and the resemblance of the enzymes of grasses to those of whales is a family resemblance.

The viruses, instead of being single-minded agents of disease and death, now begin to look more like mobile genes. Evolution is still an infinitely long and tedious biologic game, with only the winners staying at the table, but the rules are beginning to look more flexible. We live in a dancing matrix of viruses; they dart, rather like bees, from organism to organism, from plant to insect to mammal to me and back again, and into the sea, tugging along pieces of this genome, strings of genes from that, transplanting grafts of DNA, passing around heredity as though at a great party. They may be a mechanism for keeping new, mutant kinds of DNA in the widest circulation among us. If this is true, the odd virus disease, on which we must focus so much of our attention in medicine, may be looked on as an accident, something dropped.

Item. I have been trying to think of the earth as a kind of organism, but it is no go. I cannot think of it this way. It is too big, too complex, with too many working parts lacking visible connections. The other night, driving through a hilly, wooded part of southern New England, I wondered about this. If not like an organism, what is it like, what is it most like? Then, satisfactorily for that moment, it came to me: it is *most* like a single cell.

ANNIE DILLARD

Annie Dillard (1945–) has been a major figure in American nonfiction ever since her prose debut, Pilgrim at Tinker Creek, *which explored the area around her home in Virginia's Blue Ridge Mountains, and continuing with the essays in her collection* Teaching a Stone to Talk, *which rambled over different climates. Dillard has kept exploring the mysteries of the natural world and our subjective ways of taking them in; how and what we see, the very nature of perception, is a preoccupation of hers. In reading Dillard, we feel her urgency to convey with vivid images and metaphors the material present while sensing another, more elusive spiritual meaning just beneath the surface of her prose. Explaining her attachment to the essay, she commented: "The essayist does what we do with our lives; the essayist thinks about actual things. He can make sense of them analytically or artistically. In either case he renders the real world coherent and meaningful, even if only bits of it, and even if that coherence and meaning reside only inside small texts."*

On Foot in Virginia's Roanoke Valley

(1974)

I used to have a cat, an old fighting tom, who would jump through the open window by my bed in the middle of the night and land on my chest. I'd half awaken. He'd stick his skull under my nose and purr, stinking of urine and blood. Some nights he kneaded my bare chest with his front paws, powerfully, arching his back, as if sharpening his claws, or pummeling a mother for milk. Some mornings I'd wake in daylight to find my body covered with paw prints in blood; it looked as though I'd been painted with roses.

It was hot, so hot the mirror felt warm. I washed before the mirror in a daze, my twisted summer sleep still hung about me like sea kelp. What blood was this, and what roses? It could have been the rose of union, the blood of murder, or the rose of beauty bare and the blood of some unspeakable sacrifice or birth. The sign on my body could have been an emblem or a stain, the keys to the kingdom or the mark of Cain. I never knew. I never knew as I washed, and the blood streaked, faded, and finally disappeared, whether I'd purified myself or ruined the blood sign of the Passover. We wake, if we ever wake at all, to mystery, rumors of death, beauty, violence. . . . "Seem like we're just set down here," a woman said to me recently, "and don't nobody know why."

These are morning matters, pictures you dream as the final wave heaves you up on the sand to the bright light and drying air. You remember pressure, and a curved sleep you rested against, soft, like a scallop in its shell. But the air hardens your skin; you stand; leave the lighted shore to explore some dim headland, and soon you're lost in the leafy interior, intent, remembering nothing.

I still think of that old tomcat, mornings, when I wake. Things are tamer now; I sleep with the window shut. The cat and our rites are gone and my life is changed, but the memory remains of something powerful playing over me. I wake expectant, hoping to see a new thing. If I'm lucky I might be jogged awake by a strange birdcall. I dress in a hurry, imagining the yard flapping with auks, or flamingos. This morning it was a wood duck, down at the creek. It flew away.

I live by a creek, Tinker Creek, in a valley in Virginia's Blue Ridge. It's where I make myself scarce. An anchorite's hermitage is called an anchor-hold; some anchor-holds were simple sheds clamped to the side of a church like a barnacle to a rock. I think of this house clamped to the side of Tinker Creek as an anchor-hold. It holds me at anchor to the rock bottom of the creek itself and it keeps me steadied in the current, as a sea anchor does, facing the stream of light pouring down. It's a good place to live; there's a lot to think about.

The creeks—Tinker and Carvin's—are an active mystery, fresh every minute. Theirs is the mystery of the continuous creation and all that providence implies: the uncertainty of vision, the horror of the fixed, the dissolution of the present, the intricacy of beauty, the pressure of fecundity, the elusiveness of the free, and the flawed nature of perfection. The mountains—Tinker and Brushy, McAfee's Knob and Dead Man—are a

passive mystery, the oldest of all. Theirs is the one simple mystery of creation from nothing, of matter itself, anything at all, the given. Mountains
are giant, restful, absorbent. You can heave your spirit into a mountain
and the mountain will keep it, folded, and not throw it back as some
creeks will. The creeks are the world with all its stimulus and beauty; I
live there. But the mountains are home.

The wood duck flew away. I caught only a glimpse of something like a
bright torpedo that blasted the leaves where it flew. Back at the house I eat
a bowl of oatmeal; much later in the day will come the long slant of light
that means good walking.

If the day is fine, any walk will do; it all looks good. Water in particular looks its best, reflecting blue sky in the flat, and chopping it into
graveled shallows and white chute and foam in the riffles. On a dark day,
or a hazy one, even when everything else is washed-out and lackluster, the
water carries its own lights. I set out for the railroad tracks, for the hill
the flocks fly over, for the woods where the white mare lives. But first I go
to the water.

Today is one of those excellent January partly cloudies in which light
chooses an unexpected part of the landscape to trick out in gilt, and then
shadow sweeps it away. You know you're alive. You take huge steps, trying to feel the planet's roundness arc between your feet. Kazantzakis says
that when he was young he had a canary and a globe. When he freed the
canary, it would perch on the globe and sing. All his life, wandering the
earth, he felt as though he had a canary on top of his head, singing.

West of the house, Tinker Creek makes a sharp loop, so that the creek
is both in back of the house, south of me, and also on the other side of
the road, north of me. I like to go north. There the afternoon sun hits
the creek just right, deepening the reflected blue and lighting the sides of
trees on the banks. Steers from the pasture across the creek come down
to drink; I always flush a rabbit or two there. I sit on a fallen trunk in the
shade and watch the squirrels in the sun. There are two separated wooden
fences suspended from cables that cross the creek just upstream from my
tree-trunk bench. These fences keep the steers from escaping up or down
the creek when they come to drink. Squirrels, the neighborhood children,
and I use the downstream fence as a swaying bridge across the creek. But
the steers are there today.

I sit on the downed tree and watch the black steers slip on the creek
bottom. They are all bred beef: beef heart, beef hide, beef hocks. They're
a human product, like rayon. They're like a field of shoes. They have cast-
iron shanks and tongues like foam insoles. You can't see through to their
brains as you can with other animals; for there is beef fat behind their
eyes, beef stew.

I cross the fence six feet above the water, walking my hands down the rusty cable and tightroping my feet along the narrow edge of the planks. When I hit the other bank and terra firma, some steers are bunched in a knot between me and the barbed-wire fence I want to cross. So I suddenly rush at them in a wild sprint, flailing my arms and hollering, "Lightning! Copperhead! Swedish meatballs!" They flee, still in a knot, stumbling across the flat pasture. I stand with the wind on my face.

When I slide under the barbed-wire fence, cross a field, and run over a sycamore trunk felled across the water, I'm on a little island shaped like a tear in the middle of Tinker Creek. On one side of the creek is a steep forested bank; the water is swift and deep on that side of the island. On the other side is the level field I walked through next to the steers' pasture; the water between the field and the island is shallow and sluggish. In summer's low water, flags and bulrushes grow along a series of shallow pools cooled by the lazy current. Water striders patrol the surface film, crayfish hump along the silt bottom eating filth, frogs shout and glare, and shiners and small bream hide among roots from the sulky green heron's eye. I come to this island every month of the year. I walk around it, stopping and staring, or I straddle the sycamore log over the creek, curling my legs out of the water in winter, trying to read. Today I sit on dry grass at the end of the island by the slower side of the creek. I'm drawn to this spot. I come to it as to an oracle; I return to it as a man years later will seek out the battlefield where he lost a leg or an arm.

A couple of summers ago I was walking along the edge of the island to see what I could see in the water, and mainly to scare frogs. Frogs have an inelegant way of taking off from invisible positions on the bank just ahead of your feet, in dire panic, emitting a froggy "Yike!" and splashing into the water. Incredibly, this amused me, and, incredibly, it amuses me still. As I walked along the grassy edge of the island, I got better and better at seeing frogs in and out of the water. I learned to recognize, slowing down, the difference in texture of the light reflected from mudbank, water, grass, or frog. Frogs were flying all around me. At the end of the island I noticed a small green frog. He was exactly half in and half out of the water, looking like a schematic diagram of an amphibian. He didn't jump.

I crept closer. At last I knelt on the island's dead grass, lost, dumbstruck, staring at the frog in the creek not four feet away. He was a very small frog, with wide, dull eyes. And just as I looked at him, he slowly crumpled and began to sag. The spirit vanished from his eyes as if snuffed. His skin emptied and drooped; his skull itself seemed to collapse and settle like a kicked tent. He was shrinking before my eyes like a deflating football. I watched the taut, glistening skin on his shoulders ruck, and rumple, and fall. Soon, part of his skin, formless as a pricked balloon, lay in floating folds like bright scum on top of the water: It was a monstrous and terrifying thing. I gaped bewildered, appalled. An oval shadow hung in the water just behind the drained frog; then the shadow glided away. The frog skin bag started to sink.

I had read about the giant water bug, but never seen one. "Giant water bug" is in fact the name of the creature, which is an enormous, heavy-bodied brown bug. It eats insects, tadpoles, fish, and frogs. Its grasping forelegs are mighty and hooked inward. It seizes a victim with these legs, hugs it tight, and paralyzes it with enzymes injected during a vicious bite. That one bite is the only bite it ever takes. Through the puncture shoot the poisons that dissolve the victim's muscles and bones and organs— all but the skin. Then the giant water bug sucks out the victim's body, reduced to a juice. This event is quite common in warm freshwater. And now I'd seen it myself. I was still kneeling on the island grass when the unrecognizable flag of frog skin settled on the creek bottom, swaying. I stood up and brushed the knees of my pants. I couldn't catch my breath.

Many carnivorous animals, of course, devour their prey alive. The usual method seems to be to subdue the victim by downing or grasping it so it can't flee, then eating it whole or in a series of bloody bites. Frogs eat everything whole, stuffing prey in their mouth with their thumbs. People have seen frogs with their wide jaws so full of live dragonflies they couldn't close them. Ants don't even have to catch their prey: In the spring they swarm over newly hatched, featherless birds in the nest and eat them, tiny bite by tiny bite.

That it's rough out there and chancy is no surprise. Every live thing is a survivor on a kind of extended emergency bivouac. But at the same time we are also created. In the Qur'an, Allah asks, "The heaven and the earth and all in between, thinkest thou I made them *in jest?*" It's a good question. What do we think of the created universe, spanning an unthinkable void with an unthinkable profusion of forms? And what do we think of nothingness, those sickening reaches of time in either direction?

If the giant water bug was not made in jest, was it then made in earnest? Pascal uses a nice term to describe the notion of the creator's once having called forth the universe, turning his back to it: *Deus absconditus.* Is this what we think happened? Was the sense of it there, and God absconded with it, ate it, like a wolf who disappears round the edge of the house with the Thanksgiving turkey? "God is subtle," Einstein said, "but not malicious." Einstein also said that "nature conceals her mystery by means of her essential grandeur, not by her cunning."

It could be that God has not absconded but spread, as our vision and understanding of the universe have spread, to a fabric of spirit and sense so grand and subtle, so powerful in a new way, that we can only feel blindly of its hem. In making the thick darkness a swaddling band for the sea, God "set bars and doors" and said, "Hitherto shalt thou come, but no further." But have we come even that far? Have we rowed out to the thick darkness, or are we all playing pinochle in the bottom of the boat?

Cruelty is a mystery, and the waste of pain. But if we describe a world to encompass these things, a world that is a long, brute game, then we bump against another mystery: the inrush of power and light, the canary that sings on the skull. For unless all ages and races of men have been deluded by the same mass hypnotist (who?), there seems to be such a thing as beauty, a grace wholly gratuitous.

About five years ago I saw a mockingbird make a straight vertical descent from the roof gutter of a four-story building. It was an act as careless and spontaneous as the curl of a stem or the kindling of a star. The mockingbird took a single step into the air and dropped. His wings were still folded against his sides as though he were singing from a limb and not falling, accelerating thirty-two feet per second per second, through empty air. Just a breath before he would have been dashed to the ground, he unfurled his wings with exact, deliberate care, revealing the broad bars of white, spread his elegant, white-banded tail, and so floated onto the grass. I had just rounded a corner when his insouciant step off the gutter caught my eye; there was no one else in sight. The fact of his free fall was like the old philosophical conundrum about the tree that falls in the forest. The answer must be, I think, that beauty and grace are performed whether or not we will or sense them. The least we can do is try to be there.

Another time I saw a different wonder: sharks off the Atlantic coast of Florida. There is a way a wave rises above the ocean horizon, a triangular wedge against the sky. If you stand where the ocean breaks on a shallow beach, you see the raised water in a wave is in fact translucent, shot with lights. One late afternoon at low tide a hundred big sharks passed the beach near the mouth of a tidal river in a feeding frenzy. As each green wave rose from the churning water, it illuminated within itself the six- or eight-foot-long bodies of twisting sharks. The sharks disappeared as each wave rolled toward me; then a new wave swelled above the horizon, containing in it, like scorpions in amber, sharks that roiled and heaved. The sight held power and beauty, grace tangled in a rapture with violence.

We don't know what's going on here. If these tremendous events are random combinations of matter run amok, the yield of millions of monkeys at millions of typewriters, then what is it in us, hammered out of those same typewriters, that they ignite? We don't know. Our life is a faint tracing on the surface of mystery, like the idle, curved tunnels of leaf miners on the face of a leaf. We must somehow take a wider view, look at the whole landscape, really see it, and try to describe what's going on here. Then we can at least wail the right question into the swaddling band of darkness, or, if it comes to that, choir the proper praise.

At the time of Lewis and Clark, setting the prairies on fire was a well-known signal that meant "Come down to the water." It was an extravagant gesture, but we can't do less. If the landscape reveals one certainty, it is that the extravagant gesture is the very start and stuff of creation. The universe has continued to deal in extravagances, flinging intricacies and colossi down eons of emptiness, heaping profusions on profligacies with ever-fresh vigor. The whole show has been on fire from the word go. I come down to the water to cool my eyes. But everywhere I look I see fire; that which isn't flint is tinder and the whole world sparks and flames.

I have come to the grassy island late in the day. The creek is up; icy water sweeps under the sycamore log bridge. The frog skin, of course, is utterly gone. I have stared at that one spot on the creek bottom for so long, focusing past the rush of water, that when I stand, the opposite bank seems to stretch before my eyes and flow grassily upstream. When the bank settles down I cross the sycamore log and enter again the big plowed field next to the steers' pasture.

The wind is terrific out of the west; the sun comes and goes. I can see the shadow on the field before me deepen uniformly and spread like a plague. Everything seems so dull now I am amazed I can even distinguish objects. And suddenly the light runs across the land like a great comber, and up the trees, only to go again in a wink: I think I've gone blind or died. When it comes again, the light, you hold your breath, and if it stays you forget about it until it goes again.

It's the most beautiful day of the year. At four o'clock the eastern sky is a dead stratus black flecked with low white clouds. The sun in the west illuminates the ground, the mountains, and especially the bare branches of trees, so that everywhere silver trees cut into the black sky like a photographer's negative of a landscape. The air and the ground are dry; the mountains are flashing on and off like neon signs. Clouds slide east if pulled from the horizon, like a tablecloth whipped off a table. The hemlocks by the barbed-wire fence are flinging themselves east as though their backs would break. Purple shadows are racing east; the wind makes me face east, and again I feel dizzied and drawn, as I felt when the creek bank reeled.

At four-thirty the sky in the east is clear; how could that big blackness be blown? Fifteen minutes later another darkness comes overhead from the northwest; and it's here to stay. Everything drains of its light as if sucked. Only at the horizon do inky black mountains give way to distant, lighted mountains—lighted not by direct illumination but rather by paled glowing sets of mist hung before them. Now the blackness is in the east; everything is half in shadow, half in sun, every cloud, tree, mountain, and hedge. I can't see Tinker Mountain through the line of hemlock, till it comes on like a streetlight, ping, *ex nihilo*. Its sandstone cliffs pink and swell. Suddenly the light goes; the cliffs recede as if pushed. The sun hits a clump of sycamores between me and the mountains; the sycamore arms light up, and I can't see the cliffs. They're gone. The pale network of sycamore arms, which a second ago was transparent as a screen, is suddenly opaque, glowing with light. Now the sycamore arms snuff out, the mountains come on, and there are the cliffs again.

I walk home. By five-thirty the show has pulled out. Nothing is left but an unreal blue and a few banked clouds low in the north. Some sort of carnival magician has been here, some fast-talking worker of wonders who has the act backwards. "Something in this hand," he says, "something in this hand, something up my sleeve, something behind my back . . ." and abracadabra, he snaps his fingers: and it's all gone. Only the bland, blank-faced magician remains, in his unruffled cot, bare-handed, nodding at a smattering of baffled applause. When you look again the whole show has pulled up stakes and moved on down the road. It never stops. New shows roll in from over the mountains and the magician reappears unannounced from a fold in the curtain you never dreamed was an opening. Scarves of clouds, rabbits in plain view, disappear into the black hat forever. Presto chango. The audience, if there is one, is dizzy from head-turning, dazed.

Like the bear who went over the mountain, I went out to see what I could see. And, I might as well warn you, like the bear, all that I could see was the other side of the mountain: more of same. On a good day I might catch a glimpse of another wooded ridge rolling under the sun like water, another bivouac. I propose to keep here what Thoreau called "a meteorological journal of the mind," telling some tales and describing some of the sights of this rather tamed valley, and exploring, in fear and trembling, some of the unmapped dim reaches and unholy fastnesses to which those tales and sights so dizzyingly lead.

I am no scientist. I explore the neighborhood. An infant who has just learned to hold his head up has a frank and forthright way of gazing about him in bewilderment. He hasn't the faintest clue where he is, and he aims to learn. In a couple of years, what he will have learned instead is how to fake it: He'll have the cocksure air of a squatter who has come to feel he owns the place. Some unwonted, taught pride diverts us from our original intent, which is to explore the neighborhood, view the landscape, to discover at least *where* it is that we have been so startlingly set down, if we can't learn why.

So I think about the valley. It is my leisure as well as my work, a game. It is a fierce game I have joined because it is being played anyway, a game of both skill and chance, played against an unseen adversary—the conditions of time—in which the payoff, which may arrive at any moment in a blast of light, might as well come to me as anyone else. I stake the time I'm grateful to have, the energies I'm glad to direct. I risk getting stuck on the board, so to speak, unable to move in any direction, which happens enough, God knows; and I risk the searing, exhausting nightmares that plunder rest and force me facedown all night long in some muddy ditch seething with hatching insects and crustaceans.

But if I can bear the nights, the days are a pleasure. I walk out; I see something, some event I'd otherwise have utterly missed and lost; or something sees me, some enormous power brushes me with its clean wing, and I resound like a beaten bell.

I am an explorer, then, and I am also a stalker, or the instrument of the hunt itself. Certain Indians used to carve long grooves along the wooden shafts of the arrows. They called the grooves "lightning marks," because they resembled the curved fissure lightning slices down the trunks of trees. The function of lightning marks is this: If the arrow fails to kill the game, blood from a deep wound will channel along the lightning mark, streak down the arrow shaft, and spatter to the ground, laying a trail dripped on broad leaves, on stones, that the barefoot and trembling archer can follow into whatever deep or rare wilderness it leads. I am the arrow shaft, carved along my length by unexpected lights and gashes from the very sky, and this book is the straying trail of blood.

Something pummels us, something barely sheathed. Power broods and lights. We're played on like a pipe; our breath is not our own. James Houston describes two young Inuit girls sitting cross-legged on the ground, mouth on mouth, blowing by turns each other's throat cords, making a low, unearthly music. When I cross again the bridge that is really the steers' fence, the wind has thinned to the delicate air of twilight; it barely ruffles the water's skin. I watch the running sheets of light raised on the creek's surface. The sight has the appeal of the purely passive, like the racing of light under clouds on a field, the beautiful dream at the moment of being dreamed. The breeze is the merest puff, but you yourself sail headlong and breathless under the gale force of the spirit.

ADRIENNE RICH

Adrienne Rich (1929–2012) had established herself as one of the most skillful poets in the nation when she began writing essays that challenged the patriarchy's oppression of women. As a lesbian feminist, her object was to demonstrate how the personal and the political were joined (see her fine book on motherhood, Of Woman Born). As an essayist, she was to experiment boldly with varying approaches, such as the episodic, journal-entry format of "Women and Honor." In an explanatory note, she said: "I wrote 'Women and Honor' in an effort to make myself more honest, and to understand the terrible negative power of the lie in relationships among women. . . . It is clear that among women we need a new ethics; as women, a new morality. The problem of speech, of language, continues to be primary."

Women and Honor: Some Notes on Lying

(1975)

(These notes are concerned with relationships between and among women. When "personal relationship" is referred to, I mean a relationship between two women. It will be clear in what follows when I am talking about women's relationships with men.)

—

The old, male idea of honor. A man's "word" sufficed—to other men—without guarantee. "Our Land Free, Our Men Honest, Our Women Fruitful"—a popular colonial toast in America. Male honor also having something to do with killing: *I could not love thee, Dear, so much / Lov'd I not Honour more* ("To Lucasta, on Going to the Wars"). Male honor as something needing to be avenged: hence the duel.

Women's honor, something altogether else: virginity, chastity, fidelity to a husband. Honesty in women has not been considered important. We have been depicted as generically whimsical, deceitful, subtle, vacillating. And we have been rewarded for lying.

Men have been expected to tell the truth about facts, not about feelings. They have not been expected to talk about feelings at all.

Yet even about facts they have continually lied.

We assume that politicians are without honor. We read their statements trying to crack the code. The scandals of their politics: not that men in high places lie, only that they do so with such indifference, so endlessly, still expecting to be believed. We are accustomed to the contempt inherent in the political lie.

To discover that one has been lied to in a personal relationship, however, leads one to feel a little crazy.

Lying is done with words, and also with silence.

The woman who tells lies in her personal relationships may or may not plan or invent her lying. She may not even think of what she is doing in a calculated way.

A subject is raised which the liar wishes buried. She has to go downstairs, her parking meter will have run out. Or, there is a telephone call she ought to have made an hour ago.

She is asked, point-blank, a question which may lead into painful talk: "How do you feel about what is happening between us?" Instead of trying to describe her feelings in their ambiguity and confusion, she asks, "How do you feel?" The other, because she is trying to establish a ground of openness and trust, begins describing her own feelings. Thus the liar learns more than she tells.

And she may also tell herself a lie: that she is concerned with the other's feelings, not with her own.

But the liar is concerned with her own feelings.

The liar lives in fear of losing control. She cannot even desire a relationship without manipulation, since to be vulnerable to another person means for her the loss of control.

The liar has many friends, and leads an existence of great loneliness.

—

The liar often suffers from amnesia. Amnesia is the silence of the unconscious.

To lie habitually, as a way of life, is to lose contact with the unconscious. It is like taking sleeping pills, which confer sleep but blot out dreaming. The unconscious wants truth. It ceases to speak to those who want something else more than truth.

In speaking of lies, we come inevitably to the subject of truth. There is nothing simple or easy about this idea. There is no "the truth," "a truth"—truth is not one thing, or even a system. It is an increasing complexity. The pattern of the carpet is a surface. When we look closely, or when we become weavers, we learn of the tiny multiple threads unseen in the overall pattern, the knots on the underside of the carpet.

This is why the effort to speak honestly is so important. Lies are usually attempts to make everything simpler—for the liar—than it really is, or ought to be.

In lying to others we end up lying to ourselves. We deny the importance of an event, or a person, and thus deprive ourselves of a part of our lives. Or we use one piece of the past or present to screen out another. Thus we lose faith even with our own lives.

The unconscious wants truth, as the body does. The complexity and fecundity of dreams come from the complexity and fecundity of the unconscious struggling to fulfill that desire. The complexity and fecundity of poetry come from the same struggle.

An honorable human relationship—that is, one in which two people have the right to use the word "love"—is a process, delicate, violent, often terrifying to both persons involved, a process of refining the truths they can tell each other.

It is important to do this because it breaks down human self-delusion and isolation.

It is important to do this because in so doing we do justice to our own complexity.

It is important to do this because we can count on so few people to go that hard way with us.

I come back to the questions of women's honor. Truthfulness has not been considered important for women, as long as we have remained physically faithful to a man, or chaste.

We have been expected to lie with our bodies: to bleach, redden, unkink or curl our hair, pluck eyebrows, shave armpits, wear padding in various places or lace ourselves, take little steps, glaze finger and toe nails, wear clothes that emphasized our helplessness.

We have been required to tell different lies at different times, depending on what the men of the time needed to hear. The Victorian wife or the white southern lady, who were expected to have no sensuality, to "lie still"; the twentieth-century "free" woman who is expected to fake orgasms.

We have had the truth of our bodies withheld from us or distorted; we have been kept in ignorance of our most intimate places. Our instincts have been punished: clitoridectomies for "lustful" nuns or for "difficult" wives. It has been difficult, too, to know the lies of our complicity from the lies we believed.

The lie of the "happy marriage," of domesticity—we have been complicit, have acted out the fiction of a well-lived life, until the day we testify in court of rapes, beatings, psychic cruelties, public and private humiliations.

Patriarchal lying has manipulated women both through falsehood and through silence. Facts we needed have been withheld from us. False witness has been borne against us.

And so we must take seriously the question of truthfulness between women, truthfulness among women. As we cease to lie with our bodies, as we cease to take on faith what men have said about us, is a truly womanly idea of honor in the making?

Women have been forced to lie, for survival, to men. How to unlearn this among other women?

"Women have always lied to each other."

"Women have always whispered the truth to each other."

Both of these axioms are true.

"Women have always been divided against each other."

"Women have always been in secret collusion."

Both of these axioms are true.

In the struggle for survival we tell lies. To bosses, to prison guards, the police, men who have power over us, who legally own us and our children, lovers who need us as proof of their manhood.

There is a danger run by all powerless people: that we forget we are lying, or that lying becomes a weapon we carry over into relationships with people who do not have power over us.

I want to reiterate that when we talk about women and honor, or women and lying, we speak within the context of male lying, the lies of the powerful, the lie as false source of power.

Women have to think whether we want, in our relationships with each other, the kind of power that can be obtained through lying.

Women have been driven mad, "gaslighted," for centuries by the refutation of our experience and our instincts in a culture which validates only male experience. The truth of our bodies and our minds has been mystified to us. We therefore have a primary obligation to each other: not to undermine each other's sense of reality for the sake of expediency; not to gaslight each other.

Women have often felt insane when cleaving to the truth of our experience. Our future depends on the sanity of each of us, and we have a profound stake, beyond the personal, in the project of describing our reality as candidly and fully as we can to each other.

There are phrases which help us not to admit we are lying: "my privacy," "nobody's business but my own." The choices that underlie these phrases may indeed be justified; but we ought to think about the full meaning and consequences of such language.

Women's love for women has been represented almost entirely through silence and lies. The institution of heterosexuality has forced the lesbian to dissemble, or be labeled a pervert, a criminal, a sick or dangerous woman, etc., etc. The lesbian, then, has often been forced to lie, like the prostitute or the married women.

Does a life "in the closet"—lying, perhaps of necessity, about ourselves to bosses, landlords, clients, colleagues, family, because the law and public opinion are founded on a lie—does this, can it, spread into private life, so that lying (described as discretion) becomes an easy way to avoid conflict or complication? Can it become a strategy so ingrained that it is used even with close friends and lovers?

Heterosexuality as an institution has also drowned in silence the erotic feelings between women. I myself lived half a lifetime in the lie of that denial. That silence makes us all, to some degree, into liars.

When a woman tells the truth she is creating the possibility for more truth around her.

The liar leads an existence of unutterable loneliness.

The liar is afraid.

But we are all afraid: without fear we become manic, hubristic, self-destructive. What is this particular fear that possesses the liar?

She is afraid that her own truths are not good enough.

She is afraid, not so much of prison guards or bosses, but of something unnamed within her.

The liar fears the void.

The void is not something created by patriarchy, or racism, or capitalism. It will not fade away with any of them. It is part of every woman.

"The dark core," Virginia Woolf named it, writing of her mother. The dark core. It is beyond personality; beyond who loves us or hates us.

We begin out of the void, out of darkness and emptiness. It is part of the cycle understood by the old pagan religions, that materialism denies. Out of death, rebirth; out of nothing, something.

The void is the creatrix, the matrix. It is not mere hollowness and anarchy. But in women it has been identified with lovelessness, barrenness, sterility. We have been urged to fill our "emptiness" with children. We are not supposed to go down into the darkness of the core.

Yet, if we can risk it, the something born of that nothing is the beginning of our truth.

The liar in her terror wants to fill up the void, with anything. Her lies are a denial of her fear; a way of maintaining control.

Why do we feel slightly crazy when we realize we have been lied to in a relationship?

We take so much of the universe on trust. You tell me: "In 1950 I lived on the north side of Beacon Street in Somerville." You tell me: "She and I were lovers, but for months now we have only been good friends." You tell me: "It is seventy degrees outside and the sun is shining." Because I love you, because there is not even a question of lying between us, I take these accounts of the universe on trust: your address twenty-five years ago, your relationship with someone I know only on sight, this morning's weather. I fling unconscious tendrils of belief, like slender green threads, across statements such as these, statements made so unequivocally, which have no tone or shadow of tentativeness. I build them into the mosaic of my world. I allow my universe to change in minute, significant ways, on the basis of things you have said to me, of my trust in you.

I also have faith that you are telling me things it is important I should know; that you do not conceal facts from me in an effort to spare me, or yourself, pain.

Or, at the very least, that you will say, "There are things I am not telling you."

When we discover that someone we trusted can be trusted no longer, it forces us to reexamine the universe, to question the whole instinct and concept of trust. For awhile, we are thrust back onto some bleak, jutting edge, in a dark pierced by sheets of fire, swept by sheets of rain, in a world before kinship, or naming, or tenderness exist; we are brought close to formlessness.

—

The liar may resist confrontation, denying that she lied. Or she may use other language: forgetfulness, privacy, the protection of someone else. Or, she may bravely declare herself a coward.

This allows her to go on lying, since that is what cowards do. She does not say, *I was afraid,* since this would open the question of other ways of handling her fear. It would open the question of what is actually feared.

She may say, *I didn't want to cause pain.* What she really did not want is to have to deal with the other's pain. The lie is a short-cut through another's personality.

Truthfulness, honor, is not something which springs ablaze of itself. It has to be created between people.

This is true in political situations. The quality and depth of the politics evolving from a group depends in very large part on their understanding of honor.

Much of what is narrowly termed "politics" seems to rest on a longing for certainty even at the cost of honesty, for an analysis which, once given, need not be reexamined. Such is the deadendedness—for women—of Marxism in our time.

Truthfulness anywhere means a heightened complexity. But it is a movement into evolution. Women are only beginning to uncover our own truths; many of us would be grateful for some rest in that struggle, would be glad just to lie down with the sherds we have painfully unearthed, and be satisfied with those. Often I feel this like an exhaustion in my own body.

The politics worth having, the relationships worth having, demand that we delve still deeper.

The possibilities that exist between two people, or among a group of people, are a kind of alchemy.

They are the most interesting thing in life. The liar is someone who keeps losing sight of these possibilities.

When relationships are determined by manipulation, by the need for control, they may possess a dreary, bickering kind of drama, but they cease to be interesting. They are repetitious; the shock of human possibilities has ceased to reverberate through them.

When someone tells me a piece of truth which has been withheld from me, and which I needed in order to see my life more clearly, it may bring acute pain, but it can also flood me with a cold, sea-sharp wash of relief. Often such truths come by accident, or from strangers.

It isn't that to have an honorable relationship with you, I have to understand everything, or tell you everything at once, or that I can know, beforehand, everything I need to tell you.

It means that most of the time I am eager, longing for the possibility of telling you. That these possibilities may seem frightening, but not destructive, to me. That I feel strong enough to hear your tentative and groping words. That we both know we are trying, all the time, to extend the possibilities of truth between us.

The possibility of life between us.

ELIZABETH HARDWICK

Elizabeth Hardwick (1916–2007), literary critic, novelist, and essayist, is held in the highest esteem today, particularly by other critics, who regard her as a writer's writer. Her prose style is highly polished, angular, pithy, and flavorful. As a critic she could be harsh or favorable, but never mealy-mouthed (as she felt much book reviewing to be). Her portrait of the great jazz singer Billie Holiday was originally published as an essay in The New York Review of Books, *a periodical she helped found. Later, she incorporated it into her autobiographic novel,* Sleepless Nights, *which raises the category question: Should it be considered fiction or nonfiction? Whichever, it is a consummate example of Hardwick's commanding mind at work.*

Billie Holiday

(1976)

"The unspeakable vices of Mecca are a scandal to all Islam and constant source of wonder to pious pilgrims." As a pilgrim to Mecca, I lived at the Hotel Schuyler on West 45th Street in Manhattan, lived with a red-cheeked, homosexual young man from Kentucky. We had known each other all our lives. Our friendship was a violent one and we were as obsessive, critical, jealous, and cruel as any couple. Often I lay awake all night in a rage over some delinquency of his during the day. His coercive neatness inflamed me at times, as if his habits were not his right but instead a dangerous poison to life, like the slow seepage from the hotel stove. His clothes were laid out on the bed for the next day; and worst of all he had an unyielding need to brush his teeth immediately after dinner in the evening. This finally meant that no fortuitous invitation, no lovely possibility arising unannounced could be accepted without a concentrated uneasiness of mind. These holy habits ruined his sex life, even though he was, like the tolling of a time bell, to be seen every Saturday night at certain gay bars, drinking his ration of beer.

My friend had, back in Kentucky, developed a passion for jazz. This study seized him and he brought to it the methodical, intense, dogmatic anxiety of his nature. I learned this passion from him. It is a curious learning that cuts into your flesh, leaving a scar, a longing never satisfied, a wound of feeling hard to live with. It can be distressing to listen to jazz when one is troubled, alone, with the "wrong" person. Things can happen in your life that cause you to give it up altogether. Yet, under its dominion, it may be said that one is more likely to commit suicide listening to "Them There Eyes" than to Opus 132. What is it? ". . . the sea itself, or is it youth alone?"

We lived there in the center of Manhattan, believing the very placing of the hotel to be an overwhelming beneficence. To live in the obscuring jungle of the midst of things: close to—what? Within walking distance of all those places one never walked to. But it was history, wasn't it? The acrimonious twilight fell in the hollows between the gray and red buildings. Inside the hotel was a sort of underbrush, a swampy footing for the irregular. The brooding inconsequence of the old hotel dwellers, their delusions and disappearances. They lived as if in a house recently burglarized, wires cut, their world vandalized, by themselves, and cheerfully enough, also. Do not imagine they received nothing in return. They got a lot, I tell you. They were lifted by insolence above their car loans, their surly arrears, their misspent matrimonies.

The small, futile shops around us explained how little we know of ourselves and how perplexing are our souvenirs and icons. I remember strangers to the city, in a daze, making decisions, exchanging coins and bills for the incurious curiosities, the unexceptional novelties. Sixth Avenue lies buried in the drawers, bureaus, boxes, attics, and cellars of grandchildren. There, blackening, are the dead watches, the long, oval rings for the little finger, the smooth pieces of polished wood shaped into a long-chinned African head, the key rings of the Empire State building. And for us, there were the blaring shops, open most of the night, where one could buy old, scratched, worn-thin jazz records—Vocalion, Okeh, and Brunswick labels. Our hands sliced through the cases until the skin around our fingers bled.

Yes, there were the records, priceless flotsam they seemed to us then. And the shifty jazz clubs on 52nd Street. The Onyx, the Down Beat, the

Three Deuces. At the curb, getting out of a taxi, or at the White Rose Bar drinking, there "they" were, the great performers with their worn, brown faces, enigmatic in the early evening, their coughs, their broken lips and yellow eyes; their clothes, crisp and bright and hard as the bone-fibered feathers of a bird. And there she was—the "bizarre deity," Billie Holiday.

At night in the cold winter moonlight, around 1943, the city pageantry was of a benign sort. Young adolescents were then asleep and the threat was only in the landscape, aesthetic. Dirty slush in the gutters, a lost black overshoe, a pair of white panties, perhaps thrown from a passing car. Murderous dissipation went with the music, inseparable, skin and bone. And always her luminous self-destruction.

She was fat the first time we saw her, large, brilliantly beautiful, fat. She seemed for this moment that never again returned to be almost a matron, someone real and sensible who carried money to the bank, signed papers, had curtains made to match, dresses hung and shoes in pairs, gold and silver, black and white, ready. What a strange, betraying apparition that was, madness, because never was any woman less a wife or mother, less attached; not even a daughter could she easily appear to be. Little called to mind the pitiful sweetness of a young girl. No, she was glittering, somber, and solitary, although of course never alone, never. Stately, sinister, and absolutely determined.

The creamy lips, the oily eyelids, the violent perfume—and in her voice the tropical l's and r's. Her presence, her singing created a large, swelling anxiety. Long red fingernails and the sound of electrified guitars. Here was a woman who had never been a Christian.

To speak as part of the white audience of "knowing" this baroque and puzzling phantom is an immoderation; and yet there are many persons, discrete and reasonable, who have little splinters of memory that seem to have been *personal*. At times they have remembered an exchange of some sort. And always the lascivious gardenia, worn like a large, white, beautiful ear, the heavy laugh, marvelous teeth, and the splendid archaic head, dragged up from the Aegean. Sometimes she dyed her hair red and the curls lay flat against her skull, like dried blood.

Early in the week the clubs were *dead,* as they spoke of it. And the chill of failure inhabited the place, visible in the cold eyes of the owners. These men, always changing, were weary with futile calculations. They often held their ownership so briefly that one could scarcely believe the ink dry on the license. They started out with the embezzler's hope and moved swiftly to the bankrupt's torpor. The bartenders—thin, watchful, stubbornly crooked, resentful, silent thieves. Wandering soldiers, drunk and worried, musicians, and a few people, couples, hideously looking into each other's eyes, as if they were safe.

My friend and I, peculiar and tense, experienced during the quiet nights a tainted joy. Then, showing our fidelity, it seemed that a sort of motif would reveal itself, that under the glaze ancient patterns from a lost world were to be discovered. The mind strains to recover the blank spaces in history, and our pale, gray-green eyes looked into her swimming, dark, inconstant pools—and got back nothing.

In her presence on these tranquil nights it was possible to experience the depths of her disbelief, to feel sometimes the mean, horrible freedom of a thorough suspicion of destiny. And yet the heart always drew back from the power of her will and its engagement with disaster. An inclination bred upon punishing experiences compelled her to live gregariously and without affections. Her talents and the brilliance of her mind contended with the strength of the emptiness. Nothing should degrade this genuine nihilism; and so, in a sense, it is almost a dishonor to imagine that she lived in the lyrics of her songs.

Her message was otherwise. It was *style*. That was her meaning from the time she began at fifteen. It does not change the victory of her great effort, of the miraculous discovery or retrieval from darkness of pure style, to know that it was exercised on "I love my man, tell the world I do. . . ." How strange it was to me, almost unbalancing, to be sure that she did not love any man, or anyone. Also often one had the freezing perception that her own people, those around her, feared her. One thing she was ashamed of—or confused by, rather—that she was not sentimental.

In my youth, at home in Kentucky, there was a dance place just outside of town called Joyland Park. In the summer the great bands arrived, Ellington, Louis Armstrong, Chick Webb, sometimes for a Friday and Saturday or merely for one night. When I speak of the great bands it must not be taken to mean that we thought of them as such. No, they were part of the summer nights and the hot dog stands, the fetid swimming pool heavy with chlorine, the screaming roller coaster, the old rain-splintered picnic tables, the broken iron swings. And the bands were also part of Southern drunkenness, couples drinking coke and whisky, vomiting, being unfaithful, lovelorn, frantic. The black musicians, with their cumbersome instruments, their tuxedos, were simply there to beat out time for the stumbling, cuddling fox-trotting of the period.

The band busses, parked in the field, the caravans in which they suffered the litter of cigarettes and bottles, the hot, streaking highways, all night, or resting for a few hours in the black quarters: the Via Dolorosa of show business. They arrived at last, nowhere, to audiences large or small, often with us depending upon the calendar of the Park, the other occasions from which the crowd would spill over into the dance hall. Ellington's band. And what were we doing, standing close, murmuring the lyrics?

At our high school dances in the winter, small, cheap, local events. We had our curls, red taffeta dresses, satin shoes with their new dye fading in the rain puddles; and most of all we were dressed in our ferocious hope for popularity. This was stifling blanket, an airless tent; gasping, grinning, we stood anxious-eyed, next to the piano, hovering about Fats Waller who had come from Cincinnati for the occasion. Requests, perfidious glances, drunken teenagers, nodding teacher-chaperones: these we offered to the music, looking upon it, I suppose, as something inevitable, effortlessly pushing up from the common soil.

On 52nd Street: "Yeah, I remember your town," she said, without inflection.

And I remember her dog, Boxer. She was one of those women who admire large, overwhelming, impressive dogs and who give to them a care and courteous punctuality denied everything else. Several times we waited in panic for her in the bar of the Hotel Braddock in Harlem. (My friend, furious and tense with his new, hated work in "public relations," was now trying without success to get her name in Winchell's column. Today we were waiting to take her downtown to sit for the beautiful photographs Robin Carson took of her.) At the Braddock, the porters took plates of meat for the dog to her room. Soon, one of her friends, appearing almost like a child, so easily broken were others by the powerful, energetic horrors of her life, one of those young people would take the great dog to the street. These animals, asleep in dressing rooms, were like sculptured treasures, fit for the tomb of a queen.

The sheer enormity of her vices. The outrageousness of them. For the grand destruction one must be worthy. Her ruthless talent and the opulent devastation. Onto the heaviest addiction to heroin she piled up the rocks of her tomb with a prodigiousness of Scotch and brandy. She was never at any hour of the day or night free of these consumptions, never except when she was asleep. And there did not seem to be any pleading need to quit, to modify. With cold anger she spoke of various cures that had been forced upon her, and she would say, bearing down heavily, as sure of her rights as if she had been robbed, "And I paid for it myself." Out of a term at the Federal Women's Prison in West Virginia she stepped, puffy from a diet of potatoes, onto the stage of Town Hall to pick up some money and start up again the very day of release.

Still, even with her, authenticity was occasionally disrupted. An invitation for chili—improbable command. We went up to a street in Harlem just as the winter sun was turning black. Darkened windows with thin bands of watchful light above the sills. Inside the halls were dark and empty, filled only with the scent of dust. We, our faces bleached from the cold, in our thin coats, black gloves, had clinging to us the evangelical diffidence of bell-ringing members of a religious sect, a determination glacial, timid, and yet pedantic. Our frozen alarm and fascination carried us into the void of the dead tenement. The house was under a police ban and when we entered, whispering her name, the policeman stared at us with furious incredulity. She was hounded by the police, but for once the occasion was not hers. Somewhere, upstairs, behind another door there had been a catastrophe.

Her own records played over and over on the turntable; everything else was quiet. All of her living places were temporary in the purest meaning of the term. But she filled even a black hotel room with a stinging, demonic weight. At the moment she was living with a trumpet player who was just becoming known and who soon after faded altogether. He was as thin as a stick and his lovely, round, light face, with frightened, shiny, round eyes, looked like a sacrifice impaled upon the stalk of his neck. His younger brother came out of the bedroom. He stood before us, wavering between confusing possibilities. Tiny, thin, perhaps in his twenties, the young man was engrossed in a blur of functions. He was a sort of hectic Hermes, working in Hades, now buying cigarettes, now darting back to the bedroom, now almost inaudible on the phone, ordering or disposing of something in a light, shaking voice.

"Lady's a little behind. She's over-scheduled herself." Groans and coughs from the bedroom. In the peach-shaded lights, the wan rosiness of a beaten sofa was visible. A shell, still flushed from the birth of some crustacean, was filled with cigarette ends. A stocking on the floor. And the record player, on and on, with the bright clarity of her songs. Smoke and perfume and somewhere a heart pounding.

One winter she wore a great lynx coat and in it she moved, menacing and handsome as a Cossack, pacing about in the trap of her vitality. Quarrelsome dreams sometimes rushed through her speech, and accounts of wounds she had inflicted with broken glass. And at the White Rose Bar, a thousand cigarettes punctuated her appearances, which, not only in their brilliance but in the fact of their taking place at all, had about them the aspect of magic. Waiting and waiting: that was what the pursuit of her was. One felt like an old carriage horse standing at the entrance, ready for the cold midnight race through the park. She was always behind a closed door—the fate of those addicted to whatever. And then at last she must come forward, emerge in powders and Vaseline, hair twisted with a curling iron, gloves of satin or silk jersey, flowers—the expensive martyrdom of the "entertainer."

At that time not so many of her records were in print and she was seldom heard on the radio because her voice did not accord with popular taste then. The appearances in night clubs were a necessity. It was a burden to be there night after night, although not a burden to sing, once she had started, in her own way. She knew she could do it, that she had mastered it all, but why not ask the question: Is this all there is? Her work took on, gradually, a destructive cast, as it so often does with the greatly gifted who are doomed to repeat endlessly their own heights of inspiration.

She was late for her mother's funeral. At last she arrived, ferociously appropriate in a black turban. A number of jazz musicians were there. The late morning light fell mercilessly on their unsteady, night faces. In the daytime these people, all except Billie, had a furtive, suburban aspect, like family men who work the night shift. The marks of a fractured domesticity, signals of a real life that is itself almost a secret existence for the performer, were drifting about the little church, adding to the awkward unreality.

Her mother, Sadie Holiday, was short and sentimental, bewildered to be the bearer of such news to the world. She made efforts to *sneak* into Billie's life, but there was no place and no need for her. She was set up from time to time in small restaurants which she ran without any talent and failed in quickly. She never achieved the aim of her life, the professional dream, which was to be "Billie's dresser." The two women bore no resemblance, neither of face nor of body. The daughter was profoundly intelligent and found the tragic use for it in the cunning of destruction. The mother seemed to face each day with the bald hopefulness of a baby and end each evening in a baffled little cry of disappointment. Sadie and Billie Holiday were a violation, a rift in the statistics of life. The great singer was one of those for whom the word *changeling* was invented. She shared the changeling's spectacular destiny and was acquainted with malevolent forces.

She lived to be forty-four; or should it better be said she died at forty-four. Of "enormous complications." Was it a long or a short life? The "highs" she sought with such concentration of course remained a mystery. "Ah, I fault Jimmy for all that," someone said once in a taxi, naming her first husband, Jimmy Monroe, a fabulous Harlem club owner when she was young.

Once she came to see us in the Hotel Schuyler, accompanied by someone. We sat there in the neat squalor and there was nothing to do and nothing to say and she did not wish to eat. In the anxious gap, I felt the deepest melancholy in her black eyes, an abyss into which every question had fallen without an answer. She died in misery from the erosions and poisons of her fervent, felonious narcotism. The police were at the hospital bedside, vigilant lest she, in a coma, manage a last chemical inner migration.

Her whole life had taken place in the dark. The spotlight shone down on the black, hushed circle in a café; the moon slowly slid through the clouds. Night-working, smiling, in make-up, in long, silky dresses, singing over and over, again and again. The aim of it all is just to be drifting off to sleep when the first rays of the sun's brightness threaten the theatrical eyelids.

EDWARD ABBEY

Edward Abbey (1927–1989) cultivated an image of himself as a grizzled, cantankerous, anarchist loner unafraid to speak unpopular truths. Having worked off and on as a park ranger, he became a passionate environmentalist and defender of the unspoiled wilderness. His Desert Solitaire *is considered a classic of American nature writing, in the tradition of Henry David Thoreau, John Muir, and Aldo Leopold, though his prose style was far more earthy, jokey, and profane than theirs. Perhaps he belongs more with Hunter S. Thompson, Lester Bangs, Seymour Krim, and Tom Wolfe as another writer of the 1960s and '70s trying to crack open the decorous surface of American nonfiction prose.*

The Great American Desert

(1977)

In my case it was love at first sight. This desert, all deserts, any desert. No matter where my head and feet may go, my heart and my entrails stay behind, here on the clean, true, comfortable rock, under the black sun of God's forsaken country. When I take on my next incarnation, my bones will remain bleaching nicely in a stone gulch under the rim of some faraway plateau, way out there in the back of beyond. An unrequited and excessive love, inhuman no doubt but painful anyhow, especially when I see my desert under attack. "The one death I cannot bear," said the Sonoran-Arizonan poet Richard Shelton. The kind of love that makes a man selfish, possessive, irritable. If you're thinking of a visit, my natural reaction is like a rattlesnake's—to warn you off. What I want to say goes something like this.

Survival Hint #1: Stay out of there. Don't go. Stay home and read a good book, this one for example. The Great American Desert is an awful place. People get hurt, get sick, get lost out there. Even if you survive, which is not certain, you will have a miserable time. The desert is for movies and God-intoxicated mystics, not for family recreation.

Let me enumerate the hazards. First the Walapai tiger, also known as conenose kissing bug. *Triatoma protracta* is a true bug, black as sin, and it flies through the night quiet as an assassin. It does not attack directly like a mosquito or deerfly but alights at a discreet distance, undetected, and creeps upon you, its hairy little feet making not the slightest noise. The kissing bug is fond of warmth and like Dracula requires mammalian blood for sustenance. When it reaches you the bug crawls onto your skin so gently, so softly that unless your senses are hyperacute you feel nothing. Selecting a tender point, the bug slips its conical proboscis into your flesh, injecting a poisonous anesthetic. If you are asleep you will feel nothing. If you happen to be awake you may notice the faintest of pinpricks, hardly more than a brief ticklish sensation, which you will probably disregard. But the bug is already at work. Having numbed the nerves near the point of entry the bug proceeds (with a sigh of satisfaction) to withdraw blood. When its belly is filled, it pulls out, backs off, and waddles away, so drunk and gorged it cannot fly.

At about this time the victim awakes, scratching at a furious itch. If you recognize the symptoms at once, you can sometimes find the bug in your vicinity and destroy it. But revenge will be your only satisfaction. Your night is ruined. If you are of average sensitivity to a kissing bug's poison your entire body breaks out in hives, skin aflame from head to toe. Some people become seriously ill, in many cases requiring hospitalization. Others recover fully after five or six hours except for a hard and itchy swelling which may endure for a week.

After the kissing bug, you should beware of rattlesnakes; we have half a dozen species, all offensive and dangerous, plus centipedes, millipedes, tarantulas, black widows, brown recluses, Gila monsters, the deadly poisonous coral snakes, and giant hairy desert scorpions. Plus an immense variety and near infinite number of ants, ticks, midges, gnats, bloodsucking flies, and blood-guzzling mosquitoes. (You might think the desert would be spared at least mosquitoes? Not so. Peer in any water hole by day: swarming with mosquito larvae. Venture out on a summer's eve: The air vibrates with their mournful keening.) Finally, where the desert meets the sea, as on the coasts of Sonora and Baja California, we have the usual assortment of obnoxious marine life: sandflies, ghost crabs, stingrays, electric jellyfish, spiny sea urchins, man-eating sharks, and other creatures so distasteful one prefers not even to name them.

It has been said, and truly, that everything in the desert either stings, stabs, stinks, or sticks. You will find the flora here as venomous, hooked, barbed, thorny, prickly, needled, saw-toothed, hairy, stickered, mean, bitter, sharp, wiry, and fierce as the animals. Something about the desert inclines all living things to harshness and acerbity. The soft evolve out. Except for sleek and oily growths like the poison ivy—oh yes, indeed—that flourish in sinister profusion on the dank walls above the quicksand down in those corridors of gloom and labyrinthine monotony that men call canyons.

We come now to the third major hazard, which is sunshine. Too much of a good thing can be fatal. Sunstroke, heatstroke, and dehydration are common misfortunes in the bright American Southwest. If you can avoid the insects, reptiles, and arachnids, the cactus and the ivy, the smog of the southwestern cities and the lung fungus of the desert valleys (carried by dust in the air), you cannot escape the desert sun. Too much exposure to it eventually causes, quite literally, not merely sunburn but skin cancer.

Much sun, little rain also means an arid climate. Compared with the high humidity of more hospitable regions, the dry heat of the desert seems at first not terribly uncomfortable—sometimes even pleasant. But that sensation of comfort is false, a deception, and therefore all the more dangerous, for it induces overexertion and an insufficient consumption of water, even when water is available. This leads to various internal complications, some immediate—sunstroke, for example—and some not apparent until much later. Mild but prolonged dehydration, continued over a span of months or years, leads to the crystallization of mineral solutions in the urinary tract, that is, to what urologists call urinary calculi or kidney stones. A disability common in all the world's arid regions. Kidney stones, in case you haven't met one, come in many shapes and sizes, from pellets smooth as BB shot to highly irregular calcifications resembling asteroids, Vietcong shrapnel, and crown-of-thorns starfish. Some of these objects may be "passed" naturally; others can be removed only by means of the Davis stone basket or by surgery. Me—I was lucky; I passed mine with only a groan, my forehead pressed against the wall of a pissoir in the rear of a Tucson bar that I cannot recommend.

You may be getting the impression by now that the desert is not the most suitable of environments for human habitation. Correct. Of all the Earth's climatic zones, excepting only the Antarctic, the deserts are the least inhabited, the least "developed," for reasons that should now be clear.

You may wish to ask, Yes, okay, but among North American deserts which is the *worst*? A good question—and I am happy to attempt an answer.

Geographers generally divide the North American desert—what was once termed "the Great American Desert"—into four distinct regions or subdeserts. These are the Sonoran Desert, which comprises southern Arizona, Baja California, and the state of Sonora in Mexico; the Chihuahuan Desert, which includes west Texas, southern New Mexico, and the states of Chihuahua and Coahuila in Mexico; the Mojave Desert, which includes southeastern California and small portions of Nevada, Utah, and Arizona; and the Great Basin Desert, which includes most of Utah and Nevada, northern Arizona, northwestern New Mexico, and much of Idaho and eastern Oregon.

Privately, I prefer my own categories. Up north in Utah somewhere is the canyon country—places like Zeke's Hole, Death Hollow, Pucker Pass, Buckskin Gulch, Nausea Crick, Wolf Hole, Mollie's Nipple, Dirty Devil River, Horse Canyon, Horseshoe Canyon, Lost Horse Canyon, Horsethief Canyon, and Horseshit Canyon, to name only the more classic places. Down in Arizona and Sonora there's the cactus country; if you have nothing better to do, you might take a look at High Tanks, Salome Creek, Tortilla Flat, Esperero ("Hoper") Canyon, Holy Joe Peak, Depression Canyon, Painted Cave, Hell Hole Canyon, Hell's Half Acre, Iceberg Canyon, Tiburon (Shark) Island, Pinacate Peak, Infernal Valley, Sykes Crater, Montezuma's Head, Gu Oidak, Kuakatch, Pisinimo, and Baboquivari Mountain, for example.

Then there's The Canyon. *The* Canyon. The Grand. That's one world. And North Rim—that's another. And Death Valley, still another, where I lived one winter near Furnace Creek and climbed the Funeral Mountains, tasted Badwater, looked into the Devil's Hole, hollered up Echo Canyon, searched for and never did find Seldom Seen Slim. Looked for *satori* near Vana, Nevada, and found a ghost town named Bonnie Claire. Never made it to Winnemucca. Drove through the Smoke Creek Desert and down through Big Pine and Lone Pine and home across the Panamints to Death Valley again—home sweet home that winter.

And which of these deserts is the worst? I find it hard to judge. They're all bad—not half bad but all bad. In the Sonoran Desert, Phoenix will get you if the sun, snakes, bugs, and arthropods don't. In the Mojave Desert it's Las Vegas, more sickening by far than the Glauber's salt in the Death Valley sinkholes. Go to Chihuahua and you're liable to get busted in El Paso and sandbagged in Ciudad Juárez—where all old whores go to die. Up north in the Great Basin Desert, on the Plateau Province, in the canyon country, your heart will break, seeing the strip mines open up and the power plants rise where only cowboys and Indians and J. Wesley Powell ever roamed before.

Nevertheless, all is not lost; much remains, and I welcome the prospect of an army of lug-soled hiker's boots on the desert trails. To save what wilderness is left in the American Southwest—and in the American Southwest only the wilderness is worth saving—we are going to need all the recruits we can get. All the hands, heads, bodies, time, money, effort we can find. Presumably—and the Sierra Club, the Wilderness Society, the Friends of the Earth, the Audubon Society, the Defenders of Wildlife operate on this theory—those who learn to love what is spare, rough, wild, undeveloped, and unbroken will be willing to fight for it, will help resist the strip miners, highway builders, land developers, weapons testers, power producers, tree chainers, clear cutters, oil drillers, dam beavers, subdividers—the list goes on and on—before that zinc-hearted, termite-brained, squint-eyed, near-sighted, greedy crew succeeds in completely californicating what still survives of the Great American Desert.

So much for the Good Cause. Now what about desert hiking itself, you may ask. I'm glad you asked that question. I firmly believe that one should never—I repeat *never*—go out into that formidable wasteland of cactus, heat, serpents, rock, scrub, and thorn without careful planning, thorough and cautious preparation, and complete—never mind the expense!—*complete* equipment. My motto is: Be Prepared.

That is my belief and that is my motto. My practice, however, is a little different. I tend to go off in a more or less random direction myself, half-baked, half-assed, half-cocked, and half-ripped. Why? Well, because I have an indolent and melancholy nature and don't care to be bothered getting all those things together—all that bloody gear—maps, compass, binoculars, poncho, pup tent, shoes, first-aid kit, rope, flashlight, inspirational poetry, water, food—and because anyhow I approach nature with a certain surly ill-will, daring Her to make trouble. Later when I'm deep into Natural Bridges Natural Moneymint or Zion National Parkinglot or say General Shithead National Forest Land of Many Abuses why then, of course, when it's a bit late, then I may wish I had packed that something extra: matches perhaps, to mention one useful item, or maybe a spoon to eat my gruel with.

If I hike with another person it's usually the same; most of my friends have indolent and melancholy natures too. A cursed lot, all of them. I think of my comrade John De Puy, for example, sloping along for mile after mile like a goddamned camel—indefatigable—with those J. C. Penny hightops on his feet and that plastic pack on his back he got with five books of Green Stamps and nothing inside it but a sketchbook, some homemade jerky and a few cans of green chiles. Or Douglas Peacock, ex–Green Beret, just the opposite. Built like a buffalo, he hefts a ninety-pound canvas pannier on his back at trailhead, loaded with guns, ammunition, bayonet, pitons and carabiners, cameras, field books, a 150-foot rope, geologist's sledge, rock samples, assay kit, field glasses, two gallons of water in steel canteens, jungle boots, a case of C-rations, rope hammock, pharmaceuticals in a pig-iron box, raincoat, overcoat, two-man mountain tent, Dutch oven, hibachi, shovel, ax, inflatable boat, and near the top of the load and distributed through side and back pockets, easily accessible, a case of beer. Not because he enjoys or needs all that weight—he may never get to the bottom of that cargo on a ten-day outing—but simply because Douglas uses his packbag for general storage both at home and on the trail and prefers not to have to rearrange everything from time to time merely for the purposes of a hike. Thus my friends De Puy and Peacock; you may wish to avoid such extremes.

A few tips on desert etiquette:

1. Carry a cooking stove, if you must cook. Do not burn desert wood, which is rare and beautiful and required ages for its creation (an ironwood tree lives for over 1,000 years and juniper almost as long).

2. If you must, out of need, build a fire, then for God's sake allow it to burn itself out before you leave—do not bury it, as Boy Scouts and Campfire Girls do, under a heap of mud or sand. Scatter the ashes; replace any rocks you may have used in constructing a fireplace; do all you can to obliterate the evidence that you camped here. (The Search & Rescue Team may be looking for you.)

3. Do not bury garbage—the wildlife will only dig it up again. Burn what will burn and pack out the rest. The same goes for toilet paper: Don't bury it, *burn* it.

4. Do not bathe in desert pools, natural tanks, *tinajas,* potholes. Drink what water you need, take what you need, and leave the rest for the next hiker and more important for the bees, birds, and animals—bighorn sheep, coyotes, lions, foxes, badgers, deer, wild pigs, wild horses—whose *lives* depend on that water.

5. Always remove and destroy survey stakes, flagging, advertising signboards, mining claim markers, animal traps, poisoned bait, seismic exploration geophones, and other such artifacts of industrialism. The men who put those things there are up to no good and it is our duty to confound them. Keep America Beautiful. Grow a Beard. Take a Bath. Burn a Billboard.

Anyway—why go into the desert? Really, why do it? That sun, roaring at you all day long. The fetid, tepid, vapid little water holes slowly evaporating under a scum of grease, full of cannibal beetles, spotted toads, horsehair worms, liver flukes, and down at the bottom, inevitably, the pale cadaver of a ten-inch centipede. Those pink rattlesnakes down in The Canyon, those diamondback monsters thick as a truck driver's wrist that lurk in shady places along the trail, those unpleasant solpugids and unnecessary Jerusalem crickets that scurry on dirty claws across your face at night. Why? The rain that comes down like lead shot and wrecks the trail, those sudden rockfalls of obscure origin that crash like thunder ten feet behind you in the heart of a dead-still afternoon. The ubiquitous buzzard, so patient—but only so patient. The sullen and hostile Indians, all on welfare. The ragweed, the tumbleweed, the Jimson weed, the snakeweed. The scorpion in your shoe at dawn. The dreary wind that blows all spring, the psychedelic Joshua trees waving their arms at you on moonlight nights. Sand in the soup du jour. Halazone tablets in your canteen. The barren hills that always go up, which is bad, or down, which is worse. Those canyons like catacombs with quicksand lapping at your crotch. Hollow, mummified horses with forelegs casually crossed, dead for ten years, leaning against the corner of a barbed-wire fence. Packhorses at night, iron-shod, clattering over the slickrock through your camp. The last tin of tuna, two flat tires, not enough water and a forty-mile trek to Tule Well. An osprey on a cardón cactus, snatching the head off a living fish—always the best part first. The hawk sailing by at 200 feet, a squirming snake in its talons. Salt in the drinking water. Salt, selenium, arsenic, radon and radium in the water, in the gravel, in your bones. Water so hard it bends light, drills holes in rock and chokes up your radiator. Why go there? Those places with the hardcase names: Starvation Creek, Poverty Knoll, Hungry Valley, Bitter Springs, Last Chance Canyon, Dungeon Canyon, Whipsaw Flat, Dead Horse Point, Scorpion Flat, Dead Man Draw, Stinking Spring, Camino del Diablo, Jornada del Muerto . . . Death Valley.

Well then, why indeed go walking into the desert, that grim ground, that bleak and lonesome land where, as Genghis Khan said of India, "the heat is bad and the water makes men sick"?

Why the desert, when you could be strolling along the golden beaches of California? Camping by a stream of pure Rocky Mountain spring water in colorful Colorado? Loafing through a laurel slick in the misty hills of North Carolina? Or getting your head mashed in the greasy alley behind the Elysium Bar and Grill in Hoboken, New Jersey? Why the desert, given a world of such splendor and variety?

A friend and I took a walk around the base of a mountain up beyond Coconino County, Arizona. This was a mountain we'd been planning to circumambulate for years. Finally we put on our walking shoes and did it. About halfway around this mountain, on the third or fourth day, we paused for a while—two days—by the side of a stream which the Indians call Nasja because of the amber color of the water. (Caused perhaps by juniper roots—the water seems safe enough to drink.) On our second day there I walked down the stream, alone, to look at the canyon beyond. I entered the canyon and followed it for half the afternoon, for three or four miles, maybe, until it became a gorge so deep, narrow and dark, full of water and the inevitable quagmires of quicksand, that I turned around and looked for a way out. A route other than the way I'd come, which was crooked and uncomfortable and buried—I wanted to see what was up on top of this world. I found a sort of chimney flue on the east wall, which looked plausible, and sweated and cursed my way up through that until I reached a point where I could walk upright, like a human being. Another 300 feet of scrambling brought me to the rim of the canyon. No one, I felt certain, had ever before departed Nasja Canyon by that route.

But someone had. Near the summit I found an arrow sign, three feet long, formed of stones and pointing off into the north toward those same old purple vistas, so grand, immense, and mysterious, of more canyons, more mesas and plateaus, more mountains, more cloud-dappled sun-spangled leagues of desert sand and desert rock under the same old wide and aching sky.

The arrow pointed into the north. But what was it pointing at? I looked at the sign closely and saw that those dark, desert-varnished stones had been in place for a long, long, time; they rested in compacted dust. They must have been there for a century at least. I followed the direction indicated and came promptly to the rim of another canyon and a drop-off straight down of a good 500 feet. Not that way, surely. Across this canyon was nothing of any unusual interest that I could see—only the familiar sun-blasted sandstone, a few scrubby clumps of blackbrush and prickly pear, a few acres of nothing where only a lizard could graze, surrounded by a few square miles of more nothingness interesting chiefly to horned toads. I returned to the arrow and checked again, this time with field glasses, looking away for as far as my aided eyes could see toward the north, for ten, twenty, forty miles into the distance. I studied the scene with care, looking for an ancient Indian ruin, a significant cairn, perhaps an abandoned mine, a hidden treasure of some inconceivable wealth, the mother of all mother lodes. . . .

But there was nothing out there. Nothing at all. Nothing but the desert. Nothing but the silent world.

That's why.

WILLIAM H. GASS

*William H. Gass (1924–2017), who has been called "our greatest living champion of the sentence" (Sven Birkerts), was a novelist, philosophy professor, and essayist. As a fiction writer (*Omensetter's Luck, The Tunnel*) he is often associated with the postmodernist circle of John Barth, John Hawkes, and Donald Barthelme, which delighted in self-reflexive linguistic playfulness. In his scintillating essay collections, such as* On Being Blue *and* Habitations of the Word, *he also experimented with language, drawing attention to prose's texture and syntax the way a painter might to brushstrokes. In "On Talking to Oneself," which began as a university commencement address, he leads the reader/listener through a merry chase around his mind, in a metaconversation. Then again, are not all essays a way of talking to oneself?*

On Talking to Oneself

(1979)

Dinner, let us imagine, has reached its second wine. We are exchanging pleasantries: gossip, tittle-tattle, perilously keen remarks. Like a fine sauce, they pique the mind. They pass the time. A thought is peeled and placed upon a plate. A nearby lady lends us a small smile, and there are glances brilliant as the silver. Patiently we listen while another talks, because everyone, our etiquette instructs, must have his chance to speak. We wait. We draw upon the cloth with unused knives. Our goblets turn as slowly as the world.

At this moment, you are reading. I am absent. Still, I shall pretend to talk. Shall you pretend to listen while you read? I shall pretend to be speaking though I write. Is this a late wet lonely night? Who knows where a voice is from, any more than we know a fly's home, when it lands on type? or where your ear is, perhaps this instant barely lifted from a pillow to listen for a noise in the house? Our present circumstances—it may be I have no present circumstance—could they be more different?

I want to talk to you about talking, that commonest of all our intended activities. Talking is our public link with one another: it is a need; it is an art; it is the chief instrument of all instruction; it is the most personal aspect of our private lives. To those who have sponsored our appearance in the world, the first memorable moment to follow our inaugural bawl is the awkward birth of our first word. It is that noise, a sound that is no longer a simple signal, like the greedy squalling of a gull, but a declaration of the incipient presence of mind, that delivers us into the human sphere. Before, there was only energy, intake, and excretion; now a person has begun. And in no idle, ordinary, or jesting sense, words are what that being will become. It is language which most shows a man, Ben Jonson said. "Speake that I may see thee." And Emerson certainly supports him: "Man is only half himself," he said, "the other half is his expression." Truths like this have been the long companions of our life, and so we often overlook them, as we miss the familiar mole upon our chin, even while powdering the blemish, or running over it with a razor.

Silence is the soul's invisibility. We can, of course, conceal ourselves behind lies and sophistries, but when we speak, we are present, however careful our disguise. The creature we choose to be on Halloween says something about the creature we are. I have often gone to masquerades as myself, and in that guise no one knew I was there.

Not to speak—to be gagged, isolated, put away out of earshot—is in its way to be removed from the world—to be shouted down, censored, rendered mute. And not to be spoken to, to be sent to Coventry, hasn't that always been felt to be as hard to carry as a cross? When we wish we were elsewhere, but are powerless to leave, we sulk. To whom I will not talk, my actions say, is not.

Plato thought of the soul as an ardent debating society in which our various interests pled their causes; and there were honest speeches and dishonest ones; there was reason, lucid and open and lovely like the nakedness of the gods, where truth found its youngest friend and nobility its ancient eloquence; and there was also pin-eyed fanaticism, deceit and meanness, a coarseness like sand in cold grease; there was bribery and seduction, flattery, browbeating and bombast. Little has changed, in that regard, either in our souls or in society since; for the great Greeks were correct: life must be lived according to the right word—the *logos* they loved—and so the search for it, the mastery of it, the fullest and finest and truest expression of it, the defense of it, became the heart of a life-long educational enterprise.

To an almost measureless degree, to *know* is to possess words, and all of us who live out in the world as well as within our own are aware that we inhabit a forest of symbols; we dwell in a context of texts. Adam created the animals and birds by naming them, and we name incessantly, conserving achievements and customs, and countries that no longer exist, in the museum of human memory But it is not only the books which we pile about us like a building, or the papers we painfully compose, the exams or letters we write, the calculations we come to by means of mystic diagrams, mathematical symbols, astrological charts or other ill or well-drawn maps of the mind; it is not simply our habit of lining the streets with wheedling, hectoring, threatening signs, writing warnings on the sides of little jars and boxes, or with cajoling smoke defacing the sky, or turning on the radio to bruise with entreaty every ear, or the TV which illustrates its lies with clowns and colour; it is not alone the languages we learn to mispronounce, the lists, the arguments and rhymes, we get by heart; it is not even our tendency to turn what is unwritten into writing with a mere look, so that rocks will suddenly say their age and origin and activity, or what is numb flesh and exposed bone will cry out that cotton candy killed it, or cancer, or canoodling, the letter C like a cut across an artery; no, it is not the undeniable importance of these things which leads me to lay such weight upon the word; it is rather our interior self I'm concerned with, and therefore with the language which springs out of the most retiring and inmost parts of us, and is the image of its parent like a child: the words we use to convey our love to one another, or to cope with anxiety, for instance; the words which will convince, persuade, which will show us clearly, or make the many one; the words I listen to when I wait out a speech at a dinner party; words which can comfort and assuage, damage and delight, amuse and dismay; but, above all, the words which one burns like beacons against the darkness, and which together comprise the society of the silently speaking self; because all these words are but humble echoes of the words the poet uses when she speaks of passion, or the historian when he drives his nails through time, or when the psychoanalyst divines our desires as through tea leaves left at the bottom of our dreams.

Even if the world becomes so visual that words must grow faces to save themselves, and put on smiles made of fragrant paste; and even if we all hunker down in front of films like savages before a divinity, to have experience explained to us in terms of experiences which need to be explained; still, we shall not trade portraits of our love affairs, only of ourselves; there is no Polaroid that will develop in moments the state of our soul, or cassette to record our pangs of conscience; so we shall never talk in doodles over dinner, or call up our spirit to its struggle with a little private sit-com or a dreary soap. Could we quarrel very well in ink blots, or reach a legal understanding in the video arcade? Even if the world falls silent and we shrink in fear within ourselves; even if words are banished to the Balkans or otherwise driven altogether out of hearing (as the word "Balkans" has been), as though every syllable were subversive (as indeed each is); all the same, when we have withdrawn from any companionship with things and people, when we have collapsed in terror behind our tal-cumed skins, and we peer suspiciously through the keyholes of our eyes, when we have reached the limit of our dwindle—the last dry seed of the self—then we shall see how greatly correct is the work of Samuel Beckett, because we shall find there, inside that seed, nothing but his featureless cell, nothing but voice, nothing but darkness and talk.

How desperately, then, we need to learn it—to talk to ourselves—because we are babies about it. Oh, we have excellent languages for the secrets of nature. Wave packets, black holes, and skeins of genes: we can write precisely and consequentially of these, as well as other extraordinary phenomena; but can we talk even of trifles: for instance, of the way a look sometimes crosses a face like the leap of a frog, so little does it live there; or how the habit of anger raisins the heart, or wet leaves paper a street? Our anatomy texts can skin us without our pain, the cellular urges of trees are no surprise, the skies are driven by winds we cannot see; yet science has passed daily life like the last bus, and left it to poetry.

It is terribly important to know how a breast is made: how to touch it in order to produce a tingle, or discover a hidden cyst (we find these things written of in books); but isn't it just as important to be able to put the beauty of a body in words, words we give like a gift to its bearer; to communicate the self to another, and in that way form a community of feeling, of thought about feeling, of belief about thought: an exchange of warmth like breathing, of simple tastes and the touch of the eye, and other sensations shortly to be sought, since there is no place for the utopia of the flesh outside the utopia of talk?

It can't be helped. We are made of layers of language like a Viennese torte. We are a Freudian dessert. My dinner companion, the lady who lent me her smile, has raised her goblet in a quiet toast. It is as though its rim had touched me, and I try to find words for the feeling, and for the wine which glows like molten rubies in her glass; because if I can do that, I can take away more than a memory which will fade faster than a winter foot-print; I can take away an intense and interpreted description, a record as tough to erase as a relief, since without words what can be well and richly remembered? Yesterdays are gone like drying mist. Without our histories, without the conservation which concepts nearly alone make possible, we could not preserve our lives as were the bodies of the pharaohs, the present would soon be as clear of the past as a bright day, and we would be innocent arboreals again.

Of course we could redream the occasion, or pretend to film our feeling, but we'll need words to label and index our images anyway, and can the photograph contain the rush of colour to my face, the warmth which reminds me I also am a glass and have become wine?

We dream in images, and might we not learn to sleepwalk while awake, think in diagrams and maps and coded colour schemes? but the images of sleep are symbols, and the words we make up while awake outline our dreams and render clearly their declarations. The phrase "a photographic history" is a misnomer. Every photograph requires a thousand words.

I remember because I talk. I talk from morning to night, and then I talk on in my sleep. Our talk is so precious to us, we think we punish others when we stop, as I've remarked. So I stay at peace because I talk. *Tête-à-têtes* are talk. Shop is talk. Parties are parades of anecdotes, gossip, opinion, raillery, and reportage. There is sometimes a band and we have to shout. Out of an incredibly complex gabble, how wonderfully clever of me to hear so immediately my own name; yet at my quiet breakfast table, I may be unwilling, and thus unable, to hear a thing my wife says. When wives complain that romance has fled from their marriage, they mean that their husbands have grown quiet and unresponsive as moss. Taciturnity—long, lovely word—it is a famous tactic. As soon as two people decide they have nothing more to talk about, everything should be talked out. Silence shields no passion. Only the mechanical flame is sputterless and quiet.

Like a good husband, then, I tell my wife what went on through the day—in the car, on the courts, at the office. Well, perhaps I do not tell her *all* that went on; perhaps I give her a slightly cleaned-up and economical account. I tell my friends how I fared in New York, and of the impatient taxi which honked me through the streets. I tell my students the substance of what they should have read. I tell my children how it used to be (it was better), and how I was a hero (of a modest kind, of course) in the Great War, moving from fact to fiction within the space of a single word. I tell my neighbors pleasant lies about the beauty of their lawns and dogs and vandalizing tykes, and in my head I tell the whole world where to get off.

Those who have reputations as great conversationalists are careful never to let anyone else open a mouth. Like Napoleons, they first conquer, then rule, the entire space of speech around them. Jesus preached. Samuel Johnson bullied. Carlyle fulminated. Bucky Fuller droned. Wittgenstein thought painfully aloud like a surgeon. But Socrates talked . . . hazardously, gaily, amorously, eloquently, religiously . . . he talked with wit, with passion, with honesty; he asked; he answered; he considered; he debated; he entertained; he made of his mind a boulevard before there was even a France.

I remember—I contain a past—partly because my friends and family allow me to repeat and polish my tales, tall as they sometimes are, like the stalk Jack climbed to encounter the giant. Shouldn't I be able to learn from history how to chronicle my self? "Every man should be so much an artist," again Emerson said, "that he could report in conversation what had befallen him." Words befell Emerson often. He made speeches in public and on paper, wherever he was, and until his mind changed, he always meant what he said. Frequently his mind changed before he reached any conclusion. In his head his heart heard the language of the other side.

Talk, of course, is not always communication. It is often just a buzz, the hum the husband makes when he's still lit, but the station's gone off. We can be bores as catastrophic as quakes, causing even the earth to yawn. Talk can be cruel and injurious to a degree which is frightening; the right word wrongly used can strike a man down like a club, turn a heart dark forever, freeze the feelings; nevertheless, while the thief is threatening to take our money or our life, he has yet to do either; and while talk mediates a strike, or weighs an allegation in the press or in committee, or considers a law in Congress or argues a crime in court; while a spouse gripes, or the con man cons, while ideas are explained to a point beyond opacity by the prof; then it's not yet the dreadful day of the exam, sentence has not been passed, the crime has not yet occurred, the walkout, or the war. It may sound like a balk, a hitch in the motion, a failure to follow through, but many things recommend talk, not least its rich and wandering rhymes.

Our thoughts tend to travel like our shadow in the morning walking west, casting their outline just ahead of us so that we can see and approve, or amend and cancel, what we are about to say. It is the only rehearsal our conversation usually gets; but that is one reason we fall upon cliché as if it were a sofa and not a sword; for we have rehearsed "good morning," and "how are you?" and "have a nice day," to the place where the tongue is like a stale bun in the mouth; and we have talked of Tommy's teeth and our cold car's stalling treachery, of our slobby dog's affection and Alice's asthma and Hazel's latest honeybunny, who, thank god, is only black and not gay like her last one; we have emptied our empty jars over one another like slapstick comics through so many baggy-panted performances we can now dream of Cannes and complain of Canada with the same breath we use to spit an olive in a napkin, since one can easily do several thoughtless things at once—in fact, one ought; and indeed it is true that prefab conversation frees the mind, yet rarely does the mind have a mind left after these interconnected clichés have conquered it; better to rent rooms to hooligans who will only draw on the walls and break the furniture; for our Gerberized phrases touch nothing; they keep the head hollow by crowding out thought; they fill all the chairs with buttocks like balloons; they are neither fed nor feed; they drift like dust; they refuse to breathe.

We forget sometimes that we live with ourselves—worse luck most likely—as well as within. The head we inhabit is a haunted house. Nevertheless, we often ignore our own voice when it speaks to us: "Remember me," the spirit says, "I am your holy ghost." But we are bored by our own baloney. Why otherwise would we fall in love if not to hear that same sweet hokum from another? Still, we should remember that we comprise true Siamese twins, fastened by language and feeling, wed better than any bed; because when we talk to ourselves we divide into the self which is all ear and the self which is all mouth. Yet which one of us is which? Does the same self do most of the talking while a second self soaks it up, or is there a real conversation?

Frequently we put on plays like a producer: one voice belongs to sister, shrill and intrepidly stupid: a nephew has another (he wants a cookie); the boss is next—we've cast him as a barnyard bully; and then there is a servant or a spouse, crabby and recalcitrant. All speak as they are spoken through; each runs around in its role like a caged squirrel, while an audience we also invent (patient, visible, too easily interested, readily pleased) applauds the heroine or the hero who has righted wrongs like an avenging angel, answered every challenge like a Lancelot, every question like Ann Landers, and met every opportunity like a perfect Romeo, every romance like a living doll. If we really love the little comedy we've constructed, it's likely to have a long run.

Does it really matter how richly and honestly and well we speak? What is our attitude toward ourselves; what tone do we tend to take? Consider Hamlet, a character who escapes his circumstances and achieves greatness despite the fact his will wavers or he can't remember the injunctions of his father's ghost. He certainly doesn't bring it off because he has an Oedipus complex (we are all supposed to have that); but because he talks to himself more beautifully than anyone else almost ever has. Consider his passion, his eloquence, his style, his range, his wit: "O what a rogue and peasant slave am I," he exclaims; "now could I drink hot blood," he brags; "to be or not to be," he wonders; "O," he hopes, "that this too too solid flesh would melt," and he complains that all occasions do inform against him. For our part, what do *we* do? do we lick our own hand and play the spaniel? do we whine and wheedle or natter like a ninny? can we formulate our anger in a righteous phrase, or will we be reduced to swearing like a soldier? All of us are dramatists, but how will we receive our training? where can we improve upon the puerile theatricals of our parents, if not here among the plays and perils of Pirandello and the dialogues of Plato, the operas of Puccini and the follies of most faculties (among the many glories of the letter "p")?

If we think awareness is like water purling gaily in its stream, we have been listening to the wrong James, for our consciousness is largely composed of slogans and signs, of language of one kind or other: we wake to an alarm; we read the weather by the brightness of a streak on the ceiling, the mood of our lover by the night's cramp still clenched in her morning body; our trembling tells us we're hung over; we wipe ourselves with a symbol of softness, push an ad around over our face; the scale rolls up a number which means "overweight," and the innersoles of our shoes say "hush!" Thus, even if we haven't uttered a word, we've so far spent the morning reading. Signs don't stream. They may straggle, but they mostly march. Language allies itself with order. Even its fragments suggest syntax, wholeness, regularity, though many of us are ashamed to address ourselves in complete sentences. Rhetorically structured paragraphs seem pretentious to us, as if, to gaze at our image in a mirror, we had first to put on a tux; and this means that everything of real importance, every decision which requires care, thoughtful analysis, emotional distance, and mature judgment, must be talked out with someone else—a consequence we can't always face, with its attendant arguments, embarrassments, counterclaims, and lies. To think for yourself—not narrowly, but rather as a mind—you must be able to talk to yourself: well, openly, and at length. You must come in from the rain of requests and responses. You must take and employ your time as if it were your life. And that side of you which speaks must be prepared to say anything so long as it is so—is seen so, felt so, thought so—and that side of you that listens must be ready to hear horrors, for much of what is so *is* horrible—horrible to see, horrible to feel, horrible to consider. But at length, and honestly—that is not enough. To speak well to oneself . . . to speak well we must go down as far as the bucket can be lowered. Every thought must be thought through from its ultimate cost back to its cheap beginnings; every perception, however profound and distant, must be as clear and easy as the moon; every desire must be recognized as a relative and named as fearlessly as Satan named his angels; finally, every feeling must be felt to its bottom where the bucket rests in the silt and water rises like a tower around it. To talk to ourselves well requires, then, endless rehearsals—rehearsals in which we revise, and the revision of the inner life strikes many people as hypocritical; but to think how to express some passion properly is the only way to be possessed by it, for unformed feelings lack impact, just as unfelt ideas lose weight. So walk around unrewritten, if you like. Live on broken phrases and syllable gristle, telegraphese and film reviews. No one will suspect . . . until you speak, and your soul falls out of your mouth like a can of corn from a shelf.

There are kinds and forms of this inner speech. Many years ago, when my eldest son was about fourteen, I was gardening alongside our house one midday in mid-May, hidden as it happened between two bushes I was pruning, when Richard came out of the house in a hurry to return to school following lunch, and like a character in a French farce, skulking there, I overheard him talking to himself. "Well, racing fans, it looks . . . it looks like the question we've all been asking is about to be answered, because HERE COMES RICHARD GASS OUT OF THE PITS NOW! He doesn't appear to be limping from that bad crash he had at the race- way yesterday—what a crash that was!—and he is certainly going straight for his car . . . what courage! . . . his helmet is on his head, fans . . . yes, he is getting into his car . . . not a hesitation . . . yes, he is going to be off in a moment for the track . . . yes"—and then he went, pedaling out of my hearing, busily broadcasting his life.

My son's consciousness, in that moment, was not only thoroughly verbal (although its subject was the Indy 500, then not too many days away, and although he could still see the street he would ride on), it had a form: that given to his language and its referents by the radio sportscaster. As I remember it now, the verbal tone belonged more to baseball than to racing. In any case, Richard's body was, in effect, on the air; his mind was in the booth "upstairs," while his feelings were doubtless mixed in with his audience, both at home and in the stands. He was being seen, heard, and *spoken of,* at the same time.

Later this memory led me to wonder whether we all didn't have fash- ions and forms in which we talked to ourselves; whether some of these might be habits of the most indelible sort, the spelling out of our secret personality; and, finally, whether they might not vitally influence the way we spoke to others, especially in our less formal moments—in bed, at breakfast, at the thirteenth tee. And for men and women, might they not very likely come from those areas of greatest influence or ambition in their lives? I recognized at once that this was certainly true of me; that although I employed many styles and modes, there was one verbal form which had me completely in its grip the way Baron Munchausen was held in his own tall tales, or the *Piers Plowman* poet in his lovely alliteration. If Richard's was that of the radio broadcast, as it seemed, mine was that of the lecture. I realized that when I woke in the morning, I rose from bed as though at the end of a night of sleepless explication, already primed to ask the world if it had any questions. I was, almost from birth, and so I suppose by "bottom nature," what Gertrude Stein called Ezra Pound—a village explainer—which, she said, was all right if you were a village, but if not, not; and sooner than sunrise I would be launched on an unvoiced speechification on the art of internal discourse, a lecture I would have given many times, though rarely aloud.

I have since asked a number of people, some from very different back- grounds, what shape their internal talk took, and found, first of all (when there was not a polite amused smile which signified unalterable resistance), that they agreed to the important presence of these forms, and that one type did tend to dominate the others: it was often broadcasting—never the lecture—though I once encountered a sermon and several revival- style pray-makers; it frequently took place in the courtroom where one was conducting a fearless prosecution or a triumphant defense; it was regularly the repetition of some pattern of parental exchange, a rut full of relatives and preconditioned response; the drama appeared to be popular, as well as works of pornography, though, in this regard, there were more movies shown than words said—a pity, both modes need such improvement. There were monologues such as Browning might have penned: the vaunt, the threat, the keen, the kvetch, the eulogy for yourself when dead; there was even the bedtime story, the diary, the chronicle, and, of course, the novel, gothic in character, or at least full of intrigue and suspense: Little did William Gass realize when he rose that gentle May morning to thump his chest and touch his toes that he would soon be embarked on an adventure whose endless ramifications would utterly alter his life; otherwise he might not have set out for the supermarket without a list; otherwise he might not have done that extra push-up; he might better have stayed in bed with the bedclothes pulled thickly over his stupidly chattering head.

In my little survey, oral modes beat written ones by a mile. Obviously. They could be spoken. And the broadcast, with its apportionment of speaker into "speaker," "spectator," and "sportsman," had a formal edge over most of its competition.

There were, finally, important differences as to sex: no woman admitted she broadcast her life as though it were some sporting event, especially not the "sporting ladies" who regularly reenacted a role they imagined their mothers had starred in: giving sex and getting money.

Yet I should like to suggest (despite the undeniable sappiness of it) that the center of the self itself is this secret, obsessive, often silly, nearly continuous *voice*—the voice that is the surest sign we are alive; and that one fundamental function of language is the communication with this self which it makes feasible; that, in fact, without someone speaking, someone hearing, someone overhearing both, no full self can exist; that if society—its families and factories and congresses and schools—has done its work, then every day every one of us is a bit nearer than we were before to being one of the fortunates who have made rich and beautiful the great conversation which constitutes our life.

When Richard rode his bike to school, the rider rode, the radio approved, the world around the ride applauded his progress. We know, in truth, that it is often otherwise; that sometimes these elements are enemies, and external conflicts become internal ferocities. What might be a neutral or friendly triangle—speaker, hearer, overhearer—is habitually filled by surrogates for ourselves, for our parents and our peers, scapegoats and villains and victims, and sometimes even by judges, juries, and the police. Then we cannot talk to ourselves for fear of being overheard. But I suspect that tyrannies, and tyrannical conditions, although they frighten many into a public silence which stills the inner self as well, produce an intense, far-ranging, wildly explosive and productive internal confrontation: that initial stage in the composition of dissident and revolutionary works. The adversary attitude can move a lot of freight—some of it even along the right track.

And everywhere here in my present absence—in your, the reader's silence, where you, or something of you, sits among the scattered numbers of listening chairs like a choir before bursting into song—there is the subversive murmur of us all: our glad, our scrappy, rude, grand, small talk to ourselves, the unheard hum of our humanity; without which—think of it!—we might not be awake; without which—imagine it!—we might not be alive; since while we speak we live up there above our bodies in the mind, and there is hope as long as we continue to talk; so long as we continue to speak, to search for eloquence even over happiness or sympathy in sorrow or anger in revenge, even if all that is left to us is the omitted outcry, Christ's query, the silent condemnation: "My God, my God, why have you left me alone?"

WALLACE STEGNER

Wallace Stegner (1909–1993), author of more than a dozen books of fiction and nonfiction, and a professor of creative writing at Stanford University (which has since named a prize after him), spoke for the American West. "All my life I have been going away east and coming back west," he wrote. What it meant to be a westerner, for him, was to be "a part of the natural world and competent to belong in it." While he acknowledges that "we have spoiled a lot of the West as we have spoiled other parts of America," his love of the land and his persistent belief in the promise that the original American idea represents are manifest in "The Twilight of Self-Reliance" (the reference is clearly to Emerson's "Self-Reliance"), which synthesizes with remarkable succinctness and balance the country's history, mythology, literature, flaws, and contradictions.

The Twilight of Self-Reliance: Frontier Values and Contemporary America

(1980)

1

Henry David Thoreau was a philosopher not unwilling to criticize his country and his countrymen, but when he wrote the essay entitled "Walking" in 1862, at a time when his country was engaged in a desperate civil war, he wrote with what Mark Twain would have called the calm confidence of a Christian with four aces. He spoke America's stoutest self-confidence and most optimistic expectations. Eastward, he said, he walked only by force, but westward he walked free: he must walk toward Oregon and not toward Europe, and his trust in the future was total.

> If the moon looks larger here than in Europe, probably the sun looks larger also. If the heavens of America appear infinitely higher, and the stars brighter, I trust that these facts are symbolical of the height to which the philosophy and poetry and religion of her inhabitants may one day soar. . . . I trust that we shall be more imaginative, that our thoughts will be clearer, fresher, and more ethereal, as our sky—our understanding more comprehensive and broader, like our plains—our intellect generally on a grander scale, like our thunder and lightning, our rivers and mountains and forests—and our hearts shall even correspond in breadth and depth and grandeur to our inland seas. Perchance there will appear to the traveler something, he knows not what, of *laeta* and *glabra,* of joyous and serene, in our very faces. Else to what end does the world go on, and why was America discovered?

The question was rhetorical; he knew the answer. To an American of his generation it was unthinkable that the greatest story in the history of civilized man—the finding and peopling of the New World—and the greatest opportunity since the Creation—the chance to remake men and their society into something cleansed of past mistakes, and closer to the heart's desire—should end as one more betrayal of human credulity and hope.

Some moderns find that idea perfectly thinkable. Leslie Fiedler finds in the Montana Face, which whatever else it is is an authentically American one, not something joyous and serene, but the large vacuity of self-deluding myth. Popular books which attempt to come to grips with American values in these times walk neither toward Oregon nor toward Europe, but toward dead ends and jumping-off places. They bear such titles as *The Lonely Crowd, The Organization Man, Future Shock, The Culture of Narcissism.* This last, subtitled "American Life in an Age of Diminishing Expectations," reports "a way of life that is dying—the culture of competitive individualism, which in its decadence has carried the logic of individualism to the extreme of a war of all against all, the pursuit of happiness to the dead end of a narcissistic preoccupation with the self." It describes "a political system in which public lying has become endemic and routine," and a typical citizen who is haunted by anxiety and spends his time trying to find a meaning in his life. "His sexual attitudes are permissive rather than puritanical, even though his emancipation from ancient taboos brings him no sexual peace. . . . Acquisitive in the sense that his cravings have no limits, he does not accumulate goods and provisions against the future, in the manner of the acquisitive individualist of the nineteenth century political economy, but demands immediate gratification and lives in a state of restless, perpetually unsatisfied desire."

Assuming that Thoreau spoke for his time, as he surely did, and that Christopher Lasch speaks for at least elements and aspects of his, how did we get from there to here in little more than a century? Have the sturdiness of the American character and the faith in America's destiny that Thoreau took for granted been eroded entirely away? What happened to confidence, what happened to initiative and strenuousness and sobriety and responsibility, what happened to high purpose, what happened to hope? Are they gone, along with the Puritans' fear of pleasure? Was the American future, so clear in Thoreau's day, no more than a reflection of apparently unlimited resources, and does democracy dwindle along with the resources that begot it? Were we never really free, but only rich? In any event, if America was discovered only so that its citizens could pursue pleasure or grope for a meaning in their lives, then Thoreau and Lasch would be in agreement: Columbus should have stood at home.

Even if I knew answers, I could not detail them in an hour's lecture, or in a book. But since I believe that one of our most damaging American traits is our contempt for all history, including our own, I might spend an hour looking backward at what we were and how America changed us. A certain kind of modern American in the throes of an identity crisis is likely to ask, or bleat, "Who am I?" It might help him to find out who he started out to be, and having found that out, to ask himself if what he started out to be is still valid. And if most of what I touch on in this summary is sixth-grade American history, I do not apologize for that. History is not the proper midden for digging up novelties. Perhaps that is one reason why a nation bent on novelty ignores it. The obvious, especially the ignored obvious, is worth more than a Fourth of July or Bicentennial look.

2

Under many names—Atlantis, the Hesperides, Groenland, Brazillia, the Fortunate Isles—America was Europe's oldest dream. Found by Norsemen about the year 1000, it was lost again for half a millennium, and only emerged into reality at the beginning of the modern era, which we customarily date from the year 1500. There is even a theory, propounded by the historian Walter Webb in *The Great Frontier,* that the new world created the modern era—stimulated its birth, funded it, fueled it, fed it, gave it its impetus and direction and state of mind, formed its expectations and institutions, and provided it with a prosperity unexampled in history, a boom that lasted fully four hundred years. If Professor Webb pushes his thesis a little hard, and if it has in it traces of the logical fallacy known as *post hoc, ergo propter hoc,* it still seems to me provocative and in some ways inescapable, and Webb seems entirely justified in beginning his discussion of America in medieval Europe. I shall do the same.

Pre-Columbian Europe, then. For 150 years it has been living close to the limit of its resources. It is always short of money, which means gold and silver, fiat money being still in the future. Its land is frozen in the structures of feudalism, owned by the crown, the church, and an aristocracy whose domains are shielded by laws of primogeniture and entail from sale or subdivision—from everything except the royal whim which gave, and can take away. Its food supply comes from sources that cannot be expanded, and its population, periodically reduced by the Black Death, is static or in decline. Peasants are bound to the soil, and both they and their masters are tied by feudal loyalties and obligations. Except among the powerful, individual freedom is not even a dream. Merchants, the guilds, and the middle class generally, struggle against the arrogance of the crown and an aristocracy dedicated to the anachronistic code of chivalry, which is often indistinguishable from brigandage. Faith is invested in a politicized, corrupt, but universal church just breaking up in the Reformation that will drown Europe in blood. Politics are a nest of snakes: ambitious nobles against ambitious kings, kings against pretenders and against each other, all of them trying to fill, by means of wars and strategic marriages, the periodic power vacuums created by the cracking of the Holy Roman Empire. The late Middle Ages still look on earthly life as a testing and preparation for the Hereafter. Fed on this opium, the little individual comes to expect his reward in heaven, or in the neck. Learning is just beginning to open out from scholastic rationalism into the empiricism of the Renaissance. Science, with all it will mean to men's lives and ways of thinking, has barely pipped its shell.

Out of this closed world Columbus sails in 1492 looking for a new route to Asia, whose jewels and silks are coveted by Europe's elite, and whose spices are indispensable to nations with no means of preserving food except smoking and salting, and whose meat is often eaten high. The voyage of the three tiny ships is full of anxiety and hardship, but the end is miracle, one of those luminous moments in history: an after-midnight cry from the lookout on the *Pinta,* Columbus and his sailors crowding to the decks, and in the soft tropical night, by the light of a moon just past full, staring at a dark ambiguous shore and sniffing the perfumed breeze off an utterly new world.

Not Asia. Vasco da Gama will find one way to that, Magellan another. What Columbus has found is puzzling, of unknown size and unknown relation to anything. The imagination has difficulty taking it in. Though within ten years of Columbus' first voyage Vespucci will demonstrate that the Americas are clearly not Asia, Europe is a long time accepting the newness of the new world. Pedro de Castañeda, crossing the plains of New Mexico, Oklahoma, and Kansas with Coronado in 1541, is confident that they make one continuous land mass with China and Peru; and when Champlain sends Jean Nicolet to explore among the Nipissings on the way to Georgian Bay and the great interior lakes in 1635—133 years after Vespucci—Nicolet will take along in his bark canoe an embroidered mandarin robe, just in case, out on those wild rivers among those wild forests, he should come to the palace of the Great Khan and need ceremonial dress.

Understanding is a slow dawning, each exploration bringing a little more light. But when the dawn arrives, it is a blazing one. It finds its way through every door and illuminates every cellar and dungeon in Europe. Though the discovery of America is itself part of Europe's awakening, and results from purely European advances—foreshadowings of Copernican astronomy, a method for determining latitude, the development of the caravel and the lateen sail—the new world responds by accelerating every stir of curiosity, science, adventure, individualism, and hope in the old.

Because Europe has always dreamed westward, America, once realized, touches men's minds like fulfilled prophecy. It has lain out there in the gray wastes of the Atlantic, not only a continent waiting to be discovered, but a fable waiting to be agreed upon. It is not unrelated to the Hereafter. Beyond question, before it is half known, it will breed utopias and noble savages, fantasies of Perfection, New Jerusalems.

Professor Webb believes that to closed and limited Europe America came as a pure windfall, a once-in-the-history-of-the-world opportunity. Consider only one instance: the gold that Sir Francis Drake looted from Spanish galleons was the merest fragment of a tithe of what the Spaniards had looted from Mexico and Peru; and yet Queen Elizabeth out of her one-fifth royal share of the *Golden Hind*'s plunder was able to pay off the entire national debt of England and have enough left to help found the East India Company.

Perhaps, as Milton Friedman would insist, increasing the money supply only raised prices. Certainly American gold didn't help Europe's poor. It made the rich richer and kings more powerful and wars more implacable. Nevertheless, trickling outward from Spain as gift or expenditure, or taken from its ships by piracy, that gold affected all of Europe, stimulating trade and discovery, science, invention, everything that we associate with the unfolding of the Renaissance. It surely helped take European eyes off the Hereafter, and it did a good deal toward legitimizing the profit motive. And as the French and English, and to a lesser extent the Dutch and Swedes, began raiding America, other and more substantial riches than gold flooded back: new food plants, especially Indian corn and the potato, which revolutionized eating habits and brought on a steep rise in population that lasted more than a century; furs; fish from the swarming Newfoundland banks, especially important to countries still largely Catholic; tobacco for the indulgence of a fashionable new habit; timber for ships and masts; sugar and rum from the West Indies.

Those spoils alone might have rejuvenated Europe. But there was something else, at first not valued or exploited, that eventually would lure Europeans across the Atlantic and transform them. The most revolutionary gift of the new world was land itself, and the independence and aggressiveness that land ownership meant. Land, unoccupied and unused except by savages who in European eyes did not count, land available to anyone with the initiative to take it, made America, Opportunity, and Freedom synonymous terms.

But only later. The early comers were raiders, not settlers. The first Spanish towns were beachheads from which to scour the country for treasure, the first French settlements on the St. Lawrence were beachheads of the fur trade. Even the English on Roanoke Island, and later at Jamestown, though authentic settlers, were hardly pioneers seeking the promised land. Many were bond servants and the scourings of debtors' prisons. They did not come, they were sent. Their hope of working off their bondage and starting new in a new country was not always rewarded, either. Bruce and William Catton estimate that eight out of ten indentured servants freed to make new lives in America failed—returned to pauperism, or became the founders of a poor-white class, or died of fevers trying to compete with black slaves on tobacco or sugar plantations, or turned outlaw.

Nevertheless, for the English who at Jamestown and Plymouth and the Massachusetts Bay Colony began to take ownership of American land in the early seventeenth century, land was the transfiguring gift. The historian who remarked that the entire history of the United States could be read in terms of real estate was not simply making words.

Here was an entire continent which, by the quaint assumptions of the raiders, was owned by certain absentee crowned heads whose subjects had made the first symbolic gesture of claiming it. They had rowed a boat into a rivermouth, sighted and named a cape, raised a cross on a beach, buried a brass plate, or harangued a crowd of bewildered Indians. Therefore Ferdinand and Isabella, or Elizabeth, or Louis owned from that point to the farthest boundary in every direction. But land without people was valueless. The Spaniards imported the *encomienda* system—that is, transplanted feudalism—and used the Indians as peons. The French built only forts at which to collect the wilderness wealth of furs. But the English were another kind, and they were the ones who created the American pattern.

"Are you ignorant of the difference between the king of England and the king of France?" Duquesne asked the Iroquois in the 1750s. "Go see the forts that our king has established and you will see that you can still hunt under their very walls. . . . The English, on the contrary, are no sooner in possession of a place than the game is driven away. The forest falls before them as they advance, and the soil is laid bare so that you can scarce find the wherewithal to erect a shelter for the night."

To be made valuable, land must be sold cheap or given away to people who would work it, and out of that necessity was born a persistent American expectation. The very word "claim" that we came to use for a parcel of land reflected our feeling that free or cheap land was a right, and that the land itself was a commodity. The Virginia Company and Lord Calvert both tried to encourage landed estates on the English pattern, and both failed because in America men would not work land unless they owned it, and would not be tied to a proprietor's acres when they could go off into the woods and have any land they wanted, simply for the taking. Their claim might not be strictly legal, but it often held: hence the development of what came to be known as squatters' rights. As Jefferson would later write in *Notes on Virginia,* Europe had an abundance of labor and a dearth of land, America an abundance of land and a dearth of labor. That made all the difference. The opportunity to own land not only freed men, it made labor honorable and opened up the future to hope and the possibility of independence, perhaps of a fortune.

The consequences inform every notion we have of ourselves. Admittedly there were all kinds of people in early America, as there are all kinds in our time—saints and criminals, dreamers and drudges, pushers and con men. But the new world did something similar to all of them. Of the most energetic ones it made ground-floor capitalists; out of nearly everyone it leached the last traces of servility. Cut off from control, ungoverned and virtually untaxed, people learned to resent the imposition of authority, even that which they had created for themselves. Dependent on their own strength and ingenuity in a strange land, they learned to dismiss tradition and old habit, or rather, simply forgot them. Up in Massachusetts the idea of the equality of souls before God probably helped promote the idea of earthly equality; the notion of a personal covenant with God made the way easier for social and political agreements such as the Plymouth Compact and eventually the Constitution of the United States. In the observed freedom of the Indian from formal government there may have been a dangerous example for people who had lived under governments notably unjust and oppressive. Freedom itself forced the creation not only of a capitalist economy based on land, but of new forms of social contract. When thirteen loosely allied colonies made common cause against the mother country, the League of the Iroquois may well have provided one model of confederation.

"The rich stay in Europe," wrote Hector St. John de Crèvecoeur before the Revolution. "It is only the middling and poor that emigrate." Middle-class values emigrated with them, and middle-class ambitions. Resentment of aristocrats and class distinctions accompanied the elevation of the work ethic. Hardship, equal opportunity to rise, the need for common defense against the Indians, and the necessity for all to postpone the rewards of labor brought the English colonists to nearly the same level and imbued all but the retarded and the most ne'er-do-well with the impulse of upward mobility. And if the practical need to hew a foothold out of the continent left many of them unlettered and ignorant, that deficiency, combined with pride, often led to the disparagement of cultivation and the cultivated as effete and European. Like work, barbarism and boorishness tended to acquire status, and in some parts of America still retain it.

Land was the base, freedom the consequence. Not even the little parochial tyranny of the Puritans in Massachusetts could be made to stick indefinitely. In fact, the Puritans' chief objection to Roger Williams, when they expelled him, was not his unorthodoxy but his declaration that the Colonists had no right to their lands, the king not having had the right to grant them in the first place. Williams also expressed an early pessimistic view of the American experiment that clashed with prevailing assumptions and forecast future disillusion. "The common trinity of the world—Profit, Preferment, and Pleasure—will be here the tria omnia, as in all the world besides . . . and God Land will be as great a God with us English as God Gold was with the Spaniard." A sour prophet indeed—altogether too American in his dissenting opinions and his challenging of authority. And right besides. No wonder they chased him off to Rhode Island.

Students of the Revolution have wondered whether it was really British tyranny that lit rebellion, or simply American outrage at the imposition of even the mildest imperial control after decades of benign neglect. Certainly one of George Ill's worst blunders was his 1763 decree forbidding settlement beyond the crest of the Alleghenies. That was worse than the Stamp Act or the Navigation Acts, for land speculators were already sniffing the western wind. When Daniel Boone took settlers over the Cumberland Gap in 1775 he was working for speculators. George Washington and Benjamin Franklin, who had a good deal to do with the Revolution, both had interests in western land. Only a very revisionist historian would call our revolution a real estate rebellion, a revolt of the subdividers, but it did have that aspect.

And very surely, as surely as the endless American forests put a curve in the helves of the axes that chopped them down, the continent worked on those who settled it. From the first frontiers in Virginia and Massachusetts through all the successive frontiers that, as Jefferson said, required Americans to start fresh every generation, America was in the process of creating a democratic, energetic, practical, profit-motivated society that resembled Europe less and less as it worked westward. At the same time, it was creating the complicated creature we spent our first century as a nation learning to recognize and trying to define: the American.

3

"Who then is the American, this new man?" asked Crèvecoeur, and answered his own question in a book published in 1782 as *Letters from an American Farmer*. We were, he said, a nation of cultivators; and it was the small farmer, the independent, frugal, hard-working, self-respecting freeholder, that he idealized—the same yeoman farmer that only a little later Jefferson would call the foundation of the republic. But out on the fringes of settlement Crèvecoeur recognized another type. Restless, migratory, they lived as much by hunting as by farming, for protecting their crops and stock against wild animals put the gun in their hands, and "once hunters, farewell to the plough. The chase renders them ferocious, gloomy, and unsocial"; they exhibit "a strange sort of lawless profligacy"; and their children, having no models except their parents, "grow up a mongrel breed, half civilized, half savage."

Crèvecoeur, familiar only with the eastern seaboard, thought the frontiersman already superseded almost everywhere by the more sober and industrious farmer. He could not know that on farther frontiers beyond the Appalachians, beyond the Mississippi, beyond the Missouri and the Rocky Mountains, the breed would renew itself for another hundred years, repeating over and over the experience that had created it in the first place. The Revolutionary War was only the climax of the American Revolution, which was the most radical revolution in history because it started from scratch, from wilderness, and repeated that beginning over and over.

The pioneer farmer has a respectable place in our tradition and an equally respectable place in our literature, from Cooper's *The Pioneers* to Rölvaag's *Giants in the Earth*. But it was the border hunter who captured our imaginations and became a myth. He was never a soft or necessarily attractive figure. Ferocious he always was, gloomy often, antisocial by definition. As D. H. Lawrence and a whole school of critics have pointed out, he was a loner, often symbolically an orphan, strangely sexless (though more in literature than in fact), and a killer. We know him not only from the Boones, Crocketts, Carsons, and Bridgers of history, but from Cooper's Leatherstocking and all his literary descendants. His most memorable recent portrait is Boone Caudill in A. B. Guthrie's *Big Sky*, who most appropriately heads for the mountains and a life of savage freedom after a murderous fight with his father. Most appropriately, for according to Lawrence's *Studies in Classic American Literature,* one essential symbolic act of the American is the murder of Father Europe, and another is re-baptism in the wilderness.

We may observe those symbolic acts throughout our tradition, in a hundred variations from the crude and barbarous to the highly sophisticated. Emerson was performing them in such essays as "Self-Reliance" ("Trust thyself: every heart vibrates to that iron string") and "The American Scholar" ("We have listened too long to the courtly muses of Europe"). Whitman sent them as a barbaric yawp over the rooftops of the world. Thoreau spoke them in the quotation with which I began this lecture, and put them into practice in his year on Walden Pond.

The virtues of the frontiersman, real or literary, are Indian virtues, warrior qualities of bravery, endurance, stoical indifference to pain and hardship, recklessness, contempt for law, a hawk-like need of freedom. Often in practice an outlaw, the frontiersman in literature is likely to display a certain noble savagery, a degree of natural goodness that has a more sophisticated parallel in the common American delusion, shared even by Jefferson, who should have known better, that untutored genius is more to be admired than genius schooled. In the variants of the frontiersman that Henry Nash Smith traces in *Virgin Land*—in flatboatman, logger, cowboy, miner, in literary and mythic figures from the Virginian to the Lone Ranger and Superman—the Indian qualities persist, no matter how overlaid with comedy or occupational detail. Malcolm Cowley has shown how they emerge in a quite different sort of literature in the stiff-upper-lip code hero of Ernest Hemingway.

We need not admire them wholeheartedly in order to recognize them in their modern forms. They put the Winchesters on the gun racks of pick-ups and the fury into the arguments of the gun lobby. They dictate the leather of Hell's Angels and the whanged buckskin of drugstore Carsons. Our most ruthless industrial, financial, and military buccaneers have displayed them. The Sagebrush Rebellion and those who would open Alaska to a final stage of American continent-busting adopt them as a platform. Without them there would have been no John Wayne movies. At least as much as the sobriety and self-reliant industry of the pioneer farmer, it is the restlessness and intractability of the frontiersman that drives our modern atavists away from civilization into the woods and deserts, there to build their yurts and geodesic domes and live self-reliant lives with no help except from trust funds, unemployment insurance, and food stamps.

This mythic figure lasts. He is a model of conduct of many kinds. He directs our fantasies. Curiously, in almost all his historic forms he is both landless and destructive, his kiss is the kiss of death. The hunter roams the wilderness but owns none of it. As Daniel Boone, he served the interests of speculators and capitalists; even as Henry David Thoreau he ended his life as a surveyor of town lots. As mountain man he was virtually a bond servant to the company, and his indefatigable labors all but eliminated the beaver and undid all the conservation work of beaver engineering. The logger achieved his roughhouse liberty within the constraints of a brutally punishing job whose result was the enrichment of great capitalist families such as the Weyerhausers and the destruction of most of the magnificent American forests. The cowboy, so mythically free in books and movies, was a hired man on horseback, a slave to cows and the deadliest enemy of the range he used to ride.

Do these figures represent our wistful dream of freedom from the shackles of family and property? Probably they do. It may be important to note that it is the mountain man, logger, and cowboy whom we have made into myths, not the Astors and General Ashleys, the Weyerhausers, or the cattle kings. The lowlier figures, besides being more democratic and so matching the folk image better, may incorporate a dream not only of freedom but of irresponsibility. In any case, any variety of the frontiersman is more attractive to modern Americans than is the responsible, pedestrian, hard-working pioneer farmer breaking his back in a furrow to achieve ownership of his claim and give his children a start in the world. The freedom of the frontiersman is a form of mortal risk and contains the seed of its own destruction. The shibboleth of this breed is prowess.

The pioneer farmer is another matter. He had his own forms of self-reliance; he was a mighty coper, but his freedom of movement was restricted by family and property, and his shibboleth was not prowess but growth. He put off the present in favor of the future. Travelers on the Midwestern frontier during the 1820s, '30s, and '40s were universally moved to amazement at how farms, villages, even cities, had risen magically where only a few years before bears had been measuring their reach on the trunks of trees. British travelers such as Mrs. Trollope found the pioneer farms primitive, the towns crude, and the brag of the townsmen offensive, but Americans such as Timothy Flint, Thomas Nuttall, and John James Audubon regarded the settlement of the Midwest with a pride that was close to awe. Mormons looking back on their communal miracles in Nauvoo and Salt Lake City feel that same pride. Progress we have always measured quantitatively, in terms of acres plowed, turnpikes graded, miles of railroad built, bridges and canals constructed. I heard former Governor Pat Brown of California chortle with delight when the word came that California had passed New York in the population race. All through our history we have had the faith that growth is good, and bigger is better.

And here we may observe a division, a fault-line, in American feeling. Cooper had it right in *The Pioneers* nearly 160 years ago. Leatherstocking owns Cooper's imagination, but the town builders own the future, and Leatherstocking has to give way. *The Pioneers* is at once an exuberant picture of the breaking of the wilderness and a lament for its passing; and it is as much the last of the frontiersmen as the last of the Mohicans that the Leatherstocking series mourns. Many of Cooper's successors have felt the same way—hence the elegiac tone of so many of our novels of the settlement and the land. We hear it in Willa Cather's *A Lost Lady*, where the railroad builder Captain Forrester is so much larger than anyone in the shrunken present. We hear it in Larry McMurtry's *Horseman, Pass By*, which before it was made into the movie *Hud* was a requiem for the old-time cattleman. A country virtually without history and with no regard for history—history is bunk, said Henry Ford—exhibits an odd mournfulness over the passing of its brief golden age.

The romantic figure of the frontiersman was doomed to pass with the wilderness that made him. He was essentially over by the 1840s, though in parts of the West he lingered on as an anachronism. His epitaph was read, as Frederick Jackson Turner noted in a famous historical essay, by the census of 1890, which found no continuous line of frontier existing anywhere in the United States. He was not the only one who died of that census report. The pioneer farmer died too, for without a frontier there was no more free land. But whether the qualities that the frontier had built into both frontiersman and farmer died when the line of settlement withered at the edge of the shortgrass plains—that is not so clear.

4

Not only was free land gone by 1890, or at least any free land capable of settlement, but by the second decade of the twentieth century the population of the United States, despite all the empty spaces in the arid West, had reached the density which historians estimate congested Europe had had in 1500. The growth that Jefferson had warned against had gone on with astounding speed. The urban poor of Europe whose immigration he would have discouraged had swamped the original nation of mainly Protestant, mainly North European origins, and together with the industrial revolution, accelerated by the Civil War, had created precisely the sort of manufacturing nation, complete with urban slums and urban discontents, that he had feared. We were just at the brink of changing over from the nation of cultivators that Crèvecoeur had described and Jefferson advocated into an industrial nation dominated by corporations and capitalistic buccaneers still unchecked by any social or political controls.

The typical American was not a self-reliant and independent landowner, but a wage earner; and the victory of the Union in the Civil War had released into the society millions of former slaves whose struggle to achieve full citizenship was sure to trouble the waters of national complacency for a century and perhaps much longer. The conditions that had given us freedom and opportunity and optimism were over, or seemed to be. We were entering the era of the muckrakers, and we gave them plenty of muck to rake. And even by 1890 the note of disenchantment, the gloomy Dostoyevskyan note that William Dean Howells said did not belong in American literature, which should deal with the more smiling aspects of life, had begun to make its way into our novels.

After 1890 we could ask ourselves in increasing anxiety the question that Thoreau had asked rhetorically in 1862. To what end *did* the world go on, and why *was* America discovered? Had the four hundred years of American experience created anything new, apart from some myths as remote as Romulus and Remus, or were we back in the unbreakable circle from which Columbus had sprung us?

From 1890 to the present there have been plenty of commentators, with plenty of evidence on their side, to say that indeed we have slipped back into that vicious circle; and when we examine the products of the Melting Pot we find lugubrious reminders that it has not melted everybody down into any sort of standard American. What we see instead is a warring melee of minority groups—racial, ethnic, economic, sexual, linguistic— all claiming their right to the American standard without surrendering the cultural identities that make them still unstandard. We seem to be less a nation than a collection of what current cant calls "communi-ties": the Black Community, the Puerto Rican Community, the Chicano Community, the Chinese Community, the Gay Community, the Financial Community, the Academic Community, and a hundred others. We seem to approach not the standard product of the Melting Pot but the mosaic that Canadians look forward to, and that they think will save them from becoming the stereotypes they think we are.

With all respect to Canada, we are not a set of clones. We are the wild-est mixture of colors, creeds, opinions, regional differences, occupations, and types. Nor is Canada the permanent mosaic it says it wants to be. Both nations, I am convinced, move with glacial slowness toward that unity in diversity, that *e pluribus unum* of a North American synthesis, that is inevitable, or nearly so, no matter which end it is approached from. When we arrive there, a century or two or three hence, darker of skin and more united in mind, the earlier kind of American who was shaped by the frontier will still be part of us—of each of us, even if our ancestors came to this continent after the frontier as a fact was gone.

For as Turner pointed out, the repeated experience of the frontier through more than 250 years coalesced gradually into a package of beliefs, habits, faiths, assumptions, and values, and these values in turn gave birth to laws and institutions that have had a continuous shaping effect on every newer American who enters the society either by birth or immigration. These are the things that bind us together no matter how many other forces may be pushing us apart. Language is one thing. I believe it has to be English, for language is at the core of every culture and inseparable from its other manifestations. If we permit bilingualism or multilingualism more than temporarily as an aid to assimilation, we will be balkanized and undone, as Canada is in danger of being by the apparently irremediable division between the Anglophones and the Francophones. The Bill of Rights is another unifier. We rely on it daily—even our enemies rely on it. And the images of ourselves, including the variant myths, that we developed when we were a younger, simpler, and more hopeful nation are still another. The national character, diffuse or not, recognizable if not definable, admirable and otherwise, bends newcomers to its image and outlasts time, change, crowding, shrinking resources, and fashionable pessimism. It has bent those apparently untouched by the Melting Pot, bent them more than they may know. Thus James Baldwin, visiting Africa, discovered to his surprise that though black, he was no African: he was an American, and thought and felt like one.

Time makes slow changes in our images of ourselves, but at their best, the qualities our writers and mythmakers have perpetuated are worth our imitation. The untutored decency and mongrel smartness of Huckleberry Finn, as well as the dignity that the slave Jim salvaged out of an oppressed life, could only have been imagined in America. The innocent philistinism of Howells' Silas Lapham could have been imagined by a European observer, but the ethical worth that nearly ennobles Lapham in his financial crisis is—realistic or not—pure American. Henry James' American, significantly named Christopher Newman, has a magnanimity that matches his naïveté. And the literary archetypes of the pre-1890 period are not the only ones. We have had political leaders who have represented us in more than political ways, and two at least who have taught us at the highest level who we are and who we might be.

Washington I could never get next to; he is a noble impersonal obelisk on the Mall. But Jefferson and Lincoln are something else. Jefferson did more than any other man to shape this democracy: formulated its principles in the Declaration of Independence and insisted on the incorporation of the Bill of Rights into the Constitution; had a hand in preventing the establishment of a state church; created the monetary system; framed the rules for the government of the western territories; invented the pattern for the survey of the public domain; bought Louisiana; sent Lewis and Clark to the western ocean and back, thus fathering one of our most heroic legends and inventing Manifest Destiny. If he had a clouded love affair with the slave half-sister of his dead wife, that only winds him more tightly into the ambiguous history of his country. As for Lincoln, he gave eloquence and nobility to the homespun values of frontier democracy. He was native mind and native virtue at their highest reach, and he too, like Jefferson but more sternly, was mortally entangled in the slave question that threatened to break America apart before it came of age.

Historians in these anti-heroic times have sometimes scolded the folk mind for apotheosizing Jefferson and Lincoln; and certainly, from their temples on the Potomac, they do brood over our national life like demi-gods. But as Bernard DeVoto said in one of his stoutly American "Easy Chairs," the folk mind is often wiser than the intellectuals. It knows its heroes and clings to them stubbornly even when heroes are out of fashion. Unfortunately, it is about as unreliable in its choice of heroes as in its creation of myths. It has a dream of jackpots as well as a dream of moral nobility and political freedom; it can make a model for imitation out of Jim Fisk or a myth out of a psychopathic killer like Billy the Kid almost as readily as it makes them out of the Great Emancipator.

5

These days, young people do not stride into their future with the confidence their grandparents knew. Over and over, in recent years, I have heard the cold undertone of doubt and uncertainty when I talk with college students. The American Dream has suffered distortion and attrition; for many, it is a dream glumly awakened from.

Per Hansa, in *Giants in the Earth,* could homestead Dakota farmland, gamble his strength against nature, lose his life in the struggle, but win in the end by handing down a productive farm to his son, and insuring him a solid, self-respecting place in the world. Per Hansa's grandsons have no such chances. Only one of them can inherit the family farm, for it would not be an economic unit if divided (it barely is while still undivided), and so something like primogeniture must be invoked to protect it. The other sons cannot hope to buy farms of their own. Land is too high, money is too expensive, machinery is too costly. The products of a farm acquired on those terms could not even pay the interest on the debt. So the other sons have a choice between leaving the farm, which they know and like, and going into the job market; or hiring out as tenant farmers or hired hands to some factory in the field. All over the United States, for several decades, farms have become fewer, larger, and more mechanized, and family ownership has grown less. Though I have no statistics in the matter, I would not be surprised to hear before the end of the 1980s that investors from the Middle East, Hong Kong, and Japan own as much American farmland as independent American farmers do.

For the vast majority of American youth who are not farmers, the options of independence have likewise shrunk. What they have to consider, more likely than not, is a job—a good job, in a company with a good pay scale, preferably, and with guaranteed promotions and a sound retirement plan. The future is not a thing we want to risk; when possible, we insure against it. And for the economically disadvantaged, the core-city youth, the minorities ethnic or otherwise, the people with inferior capacities or bad training or no luck, it is as risky as it ever was in frontier times, but without the promise it used to hold, and with no safety valve such as free land used to provide.

So we return to the vision of Christopher Lasch in *The Culture of Narcissism*. With some of it, especially its glib Freudian analyses of straw men, I am not in sympathy. By some parts, even when I think accurate observations are being marshaled to a dubious conclusion, I have to be impressed. The vision is apocalyptic. Lasch sees our cities as bankrupt or ungovernable or both, our political life corrupt, our bureaucracies greedy and expanding, our great corporations pervaded by the dog-eat-dog individualism of managerial ambition, maximized profits, and "business ethics"—which bear the same relation to ethics that military intelligence bears to intelligence. He sees Americans degraded by selfishness, cynicism, and venality, religion giving way to therapy and lunatic cults, education diluted by the no-fail concept, high school graduates unable to sign their names, family life shattered and supervision of children increasingly passed on to courts, clinics, or the state. He sees sexuality rampant, love extinct, work avoided, instant pleasure pursued as the whole aim of life. He sees excellence disparaged because our expectations so far exceed our deserving that any real excellence is a threat. He sees the Horatio Alger hero replaced in the American Pantheon by the Happy Hooker, the upright sportsmanship of Frank Merriwell replaced by the sports manners of John McEnroe, and all the contradictory strains of American life beginning to focus in the struggle between a Far Right asserting frontier ruthlessness and unhampered free enterprise, and a welfare liberalism to which even the requirement of reading English in order to vote may seem like a violation of civil rights.

The culture hero of Lasch's America is no Jefferson or Lincoln, no Leatherstocking or Carson, no Huck Finn or Silas Lapham. He is no hero at all, but the limp, whining anti-hero of Joseph Heller's *Something Happened*—self-indulgent, sneaky, scared of his superiors, treacherous to his inferiors, held together only by clandestine sex and by a sticky sentiment for the children to whom he has given nothing, the wife whom he ignores and betrays, and the mother whom he filed away in a nursing home and forgot.

Not quite what Thoreau predicted. The question is—and it is a question forced by Lasch's implication that his generalizations, and Heller's character, speak for the whole culture—does the Lasch-Heller characteristic American match the Americans you know in Salt Lake City and I know in California and other people know in Omaha and Des Moines and Wichita and Dallas and Hartford and Bangor?

I doubt that we know many such limp dishrags as Heller's Bob Slocum, but we recognize elements of the world he lives in. We have watched the progress of the sexual revolution and the one-hoss-shay collapse of the family. We have observed how, in the mass media and hence in the popular imagination, celebrity has crowded out distinction. We have seen the gap widen between rich and poor, have seen crime push itself into high places and make itself all but impregnable, have watched the drug culture work outward from the ghettos into every level of American life. We are not unaware of how the Pleasure Principle, promoted about equally by prosperity, advertisers, and a certain kind of therapist, has eaten the pilings out from under dedication and accomplishment; how we have given up saving for the future and started spending for the present, because the Pleasure Principle preaches gratification, because the tax laws and inflation discourage saving and encourage borrowing. We have stood by uneasily while the Pleasure Principle invaded the schools, and teachers tried desperately to save something out of the wreck by pretending to be entertainers. Johnny can't read, but he expects his English class to be as entertaining as an X-rated movie. Increasingly he seems to be a vessel which dries out and deteriorates if it is not kept filled, and so for his leisure hours he must have a four-hundred-dollar stereo and/or a color TV, and when he walks around he carries a transistor radio, tuned loud. If he doesn't get a ski weekend during the winter term, he calls a school strike. He has never worn a tie, but he can vote, being eighteen.

We have lived through times when it has seemed that everything ran downhill, when great corporations were constantly being caught in bribery, price fixing, or the dumping of chemical wastes in the public's backyard—when corporate liberty, in other words, was indulged at the public expense. We have seen the proliferation of government bureaus, some of them designed to curb corporate abuses and some apparently designed only to inhibit the freedom of citizens. We have watched some of our greatest cities erupt in mindless violence. We have built ourselves a vast industrial trap in which, far from being the self-reliant individuals we once were, and still are in fantasy, we are absolutely helpless when the power fails.

Can any of the values left over from the frontier speak persuasively to the nation we have become? Some of the most antisocial of them still do, especially the ruthless go-getterism of an earlier phase of capitalism. Single-minded dedication, self-reliance, a willingness to work long and hard persist most visibly not in the average democratic individual but in the managers of exploitative industry and in spokesmen for the Far Right. Expressed in a modern context, they inspire not admiration but repulsion, they make us remember that some of the worst things we have done to our continent, our society, and our character have been done under their auspices. We remain a nation of real estate operators, trading increasingly small portions of the increasingly overburdened continent back and forth at increasingly inflated prices.

But I have a faith that, however obscured and overlooked, other tendencies remain from our frontier time. In spite of multiplying crises, galloping inflation, energy shortages, a declining dollar, shaken confidence, crumbling certainties, we cannot know many Americans without perceiving stubborn residues of toughness, ingenuity, and cheerfulness. The American is far less antisocial than he used to be; he has had to learn social values as he created them. Outside of business, where he still has a great deal to learn, he is very often such a human being as the future would be safe with.

I recognize Heller's Bob Slocum as one kind of contemporary American, but I do not commonly meet him in my own life. The kind I do meet may be luckier than most, but he seems to me far more representative than Bob Slocum, and I have met him all over the country and among most of the shifting grades of American life. He is likely to work reasonably hard, but not kill himself working; he doesn't have to, whether he is an electronics plant manager or a professor or a bricklayer. If he is still an individualist in many ways, he is also a belonger. If he belongs to a minority he is probably a civil rights activist, or at least sympathizer. If he belongs to that group of "middle Americans" about whom Robert Coles wrote a perceptive book, he may be confused and shaken by some equal-opportunity developments, but as often as not he understands the historical context and the necessity for increasing the access to opportunity, and if not supportive, is at least acquiescent.

He has not given up the future, as Lasch believes. He is often very generous. He gives to good causes, or causes he thinks good, and in a uniquely American way he associates himself with others in ad hoc organizations to fight for better schools, more parks, political reforms, social justice. That is the remote but unmistakable echo of the Plymouth Compact—government improvised for the occasion; government of, by, and for the people.

This American may be pinched, but he is not poor by any definition. He is lower middle, middle middle, upper middle. Whether he works for a corporation, a university, a hospital, a government bureau, whether he is a skilled laborer or a professional, he has a considerable stake in this society. He is always respectful of money, but he cannot be called money-crazy: money-craziness occurs much more commonly among the poor who have far too little or the rich who have far too much. Unless he is financially involved in growth, in which case he may be everything I have just said he is not, he is wary of uncontrolled growth and even opposed to it. Free enterprise in the matter of real estate speculation strikes him as more often fruitful of social ill than social good, just as industrialization strikes him not as the cure for our ills but the cause of many of them. He takes his pleasures and relaxations, and expects far more of them than his frontier grandparents did, but he can hardly be called a pleasure freak bent on instant gratification. He is capable, as many of us observed

during a recent California drought, of abstinence and economy and personal sacrifice in the public interest, and would be capable of much more
of those if he had leaders who encouraged them.

This sort of American is either disregarded or disparaged in the alarming books that assay our culture. Lasch, though he would like him better
than the kind he describes, seems to think him gone past retrieval. But
Lasch, like some other commentators, is making a point and selects his
evidence. To some extent also, he makes the New Yorker mistake of mistaking New York for the United States. To an even greater extent he reads
a certain class as if it were a cross section of the entire population. He
would honestly like to get us back onto the tracks he thinks we have left,
or onto new tracks that lead somewhere, and he deplores what he sees as
much as anyone would.

But in fact we may be more on the tracks than he believes we are. His
book is rather like the books of captious British travelers in the first half
of the nineteenth century. Not having experienced the potency of the
dream of starting from scratch, he sees imperfections as failures, not as
stages of a long slow effort. But there is something very American about
The Culture of Narcissism, too. We have always had a habit, when we
were not bragging, of accepting Father Europe's view that we are short
on cultural finesse and that our fabled moral superiority is a delusion. It
may be a delusion; that does not make an American a creature unworthy
of study, or American society a dismal failure. We have never given up the
habit we acquired while resisting George III: we knock government and
authority, including our own; we bad-mouth ourselves; like Robert Frost's
liberal, we won't take our own side in an argument.

It is time we did. In 1992, twelve years from now, it will be half a millennium since Columbus and his sailors poured out on deck to see the
new world. In half a millennium we should have gone at least partway
toward what we started out to be. In spite of becoming the dominant
world power, the dominant industrial as well as agricultural nation, the
dominant force for freedom in the world, in spite of the fact that historically our most significant article of export has been the principle of
liberty, in spite of the fact that the persecuted and poor of the earth still
look to the United States as their haven and their hope—ask a Mexican
wetback family, ask a family of Vietnamese boat people—many of us
have never quite got it straight what it was we started out to be, and some
of us have forgotten.

Habits change with time, but the principles have not changed. We
remain a free and self-reliant people and a land of opportunity, and if
our expectations are not quite what they once were, they are still greater
expectations than any people in the world can indulge. A little less prosperity might be good for some of us, and I think we can confidently expect
God to provide what we need. We could also do with a little less pleasure,

learn to limit it in quantity and upgrade it in quality. Like money, pleasure is an admirable by-product and a contemptible goal. That lesson will still take some learning.

Give us time. Half a millennium is not enough. Give us time to wear out the worst of the selfishness and greed and turn our energy to humane and socially useful purposes. Give us a perennial few (a few is all any society can expect, and all any society really needs) who do not forget the high purpose that marked our beginnings, and Thoreau may yet be proved right in his prophecy.

Above all, let us not forget or mislay our optimism about the possible. In all our history we have never been more than a few years without a crisis, and some of those crises, the Civil War for one, and the whole problem of slavery, have been graver and more alarming than our present one. We have never stopped criticizing the performance of our elected leaders, and we have indeed had some bad ones and have survived them. The system was developed by accident and opportunity, but it is a system of extraordinary resilience. The United States has a ramshackle government, Robert Frost told Khrushchev in a notable conversation. The more you ram us, the harder we shackle. In the midst of our anxiety we should remember that this is the oldest and stablest republic in the world. Whatever its weaknesses and failures, we show no inclination to defect. The currents of defection flow the other way.

Let us not forget who we started out to be, or be surprised that we have not yet arrived. Robert Frost can again, as so often, be our spokesman. "The land was ours before we were the land's," he wrote. "Something we were withholding made us weak, until we found that it was ourselves we were withholding from our land of living." He was a complex, difficult, often malicious man, with grave faults. He was also one of our great poets, as much in the American grain as Lincoln or Thoreau. He contained within himself many of our most contradictory qualities, he never learned to subdue his selfish personal demon—and he was never a favorite of the New York critics, who thought him a country bumpkin.

But like the folk mind, he was wiser than the intellectuals. No American was ever wiser. Listening to him, we can refresh ourselves with our own best image, and renew our vision of America: not as Perfection, not as Heaven on Earth, not as New Jerusalem, but as flawed glory and exhilarating task.

CYNTHIA OZICK

Cynthia Ozick (1928–), hailed by David Foster Wallace as one of the greatest living American writers, is equally devoted to fiction and essays. Her many essay collections have included literary criticism, memoir pieces, polemics, ruminations on Jewish themes, and usually something about Henry James, whose rigorous example not only inspired her but also, she jestingly complained, stole her youth. "When I say I 'became' Henry James, you must understand this: though I was a near-sighted twenty-two-year-old young woman infected with the commonplace intention of writing a novel, I was also the elderly bald-headed Henry James." This desire to meet the standards of great literature, combined with a wry sensitivity to the comic mortifications of daily life, have contributed to forming her original prose style. "A Drugstore in Winter" is one of two masterly essays she has written about her pharmacy upbringing, the other being the more often anthologized "A Drugstore Eden."

A Drugstore in Winter

(1982)

This is about reading; a drugstore in winter; the gold leaf on the dome of the Boston State House; also loss, panic, and dread.

First, the gold leaf. (This part is a little like a turn-of-the-century pulp tale, though only a little. The ending is a surprise, but there is no plot.) Thirty years ago I burrowed in the Boston Public Library one whole afternoon, to find out—not out of curiosity—how the State House got its gold roof. The answer, like the answer to most Bostonian questions, was Paul

Revere. So I put Paul Revere's gold dome into an "article," and took it (though I was just as scared by recklessness then as I am now) to the *Boston Globe,* on Washington Street. The Features Editor had a bare severe head, a closed parenthesis mouth, and silver Dickensian spectacles. He made me wait, standing, at the side of his desk while he read; there was no bone in me that did not rattle. Then he opened a drawer and handed me fifteen dollars. Ah, joy of Homer, joy of Milton! Grub Street bliss!

The very next Sunday, Paul Revere's gold dome saw print. Appetite for more led me to a top-floor chamber in Filene's department store: Window Dressing. But no one was in the least bit dressed—it was a dumbstruck nudist colony up there, a mob of naked frozen enigmatic manikins, tall enameled skinny ladies with bald breasts and skulls, and legs and wrists and necks that horribly unscrewed. Paul Revere's dome paled beside this gold mine! A sight—mute numb Walpurgisnacht—easily worth another fifteen dollars. I had a Master's degree (thesis topic: "Parable in the Later Novels of Henry James") and a job as an advertising copywriter (9 a.m. to 6 p.m. six days a week, forty dollars per week; if you were male and had no degree at all, sixty dollars). Filene's Sale Days—Crib Bolsters! Lulla-Buys! Jonnie-Mops! Maternity Skirts with Expanding Invisible Trick Waist! And a company show; gold watches to mark the retirement of elderly Irish salesladies; for me the chance to write song lyrics (to the tune of "On Top of Old Smoky") honoring our Store. But "Mute Numb Walpurgisnacht in Secret Downtown Chamber" never reached the *Globe.* Melancholy and meaning business, the Advertising Director forbade it. Grub Street was bad form, and I had to promise never again to sink to another article. Thus ended my life in journalism.

Next: reading, and certain drugstore winter dusks. These come together. It is an aeon before Filene's, years and years before the Later Novels of Henry James. I am scrunched on my knees at a round glass table near a plate glass door on which is inscribed, in gold leaf Paul Revere never put there, letters that must be read backward: ʏɔɒmɿɒʜꟼ wɘiV ʞɿɒꟼ There is an evening smell of late coffee from the fountain, and all the librarians are lined up in a row on the tall stools, sipping and chattering. They have just stepped in from the cold of the Traveling Library, and so have I. The Traveling Library is a big green truck that stops, once every two weeks, on the corner of Continental Avenue, just a little way in from Westchester Avenue, not far from a house that keeps a pig. Other houses fly pigeons from their roofs, other yards have chickens, and down on Mayflower there is even a goat. This is Pelham Bay, the Bronx, in the middle of the Depression, all cattails and weeds, such a lovely place and tender hour! Even though my mother takes me on the subway far, far downtown to buy my winter coat in the frenzy of Klein's on Fourteenth Street, and even though I can recognize the heavy power of a quarter, I don't know it's the Depression. On the trolley on the way to Westchester Square I see the children who live in the boxcar strangely set down in an empty lot some distance from Spy Oak (where a Revolutionary traitor was hanged—served him right for siding with redcoats); the lucky boxcar children dangle their stick-legs from their train-house maw and wave; how I envy them! I envy the orphans of the Gould Foundation, who have their own private swings and seesaws. Sometimes I imagine I am an orphan, and my father is an impostor pretending to be my father.

My father writes in his prescription book: *#59330 Dr. O'Flaherty Pow .60/ #59331 Dr. Mulligan Gtt .65/ #59332 Dr. Thron Tab .90.* Ninety cents! A terrifically expensive medicine; someone is really sick. When I deliver a prescription around the corner or down the block, I am offered a nickel tip. I always refuse, out of conscience; I am, after all, the Park View Pharmacy's own daughter, and it wouldn't be seemly. My father grinds and mixes powders, weighs them out in tiny snowy heaps on an apothecary scale, folds them into delicate translucent papers or meticulously drops them into gelatin capsules.

In the big front window of the Park View Pharmacy there is a startling display—goldfish bowls, balanced one on the other in amazing pyramids. A German lady enters, one of my father's cronies—his cronies are both women and men. My quiet father's eyes are water-color blue, he wears his small skeptical quiet smile and receives the neighborhood's life-secrets. My father is discreet and inscrutable. The German lady pokes a punchboard with a pin, pushes up a bit of rolled paper, and cries out—she has just won a goldfish bowl, with two swimming goldfish in it! Mr. Jaffe, the salesman from McKesson & Robbins, arrives, trailing two mists: winter steaminess and the animal fog of his cigar,* which melts into the coffee smell, the tarpaper smell, the eerie honeyed tangled drugstore smell. Mr. Jaffe and my mother and father are intimates by now, but because it is the 1930s, so long ago, and the old manners still survive, they address one another gravely as Mr. Jaffe, Mrs. Ozick, Mr. Ozick. My mother calls my father Mr. O, even at home, as in a Victorian novel. In the street my father tips his hat to ladies. In the winter his hat is a regular fedora; in the summer it is a straw boater with a black ribbon and a jot of blue feather.

What am I doing at this round glass table, both listening and not listening to my mother and father tell Mr. Jaffe about their struggle with "Tessie," the lion-eyed landlady who has just raised, threefold, in the middle of that Depression I have never heard of, the Park View Pharmacy's devouring rent? My mother, not yet forty, wears bandages on her ankles, covering oozing varicose veins; back and forth she strides, dashes,

---

* Mr. Matthew Bruccoli, another Bronx drugstore child, has written to say that he remembers with certainty that Mr. Jaffe did not smoke. In my memory the cigar is somehow there, so I leave it.

runs, climbing cellar stairs or ladders; she unpacks cartons, she toils behind drug counters and fountain counters. Like my father, she is on her feet until one in the morning, the Park View's closing hour. My mother and father are in trouble, and I don't know it. I am too happy. I feel the secret center of eternity, nothing will ever alter, no one will ever die. Through the window, past the lit goldfish, the gray oval sky deepens over our neighborhood wood, where all the dirt paths lead down to seagull-specked water. I am familiar with every frog-haunted monument: Pelham Bay Park is thronged with WPA art—statuary, fountains, immense rococo staircases cascading down a hillside, Bacchus-faced stelae—stone Roman glories afterward mysteriously razed by an avenging Robert Moses. One year—how distant it seems now, as if even the climate is past returning—the bay froze so hard that whole families, mine among them, crossed back and forth to City Island, strangers saluting and calling out in the ecstasy of the bright trudge over such a sudden wilderness of ice.

In the Park View Pharmacy, in the winter dusk, the heart in my body is revolving like the goldfish fleet-finned in their clear bowls. The librarians are still warming up over their coffee. They do not recognize me, though only half an hour ago I was scrabbling in the mud around the two heavy boxes from the Traveling Library—oafish crates tossed with a thump to the ground. One box contains magazines—*Boy's Life, The American Girl, Popular Mechanix*. But the other, the other! The other transforms me. It is tumbled with storybooks, with clandestine intimations and transfigurations. In school I am a luckless goosegirl, friendless and forlorn. In P.S. 71 I carry, weighty as a cloak, the ineradicable knowledge of my scandal—I am cross-eyed, dumb, an imbecile at arithmetic; in P.S. 71 I am publicly shamed in Assembly because I am caught not singing Christmas carols; in P.S. 71 I am repeatedly accused of deicide. But in the Park View Pharmacy, in the winter dusk, branches blackening in the park across the road, I am driving in rapture through the Violet Fairy Book and the Yellow Fairy Book, insubstantial chariots snatched from the box in the mud. I have never been *inside* the Traveling Library; only grownups are allowed. The boxes are for the children. No more than two books may be borrowed, so I have picked the fattest ones, to last. All the same, the Violet and the Yellow are melting away. Their pages dwindle. I sit at the round glass table, dreaming, dreaming. Mr. Jaffe is murmuring advice. He tells a joke about Wrong-Way Corrigan. The librarians are buttoning up their coats. A princess, captive of an ogre, receives a letter from her swain and hides it in her bosom. I can visualize her bosom exactly—she clutches it against her chest. It is a tall and shapely vase, with a hand-painted flower on it, like the vase on the secondhand piano at home.

I am incognito. No one knows who I truly am. The teachers in P.S. 71 don't know. Rabbi Meskin, my *cheder* teacher, doesn't know. Tessie the lion-eyed landlady doesn't know. Even Hymie the fountain clerk can't know—though he understands other things better than anyone: how to tighten roller skates with a skatekey, for instance, and how to ride a horse. On Friday afternoons, when the new issue is out, Hymie and my brother fight hard over who gets to see *Life* magazine first. My brother is older than I am, and doesn't like me; he builds radios in his bedroom, he is already W2LOM, and operates his transmitter *(da-di-da-dit, da-da-di-da)* so penetratingly on Sunday mornings that Mrs. Eva Brady, across the way, complains. Mrs. Eva Brady has a subscription to *The Writer;* I fill a closet with her old copies. How to Find a Plot. Narrative and Character, the Writer's Tools. Because my brother has his ham license, I say, "I have a license too." "What kind of license?" my brother asks, falling into the trap. "Poetic license," I reply; my brother hates me, but anyhow his birthday presents are transporting: one year *Alice in Wonderland, Pinocchio* the next, then *Tom Sawyer.* I go after Mark Twain, and find Joan of Arc and my first satire, *Christian Science.* My mother surprises me with *Pollyanna,* the admiration of her Lower East Side childhood, along with *The Lady of the Lake.* Mrs. Eva Brady's daughter Jeannie has outgrown her Nancy Drews and Judy Boltons, so on rainy afternoons I cross the street and borrow them, trying not to march away with too many—the child of immigrants, I worry that the Bradys, true and virtuous Americans, will judge me greedy or careless. I wrap the Nancy Drews in paper covers to protect them. Old Mrs. Brady, Jeannie's grandmother, invites me back for more. I am so timid I can hardly speak a word, but I love her dark parlor; I love its black bookcases. Old Mrs. Brady sees me off, embracing books under an umbrella; perhaps she divines who I truly am. My brother doesn't care. My father doesn't notice. I think my mother knows. My mother reads the *Saturday Evening Post* and the *Woman's Home Companion;* sometimes the *Ladies' Home Journal,* but never *Good Housekeeping.* I read all my mother's magazines. My father reads *Drug Topics* and *Der Tog,* the Yiddish daily. In Louie Davidowitz's house (waiting our turn for the rabbi's lesson, he teaches me chess in *cheder*) there is a piece of furniture I am in awe of: a shining circular table that is also a revolving bookshelf holding a complete set of Charles Dickens. I borrow *Oliver Twist.* My cousins turn up with *Gulliver's Travels, Just So Stories, Don Quixote,* Oscar Wilde's *Fairy Tales,* uncannily different from the usual kind.

Blindfolded, I reach into a Thanksgiving grabbag and pull out *Mrs. Leicester's School,* Mary Lamb's desolate stories of rejected children. Books spill out of rumor, exchange, miracle. In the Park View Pharmacy's lending library I discover, among the nurse romances, a browning, brittle miracle: *Jane Eyre.* Uncle Morris comes to visit (his drugstore is on the other side of the Bronx) and leaves behind, just like that, a three-volume

Shakespeare. Peggy and Betty Provan, Scottish sisters around the corner, lend me their *Swiss Family Robinson*. Norma Foti, a whole year older, transmits a rumor about Louisa May Alcott; afterward I read *Little Women* a thousand times. Ten thousand! I am no longer incognito, not even to myself. I am Jo in her "vortex"; not Jo exactly, but some Jo-of-the-future. I am under an enchantment: who I truly am must be deferred, waited for and waited for. My father, silently filling capsules, is grieving over his mother in Moscow. I write letters in Yiddish to my Moscow grandmother, whom I will never know. I will never know my Russian aunts, uncles, cousins. In Moscow there is suffering, deprivation, poverty. My mother, threadbare, goes without a new winter coat so that packages can be sent to Moscow. Her fiery justice-eyes are semaphores I cannot decipher.

Some day, when I am free of P.S. 71, I will write stories; meanwhile, in winter dusk, in the Park View, in the secret bliss of the Violet Fairy Book, I both see and do not see how these grains of life will stay forever, papa and mama will live forever, Hymie will always turn my skatekey. Hymie, after Italy, after the Battle of the Bulge, comes back from the war with a present: *From Here to Eternity*. Then he dies, young. Mama reads *Pride and Prejudice* and every single word of Willa Cather. Papa reads, in Yiddish, all of Sholem Aleichem and Peretz. He reads Malamud's *The Assistant* when I ask him to.

Papa and mama, in Staten Island, are under the ground. Some other family sits transfixed in the sun parlor where I read *Jane Eyre* and *Little Women* and, long afterward, *Middlemarch*. The Park View Pharmacy is dismantled, turned into a Hallmark card shop. It doesn't matter! I close my eyes, or else only stare, and everything is in its place again, and everyone.

A writer is dreamed and transfigured into being by spells, wishes, goldfish, silhouettes of trees, boxes of fairy tales dropped in the mud, uncles' and cousins' books, tablets and capsules and powders, papa's Moscow ache, his drugstore jacket with his special fountain pen in the pocket, his beautiful Hebrew paragraphs, his Talmudist's rationalism, his Russian-Gymnasium Latin and German, mama's furnace-heart, her masses of memoirs, her paintings of autumn walks down to the sunny water, her braveries, her reveries, her old, old school hurts.

A writer is buffeted into being by school hurts—Orwell, Forster, Mann!—but after a while other ambushes begin: sorrows, deaths, disappointments, subtle diseases, delays, guilts, the spite of the private haters of the poetry side of life, the snubs of the glamorous, the bitterness of those for whom resentment is a daily gruel, and so on and so on; and then one day you find yourself leaning here, writing at that selfsame round glass table salvaged from the Park View Pharmacy—writing this, an impossibility, a summary of how you came to be where you are now, and where, God knows, is that? Your hair is whitening, you are a well of tears, what you meant to do (beauty and justice) you have not done, papa and mama are under the earth, you live in panic and dread, the future shrinks and darkens, stories are only vapor, your inmost craving is for nothing but an old scarred pen, and what, God knows, is that?

AUDRE LORDE

Audre Lorde (1934–1992) was a poet, essayist, and self-described "Black lesbian feminist" whose writing and activism formed an inseparable whole. Her essays, suffused with eloquent passion and outrage at injustice, were a clarion call to many, and have gone on to become crucial texts in feminist theory, race studies, and queer theory. Rather than arguing that we are all alike, she stressed the importance of acknowledging difference as a means to correcting the marginality of groups suffering from majority prejudice. She taught at various universities, experiencing herself as an outsider in mostly white institutions, and used that perspective to lecture fellow feminists in the address below, whose very title has become canonical.

The Master's Tools Will Never Dismantle the Master's House

(1983)

I agreed to take part in a New York University Institute for the Humanities conference a year ago, with the understanding that I would be commenting upon papers dealing with the role of difference within the lives of American women: difference of race, sexuality, class, and age. The absence of these considerations weakens any feminist discussion of the personal and the political.

It is a particular academic arrogance to assume any discussion of feminist theory without examining our many differences, and without a significant input from poor women, Black and Third World women, and lesbians. And yet, I stand here as a Black lesbian feminist, having been invited to comment within the only panel at this conference where the input of Black feminists and lesbians is represented. What this says about the vision of this conference is sad, in a country where racism, sexism, and homophobia are inseparable. To read this program is to assume that lesbian and Black women have nothing to say about existentialism, the erotic, women's culture and silence, developing feminist theory, or heterosexuality and power. And what does it mean in personal and political terms when even the two Black women who did present here were literally found at the last hour? What does it mean when the tools of a racist patriarchy are used to examine the fruits of that same patriarchy? It means that only the most narrow parameters of change are possible and allowable.

The absence of any consideration of lesbian consciousness or the consciousness of Third World women leaves a serious gap within this conference and within the papers presented here. For example, in a paper on material relationships between women, I was conscious of an either/or model of nurturing which totally dismissed my knowledge as a Black lesbian. In this paper there was no examination of mutuality between women, no systems of shared support, no interdependence as exists between lesbians and women-identified women. Yet it is only in the patriarchal model of nurturance that women "who attempt to emancipate themselves pay perhaps too high a price for the results," as this paper states.

For women, the need and desire to nurture each other is not pathological but redemptive, and it is within that knowledge that our real power I rediscovered. It is this real connection which is so feared by a patriarchal world. Only within a patriarchal structure is maternity the only social power open to women.

Interdependency between women is the way to a freedom which allows the "I" and "be," not in order to be used, but in order to be creative. This is a difference between the passive *be* and the active *being*.

Advocating the mere tolerance of difference between women is the grossest reformism.

It is a total denial of the creative function of difference in our lives. Difference must be not merely tolerated, but seen as a fund of necessary polarities between which our creativity can spark like a dialectic. Only then does the necessity for interdependency become unthreatening. Only within that interdependency of different strengths, acknowledged and equal, can the power to seek new ways of being in the world generate, as well as the courage and sustenance to act where there are no charters.

Within the interdependence of mutual (nondominant) differences lies that security which enables us to descend into the chaos of knowledge and return with true visions of our future, along with the concomitant power to effect those changes which can bring that future into being. Difference is that raw and powerful connection from which our personal power is forged.

As women, we have been taught either to ignore our differences, or to view them as causes for separation and suspicion rather than as forces for change. Without community there is no liberation, only the most vulnerable and temporary armistice between an individual and her oppression. But community must not mean a shedding of our differences, nor the pathetic pretense that these differences do not exist.

Those of us who stand outside the circle of this society's definition of acceptable women; those of us who have been forged in the crucibles of difference—those of us who are poor, who are lesbians, who are Black, who are older—know that *survival is not an academic skill*. It is learning how to take our differences and make them strengths. *For the master's tools will never dismantle the master's house.* They may allow us temporarily to beat him at his own game, but they will never enable us to bring about genuine change. And this fact is only threatening to those women who still define the master's house as their only source of support.

Poor women and women of Color know there is a difference between the daily manifestations of marital slavery and prostitution because it is our daughters who line 42nd Street. If white American feminist theory need not deal with the differences between us, and the resulting difference in our oppressions, then how do you deal with the fact that the women who clean your houses and tend your children while you attend conferences on feminist theory are, for the most part, poor women and women of Color? What is the theory behind racist feminism?

In a world of possibility for us all, our personal visions help lay the groundwork for political action. The failure of academic feminists to recognize difference as a crucial strength is a failure to reach beyond the first patriarchal lesson. In our world, divide and conquer must become define and empower.

Why weren't other women of Color found to participate in this conference? Why were two phone calls to me considered a consultation? Am I the only possible source of names of Black feminists? And although the Black panelist's paper ends on an important and powerful connection of love between women, what about interracial cooperation between feminists who don't love each other?

In academic feminist circles, the answer to these questions is often, "We do not know who to ask." But that is the same evasion of responsibility, the same cop-out, that keeps Black women's art out of women's exhibitions, Black women's work out of most feminist publications except for the occasional "Special Third World Women's Issue," and Black women's texts off your reading lists. But as Adrienne Rich pointed out in a recent talk, which feminists have educated themselves about such an enormous amount over the past ten years, how come you haven't also educated yourselves about Black women and the differences between us—white and Black—when it is key to our survival as a movement?

Women of today are still being called upon to stretch across the gap of male ignorance and to educate men as to our existence and our needs. This is an old and primary tool of all oppressors to keep the oppressed occupied with the master's concerns. Now we hear that it is the task of women of Color to educate white women—in the face of tremendous resistance—as to our existence, our differences, our relative roles in our joint survival. This is a diversion of energies and a tragic repetition of racist patriarchal thought.

Simone de Beauvoir once said: "It is in the knowledge of the genuine conditions of our lives that we must draw our strength to live and our reasons for acting."

Racism and homophobia are real conditions of all our lives in this place and time. *I urge each one of us here to reach down into that deep place of knowledge inside herself and touch that terror and loathing of any difference that lives there. See whose face it wears.* Then the personal as the political can begin to illuminate all our choices.

> Prospero, you are the master of illusion.
> Lying is your trademark.
> And you have lied so much to me
> (Lied about the world, lied about me)
> That you have ended by imposing on me
> An image of myself.
> Underdeveloped, you brand me, inferior,
> That's the way you have forced me to see myself
> I detest that image! What's more, it's a lie!
> But now I know you, you old cancer,
> And I know myself as well.
>
> —Caliban, in Aime Cesaire's *A Tempest*

ROLANDO HINOJOSA

Rolando Hinojosa (1929–), a fiction writer, essayist, poet, professor of English at The University of Texas at Austin, and major figure in Chicano literature, has written extensively about his region, the Lower Rio Grande Valley, in a series of interconnected novels called the Klail City Death Trip Series. Bilingual, writing with equal flair in Spanish and English, he has been uniquely suited to articulate the concerns of those who live on the Border, as he does in his sage, informative essay, "This Writer's Sense of Place."

This Writer's Sense of Place

(1983)

I begin with a quote from a man imprisoned for his participation in the Texas–Santa Fe Expedition of 1841; while in his cell in Mexico City, he spurned Santa Anna's offer of freedom in exchange for renouncing the Republic of Texas. Those words of 1842 were said by a man who had signed the Texas Declaration of Independence and who had served in the Congress of the Republic. Later on, he was to cast a delegate vote for annexation and contributed to the writing of the first state constitution. He would win election to the state legislature and still later he would support secession.

And this is what he said:

> I have sworn to be a good Texan; and that I will not forswear. I will die for that which I firmly believe, for I know it is just and

right. One life is a small price for a cause so great. As I fought, so
shall I be willing to die. I will never forsake Texas and her cause.
I am her son.

The words were written by José Antonio Navarro. A Texas historian named James Wilson once wrote that Navarro's name is virtually
unknown to Texas school children and, for the most part, unknown to
their teachers as well. A lifetime of living in my native land leads me to
believe that Professor Wilson is correct in his assessment of the lack of
knowledge of this place in which we were born and in which some of us
still live.

The year 1985 marked the 100th anniversary of the birth of my father,
Manuel Guzmán Hinojosa, in the Campacuás Ranch, some three miles
north of Mercedes, down in the Valley; his father was born on that ranch
as was his father's father. On the maternal side, my mother arrived in the
Valley at the age of six weeks in the year 1887 along with one of the first
Anglo-American settlers enticed to the mid-Valley by Jim Wells, one of
the early developers on the northern bank. As you may already know, it's
no accident that Jim Wells County in South Texas is named for him.

One of the earliest stories I heard about Grandfather Smith was a supposed conversation he held with Lawyer Wells. You are being asked to
imagine the month of July in the Valley with no air conditioning in 1887;
Wells was extolling the Valley and he said that all it needed was a little
water and a few good people. My grandfather replied, "Well, that's all
Hell needs, too." The story is apocryphal; it has to be. But living in the
Valley, and hearing that type of story laid the foundation for what I later
learned was to give me a sense of place. By that I do not mean that I had a
feel for the place; no, not at all. I had a sense of it, and by that I mean that
I was not learning about the culture of the Valley, but living it, forming
part of it, and thus, contributing to it.

But a place is merely that until it is populated, and once populated,
the histories of the place and its people begin. For me and mine, history
began in 1749 when the first colonists began moving into the southern and
northern banks of the Rio Grande. That river was not yet a jurisdictional
barrier and was not to be until almost 100 years later; but, by then, the
border had its own history, its own culture and its own sense of place: it
was Nuevo Santander, named for old Santander in the Spanish Peninsula.

The last names were similar up and down on both banks of the river,
and as second and third cousins were allowed to marry, this further pro-
mulgated and propagated blood relationships and that sense of belonging
that led the Borderers to label their fellow Mexicans who came from the
interior, as *fuereños,* or outsiders; and later, when the people from the
North started coming to the Border, these were labeled *gringos,* a word

for foreigner, and nothing else, until the *gringo* himself, from all evidence, took the term as a pejorative label.

For me, then, part of a sense of the Border came from sharing: the sharing of names, of places, of a common history and of belonging to the place; one attended funerals, was taken to cemeteries, and one saw names that corresponded to one's own or to one's friends and neighbors, and relatives.

When I first started to write, and being what we call "empapado," which translates as drenched, imbibed, soaked or drunk with the place, I had to eschew the romanticism and the sentimentalism that tend to blind the unwary, that get in the way of truth. It's no great revelation when I say that romanticism and sentimentalism tend to corrupt clear thinking as well. The Border wasn't paradise, and it didn't have to be; but it was more than paradise, it was home (and as Frost once wrote, home, when you have to go there, is the place where they have to take you in).

And the Border was home; and it was also the home of the petty officeholder elected by an uninformed citizenry; a home for bossism and for old-time smuggling as a way of life for some. But, it also maintained the remains of a social democracy that cried out for independence, for a desire to be left alone and for the continuance of community.

The history one learned there was an oral one and somewhat akin to the oral religion brought by the original colonials. Many of my generation were raised with the music written and composed by Valley people, and we learned the ballads of the Border little knowing that it was a true native art form. And one was also raised and steeped in the stories and exploits of Juan Nepomuceno Cortina, in the nineteenth century, and with stories of the Texas Rangers in that century and of other Ranger stories in this century and then, as always, names, familiar patronymics: Jacinto Treviño, Aniceto Pizaña, the Seditionists of 1915 who had camped in Mercedes, and where my father would take me and show and mark for me the spot where the Seditionists had camped and barbecued their meat half a generation before. These were men of flesh and bone who lived and died there in Mercedes, in the Valley. And then there were the stories of the Revolution of 1910, and of the participation in it for the next ten years off and on by Valley *mexicanos* who fought alongside their south bank relatives, and the stories told to me and to those of my generation by exiles, men and women from Mexico, who earned a living by teaching us school on the northern bank while they bided their time to return to Mexico.

But we didn't return to Mexico; we didn't have to; we were Borderers with a living and unifying culture born of conflict with another culture and this, too, helped to cement further still the knowing exactly where one came from and from whom one was descended.

The language, too, was a unifier and as strong an element as there is in fixing one's sense of place; the language of the Border is a derivative of the Spanish language of Northern Mexico, a language wherein some nouns and other grammatical complements were no longer used in the Spanish Peninsula, but which persisted there; and the more the linguistically uninformed went out of their way to denigrate the language, the stiffer the resistance to maintain it and to nurture it on the northern bank. And the uninformed failed, of course, for theirs was a momentary diversion while one was committed to its preservation; the price that many Texas Mexicans paid for keeping the language and the sense of place has been exorbitant.

As Borderers, the north bank Border Mexican couldn't, to repeat a popular phrase, "go back to where you came from." The Borderer was there and had been before the interlopers; but what of the indigenous population prior to the 1749 settlement? Since Nuevo Santander was never under the presidio system and since its citizens did not build missions that trapped and stultified the indigenous people, they remained there and, in time, settled down or were absorbed by the colonial population and thus the phrase hurled at the Border Mexican "go back to where you came from" was, to use another popular term, "inoperative." And this, too, fostered that sense of place.

For the writer—this writer—a sense of place was not a matter of importance; it became essential. And so much so that my stories are not held together by the *peripeteia* or the plot as much as by what the people who populate the stories say and how they say it, how they look at the world out and the world in; and the works, then, become studies of perceptions and values and decisions reached by them because of those perceptions and values which in turn were fashioned and forged by the place and its history.

What I am saying here is not to be taken to mean that it is impossible for a writer to write about a place, its history and its people, if the writer is not from that particular place; it can be done, and it has been done. What I am saying is that I needed a sense of place, and that this helped me no end in the way that, I would say, Américo Paredes in *With His Pistol in His Hand,* Larry McMurtry in *Horseman, Pass By,* Fred Gipson in *Hound Dog Man,* William Owens in that fine, strong *This Stubborn Soil* and Tomás Rivera in *. . . and the earth did not part* were all helped by a sense of place. And I say this, because to me, these writers and others impart a sense of place and a sense of truth about the place and about the values of that place. Theirs isn't a studied attitude, but rather one of a certain love, to use that phrase, and an understanding for the place that they captured in print for themselves; something that was, for themselves, then, at that time and there. A sense of place, as Newark, New Jersey, is for Phillip Roth, and thus we see him surprised at himself when he tells us he dates a *schicksa,* and then, the wonderful storyteller that he is, he tells us of his Jewish traditions and conflicts, and we note that it becomes a pattern in some of his writings whenever he writes of relationships, which, after all, is what writers usually write about: relationships.

I am not making a medieval pitch for the shoemaker to stick to his last here, but if the writer places a lifetime of living in a work, the writer sometimes finds it difficult to remove the place of provenance from the writings, irrespective of where he situates his stories. That's a strong statement and one which may elicit comment or disagreement, but what spine one has is formed early in life, and it is formed at a specific place; later on when one grows up, one may mythicize, adopt a persona, become an actor, restructure family history, but the original facts of one's formation remain as facts always do.

It's clear, then, that I am not speaking of the formula novel, nor is it my intent to denigrate it or its practitioners; far from it. I consider the formula novel as a fine art, if done well, and many of us know that they do exist. I speak of something else—neither nobler nor better, no— merely different from that genre. It's a personal thing, because I found that after many years of hesitancy, and fits and spurts, and false starts, that despite what education I had acquired, I was still limited in many ways; that whatever I attempted to write, came out false and frail. Now, I know I wanted to write, had to write, was burning to write and all of those things that some writers say to some garden clubs, but the truth and heart of the matter was that I did not know where to begin; and there it was again, that adverb of place, the *where;* and then I got lucky: I decided to write whatever it was I had, in Spanish, and I decided to set it on the border, in the Valley.

As reduced as that space was, it too was Texas with all of its contradictions and its often repeated one-sided telling of Texas history. When the characters stayed in the Spanish-speaking milieu or society, the Spanish language worked well, and then it was in the natural order of things that English made its entrance when the characters strayed or found themselves in Anglo institutions; in cases where both cultures would come into contact, both languages were used, and I would employ both, and where one and only would do, I would follow that as well. What dominated, then, was the place, at first. Later on I discovered that generational and class differences also dictated not only usage but which language as well. From this came the *how* they said *what* they said. As the census rolls filled up in the works, so did some distinguishing features, characteristics, viewpoints, values, decisions, and thus I used the Valley and the Border, and the history and the people. The freedom to do this also led me to use the folklore and the anthropology of the Valley and to use whatever literary form I desired and saw fit to use to tell my stories: dialogs, duologs, monologs, imaginary newspaper clippings and whatever else I felt would be of use. And it was the Valley, but it remained forever Texas. At the same time, I could see this Valley, this border, and I drew a map, and this, too, was another key, and this led to more work and to more characters in that place.

It was a matter of luck in some ways, as I said, but mostly it was the proper historical moment; it came along, and I took what had been there for some time, but which I had not been able to see, since I had not fully developed a sense of place; I had left the Valley for the service, for formal university training and for a series of very odd jobs, only to return to it in my writing.

I have mentioned values and decisions; as I see them, these are matters inculcated by one's elders first, by one's acquaintances later on and usually under the influence of one's society which is another way of saying one's place of origin. Genetic structure may enter into holding on to certain values and perhaps in the manner of reaching decisions, for all I know. Ortega y Gasset, among others, I suspect, wrote that man makes dozens of decisions every day, and that the process helps man to make and to reach more serious, deliberate and even important decisions when the time presents itself. A preparatory stage, as it were. The point of this is that my decision to write what I write and where I choose to situate the writing is not based on anything else other than to write about what I know, the place I know, the language used, the values held. When someone mentions universality, I say that what happens to my characters happens to other peoples of the world at given times, and I've no doubt on that score. What has helped me to write has also been a certain amount of questionable self-education, a long and fairly misspent youth in the eyes of some, an acceptance of certain facts and some misrepresentations of the past which I could not change, but which led to a rejection not of those unalterable facts but of hypocrisy and the smugness of the self-satisfied. For this and other personal reasons, humor creeps into my writing once in a while, because it was the use of irony, as many of us know, that allowed the Borderer to survive and to maintain a certain measure of dignity.

Serious writing is deliberate as well as a consequence of an arrived-to decision; what one does with it may be of value or not, but I believe that one's fidelity to history is the first step to fixing a sense of place, whether that place is a worldwide arena or a corner of it, as is mine.

NANCY MAIRS

Nancy Mairs (1943–2016) has become an indispensable voice in disability studies, though she began writing and publishing her literate essays before there was any such academic field. Afflicted by multiple sclerosis, she wrote with remarkable candor, humor (sometimes bawdy), and lack of self-pity, refusing ever to play the victim. Her writing also touched frequently on spirituality, as she was a practicing Catholic, and on her experiences as a wife, mother, and teacher. The title of her signature piece, "On Being a Cripple," suggests a loyalty to the ruminative essay tradition by her invocation of the word "on," while her use of the problematic word "cripple" is explained by her as opting for a time-honored if harshly realistic term rather than a euphemistic softening.

On Being a Cripple

(1986)

> To escape is nothing. Not to escape is nothing.
>
> —Louise Bogan

The other day I was thinking of writing an essay on being a cripple. I was thinking hard in one of the stalls of the women's room in my office building, as I was shoving my shirt into my jeans and tugging up my zipper. Preoccupied, I flushed, picked up my book bag, took my cane down from the hook, and unlatched the door. So many movements unbalanced me, and as I pulled the door open I fell over backward, landing fully clothed on the toilet seat with my legs splayed in front of me: the old beetle-on-its-back routine. Saturday afternoon, the building deserted, I was free to laugh aloud as I wriggled back to my feet, my voice bouncing off the yellowish tiles from all directions. Had anyone been there with me, I'd have been still and faint and hot with chagrin. I decided that it was high time to write the essay.

First, the matter of semantics. I am a cripple. I choose this word to name me. I choose from among several possibilities, the most common of which are "handicapped" and "disabled." I made the choice a number of years ago, without thinking, unaware of my motives for doing so. Even now, I'm not sure what those motives are, but I recognize that they are complex and not entirely flattering. People—crippled or not—wince at the word "cripple," as they do not at "handicapped" or "disabled." Perhaps I want them to wince. I want them to see me as a tough customer, one to whom the fates/gods/viruses have not been kind, but who can face the brutal truth of her existence squarely. As a cripple, I swagger.

But, to be fair to myself, a certain amount of honesty underlies my choice. "Cripple" seems to me a clean word, straightforward and precise. It has an honorable history, having made its first appearance in the Lindisfarne Gospel in the tenth century. As a lover of words, I like the accuracy with which it describes my condition: I have lost the full use of my limbs. "Disabled," by contrast, suggests any incapacity, physical or mental. And I certainly don't like "handicapped," which implies that I have deliberately been put at a disadvantage, by whom I can't imagine (my God is not a Handicapper General), in order to equalize chances in the great race of life. These words seem to me to be moving away from my condition, to be widening the gap between word and reality. Most remote is the recently coined euphemism "differently abled," which partakes of the same semantic hopefulness that transformed countries from "undeveloped" to "underdeveloped," then to "less developed," and finally to "developing" nations. People have continued to starve in those countries during the shift. Some realities do not obey the dictates of language.

Mine is one of them. Whatever you call me, I remain crippled. But I don't care what you call me, so long as it isn't "differently abled," which strikes me as pure verbal garbage designed, by its ability to describe anyone, to describe no one. I subscribe to George Orwell's thesis that "the slovenliness of our language makes it easier for us to have foolish thoughts." And I refuse to participate in the degeneration of the language to the extent that I deny that I have lost anything in the course of this calamitous disease; I refuse to pretend that the only differences between you and me are the various ordinary ones that distinguish any one person from another. But call me "disabled" or "handicapped" if you like. I have long since grown accustomed to them; and if they are vague, at least they hint at the truth. Moreover, I use them myself. Society is no readier to accept crippledness than to accept death, war, sex, sweat, or wrinkles. I would never refer to another person as a cripple. It is the word I use to name only myself.

I haven't always been crippled, a fact for which I am soundly grateful. To be whole of limb is, I know from experience, infinitely more pleasant and useful than to be crippled; and if that knowledge leaves me open to bitterness at my loss, the physical soundness I once enjoyed (though I did not enjoy it half enough) is well worth the occasional stab of regret. Though never any good at sports, I was a normally active child and young adult. I climbed trees, played hopscotch, jumped rope, skated, swam, rode my bicycle, sailed. I despised team sports, spending some of the wretchedest afternoons of my life, sweaty and humiliated, behind a field-hockey stick and under a basketball hoop. I tramped alone for miles along the bridle paths that webbed the woods behind the house I grew up in. I swayed through countless dim hours in the arms of one man or another under the scattered shot of light from mirrored balls, and gyrated through countless more as Tab Hunter and Johnny Mathis gave way to the Rolling Stones, Creedence Clearwater Revival, Cream. I walked down the aisle. I pushed baby carriages, changed tires in the rain, marched for peace.

When I was twenty-eight I started to trip and drop things. What at first seemed my natural clumsiness soon became too pronounced to shrug off. I consulted a neurologist, who told me that I had a brain tumor. A battery of tests, increasingly disagreeable, revealed no tumor. About a year and a half later I developed a blurred spot in one eye. I had, at last, the episodes "disseminated in space and time" requisite for a diagnosis: multiple sclerosis. I have never been sorry for the doctor's initial misdiagnosis, however. For almost a week, until the negative results of the tests were in, I thought that I was going to die right away. Every day for the past nearly ten years, then, has been a kind of gift. I accept all gifts.

Multiple sclerosis is a chronic degenerative disease of the central nervous system, in which the myelin that sheathes the nerves is somehow eaten away and scar tissue forms in its place, interrupting the nerves' signals. During its course, which is unpredictable and uncontrollable, one may lose vision, hearing, speech, the ability to walk, control of bladder and/or bowels, strength in any or all extremities, sensitivity to touch, vibration, and/or pain, potency, coordination of movements—the list of possibilities is lengthy and, yes, horrifying. One may also lose one's sense of humor. That's the easiest to lose and the hardest to survive without.

In the past ten years, I have sustained some of these losses. Characteristic of MS are sudden attacks, called exacerbations, followed by remissions, and these I have not had. Instead, my disease has been slowly progressive. My left leg is now so weak that I walk with the aid of a brace and a cane; and for distances I use an Amigo, a variation on the electric wheelchair that looks rather like an electrified kiddie car. I no longer have much use of my left hand. Now my right side is weakening as well. I still have the blurred spot in my right eye. Overall, though, I've been lucky so far. My world has, of necessity, been circumscribed by my losses, but the terrain left me has been ample enough for me to continue many of the activities that absorb me: writing, teaching, raising children and cats and plants and snakes, reading, speaking publicly about MS and depression, even playing bridge with people patient and honorable enough to let me scatter cards every which way without sneaking a peek.

Lest I begin to sound like Pollyanna, however, let me say that I don't like having MS. I hate it. My life holds realities—harsh ones, some of them—that no right-minded human being ought to accept without grumbling. One of them is fatigue. I know of no one with MS who does not complain of bone-weariness; in a disease that presents an astonishing variety of symptoms, fatigue seems to be a common factor. I wake up in the morning feeling the way most people do at the end of a bad day, and I take it from there. As a result, I spend a lot of time *in extremis* and, impatient with limitation, I tend to ignore my fatigue until my body breaks down in some way and forces rest. Then I miss picnics, dinner parties, poetry readings, the brief visits of old friends from out of town. The offspring of a puritanical tradition of exceptional venerability, I cannot view these lapses without shame. My life often seems a series of small failures to do as I ought.

I lead, on the whole, an ordinary life, probably rather like the one I would have led had I not had MS. I am lucky that my predilections were already solitary, sedentary, and bookish—unlike the world-famous French cellist I have read about, or the young woman I talked with one long afternoon who wanted only to be a jockey. I had just begun graduate school when I found out something was wrong with me, and I have remained, interminably, a graduate student. Perhaps I would not have if I'd thought I had the stamina to return to a full-time job as a technical editor; but I've enjoyed my studies.

In addition to studying, I teach writing courses. I also teach medical students how to give neurological examinations. I pick up freelance editing jobs here and there. I have raised a foster son and sent him into the world, where he has made me two grandbabies, and I am still escorting my daughter and son through adolescence. I go to Mass every Saturday. I am a superb, if messy, cook. I am also an enthusiastic laundress, capable of sorting a hamper full of clothes into five subtly differentiated piles, but a terrible housekeeper. I can do italic writing and, in an emergency, bathe an oil-soaked cat. I play a fiendish game of Scrabble. When I have the time and the money, I like to sit on my front steps with my husband, drinking Amaretto and smoking a cigar, as we imagine our counterparts in Leningrad and make sure that the sun gets down once more behind the sharp childish scrawl of the Tucson Mountains.

This lively plenty has its bleak complement, of course, in all the things

I can no longer do. I will never run again, except in dreams, and one day I may have to write that I will never walk again. I like to go camping, but I can't follow George and the children along the trails that wander out of a campsite through the desert or into the mountains. In fact, even on the level I've learned never to check the weather or try to hold a coherent conversation: I need all my attention for my wayward feet. Of late, I have begun to catch myself wondering how people can propel themselves without canes. With only one usable hand, I have to select my clothing with care not so much for style as for ease of ingress and egress, and even so, dressing can be laborious. I can no longer do fine stitchery, pick up babies, play the piano, braid my hair. I am immobilized by acute attacks of depression, which may or may not be physiologically related to MS but are certainly its logical concomitant.

These two elements, the plenty and the privation, are never pure, nor are the delight and wretchedness that accompany them. Almost every pickle that I get into as a result of my weakness and clumsiness—and I get into plenty—is funny as well as maddening and sometimes painful. I recall one May afternoon when a friend and I were going out for a drink after finishing up at school. As we were climbing into opposite sides of my car, chatting, I tripped and fell, flat and hard, onto the asphalt parking lot, my abrupt departure interrupting him in mid-sentence. "Where'd you go?" he called as he came around the back of the car to find me hauling myself up by the door frame. "Are you all right?" Yes, I told him, I was fine, just a bit rattly, and we drove off to find a shady patio and some beer. When I got home an hour or so later, my daughter greeted me with "What have you done to yourself?" I looked down. One elbow of my white turtleneck with the green froggies, one knee of my white trousers, one white kneesock were blood-soaked. We peeled off the clothes and inspected the damage, which was nasty enough but not alarming. That part wasn't funny: The abrasions took a long time to heal, and one got a little infected. Even so, when I think of my friend talking earnestly, suddenly, to the hot thin air while I dropped from his view as though through a trap door, I find the image as silly as something from a Marx Brothers movie.

I may find it easier than other cripples to amuse myself because I live propped by the acceptance and the assistance and, sometimes, the amusement of those around me. Grocery clerks tear my checks out of my checkbook for me, and sales clerks find chairs to put into dressing rooms when I want to try on clothes. The people I work with make sure I teach at times when I am least likely to be fatigued, in places I can get to, with the materials I need. My students, with one anonymous exception (in an end-of-the-semester evaluation), have been unperturbed by my disability. Some even like it. One was immensely cheered by the information that I paint my own fingernails; she decided, she told me, that if I could go to such trouble over fine details, she could keep on writing essays. I suppose I became some sort of bright-fingered muse. She wrote good essays, too.

The most important struts in the framework of my existence, of course, are my husband and children. Dismayingly few marriages survive the MS test, and why should they? Most twenty-two- and nineteen-year-olds, like George and me, can vow in clear conscience, after a childhood of chicken pox and summer colds, to keep one another in sickness and in health so long as they both shall live. Not many are equipped for catastrophe: the dismay, the depression, the extra work, the boredom that a degenerative disease can insinuate into a relationship. And our society, with its emphasis on fun and its association of fun with physical performance, offers little encouragement for a whole spouse to stay with a crippled partner. Children experience similar stresses when faced with a crippled parent, and they are more helpless, since parents and children can't usually get divorced. They hate, of course, to be different from their peers, and the child whose mother is tacking down the aisle of a school auditorium packed with proud parents like a Cape Cod dinghy in a stiff breeze jolly well stands out in a crowd. Deprived of legal divorce, the child can at least deny the mother's disability, even her existence, forgetting to tell her about recitals and PTA meetings, refusing to accompany her to stores or church or the movies, never inviting friends to the house. Many do.

But I've been limping along for ten years now, and so far George and the children are still at my left elbow, holding tight. Anne and Matthew vacuum floors and dust furniture and haul trash and rake up dog droppings and button my cuffs and bake lasagna and Toll House cookies with just enough grumbling so I know that they don't have brain fever. And far from hiding me, they're forever dragging me by racks of fancy clothes or through teeming school corridors, or welcoming gaggles of friends while I'm wandering through the house in Anne's filmy pink babydoll pajamas. George generally calls before he brings someone home, but he does just as many dumb thankless chores as the children. And they all yell at me, laugh at some of my jokes, write me funny letters when we're apart—in short, treat me as an ordinary human being for whom they have some use. I think they like me. Unless they're faking. . . .

Faking. There's the rub. Tugging at the fringes of my consciousness always is the terror that people are kind to me only because I'm a cripple. My mother almost shattered me once, with that instinct mothers have—blind, I think, in this case, but unerring nonetheless—for striking blows along the fault-lines of their children's hearts, by telling me, in an attack on my selfishness, "We all have to make allowances for you, of course, because of the way you are." From the distance of a couple of years, I have to admit that I haven't any idea just what she meant, and I'm not sure that she knew either. She was awfully angry. But at the time, as the words thudded home, I felt my worst fear, suddenly realized. I could bear being called selfish: I am. But I couldn't bear the corroboration that those around me were doing in fact what I'd always suspected them of doing, professing fondness while silently putting up with me because of the way I am. A cripple. I've been a little cracked ever since.

Along with this fear that people are secretly accepting shoddy goods comes a relentless pressure to please—to prove myself worth the burdens I impose, I guess, or to build a substantial account of goodwill against which I may write drafts in times of need. Part of the pressure arises from social expectations. In our society, anyone who deviates from the norm had better find some way to compensate. Like fat people, who are expected to be jolly, cripples must bear their lot meekly and cheerfully. A grumpy cripple isn't playing by the rules. And much of the pressure is self-generated. Early on I vowed that, if I had to have MS, by God I was going to do it well. This is a class act, ladies and gentlemen. No tears, no recriminations, no faint-heartedness.

One way and another, then, I wind up feeling like Tiny Tim, peering over the edge of the table at the Christmas goose, waving my crutch, piping down God's blessing on us all. Only sometimes I don't want to play Tiny Tim. I'd rather be Caliban, a most scurvy monster. Fortunately, at home no one much cares whether I'm a good cripple or a bad cripple as long as I make vichyssoise with fair regularity. One evening several years ago, Anne was reading at the dining-room table while I cooked dinner. As I opened a can of tomatoes, the can slipped in my left hand and juice spattered me and the counter with bloody spots. Fatigued and infuriated, I bellowed, "I'm so sick of being crippled!" Anne glanced at me over the top of her book. "There now," she said, "do you feel better?" "Yes," I said, "yes, I do." She went back to her reading. I felt better. That's about all the attention my scurviness ever gets.

Because I hate being crippled, I sometimes hate myself for being a cripple. Over the years I have come to expect—even accept—attacks of violent self-loathing. Luckily, in general our society no longer connects deformity and disease directly with evil (though a charismatic once told me that I have MS because a devil is in me) and so I'm allowed to move largely at will, even among small children. But I'm not sure that this revision of attitude has been particularly helpful. Physical imperfection, even freed of moral disapprobation, still defies and violates the ideal, especially for women, whose confinement in their bodies as objects of desire is far from over. Each age, of course, has its ideal, and I doubt that ours is any better or worse than any other. Today's ideal woman, who lives on the glossy pages of dozens of magazines, seems to be between the ages of eighteen and twenty-five; her hair has body, her teeth flash white, her breath smells minty, her underarms are dry; she has a career but is still a fabulous cook, especially of meals that take less than twenty minutes to prepare; she does not ordinarily appear to have a husband or children; she is trim and deeply tanned; she jogs, swims, plays tennis, rides a bicycle, sails, but does not bowl; she travels widely, even to out-of-the-way places like Finland and Samoa, always in the company of the ideal man, who possesses a nearly identical set of characteristics. There are a few exceptions. Though usually white and often blonde, she may be black, Hispanic, Asian, or Native American, so long as she is unusually sleek. She may be old, provided she is selling a laxative or is Lauren Bacall. If she is selling a detergent, she may be married and have a flock of strikingly messy children. But she is never a cripple.

Like many women I know, I have always had an uneasy relationship with my body. I was not a popular child, largely, I think now, because I was peculiar: intelligent, intense, moody, shy, given to unexpected actions and inexplicable notions and emotions. But as I entered adolescence, I believed myself unpopular because I was homely: my breasts too flat, my mouth too wide, my hips too narrow, my clothing never quite right in fit or style. I was not, in fact, particularly ugly, old photographs inform me, though I was well off the ideal; but I carried this sense of self-alienation with me into adulthood, where it regenerated in response to the depredations of MS. Even with my brace I walk with a limp so pronounced that, seeing myself on the videotape of a television program on the disabled, I couldn't believe that anything but an inchworm could make progress humping along like that. My shoulders droop and my pelvis thrusts forward as I try to balance myself upright, throwing my frame into a bony S. As a result of contractures, one shoulder is higher than the other and I carry one arm bent in front of me, the fingers curled into a claw. My left arm and leg have wasted into pipe-stems, and I try always to keep them covered. When I think about how my body must look to others, especially to men, to whom I have been trained to display myself, I feel ludicrous, even loathsome.

At my age, however, I don't spend much time thinking about my appearance. The burning egocentricity of adolescence, which assures one that all the world is looking all the time, has passed, thank God, and I'm generally too caught up in what I'm doing to step back, as I used to, and watch myself as though upon a stage. I'm also too old to believe in the accuracy of self-image. I know that I'm not a hideous crone, that in fact, when I'm rested, well dressed, and well made up, I look fine. The self-loathing I feel is neither physically nor intellectually substantial. What I hate is not me but a disease.

I am not a disease.

And a disease is not—at least not singlehandedly—going to determine who I am, though at first it seemed to be going to. Adjusting to a chronic incurable illness, I have moved through a process similar to that outlined by Elizabeth Kübler-Ross in *On Death and Dying*. The major difference—and it is far more significant than most people recognize—is that I can't be sure of the outcome, as the terminally ill cancer patient can. Research studies indicate that, with proper medical care, I may achieve a "normal" life span. And in our society, with its vision of death as the ultimate evil, worse even than decrepitude, the response to such news is, "Oh well, at least you're not going to *die*." Are there worse things than dying? I think that there may be.

I think of two women I know, both with MS, both enough older than I to have served me as models. One took to her bed several years ago and has been there ever since. Although she can sit in a high-backed wheel-chair, because she is incontinent she refuses to go out at all, even though incontinence pants, which are readily available at any pharmacy, could protect her from embarrassment. Instead, she stays at home and insists that her husband, a small quiet man, a retired civil servant, stay there with her except for a quick weekly foray to the supermarket. The other woman, whose illness was diagnosed when she was eighteen, a nursing student engaged to a young doctor, finished her training, married her doctor, accompanied him to Germany when he was in the service, bore three sons and a daughter, now grown and gone. When she can, she travels with her husband; she plays bridge, embroiders, swims regularly; she works, like me, as a symptomatic-patient instructor of medical students in neurology. Guess which woman I hope to be.

At the beginning, I thought about having MS almost incessantly. And because of the unpredictable course of the disease, my thoughts were always terrified. Each night I'd get into bed wondering whether I'd get out again the next morning, whether I'd be able to see, to speak, to hold a pen between my fingers. Knowing that the day might come when I'd be physically incapable of killing myself, I thought perhaps I ought to do so right away, while I still had the strength. Gradually I came to understand that the Nancy who might one day lie inert under a bedsheet, arms and legs paralyzed, unable to feed or bathe herself, unable to reach out for a gun, a bottle of pills, was not the Nancy I was at present, and that I could not presume to make decisions for that future Nancy, who might well not want in the least to die. Now the only provision I've made for the future Nancy is that when the time comes—and it is likely to come in the form of pneumonia, friend to the weak and the old—I am not to be treated with machines and medications. If she is unable to communicate by then, I hope she will be satisfied with these terms.

Thinking all the time about having MS grew tiresome and intrusive, especially in the large and tragic mode in which I was accustomed to considering my plight. Months and even years went by without catastrophe (at least without one related to MS), and really I was awfully busy, what with George and children and snakes and students and poems, and I hadn't the time, let alone the inclination, to devote myself to being a disease. Too, the richer my life became, the funnier it seemed, as though there were some connection between largesse and laughter, and so my tragic stance began to waver until, even with the aid of a brace and a cane, I couldn't hold it for very long at a time.

After several years I was satisfied with my adjustment. I had suffered my grief and fury and terror, I thought, but now I was at ease with my lot. Then one summer day I set out with George and the children across the desert for a vacation in California. Part way to Yuma I became aware that my right leg felt funny. "I think I've had an exacerbation," I told George. "What shall we do?" he asked. "I think we'd better get the hell to California," I said, "because I don't know whether I'll ever make it again." So we went on to San Diego and then to Orange, up the Pacific Coast Highway to Santa Cruz, across to Yosemite, down to Sequoia and Joshua Tree, and so back over the desert to home. It was a fine two-week trip, filled with friends and fair weather, and I wouldn't have missed it for the world, though I did in fact make it back to California two years later. Nor would there have been any point in missing it, since in MS, once the symptoms have appeared, the neurological damage has been done, and there's no way to predict or prevent that damage.

The incident spoiled my self-satisfaction, however. It renewed my grief and fury and terror, and I learned that one never finishes adjusting to MS. I don't know now why I thought one would. One does not, after all, finish adjusting to life, and MS is simply a fact of my life—not my favorite fact, of course—but as ordinary as my nose and my tropical fish and my yellow Mazda station wagon. It may at any time get worse, but no amount of worry or anticipation can prepare me for a new loss. My life is a lesson in losses. I learn one at a time.

And I had best be patient in the learning, since I'll have to do it like it or not. As any rock fan knows, you can't always get what you want. Particularly when you have MS. You can't, for example, get cured. In recent years researchers and the organizations that fund research have started to pay MS some attention even though it isn't fatal; perhaps they have begun to see that life is something other than a quantitative phenomenon, that one may be very much alive for a very long time in a life that isn't worth living. The researchers have made some progress toward understanding the mechanism of the disease: It may well be an autoimmune reaction triggered by a slow-acting virus. But they are nowhere near its prevention, control, or cure. And most of us want to be cured. Some, unable to accept incurability, grasp at one treatment after another, no matter how bizarre: megavitamin therapy, gluten-free diet, injections of cobra venom, hypothermal suits, lymphocytopharesis, hyperbaric chambers. Many treatments are probably harmless enough, but none are curative.

The absence of a cure often makes MS patients bitter toward their doctors. Doctors are, after all, the priests of modern society, the new shamans, whose business is to heal, and many an MS patient roves from one to another, searching for the "good" doctor who will make him well. Doctors too think of themselves as healers, and for this reason many have trouble dealing with MS patients, whose disease in its intransigence defeats their aims and mocks their skills. Too few doctors, it is true, treat their patients as whole human beings, but the reverse is also true. I have always tried to be gentle with my doctors, who often have more at stake in terms of ego than I do. I may be frustrated, maddened, depressed by the incurability of my disease, but I am not diminished by it, and they are. When I push myself up from my seat in the waiting room and stumble toward them, I incarnate the limitation of their powers. The least I can do is refuse to press on their tenderest spots.

This gentleness is part of the reason that I'm not sorry to be a cripple. I didn't have it before. Perhaps I'd have developed it anyway—how could I know such a thing?—and I wish I had more of it, but I'm glad of what I have. It has opened and enriched my life enormously, this sense that my frailty and need must be mirrored in others, that in searching for and shaping a stable core in a life wrenched by change and loss, change and loss, I must recognize the same process, under individual conditions, in the lives around me. I do not deprecate such knowledge, however I've come by it.

All the same, if a cure were found, would I take it? In a minute. I may be a cripple, but I'm only occasionally a loony and never a saint. Anyway, in my brand of theology God doesn't give bonus points for a limp. I'd take a cure; I just don't need one. A friend who also has MS startled me once, by asking, "Do you ever say to yourself, 'Why me, Lord?'" "No, Michael, I don't," I told him, "because whenever I try, the only response I can think of is 'Why not?'" If I could make a cosmic deal, who would I put in my place? What in my life would I give up in exchange for sound limbs and a thrilling rush of energy? No one. Nothing. I might as well do the job myself. Now that I'm getting the hang of it.

GUY DAVENPORT

Guy Davenport (1927–2005) wrote, in addition to experimental fiction, more than four hundred essays, articles, and book reviews. A true polymath, whose curiosity and love of learning new things took him into many arcane subjects, he also made collages, painted, and translated from the ancient Greek. His essay "On Reading" is surely one of the most beautiful tributes to that practice ever written. Typically, for a Davenport essay, it ranges with effortless freedom across time periods, from the specific to the general, the personal to the universal, unpretentiously strewing cultural references along the way.

On Reading

(1987)

To my Aunt Mae—Mary Elizabeth Davenport Morrow (1881–1964), whose diary when I saw it after her death turned out to be a list of places, with dates, she and Uncle Buzzie (Julius Allen Morrow, 1885–1970) had visited over the years, never driving over thirty miles an hour, places like Toccoa Falls, Georgia, and Antreville, South Carolina, as well as random sentences athwart the page, two of which face down indifference, "My father was a horse doctor, but not a common horse doctor" and "Nobody has ever loved me as much as I have loved them"—and a Mrs. Cora Shiflett, a neighbor on East Franklin Street, Anderson, South Carolina, I owe my love of reading.

Mrs. Shiflett, one of that extensive clan of the name, all retaining to this day the crofter mentality of the Scots Lowlands from which they come, a mixture of rapacity and despair (Faulkner called them Snopes), had rented a house across the street from us formerly occupied, as long as I could remember, by another widow, Mrs. Spoone ("with an *e*"), she and her son, whom we never saw, as he was doing ten years "in the peni-tencher." But before Mrs. Shiflett's son, "as good a boy to his mother as ever was," fell into some snare of the law, he had been a great reader. And one fateful day Mrs. Shiflett, who wore a bonnet and apron to authen-ticate her respectability as a good countrywoman, brought with her, on one of her many visits to "set a spell" with my mother, a volume of the Tarzan series, one in which Tarzan saves himself from perishing of thirst in the Sahara by braining a vulture and drinking its blood. She lent it to me. "Hit were one of the books Clyde loved in particular."

I do not have an ordered memory, but I know that this work of Edgar Rice Burroughs was the first book I read. I was thought to be retarded as a child, and all the evidence indicates that I was. I have no memory of the first grade, to which I was not admitted until I was seven, except that of peeing my pants and having to be sent home whenever I was spoken to by our hapless teacher. I have even forgotten her appearance and her name, and I call her hapless because there was a classmate, now a psychiatrist, who fainted when he was called on, and another who stiffened into petit mal. I managed to control my bladder by the third grade, but the fainter and the sufferer from fits, both classmates of mine through the ninth grade, when I quit school, kept teachers edgy until graduation.

No teacher in grammar or high school ever so much as hinted that reading was a normal activity, and I had to accept it, as my family did, was part of my affliction as a retarded person. The winter afternoon on which I discovered that I could follow Tarzan and Simba and some evil Arab slave traders was the first in a series of by now fifty years of sessions in chairs with books. I read very slowly, and do not read a great deal as I would much rather spend my leisure painting and drawing, or writing, and I do not have all that much leisure. And as a teacher of literature I tend to read the same books over and over, year after year, to have them fresh in my mind for lectures.

From *Tarzan*, which I did not read efficiently (and Burroughs's vocabu-lary runs to the exotic), I moved on to available books. My father had a small library of a hundred or so, from which I tried a *Collected Writings of Victor Hugo*, mysteriously inscribed in my father's hand, "G.M. Davenport, Apr. 24, 1934, Havana, Cuba," where I am positive my father never set foot. Under this inscription, he (or somebody) drew a cube, in ink that bled through to appear on the other surface of the page, on Vic-tor Hugo's forehead in a frontispiece engraving. But Hugo is not Edgar Rice Burroughs, and I could make nothing of him.

Aunt Mae had inherited, with pride, the small library of my uncle Eugene, a soldier in World War I, buried in France a decade before my

birth. This contained a complete Robert Louis Stevenson and James Feni-
more Cooper, both of whom proved to be over my head. But there was a
picture book of Pompeii and Herculaneum, which opened a door of a different sort, giving me my first wondering gaze into history and art. Aunt
Mae was herself addicted to the novels of Zane Grey, whom I lumped in
with Victor Hugo as a writer unable to get on with what he had to say, as
bad at dawdling as Cooper.

And then I made the discovery that what I liked in reading was to learn
things I didn't know. Aunt Mae's next-door neighbor, Mrs. McNinch,
belonged to the Book-of-the-Month Club, which in 1938—I was eleven—
sent its subscribers Antonina Vallentin's *Leonardo da Vinci.* Mrs.
McNinch, a woman of fervent piety and a Presbyterian, had chosen this
book because of *The Last Supper.* She lent it to me. I had not known until
the wholly magic hours I spent reading it, all of a wet spring, that such a
man as Leonardo was possible, and I was hearing of the Renaissance for
the first time. I read this difficult book in a way I can no longer imagine. I
pretended, I think, that I was following the plot and the historical digres-
sions. I have not reread this book and yet I can in lectures cite details of
Leonardo's career from it. Or think I can. I have read some forty studies
of Leonardo since, and many books about his epoch, and may be fooling
myself as to which source I'm remembering. But I can still see all the
illustrations, the codex pages in sepia, the paintings in color.

When I returned the biography of Leonardo, the generous Mrs.
McNinch lent me Carl Van Doren's *Benjamin Franklin,* also published
in 1938 and a Book-of-the-Month Club selection. This was harder going,
with phrases like "minister plenipotentiary," which I would mutter
secretly to myself. It is a truism that reading educates. What it does most
powerfully is introduce the world outside us, negating the obstructions
of time and place. When, much later, I ran across the word *opsimathy*
in Walter Pater, I could appreciate the tragic implications of late learning. All experience is synergetic: Bucky Fuller should have written, and
probably did, about the phenomenon of Synergetic Surprise. We cannot
guess what potential lies in wait for the imagination through momentum
alone. The earlier Leonardo and Franklin enter one's mind, the greater
the possibility of their bonding and interacting with ongoing experience
and information.

My childhood was far from bookish. I spent a lot of it hunting and
fishing, searching Georgia and South Carolina fields for arrowheads,
longing to work on the Blue Ridge Railroad, playing softball in the street,
building tree houses. The hunting was done with my Uncle Broadus
Dewey on Saturdays with a bird dog named Joe. Joe was gun-shy and had
conniption fits with pitiful howls when we took a shot at game. Many
lives were spared, of squirrels and partridges and rabbits, to spare Joe's
nerves. I myself never managed to shoot anything. What I liked was the

outing and the comradeship and pretending to have Leonardo's eyes in looking at plants, rocks, the landscape. Back from hunting, I would try to imitate a page of the notebooks. On manila construction paper from Woolworth's I would draw in brown ink leaves in clusters, and rocks, and insects, hoping that the page resembled one by Leonardo.

When the first American paperbacks came along, they, too, opened other worlds: Sherlock Holmes and other detective fiction, leading me to read people in the Holmesian manner at the barbershop and on the street.

I now have ample evidence for tracing synergies in reading. A few summers ago I spent a beautiful day in Auvers-sur-Oise, standing by the graves of Vincent and Theo. The wheat field is still unmistakably there, across the road from where they are buried against the cemetery wall, the Protestant place; and Gachet's house and garden. This day began with Henry Stone's trashy and irresponsible biography and the hilariously vulgar film based on it, but one must begin somewhere. Opsimathy differs from early learning in that there are no taproots, no years of crossbreeding, no naturalization in a climate.

After I had taught myself to read, without reading friends or family, I kept at it, more or less unaware of what hunger I was feeding. I can remember when I read any book, as the act of reading adheres to the room, the chair, the season. Doughty's *Arabia Deserta* I read under the hundred-year-old fig tree in our backyard in South Carolina, a summer vacation from teaching at Washington University, having lucked onto the two volumes (minus the map that ought to have been in a pocket in vol. II) at a St. Louis rummage sale. (The missing map was given me fifteen years later by Issam Safady, the Jordanian scholar.)

I read most of Willa Cather and Mann's Joseph tetralogy in the post library at Fort Bragg. The ordnance repair shop was on one side, the stockade on the other, and I was "keeping up my education" on orders from the adjutant general of the XVIIIth Airborne Corps, who kindly gave me Wednesday afternoons off specifically to read.

Proust I began among the spring blossoms of the Sarah P. Duke gardens in Durham, North Carolina, and finished forty years later by my fireplace in Lexington, Kentucky, convalescing from a very difficult operation to remove an embedded kidney stone. These settings are not merely sentimental; they are real interrelations. The moment of reading is integral to the process. My knowledge of Griaule's *Le renard pâle* is interwoven with my reading a large part of it in the Greenville, South Carolina, Trailways bus station. Yeats's *A Vision* belongs to the Hôtel Monsieur-le-Prince, once on the street of that name, as does *Nightwood* and *Black Spring*. *The Seven Pillars*, an Oxford room; *Fanny Hill*, the Haverford cricket field. And not all readings are nostalgic: the conditions under which I made my way through the *Iliad* in Greek were the violence and paralyzing misery of a disintegrating marriage, for which abrasion, nevertheless, the meaning of the poem was the more tragic. There are texts I can never willingly return to because of the misery adhering to them.

Students often tell me that an author was ruined for them by a high-school English class; we all know what they mean. Shakespeare was almost closed to me by the world's dullest teacher, and there are many writers whom I would probably enjoy reading except that they were recommended to me by suspect enthusiasts. I wish I knew how to rectify these aversions. I tell bright students, in conference, how I had to find certain authors on my own who were ruined for me by bad teachers or inept critics. Scott, Kipling, Wells will do to illustrate that only an idiot will take a critic's word without seeing for oneself. I think I learned quite early that the judgments of my teachers were probably a report of their ignorance. In truth, my education was a systematic misleading. Ruskin was dismissed as a dull, preacherly old fart who wrote purple prose. In a decent society the teacher who led me to believe this would be tried, found guilty, and hanged by the thumbs while being pelted with old eggs and cabbage stalks. I heard in a class at Duke that Joyce's *Ulysses* was a tedious account of the death of Molly Bloom. An Oxford don assured me that Edmund Wilson is an astute critic. Around what barriers did I have to force my way to get to Pound, to Joyce, to William Carlos Williams?

All of this points to our having a society that reads badly and communicates execrably about what we read. The idea persists that writing is an activity of thoughtful, idealistic, moral people called authors and that they are committed to protecting certain values vital to a well-ordered society. Books mold character, enforce patriotism, and provide a healthy way to pass the leisurely hour. To this assumption there has been added in our day the image of the author as a celebrity, someone worth hearing at a reading or lecture even if you have no intention of parting with a dime for one of the author's books.

There is little room in this popular concept of writing for the apprehension and appreciation of style. I had all along, I would like to think, been responding to style in my earliest attempts to read. I knew that the books I failed to enjoy—Scott's *The Black Dwarf* was the worst of these—were texts that remained foggy and indeterminate, like a moving picture experienced through bad eyesight and defective hearing. Style is radically cultural both linguistically and psychologically. I couldn't read Scott, Stevenson, and Cooper because I had not developed the imaginative agility needed to close the distance between me and the style of their texts. I could read, with excitement and a kind of enchantment, the biographies I encountered so early of Leonardo and Franklin not only because my curiosity about them was great, but because these biographies were in a contemporary, if academic, English.

My discovery of style came about through various humble books.

Hendrik Van Loon's whimsical history of the world (a Pocket Book from Woolworth's) alerted me to the fact that tone makes all the difference. It was this book that began to make something of an aesthete of me, for I progressed to Van Loon's biography of Rembrandt (conflating the rich experience of the Leonardo biography with the pleasure of reading for style), a book I kept reading for the pleasure of the prose, despite my ignorance of his historical setting. In it, however, I saw the name Spinoza, which led me to dear old Will Durant, who led me to Spinoza's texts, and all fellow readers who have ever taken a book along to a humble restaurant will understand my saying that life has few enjoyments as stoical and pure as reading Spinoza's *Ethics,* evening after evening, in a strange city—St. Louis, before I made friends there. The restaurant was Greek, cozy, comfortable, and for the neighborhood. The food was cheap, tasty, and filling.

Over white beans with chopped onions, veal cutlet with a savory dressing, and eventually a fruit cobbler and coffee, I read the *De Ethica* in its Everyman edition, Draftech pen at the ready to underline passages I might want to refind easily later. Soul and mind were being fed together. I have not eaten alone in a restaurant in many years, but I see others doing it and envy them.

At some time, as a freshman in college I would guess, my pleasure in style came together with the inevitable duty of having to read for content. I became increasingly annoyed with inept styles, like James Michener's, or styles that did violence to the language (and thus knew nothing of sociology until I could read it in French), with the turkey gobble of politicians and the rev. clergy. I began to search out writers whose style, as I was learning to see, was an indication that what they had to say was worth knowing. This was by no means an efficient or intellectually respectable procedure. I found Eric Gill's writing (all of which has evaporated from my mind), Spengler (all retained), Faulkner (then unknown to my English profs), Joyce (whose name I found in Thomas Wolfe), Dostoyevsky.

A memory: I was desperately poor as an undergraduate at Duke, did not belong to a fraternity, and except for a few like-minded friends (Dan Patterson, who was to become the great student of Shaker music; Bob Loomis, the Random House editor; Clarence Brown, the translator and biographer of Osip Mandelstam) was romantically and self-indulgently lonely. I was already learning the philosophical simpleness that would get me through life, and I remember a Saturday when I was the only person in the library. I took out Faulkner's *Absalom, Absalom!* (buff paper, good typography) and went back to my room. I felt, somehow, with everybody else out partying (Dan Patterson was practicing the piano in the basement of Duke chapel), Faulkner deserved my best. I showered, washed my hair, put on fresh clothes, and with one of Bob Loomis's wooden-tipped cigars, for the wickedness of it, made myself comfortable and opened the Faulkner to hear Miss Rosa Coldfield telling Quentin Compson about Thomas Sutpen.

So it went with my education. God knows what I learned from classes; very little. I read Santayana instead of my philosophy text (the style of which sucked), I read *Finnegans Wake* instead of doing botany (in which I made an F, and sweet Professor Anderson, that great name in photosynthesis, wrote on the postcard that conveyed the F, "You have a neat and attractive handwriting"). Instead of paying attention to psychology I made a wide study of Klee and Goya.

On a grander scale I got the same kind of education at Oxford and Harvard, where I read on my own while satisfying course requirements. I can therefore report that the nine years of elementary schooling, four of undergraduate, and eight of graduate study were technically games of futility. If, now, I had at my disposal as a teacher only what I learned from the formalities of education, I could not possibly be a university professor. I wouldn't know anything. I am at least still trying. I've kept most of my textbooks and still read them (and am getting pretty good at botany).

Wendell Berry, that thoughtful man, once remarked that teachers are like a farmer dropping an acorn into the ground. Some years will pass before the oak comes to maturity. We give grades, and lecture, and do the best we can. But we cannot see what we have done for many years to come. In setting out to write about the pleasure of reading, I find that I have equated my private, venturesome reading with my education, such as it is. There's much to be learned from this. All useful knowledge is perhaps subversive, innocently and ignorantly so at first. I assumed, with the wisdom of children, that it was best not to mention to my fourth- and fifth- grade teachers, Miss Taylor (who made us all take a Pledge of Life-long Abstinence from Alcohol) and Miss Divver, that I had read Antonina Vallentin's *Leonardo* and Van Doren's *Franklin,* and wanted very much, if I could find them, to read *Frankenstein* and *Dracula.*

I also read in those grammar-school years the nine volumes of Alexander Dumas's *Celebrated Crimes,* a dozen or so volumes of E. Phillips Oppenheim, and the three-volume *Century Dictionary* (I have always accepted dictionaries and encyclopedias as good reading matter).

Last year I met a young man in his twenties who is illiterate; there are more illiterates in Kentucky than anywhere else, with the possible exception of the Philippines and Haiti. The horror of his predicament struck me first of all because it prevents his getting a job, and secondly because of the blindness it imposes on his imagination. I also realized more fully than ever before what a text is and how it can only be realized in the imagination, how mere words, used over and over for other purposes and in other contexts, can be so ordered by, say, Jules Verne, as to be deciphered as a narrative of intricate texture and splendid color, of precise meanings and values. At the time of the illiterate's importuning visits (I was trying to help him find a job) I was reading Verne's *Les enfants du capitaine Grant,* a geography book cunningly disguised as an adventure story, for French children, a hefty two-volume work. I had never before felt how lucky and privileged I am, not so much for being literate, a state of grace that might in different circumstances be squandered on tax forms or law books, but for being able, regularly, to get out of myself completely, to be somewhere else, among other minds, and return (by laying my book aside) renewed and refreshed.

For the real use of imaginative reading is precisely to suspend one's mind in the workings of another sensibility, quite literally to give oneself over to Henry James or Conrad or Ausonius, to Yuri Olyesha, Bashō, and Plutarch.

The mind is a self-consuming organ and preys on itself. It is an organ for taking the outside in. A wasp has a very simple ganglion of nerves for a brain, a receptor of color, smell, and distances. It probably doesn't think at all, and if it could write, all it would have to say would concern the delicious smell of female wasps and fermenting pears, hexagonalities in various material (wood fiber, paper) in the architecture of nests, with maybe some remarks on azimuths (for the young). Angels, to move to the other pole of being, write history and indictments only, and if Satan has written his memoirs they would read like Frank Harris, and who would want to read them?

Music is as close as we will get to angelic discourse. Literature comes next, with a greater measure than music can claim of the fully human. I am on slippery ground here, as the two arts can share natures. *Don Giovanni* and the *Mass in B Minor* are both music and literature; all of what we now call poetry was for many centuries song. Even if we had all of Sappho's texts, we would still be without the tunes to which they were sung—like having only the libretto of *The Magic Flute.*

Shakespeare's sonnets and the *Duino Elegies* are a kind of music in themselves.

By "fully human" I mean *The Miller's Tale* and the *Quixote,* Surtees and *Humphry Clinker,* Rabelais and Queneau. The fully human is suspect in our society; Kentucky high schools keep banning *As I Lay Dying.* We do not read enough to have seen that literature itself is not interested in the transcendental role society has assumed for it. The pleasure of reading has turned out not to be what our culture calls pleasure at all. The most imperceptive psychologist or even evangelist can understand that television idiotizes and blinds while reading makes for intelligence and perception.

Why? How? I wish I knew. I also wish I knew why millions of bright American children turn overnight into teenage nerds. The substitution of the automobile for the natural body, which our culture has effected in the most evil perversion of humanity since chivalry, is one cause; narcosis by drugs and Dionysian music is another. I cannot say that an indifference to literature is another cause; it isn't. It's a symptom, and one of our trivializing culture's great losses. We can evince any number of undeniable beliefs—an informed society cannot be enslaved by ideologies and fanaticism, a cooperative pluralistic society must necessarily be conversant with the human record in books of all kinds, and so on—but we will always return to the private and inviolable act of reading as our culture's way of developing an individual.

Aunt Mae didn't read the books she inherited from Uncle Eugene, slain in France fighting for my and your right to read what we want to. She read *Cosmopolitan* and *Collier's* and "the *Grit*." And Zane Grey. She knew, however, that books are important, to be kept right-side up on a shelf in the living room near her plaster-of-Paris life-size statue of Rin Tin Tin.

The world is a labyrinth in which we keep traversing familiar crossroads we had thought were miles away, but to which we are doomed to backtrack. Every book I have read is in a Borgesian series that began with the orange, black, and mimosa-green cloth-bound *Tarzan* brought to me as a kindly gift by Mrs. Shiflett in her apron and bonnet. And the name Shiflett, I know because of books, is the one Faulkner transmuted to Snopes.

And Aunt Mae, whose father was a horse doctor but not a common horse doctor, looked down her nose at the Shifletts of this world as common white trash (she was an accomplished snob, Aunt Mae). A few years ago, exploring the Cimitière des Chiens et Chats in Paris, I came upon the grave of Rin Tin Tin, Grande Vedette du Cinema, and felt the ghost of Aunt Mae, who had always intended "to visit the old country," very much with me, for I'm old enough to know that all things are a matter of roots and branches, of spiritual seeds and spiritual growth, and that I would not have been in Paris at all, not, anyway, as a scholar buying books and tracking down historical sites and going to museums with educated eyes rather than eyes blank with ignorance, if, in the accident of things, Aunt Mae and Mrs. Shiflett had not taken the responsibility of being custodians of the modest libraries of a brother and a son, so that I could teach myself to read.

N. SCOTT MOMADAY

N. Scott Momaday (1934–), poet, novelist, and essayist, is considered a major figure in the Native American literary movement. A member of the Kiowa tribe, he grew up on reservations, the son of two schoolteachers, and earned a PhD in English literature at Stanford University. His novel, House Made of Dawn, *received the Pulitzer Prize in fiction in 1969. In his essay collections, Momaday has written extensively about the Native American oral tradition, gracefully bridging the roles of scholar and creative writer, interpreter, and practitioner.*

The Native Voice in American Literature

(1988)

I

> *Write:* to draw or form by or as by scoring or incising a surface.
> —*Webster's Seventh New Collegiate Dictionary*

Imagine: somewhere in the prehistoric distance a man holds up in his hand a crude instrument—a brand, perhaps, or something like a daub or a broom bearing pigment—and fixes the wonderful image in his mind's eye to a wall or rock. In that instant is accomplished really and symbolically the advent of art. That man, apart from his remarkable creation, is all but impossible to recall, and yet he is there in our human parentage, deep in our racial memory. In our modern, sophisticated terms, he is primitive and preliterate, and in the long reach of time he is utterly without distinction, except: he draws. And his contribution to posterity is inestimable; he makes a profound difference in our lives, who succeed him by millennia. For all the stories of all the world proceed from the moment in which he makes his mark. All literatures issue from his hand.

Language and literature involve sacred matter. Among sacred places in America, places of ancient origin and deepest mystery, there is one that comes to my mind again and again. At Barrier Canyon, Utah, there are some twenty sites at which are preserved prehistoric rock art. One of these, known as the Great Gallery, is particularly arresting. Among arched alcoves and long ledges of rock is a wide sandstone wall on which are drawn large, tapering anthropomorphic forms, colored in dark red pigment. There on the geologic picture plane is a procession of gods approaching inexorably from the earth. They are informed with irresistible power; they are beyond our understanding, masks of infinite possibility. We do not know what they mean, but we know that we are involved in their meaning. They persist through time in the imagination, and we cannot doubt that they are invested with the very essence of language, the language of story and myth and primal song. They are two thousand years old, more or less, and they remark as closely as anything can the origin of American literature.

The native voice in American literature is indispensable. There is no true literary history of the United States without it, and yet it has not been clearly delineated in our scholarship. The reasons for this neglect are perhaps not far to find. The subject is formidable; the body of songs, prayers, spells, charms, omens, riddles, and stories in Native American oral tradition, though constantly and considerably diminished from the time of European contact, is large, so large as to discourage investigation. The tradition has evolved over a very long and unrecorded period of time in numerous remote and complex languages, and it reflects a social and cultural diversity that is redoubtable. Research facilities are inadequate by and large, and experts in the field are few. Notwithstanding, the need is real and apparent.

Ancestors of modern American Indians were at the top of North America as early as 25,000 years ago. They were hunters whose survival was predicated upon the principle of mobility. Their dispersal upon the continent was rapid. In the hard environment of the far north there remains little evidence of their occupation, but they knew how to make fire and tools, and they lived as we do in the element of language.

American literature begins with the first human perception of the American landscape expressed and preserved in language. *Literature* we take commonly to comprehend more than writing. If writing means visible constructions within a framework of alphabets, it is not more than six or seven thousand years old, we are told. Language, and in it the formation of that cultural record which is literature, is immeasurably older. Oral tradition is the foundation of literature.

II

> If verbal artistry is the essence of literature, then it need not be
> preserved in writing to be worthy of the name.
> —John Bierhorst, *In the Trail of the Wind*

A comparison of the written and oral traditions is of course a matter of the greatest complexity. Those who make this comparison are irrevocably committed to the written tradition. Writing defines the very terms of our existence. We cannot know what it is to exist within an oral tradition, or we cannot know entirely. But we can know more than we do, and it behooves us to learn as much as we can, if for no other reason than to gain possession of invaluable resources that are rightfully ours, to discover, that is, a great and legitimate part of our literary heritage.

Writing engenders in us certain attitudes toward language. It encourages us to take words for granted. Writing has enabled us to store vast quantities of words indefinitely. This is advantageous on the one hand but dangerous on the other. The result is that we have developed a kind of false security where language is concerned, and our sensitivity to language has deteriorated. And we have become in proportion insensitive to silence.

But in the oral tradition one stands in a different relation to language. Words are rare and therefore dear. They are jealously preserved in the ear and in the mind. Words are spoken with great care, and they are heard. They matter, and they must not be taken for granted; they must be taken seriously and they must be remembered.

With respect to the oral tradition of the American Indian, these attitudes are reflected in the character of the songs and stories themselves. Perhaps the most distinctive and important aspect of that tradition is the way in which it reveals the singer's and the storyteller's respect for and belief in language.

At the heart of the American Indian oral tradition is a deep and unconditional belief in the efficacy of language. Words are intrinsically powerful. They are magical. By means of words can one bring about physical change in the universe. By means of words can one quiet the raging weather, bring forth the harvest, ward off evil, rid the body of sickness and pain, subdue an enemy, capture the heart of a lover, live in the proper way, and venture beyond death. Indeed, there is nothing more powerful. When one ventures to speak, when he utters a prayer or tells a story, he is dealing with forces that are supernatural and irresistible. He assumes great risks and responsibilities. He is clear and deliberate in his mind and in his speech; he will be taken at his word. Even so, he knows that he stands the chance of speaking indirectly or inappropriately, or of being mistaken by his hearers, or of not being heard at all. To be careless in the presence of words, on the inside of language, is to violate a fundamental morality.

But one does not necessarily speak in order to be heard. It is sometimes enough that one places one's voice on the silence, for that in itself is a whole and appropriate expression of the spirit. In the native American oral tradition, expression, rather than communication, is often first in importance. Singing of the Yeibichai, for example, the mountain spirits of the Navajos, the singers chant in the spirits' strange and urgent language, a language that is unintelligible to us mortals. Although meaningless in the ordinary sense of the word, the chant is nonetheless deeply moving and powerful beyond question.

In this sense, silence too is powerful. It is the dimension in which ordinary and extraordinary events take their proper places. In the Indian world, a word is spoken or a song is sung not against, but within the silence. In the telling of a story, there are silences in which words are anticipated or held on to, heard to echo in the still depths of the imagination. In the oral tradition, silence is the sanctuary of sound. Words are wholly alive in the hold of silence; there they are sacred.

Properly speaking, then, language is sacred. It will not suffice to say that the verbal and the sacred are related; they are indivisible. Consider this ritual formula from the Navajo:

> Reared within the Mountains!
> Lord of the Mountains!
> Young Man!
> Chieftain!
> I have made your sacrifice.
> I have prepared a smoke for you.
> My feet thou restore for me.
> My legs thou restore for me.
> My body thou restore for me.
> My mind thou restore for me.
> My voice thou restore for me.
> Restore all for me in beauty.
> Make beautiful all that is before me.
> Make beautiful all that is behind me.
> It is done in beauty.
> It is done in beauty.
> It is done in beauty.
> It is done in beauty.

This has the formality of prayer and the measure of poetry. It is immediately and essentially religious in its tone and statement. That is to say, the attitude that informs it is holy. In such a formulaic context as this, where the words are precisely fitted into the context of religious ceremony, the oral tradition achieves a remarkable stability, an authority not unlike that of Scripture.

It is significant that in this rich, ceremonial song the singer should end upon the notion of beauty, of beauty in the physical world, of man in the immediate presence and full awareness of that beauty. And it is significant, indeed necessary, that this whole and aesthetic and spiritual sense should be expressed in language. Man has always tried to represent and even to re-create the world in words. The singer affirms that he has a whole and irrevocable investment in the world. His words are profoundly simple and direct. He acknowledges the sacred reality of his being in the world, and to that reality he makes his prayer as an offering, a pledge of his integral involvement, commitment, and belief. He aspires to the restoration of his body, mind, and soul, an aim which in his cultural and religious frame of reference is preeminently an aesthetic consideration, a perception of well-ordered being and beauty, a design of which he is the human center. And the efficacy of his prayer is realized even as he makes it; it is done in beauty.

Often the words are returned upon themselves in a notable and meaningful way. They transcend their merely symbolic value and become one with the idea they express. They are not then intermediate but primary; they are at once the names of things and the things named.

> You have no right to trouble me,
> Depart, I am becoming stronger;
> You are now departing from me,
> You who would devour me;
> I am becoming stronger, stronger.
> Mighty medicine is now within me,
> You cannot now subdue me—
> I am becoming stronger,
> I am stronger, stronger, stronger.

This magic formula from the Iroquois, like the Navajo prayer above, accomplishes its purpose in itself. The strength of which the singer stands in need is imparted in the very utterance of his words. The singer not only acknowledges and affirms his strength; indeed he brings it about, he creates it of his own breath; it is done in belief.

The power and beauty of words are sometimes inherent in the most apparently benign and understated utterance, as in this Crow charm, meant to bring sleep upon an enemy:

At night when we lie down, listening to the wind rustling through
the bleached trees, we know not how we get to sleep but we fall
asleep, don't we?

or this Chippewa love song:

A loon I thought it was
But it was my love's splashing oar.
To Sault Ste. Marie he has departed,
My love has gone on before me,
Never again can I see him.
A loon I thought it was,
But it was my love's splashing oar.

Among the most succinct and potent of American Indian verbal formulas are the warrior songs.

Let us see, is this real,
Let us see, is this real,
Let us see, is this real,
This life I am living?
Ye gods, who dwell everywhere,
Let us see, is this real,
This life I am living.

This song from the Pawnee is an epitome of the warrior ideal. The singer
means to place even his life on the line; if the life he lives is not perfectly
real, so seems the consequent meaning, then he had better know it, that
he might make a right resolution. It is a moral necessity that he put the
matter to the test. There is a quiet irony in this, a rhetorical force that
is so closely controlled as to be almost subliminal. The whole formula
underscores the quality of life, yet the attitude toward life itself is uncompromisingly rational, the pose nearly indifferent, nearly haughty.
   Or this, from the Sioux:

soldiers
you fled
even the eagle dies

In this song we have one of the most concentrated and beautiful examples
of American Indian oral tradition that I know. It is a nearly perfect formula; there is only the mysterious equation of soldiers and flight on the
one hand and the eagle and death on the other. Yet it is a profound equation in which the eternal elements of life and death and fear are defined in

terms of freedom and courage and nobility. One might well brood upon the death of eagles; I have looked at these words on the page a long time, and I have heard them grow up in the silence again and again. They do not fade or fail.

This Sioux formula embodies in seven words the essence of literature, I believe. It is significant that the song was transcribed; that is, it was not composed in writing, but it is preserved on the printed page, it exists now in written form. What was lost or gained in the process of translation and transcription? This we cannot know, but it is perhaps enough to know that the song, as we have it, is alive and powerful and beautiful, and that it is eminently worthy of being preserved for its own sake. It is literature of the highest order.

MARILYNNE ROBINSON

Marilynne Robinson (1943–), chiefly known for her four stunningly crafted novels, Housekeeping, Gilead, Home, *and* Lila, *has also written five collections of opinionated, high-minded essays, starting with* The Death of Adam. *Having taught for twenty years in the Iowa Writers' Workshop before she retired, she has championed the Midwest as an unsung seedbed of progressive intellectual thought. A practicing Congregationalist, Robinson has also made a personal cause of promoting John Calvin as a major thinker; and in her essay "Puritans and Prigs," she argues with dignity and controlled sarcasm against the caricatured denigration of Calvinist Puritanism. If her position seems at first sight counterintuitive, it should be understood that Robinson relishes a good argument, especially one that questions received opinion.*

Puritans and Prigs: An Anatomy of Zealotry

(1994)

Puritanism was a highly elaborated moral, religious, intellectual and political tradition which had its origins in the writing and social experimentation of John Calvin and those he influenced. While it flourished on this continent—it appears to me to have died early in this century—it established great universities and cultural institutions and an enlightened political order. It encouraged simplicity in dress and manner and an esthetic interest in the functional which became bone and marrow of what we consider modern. Certainly the idea that a distaste for the mannered and elaborated should be taken to indicate joylessness or an indifference to beauty is an artifact of an old polemic. No acquaintance with New England portrait or decorative art encourages the idea that Puritan tastes were somber. Even their famous headstones display a marked equanimity beside headstones in Church of England graveyards in Britain, with their naturalistic skulls with bones in their teeth and so on. Puritan civilization in North America quickly achieved unprecedented levels of literacy, longevity and mass prosperity, or happiness, as it was called in those days. To isolate its special character we need only compare colonial New England and Pennsylvania—Quakers as well as Congregationalists and Presbyterians were Puritans—with the colonial South.

Or let us compare them with ourselves. When crops failed in Northampton, Massachusetts in 1743, Jonathan Edwards of course told his congregation that they had their own wickedness to blame for it. They had failed to do justice (his word) to the poor. He said, "Christian people are to give to others not only so as to lift him above extremity but liberally to furnish him." No one bothers us now with the notion that our own failures in this line might be called sinful, though we fall far short of the standard that in Edwards' view invited divine wrath. Nor does anyone suggest that punishment might follow such failures, though the case could easily be made that our whole community is punished for them every day. In one respect at least we have rid ourselves entirely of Puritanism.

My reading of Puritan texts is neither inconsiderable nor exhaustive, so while I cannot say they yield no evidence of Puritanism as we understand the word, I can say they are by no means characterized by, for example, fear or hatred of the body, anxiety about sex, or denigration of women. This is not true of Christian tradition in general, yet for some reason Puritanism is uniquely synonymous with these preoccupations. Puritans are thought to have taken a lurid pleasure in the notion of Hell, and certainly Hell seems to have been much in their thoughts, though not more than it was in the thoughts of Dante, for example. We speak as though John Calvin invented the Fall of Man, when that was an article of faith universal in Christian culture.

For Europeans, our Puritans showed remarkably little tendency to hunt witches, yet one lapse, repented of by those who had a part in it, has stigmatized them as uniquely inclined to this practice. They are condemned for their dealings with the Indians, quite justly, and yet it is important to point out that contact between native people anywhere and Europeans of whatever sort was disastrous, through the whole colonial period and after. It is pointless to speak as if Puritanism were the factor that caused the disasters in New England, when Anglicans and Catholics elsewhere made no better account of themselves. Cortez was no Puritan, but William Penn was one. By the standards of the period in which they flourished,

American Puritans were not harsh or intolerant in the ordering of their own societies. Look a little way into contemporary British law—Dr. Johnson would never have seen a woman flayed in New England, yet it is Old England we think of as having avoided repressive extremes. As for religious intolerance, one must again consider the standards of the period. The Inquisition was not officially ended until 1837. Quakers living in Britain were deprived of their civil rights well into the 19th century, as were Catholics and Jews. It seems fair to note that such tolerance as there was in Europe was to be found in Calvinist enclaves such as Holland.

What does it matter if a tradition no one identifies with any longer is unjustly disparaged? If history does not precisely authorize the use we make of the word "Puritanism," we all know what we mean by it, so what harm is done? Well, for one thing we make ourselves ignorant and contemptuous of the first two or three hundred years of one major strain of our own civilization. I am eager to concede that in our cataclysmic world this is a little misfortune, arousing even in me only the kind of indignation that could be thoroughly vented in a long footnote somewhere. In fact it is by no means proved to my satisfaction that a society is happier or safer or more humane for having an intense interest in its own past.

Yet the way we speak and think of the Puritans seems to me a serviceable model for important aspects of the phenomenon we here are calling Puritanism. Very simply, it is a great example of our collective eagerness to disparage without knowledge or information about the thing disparaged, when the reward is the pleasure of sharing an attitude one knows is socially approved. And it demonstrates how effectively such consensus can close off a subject from inquiry. I know from experience that if one says the Puritans were a more impressive and ingratiating culture than they are assumed to have been, one will be heard to say that one finds repressiveness and intolerance ingratiating. Unauthorized views are in effect punished by incomprehension, not intentionally and not to anyone's benefit, but simply as a consequence of a hypertrophic instinct for consensus. This instinct is so powerful that I would suspect it had survival value, if history or current events gave me the least encouragement to believe we are equipped to survive.

To spare myself the discomfort of reinforcing the same negative associations I have just deplored, and for weightier reasons, I will introduce another name in the place of "Puritanism" to indicate the phenomenon we are here to discuss. I choose the word "priggishness." This fine old English word, of no known etymology and therefore fetched from the deep anonymous heart of English generations, is a virtual poem in the precision with which it expresses pent irritation. One imagines the word being spat, never shouted, which suggests it is a trait most commonly found among people at some kind of advantage. *Webster's Third New International Dictionary* defines "priggish" as "marked by overvaluing oneself or one's ideas, habits, notions, by precise or inhibited adherence to them, and by small disparagement of others." In adopting this word I hope to make the point that the very important phenomenon it describes transcends culture and history. I believe we have all heard accounts of unbridled priggishness during the Cultural Revolution in China, for example, or in Spain under the dictatorship of Franco.

Americans never think of themselves as sharing fully in the human condition, and therefore beset as all humankind is beset. Rather they imagine that their defects result from their being uniquely the products of a crude system of social engineering. They believe this is a quirk of their brief and peculiar history, a contraption knocked together out of ramshackle utilitarianism and fueled by devotion to the main chance. This engineering is performed by them and upon them negligently or brutally, or with shrewd cynicism or mindless acquiescence, all tending to the same result: shallowness, materialism, a merely ersatz humanity.

Clearly there is an element of truth in this. The error comes in the belief that they are in any degree exceptional, that there is a more human world in which they may earn a place if only they can rid themselves of the deficiencies induced by life in an invented nation and a manufactured culture. They have one story they tell themselves over and over, which is: *Once we were crude and benighted, and in fact the vast majority of us remain so, but I and perhaps certain of my friends have escaped this brute condition by turning our backs on our origins with contempt, with contempt and derision.* When anything goes wrong, the thinkers among us turn once again to the old conversion narrative: *This is a resurgence of former brutishness, which we will spurn and scorn till we have exorcised it, or at least until those whose approval we covet know this old spirit no longer has power over us, personally—though we cannot of course speak for all our friends.* In great things as in small, we are forever in a process of recovery from a past that is always being re-interpreted to account for present pathologies. When things went wrong in Calvinist America, the minister or mayor or governor or president, including of course Lincoln, would declare a Day of Fasting and Humiliation, during which businesses and offices closed and the population went to their various churches to figure out what they were doing wrong and how to repent of it.

The assumption of present responsibility for the present state of things was a ritual feature of life in this culture for two and a half centuries, and is entirely forgotten by us now. Though I cannot take time to make the argument for it here, it is my belief that a civilization can trivialize itself to death, that we have set our foot in that path, and that our relation to the issue of responsibility is one measure of our progress. No matter, it is a self-limiting misfortune—by the time the end comes the loss to the world will be very small. My point here is simply that there is a reflex in this culture of generalized disapproval, of small or great disparagement,

of eagerness to be perceived as better than one's kind, which is itself priggish, and which creates the atmosphere in which these exotic new varieties
of priggishness can flower.

The Calvinist doctrine of total depravity—depravity means warping or
distortion—was directed against casuistical enumerations of sins, against
the attempt to assign them different degrees of seriousness. For Calvinism
we are all absolutely, that is equally, unworthy of, and dependent upon,
the free intervention of grace. This is a harsh doctrine, but no harsher
than others, since Christian tradition has always assumed that rather
few would be saved, and has differed only in describing the form election
would take. It might be said in defense of Christianity that it is unusual in
a religion to agonize much over these issues of ultimate justice, though in
one form or another every religion seems to have an elect. The Calvinist
model at least allows for the mysteriousness of life. For in fact life makes
goodness much easier for some people than for others, and it is rich with
varieties of cautious or bland or malign goodness, in the Bible referred to
generally as self-righteousness, and inveighed against as grievous offenses
in their own right. The belief that we are all sinners gives us excellent
grounds for forgiveness and self-forgiveness, and is kindlier than any
expectation that we might be saints, even while it affirms the standards all
of us fail to attain.

A Puritan confronted by failure and ambivalence could find his faith
justified by the experience, could feel that the world had answered his
expectations. We have replaced this and other religious visions with an
unsystematic, uncritical and in fact unconscious perfectionism, which
may have taken root among us while Stalinism still seemed full of promise, and have been refreshed by the palmy days of National Socialism in
Germany, by Castro and by Mao—the idea that society can and should
produce good people, that is, people suited to life in whatever imagined
optimum society, who then stabilize the society in its goodness so that it
produces more good people, and so on. First the bad ideas must be weeded
out and socially useful ones put in their place. Then the bad people must
be identified, especially those that are carriers of bad ideas. Societies have
done exactly the same thing from motives they considered religious, of
course. But people of advanced views believe they are beyond that kind
of error, because they have not paused to worry about the provenance or
history of these advanced views. Gross error survives every attempt at
perfection, and flourishes. No Calvinist could be surprised. No reader of
history could be surprised.

Disallowing factors of disruption and recalcitrance called by names
like sin, what conclusion can be drawn? If human beings are wholly the
products of societies, and societies are accessible to reform, what other
recourse is there than to attempt to reform one and the other? The
question seems pressing now that the community increasingly fails its

individual members, and as it is more and more feared, abused or abandoned by them.

I depend here on the general sense that we are suffering a radical moral decline which is destroying the fabric of society, seriously threatening our sense of safety as well as of mutual respect and shared interest. Such anxieties can be dangerous and irrational—perhaps they are in most cases. But the evidence is impressive that we are now looking at real decay, so I will accept the notion for the purposes of this discussion. I take on faith Tocqueville's lapidary remark that we were great because we were good, when he knew us. Let us say, as history would encourage us to do, that one great difference between then and now is the sense of sin which then flourished, the belief that mortals are born in a state of sin, that no one is or is likely to be perfected. One implication of that belief is certainly that neither social engineering nor intellectual eugenics could produce a good society full of good people. Americans studied the example of biblical Israel, for whom God himself had legislated, and who sinned and strayed very much in the manner of people less favored. The teaching that surrounded the biblical history of Israel suggested that to do justice and love mercy made the community good, but never that the community could be so ordered as to create a population conditioned always to do justice and love mercy. The community never ceased to struggle against contrary impulses, which it did not induce in itself and from which it could not free itself. Christian individualism enforced the awareness that exactly the same impulses are always at work in one's own soul.

The Stalinist vision is much more optimistic. It can propose a solution. Society is simply other people, useful or not, capable of contributing to the general good, or not. Creatures of society, they are also the reasons for the continuing failure and suffering of society. At the same time, since society is the only possible agent of its own transformation, the victim stands revealed as the enemy, the obstacle to reform, the problem to be eliminated. Freed of those it has maimed, it might at last be perfect. This is a great solipsism, a tautology, based on a model of human being-in-the-world which, curiously, has long seemed scientific to people because it is so extremely narrow and simple and has no basis in history or experience.

It has also an attraction that Puritanism never had, Puritanism with its grand assertion and concession, In Adam's Fall / We sinned *all*. It creates clear distinctions among people, and not only justifies the disparagement of others but positively requires it. Its adherents are overwhelmingly those who feel secure in their own reasonableness, worth and goodness, and are filled with a generous zeal to establish their virtues through the whole of society, and with an inspiring hope that this transformation can be accomplished. It would seem to me unfair and extreme to liken our new zealots to Stalinists, if I did not do so with the understanding that the whole of the culture is very much influenced by these assumptions, and that in this as in other ways the zealots differ from the rest of us only as an epitome differs from a norm.

Optimists of any kind are rare among us now. Rather than entertaining visions, we think in terms of stop-gaps and improvisations. A great many of us, in the face of recent experience, have arrived with a jolt at the archaic-sounding conclusion that morality was the glue holding society together, just when we were in the middle of proving that it was a repressive system to be blamed for all our ills. It is not easy at this point for us to decide just what morality is or how to apply it to our circumstances. But we have priggishness at hand, up to date and eager to go to work, and it does a fine imitation of morality, self-persuaded as a method actor. It looks like it and it feels like it, both to those who wield it and to those who taste its lash.

(Since I am already dependent on one, I will attempt a definition of authentic morality, based on common usage. When we say someone is moral, we mean that she is loyal in her life and behavior to an understanding of what is right and good, and will honor it even at considerable cost to herself. We would never say she was not moral because she did not urge or enforce her own standards on other people. Nor would we say she was more moral for attempting to impose her standards than she would be if she made no such attempt. Similarly, we say someone is immoral because she does not govern her behavior to answer to any standard of right or good. That being true of her, we would never say she was not immoral because she tried to enforce a standard of virtue on the people around her, nor even that she was less immoral for making such an attempt. Nor would we say someone was moral because her society had one way or another so restricted her behavior that she could not, in its terms, do anything wrong.)

Though etymologically "morality" means something like social custom, as we use it it means the desire to govern oneself, expressed as behavior. People who attempt this fail, and learn in the course of failing that to act well, even to know what it is to act well, is a great struggle and a mystery. Rather than trying to reform others, moral people seem to me especially eager to offer pardon in the hope of receiving pardon, to forgo judgment in the hope of escaping judgment.

So perhaps what I have called priggishness is useful in the absence of true morality, which requires years of development, perhaps thousands of years, and cannot simply be summoned as needed. Its inwardness and quietism make its presence difficult to sense, let alone quantify, and they make its expression often idiosyncratic and hard to control. But priggishness makes its presence felt. And it is highly predictable because it is nothing else than a consuming loyalty to ideals and beliefs which are in general so widely shared that the spectacle of zealous adherence to them is reassuring. The prig's formidable leverage comes from the fact that his or her ideas, notions or habits are always fine variations on the commonplace. A prig with original ideas is a contradiction in terms, because he or she is a creature of consensus who can usually appeal to one's better nature, if only in order to embarrass dissent. A prig in good form can make one ashamed to hold a conviction so lightly, and, at the same time, ashamed to hold it at all.

I will offer an example of the kind of thing I mean. Our modern zealots have dietary laws. Puritans did not, Calvin having merely urged moderation. For him many things were "things indifferent," that is, he considered it wrong to attach importance to them. This is a concept alien to the new zealotry.

There has been much attention in recent years to diet as a factor in determining the length and quality of life. That is, the idea together with all sorts of supporting information and speculation has been more than commonplace for a very long time. So here priggishness has a natural stronghold. One codicil of these dietary laws: It is good to eat fish. It is good to eat fish because it is bad to eat beef, an inefficient way to package protein, as Ralph Nader told us years ago, and a destructive presence in the world ecology, and a source of fat and cholesterol. It is good to eat fish because breast cancer is relatively rare in Japanese women and the Japanese life expectancy is imposing and beef was associated somewhere by someone with aggressive behavior in men. Also, steers are warm and breathy and have melting eyes, while fish are merely fish.

A shift in American tastes is a shift in global ecology. The sea has been raided and ransacked to oblige our new scruple, till even some species of shark are threatened with extinction. I myself am inclined to believe that no ecology is so crucial as the sea, or so impossible to monitor or to repair. Until we have some evidence that that great icon the whale can learn to live on municipal refuse and petroleum spills, we might try a little to respect the intricate and delicate system of dependencies necessary to its survival, and already profoundly disturbed. Fish is a terribly inefficient way to package protein, if it is provided on a scale that diminishes the productivity of the sea. And consider: The sea is traditionally the great resource of the poor. We are ashamed to eat beef because only a very wealthy country could sustain such a food source. And it makes us fat, parodies of ourselves. So what is any self-respecting people to do? Why, take away the food of the poor. Then at last we will be virtuous as they are.

As for the matter of the health benefits of eating fish. I think that person is a poor excuse for an ecologist who would tax a crucial and faltering natural system to extend her life a few years, assuming so much can be hoped. People in poor countries whose coasts and fishing grounds have been ruined will give up many years for the sake of the few she will gain, losing children to lengthen her old age. But certain of us have persuaded ourselves that a life lived in accordance with sound principles will be long, so longevity is as solemnly aspired to as goodness would have been in another time.

It is not hard to raise questions about the virtue of eating fish, or about the ecological consequences of mining quartz for those crystals that make us feel so at one with the earth. Is it really worth the petroleum, the pollution, the environmental wear and tear, to import drinking water? Such questions would be inevitable, if these were not the tastes of people who are strongly identified in their own minds as virtuous, and if these were not in fact signs by which they make themselves recognizable to others and to themselves as virtuous. For a very long time this country has figured in the world as a great appetite, suddenly voracious, as suddenly sated, disastrous in either case. The second worst thing that can be said about these virtuous people is, they have not at all escaped the sins of their kind. The worst thing that can be said is, they believe they have escaped them.

People who are blind to the consequences of their own behavior no doubt feel for that reason particularly suited to the work of reforming other people. To them morality seems almost as easy as breathing. Fish-eating water-drinkers who confront their geriatric disorders in long anticipation—we could all be like them. But if there is, as I wish to suggest, little to choose between the best of us and the worst of us in terms of our ecological impact, how do the zealots command the attention they do? Why do they have no real critics?

First of all, as I have said, they are arch-defenders of the obvious, for example, of the proposition that the planet needs looking after, and that one's health needs looking after—and while their diligence may in fact be as destructive as the general lethargy, it is reassuring to all of us to think that there is a radical vanguard, girded with purpose, armed with fact, etc.

Second, there is simple snobbery. Here I am, reaching yet again into the lexicon of British dialect—no language of flatterers, in fact a reservoir of painful truth. Our zealots adopt what are in effect class markers. Recently I saw a woman correct a man in public—an older man whom she did not know well—for a remark of his she chose to interpret as ethnocentric. What he said could easily have been defended, but he accepted the rebuke and was saddened and embarrassed. This was not a scene from some guerrilla war against unenlightened thinking. The woman had simply made a demonstration of the fact that her education was more recent, more fashionable and more extensive than his, with the implication, which he seemed to accept, that right thinking was a property or attainment of hers in a way it never could be of his. To be able to defend magnanimity while asserting class advantage! And with an audience already entirely persuaded of the evils of ethnocentricity, therefore more than ready to admire! This is why the true prig so often has a spring in his step. Morality could never offer such heady satisfactions.

The woman's objection was a quibble, of course. In six months the language she provided in place of his will no doubt be objectionable—no doubt in certain quarters it is already. And that is the genius of it. In six months she will know the new language, while he is still reminding himself to use the words she told him he must prefer. To insist that thinking worthy of respect can be transmitted in a special verbal code only is to claim it for the class that can concern itself with inventing and acquiring these codes and is so situated in life as to be able, or compelled, to learn them. The more tortuous our locutions the more blood in our streets. I do not think these phenomena are unrelated, or that they are related in the sense that the thought-reforms we attempt are not extensive enough or have not taken hold. I think they are related as two manifestations of one phenomenon of social polarization.

There is more to this little incident. In fact, I must back up a considerable distance, widen the scene a little, if I am to do it any sort of justice. First of all, where did the idea come from that society should be without strain and conflict, that it could be satisfying, stable and harmonious? This is the assumption that has made most of the barbarity of our century seem to a great many people a higher philanthropy. The idea came from Plato, I suppose. Our social thought has been profoundly influenced by a categorical rejection of Periclean Athens. No point brooding over that.

Let us look at the matter scientifically. The best evidence must lead us to conclude that we are one remote and marginal consequence of a cosmic explosion. Out of this long cataclysm arose certain elements and atmospheres, which in combination and over time produced, shall we say, New York City, with all it embraces and implies. Well, all right. Imagine accident upon coincidence upon freak, heightened by mysterious phenomena of order and replication, and there you have it. That a natural process should have produced complicated animals who exist in vast aggregations is conceivable. But, I submit, that they should be suited to living happily—in vast aggregations or in farming villages or as hermits on the tops of mountains—is a stroke of thinking so remarkable in a supposedly non-theological context that it takes my breath away. Scientifically speaking, we are weird, soft, big-headed things because we adapted to the mutable world by keeping a great many options open. Biologically speaking, we are without loyalties, as ready to claim an isthmus as a steppe. In our bodies we are utterly more ancient than Hittites and Scythians, survivors of the last swarm of locusts, nerved for the next glaciation. We have left how many cities standing empty? That any condition of life should be natural and satisfactory to us is an idea obviously at odds with our nature as a species, and as clearly at odds with our history. Would not mass contentment be maladaptive? Yet so much of modern life has been taken up with this nightmare project of fitting people to society, in extreme cases hewing and lopping away whole classes and categories. Humankind has adopted and discarded civilization after civilization and remained itself. We have done the worst harm we have ever suffered by acting as if society can or should be stable and fixed, and humankind transformed by whatever means to assure that it will be.

I am making this argument in terms not natural to me. My heart is with the Puritans. I would never suggest that history, whatever that is, should be left to take its natural course, whatever that is. I accept what Jonathan Edwards might have called the "arbitrary constitution" of behests and obligations. I draw conclusions from the fact that we cannot reason our way to a code of behavior that is consistent with our survival, not to mention our dignity or our self-love. But, even in the terms of this argument, what could have been more brutal than these schemes to create happy and virtuous societies? Might we not all have been kinder and saner if we had said that discontent is our natural condition, that we are the Ishmael of species, that, while we belong in the world, we have no place in the world? And that this is true not because something went wrong, but because of the peculiar terms of our rescue from extinction? Our *angst* and our *anomie* have meant to us that society has gone wrong, which means that other people have harmed us. The corollary of this notion, that our unhappiness is caused by society, is that society can make us happy, or remove the conditions that prevent us from being happy. And if the obstacle to collective happiness is believed to be other people, terrible things seem justified.

When the woman in the episode I described rebuked and embarrassed someone for using the wrong language, she was acting on an assumption that is now very common and respectable, which is that vice, shall we call it, is perpetuated in society in words, images, narratives and so on, that when these things are weeded out vice is attacked, that where they still appear vice is flourishing. Now the crudest words and the most disturbing images have normally been discountenanced in this society, and have been cherished by those who love forbidden things, just as they are now. Formerly the society was more tolerant of racial slurs and vastly less tolerant of depictions of violence, especially against women. It was also more racist and less violent. I cannot speculate which is cause and which effect, or even if it is meaningful to describe the phenomena in those terms. In any case, the "vice" in this instance was on the order of saying Mohammedan for Muslim, Oriental for Asian. Neither of the forbidden words has a hint of aspersion in it. They are simply associated with old attitudes, which they are taken to contain and reveal. No matter that the man who mis-spoke is known to be a very generous-spirited man, who would never intend an aspersion against anyone. Social methods that have been used to restrict the expression of obscenity or aggression, shaming, for example, are slurring over to control many other forms of language (and therefore, on the short-blanket principle that is always a factor in moral progress, no longer obscenity and aggression). This is done on the grounds that they are socially destructive, as indeed in varying degrees and circumstances they may sometimes be. This would be no fit subject for an analysis of priggishness if it did not have at least one foot in safe moral territory.

But, needless to say, there are problems. One is in the binary assumption that ideas equal words and that words carry ideas in them. If the relationship between words and ideas were indeed that close, no one would be paid for writing. Words would not be transformed by use. New ideas would depend on new coinages. This is thinking of the kind I call Stalinist, because it derives moral confidence and authority from its incredible simplicity. Now, if anything in the world is complex, language is complex. But the point is not really to characterize language but to characterize society by implying that certain things are true about language. A great mythic world rests on the back of this small conceptual turtle.

Very early on I proposed that priggishness is so available to us, and that where we do not subscribe to it we are nevertheless so helpless against it, because we cherish a myth of conversion in which we throw off the character our society gives us and put on a new one in all ways vastly superior. Normally this great change is achieved by education, enhanced by travel, refined by reading certain publications, manifested in the approved array of scruples and concerns, observed ritually in the drinking of water, the eating of fish, the driving of Volvos, and otherwise. (I think to myself, if we must be so very imitative, why can we never imitate a grace or an elegance? But that is outside the range of the present discussion. Though I do note that priggishness has never shown any aptitude for such things, any more than elegance or grace have claimed an affinity with priggishness.) Among us salvation is proved by a certain fluency of disparagement and disavowal. The prig in us could not enjoy all this, or believe in it, if the distinctions made were only economic and social. They must also, first of all, be moral.

Here I will divulge a bitter thought. I will say, by way of preparation, that much of the behavior I observe in these people looks like the operations of simple fashion. Phrases and sensitivities change continuously, perhaps as a function of evolving consciousness, perhaps as a feature of intense and active peer group identification. Clearly as economic subset our zealots experience the same frissons of consumer optimism we all do, though they might be focused on fetish bears rather than video cameras, one desideratum supplanting another in the ordinary way. Traffic in moral relics is an ancient practice, and while it is not harmless, neither is much else.

But I think there might be another impetus behind all this mutation. I think because our zealots subscribe to the conversion myth, they can only experience virtuousness as difference. They do not really want to enlist or persuade—they want to maintain difference. I am not the first to note their contempt for the art of suasion. Certainly they are not open to other points of view. If it is true that the shaping impulse behind all this stylized language and all this pietistic behavior is the desire to maintain social distinctions, then the moral high ground that in other generations was held by actual reformers, activists and organizers trying to provoke debate and build consensus, is now held by people with no such intentions, no notion of what progress would be, no impulse to test their ideas against public reaction as people do who want to accomplish reform. It is my bitter thought that they may have made a fetish of responsibility, a fetish of concern, of criticism, of indignation.

More bitter still is the thought that those who are, in Edwards' terms, in need of justice, are, in contemporary terms, damaged, imperfectly humanized, across the divide. The fact is that in this generation change in the lives of the poor and the undefended is change for the worse, again for the worse, always for the worse. If serious efforts at rectification were being made, would this be true? If serious solutions were being attempted, would not someone hold them to the standard of their effect, and suggest a reconsideration?

While Calvinists spoke of an elect, Leninists and such like have spoken of an elite. The two words come from the same root and mean the same thing. Their elect were unknowable, chosen by God in a manner assumed to be consistent with his tendency to scorn the hierarchies and overturn the judgments of this world. Our elites are simply, one way or another, advantaged. Those of us who have shared advantage know how little it assures, or that it assures nothing, or that it is a positive threat to one's moral soundness, attended as it is with so many encouragements to complacency and insensitivity. I have not yet found a Puritan whose Calvinism was so decayed or so poorly comprehended that he or she would say to another soul, I am within the circle of the elect and you are outside it. But translated into the terms of contemporary understanding, and into the terms of my narrative, that is what that woman said to that man.

A small thing, foolishness, bad manners. I run the risk of being ungenerous in taking this woman so much to task, and there is a whiff of snobbery in my own scorn for her pretentions. I accept the justice of all this, yet I persist.

The American salvation myth and the Stalinist salvation myth have in common the idea that the great body of the culture is a vast repository of destructive notions and impulses, that certain people rise out of the mass in the process of understanding and rejecting all that is retrograde, and that, for those people, there is never any use for, nor even any possibility of, conversation on equal terms with those who remain behind. The history of elites is brutal and terrible. When the impact of scientific and industrial and political elites finally becomes clear—and it has been devastating in every part of the world—it will become clear also that people picked at random off the street would probably have made better decisions. It would be wonderful if there were a visible elect, a true elite, who could lead us out of our bondage, out of our wilderness. But we are not so favored. Our zealots seem to assume they do provide such leadership—that if one cannot embrace their solutions it is surely because one is indifferent to great problems, or complicit in them. This is a manifestation of their presumption of legitimacy that I find especially disturbing, not least because their solutions then become the issue while the reality of the problems is forgotten, except by the police, the courts, the coroners.

If there is any descriptive value in the definition of morality I offered above, its great feature is autonomy. Tacitus admired the morality of the Germans, Calvin admired the morality of Seneca and Cicero—anyone who considers the question knows that morality can take any number of forms, that it can exist in many degrees of refinement and so on. We all distinguish instantly between a moral lapse and a difference of standards. Whatever else it is, morality is a covenant with oneself, which can only be imposed and enforced by oneself. Society can honor these covenants or not. Historically it seems that repression often encourages them. The great antidote to morality is cynicism, which is nothing more than an understanding of how arbitrary morality is, how unpredictable and unenforceable, how insecurely grounded in self-interest. It appears to me that even very thoughtful people discover what terms they have made with themselves only as they live, which prohibitions are conditional, which absolute, and so on. So in this great matter of moral soundness or rigor or whatever, we are as great mysteries to ourselves as we are to one another. It should not be that way, of course. The human condition has an amazing wrongness about it. But if it is agreed that we are in this respect mysterious, then we should certainly abandon easy formulas of judgment. If it is true that morality is a form of autonomy, then social conditioning is more likely to discourage than to enhance it.

If, putting out of consideration the inwardness of people, and putting aside the uniqueness of the terms in which everyone's relations with the world are negotiated, and excluding the very prevalent desire of people to align themselves with what they take to be right, and ignoring the fact that people have ideas and convictions for which they cannot find words, we choose to believe all the errors of our past are stored in the minds of those who use language we have declared to embody those errors, then we make the less sophisticated tiers of the society the problem and the enemy, and effectively exonerate ourselves. We know what they mean better than they do, so we only listen to hear them condemn themselves. In the name of justice we commit a very crude injustice. We alienate a majority of our people, and exclude them from a conversation of the most pressing importance to them, having nothing but our smugness to justify the presumption. We must find a better model to proceed from.

This is John Calvin glossing the text "Love thy neighbor":

> Here, therefore, let us stand fast: our life shall best conform to God's will and the prescriptions of the law when it is in every respect most fruitful for our brethren . . . It is very clear that we keep the commandments not by loving ourselves but by loving God and neighbor; that he lives the best and holiest life who lives and strives for himself as little as he can, and that no one lives in a worse or more evil manner than he who lives and strives for himself alone, and thinks about and seeks only his own advantage . . .

Here is John Calvin answering the question "Who is our neighbor?"

> It is the common habit of mankind that the more closely men are bound together by the ties of kinship, of acquaintanceship, or of neighborhood, the more responsibilities for one another they share. This does not offend God; for his providence, as it were, leads us to it. But I say: we ought to embrace the whole human race without exception in a single feeling of love; here there is no distinction between barbarian and Greek, worthy and unworthy, friend and enemy, since all should be contemplated in God, not in themselves. When we turn aside from such contemplation, it is no wonder we become entangled in many errors. Therefore, if we rightly direct our love, we must first turn our eyes not to man, the sight of whom would more often engender hate than love, but to God, who bids us extend to all men the love we bear to him, that this may be an unchanging principle: Whatever the character of the man, we must yet love him because we love God.

Here is John Calvin explaining how we are to determine our obligation to others:

> Say, "He is contemptible and worthless"; but the Lord shows him to be one to whom he has deigned to give the beauty of his image. Say that you owe nothing for any service of his; but God, as it were, has put him in his own place in order that you may recognize toward him the many and great benefits with which God has bound you to himself. Say that he does not deserve even your least effort for his sake; but the image of God, which recommends

him to you, is worthy of your giving yourself and all your possessions. Now if he has not only deserved no good at your hand, but has also provoked you by unjust acts and curses, not even this is just reason why you should cease to embrace him in love and to perform the duties of love on his behalf . . . Assuredly there is but one way in which to achieve what is not merely difficult but utterly against human nature: to love those who hate us, to repay their evil deeds with benefits, to return blessings for reproaches. It is that we remember not to consider men's evil intention but to look upon the image of God in them, which cancels and effaces their transgressions, and with its dignity allures us to love and embrace them.

This is the theological basis for Jonathan Edwards' wonderful definition of "justice."

Whatever confronts us, it is not a resurgence of Puritanism. If we must look to our past to account for our present circumstances, perhaps we might ponder the impulse long established in it to disparage, to cheapen and deface, and to falsify, which has made a valuable inheritance worthless. Anyone who considers the profound wealth and continuing good fortune of this country must wonder, how do we make so little of so much? Now, I think, we are making little of the language of social conscience and of the traditions of activism and reform. We are losing and destroying what means we have had to do justice to one another, to confer benefit upon one another, to assure one another a worthy condition of life. If Jonathan Edwards were here, he would certainly call that a sin. I am hard pressed to think of a better word.

JAMAICA KINCAID

Jamaica Kincaid (1949–), author of such penetrating fictions as Lucy *and* Mr. Potter, *was born on the Caribbean island of Antigua (which she describes in her essay "In History" as "a small lump of insignificance, green, green, green, and green again") before coming to the United States. Using her patented rhythmic, circling style, which proceeds patiently step by step, Kincaid challenges the ignorant presumptions of Western colonials. How that colonialism has since morphed into tourism she shows unforgettably in her long essay,* A Small Place. *Here, she questions the very notion of singular identity and of assigning names (especially to plants: Kincaid is a fervent gardener). Her halting, singsong, idiosyncratically estranged voice in the essay uncannily suits the hard questions she is asking about who has the right to name things, or to utter and frame historical narratives.*

In History

(1997)

What to call the thing that happened to me and all who look like me?

Should I call it history?

If so, what should history mean to someone like me?

Should it be an idea, should it be an open wound and each breath I take in and expel healing and opening the wound again and again, over and over, or is it a moment that began in 1492 and has come to no end yet? Is it a collection of facts, all true and precise details, and, if so, when I come across these true and precise details, what should I do, how should I feel, where should I place myself?

Why should I be obsessed with all these questions?

My history began like this: in 1492, Christopher Columbus discovered the New World. Since this is only a beginning and I am not yet in the picture, I have not yet made an appearance, the word "discover" does not set off an alarm, and I am not yet confused by this interpretation. I accept it. I am only taken by the personality of this quarrelsome, restless man. His origins are sometimes obscure; sometimes no one knows just where he really comes from, who he really was. His origins are sometimes quite vivid: his father was a tailor, he came from Genoa, he as a boy wandered up and down the Genoese wharf, fascinated by sailors and their tales of lands far away; these lands would be filled with treasures, as all things far away are treasures. I am far away, but I am not yet a treasure: I am not a part of this man's consciousness, he does not know of me, I do not yet have a name. And so the word "discover," as it is applied to this New World, remains uninteresting to me.

He, Christopher Columbus, discovers this New World. That it is new only to him, that it had a substantial existence, physical and spiritual, before he became aware of it, does not occur to him. To cast blame on him now for this child-like immaturity has all the moral substance of a certificate given to a school girl for good behavior. To be a well-behaved school girl is not hard. When he sees this New World, it is really new to him: he has never seen anything like it before, it was not what he had expected, he had images of China and Japan, and, though he thought he was in China and Japan, it was not the China or Japan that he had fixed in his mind. He couldn't find enough words to describe what he saw before him: the people were new, the flora and fauna were new, the way the water met the sky was new, this world itself was new, it was the New World.

"If one does not know the names, one's knowledge of things is useless." This is attributed to Isidorus, and I do not know if this is the Greek Isidorus or the other Isidorus, the bishop of Seville; but now put it another way: to have knowledge of things, one must first give them a name. This, in any case, seems to me to have been Christopher Columbus' principle, for he named and he named: he named places, he named people, he named things. This world he saw before him had a blankness to it, the blankness of the newly made, the newly born. It had no before—I could say that it had no history, but I would have to begin again, I would have to ask those questions again: what is history? This blankness, the one Columbus met, was more like the blankness of paradise; paradise emerges from chaos, and this chaos is not history; it is not a legitimate order of things. Paradise then is the arrangement of the ordinary and the extraordinary. But in such a way as to make it, paradise, seem as if it had fallen out of the clear air. Nothing about it suggests the messy life of the builder, the carpenter, the quarrels with the contractor, the people who are late with the delivery of materials, their defense which, when it is not accepted, is met with their back chat. This is an unpleasant arrangement; this is not paradise. Paradise is the thing just met when all the troublesome details have been vanquished, overcome.

Christopher Columbus met paradise. It would not have been paradise for the people living there; they would have had the ordinary dreariness of living anywhere day after day, the ordinary dreariness of just being alive. But someone else's ordinary dreariness is another person's epiphany.

The way in which he wanted to know these things was not in the way of satisfying curiosity, or in the way of correcting an ignorance; he wanted to know them, to possess them, and he wanted to possess them in a way that must have been a surprise to him. His ideas kept not so much changing, as they kept evolving: he wanted to prove the world was round, and even that, to know with certainty that the world was round, that it did not come to an abrupt end at a sharp cliff from which one could fall into nothing, to know that is to establish a claim also. And then after the world was round, this round world should belong to his patrons, the king and queen of Spain; and then finding himself at the other side of the circumference and far away from his patrons, human and other kind, he loses himself, for it becomes clear: the person who really can name the thing gives it a life, a reality, that it did not have before. His patrons are in Spain, looking at the balance sheet: if they invest so much, will his journey yield a return to make the investment worthwhile? But he, I am still speaking of Columbus, is in the presence of something else.

His task is easier than he thought it would be; his task is harder than he could have imagined. If he had only really reached Japan or China, places like that already had an established narrative. It was not a narrative that these places had established themselves; it was a narrative that someone like him had invented, Marco Polo, for instance; but this world, China or Japan, in the same area of the world to him (even as this familiarity with each other—between China and Japan—would surprise and even offend the inhabitants of these places), had an order and the order offered a comfort (the recognizable is always so comforting). But this new place, what was it? Sometimes it was just like Seville, Spain; sometimes it was like Seville but only more so; sometimes it was more beautiful than Seville. Mostly it was "marvelous," and this word "marvelous" is the word he uses again and again, and when he uses it, what the reader (and this is what I have been, a reader of this account of the journey, and the account is by Columbus himself) can feel, can hear, can see, is a great person whose small soul has been sundered by something unexpected. And yet the unexpected turned out to be the most ordinary things: people, the sky, the sun, the land, the water surrounding the land, the things growing on the land.

What were the things growing on the land? I pause for this. What were the things growing on that land and why do I pause for this?

I come from a place called Antigua. I shall speak of it as if no one has ever heard of it before; I shall speak of it as if it is just new. In the writings, in anything representing a record of the imagination of Christopher Columbus, I cannot find any expectation for a place like this. It is a small lump of insignificance, green, green, green, and green again. Let me describe this landscape again: it is green, and unmistakably so; another person, who would have a more specific interest, a painter, might say, it is a green that often verges on blue, a green that often is modified by reds and yellows and even other more intense or other shades of green. To me, it is green and green and green again. I have no interest other than this immediate and urgent one: the landscape is green. For it is on this green landscape that, suddenly, I and the people who look like me made an appearance.

I, me. The person standing in front of you started to think of all this while really focused on something and someone else altogether. I was standing in my garden; my garden is in a place called Vermont; it is in a village situated in a place called Vermont. From the point of view of growing things, that is the gardener's, Vermont is not in the same atmosphere as that other place I am from, Antigua. But while standing in that place, Vermont, I think about the place I am from, Antigua. Christopher Columbus never saw Vermont at all; it never entered his imagination. He saw Antigua, I believe on a weekday, but if not then it would have been a Sunday, for in this life there would have been only weekdays or Sundays, but he never set foot on it, he only came across it while passing by. My world then—the only world I might have known if circumstances had not changed, intervened, would have entered the human imagination, the human imagination that I am familiar with, the only one that dominates the world in which I live—came into being as a footnote to someone just passing by. By the time Christopher Columbus got to the place where I am from, the place which forms the foundation of the person you see before you, he was exhausted, he was sick of the whole thing, he longed for his old home, or he longed just to sit still and enjoy the first few things that he had come upon. The first few things that he came on were named after things that were prominent in his thinking, his sponsors especially; when he came to the place I am from, he (it) had been reduced to a place of worship; the place I am from is named after a church. This church might have been an important church to Christopher Columbus, but churches are not important, originally, to people who look like me. And if people who look like me have an inheritance, among this inheritance will be this confusion of intent; nowhere in his intent when he set out from his point of embarkation (for him, too, there is not origin: he originates from Italy, he sails from Spain, and this is the beginning of another new traditional American narrative, point of origin and point of embarkation): "here is something I have never seen before, I especially like it because it has no precedent, but it is frightening because it has no precedent, and so to make it less frightening I will frame it in the thing I know; I know a church, I know the name of the church, even if I do not like or know the people connected to this church, it is more familiar to me, this church, than the very ground I am standing on; the ground has changed, the church, which is in my mind, remains the same."

I, the person standing before you, close the quotation marks. Up to this point I and they that look like me are not yet a part of this narrative. I can look at all these events: a man setting sail with three ships, and after many, many days on the ocean, finding new lands whose existence he had never even heard of before, and then finding in these new lands people and their things and these people and their things, he had never heard of them before, and he empties the land of these people, and then he empties the people, he just empties the people. It is when this land is completely empty that I and the people who look like me begin to make an appearance, the food I eat begins to make an appearance, the trees I will see each day come from far away and begin to make an appearance, the sky is as it always was, the sun is as it always was, the water surrounding the land on which I am just making an appearance is as it always was; but these are the only things left from before that man, sailing with his three ships, reached the land on which I eventually make an appearance.

When did I begin to ask all this? When did I begin to think of all this and in just this way? What is history? Is it a theory? I no longer live in the place where I and those who look like me first made an appearance. I live in another place. It has another narrative. Its narrative, too, can start with that man sailing on his ships for days and days, for that man sailing on his ships for days and days is the source of many narratives, for he was like a deity in the simplicity of his beliefs, in the simplicity of his actions; just listen to the straightforward way many volumes featuring this man sailing on his ships began, "In fourteen hundred and ninety-two . . . In fourteen hundred and ninety-two." But it was while standing in this other place that has a narrative mostly different from the place in which I make an appearance, that I begin to think of this.

One day, while looking at the things that lay before me at my feet, I was having an argument with myself over the names I should use when referring to the things that lay before me at my feet. These things were plants. The plants, all of them and they were hundreds, had two names: they had a common name, that is the name assigned to them by people for whom these plants have value, and then they have a proper name, or a Latin name, and that is a name assigned to them by an agreed-on group of botanists. For a long time I resisted using the proper names of the things that lay before me. I believed that it was an affectation to say "Eupatorium" when you could say "Joe Pye Weed." I then would only say "Joe Pye Weed." The botanists are from the same part of the world as the man who sailed on the three ships, that same man who started the narrative from which I trace my beginning. And the botanists are like that man who sailed on the ships in a way, too: they emptied the worlds of things animal, mineral and vegetable, of their names, and replaced these names with names pleasing to them; the recognized names are now reasonable, as reason is a pleasure to them.

Carl Linnaeus was born on the 23rd of May, in 1707 somewhere in Sweden. (I know where, but I like the high handedness of not saying so.) His father's name was Nils Ingemarsson; the Ingemarssons were farmers. Apparently, in Sweden then, surnames were uncommon among ordinary people, and so the farmer would add "son" to his name or he was called after the farm on which he lived. Nils Ingemarsson became a Lutheran minister, and on doing so he wanted to have a proper surname, not just a name with "son" attached to it. On his family's farm grew a linden tree. It had grown there for generations and had come to be regarded with reverence among neighboring farmers; people believed that misfortune would fall on you if you harmed this tree in any way. This linden tree was so well regarded that people passing by used to pick up twigs that had dropped from it and carefully place them at the base of the tree. Nils Ingemarsson took his surname from this tree: Linnaeus is the latinized form of the Swedish word *lind*. Other branches of this family who also needed a surname drew inspiration from this tree; some took the name Tiliander—the Latin word for linden is *tilia*—and then some others again who also needed a surname took the name Lindelius from the Swedish word *lind*, which means linden.

Carl Linnaeus's father had a garden. I do not know what his mother had. His father loved growing things in this garden and would point them out to the young Carl, but, when the young Carl could not remember the names of the plants, his father gave him a scolding and told him he would not tell him the names of any more plants. (Is this story true? But how could it not be?) He grew up not far from a forest filled with Beech, a forest with pine, a grove filled with oaks, meadows. His father had a collection of rare plants in his garden (but what would be rare to him and in that place, I do not know). At the time Linnaeus was born, Sweden, this small country that I now think of as filled with well-meaning and benign people interested mainly in the well-being of children, the well-being of the unfortunate no matter their age, was the ruler of an Empire; but the remains of it are only visible in the architecture of the main square of the capital of places like Estonia. And so what to make of all this, this small detail that is the linden tree, this large volume of the Swedish empire, and a small boy whose father was a Lutheran pastor? At the beginning of this narrative, the narrative that is Linnaeus, I have not made an appearance yet; the Swedes are not overly implicated in the Atlantic slave trade, not because they did not want to, only because they weren't allowed to do so; other people were better at it than they.

He was called "the little botanist" because he would neglect his studies and go out looking for flowers; if even then he had already showed an interest in, or the ability to name and classify plants, this fact is not in any account of his life that I have come across. He went to university at Uppsala; he studied there with Olaus Rudbeck. I can pause at this name, Rudbeck, and say Rudbeckia, and say, I do not like Rudbeckia, I never have it in my garden, but then I remember that a particularly stately, beautiful yellow flower in a corner of my field garden is Rudbeckia nitida growing there. He met Olaf Celsius (the Celsius scale of temperature measurement), who was so taken with Linnaeus's familiarity and knowledge of botany that he gave Linnaeus free lodging in his house. He became one of the youngest lecturers at the University. He went to Lapland and collected plants and insects native to that region of the world; he wrote and published an account of it called *Flora Lapponica*. In Lapland, he acquired a set of clothing that people native to that region of the world wore on festive occasions; I have seen a picture of him dressed in these clothes, and the caption under the picture says that he is wearing his Lapland costume. Suddenly, I am made a little uneasy, for just when is it that other people's clothes become your costume? But I am not too uneasy, I haven't really entered this narrative yet, I shall soon, in any case I do not know the Laplanders, they live far away, I don't believe they look like me.

I only enter the picture when Linnaeus takes a boat to Holland. He becomes a doctor to an obviously neurotic man (obvious, only to me, I arbitrarily deem him so; no account of him I have ever come across has described him so) named George Clifford. George Clifford is often described as a rich merchant banker; just like that, a rich merchant banker, and this description often seems to say that to be a rich merchant banker is just a type of person one could be, an ordinary type of person, anyone could be that. And now how to go on, for on hearing that George Clifford was a rich merchant in the 18th century, I now am sure I have become a part of the binomial system of plant nomenclature narrative.

George Clifford had glass houses full of vegetable materials from all over the world. This is what Linnaeus writes of it: "I was greatly amazed when I entered the greenhouses, full as they were of so many plants that a son of the North must feel bewitched, and wonder to what strange quarter of the globe he had been transported. In the first house were cultivated an abundance of flowers from southern Europe, plants from Spain, the South of France, Italy, Sicily and the isles of Greece. In the second were treasures from Asia, such as Poincianas, coconut and other palms, etc.; in the third, Africa's strangely shaped, not to say misshapen plants, such as the numerous forms of Aloe and Mesembryanthemum families, carnivorous flowers, Euphorbias, Crassula and Proteas species, and so on. And finally in the fourth greenhouse were grown the charming inhabitants of America and the rest of the New World; large masses of Cactus varieties, orchids, cruciferea, yams, magnolias, tulip-trees, calabash trees, arrow, cassias, acacias, tamarinds, pepper-plants, Anona, manicinilla, cucurbitaceous trees and many others, and surrounded by these, plantains, the most stately of all the world's plants, the most beauteous Hernandia, silver-gleaming species of Protea and camphor trees. When I then entered the positively royal residence and the extremely instructive museum, whose collections no less spoke in their owner's praise, I, a stranger, felt completely enraptured, as I had never before seen its like. My heart-felt wish was that I might lend a helping hand with its management."

In almost every account of an event that has taken place sometime in the last five hundred years, there is always a moment when I feel like placing an asterisk somewhere in its text, and at the end of this official story place my own addition. This chapter in the history of botany is such a moment. But where shall I begin? George Clifford is interesting—shall I look at him? He has long ago entered my narrative; I now feel I must enter his. What could it possibly mean to be a merchant banker in the 18th century? He is sometimes described as making his fortune in spices. Only once have I come across an account of him that says he was a director of the Dutch East India Company. The Dutch East India Company would not have been involved in the Atlantic trade in human cargo from Africa, but human cargo from Africa was a part of world trade. To read a brief account of the Dutch East India trading company in my very old encyclopedia is not unlike reading the label on an old can of paint. The entry mentions dates, the names of Dutch governors or people acting in Dutch interest; it mentions trade routes, places, commodities, incidents of war between the Dutch and other European people; it never mentions the people who lived in the area of the Dutch trading factories. Places like Ceylon, Java, the Cape of Good Hope are emptied of its people as the landscape itself was emptied of the things they were familiar with, the things that Linnaeus found in George Clifford's greenhouse.

"If one does not know the names, one's knowledge of things is useless." It was in George Clifford's greenhouse that Linnaeus gave some things names. The Adam-like quality of this effort was lost on him. "We revere the Creator's omnipotence," he says, meaning, I think, that he understood he had not made the things he was describing, he was only going to give them names. And even as a relationship exists between George Clifford's activity in the world, the world as it starts out on ships leaving the sea ports of the Netherlands, traversing the earth's seas, touching on the world's peoples and the places they are in, the things that have meant something to them being renamed and a whole new set of narratives imposed on them, narratives that place them at a disadvantage in relationship to George Clifford and his fellow Dutch, even as I can say all this in one breath or in one large volume, so too then does an invisible thread, a thread that no deep breath or large volume can contain, hang between Carolus Linnaeus, his father's desire to give himself a distinguished name, the name then coming from a tree, the Linden tree, a tree whose existence was regarded as not ordinary, and his invention of a system of naming that even I am forced to use?

The invention of this system has been a good thing. Its narrative would begin this way: in the beginning, the vegetable kingdom was chaos; people everywhere called the same things by a name that made sense to them, not by a name that they arrived at by an objective standard. But who has an interest in an objective standard? Who would need one? It makes me ask again what to call the thing that happened to me and all who look like me? Should I call it history? And if so, what should history mean to someone who looks like me? Should it be an idea, should it be an open wound and each breath I take in and expel healing and opening the wound again, over and over, or is it a long moment that begins anew each day since 1492?

VIVIAN GORNICK

Vivian Gornick (1935–), personal essayist, sublime memoirist (Fierce Attachments) *and literary critic, is instantly recognizable on the page by her lively urban voice and her assertive, often sharply funny sentences cutting ax-like through tentativeness. A lifelong feminist, her investment in psychoanalytic insight made her eager to discover the responsibility women may have had in their own disappointments, without letting patriarchy off the hook. Her feminist psychological outlook also led her to demystify the romantic narrative* (The End of the Novel of Love) *and pay tribute to a forerunner* (The Solitude of Self: Thinking About Elizabeth Cady Stanton)*. In her life-writing guide,* The Situation and the Story: The Art of Personal Narrative, *Gornick draws an important distinction between telling what has happened and revealing what the author makes of it. That dual process can be found throughout her descriptions of loneliness and resilience in* The Odd Woman and the City, *from which "The Princess and the Pea" (which originally appeared as a stand-alone essay) is taken.*

The Princess and the Pea

(1997)

I learned early that life was either Chekhovian or Shakespearean. In our house there was no contest. My mother lay on a couch, in a half-darkened room, one arm flung across her forehead, the other pressed against her breast. "I'm lonely!" she cried, and from every quarter of the tenement, women, and men also, flapped about, trying to assuage an anguish of the soul they took to be superior. But she turned away, her eyes closed in frantic dissatisfaction. She wanted a solace of the spirit none of them could provide. They were not the right people. No one around her was the right person. There had been only one right person, and now he was dead.

She had elevated love to the status of the holy grail. To find love was not simply to have sexual happiness, it was to achieve a place in the universe. When she married my father, she told me, a cloud of obscurity lifted from her soul. That's how she put it: a cloud of obscurity. Papa was magic: his look, his touch, his understanding. She leaned forward when she got to the end of this sentence. *Understanding* was the talismanic word. Without understanding, she said, she didn't know she was alive; with understanding, she felt centered and in the world. In my father's presence she responded with a depth she hadn't known she possessed to poetry, politics, music, sex: everything. She closed her eyes dramatically. *Everything.* When he died, she said, "everything" went with him. The cloud over her soul returned, blacker than ever: now it blotted out the earth.

The depression was profound and, apparently, nonnegotiable, persisting undiminished and undiluted for years on end. She could not forget the absolute *rightness* of what had once been hers. Whatever was now being offered, it would not do. Nothing was ever again exactly the right thing, no one exactly the right one. Refusal of the approximate took on a life of its own.

I became my mother's daughter. Very young, I was not able to find myself interesting without intelligent response. I required the company of minds attuned to my own, but no one around gave me back the words I needed to hear. I was forever telling the children on the block a story that had grown out of something that had just happened at school, in the grocery store, in the tenement building where I lived. I'd give them the narration, then I'd sum up, giving them the sentence that delivered the meaning of the story. After that I wanted someone to speak a sentence that would let me know my own had been received. Instead, eager looks evaporated, expressions turned puzzled or hostile, and, inevitably, someone said, "Whaddaya mean by that?"

I grew agitated, restless, and insulting, permanently aggrieved. "How can you say that!" I cried long before I could vote. I was beside myself with my mother's sense of deprivation. It was as though I'd been cheated at birth of the Ideal Friend, and now all I could do was register the insufficiency of the one at hand.

I was never going to know what Keats knew before he was twenty-five, that "any set of people is as good as any other." Now *there* was a Shakespearean life. Keats occupied his own experience to such a remarkable degree, he needed only the barest of human exchanges to connect with an inner clarity he himself had achieved. For that, almost anyone would do.

He lived inside the heaven of a mind nourished by its own conversation. I would wander for the rest of my life in the purgatory of self-exile, always looking for the right person to talk to.

This dead end led quickly to high-minded moralizing. I became the only fourteen-year-old girl on the block who pronounced regularly on the meaning and nature of Love with a capital L. Real love, true love, right love. You knew *instantly,* I declared categorically, when you were in the presence of love. If you didn't know, it wasn't love. If it *was,* whatever the obstacles, you were to give yourself to it without question, because love was the supreme intensity, the significant exaltation. It was the certainty with which I rehearsed this litany, again and again, that marked me.

At the same time that I was pontificating about Love with a capital L, I was a girl who continually daydreamed herself up on the stage of some great auditorium, or on a platform in a public square, addressing a crowd of thousands, urging it to revolution. The conviction that one day I would have the eloquence and the vision to move people to such action was my secret thrill. Sometimes I'd feel puzzled about how I would manage life both as an agent of revolution and as a devotee of Love. Inevitably, then, a picture formed itself of me on the stage, my face glowing with purpose, and an adoring man in the audience waiting for me to come down into his arms. That seemed to cover all the bases.

As I passed into my late teens, this image in my head of myself leading the revolution began, mysteriously, to complicate itself. I knew, of course, that a significant life included real work—work done out in the world— but now I seemed to imagine that an Ideal Partner was necessary in order to do the work. With the right man at my side, I posited, I could do it all. Without the right man . . . but no, that was unthinkable. There would *be* no without the right man. The emphasis began to shift away from doing the work to finding the right man in order to do the work. Slowly but surely, finding the right man seemed to become the work.

In college, the girls who were my friends were literary. Every one of us identified either with George Eliot's Dorothea Brooke, who mistakes a pedant for a man of intellect, or with Henry James's Isabel Archer, who sees the evil-hearted Osmond as a man of cultivation. Those who identified with Dorothea were impressed by her prideful devotion to "standards"; those who didn't thought her a provincial prig. Those who identified with Isabel admired her for the largeness of her emotional ambition; those who didn't thought her dangerously naïve. Either way, my friends and I saw ourselves as potential variations of one or the other. The seriousness of our concerns lay in our preoccupation with these two fictional women.

The problem, in both *Middlemarch* and *Portrait of a Lady,* was that of the protagonist—beautiful, intelligent, sensitive—mistaking the wrong man for the right man. As a problem, the situation seemed entirely reasonable to all of us. We saw it happening every day of the week. Among us were young women of grace, talent, and good looks attached, or becoming attached, to men dull in mind or spirit who were bound to drag them down. The prospect of such a fate haunted all of us. We each shuddered to think that we might become such women.

Not me, I determined. If I couldn't find the right man, I swore boldly, I'd do without.

For nearly ten years after college I knocked about in pursuit of the holy grail: Love with a capital L, Work with a capital W. I read, I wrote, I fell into bed. I was married for ten minutes, I smoked marijuana for five. Lively and animated, I roamed the streets of New York and Europe. Somehow, nothing quite suited. I couldn't figure out how to get down to work, and needless to say, I couldn't stumble on the right man. In time, a great lassitude overcame me. It was as though I'd fallen asleep on my feet and needed to be awakened.

On the very last day of my twenties I married a scientist, a man of brooding temperament who had taken eighteen years to complete his dissertation. His difficulty made him poetic in my eyes. He, of course, was remarkably sensitive to my own divided will. During our courtship we walked together by the hour while I discoursed ardently on why I could not get to Moscow. His eyes flashed with emotion as I spoke. "My dear girl!" he would exclaim. "My beautiful, marvelous girl. You are life itself!"

I became the interesting, conflicted personage and he the intelligent, responsive wife. The arrangement made us both happy. It felt like comradeship. At last, I thought, I had an Ideal Friend. Life seemed sweet then. Alone, I had been cramped up inside; now I felt myself breathing freely. It gave me pleasure to open my eyes in the morning and see my husband lying beside me. I experienced a comfort of the soul that I had not known before.

One morning I awoke desolate. Why, I could not tell. Nothing had changed. He was the same, I was the same. Just a few weeks before I'd awakened feeling festive. Now I stood in the shower stricken, spots of grief dancing in the air before my eyes, the old loneliness seeping back in.

Who is he? I thought.

He's not the right one, I thought.

If only I had the right one, I thought.

A year later we were divorced.

I was still my mother's daughter. Now she was the negative and I the print, but there we both were: alone at last with not the right one.

I did not understand until years after I'd left Gerald that I was born to find the wrong man, as were Dorothea and Isabel. That's what we were in business for. If this had not been the case, we'd all have found some useful work to do and long forgotten the whole question of the right man. But we did not forget it. We never forgot it. The elusive right man became a staple in our lives, his absence a defining experience.

It was then that I understood the fairy tale about the princess and the pea. She wasn't after the prince, she was after the pea. That moment when she feels the pea beneath the twenty mattresses, that is her moment of definition. It is the very meaning of her journey, why she has traveled so far, what she has come to confirm: the unholy dissatisfaction that will keep life permanently at bay.

So it was with my mother, who spent her years sighing for the absent right one. And so it was with me.

We were in thrall to neurotic longing, all of us—Dorothea and Isabel, my mother and I, the fairy-tale princess. Longing was what attracted us, what compelled our deepest attention. The essence, indeed, of a Chekhovian life. Think of all those Natashas sighing through three long acts for what is not, and can never be. While one (wrong) man after another listens sympathetically to the recital of a dilemma for which there is no solution.

Gerald and I were Natasha and the Doctor forever talking, talking, talking. Behind Natasha's enchanting conversation lies a passivity of monumental proportion—for which the Doctor is the perfect foil. Inevitably, Natasha and the Doctor must part. They have only been keeping each other company, spending their equally insufficient intent together.

DAVID FOSTER WALLACE

David Foster Wallace (1962–2008) is considered by many the best fiction writer of his generation; some would say the same about his nonfiction. In the two essay collections published during his lifetime, A Supposedly Fun Thing I'll Never Do Again *and* Consider the Lobster, *seemingly focused on tennis, state fairs, cruises, television, and the novel, he elaborated his conviction that American society was in a state of crisis, paralyzed by postmodernist irony and shallow cynicism. Wallace, a formidably intellectual, linguistically virtuosic, philosophically sophisticated, clinically depressed man, was increasingly drawn to simplicity, goodness, kindness, and normalcy. The tension in Wallace's vision of average Americans, whom he envied and felt humbled by but also disconcertingly superior to, is nowhere more clearly evinced than in this powerful, uncharacteristically straightforward (only a handful of footnotes, no endnotes) diary-essay about 9/11.*

The View from Mrs. Thompson's

(2001)

LOCATION: BLOOMINGTON, ILLINOIS
DATES: 11–13 SEPTEMBER 2001
SUBJECT: OBVIOUS

SYNECDOCHE In true Midwest fashion, people in Bloomington aren't unfriendly but do tend to be reserved. A stranger will smile warmly at you, but there normally won't be any of that strangerly chitchat in waiting areas or checkout lines. But now, thanks to the Horror, there's something to talk about that overrides all inhibition, as if we were somehow all standing right there and just saw the same traffic accident. Example: overheard in the checkout line at Burwell Oil (which is sort of the Nei-man Marcus of gas station/convenience store plazas—centrally located athwart both one-way main drags, and with the best tobacco prices in town, it's a municipal treasure) between a lady in an Osco cashier's smock and a man in a dungaree jacket cut off at the shoulders to make a sort of homemade vest: "With my boys they thought it was all some movie like that *Independence Day,* till then they started to notice how it was the same movie on all the channels." (The lady didn't say how old her boys were.)

WEDNESDAY Everyone has flags out. Homes, businesses. It's odd: you never see anybody putting out a flag, but by Wednesday morning there they all are. Big flags, small, regular flag-sized flags. A lot of homeown-ers here have those special angled flag-holders by their front door, the kind whose brace takes four Phillips screws. Plus thousands of the little handheld flags-on-a-stick you normally see at parades—some yards have dozens of these stuck in the ground all over, as if they'd somehow all just sprouted overnight. Rural-road people attach the little flags to their mailboxes out by the street. A good number of vehicles have them wedged in their grille or attached to the antenna. Some upscale people have actual poles; their flags are at half-mast. More than a few large homes around Franklin Park or out on the east side even have enormous multistory flags hanging gonfalon-style down over their facades. It's a total mystery where people can buy flags this big or how they got them up there, or when.

My own next-door neighbor, a retired bookkeeper and USAF vet whose home- and lawn-care are nothing short of phenomenal, has a regulation-size anodized flagpole secured in eighteen inches of reinforced cement that none of the other neighbors like very much because they feel it draws lightning. He says there's a very particular etiquette to having your flag at half-mast: you're supposed to first run it all the way up to the finial at the top and *then* bring it halfway down. Otherwise it's some kind of insult. His flag is out straight and popping smartly in the wind. It's far and away the biggest flag on our street. You can also hear the wind in the cornfields just south; it sounds roughly the way light surf sounds when you're two dunes back from the shore. Mr. N——'s pole's halyard has metal elements that clank against the pole when it's windy, which is something else the neighbors don't much care for. His driveway and mine are almost right together, and he's out here on a stepladder polishing his pole with some kind of special ointment and a chamois cloth—I shit you not—although in the morning sun it's true that his metal pole does shine like God's own wrath.

"Hell of a nice flag and display apparatus, Mr. N——."

"Ought to be. Cost enough."

"Seen all the other flags out everywhere this morning?"

This gets him to look down and smile, if a bit grimly. "Something, isn't it." Mr. N—— is not what you'd call the friendliest next-door neighbor. I really only know him because his church and mine are in the same softball league, for which he serves with great seriousness and precision as his team's statistician. We are not close. Nevertheless he's the first one I ask:

"Say, Mr. N——, suppose somebody like a foreign person or a TV reporter or something were to come by and ask you what the purpose of all these flags after what happened yesterday was, exactly—what do you think you'd say?"

"Why" (after a little moment of him giving me the same sort of look he usually gives my lawn), "to show our support towards what's going on, as Americans."*

The overall point being that on Wednesday here there's a weird accretive pressure to have a flag out. If the purpose of displaying a flag is to make a statement, it seems like at a certain point of density of flags you're making more of a statement if you *don't* have a flag out. It's not totally clear what statement this would be, though. What if you just don't happen to have a flag? Where has everyone gotten these flags, especially the little ones you can fasten to your mailbox? Are they all from the Fourth of July and people just save them, like Christmas ornaments? How do they know to do this? There's nothing in the Yellow Pages under *Flag*. At some point there starts to be actual tension. Nobody walks by or stops their car and says, "Hey, how come your house doesn't have a flag?," but it gets easier and easier to imagine them thinking it. Even a sort of half-collapsed house down the street that everybody thought was abandoned has one of the little flags on a stick in the weeds by the driveway. None of Bloomington's grocery stores turn out to stock flags. The big novelty shop downtown has nothing but Halloween stuff. Only a few businesses are actually open, but even the closed ones are now displaying some sort of flag. It's almost surreal. The VFW hall is obviously a good bet, but it can't open until noon if at all (it has a bar). The counter lady at Burwell Oil references a certain hideous KWIK-N-EZ convenience store out by I-55 at which she's pretty sure she recalls seeing some little plastic flags back in the racks with all the bandannas and NASCAR caps, but by the

---

* Plus: selected other responses from various times during the day's flag-hunt when circumstances permitted the question to be asked without one seeming like a smartass or loon:

"To show we're Americans and we're not going to bow down to nobody";

"It's a classic pseudo-archetype, a reflexive semion designed to preempt and negate the critical function" (grad student);

"For pride";

"What they do is symbolize unity and that we're all together behind the victims in this war and they've fucked with the wrong people this time, amigo."

time I get down there they all turn out to be gone, snapped up by parties unknown. The cold reality is that there is not a flag to be had in this town. Stealing one out of somebody's yard is clearly just out of the question. I'm standing in a fluorescent-lit KWIK-N-EZ afraid to go home. All those people dead, and I'm sent to the edge by a plastic flag. It doesn't get really bad until people come over and ask if I'm OK and I have to lie and say it's a Benadryl reaction (which in fact can happen).

. . . And so on until, in one more of the Horror's weird twists of fate and circumstance, it's the KWIK-N-EZ proprietor himself (a Pakistani, by the way) who offers solace and a shoulder and a strange kind of unspoken understanding, and who lets me go back and sit in the stockroom amid every conceivable petty vice and indulgence America has to offer and compose myself, and who only slightly later, over styrofoam cups of a strange kind of perfumey tea with a great deal of milk in it, suggests construction paper and "Magical Markers," which explains my now-beloved and proudly displayed homemade flag.

AERIAL & GROUND VIEWS Everyone here gets the local news organ, the *Pantagraph,* which is roundly loathed by most of the natives I know. Imagine, let's say, a well-funded college newspaper co-edited by Bill O'Reilly and Martha Stewart. Wednesday's headline is: **ATTACKED!** After two pages of AP stuff, you get to the real *Pantagraph.* Everything to follow is *sic.* Wednesday's big local headers are: STUNNED CITIZENS RUN THROUGH MANY EMOTIONS; CLERGY OPEN ARMS TO HELP PEOPLE DEAL WITH TRAGEDY; ISU PROFESSOR: B-N NOT A LIKELY TARGET; PRICES ROCKET AT GAS PUMPS; AMPUTEE GIVES INSPIRATIONAL SPEECH. There's a half-page photo of a student at Bloomington Central Catholic HS saying the rosary in response to the Horror, which means that some staff photographer came in and popped a flash in the face of a traumatized kid at prayer. The Op-Ed column for 9/12 starts out: "The carnage we have seen through the eyes of lenses in New York City and Washington, D.C., still seems like an R-rated movie out of Hollywood."

Bloomington is a city of 65,000 in the central part of a state that is extremely, emphatically flat, so that you can see the town's salients from way far away. Three major interstates converge here, and several rail lines. The town's almost exactly halfway between Chicago and St. Louis, and its origins involve being an important train depot. Bloomington is the birthplace of Adlai Stevenson and the putative hometown of Colonel Blake on *M*A*S*H.* It has a smaller twin city, Normal, that's built around a public university and is a whole different story. Both towns together are like 110,000 people.

As Midwest cities go, the only remarkable thing about Bloomington is its prosperity. It is all but recession-proof. Some of this is due to the county's farmland, which is world-class fertile and so expensive per acre that a civilian can't even find out how much it costs. But Bloomington is also the national HQ for State Farm, which is the great dark god of US consumer insurance and for all practical purposes owns the town, and because of which Bloomington's east side is now all smoked-glass complexes and Build to Suit developments and a six-lane beltway of malls and franchises that's killing off the old downtown, plus an ever-wider split between the town's two basic classes and cultures, so well and truly symbolized by the SUV and the pickup truck, respectively.*

Winter here is a pitiless bitch, but in the warm months Bloomington is a lot like a seaside community except here the ocean is corn, which grows steroidically and stretches to the earth's curve in all directions. The town itself in summer is intensely green—streets bathed in tree-shade and homes' explosive gardens and dozens of manicured parks and ballfields and golf courses you almost need eye protection to look at, and broad weedless fertilized lawns all made to line up exactly flush to the sidewalk with special edging tools.† To be honest, it's all a little creepy, especially in high summer, when nobody's out and all that green just sits in the heat and seethes.

Like most Midwest towns, B-N is crammed with churches: four full pages in the phone book. Everything from Unitarian to bug-eyed Pentecostal. There's even a church for agnostics. But except for church—plus I guess your basic parades, fireworks, and a couple corn festivals—there isn't much public community. Everybody has his family and neighbors and tight little circle of friends. Folks keep to themselves (the native term for light conversation is *visit*). They basically all play softball or golf and grill out, and watch their kids play soccer, and sometimes go to mainstream movies . . .

. . . And they watch massive, staggering amounts of TV. I don't just mean the kids, either. Something that's obvious but important to keep in mind re Bloomington and the Horror is that reality—any felt sense of a larger world—is mainly televisual. New York's skyline, for instance, is as recognizable here as anyplace else, but what it's recognizable from is TV. TV's also a more social phenomenon than on the East Coast, where in my experience people are almost constantly leaving home to go meet other people face-to-face in public places. There don't really tend to be parties or mixers per se so much here—what you do in Bloomington is all get together at somebody's house and watch something.

In Bloomington, therefore, to have a home without a TV is to become a kind of constant and Kramer-like presence in others' homes, a perpetual guest of folks who can't quite understand why somebody wouldn't own a

---

* *Pace* some people's impression, the native accent around here isn't southern so much as just rural. The town's corporate transplants, on the other hand, have no accent at all—in Mrs. Bracero's phrase, State Farm people "sound like the folks on TV."

† People here are deeply, deeply into lawn-care; my own neighbors tend to mow as often as they shave.

TV but are totally respectful of your need to watch TV, and who will offer you access to their TV in the same instinctive way they'd bend to offer a hand if you fell down in the street. This is especially true for some kind of must-see, crisis-type situation like the 2000 election or this week's Horror. All you have to do is call someone you know and say you don't have a TV: "Well shoot, boy, get over here."

TUESDAY There are maybe ten days a year when it's gorgeous in Bloomington, and 11 September is one of them. The air is clear and temperate and wonderfully dry after several weeks of what's felt very much like living in someone's armpit. It's just before serious harvesting starts, when the region's pollen is at its worst, and a good percentage of the city is stoned on Benadryl, which as you probably know tends to give the early morning a kind of dreamy, underwater quality. Time-wise, we're an hour behind the East Coast By 8:00, everybody with a job is at it, and just about everybody else is home drinking coffee and blowing their nose and watching *Today* or one of the other network AM shows that all broadcast (it goes without saying) from New York. At 8:00 on Tuesday I personally was in the shower, trying to listen to a Bears postmortem on WSCR Sports Radio in Chicago.

The church I belong to is on the south side of Bloomington, near where my house is. Most of the people I know well enough to ask if I can come over and watch their TV are members of my church. It's not one of those churches where people throw Jesus' name around a lot or talk about the End Times, but it's fairly serious, and people in the congregation get to know each other well and to be pretty tight. As far as I know, all the congregants are natives of the area. Most are working-class or retired from same. There are some small-business owners. A fair number are veterans and/or have kids in the military or—especially—in the Reserves, because for many of these families that's what you do to pay for college.

The house I end up sitting with shampoo in my hair watching most of the actual unfolding Horror at belongs to Mrs. Thompson, who is one of the world's cooler seventy-four-year-olds and exactly the kind of person who in an emergency even if her phone is busy you know you can just come on over. She lives about a mile away from me on the other side of a mobile-home park. The streets are not crowded, but they're also not as empty as they're going to get. Mrs. Thompson's is a tiny immaculate one-story home that on the West Coast would be called a bungalow and on the south side of Bloomington is called a house. Mrs. Thompson is a long-time member and a leader in the congregation, and her living room tends to be kind of a gathering place. She's also the mom of one of my very best friends here, F——, who was in the Rangers in Vietnam and got shot in the knee and now works for a contractor installing various kinds of franchise stores in malls. He's in the middle of a divorce (long story) and living with Mrs. T. while the court decides on the disposition of his house. F—— is one of those veterans who doesn't talk about the war or belong to the VFW but is sometimes preoccupied in a dark way, and goes quietly off to camp by himself over Memorial Day weekend, and you can tell that he carries some serious shit in his head. Like most people who work construction, he wakes up very early and was long gone by the time I got to his mom's, which happened to be just after the second plane hit the South Tower, meaning probably around 8:10.

In retrospect, the first sign of possible shock was the fact that I didn't ring the bell but just came on in, which normally here one would never do. Thanks in part to her son's trade connections, Mrs. T. has a forty-inch flat-panel Philips TV on which Dan Rather appears for a second in shirtsleeves with his hair slightly mussed. (People in Bloomington seem overwhelmingly to prefer CBS News; it's unclear why.) Several other ladies from church are already over here, but I don't know if I exchanged greetings with anyone because I remember when I came in everybody was staring transfixed at one of the very few pieces of video CBS never reran, which was a distant wide-angle shot of the North Tower and its top floors' exposed steel lattice in flames, and of dots detaching from the building and moving through smoke down the screen, which then a sudden jerky tightening of the shot revealed to be actual people in coats and ties and skirts with their shoes falling off as they fell, some hanging onto ledges or girders and then letting go, upside-down or wriggling as they fell and one couple almost seeming (unverifiable) to be hugging each other as they fell those several stories and shrank back to dots as the camera then all of a sudden pulled back to the long view—I have no idea how long the clip took—after which Dan Rather's mouth seemed to move for a second before any sound emerged, and everyone in the room sat back and looked at one another with expressions that seemed somehow both childlike and terribly old. I think one or two people made some sort of sound. I'm not sure what else to say. It seems grotesque to talk about being traumatized by a piece of video when the people in the video were dying. Something about the shoes also falling made it worse. I think the older ladies took it better than I did. Then the hideous beauty of the rerun clip of the second plane hitting the tower, the blue and silver and black and spectacular orange of it, as more little moving dots fell. Mrs. Thompson was in her chair, which is a rocker with floral cushions. The living room has two other chairs, and a huge corduroy sofa that F—— and I had had to take the front door off its hinges to get in the house. All the seats were occupied, meaning I think five or six other people, most women, all these over fifty, and there were more voices in the kitchen, one of which was very upset-sounding and belonged to the psychologically delicate Mrs. R——, who I don't know very well but is said to have once been a beauty of great local repute. Many of the people are Mrs. T.'s neighbors, and some are still in robes, and at various times people leave to go home and use the phone and come back, or leave altogether (one younger lady went to go take her children out of school), and other people came. At one point, around the time the South Tower was falling so perfectly-seeming down into itself (I remember thinking that it was falling the way an elegant lady faints, but it was Mrs. Bracero's normally pretty much useless and irritating son, Duane, who pointed out that what it really looked like is if you took some film of a NASA liftoff and ran it backward, which now after several re-viewings does seem dead on), there were at least a dozen people in the house. The living room was dim because in summer here everyone always keeps their drapes pulled.*

Is it normal not to remember things very well after only a couple days, or at any rate the order of things? I know at some point for a while there was the sound outside of some neighbor mowing his lawn, which seemed totally bizarre, but I don't remember if anybody remarked on it. Sometimes it seemed like nobody said anything and sometimes like everybody was talking at once. There was also a lot of telephonic activity. None of these women carry cell phones (Duane has a pager whose function is unclear), so it's just Mrs. T.'s old wall-mount in the kitchen. Not all the calls made rational sense. One side effect of the Horror was an overwhelming desire to call everyone you loved. It was established early on that you couldn't get New York—dialing 212 yielded only a weird whooping sound. People keep asking Mrs. T.'s permission until she tells them to knock it off and for heaven's sake just use the phone. Some of the ladies reach their husbands, who are apparently all gathered around TVs and radios at their various workplaces; for a while bosses are too shocked to think to send people home. Mrs. T. has coffee on, but another sign of crisis is that if you want some you have to go get it yourself—usually it just sort of appears. From the door to the kitchen I remember seeing the second tower fall and being confused about whether it was a replay of the first tower falling. Another thing about the hay fever is that you can't ever be totally sure someone's crying, but over the two hours of first-run Horror, with bonus reports of the crash in PA and Bush being moved into a SAC bunker and a car bomb that's gone off in Chicago (the latter then retracted), pretty much everybody either cries or comes very close, according to his or her relative abilities. Mrs. Thompson says less than almost anyone. I don't think she cries, but she doesn't rock in her chair as usual, either. Her first husband's death was apparently sudden and grisly,

---

* Mrs. Thompson's living room is prototypical working-class Bloomington, too: double-pane windows, white Sears curtains w/ valence, catalogue clock with a background of mallards, woodgrain magazine rack with *CSM* and *Reader's Digest,* inset bookshelves used to display little collectible figurines and framed photos of relatives and their families. There are two knit samplers w/ the Desiderata and Prayer of St. Francis, antimacassars on every good chair, and wall-to-wall carpet so thick that you can't see your feet (people take their shoes off at the door—it's basic common courtesy).

and I know at times during the war F—— would be out in the field and she wouldn't hear from him for weeks at a time and didn't know whether he was even alive. Duane Bracero's main contribution is to keep iterating how much like a movie it all seems. Duane, who's at least twenty-five but still lives at home while supposedly studying to be a welder, is one of these people who always wears camouflage T-shirts and paratrooper boots but would never dream of actually enlisting (as, to be fair, neither would I). He has also kept his hat, the front of which promotes something called SLIPKNOT, on his head indoors in Mrs. Thompson's house. It always seems to be important to have at least one person in the vicinity to hate.

It turns out the cause of poor tendony Mrs. R——'s meltdown in the kitchen is that she has either a grandniece or removed cousin who's doing some type of internship at Time, Inc., in the Time-Life Building or what-ever it's called, about which Mrs. R—— and whoever she's managed to call know only that it's a vertiginously tall skyscraper someplace in New York City, and she's out of her mind with worry, and two other ladies have been out here the whole time holding both her hands and trying to decide whether they should call her doctor (Mrs. R—— has kind of a history), and I end up doing pretty much the only good I do all day by explaining to Mrs. R—— where midtown Manhattan is. It thereupon emerges that none of the people here I'm watching the Horror with—not even the couple ladies who'd gone to see *Cats* as part of some group tour thing through the church in 1991—have even the vaguest notion of New York's layout and don't know, for example, how radically far south the Financial District and Statue of Liberty are; they have to be shown this via pointing out the ocean in the foreground of the skyline they all know so well (from TV).

The half-assed little geography lesson is the start of a feeling of alien-ation from these good people that builds in me all throughout the part of the Horror where people flee rubble and dust. These ladies are not stupid, or ignorant. Mrs. Thompson can read both Latin and Spanish, and Ms. Voigtlander is a certified speech therapist who once explained to me that the strange gulping sound that makes NBC's Tom Brokaw so distracting to listen to is an actual speech impediment called a *glottal L*. It was one of the ladies out in the kitchen supporting Mrs. R—— who pointed out that 11 September is the anniversary of the Camp David Accords, which was certainly news to me.

What these Bloomington ladies are, or start to seem to me, is innocent. There is what would strike many Americans as a marked, startling lack of cynicism in the room. It does not, for instance, occur to anyone here to remark on how it's maybe a little odd that *all three* network anchors are in shirtsleeves, or to consider the possibility that Dan Rather's hair's being mussed might not be wholly accidental, or that the constant rerunning of horrific footage might not be just in case some viewers were only now tuning in and hadn't seen it yet. None of the ladies seem to notice the president's odd little lightless eyes appear to get closer and closer together throughout his taped address, nor that some of his lines sound almost plagiaristically identical to those uttered by Bruce Willis (as a right-wing wacko, recall) in *The Siege* a couple years back. Nor that at least some of the sheer weirdness of watching the Horror unfold has been how closely various shots and scenes have mirrored the plots of everything from *Die Hard I–III* to *Air Force One*. Nobody's near hip enough to lodge the sick and obvious po-mo complaint: We've Seen This Before. Instead, what they do is all sit together and feel really bad, and pray. No one in Mrs. Thompson's crew would ever be so nauseous as to try to get everybody to pray aloud or form a prayer circle, but you can still tell what they're all doing.

Make no mistake, this is mostly a good thing. It forces you to think and do things you most likely wouldn't alone, like for instance while watching the address and eyes to pray, silently and fervently, that you're wrong about the president, that your view of him is maybe distorted and he's actually far smarter and more substantial than you believe, not just some soulless golem or nexus of corporate interests dressed up in a suit but a statesman of courage and probity and . . . and it's good, this is good to pray this way. It's just a bit lonely to have to. Truly decent, innocent people can be taxing to be around. I'm not for a moment trying to suggest that everyone I know in Bloomington is like Mrs. Thompson (e.g., her son F—— isn't, though he's an outstanding person). I'm trying, rather, to explain how some part of the horror of the Horror was knowing, deep in my heart, that whatever America the men in those planes hated so much was far more my America, and F——'s, and poor old loathsome Duane's, than it was these ladies'.

RICHARD RODRIGUEZ

Richard Rodriguez (1944–) sprang to prominence with his first book, Hunger of Memory, *a memoir in the form of essays: its flawlessly elegant literary style was as notable as its author's refusal to accept the advantages of a disadvantaged minority. Rodriguez's controversial stance against bilingual education and affirmative action was consistent with his acceptance of U.S. citizenship as inevitably if tragically producing an alienation from his family's Mexican roots. Since then, he has often found himself expected to perform as an ethnic spokesman (vide the puckish "Hispanic" from his essay collection* Brown: The Last Discovery of America*), when he is first and foremost a writer—an immensely dexterous, moral, and ironic writer with the capacity to think against himself and to see all sides of every question.*

Hispanic

(2002)

Hi.*spa´*.nick. 1. Spanish, *adjective*. 2. Latin American, *adjective*. 3. Hispano, *noun*. An American citizen or resident of Spanish descent. 4. Ducking under the cyclone fence, *noun*. 5. Seen running from the scene of the crime, *adjective*. Clinging to a raft off the Florida coast. Elected mayor in New Jersey. Elevated to bishop or traded to the San Diego Padres. Awarded the golden pomegranate by the U.S. Census Bureau: "most fertile." Soon, an oxymoron: America's largest minority. An utter absurdity: "destined to outnumber blacks." A synonym for the future (salsa having replaced catsup on most American kitchen tables). Madonna's daughter.

Sammy Sosa's son. Little Elián and his Great Big Family. A jillarioso novel about ten sisters, their sorrows and joys and intrauterine devices. The new face of American Protestantism: Evangelical minister, tats on his arms; wouldn't buy a used car from. Highest high school dropout rate; magical realism.

The question remains: Do Hispanics exist?

I tell myself, on mornings like this—the fog has burned off early—that I am really going to give it up. Hispanicism cannot interest me anymore. My desk a jumble of newspaper clippings. Look at all this! Folders. It looks like a set for *The Makropolous Case*. I will turn instead to the death agony of a moth, the gigantic shuddering of lantern-paper wings. Or I will count the wrinkles on Walden Pond. I will write some of those constipated, low-paying, fin de siècle essays about the difficulty of saying anything in this, our age. *Visi d'arte,* from now on, as Susan Sontag sang so memorably from the chapel of Sant'Andrea della Valle.

For years now I have pursued Hispanicism, as a solitary, self-appointed inspector in an old Hitchcock will dog some great hoax; amassing data; abstractedly setting down his coffee cup at a precarious angle to its saucer, to the stack of papers and books and maps on which it rests, because he is drawn to some flash-lit, spyglassed item in the morning paper. I am catching them up, slowly, inexorably, confident of the day—soon—when I shall publish my findings.

Soon. I take my collapsible double-irony on tour to hotel ballroom conferences and C-SPAN-televised luncheons and "Diversity Week" lectures at universities. For a fee, I rise to say I am not Latin American, because I am Hispanic. I am Hispanic because I live in the United States. *Thank you.* (For a larger fee, I will add there is no such thing as a Hispanic. *Thank you.*)

But this morning I have decided, after all, to join the hoax.

Hispanic has had its way with me. I suspect also with you. The years have convinced me that Hispanic is a noun that can't lose. An adjective with legs. There is money in it.

Hispanic (the noun, the adjective) has encouraged the Americanization of millions of Hispanics. But at the same time, Hispanic—the ascending tally announced by the U.S. Census Bureau—has encouraged the Latinization of non-Hispanics.

As a Hispanic, as a middle-aged noun, like Oscar Wilde descending to gaol, I now take my place in the booth provided within that unglamorous American fair devised by the Richard Nixon administration in 1973 (O.M.B. Statistical Directive 15). Within the Nixonian fair are five exposition halls:

BLACK;

WHITE;

ASIAN/PACIFIC ISLANDER;

NATIVᴱ AMERICAN/ESKIMO;
HISPA . . iC.

They aren't much, these drafty rooms—about what you'd expect of government issue. Nixon's fair attempted to describe the world that exists by portraying a world that doesn't. Statisticians in overalls moved India—*ouffff*—that heavy, spooled and whirligigged piece of Victorian mahogany, over beneath the green silk tent of Asia. Mayan Indians from the Yucatán were directed to the Hispanic pavilion (Spanish colonial), which they must share with Argentine tangoistas, Colombian drug dealers, and Russian Jews who remember Cuba from the viewpoint of Miami. Of the five ports, Hispanic has the least reference to blood. There is no such thing as Hispanic blood. *(Do I not bleed?)* Though I meet young Hispanics who imagine they descend from it.

Nixon's fair does at least succeed in portraying the United States in relation to the world. One can infer a globe from a pentagram.

Over my head, as I write these words, a New World Indian is singing in the language of the conquistador. (A Korean contractor, hired by my landlord, has enlisted a tribe of blue-jumpered Mexican Indians to reroof the apartment building where I live.) In trustworthy falsetto, the young man lodges a complaint against an intangible mistress unfond, as high above him as the stars, and as cold. Yesterday, as he was about to hoist a roll of tar paper, this same young man told me the choir of roofers, excepting *"el patrón,"* originate from a single village in a far state of Mexico. And a few minutes ago, I overheard them all—the Mexicans and the Korean contractor—negotiating their business in pidgin (Spanish, curiously; I would have expected English). Then my ceiling shook with their footfalls. And with bolts of tar paper flung upon it. My library leapt in its shelves—those ladies and gentlemen, so unaccustomed.

Tomorrow, having secured my abstractions against the rainy season, the Mexican Indians will fly away to some other rooftop in the city, while I must remain at this desk.

Why must I? Because my literary agent has encouraged from me a book that answers a simple question: *What do Hispanics mean to the life of America?* He asked me that question several years ago in a French restaurant on East Fifty-seventh Street, as I watched a waiter approach our table holding before him a shimmering *îles flottantes.*

But those were palmier days. Before there were Hispanics in America, there was another fictitious, inclusive genus: the Latin Lover. The Latin Lover was male counterpart to the vamp. He specialized in the inarticulate—"dark"—passions; perhaps a little cruel. He was mascaraed, mute, prepotent. Phantom, sheikh, or matador, he was of no philosophy but appetite. His appetite was blond.

White America's wettest perdition fantasy has always been consanguinity with some plum-colored thigh. The Latin Lover was a way of meeting the fantasy halfway. This was not a complicated scenario. Nor was Hollywood fussy about casting it. Ramon Navarro, Rudolph Valentino, Ezio Pinza, Rossano Brazzi, Ricardo Montalban, Prince Rainier, George Chakiris, all descended from the dusky isles of Cha-Cha.

Probably the last unironic Latin Lover conscripted into American fantasy was Omar Sharif, hired to seduce Peter O'Toole.

But, by then, Lucille Ball had undermined the fantasy by domesticating the Latin Lover. In the 1950s, Lucille Ball insisted upon casting her real-life husband as her fictional husband, against the advice of CBS Television executives. Desi Arnaz was not mute, nor were his looks smoldering. In fact his eyes bulged with incredulity at *la vida loca* with Lucy. Curiously, Lucy was the madcap for having married a Cuban bandleader in the first place. Curiously, Desi was the solid American citizen (though he did wear a smoking jacket at home). Soon, millions of Americans began a Monday night vigil, awaiting the birth of Little Ricky, the first Hispanic.

By the time *I Love Lucy* went to divorce court, Desi Arnaz had been replaced on our television screens by Fidel Castro. Castro was a perverted hotblood—he was a cold warrior—as was his Byronic sidekick, Ché. Our fantasy toyed for a time with what lay beneath the beards. When we eventually got a translation, we took fright. *Bad wolf!* Rhetoric too red for our fantasy.

The red wolf ripped away the Copacabana curtain—all the nightclub gaiety of Latin America in old black-and-white movies—to reveal a land of desperate want.

In the early 1960s, Mexican Americans were described by American liberals as an "invisible minority." Americans nevertheless saw farmworkers in the Central Valley of California singing and praying in Spanish. Americans later saw angry Chicanos on TV imitating the style of black militancy.

By the 1970s, even as millions of Latin Americans came north, seeking their future as capitalists, the Latin Lover faded from America's imagination.

Surviving Chicanos (one still meets them) scorn the term Hispanic, in part because it was Richard Nixon who drafted the noun and who made the adjective uniform. Chicanos resist the term, as well, because it reduces the many and complicated stories of the Mexican in America to a mere chapter of a much larger saga that now includes Hondurans and Peruvians and Cubans. Chicanos resent having to share mythic space with parvenus and numerically lesser immigrant Latin American populations. After all, Mexican Americans number more than seventy percent of the nation's total Hispanics. And, Chicanos say, borrowing a tabula rasa from American Indians, we are not just another "immigrant" population in the

United States. We were here before the *Mayflower*. Which is true enough, though "we" and "here" are blurred by imprecision. California was once Mexico, as were other parts of the Southwestern United States. So we were here when here was there. In truth, however, the majority of Mexican Americans, or our ancestors, crossed a border.

One meets Hispanics who refuse Hispanic because of its colonial tooling. Hispanic, they say, places Latin America (once more) under the rubric of Spain. An alternate noun the disaffected prefer is "Latino," because they imagine the term locates them in the Americas, which the term now does in all revised American dictionaries, because Latinos insist that it does. (What is language other than an agreement, like Greenwich Mean Time?) In fact, Latino commits Latin America to Iberian memory as surely as does Hispanic. And Latino is a Spanish word, thus also paying linguistic obeisance to Spain. For what, after all, does "Latin" refer to, if not the imperial root system?

Hispanicus sui.

My private argument with Latino is no more complicated than my dislike for a dictation of terms. I am Latino against my will: I write for several newspapers—the *Los Angeles Times* most often—papers that have chosen to warrant "Latino" over "Hispanic" as correct usage. The newspaper's computer becomes sensitive, not to say jumpy, as regards correct political usage. Every Hispanic the computer busts is digitally repatriated to Latino. As I therefore also become.

In fact, I do have a preference for Hispanic over Latino. To call oneself Hispanic is to admit a relationship to Latin America in English. *Soy* Hispanic is a brown assertion.

Hispanic nativists who, of course, would never call themselves Hispanic, nonetheless have a telling name for their next-door neighbors who are not Hispanic. The word is "Anglo." Do Irish Americans become Anglos? And do you suppose a Chinese American or an African American is an Anglo? Does the term define a group of Americans by virtue of a linguistic tie to England or by the lack of a tie to Spain? (Come now, think. Did no one in your family take a Spanish course? In high school?) In which case, the more interesting question becomes whether Hispanics who call Anglos Anglo are themselves Anglo?

Nevertheless, in a Texas high school, according to the *Dallas Morning News,* a gang of "Anglos" and a gang of "Hispanics" shed real blood in a nonfictional cafeteria, in imitation of a sixteenth-century sea battle the students doubtlessly never heard of. Who could have guessed that a European rivalry would play itself out several hundred years after Philip's Armada was sunk by Elizabeth's navie? And here? No other country in the world has been so confident of its freedom from memory. Yet Americans comically (because unknowingly) assume proxy roles within a centuries-old quarrel of tongues.

—

Englande and España divided much of the Americas between them. England gave her colonial territories a remarkable code of civil law, a spectacular literature, a taste for sweeties, and the protean pronoun that ushered in the modern age—"I"—the lodestar for Protestant and capitalist and Hispanic memoirist. Counter-Reformation Spain gave its New World possessions *nosotros*—the cupolic "we"—an assurance of orthodoxy, baroque, fugue, smoke, sunglasses, and a piquant lexicon for miscegenation. Every combination of races is accounted for in New World Spanish. (Except Hispanic.) (Or Latino.)

The numerical rise of the Hispanic in the United States occasioned language skirmishes, especially in those parts of the country where the shadow of Philip's crown once crossed Elizabeth's scepter. On the one hand, in the 1960s, Chicano neo-nationalists attempted to make "bilingual education" the cornerstone of their political agenda, since little other than tongue (and not even that oftentimes) united Hispanics. Anglo nativists distributed ballots to establish English as "the official language of the United States." In truth, America is a more complicated country than either faction dares admit.

Americans do not speak "English." Even before our rebellion against England, our tongue tasted of Indian—*succotash, succotash,* we love to say it; *Mississippi,* we love to spell. We speak American. Our tongue is not something slow arid mucous that plods like an oyster through its bed in the sea, afearing of taint or blister. Our tongue sticks out; it is a dog's tongue, an organ of curiosity and science.

The history of a people—their hungers, weathers, kinships, humors, erotic salts and pastimes—gets told by turns of phrase. Which is why the best history of the United States I ever read is not a history of battles and presidents and such, but H. L. Mencken's *The American Language,* an epic of nouns and verbs and proverbs; things we pick up or put down by name.

By 1850, William C. Fowler was describing "American dialects." Nine years later, John Russell Bartlett offered a glossary of "words and phrases usually regarded as peculiar to the United States": archaisms, et cetera. The American tongue created what Russell called "negroisms"— cadences, inflections, parodies, refusals. Our lewd tongue partook of everything that washed over it; everything that it washed—even a disreputable history. That is how young Walt Whitman heard America singing in the nineteenth century, heard the varied carols of trade in old New York harbor, heard young fellows, robust, friendly, singing with open mouths.

Nativists who want to declare English the official language of the United States do not understand the omnivorous appetite of the language they wish to protect. Neither do they understand that their protection would harm our tongue. (A restaurant in my neighborhood advertises "Harm on Rye.") Those Americans who would build a fence around American English to forestall the Trojan burrito would turn American into a brightened tongue, a shrinking little oyster tongue, as French has lately become, priested over by the Ancients of the Académie, who fret so about *le weekend*.

In an essay published in *Harper's* of April 1917, an immigrant son, M. E. Ravage, complained about the way Americans lick the oak leaves and acorns off the old monikers, so that they became "emasculated and devoid of either character or meaning. Mordecai—a name full of romantic association—had been changed to the insipid monosyllable Max. Rebecca—mother of the race—was in America Becky. Samuel had been shorn to Sam, Abraham to Abe, Israel to Izzy."

How Ricardo became rich: When I was new to this tongue I now include myself in, I learned some things that were true about America from its corn, its speed, its disinclination to be tied down, pretty much; its inclination toward shortcuts, abbreviations, sunwise turns. I learned from "hi" and "nope" and "OK." We Americans like the old, rubbed phrases; we like better the newest, sassiest, most abbreviated: Y2K. The most bubbulous American word I learned early on was the unexpected word for one's father (though not mine) and soda and what the weasel goes: pop.

I observed parents laughing over their children's coinages. I inferred the burden and responsibility of each adolescent generation to come up with neat subversions; to reinvent adolescence in a patois inscrutable to adults. The older generation expected it.

But not in my family. My mother and father (with immigrant pragmatism) assumed the American tongue would reinvent their children. Just so did several immigrant Hispanic mothers in Southern California recently remark their children's reluctance to join America. These mothers feared their children were not swimming in the American current—not in the swifts and not in the depths; not even in the pop. They blamed "bilingual education," a leaky boat theorem ostensibly designed to sink into the American current. (In fact, the theorem became a bureaucracy preoccupied with prolonging itself.) These few mothers organized an opposition to bilingual education and eventually they sank the Armada in California. Theirs was an American impulse: to engage the American flow directly and to let their children be taken by it.

But the American current always fears itself going dry—it longs, always, for a wetter wah-wah (there used to be a night club called "King Tut's Wah-Wah Hut"); yearns now to swizzle Latin America in its maw. Spanish is becoming unofficially but truly the second language of the United States. Moreover, Yankee pragmatism accomplishes the romance of the American tongue. By the 1980s, advertising executives in L.A. and Miami were the first to describe the United States as "the fifth-largest

Spanish-speaking market in the world." Pragmatism made Spanish the language of cheap labor from fishing villages in Alaska to Chinese restaurants in Georgia to my rooftop here in San Francisco.

Thus does official America now communicate in at least two "voices," like a Tuva singer; three in Eurasian San Francisco. And if it isn't entirely English, it is nevertheless entirely American.

Press ONE, if you wish to continue in English. Pragmatism leads to Spanish signage at government offices, hospitals, parking lots, bus stops, polls. Telephone instructions, prescription instructions, microwave instructions—virtually all instructions in America are in Spanish as well as English.

American politicians, too, begin to brush up their Yanqui-Dudel.

I remain skeptical of the effect pragmatic Spanish might have on the assimilation of Latin American immigrants. Working-class newcomers from Latin America do not suffer the discontinuity that previous generations used to propel themselves into the future tense. But middle-class Americans, friends of mine, composites of friends of mine, of a liberal bent, nice people, OK people, see nothing wrong with bilingual education. In fact, they wish their own children to be bilingual. In fact, they send their kids to French schools. In fact, they ask if I know of a housekeeper who might inadvertently teach their children Spanish while she dusts under the piano.

Nope.

But I marvel at the middle-class American willingness to take Spanish up. Standing in the burrito line in a Chinese neighborhood, I notice how many customers know the chopsticks of Spanish: "carnitas" and "guacamole" and "sí," "gracias," "refritos," and "caliente," and all the rest of what they need to know. And it occurs to me that the Chinese-American couple in front of me, by speaking Spanish, may actually be speaking American English.

On an American Airlines flight to New York, I listen to the recorded bilingual safety instructions. "She" speaks in cheerful, speedo, gum-scented American English. "He" partners her every unlikely event in Spanish; makes tragedy sound a tad less unlikely. (The Latin Lover speaks, I think to myself.)

Some years ago, I stood on a bluff on the San Diego side of the U.S.–Mexico border, watching Latin American peasants bent double and yet moving rapidly through the dark. I experienced something like the confounding stasis one dislikes in those Escher prints where the white birds fly east as the black birds fly west and the gray birds seem unformed daubs of marzipan. Was I watching the past become the future or the future becoming the past?

Back in the 1960s, Chicano activists referred to the "reconquista" of the United States, by which they meant the Southwest was becoming, again, Spanish-speaking, as it had been in the 1840s (history, therefore, a circle, and not, as America had always insisted, a straight line). Then again I might be watching an advance of the Spanish crown—Latin American peasants as cannon fodder for the advance of King Philip II; spies in cloaks who will insinuate themselves into Anglo households to whisper Ave Marias into baby's shell-like ear.

Sitting on American Airlines flight 64, I am not so sure. The numbers of Latin American immigrants making their way into the United States more truly honor England. Millions of Latin Americans, my parents among them, have come to the United States because of the enduring failures of Father Spain. Their coming honors England.

Her face painted white, she receives the passenger list into her gem-encrusted hand, but does not look upon it.

The Armada sank, ma'am.

There is glint in her simian eye. Lips recede from tallow teeth to speak:

They are trumped, then, My Lord Admiral.

The airplane shudders down the runway, hoisting sail.

What did Nixon know? Did he really devise to rid himself of a bunch of spic agitators by officially designating them a minority, entitled to all rights, honors, privileges, and obligations thereto appertaining: rhetorical flatteries, dollars, exploding cigars? (Maybe, by the same token, he could put blacks on notice that they were no longer such a hot ticket.)

A young Bolivian in Portland giggled, oh quite stupidly, at my question, her hand patting her clavicle as if she held a fan. I had asked her whether she had yet become Hispanic. Perhaps she didn't understand the question.

In *The Next American Nation,* Michael Lind observes that "real Hispanics think of themselves not as generic Hispanics, but as Mexicans, or Puerto Ricans or Cubans or Chileans." Lind is wrong. Well, he is right in the past tense; he is wrong in the future. You won't find Hispanics in Latin America (his point)—not in the quickening cities, not in the emasculated villages. You need to come to the United States to meet Hispanics (my point). What Hispanic immigrants learn within the United States is to view themselves in a new way, as belonging to Latin America entire—precisely at the moment they no longer do.

America's brilliance is a lack of subtlety. Most Americans are soft on geography. We like puzzles with great big pieces, piecrust coasts. And we're not too fussy about the midlands. But American obliviousness of the specific becomes a gift of prophesy regarding the approaching mass. Our impatience has created the map of the future. Many decades before Germans spoke of the EEC or the French could imagine buying french fries with Euros, Americans spoke of "Europe" (a cloud bank, the Eiffel Tower, the Colosseum, any decorative ormolu, inventing the place in novels and government reports, blurring borders and tongues and currencies and Prussians and Talleyrands into an abstraction, the largest unit, the largest parenthesis that can yet contain onion domes, Gothic spires, windmills, gondolas, bidets, and the *Mona Lisa*).

Many European men, such as the gondolier in Venice, come home from work to eat their noonday meals (according to an American social studies textbook, c. 1959).

Similarly, and for many generations, slaves and the descendants of slaves in America invented a homeland called "Africa"—a land before slave ships, a prelapsarian savanna whereupon the provocatively dressed gazelle could stroll safely after dark. Perhaps someday Africa will exist, in which case it will have been patented by African Americans in the U.S.A. from the example of the American Civil Rights movement. Yes, and lately I have begun to meet people in the United States who call themselves "Asians." A young woman (a Vietnamese immigrant) tells me, for instance, she will only "date Asian." Asians do not exist anywhere in Asia. The lovely brown woman who has cared for my parents, a Mormon born on an island in a turtle-green sea (I've guessed the Philippines or Samoa), will only admit to "Pacific Islander." A true daughter of Nixon.

It is not mere carelessness that makes Americans so careless, it is also that Americans think more about the future than the past. The past is vague to us. Tribal feuds may yet hissle and spit on the stoves of somebody's memory, but we haven't got time for that. The entry guard at Ellis Island didn't have time for that. The INS official at LAX doesn't have time for that. He is guarding the portal to individualism, the greatest abstraction the world has ever known: *One at a time, one at a time—back up, sir!* Only America could create Hispanics, Asians, Africans, Americans.

The Chinese people are like Americans in many ways. They like to laugh and be happy and play games. (Same American social studies textbook, c. 1959.)

It was only when it came to the landmass extending from Tierra del Fuego to the Aleutians that Americans refused to think in terms of hemispheric or historical mass. America (the noun) became our border against all that lay to the south and north—much to the annoyance of Mexicans, for example, or Canadians. "We are Americans, too," they said. No you're not, you are Mexicans. And you are Canadians. We are Americans©.

Whereas Miss Bolivia, having gotten over herspanic and now surreptitiously refreshing her lip gloss, does, as it turns out, understand my question. She is not Hispanic. Ha ha no. What is she then?

Her eyes flash. I mean, what do you consider yourself to be?

¡Bolivian!

Of course, but I protest she is destined for Hispanicity. Because you live in the United States, you see.

¿?

You will know more Colombians and Nicaraguans as friends, fellow religionists, than you would have known had you never left Bolivia. Spanish-language radio and TV, beamed at immigrants of provincial memory, will parlay soccer scores from an entire hemisphere. You will hear weather reports from Valparaiso to Anchorage borne on a dolphin-headed breeze. Listen, chaste Miss Bolivia: All along the dial, north and south, on Spanish-language radio stations, you can already hear a new, North American Spanish accent—akin to "accentless" California TV English—meant to be decipherable (and inoffensive) alike to Cubans, Mexicans, Dominicans, and blonds like you, because it belongs to none.

Hispanic Spanish is hybrid, uniform. Colorless, yes. I do not deplore it. If I were Miss Bolivia, I might deplore it. One should deplore any loss of uniquity in a world that has so little. But I take the bland transparent accent as an anabranch of the American tongue. We bid fond farewell to Miss Bolivia. Who's our next contestant, Johnny?

The Cuban grandfather in Miami, Dick, who persists in mocking Mexicans because we are Indians, less European than he is, the old frog. We've put him in a soundproof booth so his Hispanic grandson can mimic for us the old man's Caribbean Spanish, filigreed as a viceroy's sleeve.

I think Richard Nixon would not be surprised to hear that some of my Hispanic nieces and nephews have Scottish or German surnames. Nixon intended his Spanish'd noun to fold Hispanics into America. By the time the Sunday supplements would begin writing about the political ascendancy of a Hispanic generation, the American children of that generation would be disappearing into America. But Nixon might be surprised to hear that my oldest nephew, German-surnamed, has a restaurant in Oakland dedicated to classic Mexican cooking; the majority of his customers are not Hispanic.

In generations past, Americans regarded Latin America as an "experiment in democracy," meaning the brutish innocence of them, the negligent benevolence of us, as defined by the Monroe Doctrine. We installed men with dark glasses to overthrow men with dark glasses.

As a result of Nixon's noun, our relationship to Latin America became less remote. Within our own sovereign borders, crested with eagles, twenty-five million became twenty-seven million Hispanics; became thirty-five million. The Census Bureau began making national predictions: By the year 2040 one in three Americans will declare herself Hispanic. Leaving aside the carbonated empiricism of such predictions, they nevertheless did convince many Americans that Latin America is no longer something "down there," like an adolescent sexual abstraction. By the reckoning of the U.S. Census Bureau, the United States has become one of the largest Latin American nations in the world.

And every day and every night poor people trample the legal fiction that America controls its own destiny. There is something of inevitability, too, in what I begin hearing in America from businessmen—a hint of Latin American fatalism, a recognition of tragedy that is simply the verso of optimism, but descriptive of the same event: *You can't stop them coming* becomes *the necessity to develop a Spanish-language ad strategy.*

The mayor of San Diego, speaking to me one morning several years ago about her city's relationship to Tijuana, about the proximity of Tijuana to San Diego, used no future tense—*Here we are,* she said. She used no hand gesture to indicate "they" or "there" or "here." The mayor's omission of a demonstrative gesture in that instance reminded me of my father's nonchalance. My father never expected to escape tragedy by escaping Mexico, by escaping poverty, by coming to the United States. Nor did he. Such sentiments—the mayor's, my father's—are not, I remind you, the traditional sentiments of an "I" culture, which would formulate the same proximity as *"right up to here."* For my father, as for the mayor, the border was missing.

In old cowboy movies, the sheriff rode hell-for-leather to capture the desperados before they crossed the Rio Grande. It is an old idea, more Protestant than Anglo-Saxon: that Latin America harbors outlaws.

Some Americans prefer to blame the white-powder trail leading from here to there on the drug lords of Latin America. More Americans are beginning to attribute the rise of drug traffic to American addiction. Tentative proposals to legalize drugs, like tentative proposals to open the border, bow to the inevitable, which is, in either case, the knowledge that there is no border.

The other day I read a survey that reported a majority of Americans believe most Hispanics are in the United States illegally. Maybe. Maybe there is something inherently illegal about all of us who are Hispanics in the United States, gathered under an assumed name, posing as one family. Nixon's categorical confusion brings confusion to all categories.

Once the United States related millions of its citizens into the family Hispanic—which as a legality exists only within U.S. borders—then that relation extends back to our several origins and links them. At which juncture the U.S.A. becomes the place of origin for all Hispanics. The illegal idea now disseminated southward by the U.S. is the idea that all Latin Americans are Hispanic.

The United States has illegally crossed its own border.

WAYNE KOESTENBAUM

*Wayne Koestenbaum (1958–), a poet and cultural critic, has written about opera (*The Queen's Throat*), Jackie Onassis, Andy Warhol, Harpo Marx, and humiliation, always from the knowing viewpoint of a gay intellectual equally at home with campiness and critical theory. His poet's training has led to the writing of lyrical essays that make full use of lists, fragmentation, startling imagery, pastiche, and linguistic play. In "My 1980s," he sums up a whole decade in bite-sized recollections, with self-mocking humor and rue, revealing both the plight of a hapless graduate student expected to absorb all of world literature and a young gay man suddenly faced with the AIDS epidemic.*

My 1980s

(2003)

> Les Fleuves m'ont laissé descendre où je voulais.
> —Arthur Rimbaud

I met Tama Janowitz once in the 1980s. (Was it 1987?) She probably doesn't remember our encounter. She was a visiting fellow at Princeton, where I was a graduate student in English. At a university gathering, Joyce Carol Oates complimented the ostentatious way that Tama and I were dressed. Seeking system, I replied, "Tama is East Village. I'm West Village."

·

I had little to do with art in the eighties. I saw Caravaggio in Rome, and Carpaccio in Venice. I neglected the contemporary. For half the decade I lived in New York City, and yet I didn't go to a single Andy Warhol opening. Missed opportunities? My mind was elsewhere.

•

My mind was on *écriture feminine* as applied to homosexuals. I was big on the word *homosexual*. I read *Homosexualities and French Literature* (edited by George Stambolian and Elaine Marks). I read Hélène Cixous. On a train I read *Roland Barthes by Roland Barthes* (translated by Richard Howard); I looked out dirty windows onto dirty New Jersey fields. I began to take autobiography seriously as a historical practice with intellectual integrity. On an airplane I read Michel Leiris's *Manhood* (translated by Richard Howard) and grooved to Leiris's mention of a "bitten buttock"; I decided to become, like Leiris, a self-ethnographer. I read André Gide's *Immoralist* (translated by Richard Howard) in Hollywood, Florida, while lying on a pool deck. I read many books translated by Richard Howard. In the eighties I read *The Fantastic* by Tzvetan Todorov (translated by Richard Howard) and meditated on the relation between fantasy and autobiography. I brought Richard Howard flowers the first time I met him (1985), in his book-lined apartment. He assured me that I was a poet.

•

I discovered the word *essentialism* in the late eighties. I should have discovered it earlier. Sex-and-gender essentialism was a dread fate. I feared that it was my condition. Essentialists believed in God and trusted the government. In the early nineties, after I stopped worrying about my essentialism, I realized that I'd never been an essentialist after all.

•

Too many of these sentences begin with the first-person-singular pronoun. Later I may jazz up the syntax, falsify it.

•

I am typing this essay on the IBM Correcting Selectric III typewriter I bought in 1981 for one thousand dollars. I borrowed the money from my older brother, a cellist. It took me several years to pay him back.

•

In the eighties I worked as a legal secretary, a paralegal, and a legal proofreader. I freelanced as a typist, $1.50 per page. I temped for Kelly Girl; one pleasurable assignment was a stint at the Girl Scouts headquarters.

I taught seventh- through twelfth-grade English at a yeshiva. I tutored a man from Japan in English conversation. I didn't turn a single trick.

•

This morning I asked my boyfriend, an architect, about the 1980s. I said, "Let's make a list of salient features of our eighties." We came up with just two items: cocaine, AIDS.

•

In 1980 after Reagan was elected I began, in repulsed reaction, to read the *New York Times*. Before then, I'd never read the newspaper.

•

I remember a specific homeless woman on the Upper West Side in the 1980s. She smelled predictably of pee or shit and hung out in an ATM parlor near the Seventy-Second Street subway stop. She seemed to rule the space. Large, she epitomized. Did I ever give her money? I blamed Reagan.

•

A stranger smooched me during a "Read My Lips" kiss-in near the Jefferson Market Public Library: festive politics. 1985? I stumbled on the ceremony. Traffic stopped.

•

A cute short blond guy named Mason used to brag about sex parties; I was jealous. I didn't go to sex parties. He ended up dying of AIDS. I'm not pushing a cause-and-effect argument.

•

In 1985 I read Mario Mieli's *Homosexuality and Liberation*. I bought, but did not read, an Italian periodical, hefty and intellectually substantial, called *Sodoma: Rivista Omosessuale di Cultura*. That year, I turned to Georges Bataille for bulletins on the solar anus, for lessons on smart, principled obscenity.

•

A handsome brunet poet came to my apartment, and I dyed his hair blond. I had a crush on him. He talked a lot about Michel Foucault. The poet and I bought the dye on Sixth Avenue in the Village. In my kitchen he stripped to his undershorts, which had holes. His nipples were large and erect: impressive! I'd never seen such ready-to-go nipples. He leaned over the kitchen sink; I washed his hair and applied the dye. I kept on my undershirt during the session; I wasn't proud of my body (though in retrospect I respect its scrawniness). I continued to read Foucault through-out the eighties. Foucault never deeply moved me. I switched to Maurice Blanchot in the late nineties.

•

My boyfriend worked out downstairs. We lived above a gay gym: the Body Center, corner of Sixth and Fifteenth, now the David Barton Gym. After midnight we could hear loud music coming through our radiators: the Body Center's cleaning crew had turned up the sound system.

•

Geographical facts: during the 1980s, I lived in Cambridge, Baltimore, New York, New Haven. The important city was New York: 1984–1988. There, I worked out at the McBurney Y. I swam in its skanky, dank, tiny, cloudy, over-warm pool. I recall a not-handsome guy shaving off his body hair at the sink. Careful, I didn't once enter the Y's cramped sauna.

•

I read all of Proust in summer 1986. Proust and summer passed quickly. That same summer I reread James Schuyler's *Morning of the Poem* and experienced an AIDS-panic-related sense of life's brevity; houseguest, I sat on an Adirondack chair in Southold, Long Island. My host, hardy in the garden, was ill with AIDS. I recall wild blueberries I picked with him, and his reticence, and mine.

•

In 1986 or '87 I heard Eve Kosofsky Sedgwick give a lecture on "unknow-ing" in Diderot's *The Nun*. I had just read her *Between Men*. Her difficult lucidity gave my stumbling concepts one warm, fruitful context.

•

In 1984 I took a course in feminist theory with Elaine Showalter and decided to be a male feminist. I decided not to write a dissertation about John Ashbery and W. H. Auden. Instead, I wanted to write a flaming treatise. In a seminar on the Victorian novel, Showalter showed slides of Charcot's hysterics in *arcs-en-cercle* and of fin de siècle faces disfigured by syphilis. I flipped out with intellectual glee. Hysteria would be my open sesame.

•

In the eighties I was happiest when writing "syllabic" poems. Supersti-tiously I discovered my existence's modicum of dignity and value by counting duration in syllables, on my fingers, while I typed, on the same Selectric I am using now.

•

I saw *Taxi zum Klo* and *Diva:* two films that made a dent. I went to all the gay movies. *L'homme blessé.* On TV I saw *Brideshead Revisited* and the Patrice Chéreau production of Wagner's *Ring.* I went to Charlie Chan movies (guilty pleasure) at Theater 80 St. Marks; there, my treat was buying a blue mint from the transparent vessel on the dim-lit lobby's counter. I saw *Shoah:* only the first part. I heard Leonie Rysanek sing Elisabeth in *Tannhäuser* and Ortrud in *Lohengrin* and Kundry in *Parsifal* at the Met, and Sieglinde in *Die Walküre* in San Francisco. I heard Christa Ludwig's twenty-fifth-anniversary performance at the Met: Klytämnestra in Strauss's *Elektra,* December 20, 1984.

•

I wore a bright red Kikit baseball jacket and red espadrilles. I decided that bright blue and red—DayGlo, neon, opalescent—were passports to private revolution. I wore a paisley tux jacket and black patent-leather cowboy boots. I didn't mind looking vulgar, slutty, off-base.

I spent a lot of the eighties thinking about Anna Moffo, soprano—her career's ups and downs, and her timbre's uncanny compromise between vulnerability and voluptuousness. I regret not buying her Debussy song album, used, at Academy Records on West Eighteenth Street: on the soft-focus cover, she wore a summer hat. The LP era ended.

•

I focused on my sadness as if it were an object in the room, a discrete, dense entity, impervious to alteration. I never used the word *subjectivity* in the 1980s, though I was fond of *gap, blank page, masculine,* and *feminine.* I planned to call my first book of poems *Queer Street,* nineteenth-century British slang for shady circumstances, debt, bankruptcy, blackmail. I found the phrase in Robert Louis Stevenson's *The Strange Case of Dr. Jekyll and Mr. Hyde.*

•

In 1980 my new boyfriend gave me a 45 rpm single (blue-labeled Chrysalis) of Blondie's "Call Me" (from *American Gigolo*). We considered it our theme song. Then I stopped listening to "popular" music. Not consciously. Not programmatically. The defection happened naturally.

•

In 1981 I made an onion-bacon-apple casserole from *The Joy of Cooking.* I served it, as a main dish, to a schizophrenic friend. A few years later she sent me a letter, dated 1975. This significant confusion of chronology meant that she had cracked up. I began methodically to cook from Marcella Hazan. I tirelessly stirred risotto in a cheap aluminum saucepan with high sides. I made a *bombe aux trois chocolats* from Julia Child: a molded dessert, for which I used a beige Tupperware bowl.

•

In 1983 I served a friend a veal roast stuffed with pancetta. We agreed that the roast tasted like human baby. We blamed the pancetta.

•

Sometime in the mid-eighties I stopped swallowing cum. I don't miss its taste.

•

The first guy I knew with AIDS died at age thirty-five. His name was Metro. I've written about this death before, and I hesitate to repeat myself. I have almost no visual memory of Metro, though I recall his precision and hypercapability; we lay on a stony beach, Long Island Sound, more rock than sand. What sand there was he dusted off his body with decisive, practiced gestures.

•

I went to Paris for the first time in the eighties: I wore blue leather gloves purchased on Christopher Street. In a rue Jacob hotel bedroom I woke up, sweat-drenched, feverish; I observed the wallpaper's mesmerizing, dull pattern, its refusal to serve as reliable augury. On the flight back from Paris I read Marianne Moore's prose and picked up pointers from its ornery mannerism.

•

Despite my best efforts, I existed in history, not as agent but as frightened, introspective observer. I began to fine-tune my sentences—a fastidiousness I learned from Moore's prose. Precise sentences were my ideals, though in practice I was slipshod and sentimental. I began to seek a balance between improvisation and revision. I revised by endlessly retyping.

•

I read Freud in the eighties. He was always describing me, my likenesses, my forebears. Anna O. became my touchstone. I decided that psychoanalysis was the hysterical child born from Freud's anus.

•

In 1981 I read Susan Sontag's *On Photography*. In 1982 I read her *Under the Sign of Saturn*. I swore allegiance to the aphorism. But I didn't read Walter Benjamin until the nineties.

•

In 1981 I published for the first time: a story, "In the White Forest," in a small periodical, *The Pale Fire Review*. In 1982 I stopped writing fiction. The last story I wrote, "Liberty Baths," autobiographically reported my San Francisco bathhouse experiences of summer 1979. A guy I met at the baths took me to his loft. A commercial photographer, he shot a whole roll of me nude, from the rear. I was insulted that he didn't photograph me frontally. I should have been grateful that he found one angle comely.

•

I spent the summer of 1983 writing fifty sonnets. My stylistic model was Auden's sequence *In Time of War:* I loved his phrase "Anxiety / Receives them like a grand hotel." I put together a manuscript called, unadventurously, "Fifty Sonnets." It never got published as a book. In one of the sonnets, I rhymed "Callas" and "callous."

•

The world was doing its best to ignore the fact that I was a writer. In search of fragile legitimacy, I obsessively submitted work to periodicals. Rejection slips arrived, sometimes with a beckoning "Thanks!" or "Sorry!" or "Send more?" I always sent more; immediately, with a treacly letter, informing the hapless editor how much the invitation to send more had meant to me.

•

I was not thinking about the world. I was not thinking about history. I was thinking about my body's small, precise, limited, hungry movement forward into a future that seemed at every instant on the verge of being shut down.

•

I didn't take the HIV test until the nineties. I spent most of the eighties worried about being HIV-positive, only discovering, in the nineties, that I was negative. My attitude in the eighties was: wait and see. Wait for symptoms. When a friend suggested I get tested, I broke off the friendship. It wasn't much of a friendship. She wanted us to write a collaborative book on Verdi's Oedipus complex. A semi-invalid, she sent me on errands to buy dollhouse furniture—her hobby.

•

I heard Leontyne Price sing a recital at the Met on March 24, 1985. I still remember the sensation of her voice in my body. I think she gave "Chi il bel sogno di Doretta" from *La Rondine* as an encore.

•

I read Jacques Derrida's *Spurs* (translated by Barbara Harlow). I wondered why he didn't use male testicles—instead of vaginas and veils—as metaphors. Invaginate, indeed! In the 1980s I made snap judgments.

•

Poems I published in the eighties, in small periodicals, but never collected into a book: "Where I Lived, and What I Lived For"; "*Carmen* in Digital for a Deaf Woman"; "Teachers of Obscure Subjects"; "The Babysitter in the Ham Radio." I published my first full-length essay in 1987: its polite subtitle was "Oblique Confession in the Early Work of John Ashbery."

•

In the eighties I wrote book reviews for the *New York Native,* a now-defunct gay newspaper. Among my subjects: James Schuyler's *A Few Days,* John Ashbery's *April Galleons,* Sylvère Lotringer's *Overexposed: Treating Sexual Perversion in America.*

•

Does any of this information matter? I am not responsible for what matters and what doesn't matter. Offbeat definition of materialism: a worldview in which every detail matters, in which every factual statement is material.

•

I bought soft-core porn magazines—*Mandate, Honcho,* others—from a newsstand on Fourteenth Street. I felt guilty about my insatiably scopophilic core; culpable, it could never get its fill of images. Over the years I began to notice changes in porn bodies: the men were growing younger. Now, when I look back at those magazines (I've saved many), the men seem like old friends, guys I went to school with. Max Archer. Chad Douglas. Jesus.

•

I have always had a rather limited circle of friends; although I am superficially gregarious, most human contact makes me, eventually, uncomfortable. I didn't realize this fact in the eighties. During those years, I was intensely ill at ease.

•

I stopped using drugs (pot, cocaine) when I began to take AIDS seriously. Health suddenly mattered: I wanted always to feel tip-top, without chemical enhancement.

•

If my eighties don't match yours, chalk up the mismatch to the fact that I am profoundly out of touch with my time. I never chose to nominate myself as historical witness.

•

Notice, please, my absence of nostalgia.

•

I started dyeing my hair in 1984: reddish highlights. I stopped in 1988. I returned to nature.

•

My mission in the eighties was to develop my aestheticism. My mission in the nineties was to justify my aestheticism.

•

In 1988 I started teaching at Yale. I decided to wear bow ties. I had several: red polka-dot; blue polka-dot; amber with black triangles; neon yellow. The first semester, I taught a required core course on Chaucer, Spenser, and Donne. I also taught my first elective: a seminar decorously titled "Literature and Sexuality: Countertraditions." I was hyperconscious of authorities. In 1989, I published my first book, *Double Talk: The Erotics of Male Literary Collaboration.* When the published book first arrived in my apartment, I admired its cover—George Platt Lynes's photograph *The Second Birth of Dionysus*—but wished the book were a novel instead: same cover, different contents.

•

In New Haven, outside my apartment, 1989, I was mugged. A guy said, "Give me your wallet or I'll blow your brains out."

•

In 1989 I developed a sustaining, mood-brightening crush on the UPS man. Hundreds—thousands—of men and women in New Haven must have had a crush on that same UPS man. The first time he appeared at my doorstep with a package, I thought that a *Candid Camera* porn movie had just begun. If you want me to describe him, I will.

•

When I look back at the eighties I see myself as a small boat. It is not an important, attractive, or likable boat, but it has a prow, a sail, and a modest personality. It has no consciousness of the water it moves through. Some days it resembles Rimbaud's inebriated vessel. Other, clearer days, it is sober and undemonstrative. There are few images or adjectives we could affix to the boat; there are virtually no ways to classify it. Its only business is staying afloat. Thus the boat is amoral. It has been manu-factured in a certain style. Any style contains a history. The boat is not conscious of the history shaping its movements. The boat, undramatic, passive, at best pleasant, at worst slapdash, persistently attends to the work of flotation, which takes precedence over responsible navigation. As far as the boat is concerned, it is the only vessel on the body of water. How many times must I repeat the word *boat* to convince you that in the eighties I was a small boat with a minor mission and a fear of sinking? The boat did not sink.

LEONARD MICHAELS

Leonard Michaels (1933–2003) was a magnificent short story writer and an equally strong essayist. His original prose moves at a fast clip and pays readers the compliment of assuming they can match his mental velocity, with a concise, pungent, and pyrotechnic style that tolerates no flab. His later fiction writing evolved in an essayistic direction, increasingly receptive to aphorism and digressive reflection, or what might be called "wisdom asides." In "My Yiddish," many of his sentences exist in a syntactical exchange between English and Yiddish inflections. Michaels culminates that postwar flowering of American Jewish writing that included Saul Bellow, Bernard Malamud, Norman Mailer, and Philip Roth and that did so much to revitalize the national prose.

My Yiddish

(2003)

In Paris one morning in the seventies, walking along the rue Mahler, I saw a group of old men in an argument, shouting and gesticulating. I wanted to know what it was about, but my graduate-school French was good enough only to read great writers, not good enough for an impassioned argument or even conversation with the local grocer. But then, as I walked by the old men, I felt a shock and a surge of exhilaration. I did understand them. My God, I possessed the thing: spoken French! Just as suddenly, I crashed. The old men, I realized, were shouting in Yiddish.

Like a half-remembered dream, the incident lingered. It seemed intensely personal yet impersonal. Meaning had come alive in me. I hadn't translated what the old men said. I hadn't done anything. A light turned on. Where nothing had been, there was something.

Philosophers used to talk about "The Understanding" as if it were a distinct mental function. Today they talk about epistemology or cognitive science. As for "The Understanding," it's acknowledged in IQ tests, the value of which is subject to debate. It's also acknowledged in daily life in countless informal ways. You're on the same wavelength with others or you are not. The Paris incident, where I rediscovered The Understanding, made me wonder if Descartes' remark "I think, therefore I am" might be true in his case, but not mine. I prefer to say, "I am, therefore I think." And also, therefore, I speak.

Until I was five, I spoke only Yiddish. It did much to permanently qualify my thinking. Eventually I learned to speak English, then to imitate thinking as it transpires among English-speakers. To some extent, my intuitions and my expression of thoughts remain basically Yiddish. I can say only approximately how this is true. For example, this joke:

The rabbi says, "What's green, hangs on the wall, and whistles?"

The student says, "I don't know."

The rabbi says, "A herring."

The student says, "Maybe a herring could be green and hang on the wall, but it absolutely doesn't whistle."

The rabbi says, "So it doesn't whistle."

The joke is inherent in Yiddish, not any other language. It's funny and, like a story by Kafka, it isn't funny. I confess that I don't know every other language. Maybe there are such jokes in Russian or Chinese, but no other language has a history like Yiddish, which, for ten centuries, has survived the dispersion and murder of its speakers.

As the excellent scholar and critic Benjamin Harshav points out, in *The Meaning of Yiddish,* the language contains many words that don't mean anything: *nu, epes, tockeh, shoyn.* These are fleeting interjections, rather like sighs. They suggest, without meaning anything, "so," "really," "well," "already." Other Yiddish words and phrases, noticed by Harshav, are meaningful but defeat translation. Transparent and easy to understand, however, is the way Yiddish serves speech—between you and me—rather than the requirements of consecutive logical discourse; that is, between the being who goes by your name and who speaks to others objectively and impersonally. For example, five times five is twenty-five, and it doesn't whistle.

Yiddish is probably at work in my written English. This moment, writing in English, I wonder about the Yiddish undercurrent. If I listen, I can almost hear it: "This moment"—a stress followed by two neutral syllables—introduces a thought that hangs like a herring in the weary droop of "writing in English," and then comes the announcement, "I wonder about the Yiddish undercurrent." The sentence ends in a shrug.

Maybe I hear the Yiddish undercurrent, maybe I don't. The sentence could have been written by anyone who knows English, but it probably would not have been written by a well-bred Gentile. It has too much drama, and might even be disturbing, like music in a restaurant or elevator. The sentence obliges you to abide in its staggered flow, as if what I meant were inextricable from my feelings and required a lyrical note. There is a kind of enforced intimacy with the reader. A Jewish kind, I suppose. In Sean O'Casey's lovelier prose you hear an Irish kind.

Wittgenstein says in his *Philosophical Investigations,* "Aren't there games we play in which we make up the rules as we go along, including this one." *Nu.* Any Yiddish speaker knows that. A good example of playing with the rules might be Montaigne's essays, the form that people say he invented. *Shoyn,* a big inventor. Jews have always spoken essays. The scandal of Montaigne's essays is that they have only an incidental relation to a consecutive logical argument but they are cogent nonetheless. Their shape is their sense. It is determined by motions of his mind and feelings, not by a pretension to rigorously logical procedure. Montaigne literally claims his essays are himself. Between you and him nothing intervenes. A Gentile friend used to say, in regard to writing she didn't like, "There's nobody home." You don't have to have Jewish ancestors, like those of Montaigne and Wittgenstein, to understand what she means.

I didn't speak English until I was five because my mother didn't speak English. My father had established himself in New York in the twenties, then gone back to Poland to find a wife. He returned with an attractive seventeen-year-old who wore her hair in a long black braid. Men would hit on her, so my father wouldn't let her go take English classes. She learned English by doing my elementary-school homework with me. As for me, before and after the age of five, I was susceptible to lung diseases and spent a lot of time in a feverish bed in a small apartment on the Lower East Side of Manhattan, where nobody spoke anything but Yiddish. Years passed before I could ride a bike or catch a ball. In a playground fight, a girl could have wiped me out. I was badly coordinated and had no strength or speed, only a Yiddish mouth.

For a long time, Yiddish was my whole world. In this world family didn't gather before dinner for cocktails and conversation. There were no cocktails, but conversation was daylong and it included criticism, teasing, opinionating, gossiping, joking. It could also be very gloomy. To gather before dinner for conversation would have seemed unnatural. I experienced the pleasure of such conversation for the first time at the University of Michigan around 1956. It was my habit to join a friend at his apartment after classes. He made old-fashioneds and put music on the phonograph, usually chamber music. By the time we left for dinner, I felt uplifted by conversation and splendid music. Mainly, I was drunk, also a new experience. Among my Jews, conversation had no ritual character, no aesthetic qualities. I never learned to cultivate the sort of detachment that allows for the always potentially offensive personal note. Where I came from everything was personal.

From family conversation I gathered that, outside of my Yiddish child-world, there were savages who didn't have much to say but could fix the plumbing. They were fond of animals, liked to go swimming, loved to drink and fight. All their problems were solved when they *hut geharget yiddin*. Killed Jews. Only the last has been impossible for me to dismiss. Like many other people, I have fixed my own plumbing, owned a dog and a cat, gotten drunk, etc., but everything in my life, beginning with English, has been an uncertain movement away from my *hut geharget* Yiddish childhood. When a BBC poet said he wanted to shoot Jews on the West Bank, I thought, "*Epes.* What else is new?" His righteousness, his freedom to say it, suggests that he believes he is merely speaking English and anti-Semitism is a kind of syntax, or what Wittgenstein calls "a form of life." But in fact there is something new, or anyhow more evident lately. The *geharget yiddin* disposition now operates at a remove. You see it in people who become hysterical when their ancient right to hate Jews is brought into question. To give an example would open a boxcar of worms.

It's possible to talk about French without schlepping the historical, cultural, or national character of a people into consideration. You cannot talk that way about Yiddish unless you adopt a narrow scholarly focus, or restrict yourself to minutiae of usage. The language flourished in a number of countries. Theoretically, it has no territorial boundary. The meaning of Yiddish, in one respect, is No Boundaries. In another respect, for a people without a land, the invisible boundaries couldn't be more clear. There is mutual contempt between what are called "universalist Jews" and Jewish Jews. It's an old situation. During the centuries of the Spanish Inquisition, Jews turned on Jews. In Shakespeare's *The Merchant of Venice*—assuming the merchant Antonio is a gay converso, or new Christian, and Shylock is an Old Testament moralistic Jewish Jew—the pound of flesh, a grotesquely exaggerated circumcision, is to remind Antonio (who says, "I know not why I am so sad") of his origins.

The first time I went to a baseball game, the great slugger Hank Greenberg, during warm-up, casually tossed a ball into the stands, a gift to the crowd of preadolescent kids among whom I sat. My hand, thrusting up in a blossom of hands, closed on that baseball. I carried it home, the only palpable treasure I'd ever owned. I never had toys. On Christmas nights I sometimes dreamed of waking and finding toys in the living room. *Tockeh?* Yes, really. If there is a support group for Christmas depressives, I will be your leader. The baseball made me feel like a real American. It happened to me long before I had a romance with the mythical blond who grants citizenship to Jews. By then I was already fifteen. I had tasted *traif* and long ago stopped speaking Yiddish except when I worked as a waiter in Catskill hotels. What Yiddish remained was enough for jokes, complaints, and insults. As guests entered the dining room, a waiter might say, "Here come the *vildeh chayes,*" or wild animals. One evening in the Catskills I went to hear a political talk given in Yiddish. I understood little except that Yiddish could be a language of analysis, spoken by intellectuals. I felt alienated and rather ashamed of myself for not being like them.

Family members could speak Polish as well as Yiddish, and some Hebrew and Russian. My father worked for a short while in Paris and could manage French. My mother had gone to high school in Poland and was fluent in Polish, but refused to speak the language even when I asked her to. Her memory of pogroms made it unspeakable. In Yiddish and English I heard about her father, my grandfather, a tailor who made uniforms for Polish army officers. Once, after he'd worked all night to finish a uniform, the officer wouldn't pay. My grandfather, waving a pair of scissors, threatened to cut the uniform to pieces. The officer paid. The Germans later murdered my grandfather, his wife, and one daughter. Polish officers imprisoned in Katyn Forest and elsewhere were massacred by Stalin. This paragraph, beginning with the first sentence and concluding with a moral, is in the form of a *geshichte,* or Yiddish story, except that it's in English and merely true.

At the center of my Yiddish, lest I have yet failed to make myself clear, remains *hut geharget yiddin,* from which, like the disgorged contents of a black hole in the universe, come the jokes, the thinking, the meanings, and the meaninglessness. In 1979, American writers were sent to Europe by the State Department. I went to Poland and gave talks in Warsaw, Poznan, and Cracow. I was surprised by how much seemed familiar, and exceedingly surprised by the intelligence and decency of the Poles, a few of whom became friends and visited me later in America. One of the Poles whom I didn't see again was a woman in Cracow with beautiful blue eyes and other features very like my mother's. I was certain that she was a Jew, though she wore a cross. I didn't ask her questions. I didn't want to know her story. I could barely look at her. I detest the word "shiksa," which I've heard used more often by friendly anti-Semites than Jews, but in my personal depths it applies to her.

As suggested earlier, in Yiddish there is respect for meaninglessness. If the woman in Cracow was passing as a Catholic, was she therefore a specter of meaninglessness who haunted me, the child of Polish Jews, passing as an American writer? A familiar saying comes to mind: "If you forget you are a Jew, a Gentile will remind you," but, in the way of forgetting, things have gone much further. Lately, it might take a Jew to remind a Jew that he or she is a Jew. Then there is a risk of ruining the friendship. For an extreme example, I have had depressing arguments with Jewish Stalinists who, despite evidence from numerous and unimpeachable sources that Stalin murdered Jews because they were Jews, remain Stalinists. It's as if they would rather die than let personal identity spoil their illusions. Thus, the Jewish face of insanity says to me, "Stalin was a good guy. He just got a bad rap." A demonic parallel to this mentality is in the way Nazis used material resources, critical to their military effort, to murder Jews even as the Russian army was at the gates. They would rather die, etc. In the second century, Tertullian, a Father of the Christian church, insisted that absurdity is critical to belief. His political sophistication seems to me breathtaking, and also frightening in its implications. As believers multiply everywhere, it becomes harder to believe—rationally—in almost anything.

Paradox as a cognitive mode is everywhere in Yiddish. It's probably in the genes and may explain the Jewish love of jokes. The flight from sense to brilliance effects an instant connection with listeners. Hobbes calls laughter "sudden glory," which is a superb phrase, but I've seen the Jewish comics, Lenny Bruce and Myron Cohen, reduce a nightclub audience to convulsive and inglorious agonies of laughter. When I worked in the Catskill hotels, I noticed that it was often the *tumler,* or the hotel comic and hell-raiser, to whom women abandoned themselves. Jerry Lewis, formerly a *tumler,* said in a televised interview that at the height of his fame, he "had four broads a day." As opposed to Jerry Lewis, Hannah Arendt preferred disconnection. She used the snobbish-aesthetic word "banal" to describe the murderer of millions of Jews, and later said in a letter, despite the abuse she received for having used that word, she remained "lighthearted." Not every Jew is in the same league as Jerry Lewis, but still, with Arendt one could die laughing.

Family was uncles and aunts who escaped from Poland and immigrated to the United States. They stayed with us until they found their own apartments. I'd wake in the morning and see small Jews sleeping on the living-room floor. My aunt Molly, long after she had a place of her own, often stayed overnight and slept on the floor. She was very lonely. Her husband was dead, her children had families of their own. A couch with a sheet, blanket, and pillow was available, but she refused such comforts. She wanted to be less than no trouble. She wore two or three dresses at once, almost her entire wardrobe. She slept on the floor in her winter coat and dresses. To see Molly first thing in the morning, curled against a wall, didn't make us feel good. She was the same height as my mother, around five feet, and had a beautiful, intelligent, melancholy face. I never saw her laugh, though she might chuckle softly, and she smiled when she teased me. She used to *krotz* (scratch) my back as I went to sleep, and she liked to speak to me in rhymes. First they were entirely Yiddish. Then English entered the rhymes:

Label, gay fressen.
A fish shtayt on de tish.
Lenny, go eat.
A fish is on the table.

Shtayt doesn't exactly mean "is." "Stands on the table," or "stays on the table," or "exists on the table" would be somewhat imprecise, though I think "A fish exists on the table" is wonderful. I once brought a girl-friend home, and Aunt Molly said, very politely, "You are looking very fit." Her "fit" sounded like "fet," which suggested "fat." My girlfriend squealed in protest. It took several minutes to calm her down. The pro-nunciation of "fet" for "fit" is typical of Yiddishified English, which is almost a third language. I speak it like a native when telling jokes. The audience for such jokes has diminished over the years because most Jews now are politically liberal and have college degrees and consider such jokes undignified or racist. A joke that touches on this development tells of Jewish parents who worry about a son who studies English literature at Harvard. They go to see Kittredge, the great Shakespeare scholar, and ask if he thinks their son's Yiddish accent is a disadvantage. Kittredge booms, "Vot ekcent?"

As a child I knew only one Jew who was concerned to make a *bella figura*. He was a highly respected doctor, very handsome, always dressed in a fine suit, and, despite his appearance, fluent in Yiddish. His office was in the neighborhood. He came every morning to my father's barber shop for a shave. A comparable miracle was the chicken-flicker down the block, a boisterous man who yelled at customers in vulgar, funny Yiddish. This man's son was a star at MIT. In regard to such miracles, an expres-sion I often heard was "He is up from pushcarts." It means he went from the Yiddish immigrant poverty to money or, say, a classy professorship. The day of such expressions is past. In the sixties there were Jewish kids who, as opposed to the spirit of Irving Howe's *The World of Our Fathers,* yelled "Kill the parents." The suicidal implication is consistent with the paradoxical Yiddish they no longer spoke.

If I dressed nicely to go out, my mother would ask why I was *fapitzed,* which suggests "tarted up." Yiddish is critical of pretensions to being bet-ter than a Jew, and also critical of everything else. A man wants to have sex or wants to pee—what a scream. A woman appears naked before her husband and says, "I haven't got a thing to wear." He says, "Take a shave. You look like a bum." Henry Adams speaks of "derisive Jew laughter." It is easy to find derision produced by Jews, but Adams's words, aside from their stupid viciousness, betray the self-hate and fear that inspires anti-Semitism among the educated, not excluding Jews. Ezra Pound called his own anti-Semitic ravings "stupid." The relation of stupidity and evil has long been noted.

Jewish laughter has a liberal purview, and its numerous forms—some very silly—seem to me built into Yiddish. Sometime around puberty, I decided to use shampoo rather than hand soap to wash my hair. I bought a bottle of Breck. My father noticed and said in Yiddish, "Nothing but the best." I still carry his lesson in my heart, though I never resumed using hand soap instead of shampoo. What has shampoo to do with Yiddish? In my case, plenty, since it raises the question, albeit faintly, "Who do you think you are?"

What I have retained of Yiddish, I'm sorry to say, isn't much above the level of my aunt Molly's poems. But what good to me is Yiddish? Recently, in Rome during the High Holidays, a cordon was established around the synagogue in the ghetto, guarded by the police and local Jews. As I tried to pass I was stopped by a Jew. Couldn't he tell? I said, *"Ich bin a yid. Los mir gayen arein."* He said, "Let me see your passport." *La mia madra lingua* wasn't his. This happened to me before with Moroccan Jews in France. I've wondered about Spinoza. His Latin teacher was German, and the first Yiddish newspaper was published in Amsterdam around the time of his death. Is it possible that he didn't know Yiddish?

I'm sure of very little about what I know except that the Yiddish I can't speak is more natural to my being than English. Partly for that reason I've studied poets writing in English. There is a line in T. S. Eliot where he says words slip, slide, crack, or something. "Come off it, Tom," I think. "With words you never had no problem." Who would suspect from his hateful remark about a Jew in furs that Eliot's family, like my mother's ancestors in Vienna, was up from the fur business? Eliot liked Groucho Marx, a Jew, but did Eliot wonder when writing *Four Quartets,* with its striking allusions to Saint John of the Cross, that the small, dark, brilliant, mystical monk might have been a Jew?

"Let there be light" are the first spoken words in the Old Testament. This light is understanding, not merely seeing. The Yiddish saying "To kill a person is to kill a world" means the person is no longer the embodiment, or a mode of the glorious nothing that is the light, or illuminated world. This idea, I believe, is elaborated in Spinoza's *Ethics.* Existence—or being—entails ethics. Maybe the idea is also in Wittgenstein, who opens the *Tractatus* this way: "The world is everything that is the case." So what is the case? If it's the case that facts are bound up with values, it seems Yiddish or Spinozist. Possibly for this reason Jewish writers in English don't write about murder as well as Christians. Even Primo Levi, whose great subject is murder, doesn't offer the lacerating specificity one might expect.

In regard to my own writing, its subterranean Yiddish may keep me from being good at killing characters in my stories. The closest I've come is my story "Trotsky's Garden," where I adopt a sort of Yiddish intonation to talk about the murders that haunted his life. I'd read a psychological study that claimed Trotsky was responsible for murders only to please Lenin, his father figure. If so, his behavior was even worse than I thought. I wrote my story out of disappointment. I had wanted to admire Trotsky for his brilliant mind, courage, and extraordinary literary gifts. His description in his diaries of mowing wheat, for example, almost compares with Tolstoy's description in *Anna Karenina* and is difficult to reconcile with a life steeped in gore.

Yiddish can be brutal, as for example: *Gay koken aff yam,* which means "Go shit in the ocean," but in regard to murder, what Jewish writer compares with Shakespeare, Webster, Mark Twain, Flannery O'Connor, Cormac McCarthy, or Elmore Leonard? The Old Testament story of Abraham and Isaac, which is of profound importance to three faiths, stops short of murder, but it is relevant to children murdered in contemporary religious terrorism.

A story by Bernard Malamud begins with the death of a father whose name is Ganz. In Yiddish *ganz* means "all" or "the whole thing" or "everything." Metaphorically, with the death of Ganz, the whole world dies. Everything is killed. Malamud couldn't have named the father Ganz if he had written the story in Yiddish. It would be too funny and undermine all seriousness. The death of a father, or a world-killed-in-a-person, is the reason for Hamlet's excessive grief, a condition feared among Jews for a reason given in the play: "All the uses of this world seem to me weary, stale, flat, and unprofitable." Because Hamlet Senior is dead, Hamlet Junior is as good as dead. Early in the play he jokes about walking into his grave, and the fifth act opens, for no reason, with Hamlet in a graveyard, and then he actually jumps into a grave. On the subject of grief, in "Mourning and Melancholia," Freud follows Shakespeare. Like Hamlet, who demands that his mother look at the picture of his father, Freud makes a great deal of the residual, or cathectic, force of an image. Again, regarding my Yiddish, when I once wrote about my father's death, I restricted my grief to a few images and a simple lamentation: "He gave. I took." My short sentences are self-critical, and have no relation to writers known for short sentences. They are only Yiddish terseness seizing an English equivalent.

Shakespeare's short sentences—"Let it come down," "Ripeness is all," "Can Fulvia die?"—seem to me amazing. I couldn't write one of those. This confession brings a joke instantly to mind. The synagogue's janitor is beating his breast and saying, "Oh, Lord, I am nothing." He is overheard by the rabbi, who says, "Look who is nothing." Both men are ridiculed. A Jewish writer has to be careful. Between schmaltz and irony, there is just an itty-bitty step.

My mother sometimes switches in mid-sentence, when talking to me, from English to Yiddish. If meaning can leave English and reappear in Yiddish, does it have an absolutely necessary relation to either language?

Linguists say, "No. Anything you can say in German you can say in Swahili, which is increasingly Arabic." But no poet would accept the idea of linguistic equivalence, and a religious fanatic might want to kill you for proposing it. Ultimately, I believe, meaning has less to do with language than with music, a sensuous flow that becomes language only by default, so to speak, and by degrees. In great fiction and poetry, meaning is always close to music. Writing about a story by Gogol, Nabokov says it goes la, la, do, la la la, etc. The story's meaning is radically musical. I've often had to rewrite a paragraph because the sound was wrong. When at last it seemed right, I discovered—incredibly—the sense was right. Sense follows sound. Otherwise, we couldn't speak so easily or quickly. If someone speaks slowly, and sense unnaturally precedes sound, the person can seem too deliberative, emotionally false, boring. I can tell stories all day, but to write one that sounds right entails labors of indefinable innerness until I hear the thing I must hear before it is heard by others. A standard of rightness probably exists for me in my residual subliminal Yiddish. Its effect is to inhibit as well as to liberate.

An expression popular not long ago, "I hear you," was intended to assure you of being understood personally, as if there were a difference in comprehension between hearing and really hearing. In regard to being really heard, there are things in Yiddish that can't be heard in English. *Hazar fisl kosher*. "A pig has clean feet." It is an expression of contempt for hypocrisy. The force is in Yiddish concision. A pig is not clean. With clean feet it is even less clean. Another example: I was talking to a friend about a famous, recently deceased writer. The friend said, "He's *ausgespielt*." Beyond dead. He's played out. So forget it. Too much has been said about him.

Cultural intuitions, or forms or qualities of meaning, derive from the unique historical experience of peoples. The intuitions are not in dictionaries but carried by tones, gestures, nuances effected by word order, etc. When I understood the old men in Paris, I didn't do or intend anything. It wasn't a moment of romantic introspection. I didn't know what language I heard. I didn't understand that I understood. What comes to mind is the assertion that begins the book of John: "In the beginning was the word." A sound, a physical thing, the word is also mental. So this monism can be understood as the nature of everything. Like the music that is the meaning of stories, physical and mental are aspects of each other. Yiddish, with its elements of German, Hebrew, Aramaic, Latin, Spanish, Polish, Russian, Romanian, etc., is metaphorically everything. A people driven hither and yon, and obliged to assimilate so much, returned immensely more to the world. How they can become necessary to murder is the hideous paradox of evil.

When I was five years old, I started school in a huge gloomy Victorian building where nobody spoke Yiddish. It was across the street from

Knickerbocker Village, the project in which I lived. To cross that street meant going from love to hell. I said nothing in the classroom and sat apart and alone, trying to avoid the teacher's evil eye. Eventually, she decided that I was a moron and wrote a letter to my parents saying I would be transferred to the "ungraded class," where I would be happier and could play Ping Pong all day. My mother couldn't read the letter so she showed it to our neighbor, a woman from Texas named Lynn Nations. A real American, she boasted of Indian blood, though she was blond and had the cheekbones, figure, and fragility of a fashion model. She would ask us to look at the insides of her teeth and see how they were cupped. To Lynn this proved descent from original Americans. She was very fond of me, though we had no conversation, and I spent hours in her apartment looking at her art books and eating forbidden foods. I could speak to her husband, Arthur Kleinman, yet another furrier and a lefty union activist, who knew Yiddish.

Lynn believed I was brighter than a moron and went to the school principal, which my mother would never have dared to do, and demanded an intelligence test for me. Impressed by her Katharine Hepburn looks, the principal arranged for a school psychologist to test me. Afterward, I was advanced to a grade beyond my age with several other kids, among them a boy named Bonfiglio and a girl named Estervez. I remember their names because we were seated according to our IQ scores. Behind Bonfiglio and Estervez was me, a kid who couldn't even ask permission to go to the bathroom. In the higher grade I had to read and write and speak English. It happened virtually overnight, so I must have known more than I knew. When I asked my mother about this, she said, "Sure you knew English. You learned from trucks." She meant, while lying in my sickbed, I would look out the window at trucks passing in the street; studying the words written on their sides, I taught myself English. Unfortunately, high fevers burned away most of my brain, so I now find it impossible to learn a language from trucks. A child learns any language at incredible speed. Again, in a metaphorical sense, Yiddish is the language of children wandering for a thousand years in a nightmare, assimilating languages to no avail.

I remember the black shining print of my first textbook, and my fearful uncertainty as the meanings came with all their exotic Englishness and devoured what had previously inhered in my Yiddish. Something remained indigestible. What it is can be suggested, in a Yiddish style, by contrast with English. A line from a poem by Wallace Stevens, which I have discussed elsewhere, seems to me quintessentially goyish, or antithetical to Yiddish:

It is the word *pejorative* that hurts.

Stevens effects detachment from his subject, which is the poet's romantic heart, by playing on a French construction: "word *pejorative*," like *mot juste,* makes the adjective follow the noun. Detachment is further evidenced in the rhyme of "word" and "hurts." The delicate resonance gives the faint touch of hurtful impact without obliging the reader to suffer the experience. The line is ironically detached even from detachment. In Yiddish there is plenty of irony, but not so nicely mannered or sensitive to a reader's experience of words. Stevens's line would seem too self-regarding, and the luxurious subtlety of his sensibility would seem unintelligible if not ridiculous. He flaunts sublimities here, but it must be said that elsewhere he is as visceral and concrete as any Yiddish speaker.

I've lost too much of my Yiddish to know exactly how much remains. Something remains. If a little of its genius is at work in my sentences, it has nothing to do with me personally. Pleasures of complexity and the hilarity of idiocy, as well as an idea of what's good or isn't good, are in Yiddish. If it speaks in my sentences, it isn't I, let alone me, who speaks.

When asked what he would have liked to be if he hadn't been born an Englishman, Lord Palmerston said, "An Englishman." The answer reminds me of a joke. A Jew sees himself in a mirror after being draped in a suit by a high-class London tailor. The tailor asks what's wrong. The Jew says, crying, "Vee lost de empire." The joke assimilates the insane fury that influenced the nature of Yiddish and makes it apparent that identity for a Jew is not, as for Palmerston, a witty preference.

ZADIE SMITH

Zadie Smith (1975–) was born in London of a Jamaican mother and an English father, and continues to straddle two worlds (biracial, binational), dividing her year between the United Kingdom and the United States, where she holds a professor's chair at New York University. The acclaimed author of five novels, she has also written two superb essay collections, Changing My Mind *and* Feel Free, *which display a keen understanding of American culture from an outsider-insider's perspective. Smith has also shown a deep awareness of the game of essay writing: building up the I-speaker's persona, filling in autobiographical context when necessary, augmenting her explorations with research, and thinking against herself by entertaining opposing points of view. In "Speaking in Tongues" she summarizes the dilemma of immigrants (or semi-immigrants) in a diverse society, trying to assert a unitary self while containing inner multitudes.*

Speaking in Tongues

(2008)

1

Hello. This voice I speak with these days, this English voice with its rounded vowels and consonants in more or less the right place—this is not the voice of my childhood. I picked it up in college, along with the unabridged *Clarissa* and a taste for port. Maybe this fact is only what it seems to be—a case of bald social climbing—but at the time, I genuinely thought this was the voice of lettered people, and that if I didn't have the voice of lettered people I would never truly be lettered. A braver person, perhaps, would have stood firm, teaching her peers a useful lesson by example: not all lettered people need be of the same class nor speak identically. I went the other way. Partly out of cowardice and a constitutional eagerness to please, but also because I didn't quite see it as a straight swap, of this voice for that. My own childhood had been the story of this and that combined, of the synthesis of disparate things. It never occurred to me that I was leaving Willesden for Cambridge. I thought I was adding Cambridge to Willesden, this new way of talking to that old way. Adding a new kind of knowledge to a different kind I already had. And for a while, that's how it was: at home, during the holidays, I spoke with my old voice, and in the old voice seemed to feel and speak things that I couldn't express in college, and vice versa. I felt a sort of wonder at the flexibility of the thing. Like being alive twice.

But flexibility is something that requires work if it is to be maintained. Recently my double voice has deserted me for a single one, reflecting the smaller world into which my work has led me. Willesden was a big, colorful, working-class sea; Cambridge was a smaller, posher pond, and almost univocal; the literary world is a puddle. This voice I picked up along the way is no longer an exotic garment I put on like a college gown whenever I choose—now it is my only voice, whether I want it or not. I regret it; I should have kept both voices alive in my mouth. They were both a part of me. But how the culture warns against it! As George Bernard Shaw delicately put it in his preface to the play *Pygmalion*, "many thousands of [British] men and women . . . have sloughed off their native dialects and acquired a new tongue." Few, though, will admit to it. Voice adaptation is still the original British sin. Monitoring and exposing such citizens is a national pastime, as popular as sex scandals and libel cases. If you lean toward the Atlantic with your high-rising terminals, you're a sellout; if you pronounce borrowed European words in their original style—even if you try something as innocent as *parmigiano* for *parmesan*—you're a fraud. If you go (metaphorically speaking) down the British class scale, you've gone from Cockney to "mockney" and can expect a public tarring and feathering; to go the other way is to perform an unforgivable act of class betrayal. Voices are meant to be unchanging and singular. There's no quicker way to insult an expat Scotsman in London than to tell him he's lost his accent. We feel that our voices are who we are, and that to have more than one, or to use different versions of a voice for different occasions, represents, at best, a Janus-faced duplicity, and at worst, the loss of our very souls. Whoever changes their voice takes on, in Britain, a queerly tragic dimension. They have betrayed that puzzling dictum "To thine own self be true," so often quoted approvingly as if it represented the wisdom of Shakespeare rather than the hot air of Polonius. "What's to become of me? What's to become of me?" wails Eliza Doolittle, realizing her middling dilemma. With a voice too posh for the flower girls and yet too redolent of the gutter for the ladies in Mrs. Higgins's drawing room.

But Eliza—patron saint of the tragically double-voiced—is worthy of closer inspection. The first thing to note is that both Eliza and *Pygmalion* are entirely didactic, as Shaw meant them to be. "I delight," he wrote, "in throwing [*Pygmalion*] at the heads of the wiseacres who repeat the parrot cry that art should never be didactic. It goes to prove my contention that art should never be anything else." He was determined to tell the unambiguous tale of a girl who changes her voice and loses her self. And so she arrives like this:

> Don't you be so saucy. You ain't heard what I come for yet. Did you tell him I come in a taxi? . . . Oh, we are proud! He ain't above giving lessons, not him: I heard him say so. Well, I ain't come here to ask for any compliment; and if my money's not good enough I can go elsewhere. . . . Now you know, don't you? I'm come to have lessons, I am. And to pay for em too: make no mistake. . . . I want to be a lady in a flower shop stead of selling at the corner of Tottenham Court Road. But they wont take me unless I can talk more genteel.

And she leaves like this:

> I can't. I could have done it once; but now I can't go back to it. Last night, when I was wandering about, a girl spoke to me; and I tried to get back into the old way with her; but it was no use. You told me, you know, that when a child is brought to a foreign country, it picks up the language in a few weeks, and forgets its own. Well, I am a child in your country. I have forgotten my own language, and can speak nothing but yours.

By the end of his experiment, Professor Higgins has made his Eliza an awkward, in-between thing, neither flower girl nor lady, with one voice lost and another gained, at the steep price of everything she was and everything she knows. Almost as afterthought, he sends Eliza's father, Alfred Doolittle, to his doom, too, securing a three-thousand-a-year living for the man on the condition that Doolittle lecture for the Wannafeller Moral Reform World League up to six times a year. This burden brings the philosophical dustman into the close, unwanted embrace of what he disdainfully calls "middle class morality." By the time the curtain goes down, both Doolittles find themselves stuck in the middle, which is, to

Shaw, a comi-tragic place to be, with the emphasis on the tragic. What are they fit for? What will become of them?

How persistent this horror of the middling spot is, this dread of the interim place! It extends through the specter of the tragic mulatto, to the plight of the transsexual, to our present anxiety—disguised as genteel concern—for the contemporary immigrant, tragically split, we are sure, between worlds, ideas, cultures, voices—whatever will become of them? Something's got to give—one voice must be sacrificed for the other. What is double must be made singular. But this, the apparent didactic moral of Eliza's story, is undercut by the fact of the play itself, which is an orchestra of many voices, simultaneously and perfectly rendered, with no shade of color or tone sacrificed. Higgins's Harley Street high-handedness is the equal of Mrs. Pearce's lower-middle-class gentility, Pickering's kind-hearted aristocratic imprecision every bit as convincing as Alfred Doolittle's Nietzschean Cockney-by-way-of-Wales. Shaw had a wonderful ear, able to reproduce almost as many quirks of the English language as Shakespeare. Shaw was in possession of a gift he wouldn't, or couldn't, give Eliza: he spoke in tongues.

It gives me a strange sensation to turn from Shaw's melancholy Pygmalion story to another, infinitely more hopeful version, written by the new president of the United States of America. Of course, his ear isn't half bad either. In *Dreams from My Father,* the new president displays an enviable facility for dialogue, and puts it to good use, animating a cast every bit as various as the one James Baldwin—an obvious influence—conjured for his own many-voiced novel *Another Country.* Obama can do young Jewish male, black old lady from the South Side, white woman from Kansas, Kenyan elders, white Harvard nerds, black Columbia nerds, activist women, churchmen, security guards, bank tellers, and even a British man called Mr. Wilkerson, who on a starry night on safari says credibly British things like: "I believe that's the Milky Way." This new president doesn't just speak for his people. He can speak them. It is a disorienting talent in a president; we're so unused to it. I have to pinch myself to remember who wrote the following well-observed scene, seemingly plucked from a comic novel:

"Man, I'm not going to any more of these bullshit Punahou parties."

"Yeah, that's what you said the last time. . . ."

"I mean it this time. . . . These girls are A-1, USDA-certified racists. All of 'em. White girls. Asian girls—shoot, these Asians worse than the whites. Think we got a disease or something."

"Maybe they're looking at that big butt of yours. Man, I thought you were in training."

"Get your hands out of my fries. You ain't my bitch, nigger . . . buy your own damn fries. Now what was I talking about?"

"Just 'cause a girl don't go out with you doesn't make her a racist."

This is the voice of Obama at seventeen, as remembered by Obama. He's still recognizably Obama; he already seeks to unpack and complicate apparently obvious things ("Just 'cause a girl don't go out with you doesn't make her a racist"); he's already gently cynical about the impassioned dogma of other people ("Yeah, that's what you said the last time"). And he has a sense of humor ("Maybe they're looking at that big butt of yours"). Only the voice is different: he has made almost as large a leap as Eliza Doolittle. The conclusions Obama draws from his own Pygmalion experience, however, are subtler than Shaw's. The tale he tells is not the old tragedy of gaining a new, false voice at the expense of a true one. The tale he tells is all about addition. His is the story of a genuinely many-voiced man. If it has a moral, it is that each man must be true to his selves, plural.

For Obama, having more than one voice in your ear is not a burden, or not solely a burden—it is also a gift. And the gift is of an interesting kind, not well served by that dull publishing-house title, *Dreams from My Father: A Story of Race and Inheritance,* with its suggestion of a simple linear inheritance, of paternal dreams and aspirations passed down to a son, and fulfilled. *Dreams from My Father* would have been a fine title for John McCain's book *Faith of My Fathers,* which concerns exactly this kind of linear masculine inheritance, in his case from soldier to soldier. For Obama's book, though, it's wrong, lopsided. He corrects its misperception early on, in the first chapter, while discussing the failure of his parents' relationship, characterized by their only son as the end of a dream. "Even as that spell was broken," he writes, "and the worlds that they thought they'd left behind reclaimed each of them, I occupied the place where their dreams had been."

To occupy a dream, to exist in a dreamed space (conjured by both father and mother), is surely a quite different thing from simply inheriting a dream. It's more interesting. What did Pauline Kael call Cary Grant? "The Man from Dream City." When Bristolian Archibald Leach became suave Cary Grant, the transformation happened in his voice, which he subjected to a strange, indefinable manipulation, resulting in that heavenly sui generis accent, neither west country nor posh, American nor English. It came from nowhere; *he* came from nowhere. Grant seemed the product of a collective dream, dreamed up by moviegoers in hard times, as it sometimes feels voters have dreamed up Obama in hard times. Both men have a strange reflective quality, typical of the self-created man—we see in them whatever we want to see. "Everyone wants to be Cary Grant," said Cary Grant. "Even I want to be Cary Grant." It's not hard to imagine Obama having that same thought, backstage at Grant Park, hearing his own name chanted by the hopeful multitude. Everyone wants to be Barack Obama. Even I want to be Barack Obama.

2

But I haven't described Dream City. I'll try to. It is a place of many voices, where the unified singular self is an illusion. Naturally, Obama was born there. So was I. When your personal multiplicity is printed on your face, in an almost too obviously thematic manner, in your DNA, in your hair and in the neither-this-nor-that beige of your skin—well, anyone can see you come from Dream City. In Dream City everything is doubled, everything is various. You have no choice but to cross borders and speak in tongues. That's how you get from your mother to your father, from talking to one set of folks who think you're not black enough to another who figure you insufficiently white. It's the kind of town where the wise man says "I" cautiously, because *I* feels like too straight and singular a phoneme to represent the true multiplicity of his experience. Instead, citizens of Dream City prefer to use the collective pronoun *we*.

Throughout his campaign Obama was careful always to say *we*. He was noticeably wary of *I*. By speaking so, he wasn't simply avoiding a singularity he didn't feel; he was also drawing us in with him. He had the audacity to suggest that, even if you can't see it stamped on their faces, most people come from Dream City, too. Most of us have complicated backstories, messy histories, multiple narratives. It was a high-wire strategy, for Obama, this invocation of our collective human messiness. His enemies latched on to its imprecision, emphasizing the exotic, un-American nature of Dream City, this ill-defined place where you could be from Hawaii and Kenya, Kansas and Indonesia all at the same time, where you could jive talk like a street hustler and orate like a senator. What kind of a crazy place is that? But they underestimated how many people come from Dream City, how many Americans, in their daily lives, conjure contrasting voices and seek a synthesis between disparate things. Turns out, Dream City wasn't so strange to them.

Or did they never actually see it? We now know that Obama spoke of *Main Street* in Iowa and of *sweet potato pie* in Northwest Philly, and it could be argued that he succeeded because he so rarely misspoke, carefully tailoring his intonations to suit the sensibility of his listeners. Sometimes he did this within one speech, within one *line:* "We worship an *awesome* God in the blue states, and we don't like federal agents poking around our libraries in the red states." *Awesome God* comes to you straight from the pews of a Georgia church; *poking around* feels more at home at a kitchen table in South Bend, Indiana. The balance was perfect, cunningly counterpoised and never accidental. It's only now that it's over that we see him let his guard down a little, on *60 Minutes,* say, dropping in that culturally, casually black construction, "Hey, I'm not stupid, man, that's why I'm president," something it's hard to imagine him doing even three weeks earlier. To a certain kind of mind, it must have looked like the mask had slipped for a moment.

Which brings us to the single-voiced Obamanation crowd. They rage on in the blogs and on the radio, waiting obsessively for the mask to slip. They have a great fear of what they see as Obama's doubling ways. "He says one thing but he means another"—this is the essence of the fear campaign. He says he's a capitalist, but he'll spread your wealth. He says he's a Christian, but really he's going to empower the Muslims. And so on and so forth. These are fears that have their roots in an anxiety about voice. "Who is he?" people kept asking. I mean, who is this guy, really? He says "sweet potato pie" in Philly and "Main Street" in Iowa! When he talks to us, he sure sounds like us—but behind our backs he says we're clinging to our religion, to our guns. And when Jesse Jackson heard that Obama had lectured a black church congregation about the epidemic of absent black fathers, he experienced this, too, as a tonal betrayal; Obama was "talking down to black people." In both cases, there was the sense of a double-dealer, of someone who tailors his speech to fit the audience, who is not of the people (because he is able to look at them objectively) but always above them.

The Jackson gaffe, with its Oedipal violence ("I want to cut his nuts out"), is especially poignant because it goes to the heart of a generational conflict in the black community, concerning what we will say in public and what we say in private. For it has been a point of honor, among the civil rights generation, that any criticism or negative analysis of our community, expressed, as they often are by white politicians, without context, without real empathy or understanding, should not be repeated by a black politician when the white community is listening, even if (especially if) the criticism happens to be true (more than half of all black American children live in single-parent households). Our business is our business. Keep it in the family; don't wash your dirty linen in public; stay unified. (Of course, with his overheard gaffe, Jackson unwittingly broke his own rule.)

Until Obama, black politicians had always adhered to these unwritten rules. In this way, they defended themselves against those two bogeymen of black political life: the Uncle Tom and the House Nigger. The black politician who played up to, or even simply echoed, white fears, desires and hopes for the black community was in danger of earning these epithets—even Martin Luther King was not free from such suspicions. Then came Obama, and the new world he had supposedly ushered in, the postracial world, in which what mattered most was not blind racial allegiance but factual truth. It was felt that Jesse Jackson was sadly out of step with this new postracial world: even his own son felt moved to publicly repudiate his "ugly rhetoric." But Jackson's anger was not incomprehensible or his distrust unreasonable. Jackson lived through a bitter struggle, and bitter struggles deform their participants in subtle, complicated ways. The idea that one should speak one's cultural allegiance first and the truth second (and that this is a sign of authenticity) is precisely such a deformation.

Right up to the wire, Obama made many black men and women of Jackson's generation suspicious. How *can* the man who passes between culturally black and white voices with such flexibility, with such ease, be an honest man? How *will* the man from Dream City keep it real? Why won't he speak with a clear and unified voice? These were genuine questions for people born in real cities at a time when those cities were implacably divided, when the black movement had to yell with a clear and unified voice, or risk not being heard at all. And then he won. Watching Jesse Jackson in tears in Grant Park, pressed up against the varicolored American public, it seemed like he, at least, had received the answer he needed: only a many-voiced man could have spoken to that many people.

A clear and unified voice. In that context, this business of being biracial, of being half black and half white, is awkward. In his memoir, Obama takes care to ridicule a certain black girl called Joyce—a composite figure from his college days who happens also to be part Italian and part French and part Native American and is inordinately fond of mentioning these facts, and who likes to say:

> I'm not black . . . I'm multiracial. . . . Why should I have to choose between them? . . . It's not white people who are making me choose. . . . No—it's black people who always have to make everything racial. They're the ones making me choose. They're the ones who are telling me I can't be who I am. . . .

He has her voice down pat and so condemns her out of her own mouth. For she's the third bogeyman of black life, the tragic mulatto, who secretly wishes she "passed," always keen to let you know about her white heritage. It's the fear of being mistaken for Joyce that has always ensured that I ignore the box marked "biracial" and tick the box marked "black" on any questionnaire I fill out, and call myself unequivocally a black writer and roll my eyes at anyone who insists that Obama is not the first black president but the first biracial one. But I also know in my heart that it's an equivocation; I know that Obama has a double consciousness, is black and, at the same time, white, as I am, unless we are suggesting that one side of a person's genetics and cultural heritage cancels out or trumps the other.

But to mention the double is to suggest shame at the singular. Joyce insists on her varied heritage because she fears and is ashamed of the singular black. I suppose it's possible that subconsciously I am also a tragic mulatto, torn between pride and shame. In my conscious life, though, I cannot honestly say I feel proud to be white and ashamed to be black or proud to be black and ashamed to be white. I find it impossible to experience either pride or shame over accidents of genetics in which I had no active part. I understand how those words got into the racial discourse, but I can't sign up to them. I'm not proud to be female either. I am not even proud to be human—I only love to be so. As I love to be female and I love to be black, and I love that I had a white father.

It's telling that Joyce is one of the few voices in *Dreams from My Father* that is truly left out in the cold, outside of the expansive sympathy of Obama's narrative. She is an entirely didactic being, a demon Obama has to raise up, if only for a page, so everyone can watch him slay her. I know the feeling. When I was in college I felt I'd rather run away with the Black Panthers than be associated with the Joyces I occasionally met. It's the Joyces of this world who "talk down to black people." And so to avoid being Joyce, or being seen to be Joyce, you unify, you speak with one voice. And the concept of a unified black voice is a potent one. It has filtered down, these past forty years, into the black community at all levels, settling itself in that impossible injunction "keep it real," the original intention of which was unification. We were going to unify the concept of Blackness in order to strengthen it. Instead we confined and restricted it. To me, the instruction "keep it real" is a sort of prison cell, two feet by five. The fact is, it's too narrow. I just can't live comfortably in there. "Keep it real" replaced the blessed and solid genetic fact of Blackness with a flimsy imperative. It made Blackness a quality each individual black person was constantly in danger of losing. And almost anything could trigger the loss of one's Blackness: attending certain universities, an impressive variety of jobs, a fondness for opera, a white girlfriend, an interest in golf. And of course, any change in the voice. There was a popular school of thought that maintained the voice was at the very heart of the thing; fail to keep it real there and you'd never see your Blackness again. How absurd that all seems now. And not because we live in a post-racial world—we don't—but because the reality of race has diversified. Black reality has diversified. It's black people who talk like me, and black people who talk like Lil Wayne. It's black conservatives and black liberals, black sportsmen and black lawyers, black computer technicians and black ballet dancers and black truck drivers and black presidents. We're all black, and we all love to be black, and we all sing from our own hymn sheet. We're all surely black people, but we may be finally approaching a point of human history where you can't talk up or down to us anymore, but only *to* us. He's talking down to white people—how curious it sounds the other way round! In order to say such a thing, one would have to think collectively of white people, as a people of one mind who speak with one voice—a thought experiment in which we have no practice. But it's worth trying. It's only when you play the record backward that you hear the secret message.

3

For reasons that are obscure to me, those qualities we cherish in our artists we condemn in our politicians. In our artists we look for the many-colored voice, the multiple sensibility. The apogee of this is, of course, Shakespeare: even more than for his wordplay we cherish him for his lack of allegiance. Our Shakespeare sees always both sides of a thing; he is black and white, male and female—he is everyman. The giant lacunae in his biography are merely a convenience; if any new facts of religious or political affiliation were ever to arise, we would dismiss them in our hearts anyway. Was he, for example, a man of Rome or not? He has appeared, to generations of readers, not of one religion but of both, in truth, beyond both. Born into the middle of Britain's fierce Catholic-Protestant culture war, how could the bloody absurdity of those years not impress upon him a strong sense of cultural contingency?

It was a war of ideas that began for Will—as it began for Barack—in the dreams of his father. For we know that John Shakespeare, a civic officer in Protestant times, oversaw the repainting of medieval frescoes and the destruction of the rood loft and altar in Stratford's own fine Guild Chapel, but we also know that in the rafters of the Shakespeare home John hid a secret Catholic "Spiritual Testament," a signed profession of allegiance to the old faith. A strange experience, to watch one's own father thus divided, professing one thing in public while practicing another in private. John Shakespeare was a kind of equivocator: it's what you do when you're in a corner, when you can't be a Catholic and a loyal Englishman at the same time. When you can't be both black and white. Sometimes in a country ripped apart by dogma, those who wish to keep their heads—in both senses—must learn to split themselves in two. And this we still know, here, at a four-hundred-year distance. No one can hope to be president of these United States without professing a committed and straightforward belief in two things: the existence of God and the principle of American exceptionalism. But how many of them equivocated, and who, in their shoes, would not equivocate, too?

Fortunately, Shakespeare was an artist and so had an outlet his father didn't have—the many-voiced theater. Shakespeare's art, the very medium of it, allowed him to do what civic officers and politicians can't seem to: speak simultaneous truths. (Is it not, for example, experientially true that one can both believe and not believe in God?) In his plays he is woman, man, black, white, believer, heretic, Catholic, Protestant, Jew, Muslim.

He grew up in an atmosphere of equivocation, but he lived in freedom. And he offers us freedom: to pin him down to a single identity would be an obvious diminishment, both for Shakespeare and for us. Generations of critics have insisted on this irreducible multiplicity, though they have each expressed it different ways, through the glass of their times. Here is Keats's famous attempt, in 1817, to give this quality a name:

> At once it struck me, what quality went to form a Man of Achievement especially in Literature and which Shakespeare possessed so enormously—I mean Negative Capability, that is when man is capable of being in uncertainties, Mysteries, doubts, without any irritable reaching after fact and reason.

And here is Stephen Greenblatt doing the same, in 2004:

> There are many forms of heroism in Shakespeare, but ideological heroism—the fierce, self-immolating embrace of an idea or institution—is not one of them.

For Keats, Shakespeare's many voices are quasi-mystical, as suited the romantic thrust of Keats's age. For Greenblatt, Shakespeare's negative capability is sociopolitical at root. Will had seen too many wild-eyed martyrs, too many executed terrorists, too many wars on the Catholic terror. He had watched men rage absurdly at rood screens and write treatises in praise of tables. He had seen men disemboweled while still alive, their entrails burned before their eyes, and all for the preference of a Latin Mass over a common prayer or vice versa. He understood what fierce, singular certainty creates and what it destroys. In response, he made himself a diffuse, uncertain thing, a mass of contradictory, irresolvable voices that speak truth plurally. Through the glass of 2008, "negative capability" looks like the perfect antidote to "ideological heroism."

From our politicians, though, we still look for ideological heroism, despite everything. We consider pragmatists to be weak. We call men of balance naive fools. In England, we once had an insulting name for such people: trimmers. In the mid-1600s, a trimmer was any politician who attempted to straddle the reviled middle ground between Cavalier and Roundhead, Parliament and the Crown; to call a man a trimmer was to accuse him of being insufficiently committed to an ideology. But in telling us of these times, the nineteenth-century English historian Thomas Macaulay draws our attention to Halifax, great statesman of the Privy Council, set up to mediate between Parliament and Crown as London burned. Halifax proudly called himself a trimmer, assuming it, Macaulay explains, as a title of honour, and vindicating, with great vivacity, the dignity of the appellation. Everything good, he said, trims between extremes. The temperate zone trims between the climate in which men are roasted and the climate in which they are frozen. The English Church trims between the Anabaptist madness and the Papist lethargy. The English constitution trims between the Turkish despotism and Polish anarchy. Virtue is nothing but a just temper between propensities any one of which, if indulged to excess, becomes vice.

Which all sounds eminently reasonable and Aristotelian. And Macaulay's description of Halifax's character is equally attractive:

His intellect was fertile, subtle, and capacious. His polished, luminous, and animated eloquence . . . was the delight of the House of Lords. . . . His political tracts well deserve to be studied for their literary merit.

In fact, Halifax is familiar—he sounds like the man from Dream City. This makes Macaulay's caveat the more striking:

Yet he was less successful in politics than many who enjoyed smaller advantages. Indeed, those intellectual peculiarities which make his writings valuable frequently impeded him in the contests of active life. For he always saw passing events, not in the point of view in which they commonly appear to one who bears a part in them, but in the point of view in which, after the lapse of many years, they appear to the philosophic historian.

To me, this is a doleful conclusion. It is exactly men with such intellectual peculiarities that I have always hoped to see in politics. But maybe Macaulay is correct: maybe the Halifaxes of this world make, in the end, better writers than politicians. A lot rests on how this president turns out—but that's a debate for the future. Here I want instead to hazard a little theory, concerning the evolution of a certain type of voice, typified by Halifax, by Shakespeare, and very possibly by the president. For the voice of what Macaulay called "the philosophic historian" is, to my mind, a valuable and particular one, and I think someone should make a proper study of it. It's a voice that develops in a man over time; my little theory sketches four developmental stages. The first stage in the evolution is contingent and cannot be contrived. In this first stage, the voice, by no fault of its own, finds itself trapped between two poles, two competing belief systems. And so this first stage necessitates the second: the voice learns to be flexible between these two fixed points, even to the point of equivocation. Then the third stage: this native flexibility leads to a sense of being able to "see a thing from both sides." And then the final stage, which I think of as the mark of a certain kind of genius: the voice relinquishes ownership of itself, develops a creative sense of disassociation in which the claims that are particular to it seem no stronger than anyone else's. There it is, my little theory—I'd rather call it a story. It is a story about a wonderful voice, occasionally used by citizens, rarely by men of power. Amid the din of the 2008 culture wars it proved especially hard to hear.

In this lecture I have been seeking to tentatively suggest that the voice that speaks with such freedom, thus unburdened by dogma and personal bias, thus flooded with empathy, might make a good president. It's only now that I realize that in all this utilitarianism I've left joyfulness out of the account, and thus neglected a key constituency of my own people, the poets! Being many voiced may be a complicated gift for a president, but in poets it is a pure delight in need of neither defense nor explanation. Plato banished them from his uptight and annoying republic so long ago that they have lost all their anxiety. They are fancy-free.

"I am a Hittite in love with a horse," writes Frank O'Hara.

> I don't know what blood's
> in me I feel like an African prince I am a
> girl walking downstairs
> in a red pleated dress with heels I am a
> champion taking a fall
> I am a jockey with a sprained ass-hole I
> am the light mist in which a face
> appears
> and it is another face of blonde I am a
> baboon eating a banana
> I am a dictator looking at his wife I am a
> doctor eating a child
> and the child's mother smiling I am a
> Chinaman climbing a mountain
> I am a child smelling his father's
> underwear I am an Indian
> sleeping on a scalp
> and my pony is stamping in
> the birches,
> and I've just caught sight of the
> *Niña,* the *Pinta* and the *Santa*

Maria.
What land is this, so free?

Frank O'Hara's republic is of the imagination, of course. It is the only land of perfect freedom. Presidents, as a breed, tend to dismiss this land, thinking it has nothing to teach them. If this new president turns out to be different, then writers will count their blessings, but with or without a president on board, writers should always count their blessings. A line of O'Hara's reminds us of this. It's carved on his gravestone. It reads: "Grace to be born and live as variously as possible."

But to live variously cannot simply be a gift, endowed by an accident of birth; it has to be a continual effort, continually renewed. I felt this with force the night of the election. I was at a lovely New York party, full of lovely people, almost all of whom were white, liberal, highly educated, and celebrating with one happy voice as the states turned blue. Just as they called Iowa, my phone rang and a strident German voice said: "Zadie! Come to Harlem! It's vild here. I'm in za middle of a crazy reggae bar—it's so vonderful! Vy not come now!"

I mention he was German only so we don't run away with the idea that flexibility comes only to the beige, or gay, or otherwise marginalized. Flexibility is a choice, always open to all of us. (He was a writer, however. Make of that what you will.)

But wait: all the way uptown? A crazy reggae bar? For a minute I hesitated, because I was at a lovely party having a lovely time. Or was that it? There was something else. In truth I thought: but I'll be ludicrous, in my silly dress, with this silly posh English voice, in a crowded bar of black New Yorkers celebrating. It's amazing how many of our cross-cultural and cross-class encounters are limited not by hate or pride or shame, but by another equally insidious, less-discussed, emotion: embarrassment. A few minutes later, I was in a taxi and heading uptown with my Northern Irish husband and our half-Indian, half-English friend, but that initial hesitation was ominous; the first step on a typical British journey. A hesitation in the face of difference, which leads to caution before difference and ends in fear of it. Before long, the only voice you recognize, the only life you can empathize with, is your own. You will think that a novelist's screwy leap of logic. Well, it's my novelist credo and I believe it. I believe that flexibility of voice leads to a flexibility in all things. My audacious hope in Obama is based, I'm afraid, on precisely such flimsy premises.

It's my audacious hope that a man born and raised between opposing dogmas, between cultures, between voices, could not help but be aware of the extreme contingency of culture. I further audaciously hope that such a man will not mistake the happy accident of his own cultural sensibilities for a set of natural laws, suitable for general application. I even hope that he will find himself in agreement with George Bernard Shaw when he declared, "Patriotism is, fundamentally, a conviction that a particular country is the best in the world because you were born in it." But that may be an audacious hope too far. We'll see if Obama's lifelong vocal flexibility will enable him to say proudly with one voice, "I love my country," while saying with another voice, "It is a country, like other countries." I hope so. He seems just the man to demonstrate that between those two voices there exists no contradiction and no equivocation, but rather a proper and decent human harmony.

ACKNOWLEDGMENTS

It takes a village to edit an anthology. I needed all the help I could get, and my friends and colleagues came forward with so many tips that I had to tell them to stop after a while. Thank you so much, Peter Balakian, Halbert Barton, Carmen Boullosa, Robert Boyers, Andrew Delbanco, Chris Edling, Vivian Gornick, Mikhail Iossel, Margo Jefferson, Randall Kennedy, Jonathan Kirshner, David Lazar, Richard Locke, Honor Moore, Ross Posnock, Vijay Seshadri, Benjamin Taylor, Clifford Thompson, Brenda Wineapple. Special thanks go to two people who gave of their time and expertise unstintingly: Ned Stuckey-French and Jennifer Ratner-Rosenhagen. Ned was particularly helpful before he passed away, and I dedicate this anthology to him.

My blessedly honest preliminary readers, Shifra Sharlin and Lisa Brennan Jobs, kept me from making wrong choices, as did my wonderful students in the Columbia University graduate program, those willing canaries in the mine shaft.

I was very fortunate in having the resourceful, able assistance of graduate student Adam Schwartzman. I'd also like to thank the dean of the School of the Arts, Carol Becker, and Assistant Dean Jana Wright, for granting me a course reduction while working on the manuscript, and the Columbia University Arts & Humanities Division for their FRAP award, which enabled me to buy probably too many books.

There were certain resources I turned to often: the invaluable Library of America series, the *Encyclopedia of the Essay* (edited by Tracy Chevalier), Ned Stuckey-French's *The American Essay in the American Century,* *The Making of the American Essay* (edited by John D'Agata), *Contemporary American Essays* (edited by Maureen Howard), *Best American Essays of the Century* (edited by Joyce Carol Oates), and Patrick Madden's sterling website, Quotidiana.

My wily literary agent, Gail Hochman, steered the project to its proper home.

My splendid, forbearing editor at Pantheon/Anchor Books, Diana Secker Tesdell, had my back from the start, and is largely responsible for allowing me to expand the project beyond its original, more sensible proportions.

Finally, of course, all gratitude goes to my wife, Cheryl, and daughter, Lily: only you know how much you sustained me in this wacky venture.

imprint of Random House, a division of Penguin Random House LLC. All rights reserved.

NORA EPHRON: "A Few Words About Breasts," copyright © 1972 by Nora Ephron. First printed in *Esquire*. Reprinted by permission of ICM Partners.

M. F. K. FISHER: "Meals for Me" by M. F. K. Fisher, copyright © The Literary Trust u/w/o M. F. K. Fisher. Reprinted by permission.

F. SCOTT FITZGERALD: "My Lost City" from *The Crack-Up,* copyright © 1945 by New Directions Publishing Corp. Reprinted by permission of New Directions Publishing Corp.

WILLIAM H. GASS: "On Talking to Oneself" from *Habitations of the Word: Essays* by William Gass. Copyright © 1979, 1984, and 1985 by William Gass. Reprinted by permission of the author.

EMMA GOLDMAN: "Was My Life Worth Living?" by Emma Goldman, copyright © 1934 by *Harper's Magazine*. All rights reserved. Reproduced from the December issue by special permission.

VIVIAN GORNICK: "The Princess and the Pea," by Vivian Gornick. Reprinted by permission of the author.

CLEMENT GREENBERG: "Art and Culture" by Clement Greenberg. Copyright © 1961, 1989 by Clement Greenberg. Reprinted by permission of Beacon Press, Boston.

ELIZABETH HARDWICK: "Billie Holiday" by Elizabeth Hardwick, originally published in *The New York Review of Books*. Copyright © 1976 by Elizabeth Hardwick, used by permission of The Wylie Agency LLC.

ROLANDO HINOJOSA-SMITH: "This Writer's Sense of Place" from *A Voice of My Own* by Rolando Hinojosa-Smith is reprinted with permission from the publisher (© 2011 Arte Publico Press—University of Houston).

JOHN BRINCKERHOFF JACKSON, "The Stranger's Path" from *Selected Writings of J. B. Jackson,* reprinted by permission of The Center for Southwest Research at the University of New Mexico.

JAMAICA KINCAID: "In History" by Jamaica Kincaid. Copyright © 1997 by Jamaica Kincaid, used by permission of The Wylie Agency LLC.

MARTIN LUTHER KING JR.: "Beyond Vietnam," copyright © 1967 by Dr. Martin Luther King Jr., © renewed 1995 by Coretta Scott King. Reprinted by arrangement with The Heirs to the Estate of Martin Luther King Jr., c/o Writers House as agent for the proprietor, New York, NY.

WAYNE KOESTENBAUM: "My 1980s" from *My 1980s and Other Essays* by Wayne Koestenbaum. Copyright © 2013 by Wayne Koestenbaum. Reprinted by permission of Farrar, Straus and Giroux.

AUDRE LORDE: "The Master's Tools Will Never Dismantle the Master's House" from *Sister Outsider,* published by Crossing Press, Random House Inc. Copyright © 1984, 2007 by Audre Lorde. Used herein by permission of the Charlotte Sheedy Literary Agency, Inc.

NORMAN MAILER: "The Homosexual Villain" from *Advertisements for Myself* by Norman Mailer (Penguin Classics, 2018). Copyright © 1959,

2018 by Norman Mailer, used by permission of The Wylie Agency LLC. Reprinted by permission of Penguin Books Ltd. All rights reserved.

NANCY MAIRS: "On Being a Cripple" from *Plaintext* by Nancy Mairs. Copyright © 1986 by Arizona Board of Regents. Reprinted by permission of the University of Arizona Press.

MARY MCCARTHY: "America the Beautiful" by Mary McCarthy, reprinted by permission of The Mary McCarthy Literary Trust.

H. L. MENCKEN: "The Hills of Zion," copyright © 1926, 1949 by Penguin Random House LLC; from *A Mencken Chrestomathy* by H. L. Mencken. Used by permission of Alfred A. Knopf, an imprint of the Knopf Doubleday Group, a division of Penguin Random House LLC. All rights reserved.

LEONARD MICHAELS: "My Yiddish" by Leonard Michaels, copyright © 2019 by Katharine Ogden Michaels.

N. SCOTT MOMADAY: "The Native American Voice in American Literature," by N. Scott Momaday. Reprinted by permission of the author.

LEWIS MUMFORD: "A New York Adolescence" by Lewis Mumford. Used by permission of Gina Maccoby Literary Agency. Copyright © 1937, 1965 by Elizabeth M. Morss and James G. Morss.

CYNTHIA OZICK: "A Drugstore in Winter" from *Art & Ardor* by Cynthia Ozick. Copyright © 1983 by Cynthia Ozick. Reprinted with permission by Melanie Jackson Agency, LLC.

ADRIENNE RICH: "Women and Honor: Some Notes on Lying" from *Arts of the Possible: Essays and Conversations* by Adrienne Rich. Copyright © 2001 by Adrienne Rich. Used by permission of W. W. Norton & Company, Inc.

MARILYNNE ROBINSON: "Puritans and Prigs: An Anatomy of Zealotry" from *The Death of Adam: Essays on Modern Thought* by Marilynne Robinson. Copyright © 1998 by Marilynne Robinson. Reprinted by permission of Houghton Mifflin Harcourt Publishing Company. All rights reserved.

RICHARD RODRIGUEZ: "Hispanic" from *Brown: The Last Discovery of America* by Richard Rodriguez. Copyright © 2002 by Richard Rodriguez. Used by permission of Viking Books, an imprint of Penguin Publishing Group, a division of Penguin Random House LLC. All rights reserved.

WILLIAM SAROYAN: "Fragments" from *My Name Is Aram* by William Saroyan, reprinted by permission of Pollinger Limited (www.pollingerlimited.com) on behalf of The Board of Trustees of Leland Stanford Junior University.

ZADIE SMITH: "Speaking in Tongues" by Zadie Smith. Published by *The New York Review of Books,* 2008. Copyright © by Zadie Smith. Reproduced by permission of the author c/o Rogers, Coleridge & White Ltd., 20 Powis Mews, London W11 1JN.

SUSAN SONTAG: "Against Interpretation" from *Against Interpretation* by Susan Sontag. Copyright © 1964, 1966, renewed 1994 by Susan Sontag. Reprinted by permission of Farrar, Straus and Giroux.

WALLACE STEGNER: "The Twilight of Self-Reliance," a Tanner Lecture on Human Values given by Wallace Stegner at the University of Utah on February 25, 1980. Reprinted by permission of the University of Utah Press.

GERTRUDE STEIN: "What Are Master-pieces?" by Gertrude Stein. Reprinted by permission of David Higham Associates Limited.

LEWIS THOMAS: "The Lives of a Cell" from *Lives of a Cell* by Lewis Thomas, copyright © 1974 by Lewis Thomas; copyright © 1971, 1972, 1973 by Massachusetts Medical Society. Used by permission of Viking Books, an imprint of Penguin Publishing Group, a division of Penguin Random House LLC. All rights reserved.

JAMES THURBER: "The Nature of the American Male" from *Is Sex Necessary?* by James Thurber and E. B. White. Copyright © 1929 by James Thurber and E. B. White. Reprinted by arrangement with Rosemary A. Thurber and The Barbara Hogenson Agency, Inc. and The Estate of E. B. White and ICM. All rights reserved.

PAUL TILLICH: "The Lost Dimension in Religion" by Paul Tillich © SEPS licensed by Curtis Licensing.

DAVID FOSTER WALLACE: "The View from Mrs. Thompson's" from *Consider the Lobster* by David Foster Wallace, copyright © 2005, 2007. Reprinted by permission of Little, Brown and Company, an imprint of Hachette Book Group, Inc.

EUDORA WELTY: "Ida M'Toy" from *The Eye of the Story* by Eudora Welty. Reprinted by the permission of Russell & Volkening as agents for Eudora Welty, copyright © 1969 by Eudora Welty, renewed in 1997 by Eudora Welty.

E. B. WHITE: "Death of a Pig" from *Essays of E. B. White* by E. B. White. Copyright © 1977 by E. B. White. Reprinted by permission of HarperCollins Publishers.

EDMUND WILSON: "John Jay Chapman" from *The Triple Thinkers* by Edmund Wilson. Copyright © 1948 by Edmund Wilson. Copyright © renewed 1975 by Elena Wilson. Reprinted by permission of Farrar, Straus and Giroux.

A NOTE ABOUT THE EDITOR

Phillip Lopate is the author of *To Show and to Tell: The Craft of Literary Nonfiction* and of four essay collections, *Bachelorhood, Against Joie de Vivre, Portrait of My Body,* and *Portrait Inside My Head.* He is the editor of the anthologies *The Art of the Personal Essay, Writing New York,* and *American Movie Critics.* He was awarded a John Simon Guggenheim Fellowship, a New York Public Library Center for Scholars and Writers Fellowship, two National Endowment for the Arts grants, and two New York Foundation for the Arts grants. He is a professor of writing at Columbia University's nonfiction MFA program and lives in Brooklyn, New York.

A NOTE ON THE TYPE

The text of this book was set in Sabon, a typeface designed by Jan Tschichold (1902–1974), the well-known German typographer. Based loosely on the original designs by Claude Garamond (ca. 1480–1561), Sabon is unique in that it was explicitly designed for hot-metal composition on both the Monotype and Linotype machines as well as for filmsetting. Designed in 1966 in Frankfurt, Sabon was named for the famous Lyons punch cutter Jacques Sabon, who is thought to have brought some of Garamond's matrices to Frankfurt.

Composed by North Market Street Graphics
Lancaster, Pennsylvania

Printed and bound by LSC Communications
Crawfordsville, Indiana

Designed by Michael Collica